CALIFORNIA

UNITED STATES HISTORY
THE TWENTIETH CENTURY

 Pearson

Boston, Massachusetts   **Chandler, Arizona**
Glenview, Illinois   **New York, New York**

Social Studies Reimagined

 To start, download the free **Pearson BouncePages** app on your smartphone or tablet. Simply search for the Pearson BouncePages app in your mobile app store. The app is available for Android and IOS (iPhone®/iPad®).

Make your book come alive!

Activate your digital course interactivities directly from the page.

To launch the myStory video look for this icon.

To activate more interactivities look for this icon. **Bounce to Activate**

1. **AIM** the camera over the image so it is easily viewable on your screen.

2. **TAP** the screen to scan the page.

3. **BOUNCE** the page to life by clicking the icon.

Pearson Education, Inc. 330 Hudson Street, New York, NY 10013

ISBN-13: 978-0-32-898691-0
ISBN-10: 0-32-898691-7

Authors, Consultants, Partners

[Authors]

Emma J. Lapsansky-Werner

Emma J. Lapsansky-Werner is Professor of History and Curator of the Quaker Collection at Haverford College. After receiving her doctorate from the University of Pennsylvania, she taught at Temple University for almost two decades. Dr. Lapsansky-Werner's recent publications include *Quaker Aesthetics,* coauthored with Ann Verplanck, *Back to Africa: Benjamin Coates and the Colonization Movement in America, 1848–1880,* coedited with Margaret Hope Bacon, as well as *Struggle For Freedom,* a textbook on African American history, coauthored with Gary B. Nash and Clayborne Carson.

Peter B. Levy

Peter B. Levy is a Full Professor in the Department of History at York College of Pennsylvania, where he teaches a wide variety of courses in American history. He received his B.A. from the University of California, Berkeley, and his Ph.D. from Columbia University. Dr. Levy is the author of eight books and many articles, including: *The New Left and Labor in the 1960s; Civil War on Race Street: The Civil Rights Movement in Cambridge, Maryland;* and *100 Key Documents in American Democracy.* He lives in Towson, Maryland.

Randy Roberts

Randy Roberts is Distinguished Professor of History at Purdue University. An award-winning author, his primary research areas are sports and popular culture, and he has written, co-written, and edited more than 30 books. He has also won numerous teaching awards, including the Carnegie Foundation for the Advancement of Teaching as Indiana Professor of the Year. Among his work are books on Oscar Robertson, Joe Louis, the Alamo, and Vietnam. His most recent books include *A Team for America: The Army-Navy Game That Rallied a Nation* and *Rising Tide: Bear Bryant, Joe Namath, and Dixie's Last Quarter,* co-authored with Ed Krzemienski. Roberts has served as a consultant and on-camera commentator for PBS, HBO, and History Channel. He lives in Lafayette, Indiana, with his wife Marjie.

Alan Taylor

Alan Taylor is the Thomas Jefferson Memorial Foundation Chair at the University of Virginia. He earned his Ph.D. in history from Brandeis University and did a postdoctoral fellowship at the Institute of Early American History and Culture in Williamsburg, Virginia. He teaches courses in early American history and the history of the American West. Dr. Taylor is the author of eight books, including *The Internal Enemy: Slavery and War in Virginia, 1772–1832,* which won the 2014 Pulitzer Prize for American history, and *American Colonies* and *William Cooper's Town,* which won the Bancroft and Beveridge prizes, as well as the 1996 Pulitzer Prize for American history.

[Program Consultant]

Dr. Kathy Swan is an associate professor of curriculum and instruction at the University of Kentucky. Her research focuses on standards-based technology integration, authentic intellectual work, and documentary-making in the social studies classroom. Swan has been a four-time recipient of the National Technology Leadership Award in Social Studies Education. She is also the advisor for the Social Studies Assessment, Curriculum, and Instruction Collaborative (SSACI) at CCSSO.

[Program Partners]

 NBC Learn, the educational arm of NBC News, develops original stories for use in the classroom and makes archival NBC News stories, images, and primary source documents available on demand to teachers, students, and parents. NBC Learn partnered with Pearson to produce the myStory videos that support this program.

 Constitutional Rights Foundation is a nonprofit, nonpartisan, community-based organization focused on educating students about the importance of civic participation in a democratic society. The Constitutional Rights Foundation is the lead contributor to the development of the Civic Discussion Topic Inquiries for this program.

Pearson California United States History was developed especially for you and your students. The story of its creation began with a three-day Innovation Lab in which teachers, historians, students, and authors came together to imagine our ideal Social Studies teaching and learning experiences. We refined the plan with a series of teacher roundtables that shaped this new approach to ensure your students' mastery of content and skills. A dedicated team, made up of Pearson authors, content experts, and social studies teachers, worked to bring our collective vision into reality. Kathy Swan, Professor of Education and architect of the new College, Career, and Civic Life (C3) Framework, served as our expert advisor on curriculum and instruction.

Pearson would like to extend a special thank you to all of the teachers who helped guide the development of this program. We gratefully acknowledge your efforts to realize Next Generation Social Studies teaching and learning that will prepare American students for college, careers, and active citizenship.

[Program Advisors]

Campaign for the Civic Mission of Schools is a coalition of over 70 national civic learning, education, civic engagement, and business groups committed to improving the quality and quantity of civic learning in American schools. The Campaign served as an advisor on this program.

Buck Institute for Education is a nonprofit organization dedicated to helping teachers implement the effective use of Project-Based Learning in their classrooms. Buck Institute staff consulted on the Project-Based Learning Topic Inquiries for this program.

[California Academic Reviewers]

Robert Cleary
Temescal Canyon High School
Lake Elsinore, California

Nina Glassen
Capistrano Unified School District
San Juan Capistrano, California

Robert Hiles
Newport-Mesa Unified School District
Newport Beach, California

Sarah Nauss
Fremont Unified School District
Fremont, California

Michael Ochs
Chaminade High School
West Hills, California

Michelle Ritter
Temescal Canyon High School
Lake Elsinore, California

Gary Roldan
Orosi High School
Orosi, California

[Program Academic Consultants]

Barbara Brown
Director of Outreach
College of Arts and Sciences
African Studies Center
Boston University
Boston, Massachusetts

William Childs
Professor of History Emeritus
The Ohio State University
Columbus, Ohio

Jennifer Giglielmo
Associate Professor of History
Smith College
Northhampton, Massachusetts

Joanne Connor Green
Professor, Department Chair
Political Science
Texas Christian University
Fort Worth, Texas

Ramdas Lamb, Ph.D.
Associate Professor of Religion
University of Hawaii at Manoa
Honolulu, Hawaii

Huping Ling
Changjiang Scholar Chair Professor
Professor of History
Truman State University
Kirksville, Missouri

Jeffery Long, Ph.D.
Professor of Religion and Asian Studies
Elizabethtown College
Elizabethtown, Pennsylvania

Gordon Newby
Professor of Islamic, Jewish and
    Comparative Studies
Department of Middle Eastern and
    South Asian Studies
Emory University
Atlanta, Georgia

Mark Peterson
Associate Professor
Department of Asian and Near Eastern
    Languages
Brigham Young University
Provo, Utah

William Pitts
Professor, Department of Religion
Baylor University
Waco, Texas

Benjamin Ravid
Professor Emeritus of Jewish History
Department of Near Eastern and
    Judaic Studies
Brandeis University
Waltham, Massachusetts

Harpreet Singh
College Fellow
Department of South Asian Studies
Harvard University
Cambridge, Massachusetts

Christopher E. Smith, J.D., Ph.D.
Professor
Michigan State University
MSU School of Criminal Justice
East Lansing, Michigan

John Voll
Professor of Islamic History
Georgetown University
Washington, D.C.

Michael R. Wolf
Associate Professor
Department of Political Science
Indiana University-Purdue University
    Fort Wayne
Fort Wayne, Indiana

Social studies is more than dots on a map or dates on a timeline. It's where we've been and where we're going. It's stories from the past and our stories today. And in today's fast-paced, interconnected world, it's essential.

Welcome to California social studies!

Pearson's new California social studies program was created in collaboration with California educators, social studies experts, and students. The program is based on Pearson's CA History Social-Science Standards and Framework (CAHSS) Mastery. The System uses tested best practices, CAHSS expectations, technology, and a four-part framework—Connect, Investigate, Synthesize, and Demonstrate—to prepare students to be college-ready while mastering CAHSS.

The System includes:

- 100% coverage of the California State Standards.
- CAHSS-focused table of contents that will save teachers time and improve pacing. Higher-level content that gives support to access complex text, acquire core content knowledge, and tackle rigorous questions.
- Inquiry-focused Projects, Civic Discussions, and Document Analysis activities that develop content and skills mastery in preparation for real-world challenges.
- Digital content on Pearson Realize that is dynamic, flexible, and uses the power of technology to bring social studies to life.

» **Go online to learn more and see the program overview video.**

Connect
Make meaning personal

Demonstrate
Show understanding

Investigate
Acquire knowledge and skills

Assess CAHSS Mastery

Synthesize
Practice knowledge and skills

PEARSON
realize™

The digital course on Realize!

The program's digital course on Realize puts rich and engaging content, embedded assessments with instant data, and flexible tools at your fingertips.

Connect: Make Meaning Personal

CONNECT! Begin the Pearson CAHSS Mastery System by engaging in the topic story and connecting it to your own life.

CAHSS Preview—Each Topic opens with CAHSS, allowing you to preview what you can expect to learn. California analysis skills are closely integrated within the content.

>> Instruction begins with an **Essential Question**. These thought-provoking questions introduce the Topic.

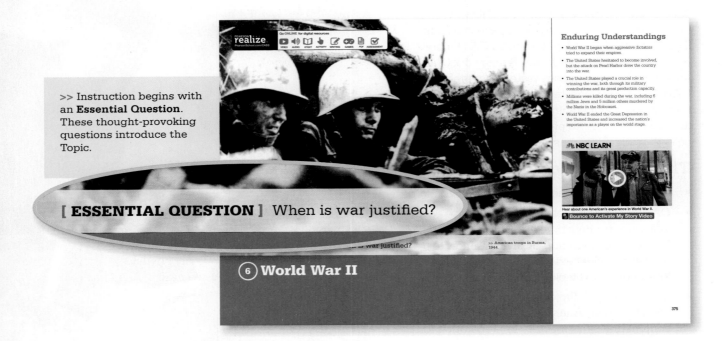

[**ESSENTIAL QUESTION**] When is war justified?

(6) World War II

>> American troops in Burma, 1944

Enduring Understandings

- World War II began when aggressive dictators tried to expand their empires.
- The United States hesitated to become involved, but the attack on Pearl Harbor drew the country into the war.
- The United States played a crucial role in winning the war, both through its military contributions and its great production capacity.
- Millions were killed during the war, including 6 million Jews and 5 million others murdered by the Nazis in the Holocaust.
- World War II ended the Great Depression in the United States and increased the nation's importance as a player on the world stage.

NBC LEARN

Hear about one American's experience in World War II.
Bounce to Activate My Story Video

375

NBC LEARN

Hear about one American's experience in World War II.

>> Developed in partnership with NBCLearn, the **My Story** videos help you connect to the Topic content by hearing the personal story of an individual whose life is related to the content you are about to learn.

INVESTIGATE! Step two of the CAHSS Mastery System allows you to investigate the topic story through a number of engaging features as you learn the content.

>> **Active Classroom Strategies** integrated in the daily lesson plans help to increase in-class participation, raise energy levels and attentiveness, all while engaging in the story. These 5-15 minute activities have you use what you have learned to draw, write, speak, and decide.

>> **Interactive Primary Source Galleries:** Use primary source image galleries throughout the lesson to see, analyze, and interact with images that tie to the topic story content.

>> Feel like you are a part of the story with **interactive 3-D models**.

>> Continue to investigate the topic story through **dynamic interactive maps**. Build map skills while covering the essential standards.

>> Learn content by reading narrative text online or in a printed Student Edition.

Synthesize: Practice Knowledge and Skills

SYNTHESIZE!

In step three of the Mastery System, pause to reflect on what you learn and revisit an essential question.

DEMONSTRATE! The final step of the CAHSS Mastery System is to demonstrate understanding of the California History-Social Science Standards and Framework.

PEARSON realize™

>> **The digital course on Realize!** The program's digital course on Realize puts engaging content, embedded assessments, instant data, and flexible tools at your fingertips.

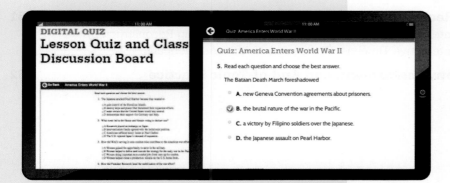

>> **CAHSS Assessment.** At the end of each lesson and topic, demonstrate understanding through Lesson Quizzes, Topic Tests, and Topic Inquiry performance assessments. The System provides remediation and enrichment recommendations based on your individual performance towards mastery.

>> **Class and Data** features on Realize make it easy for your teacher to use CAHSS mastery data to decide whether to re-teach or move ahead.

To activate your digital course interactivities download the free **Pearson BouncePages** app on your smartphone or tablet. Simply search for the Pearson BouncePages app in your mobile app store. The app is available for Android and IOS (iPhone®/iPad®).

Table of Contents

TOPIC 5

The Great Depression and the New Deal (1928–1941)

318

Content Standards

HSS 11.1.3
HSS 11.3.3
HSS 11.5.6
HSS 11.6
HSS 11.6.1
HSS 11.6.2
HSS 11.6.3
HSS 11.6.4
HSS 11.6.5
HSS 11.8.5
HSS 11.8.8
HSS 11.9.7
HSS 11.11.5
Analysis CST.4

Table of Contents

TOPIC 7   Postwar America (1945–1960)   460

🕐 **Content Standards**

HSS 11.2.3
HSS 11.4.6
HSS 11.7
HSS 11.7.8
HSS 11.8
HSS 11.8.1
HSS 11.8.2
HSS 11.8.3
HSS 11.8.4
HSS 11.8.5
HSS 11.8.7
HSS 11.8.8
HSS 11.9
HSS 11.9.2
HSS 11.9.3
HSS 11.9.4
HSS 11.9.7
HSS 11.10.1
HSS 11.11.2
HSS 11.11.3
HSS 11.11.7
Analysis CST.4

TOPIC 8   Civil Rights and Reform in the 1960s (1945–1968)   516

Content Standards

HSS 11.3
HSS 11.3.1
HSS 11.3.5
HSS 11.10
HSS 11.10.1
HSS 11.10.2
HSS 11.10.4
HSS 11.10.5
HSS 11.10.6
HSS 11.11.1
HSS 11.11.2
HSS 11.11.6
HSS 11.11.7
Analysis CST.3
Analysis CST.4

TOPIC 9

The Vietnam War Era (1954–1975)   **568**

WOODSTOCK
MUSIC & ART FAIR
presents
AN
AQUARIAN
EXPOSITION
in
WHITE LAKE, N.Y.

Table of Contents

Go online to PearsonSchool.com/CASS and use the texts, quizzes, interactivities, Interactive Reading Notepads, Flipped Videos, and other resources from this Topic to prepare for the Topic Test.

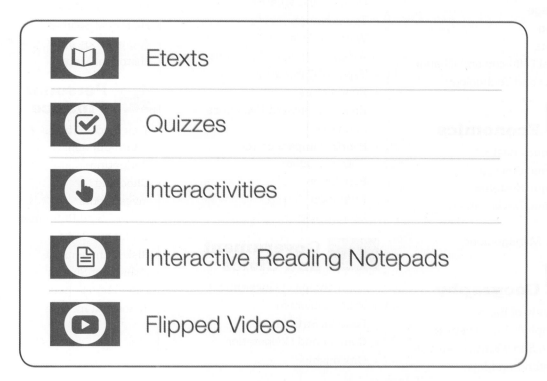

📖 Etexts

☑ Quizzes

👆 Interactivities

📄 Interactive Reading Notepads

▶ Flipped Videos

While online you can also check the progress you've made learning the topic and course content by viewing your grades, test scores, and assignment status.

Digital Resources

This course includes an online component that offers biographies, primary sources, maps, and other resources to expand your study of U.S. History and bring the content to life.

 Core Concepts

 Culture

- What Is Culture?
- Families and Societies
- Language
- Religion
- The Arts
- Cultural Diffusion and Change
- Science and Technology

 Economics

- Economics Basics
- Economic Process
- Economic Systems
- Economic Development
- Trade
- Money Management

 Geography

- The Study of Earth
- Geography's Five Themes
- Ways to Show Earth's Surface
- Understanding Maps

- Earth in Space
- Time and Earth's Rotation
- Forces on Earth's Surface
- Forces Inside Earth
- Climate and Weather
- Temperature
- Water and Climate
- Air Circulation and Precipitation
- Types of Climate
- Ecosystems
- Environment and Resources
- Land Use
- People's Impact on the Environment
- Population
- Migration
- Urbanization

 Government and Civics

- Foundations of Government
- Political Systems
- Political Structures
- Conflict and Cooperation
- Citizenship

 History

- How Do Historians Study History?
- Measuring Time
- Historical Sources
- Archaeology and Other Sources
- Historical Maps

 Personal Finance

- Your Fiscal Fitness: An Introduction
- Budgeting
- Checking
- Investments
- Savings and Retirement
- Credit and Debt
- Risk Management
- Consumer Smarts
- After High School
- Taxes and Income

Landmark Supreme Court Cases

- *Korematsu* v. *United States*
- *Marbury* v. *Madison*
- *McCulloch* v. *Maryland*
- *Gibbons* v. *Ogden*
- *Worcester* v. *Georgia*
- *Dred Scott* v. *Sandford*
- *Plessy* v. *Ferguson*
- *Schenck* v. *United States*
- *Brown* v. *Board of Education*
- *Engel* v. *Vitale*

- *Sweatt* v. *Painter*
- *Mapp* v. *Ohio*
- *Hernandez* v. *Texas*
- *Gideon* v. *Wainwright*
- *Wisconsin* v. *Yoder*
- *Miranda* v. *Arizona*
- *White* v. *Regester*
- *Tinker* v. *Des Moines School District*
- *Roe* v. *Wade*

- *Baker* v. *Carr*
- *Grutter* v. *Bollinger*
- *Edgewood* v. *Kirby*
- *Texas* v. *Johnson*
- *National Federation of Independent Businesses et al.* v. *Sebelius et al.*
- *Mendez* v. *Westminster* and *Delgado* v. *Bastrop*

Interactive Primary Sources

- Code of Hammurabi
- Psalm 23
- The Republic, Plato
- Politics, Aristotle
- Edicts, Asoka
- Analects, Confucius
- De re publica, Cicero
- First Letter to the Corinthians, Paul
- The Quran
- The Magna Carta
- Travels, Ibn Battuta
- The Prince, Niccolò Machiavelli
- The Destruction of the Indies, Bartolomé de Las Casas
- Mayflower Compact
- English Petition of Right
- English Bill of Rights
- Two Treatises of Government, John Locke
- The Spirit of Laws, Baron de Montesquieu
- The Social Contract, Jean-Jacques Rousseau
- The Interesting Narrative of the Life of Olaudah Equiano
- "Give Me Liberty or Give Me Death," Patrick Henry
- "Remember the Ladies," Abigail Adams
- Common Sense, Thomas Paine
- Declaration of Independence
- Virginia Declaration of Rights
- Virginia Statute for Religious Freedom, Thomas Jefferson
- "To His Excellency, General Washington," Phillis Wheatley
- Articles of Confederation
- Anti-Federalist Papers
- The Federalist No. 10, James Madison
- The Federalist No. 39, James Madison
- The Federalist No. 51
- The Federalist No. 78, Alexander Hamilton
- Northwest Ordinance
- Iroquois Constitution
- Declaration of the Rights of Man and the Citizen
- Farewell Address, George Washington
- Mexican Federal Constitution of 1824
- State Colonization Law of 1825
- Law of April 6, 1830
- Debate Over Nullification, Webster and Calhoun
- Turtle Bayou Resolutions
- Democracy in America, Alexis de Tocqueville
- 1836 Victory or Death Letter from the Alamo, Travis
- Texas Declaration of Independence
- Declaration of Sentiments and Resolutions
- "Ain't I a Woman?," Sojourner Truth
- Uncle Tom's Cabin, Harriet Beecher Stowe
- "A House Divided," Abraham Lincoln
- First Inaugural Address, Abraham Lincoln
- Declaration of Causes: February 2, 1861
- Emancipation Proclamation, Abraham Lincoln
- Gettysburg Address, Abraham Lincoln
- Second Inaugural Address, Abraham Lincoln
- "I Will Fight No More Forever," Chief Joseph
- How the Other Half Lives, Jacob Riis
- The Pledge of Allegiance
- Preamble to the Platform of the Populist Party
- Atlanta Exposition Address, Booker T. Washington
- "The White Man's Burden," Rudyard Kipling
- The Jungle, Upton Sinclair
- Hind Swaraj, Mohandas Gandhi
- The Fourteen Points, Woodrow Wilson
- Two Poems, Langston Hughes
- Four Freedoms, Franklin D. Roosevelt
- Anne Frank: The Diary of a Young Girl, Anne Frank
- Charter of the United Nations
- Universal Declaration of Human Rights
- Autobiography, Kwame Nkrumah
- Inaugural Address, John F. Kennedy
- Silent Spring, Rachel Carson
- "I Have a Dream," Martin Luther King, Jr.
- "Letter From Birmingham Jail," Martin Luther King, Jr.
- State of the Union address, Lyndon Johnson
- State of the Union address, Gerald Ford
- "Tear Down This Wall," Ronald Reagan
- "Freedom From Fear," Aung San Suu Kyi
- "Glory and Hope," Nelson Mandela
- State of the Union address, Bill Clinton
- State of the Union address, George W. Bush

Biographies

- Abigail Adams
- John Adams
- John Quincy Adams
- Samuel Adams
- James Armistead
- Crispus Attucks
- Moses Austin
- Stephen F. Austin
- James A. Baker III
- Emily Greene Balch
- William Blackstone
- Simón Bolívar
- Napoleon Bonaparte
- Chief Bowles
- Omar Bradley
- John C. Calhoun
- César Chávez
- Wentworth Cheswell
- George Childress
- Winston Churchill
- Henry Clay
- Bill Clinton
- Jefferson Davis
- Martin De León
- Green DeWitt
- Dwight Eisenhower
- James Fannin
- James L. Farmer, Jr.
- Benjamin Franklin
- Milton Friedman
- Betty Friedan
- Bernardo de Gálvez
- Hector P. Garcia
- John Nance Garner
- King George III
- William Gladstone
- Henry B. González
- Raul A. Gonzalez, Jr.
- Mikhail Gorbachev
- William Goyens
- Ulysses S. Grant

- José Gutiérrez de Lara
- Alexander Hamilton
- Hammurabi
- Warren Harding
- Václav Havel
- Friedrich Hayek
- Jack Coffee Hays
- Patrick Henry
- Adolf Hitler
- Oveta Culp Hobby
- James Hogg
- Sam Houston
- Kay Bailey Hutchison
- Andrew Jackson
- John Jay
- Thomas Jefferson
- Lyndon B. Johnson
- Anson Jones
- Barbara Jordan
- Justinian
- John F. Kennedy
- John Maynard Keynes
- Martin Luther King, Jr.
- Marquis de Lafayette
- Mirabeau B. Lamar
- Robert E. Lee
- Abraham Lincoln
- John Locke
- Niccolò Machiavelli
- James Madison
- John Marshall
- George Marshall
- Karl Marx
- George Mason
- Mary Maverick
- Jane McCallum
- Joseph McCarthy
- James Monroe
- Charles de Montesquieu
- Dwight L. Moody
- Edwin W. Moore

- Moses
- Benito Mussolini
- José Antonio Navarro
- Chester A. Nimitz
- Richard M. Nixon
- Barack Obama
- Sandra Day O'Connor
- Thomas Paine
- Quanah Parker
- Rosa Parks
- George Patton
- John J. Pershing
- John Paul II
- Sam Rayburn
- Ronald Reagan
- Hiram Rhodes Revels
- Franklin D. Roosevelt
- Theodore Roosevelt
- Lawrence Sullivan Ross
- Haym Soloman
- Antonio Lopez de Santa Anna
- Phyllis Schlafly
- Erasmo Seguín
- Juan N. Seguín
- Roger Sherman
- Adam Smith
- Alexander Solzhenitsyn
- Joseph Stalin
- William Graham Sumner
- Billy Sunday
- Raymond L. Telles
- Margaret Thatcher
- Alexis de Tocqueville
- Hideki Tojo
- William B. Travis
- Harry Truman
- Lech Walesa
- Mercy Otis Warren
- George Washington

- Daniel Webster
- Lulu Belle Madison White
- William Wilberforce
- James Wilson
- Woodrow Wilson
- Lorenzo de Zavala
- Mao Zedong

21st Century Skills

- Identify Main Ideas and Details
- Set a Purpose for Reading
- Use Context Clues
- Analyze Cause and Effect
- Categorize
- Compare and Contrast
- Draw Conclusions
- Draw Inferences
- Generalize
- Make Decisions
- Make Predictions
- Sequence
- Solve Problems
- Summarize
- Analyze Media Content
- Analyze Primary and Secondary Sources
- Compare Viewpoints
- Distinguish Between Fact and Opinion
- Identify Bias
- Analyze Data and Models

- Analyze Images
- Analyze Political Cartoons
- Create Charts and Maps
- Create Databases
- Read Charts, Graphs, and Tables
- Read Physical Maps
- Read Political Maps
- Read Special-Purpose Maps
- Use Parts of a Map
- Ask Questions
- Avoid Plagiarism
- Create a Research Hypothesis
- Evaluate Web Sites
- Identify Evidence
- Identify Trends
- Interpret Sources
- Search for Information on the Internet
- Synthesize
- Take Effective Notes
- Develop a Clear Thesis
- Organize Your Ideas

- Support Ideas With Evidence
- Evaluate Existing Arguments
- Consider & Counter Opposing Arguments
- Give an Effective Presentation
- Participate in a Discussion or Debate
- Publish Your Work
- Write a Journal Entry
- Write an Essay
- Share Responsibility
- Compromise
- Develop Cultural Awareness
- Generate New Ideas
- Innovate
- Make a Difference
- Work in Teams
- Being an Informed Citizen
- Paying Taxes
- Political Participation
- Serving on a Jury
- Voting

Atlas

- United States: Political
- United States: Physical
- California: Political
- California: Physical
- World Political
- World Physical
- World Climate
- World Ecosystems
- World Population Density
- World Land Use
- North Africa and Southwest Asia: Political
- North Africa and Southwest Asia: Physical
- Sub-Saharan Africa: Political
- Sub-Saharan Africa: Physical
- South Asia: Political
- South Asia: Physical

- East Asia: Political
- East Asia: Physical
- Southeast Asia: Political
- Southeast Asia: Physical
- Europe: Political
- Europe: Physical
- Russia, Central Asia, and the Caucasus: Political
- Russia, Central Asia, and the Caucasus: Physical
- North America: Political
- North America: Physical
- Central America and the Caribbean: Political
- Central America and the Caribbean: Physical
- South America: Political
- South America: Physical
- Australia and the Pacific: Political
- Australia and the Pacific: Physical

United States History and Geography: Continuity and Change in the Twentieth Century

11.1 Students analyze the significant events in the founding of the nation and its attempts to realize the philosophy of government described in the Declaration of Independence.

11.1.1 Describe the Enlightenment and the rise of democratic ideas as the context in which the nation was founded.

11.1.2 Analyze the ideological origins of the American Revolution, the Founding Fathers' philosophy of divinely bestowed unalienable natural rights, the debates on the drafting and ratification of the Constitution, and the addition of the Bill of Rights.

11.1.3 Understand the history of the Constitution after 1787 with emphasis on federal versus state authority and growing democratization.

11.1.4 Examine the effects of the Civil War and Reconstruction and of the industrial revolution, including demographic shifts and the emergence in the late nineteenth century of the United States as a world power.

11.2 Students analyze the relationship among the rise of industrialization, large-scale rural-to-urban migration, and massive immigration from Southern and Eastern Europe.

11.2.1 Know the effects of industrialization on living and working conditions, including the portrayal of working conditions and food safety in Upton Sinclair's *The Jungle*.

11.2.2 Describe the changing landscape, including the growth of cities linked by industry and trade, and the development of cities divided according to race, ethnicity, and class.

11.2.3 Trace the effect of the Americanization movement.

11.2.4 Analyze the effect of urban political machines and responses to them by immigrants and middle-class reformers.

11.2.5 Discuss corporate mergers that produced trusts and cartels and the economic and political policies of industrial leaders.

11.2.6 Trace the economic development of the United States and its emergence as a major industrial power, including its gains from trade and the advantages of its physical geography.

11.2.7 Analyze the similarities and differences between the ideologies of Social Darwinism and Social Gospel (e.g., using biographies of William Graham Sumner, Billy Sunday, Dwight L. Moody).

11.2.8 Examine the effect of political programs and activities of Populists.

11.2.9 Understand the effect of political programs and activities of the Progressives (e.g., federal regulation of railroad transport, Children's Bureau, the Sixteenth Amendment, Theodore Roosevelt, Hiram Johnson).

11.3 Students analyze the role religion played in the founding of America, its lasting moral, social, and political impacts, and issues regarding religious liberty.

11.3.1 Describe the contributions of various religious groups to American civic principles and social reform movements (e.g., civil and human rights, individual responsibility and the work ethic, antimonarchy and self-rule, worker protection, family-centered communities).

11.3.2 Analyze the great religious revivals and the leaders involved in them, including the First Great Awakening, the Second Great Awakening, the Civil War revivals, the Social Gospel Movement, the rise of Christian liberal theology in the nineteenth century, the impact of the Second Vatican Council, and the rise of Christian fundamentalism in current times.

11.3.3 Cite incidences of religious intolerance in the United States (e.g., persecution of Mormons, anti-Catholic sentiment, anti-Semitism).

11.3.4 Discuss the expanding religious pluralism in the United States and California that resulted from large-scale immigration in the twentieth century.

11.3.5 Describe the principles of religious liberty found in the Establishment and Free Exercise clauses of the First Amendment, including the debate on the issue of separation of church and state.

11.4 Students trace the rise of the United States to its role as a world power in the twentieth century.

11.4.1 List the purpose and the effects of the Open Door policy.

11.4.2 Describe the Spanish-American War and U.S. expansion in the South Pacific.

11.4.3 Discuss America's role in the Panama Revolution and the building of the Panama Canal.

11.4.4 Explain Theodore Roosevelt's Big Stick diplomacy, William Taft's Dollar Diplomacy, and Woodrow Wilson's Moral Diplomacy, drawing on relevant speeches.

11.4.5 Analyze the political, economic, and social ramifications of World War I on the home front.

11.4.6 Trace the declining role of Great Britain and the expanding role of the United States in world affairs after World War II.

11.5 Students analyze the major political, social, economic, technological, and cultural developments of the 1920s.

11.5.1 Discuss the policies of Presidents Warren Harding, Calvin Coolidge, and Herbert Hoover.

11.5.2 Analyze the international and domestic events, interests, and philosophies that prompted attacks on civil liberties, including the Palmer Raids, Marcus Garvey's "back-to-Africa" movement, the Ku Klux Klan, and immigration quotas and the responses of organizations such as the American Civil Liberties Union, the National Association for the Advancement of Colored People, and the Anti-Defamation League to those attacks.

11.5.3 Examine the passage of the Eighteenth Amendment to the Constitution and the Volstead Act (Prohibition).

11.5.4 Analyze the passage of the Nineteenth Amendment and the changing role of women in society.

11.5.5 Describe the Harlem Renaissance and new trends in literature, music, and art, with special attention to the work of writers (e.g., Zora Neale Hurston, Langston Hughes).

11.5.6 Trace the growth and effects of radio and movies and their role in the worldwide diffusion of popular culture.

11.5.7 Discuss the rise of mass production techniques, the growth of cities, the impact of new technologies (e.g., the automobile, electricity), and the resulting prosperity and effect on the American landscape.

11.6 Students analyze the different explanations for the Great Depression and how the New Deal fundamentally changed the role of the federal government.

11.6.1 Describe the monetary issues of the late nineteenth and early twentieth centuries that gave rise to the establishment of the Federal Reserve and the weaknesses in key sectors of the economy in the late 1920s.

11.6.2 Understand the explanations of the principal causes of the Great Depression and the steps taken by the Federal Reserve, Congress, and Presidents Herbert Hoover and Franklin Delano Roosevelt to combat the economic crisis.

11.6.3 Discuss the human toll of the Depression, natural disasters, and unwise agricultural practices and their effects on the depopulation of rural regions and on political movements of the left and right, with particular attention to the Dust Bowl refugees and their social and economic impacts in California.

11.6.4 Analyze the effects of and the controversies arising from New Deal economic policies and the expanded role of the federal government in society and the economy since the 1930s (e.g., Works Progress Administration, Social Security, National Labor Relations Board, farm programs, regional development policies, and energy development projects such as the Tennessee Valley Authority, California Central Valley Project, and Bonneville Dam).

11.6.5 Trace the advances and retreats of organized labor, from the creation of the American Federation of Labor and the Congress of Industrial Organizations to current issues of a postindustrial, multinational economy, including the United Farm Workers in California.

11.7 Students analyze America's participation in World War II.

11.7.1 Examine the origins of American involvement in the war, with an emphasis on the events that precipitated the attack on Pearl Harbor.

11.7.2 Explain U.S. and Allied wartime strategy, including the major battles of Midway, Normandy, Iwo Jima, Okinawa, and the Battle of the Bulge.

11.7.3 Identify the roles and sacrifices of individual American soldiers, as well as the unique contributions of the special fighting forces (e.g., the Tuskegee Airmen, the 442nd Regimental Combat team, the Navajo Code Talkers).

11.7.4 Analyze Roosevelt's foreign policy during World War II (e.g., Four Freedoms speech).

11.7.5 Discuss the constitutional issues and impact of events on the U.S. home front, including the internment of Japanese Americans (e.g., *Fred Korematsu* v. *United States of America*) and the restrictions on German and Italian resident aliens; the response of the administration to Hitler's atrocities against Jews and other groups; the roles of women in military production; and the roles and growing political demands of African Americans.

11.7.6 Describe major developments in aviation, weaponry, communication, and medicine and the war's impact on the location of American industry and use of resources.

11.7.7 Discuss the decision to drop atomic bombs and the consequences of the decision (Hiroshima and Nagasaki).

11.7.8 Analyze the effect of massive aid given to Western Europe under the Marshall Plan to rebuild itself after the war and the importance of a rebuilt Europe to the U.S. economy.

11.8 Students analyze the economic boom and social transformation of post-World War II America.

11.8.1 Trace the growth of service sector, white collar, and professional sector jobs in business and government.

11.8.2 Describe the significance of Mexican immigration and its relationship to the agricultural economy, especially in California.

11.8.3 Examine Truman's labor policy and congressional reaction to it.

11.8.4 Analyze new federal government spending on defense, welfare, interest on the national debt, and federal and state spending on education, including the California Master Plan.

11.8.5 Describe the increased powers of the presidency in response to the Great Depression, World War II, and the Cold War.

11.8.6 Discuss the diverse environmental regions of North America, their relationship to local economies, and the origins and prospects of environmental problems in those regions.

11.8.7 Describe the effects on society and the economy of technological developments since 1945, including the computer revolution, changes in communication, advances in medicine, and improvements in agricultural technology.

11.8.8 Discuss forms of popular culture, with emphasis on their origins and geographic diffusion (e.g., jazz and other forms of popular music, professional sports, architectural and artistic styles).

11.9 Students analyze U.S. foreign policy since World War II.

11.9.1 Discuss the establishment of the United Nations and International Declaration of Human Rights, International Monetary Fund, World Bank, and General Agreement on Tariffs and Trade (GATT) and their importance in shaping modern Europe and maintaining peace and international order.

11.9.2 Understand the role of military alliances, including NATO and SEATO, in deterring communist aggression and maintaining security during the Cold War.

11.9.3 Trace the origins and geopolitical consequences (foreign and domestic) of the Cold War and containment policy, including the following:

    o The era of McCarthyism, instances of domestic Communism (e.g., Alger Hiss) and blacklisting

    o The Truman Doctrine

    o The Berlin Blockade

    o The Korean War

    o The Bay of Pigs invasion and the Cuban Missile Crisis

    o Atomic testing in the American West, the "mutual assured destruction" doctrine, and disarmament policies

    o The Vietnam War

    o Latin American policy

11.9.4 List the effects of foreign policy on domestic policies and vice versa (e.g., protests during the war in Vietnam, the "nuclear freeze" movement).

11.9.5 Analyze the role of the Reagan administration and other factors in the victory of the West in the Cold War.

11.9.6 Describe U.S. Middle East policy and its strategic, political, and economic interests, including those related to the Gulf War.

11.9.7 Examine relations between the United States and Mexico in the twentieth century, including key economic, political, immigration, and environmental issues.

11.10 **Students analyze the development of federal civil rights and voting rights.**

11.10.1 Explain how demands of African Americans helped produce a stimulus for civil rights, including President Roosevelt's ban on racial discrimination in defense industries in 1941, and how African Americans' service in World War II produced a stimulus for President Truman's decision to end segregation in the armed forces in 1948.

11.10.2 Examine and analyze the key events, policies, and court cases in the evolution of civil rights, including *Dred Scott* v. *Sandford*, *Plessy* v. *Ferguson*, *Brown* v. *Board of Education*, *Regents of the University of California* v. *Bakke*, and California Proposition 209.

11.10.3 Describe the collaboration on legal strategy between African American and white civil rights lawyers to end racial segregation in higher education.

11.10.4 Examine the roles of civil rights advocates (e.g., A. Philip Randolph, Martin Luther King, Jr., Malcolm X, Thurgood Marshall, James Farmer, Rosa Parks), including the significance of Martin Luther King, Jr.'s "Letter from Birmingham Jail" and "I Have a Dream" speech.

11.10.5 Discuss the diffusion of the civil rights movement of African Americans from the churches of the rural South and the urban North, including the resistance to racial desegregation in Little Rock and Birmingham, and how the advances influenced the agendas, strategies, and effectiveness of the quests of American Indians, Asian Americans, and Hispanic Americans for civil rights and equal opportunities.

11.10.6 Analyze the passage and effects of civil rights and voting rights legislation (e.g., 1964 Civil Rights Act, Voting Rights Act of 1965) and the Twenty-Fourth Amendment, with an emphasis on equality of access to education and to the political process.

11.10.7 Analyze the women's rights movement from the era of Elizabeth Stanton and Susan Anthony and the passage of the Nineteenth Amendment to the movement launched in the 1960s, including differing perspectives on the roles of women.

11.11 Students analyze the major social problems and domestic policy issues in contemporary American society.

11.11.1 Discuss the reasons for the nation's changing immigration policy, with emphasis on how the Immigration Act of 1965 and successor acts have transformed American society.

11.11.2 Discuss the significant domestic policy speeches of Truman, Eisenhower, Kennedy, Johnson, Nixon, Carter, Reagan, Bush, and Clinton (e.g., with regard to education, civil rights, economic policy, environmental policy).

11.11.3 Describe the changing roles of women in society as reflected in the entry of more women into the labor force and the changing family structure.

11.11.4 Explain the constitutional crisis originating from the Watergate scandal.

11.11.5 Trace the impact of, need for, and controversies associated with environmental conservation, expansion of the national park system, and the development of environmental protection laws, with particular attention to the interaction between environmental protection advocates and property rights advocates.

11.11.6 Analyze the persistence of poverty and how different analyses of this issue influence welfare reform, health insurance reform, and other social policies.

11.11.7 Explain how the federal, state, and local governments have responded to demographic and social changes such as population shifts to the suburbs, racial concentrations in the cities, Frostbelt-to-Sunbelt migration, international migration, decline of family farms, increases in out-of-wedlock births, and drug abuse.

Historical and Social Sciences Analysis Skills

Chronological and Spatial Thinking

CST.1 Students compare the present with the past, evaluating the consequences of past events and decisions and determining the lessons that were learned.

CST.2 Students analyze how change happens at different rates at different times; understand that some aspects can change while others remain the same; and understand that change is complicated and affects not only technology and politics but also values and beliefs.

CST.3 Students use a variety of maps and documents to interpret human movement, including major patterns of domestic and international migration, changing environmental preferences and settlement patterns, the frictions that develop between population groups, and the diffusion of ideas, technological innovations, and goods.

CST.4 Students relate current events to the physical and human characteristics of places and regions.

Historical Research, Evidence, and Point of View

HRE.1 Students distinguish valid arguments from fallacious arguments in historical interpretations.

HRE.2 Students identify bias and prejudice in historical interpretations.

HRE.3 Students evaluate major debates among historians concerning alternative interpretations of the past, including an analysis of authors' use of evidence and the distinctions between sound generalizations and misleading oversimplifications.

HRE.4 Students construct and test hypotheses; collect, evaluate, and employ information from multiple primary and secondary sources; and apply it in oral and written presentations.

Historical Interpretation

HI.1 Students show the connections, causal and otherwise, between particular historical events and larger social, economic, and political trends and developments.

HI.2 Students recognize the complexity of historical causes and effects, including the limitations on determining cause and effect.

HI.3 Students interpret past events and issues within the context in which an event unfolded rather than solely in terms of present-day norms and values.

HI.4 Students understand the meaning, implication, and impact of historical events and recognize that events could have taken other directions.

HI.5 Students analyze human modifications of landscapes and examine the resulting environmental policy issues.

HI.6 Students conduct cost-benefit analyses and apply basic economic indicators to analyze the aggregate economic behavior of the U.S. economy.

COURSE INTRODUCTION

Questions from the History–Social Science Framework for California Public Schools to guide your study of United States History

Over its history as a nation, the United States has remained a representative democracy with a federalist government and a diverse population. In modern times, the role of the federal government has evolved, and the demographics of the country's citizens have been constantly shifting. Studying changes and trends in the country's history gives us a better idea of what it means to be an American today.

GUIDING QUESTION

How did the federal government grow between the late nineteenth and twenty-first centuries?

The United States set up its government based on the concept of federalism, a system that divides power between the national and state governments. For much of the country's early history, the federal, or national, government played a smaller role, leaving the states greater power. In modern times, however, the power of the federal government has grown.

Industry and Regulations

>> In the late 1800s, the nature of American business changed dramatically with the rise of corporations, businesses owned by a number of people. The people in charge of corporations used many strategies to increase profit, such as consolidating firms in order to gain a monopoly, or complete control of a market or service. Their business practices allowed a few people to gain incredible wealth but hurt smaller businesses and consumers. Traditionally, the federal government had operated under a mostly laissez-faire policy, in which government stays out of business dealings. The new business practices ushered in a new era, however, as the government stepped in with regulations to manage corporate growth.

See Topic 1, Lessons 1 and 2, to learn more about the shift in federal government's role in business dealings.

The New Deal

>> The Great Depression, which lasted from 1929 to 1941, was the largest economic downturn in modern times. With banks and businesses failing throughout the country, Americans of all classes suffered. President Franklin D. Roosevelt enacted the New Deal, a plan for fighting the crisis with federal resources. The New Deal increased the range and power of the federal government, and many of the programs that were introduced at the time, such as Social Security, have endured to this day.

See Topic 5 to learn more about the federal government's actions during the New Deal.

New Federalism

>> In 1968, Richard M. Nixon won the presidency on a campaign promise of "new federalism." He believed that the national government needed to provide the resources for state governments to function. Though this helped return power to the states, Nixon also increased the role of the federal government, forming many new agencies. Some of the agencies he started, such as the Occupational Safety and Health Administration (OSHA) and the Drug Enforcement Administration (DEA) have a great deal of power today.

See Topic 10, Lesson 5, to learn more about Nixon's role in increasing the size of government.

CONNECTING TO THE GUIDING QUESTION

1. How did the rise of corporations lead to an increase in the federal government's power?
2. Why did Roosevelt feel that the power of federal government needed to be increased?
3. What is the legacy of Nixon's "new federalism" on today's government?

GUIDING QUESTION

What does it mean to be an American in modern times?

The civic values of the United States are expressed in its founding documents—the Declaration of Independence and the U.S. Constitution. Ever since Thomas Jefferson, in the Declaration of Independence, championed values of equality and the human right to "life, liberty, and the pursuit of happiness," America's civic values have remained an important part of every citizen's identity. The United States is a very different nation than it was in Jefferson's time, but these values continue to define what it means to be an American. Although we live in a time of greater diversity and stronger global connections, Americans still adhere to the civic values first defined by the country's founders.

SAVE FREEDOM OF SPEECH

BUY WAR BONDS

Civic Values

>> Through centuries of change, the basic civic values outlined by the country's founders have endured, providing a firm foundation for an American identity. In modern times, what it means to be an American remains firmly linked to the ongoing interpretation of the Constitution, as voting rights have been extended to every citizen, regardless of race or gender. The Constitution continues to provide guidance, especially during times of worldwide instability, when Democracy itself seems under threat. As World War II raged, President Franklin D. Roosevelt gave a speech about the "four freedoms" that are fundamental to American democracy and that people everywhere should have the right to enjoy: freedom of speech, freedom of worship, freedom from want, and freedom from fear. Today, as we live through another time of instability and rapid technological change, Americans continue to find strength and civic identity in the political principles that are embodied in the Constitution.

See Topic 6, Lesson 2, to read Roosevelt's "Four Freedoms" speech, and Topic 12, Lesson 4, to learn about the civic values that form the basis of American identity.

Diversity

>> From its founding, the United States has always been a nation of immigrants. Except for American Indians, every ethnic group in the country immigrated here relatively recently. Immigration policies over the years have changed the demographics of the country, and the United States today is a place of great diversity. People of different ethnic, racial, and religious backgrounds live side by side, while in recent decades members of the LGBT community have become more active politically. Although differences between groups often cause conflict, Americans benefit from the variety of viewpoints and traditions brought together in the country.

See Topic 12, Lesson 4, to learn more about diversity in America today.

Global Connections

>> Technology has allowed global connections in the twenty-first century that earlier generations could not have imagined. Instant communication and rapid travel have decreased the distance between nations. The United States economy has followed suit, as it is increasingly linked to the fortunes of the rest of the world. Globalization, the process by which national economies, politics, cultures, and societies mix with those of other nations around the world, affects the lives of all Americans today. Although people disagree about the extent to which this process benefits or harms individual societies, globalization plays a central role in most aspects of our lives, from our consumer habits to our political policies.

See Topic 11, Lesson 5, and Topic 12, Lesson 1, to learn about America's role in the global economy and the effects of technology on globalization.

CONNECTING TO THE GUIDING QUESTION

1. Assess the extent to which the United States is a diverse nation based on the three topics presented.

2. Summarize the role of globalization in the United States today.

3. Apply the "four freedoms" to your life today. What actions do you take on a daily basis and why?

GUIDING QUESTION

How did the United States become a superpower?

In its short history as a nation, the United States quickly grew from a loose federation of former colonies to the world's preeminent superpower. A superpower is a nation that dominates world politics and economies and whose actions shape the future of the world. During the United States' time as a superpower, only its Cold War rival the Soviet Union came close to matching America's influence.

The United States Becomes a World Power

>> The United States first emerged as a world power at the end of the nineteenth century. In the Spanish-American War of 1898, the United States defeated the Spanish on two fronts: Cuba and the Philippines. With victory came American expansion into new territories, as the United States took control of the Philippines and the island of Guam and intervened in the affairs of Cuba and Puerto Rico. The Spanish-American War signaled the beginning of America's role as a world power. The country's foreign policy shifted, with intervention in the affairs of East Asian and Latin American countries.

See Topic 3, Lessons 6 and 7, to learn more about the emergence of the United States as a world power.

UNITED KINGDOM

London

Thames River

Dover

Portsmouth   Shoreham

Strait of Dover

Calais

BELGIUM

Weymouth

Torquay

50°N

52°N

2°E

English Channel

Cherbourg

Seine River

① ② ③ ④ ⑤

NORMANDY

FRANCE

0   50 mi
0   50 km
Albers Conic
Equal-Area Projection

4°W   2°W

KEY
→ American
→ British
→ Canadian

Landing Beaches
❶ Utah
❷ Omaha
❸ Gold
❹ Juno
❺ Sword

Alliances and Conflict

>> At the start of both World War I and World War II, the United States tried to stay isolated, but events eventually pulled it into the conflict. In both cases, the United States, with its massive military power, played a major role in deciding the course of war. The world wars were conflicts between alliances, and the United States allied itself with the United Kingdom and the Soviet Union. With its mainland located far from the battlefronts, the United States suffered much less physical damage. Because of this, the nation emerged from World War II better able to assist with economic recovery in devastated parts of the world.

See Topics 4 and 6 to learn more about the United States' role in the two world wars.

Cold War

>> After World War II, former allies the United States and the Soviet Union became fierce rivals. The 46-year struggle between the two was known as the Cold War because the two nations never fought each other directly in a "hot" war. Tension between the two powers led to conflicts all over the world however, prompting intervention in countries such as Cuba, Vietnam, and Afghanistan. To protect themselves, the rival superpowers increased their supplies of nuclear weapons in an arms race.

See Topic 7 to learn more about the start of the Cold War.

CONNECTING TO THE GUIDING QUESTION

1. What event signaled the emergence of the United States as a world power?

2. How did America use its power during and after the two world wars?

3. Summarize three key ideas about the United States as a superpower.

GUIDING QUESTION

How did the United States' population become more diverse over the twentieth century?

From the nation's founding, the United States has been a country of great ethnic and religious diversity. Different immigration policies over the years have changed the racial and ethnic demographics of the population, creating an even more diverse nation. Over the course of the twentieth and into the twenty-first century, Americans have become more conscious of this diversity as minorities have campaigned for civil rights and greater representation in political life and the media.

Minorities Become More Visible

>> Although the United States has always had a racially diverse population, until the 1960s, minorities were generally excluded from participation in government and society. Segregation in housing, education, and employment kept African Americans and other minorities from integration with the larger population, while media representation of ethnic and sexual minorities reinforced distorted stereotypes and assumptions. However, in the 1960s, this situation began to change dramatically as the civil rights movement drew attention to the diversity of American society.

See Topic 8 Lessons 1–3 and Topic 10, Lesson 3 to learn more about how the struggle for civil rights drew attention to issues of justice and equality in a diverse society.

Immigration in California

>> The quota system of the 1920s, which limited immigration based on ethnicity, did not apply to Mexico, and many Mexican immigrants came to the American Southwest and California as farm workers. Immigration (both legal and illegal) of Spanish speakers to California boomed in the 1970s, and by 2000, more than one third of California's population were Latinos. The majority of Asian immigrants to the United States have also settled in California. People with family roots in Latin America and Asia have contributed to California's diverse culture.

See Topic 12, Lesson 4, to learn more about Latin American and Asian immigration to California.

Changing Demographics

>> As the United States moved into the twenty-first century, immigration restrictions further decreased with policies such as the Immigration Act of 1990. As a result, immigrants now account for 10 percent of the nation's population. This diversity has led to changes such as a rise in bilingual education. As the racial, ethnic, and religious demographics of the United States have changed, the country has also seen increased visibility of the LGBT (Lesbian, Gay, Bisexual, and Transgender) community. Expanding and protecting the rights of all Americans has allowed more people to live freely and contribute their viewpoints to society.

See Topic 12, Lesson 4, to learn more about recent changes to American society.

CONNECTING TO THE GUIDING QUESTION

1. How have quotas affected the demographics of the United States?
2. Summarize how California is shaped by immigration.
3. How is diversity reflected in your community? Make a connection to history.

> "We hold these Truths to be self-evident, that all Men are created equal, that they are endowed by their Creator with certain unalienable Rights, that among these are Life, Liberty and the Pursuit of Happiness. That to secure these Rights, Governments are instituted among Men, deriving their just Powers from the Consent of the Governed."
>
> —Declaration of Independence

Declaration of Independence

When it issued the Declaration of Independence in 1776, the Continental Congress did more than announce the separation of the 13 American colonies from Great Britain. It also summed up the most basic principles that came to underlie American government. This section, the preamble, is sometimes called the "social contract" section. You can read the words at left.

The Declaration, largely written by Thomas Jefferson, is one of the most important documents in the history of the world. It not only declared the independence of a colony from its mother country—thereby setting a precedent for other oppressed peoples around the world to do the same—it also established the first government of, by, and for the people.

The ideas expressed in the Declaration of Independence also had a profound effect on later developments in American history. You will notice the relationship of the ideas behind the Declaration of Independence to the American Revolution, the writing of the U.S. Constitution, including the Bill of Rights, and the movements to end slavery and to give women the right to vote. You'll see how the United States became a nation of immigrants, with its rich diversity of people, and the ways this development relates to the ideas of the Declaration of Independence.

Read the first three paragraphs of the Declaration of Independence. Then recite words from the Declaration of Independence quoted at left. Consider their meaning and then answer these questions.

☑ ASSESSMENT

1. **Identify Central Idea** According to the preamble (left) of the Declaration of Independence, why do people form governments?

2. **Predict** What concepts in this passage would eventually be used to justify ending the practice of slavery in the United States?

3. **Apply Information** Identify two ways that your federal, state, or local government protect the rights to life, liberty, or the pursuit of happiness.

Constitution Day Assembly

September 17 is Constitution Day, and your school may hold an assembly or other celebration in honor of the day. As part of this celebration, your teacher may ask you to participate in planning and holding a Constitution Day assembly.

Organize As a class, create the basic plan for your assembly. Discuss the following:

1. When and where should the assembly take place?

2. How long should it take? Should you plan on a short program taking a single class period or a longer program?

3. Who should be involved? Will other classes or other grades take part? Will you invite outsiders, such as parents or people from the community?

4. What activities might be included?

Plan After your discussion, divide the class into committees to complete jobs such as getting permission from the school administration, preparing a program, inviting any guests, advertising the plan beforehand, and blogging about it afterward.

Give thought to the types of activities that might be included in the assembly. You might invite a guest speaker from your community. You might run an essay contest among students and have the winners read their essays during the assembly. Some students might prepare a video presentation about the Bill of Rights. Others might write and perform a skit about what the Declaration of Independence or U.S. Constitution mean to them.

Consider asking those who present speeches, essays, videos, or skits to address this question: What are the key tenets or principles of American democracy?

>> Your school may hold a Constitution Day assembly like the one shown here.

Communicate Present your Constitution Day assembly. After the assembly is over, discuss the event with the class. Ask yourselves questions such as these:

1. How well was the assembly planned and organized? What improvements could we have made?

2. How would you rate each of the presentations or other activities of the assembly?

3. Was the audience engaged?

4. How effectively did the class work together?

[ESSENTIAL QUESTION] How much does geography affect people's lives?

⓪ Connecting with Past Learnings

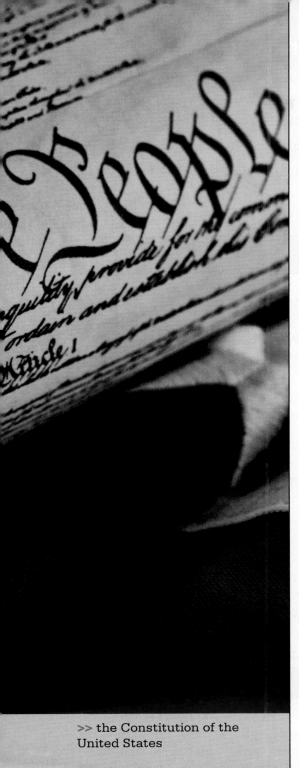

Enduring Understandings

- Christopher Columbus's arrival in the Western Hemisphere launched European colonization of the Americas.

- Colonization brought conflict between Europeans and indigenous peoples and the transportation of enslaved Africans to the Americas.

- In North America, 13 colonies established the United States before winning independence from Great Britain.

- Conflict over slavery led to a civil war in which the Confederacy of the southern states was defeated.

- After the Civil War came a period of Reconstruction, followed by a loss of rights for African Americans.

California Topic 0 Overview

In this Topic, you'll refresh your memory about American history up to the end of Reconstruction. Look at the lesson outline and explore the timeline. As you study this Topic, you'll complete the Quest team project.

LESSON OUTLINE

0.1 Colonies and Revolution
HSS 11.1, HSS 11.1.1, HSS 11.1.2, HSS 11.3, HSS 11.3.1, HSS 11.3.2, HSS 11.8.6, Analysis CST.4

0.2 Founding a New Nation
HSS 11.1, HSS 11.1.1, HSS 11.1.2, HSS 11.3, HSS 11.3.1, HSS 11.3.5

0.3 America in the Early 1800s
HSS 11.1.3, HSS 11.1.4, HSS 11.2.2, HSS 11.3.2, HSS 11.10.7, Analysis CST.4

0.4 The Union in Crisis
HSS 11.10.2

0.5 The Civil War
HSS 11.1.4, HSS 11.3, HSS 11.3.1, HSS 11.3.2

0.6 The Reconstruction Era
HSS 11.1.3, HSS 11.3.1, HSS 11.10.2

Key Events Before End of Reconstruction

1513 Ponce de León claims Florida for Spain

1607 Jamestown settled

1620 Plymouth Settled

1775 American Revolution begins

1783 Treaty of Paris ends Revolution

1861 Confederacy is formed, and Civil War begins

1865 Civil War ends; Reconstruction begins

1877 Reconstruction ends

1500   1600   1700   1800   1900

QUEST!

Civic Discussion: Andrew Johnson's Impeachment

Was the impeachment of President Andrew Johnson justified? How did significant people or groups influence this event during Reconstruction? In this Quest you'll explore this question by examining the sources, the evidence and by holding a civic discussion.

STEP 1
Read the discussion launch and discuss the major points with your classmates.

STEP 2
Examine the sources to understand the various authors' perspectives on the main question. Assess the author's claims, reasoning and evidence.

STEP 3
Join either the YES or NO group to work on your answer to the question. As a group present your arguments and evidence before switching sides.

STEP 4
Present your own opinion and record your point of view on the Information Organizer. Reflect on what you've learned about the divisive issues of Reconstruction.

5

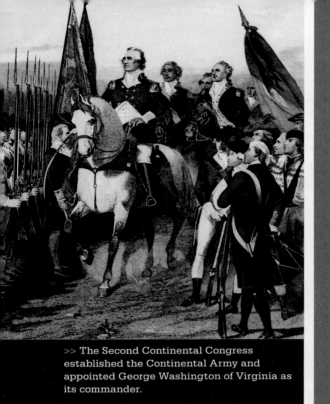

>> The Second Continental Congress established the Continental Army and appointed George Washington of Virginia as its commander.

Bounce to Activate Flipped Video

0.1 In 1492, the European explorer Christopher Columbus landed on the island of Hispaniola in the Caribbean Sea. Columbus called the Native Americans he met there "Indians," thinking he had landed in the Indies. Following Columbus's landing, Europeans began to slowly make contact with the many peoples already living in North and South America. The arrival of the Europeans dramatically affected these native peoples. One consequence was the rapid spread of diseases among the Indian population that not only claimed lives but demoralized survivors.

>> Objectives

Describe the early European settlement of North America.

Identify the factors that influenced the development of colonial democratic ideals.

Explain the colonists' reaction to new taxes.

Assess why Congress declared independence and the ideas underlying the Declaration of Independence.

>> Key Terms

George Washington
Mayflower Compact
Magna Carta
English Bill of Rights
Enlightenment
Great Awakening
Thomas Jefferson
John Locke
John Hancock
House of Burgesses

Colonies and Revolution

European Colonies in the Americas

Over the next two centuries European nations explored the Americas and began establishing colonies, often taking control of land from Native Americans in the process. Spain, which had sponsored Columbus's voyage, rapidly conquered a vast empire around the Caribbean and in Central and South America, with a few holdings in North America, including Florida, where Juan Ponce de León had landed in 1513. France established smaller colonies in what is now Canada. England established 13 colonies along the mid-Atlantic coast of North America. Eventually, these colonies would declare their independence from England and become a new nation: the United States of America.

Wealth flowed into Spain from its colonies in Mexico, Central America, and South America. The population was thin and life was hard in the borderland regions in the present-day Southwest and in Florida. To encourage settlements and protect these outposts, Spain established presidios, or forts. Priests and nuns established dozens of missions to convert Native Americans to Christianity. St. Augustine, Florida, was the main northern fort of the Spanish colonial empire. Founded in 1565 by Pedro Menéndez de Avilés,

St. Augustine played a key role in protecting the route of the Spanish treasure fleet and is the oldest continuously inhabited European-founded city in the United States.

American Indians were eager to exchange beaver pelts for European-made metal axes, knives, and kettles. During the 1690s, the French founded Louisiana, along the Mississippi River valley and the Gulf Coast.

The French established colonies in Canada along the coast of Nova Scotia and the St. Lawrence River. Besides exploiting rich fishing off the coast, they found a fortune in furs.

The Virginia Colonies In 1607, the English established their first enduring settlement, Jamestown, in Virginia. Despite enormous losses from disease, starvation, and war with local Native Americans, the English expanded around the Chesapeake Bay. The colonists prospered by raising tobacco for export. Claiming the political rights of Englishmen, the Virginia planters elected a legislature, known as the **House of Burgesses**. It governed the colony in partnership with a royal governor appointed by the king of England.

New England To the north, the English established more colonies, which they called New England. The first colonists were devout Protestants called "Puritans," who hoped to create model moral communities. They settled first in 1620 at Plymouth, where they adopted the **Mayflower Compact**. The Mayflower Compact provided a framework for self-government. By 1700, New England had four colonies: Massachusetts, Rhode Island, Connecticut, and New Hampshire.

Adapting to the cold climate and short growing season, the New Englanders supplemented farming with lumber harvested from the forests and fish from the sea. By building ships, they were able to trade with the other colonies and with Europe. These colonies were originally settled by English families and communities that crossed the Atlantic together. As family-based communities, they had a high regard for work, which they regarded as a moral responsibility to honor God. The Puritans' high regard for individual responsibility and the work ethic became one of the foundations of American culture and character.

The Middle and Southern Colonies The English developed a third cluster of colonies between Maryland and New England. They conquered Dutch New Netherland and renamed it New York, then added New Jersey and Pennsylvania, a haven for Quaker immigrants. The Middle Colonies offered religious toleration and a prospering economy based on exporting wheat.

South of Virginia, the English developed a fourth cluster of colonies. The Southern Colonies consisted of North Carolina, South Carolina, and Georgia

Areas Settled by Colonial Powers, late 1600s

KEY
- Dutch settlements
- English settlements
- French settlements
- Spanish settlements

Great Lakes

Hudson R.

Chesapeake Bay

ATLANTIC OCEAN

St. Augustine

0   400 mi
0   400 km
Albers Conic Equal-Area Projection

>> By 1660, several European nations had established colonies scattered along the mid-Atlantic coast of North America. **Analyze Maps** Why were the first settlements founded near bodies of water?

Bounce to Activate Map

in addition to Virginia. The colonists raised rice on coastal plantations and cattle on farms in the backcountry. The plantations relied on the labor of enslaved Africans.

☑ **IDENTIFY** Where and when did the English establish their first colonial settlement?

Democratic Ideals in the American Colonies

The English colonists brought ideas about democracy and republican government with them to America. Some of these ideas came from ancient Greece and Rome, others from Judeo-Christian roots, and still others came from traditions and thinkers from Europe's relatively recent past.

Political Traditions From England As English citizens, the colonists believed that they were entitled to the same rights as English citizens in Britain. Many of these rights were contained in two important documents: the Magna Carta and the English Bill of Rights. The **Magna Carta**, signed by King John in 1215, limited the power of the English monarch. It protected the right of people to own private property and guaranteed the right to trial by jury. The **English Bill of Rights**, signed by King William and Queen Mary in 1688, was a written list of freedoms that the government promised to protect.

The English Bill of Rights required Parliament, England's lawmaking body, to meet regularly. It also stated that the monarch could not raise taxes or build an army without Parliament's consent.

The Influence of the Enlightenment and the Great Awakening During the 1700s, ideas based on the **Enlightenment** circulated among well-educated American colonists. The Enlightenment was a European intellectual movement. Enlightenment philosophers believed that all problems could be solved by human reason. Frenchman Baron de Montesquieu and Englishman **John Locke** were two thinkers who applied reason to government and politics. Locke believed that people had natural rights that came from God, not from monarchs. Locke's ideas would have an enormous influence on American political leaders in the late 1700s.

While Enlightenment thinkers promoted the value of human reason, in the 1740s a religious movement called the **Great Awakening** developed in response to the colonists' emotional and spiritual needs.

Evangelical preachers such as Jonathan Edwards and George Whitefield toured the colonies promoting revivals where people felt a direct and transforming contact with an overwhelming Holy Spirit. The Great Awakening challenged established religious authority and led to the birth of new churches. This eventually increased tolerance of religious differences. Evangelical preachers stressed that salvation and belief were open to everyone, not only to a privileged elite. Religious ideas like this helped popularize the ideal of equality and prepared the ground for a political transformation.

The Enlightenment and the Great Awakening would later combine to influence the American Revolution. Despite their differences, both movements prepared the way for self-rule by encouraging independent thinking and challenging authority. Both movements also valued civil and human rights. In this way, the Enlightenment

THE FOUNDATIONS OF AMERICAN DEMOCRACY

Founding Documents	Fundamental Principles	State constitutions, the United States Constitution and Bill of Rights
• Magna Carta • English Bill of Rights • Commentaries on the Laws of England	• Government authority comes from the consent of the governed • The power of government should be limited • Government exists to protect individual rights and freedoms	• Guarantee due process • Establish rule of law • Guarantee free elections and free speech • Establish checks on governmental authority

>> Colonial government in the English colonies was influenced by European thought.
Analyze Charts Which of these principles is protected by the Bill of Rights?

>> **Analyze Maps** Which European power had lost almost all its colonial territory by 1763?

and the Great Awakening fostered the civic principles that would become the foundation of the United States.

☑ **IDENTIFY** The followers of which intellectual movement believed all problems could be solved with reason?

Causes of the American Revolution

The tradition of a limited English monarchy, experience with self-government, and exposure to Enlightenment ideas influenced the leading American colonists. A European war and a spirit of independence in the colonies prompted the colonists to take action that would change the course of world history.

Between 1689 and 1763, the British and French fought a series of wars in Europe. (In 1707, a treaty joined England and Scotland to form Great Britain.) These conflicts spread to North America and involved the French and British colonists and their Native American allies.

The last of these wars, called the French and Indian War, erupted in 1754 and ended in 1763 with a British victory. The peace treaty gave Canada, Florida, and a portion of French Louisiana to Britain. British colonists were eager to move into Louisiana, but Britain wished to keep peace with the Indians who lived on this territory. British limits on westward expansion angered the colonists.

Violation of the Rights of Englishmen The British victory was expensive, nearly doubling Britain's national debt. During the 1760s, the British Parliament asserted that the colonists should pay new taxes to help the empire. The proposed taxes and tighter trade regulations shocked the colonists. Certain parliamentary acts in the 1760s and 1770s violated other rights enjoyed by men in Britain, including the principles of no standing army in peacetime without consent and trial by jury.

Many colonists believed that since they were not directly represented in Parliament, new taxes and trade regulations denied them their rights as Englishmen. They cited the Magna Carta and the English Bill of Rights, which blocked the king from levying taxes without the permission of Parliament. During the 1760s, their problem was with Parliament, rather than with King George III. Professing loyalty to the king, the colonists hoped to be free from Parliament's efforts to tax them. They would pay taxes levied only by their own elected assemblies in the colonies.

>> In this political cartoon, some angry colonists protest the unpopular taxes required by the Stamp Act by tarring and feathering tax collectors and pouring hot tea down their throats.

>> The Declaration of Independence, signed by the delegates to the Second Continental Congress, served notice to King George III that the 13 colonies had separated from Great Britain.

Bounce to Activate Gallery

Pressuring Parliament Valuing the prosperity and protection of the empire, the colonists did not immediately seek independence. Instead, they wanted to remain part of the empire that for so long had produced so many benefits at so little cost to them. They also wanted to enjoy the traditional rights of Englishmen.

To pressure Parliament, colonists boycotted British goods. Local committees enforced this boycott, which threatened the British economy. Angry crowds harassed colonists who helped to collect the new taxes. Colonists who refused to honor the boycotts or who spoke out in favor of the taxes were considered Loyalists. Representing a large minority, the Loyalists preferred to pay the taxes and honor Parliament and the king. They also feared that the resistance would lead to a war that Britain seemed certain to win.

☑ **EXPLAIN** Why did many American colonists oppose an increase in taxes?

The American Revolution

In 1774, leading colonists held a convention, called the First Continental Congress. Delegates from 12 of the colonies (all except Georgia) met in Philadelphia to discuss what to do next. The delegates sent a list of complaints to the British government. The letter was ignored.

Americans Declare Their Independence In 1775, war began when British troops tried to seize arms and ammunition stored at Concord, Massachusetts. New Englanders quickly organized an army, which the Continental Congress adopted as the army for all the colonies.

That year, the Second Continental Congress assembled. Another letter of complaint was sent to the British government. When this letter was also ignored, Congress decided to declare the colonies' independence from Britain. A committee made up of Benjamin Franklin, John Adams, Roger Sherman, Robert Livingston, and Thomas Jefferson was given the task of drafting an official declaration.

The Declaration of Independence was mainly written by **Thomas Jefferson** with help from Adams and Franklin. After it was approved by the delegates at the Continental Congress, the first person to sign the document was **John Hancock**, a wealthy merchant and leader of the Patriots in Massachusetts who later served nine terms as governor of the Commonwealth of Massachusetts.

Continental vs. British Forces

	CONTINENTAL	BRITISH
TOTAL FORCES	about 90,000 as a peak estimate	more than 70,000
COMPOSITION OF FORCES	Continental Army, State Militias	Army, Navy, hired mercenaries
ALLIES	France, Spain	Native Americans, Loyalists
QUALITY OF FORCES	untrained, unconventional	trained, disciplined
MOTIVATION	freedom from British control	regain British control
SUPPLIES	very limited weapons, food, and clothing	better availability of weapons, food, and clothing, but moving supplies was difficult

>> **Analyze Charts** Compare the advantages and disadvantages of the Continental forces versus the British forces.

Other signers included the well-known doctor Benjamin Rush, of Philadelphia, who later served as treasurer of the U.S. Mint.

The Intent and Meaning of the Declaration

The intent of the Declaration of Independence was to state that the 13 American colonies were now independent from Britain and to give reasons why the Patriots felt this step was necessary. But it had more meaning than a statement of independence. It expressed Enlightenment ideas about the natural rights of people and the purposes of government.

> We hold these truths to be self-evident, that all men are created equal; that they are endowed by their Creator with certain unalienable rights; that among these are life, liberty, and the pursuit of happiness.
>
> —Declaration of Independence, July 4, 1776

In this passage, Jefferson presents the Founding Father's philosophy of divinely bestowed unalienable natural rights—God-given rights that cannot be taken away. Jefferson also makes the argument that the purpose of the government is "to secure these rights," a position influenced by Enlightenment thinkers. He asserted that when a government fails to respect or protect the rights of its people, the people have the right to replace that government with a new government of their own making.

The importance of the Declaration of Independence lay in both how it captured the ideals of the revolution, inspiring the struggle, and how it laid the groundwork for the creation of the United States Constitution. Revolutionary movements in other countries drew inspiration from the document and its enduring ideals.

The Declaration went on to list the reasons why the colonists felt that they had no other choice but rebellion. The colonists had not come to the decision to rebel lightly. Once they did, they fought hard for victory.

Patriot Leaders During the war, the British made many military mistakes because they underestimated the Patriots, who were highly motivated by their cause. Colonists of all kinds gave up their lives to fight for the cause of independence. John Peter Muhlenberg, a Virginia minister, gave up preaching to recruit and lead a troop of 300 men. He proclaimed, "There is a time to pray and a time to fight, and that time has now come!" Another minister, John Witherspoon of New Jersey, was elected to the Continental Congress and was one of only a few clergymen to sign the Declaration of Independence.

The Patriots greatly benefited from the leadership of **George Washington**, who had gained valuable military experience during the French and Indian War. They also owed much to the resourcefulness

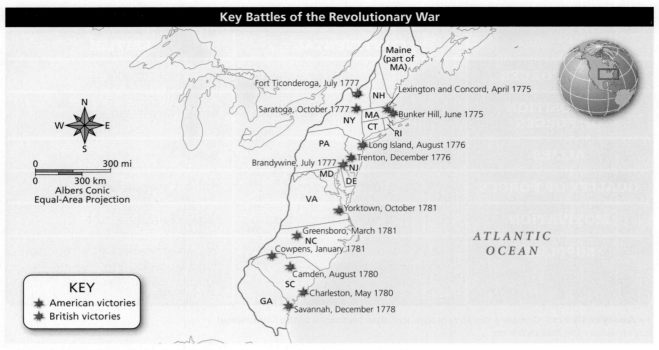

Key Battles of the Revolutionary War

Maine (part of MA)

Fort Ticonderoga, July 1777

Lexington and Concord, April 1775

Saratoga, October 1777

NH

Bunker Hill, June 1775

NY   MA

CT

RI

PA

Long Island, August 1776

Brandywine, July 1777

Trenton, December 1776

MD   NJ

DE

VA

Yorktown, October 1781

Greensboro, March 1781

NC

Cowpens, January 1781

ATLANTIC
OCEAN

Camden, August 1780

SC

Charleston, May 1780

GA

Savannah, December 1778

N
W   E
S

0   300 mi
0   300 km
Albers Conic
Equal-Area Projection

KEY
⭑ American victories
⭑ British victories

>> **Analyze Maps** Based on the information in the map, is it surprising that the Americans were able to defeat the British and gain independence?

of leaders such as Jonathan Trumbull, Sr., who was a close friend and advisor to Washington. Trumbull, a former merchant, was the colonial governor of Connecticut. He made a key contribution to the revolution's success by helping to organize the supply of food, clothing, shoes, guns, and ammunition for the Continental Army.

French Assistance In 1776, the colonists sent a small delegation led by Maryland planter Charles Carroll to seek the assistance of French Canadians in the fight against the British. Carroll was the only Catholic signer of the Declaration of Independence and was the last survivor of the 56 signers, dying in 1832. The mission failed, but by 1778, the Patriots began receiving military assistance from France itself. In 1781, a French fleet trapped the British army at Yorktown in Virginia, where Washington's army completed the victory.

The Treaty of Paris The treaty of Paris, signed in 1783, gave the new nation very favorable boundaries, stretching to Florida in the south; to the Great Lakes to the north; and to the Mississippi River in the west. The British retreated to Canada, while the Spanish claimed Florida and everything west of the

Mississippi. Most of Florida would remain under Spanish rule until the Adams-Onís Treaty of 1821, when the territory became part of the United States.

☑ **EXPLAIN** How did Thomas Jefferson justify writing the Declaration of Independence?

☑ ASSESSMENT

1. **Identify Cause and Effect** Explain how the arrival of European colonists affected Native Americans.

2. **Integrate Information** Explain how the philosophies of the Enlightenment affected American colonists.

3. **Generate Explanations** Explain why many colonists opposed Britain's proposition to introduce new taxes.

4. **Summarize** the main principles of the Declaration of Independence.

5. **Describe** the contributions of leaders such as George Washington and Jonathan Trumbull, Sr., during the Revolutionary War.

0.2 Dissatisfied with living under colonial rule, the American colonists rebelled and declared independence from Britain. In addition to fighting a war to win their independence, the leaders of the new nation faced the task of creating a system of government for themselves.

>> Benjamin Franklin (with cane, center) and George Washington (raising hat, right) were among the delegates to the Constitutional Convention in 1787.

Bounce to Activate Flipped Video

Founding a New Nation

A Confederation of States

States Establish Republican Governments By declaring their independence, the former colonies became states. Each of the 13 new states wrote a constitution that created a **republican government**, or a government in which officials are representatives elected by the people. Most state constitutions also included a **bill of rights**, a list of freedoms guaranteed by the state government. Many of them guaranteed freedom of religion, freedom of the press, and the right to trial by jury.

At the time, voting rights were very limited. Only white male property owners could vote, except in New Jersey, where women had the right to vote until 1807. African Americans—whether free or enslaved—and Native Americans were not permitted to vote. Democratic and conservative Patriots disagreed about who should have the right to vote. Patriots who were more democratic wanted equal political rights for almost all free men, even those who had little or no property. In most states, however, more conservative Patriots restricted voting rights to those who had enjoyed those rights in colonial times—free men who owned property.

>> **Objectives**

Describe the weaknesses of the Articles of Confederation.

Describe the compromises made in order to reach agreement on the Constitution.

Summarize the arguments for and against ratification of the Constitution.

Explain the principles of the Constitution.

>> **Key Terms**

republican
  government
bill of rights
Shays' Rebellion
James Madison
ratify
federalism
limited government
separation of
  powers

Northwest Territory
Articles of
  Confederation
confederation
*The Federalist
  Papers*
Antifederalists
checks and
  balances

Go **ONLINE** for digital resources

VIDEO   AUDIO   ACTIVITY   ETEXT   WRITING   ASSESSMENT

Religious Liberty In the colonial period, many colonies collected taxes to support religious establishments. For example, in colonial Virginia the Anglican Church was the official established church of the colony, so colonists were obliged to pay taxes to support the Anglican establishment. The practice of government giving preferential treatment to a particular Christian denomination did not make sense as the colonies filled up with people belonging to different denominations. So after the Revolution, religious liberty and pluralism became the norm. These principles were codified in the Virginia Statute for Religious Freedom, drafted by Thomas Jefferson and passed in 1786. Massachusetts and Connecticut were exceptions. They kept their Congregational established churches, which continued to draw fire from Baptists and Methodists.

The First Plan of Government In November 1777, the Continental Congress adopted the first national constitution, the **Articles of Confederation**. The Articles officially created the United States of America. Ratification by all 13 states did not occur until March 1781.

>> Shays' Rebellion resulted in bloodshed when state militia attacked angry rioters led by Daniel Shays. **Describe** How did Shays' Rebellion test the strength of the new national government?

The Patriots feared the creation of another tyrannical or abusive government, so they refused to entrust the new union with much power. As a result, under the Articles of Confederation, most power remained with the states. The Articles created a national government without a President or a judicial branch. The legislative branch had only very limited powers. Congress could declare and conduct war. It could also regulate trade with foreign countries and with Indian nations. But it could not raise troops or levy taxes, and there was no way to enforce trade regulations. The United States government could only collect money and muster an army with voluntary contributions from the states.

Weaknesses of the Articles Under the Articles, the national government had no say over the rules of interstate commerce. Each state set its own trade policy. Most states tried to protect their industries and agriculture from competition by taxing goods imported from other states. This practice discouraged trade among the states and led to competition that had the potential to become destructive.

The national debt was also a problem. Because the Continental Congress had borrowed money and issued paper currency during the Revolutionary War, the new government was deeply in debt. However, it had no way to raise the money to pay off this debt. The states were all paying off their own war debts and were largely unwilling or unable to contribute money to the national government.

The national government also suffered from structural weaknesses. There was no President. Each state, no matter how large or small, had a single vote in a unicameral, or one-house, Congress. On the major issues, including declaring war and making treaties, two thirds of the states (9 out of 13) had to approve. Amending the Articles was almost impossible, because every single one of the states had to endorse any change.

Increasing Troubles During the mid-1780s, an economic depression reduced the prices paid to farmers for their produce. Unable to pay their debts, farmers faced losing their crops, livestock, and even their homes. In Massachusetts, matters worsened when the courts seized farms from farmers who did not pay taxes to the state or their loans. In rural Massachusetts in 1786, armed farmers led by Daniel Shays shut down the courts, blocking foreclosures. The state of Massachusetts sent troops to suppress this revolt, known as **Shays' Rebellion**. The rebellion highlighted the weaknesses of the national

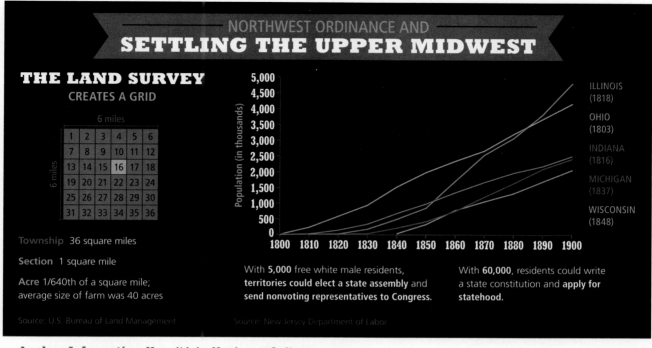

NORTHWEST ORDINANCE AND
SETTLING THE UPPER MIDWEST

THE LAND SURVEY
CREATES A GRID

6 miles

1	2	3	4	5	6
7	8	9	10	11	12
13	14	15	16	17	18
19	20	21	22	23	24
25	26	27	28	29	30
31	32	33	34	35	36

6 miles

Township 36 square miles

Section 1 square mile

Acre 1/640th of a square mile; average size of farm was 40 acres

Source: U.S. Bureau of Land Management

Population (in thousands)

ILLINOIS (1818)
OHIO (1803)
INDIANA (1816)
MICHIGAN (1837)
WISCONSIN (1848)

With **5,000** free white male residents, territories could **elect a state assembly** and send nonvoting representatives to Congress.

With **60,000**, residents could write a state constitution and **apply for statehood**.

Source: New Jersey Department of Labor

>> **Analyze Information** How did the Northwest Ordinance ensure the orderly incorporation of new territory into the United States?

government set up by the Articles of Confederation. Lacking an army, the weak **confederation** could not defend American interests on the frontier. The Spanish in Louisiana tried to constrain western American settlements by closing the port of New Orleans. Along the Great Lakes, the British refused to abandon frontier forts on the American side of the boundary set by the terms of the peace treaty that ended the American Revolution.

Managing the Northwest Territory Despite its weaknesses under the Articles of Confederation, the national government took up the task of fulfilling its duties as best it could. The Articles gave Congress authority over the vast **Northwest Territory**, which lay north of the Ohio River and stretched west from Pennsylvania to the Mississippi River. In 1785 and 1787, Congress passed two laws to manage this land. The first, the Land Ordinance, created a system for surveying and selling the land to settlers. The second, the Northwest Ordinance, described how territories should be governed and how they could become full-fledged states. This law also banned slavery in the territory and provided for public education.

☑ **RECALL** What were the main weaknesses of the Articles of Confederation?

The Constitutional Convention

By 1787, many Americans agreed that the Articles of Confederation were flawed. In May 1787, the states sent delegates to a special convention in Philadelphia to draft proposed amendments to the Articles. However, once there, the delegates decided not to revise the Articles of Confederation. Instead, they agreed to undertake a complete restructuring of the national government. The convention came to be known as the Constitutional Convention. The Convention would go on to produce a completely new, much stronger plan of government. That plan, the United States Constitution, has endured to this day with relatively few significant changes.

Two Opposing Plans While the delegates agreed that the Articles of Confederation were deeply flawed, it was much harder for them to reach an agreement on the best solution.

The first proposal put forth was the Virginia Plan, designed by **James Madison**. The Virginia Plan advocated a national union that was both strong and republican. Madison insisted that a large republic could be more stable than a small one, because in a large republic, the diverse interests would provide **checks and balances** to preserve the common good.

>> Despite the fact that some delegates from northern states urged that slavery be banned throughout the nation, the Constitutional Convention did not succeed in ending slavery or the slave trade.

In addition to securing the power to tax and to regulate commerce, this plan proposed a government that divided power among three branches—the legislative, the executive, and the judicial. The nation would have a bicameral legislature: a House of Representatives and a Senate. In both houses, the states with larger populations would have more members. Madison's plan also included a daring feature—the national Congress would have the power to veto any state law, just as Parliament had done with colonial laws. The Virginia Plan also featured a President to command the armed forces and to manage foreign relations. He would appoint all executive and judicial officers, subject only to approval by the Senate. A critic of the plan, Patrick Henry, worried that such a powerful President could "easily become a king."

William Paterson offered a counterproposal called the New Jersey Plan. This plan, favored by the small states, would give Congress the power to regulate commerce and to tax while keeping the basic structure of the Confederation. The plan retained a unicameral legislature representing the states as equals—no matter how large or small. The states remained sovereign except for those few powers specifically granted to the national government. Under the New Jersey Plan, the United States would stay a loose confederation of states, rather than become a unified nation.

The Great Compromise The delegates worked throughout the hot Philadelphia summer to resolve their differences. Roger Sherman proposed what has come to be called the Great Compromise. It settled the differences between the Virginia and the New Jersey plans by creating a bicameral, or two-house, legislature. In a concession to the smaller states, the Senate would equally represent every state by allowing just two senators per state.

In keeping with the Virginia Plan, the House of Representatives, in which representation was based on population, granted more power to the larger states.

In another concession, Madison abandoned his cherished national veto over state laws. Instead, the compromise simply forbade the states from enacting the sorts of laws that offended many during the 1780s. For instance, the states could no longer issue their own money or provide debtor relief at creditors' expense. By compromising between the Virginia and the New Jersey plans, the delegates supported a system known as **federalism**, which divided power between the federal and state governments.

The Slavery Issue Another major compromise appeased the southern states. Their delegates feared domination by the northern states, which had a larger white population. They worried that northern domination would threaten the slave system, which they viewed as essential to the southern economy and society. The delegates from South Carolina and Georgia threatened to walk out unless the Constitution protected the institution of slavery. To reassure the South, the delegates adopted the three-fifths clause. It counted each enslaved person as three fifths of a person, to be added to a state's free population, which boosted the number of the South's seats in Congress. The three-fifths clause, however, gave no rights to enslaved African Americans. In fact, Article IV of the Constitution obliged all states to return slaves to their owners. In other words, running away to a free state did not free a slave. Northerners were required to help enforce the slave system as a price of union.

☑ **CHECK UNDERSTANDING** What was the basic principle of the Great Compromise?

The Struggle Over Ratification

The Constitution was now written, but it was not yet the law of the land. Before it could go into effect, 9 of the 13 states had to **ratify**, or officially approve, it.

Federalists Argue for Ratification Supporters of the Constitution were called Federalists. They wanted the United States to have a strong central government. Three leading Federalists—James Madison, Alexander Hamilton, and John Jay—wrote a series of letters to newspapers in support of the Constitution. These letters, collectively called *The Federalist Papers*, explained why they believed the Constitution was vital to the survival of the new nation. They also explained how the new system of government would work.

The essays argued that the **separation of powers** in three branches of government would prevent the concentration of power dreaded by the Antifederalists. They argued, in *The Federalist*, No. 51, that the checks and balances in the Constitution prevented any of the three branches from gaining too much power. The authors insisted that the real threat to liberty came from the state legislatures, which lacked sufficient checks and balances. Today, the *Federalist* essays are recognized as perhaps the most sophisticated explanation of the new American political system ever written, which helps scholars, judges, and lawyers understand the meaning of the Constitution

The Federalists enjoyed popular support in key places—the seaports—which hosted many of the ratifying conventions. Most urban artisans also supported the Constitution. Hurt by the depression of the 1780s, the artisans hoped that a strong national government would expand American commerce. The seaports also had most of the nation's newspapers, the printers of which strongly endorsed the Constitution.

Antifederalists Argue Against Ratification Opponents of the proposed Constitution were called **Antifederalists**. They included some leading Americans, such as Patrick Henry and Samuel Adams. The Antifederalists objected to the Constitution because they thought it gave the national government far too much power at the expense of the states. They believed that the President had too much power, that Congress was too small and could not represent voters, and that a federal court system interfered with local courts.

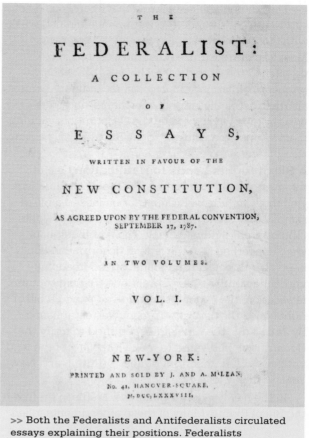

>> Both the Federalists and Antifederalists circulated essays explaining their positions. Federalists supported ratification and Antifederalists opposed it.

Bounce to Activate Gallery

From the Independent Chronicle and Universal Advertiser, Boston, Thursday June 26, 1788.

>> In this cartoon about ratification, states are represented by pillars; some are standing and others are not. **Analyze Political Cartoons** What does the cartoon suggest about ratification?

Bounce to Activate Chart

The Antifederalists believed that liberty could not survive unless the federal government remained weak, with most power belonging to state governments. Most farmers recognized that the Constitution threatened the state debtor-relief laws that had rescued their farms from foreclosure. Ordinary farmers also distrusted the lawyers, merchants, and other wealthy men who promoted the Constitution, viewing them as aristocrats hostile to the Republic.

A Bill of Rights Leads to Ratification One of the most powerful arguments of the Antifederalists was that the proposed Constitution lacked a bill of rights. Most of the states already had bills of rights protecting individual liberty. The Antifederalists were concerned that the federal government would become a threat to Americans' prized freedoms without a similar set of protections. To help secure ratification, the Federalists promised to add a bill of rights once the new government was established. By June 1788, the nine states required to ratify the Constitution had voted to make it the law of the land, with two other important states—Virginia and New York—quickly following.

In the newly elected Congress, Madison drafted the Bill of Rights. Many of these amendments relied on the **Virginia Declaration of Rights**. Madison limited the amendments to guarantees of individual rights, leaving the federal framework the same. He also avoided any sweeping preamble that declared all men equal in their creation and rights. That omission enabled slave owners to persist in denying rights to their slaves.

In 1789, Congress approved the 10 constitutional amendments that became the federal Bill of Rights. The states ratified these amendments in 1791.

Importance of the Bill of Rights The Bill of Rights protects a wide range of personal freedoms, including freedom of speech, freedom of religion, freedom of the press and of assembly, the right to bear arms as part of "a well-regulated militia," and protections against arbitrary intrusions and arrests, unfair trials, and "cruel and unusual" punishments. The personal freedoms established by the Bill of Rights have been cherished by Americans ever since. The protection they provide against abuses of power by the government are as important today as they were when they were originally written, perhaps even more so.

Separation of Church and State Principles of religious liberty are found in the Establishment

>> New Yorkers celebrate ratification. **Analyze Political Cartoons** What does the float suggest about the political leanings of most New Yorkers?

and Free Exercise clauses of the First Amendment: "Congress shall make no law respecting an establishment of religion, or prohibiting the free exercise thereof."

While the establishment clause reflects Jefferson's belief that the state, or government, should not promote religion, the exercise clause makes it clear that the government should not prevent religious practice. The tension between these two clauses continues to fuel debate on the issue of separation of church and state.

☑ **CHECK UNDERSTANDING** Why was the Bill of Rights added to the Constitution?

Principles of the Constitution

The intent of the Constitution was to create the framework for a republican form of government that strengthened the federal government from what it had been under the Articles of Confederation while balancing the interests of the large and small states.

The Meaning of the Constitution The authors of the Constitution established a representative government based on these basic principles: popular sovereignty, separation of powers, **limited government**, federalism, checks and balances, and representative government.

Popular Sovereignty The government derives its political authority from the people. This sentiment is reflected in the Constitution's opening words, "We the People of the United States . . ."

Separation of Powers The Constitution defined distinct legislative, executive, and judicial branches with different powers and responsibilities to prevent misuses of power by any of the three branches.

Limited Government Popular sovereignty ensures that a government's power is restricted, or limited. The Constitution specifically defined and limited the powers of government. Government leaders are not above the law.

Federalism To create a national government stronger than the one under the Articles of Confederation, the framers created a new form of federalism to share power between the national and state governments. The states could no longer issue their own paper money or regulate trade

>> On average, almost 55 percent of registered voters have participated in recent presidential elections.

with other states. These powers, known as the delegated powers, now belonged only to the federal government. Certain reserved powers continued to belong to the states alone, including the power to regulate and conduct elections. The federal and state governments also held some overlapping, or concurrent, powers, among them parallel court systems and the right to collect taxes.

Checks and Balances The three branches were given separate and sometimes overlapping responsibilities, along with specific ways to override, or check and balance, the decisions of the other branches. This distribution of power was intended to prevent the emergence of a single center of power and to provide remedies for abuses of power by the members of any one branch. For example, only Congress has the power to enact laws, but the President may veto those laws. However, a two-thirds majority in both houses of Congress can override the President's veto. The President nominates judges, but the Senate must approve them.

Representative Government The writers of the Constitution had misgivings about the democratic rule of the majority. Many feared democracy as something that would lead to mob rule. So instead of forming a direct democracy in which all citizens vote on every matter, the writers created an indirect democracy in which voters elect representatives to be their voice in government. The Constitution stipulated that citizens would directly elect only the representatives to the House of Representatives. The state legislatures rather than the voters would choose the members of the Senate. Similarly, an electoral college, or group of persons chosen from each state, would indirectly elect the President.

In addition, the indirectly elected President and senators would choose the least democratic branch of all: the judiciary. The delegates intended to insulate judges from political influence or interference.

The Importance of the Constitution The Republic established by the Constitution of the United States became a symbol of freedom not only to Americans but to countries in Europe and republics in Latin America as well. The 13 colonies were now forged together into a single nation with a strong central government to bind it together.

E pluribus unum This unity had already been suggested by the phrase "E pluribus unum," which is Latin for "Out of many, one." This phrase was first suggested as a motto for the young nation by the committee appointed in 1776 to design an official seal for what political leaders were beginning to call "the United States of America." As the United States grew and developed into a more diverse nation, it began to take on a second meaning. "Out of many, one" is now commonly taken to signify that a single, unified people has grown out of people with many different backgrounds, ethnicities, and beliefs.

☑ **CHECK UNDERSTANDING** What is the division of government between the states and the national government?

☑ ASSESSMENT

1. **Generate Explanations** Explain why the national government was weaker than individual states under the Articles of Confederation.

2. **Support a Point of View With Evidence** Explain why the Antifederalists opposed the Constitution.

3. **Compare and Contrast** Describe the similarities and differences between the Articles of Confederation and the Constitution.

4. **Analyze Context** Explain the significance of the phrase "E pluribus unum" and account for changes in its meaning over time.

5. **Discuss** the idea of the separation of powers and explain how the Constitution enacted this principle.

As the new federal government gathered in New York City for the first time in 1789, the nation faced a number of pressing problems. The unity of the Revolutionary era was being replaced by differences of opinion about the direction the new nation should take.

>> This portrait of Andrew Jackson was painted during his first year in office. It is the model for his image on the $20 bill.

Bounce to Activate Flipped Video

America in the Early 1800s

The New Republic and the War of 1812

Political Parties Develop Secretary of the Treasury Alexander Hamilton wanted the United States to develop a commercial and industrial economy. In order to promote economic development, Hamilton proposed issuing government bonds, creating new taxes, and creating a Bank of the United States. Hamilton's proposals were embraced by the newly formed **Federalist Party** but opposed by leaders such as Thomas Jefferson and James Madison, who wanted a limited government and an agrarian society. Jefferson and Madison and their mostly southern supporters formed the **Democratic Republican Party** to oppose Hamilton's agenda.

The Struggle Over Foreign Policy The two parties differed on foreign policy issues as well. The Federalists supported strong trade ties with Great Britain, while the Democratic Republicans wanted close ties with Britain's enemy, France.

>> **Objectives**

Describe the early years of the federal government, including the development of the two-party system and the importance of the Louisiana Purchase and War of 1812.

Summarize the key issues and events of the presidency of Andrew Jackson.

>> **Key Terms**

Federalist Party
Democratic
   Republican Party
John Marshall
judicial review
Louisiana Purchase
Monroe Doctrine
Andrew Jackson
Jacksonian
   democracy
Indian Removal Act
Trail of Tears
Whig Party
Panic of 1837
Alexis de Tocqueville
populism
Industrial Revolution
cotton gin

underground railroad
abolitionists
Frederick Douglass
Second Great
   Awakening
Lucretia Mott
Elizabeth Cady
   Stanton
women's rights
   movement
Declaration of
   Sentiments
Susan B. Anthony
suffrage
Manifest Destiny
Sam Houston
James K. Polk

President Washington wanted the United States to continue to trade with both Britain and France. In 1793, the British navy tested American neutrality by seizing U.S. merchant ships trading with French colonies. This added to U.S. outrage at the continued presence of British forts on the American side of the Great Lakes. To avoid war, Washington sent Chief Justice John Jay to London to negotiate with the British. In the Jay Treaty of 1794, the British gave up the forts but kept most of their restrictions on U.S. shipping.

New Powers and New Territory As the nation was struggling to find its footing in foreign affairs, the federal government took steps that expanded the government's powers and enlarged the nation's territory.

In 1803, Chief Justice **John Marshall** used a partisan dispute in the case of *Marbury* v. *Madison*. to assert that the Supreme Court had the power of **judicial review**. That meant that the judicial branch could now decide the constitutionality of congressional actions.

That same year, France's new ruler, Napoleon Bonaparte, agreed to sell the vast Louisiana Territory west of the Mississippi to the United States. The **Louisiana Purchase** nearly doubled the size of the United States and cost the country only $15 million. In 1804, President Jefferson sent Meriwether Lewis and William Clark to explore the new territory, in what became known as the Lewis and Clark expedition.

The War of 1812 By the early 1800s, the British navy had resumed seizing American merchant ships trading with France. In order to pressure the British to stop, the United States declared an **embargo** on British goods, but the embargo ended up hurting Americans more than it hurt the British. Congress lifted the embargo in 1809. The next President, James Madison, was unable to end the problems with Britain, and in 1812, Congress declared war. Some Americans hoped for a quick victory and the capture of British Canada.

During the two-and-a-half years of war, little progress was made by either side. In 1815, both sides agreed to end the fighting and sign a peace treaty. Although the treaty did not change any boundaries, the war was hailed as a victory by many Americans. They felt that the war proved the strength of their young nation. Twice in two generations, a young, upstart nation had fought successfully against one of the world's greatest powers. Some called it "The Second American Revolution" because it proved the stability of the country's republican form of government.

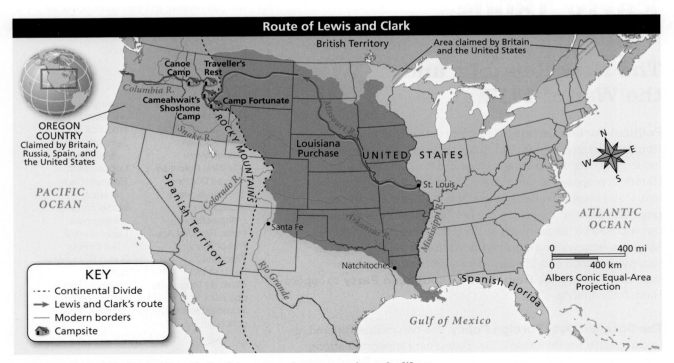

Route of Lewis and Clark

>> The Lewis and Clark expedition helped Americans learn more about the West.
Make Predictions How might westward expansion lead to conflict with other nations?

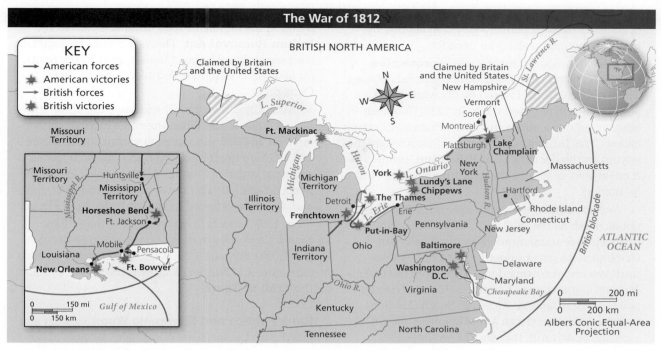

KEY
→ American forces
✳ American victories
→ British forces
✳ British victories

BRITISH NORTH AMERICA

Claimed by Britain and the United States

Missouri Territory

Missouri Territory

Huntsville

Mississippi Territory

Horseshoe Bend

Ft. Jackson

Mobile

Pensacola

Louisiana

New Orleans

Ft. Bowyer

Gulf of Mexico

0 150 mi
0 150 km

L. Superior

Ft. Mackinac

L. Huron

L. Michigan

Michigan Territory

Illinois Territory

Detroit

Frenchtown

York

L. Ontario

Lundy's Lane

Chippews

The Thames

L. Erie

Erie

Put-in-Bay

Indiana Territory

Ohio

Kentucky

Tennessee

Ohio R.

North Carolina

Claimed by Britain and the United States

New Hampshire

Vermont

Sorel

Montreal

Plattsburgh

Lake Champlain

New York

Massachusetts

Hartford

Rhode Island

Connecticut

New Jersey

Pennsylvania

Baltimore

Washington, D.C.

Virginia

Maryland

Chesapeake Bay

Delaware

British blockade

ATLANTIC OCEAN

0 200 mi
0 200 km

Albers Conic Equal-Area Projection

St. Lawrence R.

Hudson R.

Mississippi R.

>> Both sides won victories in the War of 1812, with no clear overall winner. **Analyze Maps** Where did Andrew Jackson's forces win victories on their route to New Orleans?

In 1817, James Monroe of Virginia succeeded Madison as President. Monroe and his Secretary of State John Quincy Adams made another foreign policy statement by issuing the **Monroe Doctrine**. In this declaration, the United States asserted that the monarchies of Europe had no business meddling with American republics, including those in Latin America. In turn, the United States promised to stay out of European affairs.

☑ **DEFINE** What is the principle of judicial review?

The Age of Jackson

The rise of war hero General **Andrew Jackson** in the 1820s shifted the politics of the nation. While the age of **Jacksonian democracy** expanded the concept of democracy, some policies of the Jackson era resulted in long-term political strife.

The End of an Era The conclusion of the War of 1812 brought on a period of relative political unity in the United States. Some historians call this the "Era of Good Feeling." However, during the early 1820s, internal differences among Democratic Republicans began emerging. These differences resulted in a four-way presidential race in 1824.

Jackson was the clear winner of the popular vote, but in a four-way race, no candidate was able to win a majority of electoral votes. Therefore, under the Constitution, the election was decided by the House of Representatives. Fourth-place finisher Henry Clay threw his support to John Quincy Adams, who became President.

Aided by his party's organization, Jackson triumphed over Adams in 1828. Jackson's victory split the Democratic Party when Democrats who opposed Jackson founded a new political party known as the Whigs. The Era of Good Feelings was at an end.

Jacksonian Democracy Jackson rose to prominence at a time when national politics was becoming increasingly democratic. More states chose presidential electors by popular vote, rather than by state legislatures, and many states abolished property requirements for voting. Participation in elections grew from less than 30 percent of white men in the early 1800s to almost 80 percent in 1840.

Jacksonian democracy had serious limits. Most state constitutions took the vote away from free blacks, even those with property. Native Americans, who were not citizens, and women could not vote in any state.

The Nullification Crisis Jackson was at the center of conflicts over economic policy that shaped the tone of American politics for decades.

The federal government's use of **protective tariffs** had long been a source of sectional debate. The industrial North favored tariffs while the agrarian South opposed them. In 1828, Congress adopted an especially high tariff, which southerners called "The Tariff of Abominations." South Carolina, relying on the doctrine of **nullification**, claimed that it could void, or nullify, unconstitutional laws within its borders.

Jackson signed into law a new tariff that was not as harsh as the 1828 tariff, but it was still unacceptable to many southerners. The South Carolina state government voted to nullify the tariff law and threatened to secede from the Union. Jackson threatened to use troops to enforce federal law in South Carolina. Although South Carolina eventually backed down after Congress passed a compromise tariff, this showdown between proponents of the states' rights view and the federal government hinted at thorny future conflicts.

Jackson Pushes Indian Removal Despite his stand against nullification, Jackson's political base was in the South, and those voters expected him to help them remove the 60,000 Native Americans living in the region. In 1830 Congress passed the **Indian Removal Act**. This law sought to negotiate the peaceful exchange of Indian lands in the South for new lands in Indian Territory (present-day Oklahoma).

Most Choctaws and Chickasaws did agree to accept lands in the West. But other groups resisted removal. In 1836, after several violent conflicts, the U.S. military forcibly removed the Creeks from their southern lands. In Florida, the Seminoles fought the Second Seminole War between 1835 and 1842. In the end, U.S. troops forced most Seminoles from Florida.

In 1838, federal troops compelled more than 15,000 Cherokees to travel from the Southeast to Oklahoma. At least 4,000 Cherokees died of disease, exposure, and hunger along what came to be called the **Trail of Tears**.

Bank Politics and Economic Woes Jackson also sided with the interests of southern farmers in his opposition to the second Bank of the United States, which Congress had chartered in 1816. Business leaders argued that the Bank fostered economic growth and confidence, but Jacksonian Democrats felt that it favored a small number of rich investors. In 1832, Jackson vetoed the renewal of the Bank's charter.

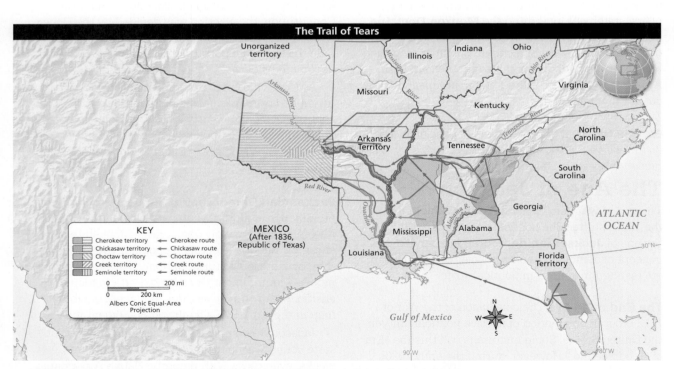

>> This map shows the Trail of Tears and its outcome. **Interpret** Using the scale bar, find the distance the Cherokee walked. How might this explain why so many died on the journey?

FUNCTIONS OF THE SECOND BANK
OF THE UNITED STATES

BANK OF THE FEDERAL GOVERNMENT
- Holds the government's money
- Pays the government's bills

MONEY CREATOR
Issues paper money that people can use throughout the United States, unlike state money

REGULATOR
- Issues or redeems national money to keep economy stable
- Monitors amount of money from state banks

COMMERCIAL BANK
- Accepts deposits and makes loans
- Provides access to businesses and individuals at branches across the country

>> The second National Bank was founded to help the federal government manage its income and expenses. **Analyze Charts** How was the Bank involved in the nation's economy?

Supporters of the Bank formed the **Whig Party** to oppose Jackson's policies. After Jackson won re-election in 1832, he took steps to finish off the Bank. Relieved from federal regulation, state and private banks flooded the nation with paper money of uncertain value. Jackson's decision to stop accepting paper money for the purchase of federal land eventually let to the **Panic of 1837**, the nation's worst economic depression to that date.

The Young Republic The United States in the early 1800s had its share of political disputes and economic hiccups, but these problems only served to prove the stability and strength of the United States.

By the 1830s, the United States was a rising economic power and a model of democratic stability. Beginning in 1831, French aristocrat **Alexis de Tocqueville** undertook a study of American society and politics. His findings were published in a now-classic work of political science, *Democracy in America*. Tocqueville was impressed with the young nation's commitment to the ideals of liberty and individualism expressed in the Declaration of Independence and Constitution.

Tocqueville was particularly astonished by American individualism and populism, or the widespread participation of ordinary citizens in the political process. These traits were largely absent in the older social systems of Europe, where class identity determined an individual's place in society and the upper classes dominated politics to the exclusion of nearly everyone else.

☑ **DEFINE** What event did the federal government's use of a strong protective tariff lead to?

Growing Differences Between North and South

In the United States, the **Industrial Revolution** took hold first in the Northeast, which had more water power than any other region. The new factories attracted European immigrants seeking work. With more labor power available, even more factories were built and cities grew.

While the Northeast industrialized, the southern states became more reliant on an agricultural economy fueled by slave labor. The invention of the **cotton gin** in 1793 made cotton the South's leading crop and increased the need for, and the profitability of, slaves.

Growing Demand for Cotton Because of demand for cotton from textile mills in both Europe and the North, cotton prices increased. This encouraged southern planters to expand their fields and increase the number of enslaved African Americans they owned.

As the northern and southern economies diverged, their political differences increased as well. Many northerners objected to slavery on moral grounds, and by 1804, every state north of Maryland had passed laws to end slavery gradually. Because of the importance of slavery to the southern economy, southerners grew stronger in their defense of slavery.

Resistance to Slavery Many enslaved people did whatever they could to fight back against their oppressors. Resistance often took the form of sabotage, such as breaking tools or outwitting overseers.

Sometimes, resistance became violent. Historians estimate that nearly 200 significant slave revolts took place in the first half of the 1800s. Terrified by the idea of a successful slave revolt, southerners passed harsher laws and controls regarding slavery. Enslaved people were forbidden to gather in groups unless an overseer was present. In addition, it became illegal to teach enslaved people to read.

The increasingly harsh conditions faced by slaves inspired some people in the North to work against slavery. Some northern abolitionists and free blacks organized a network known as the **underground railroad** to help slaves escape from the South. A secret network of "conductors" hid runaway slaves in farm wagons and on riverboats and then moved them to destinations in the North or in Canada. Using complex signals and hiding places, the underground railroad carried its passengers over hundreds of miles of dangerous terrain.

The Voices of Abolitionism By the early 1800s, a growing number of **abolitionists** began to speak out against slavery. One of the most influential abolitionists was **Frederick Douglass**. As a former slave with direct experience of the harsh conditions the enslaved endured in the South, Douglass became a powerful speaker at abolitionist meetings. In 1852, Douglass was invited to speak at an Independence Day celebration.

Fellow citizens, pardon me, and allow me to ask, why am I called upon to speak here today? What have I or those I represent to do with your national independence? Are the great principles of political freedom and of natural justice, embodied in that Declaration of Independence,

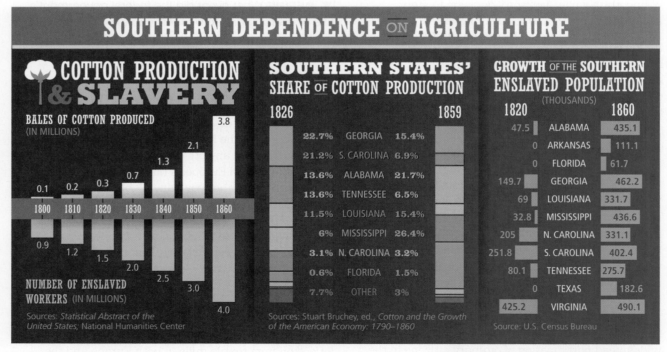

SOUTHERN DEPENDENCE ON AGRICULTURE

COTTON PRODUCTION & SLAVERY

BALES OF COTTON PRODUCED (IN MILLIONS)

1800	1810	1820	1830	1840	1850	1860
0.1	0.2	0.3	0.7	1.3	2.1	3.8

NUMBER OF ENSLAVED WORKERS (IN MILLIONS)

| 0.9 | 1.2 | 1.5 | 2.0 | 2.5 | 3.0 | 4.0 |

Sources: *Statistical Abstract of the United States*; National Humanities Center

SOUTHERN STATES' SHARE OF COTTON PRODUCTION

1826		1859
22.7%	GEORGIA	15.4%
21.2%	S. CAROLINA	6.9%
13.6%	ALABAMA	21.7%
13.6%	TENNESSEE	6.5%
11.5%	LOUISIANA	15.4%
6%	MISSISSIPPI	26.4%
3.1%	N. CAROLINA	3.2%
0.6%	FLORIDA	1.5%
7.7%	OTHER	3%

Sources: Stuart Bruchey, ed., *Cotton and the Growth of the American Economy: 1790–1860*

GROWTH OF THE SOUTHERN ENSLAVED POPULATION (THOUSANDS)

1820		1860
47.5	ALABAMA	435.1
0	ARKANSAS	111.1
0	FLORIDA	61.7
149.7	GEORGIA	462.2
69	LOUISIANA	331.7
32.8	MISSISSIPPI	436.6
205	N. CAROLINA	331.1
251.8	S. CAROLINA	402.4
80.1	TENNESSEE	275.7
0	TEXAS	182.6
425.2	VIRGINIA	490.1

Source: U.S. Census Bureau

>> **Analyze Charts** Which state experienced the largest growth in cotton production between 1826 and 1859?

 Bounce to Activate Map

The Reform Movement

Political Origins

- The ideals of liberty and equality in the Declaration of Independence inspire people to try to improve society
- During Jackson era, more people can vote than ever before
- Critics say slavery and other injustices violate democratic ideals

Religious Influences

- Second Great Awakening stresses free will rather than predestination
- Revivals encourage people to reform their lives
- Finney teaches that individual salvation is the first step to the reform of a society

>> **Analyze Charts** Based on the information in the chart, how were the reform movements of the nineteenth century rooted in American cultural and political ideals?

extended to us? . . . What, to the American slave, is your Fourth of July? I answer: a day that reveals to him, more than all other days in the year, the gross injustice and cruelty to which he is the constant victim.

—Frederick Douglass, speech at Rochester, 1852

Slavery Divides the Nation In cities across the Northeast and the Midwest, abolitionist societies sprang up, yet most Americans did not support the abolition of slavery. White workers in the North feared that free African Americans would take their jobs, and wealthy industrialists worried that the end of slavery would cut off the supply of southern cotton and reduce the demand for ships and shipyards.

Defenders of slavery maintained that slave labor was superior to the wage labor of the North. They argued that northern employers and laborers were inevitably at odds, since employers wanted workers to work more for less money while workers wanted to work less for more money.

Despite the interdependence of the northern and southern economies, the issue of slavery above all others increasingly divided Americans.

☑ **DEFINE** What is an abolitionist?

Reform in the Early 1800s

Abolitionism was part of a drive to reform American society in the early 1800s. This reform movement was partly created by the **Second Great Awakening**, a revival of religious feeling that led to an increase in participation in evangelical Protestant movements. This reform movement provided new opportunities for women. In the early 1800s, American women lacked many basic legal and economic rights. Education beyond grade school was almost unheard-of, and they rarely took part in public life.

Women Lead Reform Efforts Women, however, were welcomed by the emerging reform movements. They worked in the temperance movement, the abolition movement, and other reform movements. Sisters Angelina and Sarah Grimké spoke and wrote against slavery. Dorothea Dix campaigned to win better, more humane treatment for people with mental illness. Emma Willard established schools for women in Connecticut, Ohio, and New York. Soon, some of these reformers began to work to gain equality for women as well. Their efforts would lay the groundwork for women's struggle for equal rights—especially the right to vote—over the next hundred years.

A Women's Rights Movement Emerges The industrialization of the 1820s and 1830s provided the first real economic opportunity for women outside the home in the nation's history. Thousands of young women who would have stayed in the family home instead went to work in mills and factories. This gave them a small degree of economic independence and a larger degree of social independence.

Although many women became leading reformers and many others entered the workforce, there had still been virtually no progress in women's rights. As more women became involved in the abolitionist movement, they began to see their own social restrictions as being comparable to slavery. They began to call for increased rights of their own. Women's rights reformers began to publish their ideas in pamphlets and books.

The Seneca Falls Convention In 1848, **Lucretia Mott** and **Elizabeth Cady Stanton**, two prominent abolitionists, helped organize the **Seneca Falls Convention**. This meeting, the first of the **women's rights movement** in the United States, attracted hundreds of men and women. One of the most illustrious attendees was Frederick Douglass.

The delegates to the convention adopted a **Declaration of Sentiments**, modeled after the language of the Declaration of Independence.

> We hold these truths to be self-evident: that all men and women are created equal. . . . The history of mankind is a history of repeated injuries and usurpations on the part of man toward woman, having in direct object the establishment of an absolute tyranny over her.
>
> —Elizabeth Cady Stanton, Declaration of Sentiments

The Declaration called for greater educational opportunities for women, as well as for the right of women to control their own wages and property.

The convention inspired a generation of leaders who carried on the struggle. Among them was **Susan B. Anthony**, whose involvement in the temperance and abolition movements inspired her to work for greater rights for women as well. By the mid-1800s, women reformers had laid the foundation for a future in which equality seemed a real possibility. However, the most coveted goal of the women's rights movement—**suffrage**—was not achieved until 1920.

☑ **IDENTIFY MAIN IDEAS** What was the outcome of the Seneca Fall Convention?

The Nation Expands

By 1830, the United States had grown beyond its original territory along the Atlantic Coast to include the Louisiana Purchase and Florida. American **expansionists** coveted the Oregon Territory in the Northwest and the Mexican provinces of New Mexico, Texas, and California.

Manifest Destiny In an influential editorial, journalist John L. O'Sullivan expressed the ideals that motivated many American expansionists.

Roots of Manifest Destiny

SOCIAL	POLITICAL	ECONOMIC
• Belief in America as an exceptional nation • Desire to spread American democracy and ideals • Belief that it was God's will for America to expand • View that white Americans were superior to Native Americans	• Monroe Doctrine warning against European colonization in the Western hemisphere • Desire to acquire Oregon from Britain • Desire to acquire Texas from Mexico • Success of Democrats, who supported expansion, over Whigs, who did not	• Farmland for settlers • Access to rich resources • Land for southern crops such as cotton

>> People had different reasons for supporting the idea of Manifest Destiny. **Analyze Charts** How might people's values lead them to support Manifest Destiny?

 Bounce to Activate Map

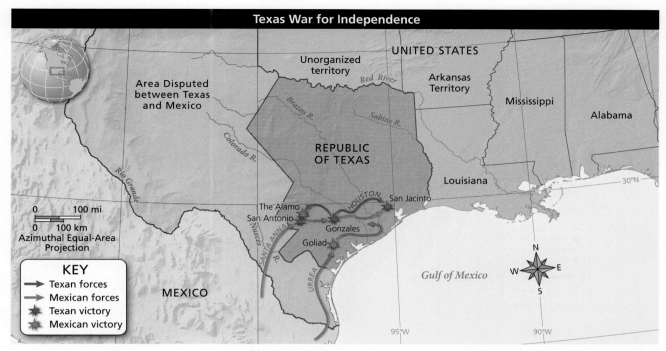

>> After a brief yet bloody war, the Republic of Texas won its independence from Mexico. **Analyze Maps** Describe the movement of Mexican and Texan forces after the battle at the Alamo.

The American claim is by the right of our manifest destiny to overspread and possess the whole of the continent which Providence has given us for the development of the great experiment of liberty and . . . self-government entrusted to us.

—John L. O'Sullivan, *New York Morning News,* December 27, 1845

The phrase **Manifest Destiny** soon became a rallying cry for expansionists. During the 1840s alone, nearly 20,000 Americans migrated to California, Oregon, and Utah along the major overland trails. The trails also became trade routes, carrying merchants and goods in both directions.

The Texas Revolution During the 1820s, farmers from the South had begun to settle in Texas, becoming Mexican citizens. By 1835, Texas was home to about 30,000 colonists from the United States known as Anglo-Texans. In 1835, Anglo-Texans rebelled against the Mexican government, and in 1836, Texas declared its independence and adopted a republican constitution. In response, Mexican forces attacked the Texan rebels. Led by

Sam Houston, Texan forces crushed the Mexican army at the Battle of San Jacinto, forcing the Mexican general to sign a treaty recognizing Texan independence and conceding generous boundaries that stretched south and west to the Rio Grande. The government in Mexico City refused to honor the terms of the treaty, and a border war persisted between Texas and Mexico.

After achieving independence, Texas quickly asked to be annexed by the United States. President Jackson favored annexation, as did American expansionists from the South. However, northern representatives in Congress balked at adding another slave state, especially one so large and potentially powerful. Texas was not annexed until 1845.

War With Mexico In 1844, **James K. Polk**, a slaveholder and expansionist, was elected President. Polk favored the annexation of Texas, and he vowed to fight Britain if it did not give up its claims to the Oregon Territory. Despite his strong words, Polk compromised with the British, agreeing to split the Oregon Territory at the 49th parallel of latitude.

Polk took a harder line on the Texas question. He endorsed a Texan border claim that was still disputed by Mexico and sent troops to occupy the

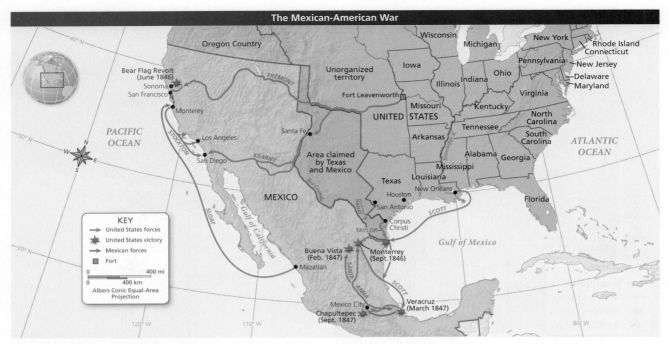

>> Analyze Maps What region on the map was the subject of the land dispute that sparked the war? Describe the U.S. troop movements in the final month of the war.

contested territory. After a Mexican patrol clashed with U.S. soldiers in May 1846, Polk asked for and received a declaration of war against Mexico.

Democrats, especially those from the South, were enthusiastically in favor of the war. Whigs suspected Polk of deliberately provoking the conflict in order to annex New Mexico and California, which might then enter the Union as slave states.

A Decisive Victory Expands U.S. Territory The war with Mexico was extremely one-sided. During the next year and a half, the United States won every major battle, and by September 1847, U.S. forces had captured the Mexican capital of Mexico City, forcing the Mexicans to sign the **Treaty of Guadalupe Hidalgo**. This treaty gave the United States possession of New Mexico and California for the price of $18 million and secured the Rio Grande as the southern boundary of Texas. The Mexican-American War, together with the annexation of Texas, increased the size of U.S. territory by a third.

The slavery debate was rekindled when California applied for statehood a year later. In 1849, the nation had an equal number of free and slave states—15 each—maintaining the sectional balance in the Senate. The admission of California would tip that balance in favor of the free states. Thus, the U.S. victory over Mexico ultimately contributed to the growing conflict between North and South.

☑ **DEFINE** What was Manifest Destiny?

☑ ASSESSMENT

1. **Describe** the positive and negative aspects of Jacksonian democracy.

2. **Identify Central Issues** Explain how President Jackson's administration dealt with the Native Americans in the South.

3. **Generate Explanations** Explain how the United States government differed from foreign governments at the time of Alexis de Tocqueville's visit.

4. **Make Generalizations** How did the women's rights movement begin in the United States?

5. **Generate Explanations** Explain how the Texas Revolution and the Mexican-American War expanded the territory of the United States.

Democracy in America: Alexis de Tocqueville

Alexis de Tocqueville, a young French writer, visited the United States in 1831. During his travels, he observed firsthand the impact of Jacksonian democracy. After returning to France, Tocqueville began writing *Democracy in America*, a detailed look at American politics, society, economics, religion, and law. In these excerpts from *Democracy in America*, Tocqueville discusses the role of the American people in their government and gives his view of the American character.

>> *The County Election* George Caleb Bingham

In America the principle of the sovereignty of the people is not either barren or concealed, as it is with some other nations; it is recognized by the customs and proclaimed by the laws; it spreads freely, and arrives without impediment at its most remote consequences. If there be a country in the world where the doctrine of the sovereignty of the people can be fairly appreciated, where it can be studied in its application to the affairs of society, and where its dangers and its advantages may be foreseen, that country is assuredly America.

I have already observed that, from their origin, the sovereignty of the people was the fundamental principle of the greater number of British colonies in America. It was far, however, from then exercising as much influence on the government of society as it now does. Two obstacles, the one external, the other internal, checked its invasive progress. It could not ostensibly disclose itself in the laws of colonies which were still constrained to obey the mother-country: it was therefore obliged to spread secretly, and to gain ground in the provincial assemblies, and especially in the townships.

☑ **SUMMARIZE** According to Tocqueville, how did the principle of popular sovereignty spread throughout the British colonies?

. . . it is at least true that in the United States the county and the township are always based upon the same principle, namely, that everyone is the best judge of what concerns himself alone, and the most proper person to supply his private wants.

☑ **DETERMINE CENTRAL IDEAS** Recall that laissez-faire is the economic principle that says business should be free from government interference. How is the principle of laissez-faire represented in this section of Tocqueville's text?

In America the people appoints the legislative and the executive power, and furnishes the jurors who punish all offences against the laws. The American institutions are democratic, not only in their principle but in all their consequences; and the people elects its representatives directly, and for the most part annually, in order to ensure their dependence. The people is therefore the real directing power; and although the form of government is representative, it is evident that the opinions, the prejudices, the interests, and even the passions of the community are hindered by no durable obstacles from exercising a perpetual influence on society. In the United States the majority governs in the name of the people, as is the case in all the countries in which the people is supreme. The majority is principally composed of peaceful citizens who, either by inclination or by interest, are sincerely desirous of the welfare of their country. But they are surrounded by the incessant agitation of parties, which attempt to gain their co-operation and to avail themselves of their support.

☑ **EXPLAIN AN ARGUMENT** What does Tocqueville mean when he says that American institutions are "democratic" both in their "principle" and their "consequences"?

The inhabitants of the United States are never fettered by the axioms of their profession; they escape from all the prejudices of their present station; they are not more attached to one line of operation than to another; they are not more prone to employ an old method than a new one; they have no rooted habits, and they easily shake off the influence which the habits of other nations might exercise upon their minds from a conviction that their country is unlike any other, and that its situation is without a precedent in the world. America is a land of wonders, in which everything is in constant motion, and every movement seems an improvement. The idea of novelty is there indissolubly connected with the idea of amelioration. No natural boundary seems to be set to the efforts of man; and what is not yet done is only what he has not yet attempted to do.

This perpetual change which goes on in the United States, these frequent vicissitudes of fortune, accompanied by such unforeseen fluctuations in private and in public wealth, serve to keep the minds of the citizens in a perpetual state of feverish agitation, which admirably invigorates their exertions, and keeps them in a state of excitement above the ordinary level of mankind. The whole life of an American is passed like a game of chance, a revolutionary crisis, or a battle. As the same causes are continually in operation throughout the country, they ultimately impart an irresistible impulse to the national character. The American, taken as a chance specimen of his countrymen, must then be a man of singular warmth in his desires, enterprising, fond of adventure, and, above all, of innovation. The same bent is manifest in all that he does; he introduces it into his political laws, his religious doctrines, his theories of social economy, and his domestic occupations; he bears it with him in the depths of the backwoods, as well as in the business of the city. . .

☑ **DRAW CONCLUSIONS** What explains the qualities of adaptability that Tocqueville perceives in the American character?

☑ ASSESSMENT

1. **Explain an Argument** Explain why Tocqueville regards the principle of individualism as such a crucial social value.

2. **Summarize** What impressed Tocqueville during his time in America? Cite examples to support your answer.

3. **Draw Conclusions** In what way could Tocqueville's book be relevant today?

Regional differences between the North and the South had existed since colonial times. These differences widened in the 1800s as the North developed an industrial economy while the South continued to depend on plantation agriculture and slavery. In time, conflict over the issue of slavery led to an armed struggle that would forever change the nation: the Civil War.

>> John Brown led fellow antislavery settlers on a murderous raid in Kansas against proslavery settlers in 1856. **Infer** What conditions led Brown to take this action?

Bounce to Activate Flipped Video

The Union in Crisis

Slavery and Western Expansion

During the Mexican-American War, the question of slavery in the West emerged as a major issue. To prevent the South from extending slavery into the western territories, in 1846 Pennsylvania congressman David Wilmot proposed an amendment, or proviso, to an appropriations bill. The **Wilmot Proviso** called for a ban on slavery in any territory that the United States gained from Mexico as a result of the war.

Southern leaders angrily denounced the proposal.

The amendment passed the northern-dominated House of Representatives, but it was defeated in the Senate. Although it never became law, the Wilmot Proviso contributed to the increasing tension between the North and South over the slavery issue.

The Formation of the Free-Soil Party The Wilmot Proviso helped spur the rise of antislavery political parties. In 1848, northern opponents of slavery formed the **Free-Soil Party**. The Free-Soil Party wanted to prevent the expansion of slavery into the western territories. The party nominated former President Martin Van Buren as their presidential candidate in the election of 1848. Van Buren did not win, but he and other Free-Soil candidates

>> Objectives

Analyze why slavery in the territories was a divisive issue and how Congress tried to settle the issue in 1850.

Assess how the Kansas-Nebraska Act and John Brown's raid affected the tensions between North and South.

Compare the candidates in the election of 1860, and analyze the results.

Analyze why southern states seceded from the Union.

>> Key Terms

Wilmot Proviso
Free-Soil Party
Compromise of 1850
popular sovereignty
Fugitive Slave Act
Harriet Beecher Stowe
Kansas-Nebraska Act

John Brown
Dred Scott v. *Sandford*
Roger Taney
Abraham Lincoln
John C. Breckinridge
Confederate States of America
Jefferson Davis

>> Harriet Tubman (far left) poses with a group of enslaved people she helped escape to the North along the underground railroad—a loosely organized network of hiding places created by northern abolitionists and free blacks.

garnered enough votes to show that the party's motto of "Free soil, Free speech, Free labor, and Free men" would not be silenced.

Another Compromise In 1850, California applied to enter the Union as a free state, threatening the balance of power between slave and free states in the Senate. To ease southern concerns, Congress debated and then passed the **Compromise of 1850**.

According to this measure, California was admitted as a free state, but in the other territory acquired from Mexico, voters would decide the slavery issue for themselves. This approach became known as **popular sovereignty**, an application of that founding principle enshrined in the Constitution. But by permitting slavery north of 36°30'N latitude, the Compromise of 1850 undid the Missouri Compromise.

The Compromise of 1850 included a **Fugitive Slave Act**. This law allowed officials to arrest any person accused of being a runaway slave, denied fugitives the right to a jury trial, and required all citizens to help capture runaway slaves. The Fugitive Slave Act outraged many Northerners, who resented being legally forced to support the slave system.

Some northern states fought back by passing personal liberty laws. These laws nullified the Fugitive Slave Act, allowing the states to arrest slave catchers for kidnapping. Northern opponents of the law also mounted an intense resistance. In 1851, at Christiana, Pennsylvania, a small band of African Americans gathered to protect several runaways from southern slave catchers. Local white bystanders refused to help the slave-hunting party. Then, after the slave owner died in the scuffle, a white jury refused to convict the killers.

☑ **RECALL** Which piece of legislation kept the balance between free states and slave states?

The Road to Disunion

Resentment against the Fugitive Slave Act spurred **Harriet Beecher Stowe** to write the novel *Uncle Tom's Cabin*, a powerful condemnation of slavery. Stowe's sympathetic main character, Uncle Tom, put a human face on slavery for readers who had never witnessed slavery firsthand. *Uncle Tom's Cabin* sold 300,000 copies in its first year, increasing antislavery sentiment in the North. But it angered Southerners, who argued that Stowe's book presented a false picture of slavery and the South.

>> Harriet Beecher Stowe came from a family of well-known abolitionists, ministers, and education reformers.

Published in 1852, *Uncle Tom's Cabin* was so influential that years later, when Stowe visited President Lincoln at the White House during the Civil War, Lincoln reportedly greeted the author by saying, "So you are the little woman who wrote the book that made this great war."

Popular Sovereignty in Kansas and Nebraska

In 1854, Congress again tried to settle the issue of slavery in the West. When Senator Stephen Douglas introduced a bill to establish a government for the Nebraska Territory, his proposal was defeated by southern senators who objected to allowing Nebraska to enter the Union as a free state. To accommodate Southerners, Douglas rewrote the bill. After much debate, Congress passed the **Kansas-Nebraska Act**, which divided the Nebraska Territory into Kansas and Nebraska. Voters in each territory would decide the issue of slavery by popular sovereignty. Many Northerners complained that this plan allowed slavery in areas where it had been banned by the Missouri Compromise.

Soon, both proslavery and antislavery settlers were flocking to Kansas, each hoping to outnumber the other when the time came to vote on slavery. In 1855, proslavery supporters set up a territorial government at Shawnee Mission. Free-state settlers responded by establishing an antislavery government in Topeka. Kansas now had two governments—a formula for disaster.

"Bleeding Kansas" On May 21, 1856, southern proslavery forces attacked the free-state town of Lawrence, Kansas. They looted homes, burned down the hotel, and destroyed the presses of *The Kansas Free State* newspaper. Swift retaliation came from New York abolitionist **John Brown**, who had moved his family to Kansas in pursuit of an opportunity to confront the slavery issue. A few days after the sack of Lawrence, Brown, along with his sons and a few friends, conducted a midnight raid on the proslavery settlement at nearby Pottawatomie Creek. During the raid, they brutally murdered five proslavery settlers. These killings led to even more violence. Throughout the fall of 1856, there was so much violence perpetrated by both sides that the territory became known as "Bleeding Kansas." Finally, in 1861, Kansas entered the Union as a free state.

The Formation of the Republican Party

Opposition to slavery led to the creation of the new Republican Party in 1854. Republicans included abolitionists, antislavery business leaders, and Northerners who argued that the Fugitive Slave Act

>> Dred Scott, having once lived in a free state, sued for his freedom after his owner died.

intruded into state politics. The Republican Party quickly became a powerful political force, winning 105 seats in the House of Representatives in the 1854 congressional elections.

The presidential election of 1856 pitted Democrat James Buchanan against John C. Frémont, the candidate of the new Republican Party. Buchanan, who promised that as President he would stop "the agitation of the slavery issue," was supported by a large majority of Southerners. He won the election, but Frémont, who opposed the spread of slavery, made a strong showing. Frémont won one third of the popular vote and 11 northern states.

A Controversial Supreme Court Ruling In 1857, a controversial Supreme Court ruling widened the growing divisions over slavery. The ruling concerned the case of Dred Scott, an enslaved African American from Missouri who had sued for his freedom in 1846. Scott's lawyers argued that he should be considered free because he had lived with his master in the free state of Illinois between 1834 and 1838. After a series of appeals, Scott's case reached the Supreme Court.

In ***Dred Scott* v. *Sandford***, the Court ruled against Scott. But the Court's sweeping ruling went far beyond the particulars of Scott's case. The Court

>> In 1858, Abraham Lincoln and Stephen Douglas debated over the spread of slavery. While both men disliked slavery, Lincoln opposed its spread and Douglas favored settling the issue by popular sovereignty.

>> An eloquent speaker, former slave Frederick Douglass became a powerful spokesperson for the abolition of slavery. He also published an autobiography in which he described the brutality of slavery.

declared that African Americans were not citizens and, therefore, were not entitled to sue in the courts.

Chief Justice **Roger Taney** stated that since African Americans had not been part of the political community when the Constitution was adopted, they did not have the same rights as groups that were included in that community. He wrote that slaves "are not included, and were not intended to be included, under the word 'citizens' in the Constitution, and can therefore claim none of the rights and privileges which that instrument provides for and secures to citizens of the United States."

The Court went beyond the question of slaves' citizenship and stated that Congress did not have the power to ban slavery in any territory. Taney pointed out that such a ban deprived citizens of their property without due process of law, a violation of the Fifth Amendment. This meant that the Missouri Compromise was unconstitutional, as would be any future attempt by Congress to decide the slavery status of a new state.

Reaction to the *Dred Scott* Decision The language of the Court's ruling seemed to indicate that the Constitution itself settled the issue: slaves were not citizens, and states had the right to decide on the issue of slavery themselves. However, the *Dred Scott* decision only intensified the slavery debate rather than helping settle it, and public reactions drove the North and the South further apart than ever. Southerners were delighted with the Court's ruling while Northerners viewed it with alarm. Some abolitionists, however, felt that such an unfair decision would bring the crisis to a head more quickly, actually hastening the end of slavery. As leading black abolitionist Frederick Douglass said, "This very attempt to blot out forever the hopes of an enslaved people may be one necessary link in the chain of events preparatory to the complete overthrow of the whole slave system."

☑ **APPLY CONCEPTS** What was the result of the *Dred Scott* decision?

The Lincoln-Douglas Debates

The 1858 Senate race in Illinois crystallized the slavery issue for many Americans. Republican **Abraham Lincoln** challenged Senator Stephen Douglas, a Democrat and the architect of the Kansas-Nebraska Act, to a series of debates.

THE CHANGING PERCEPTION OF SLAVERY

1854
SUPPORT FOR THE
KANSAS-NEBRASKA ACT

HOUSE VOTE

100 AGAINST

113 FOR

SENATE VOTE

14

37

Source: Library of Congress

1855
KANSAS ELECTION FOR
TERRITORIAL LEGISLATURE

2,905 LEGALLY-REGISTERED VOTERS

6,218 ACTUAL VOTES CAST

791 VOTES FOR ANTI-SLAVERY CANDIDATES

5,427 VOTES FOR PRO-SLAVERY CANDIDATES

Source: John Lalor, *Cyclopaedia of Political Science, Political Economy, and of the Political History of the United States* (1883)

1858
ILLINOIS SENATE ELECTION

54% DOUGLAS
(WON ALL DEMOCRATIC LEGISLATORS' VOTES)

46% LINCOLN
(WON ALL REPUBLICAN LEGISLATORS' VOTES)

Source: Northern Illinois University

>> **Analyze Data** Why did Abraham Lincoln lose the 1858 senatorial election even though he won the popular vote?

The Lincoln-Douglas Debates Both Lincoln and Douglas were excellent speakers whose political differences were underscored by their contrasting physical appearances. Lincoln, tall and thin, had a reputation for integrity that had earned him the nickname "Honest Abe." Senator Douglas, short and stout, with a deep voice, was known as the "Little Giant."

Lincoln, a self-educated lawyer, had begun his political career as a representative to the Illinois state legislature. From 1847 to 1849, Lincoln served one term in the House of Representatives and then returned to his law practice in Springfield. His opposition to the Kansas-Nebraska Act and popular sovereignty inspired Lincoln to resume his political career.

The politically ambitious Douglas believed that popular sovereignty was the implied intent of the Constitution. But many questioned his motives, saying that Douglas favored popular sovereignty in order to gain southern support for a future presidential run. Others claimed that Douglas was eager for Kansas and Nebraska to achieve statehood, because railroad lines built through the new states would benefit Chicago, the largest city in Douglas's state, by making it a hub for economic development of the West.

Thousands of Americans attended the Lincoln-Douglas debates and listened intently as the candidates presented opposing views of slavery and its role in America. Lincoln did not call for the immediate abolition of slavery or for political equality for African Americans. Still, he argued:

> There is no reason in the world why the negro is not entitled to all the natural rights enumerated in the Declaration of Independence, the right to life, liberty and the pursuit of happiness. . . . In the right to eat the bread, without leave of anybody else, which his own hand earns, he is my equal and the equal of Judge Douglas, and the equal of every living man.
>
> —Abraham Lincoln, debate at Ottawa, Illinois, 1858

Douglas, meanwhile, promoted popular sovereignty as the solution to regional tensions. "This Union was established on the right of each State to do as it pleased on the question of slavery, and every other question," he insisted. Douglas won the Senate race, but the debates, covered by newspapers throughout the country, brought Lincoln national attention.

>> Disagreement over slavery turned into violence on the Senate floor in 1856. Abolitionist Senator Charles Sumner of Massachusetts was beaten by Congressman Preston Brooks of South Carolina in retaliation for an anti-slavery speech Sumner gave in which he criticized Brooks's uncle, a senator from South Carolina.

Bounce to Activate Gallery

>> In this abolitionist painting, John Brown pauses on his way to his execution to kiss an enslaved woman's baby.

Trying to Spark a Slave Rebellion While Lincoln and Douglas used the political process to address the slavery issue, radical abolitionist John Brown concluded that using violence was the best way to defeat slavery. In the fall of 1859, Brown and a small band of followers seized the federal arsenal at Harpers Ferry, Virginia (now West Virginia). He hoped to inspire and arm local slaves for an uprising that would spread into a general slave rebellion, eventually ending slavery. But no slaves joined Brown's revolt. Instead, troops under the command of Colonel Robert E. Lee retook the arsenal, wounding Brown and killing or capturing most of his men.

Put on trial for treason and murder, Brown proclaimed his willingness to "mingle my blood . . . with the blood of millions in this slave country whose rights are disregarded by wicked, cruel, and unjust enactments." After a brief trial, the court found him guilty and sentenced him to death by hanging.

Brown's defense of his actions and the dignified calm with which he faced execution made him a heroic martyr to the antislavery cause. Although most Northerners had condemned the raid, Brown's death touched many, increasing northern opposition to slavery. But northern sympathy for a man who had tried to lead a slave revolt further inflamed southern anger and suspicion.

☑ **CHECK UNDERSTANDING** Why did John Brown seize the arsenal at Harpers Ferry?

The Union Collapses

Despite repeated attempts at compromise, disagreement between the North and the South over the issue of slavery continued to deepen. With ill will running so deep, the upcoming elections posed a serious dilemma. It was hard to imagine that either Northerners or Southerners would accept a President from the other region. Could the Union survive?

A Divide Among Democrats The Democrats held their nominating convention in Charleston, South Carolina. The southern Democrats called for a platform supporting federal protection of slavery in the territories. The northern Democrats supported the doctrine of popular sovereignty.

When the northern forces prevailed, the delegates from eight southern states walked out and formed a separate convention.

The Democrats were now split into two parties. The northern Democrats nominated Stephen A.

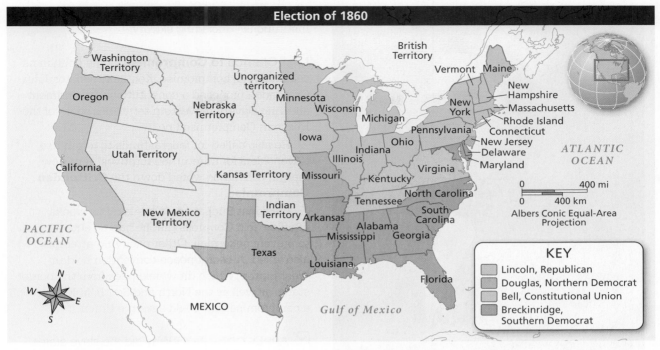

Election of 1860

KEY
- Lincoln, Republican
- Douglas, Northern Democrat
- Bell, Constitutional Union
- Breckinridge, Southern Democrat

>> **Analyze Maps** Would the results of the election have been any different if the Democratic Party had not split into three factions?

Douglas. The southern Democrats nominated the Vice President, **John C. Breckinridge** of Kentucky. Breckinridge was committed to expanding slavery into the territories.

In the meantime, the few remaining Whigs teamed up with the Know-Nothings to create the Constitutional Union Party. They nominated John Bell of Tennessee, and their platform condemned sectional parties and promised to uphold "the Constitution of the country, the Union of the States and the enforcement of the laws."

Lincoln's Nomination The Republican platform called for the end of slavery in the territories. At the same time, the Republicans defended the constitutional principle of federalism. They asserted the right of each state to control its own institutions and stipulated that there should be no interference with slavery in the states where it already existed. At their convention held in Chicago, Abraham Lincoln—with his great debating skills, his moderate views, and his reputation for integrity—was chosen as the candidate to carry the Republican party to victory.

Lincoln's Victory Benefiting from the fracturing among the other political parties, Lincoln won the election handily but did not receive a single southern

electoral vote. In fact, he was not even on the ballot in most southern states.

Southerners were outraged at Lincoln's election. As they had during the Nullification Crisis of Andrew Jackson's presidency, many believed that the Constitution gave the states sovereign power over their own affairs, including the decision to leave the Union if the federal government wasn't protecting their rights. Lincoln and most Northerners disagreed.

The First Wave of Secession As soon as Lincoln's election was confirmed, the South Carolina legislature summoned a state convention.

Meeting in Charleston on December 20, 1860, the convention declared that "the union now subsisting between South Carolina and the other States, under the name of the 'United States of America,' is hereby dissolved." They cited as their reason for seceding the election of a President "whose opinions and purposes are hostile to slavery."

The Southern States Band Together In the next few weeks, six other states of the Deep South seceded from the Union. In February 1861, the seven seceding states established the **Confederate States of America**.

>> Jefferson Davis was a veteran of the Mexican-American War and former Secretary of War under Franklin Pierce. In 1861 he would become president of the Confederate States of America.

Bounce to Activate Chart

They then proceeded to frame a constitution for the new government. The Confederate constitution closely resembled the U.S. Constitution. However, it stressed the independence of each state and implied that states had the right to secede. It also guaranteed the protection of slavery.

Not all Southerners backed the Confederacy. Some large planters with economic ties to the North still hoped for a compromise. So, too, did many small farmers with no vested interest in slavery. To gain the loyalty of such citizens, the Confederacy chose former Mississippi senator **Jefferson Davis** as their president. Davis had supported the Compromise of 1850, but he had also insisted that the South

should be left alone to manage its own culture and institutions—including slavery.

Last Chance to Compromise Some politicians sought a final compromise. Kentucky senator John Crittenden proposed a constitutional amendment allowing slavery in western territories south of the Missouri Compromise line.

He also called for federal funds to reimburse slaveholders for unreturned fugitives. A narrow margin of senators voted down the **Crittenden Compromise**.

President Buchanan, in his last few weeks in office, told Congress that he had no authority to prevent secession. Other pacifying attempts also failed. A secret peace convention held in Washington, which drew delegates from the border states as well as the North and South, failed to reach a compromise that could save the Union.

APPLY CONCEPTS Why did the slave states secede from the Union after Lincoln was elected?

✓ ASSESSMENT

1. **Compare and Contrast** the positions of Abraham Lincoln and Stephen Douglas during the 1858 Senate race.

2. **Describe** the American public's reaction to the *Dred Scott* v. *Sandford* Supreme Court case.

3. **Compare Points of View** Explain how John Brown's approach to abolitionism differed from the approaches of other abolitionists at the time.

4. **Generate Explanations** Explain why the Democratic Party separated into two different groups, and analyze the effect of this split.

5. **Compare and Contrast** the main ideas of the Confederate constitution with those of the U.S. Constitution.

Amid the turmoil of southern states seceding from the Union, forming a new nation, and preparing for war, Abraham Lincoln took office as the new President. Lincoln had no illusions about the challenges he faced in the coming months. He confronted "a task," he feared, "greater than that which rested upon [President George] Washington."

>> At the start of his first term as President, Lincoln gained the respect of those around him. He was admired for his leadership as well as his good nature and sense of humor.

Bounce to Activate Flipped Video

The Civil War

The Civil War Begins

Lincoln Challenges Secession Lincoln was sworn in as President on March 4, 1861. In his inaugural address, he took a firm but conciliatory tone toward the South. "I have no purpose, directly or indirectly, to interfere with the institution of slavery in the states where it exists," he began. But he *did* intend to preserve the Union. "No state, upon its own mere action, can lawfully get out of the Union," he said. Still, he would avoid violence. There would be no war, he pledged, unless the South started it. He concluded with an appeal to the South to live in peace.

> We are not enemies, but friends. We must not be enemies. Though passion may have strained, it must not break our bonds of affection. The mystic chords of memory, stretching from every battle-field, and patriot grave, to every living heart and hearthstone, all over this broad land, will yet swell the chorus of the Union, when

>> Objectives

Assess the events that led to the outbreak of war.

Compare and contrast the resources and strategies of the North and South.

Analyze why Lincoln decided to issue the Emancipation Proclamation and what it achieved.

Analyze how the war changed the economy and society in the North and South.

>> Key Terms

Fort Sumter
Robert E. Lee
Anaconda Plan
Emancipation
  Proclamation
draft law
habeas corpus
inflation

Ulysses S. Grant
Battle of Gettysburg
Gettysburg Address
William T. Sherman
total war
Thirteenth
  Amendment
freedmen

>> When Confederate troops fired across the Charleston Harbor at Fort Sumter, one of only three remaining federal forts in the South, it sparked the beginning of the American Civil War.

>> At the outbreak of hostilities, Washington, D.C., became a staging area for Union troops such as these in 1861. Troops gathered and trained for invasion of the South, part of the Union's aggressive strategy to win the war.

again touched, as surely they will be, by the better angels of our nature.

—Abraham Lincoln, March 4, 1861

Lincoln Makes the First of Many Difficult Decisions

When the southern states seceded, they seized the federal forts and arsenals within their borders. Only four forts remained in Union hands. The most important of these was **Fort Sumter**, which guarded the harbor at Charleston, South Carolina. In January1861, President Buchanan tried to send troops and supplies to the fort, but the unarmed supply ship sailed away when Confederate guns fired on it. Upon taking office, Lincoln had to decide whether to take the risk required to hold on to these forts or yield to Confederate demands that they be surrendered.

By April, the troops at the fort desperately needed food and supplies. Lincoln, who still hoped to bring back the South without bloodshed, faced a dilemma. Should he try to resupply the fort? Or should he let the Confederates take it? Lincoln struggled to make a decision. During his inaugural address, he had promised Southerners that "the government will not assail you." But as President, he was sworn to defend the property of the United States. A wrong move could touch off a war. At last, trying to steer a middle course, Lincoln notified South Carolina that he was sending supplies—food only, no arms—to the fort.

The Surrender of Fort Sumter

South Carolinians were suspicious of Lincoln's motives and ordered the Fort Sumter garrison to surrender to the Confederacy. When the Union troops refused, the Confederates fired on the fort. The Union troops eventually ran out of ammunition, forcing the commander to surrender.

President Lincoln called for 75,000 volunteers to fight against the Confederacy. The South responded just as strongly. As in the North, the South raised troops quickly and struggled to equip and train them before sending them into battle. Both sides predicted a short skirmish, with victory only a few days or months away. These predictions were unfounded. Americans faced years of terrible suffering before the fighting that had begun at Fort Sumter would finally end.

Northerners responded to the attack on Fort Sumter with shock and anger. A few days later, on April 15, President Lincoln declared that "insurrection" existed. The Civil War had officially begun. The slave states that had remained in

ECONOMIC DEVELOPMENT IN THE NORTH & SOUTH

POPULATION IN 1860

NORTH	27.71 MILLION
SOUTH	8.73 MILLION

50 U.S. CITIES WITH LARGEST POPULATIONS 1860

NORTH 38

5 BORDER STATES

SOUTH 7

Source: U.S. Census Bureau

TOTAL VALUE OF MANUFACTURED PRODUCTS 1860
TOP 5 NORTHERN & SOUTHERN STATES

NY	$378,870,939	$50,652,124	VA
PA	$290,121,188	$17,987,225	TN
MA	$255,545,922	$16,925,564	GA
OH	$121,691,148	$16,678,698	NC
CT	$81,924,555	$15,587,473	LA

Source: Historical Census Browser, University of Virginia

UNION & CONFEDERATE RESOURCES 1861

RAILROADS	71%	29%
FARM ACREAGE	65%	35%
MANUFACTURING WORKERS	92%	8%
FACTORIES (THOUSANDS)	110	18

Source: U.S. Census Bureau

>> **Analyze Data** What advantages did the North have over the South at the start of the Civil War?

Bounce to Activate Chart

the Union now had to choose sides. Within two months of the surrender at Fort Sumter, Virginia, Arkansas, Tennessee, and North Carolina joined the Confederacy. Delaware, Kentucky, Maryland, and Missouri remained in the Union.

☑ **SEQUENCE EVENTS** What event marked the beginning of the Civil War?

Resources, Strategies, and Early Battles

With the election of Lincoln, the slavery issue that had long divided North from South finally split the nation in two. From April 1861 to April 1865, the United States of America and the Confederate States of America faced each other in the bloody Civil War. At stake was the future not only of slavery but of the Union itself.

As the Civil War began, each side had a clear goal. The North was determined to preserve the Union, arguing that no state had the right to secede. The southern states that formed the Confederacy aimed to gain their independence from a Union that they felt had become hostile to their interests.

Advantages Enjoyed by the North Although each side faced challenges, a variety of factors favored the Union. In the Northeast, growing urban populations supported a wide range of manufacturing. Replenished by a continuing influx of immigrant workers from Europe, northern factories were able to increase production of the supplies needed to wage war: ammunition, arms, uniforms, medical supplies, food, ships, and railroad cars.

Across the North, the railroad network was well developed, as were systems for farming, mining, and processing raw materials. Banking, insurance, and financing industries were also clustered in the urbanized North. The federal government had a well-organized navy. By the end of 1861, the Union navy had outfitted and launched more than 250 warships and was constructing dozens more. Naval superiority allowed the Union to blockade the South's few vital ports.

Advantages Enjoyed by the South Given such advantages, Northerners anticipated a quick victory. But the South had distinct advantages as well. When the war began, the Union army consisted of only about 16,000 men. Although the South had an even smaller army, its troops at the outset of the war were more highly motivated, and they were led by some of the nation's finest and most experienced officers. The experienced and inspiring **Robert E. Lee** had originally been offered command of Union forces but chose instead to remain loyal to his native Virginia. Throughout the war, General Lee provided the Confederacy with expert military leadership. The North struggled for much of the war to find a commander of comparable skill and daring.

Perhaps the biggest advantage the Confederates enjoyed was the fact that they were fighting a defensive war on their own territory. All they had to do was outlast the Union to achieve victory. The Union had the much more difficult task of conquering the South. They had to do this fighting in unfamiliar territory against an enemy that had a lot more at stake.

Early Strategies Each side had a clear military goal. The Confederacy simply had to survive, keeping their armies in the field until Northerners became tired of fighting. The Union, however, had to crush and conquer the Confederacy.

The North adopted a strategy designed to starve the South into submission. It was called the **Anaconda Plan** after the snake that slowly squeezes its prey to death. The plan involved seizing the Mississippi River and the Gulf of Mexico so that the South could not send or receive shipments. By the middle of 1862, with victories in Mississippi and New Orleans, the North had captured the Mississippi Valley. Union soldiers also seized the strategic railroad juncture at Chattanooga, Tennessee, and scored victories in battles as far west as New Mexico.

Stalemate On the East Coast, though both sides won battles, neither side could gain a clear and decisive victory in the early part of the war. Union armies hoped to capture the Confederate capital of Richmond, Virginia. But troops outside Washington, D.C., could not seem to make progress toward that goal. Confederate troops were equally unsuccessful in pushing the war north toward Washington, D.C.

Thanks to efficient new weapons—especially more accurate rifles and deadlier bullets—a single day's battle might produce more than 10,000 casualties. This new lethal warfare stung the public consciousness. Battle sites such as Bull Run (July 1861), Shiloh (April 1862), Antietam (September 1862), and Fredericksburg (December 1862) are still remembered as the scenes of some of the deadliest encounters in American history. Limited medical care ensured that many of the wounded died of infection rather than of the wounds themselves. Faced with constant reminders of death and mortality, soldiers on both sides experienced surges in religious faith. Religious revival meetings among the troops became a constant aspect of life during the Civil War.

☑ **DESCRIBE** Which side had more advantages when the war began?

The Emancipation Proclamation

Early in the war, President Lincoln insisted that he did not have the authority to end slavery. In his public statements, he emphasized the fact that his chief goal was to preserve the Union, not end slavery. Although Lincoln personally opposed slavery, he did not want to lose the support of the four slave states—Maryland, Delaware, Kentucky, and Missouri—that had remained loyal to the Union.

However, by the autumn of 1862, with the military situation beginning to look better for the Union, Lincoln decided to take a first step toward the end of slavery. In January 1863, he issued the **Emancipation Proclamation**. This presidential decree declared that "all persons held as slaves

>> General Robert E. Lee of Virginia rejected Lincoln's offer to command the Union army. The decision would prove costly for the Union due to Lee's exceptional military skills.

within any State or designated part of a State, the people whereof shall then be in rebellion against the United States, shall be then, thenceforward, and forever free."

The Emancipation Proclamation did not apply to the loyal slave states or to those areas of the South already under Union control. As a result, it did not immediately free a single slave. Nevertheless, it was an important turning point because it encouraged enslaved African Americans in the South to run away to Union army encampments and to aid the Union cause. It also symbolically redefined the war as being "about slavery."

African Americans had always believed that the war should be about slavery, and they had volunteered to fight as soon as the war began. But at first they were turned away and told "this is a white man's war." After the Emancipation Proclamation, however, the Union began to actively recruit both free blacks from the North and newly freed African Americans from the South. Eventually, some 180,000 African American men served in the Union Army.

☑ **DESCRIBE** What were the effects of the Emancipation Proclamation?

War Affects Daily Life

The Civil War not only engaged the nation in a prolonged and violent conflict, it also transformed the nation's civilian life. In the North, mines and factories stepped up production to supply military needs such as ships, railroads, weapons, uniforms, provisions, and fuel. To pay for the war, the federal government raised tariffs, imposed income taxes, and printed money. Congress also encouraged western settlement and offered free land to soldiers who would give two years of military service. Such land grants sparked agricultural growth, which helped feed Union troops.

The Union Takes Extraordinary Measures As the war dragged on, the Union army experienced a shortage of volunteers. When Congress passed a **draft law** in 1863, requiring all able-bodied men between the ages of 20 and 45 to serve in the military if called, riots broke out in several northern cities. The most severe rioting took place in New York City in July 1863. White workers attacked free African Americans as well as wealthy New Yorkers who were able to pay a fee to avoid military service.

Some Northerners opposed Lincoln's conduct of the war and demanded immediate peace. To deal with dissent, Lincoln suspended the Constitutional right of **habeas corpus** which guarantees that no one can be held in prison without specific charges being

>> The South had claimed that the war was being fought over states' rights. The Emancipation Proclamation focused the war on the ending of slavery.

>> African Americans celebrated the Emancipation Proclamation. However, freedom for African Americans in the South would only become a reality if the Union defeated the Confederacy.

>> During the Civil War, women helped by caring for the sick and wounded. They were so successful that nursing became an accepted profession for women following the war.

>> The Union army was able to secure the high ground on the first day of the Battle of Gettysburg. After three days of Confederate attacks, the Union army forced their retreat.

 Bounce to Activate Map

filed. Union troops arrested many people suspected of disloyalty. Although Lincoln felt such measures were necessary to preserve the Union, others criticized his actions as unconstitutional.

Hardships in the South Almost all of the battles took place on southern soil. The fighting destroyed some of the South's traditional strengths, such as large-scale agriculture, and stripped the Confederacy of the resources it might have used to rebuild. By 1863, the Union plan to starve the South into submission seemed to be on the verge of succeeding.

The South seized every opportunity to ease its economic problems. As Lincoln had done, Confederate President Jefferson Davis authorized the Confederacy to issue paper money, backed only by the government's promise to pay.

Doubts about the true value of Confederate money led to severe **inflation**, or price increases. The combination of rising prices and food shortages sparked food riots in some parts of the South.

A Time of Social Change On both sides, the war gave women new tasks. Women set up field hospitals and nursed wounded soldiers. Many Confederate women took to the fields to harvest crops. White and black teachers from the North went south to become teachers of newly freed slaves.

Churches in both the North and South supported the war effort. Confederate soldiers often held revival meetings near the field of battle. One Virginia chaplain claimed that many southern men "have come out of this war Christian soldiers."

☑ **ANALYZE INFORMATION** How did the Civil War affect the northern and southern economies?

The Union Prevails

In the summer of 1863, the Union succeeded in capturing Vicksburg, Mississippi. Advancing from the Louisiana side of the Mississippi River, Union General **Ulysses S. Grant** scored five victories in three weeks, ending with the surrender of 30,000 Confederate troops. The Anaconda Plan had achieved one of its major goals: Confederate territory was split apart.

The Battle of Gettysburg Meanwhile, in the East, General Lee marched into Pennsylvania. He hoped to win a surprise victory, then swing south to Washington, D.C. But in July 1863, Union troops

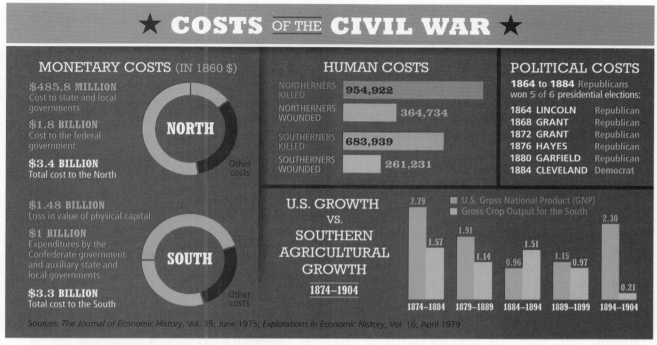

★ COSTS OF THE CIVIL WAR ★

MONETARY COSTS (IN 1860 $)

$485.8 MILLION
Cost to state and local governments

$1.8 BILLION
Cost to the federal government

$3.4 BILLION
Total cost to the North

NORTH

Other costs

$1.48 BILLION
Loss in value of physical capital

$1 BILLION
Expenditures by the Confederate government and auxiliary state and local governments

$3.3 BILLION
Total cost to the South

SOUTH

Other costs

HUMAN COSTS

NORTHERNERS KILLED	954,922
NORTHERNERS WOUNDED	364,734
SOUTHERNERS KILLED	683,939
SOUTHERNERS WOUNDED	261,231

POLITICAL COSTS

1864 to **1884** Republicans won 5 of 6 presidential elections:

1864	LINCOLN	Republican
1868	GRANT	Republican
1872	GRANT	Republican
1876	HAYES	Republican
1880	GARFIELD	Republican
1884	CLEVELAND	Democrat

U.S. GROWTH VS. SOUTHERN AGRICULTURAL GROWTH
1874–1904

■ U.S. Gross National Product (GNP)
■ Gross Crop Output for the South

	1874–1884	1879–1889	1884–1894	1889–1899	1894–1904
GNP	2.79	1.91	0.96	1.15	2.30
Crop	1.57	1.14	1.51	0.97	0.21

Sources: *The Journal of Economic History*, Vol. 35, June 1975; *Explorations in Economic History*, Vol. 16, April 1979

>> **Evaluate Data** Why do you think the North suffered significantly more casualties than the South?

defeated Lee at the town of Gettysburg. The **Battle of Gettysburg** destroyed one third of Lee's forces and marked the last major Confederate attempt to invade the North.

A few months later, the President went to Gettysburg to help dedicate a battle cemetery by giving a speech that would come to be known as the **Gettysburg Address**. In the speech, Lincoln referred to the Declaration of Independence and its founding principles of liberty and equality. He applied these principles to the current struggle and asked that the Union remember the men who died at Gettysburg as they fought for a "new birth of freedom."

> Four score and seven years ago our fathers brought forth on this continent, a new nation, conceived in Liberty, and dedicated to the proposition that all men are created equal.
>
> —Abraham Lincoln, *Gettysburg Address*, November 19, 1863

The Confederacy Surrenders In the fall of 1864, Union General **William T. Sherman** led more than 60,000 troops on a 400-mile march of destruction through Georgia and South Carolina. The march was part of a strategy of **total war**, which targeted not only troops but all of the resources needed to feed, clothe, and support an army. Sherman's troops burned crops in fields, tore up railroad tracks, and destroyed homes, plantations, and public buildings.

By spring 1865, the Confederacy was exhausted. Union troops captured the Confederate capital of Richmond, Virginia. On April 9, in the small Virginia town of Appomattox Court House, Lee surrendered to Grant.

The Lasting Impact of the War The Civil War ushered in the harsh reality of modern warfare. More than one third of northern and southern soldiers were killed or disabled.

The southern landscape and economy were in shambles. Millions of dislocated Southerners drifted north in search of new lives in Illinois, Indiana, Missouri, or other points north. Others joined the increasing migration to the West, becoming cowboys or farmers. The war ended an era in American political life. Although debates about states' rights and federal authority continue to this day, never again would states attempt to secede. More and more, Americans would see themselves not just as citizens of a state, but of a united nation.

Full Emancipation The Emancipation Proclamation had only applied to the states that left the Union, and it only freed slaves in Confederate territory that the Union was able to control. With the final Union victory, Congress and the President were ready to abolish slavery throughout the nation. Even before the Civil War ended, Congress passed the **Thirteenth Amendment**, making slavery unconstitutional. However, this amendment had to be ratified by three fourths of the states to go into effect. This process took until December 1865, over six months after the fighting ended. The southern states that had seceded were now occupied by the Union army. They now had to accept the Thirteenth Amendment even though they had fought the war to preserve slavery.

For African Americans in the South, emancipation promised them new opportunities, including a chance to work for wages and to control their own lives. Some joined the migration to the North and West while others remained in the South, hoping to work as **freedmen** the land they had worked as slaves. The Thirteenth Amendment was a victory for the abolitionist movement and a milestone in the development of the civil rights movement in the nineteenth century. It further applied the founding principles of equality and liberty underlying our nation. But the freedmen and other African Americans had a long struggle ahead of them for full equality.

☑ **DESCRIBE** What was the effect of the Thirteenth Amendment?

☑ ASSESSMENT

1. **Determine Point of View** Explain how the outcome of the Civil War differed from many initial predictions.

2. **Compare and Contrast** the advantages of both the North and the South during the Civil War.

3. **Describe** the literal and symbolic significance of the Emancipation Proclamation.

4. **Generate Explanations** Explain how the war affected women in both the North and South.

5. **Draw Conclusions** Discuss African American contributions to the war effort.

Emancipation Proclamation: Abraham Lincoln

President Abraham Lincoln's Emancipation Proclamation freed all enslaved persons in states under Confederate control as of January 1, 1863. The Proclamation changed the nature of the Union cause and paved the way for the eventual abolition of slavery by the Thirteenth Amendment in 1865.

The second primary source is President Lincoln's speech at the dedication of the Gettysburg National Cemetery on November 19, 1863. The address is considered one of the most eloquent and moving speeches in American history.

>>An abolitionist illustration in praise of emancipation

Whereas on the twenty-second day of September, in the year of our Lord one thousand eight hundred and sixty-two, a proclamation was issued by the President of the United States, containing, among other things, the following, to wit [namely]:

That on the first day of January, in the year of our Lord one thousand eight hundred and sixty-three, all persons held as slaves within any State or designated part of a State, the people whereof shall then be in rebellion against the United States, shall be then, thenceforward [from then on], and forever free; and the Executive Government of the United States, including the military and naval authority thereof, will recognize and maintain the freedom of such persons, and will do no act or acts to repress such persons, or any of them, in any efforts they may make for their actual freedom. . . .

☑ DETERMINE CENTRAL IDEAS In what parts of the nation were enslaved people freed by this proclamation?

That the Executive will, on the first day of January aforesaid, by proclamation, designate the States and parts of States, if any, in which the people thereof, respectively, shall then be in rebellion against the United States; and the fact that any State, or the people thereof, shall on that day be, in good faith,

represented in the Congress of the United States by members chosen thereto at elections wherein a majority of the qualified voters of such State shall have participated, shall, in the absence of strong countervailing testimony, be deemed conclusive evidence that such State, and the people thereof, are not then in rebellion against the United States. . . .

And by virtue of the power, and for the purpose aforesaid, I do order and declare that all persons held as slaves within said designated States, and parts of States, are, and henceforward shall be free; and that the Executive government of the United States, including the military and naval authorities thereof, will recognize and maintain the freedom of said persons.

And I hereby enjoin [direct; order] upon the people so declared to be free to abstain from all violence, unless in necessary self-defence; and I recommend to them that, in all cases when allowed, they labor faithfully for reasonable wages.

And I further declare and make known, that such persons of suitable condition, will be received into the armed services of the United States to garrison [occupy with troops] forts, positions, stations, and other places, and to man vessels of all sorts in said service.

☑ SUMMARIZE In what way would freed people now be able to support the Union cause?

And upon this act, sincerely believed to be an act of justice, warranted [authorized; justified] by the Constitution, upon military necessity, I invoke the considerate judgment of mankind, and the gracious favor of Almighty God. . . .

☑ **IDENTIFY SUPPORTING DETAILS** Under what extraordinary conditions was the president able to authorize this act?

Gettysburg Address: Abraham Lincoln

Four score [a group of twenty] and seven years ago our fathers brought forth on this continent, a new nation, conceived [planned] in Liberty, and dedicated to the proposition [judgment or opinion] that all men are created equal.

Now we are engaged in a great civil war, testing whether that nation, or any nation so conceived and so dedicated, can long endure. We are met on a great battle-field of that war. We have come to dedicate a portion of that field, as a final resting place for those who here gave their lives that the nation might live. It is altogether fitting and proper that we should do this.

☑ **DETERMINE CENTRAL IDEAS** Why does Lincoln begin his speech by referencing the nation's founding?

But, in a larger sense, we can not dedicate—we can not consecrate [make sacred]—we can not hallow [honor as holy]—this ground. The brave men, living and dead, who struggled here, have consecrated it, far above our poor power to add or detract. The world will little note, nor long remember what we say here, but it can never forget what they did here. It is for us the living, rather, to be dedicated here to the unfinished work which they who fought here have thus far so nobly advanced. It is rather for us to be here dedicated to

the great task remaining before us—that from these honored dead we take increased devotion to that cause for which they gave the last full measure of devotion—that we here highly resolve [decide] that these dead shall not have died in vain—that this nation, under God, shall have a new birth of freedom—and that government of the people, by the people, for the people, shall not perish from the earth.

☑ **DETERMINE MEANING** What is the "unfinished work" for which these soldiers have fought?

☑ ASSESSMENT

1. **Draw Conclusions** The number of enslaved people who were freed because of the Emancipation Proclamation increased gradually over time. Why do you think that was?

2. **Determine Author's Purpose** Why do you think President Lincoln issued the proclamation? Explain your answer.

3. **Determine Author's Purpose** Why did Lincoln deliver this speech at Gettysburg, and what effect did he hope it would have on the nation?

4. **Integrate Information from Diverse Sources** How do the ideas expressed in the Emancipation Proclamation relate to the ideas expressed in both the Declaration of Independence and the U.S. Constitution? Is the proclamation an extension of these documents, a rebuttal to them, or something else? Explain your answer.

5. **Compare and Contrast** How might Northerners and Southerners have responded to this address by Lincoln?

6. **Draw Conclusions** What is it about the structure and key sentences of this speech that make it so powerful, and why is it considered so important in American history?

The Civil War ended in April 1865 with the Union victory, but this was only the beginning of healing the rift between the North and South. Both regions faced the challenges of reuniting and rebuilding. The political decisions made in the decades that followed the Civil War helped shape the modern South. Constitutional amendments passed during this period redefined American ideas of citizenship and civil rights.

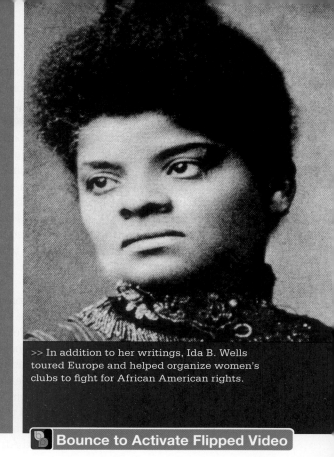

>> In addition to her writings, Ida B. Wells toured Europe and helped organize women's clubs to fight for African American rights.

Bounce to Activate Flipped Video

The Reconstruction Era

The Nation Moves Toward Reunion

When the **Civil War** ended, Congress turned its attention to reuniting the nation and to rebuilding the devastated South. Parts of the South lay in ruins—homes had been burned, businesses closed, and many properties abandoned. African Americans, though emancipated, lacked full citizenship and the means to make a living. During the era of **Reconstruction** (1865–1877), the federal government struggled with how to return the eleven southern states to the Union, rebuild the South's ruined economy, and promote the rights of former slaves.

Peace may have come, but tensions between federal power and state authority continued. The bitterness between the North and South was compounded by a power struggle between the executive and legislative branches of government. The issues that arose during this struggle and how they were dealt with would have consequences for generations to come.

>> **Objectives**

Describe the Reconstruction plans of Lincoln, Johnson, and Congress.

Describe the Thirteenth, Fourteenth, and Fifteenth Amendments.

Analyze how freedmen adjusted to freedom and the role of the Freedmen's Bureau.

Explain *de jure* segregation and the effect of Jim Crow laws on southern African Americans.

Explain the viewpoints of post-Reconstruction African American civil rights leaders.

>> **Key Terms**

Reconstruction
Freedmen's Bureau
Andrew Johnson
Thirteenth
  Amendment
Radical Republicans
impeach
Fourteenth
  Amendment
Fifteenth
  Amendment

Ku Klux Klan
de jure segregation
disenfranchise
Jim Crow laws
poll tax
literacy tests
grandfather clauses
de facto segregation
Booker T.
  Washington
W.E.B. Du Bois

Go ONLINE for digital resources

VIDEO   AUDIO   ACTIVITY   ETEXT   WRITING   ASSESSMENT

Conflict Over Reconstruction Policy Even before the war ended, Union politicians began debating the policies that would guide Reconstruction. For President Lincoln, the major goal of Reconstruction was reunifying the nation and reconciliation.

Not all Republicans had the same ideas about Reconstruction as the President. Some congressional leaders wanted to punish the South. They favored a harsh Reconstruction plan designed to make the South pay for the devastation of the war. The next several years would bring sharp differences between congressional leaders bent on imposing their will on the South and two Presidents who wanted to make Reconstruction as painless as possible.

Aid for Emancipated Slaves Shortly before the war ended, Lincoln and Congress did agree on the creation of the **Freedmen's Bureau**, a federal agency designed to aid freed slaves and relieve the South's immediate needs. The black and white agents of the Bureau delivered food and healthcare and began to develop a public school system for both black and white Southerners. It also helped to reunite families separated by slavery and to negotiate fair labor contracts between formerly enslaved African Americans and white landowners.

Lincoln's Ten Percent Plan Throughout the war, Lincoln had felt some sympathy for the South and hoped that southern states might easily rejoin the

Union after the war. To this end, in 1863 he issued a Proclamation of Amnesty and Reconstruction, known as the "Ten Percent Plan." According to its terms, as soon as ten percent of a state's voters took a loyalty oath to the Union, the state could set up a new government. If the state's constitution abolished slavery and provided education for African Americans, the state would regain representation in Congress.

Rejecting Lincoln's Ten Percent Plan, Congress passed the Wade-Davis Bill in 1864. It required that a majority of a state's prewar voters swear loyalty to the Union before the process of restoration could begin. The bill also demanded guarantees of African American equality.

A New President Meanwhile, debate over Reconstruction continued. Before he could gain support for his moderate plan of Reconstruction, Abraham Lincoln was assassinated on April 14, 1865. As the nation mourned, Vice President **Andrew Johnson** became President.

As a Southerner who had remained loyal to the Union, Johnson was similarly in favor of a relatively forgiving approach to Reconstruction. In fact, Johnson expected the United States to have a "government for white men." He did not want African Americans to have the vote and had little sympathy for their plight. Johnson supported states' rights, which would allow the laws and customs of the state to outweigh federal regulations. States would, therefore, be able to limit

Rival Plans for Reconstruction

PLAN	TEN PERCENT PLAN	WADE-DAVIS BILL	JOHNSON PLAN	RECONSTRUCTION ACT
Proposed by	President Abraham Lincoln (1863)	Republicans in Congress (1864)	President Andrew Johnson (1865)	Radical Republicans (1867)
Conditions for Former Confederate States to Rejoin Union	• 10 percent of voters must swear loyalty to Union • Must abolish slavery	• Majority of white men must swear loyalty • Former Confederate volunteers cannot vote or hold office • Wartime debts by states will not be recognized	• Majority of white men must swear loyalty • Must ratify Thirteenth Amendment • Former Confederate officials may vote and hold office • Each state would be appointed a governor chosen by the President	• Must disband state governments • Must write new constitutions • Must ratify Fourteenth Amendment • African American men must be allowed to vote • Must disqualify former officials of the Confederacy from holding public office

>> **Analyze Charts** In what ways did the Reconstruction Act of 1867 place more restrictions on former Confederate states than previous plans?

Bounce to Activate Chart

RECONSTRUCTION POLITICS

CONGRESSIONAL VOTES ON KEY AMENDMENTS

14TH

KEY
- YAY
- NAY
- DID NOT VOTE

SENATE: 33, 11, 5
HOUSE: 120, 32, 32

15TH

SENATE: 39, 13, 14
HOUSE: 144, 44, 35

Sources: Library of Congress; Congressional Record

IMPEACHMENT OF PRESIDENT ANDREW JOHNSON

SENATE: 36, 19
HOUSE: 126, 47

Source: U.S. House and Senate

THE SENATE WAS ONE VOTE SHORT OF THE TWO-THIRDS MAJORITY NEEDED TO CONVICT PRESIDENT JOHNSON

ULYSSES S. GRANT **214**

ELECTION OF 1868
ELECTORAL VOTES EARNED

HORATIO SEYMOUR **80**

Source: The American Presidency Project

>> **Analyze Graphs** How would you describe congressional support for the Fourteenth and Fifteenth Amendments?

the freedoms of former slaves. He put forth a plan that restored political power to Southerners if they swore allegiance to the United States and ratified the Thirteenth Amendment. In return, the new President promised to uphold states' rights.

Radical Republicans in Congress favored punishment and a harsh reorganization for the South. Radicals also advocated full citizens' rights for African Americans and wanted states' authority to be subordinate to federal power. When southern legislatures passed laws to restrict the activities of African Americans, Radicals became even more determined to impose a harsh Reconstruction policy on the South.

Black Codes in the South All of the southern states instituted black codes—laws that sought to limit the rights of African Americans and keep them as landless workers. The codes required African Americans to work in only a limited number of occupations, most often as servants or farm laborers. Some states prohibited African Americans from owning land, and all set up vagrancy laws. These laws stipulated that any African American person who did not have a job could be arrested and sent to work as prison labor. Even though the South remained under Union military occupation, white Southerners openly used violence and intimidation to enforce the black codes.

Conflict Between Johnson and Congress
Both Radical and moderate Republicans were infuriated by the South's disregard of the spirit of Reconstruction. Through the spring of 1866, the political situation grew worse. While the Radicals insisted that federal intervention was needed to advance African American political and civil rights, President Johnson accused them of trying "to Africanize the southern half of our country."

When Congress passed a bill that not only allowed the Freedmen's Bureau to continue its work, but provided it with the authority to punish state officials who failed to extend civil rights to African Americans, Johnson vetoed it. Undaunted, Congress sought to overturn the black codes by passing the Civil Rights Act of 1866. This measure created federal guarantees of civil rights and superseded any state laws that limited them. But once again, Johnson used his veto power to block the law, because he thought Reconstruction measures were against constitutional principles. Congress then did something unprecedented. For the first time ever, it passed major legislation over a President's veto. The Civil Rights Act of 1866 became law.

Johnson and the Radicals in Congress clashed repeatedly. In 1868, Congress voted to **impeach** Johnson. Johnson won his impeachment trial by a single vote in the Senate, but this victory did him little good. By that time he had lost control of

Reconstruction. A few months later, Civil War hero Ulysses S. Grant was elected President.

☑ **CHECK UNDERSTANDING** Why did the Radical Republicans oppose President Johnson's approach to Reconstruction?

The Reconstruction South

With Congress firmly under their control, Radical Republicans designed a sweeping Reconstruction plan that in many ways violated the constitutional rights of southern citizens. For example, they divided the South into five military districts under the command of Union generals. As a condition of readmission to the Union, all southern states were required to grant voting rights to African American men.

Perhaps most important, Radicals passed the **Fourteenth Amendment**, which guaranteed full citizenship status and rights to every man born in the United States, including African Americans. The Bill of Rights would now apply to all Americans no matter their race. The Amendment was ratified in 1868.

Under the amendment, any state that refused to allow African Americans to vote would risk losing the number of seats in the House of Representatives that were represented by its African American population. The amendment states that this representation was based on "counting the whole number of persons in each State," specifically

undoing the Three-Fifths Compromise that had emerged during the debates over ratification of the Constitution. As you may recall, this had allowed the southern states to boost their number of seats in Congress by counting each enslaved person as three-fifths of a person.

Voting Rights for African Americans Under Radical Reconstruction, many white Southerners were not eligible to vote or chose to stay away from the polls. African American men, on the other hand, eagerly signed up to exercise their new right of suffrage. Most new African American voters voted for the Republican Party. Thus, by 1868, many southern states had black elected officials and were dominated by a strong Republican Party. South Carolina—the first state to secede—became the only state where, for a short time, an African American majority dominated the legislature.

At this time, no laws guaranteed the vote to African Americans in the North. To remedy this imbalance, Congress passed the **Fifteenth Amendment**, which guaranteed that no male citizen could be denied the right to vote on the basis of "race, color, or previous condition of servitude." It was ratified in 1870.

Both the Fourteenth and Fifteenth amendments contained loopholes that left room for evasion. States could still impose voting restrictions based on literacy or property qualifications, which in effect would exclude most African Americans. Soon the southern states would do just that.

New Lives for Freedmen In the South, formerly enslaved African Americans worked to carve out new lives. Some struck out for the North or West. But many more stayed in the South. They assembled their scattered families and built strong churches that also served as community centers, employment agencies, schoolhouses, and—in later years—centers of protest.

For the first time, many African American men and women could legalize and celebrate their marriages, set up housekeeping with their families and make choices about where they would reside. Some freed women could leave field labor and care for their families at home.

Freed people also realized the importance of learning to read and do basic math. So the Freedmen's Bureau schools quickly filled. By 1869, as many as 300,000 African American adults and children were acquiring basic literacy.

>> Radical Republican members of South Carolina's first legislature after the Civil War.

Land Distribution in the South After the war, millions of landless southern white people found themselves competing with millions of landless African American people for work as farm laborers on the land of others. But even large land owners had no money to purchase supplies or pay workers. As a result, many Southerners adopted one of three arrangements: sharecropping, share-tenancy, or tenant-farming.

Under the sharecropping system, a landowner dictated the crop and provided the sharecropper with a place to live, as well as seeds and tools, in return for a "share" of the harvested crop. Share-tenancy was much like sharecropping, except that the farmworker chose what crop he would plant and bought his own supplies. Then, he gave a share of the crop to the landowner. He might be able to grow a variety of crops or use some of the land to grow food for his family.

In tenant farming the tenant paid cash rent to a landowner and then was free to choose and manage his own crop—and free to choose where he would live.

Scalawags and Carpetbaggers The Republican Party attracted not only African American Southerners but also others who sought change. Scalawags, as southern white critics called them, were white men who had been locked out of pre–Civil War politics by their wealthier neighbors. The new Republican Party invited them in.

Scalawags found allies in northern whites or African Americans who relocated to the South. These Northerners came seeking to improve their economic or political situations, or to help make a better life for freedmen. Many southern white people resented what they felt was the invasion of opportunists, come to make their fortunes from the South's misfortune. Southerners labeled the newcomers "carpetbaggers," after the inexpensive carpet-cloth suitcases often carried by Northerners.

Terrorism in the Reconstruction South Even though the South remained under military occupation, organized secret societies, such as the **Ku Klux Klan**, used terror and violence against African Americans and their white supporters. A federal grand jury concluded that the chief goal of the Klan attacks was to keep African Americans from voting.

The Klan . . . inflicted summary vengeance on the colored citizens of these counties by breaking into their houses at the dead of night, dragging them from their beds, torturing them in the most inhuman manner, and

>> A woman representing the Solid South carries President Grant, who is sitting atop a carpetbag. "Carpetbagger" was a negative term Southerners called Northerners who exploited the South during Reconstruction. **Analyze Political Cartoons** How does this cartoon show Southerners' feelings about northern rule during Reconstruction?

in many instances murdering them; and this, mainly, on account of their political affiliations.

—42nd Congress, House Report No. 22, 1871

The Radical Republicans in Congress responded by passing laws making it a crime to use violence to prevent people from voting. Although Klan activities lessened somewhat, the threat of violence kept many southern African Americans from the polls.

☑ **RECALL** How did the Fourteenth Amendment affect the Three-Fifths Compromise?

Reconstruction Comes to an End

After a decade of Reconstruction, Northerners turned their focus to other social, political, and economic issues. In the fall of 1873, a series of bank failures sparked a severe economic downturn. At the same time, a series of political scandals in the Grant administration damaged the Radical Republicans.

>> An African American man is asked by a white passenger to give up his seat on a railway car in Philadelphia. **Infer** What does this image suggest about segregation in the North?

Under these circumstances, Reconstruction began to fade. Gradually and quietly, beginning in 1871, troops were withdrawn from the South. In 1872, Congress dissolved the Freedmen's Bureau.

The Return of Southern Democrats Meanwhile, southern white Democrats devised a strategy for regaining political control. They argued that Republican programs for public schools and road building resulted in higher taxes. Southern Democrats grasped every opportunity to paint African American politicians as corrupt and incompetent. At the same time, the ever-present threat of violence kept African Americans from voting, thus depriving the Republicans of a large segment of their political base.

One by one, southern states reinstated wealthy white southern men as governors and sent former Confederate leaders to the U.S. Congress. In the 1874 elections, the Republicans lost control of the House of Representatives. By 1876, only South Carolina, Florida, and Louisiana—three states with large African American populations—still had Reconstruction governments and remained under military occupation.

The Disputed Election of 1876 The presidential election of 1876 brought a final end to Reconstruction. Democratic candidate Samuel Tilden won more popular votes than Republican candidate Rutherford B. Hayes, but the electoral vote was in dispute.

In an informal compromise intended to end the dispute, a congressional committee declared the Republican candidate the winner. In return, Hayes promised to pull all remaining federal troops from the South. In effect, the election of Hayes ended Reconstruction.

Evaluating Reconstruction Was Reconstruction a success or a failure? Southerners and Northerners, black and white, then and now would give different answers. All will agree, however, that some things were changed forever by those dozen years during which the victorious North tried to remake the vanquished South.

Certainly, Radical Reconstruction failed in most of its aims. It had violated the Constitution in several ways for years at a time. By the end of the century, the political rights of African Americans in the South had eroded. Southern states slowly took away the voting rights of African Americans. All of the former Confederate states created systems of **de jure segregation**—laws that made African Americans second-class citizens. Support for African Americans was not abundant in the North either.

Still, Reconstruction did mark the beginning of the physical and economic rebuilding of the South. Despite continuing conflicts and resentments, the nation was permanently reunited. And the constitutional amendments passed during Reconstruction, especially the Fourteenth Amendment, would eventually form the basis for a revived civil rights movement in the twentieth century that sought political equality for all citizens.

Questions of State vs. Federal Power Which political unit has more power—the federal government or the individual states? In cases of disputes about public policy, which branch of the federal government has the last word? These questions have perplexed American lawmakers since the drafting of the Constitution. During Reconstruction, these questions acquired deeper meaning as the federal government asserted its authority not only over southern states but also over state laws in other regions.

In the end, American voters and their representatives in government opted for a balance of power, at the expense of protecting freed people in the South. With the demise of the Radical Republicans, most congressmen concluded that it was better to let the South attend to its own affairs than to leave a whole region under the control of federal military power and political control. That choice would have far-reaching social, political, and economic implications.

☑ **DEFINE** Define de jure segregation.

African Americans in the Late 1800s

After Reconstruction ended, many white politicians in the North and South turned their attention from racial issues, allowing racist laws and segregation to spread in the South, and, to a lesser extent, in the North. This turn away from equality for all had a lasting impact on society in the United States.

During the Gilded Age (1877 to 1900), southern state governments enacted various measures intended to **disenfranchise** African Americans and enacted **Jim Crow laws** to keep blacks and whites apart as much as possible.

Methods of Restricting Voting Rights The Fifteenth Amendment prohibited state governments from denying someone the right to vote because of "race, color, or previous condition of servitude." After Reconstruction, southern states got around this amendment by passing a number of other restrictive measures. They enacted a **poll tax** requiring voters to pay a tax to vote. Poor African Americans could scarcely afford such a fee. The states also required voters to pass **literacy tests** and "understanding" tests. Because African Americans had been exploited economically and denied an education, these restrictions disqualified many of them as voters.

Southern states got around the Fifteenth Amendment's restriction on the use of "previous condition of servitude" with **grandfather clauses** that allowed a person to vote as long as his ancestors had voted prior to 1866. Some southern states also established all-white primaries, meaning only whites had a voice in selecting who got to run in general elections. In addition, whites resorted to violence to keep African Americans from participating in the political process.

As a result of these actions, throughout the Deep South, black participation in politics fell dramatically.

Similarly, in northern states, including those that had civil rights laws that outlawed legal segregation, black migrants found many examples of **de facto segregation**—customs or practices limiting where they could live, work, and socialize.

Civil Rights and the Supreme Court The Civil Rights Act of 1875 guaranteed African American citizens the right to ride trains and use public facilities, such as hotels. Yet it was left to the courts to interpret how these new amendments and laws would be applied.

In the 1870s, in a series of landmark cases, the Supreme Court chipped away at African American freedoms. In what became known as the *Slaughterhouse Cases* (1873), the Court restricted the scope of the Fourteenth Amendment. It concluded that although a citizen had certain national rights, the federal government had no control over how a state chose to define rights for its citizens.

The ruling also stated that the protection of civil rights did not include property rights of businesses and weakened the protections of the Fourteenth Amendment.

>> Jim Crow laws made it legal to segregate nonwhites and whites in places such as this school. **Predict Consequences** What impact did these laws have on the equality of educational opportunities for African Americans?

>> Booker T. Washington was born a slave in Virginia. After the war he attended college and in 1881 became the first president of the newly founded black college, the Tuskegee Institute in Alabama.

Bounce to Activate Map

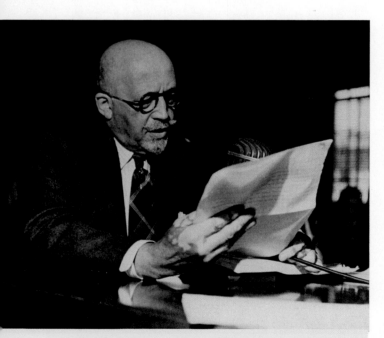

>> W.E.B. Du Bois's collection of essays, *The Souls of Black Folk*, underscored the unique African American identity of being both American and black that resulted in, "doubleconsciousness, this sense of always looking at one's self through the eyes of others."

Two years later, the Supreme Court heard the case of *United States* v. *Cruikshank*. This case involved a white mob in Louisiana who had killed a large group of African Americans at a political rally. The Court ruled that the due process and equal protection clauses of the Fourteenth Amendment protected citizens only from the action of the state and not from the action of other citizens.

Later Supreme Court rulings would build on these early precedents to further restrict African American and other minorities' rights. In *Plessy* v. *Ferguson* (1896), the Supreme Court upheld the constitutionality of Jim Crow laws. It did so by arguing that as long as states maintained "separate but equal" facilities, they did not violate the Fourteenth Amendment. Yet, in reality, separate facilities were rarely equal.

African Americans Oppose Injustice Even during the darkest days of Jim Crow, African Americans refused to accept this inferior legal and social status. They established black newspapers, women's clubs, fraternal organizations, schools and colleges, and political associations with the goal of securing their freedom. They did not always agree on the best strategies for achieving their goals, but they were united in their determination to "never turn back" until they had achieved equality.

One of the most famous black leaders of the late-nineteenth century was **Booker T. Washington**. Born a slave in 1856, Washington argued that African Americans needed to accommodate themselves to segregation, meaning they should *not* focus their energies on seeking to overturn Jim Crow. Instead, he called for blacks to "pull themselves up from their own bootstraps" by building up their economic resources and establishing their reputations as hardworking and honest citizens.

Washington's ideas about accommodation were opposed by **W.E.B. Du Bois**, a man who by many measures was a living example of Washington's hopes. Du Bois earned his Ph.D. from Harvard University in 1896, and he lived in a relatively tolerant community. Du Bois, however, criticized Washington's willingness to accommodate southern whites. Echoing the spirit of the abolitionists, he argued that blacks should demand full and immediate equality and not limit themselves to vocational education. The dispute between gradual progress and radicalism that characterized the Washington-Du Bois debate would define the civil rights movement throughout much of its history.

One African American woman who fought for justice was Ida B. Wells. Born into slavery in 1862, Wells moved to Memphis, Tennessee, as a young adult. There she worked as a schoolteacher and became active in the African Methodist Episcopal Church. Wells bought a local newspaper, renamed it *Free Speech*, and wrote numerous articles that condemned the mistreatment of blacks.

The contributions of leaders like Wells, Washington, and Du Bois, as well as the organizations they founded, would help direct the struggle for equality for African Americans as the United States entered a new era following the Civil War.

☑ **IDENTIFY** What was the main difference between Booker T. Washington's and W.E.B. Du Bois's approach to the early African American civil rights movement?

☑ ASSESSMENT

1. **Contrast** the goals of Radical Republicans with those of more moderate Republicans such as President Lincoln.

2. **Describe** the factors that led to the decline of Reconstruction.

3. **Draw Conclusions** Analyze the successes and failures of Reconstruction.

4. **Generate Explanations** Explain how de jure segregation affected African Americans in the South.

5. **Compare and Contrast** the ideas of Booker T. Washington, W.E.B. Du Bois, and Ida B. Wells.

Second Inaugural Address: Abraham Lincoln

Lincoln delivered his second inaugural address just over a month before his death. He spoke about the war, slavery, and the need "to bind up the nation's wounds." The speech's closing words of reconciliation and healing are today carved in the walls of the Lincoln Memorial.

>> President Abraham Lincoln

At this second appearing to take the oath of the Presidential office there is less occasion for an extended address than there was at the first. Then a statement somewhat in detail of a course to be pursued seemed fitting and proper. Now, at the expiration of four years, during which public declarations have been constantly called forth on every point and phase of the great contest which still absorbs the attention and engrosses the energies of the nation, little that is new could be presented. The progress of our arms, upon which all else chiefly depends, is as well known to the public as to myself, and it is, I trust, reasonably satisfactory and encouraging to all. With high hope for the future, no prediction in regard to it is ventured.

☑ **DETERMINE MEANING** Why does the President say this second inaugural address will be shorter than the first inaugural address?

. . . On the occasion corresponding to this four years ago all thoughts were anxiously directed to an impending civil war. All dreaded it, all sought to avert it. While the inaugural address was being delivered from this place, devoted altogether to saving the Union without war, insurgent [rebelling against authority or government] agents were in the city seeking to destroy it without war—seeking to dissolve the Union and divide effects by negotiation.

Both parties deprecated [expressed disapproval of] war, but one of them would make war rather than let the nation survive, and the other would accept war rather than let it perish, and the war came.

☑ **COMPARE AND CONTRAST** Whom does Lincoln blame for the outbreak of the war?

One-eighth of the whole population were colored slaves, not distributed generally over the Union, but localized in the southern part of it. These slaves constituted a peculiar [special] and powerful interest. All knew that this interest was somehow the cause of the war. To strengthen, perpetuate, and extend this interest was the object for which the insurgents would rend [tear apart] the Union even by war, while the Government claimed no right to do more than to restrict the territorial enlargement of it. Neither party expected for the war the magnitude or the duration which it has already attained. Neither anticipated that the cause of the conflict might cease with or even before the conflict itself should cease. Each looked for an easier triumph, and a result less fundamental and astounding. Both read the same Bible and pray to the same God, and each invokes His aid against the other.

☑ **DETERMINE CENTRAL IDEAS** What, according to the President, was the cause of the Civil War?

It may seem strange that any men should dare to ask a just God's assistance in wringing their bread from the sweat of other men's faces, but let us judge not, that we be not judged. The prayers of both could not be answered. That of neither has been answered fully. The Almighty has His own purposes. "Woe unto the world because of offenses; for it must needs be that offenses come, but woe to that man by whom the offense cometh." If we shall suppose that American slavery is one of those offenses which, in the providence of God, must needs come, but which, having continued through His appointed time, He now wills to remove, and that He gives to both North and South this terrible war as the woe due to those by whom the offense came, shall we discern therein any departure from those divine attributes which the believers in a living God always ascribe to Him?

☑ **DETERMINE MEANING** What are the "offenses" discussed in this passage?

Fondly [with trust] do we hope, fervently [with strong emotion] do we pray, that this mighty scourge of war may speedily pass away. Yet, if God wills that it continue until all the wealth piled by the bondsman's two hundred and fifty years of unrequited [with nothing given in return] toil shall be sunk, and until every drop of blood drawn with the lash shall be paid by another drawn with the sword, as was said three thousand years ago, so still it must be said "the judgments of the Lord are true and righteous [morally correct] altogether."

☑ **DRAW INFERENCES** Why might this passage have been particularly inspiring to Radical Republicans?

With malice toward none, with charity for all, with firmness in the right as God gives us to see the right, let us strive on to finish the work we are in, to bind up the nation's wounds, to care for him who shall have borne the battle and for his widow and his orphan, to do all which may achieve and cherish a just and lasting peace among ourselves and with all nations.

☑ **PARAPHRASE** Rewrite this paragraph in your own words.

☑ ASSESSMENT

1. **Analyze Structure** What examples can you find in Lincoln's address of organizing ideas into groups of three?

2. **Draw Conclusions** Based on this address, how do you think Lincoln would have dealt with southern states returning to the Union if he had lived to complete his second term? Explain your answer.

3. **Make Inferences** How does this address reveal the mixed emotions that Lincoln and many Northerners had toward the South during the end of the war?

PEARSON
realize™
PearsonSchool.com/CASS

Go ONLINE for primary sources
ACTIVITY   ETEXT   WRITING   ASSESSMENT

0.6 The Reconstruction Era **61**

LESSON SUMMARIES

Use these Lesson Summaries, and the longer versions available online, to review the key ideas for each lesson in this Topic.

Lesson 0.1: Colonies and Revolution

Spain and France set up colonies in North America. In the English colonies, settlers brought over English traditions of self-government and legal rights. After Great Britain defeated France in a war for control of North America, the British government imposed taxes on the colonists. The War of Independence began in 1775, continuing until the colonists defeated the British and a peace treaty was signed in 1783.

Lesson 0.2: Founding a New Nation

After winning their independence from Britain, the former American colonies became states. The 13 states had adopted a national constitution called the Articles of Confederation creating a weak federal government. However, a new Constitution divided power between the states and the nation, separated powers within the federal government, and included a Bill of Rights.

Lesson 0.3: America in the Early 1800s

The Louisiana Purchase enlarged the nation's boundaries. After the War of 1812 between United States and Britain, the United States became more self-confident. President Andrew Jackson came to power during a period of expanding democracy, but also oversaw the tragic removal of American Indians from the Southeast. War between the U.S. and Mexico led to the annexation of Texas by the U.S. As the northern and southern sections

of the country developed different economies, tensions over slavery increased, and new movements for the abolition of slavery and women's rights emerged.

Lesson 0.4: The Union in Crisis

Disputes between northern and southern states over the issue of slavery shaped U.S. politics during the 1840s and '50s. The Compromise of 1850 allowed voters in new territories to decide the slavery issue, but required all citizens to capture runaway slaves. Kansas saw bloodshed as pro- and anti-slavery settlers battled each other. A Supreme Court decision asserting that African Americans were not citizens further enraged Abolitionists. When Abraham Lincoln was elected president, the southern states began to secede from the Union.

Lesson 0.5: The Civil War

Civil War broke out when Fort Sumter was fired upon in Charleston harbor. Between 1861 and 1865, the Union and the Confederacy fought each other, with the Union succeeding in its "Anaconda Plan" of seizing control of the Mississippi River and the Gulf of Mexico. As the Union, with its larger population and industrial strength, overcame the Confederacy, Lincoln issued the Emancipation Proclamation, which freed slaves in rebel areas. In the Thirteenth Amendment, slavery was made unconstitutional. With the defeat of the Confederacy the Union was restored.

Lesson 0.6: The Reconstruction Era

During the era of Reconstruction (1865–1877), the federal government debated how to return the southern states to the Union, rebuild the South's ruined economy, and promote the rights of former slaves. After President Lincoln's assassination in 1865, Andrew Johnson became President and struggled with "Radical Republicans" in Congress who wanted African Americans to have full citizenship, including the right to vote. However, the rights of African Americans were slowly curtailed, as southern states passed Jim Crow laws that enforced segregation and limited voting rights.

VISUAL REVIEW

Use these graphics to review some of the key terms, people, and ideas from this Topic.

America's Early History: Key Events

1492	Columbus lands in the Bahamas.
1607	Jamestown is settled.
1620	Plymouth is settled.
1763	French and Indian War ends.
1775	American Revolution begins.
1783	The Treaty of Paris is signed, which ends the American Revolution.

The American Revolution

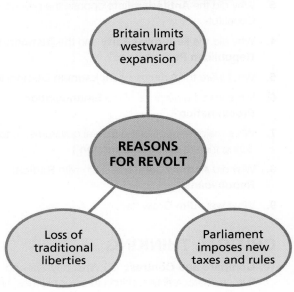

Britain limits westward expansion

REASONS FOR REVOLT

Loss of traditional liberties

Parliament imposes new taxes and rules

The New Constitution

FEDERALISTS

wanted strong central government

COMPROMISE

Bill of Rights; states share power with federal government

ANTI-FEDERALISTS

wanted power for states and protection of rights

Advantages of Opposing Sides in the Civil War

UNION	CONFEDERACY
• Large urban populations	• Highly motivated troops
• Factories to produce war supplies	• Excellent military leaders
• Well developed railroad network	• Fighting a defensive war on own territory
• Strong navy	
• Banking, insurance, financing industries	

KEY TERMS AND IDEAS

1. What important political traditions were established by the **Magna Carta** and the **English Bill of Rights**?

2. What issues led to the American Revolution?

3. Why did the **Antifederalists** oppose the proposed Constitution?

4. Why did the **Federalist Party** and the **Democratic Republican Party** develop?

5. What were the features of **Jacksonian Democracy**?

6. What was the purpose of the **Emancipation Proclamation**?

7. What major issues did the federal government face during the era of **Reconstruction**?

8. Why did **Andrew Johnson** clash with **Radical Republicans**?

9. What were **Jim Crow** laws?

CRITICAL THINKING

10. **Compare and Contrast** (a.) What physical and human characteristics, dating to colonial times, helped define the northern and southern regions of the United States? (b.) How did these characteristics help divide the northern and southern regions?

11. **Identify Cause and Effect** How did both the Enlightenment and the Great Awakening prepare colonists to declare independence from Great Britain?

12. **Summarize** How did colonial practices and the British political tradition influence democratic ideals in the American colonies?

13. **Find the Main Idea** (a.) What were the flaws in the Articles of Confederation? (b.) How was the Constitution designed to correct these flaws?

14. **Draw Inferences** What common concerns were shared by the Abolition and Women's Rights movements?

15. **Identify Cause and Effect** How did the issue of slavery divide the nation in the 1800s?

16. **Draw Conclusions** What role did industry play in the Union's victory in the Civil War?

17. **Analyze Maps** Describe the route and estimate the distance that the Seminoles were forced to travel from Florida to Indian Territory.

18. **Writing Activity: Use Primary Sources** Identify which paragraph of the Declaration of Independence is shown in the excerpt below, analyze the purpose of the text, and evaluate why the paragraph is important.

> When in the Course of human events, it becomes necessary for one people to dissolve the political bands which have connected them with another, and to assume among the powers of the earth, the separate and equal station to which the Laws of Nature and of Nature's God entitle them, a decent respect to the opinions of mankind requires that they should declare the causes which impel [force] them to the separation.
>
> —*Declaration of Independence*

DOCUMENT-BASED QUESTIONS

The debate over the ratification of the Constitution was lively and prolonged, pitting Federalists against Antifederalists. Read the documents below, then answer the questions that follow.

DOCUMENT A

In this excerpt, from *The Federalist Papers: No. 10*, James Madison argues that only a strong government, or "State" can defeat the divisive power of "faction." Use context clues to help you define this term.

> AMONG the numerous advantages promised by a well constructed Union, none deserves to be more accurately developed than its tendency to break and control the violence of faction. . . . By a faction, I understand a number of citizens, whether amounting to a majority or a minority of the whole, who are united and actuated by some common impulse of passion, or of interest, adversed to the rights of other citizens, or to the permanent and aggregate interests of the community. . . . A rage for paper money, for an abolition of debts, for an equal division of property, or for any other improper or wicked project, will be less apt to pervade the whole body of the Union than a particular member of it; in the same proportion as such a malady is more likely to taint a particular county or district, than an entire State.
> —*Federalist Papers, No. 10*

DOCUMENT B

This political cartoon appeared as the Antifederalists and Federalists argued about ratification of the Constitution.

DOCUMENT C

This excerpt from a speech by Patrick Henry explains his view of the new Constitution.

> Here is a resolution as radical as that which separated us from Great Britain. It is radical in this transition; our rights and privileges are endangered, and the sovereignty of the states will be relinquished: and cannot we plainly see that this is actually the case? The rights of conscience, trial by jury, liberty of the press, all your immunities and franchises, all pretensions to human rights and privileges, are rendered insecure, if not lost, by this change, so loudly talked of by some, and inconsiderately by others. Is this tame relinquishment of rights worthy of freemen?
> —*Patrick Henry, June 5, 1788*

DOCUMENT D

In this excerpt from a letter of 1787, Samuel Adams expresses his concerns about the new Constitution.

> And can this National Legislature be competent to make Laws for the free internal Government of one People, living in Climates so remote and whose "Habits & particular Interests" are and probably always will be so different. Is it to be expected that General Laws can be adapted to the Feelings of the more Eastern and the more Southern Parts of so extensive a Nation? It appears to me difficult if practicable. Hence then may we not look for Discontent, Mistrust, Disaffection to Government and frequent Insurrections, which will require standing Armies to suppress them in one Place & another where they may happen to arise.
> —*Samuel Adams, 1787*

19. In Document A, Madison defines faction as
A. a religious organization.
B. a special interest group.
C. a group of Antifederalists.
D. people opposed to states' rights.

20. Analyze Political Cartoons Does Document B oppose or support the new Constitution?

21. In Document C, Patrick Henry is worried that the new Constitution
A. gives too much power to the states.
B. gives too little power to the states.
C. will transfer power to the courts.
D. will not protect individual rights.

22. In Document D, Samuel Adams fears that the new Constitution will
A. lead to regionalism and civil war.
B. not protect individual rights.
C. encourage unity among regions.
D. destroy American independence.

23. Writing Activity: Primary Source Write a paragraph explaining whether you think the worries and concerns expressed here were addressed and the problems solved. Use the sources as well as additional information you have learned.

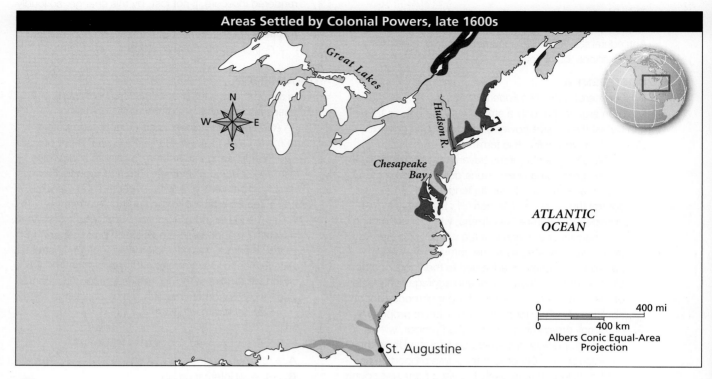

Areas Settled by Colonial Powers, late 1600s

Great Lakes

N
W E
S

Hudson R.

Chesapeake Bay

ATLANTIC OCEAN

0   400 mi
0   400 km
Albers Conic Equal-Area Projection

•St. Augustine

1 How would you label the European settlements at the far south of this map?

A Dutch settlements.

B English settlements.

C Spanish settlements.

D French settlements.

2 Study the map shown in item 1. What can you deduce about most of the colonies from studying their placement on the map?

F They were hemmed in by hostile Native American groups.

G They used waterways for trade and communication.

H They were centers of manufacturing.

I They traded with one another more than with Europe.

VIRGINIA PLAN

A bicameral legislature of a House and Senate. In both, the states with large populations would have more members.

THE GREAT COMPROMISE

_____

_____

_____

NEW JERSEY PLAN

Unicameral legislature of one house would treat all states as equal, regardless of population.

3 What does each plan reveal about the state that proposed it?

A Virginia's population was larger than New Jersey's.

B Unlike Virginians, people of New Jersey valued social equality.

C New Jersey's population was larger than Virginia's.

D Both Virginia and New Jersey had large populations.

4 What were the implications for enslaved people when the founding principle of citizenship as defined in the U.S. Constitution was clarified by the Dred Scott Supreme Court ruling to mean that slaves were not citizens?

F It meant that enslaved people could be deported.

G It meant that even free African Americans could be enslaved.

H It meant that they had special civil rights and protections.

I It meant that only free men were citizens.

If you have trouble with...				
Question	1	2	3	4
See Lesson	0.1	0.1	0.2	0.4

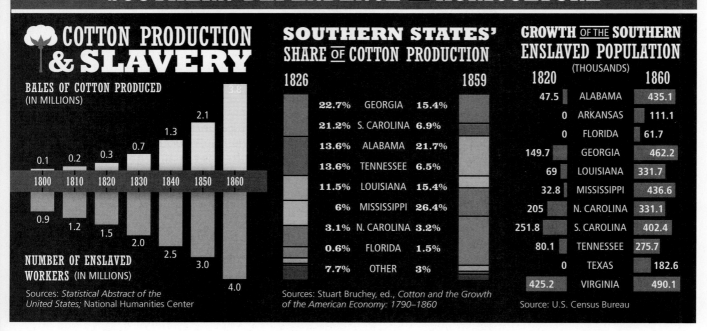

SOUTHERN DEPENDENCE ON AGRICULTURE

COTTON PRODUCTION & SLAVERY

BALES OF COTTON PRODUCED (IN MILLIONS)

1800	1810	1820	1830	1840	1850	1860
0.1	0.2	0.3	0.7	1.3	2.1	3.8

NUMBER OF ENSLAVED WORKERS (IN MILLIONS)

| 0.9 | 1.2 | 1.5 | 2.0 | 2.5 | 3.0 | 4.0 |

Sources: *Statistical Abstract of the United States;* National Humanities Center

SOUTHERN STATES' SHARE OF COTTON PRODUCTION

1826		1859
22.7%	GEORGIA	15.4%
21.2%	S. CAROLINA	6.9%
13.6%	ALABAMA	21.7%
13.6%	TENNESSEE	6.5%
11.5%	LOUISIANA	15.4%
6%	MISSISSIPPI	26.4%
3.1%	N. CAROLINA	3.2%
0.6%	FLORIDA	1.5%
7.7%	OTHER	3%

Sources: Stuart Bruchey, ed., *Cotton and the Growth of the American Economy: 1790–1860*

GROWTH OF THE SOUTHERN ENSLAVED POPULATION (THOUSANDS)

1820		1860
47.5	ALABAMA	435.1
0	ARKANSAS	111.1
0	FLORIDA	61.7
149.7	GEORGIA	462.2
69	LOUISIANA	331.7
32.8	MISSISSIPPI	436.6
205	N. CAROLINA	331.1
251.8	S. CAROLINA	402.4
80.1	TENNESSEE	275.7
0	TEXAS	182.6
425.2	VIRGINIA	490.1

Source: U.S. Census Bureau

5 What does the graph of cotton production and slavery reveal about the slave economy during the first half of the 1800s?

A The southern economy was becoming less dependent on slavery.

B Slavery was becoming an essential part of the southern economy.

C The amount of cotton produced had no relation to the number of slaves.

D Both the amount of cotton produced and the number of enslaved workers fell.

6 During Reconstruction, who were the Radical Republicans?

F Supporters of Lincoln's One-Tenth Plan.

G Supporters of Andrew Johnson's presidency.

H Congressmen who believed that federal intervention was needed to protect African American rights.

I Congressmen who believed that Southerners needed to be forgiven and brought back into the Union.

ECONOMIC DEVELOPMENT IN THE NORTH & SOUTH

POPULATION IN 1860

NORTH	27.71 MILLION
SOUTH	8.73 MILLION

50 U.S. CITIES WITH LARGEST POPULATIONS 1860

NORTH 38

5 BORDER STATES

SOUTH 7

Source: U.S. Census Bureau

TOTAL VALUE OF MANUFACTURED PRODUCTS 1860
TOP 5 NORTHERN & SOUTHERN STATES

NY	$378,870,939	$50,652,124	VA
PA	$290,121,188	$17,987,225	TN
MA	$255,545,922	$16,925,564	GA
OH	$121,691,148	$16,678,698	NC
CT	$81,924,555	$15,587,473	LA

Source: Historical Census Browser, University of Virginia

UNION & CONFEDERATE RESOURCES 1861

	Union	Confederate
RAILROADS	71%	29%
FARM ACREAGE	65%	35%
MANUFACTURING WORKERS	92%	8%
FACTORIES (THOUSANDS)	110	18

Source: U.S. Census Bureau

7 What does the infographic show about the country in 1860?

A The South was much wealthier than the North.

B The South had as many factories as the North.

C Fewer people were living in the North than in the South.

D Northern and southern economies differed dramatically.

8 How did the Fifteenth Amendment change the United States forever?

F The amendment struck down segregation throughout the United States.

G The amendment made slavery illegal throughout the entire United States.

H The amendment declared that all freedmen were full citizens of the United States.

I The amendment extended voting rights to all African American men in the United States.

If you have trouble with...				
Question	5	6	7	8
See Lesson	0.3	0.6	0.5	0.6

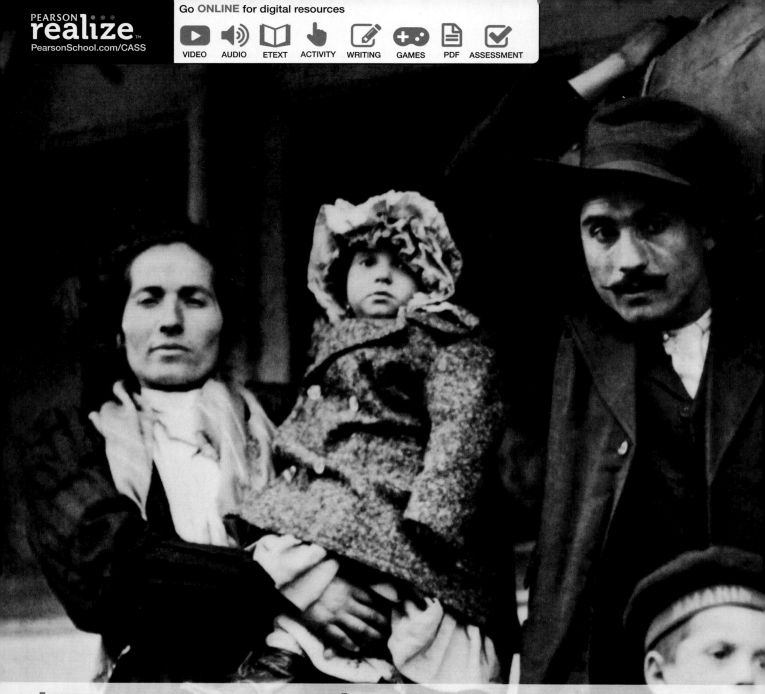

[ESSENTIAL QUESTION] How do science and technology affect society?

① Industry and Immigration

Enduring Understandings

- In the late 1800s, rapid industrialization, driven by entrepreneurs and innovators, transformed daily life in positive and negative ways.

- Americans tried to address some of the negative effects of industrialization.

- In the late 1800s, immigrants from southern and eastern Europe and Asia changed American culture as they fought to establish lives in their new homes.

- Cities grew quickly as a result of industrialization and immigration.

- New technology, urbanization, and industrialization created new ways of life and mass cultural movements in the United States.

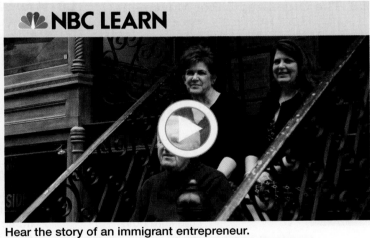

Hear the story of an immigrant entrepreneur.

Bounce to Activate My Story Video

>> An immigrant family arrives at Ellis Island.

In this Topic, you'll learn about industry and immigration in America between 1865 and 1914. Look at the lesson outline and explore the timeline. As you study this Topic, you'll complete the Quest team project.

LESSON OUTLINE

1.1 Innovation Boosts Growth
HSS 11.1.4, HSS 11.2.2, HSS 11.2.6, HSS 11.8.6; Analysis CST.4

1.2 Big Business Rises
HSS 11.2.5, HSS 11.2.6

1.3 The Organized Labor Movement
HSS 11.2.1, HSS 11.2.5, HSS 11.6.5

1.4 The New Immigrants
HSS 11.1.4, HSS 11.2, HSS 11.3.3; Analysis CST.4

1.5 A Nation of Cities
HSS 11.2, HSS 11.2.1, HSS 11.2.2

1.6 New Ways of Life
HSS 11.2.2, HSS 11.8.8

Industry and Immigration (1865–1914)

1871
Fire destroys Chicago

1880
Edison invents the light bulb

1894
Pullman strike halts railroad traffic

1870   1880   1890   1900   1910

1872
Yellowstone Park established

1886
American Federation of Labor is founded

1910
Angel Island opens

QUEST! TEAM PROJECT

Civic Discussion: Andrew Carnegie

What do you think about the success of industrialists like Carnegie, who grew rich during the second Industrial Revolution? In this Quest you'll participate in a group discussion about Carnegie's influence on America.

STEP 1
Join a small group and read the discussion launch. Take notes as you read and discuss the major points with your group.

STEP 2
Read and analyze the sources that give different perspectives on the main question. As you analyze each source, fill in step 2 of the Information Organizer.

STEP 3
After your group has been assigned a YES or NO position on the main question, prepare the most compelling arguments in support of your position. Present your arguments and then switch sides.

STEP 4
Discuss the question from your own point of view. Think about what you have learned through the discussion and answer the questions in Step 4 of the Information Organizer.

PearsonSchool.com/CASS

Go **ONLINE** for complete Quest materials

 VIDEO ETEXT WRITING RUBRIC PDF ASSESSMENT

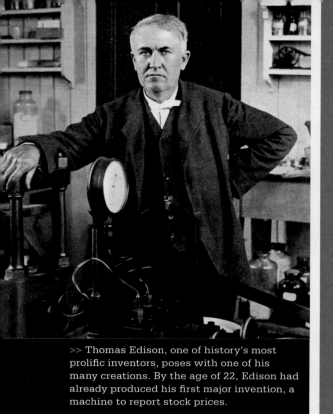

>> Thomas Edison, one of history's most prolific inventors, poses with one of his many creations. By the age of 22, Edison had already produced his first major invention, a machine to report stock prices.

Bounce to Activate Flipped Video

1.1 The Industrial Revolution began in the British textile industry in the 1700s. Within a few decades, it spread to other European countries and the new country of the United States, which had the greatest number of resources to expand the revolution. The first Industrial Revolution was marked by the introduction of steam power and the factory system. Coal and iron became key resources. Around the 1850s, the Industrial Revolution entered a new phase, dominated by steel, oil, and a major new power source—electricity. These new energy sources significantly improved the standard of living throughout the country. This second Industrial Revolution also had a distinctly American character.

>> Objectives

Analyze the factors that encouraged industrialization in the United States in the late 1800s.

Explain how new inventions, scientific discoveries, and technological innovations fueled growth and improved the standard of living.

Explain the challenges faced by the South in industry and agriculture in the late 1800s.

Describe the impact of industrialization in the late 1800s.

>> Key Terms

entrepreneurs
laissez-faire
protective tariffs
patent
Thomas Edison
Bessemer process
suspension bridges
time zones
mass production
cash crop
free enterprise

Innovation Boosts Growth

American Industry Grows

The Civil War challenged industries to make goods more quickly and efficiently, especially in the North, which already had an industrial base. Using new tools and methods, factories stepped up production of guns, ammunition, medical supplies, and uniforms. The food industry developed ways to process foods so they could be shipped long distances. Railroads expanded, and more efficient methods of creating power were developed. Meanwhile, the government encouraged immigration to meet the increasing demand for labor in the nation's factories.

Natural Resources Fuel Economic Development The country's growth was fueled, in part, by its vast supply of natural resources. Numerous coal mines along the eastern seaboard provided fuel to power steam locomotives and factories. Thick forests were cut into lumber for construction.

Iron ore was converted into iron and later into steel to build bridges, railroad tracks, and machines. The nation's many navigable riverways transported these and other resources to cities and factories.

Many technological innovations expanded the country's natural resource base even further. In 1859, Edwin Drake used a steam engine to drill the world's first successful oil well near Titusville, Pennsylvania. Before Drake's innovation, oil, which was used for light and fuel, was mainly obtained from boiling down whale blubber. But whale hunting was time-consuming, and whales were becoming scarce. Drilled oil was relatively cheap to produce and easy to transport. The oil industry grew quickly after 1859 and encouraged the growth of related industries such as kerosene and gasoline.

Another technological innovation of the 1850s made it easier to process iron ore into steel. Steel production soon skyrocketed as boatloads of iron ore moved across the Great Lakes from cities in Minnesota to Pittsburgh, Pennsylvania, and other cities that became steel-making centers. The steel rails produced by these new steel-making cities encouraged economic development by allowing railroads to bring distant natural resources to eastern cities and factories.

The Workforce Grows Population changes also promoted the growth of industry. After the Civil War, large numbers of Europeans, and some Asians, immigrated to the United States. They were pushed from their homelands by factors such as political upheaval, religious discrimination, and crop failures.

In 1881 alone, nearly three quarters of a million immigrants arrived in America. That number climbed steadily, reaching almost one million per year by 1905.

Immigrants were willing to work for low wages because competition for jobs was fierce. And they were prepared to move frequently in pursuit of economic opportunity. All of these factors meant that industries had a huge, and willing, workforce to fuel growth. The potential workforce grew even larger in the 1890s, when droughts and competition from foreign farmers drove American farmers in large numbers to seek jobs in the cities.

Free Enterprise Encourages the Rise of Entrepreneurship In 1868, Horatio Alger published his first novel, *Ragged Dick or Street Life in New York*. This wildly successful novel told the story of a poor boy who rose to wealth and fame by working hard. Alger's novels stressed the possibility that anyone could vault from poverty and obscurity to wealth and fame.

In this excerpt, he describes how Ragged Dick starts his climb to success.

Growth in Mineral Production, 1870–1910

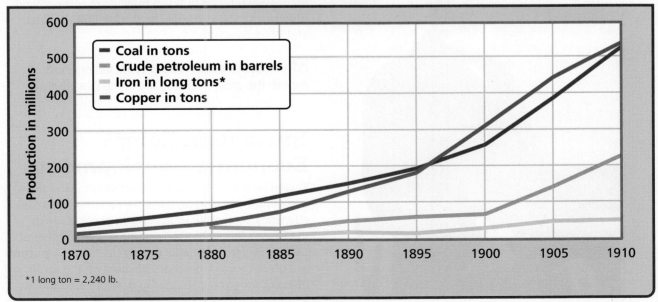

SOURCE: *Historical Statistics of the United States*

>> Technological innovation prompted the country's production of natural resources to increase significantly. **Analyze Graphs** What relationship do you see between natural resources and economic growth?

Ten dollars a week was to him a fortune. . . . Indeed, he would have been glad, only the day before, to get a place at three dollars a week. . . . Then he was to be advanced if he deserved it. It was indeed a bright prospect for a boy who, only a year before, could neither read nor write. . . . Dick's great ambition to "grow up 'spectable'" seemed likely to be accomplished after all.

—Horatio Alger, 1868

The "rags to riches" idea depended on the system of capitalism, in which individuals own most businesses.

The heroes of this system were **entrepreneurs**, or people who build and manage businesses or enterprises in order to make a profit. Entrepreneurs invest time, money, or both in a product or service, often risking their own livelihoods on the chance of success.

>> Andrew Carnegie was an entrepreneur who thrived in the American free enterprise system. He built successful businesses and contributed much of his wealth to philanthropic causes.

The rise of entrepreneurship fueled industrialization and economic growth in the late 1800s. Entrepreneurs thrived under the idea of **free enterprise**, or the freedom to run a business for profit with minimal regulation beyond what is necessary to protect the public interest. Entrepreneurs competed among themselves for consumers' dollars. If one business priced a certain product too high, consumers might buy a similar product from a competitor. So entrepreneurs found innovative ways to increase efficiency, cut costs, and lower prices, which enabled them to compete and survive in the free enterprise system. The factories, railroads, and mines they established created jobs and also attracted foreign investment.

Laissez-Faire Policies Encourage Growth The government encouraged **laissez-faire** policies, which allowed businesses to operate under minimal government regulation. Without government regulation, workplace conditions were sometimes challenging. However, laissez-faire policies, along with a strong legal system that enforced private property rights, provided the predictability and security that businesses and industries desired and encouraged investment and growth. These factors created an economic environment in which entrepreneurs could flourish.

To promote the buying of American goods, Congress enacted **protective tariffs**, or taxes that made imported goods cost more than those made in the United States. The government also gave innovative railroad builders millions of acres of land in return for their promise to quickly link the East and West coasts.

☑ **IDENTIFY MAIN IDEAS** What factors help explain the growth of industry in the late 1800s?

Innovation Drives Economic Development

Fueled by entrepreneurship, competition, and the free enterprise system, the drive for innovation and efficiency seemed to touch every sphere of life in the United States by the late 1800s. The number of patents increased rapidly during this time. A **patent** is a grant by the federal government giving an inventor the exclusive right to develop, use, and sell an invention for a set period of time. Business leaders invested heavily in these new scientific discoveries and innovations, hoping to create new industries and expand old ones. Eager consumers welcomed new

THE BIRTH OF MODERN TELECOMMUNICATION

SENDING A LETTER ✉ FROM MISSOURI TO ➤ CALIFORNIA

REGULAR MAIL 2 DAYS TO 2 MONTHS

PONY EXPRESS 10 DAYS

TELEGRAPH MESSAGE 1 HOUR

THE TELEGRAPH CATCHES ON

1844 Samuel Morse sends a message by telegraph from Washington D.C. to Baltimore.

1851 There are **75** telegraph companies and **21,147** miles of telegraph wire.

Sources: Western Union, *Historical Statistics of the United States*, National Museum of American History Archives Center

1866 Mergers and acquisitions leave Western Union as the sole survivor: transatlantic cables are successfully laid and global communication begins.

1867 There are **2,500** telegraph offices, **76,000** miles of wire, **5.8** million messages sent

EFFECTS

The Associated Press (AP) embraces the telegraph and newspaper reporting changes radically.

Foreign policy changes as leaders have timely information about international crisis.

>> The telegraph could send a message exponentially faster than standard mail. **Infer** How did telecommunication innovations improve the standard of living in the United States?

Bounce to Activate Gallery

---

inventions to the market, helping to spur the nation's economic development.

Electricity Improves Standards of Living With support from wealthy industrialists like J.P. Morgan, inventor **Thomas Edison** established a research laboratory at Menlo Park, New Jersey in 1876. Edison, a creative genius who had only a few months of formal education, would receive more than 1,000 patents for new inventions and scientific discoveries. In 1880, for example, with the goal of developing affordable lighting for homes, Edison and his team invented the light bulb, experimenting with thousands of different types of materials to find one that worked. Within a few years, they had also developed plans for central power plants to light entire sections of cities. Other inventors, such as the African American Lewis Latimer, improved upon Edison's work, and other uses for electricity improved Americans' standard of living. George Westinghouse, for example, developed technology to send electricity over long distances. Electricity lit city streets and powered homes and factories, extending the number of hours in the day when Americans could work and play.

Innovation in Communications In 1844, inventor Samuel Morse perfected telegraph technology, or the process of sending messages over wire. In 1876,

Alexander Graham Bell patented the telephone. The two inventions attracted investors. Within a few years, 148 telephone companies had strung more than 34,000 miles of wire, and long-distance lines linked several cities in the Northeast and Midwest. By 1900, there were more than one million telephones in the United States, and more than 100,000 miles of telegraph wire linked users across the land. In 1896, Guglielmo Marconi invented the wireless telegraph. Innovative entrepreneurs later built on Marconi's achievement and developed the radio. All of these inventions improved communication between Americans. Instead of waiting days for a letter to arrive, Americans could receive telegraphs in a matter of minutes or hear loved ones' voices immediately on the telephone. Improved communication also meant that news of public events spread quickly.

Steel, Innovation, and Economic Development In the 1850s in England, a man named Henry Bessemer developed a process for purifying iron to make strong, but lightweight, steel. American industries quickly adopted the **Bessemer process**, and by 1890 the United States was outproducing British steel manufacturers. Strong steel made possible a host of innovations, including skyscrapers and the elevators to service them. One of its most dramatic uses was in the construction of **suspension bridges**, bridges in which the roadway is suspended by steel cables. The first suspension bridge was the Brooklyn Bridge, spanning the East River in New York City. Completed in 1883, it was at the time of its construction the longest bridge in the world.

Technology Affects Travel As railroads expanded, they made other use of new technologies and also encouraged innovation. George Westinghouse patented air brakes for trains in 1869, while Granville Woods patented a telegraph system for trains in 1887.

Woods was one of many African Americans who developed and patented new inventions. Meanwhile, meatpacker Gustavus Swift developed refrigerated cars for transporting food. By 1883, there were three transcontinental railroad lines in the United States.

The expanding transportation network caused some problems, however. Throughout most of the 1800s, most towns set their clocks independently. When trains started regular passenger service between towns, time differences made it hard to set schedules. In 1884, delegates from 27 countries divided the globe into 24 **time zones**, one for each hour of the day. The railroads adopted this system, which is still used today.

Technology also affected how Americans traveled and where they lived. Electric streetcars, commuter

trains, and subways appeared in major cities. As a result, Americans could live in neighborhoods outside the city and commute to work. Factory production of automobiles with gas-powered engines began in 1902. Experiments in manned flight in a heavier-than-air craft by Orville and Wilbur Wright, among others, in the early 1900s marked the birth of aeronautics, another new industry. Women, too, introduced new inventions. For example, Mary Anderson invented a windshield wiper for streetcars that was patented in 1903.

An Upward Spiral of Growth Railroads played a key role in transforming American industries and businesses. They could transport large amounts of goods long distances quickly, cheaply, and efficiently. Because they linked the nation, they allowed businesses to obtain raw materials easily and to sell finished goods to larger numbers of people. They encouraged new methods for management and administration, which were soon adopted by the rest of the business community. In addition, the expanding railroad network stimulated innovation in many other industries.

An abundance of natural resources and an efficient transportation system to carry raw materials and finished goods set up a spiral of related growth. For example, factories turned out plate glass for windows of passenger rail cars. The factories

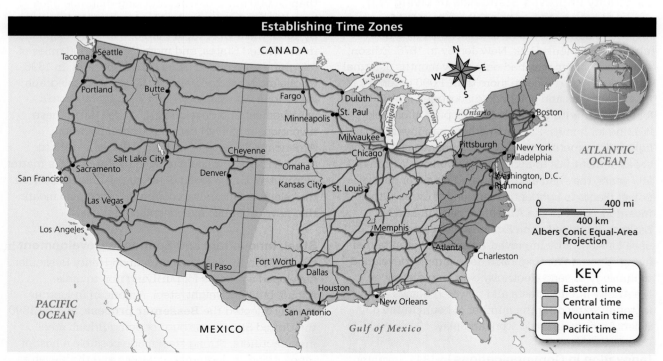

>> Railroads expanded across the country in the mid-nineteenth century. **Analyze Maps** What effect did railroads have on the production and distribution of goods?

Bounce to Activate Map

needed freight cars to carry the windows to their destinations.

Those freight cars were created in factories that used railroads to transport fuel to supply the furnaces that turned out more railroad cars. In this way, factory production generated more factory production.

To meet the growing demand, factory owners and other innovators developed systems for turning out large numbers of products quickly and inexpensively. Known as **mass production**, these systems depended upon machinery to carry out tasks that were once done with hand tools. In addition, Frederick Taylor and others studied the flow of work and workers' places in it to develop a system of industrial management that found the most efficient ways for workers to use new machinery. These technological and management innovations improved the standard of living for some Americans by increasing the development of an economic middle class. Middle-class Americans, especially those that lived in the industrialized North, could afford less expensive products produced by companies utilizing new technology.

☑ **CHECK UNDERSTANDING** How did new technologies influence industrialization?

Industrialization and the New South

While industry boomed in the North after the Civil War and Reconstruction, the South fell behind. The South struggled to develop its industry, and there were some pockets of success, especially in tobacco-processing, stone-quarrying, and furniture-making. In the 1890s, Altanta, Georgia, for example, was one of the earliest cities to develop an electric trolley system. But even though cities like Atlanta and Knoxville, Tennessee, grew strongly, the South struggled to overcome economic and social obstacles to broad industrial and urban development. As a result, the South remained largely agricultural and developed a smaller middle class than the North.

However, some post-Reconstruction industrial growth was led by many southern white leaders who envisioned a modernized economy that included not only agriculture but also mills and factories. Atlanta newspaper editor Henry Grady was among those who called for a "New South." A gifted orator, Grady thought the South should use its resources to develop industry:

>> A worker does her job in a typical Alabama textile mill in the early 1900s. **Interpret** In what way is this worker a symbol of the "New South"?

There was a South of slavery and secession—that South is dead. There is a South of union and freedom— that South, thank God, is living, breathing, growing every hour. . . . The old South rested everything on slavery and agriculture, unconscious that these could neither give nor maintain healthy growth. The new South presents a perfect democracy. . . a social system compact and closely knitted, less splendid on the surface, but stronger at the core. . . and a diversified industry that meets the complex needs of this complex age.

—Henry Grady, 1886

New Industries Develop Before the Civil War, the South had shipped its raw materials—including cotton, wood, and iron ore—abroad or to the North for processing into finished goods. In the 1880s, northern investors and entrepreneurs backed textile factories in North Carolina, South Carolina, and Georgia, as well as cigar and lumber production, especially in North Carolina and Virginia. In Florida, Vicente Martinez Ybor, an immigrant from Cuba, set up cigar manufacturing in Ybor City, which became part of Tampa. Other private investment in coal-, iron-, and steel-processing created urban centers in Nashville, Tennessee, and Birmingham, Alabama.

During this time, farming also became somewhat more diversified, with an increase in grain, tobacco, and fruit crops. Even the landscape of farming changed as smaller farms replaced large plantations.

Railroads Connect Cities and Towns The South needed reliable transportation to aid its industrial growth. To meet this need, southern rail lines expanded, joining rural areas with urban hubs such as Mobile and Montgomery in Alabama and the bustling ports of New Orleans, Louisiana, and Charleston, South Carolina. Yet, by the 1880s, only two rail lines—from Texas to Chicago and from Tennessee to Washington, D.C.—linked southern freight to northern markets.

To combat economic isolation, southerners lobbied the federal government for economic help and used prison labor to keep railroad construction costs down. Gradually, rail connections helped expand small hubs such as Meridian, Mississippi, and Americus, Georgia. The newer cities of Atlanta, Dallas, and Nashville developed rapidly and began rivaling older cities.

The Southern Economy Lags Behind Despite these changes, the southern economy continued to lag behind the rest of the country. While the North was able to build on its strong industrial base, the South first had to repair the damages of war. Moreover, industry rests on a three-legged stool: natural resources, labor, and capital investment, or money invested to start or improve the business. The South had plenty of the first but not enough of the second and third.

Sustained economic development also requires workers who are well trained and productive, but public education in the South was limited.

In fact, the South spent less than any other part of the country on education, and it lacked the technical and engineering schools that could have trained the people needed by industry. At the same time, low wages discouraged skilled workers from coming to the South, and the lure of higher wages or better conditions elsewhere siphoned off southern workers.

Additionally, very few southern banks had survived the war, and those that were functioning had fewer assets than their northern competitors. Most of the South's wealth was concentrated in the hands of a few people. Poor tenant farmers and factory workers did not have cash to deposit. With

Wholesale Price of Cotton, 1865–1890

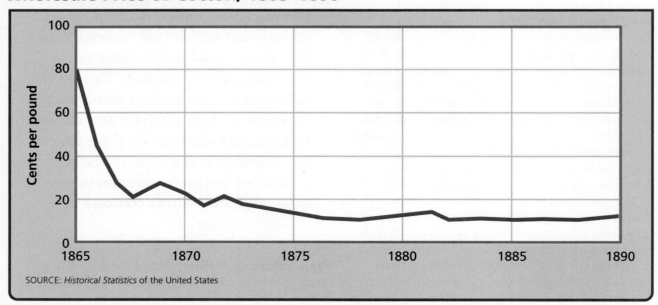

SOURCE: *Historical Statistics* of the United States

>> The price of cotton fell dramatically following the Civil War. **Analyze Graphs** What factors contributed to cotton's declining value?

few strong banks, southern financiers were dependent on northern banks to start or expand businesses or farms. The southern economy suffered from this lack of labor and capital.

Farm Issues in the South Before the Civil War, most southern planters had concentrated on such crops as cotton and tobacco, which were grown not for their own use but to be sold for cash. The lure of the **cash crop** continued after the war, despite efforts to diversify. Cotton remained the centerpiece of the southern agricultural economy. However, during the war, many European textile factories had found suppliers outside the South, and the price of cotton had fallen. Now, the South's abundance of cotton simply depressed the price further.

Dependence on one major crop was extremely risky. In the case of southern cotton, it was the boll weevil that heralded disaster. The boll weevil, a beetle which could destroy an entire crop of cotton, appeared in Texas in the early 1890s. Over the next decade, the yield from cotton cultivation in some states dropped by more than 50 percent. Fortunately, the African American inventor George Washington Carver introduced crop rotation as a way to replenish soil that had been worn out by cotton production.

☑ **IDENTIFY SUPPORTING DETAILS** What factors inhibited southern economic recovery?

The Effects of Industrialization

Free enterprise and industrialization touched every aspect of American life in the late 1800s, from the way businesses and farms operated to the kinds of products Americans used. They also affected the country's relationship with the world and with its own environment.

Dominating World Markets By the 1880s, American exports of grain, steel, and textiles dominated international markets. Although Britain was building railroads to access natural resources in Africa, Asia, and other places across the world, by 1900, the United States had almost as many miles of railroad track as the rest of the world combined. The United States could easily transport goods from where they were made or grown to ports where they could be shipped around the world. Exports of food and goods greatly expanded the American economy. As the United States grew as a world economic power, it often clashed with the economic policies of other countries.

>> A manager on a late nineteenth-century cotton plantation weighs the amount of cotton picked by laborers.

>> From freight yards such as this massive complex in New York City, American industry transported food and other goods nationwide, greatly increasing Americans' access to consumer products.

>> Factories, with their multitude of smoke stacks, created a great deal of air pollution. Industrial waste was a byproduct of the Industrial Revolution.

Daily Life Changes Massive changes in industry altered how Americans lived and worked. As farms became mechanized, fewer farm laborers were needed to feed the nation. Out-of-work farmers and their families moved to urban areas to find work, especially in the increasingly industrial North. The mass production of goods meant that these new urban dwellers had easy access to clothing and supplies that they would have had to make by hand in the past. Yet they faced higher costs of living, were dependent upon cash wages to buy food, and performed repetitive work in factories.

Concerns About the Environment In the early 1800s, few worried about how industry might affect the environment. However, by the late 1800s, industrial waste had risen dramatically and mining had begun to damage the land. In the Midwest, increasing agricultural production had led to soil erosion and dust storms. People began to raise concerns about protecting natural resources. Congress responded by setting aside protected lands that would eventually become part of the National Park Service. Its creation of Yellowstone Park in 1872 was one of the first federal responses to concerns about the environment, and Yellowstone was the first such national park established anywhere in the world. Over the next decades, many more square miles of American land would be set aside to be protected.

☑ **IDENTIFY CENTRAL IDEAS** Explain how industrialization impacted the lives of Americans.

☑ ASSESSMENT

1. **Compare and Contrast** the risks and goals of entrepreneurs and inventors.

2. **Identify Central Issues** Why was the South slower to industrialize than the North?

3. **Cite Evidence** that there were some negative effects of industrialization.

4. **Infer** why the free enterprise system was so important to entrepreneurs and why entrepreneurs were crucial to the free enterprise system.

5. **Support Ideas with Evidence** What did the United States have that made it so successful during the second Industrial Revolution? Include as many factors as you can think of.

1.2 The rapid industrial growth that occurred after the Civil War transformed American business and society. Yet it was only the beginning. The rise of big business, characterized by the investment of huge amounts of private financial resources, helped the United States push aside strong economies like Britain's, to become one of the most economically powerful countries in the modern world.

>> The Standard Oil Company continued to refine its production processes with new technologies in its many refineries.

Bounce to Activate Flipped Video

Big Business Rises

Corporations Find New Ways of Doing Business

Until the mid-nineteenth century, most businesses were run by one person or family. This meant that no business could grow bigger than one family's ability to invest in it or run it. Businesses were also local, buying and selling to customers who lived nearby. Industrialization changed all this. Railroads provided businesses with access to raw materials and customers from farther and farther away. Business leaders, desiring the profits offered by these larger markets, responded by combining funds and resources.

The Corporation Meets New Needs To take advantage of expanding markets, investors developed a form of group ownership known as a **corporation**. In a corporation, a number of people share the ownership of a business. If a corporation experiences economic problems, the investors lose no more than they had originally invested in the business. The corporation was the perfect solution to the challenge of expanding business, especially for risky industries such as railroads or mining. A corporation had the same rights as an individual: it could buy and sell property, and it could sue in the courts. If one person chose to leave the group, others could buy his interests.

>> **Objectives**

Analyze different management innovations that businesses used to increase their profits.

Describe the public debate over the pros and cons of big business.

Explain how the government took steps to block abuses of corporate power.

>> **Key Terms**

corporation
monopoly
cartel
John D. Rockefeller
horizontal integration
trust
Andrew Carnegie
vertical integration
Social Darwinism
Interstate
   Commerce
   Commission (ICC)
Sherman Antitrust
   Act

Corporations were perfectly suited to expanding markets. They had access to huge amounts of capital, or invested money, allowing them to fund new technology, enter new industries, or run large plants across the country. Aided by railroads and the telegraph, corporations had the ability to operate in several different regions. After 1870, the number of corporations in America increased dramatically. They were an important part of industrial capitalism. The economic free-market system centered around industries.

Finding New Ways to Gain Advantage

Corporations worked to maximize profits in several ways. They advertised their products widely, which enabled them to reach more potential customers. They paid low wages to workers and tried to obtain raw materials as cheaply as possible. They adopted forms of business organization, such as horizontal or vertical integration, and applied other innovations in production management to seek out efficiencies that would in turn decrease their cost of producing goods or services. Like J. P. Morgan, the heads of some corporations supported research laboratories where inventors could experiment with new processes that could lower production costs or new products that could bring future profits.

Others thought of new ways to make their businesses profitable. Cornelius Vanderbilt, an entrepreneur in the railroad industry, got his start in the steamboat business. He succeeded in getting his competitors to pay him to relocate because his low fares were driving them out of business. Some corporations worked to eliminate competition by forming a **cartel**. In this arrangement, businesses making the same product agree to limit their production and thus keep prices high. **John D. Rockefeller**, an Ohio oil tycoon, made agreements with railroads that made it difficult for his competitors to ship their products:

> [Rockefeller's company] killed its rivals, in brief, by getting the great trunk lines to refuse to give them transportation. Vanderbilt is reported to have said that there was but one man—Rockefeller—who could dictate to him.
>
> —H. D. Lloyd, *The Atlantic*, 1881

Business Management Innovations Business leaders continued to develop ever more effective ways to decrease costs and increase profits. One way was to merge competing firms into a giant company whose size would lead to lower production costs. This system of consolidating many firms in the same business is called **horizontal integration**. Some corporations used horizontal integration to gain a **monopoly**, or complete control of a product

Economic Advantages of Being Big

>> Production costs usually decrease as more goods are produced. **Analyze Graphs**
What competitive advantages do larger businesses have over smaller ones?

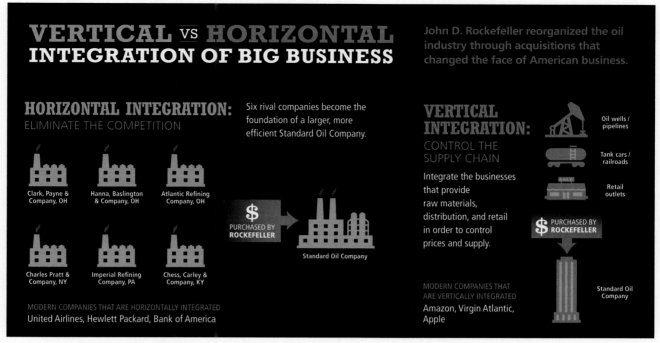

VERTICAL VS HORIZONTAL
INTEGRATION OF BIG BUSINESS

John D. Rockefeller reorganized the oil industry through acquisitions that changed the face of American business.

HORIZONTAL INTEGRATION:
ELIMINATE THE COMPETITION

Six rival companies become the foundation of a larger, more efficient Standard Oil Company.

Clark, Payne & Company, OH

Hanna, Baslington & Company, OH

Atlantic Refining Company, OH

Charles Pratt & Company, NY

Imperial Refining Company, PA

Chess, Carley & Company, KY

PURCHASED BY ROCKEFELLER

Standard Oil Company

MODERN COMPANIES THAT ARE HORIZONTALLY INTEGRATED
United Airlines, Hewlett Packard, Bank of America

VERTICAL INTEGRATION:
CONTROL THE SUPPLY CHAIN

Integrate the businesses that provide raw materials, distribution, and retail in order to control prices and supply.

Oil wells / pipelines

Tank cars / railroads

Retail outlets

PURCHASED BY ROCKEFELLER

Standard Oil Company

MODERN COMPANIES THAT ARE VERTICALLY INTEGRATED
Amazon, Virgin Atlantic, Apple

>> Management innovations such as horizontal and vertical integration allowed American businesses to remain competitive in the age of industrialization. **Contrast** What differences do you see between horizontal and vertical integration?

or service. To do this, a company either bought its competitors or drove them out of business. With no remaining competition and an efficient production process, the company was free to set its own prices based on demand for its products. This power did not always mean higher prices for consumers, but the potential for setting high prices was there. The management innovation of horizontal integration made business more efficient but occasionally had a negative impact on labor, because workers at smaller companies driven out of business would need to find employment elsewhere.

Production management, a management innovation designed to maximize the efficiency of a production process, also impacted labor. Business owners were understandably interested in controlling labor costs and continually looked for ways to improve worker productivity in conjunction with new machines. As a result, business owners could often meet production goals with fewer skilled workers. Those without the required skills to work with the new technologies and those unable to maintain the pace of a regimented workflow on factory floors oftentimes found themselves without work.

Rockefeller was one of the first businessmen to use horizontal integration. However, Ohio state law

prevented one company from owning the stock of another. This meant that Rockefeller could not buy out his competitors. Instead he found a way to get around the law by forming a new type of business organization called a **trust**. In a trust, companies assigned their stock to a board of trustees, who combined them into a new organization that the trustees ran. By the early 1880s, Rockefeller and his Standard Oil trust controlled most of the oil refined in the United States.

In Ohio and elsewhere, trusts arose, in part, because state laws governing corporations were inadequate. In many states in the mid-1800s, corporations could only be chartered by the state legislature passing an act. Business leaders looked for more flexible ways to build their businesses. For some business leaders, trusts were also a way to bring efficiency and stability to a free market where competition could be fierce and unpredictable. As state laws changed, trusts were replaced by other types of business mergers. However, the public continued to apply the term "trust" to any form of monopolistic business association.

Rockefeller, steel tycoon **Andrew Carnegie**, and other business leaders also strengthened their companies and made the workplace more efficient by gaining control of the different businesses that were involved in all stages of manufacturing their products. Carnegie, for example, owned the coal mines and iron-ore fields that provided the raw materials for his steel, as well as the ships and railroads that brought them to his steel mills. This process, called **vertical integration**, allowed companies to reduce their costs of production.

☑ **IDENTIFY MAIN IDEAS** How were corporations able to decrease costs and increase profits?

The Pros and Cons of Big Business

Throughout the 1880s, business mergers created powerful empires for those who controlled steel, railroads, meat, farm equipment, sugar, lumber, and a number of other enterprises. However, many smaller companies and consumers began to question the goals and tactics of those who led these businesses.

"Robber Barons" or "Captains of Industry"?

Many small businesses were bought up or squeezed out of competition. Those that joined trusts

THE PROTECTORS OF OUR INDUSTRIES.

>> "The Protectors of Our Industries" shows Cornelius Vanderbilt II and other business leaders. **Analyze Political Cartoons** What point of view about these leaders does this cartoon express?

Bounce to Activate Gallery

often found that they received few profits. Some consumers were alarmed by the high prices that monopolies and cartels sometimes set on their products. Gradually, many consumers, workers, and the federal government came to believe that systems like trusts, cartels, and monopolies gave powerful business leaders unfair advantages. They believed that perhaps the government's laissez-faire policies had been too hands off and costly in terms of hurting workers and consumers. People who held these views began to refer to these leaders as "robber barons."

At the same time, other people believed that these industrialists served the nation positively. They believed that laissez-faire policies had benefited the nation by allowing business to flourish and regulate itself according to free enterprise principles. They recognized that the spread of factories, steel mills, and railroads provided jobs for an ever-growing labor force. Large, efficient corporations often lowered prices for consumers. Business supporters also noted that the industrialists' efficient business practices and support for developing technology benefited the nation's economy, stimulating innovation and shaping the United States into a strong international leader. Furthermore, many business leaders, like Carnegie, Rockefeller, and Vanderbilt, were important philanthropists.

They established universities, museums, and libraries, believing that such institutions made it possible for the disadvantaged to rise to wealth. For these reasons, people who took this point of view thought of business leaders as "captains of industry."

The Causes and Effects of Social Darwinism

In 1859, biologist Charles Darwin published *On the Origin of Species*, arguing that animals evolved by a process of "natural selection" and that only the fittest survived to reproduce. Yale professor William Graham Sumner soon applied this theory to the rough-and-tumble world of American capitalism, calling it **Social Darwinism**. He declared that wealth was a measure of one's inherent value and those who had it were the most "fit."

The theory of Social Darwinism, caused by this modification of Darwin's scientific findings, became a social issue when it was used to justify a wide variety of beliefs and conditions. Supporters of the laissez-faire economic system argued that the government should stay out of private business, because interference would disrupt natural selection.

Many Social Darwinists believed that the nation would grow strong by allowing its most vigorous members to rise to the top, and that it was wrong to use public funds to assist the poor. Social Darwinism was often used to fuel discrimination. Social Darwinists pointed to the poverty-stricken condition of many minorities as evidence of their unfitness.

☑ **CHECK UNDERSTANDING** How did people explain their support or opposition to big business?

The Changing Relationship Between Government and Business

The great industrialists' methods and their influence on the nation's economy worried some Americans. Competing railroads took part in practices such as fixing rates and pooling, or entering into secret agreements to divide up the nation's freight. Many Americans felt that price fixing and pooling drove up rates and were unfair to consumers. They also thought that unfair business practices and poor wages and working conditions for the labor force had made the costs of the government's laissez-faire policies too high. They wanted the federal government to take action.

Attempts to Regulate Business Finally, in 1887, Congress responded by creating the **Interstate Commerce Commission (ICC)** to monitor railroad shipping rates. However, it could only keep watch on railroads that crossed state lines. Also, it could not make laws or control the railroads' transactions. Although court rulings favoring states and railroads weakened even these few powers, the ICC was the first federal agency to monitor business practices. Over the next several decades, the government would create many other federal bodies to regulate American businesses.

Similarly, the federal government slowly became involved in regulating trusts. In 1890, the Senate passed the **Sherman Antitrust Act**, which outlawed any trust that operated "in restraint of trade or commerce among the several states." The government claimed that it had a constitutional right to regulate such commerce. But for more than a decade, the law was seldom enforced because court rulings generally favored business owners.

In fact, it was often used in businesses' favor because they successfully argued in court that labor unions restrained trade. However, the ICC and the Sherman Antitrust Act began a trend toward federal limitations on corporations' power.

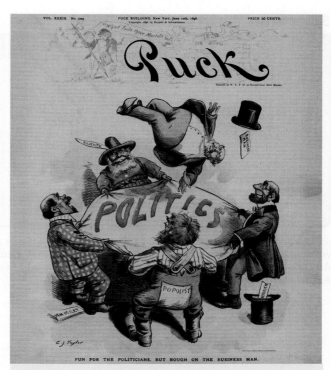

>> In this cartoon, men labeled *Populist*, *Democrat*, *Republican*, and *Silverite* toss a Business Man around on a sheet. **Analyze Political Cartoons** According to this artist, who is in control of business?

>> Railroads all travel to one destination. **Analyze Political Cartoons** What does the "robber baron" in this cartoon represent?

Sherman Antitrust Act, 1890

ADVANTAGES	DISADVANTAGES
• Enabled Congress to regulate trade between states and end monopolistic practices • Tried to eliminate hidden monopolies (trusts) that affected trade • Enabled competitors to sue trustees of rival companies for loss of revenue • Levied fines against those forming trusts	• Difficult to enforce • Lacked clear definition of the practices that resulted in a restraint of trade • More often used successfully against labor unions than monopolies

>> The Sherman Antitrust Act tried to create a fair marketplace in which the needs of businesses, workers, and consumers were addressed. **Analyze Charts** Why might some businesses disagree with the Sherman Antitrust Act?

 Bounce to Activate Chart

A Difficult Balance Between Business, Government, and Consumer These limits on corporations' power were made in an attempt to create a fair environment for competition. They sought to prevent any one company from undercutting market forces by driving its competition out of the market, which would allow the company rather than the market to determine the best price for its products. To this end, the federal government tried many kinds of legislation and regulation—with a mixture of costs and benefits. Often neither businesses nor consumers felt that their interests were well-served by government policies and actions.

The costs and benefits of anti-trust acts continued to be debated. Over the course of 50 years, corporations, federal regulatory agencies, consumers, unions, and the courts struggled to find an acceptable balance between fair prices and wages, as well as workers' safety and dignity and the corporations' legitimate quest for efficiencies that would provide a fair return on the investment and risk involved in doing business in a free-market system. Historians continue to assess the ways in which—and the degree to which—that attempt at balance was met. Historians and economists also debate the question of who should have the responsibility for developing the policies to achieve

that balance. Indeed, these issues are still part of the relationship between business, government, and the consumer in our own time.

☑ **IDENTIFY SUPPORTING DETAILS** How did the federal government attempt to regulate business?

☑ ASSESSMENT

1. **Generate Explanations** Why did forming corporations allow big business to increase in power and profitability?

2. **Interpret** the effects of monopolies and cartels on the consumer.

3. **Summarize** what made John D. Rockefeller such a successful businessman.

4. **Compare Points of View** Why would one person use the term "robber baron" and another "captain of industry" to describe the same person?

5. **Support Ideas with Examples** Cite arguments for and against increased federal regulatory power of private business using specific examples to support your answer.

1.3 As industrialization intensified, the success of the booming American economy relied heavily on its workers. But struggles between business owners and workers also intensified, as workers rebelled against low pay and unsafe working conditions. To keep the economy thriving, Americans had to find ways to ease the tensions between business owners and workers.

>> This riot in Haymarket Square is still remembered today.

Bounce to Activate Flipped Video

The Organized Labor Movement

Workers Endure Difficulties

The industrial expansion in the United States produced great wealth for the owners of factories, mines, railroads, and large farms. It also brought general improvements to American society in the form of a higher standard of living, wider availability of cheap goods, and increased access to public institutions like museums and schools. However, the economic growth of the late 1800s caused domestic issues. Many of the people who performed the work in the nation's great industries struggled to survive. In addition, workers—especially immigrants, women, and minorities—often faced ridicule and discrimination.

The Hardships of Factory Work In the 1880s and 1890s, factory owners, seeking to keep down production costs, employed people who would work for low wages. Immigrants made up a large percentage of the workforce. Far from home, lacking good English-speaking skills, and often very poor, immigrants would generally take almost any job. Factory workers toiled long hours—12 hours a day, 6 days a week. Countless thousands of others worked similar hours in small, hot, dark, and dirty workhouses known as

>> **Objectives**

Assess the impact of business practices on workers in the late 1800s.

Compare the goals and strategies of the first labor unions.

Analyze the causes and effects of strikes in the late 1800s.

>> **Key Terms**

sweatshops
company towns
collective bargaining
socialism
Knights of Labor
Terence V. Powderly
Samuel Gompers
American Federation
  of Labor (AFL)
Haymarket Riot
Homestead Strike
Eugene V. Debs
Pullman Strike

>> Work in the textile mills could be very dangerous, and it was not unheard of for an inexperienced, young worker (some as young as eight years old) to lose a finger in an accident.

>> A surplus of immigrant labor made it difficult for sweatshop workers, such as these women, to demand fair wages and safe working conditions.

sweatshops. Sweatshop workers, mainly women, labored long hours at machines making mass-produced items. Owners ensured productivity by strictly regulating workers' days. They clocked work and break hours and fined workers for breaking rules or working slowly.

Factory work was often dangerous. Workspaces were poorly lit, often overheated, and badly ventilated. Some workers lost their hearing from the noisy machines. Accidents were common, both from faulty equipment and from lack of proper training. Despite the harsh conditions, employers suffered no shortage of labor. There were always more people than jobs.

Children in the Workplace As industrialization advanced, more jobs opened up for women. They worked as laundresses, telegraph operators, and typists. But most women—and their families—worked in the factories. Since low wages meant that both parents needed jobs, bringing children to work kept them off the streets and close to their parents. It also meant that the children could earn a wage, which helped the family to survive.

By the end of the 1800s, nearly one in five children between the ages of 10 and 16 worked rather than attending school. Harsh conditions stunted their physical and mental growth. By the 1890s, social workers began to recognize the social issues caused by child labor. They lobbied to get children out of factories and into child care or schools. Eventually, the efforts of social workers and other reformers prompted states to pass legislation to stop child labor.

Company Towns and Wage Slavery As immigrants flooded into manufacturing centers, employers had to house them. In Florida, Vicente Martinez Ybor offered the workers in his cigar factories new houses that could be purchased over time. Elsewhere, however, workers were not so lucky. Many laborers, especially those who worked in mines, were forced to live in isolated communities near their workplaces. The housing in these communities, known as **company towns**, was owned by the business and rented out to employees. The employer also controlled the "company store," where workers were forced to buy goods. The company store sold goods on credit but charged high interest. As a result, by the time the worker was paid, most of the wages were owed back to the employer. Since workers could be arrested if they left their jobs before they completely repaid these debts, employers could hold onto workers through a system that workers' advocates called "wage slavery." Through management of their company towns, employers could also reinforce ethnic competition and distrust. For example, Mexican, African American, or Chinese workers could be segregated in separate towns.

☑ **IDENTIFY CENTRAL IDEAS** In what ways did labor conditions affect families?

The Growth of Labor Unions

Industrialization and free enterprise lowered the prices of consumer goods but helped business investors gain large profits. Workers usually did not object to their employer making a profit from their work. After all, if the business was not profitable, it could close and leave workers jobless.

However, workers were understandably frustrated that their wages did not earn enough to buy many consumer goods, even at lower prices. They also resented working in unsafe conditions that in some cases ruined their health and therefore their ability to earn a living. Increasingly, workers organized to demand better wages and working conditions. Employers usually opposed the growing labor movement, which they saw as a threat to their businesses and profits. Employers tended to view efforts to improve wages or working conditions as a violation of their property rights—their right to run their businesses as they saw fit.

Early Labor Protests As early as the 1820s, factory workers tried to gain more power by using the technique of **collective bargaining**, or negotiating as a group with their employer for higher wages or better working conditions. A related tool to collective bargaining was the strike, in which workers refused to work until certain demands were met. Most strikes were local, but sometimes they involved workers in a whole industry across a state, a region, or the country.

The first national labor union, founded in 1834, was the National Trades Union, open to workers from all trades. It lasted only a few years. However, strikes succeeded in reducing the length of the workday in some regions. By the mid-1800s, a six-day work week with a 10-hour workday became the standard in most New England factories. Gradually, national unions began to reappear.

>> Many working-class families struggled to get by on low wages.

Socialism Influences Labor In the 1830s, a movement called **socialism** spread throughout Europe. Socialism is an economic and political philosophy that favors public, instead of private, control of property and income. Socialists believe that society, not just private individuals, should control a nation's wealth. That wealth, they argue, should be distributed equally to everyone.

In 1848, the German philosophers Karl Marx and Friedrich Engels expanded on the ideas of socialism in a treatise titled *The Communist Manifesto*. This pamphlet denounced capitalism and predicted that workers would overturn it. Most Americans rejected these ideas, believing that they threatened the American ideals of free enterprise, private property, and individual liberty. The wealthy in particular opposed socialism because it threatened their fortunes. But many labor activists borrowed ideas from socialism to demand social reform.

The Knights of Labor In 1869, Uriah Stephens founded a labor union called the **Knights of Labor**. Stephens, a tailor who had worked around the country, included all workers of any trade, skilled or unskilled, in his union. The Knights also recruited women and African Americans. Under Stephens, the union functioned largely as a secret society, devoted

>> The Knights of Labor were sometimes portrayed in a comical fashion in the media.

Bounce to Activate Cartoon

>> Many laborers sought better working conditions and better pay through unionization.

to broad social reform such as replacing capitalism with workers' cooperatives. The Preamble to the Knights' Constitution, written in 1878, read:

> The recent alarming development and aggression of aggregated wealth, which, unless checked, will inevitably lead to the pauperization and hopeless degradation of the toiling masses, render it imperative, if we desire to enjoy the blessings of life, that a check should be placed upon its power . . . and a system adopted which will secure to the laborer the fruits of his toil. . . .
>
> —Preamble to the Knights' Constitution, 1878

In 1879, **Terence V. Powderly** took on the leadership of the Knights. Powderly abandoned the secretive nature of the Knights. Under his leadership the union used collective bargaining, boycotts, and the threat of strikes to win gains for workers. But like Stephens, Powderly also pursued reforms intended to free workers from wage labor. He planned large-scale manufacturing cooperatives which members workers would operate and take a share in the profits. By 1885, the Knights had grown to include some 700,000 men and women nationwide, of every race and ethnicity. By the 1890s, however, after a series of failed strikes, the Knights had largely disappeared. Many Knights who worked in skilled crafts or trades abandoned the union for a new, rival labor organization, the American Federation of Labor.

A New Organization for Workers Samuel Gompers was a poor Jewish immigrant from England who had worked his way up to head the Cigarmakers' Union in New York. In 1886, Gompers helped found the **American Federation of Labor (AFL)** and served as its president for nearly 40 years. While the Knights of Labor was open to nearly all workers, the AFL was a loose organization of some 100 unions of skilled workers devoted to specific crafts. These trade unions retained their individuality but gained strength in bargaining through their affiliation with the AFL.

Gompers set high dues for membership in the AFL, pooling the money to create a strike and pension fund to assist workers in need. Unlike the Knights of Labor, the AFL did not aim for larger social gains for workers. Instead, it focused on specific workers' issues such as wages, working

Influential Labor Unions

NAME	DATE FOUNDED	SIGNIFICANCE
National Trades Union	1834	First national union; open to workers from all trades
Knights of Labor	1869	Sought general ideological reform; open to workers of all trades
American Federation of Labor	1886	Focused on specific workers' issues; organization of skilled workers from local craft unions
American Railway Union	1893	First industrial union; open to all railway workers

>> Different labor unions continued to advocate for worker's rights. **Analyze Tables** How were all of these labor unions similar? What were some ways in which they differed?

hours, and working conditions. In testimony before a government labor commission, Gompers argued in fact that unions and strikes were the only way workers' issues such as these could be addressed:

> We recognize that peaceful industry is necessary to successful civilized life, but the right to strike and the preparation to strike is the greatest preventive to strikes.
>
> If the workmen were to make up their minds tomorrow that they would under no circumstances strike, the employers would do all the striking for them in the way of lesser wages, and longer hours of labor.
>
> —Report on the (U.S.) Industrial Commission on Capital and Labor, 1890

The AFL also pressed for workplaces in which only union members could be hired. Because of its narrow focus on workers' issues, the AFL was often called a "bread and butter" union.

The AFL was not as successful as the Knights in rapidly gaining the widespread support of workers, partly because of its own policies. It opposed union membership for women because Gompers

believed their presence in the workplace drove wages down. While it was theoretically open to African Americans, member unions usually found ways to exclude them. Nevertheless, by 1910 AFL membership had reached two million workers.

☑ **IDENTIFY** What similarities and differences existed in the goals of various labor unions?

Labor Unions Lead Protests

As membership in labor unions rose and labor activists became more skilled in organizing large-scale protests, a wave of bitter confrontations between labor and management hit the nation. The first major strike occurred in the railroad industry in 1877. Striking workers, responding to wage cuts, caused massive property destruction in several cities. State militias were called in to protect strikebreakers, or temporary workers hired to perform the jobs of striking workers. Finally, the federal government sent in troops to restore order. In the decades to follow, similar labor disputes would affect businesses, the government, and the organization of labor unions themselves.

Workers Protest in Chicago In May 1886, thousands of workers mounted a national demonstration for an eight-hour workday. Strikes erupted in several cities, and fights broke out between strikers and strikebreakers. Conflict then escalated between strikers and police who were brought in to halt the violence. On May 4, protesters gathered at Haymarket Square in Chicago. The diverse crowd included anarchists, or radicals opposed to all government. A protester threw a bomb, killing a policeman. In the subsequent frenzy, dozens of people, both protesters and policemen, were killed. Eight anarchists were tried for murder, and four were executed.

The **Haymarket Riot** left an unfortunate legacy. The Knights of Labor fizzled out as people shied away from radicalism. Employers and much of the American public became even more suspicious of union activities, associating them with violence.

Steelworkers Clash with the Pinkertons In the summer of 1892, a Carnegie Steel plant in Homestead, Pennsylvania, cut workers' wages. The union immediately called a strike. Andrew Carnegie's partner, Henry Frick, responded by bringing in the Pinkertons, a private police force known for their ability to break up strikes. The Pinkertons killed several strikers and wounded many others in a standoff that lasted some two weeks. Then, on July 23, an anarchist who had joined the

protesters tried to assassinate Frick. The union had not backed his plan, but the public associated the two. Recognizing that public opinion was turning against unions, the union called off the strike in November. The **Homestead Strike** was part of an epidemic of steelworkers' and miners' strikes that took place as economic depression spread across America. In each case, troops and local militia were called in to suppress the unrest.

A Union Addresses Social Issues in a Pullman Town In 1893, inventor George Pullman, whose Pullman Palace Car Company produced luxury railroad passenger cars, laid off many of his workers and cut wages by 25 percent. Although the economic slowdown plaguing the nation at the time justified this action to some degree, Pullman did not reduce the rents in his company town near Chicago, where his workers lived. In May 1894, workers sent a delegation to discuss their situation with Pullman. He refused to negotiate and fired three workers. His other workers responded by going on strike.

When Pullman brought in strikebreakers, the workers turned to the newly organized American Railway Union (ARU) for help. Founded by former railroad worker **Eugene V. Debs,** the ARU was organized as an industrial union, grouping all railroad workers together rather than into separate

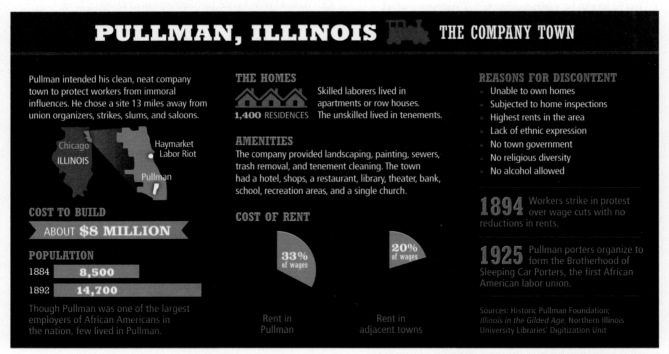

PULLMAN, ILLINOIS THE COMPANY TOWN

Pullman intended his clean, neat company town to protect workers from immoral influences. He chose a site 13 miles away from union organizers, strikes, slums, and saloons.

Chicago
ILLINOIS

Haymarket Labor Riot

Pullman

COST TO BUILD
ABOUT **$8 MILLION**

POPULATION
1884	8,500
1892	14,700

Though Pullman was one of the largest employers of African Americans in the nation, few lived in Pullman.

THE HOMES
1,400 RESIDENCES
Skilled laborers lived in apartments or row houses. The unskilled lived in tenements.

AMENITIES
The company provided landscaping, painting, sewers, trash removal, and tenement cleaning. The town had a hotel, shops, a restaurant, library, theater, bank, school, recreation areas, and a single church.

COST OF RENT
33% of wages
Rent in Pullman

20% of wages
Rent in adjacent towns

REASONS FOR DISCONTENT
- Unable to own homes
- Subjected to home inspections
- Highest rents in the area
- Lack of ethnic expression
- No town government
- No religious diversity
- No alcohol allowed

1894 Workers strike in protest over wage cuts with no reductions in rents.

1925 Pullman porters organize to form the Brotherhood of Sleeping Car Porters, the first African American labor union.

Sources: Historic Pullman Foundation; *Illinois in the Gilded Age,* Northern Illinois University Libraries' Digitization Unit

>> Company towns like this one provided everything workers would need, but at a significant cost. **Analyze Graphs** What reasons account for the workers' complaints about Pullman?

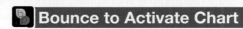
Bounce to Activate Chart

trade unions according to the job they held. Debs believed that industrial unions allowed workers to exert united pressure on employers.

The ARU ordered a nationwide strike against Pullman. By June 1894, nearly 300,000 railworkers were refusing to work on, handle, or move any trains that had Pullman cars on them. As the **Pullman Strike** escalated, the nation's railroad traffic came to a halt. Railroad owners cited the Sherman Antitrust Act to argue that the union was illegally disrupting free trade. Since the nation's mail moved by train, the federal government took action to end the strike. A federal court ordered a halt to the strike. When Debs defied the court order, President Grover Cleveland sent in federal troops to force the strikers back to work. Debs was jailed for conspiring against interstate commerce. Debs appealed his conviction, claiming that the government had no authority to halt the strike. However, the Supreme Court upheld Debs' conviction in the case *In re Debs* in 1895, ruling that protecting interstate commerce and the private property rights of the railroads was a lawful exercise of government power.

The Impact of Labor Unions The outcome of the Pullman Strike set an important trend. Employers, hoping to maintain profitability and thus create more jobs, appealed frequently for court orders against unions, citing legislation like the Sherman Antitrust Act. The federal courts and other federal officials routinely supported these appeals, denying unions recognition as legally protected organizations and limiting union gains for more than 30 years. As the twentieth century opened, industrialists, workers, and government continued to battle over numerous labor issues. Collective bargaining, strikes, and legislation would become the way of life for American industry.

In the decades after Pullman, the labor movement split into different factions, some increasingly influenced by socialism. By the end of the 1800s, Debs had become a Socialist. He helped organize the American Socialist Party in 1897, running for President in 1900. In 1905, he helped found the Industrial Workers of the World (IWW), or Wobblies. The IWW was a radical union of unskilled workers with many Socialists among its leaders. In the first few decades of the 1900s, the IWW led a number of strikes, many of them violent.

☑ **CHECK UNDERSTANDING** Why did workers turn to the strike as a tactic to win labor gains?

>> Eugene V. Debs, leader of the American Railroad Union, speaks to a crowd. Debs was known as a fiery and inspirational speaker.

☑ ASSESSMENT

1. **Support a Point of View with Evidence** In the late 1800s, sweatshops and other factories were horrible places to work. What evidence supports this point of view?

2. **Determine Point of View** Why does the concept of child labor in factories seems so terrible to us today when it was a widely accepted practice in the 1800s?

3. **Compare** life in a company town with life today for a low-paid worker.

4. **Generate Explanations** Someone's "bread and butter" is his or her means of support, or livelihood. Why was the AFL called a "bread and butter" union while the Knights of Labor was not?

5. **Express Problems Clearly** Why did labor unions such as the Knights of Labor, the AFL, and the ARU have such a difficult time carrying out a successful strike?

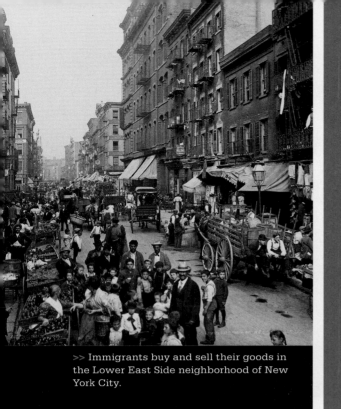

>> Immigrants buy and sell their goods in the Lower East Side neighborhood of New York City.

Bounce to Activate Flipped Video

1.4 Immigration has been a central theme in American history. However, when the foreign-born population of the United States nearly doubled between 1870 and 1900, some Americans feared that the newcomers would damage American culture. Instead, Americans adopted parts of immigrants' cultures, while immigrants adopted parts of American culture. The contributions of immigrants, combined with the existing culture, helped shape American culture into a diverse and unique whole.

>> Objectives

Compare the "new immigrants" of the late 1800s to earlier immigrants.

Explain the push and pull factors leading immigrants to America.

Describe the challenges that immigrants faced establishing new lives in America.

Analyze how immigrants adapted to American life while contributing to American culture.

>> Key Terms

"new" immigrants
steerage
Ellis Island
Angel Island
Americanization
"melting pot"
nativism
Chinese Exclusion
    Act

The New Immigrants

New Immigrants Seek Better Lives

A Rush of "New" Immigrants Immigrants had always come to America for economic opportunity and religious freedom. Until the 1870s, the majority had been Protestants from northern and western Europe. They came as families to settle in the United States, often on farms with family or friends who had come previously. Many had saved some money for the journey, had a skill or trade, or had a formal education.

Many German and Irish Catholics had immigrated in the 1840s and 1850s, and more arrived after the Civil War. Some Americans had prejudices against Catholics, but the Irish spoke English and the German Catholics benefited from the good reputation of their Protestant countrymen. Although many lacked skills and money, the children of these immigrants were often able to blend into American society. Beginning in the 1870s, Irish and Germans were joined by **"new" immigrants** from southern and eastern Europe. They arrived in increasing numbers until the outbreak of World War I.

In contrast to "old" immigrants who had come before the Irish and Germans, "new" immigrants were often Catholic or Jewish, and likely to settle in cities rather than on farms. Many came alone, planning to save some money in the United States and return home to live. They came from Italy, Greece, Poland, Hungary, and Russia in large numbers. After 1900, immigrants from Southern and Eastern Europe made up more than 70 percent of all immigrants, up from about 1 percent in the mid-1800s. Many native-born Americans felt threatened by these newcomers with different cultures and languages.

Causes of Immigration The legal immigration of these immigrants changed demographic patterns in the United States. Two types of factors caused this immigration, as they have caused people to immigrate before and after the rush at the turn of the twentieth century. Push factors are those that compel people to leave their homes, such as famine, war, or persecution. For example, in the 1880s, farmers had a difficult time in many parts of the world. In Mexico, Poland, and China, land reform and low prices for crops forced many farmers off their land. Some chose to come to America to make a new start. Beginning in the 1840s, China and eastern Europe experienced repeated wars and political revolutions. These events disrupted economies and created political refugees. One of the largest groups to settle in America were Russian and eastern European Jews. Beginning in the 1880s, they fled religious persecution and came to the United States to live in safety, and hopefully, achieve a better life.

Another type of factor that leads to immigration is a pull factor. Pull factors are those that draw people *to* a new place, such as economic opportunity or religious freedom. In addition to a vague hope for opportunity, the United States offered special attractions, including plentiful land and employment. The 1862 Homestead Act and aid from railroad companies made western farmland inexpensive. The railroads even offered reduced fares to get there because they needed customers in the West for their own businesses to succeed. Until 1885, immigrants were recruited from their homelands to build railroads, dig in mines, work in oil fields, harvest produce, or toil in factories. Others hoped to strike it rich by finding gold in the West.

Many others were "chain immigrants," joining family or friends who had already settled in America. The immigrants who had arrived earlier promised to help the newcomers find work and housing, and sometimes they even sent them tickets for the journey. Immigrants may have lured their families and friends to America with the promise of religious

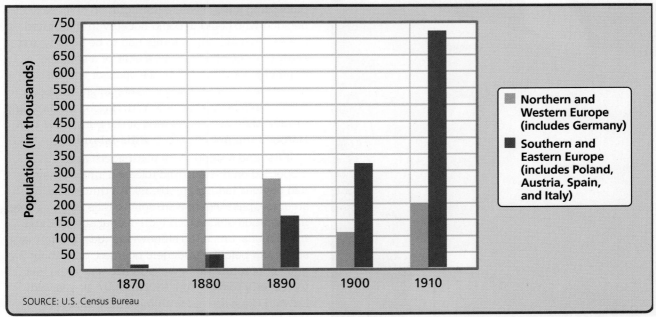

Immigration from Europe, 1870-1910

Population (in thousands)

Legend:
- Northern and Western Europe (includes Germany)
- Southern and Eastern Europe (includes Poland, Austria, Spain, and Italy)

SOURCE: U.S. Census Bureau

>> The number of immigrants increased at the turn of the twentieth century. **Analyze Graphs** Which region shows the greatest increase in immigration during the time period shown on the graph?

Bounce to Activate Chart

and political freedom. In America, one could worship and vote as one chose without fear of persecution by the government. Many immigrants in the late nineteenth century had both push and pull factors that helped them decide to leave the familiar for the unknown. For example, Cuban immigrants in Florida were both "pulled" by the attraction of work in industries like cigar manufacturing, and "pushed" out of Cuba by the political turbulence of the revolutionary struggle against Spain in the 1860s and 1870s.

☑ **IDENTIFY SUPPORTING DETAILS** What details from the reading help explain why immigrants came to America?

Optimism and the Immigrant Experience

Immigrant experiences varied greatly. However, there were common themes: a tough decision to leave home and family, a hard and costly journey with an uncertain end, and the difficulties of learning a new language and adjusting to a foreign culture. Nevertheless, many immigrants were optimistic that moving to America would lead to better lives. As one young Russian Jewish woman explained, "America means for an Immigrant a fairy promised land that came out true, a land that gives all they need for their work, a land which gives morality through her churches and education through her free schools and libraries." Millions of people decided that such possibilities outweighed the risks and set out for the United States.

The Long Journey to America Coming to America was a big task. Travelers needed money for passage and to make a new start, although some had only enough for a ticket. Usually, they brought only what they could carry. Reaching a port of departure was often difficult. In war-torn areas, just getting to the ship could be dangerous.

By the 1870s, steamships made the trip across the Atlantic safer and faster than ever before. However, it could be an awful voyage. Most immigrants traveled in **steerage**, the worst accommodations on the ship. Located on the lower decks with no private cabins, steerage was crowded and dirty. Illness spread quickly, while rough weather could force seasick passengers to stay in cramped quarters for days at a time. Under these conditions, even healthy immigrants fell ill, while frail passengers sometimes died. On other voyages, passengers were fortunate to have beautiful weather and no illness onboard.

Immigrants Arrive at Ellis and Angel Islands The first stop for ships at American ports was a processing station where immigration officials decided who could or could not stay in the United States. To enter, immigrants had to be healthy and show that they had money, a skill, or a sponsor to provide for them. Often the sponsor was an industrialist who needed workers. Most European immigrants arrived in New York Harbor. Beginning in 1892, they were processed at the busy, New York Harbor immigration station **Ellis Island**.

First and second-class passengers were inspected on the ship and released, unless they had obvious medical problems. All third-class, or steerage, passengers were sent to Ellis Island. There, immigration officers conducted legal and medical inspections. Since the shipowners did a preliminary screening before passengers boarded, only about 2 percent of immigrants were denied entry; the rest took a ferry to New York City. In 1907, 10-year-old Edward Corsi arrived with his family from Italy. Years later, when he had become an immigration official, he remembered his first impressions:

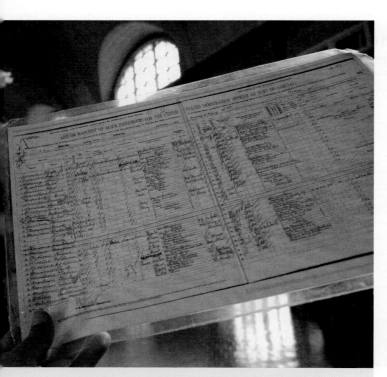

>> Passenger manifests such as this tracked the vital information of immigrants who entered U.S. ports to begin their lives as Americans.

I realized that Ellis Island could inspire both hope and fear. Some of the passengers were afraid . . . ; others were impatient, anxious to get through the inspection and be off to their destinations.

—Edward Corsi, *In the Shadow of Liberty,* 1935

Chinese and other Asian immigrants crossed the Pacific Ocean, many arriving in San Francisco Bay. Chinese immigrants came in larger numbers in the 1850s to work in mines, on railroads, and on farms and fisheries. After 1882, Chinese immigrants were turned away unless they could prove that they were American citizens or had relatives living in America. **Angel Island**, a processing center for Chinese immigrants, opened in San Francisco Bay in 1910. If Ellis Island was welcoming to some, Angel Island was always formidable. It was designed to filter out Chinese immigrants. Officials often assumed that Chinese newcomers would misrepresent themselves in order to gain entry.

While most immigrants left Ellis Island within hours, Chinese immigrants at Angel Island were often held for weeks or even months in poor conditions waiting for permission to stay in the United States. To pass the time and express their frustrations, many carved poems into the walls at Angel Island. One detainee wrote:

Lin, upon arriving in America,

Was arrested, put in a wooden building,

And made a prisoner.

I was here for one autumn.

The Americans did not allow me to land.

I was ordered to be deported.

—*Taoist from the Town of Iron*

In addition to San Francisco and New York, thousands of immigrants arrived during this period through other ports on the East Coast such as Boston, Baltimore, and Philadelphia, southern ports such as New Orleans and Galveston, or western ports such as Los Angeles.

☑ **CHECK UNDERSTANDING** What factors made the trip to America difficult for many immigrants?

>> The experience of Asian immigrants like these ones on the West Coast was often less welcoming than that of European immigrants in the East.

Social Issues Affecting Immigrants

Passing immigration inspections was just the first step. Once in America, immigrants immediately faced tough decisions such as where to settle and how to find work. On top of that, most had to learn a new language and new customs. Sometimes immigrants worked with an agent who spoke their language for help finding work and housing, but many agents took advantage of the newcomers to make money. Lucky immigrants had contacts through family and friends who could help them navigate a new and strange world.

Americanization Movement Most new immigrants stayed in cities, close to industrial jobs in factories. There, they often lived in ethnic neighborhoods with people who shared their native language, religion, and culture. Neighbors might have come from the same country, region, or even village.

By 1890, many cities had huge immigrant populations. In San Francisco and Chicago, immigrants made up more than 40 percent of the population. Four out of five inhabitants of New York City were foreign born or had foreign-born parents. While exclusionist policies forced some people to live in ghettoes, these neighborhoods also provided familiarity. Specialty shops, grocers, and clothing stores provided a taste of the food and culture that immigrants had left behind.

In many cities, volunteer institutions known as settlement houses ran **Americanization** programs, helping newcomers learn English and adopt American dress and diet. At the same time, immigrants helped one another through fraternal associations, such as the Polish National Alliance and the Ancient Order of Hibernians (an Irish Catholic organization). These organizations, based on ethnic or religious identity, provided social services and financial assistance to encourage people to pursue economic opportunity while making them feel more at home in the United States. Many settlement workers and immigrants alike believed that American society was a **"melting pot"** in which white people of all different nationalities blended to create a single culture. The

term came from the name of a play that opened in 1908. This model excluded Asian immigrants, who became targets of social and legal discrimination.

Despite the hopes of settlement workers, immigrants often held on to their traditions. Their children, however, became more Americanized, without memories of homes and families left behind. Some adults reported that they dreamed of returning to their homelands, but most immigrants did not return to their country of origin. Instead, they established fraternal lodges and religious institutions that made them feel more comfortable in their new surroundings.

Catholics, in particular, established churches and parochial schools. In many cities, Irish Catholic churches stood side by side with Italian Catholic churches—each built to serve the needs of its own community. The immigrants' churches, schools, and institutions reminded native-born Americans that new cultures were changing American society.

New Immigrants Face Hostility Accepting immigrants into American society was not always easy. Newcomers often faced **nativism**, which was a tendency towards preferring native-born, white Americans over "new" immigrants. During the economic recessions of the late nineteenth century, competition for jobs and housing fueled resentment. Many native-born workers worried that immigrants would work for lower pay. Nativist intellectuals backed up their beliefs with dubious scientific rhetoric that linked immigrants' physical characteristics to criminal tendencies or lesser intellectual abilities. Social Darwinism also played a role in nativism.

Religious and cultural differences sparked suspicion between native-born Americans and immigrants, as well as between different immigrant ethnic groups. Many Irish, German, Italian, and Polish immigrants practiced Roman Catholicism, and some Protestants feared that Catholics' first loyalty was to the Pope rather than to American ideals. Anti-semitism in the United States was nothing new—the U.S. Army had briefly expelled all Jews from Grant's military department in 1862—and the arrival of Jews fleeing persecution in Eastern Europe only complicated the issue. Some native-born Jews worried that these Eastern European immigrants, who were culturally quite different than American or German Jews, would fuel anti-Jewish attitudes and that the newcomers would not be able to Americanize. Some native-born white Protestants would not hire, vote for, or work with Catholics or Jews. Some Americans even signed restrictive

>> "Looking Backward" shows a man carrying his possessions being confronted by a group of well-dressed men. **Analyze Political Cartoons** What do the shadows behind the well-dressed men represent?

contracts agreeing not to rent or sell property to Catholics, Jews, African Americans, or other groups they considered "non-native."

Policies Restrict Some Immigration Extreme hostility toward Chinese laborers had led Congress to pass the **Chinese Exclusion Act** in 1882. The act prohibited immigration by Chinese laborers, limited the civil rights of Chinese immigrants already in the United States, and forbade the naturalization of Chinese residents. The act had unintended negative consequences on the economy, especially in states such as California that relied on cheap Chinese labor. Restricting the immigration of Chinese laborers made it difficult for large single-crop ranches to be profitable. The act also prevented many Chinese in the United States from visiting their families in China, fearing they would not be permitted to return. In 1898, a court case established that Chinese people born in America were United States citizens and could, therefore, come and go freely. However, many immigration officials ignored this ruling.

In the same year, Congress passed another act that prohibited the entry of anyone who was a criminal, immoral, a pauper, or likely to need public assistance. In practice, the law was used to bar many poor or handicapped immigrants. These acts marked the beginning of legislation restricting immigration in the United States. Until then, anti-immigrant activity had been episodic and often short-lived. Immigration became a constant topic of conversation throughout America.

☑ **IDENTIFY CENTRAL IDEAS** Why did some Americans want to restrict immigration?

Immigrants Affect American Society

Despite anti-immigrant sentiment, immigrants of many racial and ethnic groups transformed American society. They fueled industrial growth, acquired citizenship, participated in the democratic process, and made their traditions part of American culture. Mexican Americans in the Southwest developed effective ranching techniques, while Chinese, Irish, and Mexican laborers built the railroads. Equally important, immigrants labored in coal mines, steel mills, textile mills, and factories. Immigrant women worked in factories, as seamstresses, as laundresses, and doing piecework. Others became domestic servants. Though the

>> Immigrants arrive at Ellis Island. The labor provided by immigrants like these helped fuel the burgeoning U.S. economy.

Bounce to Activate Gallery

conditions were harsh and immigrants received few benefits, their labor helped the United States become an economic world power.

Immigrants' Contributions to American Culture Immigrants not only helped propel the American economic engine; they also helped shape the evolving American culture. Immigrants from around the world brought their languages, religions, and cuisines to the United States. New foods and the words to describe them quickly became part of the American vocabulary. European Jews introduced bagels; Italian immigrants popularized pasta dishes like spaghetti; German immigrants brought sausages called wieners and Frankfurters. The Chinese introduced a vast knowledge of how to use plants for medicinal purposes as well as foods such as chow mein.

Many individual immigrants made valuable contributions to American culture. Andrew Carnegie, a Scottish immigrant, turned to philanthropy following the sale of his steel empire. He donated some $288 million to social and educational causes in the United States. James Naismith, who moved from Canada to Massachusetts, invented the sport of basketball in the late 1800s. In addition, Alexander Graham

Bell, also born in Scotland, revolutionized modern communications with his patent of the telephone in 1876. Belgian immigrant Leo Baekeland transformed technology with the development of modern plastics. Inventor Nikola Tesla, born in what is now Croatia, pioneered discoveries in the generation and transmission of electricity.

Immigrants Lead Labor and Social Movements
The lives of many immigrants in the 1800s were very hard. Many lived in overcrowded slums and unhealthy and unsafe tenement housing. Others took dangerous jobs in mines and factories. Increasingly, immigrants demanded a voice, becoming active in labor unions and politics. They lobbied for policies to protect the poor and powerless and used their votes to elect governments favorable to those goals. Some of the political leaders they supported became powerful.

Among these influential activists was Irish immigrant Mary Harris Jones, also known as Mother Jones. She fought for the union rights of coal miners. Samuel Gompers was a Jewish cigar maker from England who became an influential labor organizer and leader. Gompers' leadership of the American Federation of Labor, through which he organized national unions comprised of local chapters, became the model for unionism in the United States. Union leaders like Gompers and Mother Jones demanded reforms that helped immigrants as well as all laborers. Immigrants expanded the definition of *American*.

☑ **IDENTIFY** In what ways did immigrants assimilate to and change American culture?

☑ **ASSESSMENT**

1. **Summarize** What are the push and pull factors that motivate immigration? Give two examples of each.

2. **Infer** What was the most likely reason that healthy first and second-class passengers were admitted to the U.S. without being processed at Ellis Island, while those in steerage had to go through processing?

3. **Compare and Contrast** How were the roles of settlement houses and fraternal organizations the same? Different?

4. **Summarize** How were Chinese immigrants treated in the late 1800s?

5. **Identify Central Issues** How did immigrants help the United States become the country it is today?

1.5 As one historian has noted, America was born on the farm and moved to the city. In 1860, most Americans lived in rural areas, with only 16 percent living in towns or cities with a population of 8,000 or more. By 1900, that percentage had doubled, and nearly 15 million Americans lived in cities with populations of more than 50,000. Migration to urban areas during this time changed the demographics, or statistical characteristics, of the population of the United States. This period was the beginning of an upsurge in urbanization that both reflected and fueled massive changes in the way Americans lived.

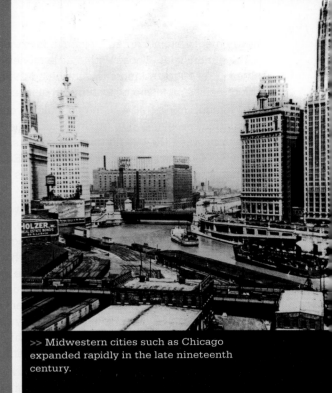

>> Midwestern cities such as Chicago expanded rapidly in the late nineteenth century.

Bounce to Activate Flipped Video

A Nation of Cities

Americans Migrate to Cities

In the late nineteenth century, America experienced a period of **urbanization** in which the number of cities and people living in them increased dramatically. Still, numbers and statistics do not tell the whole story of how Americans became city folk. Urban people lived differently from rural people.

People in the country lived and worked on farms, either owned by their family or rented from a larger landowner. Their work was driven by the growing cycle. They did a lot of their work outside when weather permitted. In contrast, many people in cities worked for large companies inside factory buildings or sweatshops, rode trolley cars or walked to work, and lived in apartment buildings. Unlike farming, factory work was a year-round, daily grind, and workers had no control over their schedules. Over time, this structured scheduling, combined with the urban way of life, became part of American culture.

City Life Beckons to Immigrants and Migrants America's major cities were manufacturing and transportation centers clustered in the northeast, on the Pacific coast, and along the waterways of the midwest. Connected by the new railroad lines, cities became magnets for immigrants and rural Americans. The

>> **Objectives**

Analyze urban growth in the late 1800s.

Explain how technology improved city life.

Evaluate the problems caused by rapid urban growth and ways that city dwellers tried to solve them.

>> **Key Terms**

urbanization
rural-to-urban
  migrants
skyscrapers
Elisha Otis
mass transit
suburbs
Frederick Law
  Olmsted
tenements
cholera

newcomers were attracted by jobs in factories or the service industries. Those with a little money opened shops. The educated increasingly joined the new middle-class professions, working in offices.

Women's opportunities, in particular, were dramatically expanded in urban areas. In addition to factory work, they could take in boarders, do piecework, or become domestic servants. Educated women found work as teachers or in offices as secretaries and typists.

While many city jobs offered only hard work for little reward, cities offered variety, promise, and even a bit of glamour. By saving part of their wages, city workers might attain some comforts or perhaps even move into the growing middle class. At the least, they could increase their children's opportunities by sending them to school. While some laborers were trapped in an endless cycle of poverty, only the very poorest were unable to enjoy a somewhat higher standard of living in the late nineteenth century.

Life was hard in the city, but many still loved it. Horace Greeley, a politician and New York City newspaper editor, wrote in the 1860s, "We cannot all live in cities, yet nearly all seem determined to do so." City churches, theaters, social clubs, and museums offered companionship and entertainment.

>> City streets became crowded as more and more people of various incomes and classes sought their fortunes in big cities.

Bounce to Activate Gallery

Cities Attract Immigrants The demographics of many cities changed very quickly as legal immigrants arrived. By 1900, some urban populations were more than 40 percent foreign born. Some immigrants found their way to a city through happenstance, while others joined relatives or were recruited by companies needing labor. In this way, neighborhoods, cities, regions, and industries often acquired a majority of workers from a particular locale. For example, employees at the steel mills of western Pennsylvania were predominantly Polish, while the textile factories of New York became a center for eastern European Jewish people. Domestic servants in the Northeast were primarily Irish women, while Scandinavians worked in the fish-packing industry of the Pacific Northwest.

Farmers Migrate to Urban Areas Demographic patterns also changed in response to the many **rural-to-urban migrants** who moved to cities in the 1890s. For many rural Americans, making a living on a farm had become increasingly difficult. In addition to unpredictable weather conditions, isolation, and limited opportunities, farmers faced economic struggles that hindered their livelihoods. New technologies enabled farmers to produce more crops, but the greater supply caused prices to drop. These factors, combined with the excitement and variety of city life, sparked widespread rural-to-urban migration. However, the move from farm to factory could be wrenching. Former agricultural workers often found themselves working in dim light and narrow confines. The pace of work was controlled by rigid schedules, with no slow seasons. However, factory work paid wages in cash, which was sometimes scarce on family farms.

Midwestern cities such as Minneapolis–St. Paul and Chicago exploded in the decade between 1880 and 1890. Many of the newcomers were immigrants or migrants from the rural West.

African Americans moving out of the rural South were also part of the migration, although on a smaller scale. The majority of the migrating African Americans stayed in southern cities, but the few black migrants to northern and western cities paved the way for a much larger migration after World War I.

Urban Subcultures Emerge The combination of massive migration from rural areas and immigration from abroad transformed life in urban areas. Many new arrivals were young unmarried men and women free from the control of their families and communities. In their leisure time they flocked to amusement parks and dance halls to meet one another and date. The more anonymous environment

Comparison of Rural and Urban Populations

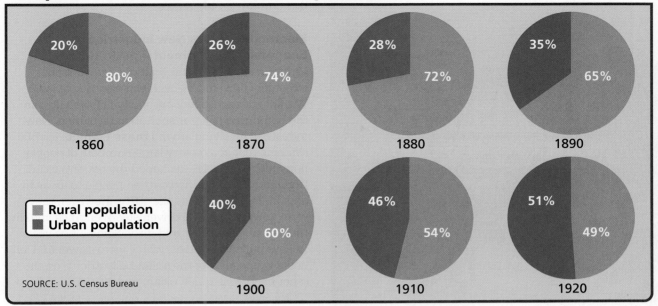

Rural population
Urban population

20% / 80% 1860	26% / 74% 1870	28% / 72% 1880	35% / 65% 1890
40% / 60% 1900	46% / 54% 1910	51% / 49% 1920	

SOURCE: U.S. Census Bureau

>> The percentage of the population living in urban areas increased relative to those living in rural areas over several decades. **Analyze Graphs** What factors account for the demographic shift from rural to urban areas over these decades?

of cities also made it easier for migrants to seek out same-sex partners. By the 1890s, certain urban neighborhoods had "gay" bars or meeting places. Not coincidentally, this was also the time when our modern concepts of homosexuality and heterosexuality emerged as discrete categories of identity.

Meanwhile, some of the larger American cities developed so-called "bohemian" racially-mixed neighborhoods that attracted artists, writers, political radicals, gays and lesbians and others whose lives defied social conventions. The bohemian neighborhood of Greenwich Village in New York City was home to Emma Goldman, the feminist anarchist whose lecture tour of 1915 included speeches in favor of homosexual rights—a shocking demand at the time but a foretaste of things to come.

☑ **CHECK UNDERSTANDING** Why did many people choose to move to cities?

Technology Improves City Life

As cities swelled in size, politicians and workers struggled to keep up with the demands of growth to provide water, sewers, schools, and safety. American innovators stepped up to the task by developing new technologies to improve living conditions. The middle and upper classes benefited most from the innovations, but every city dweller was affected. Electric trolleys and subways, building codes, and other innovations increased the pace of urbanization and economic development in cities across the country.

Engineers Build Skyward with Steel The cities of the late nineteenth century began to take their modern form. For the first time, skylines became recognizable by their **skyscrapers**. Steel was first mass-produced to create railroad rails, but architects and engineers realized the possibilities of using this strong and resilient metal for the construction of buildings. Skyscrapers of ten stories and taller had steel frames and used artistic designs to magnify their imposing height. Inside, they provided office space in cities that had no room left on the ground. Increased office space in turn allowed more businesses to establish themselves and more people to live in closer proximity to each other, which further stimulated economic development in urban areas. But tall buildings were only realistic because of other new technology. In the 1850s, **Elisha Otis** developed a safety elevator that would not fall if the lifting rope broke. Central heating systems were also improved in the 1870s. Technological innovations

>> Electric cable cars carried passengers all around the city.

Bounce to Activate Illustration

>> Architect Daniel Burnham designed the "White City" for the 1893 World's Fair Columbian Exhibition in Chicago, Illinois.

like these, dramatically improved the standard of living in the United States.

Electricity Powers New Industries and Economic Development In 1888, Richmond, Virginia, introduced a revolutionary invention: streetcars powered by overhead electric cables. Within a decade, every major city followed. It was the beginning of a transportation revolution. New industries revolving around **mass transit**—public systems that could carry large numbers of people fairly inexpensively—reshaped the nation's cities. Commuter rail lines had carried people to areas in and around cities since the 1870s. However, they were powered by coal-driven steam engines, making them slow, unreliable, and dirty. Some cities used trolleys pulled by horses, which were slower and left horse waste all over the streets. Electricity, on the other hand, was quiet, clean, and efficient.

Electric cars also ran on a reliable schedule and could carry many more people than horse-drawn carts. These advances in transportation were all made possible by the free enterprise system, which applied technological innovation to the needs of daily life.

Electric cable cars were not practical in every city, however. Cables strung in narrow streets could block fire trucks, and traffic congestion often prevented streetcars from running on schedule. In 1897, Boston solved this problem by running the cars underground in the nation's first subway system. New York City followed in 1904. Electric cable cars and subways allowed urban economies to expand even faster. These new industries efficiently moved people in and around cities, making it possible for urban populations to grow at an increasingly rapid pace.

Middle and upper class people who could afford transit fares moved away from the noise and dirt of the industrial city. They built housing in the cleaner, quieter perimeter, known as streetcar **suburbs**. From there, they rode mass transit into the center of the city to work, shop, or be entertained, returning to their homes in the evening. Poorer people remained in city centers so that they could walk to work.

City Planners Lay Out Cities As cities grew larger and more complex, architectural firms expanded to offer city-planning services designed to make cities more functional and beautiful, even as their populations skyrocketed. Architect Daniel Burnham designed his version of the ideal city for Chicago's 1893 World's Fair Columbian Exhibition, a fair held to commemorate Columbus's arrival in the Americas on the event's 400th anniversary. Called the White City, the integrated design included boulevards, parks, buildings, and even electric streetlights.

Mass transit allowed city planners to segregate parts of the city by zoning, or designating certain areas for particular functions. Through the 1890s, cities embraced designs that had separate zones for heavy industry, financial institutions, and residences. They also built public spaces, such as public libraries, government buildings, and universities.

Parks and recreational spaces were one of the most important aspects of city planning. Since the 1850s, cities had built parks as a solution to some of the problems of urban growth. Philadelphia purchased areas along the Schuylkill River to protect the city's water supply from industrial pollution. They hired landscape engineer **Frederick Law Olmsted** to design Fairmount Park. Olmsted had also designed New York City's Central Park and similar parks in Detroit, Michigan; Washington, D.C.; and Palo Alto, California.

☑ **IDENTIFY CENTRAL IDEAS** How did public transportation change urban areas?

>> Most immigrants and rural migrants could only afford to live in poorer urban neighborhoods. **Infer** Why would life in an urban setting be both a blessing and a curse for new arrivals?

🅑 **Bounce to Activate 3D Model**

Urban Living Creates Social Issues

Urbanization led to many social issues caused by overcrowding and poverty. In 1890, New York's Lower East Side had a population of more than 700 people per acre. As immigrants and rural migrants arrived, they crowded into neighborhoods that already seemed to be overflowing.

Housing Conditions Worsen As newcomers moved into urban areas, those who could not afford to ride mass transit had to live within walking distance of the industrial plants and factories where they worked. Housing in densely populated neighborhoods was often aging and usually overcrowded. Most urban workers lived in **tenements**: low-cost multifamily housing designed to squeeze in as many families as possible. Sometimes, several families lived in one apartment or even one room. They used the space for sewing clothes or doing other piecework to earn money. For those who had moved from rural areas, adapting to city life could be difficult. Typical rural areas had a small town or village with several small family farms located in the surrounding few miles. People had little contact with others from outside the

community, but had daily access to acres of land and open air.

Tenement owners usually lived in the suburbs or in fashionable downtown areas, away from the industrial grime. However, they built apartments for desperate people who had little choice about where they lived. With few windows and little sanitation, tenements were unhealthy and dangerous. In 1890, journalist Jacob Riis drew attention to the plight of New York tenement dwellers:

Go into any of the 'respectable' tenement neighborhoods . . . you shall come away agreeing [that] . . . life there does not seem worth living. . . . [T]he airshaft . . . seems always so busy letting out foul stenches . . . that it has no time to earn its name by bringing down fresh air.

—Jacob Riis, *How the Other Half Lives*

Public Health Concerns Cities in the late 1800s were filthy. Unpaved streets were snarled with

>> The Great Chicago Fire blazes across land and water.

Safety in Cities In addition to public health concerns, cities also faced the dangers of fire, crime, and conflict. Even one careless act could have devastating consequences in crowded housing.

Open fireplaces and gas lighting started fires that quickly swept through a city. A fire destroyed Chicago in 1871, killing between 200 to 300 people. It also left more than 100,000 people homeless. As the nineteenth century drew to a close, many cities developed professional firefighting teams.

At night, the streets were dangerous, yet many factory workers had to travel to and from work in the dark. In response to this challenge, professional, uniformed city police forces replaced the lone constable and the decentralized neighborhood watch. The new officers were civil servants who took exams and regularly patrolled city neighborhoods. They were aided in their task of ensuring safety by new electric streetlights.

However, the police were unable to overcome the challenge of tension between urban groups. In every big city, communities clashed along ethnic and racial fault lines. Police allowed immigrants to sleep in the station houses to avoid the violence in the streets. Even very young boys joined neighborhood gangs for safety.

Race, class, and neighborhood loyalties and conflicts continued to define neighborhood life for many generations.

☑ **IDENTIFY SUPPORTING DETAILS** What issues created by urban living made life difficult for many city dwellers?

ruts and littered with trash and even dead horses that were left to rot. Alleys between tenements were clogged with food waste and trash. Only the newest urban dwellings had indoor toilets, and the shared toilets in tenements often overflowed. These conditions were perfect for breeding epidemics, posing danger to everyone. For example, **cholera**, a particularly dangerous illness, reached epidemic proportions several times in the United States in the 1800s, killing thousands.

Cholera spreads when people drink contaminated water. Fresh water supplies and less burdened sanitary systems in rural areas often prevented these epidemics from happening. In urban areas, governments and city planners began to take steps to improve living conditions.

During the 1880s, planners attempted to regulate housing, sanitation, sewers, and public health. They began to take water from reservoirs that were separate from the polluted rivers and lakes. In the next decade, urban standards of living improved as a new filtration system improved water quality even more. Private companies competed for lucrative contracts to manage water distribution. Especially in the Southwest, where water was in short supply, questions of who should profit from water delivery sent city planners into a frenzy.

☑ **ASSESSMENT**

1. **Support Ideas with Examples** Use examples to support the claim that women had a number of options for work in cities.

2. **Identify Central Ideas** What factors encouraged the rural-to-urban migration of farmers in the 1890s?

3. **Draw Conclusions** Why was it important for architecture to become a specialized, professional career in the late 1800s?

4. **Generate Explanations** Why was public health a major concern in large cities during the 1880s?

5. **Analyze Information** How did urban gangs that were such a source of tension in the late 1800s reflect wider social problems?

1.6 Novelist Mark Twain satirized American life in his 1873 novel, *The Gilded Age*. He depicted American society as gilded, or having a rotten core covered with gold paint. Most Americans were not as cynical. The dizzying array of things to do and buy convinced the growing middle class that modern America was in a true golden age.

>> Once the bicycle was mass-produced, it became a popular mode of transportation for people who lived in the city.

Bounce to Activate Flipped Video

New Ways of Life

Free Enterprise Improves Life

Still, Twain's label stuck, and historians refer to the last decades of the nineteenth century as "the **Gilded Age**." The new lifestyle that middle-class Americans adopted during this period—shopping, sports, and reading popular magazines and newspapers—contributed to the development of a commonly shared American culture that would persist for the next century.

Industrialization and urbanization changed the lives of American workers. The application of scientific discoveries and technological innovations by the free enterprise system improved the standard of living in the United States. Driven by entrepreneurs, American businesses were able to create products and services that made daily life easier and more fun for many people. Mass produced materials and products lowered the prices of many goods, enabling ordinary Americans to purchase items that previously had been out of reach.

In addition, more people began to work for wages —in offices, on public transportation systems, or in factories as laborers and foremen. Even some farmers found themselves with extra time and cash as machinery improved and they were easily able to grow and sell more crops. At the same time, more products were available than ever before and at lower prices. This led to a culture

>> **Objectives**

Explain how technology, new types of stores, and marketing changed Americans' standard of living.

Analyze mass culture and education in the late 1800s.

Describe new popular cultural movements in the late 1800s.

>> **Key Terms**

Mark Twain
Gilded Age
conspicuous
  consumerism
mass culture
Joseph Pulitzer
William Randolph
  Hearst
Horatio Alger
vaudeville
Tin Pan Alley

of **conspicuous consumerism**, in which people wanted and bought the many new products on the market. All but the very poorest working-class laborers were able to do and buy more than they would have in the past.

New Ways of Shopping Expanding on a trend that was developing in Britain, France, Russia, and other countries, Rowland H. Macy opened what he called a department store in New York in 1858. It soon became the largest single store in America and served as a model for many more U.S. stores. Its sales methods—widespread advertising, a variety of goods organized into "departments," and high-quality items at fair prices—became the standard in large urban stores. By the 1870s, many big cities had department stores: Jordan Marsh in Boston, Marshall Field in Chicago, and Wanamaker's in Philadelphia.

John Wanamaker developed innovative ways to keep customers satisfied. He was the first to offer a money back guarantee. In addition, he placed large newspaper advertisements to attract customers. Later, Wanamaker became Postmaster General. In that position, he lowered the bulk shipping rates and began free delivery to rural areas, which led to a boom in the mail-order catalog business.

>> The carpet sweeper was a new invention of the Gilded Age and a status symbol among the middle class.

Bounce to Activate Illustration

While department stores pioneered new marketing and sales techniques, companies began to create trademarks with distinctive logos that consumers would recognize. For the first time, consumers began to notice and buy brand name goods. Long-distance shipping allowed consumers in Atlanta, Cincinnati, and San Francisco to purchase the same products.

Technology and Free Enterprise Lead to Higher Standards of Living After the Civil War, Americans began to measure success by what they could buy. Equating purchasing power with a higher social status, middle-class and some working-class consumers rushed to update their wardrobe with new clothing styles and to modernize their homes with new technologies, such as the carpet sweeper and the telephone. Technological innovations drove the development of new industries, which in turn created more jobs; wealth; and discretionary, or extra, income in consumers' hands. The cost of living decreased in part because factory-manufactured products often cost less than old-style handmade goods. Scientific discoveries, including better sanitation and medical care, contributed to better health, causing life expectancy to climb. The result was more middle-class Americans with more money to spend and greater opportunities to spend it on things they *chose* rather than just on things they *needed*.

The end of the nineteenth century is sometimes called the Victorian Era, after the queen of England. The rich were richer than ever before, and the middle class tried to imitate their lifestyle. Factory-produced clothing and prepackaged food gave homemakers a break from some activities, but rising expectations of cleanliness and more complicated meals meant that they spent more time on those tasks.

Other luxuries, like indoor plumbing, also became common. On the other hand, many women had to work outside their homes to achieve a middle-class lifestyle.

Life changed for men, as well. Innovations in public transportation allowed families to live at a distance from the dirt, noise, and bustle of industry. However, it often meant that men became commuters, leaving home early in the morning and returning late in the evening. Still, their culture taught them that hard work would bring the reward of more discretionary income with which to purchase the exciting products newly available on the market.

☑ **IDENTIFY MAIN IDEAS** How did consumption patterns change in the late nineteenth century?

A Mass Culture Develops

One of the effects of the spread of transportation, communication, and advertising was that Americans all across the country became more and more alike in their consumption patterns. Rich and poor could wear the same clothing styles, although the quality of that clothing varied. Household gadgets, toys, and food preferences were often the same from house to house. This phenomenon is known as **mass culture**.

The Newspaper Industry Expands The newspapers of the Gilded Age both reflected and helped create mass culture. Between 1870 and 1900, the number of newspapers increased from about 600 to more than 1,600. No one knew more about newspapers than **Joseph Pulitzer**, a Hungarian immigrant who had fought in the Civil War. Active in Missouri politics in the 1870s, Pulitzer moved to New York in the 1880s, where he started a morning paper, the *World*. It was so successful that Pulitzer soon started publishing the *Evening World*. The papers were inexpensive because they were supported in part by businesses that placed advertisements in their pages.

The job of a newspaper, Pulitzer believed, was to inform people and to stir up controversy. His newspapers were sensationalistic, filled with exposés of political corruption, comics, sports, and illustrations. They were designed to get the widest possible readership, rather than simply to report the news. Pulitzer soon found a competitor in **William Randolph Hearst**, whose *Morning Journal* employed the same tactics. Their sensational styles sold many papers.

At the same time, ethnic and special-interest publishers catered to the array of urban dwellers, especially immigrants. The *Philadelphia Tribune*, begun in the 1880s, targeted the African American market. In New York, there were six Italian-language papers by 1910. Each sold more than 10,000 copies daily. The Yiddish-language daily paper, *The Forward,* sold 120,000 copies.

The Arts Reflect the Characteristics and Issues of the Times Mark Twain was not the only author to take a critical look at society during the Gilded Age. Novels that explored harsh realities were popular. Stephen Crane exposed the slums of New York in his *Maggie: A Girl of the Streets* (1893). He later wrote *The Red Badge of Courage*, which explored the psychological aspects of war. Other novelists focused on moral issues. **Horatio Alger** wrote about characters who succeeded by hard work, while Henry James and Edith Wharton

>> Joseph Pulitzer's *Evening World* enjoyed a large readership.

questioned a society based upon rigid rules of conduct. Playwrights such as John Augustin Daly mirrored Twain's disapproval of the Gilded Age.

Musicians and songwriters, who explored the realities of everyday life, also flourished in the Gilded Age. A section of New York City, which would eventually be named **Tin Pan Alley**, became the center of the music publishing industry and the name of the style of popular music developed there. These music publishers provided sheet music that Americans throughout the country could enjoy in their homes. Ragtime, a forerunner to jazz music, was also gaining popularity. Developed by African Americans, ragtime was upbeat and highly rhythmic, which some people found disturbing.

The vitality of city life also inspired graphic artists. Philadelphia's Thomas Eakins painted a larger-than-life illustration of a medical operation, complete with exposed flesh. Painter Robert Henri and his associates developed a style of painting known as the Ashcan School that dramatized the starkness and squalor of New York City slums and street life.

The Growth of Public Schools Newspapers and literature flourished, in part, because more Americans could read. Public education expanded

>> African American children had new opportunities as students in the Gilded Age. However, they were in segregated classrooms with resources that lagged behind those available to white children.

>> Amusement parks attracted large crowds. **Compare** How do you think today's amusement parks compare to those of the Gilded Age?

Bounce to Activate Gallery

rapidly. Slowly in the South and rapidly in the North, grade-school education became compulsory. Many locales provided public high schools, although only a small percentage of young people attended. In 1870, the nation had only a few hundred high schools; in 1910, there were more than 5,000. Kindergartens also appeared as a way to help working-class mothers. As a result, the literacy rate climbed to nearly 90 percent by 1900.

Schools taught courses in science, woodworking, and drafting, providing skills that workers needed in budding industries. The curriculum also included civics and business training. Urban leaders counted on schools to help Americanize immigrants, teaching them English and shaping them into good citizens.

Teacher-training schools responded to the call. Not only did they grow in number, but they also developed more sophisticated ideas about teaching and learning. Reformer John Dewey sought to enhance student learning by introducing new teaching methods.

Institutions of higher education also began to provide specialized training for urban careers. Today's liberal arts curriculum was largely designed during this era. A few of the new careers—teaching, social work, and nursing—were open to middle-class women. This led to an upsurge in women's colleges, since women were barred from many men's colleges. However, many state universities began to accept women into their classes.

Limited access to white institutions led to a growth in schools and colleges for African Americans. Across the South, the number of normal schools, agricultural colleges, and industrial-training schools mushroomed as the children of newly freed slaves set out to prepare to compete as free people.

☑ **IDENTIFY SUPPORTING DETAILS** What details can you use to identify the changes in mass culture that occurred in the late nineteenth century?

A Boom in Popular Entertainment

Urban areas with thousands of people became centers for new types of entertainment in the Gilded Age. Clubs, music halls, and sports venues attracted large crowds with time and money to spend. The middle class began to take vacations at this time, while the working classes looked for opportunities to escape from the busy city, even if just for a day.

Amusement Parks Attract City Dwellers In 1884, Lamarcus Thompson opened the world's first roller coaster. At ten cents a ride, Thompson averaged more than $600 per day in income. The roller coaster was the first ride to open at Coney Island—the nation's best-known amusement park—at the edge of the Atlantic Ocean in New York City. Soon, Coney Island added a hotel and a horseracing track. Similar amusement parks, located within easy reach of a city, were built around the country.

While earlier generations had enjoyed a picnic in the park, the new urbanite—even those with limited means—willingly paid the entry fees for these new, more thrilling, entertainments. Urban residents of all ethnicities and races could be found at these amusement spots, though each group was usually relegated to a particular area of the parks. The parks represented a daylong vacation for city laborers who could not afford to take the long seaside vacations enjoyed by the wealthy.

Audiences Flock to Outdoor Events In 1883, "Buffalo Bill" Cody threw a Fourth of July celebration near his ranch in Nebraska. He offered prizes for competitions in riding, roping, and shooting. So many people attended that Cody took his show on the road, booking performances at points along railroad lines. Buffalo Bill's Wild West Show toured America and Europe, shaping the world's romantic notion of the American West. The show included markswoman Annie Oakley and the Sioux leader Sitting Bull, as well as displays of riding, roping, and horse-and-rider stunts.

Religious-inspired entertainment also grew in popularity. The Chautauqua Circuit, a kind of summer camp that opened in 1874, sponsored lectures and entertainment along New York's Chautauqua Lake. It began as a summer school for Methodist Sunday school teachers but soon became—and remains today—something of a cross between community college and a country fair, with lectures on intellectual subjects, music, exotic food, and crowd-pleasing special attractions. Soon, Chautauqua leaders were transporting their tents to small towns all across America to deliver comic storytelling, bands and singers, and lectures on politics or morals. A family might stay at a camp for as long as two weeks. Many people saw their first "moving pictures," or movies, in a Chautauqua tent. Theodore Roosevelt called Chautauqua "the most American thing in America."

>> Buffalo Bill's Wild West Show was a popular outdoor show in the late nineteenth century.

New Forms of Urban Entertainment Cities, with their dense populations, offered many glitzy shows and various types of entertainment. At first, **vaudeville** shows were a medley of musical drama, songs, and off-color comedy. In 1881, an entrepreneur named Tony Pastor opened a theater in New York, aiming to provide families with a "straight, clean variety show." By 1900, a few companies owned chains of vaudeville theaters, stretching all across the country.

Performance theater was not the only option. Movie theaters, called nickelodeons, soon introduced motion pictures, charging a nickel for admission. Films such as *The Great Train Robbery* became wildly popular. In music halls, ragtime bands created a style of music that would later evolve into jazz.

Some cities—including Philadelphia, Chicago, Atlanta, Buffalo, and Omaha—hosted exhibitions of new technology and entertainment. These extravaganzas stretched Americans' imaginations to see a future filled with machines and gadgets and other technological innovations that would continue to improve their lives. Millions of visitors saw everything from steam engines to typewriters and telephones. In many ways, the new amusements mirrored urban life, filled with variety, drama, bright colors, and a very fast pace.

>> Pitcher Cy Young won 511 games over his career and helped the Boston Red Sox win the 1903 World Series.

Organized Sports Attract New Fans Baseball—America's national sport—had been around for a number of years before the National League organized it into a business in 1876. After that, baseball soon became a public show. Major cities built stadiums that seated thousands, like Boston's Fenway Park. Stadium billboards advertising everything from other sports to toothpaste and patent medicines helped pay for the extravaganza. There were even baseball songs. The most famous—*Take Me Out to the Ball Game*—was written in 1908. Until 1887, teams sometimes included African American players. After the Chicago White Stockings refused to play against a team that had a black player, separate African American teams emerged by 1900.

Like baseball, horse racing, bicycle racing, boxing, and football became popular spectator sports. University football clubs formed on campuses around the country, but they faced a public outcry at the violence of the game. Rule changes made it into the sport we know today. Meanwhile, James Naismith invented basketball at the Springfield, Massachusetts, YMCA in 1891. Heroes emerged in major sports, particularly in boxing, as immigrants and ethnic Americans rooted for the boxers who shared their background.

☑ **CHECK UNDERSTANDING** Identify changes that redefined popular entertainment in the late nineteenth century.

☑ ASSESSMENT

1. **Infer** Why was Mark Twain so cynical about American society in the 1870s that he called this period "the Gilded Age?"

2. **Identify Central Issues** How did the middle-class life change during the Victorian Era?

3. **Cite Evidence** What evidence can you cite to support the idea that the growth of the newspaper industry is related to increasing public school attendance?

4. **Generate Explanations** What factors led to the increase in the number of colleges and universities during the Gilded Age?

5. **Identify Cause and Effect** Why were amusement parks so successful during the Gilded Age?

Go online to PearsonSchool.com/CASS and use the texts, quizzes, interactivities, Interactive Reading Notepads, Flipped Videos, and other resources from this Topic to prepare for the Topic Test.

Etexts

Quizzes

Interactivities

Interactive Reading Notepads

Flipped Videos

While online you can also check the progress you've made learning the topic and course content by viewing your grades, test scores, and assignment status.

LESSON SUMMARIES
Use these Lesson Summaries, and the longer versions available online, to review the key ideas for each lesson in this Topic.

Lesson 1: Innovation Boosts Growth

After the Civil War, industrialization transformed American life. Mass production helped the United States' economic growth, while the nation's factories attracted immigrant workers. Government encouraged the success of businesses and capitalism flourished. But while industry boomed in some parts of the United States, the South grew more slowly. In the North, workers began forming labor unions.

Lesson 2: Big Business Rises
Investors developed a form of group ownership known as a corporation. Corporations worked to maximize profits in several ways. Although many believed business leaders benefited the nation's economy, others persuaded the federal government to limit the power of big business with the Sherman Antitrust Act of 1890.

Lesson 3: The Organized Labor Movement
As industries grew, conflict developed between workers and employers. Many activists were influenced by socialism, which favors public, instead of private, control of property. Labor unions seeking better wages, working hours, and conditions began organizing massive protests and strikes, which often led to violence. After the Pullman Strike of 1894, the federal government supported businesses over labor.

Lesson 4: The New Immigrants
The 1870s saw a surge in immigration from southern and eastern Europe. Many of the new immigrants were fleeing famine, war and persecution and were drawn to America's economic opportunities and religious freedom. Although they helped fuel industrial growth, they faced hostility by native-born Americans and anti-immigrant laws passed by Congress.

Lesson 5: A Nation of Cities
In the late 1800s, American cities grew dramatically, due to migration from rural areas and immigration from abroad. New technologies introduced new means of transportation and taller buildings. Problems of overcrowding, poor sanitation and crime developed, forcing wealthier people to move to the suburbs and encouraging city planning.

Lesson 6: New Ways of Life
As Americans grew wealthier, consumerism increased. Department stores sold goods at fair prices. Advertising and communication helped create a mass culture of new products and entertainment. Public education expanded and helped raise literacy, while newspapers and magazines increased sales.

VISUAL REVIEW

Use these graphics to review some of the key terms, people, and ideas from this Topic.

Cities Change in the late 1800s

| Factories expand in cities. | → | Factory work attracts immigrants and migrants. | → | Poor population settles in city centers. | → | Wealthier classes move to suburbs. | → | Growing Population demands better water, sewers, and schools. |

America's Second Industrial Revolution

- Immigration enlarges workforce.
- improved transportation
- Civil War production encourages greater factory efficiency.
- technological innovations
- vast supply of natural resources

INDUSTRIALIZATION

Causes of Increased Immigration in Late 1800s

PUSH FACTORS	PULL FACTORS
Famine, land reform, and low crop prices in Mexico, Poland, and China	Economic Opportunity; availability of cheap land
War and Political Conflict in China Eastern Europe, and Cuba	Peaceful, orderly and democratic political system in U.S.
Religious Persecution: Russian and Eastern European Jews flee homelands.	Religious freedom

KEY TERMS, PEOPLE, AND IDEAS

1. How did **laissez-faire** government policies encourage growth?

2. How did **Thomas Edison** transform American life?

3. What are some features of a **corporation**?

4. What kind of issues led to **collective bargaining**?

5. Why were American Protestants afraid of increased Catholic immigration?

6. What new technologies helped create **skyscrapers**?

7. How did the introduction of zoning change cities?

8. Why did Mark Twain describe the late 1800s as **"the Gilded Age"**?

9. Which businessmen were responsible for the establishment of department stores?

CRITICAL THINKING

10. **Compare and Contrast** How did the experience of Asian immigrants in the west differ from that of European immigrants in the east?

11. **Cite Evidence** (a.) Was the labor movement inevitable? (b.) Explain your answer.

12. **Identify Cause and Effect** How did the United States change as it shifted from an agrarian to an industrial society?

13. **Compare and Contrast** (a.) Compare the resources essential to the first and second Industrial Revolutions in the United States. (b.) What effect did the second Industrial Revolution have on Americans' lives?

14. **Summarize** How did American farmers respond to new challenges in the mid to late 1800s?

15. **Draw Conclusions** How did the art of the Gilded Age reflect society?

16. **Analyze Graphs** Look at the bar graph at the top of the next column. What does the graph reveal? Then use a graphing calculator to help you change the bar graph into a line graph.

Immigration from Europe, 1890–1910

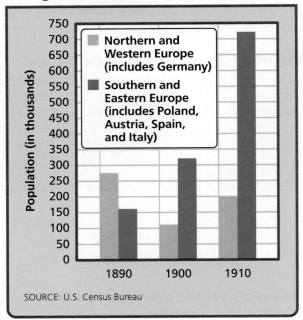

SOURCE: U.S. Census Bureau

17. **Writing Activity: Use Primary Sources** Use the excerpt below from The Chinese Exclusion Act of 1882 and your knowledge of immigration history to explain the cause and negative consequences of this law.

> Whereas, in the opinion of the Government of the United States the coming of Chinese laborers to this country endangers the good order of certain localities within the territory thereof: Therefore,
>
> Be it enacted by the Senate and House of Representatives of the United States of America in Congress assembled, That . . . the coming of Chinese laborers to the United States be, and the same is hereby, suspended; and during such suspension it shall not be lawful for any Chinese laborer to come, or having so come after the expiration of said ninety days, to remain within the United States.
>
> SEC. 2. That the master of any vessel who shall knowingly bring within the United States on such vessel, and land or permit to be landed, any Chinese laborer, from any foreign port or place, shall be deemed guilty of a misdemeanor. . .
>
> —*Chinese Exclusion Act, 1882*

DOCUMENT-BASED QUESTIONS

Read the documents below, then answer the questions that follow.

DOCUMENT A

This excerpt is from a letter written by the president of the American Federation of Labor.

> There was a time when workmen were denied the right of leaving their employers, when they were part of the soil, owned by their employers. . . . Not many years ago, when workmen counseled with each other for the purpose of resisting a reduction in their wages or making an effort to secure an increase, it was held to be a conspiracy punishable by imprisonment. Through the effort of organized labor, an enlightened public sentiment changed all this until to-day the right to unite for material, moral, and social improvement on the part of workers is accepted by all.
>
> —Samuel Gompers to Editor, Washington Evening Star, May 15, 1900

DOCUMENT B

This political cartoon, titled "The Protectors of Our Industries" appeared in 1883.

THE PROTECTORS OF OUR INDUSTRIES.

DOCUMENT C

This excerpt from Andrew Carnegie's autobiography records a dispute between workers and management.

> Gentlemen of the Blast Furnace Committee, you have threatened our firm that you will break your agreement and that you will leave these blast furnaces . . . unless you get a favorable answer to your threat by four o'clock today. It is not three but your answer is ready. You may leave the blast furnaces. . . . The worst day that labor has ever seen in this world is that day in which it dishonors itself by breaking its agreement. You have your answer.
>
> —The Autobiography of Andrew Carnegie August 1920

DOCUMENT D

This article, condemning the actions of a miners' union, was published in 1902.

> I am not exaggerating when I say that since the concessions demanded in 1900 were granted the management of the vast industries centered in the anthracite districts has been hampered by a condition which can only be termed anarchy. An example of the course pursued by the labor agitators is the mandate issue by the United Mine Workers, that no member thereof should work with a non-union man. The United Mine Workers have been endeavoring to enforce that order on our property and the properties of all other coal operators whom I have seen. I know of workmen, on our own property and on others, who assert that they cannot possibly do an honest day's work if they comply with the existing regulations of the United Mine Workers.
>
> —John Markle, Collier's Weekly 1902

18. Document A suggests that by 1900,
    A. unions were weak and discredited.
    B. the courts had destroyed union power.
    C. labor had won the right to organize.
    D. collective bargaining was not working.

19. **Analyze Political Cartoons** Document B criticizes
    A. unions that interfere with productivity.
    B. business leaders who exploit their workers.
    C. government officials who oppose unions.
    D. the tension between unions and management.

20. In Document C, what is Carnegie's view of organized labor?
    A. Businesses should bargain with employees.
    B. Workers should be paid fair wages.
    C. Employees should honor work agreements.
    D. Labor should have the right to strike.

21. In Document D, the writer describes unions as
    A. anarchists and bullies.
    B. defenders of workers' interests.
    C. reasonable and moderate.
    D. effective and powerful.

22. **Writing Activity: Primary Source** Write a paragraph explaining which side you would have supported in the labor conflicts of this time. Use the sources as well as additional information you have learned.

1 Which of the following represents a benefit of the United States government's laissez-faire policies toward business during the late 1800s?

A Strong government regulation spurred the rise of entrepreneurship.

B Minimal government regulation encouraged investment and growth.

C Strong government regulation increased wages for unskilled workers.

D Minimal government regulation encouraged Congress to ban protective tariffs.

Per Capita Income in the South, 1860 and 1880

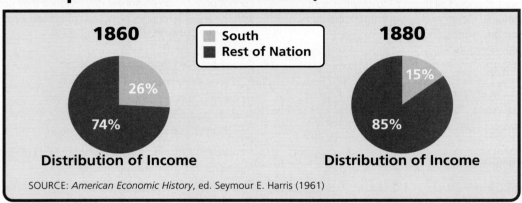

SOURCE: *American Economic History*, ed. Seymour E. Harris (1961)

2 Which of these economic conditions contributed to the change in the distribution of income in the South between 1860 and 1880 shown on the graphs above?

F falling prices for cotton

G increasing economic diversity

H increasing number of large plantations

I declining natural resources for industry

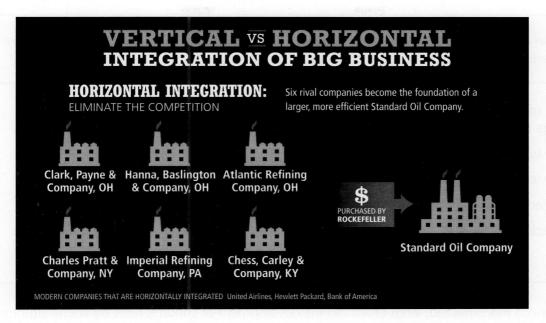

VERTICAL vs **HORIZONTAL**
INTEGRATION OF BIG BUSINESS

HORIZONTAL INTEGRATION:
ELIMINATE THE COMPETITION

Six rival companies become the foundation of a larger, more efficient Standard Oil Company.

Clark, Payne & Company, OH

Hanna, Baslington & Company, OH

Atlantic Refining Company, OH

Charles Pratt & Company, NY

Imperial Refining Company, PA

Chess, Carley & Company, KY

$
PURCHASED BY
ROCKEFELLER

Standard Oil Company

MODERN COMPANIES THAT ARE HORIZONTALLY INTEGRATED   United Airlines, Hewlett Packard, Bank of America

3 Which statement describes the impact of the management innovation shown in this illustration?

A The use of horizontal integration enabled Standard Oil to control the price of oil.

B The use of horizontal integration enabled Standard Oil to control labor costs.

C The use of monopoly trusts enabled Standard Oil to control the supply chain.

D The use of monopoly cartels enabled Standard Oil to control production costs.

4 Which of these practices is most closely associated with the growth of labor unions?

F price fixing

G protective tariffs

H collective bargaining

I vertical integration

If you have trouble with...				
Question	1	2	3	4
See Lesson	1.1	1.1	1.2	1.3

Some people in the late nineteenth century believed that certain nations and races were superior to others and therefore destined to rule over them.

5 Which of these groups of people would have been most likely to apply this idea to their feelings toward immigrants?

A nativists who opposed anti-semitism

B nativists who believed in Social Darwinism

C settlement-house workers who ran Americanization programs

D people who believed that American society was a "melting pot"

6 As America industrialized, what effect did the development of suburbs have on social structure in the cities?

F There was less contact among different social classes.

G The middle class expanded dramatically.

H The upper class grew wealthier.

I The gap between the rich and poor widened.

African American Farm Ownership, 1870–1910

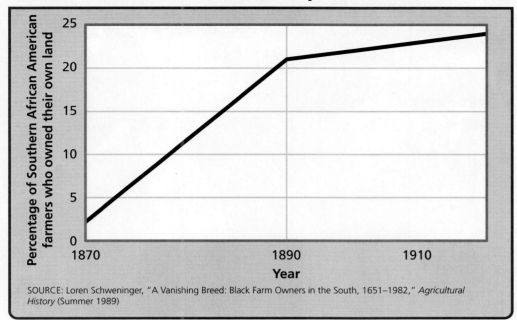

SOURCE: Loren Schweninger, "A Vanishing Breed: Black Farm Owners in the South, 1651–1982," *Agricultural History* (Summer 1989)

7 What does the graph reveal about African American farm ownership?

A It decreased between 1870 and 1910.

B It increased most dramatically between 1870 and 1890.

C It decreased between 1870 and 1890.

D It decreased between 1890 and 1910.

8 The Reconstruction struggle over Civil Rights was a replay of which of these recurring conflicts?

F protectionism versus free trade

G urban interests against rural priorities

H workers' rights against management

I states' rights versus federal power

If you have trouble with...				
Question	5	6	7	8
See Lesson	1.4	1.5	0.2	0.3

[**ESSENTIAL QUESTION**] What are the challenges of diversity?

② Challenges in the Late 1800s

Enduring Understandings

- As Americans continued to migrate, Native Americans and Mexican Americans already living in the West were pressured and pushed aside.

- Mining, ranching, and farming drew people to settle in the Great Plains and other parts of the West, helped by the growth of the railroad.

- Different groups of people in the West used land and resources differently, leading to conflict in some places.

- Corruption and difficult conditions for farmers led to a push to reform.

Learn about the Lakota Sioux in the late 1800s.

Bounce to Activate My Story Video

>> A crowd watches the completion of the transcontinental railroad.

California Topic 2 Overview

In this Topic, you'll learn about the challenges that Americans faced in the late 1800s. Look at the lesson outline and explore the timeline. As you study this Topic, you'll complete the Quest team project.

LESSON OUTLINE

2.1 American Indians Under Pressure
HSS 11.2.3; Analysis CST.4, HI.1

2.2 The West is Transformed
HSS 11.2.2, HSS 11.2.6;
Analysis CST.4, HI.5

2.3 Corruption Plagues the Nation
HSS 11.2.4

2.4 Farm Issues and Populism
HSS 11.2.8; Analysis CST.4, HI.1

Challenges in the Late 1800s (1865–1900)

1869 Transcontinental railroad connects East and West

1876 Sioux defeat U.S. troops in Battle of Little Bighorn

1883 Civil Service Commission is established

1887 Dawes Act breaks up Indian reservations

1892 The Populist Party forms

1893 Economic depression begins

1865 — 1875 — 1885 — 1895

QUEST! TEAM PROJECT

Creating a Layered Map of the American West

What was life like in the American West of the late 1800s? In this Quest you'll investigate the political, social, and economic aspects of the West in this period and then create a layered map to display your findings.

STEP ①
With your group, research either a set of states or a group of layers in the Information Organizer. Prepare to investigate by breaking down the Guiding Question into smaller questions.

STEP ②
Identify which themes or human characteristics, your group will show on the map. Gather information and decide how to present this information on the map.

STEP ③
Create the map layers and review the final map. With your group, come up with a list of questions and answers on the information you can identify in the databases and map layers.

STEP ④
Present your layered map to an audience. Reflect on what you have learned and how your group worked together as a team.

PearsonSchool.com/CASS

Go **ONLINE** for complete Quest materials

VIDEO   ETEXT   WRITING   RUBRIC   PDF   ASSESSMENT

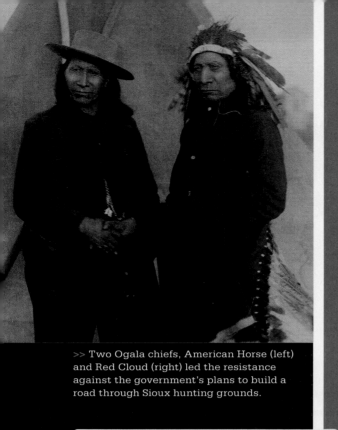

>> Two Ogala chiefs, American Horse (left) and Red Cloud (right) led the resistance against the government's plans to build a road through Sioux hunting grounds.

Bounce to Activate Flipped Video

2.1

In 1787, the Constitution granted sole power for regulating trade with the Native Americans to the federal government. This began the long, strained relationship between the federal government and Native Americans. During the 1830s, the federal government forced Native Americans from the east to resettle west of the Mississippi River and promised them the land there forever. In the 1840s through the 1860s, pressure from white settlers weakened this promise. The conflicts between settlers and Native Americans continued during and after the Civil War. The interaction changed both cultures, but irrevocably damaged Native American cultures.

>> Objectives

Compare the ways Native Americans and white settlers viewed and used the land.

Describe the conflicts between white settlers and Indians.

Analyze the impact of the Indian Wars.

Evaluate the effectiveness of the government's Americanization and reservation policies towards American Indians.

>> Key Terms

reservations
Sand Creek
  Massacre
Sitting Bull
Battle of the Little
  Big Horn
Chief Joseph
Wounded Knee
assimilated
Dawes General
  Allotment Act

American Indians Under Pressure

Cultures Forced to Adapt

By the end of the Civil War, most Native Americans—about 250,000 of them—lived in the region west of the Mississippi River referred to as "The Great American Desert." Although they were lumped together in the minds of most Americans as "Indians," Native Americans embraced many different belief systems, languages, and ways of life.

Cultural Similarities and Differences Geography influenced the cultural diversity of Native Americans. In the Pacific Northwest, the Klamaths, Chinooks, and Shastas benefited from abundant supplies of fish and forest animals. Farther south, smaller bands of hunter-gatherers struggled to exist on diets of small game, insects, berries, acorns, and roots. In the arid lands of New Mexico and Arizona, the Pueblos irrigated the land to grow corn, beans, and squash. They built adobe homes high in the cliffs to protect themselves from aggressive neighbors. The more mobile Navajos lived in homes made of mud or in hogans that could be moved easily.

The most numerous and nomadic Native Americans were the Plains Indians, including the Sioux, Blackfeet, Crows, Cheyenne, and Comanches. Some of these groups included Indians from east of the Appalachians, who had blended into the Plains Indian groups. The Plains Indians were expert horsemen and hunters. The millions of buffalo that roamed the Plains provided a rich source for lodging, clothing, food, and tools.

Indian cultures shared a common thread—they saw themselves as part of nature and respected the natural world. Many white people valued and respected nature, too. However, many also viewed the land as a resource that could be used to produce wealth. These differing views sowed the seeds of conflict.

American Settlers Move West In the early 1800s, the government carried out a policy of moving Native Americans out of the way of white settlers.

President Jackson moved the Cherokees off their land in Georgia and onto the Great Plains. To white settlers, Native Americans were welcome to what they called the Great American Desert as they thought it was uninhabitable. To limit conflict, an 1834 law regulated trade relations with Indians and strictly limited the access of white people to this Indian Territory. New European-American settlement generally paused at the eastern rim of the territory and resumed in the Far West.

By the 1850s, however, federal policy toward Native Americans was again challenged: gold and silver had been discovered in Indian Territory as well as settled regions farther west. Americans also wanted a railroad that crossed the continent. In 1851, therefore, the federal government began to restrict Indians to smaller areas. By the late 1860s, many Indian peoples had been placed on **reservations**, specific areas set aside by the government for the Indians' use. This change in their demographic patterns, a direct result of being forced to migrate to reservations, made their previous ways of life difficult if not impossible to sustain. Indians often faced poverty and the loss of their traditional ways of life on reservations.

Two more developments also threatened Native American civilizations: White settlers introduced diseases to which Indians had no immunity, and the vitally important buffalo herds were destroyed. In the 1870s, hunters would kill hundreds of buffaloes in a single day for their hides. They skinned the animals and left the meat to rot. In addition, trainloads of tourists arrived to kill buffaloes purely for sport. They left both the meat and the valuable hides behind.

☑ **IDENTIFY SUPPORTING DETAILS** How were Native American cultures threatened in the 1800s?

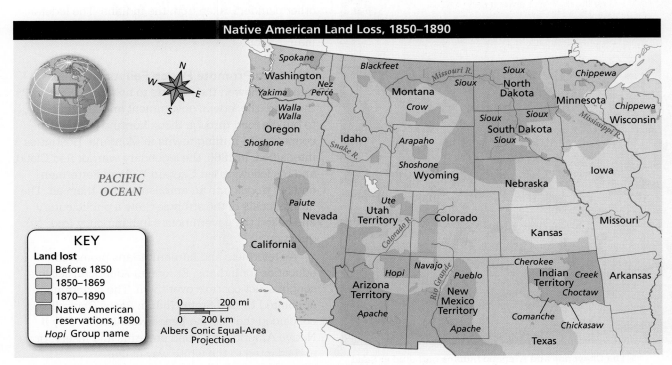

Native American Land Loss, 1850–1890

KEY

Land lost
- Before 1850
- 1850–1869
- 1870–1890
- Native American reservations, 1890

Hopi Group name

>> The U.S. government relocated many Native American groups following the Civil War. **Analyze Maps** Describe the process of how Native Americans lost their land.

Settlers and Native Americans Collide

The rapid industrial development and economic expansion that followed the Civil War set Native Americans and white settlers on a path to conflict. Advances in communication and transportation that supported industrial growth also reinforced white Americans' faith in manifest destiny. Horace Greeley, editor of the New York Tribune, encouraged the poor to move west.

> If you strike off into the broad, free West, and make yourself a farm from Uncle Sam's generous domain, you will crowd nobody, starve nobody, and neither you nor your children need evermore beg. . . .
>
> —New York Tribune, February 5, 1867

Greeley, and many others, ignored the fact that Native Americans inhabited half of the area of the United States. Indians often fought to retain or regain whatever they could.

>> The Cheyenne and Arapaho Indians gathered at Sand Creek on November 29, 1864. Many women and children died in the massacre.

Conflict Throughout the Plains In 1862, while the Civil War raged in the East, a group of Sioux Indians resisted threats to their land rights by attacking European-American settlements in eastern Minnesota. In several attacks, the Sioux killed more than 400 settlers, including many women and children. In response, the government waged a full-scale war against the Sioux, who then were pushed west into the Dakotas.

The Sioux rebellion sparked a series of attacks on settlements and stagecoach lines as other Plains Indians also saw their way of life slipping away. Each battle took its toll, raising the level of distrust on all sides. In the fall of 1864, a band of Colorado militia under commanding officer John Chivington came upon a camp of Cheyenne and Arapaho Indians near Fort Lyons at Sand Creek. The fort's commander had given the Cheyenne leader permission to stay there temporarily. Chivington's troops opened fire, killing between 150 to 200 Cheyenne and Arapaho men, women, and children.

The incident became known as the **Sand Creek Massacre**. It spawned another round of warfare as Plains Indians joined forces to repel white settlement.

Once the Civil War ended, regiments of Union troops—both white and African American—were sent to the West to bring peace to the plains. Recruitment posters for volunteer cavalry promised that soldiers could claim any "horses or other plunder" taken from the Indians. The federal government asserted that the troops were needed to maintain order.

Efforts to Promote Peace Fail As the Plains Indians renewed their efforts to hold onto what they had, the federal government announced plans to build a road through Sioux hunting grounds to connect gold-mining towns in Montana. Hostilities intensified. In 1866, the legendary warrior Red Cloud and his followers led Captain William Fetterman and his troops into an ambush, killing them all. The human costs of the struggle drew a public outcry and called the government's Indian policy into question.

As reformers and humanitarians promoted education for Indians, European-American settlers sought strict controls over them. The government-appointed United States Indian Peace Commission concluded that lasting peace would come only if Native Americans settled on farms and reservations and adapted to the white way of life.

In an effort to pacify the Sioux, the government offered the Fort Laramie Treaty of 1868. The

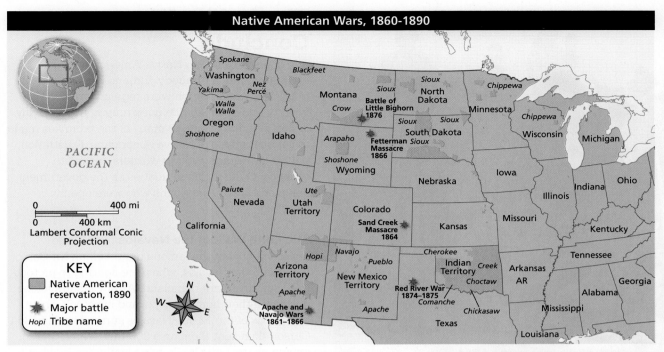

Native American Wars, 1860-1890

KEY
- Native American reservation, 1890
- Major battle
- *Hopi* Tribe name

>> **Analyze Maps** What do the locations of the clashes between Native Americans and the U.S. government suggest about westward expansion?

Bounce to Activate Map

government agreed not to build the road through Sioux territory and to abandon three forts. The treaty included the Black Hills in the Sioux reservation, and it also promised a school and other communal buildings. The Sioux and other Indians who signed the treaty agreed to live on a reservation under federal supervision with support from the federal government.

This type of promise of government support to Native Americans was part of many agreements between the government and Native American groups who were going onto reservations in various parts of the West.

The Bureau of Indian Affairs, established in 1824, handled affairs between Native Americans and the government. The agency appointed an agent who was responsible for distributing land and adequate supplies to anyone willing to farm as well as for maintaining peaceful relations between a reservation and its neighbors.

The government's plans and policies for peace did not always work out, however. Most Native Americans were disappointed with the reservations on which they were living and had little trust that the government would keep its promises. Chief Piapot, an Indian leader in Canada facing a similar situation with the government there, offered his viewpoint:

> In order to become sole masters of our land they relegated us to small reservations as big as my hand and make us long promises, as long as my arm; but the next year the promises were shorter and got shorter every year until now they are the length of my finger, and they keep only half of that.

—Chief Piapot, 1895

Unfortunately, in the United States, many Indian agents were unscrupulous and stole funds and resources that were supposed to be distributed to the Indians. Even the most well-meaning agents often lacked support from the federal government or the military to enforce the terms of the treaties that were beneficial to Native Americans. Not unexpectedly, some Indians refused to live under such conditions.

☑ **CHECK UNDERSTANDING** Why did tensions exist between settlers and Native Americans?

>> These Navajo Indians were forced to relocate from the lands they knew and relegated to the Bosque Redondo reservation in present-day Arizona and eastern New Mexico.

>> The Plains Indians fought the Red River War to protect their tradition of buffalo hunting. Here, braves leave camp to hunt buffalo.

The Indian Wars Conclude

The conditions facing Native Americans had all the ingredients for tragedy. Indians were confined to isolated areas, which were regularly ravaged by poverty and disease. The government, intentionally or not, failed to live up to many of the promises made to various groups of Native Americans. Frustration, particularly among young warriors, turned to violence. Guns replaced treaties as the government defeated Native Americans who were openly rebelling.

The Long Walk of the Navajos In 1863 the government sent the famous frontiersman Kit Carson to subdue the Navajos, who were fighting to protect their southwestern homeland. After Carson's forces destroyed their homes, crops, and livestock, about two thirds of the 12,000 Navajos surrendered in 1864. Carson then sent them on a 300-mile forced march, known as the Long Walk, to a reservation in what is now eastern New Mexico.

The poor soil on the small reservation was not suited to the kinds of agriculture the Navajos practiced. In addition, they were forced to live alongside their Apache enemies. Finally, after four years of death, disease, and starvation, the government relented. The surviving Navajos were allowed to return to a new reservation in their homeland.

The Southern Plains Indians Surrender The Red River War, a series of major and minor incidents, led to the final defeat of the powerful southern Plains Indians, including the Kiowas and Comanches. It marked the end of the southern buffalo herds and the opening of the western panhandle of Texas to white settlement. At the heart of the matter was the failure of the United States government to abide by and enforce the terms of the 1867 Treaty of Medicine Lodge. White buffalo hunters were not kept off Indian hunting grounds, food and supplies from the government were not delivered, and white lawlessness was not punished. Hostilities began with an attack by Indians on a group of Texans near the Red River in June 1874. Hostilities ended a year later, after the last Comanche holdouts surrendered to U.S. troops.

Battle of the Little Big Horn It was the lure of gold that led to the defeat of the Indians on the northern Plains. The Black Hills Gold Rush of 1875 drew prospectors onto Sioux hunting grounds in the

Dakotas and neighboring Montana. Some of this area was supposed to be protected by the 1868 Treaty of Fort Laramie. When the Sioux, led by chiefs Crazy Horse and **Sitting Bull**, assembled to drive them out, the U.S. Army sent its own troops against the Native Americans.

In June 1876, a colonel named George Custer rushed ahead of the other columns of the U.S. cavalry and arrived a day ahead of the main force. Near the Little Bighorn River, in present-day Montana, Custer and his force of about 250 men unexpectedly came upon a group of at least 2,000 Indians. Crazy Horse led the charge at what became known as the **Battle of the Little Big Horn**, killing Custer and all of his men.

Cries for revenge motivated army forces to track down the Indians. Sitting Bull and a small group of followers escaped to Canada. Crazy Horse and his followers surrendered, beaten by weather and starvation. By then, their will and the means to wage major resistance had been crushed.

The Fighting Concludes Further West Farther west, in Idaho, another powerful drama played out. In 1877, the federal government decided to move the Nez Percés to a smaller reservation to make room for white settlers. Many of the Nez Percés were Christians and had settled down and become successful horse and cattle breeders. They had a great deal to lose.

Trying to evade U.S. troops who had come to enforce their relocation, the Nez Percés's leader **Chief Joseph** led a group of refugees on a trek of more than 1,300 miles to Canada. Stopped just short of the border, Chief Joseph surrendered with deeply felt words: "I will fight no more forever." Banished with his group to a barren reservation in Oklahoma, he later traveled twice to Washington, D.C., to unsuccessfully appeal for his people's return to their homeland.

Indian Resistance Comes to an End With the loss of many leaders and the destruction of their economy, Native Americans' ability to resist diminished.

In response, many Indians welcomed a religious revival based on the Ghost Dance. Practitioners preached that the ritual would banish white settlers and restore the buffalo to the Plains. As the popularity of the movement spread, government officials became concerned about where it might lead.

In 1890, in an effort to curtail these activities, the government ordered the arrest of Sitting Bull. In

>> Sitting Bull was a famed fighter and Hunkpapa war chief. By the late 1860s, his reputation was so great that the Lakota Sioux chose him as the first-ever chief of all seven Lakota tribes.

>> A group portrait of a Sioux group by the Cheyenne River. Nearly all these men were killed in the battle at Wounded Knee.

> "There is not among these three hundred bands of Indians one which has not suffered cruelly at the hands either of the Government or of white settlers. The poorer, the more insignificant, the more helpless the band, the more certain the cruelty and outrage to which they have been subjected . . . . It makes little difference where one opens the record of the history of the Indians; every page and every year has its dark stain . . . ."
>
> —Helen Hunt Jackson, 1881

>> A Native American family poses unhappily at the Warm Springs Reservation in Oregon, visual evidence of the discontent created by the policy of relocating Indians to reservations.

the confrontation, he and several others were killed. In response, a group of Sioux left their reservation, hoping to hide out in the Badlands region. Troops then set out after the group of Indians as they fled. The cavalry finally caught up with them at Wounded Knee, in present-day South Dakota. Having been partially disarmed by U.S. troops, the Sioux were badly outgunned in the fight that followed. In the end, more than 100 men, women, and children died. The end of the Ghost Dance War at **Wounded Knee** also marked the end of major Indian resistance to white expansion and large-scale resistance to the Indian policies of the United States government.

☑ **LIST** What conflicts ended major Indian resistance?

The Government Encourages Assimilation

The reservation policy was a failure. Making Indians live in confined areas as wards of the government was costly in human and economic terms. Policy makers hoped that as the buffalo became extinct, Indians would become farmers and be **assimilated** into national life by adopting the culture and civilization of whites.

Critics Disagree with Indian Policies

A few outspoken critics defended the Indians' way of life. In *A Century of Dishonor*, Helen Hunt Jackson decried the government's treatment of Native Americans. Susette La Flesche, the granddaughter of a French trader and an Omaha Indian woman, also used her writing and lecturing talents to fight for recognition of the Indians and Indian rights in the courts. Born on the Omaha reservation in Nebraska, she studied in the East and returned to the reservation to teach.

The Americanization Movement

In 1871, Congress had passed a law stating that "no Indian nation or tribe within the United States would be recognized as an independent nation, tribe, or power with whom the United States may contract by treaty." Indians were now to be dealt with as individuals. One reason for this change was to weaken Native Americans' tribal cultures.

Reformers believed that Indians had to give up tribal loyalties and behaviors before they could adopt mainstream American values and assimilate into American society. The Americanization movement aimed at Native Americans was also aimed at new immigrants from other countries.

One way reformers thought assimilation and Americanization could be accomplished was with the passage of the **Dawes General Allotment Act** (sometimes known as the Dawes Severalty Act) by Congress in 1887, which encouraged Indians to become private property owners and farmers. The Dawes Act ended the reservations' tribal landholding system. Each Indian family was allotted, or assigned, 160-acres of the tribe's reservation to own as a farmstead. The size of these allotments was based on the eastern experience of how much land was needed to support a family. In the arid West, however, the allotment was often not big enough.

To protect Indian landowners from unscrupulous land speculators, the Dawes Act specified that the land could not be sold or transferred from its original family for 25 years. Congress hoped that by the end of that time, younger Indians would embrace the values of farming and individual land ownership.

Traditional tribal feasts, dances, and even funeral practices were outlawed, and Native American religions were discouraged. To further speed assimilation, missionaries and other reformers established boarding schools, to which Indian parents were pressured to send their children. There Indian children were to learn and live by the rules, dress, customs, and culture of white America. Ultimately, the struggle to retain their homelands, freedom, and culture proved tragic. Although many Indian peoples faced these challenges with courage and determination, tens of thousands died in war or on poverty-stricken reservations. Only a small number were left to carry on their legacy.

☑ IDENTIFY MAIN IDEAS What was the main idea of the Americanization movement, and how did the Dawes Act promote that idea?

>> As their old way of life was taken from them, many Native Americans were forced to assimilate into contemporary American life.

ᵇᵈ Bounce to Activate Timeline

☑ ASSESSMENT

1. **Summarize** the reasons Native American culture was irrevocably changed by the end of the 1800s.

2. **Compare and Contrast** how white settlers and Native Americans viewed nature.

3. **Support a Point of View with Evidence** Determine why Chief Piapot asserted that the European-led government "keep[s] only half" of the promises made to Native Americans.

4. **Compare and Contrast** the relocations and outcomes for the Navajo and Nez Percés.

5. **Hypothesize** What lasting effects did the removal to reservations have on the various Native American tribes, including the efforts of the U.S. government to abolish their practices and beliefs?

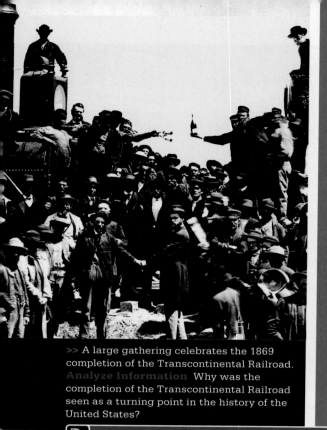

>> A large gathering celebrates the 1869 completion of the Transcontinental Railroad. Analyze Information Why was the completion of the Transcontinental Railroad seen as a turning point in the history of the United States?

Bounce to Activate Flipped Video

2.2 The West was swept by enormous change after the Civil War. As railroads increased access, settlers, ranchers, and miners permanently transformed millions of acres of western land. Mining was the first great boom in the West. Gold and silver were the magnets that attracted a vast number of people. Prospectors from the East were just a part of a flood that included people from all around the world.

>> Objectives

Analyze the impact of mining and railroads on the settlement of the West.

Explain the impact of physical and human geographic factors on the settlement of the Great Plains.

Analyze treatment of Chinese immigrants and Mexican Americans in the West.

Discuss the ways various groups used land in the West and conflicts among them.

>> Key Terms

vigilantes
Transcontinental
　Railroad
land grants
open-range system
Homestead Act
Exodusters
Las Gorras Blancas

The West Is Transformed

Mining and the Growth of Railroads

Mining Towns Expand Across the West From the Sierra Nevada to the Black Hills, there was a similar pattern and tempo to the development of mining regions. First came the discovery of gold or silver.

Then, as word spread, people began to pour into areas such as Pikes Peak in Colorado and the Yukon river near what is now Alaska. During the Klondike Gold Rush, mining camps sprang up quickly to house the thousands of people who flooded the region near the Yukon river. They were followed by more substantial communities. Miners dreamed of finding riches quickly and easily. Others saw an opportunity to make their fortune by supplying the needs of miners for food, clothing, and supplies.

The rough-and-tumble environment of these communities called out for order. To limit violence and administer justice in areas without judges or jails, miners set up rules of conduct and procedures for settling disputes. In extreme situations, self-appointed law enforcers known as **vigilantes** punished lawbreakers. As towns developed, they hired marshals and sheriffs, like Wyatt Earp and Bat Masterson, to keep the peace. Churches set up committees to address social problems.

Some mining towns—like Leadville, Colorado, and Nevada City, Montana—were "boomtowns." They thrived only as long as the gold and silver held out.

Even if a town had developed churches and schools, it might become a ghost town, abandoned when the precious metal disappeared. In contrast, Denver, Colorado; Boise, Idaho; and Helena, Montana, were among the cities that diversified and grew.

Mining Becomes Big Business The first western mining was done by individuals, who extracted the minerals from the surface soil or a stream bed. By the 1870s, the remaining mineral wealth was located deep underground. Big companies with the capital to buy mining equipment took over the industry. Machines drilled deep mine shafts. Tracks lined miles of underground tunnels. Crews—often recruited from Mexico and China—worked in dangerous conditions underground.

The arrival of the big mining companies highlighted an issue that would relentlessly plague the West: water and its uses. Large-scale mining required lots of water pumped under high pressure

to help separate the precious metals from silt. As the silt washed down the mountains, it fouled water being used by farmers and their livestock.

Despite these concerns, the federal government continued to support large mining companies by providing inexpensive land and approving patents for new inventions. Mining wealth helped fuel the nation's industrial development.

The Transcontinental Railroad Impacts the Frontier As industry in the West grew, the need for a railroad to transport goods increased as well. The idea of a **transcontinental railroad**, a rail link between the East and the West, was not new. Arguments over the route it should take, however, had delayed implementation. While the Civil War kept the South out of the running, Congress finally took action.

Unlike Europe, where railroads were built and owned by governments, in the United States, not all railroads were built with government support; they were built by private enterprise. However, Congress encouraged construction of the transcontinental railroad in two ways: It provided money in the form of loans and made **land grants**, giving builders wide stretches of land, alternating on each side of the track route.

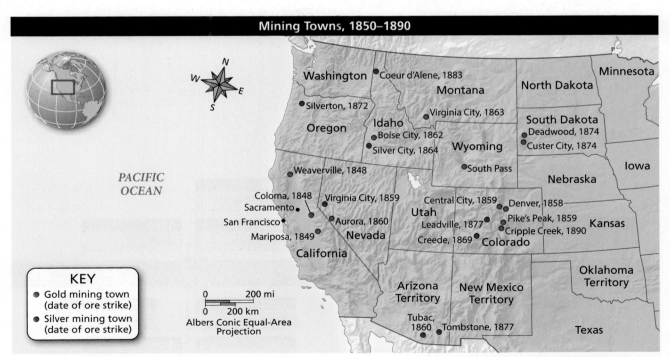

Mining Towns, 1850–1890

KEY
- Gold mining town (date of ore strike)
- Silver mining town (date of ore strike)

0   200 mi
0   200 km
Albers Conic Equal-Area Projection

>> The hope of wealth from gold and silver drew many Americans west. **Analyze Maps** Where were the biggest gold mining regions? How do you think gold discoveries affected migration?

Bounce to Activate Chart

Simultaneously in 1863, the Central Pacific started laying track eastward from Sacramento, California, while the Union Pacific headed westward from Omaha, Nebraska. Construction proved to be both difficult and expensive.

The human cost of building the railroad was also high. Starved for labor, the Central Pacific Company brought recruits from China and set them to work under harsh contracts and with little regard for their safety. Inch by inch, they chipped and blasted their way through the granite-hard Sierra Nevada and Rockies. Meanwhile, working for the Union Pacific, crews of Irish immigrants crossed the level plains from the East. The two tracks eventually met at Promontory, Utah, in 1869, the same year that the Suez Canal was completed in Egypt. The continent and the world seemed to be shrinking in size.

Railroads Spur Settlement and Growth The completion of the Transcontinental Railroad inspired a flurry of similar railroad building. By 1883, the Northen Pacific Railroad had connected St. Paul, Minnesota, with Seattle in Washington Territory.

Ten years later, James J. Hill completed a competing railroad line between St. Paul and Everett, Washington. Hill and his business partners built the Great Northern Railway without any government support. His low fares drew thousands of immigrants and other Americans to migrate west and settle along his tracks. His success allowed him to eventually gain control of the Northern Pacific, too.

The effects of the railroads were far reaching. They tied the nation together, moved products and people, and spurred industrial development. They brought western meat and farm products to the tables of eastern consumers. In turn, goods manufactured in eastern factories moved west by train and improved the lives of settlers on the frontier. Once again, the application of technological innovation by the free enterprise system was clearly raising the standard of living in the United States.

The growth of railroads also stimulated the growth of towns and cities. Speculators vied for land in places where a new railroad might be built, and towns already in existence petitioned to become a stop on the western rail route. Railroads intensified the demand for Indians' land and brought white settlers who overwhelmed Mexican American communities in the Southwest. The economic impact of the transcontinental railroads helped lead to the closing of the frontier in the late nineteeth century. There was no turning back the tide as waves of pioneers moved west. The arrival of masses of new residents led to changes in political boundaries, as territories became states.

The addition of states to the Union exemplifies the West's growth. Requirements for statehood included a population of at least 60,000 inhabitants. Between 1864 and 1896, ten territories met those requirements and became states.

☑ **IDENTIFY SUPPORTING DETAILS** How did the railroads encourage economic growth in the West?

Statehood Achieved, 1864-1896

>> **Analyze Data** Based on the dates of admission in this timeline, during which decade did the most population growth in the West probably take place?

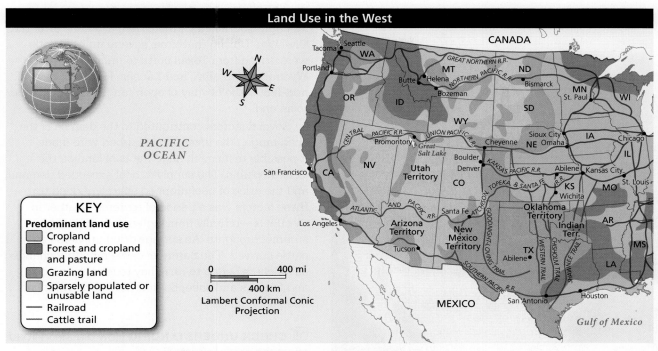

KEY
Predominant land use
- Cropland
- Forest and cropland and pasture
- Grazing land
- Sparsely populated or unusable land
— Railroad
— Cattle trail

0   400 mi
0   400 km
Lambert Conformal Conic Projection

>> Ranching was an important economic activity throughout much of the West.
Analyze Maps How might the physical geography of the West have affected where ranching most flourished?

The Cattle Industry Boom

Cattle ranching fueled another western boom. This was sparked by the vast acres of grass suitable for feeding herds of cattle. Once the railroad provided the means to move livestock to eastern markets, the race was on for land and water.

Longhorns and Vaqueros Long before the arrival of eastern settlers in the West, Mexicans in Texas had developed an efficient system for raising livestock. The Texas longhorn, which originated in Mexico, roamed freely and foraged for its own feed. Each owner marked—or "branded"—the cattle so they could be identified. Under this **open-range system**, property was not fenced in. Though ranchers claimed ownership and knew the boundaries of their property, cattle from any ranch grazed freely across those boundaries. When spring came, the ranchers would hire cowboys to comb thousands of acres of open range, "rounding up" cattle that had roamed all winter.

The culture of the cowboy owed its very existence to the Mexican vaqueros who had learned to train horses to work with cattle and had developed the roping skills, saddle, lariat, and chaps needed to do the job.

Cowboys and Cattle Drives Once the cattle were rounded up, cowboys began the long cattle drive to take the animals to a railroad that would transport them to eastern markets. The trek from Texas, Colorado, or Montana to the nearest junction on the transcontinental railroad could take weeks or even months.

The cowboys' work was hard, dangerous, low-paying, and lonely—often involving months of chasing cattle over the countryside. A band of cowboys often included a mix of white, Mexican, and African American men.

Cow Towns Cattle drives concluded in such railroad towns as Dodge City, Kansas, where the cattle were sold and the cowboys were paid. These "cow towns" gave rise to stories about colorful characters, often outlaws, such as Wild Bill Hickok, Doc Holliday, Wyatt Earp, and Jesse James. They were also the site of rodeos, competitions based on the cowboys' skills of riding, roping, and wrestling cattle. Bill Pickett, an African American cowboy, is credited with inventing bulldogging, in which a cowboy leaps from his horse onto a steer's horns and wrestles the steer to the ground.

The Open Range Comes to a Close

Open-range ranching flourished for more than a decade after the Civil War. During that time, several million cattle were driven from Texas north to railroad stops in Wyoming, Nebraska, and Kansas. However, by the mid-1880s, the heyday of open-range ranching came to an end.

Several factors contributed to the demise of the open range. The invention of barbed wire made it possible to fence in huge tracts of land on the treeless plains. The supply of beef exceeded demand, and the price of beef dropped sharply. Added to these factors was a period of extreme weather in the 1880s—brutally freezing winters followed by summer droughts. As springs dried up, herds of cattle starved. The nature of cattle ranching changed as ranchers began to raise hay to feed their stock, and farmers and sheepherders settled on what had been open range.

☑ **CHECK UNDERSTANDING** How did the railroad affect the cattle industry?

>> Settlers on the relatively dry, treeless Great Plains used the available sod to build homes for their families.

Bounce to Activate 3D Model

>> African Americans welcome new migrants from the South to St. Louis. **Hypothesize** Why might the lands and opportunities of the Great Plains have been especially appealing to African Americans following the Civil War?

Farmers Settle the Plains

The Great Plains were the last part of the country to be heavily settled by white people. The region was originally set aside for Indians because it was viewed as too dry for agriculture. Yet, with the coming of the transcontinental railroad, millions of farmers moved into the West in the last huge westward migration of European Americans in the mid to late 1800s.

The push-and-pull factors that encouraged settlement were varied. Like the miners and cattle ranchers, farmers were looking for a better life.

Railroads advertised land for sale, even sending agents to Europe to lure new immigrants, especially from Scandinavia. Other immigrants fled political upheavals in their native lands.

Westward Migration and Settlement Throughout its history, the nation's westward expansion had been marked by migrants settling on public land they did not own. These settlers, called "squatters," pressured the government to allow them to gain ownership of this land. In 1841, Congress passed the Preemption Act, giving squatters the right to buy up to 160 acres for $1.25 per acre before the land was offered for sale to other buyers. This law set the stage for the **Homestead Act**, passed in 1862. Under the Homestead Act, the government offered farm plots of 160 acres to anyone willing to live on the land for five years, dig a well, and build a road. These two laws

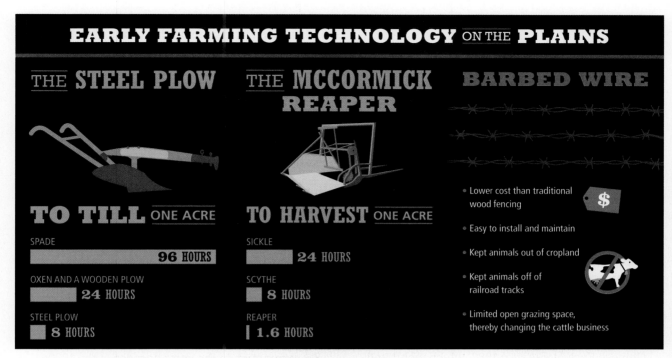

EARLY FARMING TECHNOLOGY ON THE PLAINS

THE STEEL PLOW

TO TILL ONE ACRE

SPADE
96 HOURS

OXEN AND A WOODEN PLOW
24 HOURS

STEEL PLOW
8 HOURS

THE MCCORMICK REAPER

TO HARVEST ONE ACRE

SICKLE
24 HOURS

SCYTHE
8 HOURS

REAPER
1.6 HOURS

BARBED WIRE

- Lower cost than traditional wood fencing
- Easy to install and maintain
- Kept animals out of cropland
- Kept animals off of railroad tracks
- Limited open grazing space, thereby changing the cattle business

>> **Analyze Data** How did the growth of innovative technology allow the Great Plains to support a larger population and more profitable economic activities?

encouraged further settlement and farming in the West, eventually leading to the close of the frontier.

Opportunities in the West such as mining and cattle herding were generally male occupations, so much of the western migration was led by men. But as farming expanded, more women arrived, too. They all had a job to do, such as tending the family and farm or working as an entrepreneur running a boardinghouse, laundry, or bakery.

Some of the new settlers were former slaves who fled the South after the end of Reconstruction. Benjamin Singleton, a black businessman from Tennessee, helped organize a group of African Americans called the "**Exodusters**." They took their name from the biblical story of Moses leading the exodus of the Jews out of bondage and into a new life in the "Promised Land." The Exodusters' "promised land" was in Kansas and Oklahoma, where they planted crops and founded several enduring all-black towns.

Homesteading the Plains Physical and human geographic factors made the lives of homesteaders on the Plains difficult. Windstorms, blizzards, droughts, plagues of locusts, and heart-rending loneliness tested their endurance. On the treeless plains, few new arrivals could afford to buy lumber to build a home. Instead, they cut 3-foot sections of

sod and stacked them like bricks, leaving space for a door and one window. The resulting home was dark, dirty, and dingy.

Necessity is the mother of invention, and farmers on the Plains had many needs beyond housing. The development of barbed wire, a length of wire with twisted barbs, enabled a farmer to fence land cheaply to keep out wandering livestock. The development of a plow that could tackle the sod-covered land, the grain drill that opened furrows and planted seed, the windmill that tapped underground water, and dry-farming techniques were some of the innovations that enabled farmers to succeed. To spur development of better ways to farm, Congress passed the Morrill Act in 1862, which made land grants to states for the purpose of establishing agricultural colleges.

Nothing, however, prepared farmers for a series of blizzards and droughts in the 1880s and 1890s that killed animals and ruined harvests. Some of the discouraged and ill-prepared settlers headed back east. The farmers who remained became more commercial and depended more on scientific farming methods.

☑ **IDENTIFY MAIN IDEAS** Why did farmers move to the Plains?

Minorities Encounter Difficulties

From the 1850s onward, the West had the widest diversity of people in the nation. With fewer than 20 percent of the nation's total population, it was home to more than 80 percent of the nation's Asian, Mexican and Mexican American, and Native American residents. Almost all of the nation's 100,000 Chinese immigrants lived in the West.

Economic Issues Challenge Chinese Immigrants
During the same time that Jim Crow arose in the South, Chinese immigrants faced racial prejudice on the West Coast. In 1879, California barred cities from employing people of Chinese ancestry. Several years later, San Francisco established a segregated "Oriental" school. Elsewhere, mobs of whites attacked Chinese workers, saying they had taken "white" jobs. Congress responded to these attacks by passing the Chinese Exclusion Act in 1882, which prohibited Chinese laborers from entering the country.

Brave Chinese immigrants challenged discrimination. Saum Song Bo questioned why he should support a fund-raising drive to build the Statue of Liberty. "That statue represents Liberty holding a torch which lights the passage of those of all nations who come into this country," Bo wrote in a letter published in *American Missionary* in 1898. "But are the Chinese allowed to come? As for the Chinese who are here, are they allowed to enjoy liberty as men of all other nationalities enjoy it?"

Chinese immigrants also turned to the federal courts to protect their rights but with mixed results. In 1886, in the case of *Yick Wo* v. *Hopkins*, the U.S. Supreme Court sided with a Chinese immigrant who challenged a California law that banned him and other Chinese from operating a laundry. In 1898, the Court ruled that individuals of Chinese descent, born in the United States, could not be stripped of their citizenship. Yet the Court upheld the Chinese Exclusion Act and several other discriminatory measures.

Land Ownership Proves Difficult for Mexican Americans
Like African Americans and Asian Americans, Mexican Americans struggled against discrimination in the latter decades of the 1800s. One historian has described Mexican Americans as "foreigners in their own land." At the center of their struggle stood land. The Treaty of Guadalupe Hidalgo, signed at the end of the Mexican-American War, guaranteed the property rights of Mexicans who lived in the Southwest prior to the war. Still, four out of five Mexican Americans who lived in New Mexico lost their land, as did Mexican Americans in other southwestern states.

This land loss resulted from several factors. When Anglo Americans and Mexican Americans laid claim to the same land, U.S. courts put the burden of proof on Mexican Americans to show that they really owned the land. Differences in legal customs, and the fact that much of the land was held communally, not individually, made it difficult for many Mexican Americans to do so.

In addition, Anglo Americans used political connections to take land away from Mexican Americans. The "Sante Fe Ring," an association of prominent white businessmen and government officials, got the federal government to grant the group control of millions of acres of land in New Mexico. Thousands of Mexican Americans had lived on and farmed this land for many years. Since New Mexico was a territory, not a state, however, Mexican Americans, who comprised the majority of the population, had no representatives in Washington, D.C., to challenge this deal.

Mexican Americans Defend Property Rights
Throughout the Southwest—in Texas, New Mexico,

>> Surviving harsh conditions, these Mexican-American women in San Antonio, Texas, prepare a meal outside their dwelling.

Bounce to Activate Gallery

Arizona, and California—Mexican Americans fought to maintain their rights. Many especially resented the loss of their land. One group, **Las Gorras Blancas**, targeted the property of large ranch owners by cutting holes in barbed-wire fences and burning houses. The group declared: "Our purpose is to protect the rights and interests of the people in general; especially those of the helpless classes." Supported by a national labor organization, the Knights of Labor, the group also had a newspaper to voice their grievances.

As anti-Mexican feelings increased, a group of Hispanic citizens in Tucson, Arizona, formed the Alianza Hispano-Americana in 1894 to protect the culture, interests, and legal rights of Mexican Americans. Within two years, new branches of the organization opened in other cities.

☑ **IDENTIFY SUPPORTING DETAILS** During this period, what impact did the Supreme Court have on people of Chinese descent?

Struggles and Change Across the West

There is a sharp contrast between the picture of the West depicted in novels and movies and the reality of life on the Plains. The West was a place of rugged beauty, but it was also a place of diversity and conflict.

Tension Over Economic Resources The various ways that settlers sought to use western land were sometimes at odds with one another. Conflicts between miners, ranchers, sheepherders, and farmers led to violence and acts of sabotage. Grazing cattle ruined farmers' crops, and sheep gnawed grass so close to the ground that cattle could not graze the same land. Although miners did not compete for vast stretches of grassland, runoff from large-scale mining polluted water that ran onto the Plains—and everyone needed water. And no matter who won, Native Americans lost.

Early on, geologist John Wesley Powell recognized water as an important but limited resource. He promoted community control and distribution of water for the common good. Despite his efforts, water usage remained largely unregulated, a system that benefited some but disadvantaged others.

Prejudices and Discrimination Conflict came in many guises. For example, ranchers often

>> Miners used a great deal of water in their mining operations, often with negative consequences for farmers and ranchers.

belittled homesteaders, labeling them "sodbusters" to mock their work in the soil and their modest houses. Conflict also arose because the view of the ownership of natural resources varied. For many generations, Mexicans had mined salt from the salt beds of the El Paso valley. Mexicans viewed these areas as public property, open to all. However, when Americans arrived in the 1870s, they laid claim to the salt beds and aimed to sell the salt for profit. In 1877, in what became known as the El Paso Salt War, Americans and Mexicans clashed over access to this crucial commodity. When the battles ended, the salt beds were no longer communal property. Now, users would have to buy this natural product.

Ethnic tensions often lurked beneath the surface. Many foreign-born white people sought their fortunes on the American frontier, especially in the years following the mid-century revolutions in Europe. Their multiple languages joined the mix of several dozen Native American language groups. Differences in food, religion, and cultural practices reinforced each group's fear and distrust of the others. But mostly it was in the larger cities or towns that discrimination was openly displayed. Chinese immigrants, Mexicans, and Mexican Americans were most often its targets.

Population Growth Ends the Frontier The last major land rush took place in 1889 when the federal government opened the Oklahoma Territory to homesteaders. On April 22, thousands of "boomers" gathered along the border. When the signal was given, they charged in to stake their claims. However, they found that much of the best land had already been taken by "sooners," who had sneaked into the territory and staked their claims before the official opening.

The following year, the 1890 national census revealed the extent of population growth in the West when it concluded that there was no longer a square mile of the United States that did not have at least a few white residents. The great American frontier was closed. This was in part due to completion of transcontinental railroads, which made it easier for people to migrate across the country. The country, the report said, no longer had a "frontier," which at the time was considered an uninhabited wilderness where no white person lived. The era of free western land had come to an end.

However, the challenges and tensions were far from over. Controversies over Indians' land rights were still to come. So, too, were more battles over water and over the mistreatment of minority citizens—especially Chinese and Mexican Americans. As African Americans migrated west and claimed places among the farmers, miners, railroad workers, entrepreneurs, inventors, and public servants, they indeed found new opportunities, but often these new opportunities were intertwined with discrimination.

☑ **IDENTIFY** What reasons can you identify to help explain prejudice and discrimination in the West?

☑ ASSESSMENT

1. **Support Ideas with Examples** Explain the ways mining shaped the West.

2. **Identify Cause and Effect** Describe the effects of large companies mining for minerals in the West.

3. **Summarize** the effects of the Transcontinental Railroad on the United States.

4. **Identify Patterns** in the effects of white settlers' westward expansion on other cultures.

5. **Hypothesize** Why did settlers expand westward despite the challenges of the physical environment there?

2.3 While Congress enacted many major reforms during Reconstruction, it passed very few measures between 1877 and 1900. Instead, inaction and corruption were serious political issues during the Gilded Age. This raised questions of whether or not democracy could succeed in a time dominated by large and powerful industrial corporations and men of great wealth.

>> Former Civil War general Ulysses S. Grant proved unable to keep corruption and scandal from troubling his presidential administration.

Bounce to Activate Flipped Video

Corruption Plagues the Nation

Political Power Proves Difficult to Keep

Party loyalties were so evenly divided that no faction or group gained control for any period of time. After Grant left office, only twice between 1877 and 1897 did either the Republicans or Democrats gain control of the White House and both houses of Congress at the same time. Furthermore, neither held control for more than two years in a row. This made it very difficult to pass new laws. Most of the elections were very close as well, allowing those who lost to block new legislation until they got back in power.

Political Corruption Under President Grant Ulysses S. Grant was a popular war hero but a disappointing President. Allied with the Radical Republicans, he promised to take a strong stand against southern resistance to Reconstruction. But Grant's ability to lead was marred by scandal. He gave high-level advisory posts to untrustworthy friends and acquaintances who used their positions to line their own pockets. His own Vice President, Schuyler Colfax, was investigated and implicated in a scheme to steal profits from the Union Pacific Railroad. In addition, a plan by

>> **Objectives**

Analyze the issues of weak leadership and corruption in national politics in the 1870s through 1890s.

Discuss civil service reform in the late 1800s.

Assess the importance of economic issues in the late 1800s.

>> **Key Terms**

spoils system
civil service
Pendleton Civil
   Service Act
gold standard
political machines
fiat money

railroad developer and financier Jay Gould to corner the gold market actually included President Grant's brother-in-law.

When Grant ran for reelection in 1872, some reform-minded Republicans withdrew their support and teamed up with some Democrats to create the Liberal Republican Party. The Liberal Republicans advocated civil service reform, removal of the army from the South, and an end to corruption in southern and national governments. Grant easily defeated their presidential candidate, the *New York Tribune* editor Horace Greeley.

Not long after the election, however, Americans sensed the aura of greed surrounding American politics. When scandal swirled around the members of his administration including his private secretary, the Secretary of War, and members of Congress, Grant seemed to look the other way. Even though he had stated, "Let no guilty man escape," he seemed to lack the will to root out this corruption. Confidence in public officials plummeted.

Across the nation, local scandals came to light. Many city officials sold lucrative public construction contracts to their friends or diverted money from city accounts. The most notorious of these scandals involved a band of New York City Democratic politicians led by state senator William "Boss" Tweed. The "Tweed Ring," as it came to be known, plundered millions of dollars from the city's treasury. By 1873, when Tweed was convicted and sentenced to prison, the public's confidence in its leaders was at a low ebb.

Corruption Continues in Subsequent Administrations In comparison to Lincoln, Grant and the other Presidents of the Gilded Age that followed him appeared particularly weak. Although they, like Lincoln, won by slim margins that reflected the nation's diversity of opinion on important issues, these presidents differed from Lincoln in that, once in office, they lacked integrity. Rutherford B. Hayes owed his election in 1876 to a secret deal to end Reconstruction. Benjamin Harrison became only the second President in history to lose the popular vote but win the electoral college vote. Chester Arthur, who took the helm following James Garfield's assassination, upset so many of his fellow Republicans that he failed to win his own party's presidential nomination in 1884.

The most noteworthy President of the era was Grover Cleveland. In an era known for its corruption, Cleveland maintained a reputation for integrity. He once observed, "A Democratic thief is as bad as a Republican thief." Cleveland enjoyed an extremely rapid rise to political prominence. In 1881, running as a reformer, he won the race for mayor in Buffalo, New York. A year later, he became the governor of New York, and in 1884, he became the first Democrat to win the White House in 24 years.

In 1888, even though he won the popular vote, Cleveland lost to Benjamin Harrison. But Cleveland came back to rewin the presidency in 1892.

☑ **IDENTIFY MAIN IDEAS** Why did the public lose trust in the federal government?

>> Scandals such as the secret deal that gave Republican Rutherford B. Hayes (on left) the presidency troubled Gilded Age politics. A number of administrations from this era suffered under weak or corrupt leadership.

🅑 **Bounce to Activate Gallery**

Growth of Political Machines and Corruption

Grover Cleveland's reputation for honesty was the exception. Many government officials routinely accepted bribes. As Henry Adams, the great-grandson of John Adams, observed, "One might search the whole list of Congress, Judiciary, and Executive . . . [from] 1870 to 1895, and find little but damaged reputation."

Voter Turnout in Selected Presidential Elections, 1872-1916

YEAR	TOTAL TURNOUT	REPUBLICANS	DEMOCRATS	VOTER TURNOUT PERCENTAGE	RESULT
1872	6,460,000	3,597,000	2,843,000	71.3	Ulysses S. Grant, Republican
1876	8,422,000	4,037,000	4,284,000	81.8	Rutherford B. Hayes, Republican
1880	9,217,000	4,453,000	4,414,000	79.4	James A. Garfield, Republican
1884	10,053,000	4,850,000	4,880,000	77.5	Grover Cleveland, Democrat
1892	12,061,000	5,183,000	5,555,000	74.7	Grover Cleveland, Democrat
1900	13,968,000	7,218,000	6,357,000	73.2	Theodore Roosevelt, Republican
1908	14,884,000	7,675,000	6,412,000	65.4	William Howard Taft, Republican
1916	18,531,000	8,534,000	9,128,000	61.6	Woodrow Wilson, Democrat

SOURCE: *Historical Statistics of the United States,* U.S. Census Bureau

>> **Analyze Data** Is it probable that the presidents of the Gilded Age enjoyed strong popular support for their ideas? Why or why not?

Bounce to Activate Chart

Political Supporters Are Given Jobs Political parties and the spoils system were central components of politics during the Gilded Age.

Under the **spoils system**, which was first used by President Andrew Jackson as far back as the 1820s, politicians awarded government jobs to loyal party workers, with little regard for their qualifications. Parties held elaborate rallies and parades to get out the vote. However, candidates for the presidency did not take part in the campaign. They felt it lowered the reputation of the presidency.

Parties developed sophisticated **political machines** that reached virtually into every ward, in every precinct, in many cities in the nation. In large cities, political machines were often run by "bosses" or a small group of people. These groups, like Tammany Hall in New York City or the Pendergast machine in Kansas City, controlled cities for decades. The political machines worked by winning the loyalty of large immigrant groups by promising, and in some cases, delivering, solutions to problems like poor sanitation or transportation. The spoils system also played a role, with political machines rewarding loyal organizers with city jobs. With voter loyalty secured, the political machine was assured of its political power and often became very corrupt.

The spoils system served as the glue that helped make the parties so powerful. The Postmaster General, who headed the U.S. Postal Service, for example, could reward thousands of supporters with jobs. Likewise, other officials could and did use federal contracts to convince people to vote for their candidates. Ironically, political participation probably got a boost from the spoils system and the fierce partisanship of the era. About 75 to 80 percent of all those who could vote did vote in presidential elections during the Gilded Age.

Political Cartoons Alert the Public Though many Americans saw nothing wrong with politicians rewarding their friends, writers such as Mark Twain, political cartoonists, and others who thought about American politics expressed their concern about the damaging effects of corruption.

"The Bosses of the Senate," one of the most famous political cartoons of the time, drawn by Joseph Keppler, showed a cluster of businessmen representing various trusts, glaring down on the chambers of the Senate.

Thomas Nast created a series of cartoons which exposed the illegal activities of Boss Tweed and the Tammany Hall political machine in New York City. Eventually, Tweed was arrested. He escaped and fled to Spain. While there, Tweed was identified through one of Nast's cartoons. The Tammany Hall machine, however, lived on.

Civil Service Reform Efforts The feeling that the spoils system corrupted government, or at least made it terribly inefficient, prompted a number of prominent figures to promote civil service reform. The **civil service** is a system that includes federal jobs in the executive branch. In a reformed system, most government workers would get their jobs due to their expertise and maintain them regardless of which political party won the election.

Reforming the spoils system did cause controversy. Without the spoils system, politicians felt they would not attract the people needed to run their parties. Independent attempts by politicians to change the system failed. For example, when Rutherford B. Hayes became President in 1877, he worked for civil service reform. He even placed well-known reformers in high offices. However, the Republican Party did not support his reform efforts. It took the 1881 assassination of President James Garfield by Charles J. Guiteau to make civil service reform a reality. Guiteau shot Garfield because he believed that the Republican Party had not fulfilled its promise to give him a government job.

The Pendleton Civil Service Act Chester A. Arthur became President after the assassination of

>> Charles J. Guiteau, an unstable individual who felt he was owed a government position, assassinated President Garfield in 1881. **Infer** What effect did Garfield's assassination have on civil service reform?

Garfield. While Arthur defended the spoils system, he supported the movement for civil service reform, which had been strengthened because of public indignation over Garfield's assassination. Arthur signed the **Pendleton Civil Service Act** in 1883. This act established a Civil Service Commission, which wrote a civil service exam. Individuals who wanted to work for the government had to take the exam, and getting a job depended on doing well on the exam, not on manipulating one's political connections. Initially, the act covered only a small percentage of federal employees, but its reach grew over time, reducing the power of the spoils system.

☑ **CHECK UNDERSTANDING** How did the spoils system encourage government corruption and, eventually, government reform?

Economic Policy Challenges Continue

The public's discontent was worsened by economic turmoil and uncertainty. In the fall of 1873, one of the nation's most influential banks failed, apparently as a result of overextended loans to the expanding railroad industry. A wave of fear known as the Panic of 1873 spread through the financial industry and across the nation. Bank failures, job losses, and the uncertain economy added to the array of the nation's concerns. Events such as this prompted political leaders to debate the best ways to keep the economy moving forward.

The tariff and monetary policy were critical economic issues during this time. Leaders looked to these two areas for ways to stabilize the economy, but both issues were divisive. The tariff issue sharply split the Democrats and Republicans.

Monetary policy gave rise to independent political parties or movements that disagreed with the major parties' commitment to the **gold standard**. Using the gold standard meant that the government would use gold as the basis of the nation's currency. Paper money was backed by the government's gold reserves, and could, in theory, be redeemed for actual gold.

Americans Continue to Discuss Tariffs The debate over the tariff had deep roots in American history. The tariff, or the tax on imports of manufactured goods and some agricultural products, was created as early as 1810 to protect newly developed industries. Since then, the debate to lower or increase tariffs continued. Differences over the tariff had divided the Federalists and Jeffersonians and the Democrats and Whigs. During the Gilded Age, it divided the Republicans and Democrats. The tariff question became a major issue during the presidential election of 1888. The Republicans favored a high tariff, arguing that it would allow American industries to grow and promote jobs in manufacturing. Democrats countered that high tariffs increased the costs of goods to consumers and made it harder for American farmers to sell their goods abroad.

Different Ideas About Monetary Policy Two related factors turned monetary policy into a bitter issue during the Gilded Age. During the Civil War, the federal government issued paper money, known as greenbacks. The greenbacks were **fiat money,** or currency not backed by gold or silver. After the war, because the fiat money had contributed to wartime inflation (a rise in prices), the government retired, or got rid of, the greenbacks. Over the next century, the United States and other major world economies would edge towards going off a metallic standard and onto fiat money gradually, making the final move in the 1970s. However, in the 1870s, the debate centered on whether to use gold or gold *and* silver to back the paper money.

In 1873, Congress passed the Coinage Act of 1873. This law reversed the government policy of backing money with both gold and silver. Using only gold meant that the money supply was smaller and each dollar would be worth more. Bankers and others involved in international trade favored the gold standard because it discouraged inflation and made dollars worth more overseas. In contrast, most farmers favored keeping silver to create inflation.

Already struggling, they hoped the rise in prices would increase their income. Those who favored the minting of silver—in other words, considering silver as money—protested against what they termed the "Crime of 1873" and prompted Congress to mint silver dollars. The Bland-Allison Act, passed in 1878, specified that the U.S. Treasury make a certain amount of silver-backed dollars each month, but not as many as the Free Silver advocates would have liked. The debate over whether to consider silver as money alongside gold continued until the passage of the Gold Standard Act in 1900, which set gold as the only metal backing paper dollars.

☑ **CHECK UNDERSTANDING** Why did Republicans and Democrats differ in their view of the tariff issue?

☑ **ASSESSMENT**

1. **Summarize** the reasons why President Cleveland's reputation was considered the exception to the rule for presidents from the 1870s through the 1890s.

2. **Interpret** Why do you think that party loyalties were so evenly divided after the end of the Civil War?

3. **Cite Evidence** of the corruption of the spoils system.

4. **Compare Points of View** Describe the debate pertaining to tariffs during the Gilded Age.

5. **Draw Conclusions** Why were political cartoons such an effective weapon against corruption?

>> Life was difficult for prairie farmers, who faced the difficulties of nature as well as unpredictable prices and rising debts. **Hypothesize** Why were farmers willing to put up with the hardships that came with their way of living?

 Bounce to Activate Flipped Video

2.4 Following the Civil War, millions of men and women migrated west in search of the American dream. However, in the late 1880s and early 1890s, their dream began to turn into a nightmare, which, in turn, sparked a social and political movement known as populism. This movement displayed the dissatisfaction of millions of ordinary Americans—poor farmers, small landholders, and urban workers—and produced one of the largest third-party movements in American history.

>> Objectives

Analyze the economic issues farmers faced in the late 1800s.

Describe the groups farmers formed to address their problems and what they accomplished.

Evaluate the impact of the Populist Party, and explain why the party did not last.

>> Key Terms

Oliver H. Kelley
Grange
Populist Party
William Jennings
  Bryan
William McKinley
Farmers' Alliance

Farm Issues and Populism

Farmers Face Economic Difficulty

The farmers of the West and the South were willing to accept the difficulties of farm life. Yet farmers discovered that other enormous obstacles stood in the way of realizing their dreams.

They received low prices for their crops, but they had to pay high costs for transportation. Debts mounted while their influence on the political system declined.

Farm Issues Result in Rising Debt Between 1870 and 1895, farm prices plummeted. Cotton, which sold for about 15 cents a pound in the early 1870s, sold for only about 6 cents a pound in the mid-1890s. Corn and wheat prices declined nearly as rapidly. One study estimated that by the early 1890s, it was costing farmers more to produce corn than they could get by selling it, so they burned it to use as fuel. Planting more crops did not help. On the contrary, the more crops farmers produced, the more prices declined.

During the same time period, the cost of doing business rose. To pay for new machinery, seed, livestock, and other needs, farmers went into debt. An increasing number of farmers mortgaged their farms to raise funds to survive and became tenant farmers—meaning they no longer owned the farm where they worked.

Big Business Practices Affect Farmers Farmers blamed big business, especially the railroads and the banks, for their difficulties. They protested that railroads, as monopolies, charged whatever rates they wanted. Likewise, they complained that banks set interest rates at unfairly high levels. Southern farmers, especially black sharecroppers, faced the added problem of having to deal with dishonest merchants and landlords who paid less for crops and charged more for supplies than promised.

In addition, farmers grew angry because they felt the nation had turned its back on them. The United States had a long tradition of electing leaders from farm states with agricultural backgrounds, like Thomas Jefferson. Yet it now appeared that most of the nation's leaders came from urban industrial states. Moreover, farmers felt that they performed honest labor and produced necessary goods, while bankers and businessmen were the ones who got rich. One editor for a farmers' newspaper explained:

> There are three great crops raised in Nebraska. One is the crop of corn, one a crop of freight rates, and one a crop of interest. One is produced by farmers who sweat and toil to farm the land. The other two are produced by men who sit in their offices and behind their bank counters and farm the farmers.
>
> —*Farmers' Alliance*, 1890

Farmers, however, refused to accept these circumstances. They took action.

☑ **DESCRIBE** What concerns did many farmers share about their businesses?

Farmers Seek Change Through Alliances

Farmers created a network of organizations, first in the Midwest and then in the South and West, to address their problems. The Granger movement, also known as the "Patrons of Husbandry," was the first.

The Courts Have Their Say Organized in 1867 by **Oliver H. Kelley**—a Minnesota farmer, businessman, journalist, and government clerk—the organization popularly known as the **Grange** attracted about a million members. The goals of the Grange included providing education on new farming techniques and calling for the regulation of railroad and grain elevator rates.

In the mid-1870s, the states of Illinois, Wisconsin, and Minnesota enacted laws that set maximum

Falling Prices of Farm Crops

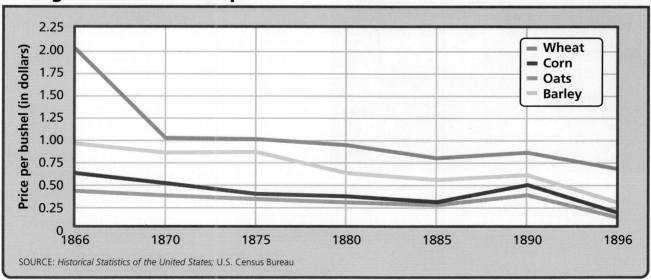

SOURCE: *Historical Statistics of the United States;* U.S. Census Bureau

>> Over this 30-year period, falling commodity prices hit American farmers hard.
Analyze Charts What trend does the graph show? What might explain that trend?

>> The Granger movement, which promoted the rights and interests of farmers, inspired this illustration. **Determine Point of View** How does the illustrator view the importance of American farmers?

>> Farmers plowed through difficult soil, often with no family members or hired workers to help them, just one of the many hardships they faced.

rates for shipping freight and for grain storage. The railroad companies challenged these "Grange Laws" in the courts. The Supreme Court upheld some decisions and overturned others, depending on the context of individual cases. In one of the significant "Granger Cases," *Munn* v. *Illinois*, the Court ruled against a Chicago grain-storage facility that challenged the constitutionality of an 1871 Illinois law setting maximum rates for shipping freight. This decision upheld the right of states to regulate private industries in some circumstances. However, in *Wabash* v. *Illinois* (1886) the Court ruled against state regulation. In this decision, the Court overturned an Illinois law by declaring that individual states did not have the power to regulate interstate commerce. Eventually, the Grangers helped to prompt the federal government to establish the Interstate Commerce Commission (ICC) to oversee interstate transportation.

Farmers and the Railroads Disagree Although the Grange declined in the late 1870s, farm protest remained strong. Faced with serious difficulties, Texas farmers in the 1870s began to organize and to negotiate as a group for lower prices for supplies.

The idea spread. Local organizations linked together in what became known as the **Farmers' Alliance**. These organizations soon connected farmers not only in the South but also in the West, and for a brief period farmers of all races and ethnicities banded together for their common cause. Because of regularly rising rates, the Alliances wanted the government to regulate the interest that banks could charge for loans. Farmers' Alliance members also tried to convince the government to force railroads to lower freight prices so members could get their crops to markets outside the South at reduced rates.

The railroads, however, argued that their prices were justified by the expense of building the railroads to begin with and by intense competition between rail companies. They had to charge high prices to earn profits and create more jobs. Often railroads would offer rebates or other incentives to larger shippers who used their rails. In addition, they would charge more to ship freight short distances than they would for long trips because they had competitors for long hauls, but not for short hauls. This was known as the "short haul and long haul" practice.

The Interstate Commerce Act, passed in 1887, prohibited several of these practices, although it proved hard to enforce.

Alliances Encourage Reform Farmers' Alliances, such as the Southern Farmers' Alliance, became important reform organizations. They formed cooperatives to collectively sell their crops, and they called on the federal government to establish "sub-treasuries," or postal banks, to provide farmers with low-interest loans. They hoped the cooperatives would push the costs of doing business down and the prices for crops up. Some of the cooperative efforts succeeded. The Georgia Alliance led a boycott against manufacturers who raised the price of the special cord that farmers used to wrap bundles of cotton.

Farmers' alliances organized across racial lines were short-lived. Soon, the Southern Farmers' Alliance organized only white farmers.

There was also an Alliance network for African American farmers. R. M. Humphrey, a white Baptist minister, headed the Colored Farmers' Alliance, which had been organized by African American and white farmers.

Nearly one million African American farmers joined the group by 1891. The Colored Farmers' Alliance recognized that both white and African American farmers shared the same difficulties, but racial tensions prevented any effective cooperation between the groups.

☑ **IDENTIFY SUPPORTING DETAILS** What reforms did the farmers' organizations introduce?

The Beginnings of Populism

The spread of the Farmers' Alliances culminated with the formation of the **Populist Party**, or People's Party, in 1892. These Populists sought to build a new political party from the grass roots up. They ran entire slates of candidates for local, state, and national positions. Like a prairie fire, the Populist Party spread rapidly, putting pressure on the two major political parties to consider their demands.

Populist Goals The Populist Party spelled out their views in their platform, which they adopted in Omaha, Nebraska, in July 1892. The platform warned about the dangers of political corruption, an inadequate monetary supply, and an unresponsive government. The Populist Party proposed specific remedies to these political issues. To fight low prices, they called for the coinage of silver, or "free silver." To combat high costs, they demanded government ownership of the railroads. Mary Elizabeth Lease, a

>> Many African American farmers joined the Colored Farmers' Alliance.

>> The Populists, or People's Party, fielded candidates for office in local, state, and national elections in 1892. **Interpret** What Populist political goals does the slogan shown here suggest?

fiery Populist Party spokesperson, also advanced the cause of women's suffrage.

The Populist Party nominated James B. Weaver of Iowa as their presidential candidate and James Field of Virginia as his running mate. Both had risen to the rank of general in the United States and Confederate armies, respectively, and their nominations represented the party's attempt to overcome the regional divisions that had kept farmers apart since the end of the Civil War. (Southern white voters had supported the Democrats; northerners, the Republicans.) The Populist Party also sought to reach out to urban workers, to convince them that they faced the same enemy: the industrial elite.

Early Impacts of the Populist Party For a new political party, the Populists did quite well in 1892. Weaver won more than one million votes for the presidency, and the Populists elected three governors, five senators, and ten congressmen. In 1894, the Populist Party continued to expand its base, gaining seats in the state legislatures and prompting the major political parties to consider endorsing its ideas.

In the South, the Populist Party had to unite black and white voters if it hoped to succeed politically.

Tom Watson, Georgia's most famous Populist Party leader, made a strong case for casting aside racial prejudice in favor of a political alliance between the races. However, the Democratic Party successfully used racist tactics, such as warning that a Populist victory would lead to "Negro supremacy," to diminish the appeal of the Populist Party.

☑ **IDENTIFY** What did the Populist Party hope to accomplish?

Populism's Declining Influence

In 1893, a four-year-long depression began that worsened conditions not only for already-suffering farmers but for other Americans as well. Labor unrest and violence engulfed the nation. The major parties failed to satisfactorily respond to the nation's distress.

In the midst of national discontent, the Populist Party's dream of forging a broad coalition with urban workers grew. The Populists' relative success at the polls in 1892 and 1894 raised their hopes further. The decision of the Democratic Party to nominate **William Jennings Bryan** as their presidential

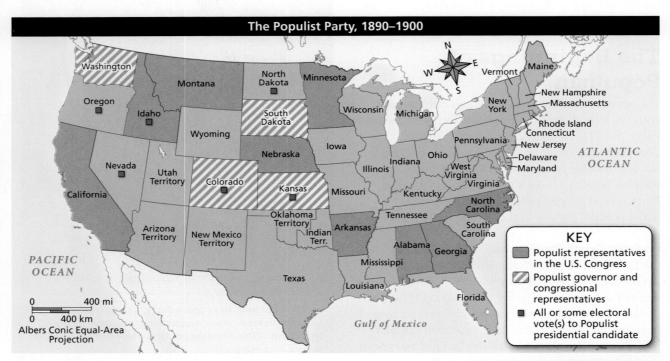

The Populist Party, 1890–1900

KEY
- Populist representatives in the U.S. Congress
- Populist governor and congressional representatives
- All or some electoral vote(s) to Populist presidential candidate

>> Around the turn of the century, the Populist Party became a viable alternative to the two established political parties. **Analyze Maps** What does the map show about the popularity of the Populist Party?

Bounce to Activate Chart

candidate put the election for the Populists on an entirely different plane, leading some to believe they could win the White House that year.

The Impact of William Jennings Bryan Born in Salem, Illinois, William Jennings Bryan moved to Lincoln, Nebraska, where he set up a law practice in 1887. He earned the nickname the "boy orator," in part by displaying his strong debating skills during his successful run for the United States Congress in 1890. In 1896, Bryan addressed the national Democratic convention on the subject of the gold standard, attacking Grover Cleveland and others in the party who opposed coining silver. The audience listened and cheered as Bryan spoke for "the plain people of this country," for "our farms," and declared "we beg no longer." The speech became known as the "Cross of Gold" speech because it ended with the following line: "You shall not press down upon the brow of labor this crown of thorns, you shall not crucify mankind upon a cross of gold."

The speech so moved the Democratic delegates that they nominated Bryan as their party's presidential candidate. He was just 36 years old and had not been a contender for the nomination until then. Bryan's advocacy of "free silver," or the coinage of silver as well as gold, and his support of a number of other Populist Party proposals, placed the Populists in a difficult situation.

Holding their convention after the Democrats, the Populists had to decide whether to nominate their own presidential candidate and continue to focus on building a broad-based movement from the bottom up or to endorse Bryan with the hope that they could capture the White House in 1896. They chose the latter course.

Bryan's campaign was like none other before. For the first time, a presidential candidate toured the nation, speaking directly to the people. In contrast, **William McKinley**, the Republican candidate, accumulated approximately $15 million, 30 times the amount Bryan had, and allowed party regulars to do the campaigning for him. Marcus Hanna, the political powerhouse who orchestrated McKinley's run, cast Bryan and his Populist Party supporters as a potential dictator and a threat to the Republic. For instance, one cartoon published in the pro-Republican *Los Angeles Times* depicted the Democratic-Populist coalition as a collection of evil witches, who fed the fires of sectionalism, discontent, and prejudice in order to win the election.

>> William Jennings Bryan, a gifted orator and Populist Party stalwart, gives a speech to his supporters.

Bounce to Activate Gallery

>> This cartoon depicts William Jennings Bryan as a large snake swallowing the Democratic donkey. **Analyze Cartoons** Was this cartoon's creator a Populist supporter? How can you tell?

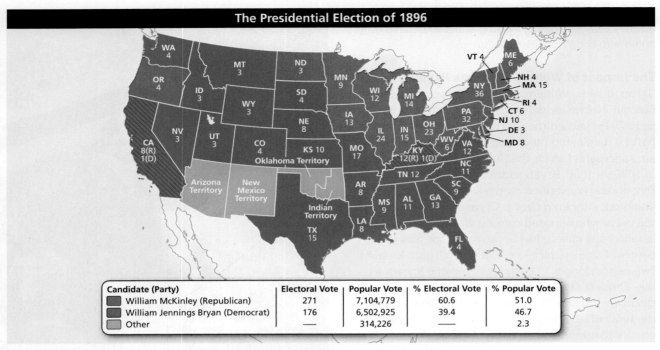

The Presidential Election of 1896

Candidate (Party)	Electoral Vote	Popular Vote	% Electoral Vote	% Popular Vote
William McKinley (Republican)	271	7,104,779	60.6	51.0
William Jennings Bryan (Democrat)	176	6,502,925	39.4	46.7
Other	—	314,226	—	2.3

>> In the presidential election of 1896, William Jennings Bryan won more states but fewer electoral votes than the victorious William McKinley. **Analyze Maps** In which regions was Bryan the most popular?

Populism's Long-Term Impact McKinley won the election of 1896 and went on to win reelection, again over Bryan, in 1900. Bryan's emphasis on monetary reform, especially free silver, did not appeal to urban workers, and the Populist Party failed to win a state outside of the South and West. Moreover, the decision to endorse Bryan weakened the Populists at the local and state levels, and the party never recovered from its defeat in 1896. The Populist Party lingered for nearly a decade. By the early 1900s, it had disappeared as a feasible alternative to the two major political parties. Most of the voters who supported the Populist Party returned to the Democratic Party in 1896.

Even though the Populist Party fell apart, its impact as a third party inspired other third parties, notably the Progressive Party in the early 1900s. Many of the specific reforms that it advocated became a reality in the early decades of the 1900s. The Progressives supported a graduated income tax, regulation of the railroads, and a more flexible monetary system. Moreover, populism had a lasting effect on the style of politics in the United States. For a brief time, there was even a coalition of whites and blacks in Texas. They were able to find a common political ground.

Increasingly, candidates campaigned directly to the people, and, like Bryan, they emphasized their association with ordinary Americans.

☑ **RECALL** How did some of the ideas of the Populist Party influence twentieth century politics?

☑ ASSESSMENT

1. **Generate Explanations** Why did farmers blame big business for their hardships?

2. **Summarize** the strategies by which farmers sought economic change at the end of the nineteenth century.

3. **Draw Conclusions** Determine the reasoning behind the Democratic Party's decision to nominate William Jennings Bryan as their presidential candidate.

4. **Compare and Contrast** the positions of the Democratic Party and the Populist Party with regard to racial equality.

5. **Identify Patterns** Explain how the Populist Party influenced twentieth-century politics, even after its decline.

Preamble to the Platform of the Populist Party

The People's, or Populist, Party adopted its party platform in 1892 at its national convention in Omaha, Nebraska. The movement, which emerged from the Farmer's Alliance in the 1880s, sought political reforms and a redistribution of political and economic power.

>> Farmers on the prairie

The conditions which surround us best justify our co-operation; we meet in the midst of a nation brought to the verge of moral, political, and material [financial] ruin. Corruption dominates the ballot-box, the Legislatures, the Congress, and touches even the ermine of the bench.

The people are demoralized; most of the States have been compelled to isolate the voters at the polling places to prevent universal intimidation and bribery. The newspapers are largely subsidized or muzzled, public opinion silenced, business prostrated, homes covered with mortgages, labor impoverished, and the land concentrating in the hands of capitalists. The urban workmen are denied the right to organize for self-protection, imported pauperized labor beats down their wages, a hireling standing army, unrecognized by our laws, is established to shoot them down, and they are rapidly degenerating into European conditions.

☑ **DETERMINE CENTRAL IDEAS** What is the party's view of democracy in America?

The fruits of the toil [labor] of millions are boldly stolen to build up colossal fortunes for a few, unprecedented [never having happened or existed before] in the history of mankind; and the possessors of these, in turn, despise the Republic and endanger liberty. From the same prolific [producing a lot of something] womb of governmental injustice we breed the two great classes—tramps and millionaires. . . .

. . . Silver, which has been accepted as coin since the dawn of history, has been demonetized to add to the purchasing power of gold by decreasing the value of all forms of property as well as human labor, and the supply of currency is purposely abridged to fatten usurers, bankrupt enterprise, and enslave industry. A vast conspiracy against mankind has been organized on two continents, and it is rapidly taking possession of the world. If not met and overthrown at once it forebodes terrible social convulsions, the destruction of civilization, or the establishment of an absolute despotism.

We have witnessed for more than a quarter of a century the struggles of the two great political parties for power and plunder [loot], while grievous [causing grief or suffering] wrongs have been inflicted upon the suffering people. We charge that the controlling influences dominating both these parties have permitted the existing dreadful conditions to develop without serious effort to prevent or restrain them.

☑ **DETERMINE MEANING** To which two parties does "the two great political parties" refer?

Neither do they now promise us any substantial reform. They have agreed together to ignore, in the coming campaign, every issue but one. They propose to drown the outcries of a plundered people with the uproar of a sham battle over the tariff, so that capitalists, corporations, national banks, rings, trusts, watered stock, the demonetization of silver and the oppressions of the usurers may all be lost sight of. They propose to sacrifice our homes, lives, and children on the altar of mammon; to destroy the multitude in order to secure corruption funds from the millionaires.

Assembled on the anniversary of the birthday of the nation, and filled with the spirit of the grand general and chief who established our independence, we seek to restore the government of the Republic to the hands of "the plain people," with which class it originated. We assert our purposes to be identical with the purposes of the National Constitution; to form a more perfect union and establish justice, insure domestic tranquility, provide for the common defence, promote the general welfare, and secure the blessings of liberty for ourselves and our posterity.

We declare that this Republic can only endure as a free government while built upon the love of the whole people for each other and for the nation; that it cannot be pinned together by bayonets; that the civil war is over, and that every passion and resentment which grew out of it must die with it, and that we must be in fact, as we are in name, one united brotherhood of free men.

Our country finds itself confronted by conditions for which there is no precedent in the history of the world; our annual agricultural productions amount to billions of dollars in value, which must, within a few weeks or months, be exchanged for billions of dollars' worth of commodities consumed in their production; the existing currency supply is wholly inadequate to make this exchange; the results are falling prices, the formation of combines and rings, the impoverishment of the producing class. We pledge ourselves that if given power we will labor to correct these evils by wise and reasonable legislation, in accordance with the terms of our platform.

We believe that the power of government—in other words, of the people—should be expanded . . . to the end [result] that oppression, injustice, and poverty shall eventually cease in the land. . . .

☑ **DETERMINE MEANING** According to the preamble, who controls power in the nation?

☑ ASSESSMENT

1. **Paraphrase** In your own words, describe what the Populist Party views as the failings of the two major parties.

2. **Identify Supporting Details** List three details from the platform that support the Populist Party's position.

3. **Draw Conclusions** What types of laws do you think the Populist Party might support? Give specific examples.

Go online to PearsonSchool.com/CASS and use the texts, quizzes, interactivities, Interactive Reading Notepads, Flipped Videos, and other resources from this Topic to prepare for the Topic Test.

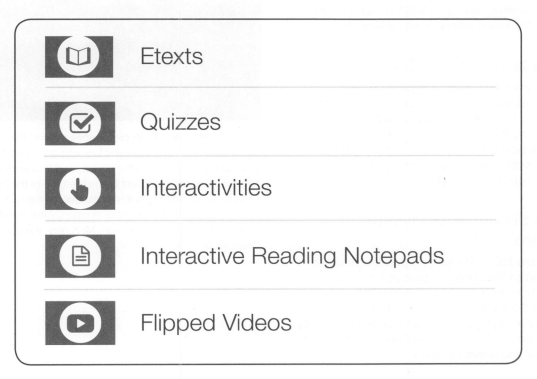

Etexts

Quizzes

Interactivities

Interactive Reading Notepads

Flipped Videos

While online you can also check the progress you've made learning the topic and course content by viewing your grades, test scores, and assignment status.

LESSON SUMMARIES

Use these Lesson Summaries, and the longer versions available online, to review the key ideas for each lesson in this Topic.

Lesson 1: American Indians Under Pressure

As white settlers moved west in the late 1800s, pressure mounted on American Indians, who resisted the seizure of their lands. In 1887, Congress granted farmsteads to Indian families while reformers established schools to help Indian children to assimilate into white society.

Lesson 2: The West is Transformed

The transcontinental railroad, completed in 1869, linked the East and West, moving products and people while spurring industrial and urban growth in the West. Cattle ranching and mining boomed. The government offered farm plots to homesteaders on the Great Plains. Meanwhile, both Chinese immigrants and Mexican Americans faced racial prejudice and discrimination.

Lesson 3: Corruption Plagues the Nation

During the late 1800s, inaction and political corruption plagued political life. Politicians gave government jobs to loyal party workers. However, in 1883 Congress established a civil service commission that based employment on qualifications rather than on party loyalty. During this period, Democrats and Republicans argued over the tariff and monetary policy.

Lesson 4: Farm Issues and Populism

Between 1870 and 1895 crop prices fell and the cost of doing business rose, plunging farmers into debt. Farmers blamed the railroad and the banks, and formed Farmers' Alliances, which in turn led to the creation of the Populist Party in 1892. The Populists endorsed Williams Jennings Bryan in the 1896 presidential election. After the defeat of Bryan by Republican William McKinley, the party never recovered.

VISUAL REVIEW

Use these graphics to review some of the key terms, people, and ideas from this Topic.

Native American Experience in the West

CONFLICT	OUTCOME
1862 Sioux Rebellion in Minnesota	U.S. pushes Sioux into the Dakotas.
1864 Sand Creek Massacre in Colorado	Plains Indians unite to resist white settlement.
1874 Red River War	Comanches and Kiowas surrender.
1876 Custer and his men killed at Battle of the Little Big Horn.	U.S. takes revenge on Sioux.
1877 Nez Percés try to flee to Canada.	Nez Percés sent to reservation in Oklahoma.
1890 Ghost Dance War	Sioux crushed at Wounded Knee in South Dakota.

Railroads Transform the West

The Tariff Question

Republicans	supported a high tariff	to encourage industries to grow and increase manufacturing jobs.
Democrats	opposed a high tariff	believing it would increase cost of goods and make it harder for farmers to sell goods abroad.

Economic Challenges to Farmers

KEY TERMS, PEOPLE, AND IDEAS

1. What was the purpose of the **Dawes General Allotment Act**?

2. For what reasons were Native Americans forced from their lands?

3. Why did the **open-range system** come to an end?

4. What factors helped create ethnic diversity in the West?

5. How did the **Pendleton Civil Service Act** undermine the **spoils system**?

6. How did **political machines** contribute to corruption in the late 1800s?

7. Why did farmers support backing money with silver?

8. What were the goals of the **Populist Party**?

9. Why did farmers blame the banks and railroads for their economic problems?

CRITICAL THINKING

10. **Draw Conclusions** What were the consequences of the 1871 law banning recognition of Indian nations or tribes?

11. **Compare and Contrast** Why was the Americanization movement aimed at both immigrants and Indians?

12. **Identify Cause and Effect** (a.) How did railroads change the West? (b.) How did these railroads affect the economy?

13. **Summarize** What kinds of discrimination did ethnic minorities face in the West?

14. **Cite Evidence** Why was it so difficult to pass laws in the late 1800s?

15. **Identify Cause and Effect** Why did farmers suffer economically as the U.S. became more industrialized?

16. **Analyze Graphs** Study the graph below. Which crop suffered the sharpest decline after 1866?

Falling Prices of Farm Crops

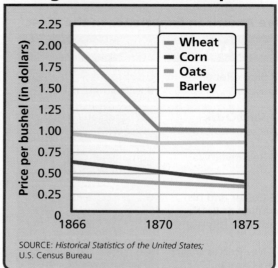

SOURCE: *Historical Statistics of the United States;* U.S. Census Bureau

17. **Writing Activity: Use Primary Sources** Evaluate how Chief Joseph's argument reflects the experience of Native Americans and the clash of cultures in the West during the late 1800s.

> All men were made by the same Great Spirit Chief. They are all brothers. The earth is the mother of all people, and all people should have equal rights upon it. You might as well expect all rivers to run backward as that any man who was born a free man should be contented penned up and denied liberty to go where he pleases. If you tie a horse to a stake, do you expect he will grow fat? If you pen an Indian up on a small spot of earth and compel him to stay there, he will not be contented nor will he grow and prosper. I have asked some of the Great White Chiefs where they get their authority to say to the Indian that he shall stay in one place, while he sees white men going where they please. They cannot tell me.
>
> —*Chief Joseph of the Nez Percés*

DOCUMENT-BASED QUESTIONS

The Populist Movement emerged as America was rapidly moving from an agrarian to an ever more industrialized society. Read the documents below, then answer the questions that follow.

DOCUMENT A

This excerpt is from a speech by the Populist campaigner Mary Elizabeth Lease.

> This is a nation of inconsistencies. The Puritans fleeing from oppression became oppressors. We fought England for our liberty and put chains on four millions of blacks. We wiped out slavery and our tariff laws and national banks began a system of white wage slavery worse than the first. . . . Wall Street owns the country. . . . The West and South are bound and prostrate before the manufacturing East. . . . We will stand by our homes and stay by our fireside by force if necessary, and we will not pay our debts to the loan-shark companies until the government pays its debts to us.
>
> —*Mary Elizabeth Lease*

DOCUMENT B

This illustration was produced by the Grange, an organization formed to support farmers.

I FEED YOU ALL!

DOCUMENT C

This excerpt is from a speech by William Jennings Bryan.

> The man who is employed for wages is as much a businessman as his employer; . . . the merchant at the crossroads store is as much a business man as the merchant of New York; the farmer who goes forth in the morning and toils all day, . . . is as much a business man as the man who goes upon the board of Trade and bets upon the price of grain; the miners who go down a thousand feet into the earth, or climb two thousand feet upon the cliffs, and bring forth from their hiding places the precious metals . . . are as much business men as the few financial magnates who, in a back room, corner the money of the world. We come to speak of this broader class of business men.
>
> —*William Jennings Bryan, Democratic National Convention, 1896*

DOCUMENT D

This excerpt is from a secondary source about Populism.

> As the People's party died, many of the disillusioned dropped out of politics. This is part of the reason the percent of eligible voters to cast ballots in presidential races dropped thirty percent between 1896 and 1924. Others continued the egalitarian struggle by joining Eugene V. Debs in the Socialist party. Many, however, returned to the reform wings of their own parties. Several farmer demands [later] became law, . . . namely monopoly regulation, banking/currency reform, and the graduated income tax. Populists had also advocated direct democracy with reforms such as the initiative and referendum. . . . America, however, adopted Populist reforms selectively and piecemeal. The result was hardly the egalitarian vision of Populism in its heyday.
>
> —*Worth Robert Miller, The Gilded Age: Essays on the Origin of Modern America*

18. In Document A, the country is suffering because of
    - **A.** the government.
    - **B.** the people of the South and West.
    - **C.** tariffs and the banks.
    - **D.** the two-party system.

19. **Analyze Images** What do you think is the political message of the Document B image?

20. In Document C, Bryan's use of repetition is to emphasize that people who are not in business
    - **A.** should be valued as much as businessmen.
    - **B.** should not have the power of businessmen.
    - **C.** control the political system.
    - **D.** should be running the country.

21. **Writing Activity: Primary Source** Write a paragraph explaining whether you think Populism was a product of its time or was addressing issues relevant to other periods of American history.

1 What assumption lay behind the Dawes General Allotment Act, which promoted private property?

  A Native American culture should be preserved.

  B White cultural practices are superior.

  C The land has always belonged to Native Americans.

  D Native Americans would be better land managers if they owned the land.

2 In what way does the photograph above illustrate the impact of population distribution on the physical environment?

  F Mining competed with the transcontinental railroad for workers to transform the physical environment.

  G Damage to the environment caused by large-scale mining prevented the growth of towns in mining regions.

  H Runoff from mining operations polluted the already limited water resources needed by farmers and ranchers.

  I Mining competed for great stretches of grassland that ranchers wanted for grazing and farmers wanted for crops.

3 What does the photograph illustrate about the impact of the physical geography of the Great Plains on the lives of settlers?

A Settlers came to the Great Plains with few possessions and livestock.

B Frequent dust storms meant that the settlers' homes were dark and dingy.

C The lack of trees meant that lumber houses were too expensive for most settlers.

D The distances between homesteads meant that settlers lived isolated lives.

4 Which of the following was an important element in the growth of political machines?

F Tariffs

G Morrill Act

H Spoils system

I Gold standard

If you have trouble with...				
Question	1	2	3	4
See Lesson	2.1	2.2	2.2	2.3

5 Which of the following groups would support the monetary policy that led to the money shown above?

A supporters of flat money

B farmers who favored high inflation

C supporters of the Coinage Act of 1873

D bankers who wanted dollars to be worth more overseas

---

6 Why did the Populist Party call for government ownership of the railroads?

F to protect farmers from exploitation by railroad companies

G to promote Socialism

H to provide cheaper railroad journeys for passengers

I to monitor railroad shipping rates

7 What political position was Social Darwinism used to justify?

    A the imposition of trade barriers

    B the use of public funds to improve the conditions of the urban poor

    C the attempt to regulate trusts

    D the refusal to help the poor

---

8 What does the late nineteenth-century boom in popular entertainment reveal about the effects of industrialization?

    F It was creating more wealth and leisure time.

    G It was creating a grim life that could only be relieved through distractions.

    H It was creating greater diversity in the cities.

    I It was creating a wide range of cheap products.

If you have trouble with...				
Question	5	6	7	8
See Lesson	2.3	2.4	1.2	1.6

[ESSENTIAL QUESTION] What can individuals do to affect society?

③ America Comes of Age

>> Theodore Roosevelt

Enduring Understandings

- At the turn of the century, reformers worked for equality in political rights and economic opportunities in the United States.

- Political organizations dedicated to various causes won significant gains, while several presidents worked to enforce fair business practices and protect the environment.

- In the same period, the United States worked to expand trade and territory around the world.

- The United States emerged as a world power after the Spanish-American War and diplomatic measures with East Asia and Latin America.

Learn about the life of Jane Addams, an important reformer.

Bounce to Activate My Story Video

In this Topic, you'll learn about the decades when America emerged as a World Power. Look at the lesson outline and explore the timeline. As you study this Topic, you'll complete the Quest team project.

LESSON OUTLINE

3.1 Progressives Drive Reform
HSS 11.2.4, HSS 11.2.5, HSS 11.2.7,
HSS 11.2.9, HSS 11.3.1, HSS 11.3.2

3.2 Women Gain Rights
HSS 11.5.4, HSS 11.10.7

3.3 Striving for Equality
HSS 11.2.3; Analysis CST.4

3.4 Reformers in the White House
HSS 11.2.4, HSS 11.2.5, HSS 11.2.9,
HSS 11.6.1, HSS 11.6.5, HSS 11.11.5

3.5 American Influence Grows
HSS 11.2.6, HSS 11.2.7;
Analysis CST.4

3.6 The Spanish-American War
HSS 11.4.2; Analysis CST.4

3.7 The United States Emerges as a World Power
HSS 11.1.4, HSS 11.2.6, HSS 11.4,
HSS 11.4.1, HSS 11.4.2, HSS 11.4.3,
HSS 11.4.4, HSS 11.9.7

America Comes of Age (1890–1920)

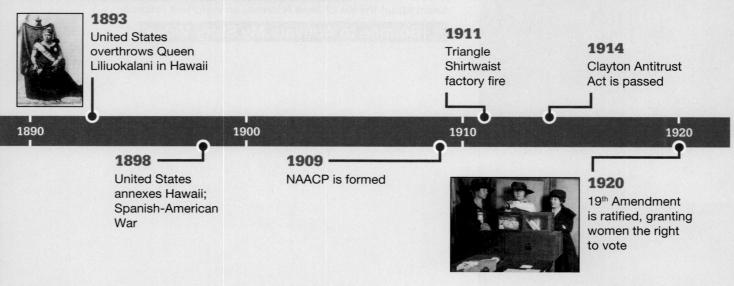

1893
United States overthrows Queen Liliuokalani in Hawaii

1898
United States annexes Hawaii; Spanish-American War

1909
NAACP is formed

1911
Triangle Shirtwaist factory fire

1914
Clayton Antitrust Act is passed

1920
19th Amendment is ratified, granting women the right to vote

1890   1900   1910   1920

QUEST!

Analyzing Historians' Viewpoints on the Spanish-American War

How does historiography influence our view of an event? In this Quest you'll investigate historians' views of the causes, course, and consequences of the Spanish-American War before writing an essay on this subject.

STEP ❶

With your team, watch a video about the Spanish-American War and discuss it with a partner.

STEP ❷

Examine the six sources relating to the U.S. Intervention in Cuba and answer the questions that follow each document.

STEP ❸

Write an essay comparing the historians' viewpoints. Use evidence from the documents and support your argument with facts.

STEP ❹

Reflect on the process of analyzing the documents and writing the essay and then complete the Self-Assessment.

PEARSON
realize™
PearsonSchool.com/CASS

Go **ONLINE** for complete Quest materials

VIDEO   ETEXT   WRITING   RUBRIC   PDF   ASSESSMENT

>> Some child laborers such as these young coal miners endured difficult and dangerous working conditions during the early 1900s.

Bounce to Activate Flipped Video

Industrialization, urbanization, and immigration brought many benefits to America, but they also produced challenging social problems. In response, a movement called Progressivism emerged in the 1890s. Progressives believed that new ideas and honest, efficient government could bring about social justice. Progressive ideas brought lasting reforms that still affect society today.

>> **Objectives**

Identify the causes of Progressivism and compare it to Populism.

Analyze the role that journalists and novelists played in the Progressive Movement.

Evaluate some of the social reforms that Progressives tackled.

Explain what Progressives hoped to achieve through political reforms.

>> **Key Terms**

Progressivism
muckraker
Lincoln Steffens
Jacob Riis
Social Gospel
settlement house
Jane Addams
direct primary
initiative
referendum
recall
Upton Sinclair
Seventeenth
  Amendment

Progressives Drive Reform

The Progressive Era Begins

The people who made up the Progressive Movement came from many walks of life. They came from all political parties, social classes, ethnic groups, and religions. Many Progressive leaders emerged from the growing middle class, whose power and influence was rapidly spreading. Dissatisfied industrial workers also joined the Progressive Movement. So did wealthy Americans driven by a desire to act for the good of society.

Progressive Beliefs and Influences What the Progressives shared in common was a belief that industrialization and urbanization had created troubling social and political problems. Progressives wanted to bring about reforms that would correct what they saw as problems and injustices. They encouraged their state legislatures and the federal government to enact laws to address the issues faced by the poor. Progressives wanted to use logic and reason to make society work in a more efficient and orderly way. Many, motivated by religious faith, sought social justice.

Progressivism was similar to the Populist Movement of the late 1800s. Both were reform movements that wanted to get rid of corrupt government officials and make government more responsive to people's needs. Both sought to eliminate the perceived abuses of big business. Despite these similarities, the two movements differed. At the forefront of Progressivism were middle-class people. They believed that highly educated leaders should use modern ideas and scientific techniques to improve society. Leaders of the Populist Movement, on the other hand, consisted mostly of farmers and workers.

Progressive Goals Some Progressives thought that political reform was the most urgent need. For many women, the number one goal was winning the right to vote. Other Progressives considered honest government to be the most important goal.

Reformers targeted city officials who built corrupt organizations, called political machines. The bosses of these political machines used bribery and violence to influence voters and win elections. They counted on the loyalty of city workers who looked the other way when they took public money for themselves. Bosses also helped people solve personal problems, which often kept voters loyal.

Corrupt and ineffective government combined with the booming growth of cities produced other problems. The people living in America's crowded cities needed paved streets, safe drinking water, decent housing, and adequate municipal services. The lack of adequate services led to wretched living conditions for the urban poor. Too often, dishonest business owners and politicians controlled municipal services. Bribes and shady deals made them rich while conditions for urban residents remained unsafe and little changed.

While some Progressives focused on government, others were worried about big business. As you have learned, wealthy industrialists built huge companies that limited competition and sometimes raised prices. Middle-class Progressives wanted the government to "bust the trusts" and so create more economic opportunities for smaller businesses. Progressives complained that the Sherman Antitrust Act of 1890 was inadequate and ineffective in limiting the abuses of big business. Business leaders, in contrast, argued that big companies produced goods more efficiently and therefore consumers could buy them at lower prices, which benefited everyone. They feared that government regulation would hurt these efficiencies and the economy as a whole.

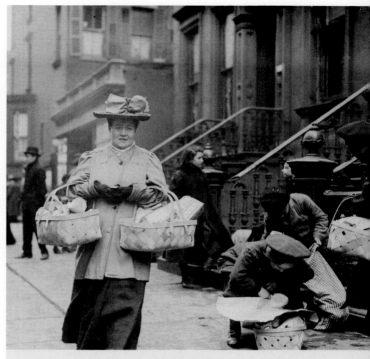

>> During the Progressive Era, volunteers like this one from the Salvation Army helped those less fortunate in many ways.

>> **Analyze Political Cartoons** According to the artist, what is the effect of the street railroad monopoly on the taxpayer?

>> Progressives worried about the unhealthy conditions facing children who lived in urban slums. These children are playing near a dead horse.

Bounce to Activate Illustration

>> Muckrakers such as Nelly Bly wrote news articles that stirred public opinion in favor of Progressive causes.

Other Progressive reformers focused on the class system. Often motivated by religious faith, they sought to reduce the gap between the rich and the poor. They attacked the harsh conditions endured by miners, factory workers, children forced to work, and other laborers. They wanted to improve conditions in city slums. They wanted social welfare laws to help children, workers, and consumers.

☑ **LIST** Which areas of society did Progressive reformers wish to change?

The Impact of Muckrakers

Socially conscious journalists and other writers dramatized the need for reform. Their sensational investigative reports uncovered a wide range of ills afflicting America in the early 1900s. Even though Theodore Roosevelt agreed with much of what they said, he called these writers **muckrakers** because he thought them too fascinated with the ugliest side of things. (A muckrake is a tool used to clean manure and hay out of animals' stables.) The writers were angry at first but in time took up Roosevelt's taunting name as a badge of honor.

The muckrakers' articles appeared in magazines and newspapers that entered millions of American homes. People across the nation were horrified by the conditions that muckrakers revealed. Muckrakers' accounts prompted Americans to push for reforms to correct these ills.

Journalists Uncover Injustices One leading muckraker was **Lincoln Steffens**. He was the managing editor at *McClure's*, a magazine known for uncovering social problems. In 1903, Steffens published *The Shame of the Cities*, a collection of articles on political corruption in the nation's cities. His reports exposed how the government of Philadelphia let utility companies charge their customers excessively high fees. He showed how corrupt politicians won elections by bribing and threatening voters, and revealed how political corruption affected all aspects of life in a city.

> The visitor [to St. Louis] is told of the wealth of the residents, of the financial strength of the banks, and of the growing importance of the industries; yet he sees poorly paved, refuse-burdened streets, and dusty or mud-covered alleys; he passes a

ramshackle firetrap crowded with the sick and learns that it is the City Hospital. . . . Finally, he turns a tap in the hotel to see liquid mud flow into [the] wash basin or bathtub.

—Lincoln Steffens and Claude Wetmore, "Corruption and Reform in St. Louis," *McClure's Magazine*, October 1902

Another influential muckraker was **Jacob Riis**, a photographer for the *New York Evening Sun*. Riis turned his camera on the crowded, unsafe, rat-infested tenement buildings where the urban poor lived. Between 1890 and 1903, he published several works, including *How the Other Half Lives*, that shocked the nation's conscience and led to reforms.

Other outraged writers joined Riis and Steffens. In *The History of Standard Oil*, Ida Tarbell reported that John D. Rockefeller used ruthless methods to ruin his competitors, charge higher prices, and thereby reap huge profits. Some writers proclaimed the need to improve schools or warned of the breakdown of family life because mothers had to work long hours in factories. John Spargo focused attention on the dangerous and difficult lives of child workers.

Novelists Highlight Social Issues Fiction writers put a human face on social problems. They developed a new genre — the naturalist novel — that portrayed human misery and the struggles of common people. Theodore Dreiser, a midwesterner raised in poverty, published *Sister Carrie* in 1900. His provocative novel traces the fate of a small-town girl drawn into the brutal urban worlds of Chicago and New York.

Naturalist novels became very popular. Frank Norris's *The Octopus* fascinated readers by dramatizing the Southern Pacific Railroad's stranglehold on struggling California farmers.

In *The Jungle*, **Upton Sinclair** related the despair of immigrants working in Chicago's stockyards and revealed the unsanitary conditions in the industry. Sinclair's account eventually prompted regulations to protect food safety. African American author Frances Ellen Watkins portrayed the struggles of black Americans in her 1892 novel *Iola Leroy*.

☑ **RECALL** Who were the muckrakers and what did they accomplish?

Reformers Impact Society

The work of the muckrakers increased popular support for Progressivism. Progressive activists

>> Walter Rauschenbusch became the leading proponent of the Social Gospel movement with the publication of his 1907 work *Christianity and the Social Crisis*.

promoted laws to improve living conditions, public health, and schools. They urged government to regulate businesses. They worked as volunteers living among the people they sought to help. They believed that careful social planning would make American life better.

Issues Affecting the Social Gospel Many reformers, like Walter Rauschenbusch, thought that Christianity should be the basis of social reform. A child of German immigrants, Rauschenbusch had become a Baptist minister. He blended ideas from German socialism and American Progressivism to form what he called the **Social Gospel**. By following Bible teachings about charity and justice, he explained, people could make society "the kingdom of God;" that is, make life on earth closer to the promised paradise of heaven by helping others and making the world more just. However, Social Darwinists like William Graham Sumner believed that society was governed by the "survival of the fittest," and opposed the Social Gospel movement.

Many Protestant leaders followed Rauschenbusch's program. Many churches already provided community support and help. Issues such as child labor and long working hours led social

Gospel adherents to call for the end of child labor and a shorter workweek. They also urged the government to limit the power of corporations and trusts.

Jane Addams Contributes to the Settlement House Movement

An important goal of many Progressives, including those influenced by religious ideals, was to improve the lives of poor people in the cities. One approach was the **settlement house**, a community center that provided social services to the urban poor. Most settlement houses were privately funded and run by volunteers, many of whom were women. Quite a few of these women formed long-term same-sex partnerships that became known as "Boston marriages," a term inspired by a couple in Henry James's novel *The Bostonians*. Settlement house workers gave mothers classes in child care and taught English to immigrants. They ran nursery schools and kindergartens.

A woman named **Jane Addams** became a leading figure in the settlement house movement. While visiting Europe, she was inspired by the work at Toynbee Hall, a settlement house in London. In 1889, Addams opened Hull House, a settlement house in Chicago. Over the years, Hull House grew to include 13 buildings. Through Hull House's programs, Addams made significant social and economic contributions to the lives of the local poor.

By educating children and adults, these programs increased their earning power.

Furthermore, the success of Hull House inspired other college-educated, middle-class women to become social workers. By 1911, the country had more than 400 settlement houses. Addams was also politically active. She supported the Progressive party candidacy of Theodore Roosevelt in 1912 and later helped found the American Civil Liberties Union. She worked closely with labor and other reform groups seeking to use political means to improve working conditions for the urban poor.

Using Hull House as a base, Addams also worked for laws regulating labor and tenement houses. In addition, she worked for women's suffrage and world peace, sharing the Nobel Peace Prize in 1931.

Religious organizations such as the Young Men's Christian Association (YMCA) also provided services to the urban poor. In addition to its goal of promoting Christian values, the YMCA offered classes, dances, and sports. Christian missionaries like Dwight L. Moody were very active in the YMCA.

Progressive-Era Issues Affecting Children

Progressives also tried to help children. A lawyer named Florence Kelley helped ban child labor in the state of Illinois, and other states soon passed similar laws. In 1902, Kelley helped form the National Child Labor Committee, which successfully lobbied

Improvements for Children in the Progressive Era

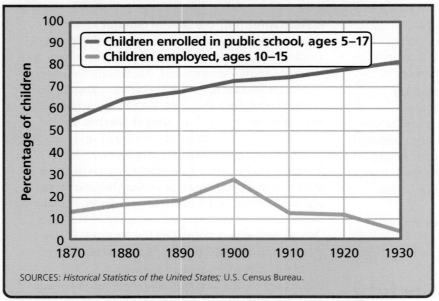

SOURCES: *Historical Statistics of the United States;* U.S. Census Bureau.

>> **Analyze Information** How did child labor laws affect children's employment levels during the Progressive Era?

the federal government to create the U.S. Children's Bureau in 1912. This new agency examined any issue that affected the health and welfare of children. The agency still works to protect children today.

But progress in children's rights had a long way to go. In 1916, Congress passed the Keating-Owens Act, which banned child labor in all states. However, two years later, the Supreme Court ruled the law unconstitutional. It was not until 1938 that Congress would end child labor for good.

Progressives also tried to better children's lives by improving education. A number of states passed laws that required children to attend school until a certain age. However, there were heated debates about what children should learn and how they should learn. Some argued that they should be taught only work skills. Others said they should learn to appreciate literature and music. Most educators agreed that girls should learn different things from boys.

Educator John Dewey criticized American schools for teaching children to memorize facts but not to think creatively. Dewey wanted schools to teach new subjects such as history and geography, as well as practical skills like cooking and carpentry. His ideas were not adopted at once, but in later years, many states put them into effect.

Reforms in the Workplace In the early 1900s, the United States had the highest rate of industrial accidents in the world. Long hours, poor ventilation, hazardous fumes, and unsafe machinery threatened not only workers' health but also their lives. Each year some thirty thousand workers died on the job, while another half a million were injured.

In March 1911, a fire at the Triangle Shirtwaist Factory in New York City shocked Americans and focused attention on the need to protect workers. Workers in the factory had little chance to escape the raging fire because managers had locked most of the exits. The fire killed 146 workers, most of them young Jewish women. Many jumped from the windows in desperation. Inside the smoldering ruins, firefighters found many more victims, "skeletons bending over sewing machines."

After the blaze, outraged Progressives intensified their calls for reform. New York passed laws to make workplaces safer, and other cities and states followed suit. Many states also adopted workers' compensation laws, which set up funds to pay workers who were hurt on the job.

Progressives also persuaded some states to pass laws limiting the workday to ten hours. However, their efforts suffered a blow in 1905 when the Supreme Court ruled in *Lochner* v. *New York* that such laws

>> Jane Addams founded one of the nation's first settlement houses, Hull House, in 1889. Here, she sits with a group of children visiting Hull House in 1935.

>> Firefighters fought to extinguish the catastrophic Triangle Shirtwaist Fire. **Draw Conclusions** How did accidents like this fire at the Triangle Shirtwaist Factory in 1911 lead to improvements in working conditions?

Bounce to Activate Gallery

were unconstitutional. Until the 1930s, the court ruled against many labor laws, but Progressives continued to work towards the goal of protecting workers.

☑ **RECALL** How did Progressives work to help the urban poor?

Progressive Reforms Impact Government

Progressive reformers sought to reform the political process in order to reform society. They wanted to free government from the control of political bosses and powerful business interests. They wanted to give people more control over their government and make government more effective and efficient in serving the public.

Reformers Change City Government Just as the Triangle Shirtwaist Factory fire spurred reformers to action, so did another disaster. In 1900, a massive hurricane left the city of Galveston, Texas, in ruins. One of the greatest national calamities in American history, the hurricane killed more than 8,000 people. As an emergency measure, Galveston replaced its mayor and board of aldermen with a five-person

>> The Galveston Hurricane of 1900 destroyed countless structures, such as this public school.

commission. Each commissioner was an expert in a different area of city affairs, such as public safety or streets and sewers, and headed the departments responsible for that area.

The commission form of government proved very efficient as the city carried out a tremendous rebuilding effort. The following year, Galveston decided to permanently adopt the commission form of government.

Known as the Galveston plan, many other cities decided to take up the commission form of government. By 1918, nearly 500 cities had adopted some form of the Galveston plan. Dayton, Ohio, and other cities modified the plan by empowering the city council or commission to hire a professional city manager to oversee all of city government. The new city governments curbed the power of bosses and their political machines. The reform governments purchased public utilities so that electric, gas, and water companies could not charge city residents unfairly high rates.

Progressive Reforms Impact Political Process
Progressives also pushed for election reforms, taking up some Populist ideas. Traditionally, party leaders picked candidates for state and local offices.

But in Wisconsin, reform governor Robert M. La Follette established a **direct primary,** an election in which citizens themselves vote to select nominees for upcoming elections. By 1916, all but four states had direct primaries.

Progressives also wanted to make sure that elected officials would follow citizens' wishes. To achieve this goal, they worked for three other political reforms: the initiative, the referendum, and the recall. The **initiative** gave people the power to put a proposed new law directly on the ballot in the next election by collecting citizens' signatures on a petition. This meant that voters themselves could suggest laws instead of waiting for elected officials to act. The **referendum** allowed citizens to approve or reject laws passed by a legislature. The **recall** gave voters the power to remove public servants from office before their terms ended.

Progressives won yet another political reform: They adopted the Populist call for the direct election of senators by voters, not state legislators.

Progressives believed that Americans should choose their own senators rather than allowing state legislatures to do so. Several states already held elections in which voters advised their legislature about which person to name, although states formally retained this decision under the U.S. Constitution. However, the proposed reform was

PROGRESSIVES AND ELECTION REFORMS

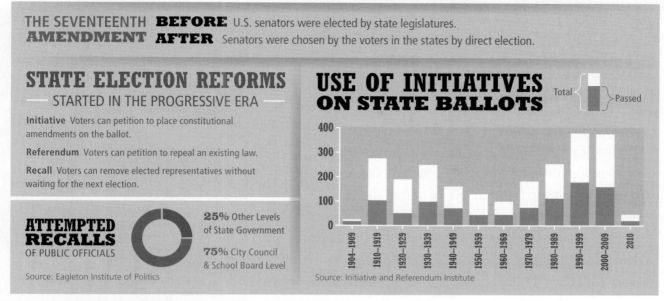

THE SEVENTEENTH AMENDMENT **BEFORE** U.S. senators were elected by state legislatures. **AFTER** Senators were chosen by the voters in the states by direct election.

STATE ELECTION REFORMS
— STARTED IN THE PROGRESSIVE ERA —

Initiative Voters can petition to place constitutional amendments on the ballot.

Referendum Voters can petition to repeal an existing law.

Recall Voters can remove elected representatives without waiting for the next election.

ATTEMPTED RECALLS OF PUBLIC OFFICIALS

25% Other Levels of State Government

75% City Council & School Board Level

Source: Eagleton Institute of Politics

USE OF INITIATIVES ON STATE BALLOTS

Total | Passed

Source: Initiative and Referendum Institute

>> **Analyze Information** What was the most significant Progressive election reform? Cite two pieces of information to support your answer.

not universally popular. Some members of Congress argued that direct election would weaken the states' power to block actions of the federal government, an important constitutional check. With the support of 31 state legislatures, however, Congress passed a constitutional amendment to enact this change in 1911. The states ratified the **Seventeenth Amendment** two years later.

States Lead the Progressive Movement

Dynamic Progressives became the leaders of several states, and chief among them was Robert La Follette of Wisconsin. Elected governor in 1900, "Fighting Bob" won the passage of many reform laws. Under his leadership, the Wisconsin state government forced railroads to charge lower fees and pay higher taxes. La Follette helped his state to improve education, make factories safer, and adopt the direct primary. Progressives called Wisconsin the "laboratory of democracy."

Hiram Johnson, governor of California, shattered the Southern Pacific Railroad's stranglehold on state government. He put in place the direct primary, initiative, referendum, and recall. He also pushed for another goal of some Progressives—planning for the careful use of natural resources such as water, forests, and wildlife.

Other Progressive governors included Theodore Roosevelt of New York and Woodrow Wilson of New Jersey. Roosevelt worked to develop a fair system for hiring state workers and made some corporations pay taxes. Wilson reduced the railroads' power and pushed for a direct primary law. Both Roosevelt and Wilson later became President and brought reforms to the White House.

☑ **CHECK UNDERSTANDING** How did Progressive reformers change local and state governments?

☑ ASSESSMENT

1. **Compare and Contrast** the Populist and Progressive movements.

2. **Summarize** the ways in which Progressives tried to help children.

3. **Generate Explanations** How did the development of settlement houses affect urban American society?

4. **Identify Cause and Effect** Explain how the Triangle Shirtwaist Factory fire affected workers' rights.

5. **Draw Conclusions** How did muckrakers influence efforts to enact social reform?

How the Other Half Lives: Jacob Riis

Jacob Riis immigrated to the United States from Denmark in 1870. After living for several years in extreme poverty, he found a job as a police reporter for the *New York Tribune*. He became one of the leading muckrakers of the Progressive Era. Riis's writing and photographs helped expose the harsh living conditions in the crowded tenements of New York City. This excerpt is from Riis's 1890 book, *How the Other Half Lives*.

>> A tenement of the late 1800s

The problem of the children becomes, in these swarms, to the last degree perplexing. Their very number make one stand aghast [horrified]. I have already given instances of the packing of the child population in East Side tenements. They might be continued indefinitely until the array [orderly arrangement] would be enough to startle any community. For, be it remembered, these children with the training they receive—or do not receive— with the instincts they inherit and absorb in their growing up, are to be our future rulers, if our theory of government is worth anything. More than a working majority of our voters now register from the tenements.

☑ **DETERMINE CENTRAL IDEAS** According to Riis, why should all Americans be concerned about tenement children?

I counted the other day the little ones, up to ten years or so, in a Bayard Street tenement that for a yard has a triangular space in the center with sides fourteen or fifteen feet long, just room enough for a row of ill-smelling closets [toilets] at the base of the triangle and a hydrant at the apex [highest point]. There was about as much light in this "yard" as in the average cellar. I gave up my self-imposed task in despair when I had counted one hundred and twenty-eight in forty families.

☑ **SUMMARIZE** What is the tenement like on Bayard Street that Riis describes?

Bodies of drowned children turn up in the rivers right along since summer whom no one seems to know anything about. When last spring some workmen, while moving a pile of lumber on a North River pier, found under the last plank the body of a little lad crushed to death, no one had missed a boy, though his parents afterward turned up. The truant [a pupil who misses school without permission] officer assuredly does not know, though he spends his life trying to find out, somewhat illogically, perhaps, since the department that employs him admits that thousands of poor children are crowded out of the schools year by year for want of room.

☑ **SUMMARIZE** What is Riis's complaint about the education received by tenement children?

The law has done what it could. That was not always a great deal, seldom more than barely sufficient for the moment. An aroused municipal conscience endowed the Health Department with almost autocratic powers in dealing with this subject, but the desire to educate rather than force the community into a better way dictated their exercise with a slow conservatism that did not always seem wise to the impatient reformer. . . Tenements quite as bad as the worst are too numerous yet; but one tremendous factor for evil in the lives of the poor has been taken by the throat, and something has unquestionably been done, where that was possible, to lift those lives out of the rut where they were equally beyond the reach of hope and of ambition. It is no longer lawful to construct barracks to cover the whole of a lot. Air and sunlight have a legal claim, and the day of rear tenements is past. Two years ago a hundred thousand people burrowed in these inhuman dens; but some have been torn down since. Their number will decrease steadily until they shall have become a bad tradition of a heedless past. The dark, unventilated bedroom is going with them, and the open sewer. The day is at hand when the greatest of all evils that now curse life in the tenements—the dearth of water in the hot summer days—will also have been remedied, and a long step taken toward the moral and physical redemption of their tenants.

☑ SUMMARIZE Why has the problem of overcrowded tenements begun to change?

The sea of a mighty population, held in galling fetters, heaves uneasily in the tenements. Once already our city, to which have come the duties and responsibilities of metropolitan greatness before it was able to fairly measure its task, has felt the swell of its resistless flood. If it rise once more, no human power may avail to check it. The gap between the classes in which it surges, unseen, unsuspected by the thoughtless, is widening day by day. No tardy enactment of law, no political expedient, can close it. Against all other dangers our system of government may offer defence and shelter; against this not. I know of but one bridge that will carry us over safe, a bridge founded upon justice and built of human hearts. I believe that the danger of such conditions as are fast growing up around us is greater for the very freedom which they mock. The words of the poet, with whose lines I prefaced this book, are truer to-day, have far deeper meaning to us, than when they were penned forty years ago:

"—Think ye that building shall endure
Which shelters the noble and crushes the poor?"

☑ ASSESSMENT

1. **Identify Supporting Details** What details in this excerpt may have shocked readers of the time? Why do you think muckrakers sought to shock their audience?

2. **Determine Meaning** To whom does the "Other Half" in the title refer? Why do you think Riis uses this phrase?

3. **Identify Cause and Effect** How do you think Riis's account might have contributed to social reforms for tenement housing?

>> Women often used protests to demand suffrage. **Draw Conclusions** Why did activists in the women's suffrage movement draw criticism from some groups of American women?

Bounce to Activate Flipped Video

3.2 In the early 1900s, a growing number of women were no longer content to have a limited role in society. Women activists helped bring about Progressive reforms and won the right to vote. In the years ahead, women would continue the struggle to expand their roles and rights.

>> Objectives

Analyze actions taken by women to address social issues affecting workers and families.

Explain actions taken during the Progressive era to expand opportunities for women, including the right to vote.

Evaluate the tactics reform leaders used to win passage of the Nineteenth Amendment.

>> Key Terms

Florence Kelley
National Consumers
 League (NCL)
temperance
 movement
Margaret Sanger
Ida B. Wells
Carrie Chapman
 Catt
National American
 Woman Suffrage
 Association
 (NAWSA)
Alice Paul

Nineteenth
 Amendment
Frances Willard
suffrage
Susan B. Anthony

Women Gain Rights

Expanding Opportunities for Women

In the early 1900s, more middle-class women wanted to do more than fulfill their roles as wives and mothers. They were ready to do other tasks besides the important ones of raising children, cooking meals, cleaning the home, and caring for family members. They wanted to expand their role in the community.

Education helped many women achieve their goals. By the 1890s, a rising number of women's colleges prepared them for careers as teachers or nurses. Some, such as Bryn Mawr College in Pennsylvania and the School of Social Work in New York, trained them to lead the new organizations working for social reform. The number of women attending college jumped. By 1900, one third of all college students, nationwide, were women. By attending college, women expanded their own economic opportunities. Armed with education and modern ideas, many middle-class white women began to tackle problems they saw in society.

Economic and Social Issues for Women Working-class women had worked outside of the home for decades, taking difficult jobs with long hours and dangerous conditions. They were usually expected to hand over their wages to their husbands, fathers, or brothers. Many women labored in factories that made cigars or clothing. Others toiled as laundresses or servants. Immigrants, African Americans, and women from rural areas filled these jobs, and most of them had little or no education.

As a result, they could easily be cheated or bullied by their employers. Without being able to vote, women had little influence on the politicians who could look after their interests.

Addressing Economic Issues A key goal of women reformers was to limit the number of work hours. They succeeded in several states. For example, a 1903 Oregon law capped women's workdays at ten hours. Five years later, in *Muller* v. *Oregon*, the Supreme Court reviewed that law. Lawyer Louis D. Brandeis argued that long working hours harmed working women and their families.

The Supreme Court agreed with Brandeis. Based on their role as mothers, it said, women could be "properly placed in a class" by themselves. As a result, laws could limit their work hours, even if similar laws would not be allowed for men. At the time, Progressives viewed this decision as a victory for women workers. In later years, however, this ruling was used to justify paying women less than men for the same job.

Florence Kelley believed that women were hurt by unfair prices for goods they had to buy to run their homes. In 1899, she helped found the **National Consumers League (NCL),** which is still active today. The NCL gave special labels to "goods produced under fair, safe, and healthy working conditions" and urged women to buy them and avoid products that did not have these labels. The NCL pushed for other reforms as well. It backed laws calling for the government to inspect meatpacking plants, to make workplaces safer, and to make payments to the unemployed.

Florence Kelley also helped form the Women's Trade Union League (WTUL), another group that tried to improve conditions for female factory workers. It was one of the few groups in which upper-class and working-class women served together as leaders. The WTUL pushed for federal laws that set a minimum wage and an eight-hour workday. It also created the first workers' strike fund, which could be used to help support families who refused to work in unsafe or unfair conditions.

Women Address Social Issues A main goal of Progressive women was to improve family life. They pushed for laws that could help mothers keep families healthy and safe. One focus of this

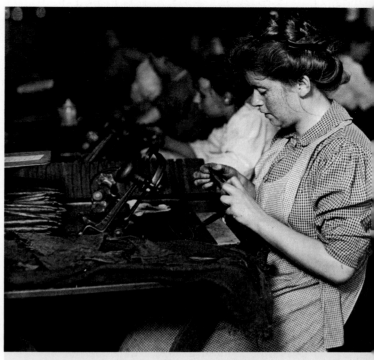

>> Like their male counterparts, women workers, like these women in a cigar factory near Pittsburgh, Pennsylvania, struggled with unpleasant and sometimes unhealthy working conditions.

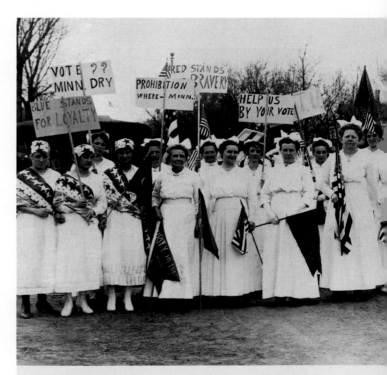

>> Women protested the production and sale of alcohol to generate support for the Eighteenth Amendment.

effort was the **temperance movement** led by the Women's Christian Temperance Union (WCTU). The WCTU, along with other groups such as the Anti-Saloon League promoted temperance, the practice of never drinking alcohol. Members felt that alcohol often led men to squander their earnings on liquor and neglect or abuse their families. Formed in the 1870s, the WCTU gained strength during the Progressive Era. The WCTU was led by the influential speaker **Frances Willard** from 1879 until her death in 1898. Her work contributed to the passage of the Eighteenth Amendment in 1919, which outlawed the production and sale of alcohol.

Temperance was Willard's primary goal, but she also supported women's **suffrage**—the right to vote. She argued that women needed the vote to prohibit the sale of alcohol. Like many WCTU members, Willard also promoted other social causes, such as public health and welfare reform.

Nurse **Margaret Sanger** thought that family life and women's health would improve if mothers had fewer children. In 1916, Sanger, herself one of 11 children, opened the country's first birth-control clinic. Very controversial at the time, Sanger was jailed several times as a "public nuisance" for distributing information about birth control. But federal courts eventually said doctors could give out information about family planning. In 1921, Sanger founded the American Birth Control League to make this information available to more women.

African American women also worked for social change. In 1896, **Ida B. Wells**, an African American teacher and journalist, helped form the National Association of Colored Women (NACW). Wells was well-known for leading an anti-lynching campaign through her writing and speaking tours. The NACW's goal was to help families strive for success and to assist those who were less fortunate. With money raised from educated black women, the NACW set up daycare centers to protect and educate black children while their parents went to work.

☑ **RECALL** What steps did women take to win workers' rights?

Women Seek Equal Political Rights

One of the boldest goals of Progressive women was suffrage. They argued that women participating in the democratic process through voting was the only way to make sure that the government would protect children, foster education, and support family life. As Jane Addams explained, women needed the vote because political issues reached inside people's homes.

> If the street is not cleaned by the city authorities no amount of private sweeping will keep the tenement free from grime; if the garbage is not properly collected and destroyed a tenement-house mother may see her children sicken and die of diseases from which she alone is powerless to shield them, although her tenderness and devotion are unbounded.
>
> She cannot even secure untainted meat for her household, . . . unless the meat has been inspected by city officials.
>
> —Jane Addams, *Ladies Home Journal*, 1910

>> Ida B. Wells, who was born into slavery, became a prominent Progressive activist promoting freedom from violence and equal opportunities for African Americans.

Bounce to Activate Gallery

Major Organizations of the Progressive Era With High Female Participation

NCL	National Consumers League	The nation's oldest consumer advocacy organization; it represents consumers on marketplace and workplace issues.
WTUL	Women's Trade Union League	The WTUL strove to reform working conditions by supporting women in labor unions and strikes.
WCTU	Women's Christian Temperance Union	The WCTU conducted "Women's Crusades" to "agitate, educate, and legislate" against the destructive power of alcohol.
NACW	National Association of Colored Women	The NACW promoted the moral, mental, and material progress by women of color, through women's suffrage and education.
NAWSA	National American Woman Suffrage Association	The NAWSA lobbied for state suffrage amendments that would lead to a federal amendment.
NAOWS	National Association Opposed to Woman Suffrage	Until passage of the 19th Amendment, the NAOWS argued that woman suffrage would impede women from making social changes.
NWP	National Woman's Party	Grown out of the NAWSA, the NWP used more militant methods to enfranchise women nationally.
NAACP	National Association for the Advancement of Colored People	The NAACP aims to educate citizens on civil rights, eliminate race prejudice, and ensure political, educational, social, and economic equality.

>> **Hypothesize** Why would an organization such as NAOWS oppose woman suffrage?

The Early Fight for a Constitutional Amendment Since the 1850s, reformers such as **Susan B. Anthony** and Elizabeth Cady Stanton had tirelessly struggled for the right for women to have a voice in political issues. Although Anthony and other women's right activists had favored ending slavery, they felt betrayed when Radical Republicans did not include women in the Fourteenth and Fifteenth amendments.

In 1869, Anthony and Stanton formed the National Woman Suffrage Association to fight for a constitutional amendment that would grant women the right to vote. They argued that just as the Constitution had been amended to extend the vote to African Americans, it should be amended to extend the vote to women.

In 1872, Anthony voted in an election in Rochester, New York, an illegal act for which she was tried and ultimately convicted in federal court. While awaiting trial, she toured the nation, delivering a speech titled "Is It a Crime for a Citizen of the United States to Vote?" Anthony declared, "Our . . . government is based on . . . the natural right of every individual member . . . to a voice and a vote in making and executing the laws." However, her speech failed to convince the nation to enact a women's suffrage amendment. An amendment was introduced in Congress and rejected in 1887. By the time of Anthony's death in 1906, only four western states—Wyoming, Utah, Colorado, and Idaho—had granted women the right to vote.

Women Lobby for Expanded Rights In the 1890s, the national suffrage effort was reenergized by **Carrie Chapman Catt**. Catt had studied law and worked as one of the country's first female school superintendents.

A captivating speaker, Catt traveled around the country urging women to join the **National American Woman Suffrage Association (NAWSA)**, created in 1890 by the merger of Anthony's organization and a rival women's suffrage group. In 1900, Catt became the president of the NAWSA. She promoted what became known as her "winning plan," which called for action on two fronts to expand women's right to participate in the democratic process. Some teams of women lobbied Congress to pass a constitutional amendment giving women the right to vote. Meanwhile, other teams used the new referendum process to try to pass state suffrage laws. The strategy at the state level eventually helped women win the right to vote in New York, Michigan, and Oklahoma.

Catt introduced a "society plan" to recruit wealthy, well-educated women. She and her army of workers signed on women from all levels of society, including African Americans, Mexican Americans, and Jewish immigrants. All these women, called "suffragettes," helped promote suffrage in their own areas.

Activists Use Nonviolent Protests By 1910, as Progressivism was nearing its height, the women's suffrage movement was growing stronger too. A new generation of leaders had emerged. Besides Catt, they included Jane Addams and Harriet Stanton Blatch, the daughter of Elizabeth Cady Stanton. The movement's new leaders expanded its goals to include calls for improvements in education, reforms of corrupt government, and labor reforms such as the passage of child labor laws. These activists presented suffrage as not only an expansion of the democratic process but also as a way to help solve many of society's other ills.This strategy linked the women's suffrage movement with the powerful wave of Progressive reform.

The suffrage movement's new goals also helped it grow by making it more appealing to working women. The rising number of college-educated women flooded into the movement as well. Some women, known as social activists, took to the streets, organizing mass parades and rallies. Catt, while cautious about these new methods, added them to her tactics at the NAWSA. Some women social activists grew even more daring in their strategies to win the vote.

Alice Paul, their best known leader, was raised in a Quaker home where she was encouraged to be independent. Paul attended a Quaker college and

the New York School of Social Work before earning a Ph.D. from the University of Pennsylvania in 1912. She believed that drastic steps were needed to win the vote. By 1913, she was organizing women to recruit others across the nation. They drew in women of many backgrounds, from Maud Younger, known as the "millionaire waitress" because she organized California's first waitresses' union, to Nina Otero-Warren, a Hispanic woman who headed New Mexico's State Board of Health.

By 1917, Paul had formed the National Woman's Party (NWP), which used public protest marches. The NWP became the first group to march with picket signs outside the White House. Hundreds of women were arrested in these protests. Some went on hunger strikes, stating that they would not eat until they could vote. While in jail, some women, including Paul, were force-fed to end their hunger strikes. The NWP methods angered many people, including women in other suffrage groups. Nevertheless, they did help women the right to vote because the NWP's actions drew attention to their cause and made less-radical groups like the NAWSA look tame by comparison.

The Nineteenth Amendment Expands Political Rights In the 1916 presidential election, both the Democratic and the Republican parties called

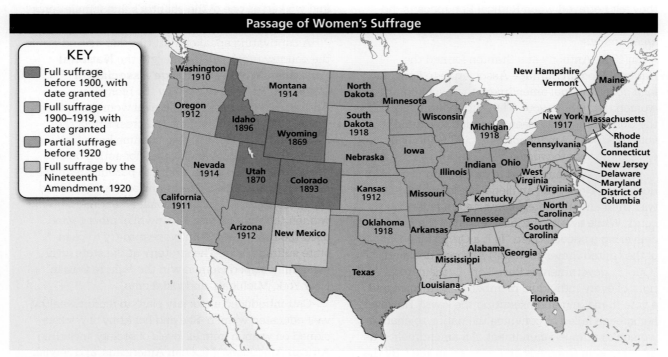

Passage of Women's Suffrage

KEY
- Full suffrage before 1900, with date granted
- Full suffrage 1900–1919, with date granted
- Partial suffrage before 1920
- Full suffrage by the Nineteenth Amendment, 1920

Washington 1910
Montana 1914
North Dakota
Minnesota
Oregon 1912
Idaho 1896
South Dakota 1918
Wisconsin
New Hampshire
Vermont
Maine
New York 1917
Massachusetts
Wyoming 1869
Michigan 1918
Rhode Island
Connecticut
Nevada 1914
Utah 1870
Colorado 1893
Nebraska
Iowa
Indiana
Ohio
Pennsylvania
New Jersey
Delaware
California 1911
Kansas 1912
Missouri
Illinois
West Virginia
Virginia
Maryland
District of Columbia
Kentucky
North Carolina
Arizona 1912
New Mexico
Oklahoma 1918
Arkansas
Tennessee
South Carolina
Texas
Mississippi
Alabama
Georgia
Louisiana
Florida

>> **Analyze Maps** In which region of the United States did the majority of states achieve full suffrage for women before the passage of the Nineteenth Amendment?

for extending the right to vote to women. As the movement gained support, however, opposition to it also increased. The liquor industry strongly opposed women's suffrage because of women's support for temperance. The textile industry also opposed suffrage because it feared women would favor laws limiting child labor. Even some women worked against the movement. The National Association Opposed to Woman Suffrage (NAOWS) believed that the effort to win the vote would take women's attention away from family and volunteer work that benefited society in many ways. But as pressure for women's suffrage grew, the NAOWS faded away.

When the United States entered World War I in April 1917, President Woodrow Wilson proclaimed that "the world must be made safe for democracy." Suffragists were astounded.

How could America be a democracy, they wondered, if women could not vote? Nevertheless, Carrie Catt and Florence Kelley led the NAWSA to support the war effort. Their actions and those of the NWP convinced a growing number of legislators to support a women's suffrage amendment.

In June 1917, envoys from Russia visited President Wilson. Alice Paul and her activists saw a golden opportunity. The Russians had just overthrown their czar, established a republic, and granted women the right to vote. As the envoys neared the White House, the suffragists stunned an embarrassed Wilson by unveiling a banner that proclaimed America was not a democracy. In 1918, an amendment to extend the vote to women was once again considered by Congress. It passed in the House of Representatives but was narrowly rejected in the Senate.

The following year, the amendment was offered in Congress once again. In June 1919, Congress finally approved the **Nineteenth Amendment,** which stated that the right to vote "shall not be denied or abridged on account of sex."

On August 18, 1920, the Tennessee State House of Representatives passed the amendment by one vote. With Tennessee's ratification, enough states had passed the amendment that it became official. Alice Paul and Carrie Catt both claimed responsibility for the victory. In fact, according to historian Nancy Cott, "neither the shocking militancy of the National Women's Party nor the ladylike moderation of NAWSA was so solely responsible for victory as each group publicly claimed." The rival groups both contributed to the triumph of the women's suffrage movement, which also gave a boost to the budding civil rights movement of the twentieth century. The impact of the Nineteenth Amendment was felt immediately.

>> Women who protested their lack of suffrage often landed in jail, where they continued to protest despite the limitations of their environment.

Bounce to Activate Timeline

>> Millions of women voted for the first time after the passage of the Nineteenth Amendment prohibited states from denying the right to vote based on sex.

On November 2, 1920, Catt, Paul, and millions of other American women voted for the first time in a U.S. presidential election.

☑ **CHECK UNDERSTANDING** How did the Nineteenth Amendment expand participation in the democratic process?

☑ ASSESSMENT

1. **Generate Explanations** Explain how *Muller v. Oregon* represented a victory for women reformers during the Progressive Era but presented a setback for them in later years.

2. **Determine Point of View** Explain why some women's rights activists were angry when the rights of African Americans were expanded after the Civil War.

3. **Summarize** Discuss the strategies of Carrie Chapman Catt's "winning plan."

4. **Generate Explanations** Explain how the women's suffrage movement changed with the rise of Progressivism.

5. **Compare and Contrast** the strategies of the National American Woman Suffrage Association and the National Woman's Party.

Prejudice and discrimination against minorities continued even as the Progressive Movement got underway. But in the spirit of Progressivism, African Americans, Latinos, Catholics, Jews, and new immigrant groups worked to help themselves. Their efforts paved the way for the era of civil rights that would follow decades later.

>> Segregation remained common throughout the Progressive Era. This one-room school in Anthoston, Kentucky, was for African Americans only. Many students are absent to harvest tobacco.

Bounce to Activate Flipped Video

Striving for Equality

Minorities Face Challenges in the Progressive Era

The Progressive Era was not so progressive for nonwhite and immigrant Americans. Most Progressives were white Anglo-Saxon Protestant reformers who were indifferent or actively hostile to minorities. They tried to make the United States a model society by encouraging everyone to follow white, middle-class ways of life.

The Americanization Movement Settlement houses and other civic groups played a prominent role in the **Americanization** efforts of many Progressives. While they taught immigrants English, their programs also tried to change how immigrants lived. They advised immigrants how to dress like white middle-class Americans and pushed them to replace the foods and customs of their homelands with Protestant practices and values. These reformers believed that assimilating immigrants into American society would make them more loyal and moral citizens.

Many Progressives found the immigrants' use of alcohol especially alarming. In many European countries, it was customary for families to serve wine or beer with meals. Many reformers, however, believed that these practices showed moral

>> **Objectives**

Analyze Progressives' attitudes toward minority rights.

Describe the political organizations formed by African Americans to promote civil rights.

Examine the actions taken by other minority groups to expand their rights.

>> **Key Terms**

Americanization
Booker T.
  Washington
W.E.B. Du Bois
Niagara Movement
National Association
  for the
  Advancement of
  Colored People
  (NAACP)
Urban League
Anti-Defamation
  League
mutualistas

American Indian
  Citizenship Act of
  1924
Anti-Defamation
  League

faults. As a result, prejudice against immigrants was one of the forces behind the temperance movement.

Effects of Racism and *Plessy* v. *Ferguson* Many Progressives shared the same prejudice against nonwhites held by other white Americans of the time. They believed that some people were more fit than others to play a leading role in society. They agreed with invalid scientific theories that said that dark-skinned peoples had less intelligence than whites. In the late 1800s, southern Progressives used these misguided theories to justify the passage of laws that kept African Americans from voting.

Some southern Progressives urged an end to the violence and terrorism waged against African Americans but still did not advocate equal rights. Edgar Gardner Murphy, an Episcopal minister and a leading Alabama Progressive, advised that African Americans "will accept in the white man's country the place assigned him by the white man, . . . not by stress of rivalry, but by genial cooperation with the white man's interests."

After the Supreme Court issued its *Plessy* v. *Ferguson* decision, which upheld Jim Crow laws, states across the North and the South had passed segregation laws. By 1910, segregation was the norm across the nation. After 1914, even the offices of the federal government in Washington, D.C., were segregated as a result of policies approved by President Woodrow Wilson, a Progressive.

☑️ **CHECK UNDERSTANDING** What attitudes did most Progressives hold about minorities and immigrant groups?

African Americans Promote Civil Rights

In the face of these injustices, the nation's most visible African American leader urged patience. **Booker T. Washington** told blacks to move slowly toward racial progress. By working hard and waiting patiently, he believed, African Americans would gradually win white Americans' respect and eventually would be able to exercise their full voting and citizenship rights.

Other African Americans rejected this view. The most outspoken among them were **W.E.B. Du Bois** and William Monroe Trotter. Both men had been raised in New England and educated at Harvard University. Both urged African Americans to demand immediately all the rights guaranteed by the Constitution.

A New Civil Rights Organization Du Bois and Trotter were especially concerned that all across the South, black men were being denied the right to vote. In the summer of 1905, they and other leading African American thinkers met at Niagara Falls. They had to meet in Canada because no hotel on the New York side of the border would give them rooms.

The **Niagara Movement,** as the group called itself, denounced the idea of gradual progress. Washington, they said, was too willing to compromise African Americans' basic rights. They also condemned his notion of teaching only trade skills. This kind of education, Du Bois said, "can create workers, but it cannot make *men*." Talented blacks should be taught history, literature, and philosophy, so they could think for themselves. DuBois had a significant impact on the ways African Americans and concerned white people thought about equality.

Two Views on Civil Rights

BOOKER T. WASHINGTON 1856–1915	W.E.B. DU BOIS 1868–1963
"[The Negro must] live peaceably with his white neighbors ... the Negro [must] deport himself modestly ... depending upon the slow but sure influences that proceed from the possessions of property, intelligence, and high character for the full recognition of his political rights."	"We claim for ourselves every single right that belongs to a freeborn American ... and until we get these rights we will never cease to protest ... How shall we get them? By voting where we may vote, by persistent, unceasing agitation, by hammering at the truth, by sacrifice and work."
Washington believed that African Americans had to achieve economic independence before civil rights. Black people must tolerate discrimination while they proved themselves equal to white people. Slowly, civil rights would come.	Du Bois believed that black Americans had to demand their social and civil rights or else become permanent victims of racism. African Americans must fight every day for the rights given to them in the Constitution.

>> **Analyze Information** How did the views of these two leaders on the ways in which African Americans should secure civil rights differ?

 Bounce to Activate Timeline

NAACP Promotes Civil Rights In the summer of 1908, a white mob in Springfield, Illinois, attempted to lynch two African American prisoners in the city jail. Upon learning that the prisoners had been removed to safety, the rioters turned their anger against the city's black residents, killing two people and burning 40 homes. The Niagara Movement members were outraged that such an attack could happen in Abraham Lincoln's hometown.

The Springfield riot also got the attention of a number of white reformers. They now acknowledged the need to help African Americans protect their lives, win the right to vote, and secure their civil rights. In 1909, several white reformers joined with leaders of the Niagara Movement to form the **National Association for the Advancement of Colored People (NAACP).** The NAACP was a political organization that aimed to help African Americans be "physically free from peonage [forced, low-paid labor], mentally free from ignorance, politically free from disfranchisement, and socially free from insult."

NAACP leaders included white and black Progressives who had worked in other areas of social reform. Among them were Jane Addams, Ray Stannard Baker, and Florence Kelley. Ida B. Wells, owner of a Tennessee newspaper, used her publication to make clear the horror of lynching at great risk to her own safety. She and the others planned the group's strategy—to use litigation in the courts to challenge unfair laws and expand the right to participate in the democratic process. In the early 1900s, the NAACP focused on the battle for equal access to decent housing and professional careers like teaching. It drew strength from members like W.E.B. DuBois, who edited the NAACP's magazine, *The Crisis*, and the lawyer, teacher, and former diplomat James Weldon Johnson.

Urban League Seeks to Expand Economic Opportunities Across the country, African Americans were migrating from rural to urban areas during this period. Local black clubs and churches set up employment agencies and relief efforts to help African Americans get settled and find work.

In 1911, more than 100 of these groups in many cities joined into a network called the **Urban League.** While the NAACP helped middle-class blacks struggle for political and social justice, the Urban League focused on poorer workers. It helped families buy clothes and books and send children to school. It also helped factory workers and domestic servants find jobs. Both the NAACP and the Urban League still aid African Americans today.

>> W.E.B. Du Bois (center) and other founding members of the Niagara Movement attended the Niagara Conference in 1905.

Bounce to Activate Gallery

☑ **RECALL** Why did African Americans and others decide it was time to organize against discrimination?

Protecting Rights for Ethnic and Religious Minorities

African Americans were not alone in seeking rights. Individuals and organizations of diverse ethnic and religious groups spoke out against unfair treatment and took action by creating self-help agencies. For example, in northern cities, Catholic parishes offered a variety of social services to immigrants. In Chicago, a network of Polish Catholic groups grew so strong that it earned the nickname American Warsaw.

Expanding Rights and Opportunities for Jews Jews in New York had formed the B'nai B'rith in 1843 to provide religious education and to help Jewish families. In response to growing anti-Semitism, the group founded the **Anti-Defamation League** in 1913. Its goal was— and still is—to defend Jews and others against physical and verbal attacks, false statements, and "to secure justice and fair treatment to all citizens alike. . . ." In this way, the group expanded political rights for Jews and others. During the late 1800s and early 1900s, some business refused to hire or serve Jewish people. The Anti-Defamation League led efforts to expand economic opportunities for Jews and other minorities by fighting this form of discrimination.

Expanding Rights and Opportunities for Mexican Americans
Mexican Americans also organized to help themselves. Those living in Arizona formed the Partido Liberal Mexicano (PLM), which offered Mexican Americans many of the same services that the Urban League gave to African Americans. In several states, Mexican Americans formed **mutualistas,** groups that made loans and provided legal assistance. The mutualistas also had insurance programs to help members if they were too sick to work.

Many Mexican Americans were forced to sign unfair labor contracts that kept them in debt to people whose land they worked. In 1911, the Supreme Court struck down a law that enforced that system.

Native Americans Gain Citizenship
Progressives did little to help Native Americans. The Dawes Act,

passed in 1887, had divided reservations into plots for individuals to farm. But the law also said that lands not given to individual Indians could be sold to the general public. By 1932, nearly two thirds of the lands held by tribes in 1887 were in the hands of whites.

Carlos Montezuma, a Native American from Arizona, helped establish the Society of American Indians in 1911, the first organization formed to promote Indian rights and protest federal Indian policy. A doctor, Montezuma treated Native Americans living on reservations. He urged Native Americans to preserve their cultures and avoid being dependent on the government. Many reformers, who hoped that Indians could be assimilated into American society like immigrants, found this position troubling.

The Dawes Act barred Native Americans from selling their plots of land for 25 years. The law provided that they would then get the title to the land and become citizens. This policy was intended to speed Native Americans' assimilation into white society. By the 1920s, however, it was clear that the policy was not achieving this goal. So Congress tried another approach. The congressional act **American Indian Citizenship Act of 1924** made all Native Americans citizens of the United States, with full voting rights. For Native Americans, this law was an important step toward political equality with other Americans.

The official reason for granting citizenship and voting rights was to reward Native Americans for their service in World War I. However, supporters also hoped that the reform would help the Americanization process.

Fighting for Rights and Opportunities for Asian Americans
Asian Americans also had to protect themselves and struggled to expand their political rights. In 1907, in an informal agreement between the United States and Japan—known as the "Gentlemen's Agreement"—the United States promised not to impose restrictions on Japanese immigration and Japan promised not to allow further emigration to the U.S. Of course, many Japanese immigrants were already in California, where they were forced to send their children to segregated schools. A 1913 California law said that only American citizens could own land. Because Japanese immigrants could not become citizens, the law forced them to sell their land. Japanese Americans found a way around this, however, by putting the land in their children's names. Because their children had been born in the United States,

>> Asian Americans faced widespread discrimination. California state laws placed barriers to the property rights of Japanese immigrant farmers, for example.

they were American citizens. The law also affected immigrants from China and India, who were also not allowed to become citizens.

Japanese immigrant Takao Ozawa fought the law in court that blocked Asian Americans from becoming citizens. In 1922, however, the Supreme Court ruled against him. A newspaper read by Japanese Americans commented, "The slim hope that we had entertained . . . has been shattered completely."

☑ **IDENTIFY** What strategies did other minority groups use to defend their rights?

☑ **ASSESSMENT**

1. **Generate Explanations** Discuss the contradictions of the Progressive Movement.

2. **Compare and Contrast** the ideologies of Booker T. Washington and W.E.B. Du Bois.

3. **Draw Conclusions** Discuss both the positive and negative implications of the American Indian Citizenship Act of 1924.

4. **Summarize** What were the goals of the National Association for the Advancement of Colored People (NAACP)?

5. **Compare** the efforts of Mexican Americans, Native Americans, Asian Americans, and Jews to fight against discrimination during the Progressive Era.

Atlanta Exposition Address: Booker T. Washington

In 1895, African American leader Booker T. Washington addressed a predominantly white audience in Atlanta. He urged fellow blacks to build friendly relations with whites and to start "at the bottom" by working at "the common occupations of life." Other black leaders rejected Washington's plan and called it the "Atlanta Compromise."

>> Booker T. Washington

One-third of the population of the South is of the Negro race. No enterprise seeking the material, civil, or moral welfare of this section can disregard this element of our population and reach the highest success. I but convey to you, Mr. President and Directors, the sentiment of the masses of my race when I say that in no way have the value and manhood of the American Negro been more fittingly and generously recognized than by the managers of this magnificent Exposition at every stage of its progress. It is a recognition that will do more to cement the friendship of the two races than any occurrence since the dawn of our freedom.

Not only this, but the opportunity here afforded will awaken among us a new era of industrial progress. Ignorant and inexperienced, it is not strange that in the first years of our new life we began at the top instead of at the bottom; that a seat in Congress or the state legislature was more sought than real estate or industrial skill; that the political convention or stump [political] speaking had more attractions than starting a dairy farm or truck garden [garden where vegetables are grown to be sold]. . . .

☑ **DRAW INFERENCES** What do you think Washington meant by "the first years in our new life"?

Our greatest danger is that in the great leap from slavery to freedom we may overlook the fact that the masses of us are to live by the productions of our hands, and fail to keep in mind that we shall prosper in proportion as we learn to dignify and glorify common labour, and put brains and skill into the common occupations of life; shall prosper in proportion as we learn to draw the line between the superficial and the substantial, the ornamental gewgaws of life and the useful. No race can prosper till it learns that there is as much dignity in tilling a field as in writing a poem. It is at the bottom of life we must begin, and not at the top. Nor should we permit our grievances to overshadow our opportunities.

☑ **EXPLAIN AN ARGUMENT** What does Washington mean by beginning "at the bottom of life"?

To those of my race who depend on bettering their condition in a foreign land or who underestimate the importance of cultivating [developing] friendly relations with the Southern white man, who is their next-door neighbor, I would say: "Cast down your bucket where you are" [make use of the resources that you don't realize are all around you]— cast it down in making friends in every manly way of the people of all races by whom we are surrounded.

✓ UNDERSTAND MEANING What was Washington calling a "foreign land"? Why was it foreign?

Cast it down in agriculture, mechanics, in commerce, in domestic service [working as a servant in the employer's home], and in the professions [occupations that require special education, such as medicine or law]. And in this connection it is well to bear in mind that whatever other sins the South may be called to bear, when it comes to business, pure and simple, it is in the South that the Negro is given a man's chance in the commercial world. . . . Our greatest danger is that in the great leap from slavery to freedom we may overlook the fact that the masses of us are to live by the productions of our hands, and fail to keep in mind that we shall prosper in proportion as we learn to dignify and glorify common labour, and put brains and skill into the common occupations of life. . . . No race can prosper till it learns that there is as much dignity in tilling [plowing] a field as in writing a poem. It is at the bottom of life we must begin, and not at the top. Nor should we permit our grievances to overshadow our opportunities. . . .

✓ ANALYZE STYLE AND RHETORIC How did Washington make use of repetition in this paragraph and the previous one? What purpose does the repetition serve?

. . . While we take pride in what we exhibit as a result of our independent efforts, we do not for a moment forget that our part in this exhibition would fall far short of your expectations but for the constant help that has come to our educational life, not only from the Southern states, but especially from Northern philanthropists, who have made their gifts a constant stream of blessing and encouragement.

The wisest among my race understand that the agitation of questions of social equality is the extremest folly, and that progress in the enjoyment of all the privileges that will come to us must be the result of severe and constant struggle rather than of artificial forcing. No race that has anything to contribute to the markets of the world is long in any degree ostracized. It is important and right that all privileges of the law be ours, but it is vastly more important that we be prepared for the exercise of these privileges. The opportunity to earn a dollar in a factory just now is worth infinitely more than the opportunity to spend a dollar in an opera-house.

✓ DRAW INFERENCES In the final paragraph what idea or political position is Washington arguing against?

✓ ASSESSMENT

1. **Determine Central Ideas** What is the main idea of the speech as excerpted here?

2. **Draw Conclusions** Do you agree with the central idea expressed in the address? Cite examples to support your answer.

3. **Analyze Interactions** Why do you think some black leaders rejected the ideas Washington expressed in this address?

>> President Theodore Roosevelt dedicated his considerable energy and abilities to achieving Progressive reforms.

 Bounce to Activate Flipped Video

3.4 In the late 1800s, the United States had several weak and ineffective Presidents. The arrival of Theodore Roosevelt, a charismatic figure who embraced Progressive ideals, ushered in a new era. Roosevelt pushed for many Progressive reforms and expanded the powers of the presidency. He changed the way Americans viewed the roles of the President and the government.

>> Objectives

Analyze how Theodore Roosevelt influenced the changing relationship between the federal government and private business.

Explain the impact of Roosevelt's actions towards managing the environment.

Compare and contrast Roosevelt's policies with Taft's and Wilson's policies.

Describe Wilson's efforts to regulate the economy.

Assess the legacy of the Progressive Era.

>> Key Terms

Square Deal
Hepburn Act
Meat Inspection Act
Pure Food and Drug
  Act
John Muir
Gifford Pinchot
National
  Reclamation Act
New Nationalism
Progressive Party

Woodrow Wilson
Sixteenth
  Amendment
Federal Reserve Act
Clayton Antitrust Act
Theodore Roosevelt

Reformers in the White House

Roosevelt Changes the Relationship Between Government and Business

In 1901, when Theodore Roosevelt became President of the United States, he was only 43 years old.

However, he had packed quite a lot into those years, gaining a reputation for being smart, energetic, and opinionated. The sickly child of wealthy parents, he had used his family's resources to develop both his strength and his mind. Observers said Theodore Roosevelt generated so much energy that if you met him, you left the event with bits of his personality "stuck to your clothes."

Roosevelt's Path to the Presidency Roosevelt had graduated with honors from Harvard University in 1880. He spent only a few months studying law at Columbia University before being elected to the New York State Assembly. After three years' service there, and after the deaths of both his mother and his wife, Alice, Roosevelt retired to a ranch in the West. There he developed a love of the wilderness.

Theodore Roosevelt could not remain long out of the spotlight, however. By 1889, he had returned to politics. As president of New York City's Board of Police Commissioners, he gained fame by fighting corruption. President William McKinley noticed him and named him Assistant Secretary of the Navy. When the Spanish-American War broke out in 1898, Roosevelt resigned the post to form the Rough Riders, a volunteer cavalry unit that became famous during the war.

After the end of the conflict, the young war hero was elected governor of New York, where he pushed for Progressive reforms. His reform efforts annoyed Republican leaders in the state, however. They convinced McKinley to choose Roosevelt as his running mate so Roosevelt would leave New York—and them—alone. McKinley was reelected President in 1900, but within a few months he was assassinated, and Roosevelt became President. He soon dominated public attention. Journalists vied for interviews with him and children begged their parents for a teddy bear, the new stuffed animal named for him.

Progressive reformers were pleased to see the benefits of the ICC spreading, namely that the powerful railroads were finally under control. This pleased farmers as well, who had long sought such regulation. But the Elkins Act and the ICC in general had costs.

He called his program the **Square Deal**. Its goals were to keep the wealthy and powerful from taking advantage of small business owners and the poor. Roosevelt's idea of fair government did not mean that everyone would get rich or that the government should take care of the lazy. He compared his Square Deal to a hand of cards.

> When I say I believe in a square deal, I do not mean to give every man the best hand. If good cards do not come to any man, or if they do come, and he has not got the power to play them, that is his affair. All I mean is that there shall be no crookedness in the dealing.

—Theodore Roosevelt, 1905

Intervening Between Owners and Workers
Roosevelt often stepped in to labor disputes with the authority and power of the federal government. One example was in 1902, when Pennsylvania coal miners went on strike. The miners wanted a pay raise and a shorter workday. Roosevelt sympathized with the overworked miners, but he knew that a steady supply of coal was needed to keep factories running and homes warm. He wanted the strike ended quickly.

First, Roosevelt tried to get mine owners to listen to workers' concerns. When this failed, he threatened to send federal troops to take control of the mines and to run them with federal employees. His threat forced the mine owners to give the miners a small pay raise and a nine-hour workday. For the first time, the federal government had stepped in to help workers in a labor dispute.

This coal strike intervention was one of many steps Roosevelt took to control the power of corporations. Within a year, Roosevelt convinced Congress to establish the Department of Commerce and Labor to monitor businesses engaged in interstate commerce.

The ICC Takes on the Railroads The cost of shipping freight on railroads had been an issue since the 1870s. Railroad companies often could charge whatever they wanted. The railroads' power was especially troublesome for western farmers. They had no other way to move their products to eastern markets.

>> People seize coal from a stalled train during the 1902 coal strike. **Analyze Images** How does this image reinforce Roosevelt's belief that it was important for the coal strike to end quickly?

In 1887, Congress had created the Interstate Commerce Commission (ICC) to oversee rail charges for shipments that passed through more than one state. The ICC was supposed to make sure that all shippers were charged the same amounts. By 1900, though, the Supreme Court had stripped away most of the ICC's power. So Roosevelt pushed Congress to pass the Elkins Act in 1903, which imposed fines on railroads that gave special rates to favored shippers. In 1906, he got Congress to pass the **Hepburn Act**, which gave the ICC even greater powers. This law allowed ICC for the first time to set maximum shipping rates. The act also set maximum rates for ferries, toll bridges, and oil pipelines. Finally, it gave any ruling by the ICC the legal force of a court order.

Progressive reformers were pleased to see the powerful railroads finally brought under control. Farmers who had long sought such regulation especially felts its benefits. But the Elkins Act and the ICC in general had costs, as its critics pointed out. The ICC's five commissioners were not elected to their positions. Once appointed by the President and approved by the Senate, they could not be removed during their term.

Some Americans found the ICC's independence from the public will and from all three branches of government to be troubling. In addition, when the ICC exercised its new power and limited railroad rates, its action harmed the economy. The value of railroad stocks plummeted, which helped to bring on the financial panic that swept the nation in 1907.

A Trustbuster Enforces Legislation It did not take long for the President and his administration to earn a reputation as "trustbusters." In response to an antitrust suit filed by Roosevelt's attorney general, the Supreme Court ruled in 1904 that the Northern Securities Company—a big railroad company—was an illegal trust. The decision forced the company to split into smaller companies. The next year, the Court found that a beef trust and several powerful agricultural companies had broken antitrust laws.

Roosevelt was not interested in bringing down all large companies. He saw a difference between "good trusts" and "bad trusts." Big businesses could often be more efficient than small ones, he believed. Big business was bad, he said, only if it bullied smaller companies or cheated consumers.

So he supported powerful corporations as long as they did business fairly. His supporters called him a "trust-tamer," but some wealthy Progressives criticized his trustbusting. Other critics claimed that his good trust-bad trust distinction meant that antitrust laws were being applied unevenly and thus unfairly. This practice may even have been unconstitutional—a violation of the private property protections in the Fifth and Fourteenth Amendments.

Despite such criticisms, most Americans were pleased with the antitrust prosecutions. However, they were also conflicted. They deeply distrusted and feared the big corporations' huge concentrations of wealth and power. But at the same time, they

Early Progressive Legislation

LEGISLATION	EFFECT
Sherman Antitrust Act (1890)	Outlawed monopolies and practices that restrained trade, such as price fixing
National Reclamation Act (1902)	Provided for federal irrigation projects by using money from the sale of public lands
Elkins Act (1903)	Imposed fines on railroads that gave special rates to favored shippers
Hepburn Act (1906)	Authorized the federal government to regulate railroad rates and set maximum prices for ferries, bridge tolls, and oil pipelines
Meat Inspection Act (1906)	Allowed the federal government to inspect meat sold across state lines and required inspections of meat-processing plants
Pure Food and Drug Act (1906)	Allowed federal inspection of food and medicine and banned the shipment and sale of impure food and the mislabeling of food and medicine

>> **Analyze Charts** Which of these acts do you believe was the most important? Why?

treasured the consumer benefits the companies' size often provided.

Regulating the Food and Drug Industries In 1906, muckraker Upton Sinclair published his novel *The Jungle*. His descriptions of the filthy, unhealthy conditions in meatpacking plants revolted the public and infuriated the President, having an immediate impact. Roosevelt urged Congress to pass the **Meat Inspection Act** that same year.

It provided federal agents with the power to inspect any meat sold across state lines and required federal inspection of meat-processing plants. Today, when we eat lunchmeat or grilled chicken, we trust that federal inspectors have monitored the plant where it is produced. If there is a serious problem, the government can force the meatpacker to pull the product off the shelves before many people become sick. This regulation is one lasting result of Progressives' insistence that the government take responsibility for food safety.

The **Pure Food and Drug Act** benefited the public by placing the same controls on other foods and on medicines. Although there was some concern that here again the federal government was taking on too much of the states' constitutional police power, most Americans felt like the benefits outweighed the costs. The act also banned the interstate shipment of impure food and the mislabeling of food and drugs. Today, the Food and Drug Administration (FDA) still enforces this law and others. The FDA monitors companies to make sure people are not hurt by dangerous substances or dishonest labels. For example, before a drug can be sold, it must be tested and approved by the FDA.

☑ **RECALL** What was the purpose of such legislation as the Hepburn Act and the Meat Inspection Act?

Managing the Environment

Roosevelt's deep reverence for nature also shaped his policies. The books he published on hunting and the rugged West reflected his fascination with the competition between humans and the wilderness. He was pleased that the federal government had established Yellowstone National Park in 1872 to protect wildlife, and he admired California naturalist **John Muir**, whose efforts had led Congress to create Yosemite National Park in 1890.

>> **Analyze Political Cartoons** What does this cartoon suggest about Roosevelt's differing approaches to regulating trusts?

>> President Roosevelt met with John Muir in Yosemite National Park, California, in 1903. **Contrast** How did Roosevelt's views on preserving wilderness areas differ from Muir's?

Bounce to Activate Gallery

Conservation or Preservation? In 1891, Congress had given the President the power to protect timberlands by setting aside land as federal forests. Following Muir's advice, Roosevelt closed off more than 100 million acres of forestland. However, the President did not agree with Muir that all wild areas should be preserved, or left untouched. Some wild lands held valuable resources, and Roosevelt thought those resources were meant to be used. This view became clear in his forest policy. In typical Progressive style, he called on experts to draw up plans for both conserving and using the forests.

Roosevelt drew on the "rational use" ideas of **Gifford Pinchot**, who led the Division of Forestry in the U.S. Department of Agriculture. Pinchot recommended a different approach—that forests be preserved for public use. By this, he meant that forests should be protected so that trees would have time to mature into good lumber. Then the protected areas should be logged for wood to build houses and new areas placed under protection. "The object of our forest policy," explained Pinchot, "is not to preserve the forests because they are refuges for the wild creatures of the wilderness, but rather they are the making of prosperous homes."

Pinchot's views came to dominate American policies toward natural resources. Conservation, or the planned management of natural resources, became government policy for managing public lands. But private ownership inspired conservation, too. In some cases, private ownership gave people the incentive to handle the natural resources on their land wisely so they would not damage the long-term value of their property.

In all, Roosevelt worked with Congress to establish five national parks and established 18 national monuments or historical landmarks under the Antiquities Act of 1906. Together, these unique places formed the core of the National Park Service, which was established in 1916 and still works today to conserve and share many natural and historic landmarks in the United States.

Roosevelt's views on land use went beyond the belief that public lands should, in some cases, be preserved or put to use for wider societal benefit. In 1908, the Supreme Court of the State of Maine handed down a decision saying, essentially, that the government could restrict the cutting of trees on private land in order to prevent erosion. Roosevelt backed up this governmental action, publicly stating his view that the needs of the community outweighed the private property rights of individuals or industries.

This was a controversial stance. The idea that private property, whether a person's own personal property or that of his or her business, is protected

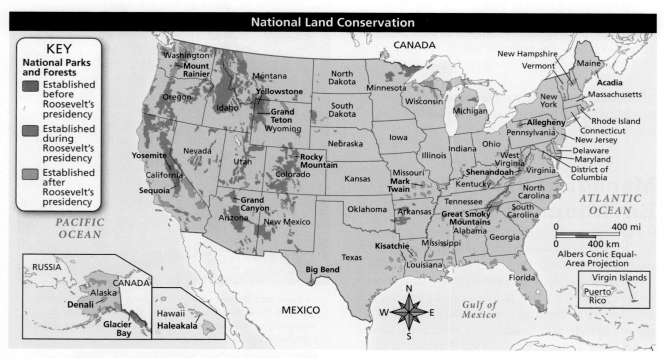

>> **Analyze Maps** Based on the information in the map, when were the majority of national parks established? What region of the country holds the largest parks?

by the Fifth Amendment to the Constitution is one of the bedrock ideals of American society and industry. The Fifth Amendment states that no "private property [shall] be taken for public use, without just compensation." Many individuals and busines owners felt that restrictions on the use of their property, such as those imposed by antitrust regulation or environmental protection regulation, violated this right. This tension between private property rights and public use for the good of the community is still present today.

Changes in Population Affect Water Policy

Another highly controversial natural resource issue was water. Over centuries, Native Americans had used various irrigation methods to bring water to the arid Southwest. The situation changed in the late 1800s, when newcomers began mining and farming in Utah, New Mexico, Colorado, Nevada, and California. Mining machinery required a great deal of water, and water-sharing systems long used by those states' Mexican American residents were challenged by the new people and businesses who arrived. Private irrigation companies came to the area, staked claims to sections of riverbeds, and redirected the water so farmers could revive— or "reclaim"— dried-up fields. As increases in population strained environmental resources, bitter fights developed over who should own water rights and how the water should be shared.

Roosevelt sprang into action on this issue. He listened to Nevada representative Francis Newlands, who wanted the federal government to help western states build huge reservoirs to hold and to conserve water. Roosevelt pushed Congress for a law that would allow it.

In 1902, Congress passed the **National Reclamation Act**, which gave the federal government the power to decide where and how water would be distributed. The government would build and manage dams that would create reservoirs, generate power, and direct water flow. This would make water from one state's rivers and streams available to farmers in other states. The full effect of the Reclamation Act was felt over the next few decades, as water management projects created huge reservoirs and lakes where there had been dry canyons. Examples include the Salt Valley Project in Arizona and the Roosevelt Dam and Hoover Dam on the Colorado River.

☑ **RECALL** What was the purpose of the National Reclamation Act?

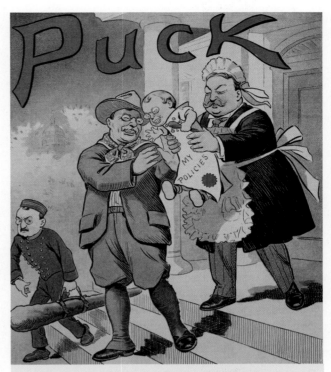

>> **Analyze Political Cartoons** What clues in this cartoon reveal what type of policies the author believes Taft will enact as president?

A New Direction In Presidential Politics

Roosevelt left the presidency after two terms in office, saying he wished to enjoy private life. He was still a powerful force in the Republican Party, however, and he used that power to help his Secretary of War William Howard Taft win the presidency in 1908. Roosevelt expected Taft to continue his programs of managing business and natural resources. Political cartoonists made caricatures of Roosevelt handing over what he called "my policies" to Taft, who seemed to have no ideas of his own.

Taft's Agenda Differs But Taft soon set his own agenda. He approved the Payne-Aldrich Act (1909), which did not lower tariffs as much as Roosevelt had wanted. He also pushed Congress to pass the Mann-Elkins Act (1910), which gave the government control over telephone and telegraph rates. He encouraged Congress to propose an income tax. Perhaps most importantly, he dropped Roosevelt's distinction between good trusts and bad trusts.

Taft's Justice Department brought lawsuits against twice as many corporations as Roosevelt's had done. One result was that in 1911, the Supreme Court "busted" the trust built by the Standard Oil Company. But Taft also supported what the Court called its "rule of reason," which relaxed the hard line set by the Sherman Antitrust Act. The rule of reason allowed big monopolies so long as they did not "unreasonably" squeeze out smaller companies. Roosevelt publicly criticized these decisions. Then Taft's attorney general sued to force U.S. Steel to sell a coal company it had bought. Roosevelt, who had earlier approved the purchase of the company, fumed.

Taft further infuriated Roosevelt and other Progressives in the Republican Party when he fired Gifford Pinchot for publicly criticizing Secretary of the Interior Richard Ballinger. Pinchot charged that Ballinger, who opposed Roosevelt's conservation policies, had worked with business interests to sell federal land rich in coal deposits in Alaska. Although a congressional investigation later cleared Ballinger of these charges, the damage had been done.

Roosevelt's Response Roosevelt began traveling the country speaking about what he called the **New Nationalism**—a program to restore the government's trustbusting power. Declaring himself as "strong as a bull moose," Roosevelt vowed to tackle the trusts in a third presidential term. The Taft-Roosevelt battle split the Republican Party as an election neared: progressives bolted from the party and set up the **Progressive Party**. Reformer Jane Addams nominated Roosevelt as the Progressive Party's candidate for the 1912 presidential election.

The Republicans nominated Taft. The question was whether a third party like the Progressive Party could have an impact in a national election. A bitter election loomed.

Wilson Takes Advantage of Republican Discord The split created an opportunity for the Democrats and their candidate, **Woodrow Wilson**, to win the White House. Wilson's ideas had caught the attention of William Jennings Bryan, who helped Wilson win the Democratic nomination. As a student and later as a professor, Wilson had thought a great deal about good government. His doctoral thesis, *Congressional Government,* had launched him on a career teaching in college before he became the reforming governor of New Jersey.

Wilson shaped his ideas into a program he called the **New Freedom**. His plan looked much like Roosevelt's New Nationalism. It, too, would place strict government controls on corporations. In a speech on the New Freedom, Wilson outlined his aim to provide more opportunities—more freedom—for small businesses.

The man with only a little capital is finding it harder and harder to get into the field, more and more impossible to compete with the big

Taft and Roosevelt

TAFT
- Offended Progressives
- Sought to rein in presidential power
- Conservative Republican
- Promoted foreign policy through trade and investment (dollar diplomacy)

- Trustbuster
- Republican
- Promoted conservation

ROOSEVELT
- Became head of Progressive Party
- Sought to increase presidential power
- Progressive Republican
- Promoted assertive foreign policy (big stick diplomacy)

>> **Analyze Information** How did Taft's and Roosevelt's views on government and politics differ?

Bounce to Activate Chart

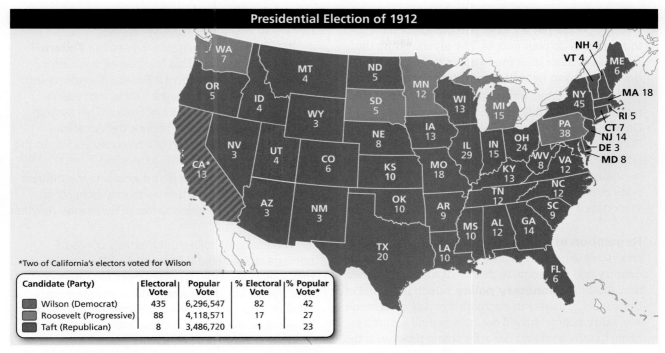

Presidential Election of 1912

Candidate (Party)	Electoral Vote	Popular Vote	% Electoral Vote	% Popular Vote*
Wilson (Democrat)	435	6,296,547	82	42
Roosevelt (Progressive)	88	4,118,571	17	27
Taft (Republican)	8	3,486,720	1	23

*Two of California's electors voted for Wilson

>> **Analyze Maps** What evidence shown on the map supports the conclusion that divisions within the Republican party made the Democrats more likely to win the 1912 election?

fellow. Why? Because the laws of this country do not prevent the strong from crushing the weak.

— Woodrow Wilson, "The New Freedom," 1913

Though he did not win the majority of the popular vote, Wilson received more than four times the number of Electoral College votes that went to Roosevelt or to Taft. The Progressive Party had indeed had an impact on the election. By splitting the Republican vote, the Progressive Party helped the Democrat Wilson to win the White House. The pious and intellectual son of a Virginia minister, Wilson was the first man born in the South to win the presidency in almost 60 years.

☑ **CHECK UNDERSTANDING** How did President Taft influence Roosevelt's decision to run for a third term?

Wilson Endorses Further Regulation

Republicans Theodore Roosevelt and William Howard Taft introduced the country to forceful Progressive Presidents. Democrat Woodrow Wilson

used the expanded power of the presidency to promote a far-reaching reform agenda. Some of Wilson's economic and antitrust measures are still important in American life today.

President Wilson attacked what he called the "triple wall of privilege"—the tariffs, the banks, and the trusts—that blocked businesses from being free. Early in his first term, he pushed for new laws that would bring down those three walls and give the government more control over the economy.

A New Tax on Income First, Wilson aimed to prevent big manufacturers from possibly charging unfairly high prices to their customers. One way to do this was to lower the tariffs on goods imported from foreign countries so consumers could buy foreign goods if American companies' prices were too high. Wilson called a special session of Congress and convinced its members to pass the Underwood Tariff Bill, which cut tariffs.

Tariffs had been one of the main sources of revenue, or money coming in, for the federal government. To make up for the loss of tariff revenue, the Underwood Tariff Act of 1913 included a provision to create a graduated income tax. The recently passed **Sixteenth Amendment** gave Congress the power to collect an income tax without restrictions. A graduated income tax means that wealthy people pay a higher percentage of their income than do poor people. The revenue from the income tax more than made up for the money the government lost by lowering tariffs on imports.

Taxing incomes proved to be a very controversial reform. Both Republicans and conservative Democrats strongly opposed ratification of the Sixteenth Amendment, as did prominent business leaders. The graduated tax became and continues to be the battleground between those who favor lower rates to stimulate economic growth and those who view it as a means to further public investment.

Regulation of Commercial Banks Next, Wilson tried to change the banking system. At the time, the country had no central authority to supervise banks and establish **monetary policy**, which is control of the supply of money in circulation at any given time. Monetary policy, carried out by a central authority, helps to influence and control interest rates with the goal of promoting economic growth and stability and controlling inflation and deflation. Without such a central authority, interest rates for loans could fluctuate wildly, and a few wealthy bankers had a great deal of control over national, state and local banks' reserve funds. This meant that a bank might

not have full access to its reserves when customers needed to withdraw or borrow money.

Wilson pushed Congress to pass the **Federal Reserve Act** (1913). This law placed commercial banks under the control of a Federal Reserve Board, which set up regional banks to hold the reserve funds from those commercial banks. This system, still in place today, helps protect the American economy from having too much money end up in the hands of one person, bank, or region.

The Federal Reserve Board also sets the interest rate that banks pay to borrow money from other banks, and it supervises banks to make sure they are well run.

The financial community bitterly opposed passage of the Federal Reserve Act. Critics claimed that it gave the federal government too much control over the nation's economy and banking system, a point of view that some Americans still hold today. However, some historians have called the Federal Reserve Act the most important piece of economic legislation before the 1930s.

Wilson and Congress Strengthen Antitrust Regulation Like Presidents before him, Wilson focused on trusts. He agreed with Roosevelt that trusts were not dangerous as long as they did not engage in unfair practices.

GOVERNMENT AUTHORITY *AND* PROPERTY RIGHTS

IN THE PROGRESSIVE ERA, **COMPREHENSIVE ZONING** GAVE THE GOVERNMENT POWER TO REGULATE USES OF PRIVATELY-OWNED LAND.

NEW YORK CITY BEFORE
THE 42-STORY
EQUITABLE BUILDING
WAS BUILT WITHOUT REGARD TO THE NEIGHBORING AREA.

The building's 7-acre shadow affected the value of neighboring buildings.

NEW YORK CITY
AFTER COMPREHENSIVE ZONING ORDINANCES
REGULATE LAND USE

In a residential district, no building could be erected unless it was a family dwelling, club, church, school, library, public museum, philanthropic institution, hospital, or railroad passenger station.

68 CITIES
ADOPT
ZONING ORDINANCES

Some state courts held that zoning encroached upon the rights of property owners.

In 1926, the U.S. Supreme Court ruled against a property owner to sustain the validity of a zoning ordinance.

1910 1911 1912 1913 1914 **1915 1916** 1917 1918 1919 1920 1921 1922 1923 1924 1925 **1926** 1927 1928 1929 1930

>> **Analyze Information** How did comprehensive zoning both protect and possibly violate property rights?

Progressive Legislation During Wilson's Presidency

LEGISLATION	EFFECT
Underwood Tariff Act (1913)	Lowered tariffs on imported goods and established a graduated income tax
Federal Reserve Act (1913)	Created the Federal Reserve Board to oversee banks and manage reserve funds
Federal Trade Commission Act (1914)	Established the Federal Trade Commission to monitor business practices, false advertising, and dishonest labeling
Clayton Antitrust Act (1914)	Strengthened the Sherman Antitrust Act by spelling out specific activities businesses could not do

>> **Analyze Charts** Which of these pieces of legislation do you think is the most important?

In 1914, Wilson persuaded Congress to create the **Federal Trade Commission (FTC)**. Members of this group were named by the President to monitor business practices that might lead to monopoly. The FTC was also charged with watching out for false advertising or dishonest labeling. Congress also passed the **Clayton Antitrust Act** (1914), which strengthened earlier antitrust laws by spelling out those activities in which businesses could not engage.

These laws are still in effect today, protecting both businesses and consumers from abusive business activities. In recent years, the FTC has prosecuted companies that traded stocks dishonestly and fined companies that published false ads. The FTC also regulates buying on the Internet. Some Americans argue, however, that such government regulation interferes with the workings of a free enterprise system and sometimes hurts competition.

Workers Gain Rights The Clayton Antitrust Act also ushered in a new era for workers by protecting labor unions from being attacked as trusts. Now, workers could organize more freely. Samuel Gompers of the American Federation of Labor (AFL) praised the new law as the "Magna Carta" of labor.

On the heels of these protections came the Workingman's Compensation Act (1916), which gave wages to temporarily disabled civil service employees. That same year, Wilson pushed for the Adamson Act to prevent a nationwide railroad strike, which would have stopped the movement of coal and food, leaving millions of Americans cold and hungry. Railroad union leaders insisted on the eight-hour day,

but railroad managers would not accept it. Wilson called many company leaders to the White House, pleading with them to change their minds and avert a strike. When those efforts failed, he worked with Congress to pass the Adamson Act, which limited railroad employees' workdays to eight hours.

However, Wilson did not always support organized labor, as a tragic incident known as the Ludlow Massacre showed. In the fall of 1913, coal miners in Ludlow, Colorado, demanded safer conditions, higher pay, and the right to form a union. When the coal company refused, they walked off the job. Evicted from company housing, the miners and their families set up in a tent city near the mines. The strike continued through the winter. Then, on April 20, 1914, the Colorado National Guard opened fire on the tent city and set fire to the tents, killing some 26 men, women, and children. In the end, Wilson sent federal troops to restore order and break up the strike. The miners' attempt to form a union had failed.

☑ **IDENTIFY SUPPORTING DETAILS** How did the government regulate commercial banks?

The Progressives' Legacy

The political reforms of the Progressives had a lasting effect on the American political system. The initiative, referendum, and recall and the Seventeenth and Nineteenth amendments expanded voters' influence. Progressive reforms also paved the way for future trends. Starting in this period, the federal government grew to offer more protection to Americans, but at the same time gaining more control over people's lives.

The American economy today showcases the Progressives' legacy. Antitrust laws, the Federal Reserve Board, and the other federal agencies watch closely over the economy. Controls that Roosevelt and Wilson put in place continue to provide consumer protections. In later years, the government, for better or worse, built on those actions to extend regulation over other aspects of business.

The Progressive years also greatly expanded the government's role in managing natural resources. However, federal action on dams, national parks, and resource use remain major areas of debate, especially in the West. Those debates and decisions affect people in other regions as well. For example, while farmers in California, Arizona, or New Mexico worry about getting enough water to grow crops, the rest of the nation awaits the delivery of the food they grow.

It is true that many of the problems identified by the Progressives still plague us today. There are still dishonest sellers, unfair employment practices, and problems in schools, cities, the environment, and public health. However, the Progressive reformers passed on the idea that government can take action to help people and private enterprise fix those problems.

☑ **IDENTIFY MAIN IDEAS** What is the essential legacy of Progressive political reform movements?

☑ **ASSESSMENT**

1. **Compare and Contrast** the domestic policies of President Roosevelt and President Taft.

2. **Compare Points of View** Explain why some people supported President Wilson's graduated income tax and why others opposed it.

3. **Generate Explanations** Explain the purpose of the Federal Trade Commission and discuss the criticism it has received.

4. **Contrast** Explain how President Roosevelt disagreed with John Muir about environmental preservation.

5. **Generate Explanations** Explain how President Wilson affected workers' rights.

The Jungle: Upton Sinclair

When Upton Sinclair published *The Jungle* in 1906, he meant to open America's eyes to the plight of workers in the filthy, dangerous Chicago stockyards. Instead, popular outrage focused on the wider-reaching threat of spoiled meat. Congress quickly passed the nation's first legislation regulating the meat, food, and drug industries. Sinclair, disappointed by his failure to provoke more sympathy for the overworked, underpaid workers, noted "I aimed at the public's heart, and by accident I hit it in the stomach."

>> A slaughterhouse in the late 1800s

There was never the least attention paid to what was cut up for sausage. . . . There would be meat that had tumbled out on the floor, in the dirt and sawdust, where the workers had tramped [walked heavily] and spit uncounted billions of consumption [tuberculosis] germs. There would be meat stored in great piles in rooms; and the water from leaky roofs would drip over it, and thousands of rats would race about on it. It was too dark in these storage places to see well, but a man could run his hand over these piles of meat and sweep off handfuls of the dried dung of rats. These rats were nuisances, and the packers would put poisoned bread out for them; they would die, and then rats, bread, and meat would go into the hoppers [containers] together.

☑ **DETERMINE AUTHOR'S POINT OF VIEW** What does Sinclair describe in this passage, and what is his viewpoint on the subject?

This is no fairy story and no joke; the meat would be shoveled into carts, and the man who did the shoveling would not trouble to lift out a rat even when he saw one—there were things that went into the sausage in comparison with which a poisoned rat was a tidbit [small piece of food]. There was no place for the men to wash their hands before they ate their dinner, and so they made a practice of washing them in the water that was to be ladled into the sausage. There were the butt-ends of smoked meat, and the scraps of corned beef, and all the odds and ends of the waste of the plants, that would be dumped into old barrels in the cellar and left there. Under the system of rigid economy which the packers enforced, there were some jobs that it only paid to do once in a long time, and among these was the cleaning out of the waste barrels.

Every spring they did it; and in the barrels would be dirt and rust and old nails and stale water—and cartload after cartload of it would be taken up and dumped into the hoppers with fresh meat, and sent out to the public's breakfast.

☑ **EXPLAIN AN ARGUMENT** According to Sinclair, why are the waste barrels not cleaned more often?

The winter was coming on again, more menacing and cruel than ever. It was October, and the holiday rush had begun. It was necessary for the packing machines to grind till late at night to provide food that would be eaten at Christmas breakfasts; and Marija and Elzbieta and Ona, as part of the machine, began working fifteen or sixteen hours a day. There was no choice about this—whatever work there was to be done they had to do, if they wished to keep their places; besides that, it added another pittance to their incomes. So they staggered on with the awful load. They would start work every morning at seven, and eat their dinners at noon, and then work until ten or eleven at night without another mouthful of food. Jurgis wanted to wait for them, to help them home at night, but they would not think of this; the fertilizer mill was not running overtime, and there was no place for him to wait save in a saloon. Each would stagger out into the darkness, and make her way to the corner, where they met; or if the others had already gone, would get into a car, and begin a painful struggle to keep awake. When they got home they were always too tired either to eat or to undress; they would crawl into bed with their shoes on, and lie like logs. If they should fail, they would certainly be lost; if they held out, they might have enough coal for the winter. . . .

. . . He crossed a long bridge over a river frozen solid and covered with slush. Not even on the river bank was the snow white—the rain which fell was a diluted solution of smoke, and Jurgis' hands and face were streaked with black. Then he came into the business part of the city, where the streets were sewers of inky blackness, with horses sleeping and plunging, and women and children flying across in panic-stricken droves. These streets were huge canyons formed by towering black buildings, echoing with the clang of car gongs and the shouts of drivers; the people who swarmed in them were as busy as ants—all hurrying breathlessly, never stopping to look at anything nor at each other. The solitary trampish-looking foreigner, with water-soaked clothing and haggard face and anxious eyes, was as much alone as he hurried past them, as much unheeded and as lost, as if he had been a thousand miles deep in a wilderness.

A policeman gave him his direction and told him that he had five miles to go. He came again to the slum districts, to avenues of saloons and cheap stores, with long dingy red factory buildings, and coal-yards and railroad tracks; and then Jurgis lifted up his head and began to sniff the air like a startled animal—scenting the far-off odor of home. It was late afternoon then, and he was hungry, but the dinner invitations hung out of the saloons were not for him. . . .

☑ **ANALYZE STYLE AND RHETORIC** In a few words, how would you describe the world that Sinclair has represented in these paragraphs?

☑ ASSESSMENT

1. **Draw Conclusions** What reforms is the author calling for by describing these scenes?

2. **Draw Conclusions** What do you think it would have been like to work in this factory?

3. **Identify Cause and Effect** What effect do you think reading this selection from *The Jungle* would have had on Americans during this time period?

4. **Analyze Style and Rhetoric** How would you describe Sinclair's writing style, and how does it make his writing more convincing?

(3.5) For most of its early history, America played a small role in world affairs, mostly by choice. But in the late 1800s, this began to change. With leading spokesmen calling for the United States to join the ranks of the world's major powers, the United States began to acquire influence and territories outside its continental borders. The United States was abandoning isolationism and emerging as a new power on the global stage.

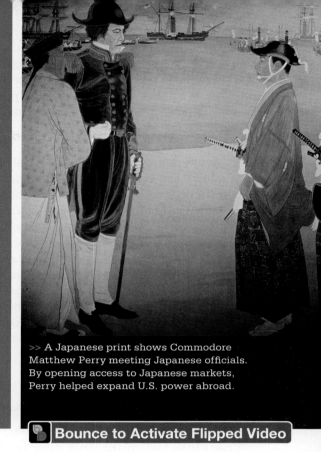

>> A Japanese print shows Commodore Matthew Perry meeting Japanese officials. By opening access to Japanese markets, Perry helped expand U.S. power abroad.

Bounce to Activate Flipped Video

American Influence Grows

America on the World Stage

During the Age of Imperialism, from the mid-1800s through the early 1900s, powerful nations engaged in a mad dash to extend their influence across much of the world. European nations added to colonies they had established during the Age of Exploration by acquiring new colonies in Africa and Asia.

Following European success, Japan and the United States also began to consider the benefits of **imperialism**, the policy by which strong nations extend their political, military, and economic control over weaker territories. Although imperialism would prove an awkward fit for the United States, the nation's desire to take its place on the world stage spurred some territorial expansion and a larger increase in influence.

Economic Causes of Imperialism One reason why European nations and Japan rushed to grab colonies was the desire for raw materials and natural resources. They sought colonies to provide tea, rubber, iron, petroleum, and other materials for their industries at home. These colonial economies were examples of **extractive economies**. The imperial country extracted, or

>> **Objectives**

Identify the key factors that caused Americans to want to take a greater role overseas.

Explain how the United States took its first steps toward the position of a world power.

Evaluate the acquisition of Hawaii by the United States.

>> **Key Terms**

imperialism
extractive
  economies
Alfred T. Mahan
Social Darwinism
Frederick Jackson
  Turner
Matthew Perry
Queen Liluokalani
Sanford B. Dole

Go ONLINE for digital resources

VIDEO   AUDIO   ACTIVITY   ETEXT   WRITING   ASSESSMENT

removed, raw materials from the colony and shipped them to the home country. Possession of colonies gave nations an edge in the competition for global resources. In contrast to those other world powers, however, the resource-rich United States had fewer concerns about shortages of raw materials in the nineteenth century.

For Americans, the problem was not a shortage of materials, but a surplus of goods. The booming U.S. economy of the late 1800s was producing more goods than Americans could consume. Farmers complained that excess production resulted in declining crop prices and profits. Industrialists urged expanding trade into new overseas markets where American commodities could be sold. Otherwise, they warned, American factories would close and unemployment would rise. Senator Albert J. Beveridge, a Progressive and friend of Theodore Roosevelt, explained why the United States needed to become a world power:

> Today we are raising more [crops] than we can consume. Today we are making more than we can use. . . . Therefore we must find new markets for our produce, new occupation for our capital, new work for our labor.

—Senator Albert J. Beveridge, "The March of the Flag," 1898

Alfred T. Mahan Stresses U.S. Military Strength

To expand and protect their interests around the world, nations built up their military strength. **Alfred T. Mahan**, a military historian and an officer in the United States Navy, played a key role in transforming America into a naval power. In *The Influence of Sea Power Upon History*, Mahan asserted that since ancient times, many great nations had owed their greatness to powerful navies. Mahan believed strongly that control of the seas during wartime was crucial to a nation's success. He called upon America to build a modern fleet. Mahan also argued that the United States would need to acquire foreign bases where American ships could refuel and gather fresh supplies.

Influenced by the ideas of Mahan and others, the United States expanded and modernized its navy by building new steel-plated, steampowered battleships such as the USS *Maine*. By 1900, the United States had the third-largest navy in the world. Leaders such as U.S. Senator Henry Cabot Lodge, a strong supporter of American expansionism, continued to encourage a naval build-up into the early twentieth century. Lodge and others believed that the a strong navy was vital to the protection of U.S. interests both at home and abroad.

Social Darwinism, Missionaries, and National Superiority

European and Japanese imperialists used ideas of racial, national, and cultural superiority to justify taking over colonies. One of these ideas was **Social Darwinism,** the belief that life consists of competitive struggles in which only the fittest survive. Social Darwinists felt that certain nations and races were superior to others and therefore were destined to rule over inferior peoples and cultures. Some prominent Americans embraced these ideas and began to worry that if the United States remained isolated while European nations gobbled up the rest of the world, America would not survive.

One reason that these Americans embraced Social Darwinism was that they had long believed that God had granted them the right and responsibility to settle the frontier. They spoke of America's "Manifest Destiny" to expand all the way to the Pacific Ocean. In a best-selling work titled *Our Country,* Josiah Strong picked up on this theme. A religious missionary, Strong argued that Americans

>> The USS *Brooklyn* played a substantial role in American naval operations in the Caribbean Sea and in Asia. U.S. leaders believed in the value of a strong military during the late 1800s.

Bounce to Activate Chart

had a responsibility to spread their Western values. "God is training the Anglo-Saxon race," he asserted, "for its mission [to civilize] weaker races." Influenced by Strong, many American missionaries journeyed to foreign lands to gain converts to Christianity. Although missionaries were often motivated by a sincere desire to spread their faith, the linking of missionary work to the concept of U.S. expansionism strengthened American presence in these territories.

In *The Significance of the Frontier in American History,* historian **Frederick Jackson Turner** noted that the frontier had been closed by gradual settlement in the nineteenth century. Throughout American history, he continued, the frontier had traditionally supplied an arena where ambitious Americans could pursue their fortunes and secure a fresh start. It had thus served as a "safety valve," siphoning off potential discontent.

Now that America had spanned the continent, advocates of Turner's thesis urged overseas expansion as a way to keep the "safety valve" open and avoid internal conflict.

☑ **IDENTIFY** What factors influenced Americans to play a more active role in the world?

>> **Draw Conclusions** What part of the Salvation Army's mission do the blue-jacketed people seem to be carrying out in this illustration?

America Begins to Expand

Beginning in the mid-1800s, with little fanfare, America focused more and more on expanding its trade and acquiring new territories. One of America's first moves toward world power came before the Civil War.

American Expansionism in the Pacific Begins

In 1853, Commodore **Matthew Perry** sailed a fleet of American warships into present-day Tokyo Bay, Japan. Prior to Perry's arrival, Japan had denied the rest of the world access to its ports. In fact, because most Japanese people had never seen steamships before, they thought the ships in Perry's fleet were "giant dragons puffing smoke." Perry cleverly won the Japanese emperor's favor by showering him with lavish gifts. Japanese leaders also realized that by closing off their nation to the outside world, they had fallen behind in military technology. Within a year, Perry negotiated a treaty that opened Japan to trade with America.

Perry's journey set a precedent for further expansion across the Pacific Ocean. In 1867, the United States took possession of the Midway Islands.

Treaties in 1875 and 1887 increased trade with the Hawaiian Islands and gave the United States the right to build a naval base at Pearl Harbor.

The Klondike Gold Rush In 1867, Secretary of State William Seward bought Alaska from Russia for $7.2 million. Journalists scoffed at the purchase and referred to Alaska as "Seward's Folly" and "Seward's Icebox." They wondered why the United States would want a vast tundra of snow and ice 1,000 miles north of its border. But Seward's purchase almost doubled the country's size, and the "icebox" turned out to be rich in timber, oil, and other natural resources. Alaska also greatly expanded America's reach across the Pacific. Scholars today see Seward's purchase as a key milestone on America's road to power.

By the mid-1880s, gold had been discovered in several locations near Alaska, sparking the Klondike Gold Rush. The stampede to the Klondike goldfields in British Columbia and Yukon territory led to the development of new towns in Alaska. However, the human geography challenges of sparse settlement and lack of transportation routes and the physical geography challenges caused by nearby mountains and a frigid climate ended the rush by 1899.

>> In Hawaii, American owners of sugar plantations, such as this one, exerted broad and increasing influence over local affairs.

Bounce to Activate Gallery

>> Hawaiian Queen Liluokalani unsuccessfully resisted U.S. influence in Hawaii.

American Expansionism in Latin America U.S. business leaders saw Latin America as a natural place to expand their trade and investments. Secretary of State James Blaine helped them by sponsoring the First International Pan-American Conference in 1889. Blaine preached the benefits of economic cooperation to delegates of 17 Latin American countries. The conference also paved the way for the construction of the Pan-American Highway system, which linked the United States to Central and South America.

In 1895, tensions rose between America and Great Britain because of a border dispute between British Guiana and Venezuela. Claiming that Britain was violating the Monroe Doctrine, President Cleveland threatened U.S. intervention. After some international saber-rattling, the British accepted a growing U.S. sphere of influence in Latin America. Relations between Britain and the United States soon improved.

☑ **RECALL** Why did journalists criticize Seward for his purchase of Alaska?

The Acquisition of Hawaii

By the 1890s, the Hawaiian Islands had been economically linked to the United States for almost a century. Since the 1790s, American merchant ships had stopped at Hawaii on their way to East Asia. Missionaries had established Christian churches and schools on the islands. Americans had also established sugar cane plantations there. In 1887, American planters convinced King Kalakaua (kah LAH kah oo ah) to amend Hawaii's constitution so that voting rights were limited to only wealthy landowners, who were, of course, the white planters.

Influence of Dole and Other Americans in Hawaii In the early 1890s, American planters in Hawaii faced two crises. First, a new U.S. tariff law imposed duties on previously duty-free Hawaiian sugar. This made Hawaiian sugar more expensive than sugar produced in the United States. The sugar growers in Hawaii therefore feared that they would suffer decreasing sales and profits.

The other problem was that in 1891, Kalakaua died and his sister Liliuokalani (lih lee oo oh kah LAH nee) was his successor. A determined Hawaiian nationalist, **Queen Liluokalani** resented the increasing power of the white planters, who owned much of Hawaiian land. She abolished the constitution that had given political power to the white minority.

With the backing of U.S. officials, the American planters responded quickly and forcefully. In 1893, they overthrew the queen. John Stevens, U.S. minister to Hawaii, ordered United States Marines to help the rebels seize power. The new government, led by influential lawyer **Sanford B. Dole**, asked President Benjamin Harrison to annex Hawaii to the United States.

Dole, born in Hawaii of missionary parents, was a well-respected lawyer and jurist who was connected to Hawaii's planter elite. His cousin, James Dole, moved to Hawaii in 1899 and helped build a pineapple company that still exists today.

The United States Annexes Hawaii After Liluokalani's overthrow, President Harrison signed the treaty of annexation but could not get the required Senate approval before Grover Cleveland became President. Cleveland ordered a full investigation, which revealed that the majority of the Hawaiian people did not approve of the treaty. Cleveland refused to sign the agreement and apologized for the "flagrant wrong" done by the "reprehensible conduct of the American minister."

However, American sentiment for annexation remained strong, especially on the West Coast, where California business interests had close ties with the planters in Hawaii. In 1897, a new President entered the White House. William McKinley's administration favored annexation, and in 1898, after the outbreak of the Spanish-American War, Congress proclaimed Hawaii an official U.S. territory with Sanford B. Dole as its first governor.

☑ **CHECK UNDERSTANDING** How did American planters react to Queen Liluokalani's actions when she gained power?

☑ ASSESSMENT

1. **Generate Explanations** Explain why many world powers developed extractive economies during the 1800s, and why this was less important for the United States.

2. **Draw Conclusions** Explain why the United States needed to expand its trade into new markets.

3. **Evaluate Arguments** Explain how some used Social Darwinism to justify imperialism.

4. **Summarize** the concept of Manifest Destiny.

5. **Generate Explanations** Explain how the United States gained influence in Latin America.

>> African Americans made up approximately 10 percent of U.S. forces during the Spanish-American War. **Infer** What do you think motivated African Americans to join the armed forces during the Spanish-American War?

Bounce to Activate Flipped Video

3.6

American power and economic interests around the world were growing. Still, the United States remained reluctant to risk war with other powers to acquire colonies. That changed, however, in 1898, when America went to war against Spain. The United States acquired colonies and became a world power.

>> Objectives

Explain the causes of the Spanish-American War.

Identify the major battles of the Spanish-American War.

Describe the consequences of the war, including the debate over imperialism.

Examine the causes and consequences of the Philippine insurrection.

>> Key Terms

José Martí
William Randolph
  Hearst
Yellow Press
jingoism
George Dewey
Emilio Aguinaldo
Rough Riders
Treaty of Paris
insurrection
guerrilla warfare
William Howard Taft

The Spanish-American War

Causes of the Spanish-American War

U.S. Sympathies for Cuban Rebels At the end of the nineteenth century, Spain was an imperial nation in decline. Its formerly vast empire had dwindled to a small number of possessions, including the Philippine Islands in the Pacific and the Caribbean islands of Puerto Rico and Cuba.

By 1897, American entrepreneurs had invested $50 million in sugar cane plantations and other ventures in Cuba, which lay just 90 miles off the Florida coast. These businessmen saw Cuba as a growing market for American products. However, the island was very unstable. Yearning for freedom, the Cubans repeatedly rebelled against Spanish rule.

In 1895, Cuban patriot **José Martí** launched a war for independence from Spain. With cries of *"Cuba Libre!"* ("Free Cuba!"), rebel fighters used guerrilla tactics of hit-and-run raids against Spanish forces. In response, Spanish General Valeriano Weyler devised a plan to deprive the rebels of food and recruits.

He herded the rural population into reconcentration camps, where tens of thousands died from disease and starvation. Meanwhile, the Cubans and Spanish destroyed American property.

Many Americans favored the Cubans, whose struggle for freedom and democracy reminded Americans of their own revolutionary heritage. José Martí had also been campaigning through the Cuban immigrant communities of Florida to raise money for the rebellion. The brutality of Spanish tactics intensified American affection and sympathy for the rebels. But other Americans, especially business people, were worried about U.S. economic interests in Cuba and hoped that Spain would quickly put down the rebellion.

Influence of Mass Media Rival newspaper publishers Joseph Pulitzer and **William Randolph Hearst** heightened the public's dislike of the Spanish government. Their publications were called the **Yellow Press** because they featured a popular comic-strip character called The Yellow Kid. To boost readership, Pulitzer's *New York World,* Hearst's *New York Journal,* and similar newspapers pasted sensational headlines and pictures on their front pages. Their stories exaggerated Spanish atrocities and compared Cuban rebels to the patriots of the American Revolution.

President William McKinley warned the Spanish to quickly establish peace, or the United States would take whatever steps it "should deem necessary to procure this result." Spain recalled General Weyler and offered the Cuban rebels some reforms. But the rebels insisted on independence, which Spain refused to grant. McKinley ordered the battleship *Maine* to Havana harbor to protect American citizens in Cuba.

Then, in February 1898, the *Journal* published a private letter written by Enrique Dupuy de Lôme, Spain's ambassador to Washington, D.C. The letter, stolen by Cuban rebels and leaked to Hearst, called McKinley a weak and stupid politician. Hearst published the letter under the sensational headline, "Worst Insult to the United States in Its History." The letter fueled American **jingoism,** or aggressive nationalism, and inflamed relations with Spain.

The Explosion of the *Maine* Soon after the *Journal* published de Lôme's letter, the *Maine* exploded in Havana harbor. Of the 350 officers and crew on board at the time, 266 died. The Yellow Press promptly accused Spain of blowing up the battleship. One *Journal* headline even declared: "War? Sure!"

President McKinley ordered a special naval board of inquiry to investigate the cause of the explosion.

>> A group of Cuban rebels attacked a Spanish plantation overseer.

>> Graphic illustrations such as this one depicting the explosion of the USS *Maine* had a profound influence on attitudes in the United States.

Bounce to Activate Gallery

On March 28, 1898, the board concluded that a mine had destroyed the battleship. Years later, follow-up investigations raised doubts about the naval board's findings, but, at the time, most people blamed Spain.

The Spanish-American War Begins War fever gripped the nation. In newspapers, speeches, and songs, patriotic Americans implored their fellow citizens to "Remember the *Maine*!" In response to American demands, Spain agreed to abolish the reconcentration camps and make other concessions, but it was too little too late. On April 11, 1898, McKinley asked Congress for the authority to use force against Spain to end the fighting in Cuba "in the name of humanity, in the name of civilization, in behalf of endangered American interests."

Eight days later, Congress enacted four resolutions that amounted to a declaration of war on Spain. The fourth resolution—the Teller Amendment—stipulated that the United States had no intention of annexing Cuba. The navy quickly blockaded Cuban ports, and McKinley called for more than 100,000 volunteers to join the army. In response, Spain declared war on the United States.

☑ **RECALL** Why did Americans object to Spanish actions in Cuba?

American Forces Defeat the Spanish

Americans responded enthusiastically to the war. About 200,000 men enlisted in the army, up from the 25,000 that enlisted at the beginning of 1898. In early May, as the United States Army prepared to attack, Americans heard news of a great naval victory over Spain. But, surprisingly, the victory was not in Cuba. Rather, it was in the Pacific Ocean, on the opposite side of the world.

Acquiring the Philippines On May 1, 1898, Commodore **George Dewey** steamed his squadron of vessels into Manila Bay, in the Spanish-held Philippines. The Americans completely surprised the Spanish fleet that was stationed in the bay.

Upon issuing the order to "fire when ready," Dewey watched his ships quickly destroy the Spanish force. While no Americans died during the naval battle, nearly 400 Spanish sailors lost their lives. American gleefully received news of the victory and proclaimed Dewey a hero.

While Dewey was winning an astounding victory over the Spanish navy, Filipino nationalists led by **Emilio Aguinaldo** (ahg ee NAHL doh) were defeating the Spanish army. Like the Cubans, the Filipinos were fighting for freedom from Spain. In

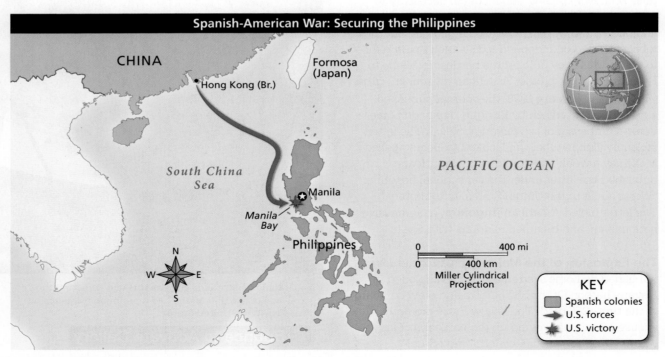

>> **Analyze Maps** Why did American forces likely launch their attack on the Philippines from the British port city of Hong Kong?

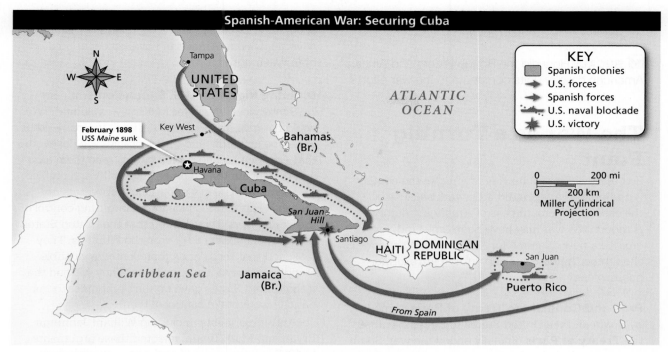

Spanish-American War: Securing Cuba

KEY
- Spanish colonies
- U.S. forces
- Spanish forces
- U.S. naval blockade
- U.S. victory

February 1898
USS *Maine* sunk

0   200 mi
0   200 km
Miller Cylindrical Projection

UNITED STATES
Tampa
Key West
ATLANTIC OCEAN
Bahamas (Br.)
Havana
Cuba
San Juan Hill
Santiago
HAITI
DOMINICAN REPUBLIC
San Juan
Puerto Rico
Caribbean Sea
Jamaica (Br.)
From Spain

>> **Analyze Maps** How do you think the U.S. naval blockade affect Spain's troop shipments to Cuba during the Spanish-American War?

August, after some 15,000 U.S. soldiers had landed on the islands, Spanish troops surrendered to the United States.

Victory in Cuba Meanwhile, American troops landed in Cuba in June 1898. U.S. Marines captured Guantánamo Bay, and a force of 17,000 soldiers under U.S. Army General William Shafter stormed ashore east of Santiago.

In spite of their excitement for the war, the troops faced deplorable conditions. They were poorly trained and supplied.

As they assembled for duty around Tampa, Florida, the soldiers were issued obsolete weapons and heavy wool uniforms that were unsuitable for Cuba's tropical climate. Corrupt and inefficient officials provided the men with rotting and contaminated food.

General Shafter's army consisted of state National Guard units and regular army units, including the African American Ninth and Tenth Cavalry regiments from the western frontier. Another cavalry unit was organized and commanded by the future President Theodore Roosevelt. His **Rough Riders** consisted of rugged westerners and upper-class easterners who relished what Roosevelt called the "strenuous life."

The Rough Riders and Roosevelt gained fame for the role they played in the battles for Kettle and San Juan hills outside Santiago, Cuba. Joined by African American soldiers from the Ninth and Tenth Cavalries, the Riders stormed up those hills to secure high ground surrounding Santiago. One war correspondent described a charge of the African American soldiers:

> [T]hey followed their leader up the terrible hill from whose crest the desperate Spaniards poured down a deadly fire of shell and musketry. They never faltered. . . . [T]heir aim was splendid, their coolness was superb. . . . The war had not shown greater heroism.

—War correspondent, 1898

Two days after the battle of San Juan Hill, the Spanish navy made a desperate attempt to escape from Santiago's harbor. U.S. forces, which had blockaded the harbor, destroyed the Spanish fleet as it tried to break out. Surrounded, outnumbered, and dispirited, Spanish forces in Santiago surrendered. Although a few battles followed when U.S. forces occupied the island of Puerto Rico, another Spanish possession, the fighting had come to an end. Although almost 3,000 Americans died during the war, only around 380 died in combat. Disease, especially malaria and yellow fever, caused most of the deaths.

☑ **RECALL** How did the Rough Riders and African American cavalry units contribute to the war effort?

The War as a Turning Point

Secretary of State John Hay referred to the conflict with Spain as a "splendid little war" because of the ease and thoroughness of America's victory. Although the war may have been "splendid," it created a new dilemma for Americans: What should the United States do with Spain's former possessions?

Pros and Cons of the Treaty of Paris Signed by Spain and the United States in December 1898, the **Treaty of Paris** officially ended the war. Spain gave up control of Cuba, Puerto Rico, and the Pacific island of Guam. It also sold the Philippines to the United States for $20 million.

The Teller Amendment, passed by Congress when it declared war on Spain, prevented the United States from taking possession of Cuba. The amendment did not, however, apply to the Philippines. Americans disagreed over whether to grant the Philippines independence or take full control of the Pacific nation.

Guam, with its excellent harbor and mid-Pacific location, was desired as a coaling station to fuel U.S. Navy and merchant ships traveling to the Far East.

Between 1898 and 1950 (aside from the period of its occupation by Japan during World War II), Guam's governor was an American naval officer appointed from Washington, D.C.

Differing Views on U.S. Expansionism In an 1899 interview, President McKinley explained, "We could not give [the Philippines] back to Spain—that would be cowardly and dishonorable." He believed that America had no choice but to "take them all, and to educate the Filipinos, and uplift and civilize . . . them." McKinley's imperialist supporters presented similar reasons for maintaining control of the Philippines. They argued that the United States had a responsibility to govern the Filipinos. They reasoned that the islands represented a valuable stepping stone to trade in China. They warned that if the United States gave up the Philippines, other nations would take control of them.

Anti-imperialists, including William Jennings Bryan and Mark Twain, rejected these arguments. In 1899, a large group of anti-imperialists formed the American Anti-Imperialist League. The league condemned imperialism as a crime and attacked it as "open disloyalty to the distinctive principles of our government."

The debate reached its climax in the U.S. Senate, where senators had to consider ratifying the Treaty of Paris. In February 1899, the Senate voted 57 to 27 in favor of the treaty. By a single "yes" ballot, the vote met the two-thirds majority necessary to ratify the treaty.

Although the military conflict had been expensive, its economic effects on the United States were mainly positive. There was much more

Pros and Cons of the Treaty of Paris, 1898

PROS	CONS
• U.S. acquires the Philippines • Treaty benefits U.S. much more than Spain • Guam and Puerto Rico become part of U.S. territory • U.S. expands influence and becomes new player in world politics	• Guerilla fighting against U.S. troops in the Philippines lasts three years • U.S. loses ten times more troops in the Philippines than in the Spanish-American War • Public opinion in U.S. divided over the issue of imperialism in Philippines • Because of its rising global influence, U.S. clashes with China and Japan

>> **Analyze Information** How did the Spanish-American War contribute to the rise of the United States as a world power?

agreement about the war's effects among the U.S. business community than in Congress.

The acquisition of Puerto Rico, Guam, and the Philippines gave the U.S. Navy secure bases and coaling stations for its ships. The westward move of American power and influence was desired by farmers and industrialists who saw Asia, and China especially, as an untapped market for their goods.

After the war, tropical agriculture, mostly in sugar, became big business for U.S. companies in Puerto Rico and Cuba. By 1895, U.S. interests already had more than $50 million invested in Cuba, and trade with the island, mostly in sugar, was worth twice that. These interests certainly welcomed the increased American intervention and control after the Spanish-American War. In 1901, U.S. legislation known as the Platt Amendment put the internal, external, and economic affairs of Cuba under the control of the United States. It also established the U.S. naval base at Guantánamo Bay. The amendment was mostly repealed in 1934, but the naval base remains even today.

☑ **CHECK UNDERSTANDING** Why did American leaders think it was important to keep the Philippines?

Effects of U.S. Expansionism in the Philippines

America's decision to keep the Philippines reflected a desire to expand its influence, compete with European colonial powers, and gain new trade in Asia.

The Filipino nationalist leader Emilio Aguinaldo had thought that the United States was an ally in the Filipino struggle for independence. His forces had fought side by side with the Americans against the Spanish. However, after the United States decided to maintain possession of the Philippines, Aguinaldo grew disillusioned with America. He helped organize an **insurrection**, or rebellion, against U.S. rule. The rebels believed they were fighting for the same principle of self-rule that had inspired America's colonial patriots during the American Revolution.

Guerrilla War Erupts in the Philippines

Outgunned by American troops, Filipino insurgents relied on **guerrilla warfare,** a form of nontraditional warfare generally involving small bands of fighters attacking behind enemy lines. In turn, the American

>> **Analyze Political Cartoons** What does the portrayal of the territories on the wall poster imply about American involvement in those regions?

🅑 **Bounce to Activate Chart**

>> Emilio Aguinaldo fought first as an American ally against the Spanish, then led an insurrection against America in favor of Filipino self-rule.

military used extraordinary measures to crush the rebellion. Like the Spanish in Cuba, U.S. soldiers gathered civilians into overcrowded concentration camps. General Jacob Smith ordered his soldiers not to take prisoners. "I wish you to kill and burn, the more you kill and burn the better you will please me," he commented. A California newspaper defended such actions:

> Let us all be frank. WE DO NOT WANT THE FILIPINOS. WE WANT THE PHILIPPINES. All of our troubles in this annexation matter have been caused by the presence in the Philippine Islands of the Filipinos. . . . The more of them killed the better. It seems harsh. But they must yield before the superior race.
>
> —San Francisco *Argonaut,*1902

In the spring of 1901, the Americans captured Aguinaldo. Although the fighting did not end immediately, his capture marked the beginning of the end of the insurrection. The war in the Philippines took more lives than the Spanish-American War. Nearly 5,000 Americans and 200,000 Filipinos died in the fighting. The U.S. government sent more than 100,000 troops to fight in the war and spent upwards of $400 million to defeat the insurgency. The conflict highlighted the rigors of fighting against guerrilla insurgents.

The Philippines Begin Limited Self-Rule In 1901, **William Howard Taft**—a future President of the United States—became governor of the Philippines. Taft had large ambitions for helping the islands recover from the rebellion. He censored the press and placed dissidents in jail to maintain order and to win the support of the Filipino people. At the same time, he began several policies to improve the situation of the Filipinos. He extended limited self-rule, with the Philippine Assembly convening in Manila in 1907. He alsoordered the construction of roads, bridges, and schools. He established a public health system to care for Filipinos.

In 1916, Congress passed the Jones Act, which pledged that the Philippines would ultimately gain their independence. Thirty years later, after U.S. forces liberated the islands from Japanese occupation at the end of World War II, the Philippines finally became an independent nation.

Growing U.S. Position as a World Power In 1900, William Jennings Bryan ran against William

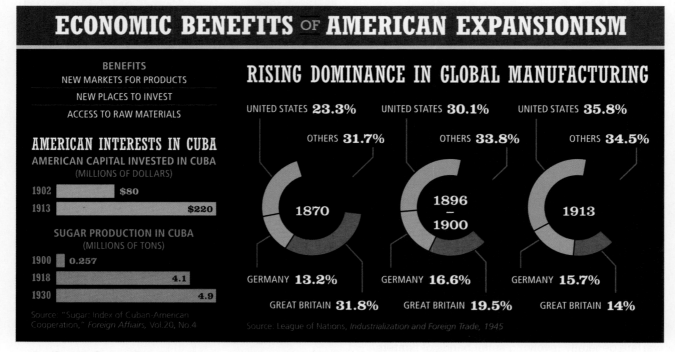

>> **Analyze Information** How did American investment in Cuba in the early 1900s affect the level of sugar production in Cuba?

McKinley for the presidency. To bolster his chances of winning reelection, the Republican McKinley named Theodore Roosevelt, the "hero of San Juan Hill," as his vice-presidential running mate. Emphasizing the overwhelming U.S. victory over Spain, McKinley soundly defeated Bryan. The President's reelection signaled America's continuing faith in his expansionist policies.

The Spanish-American War was a significant event in the emergence of the United States as a world power. As a result of the war, the United States had an empire and a new stature in world affairs. The war marked a turning point in the history of American foreign policy.

☑ **RECALL** Why did hostilities erupt in the Philippines after the Spanish-American War?

☑ ASSESSMENT

1. **Identify Cause and Effect** Explain how the Yellow Press affected relations between the United States and Spain.

2. **Compare Points of View** Discuss how Emilio Aguinaldo's opinion of the United States changed after the Spanish-American War.

3. **Summarize** the results of the Treaty of Paris and the Teller Amendment, and explain why these proved to be complicated for the United States.

4. **Draw Conclusions** Discuss the role of the Spanish-American War in determining the winner of the 1900 U.S. presidential election.

5. **Make Generalizations** Describe the conditions that U.S. troops faced during the Spanish-American War, and how they affected the war's outcome.

>> These U.S. troops in Beijing, China, were part of a multinational force deployed to put down the Boxer Rebellion in 1900.

Bounce to Activate Flipped Video

(3.7) As the United States emerged as a world power following the Spanish-American War, American leaders looked to strengthen economic and military interests in Latin America and East Asia. In East Asia, American leaders devised policies to open China and other Asian markets to U.S. producers. Meanwhile, Americans called for a more substantial role in Latin America, viewing the region as the nation's backyard. Increasing influence in both regions brought economic benefits, but also increased international tensions.

>> Objectives

Analyze how economic concerns influenced the Open Door Policy and U.S. relations with Japan.

Examine what happened to Puerto Rico and Cuba after the Spanish-American War.

Analyze the effects of Roosevelt's "big stick" diplomacy and Taft's "dollar diplomacy."

Compare Wilson's "moral diplomacy" with the foreign policies of his predecessors.

>> Key Terms

spheres of influence
John Hay
Boxer Rebellion
Open Door Policy
Russo-Japanese War
"Gentlemen's Agreement"
Great White Fleet
Foraker Act
Platt Amendment
"big stick" diplomacy
Panama Canal
Roosevelt Corollary
"dollar diplomacy"
"moral diplomacy"
Francisco "Pancho" Villa

The United States Emerges as a World Power

U.S. Trade and Intervention in China

By 1899, once-mighty China had fallen into political, economic, and military disarray. Its huge population, however, was a tempting target for other nations' imported goods. Rather than compete for Chinese trade, Britain, France, Germany, and Russia carved China into distinct **spheres of influence**. Within its zone, each power had privileged access to Chinese ports and markets. Japan also expanded its regional influence, grabbing territory in China and Korea. Since the United States did not have a zone, this system of "special privileges" threatened to limit American trade in China.

A Call for Equality in Commerce In order to overcome these barriers, U.S. Secretary of State **John Hay** issued the first of a series of notes to foreign diplomats in 1899. He notified the leaders of imperialist nations that the United States expected "perfect equality of treatment for commerce" in China. Hay's note had little immediate impact on the actions of European nations or Japan. However, it served as a guiding principle of American foreign policy in Asia for years to come.

The U.S. Intervenes in the Boxer Rebellion In response to the growing influence of outsiders in their country, some Chinese joined secret societies. One such society, the Righteous and Harmonious Fists, won the nickname "Boxers" from Europeans because its members trained in martial arts. The secret societies celebrated traditional Chinese customs and criticized Western ways. They also condemned Chinese converts to Christianity. Over time, simmering anger exploded into an outright rebellion against the "foreign devils."

In May 1900, the Boxers killed foreign missionaries and besieged the foreign diplomats' district in Beijing. A multinational force of European, American, and Japanese troops was sent to the Chinese capital to quash the **Boxer Rebellion**. An initial force of 2,100 soldiers grew to more than 20,000, including 2,000 Americans. After putting down the rebellion, European powers compelled China's imperial government to pay an indemnity, or money to repair damage caused by the rebellion. This poured more fuel onto the nationalist fire. Chinese nationalists would eventually revolt and overthrow the emperor in 1911.

The Open Door Policy As the Boxer Rebellion engulfed China, Secretary of State Hay reasserted America's **Open Door Policy**, which argued for equal privileges among countries trading with China. In a second note to European powers, Hay stated that the United States wanted to "preserve Chinese territorial and administrative entity." In other words, America did not want colonies in China; it just wanted free trade there. As an act of goodwill, the United States used some of the indemnity money it received from China to fund scholarships for Chinese students to study in America. Hay and others strongly believed that access to the markets in China was crucial to rebounding from an economic depression in the 1890s. The goal of the Open Door Policy was to bring American businesses the new foreign markets they needed.

☑ **IDENTIFY** What was the purpose of the Open Door Policy?

Spheres of Influence in China

KEY
— China border
Spheres of Influence
- British
- French
- German
- Japanese
- Russian

>> **Analyze Maps** What can you conclude about the influence of the United States in China during the early twentieth century?

Roosevelt Works With Japan

Like the United States, Japan wanted to expand its influence in China. Japan also disapproved of the European "carve-up" of the region. Furthermore, the Japanese took offense to the presence of Russian troops in Manchuria, a region of China that bordered Russia. In February 1904, without a declaration of war, Japan attacked and bottled up Russia's Pacific fleet stationed at Port Arthur, China. The Japanese followed up on this victory with a series of major land engagements in Manchuria that caused more than 100,000 Russian casualties. However, Japan also suffered heavy losses in the fighting.

Resolving the Russo-Japanese War In 1905, representatives from Russia and Japan met in Portsmouth, New Hampshire, to negotiate an end to the **Russo-Japanese War**. When the talks stalled, Theodore Roosevelt, now President, intervened and convinced the two sides to sign a peace treaty. For his efforts, Roosevelt won the Nobel Peace Prize. The President's intervention—and his receipt of the famous award—prominently displayed America's growing role in world affairs.

Racial Prejudice Affects Foreign Relations Despite Roosevelt's achievement, America entered troubled waters in its relations with Japan. A root cause of this trouble was anti-Asian sentiment on the West Coast of the United States. In the fall of 1906, the San Francisco School Board banned Japanese, Chinese, and Korean children from attending public schools with white children. The incident drew Japan's immediate wrath. One Tokyo journal demanded that Japan retaliate. "Stand up Japanese nation! Our countrymen have been HUMILIATED on the other side of the Pacific," the newspaper cried out.

Roosevelt disapproved of the decision to segregate Asian children in the San Francisco schools. He understood Japan's anger with America. To calm tensions, he negotiated a **"Gentlemen's Agreement"** with Japan. According to the pact, the school board pledged to end its segregation policy. In return, Japan agreed to limit the emigration of its citizens to the United States.

The Great White Fleet Shows Naval Power While Roosevelt used diplomacy to ease tensions with Japan, he also promoted military preparedness to protect U.S. interests in Asia. Expressing rising concerns about Japan's territorial expansion at the expense of China, Korea, and Russia—the President won congressional support for a new force of navy ships, known as the **Great White Fleet**. In 1907, Roosevelt sent this armada of 16 white battleships on a "good will cruise" around the world. The voyage of the Great White Fleet demonstrated America's increased military power to the world.

☑ **SUMMARIZE** What conditions led to the Russo-Japanese War?

American Foreign Policy in Latin America

As the United States tentatively asserted its interests in East Asia, Americans called for a more aggressive role in Latin America. American entrepreneurs and government leaders wanted the region to be a sphere of influence from which other great powers were excluded. American influence in Latin America brought obvious benefits to the United States, but it also contributed to anti-American hostility and instability in the region.

>> The Great White Fleet, part of Roosevelt's plan to protect American interests in Asia, departs from a U.S. port in 1907. **Analyze Information** Explain why Asian nations might have not have believed that the voyage of the fleet was a "good will cruise."

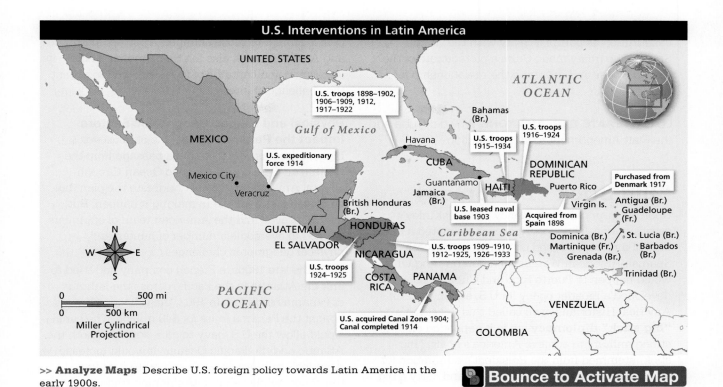

U.S. Interventions in Latin America

U.S. troops 1898–1902, 1906–1909, 1912, 1917–1922

U.S. troops 1915–1934

U.S. troops 1916–1924

U.S. expeditionary force 1914

U.S. leased naval base 1903

Acquired from Spain 1898

Purchased from Denmark 1917

U.S. troops 1909–1910, 1912–1925, 1926–1933

U.S. troops 1924–1925

U.S. acquired Canal Zone 1904; Canal completed 1914

UNITED STATES

MEXICO

Mexico City

Veracruz

Gulf of Mexico

Havana

CUBA

Guantanamo

Jamaica (Br.)

British Honduras (Br.)

GUATEMALA

EL SALVADOR

HONDURAS

NICARAGUA

COSTA RICA

PANAMA

Bahamas (Br.)

HAITI

DOMINICAN REPUBLIC

Puerto Rico

Virgin Is.

Antigua (Br.)

Guadeloupe (Fr.)

Dominica (Br.)

Martinique (Fr.)

Grenada (Br.)

St. Lucia (Br.)

Barbados (Br.)

Trinidad (Br.)

VENEZUELA

COLOMBIA

Caribbean Sea

ATLANTIC OCEAN

PACIFIC OCEAN

N W E S

0   500 mi
0   500 km
Miller Cylindrical Projection

>> **Analyze Maps** Describe U.S. foreign policy towards Latin America in the early 1900s.

Bounce to Activate Map

America's victory over Spain liberated the Puerto Rican and Cuban people from Spanish rule. But victory left the fates of these islands unresolved. Would Puerto Rico and Cuba become independent nations? Or would they become colonies of the United States? As questions lingered in the aftermath of war, the United States assumed control in Puerto Rico and Cuba.

Foreign Policy Decisions in Puerto Rico As the smoke from the Spanish-American War cleared, America's new acquisition of Puerto Rico remained under direct U.S. military rule. In 1900, Congress passed the **Foraker Act**, which established a civil government in Puerto Rico. The act authorized the President of the United States to appoint a governor and part of the Puerto Rican legislature. Puerto Ricans could fill the rest of the legislature in a general election.

Whether Puerto Ricans could enjoy citizenship rights in the United States, however, remained unclear. This unusual situation led to a series of court cases, known as Insular Cases, in which the Supreme Court determined the rights of Puerto Ricans. One case examined whether the U.S. government could assess taxes on Puerto Rican goods sold in the United States. The Supreme Court

ruled the taxes legal and determined that Puerto Ricans did not enjoy the same rights as U.S. citizens.

In 1917, President Woodrow Wilson signed the Jones-Shafroth Act. It granted Puerto Ricans more citizenship rights and gave the islanders greater control over their own legislature. Still, many Puerto Ricans expressed their discontent because they did not enjoy all of the same rights as Americans.

Relations with Cuba Although the Treaty of Paris granted Cuban independence, the United States Army did not withdraw from the island until 1902. But before the U.S. military left, Congress obliged Cuba to add to its constitution the **Platt Amendment**. The amendment restricted the rights of newly independent Cubans and effectively brought the island within the U.S. sphere. It prevented Cuba from signing a treaty with another nation without American approval. It also required Cuba to lease naval stations to the United States. Additionally, the Platt Amendment granted the United States the "right to intervene" to preserve order in Cuba.

Many Cubans strongly disliked the Platt Amendment but soon realized that America would not otherwise end its military government of the island. The United States, for its part, was unwilling to risk Cuba's becoming a base for a potentially hostile great power.

Cuba thus added the Platt Amendment to its constitution as part of a treaty with the United States. The treaty made Cuba a protectorate of the United States and governed their relationship for decades.

☑ **GENERATE EXPLANATIONS** Why did Cuba add the Platt Amendment to its constitution?

"Big Stick" Diplomacy

Upon assuming the presidency after McKinley's assassination, Theodore Roosevelt promoted a new kind of diplomacy based on America's success in the Spanish-American War. Beyond determining what would happen to Puerto Rico and Cuba, Roosevelt developed a broader policy for U.S. action in Latin America. Historians have called this Roosevelt's **"big stick" diplomacy** since it depended on a strong military to achieve America's goals. "Big stick" stemmed from the President's admiration for an old African saying, "Speak softly and carry a big stick; you will go far."

Roosevelt's view that America needed to carry a big stick during the Age of Imperialism flowed from his adherence to balance-of-power principles and from his view of the United States as a special nation with a moral responsibility to "civilize," or uplift, weaker nations. In this sense, the new President held beliefs similar to those of imperial powers in Europe and Asia. Roosevelt also felt that America's elite—its statesmen and captains of industry—had to accept the challenge of international leadership.

Physical and Human Geographic Factors Impact the Panama Canal One of Roosevelt's biggest dreams was to create a passage from the Caribbean Ocean to the Pacific Ocean through Central America. He did not originate the plan, but he played a crucial role in making it happen. But first, Roosevelt and the American team of engineers worked to overcome a number of human and physical geographic challenges.

In the late 1800s, a French company had tried to link the Atlantic to the Pacific across the Isthmus of Panama but failed. In 1903, the U.S. government bought the Panama route for $40 million. The canal would allow the U.S. navy to gain control of both the Atlantic and the Pacific Oceans. It would increase America's military security and protect its new territories, while helping its shipping trade reach overseas markets more easily and cheaply.

Before it could build a canal through Panama, however, the United States needed the consent of the Colombian government. At the time, Panama was part of independent Colombia. American efforts to negotiate a purchase of land across the isthmus

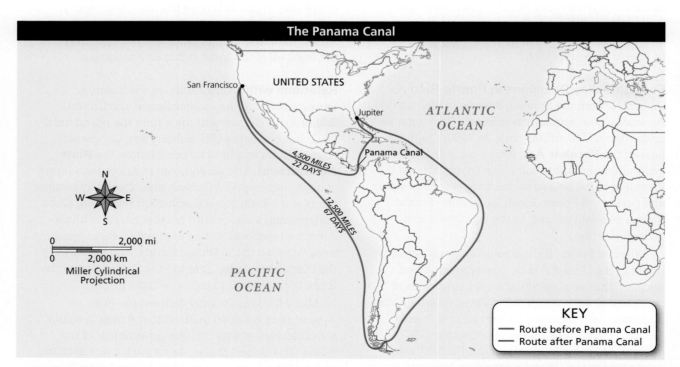

The Panama Canal

San Francisco · UNITED STATES

ATLANTIC OCEAN

Jupiter

4,500 MILES 22 DAYS

Panama Canal

12,500 MILES 67 DAYS

0 — 2,000 mi
0 — 2,000 km
Miller Cylindrical Projection

PACIFIC OCEAN

KEY
— Route before Panama Canal
— Route after Panama Canal

>> **Analyze Maps** How did the construction of the Panama Canal benefit long-distance shippers?

Bounce to Activate Gallery

★ DOLLAR DIPLOMACY IN THE EARLY 1900S ★

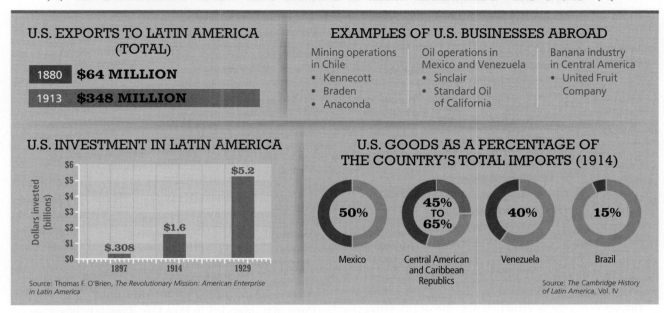

U.S. EXPORTS TO LATIN AMERICA (TOTAL)

1880 **$64 MILLION**

1913 **$348 MILLION**

EXAMPLES OF U.S. BUSINESSES ABROAD

Mining operations in Chile
- Kennecott
- Braden
- Anaconda

Oil operations in Mexico and Venezuela
- Sinclair
- Standard Oil of California

Banana industry in Central America
- United Fruit Company

U.S. INVESTMENT IN LATIN AMERICA

Dollars invested (billions)

1897 $.308
1914 $1.6
1929 $5.2

Source: Thomas F. O'Brien, *The Revolutionary Mission: American Enterprise in Latin America*

U.S. GOODS AS A PERCENTAGE OF THE COUNTRY'S TOTAL IMPORTS (1914)

50% Mexico

45% TO 65% Central American and Caribbean Republics

40% Venezuela

15% Brazil

Source: *The Cambridge History of Latin America*, Vol. IV

>> **Analyze Information** How did U.S. involvement in Latin American economies illustrate "dollar diplomacy"?

stalled when Colombia demanded more than the United States was willing to provide.

So Roosevelt stepped in. The President dispatched U.S. warships to the water off Panama to support a Panamanian rebellion against Colombia. The appearance of the United States Navy convinced the Colombians not to suppress the uprising. Panama soon declared its independence from Colombia. The new nation immediately granted America control over the "Canal Zone." To secure this land for its vital trade link, America agreed to pay Panama $10 million and an annual rent of $250,000.

More than 35,000 workers helped dig the **Panama Canal**. The physical geography and climate of the region were both factors that impacted the enormous project. Workers built a series of locks to raise ships to the level of Gatún Lake, 85 feet above sea level, to cross the isthmus. Completion of the canal depended on scientific breakthroughs by doctors as they learned how to combat tropical diseases. Still, more than 5,000 canal workers died from disease or accidents while building the canal. When the finished waterway opened in 1914, it cut some 8,000 nautical miles off the trip from the west coast to the east coast of the United States.

American Expansionism Requires an Updated Monroe Doctrine In the early 1900s, the inability of Latin American nations to pay their debts to

foreign investors raised the possibility of European intervention. In 1903, for example, Germany and Britain blockaded Venezuelan ports to ensure that debts to European bankers were repaid. Roosevelt concluded: "If we intend to say hands off to the powers of Europe, then sooner or later we must keep order ourselves." So in a 1904 message to Congress, he announced a new Latin American policy.

The President's **Roosevelt Corollary** updated the Monroe Doctrine for an age of expansionism and economic influence. In the case of "chronic wrongdoing" by a Latin American nation—the kind that Europeans might use to justify military intervention—the United States would assume the role of police power, restoring order and depriving other creditors of the excuse to intervene. This change, Roosevelt argued, merely reasserted America's long-standing policy of keeping the Western Hemisphere free from European intervention.

The Latin American Response Many Latin Americans resented America's role as the hemisphere's police force. They disagreed with Roosevelt's belief that Latin Americans could not police themselves. Francisco García Calderón, a Peruvian diplomat, contended that the Monroe Doctrine had taken on an "aggressive form with Mr. Roosevelt." Like Calderón, Nicaraguan spokesman Augusto Sandino felt that the United States threatened the "sovereignty and liberty" of his people. Sandino eventually led an army of guerrillas against U.S. Marines in Nicaragua in the 1920s.

Taft's Foreign Policies Lead to "Dollar Diplomacy" Roosevelt handpicked William Howard Taft to succeed him as the Republican candidate for President in 1908. Taft shared Roosevelt's basic foreign policy objectives. After defeating William Jennings Bryan in the general election, Taft wanted to maintain the Open Door Policy in Asia and ensure ongoing stability in Latin America. The new President pursued both goals with the aim of affecting economic issues such as expanding American trade through foreign policy.

Taft hoped to achieve these ends by relying less on the "big stick" and more on **"dollar diplomacy."** As Taft commented in 1912, he looked to substitute "dollars for bullets." The policy aimed to increase American investments in businesses and banks throughout Central America and the Caribbean. Americans busily invested in plantations, mines, oil wells, railways, and other ventures in those regions. Of course, "dollar diplomacy" sometimes required a return to the "big stick" and military intervention. Such was the case when President Taft dispatched troops to Nicaragua in 1909—and again in 1912—to protect the formation of a pro-American government there.

☑ **IDENTIFY MAIN IDEAS** How did "dollar diplomacy" affect American foreign policy?

Wilson's "Moral Diplomacy"

During the 1912 presidential election campaign, Democratic candidate Woodrow Wilson criticized the foreign policies of his Republican predecessors Theodore Roosevelt and William Howard Taft. After his election victory, Wilson appointed the anti-imperialist William Jennings Bryan as Secretary of State, which sent a strong message to the American people.

A New Emphasis on Foreign Policy The new President intended to take U.S. foreign policy in a different direction. He promised that the United States would "never again seek one additional foot of territory by conquest" but would instead work to promote "human rights, national integrity, and opportunity." Wilson spelled out his new **"moral diplomacy"** in a message to the American people:

DIFFERENT APPROACHES TO FOREIGN POLICY

Roosevelt	Taft	Wilson
Big stick diplomacy • Believed American military should be used to achieve goals • Wanted to "civilize" other countries • Did not believe nations should be self-governing • Supported rebellion in Panama • Opposed European intervention in the Western Hemisphere (Roosevelt Corollary)	Dollar diplomacy • Believed U.S. should invest in foreign economies to increase American influence • Continued Roosevelt's foreign policy but with less aggression • Worked for stability in Latin America • Worked to expand economic opportunities in China	Moral diplomacy • Believed U.S. should spread peace and democracy rather than colonize foreign countries • Believed other nations should be self-governing • Continued to use American military in Latin America • Wished to cultivate a friendship with Latin America

>> **Contrast** How did Roosevelt and Wilson differ in their approach to governing colonial territories?

> We must prove ourselves [Latin America's] friends and champions upon terms of equality and honor. . . .
>
> We must show ourselves friends by comprehending their interest, whether it squares with our own interest or not. . . . Comprehension must be the soil in which shall grow all the fruits of friendship. . . . I mean the development of constitutional liberty in the world.

—Woodrow Wilson, October 27, 1913

In spite of his stated preference for "moral diplomacy" over "big stick" or "dollar diplomacy," Wilson used the military on a number of occasions to guide Latin Americans in the directions that he thought proper. In 1915, Wilson sent marines to Haiti to protect American investments and to guard against the potential of German or French aggression in the nation. Wilson prodded the government of Haiti to sign an agreement that essentially gave the United States the right to control its financial and foreign affairs. The marines did not leave until 1934. Under Wilson, U.S. soldiers and sailors also intervened in the Dominican Republic and in Mexico.

Revolution Grips Mexico For decades, Mexican dictator Porfirio Díaz had followed policies that benefited his country's small upper class of wealthy landowners, clerics, and military men. With Díaz's encouragement, foreign investments in Mexico grew. As a result, American business leaders owned large portions of Mexico's industries. While foreign investors and Mexico's aristocracy grew rich, Mexico's large population of farmers struggled in poverty.

In 1911, Francisco Madero led the Mexican Revolution that toppled Díaz. Madero was committed to reforms but was a weak administrator. In 1913, General Victoriano Huerta seized power and executed Madero. Under "dollar diplomacy," Taft likely would have recognized Huerta as the leader of Mexico because Huerta pledged to protect American investments. But under "moral diplomacy," Wilson refused to do so, declaring that he would not accept a "government of butchers." Instead, Wilson favored Venustiano Carranza, another reformer, who had organized anti-Huerta forces.

>> The United States supported Mexican rebel leader Pancho Villa's insurrection against the Mexican government until his forces conducted an attack in the United States in 1916.

Intervention in Mexico In 1914, the President used the Mexican arrest of American sailors as an opportunity to help Carranza attain power. Wilson sent marines to occupy the Mexican port of Veracruz. The action caused Huerta's government to collapse, and Carranza assumed the presidency.

Huerta's fall from power cheered many Mexicans and appeared to validate Wilson's "moral diplomacy." However, Wilson soon discovered that he faced more trouble in Mexico. The new Carranza government was slow in bringing about reforms, and rebels again rose up, this time under the leadership of **Francisco "Pancho" Villa**. For a while, Wilson courted Villa. After American support disappeared in 1916, Villa's forces crossed into New Mexico and raided the town of Columbus, leaving 18 Americans dead. President Wilson responded by sending General John J. Pershing and more than 10,000 troops on a "punitive expedition" to Mexico.

Pershing's forces chased Villa for several months but failed to capture the rebel leader. Wilson eventually withdrew American troops from Mexico in 1917, mostly because of his concerns about World War I raging in Europe.

Not long afterward, the United States declared war on Germany. Free from hunting Villa, Pershing took command of the American Expeditionary Force in France.

A generation earlier, few would have believed it possible that more than one million American troops would engage in a large-scale war in Europe. But the triumph over Spain and U.S. actions in Asia and Latin America demonstrated that America had emerged as a world power. Now, World War I would test that new global strength.

☑ **IDENTIFY CENTRAL IDEAS** What effect would "moral diplomacy" have on American foreign policy decisions?

☑ ASSESSMENT

1. **Summarize** What was the impact of the Platt Amendment?

2. **Sequence Events** Discuss the events that led to the Boxer Rebellion.

3. **Identify Cause and Effect** What events that contributed to a hostile relationship between Japan and the United States?

4. **Draw Conclusions** How did Puerto Rico pose a problem for the United States after the Spanish-American War?

5. **Generate Explanations** Explain the purpose of the Roosevelt Corollary.

Go online to PearsonSchool.com/CASS and use the texts, quizzes, interactivities, Interactive Reading Notepads, Flipped Videos, and other resources from this Topic to prepare for the Topic Test.

Etexts

Quizzes

Interactivities

Interactive Reading Notepads

Flipped Videos

While online you can also check the progress you've made learning the topic and course content by viewing your grades, test scores, and assignment status.

LESSON SUMMARIES

Use these Lesson Summaries, and the longer versions available online, to review the key ideas for each lesson in this Topic.

Lesson 1: Progressives Drive Reform

Progressivism rose in the 1890s to tackle problems brought by industrialization, urbanization, and immigration. Journalists helped pass laws ending child labor and ensuring worker safety. New laws also targeted political corruption and limited the power of business interests. Political practices such as the ballot initiative, the referendum and the recall were introduced.

Lesson 2: Women Gain Rights

In the early 1900s, the number of women attending college increased. Women fought for the right to vote and to own property. Some women campaigned against the consumption of alcohol, while others established charitable organizations. In several states, women's groups used the referendum process to gain the right to vote. In 1920 the Nineteenth Amendment extended the vote to women.

Lesson 3: Striving for Equality

The Progressive Era did not bring much progress for minorities and immigrants. However, African Americans continued to oppose segregation and discrimination, founding the National Association for the Advancement of Colored People, which fought for civil rights and the right to vote. Meanwhile, Jews formed the Anti-Defamation League to fight verbal attacks and false statements.

Lesson 4: Reformers in the White House

Progressive reforms marked the presidencies of both Theodore Roosevelt and Woodrow Wilson. Roosevelt took on big business and extended federal protection of natural resources. The 1912 presidential election was won by Wilson, who believed the government should play an active role in the economy.

Lesson 5: American Influence Grows

During the late 1800s, the United States was emerging as a new power on the global stage, extending its economic, political, and military influence over weaker nations. A large naval force opened up Japan to American trade. The United States purchased Alaska and annexed Hawaii.

Lesson 6: The Spanish-American War

Cuban patriot José Martí launched a war for independence from Spain. After the American battleship USS *Maine* exploded in Havana Harbor, Congress declared war on Spain. Spanish troops in the Philippines and Cuba surrendered to the United States. However, in the Philippines, nationalists rebelled against U.S. rule.

Lesson 7: The United States Emerges as a World Power

By 1900, the United States was becoming more active internationally. The U.S. helped put down an uprising in China and negotiated and end to the Russo-Japanese War. In 1907, America sent a fleet of ships around the world as a display of power. The U.S. also built the Panama Canal.

VISUAL REVIEW

Use these graphics to review some of the key terms, people, and ideas from this Topic.

The Spanish-American War Begins

1868–1878 First struggle for Cuban independence; Cubans flee to Florida.

↓

José Martí travels through Florida, raising money for Cuban rebels.

↓

1895 Martí launches Cuban war for independence.

↓

U.S. sympathy for Cuban rebels grows.

↓

1898 USS *Maine* explodes in Havana harbor; U.S. declares war on Spain.

Progressive Goals:
- End political corruption
- Provide social welfare
- Grant voting rights to women
- Improve working conditions
- Improve municipal services
- Limit abuses of big business

Municipal Reforms

GOVERNMENT REFORMS	ELECTION REFORMS
• Commission form of government • City managers • Trained administrators • City-owned public utilities	• Direct primary • Initiative • Referendum • Recall

Minorities Organize

African Americans	1905 Niagara Movement formed 1909 NAACP organized 1911 Urban League founded
Jews	1913 Anti-Defamation League formed
Mexican Americans	PLM formed in Arizona Mutualistas formed in several states
Native Americans	1911 Society of American Indians formed
Asian Americans	Takao Ozawa fights law that blocks Asian Americans from becoming citizens.

KEY TERMS, PEOPLE, AND IDEAS

1. How did the **Social Gospel** movement contribute to reform?

2. How did the **settlement house** improve the lives of the poor?

3. How did Progressives shape public policy?

4. Describe ways that women fought to gain the right to vote.

5. What role did **Americanization** play in the Progressive Movement?

6. Why was the **Sixteenth Amendment** introduced?

7. How did **Alfred T. Mahan** influence American expansionism?

8. What role did Florida play in the Spanish-American War?

9. Why did the United States acquire territories?

CRITICAL THINKING

10. **Compare and Contrast** (a.) What were the similarities and differences between the goals of the Populist and the Progressive movements? (b.) Compare and contrast the kinds of voters who supported these parties.

11. **Cite Evidence** Cite evidence of women's increasing confidence and freedom in the Progressive Era.

12. **Draw Conclusions** Why did so many Progressives ignore the plight of racial and ethnic minorities?

13. **Make Generalizations** (a.) Why were Theodore Roosevelt's views on land use so controversial? (b.) How did these views reflect his Progressive politics?

14. **Identify Cause and Effect** Analyze the major factors that drove United States imperialism.

15. **Draw Inferences** What were the economic, military, and security motivations behind the building of the Panama Canal?

16. **Analyze Maps** Look at the map below. Why was Florida so strategically important during the Spanish-American War? (Use an appropriate tool to judge distances.)

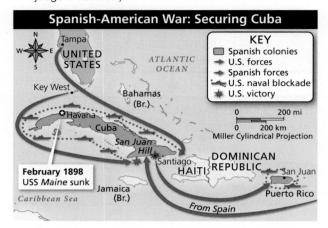

Spanish-American War: Securing Cuba

KEY
- Spanish colonies
- U.S. forces
- Spanish forces
- U.S. naval blockade
- U.S. victory

February 1898 USS *Maine* sunk

17. **Writing Activity: Use Primary Sources** Analyze this excerpt from an editorial written during the Filipino insurrection. What does it reveal about the attitudes and goals behind U.S. expansionism?

> Let us all be frank. WE DO NOT WANT THE FILIPINOS. WE WANT THE PHILIPPINES. . . . The islands are enormously rich; they abound in dense forests of valuable hardwood timber; they contain mines of the precious metals; their fertile lands will produce immense crops of sugar cane, rice and tobacco. Touched by the wands of American enterprise, fertilized with American capital, these islands would speedily become richer than Golconda was of old.
>
> But unfortunately, they are infested by Filipinos. There are many millions of them there, and it is to be feared that their extinction will be slow.
>
> —*San Francisco Argonaut, 1902*

DOCUMENT-BASED QUESTIONS

The economic policies of progressive presidents such as Theodore Roosevelt and Woodrow Wilson were controversial. Read the documents below, then answer the questions that follow.

DOCUMENT A

In this document, Woodrow Wilson discusses the nature and formation of trusts.

> I take my stand absolutely, where every progressive ought to take his stand, on the proposition that private monopoly is indefensible and intolerable. And there I will fight my battle. And I know how to fight it. Everybody who has even read the newspapers knows the means by which these men built up their power and created these monopolies. Any decently equipped lawyer can suggest to you statutes by which the whole business can be stopped. . . . I know they can be stopped by law.
> —*Woodrow Wilson, 1913*

DOCUMENT B

This political cartoon shows President Theodore Roosevelt with the good and bad trusts.

DOCUMENT C

This excerpt is from the Progressive Party platform.

> This country belongs to the people who inhabit it. Its resources, its businesses, its institutions, and its laws should be utilized, maintained, or altered in whatever manner will best promote the general interest. It is time to set the public welfare in the first place. . . .

> We demand . . . that those who profit by control of business affairs shall justify that profit and that control by sharing with the public the fruits thereof. We therefore demand a strong national regulation of interstate corporations. . . .
> —*Progressive "Bull Moose" Party Platform, 1912*

DOCUMENT D

This excerpt is from a speech against government regulation.

> What effect is what you may do here going to have upon the future welfare, productiveness, and value of the greatest single industrial interest in the country? . . . . Gentlemen, you may pass an act that will so compromise the value of the property and the prosperity of the communities of this country that it will bring widespread disaster. . . .

> What I say, gentlemen, is that [it] is a very, very serious moment when an Anglo-Saxon government undertakes the charge of the people's money and says how much they shall earn by the exercise of their constitutional rights of liberty and property.
> —*David Wilcox, President of Delaware and Hudson Railroad, testimony to Congress, 1905*

18. In Document A, Woodrow Wilson promises that he will
    A. defend big business against regulation.
    B. introduce government regulation.
    C. not interfere with the economy.
    D. create a fairer tax system.

19. **Analyze Images** In Document B, what issue does this political cartoon illustrate?

20. In Document C, the Progressive Party is calling for
    A. increased taxation of the rich.
    B. forced distribution of wealth.
    C. the lifting of all economic regulation.
    D. a fairer balance of public and private interests.

21. In Document D, the speaker is saying that government regulation of earnings is
    A. dangerous to prosperity and productivity.
    B. completely justified.
    C. guaranteed by the constitution.
    D. consistent with rights of liberty and property.

22. **Writing Activity: Primary Source** Write a paragraph explaining whether or not you think the progressive movement's calls for government regulation of business was justified. Use the sources as well as additional information you have learned.

1 How did settlement houses reflect the ideals of the Social Gospel movement?

A by helping people settle on western lands

B by attempting to reform rather than punish offenders

C by providing social services to the urban poor

D by providing religious instruction in the schools

2

> *Our . . . government is based on . . . the natural right of every individual member . . . to a voice and a vote in making and executing the laws.*
>
> —Susan B. Anthony, 1872

What reform movement was Susan B. Anthony promoting when she gave this speech?

F She was promoting the right of female landowners to run for elected office.

G She was promoting the right of female citizens to vote only in state elections.

H She was promoting expanding the right to vote to all female American citizens.

I She was promoting expanding the right to vote to all female American college graduates.

3 What did the American Indian Citizenship Act of 1924 reveal about the motives of Congress?

A Congress wanted to Americanize Native Americans.

B Congress wanted to create social equality for Native Americans.

C Congress wanted to stop Native Americans from selling their lands.

D Congress wanted to encourage Native Americans to sign up for military service.

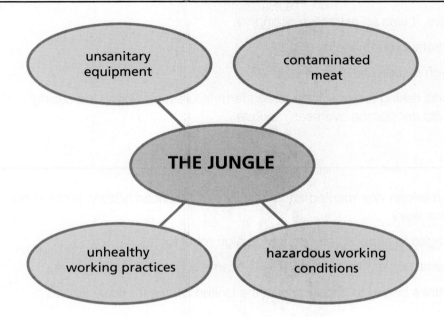

4 Upton Sinclair's book *The Jungle* embodied which belief of the Progressive Movement?

F Government intervention can solve social problems.

G Government should be more responsive to the people.

H Science can help improve society.

I The gap between rich and poor should be reduced.

If you have trouble with...				
Question	1	2	3	4
See Lesson	3.1	3.2	3.3	3.4

5

> *Today we are raising more [crops] than we can consume. Today we are making more than we can use. . . . Therefore we must find new markets for our produce, new occupation for our capital, new work for our labor.*
>
> —*Senator Albert J. Beveridge, "The March of the Flag," 1898*

What does Senator Beveridge's statement reveal about the nature of United States imperialism?

A Like European powers, it was an extractive economy.

B It needed world markets to purchase its goods.

C It depended on foreign resources.

D The United States was risking factory closings and farm failures, as well as increasing unemployment, if it did not pursue overseas markets.

---

6 In 1898, the Spanish-American War marked a turning point in American history. What ironic change resulted from this war?

F The United States began to support the rights of foreign rebel forces.

G By defeating an imperial power, the United States became an imperial power itself.

H Latin American countries began to depend upon the United States for financial and political support.

I American investors began to feel confident about putting money into businesses in foreign countries.

7 Why would the growing support for the Populist Party have forced the other two parties to consider Populist demands?

A The Populists lobbied for the other two parties to support the farmers.

B The two main parties feared that they would lose their voters to the Populists.

C Populist voters switched to one of the two major parties in order to influence party platforms.

D The other two parties realized that they were not addressing farmers' concerns.

8

> *You shall not press down upon the brow of labor this crown of thorns, you shall not crucify mankind upon a cross of gold.*
>
> —*William Jennings Bryan*

Why did this sentence from Bryan's speech have such a powerful effect?

F It used simple, religious language to describe an economic problem.

G It convinced Bryan's audience that he was sincere.

H It showed that Democrats believed in a Populist cause.

I It showed that the Populist Party was splitting the vote.

If you have trouble with...				
Question	5	6	7	8
See Lesson	4.5	4.6	3.4	3.4

[ESSENTIAL QUESTION] How should we handle conflict?

④ World War I and the 1920s

Enduring Understandings

- The United States was drawn into World War I on the side of the Allies.

- Americans rallied around the war effort, although some dissenters were treated harshly.

- President Wilson's vision for a peace was dashed when the U.S. Senate refused to support the League of Nations.

- In the 1920s, the nation saw an economic boom, spurred by technological innovation.

- While many prospered, tensions created an unsettled society.

- During the 1920s, a new mass culture emerged, women assumed new roles, and African Americans enjoyed a flowering in the arts in Harlem.

Learn about the life of film star Louise Brooks.

Bounce to Activate My Story Video

>> Dancers on the cover of a 1926 *Life* magazine

California Topic 4 Overview

In this Topic, you'll learn about World War I and the 1920s. Look at the lesson outline and explore the timeline. As you study this Topic, you'll complete the Quest team project.

LESSON OUTLINE

4.1 America Enters World War I
HSS 11.4.5; Analysis HRE.2, HI.2

4.2 The Home Front During World War I
HSS 11.3, HSS 11.4.5, HSS 11.9.7; Analysis CST.4

4.3 The End of World War I
HSS 11.4.4, HSS 11.4.5

4.4 The Postwar Economy Booms
HSS 11.2.2, HSS 11.2.6, HSS 11.4, HSS 11.5.7; Analysis CST.4

4.5 Government in the 1920s
HSS 11.5, HSS 11.5.1, HSS 11.6.1

4.6 An Unsettled Society
HSS 11.2.7, HSS 11.3, HSS 11.3.2, HSS 11.5, HSS 11.5.2, HSS 11.5.3, HSS 11.9.7

4.7 The Roaring Twenties
HSS 11.11.3, HSS 11.5, HSS 11.5.4, HSS 11.5.6, HSS 11.8.8

4.8 The Harlem Renaissance
HSS 11.5, HSS 11.5.5, HSS 11.8.8; Analysis CST.4

Key Events of World War I and the 1920s

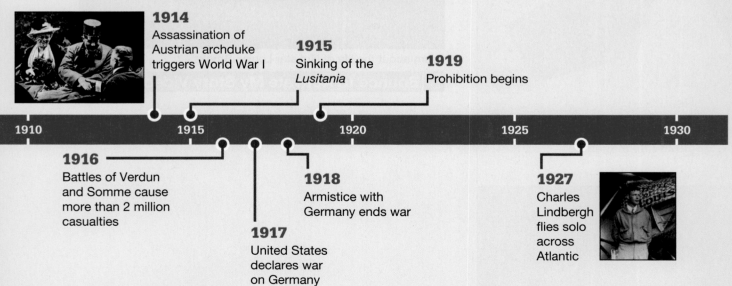

1914 Assassination of Austrian archduke triggers World War I

1915 Sinking of the *Lusitania*

1919 Prohibition begins

1916 Battles of Verdun and Somme cause more than 2 million casualties

1917 United States declares war on Germany

1918 Armistice with Germany ends war

1927 Charles Lindbergh flies solo across Atlantic

1910   1915   1920   1925   1930

QUEST!

Civic Discussion:
The League of Nations

Should the United States have joined the League of Nations or would that organization have undermined American sovereignty? In this Quest you'll explore the refusal of the United States to support the League of Nations.

STEP
Read the Discussion Launch and take notes. Then discuss the major points with the other members of your group. Write the points that your group agreed with in the Information Organizer.

STEP
Study several sources to understand different people's perspectives on the main question. As you read and analyze each source, fill in Step 2 of the Information Organizer.

STEP
After your group has been assigned a YES or NO position on the main question, prepare the most compelling arguments in support of your position. Present your arguments and then switch sides.

STEP
Discuss the main question from your own point of view. Reflect on what you've read and heard about the question and how different perspectives have broadened your understanding.

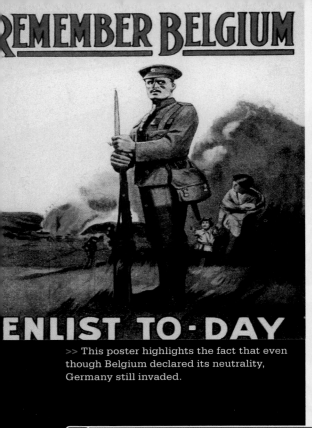

REMEMBER BELGIUM

ENLIST TO·DAY

>> This poster highlights the fact that even though Belgium declared its neutrality, Germany still invaded.

Bounce to Activate Flipped Video

4.1 In 1914, nationalism, militarism, imperialism, and entangling alliances combined with other factors to lead the nations of Europe into a brutal war. The war quickly spread around the globe. The United States remained neutral at first but ended up abandoning its long tradition of staying out of European conflicts.

>> Objectives

Identify the causes of World War I.

Analyze the impact of technological innovations in weaponry that resulted in stalemate on the Western Front.

Analyze reasons behind isolationism and neutrality in the United States before 1917.

Explain why the United States entered the conflict on the side of the Allies.

>> Key Terms

Alsace-Lorraine
militarism
Francis Ferdinand
William II
Western Front
casualty
contraband
U-boats
Lusitania
Zimmermann note

America Enters World War I

The Causes of World War I

Until 1914, there had not been a large-scale European conflict for nearly one hundred years. However, bitter, deep-rooted problems simmered beneath the surface of polite diplomacy. Europe was sitting on a powder keg of nationalism, regional tensions, economic rivalries, imperial ambitions, and militarism.

Nationalism Escalates Tension in Europe Nationalism, or devotion to one's nation, kick-started international and domestic tension. In the late 1800s, many Europeans began to reject the earlier idea of a nation as a collection of different ethnic groups. Instead, they believed that a nation should express the nationalism of a single ethnic group.

This belief evolved into an intense form of nationalism that heightened international rivalries. For example, France longed to avenge its humiliating defeat by a collection of German states in 1871 and regain **Alsace-Lorraine**, the territory it lost during that conflict. Nationalism also threatened minority groups within nation states. If a country existed as the expression of "its people," the majority ethnic group, where did ethnic minorities fit in?

The spread of the theory of Social Darwinism did not help soothe the competitive instinct. Social Darwinism applied biologist Charles Darwin's ideas of natural selection and "survival of the fittest" to human society. Social Darwinists believed that the fittest nation would come out ahead in the constant competition among countries.

Nationalism also destabilized old multinational empires such as Austria-Hungary and the Ottoman Empire. This was particularly true in the Balkan region of southeastern Europe.

For example, when Serbia emerged as an independent nation in 1878, it challenged the nearby empire of Austria-Hungary in two ways: by trying to gain territory controlled by the empire, where Serbs lived, and by the example it offered to Austria-Hungary's diverse peoples.

The nationalist sentiments of the period sometimes spilled over into the economic goals of each nation. Industrial output, trade, and the possession of an overseas empire were the yardsticks of wealth and greatness. The leading industrial nations competed for lands rich in raw materials as well as for places to build military bases to protect their empires. Britain already had a large empire, and France commanded a smaller one. But Germany, Italy, Belgium, Japan, and the United States also rushed to join the race to expand. Together, industrialized nations jostled among

themselves as they carved colonies out of Africa, claimed islands in the Pacific, and began to nibble away at China.

Militarism Increases Arms Production For some European leaders, the question was not so much *if* a great war would start but *when*. To prepare, leaders increased the size of their armies and stockpiles of weapons. No nation readied its war machinery more than Germany. By 1914, it had a huge standing army and the largest, deadliest collection of guns in the world. It also built up its navy enough to rival Britain's, the world's strongest at that time. To keep up, Britain, too, increased the size of its navy. A spirit of **militarism**, or glorification of the military, grew in the competing countries and fueled this arms race even more.

The contest between Germany and Britain at sea and between Germany, France, and Russia on land guaranteed one important thing: The next major war would involve more troops and more technologically advanced weapons than ever before. Machine guns, mobile artillery, tanks, submarines, and airplanes would change the nature of warfare.

Alliances Between Nations Increase the Potential for War European leaders also prepared for war by forming alliances. Before 1914, two major ones emerged.

>> **Analyze Maps** Based on the map, describe one possible disadvantage the Central Powers of Germany and Austria-Hungary face.

Germany, Austria-Hungary, and Italy joined together in the Triple Alliance (although Italy never fought with it). Opposed to the Triple Alliance was the Triple Entente, made up of France, Russia, and Great Britain. Alliances emboldened leaders to act recklessly. They knew that if they did declare war, powerful allies were obligated to fight along with them. No country wanted to be seen as an unreliable partner. As years passed, European leaders thought less of the advantages of peace and more of the possible benefits of war. Some also hoped that a foreign war would help to smooth over domestic problems.

A Significant Assassination On June 28, 1914, Archduke **Francis Ferdinand**, heir to the throne of Austria-Hungary, and his wife Sophie left for what they thought would be a routine visit to Sarajevo (sar uh YAY voh), the capital city of the Austro-Hungarian province of Bosnia. But a handful of young Bosnians had other plans for the archduke and his wife. These men were ethnic Serbs who believed that Bosnia rightfully belonged to Serbia, and they saw Francis Ferdinand as a tyrant.

After the archduke's driver made a wrong turn, Gavrilo Princip, one of the conspirators, noticed the couple in the car, pulled a pistol from his pocket, and fired it twice. First Sophie and then Francis Ferdinand died. People around the world were shocked by the senseless murders. But no one expected that they would lead to a great world war.

☑ **RECALL** What countries formed the Triple Entente?

The Great War Begins

Everything was in place for a great conflict—nationalist ambitions, large armies, stockpiles of weapons, alliances, and military plans. The nations of Europe were hurtling like giant trains toward a great collision. Archduke Francis Ferdinand's assassination was the incident that triggered this conflict.

Alliances Cause a Chain Reaction Soon after the assassination, Kaiser **William II**, the German emperor, assured Austria-Hungary that Germany would stand by its ally if war came. Confident in Germany's support, Austria-Hungary then sent a harsh ultimatum to Serbia demanding Serbia's total cooperation in an investigation into the assassination. When Serbia did not agree to all of the demands, Austria-Hungary declared war on July 28, 1914.

Because of the alliance system, what otherwise might have been a localized quarrel quickly spread. In early August, Russia mobilized for war to help its ally Serbia against Austria. This caused Germany to declare war against Russia.

Major Players in World War I

ALLIED POWERS	NEUTRAL POWERS	CENTRAL POWERS
France	Switzerland	Germany
Britain	Spain	Austria-Hungary
Russia	The Netherlands	Ottoman Empire
Serbia	Denmark	
Italy	Sweden	
Japan	Norway	
United States	Albania	

SOURCE: *Britannica Encyclopedia*

>> **Analyze Charts** Why was one alliance called "The Central Powers"? (Consulting a map may help you answer.)

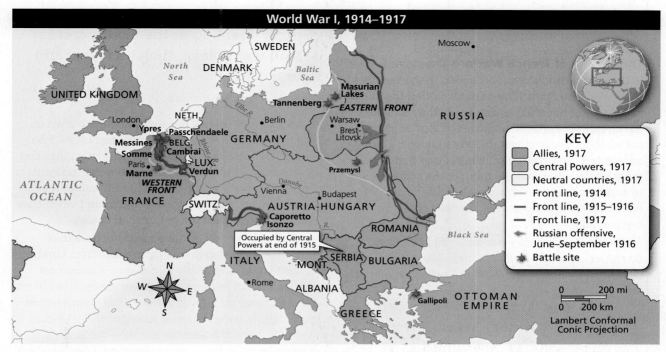

World War I, 1914–1917

KEY
- Allies, 1917
- Central Powers, 1917
- Neutral countries, 1917
- Front line, 1914
- Front line, 1915–1916
- Front line, 1917
- Russian offensive, June–September 1916
- Battle site

Occupied by Central Powers at end of 1915

0 ____ 200 mi
0 ____ 200 km
Lambert Conformal Conic Projection

>> **Analyze Maps** What challenge did Germany's location present to its pursuit of victory in the war?

France, Russia's ally, promptly declared war against Germany. The very next day, Germany declared war against neutral Belgium, so that it could launch an invasion of France through that small country. Great Britain, which had treaties with France and Belgium, immediately declared war against Germany. In less than one week, the Central Powers of Germany, Austria-Hungary, and Bulgaria were at war against the Allied Powers of Britain, France, Russia, and Serbia. The Ottoman Empire later joined the Central Powers.

German soldiers fought through Belgium and moved southwest into France, toward Paris. Then in September, with the German advance only 30 miles from Paris, the French and the British counterattacked and stopped the German forces near the Marne River.

Technological Innovations Lead to Stalemate

After the Battle of the Marne, the Germans settled onto high ground, dug trenches, and fortified their position. When the French and British attacked, the German troops used machine guns and artillery to kill thousands of them. The French and British then dug their own trenches and used the same weapons to kill thousands of counterattacking Germans.

Soon, 450 miles of trenches stretched like a huge scar from the coast of Belgium to the border of Switzerland. Although fighting went on in Eastern Europe, the Middle East, and in other parts of the world, this **Western Front** in France became the critical battle front. The side that won there would win the war.

The war dragged on for years, and it was hideously deadly—much more so than anyone had expected. The primary reason for the length of the war and its deadly nature was the simple fact that the defensive weapons of the time were better and more devastating than the offensive ones. Generals on each side threw their soldiers into assaults against the enemy without fully considering the new technology. Charging toward trenches that were defended by artillery, machine guns, and rifles was futile. In virtually every battle on the Western Front, the attacking force suffered terribly.

Even the use of poison gas did nothing to benefit the offense, despite its horrifying effects. Airplanes and tanks were both first used during World War I, but neither broke the stalemate.

Airplanes were mostly used for reconnaissance, or observing an area for military purposes. The torn-up ground caused by endless shelling created a need for a new military technology—the tank. Military leaders hoped tanks could plow through devastated battlefield areas, but the first tanks weren't able to ride over such uneven terrain and often broke down during crucial battles. Ineffective offensives and effective defenses produced only a deadly stalemate.

The Reality of Trench Warfare The stalemate led to gruesome conditions for the men in the trenches of the Western Front. The soldiers battled the harsh conditions of life often as fiercely as they attacked the enemy. They developed "trench foot" from standing for hours in wet, muddy trenches. They contracted lice from the millions of rats that infested the trenches. Dug into the ground, the soldiers lived in constant fear, afraid to pop their heads out of their holes and always aware that the next offensive might be their last.

Even on a quiet day, soldiers could be killed by snipers or a surprise gas attack, like the one described by French officer Paul Truffaut at Verdun:

> The special shells the men call "shells on wheels" [shells filled with poison gas] are whizzing by continuously. They explode silently and have no smell but can be deadly. They killed several men yesterday. One of my men refused to put his mask on because he couldn't smell anything. All of a sudden, he was dizzy, foaming at the mouth and his skin went black, then he went rigid and died.
>
> —Paul Truffaut, March 5, 1917

In between enemy lines was an area known as "no man's land." Artillery barrages had blasted no man's land until any fields, trees, or homes, that had once existed there, were charred beyond recognition. Soldiers went "over the top" of their trenches into this muddy, nearly impassable wasteland when they attempted to attack the entrenched enemy.

Casualties—or soldiers killed, wounded, or missing—mounted first in thousands, then hundreds of thousands, and finally in millions. Almost one million French soldiers were killed or wounded in just the first three months of the war. The Germans lost only slightly fewer. In two battles in 1916—Verdun (ver DUHN) and the Somme (suhm)—the British, French, and Germans sustained more than 2 million casualties. The British suffered 60,000 casualties on the first day alone at the Somme and achieved virtually nothing. And still the stalemate dragged on.

☑ **IDENTIFY SUPPORTING DETAILS** What technologies encouraged a stalemate between opposing armies?

Deadly Technology of World War I

TECHNOLOGY	APPLICATION
POISON GAS	Gases such as chlorine, phosgene, and mustard gas could kill, blind, or burn their victims.
MACHINE GUNS	Improved machine guns could fire 600 bullets per minute.
FLAMETHROWER	A new technology, flamethrowers consisted of a backpack and a gun that could shoot flames as far as 60 feet.
ARTILLERY FIELD GUNS	These long-range cannons caused more casualties than any other type of weapon.
TANKS AND ARMORED CARS	Both sides tried to develop vehicles that could go over rough ground and barbed-wire no, with limited success.
AIRPLANES	Planes were used for reconnaissance, bombing, and fighting but did not prove decisive.
SUBMARINES	German U-boats, or submarines, used torpedoes as well as on-deck guns to sink ships.

>> **Analyze Charts** Based on the types of weapons listed in the chart, what can you conclude about either side's ability to inflict casualties on the other side?

The United States Remains Neutral

As the war spread in Europe, President Woodrow Wilson called for Americans to be "impartial in thought as well as action." In a "melting pot" nation that tried to make Americans of peoples from diverse origins, Wilson did not want to see the war set Americans against one another. At first, most Americans viewed the conflict as a distant European quarrel for land and influence. Unless the nation's interests were directly threatened, Americans wanted no part of it. They preferred to maintain what they viewed as traditional American isolation from European disputes. Still, many Americans felt the war's effects and few were truly impartial in thought. Most held a preference for one or another combatant, and many businesses benefited from the increased demand by warring nations for American goods.

Many Americans Choose Sides In 1914, one third of Americans were foreign-born. Many still thought of themselves in terms of their former homelands—as German Americans, Irish Americans, Polish Americans, and so on. With relatives in Europe, many people supported the nation in which they were born.

Some German Americans in the Midwest and some Irish Americans along the East Coast felt strongly that the Central Powers were justified in their actions. Many Americans had emigrated from Germany or Austria-Hungary. Millions of Irish Americans harbored intense grudges over the centuries of Great Britain's domination of their homeland. They hoped that Ireland would gain its independence as Britain became entangled in the war. Many Jewish Americans who had fled Russia to escape the Czarist regimes' murderous pogroms against Jews hoped for Russia's defeat.

Most Americans, however, sided with Britain and France, both of which had strong historic ties with the United States. America's national language was English, its cultural heritage was largely British, and its leading trading partner was Britain. France had aided the American cause during the Revolutionary War.

U.S. Opinion Solidifies No event at the beginning of the war swayed American opinion more than the vicious German invasion of neutral Belgium. German soldiers marching through Belgium committed numerous atrocities, killing unarmed civilians, and destroying entire towns. British journalists and propagandists stressed, and sometimes exaggerated,

>> Soldiers took cover in trenches during gas attacks. **Hypothesize** Why do you think many people consider poisonous gas attacks to be morally wrong while accepting attacks by machines guns, artillery, and tanks?

Bounce to Activate 3D Model

>> **Analyze Political Cartoons** Based on the cartoon, what can you infer about President Wilson's attitude toward the war?

Bounce to Activate Chart

>> The British Navy was the strongest in the world. **Draw Conclusions** Why was naval superiority so important to Great Britain's war effort?

>> After German U-boats sank the British passenger ship *Lusitania* near the Irish coast, it became clear to many Americans that even ships carrying civilians were potential targets.

the brutality of the Germans' actions. Americans might have only dimly understood the causes of the war, but they clearly perceived the human cost of the war for Belgium.

Eventually, three distinct positions on the war crystallized among Americans. One group, the isolationists, believed that the war was none of America's business and that the nation should isolate itself from the hostilities. A second group, the interventionists, felt that the war did affect American interests and that the United States should intervene in the conflict on the side of the Allies. A third group, the internationalists, occupied the middle ground. Internationalists believed that the United States should play an active role in world affairs and work toward achieving a just peace but not enter the war.

☑ **CHECK UNDERSTANDING** Into what three positions did U.S. opinion generally fall?

Reasons for U.S. Entry into the War

An internationalist, President Wilson sincerely desired peace in his country and around the world. Between the start of the war in 1914 and America's entry into it in 1917, Wilson attempted to use his influence to end the conflict among the warring countries. He failed in this great effort. Ultimately, he also failed to keep the United States out of the war.

Britain Blockades German Ports Early in the war, British leaders decided to use their navy to blockade Germany to keep essential goods from reaching the other country. International law generally allowed **contraband** goods, usually defined as weapons and other articles used to fight a war, to be confiscated legally by any belligerent nation. Noncontraband goods, such as food, medical supplies, and other nonmilitary items, could not be confiscated. Britain, however, contested the definition of noncontraband articles. As the war continued, Britain expanded its definition of contraband until it encompassed virtually every product, including gasoline, cotton, and even food—in spite of international law.

Passenger Ships Fall Victim to the War at Sea Germany responded by attempting to blockade Britain—even though it lacked the conventional naval forces to do so. Instead, in February 1915, Germany began sinking Allied ships using its

Ships Sunk by U-boats, May 1917–January 1918

KEY
• Ship sunk

>> German U-boats destroyed more than 11 million tons of Allied shipping and killed nearly 14,000 people. **Analyze Maps** Why were U-boat attacks clustered in particular areas?

U-boats, or submarines. The reality of the German blockade struck America on May 7, 1915, when a German U-boat sank the British passenger liner **Lusitania** off the coast of Ireland.

Nearly 1,200 people perished. German officials correctly claimed that the ship was carrying ammunition and other contraband. Americans protested that an unarmed and unresisting ship should not be sunk without first being warned and provided with safety for its passengers. President Wilson was stunned but still wanted peace. "There is such a thing as a man being too proud to fight," he told his fellow citizens. "There is such a thing as a nation being so right that it does not need to convince others by force that it is right."

Germany helped to keep the United States out of the war by eventually promising not to sink any more passenger ships. But in 1916, Germany violated that promise by sinking the unarmed French passenger ship *Sussex*. Another storm of protest erupted in America. Again, Germany pledged not to sink unarmed ships. This promise, called the Sussex Pledge, would not last long.

Preparations for War President Wilson wanted to remain at peace, but even he must have realized the futility of that hope. At the end of 1915, Wilson began to prepare the nation for war.

Many believed that "preparedness" was a dangerous course that could actually provoke war. Even so, Congress passed two pieces of legislation in 1916 to prepare for the possibility of U.S. involvement. The National Defense Act expanded the size of the army, and the Naval Construction Act ordered the building of more warships.

Still, Wilson hoped to avoid conflict. In 1916, he ran for reelection with the slogan "He kept us out of war." It was a close election, but Wilson won a narrow victory over Republican Charles Evans Hughes.

The United States Is Neutral No Longer Wilson did not have much time to enjoy his victory. In early 1917, two events occurred that helped to push the United States into the war. Both events showed Germany's increasing aggression, the main reason why the United States ultimately entered the war.

American trade with the Allies had sustained Britain and France in the war, while the British blockade of Germany had stopped the flow of American goods to the Central Powers. As far as Germany was concerned, desperate times demanded desperate measures.

>> Discovery of the Zimmermann note (a coded telegram) along with unrestricted submarine warfare by Germany led Wilson to ask Congress for a declaration of war.

Bounce to Activate Timeline

In January 1917, suffering severe supply shortages due to the blockade, Germany took action. First, German Foreign Minister Arthur Zimmermann sent a telegram to Mexico. The **Zimmermann note** proposed an alliance with Mexico, stating that if the United States declared war on Germany, Mexico should declare war on the United States. In return, after a German victory, Mexico would get back the states of Texas, New Mexico, and Arizona, which it had lost in 1848 after its defeat in the Mexico-American War. The telegram was intercepted by the British, who gave it to American authorities. Next, Germany once again announced unrestricted submarine warfare against Britain.

Although most leaders knew Mexico had no intention of attacking the United States, Americans were shocked by the publication of the Zimmermann note. Even Wilson no longer called for peace. On April 2, 1917, he asked Congress for a declaration of war against Germany:

The world must be made safe for democracy. Its peace must be planted upon the tested foundations of political liberty. . . . We are but one of the champions of the rights of mankind. We shall be satisfied when those rights have been made as secure as the faith and the freedom of nations can make them.

—Woodrow Wilson, April 2, 1917

Congress responded on April 6, 1917, with a declaration of war. Wilson's long struggle to keep America at peace was over.

☑ **IDENTIFY** What two events finally led to U.S. involvement in World War I?

☑ ASSESSMENT

1. **Analyze Information** Discuss the form of nationalism that prevailed in Europe before World War I, and explain how it contributed to the start of the war.

2. **Identify Cause and Effect** Explain why the assassination of Francis Ferdinand led to more than a localized quarrel.

3. **Generate Explanations** Explain why President Wilson initially opposed U.S. involvement in World War I, and why he later changed his mind.

4. **Make Decisions** World War I is generally considered to be the first instance of total war, where every of-age citizen and all possible resources are mobilized in the war effort. In light of this, do you believe Britain's blockade of Germany—which eventually extended to all goods, thereby violating international law—was justified? Explain your opinion.

5. **Compare and Contrast** Discuss the ways in which World War I differed from previous wars.

Before the war, the federal government played a minor role in the daily lives of most Americans. But during World War I, the government assumed new powers. It regulated industrial and agricultural production, worked to shape public opinion, and established a new military draft. While war required sacrifice, it also brought new economic opportunities, and many Americans migrated to other parts of the country in search of these opportunities. The war permanently changed Americans' relationship with their government.

>> As the United States went to war, many women joined the workforce. This defense worker is welding the shell casing of a depth charge—an antisubmarine explosive.

 Bounce to Activate Flipped Video

The Home Front During World War I

Mobilizing for War

War affects many things, but its greatest impact is on the lives of ordinary people. People fight, sacrifice, and sometimes die in war. People work to produce the food that soldiers eat and the guns that soldiers fire. People shape the information that others receive about the war. War may be the result of conflicts between nations, but it touches the lives of millions of individuals.

Expanding the Army When the United States entered World War I, the U.S. Army was only a small fraction of the size of European armies. To build the army, President Wilson encouraged Americans to volunteer for service and pushed Congress to pass the **Selective Service Act**. The act, which Congress passed in May 1917, authorized a draft of young men for military service in Europe. On the first day of its enactment, June 5, 1917, more than 9.6 million Americans registered for the draft and were assigned a number. The government held a "great national lottery" in July to decide the order in which the first draftees would be called into service. Blindfolded, Secretary of War Newton D. Baker pulled number 258 out of a jar. The group of men assigned that number became the very first draftees.

>> **Objectives**

Analyze how the U.S. government mobilized the public to support the war effort.

Describe opposition to World War I and how the federal government responded to it.

Analyze the causes and effects of migration and social changes that occurred during World War I.

>> **Key Terms**

Selective Service
    Act
Bernard Baruch
Committee on
    Public Information
    (CPI)
George Creel
conscientious
    objector
Espionage Act
Great Migration
Bernard Baruch

Over the course of the war, more than 24 million Americans registered for the draft. Of these, about 2.8 million were actually drafted into the armed forces. Including volunteers, the total number of American men in uniform during World War I reached nearly 4.8 million. More than 4 million of these were sent to help the Allies in France.

Managing Economic Effects The economic effects of the international military conflict of World War I on the United States were significant. While the Selective Service Commission raised an army, President Wilson worked to shift the national economy from peacetime to wartime production. This process proved slow and frustrating. First, the Council of National Defense, which was formed in August 1916, created an array of new federal administrative agencies to oversee different phases of the war effort. Individual agencies regulated food production, coal and petroleum distribution, and railway use. The government determined what crops farmers grew, what products industries produced, and how supplies moved around on the nation's trains.

Problems and administrative overlap soon led to the creation of the War Industries Board (WIB). The WIB eventually became independent of the Council of National Defense. Headed by **Bernard Baruch** (buh ROOK), an influential Wall Street investment broker who reported directly to the President, the WIB regulated all industries engaged in the war effort. Baruch's agency determined what products industries would make and how much they would cost. The system of free enterprise was curtailed to fulfill the nation's acute need for war materials. Americans decided to cooperate rather than compete in order to defeat the Central Powers. They also bought war bonds to help the war effort.

What Baruch did for industry, future U.S. president Herbert Hoover achieved for agriculture. As head of the Food Administration, he set prices high for wheat and other foodstuffs to encourage farmers to increase production. He also asked Americans to conserve food as a patriotic gesture. If the American people ate less, then more food could be shipped to American and other Allied soldiers. To this end, Hoover instituted wheatless Mondays and Wednesdays, meatless Tuesdays, and porkless Thursdays and Saturdays.

Convincing the American People Hoover's efforts would have been fruitless if the American people did not believe in supporting the war. Most Americans did not understand the reasons for the war in 1914, and many questioned why the United States became involved in 1917. It was the job of the **Committee on Public Information (CPI)** to educate the public

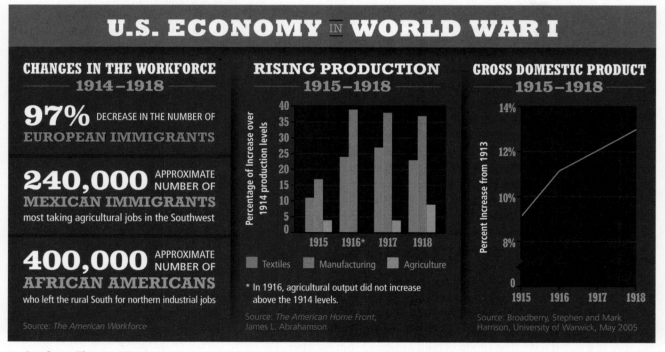

>> **Analyze Charts** Which segment of the U.S. economy was strongest from 1914-1918? Why?

about the causes and nature of the war. The CPI had to convince Americans that the war effort was a just cause.

Wilson appointed **George Creel** as the director of the CPI. A former journalist and a passionate admirer of American institutions, Creel combined education and a widespread advertising campaign to "sell America." The CPI distributed 75 million pamphlets and 6,000 press releases, and it assembled an army of 75,000 speakers who gave lectures and brief speeches on America's war aims and the nature of the enemy. In addition, the CPI designed, printed, and distributed millions of posters that dramatized the needs of America and its allies. The CPI also stressed the cruelty and wickedness of the enemy, particularly Germany, which in some cases aggravated resentment toward German Americans. Still, using these methods, Creel and the CPI earned widespread support for the American war effort.

☑ **RECALL** What cornerstone of U.S. business philosophy was partially abandoned to aid the war effort?

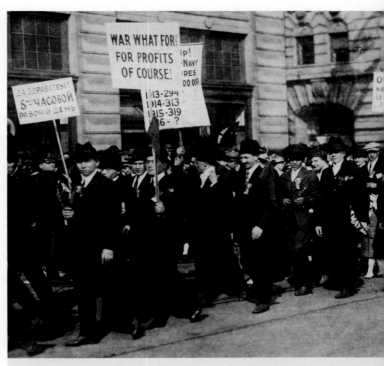

>> Some citizens showed their opposition to the war and the draft by staging protests.

Opposition to the War

The CPI's work was important because Americans did not always peacefully agree with one another about the war. Members of two large ethnic groups, German Americans and Irish Americans, tended to oppose the Allies for different reasons. Swept up in patriotic fervor, some people treated German Americans with prejudice, or intolerance. Other Americans were pacifists who opposed war for any reason. One major issue raised by U.S. involvement in World War I was that the government acted in ways that sometimes trespassed on individual liberties to quiet dissent, or differing opinions.

Opposition to the Draft Without a doubt, the draft created controversy. Some Americans believed it was an illegal intrusion of the federal government into their private lives. Some men refused to cooperate with the Selective Service process.

They were often court-martialed and imprisoned. Others simply tried to avoid the draft. Perhaps as many as 12 percent of men who received draft notices never responded to them.

Many Americans were **conscientious objectors**, people whose moral or religious beliefs forbid them to fight in wars. In theory, the Selective Service Act exempted from combat service members of "any well recognized religious sect or organization . . . whose existing creed or principles forbid its members to participate in war." In practice, this policy was widely ignored. This was a constitutional issue, because the First Amendment guarantees freedom of religion. In addition, some conscientious objectors were treated badly by their local draft boards, and others were humiliated in training camps. As America's participation in the war increased, however, the government improved its treatment of conscientious objectors.

Women Oppose the War Some American women also opposed the war. Before the war, a number of leading American feminists, including reformer Jane Addams, formed the Women's Peace Party and, with pacifist women from other countries, the Women's International League for Peace and Freedom. Jeannette Rankin, the first woman to serve in the U.S. House of Representatives, voted against the declaration of war. After America joined the Allies, some women continued to oppose the war, but most supported American war efforts. For example, the influential National American Woman Suffrage Association (NAWSA) dropped its initial peace initiatives and supported America's war objectives. After adopting this new policy, NAWSA doubled in size.

The Federal Government Stifles Dissent

Constitutional issues raised by federal government policy during World War I also centered on the First Amendment rights of free speech. The work of the CPI created a mood in America that did not welcome open debate. Some felt the CPI stifled the free expression of controversial opinions and worried about the impact of a rigorous military campaign on democracy. They did not want the freedoms that Americans held most dear to become victims of the conflict. Americans treasured their Constitution and the Bill of Rights.

And were not U.S. soldiers fighting for freedom? At the same time, since so much depended on individuals doing their part in the military or on the home front, retaining national unity was vital to America's success in the war. As in previous and future wars, the government navigated a difficult path between respecting and restricting individual rights. Authorities tended to treat harshly individuals who worked against U.S. participation in the war.

In June 1917, Congress passed the **Espionage Act**, allowing postal authorities to ban treasonable or seditious newspapers, magazines, or printed materials from the mail. Thus, another First Amendment freedom, the freedom of the press, was compromised. It also enacted severe penalties for anyone engaged in disloyal or treasonable activities. Anyone found obstructing army recruiters, aiding the enemy, or generally interfering with the war effort could be punished with up to a $10,000 fine and 20 years of imprisonment.

In 1918, Congress limited freedom of speech even further with the passage of the Sedition Act. The act made it unlawful to use "disloyal, profane, scurrilous, or abusive language" about the American form of government, the Constitution, or the military forces. The government employed the Sedition Act to prosecute socialists, political radicals, and pacifists. Eugene V. Debs, the leader of the Socialist Party in America, was imprisoned under the act. For his crime—giving a mildly antiwar speech to a convention of socialists in Canton, Ohio—he was sentenced to a 10-year term in a federal prison.

The Supreme Court upheld the constitutionality of the Sedition Act in the case of *Schenck* v. *United States* (1919). The Court ruled that there are times when the need for public order is so pressing that First Amendment protections of speech do not apply. The Debs case and others like it show that the war did lead the federal government to follow policies that raised important constitutional issues about the suppression of personal freedoms and individual rights.

Espionage and Sedition Court Cases During World War I

DEFENDANT	ACCUSATIONS	ARGUMENT
KATE RICHARDS O'HARE	Claimed U.S. involvement in World War I was only to protect U.S. corporate interests and criticized soldiers; accused of violating the Espionage Act of 1917 and the Sedition Act of 1918	First Amendment (freedom of speech)
EUGENE V. DEBS	Criticized U.S. government for prosecuting those who violated the Espionage Act of 1917 and made a speech opposing the war; accused of violating the Espionage Act of 1917 and the Sedition Act of 1918	First Amendment (freedom of speech); led to the Supreme Court case *Debs* v. *United States* in 1919
CHARLES T. SCHENCK	Opposed military draft; accused of violating the Espionage Act of 1917 and Sedition Act of 1918	First Amendment (freedom of speech); led to the Supreme Court case *Schenck* v. *United States* in 1919
EMMA GOLDMAN	Opposed U.S. involvement in the war; accused of conspiring against the draft law in 1917	First Amendment (freedom of speech)

>> **Analyze Charts** Do you think Eugene V. Debs should have been arrested during World War I? Why or why not?

 Bounce to Activate Gallery

Prejudice Against German Americans

Sometimes, the war enthusiasm created by the CPI and other groups took an ugly turn. Some German Americans were treated harshly during the war. Largely because of CPI efforts, Americans regarded Germany's kaiser as arrogant, its generals as ruthless, and its soldiers as spike-helmeted brutes. Germany was seen as the primary foe among the Central Powers. Popular movies, such as *The Kaiser, the Beast of Berlin*, as well as some CPI posters and speeches intensified this feeling by portraying Germany as a cruel enemy. Some Americans wrongly generalized that if Germany was cruel, then all German people were cruel.

As a result, Americans stopped teaching German in public schools and discontinued playing the music of Beethoven and Brahms. They renamed German measles "liberty measles," cooked "liberty steaks" instead of hamburgers, and walked their "liberty pups" instead of dachshunds.

German Americans were pressured to prove their loyalty to America by condemning the German government, giving up speaking German and reading German-language newspapers, and participating enthusiastically in any patriotic drive. Occasionally, hatred of the German enemy boiled over into violence against German Americans. Some German Americans were harassed, others were beaten, and a few were killed for no other reason than they were born in Germany or spoke with a German accent.

☑ **GENERATE EXPLANATIONS** Why was the status of conscientious objectors a constitutional issue?

The War Changes American Society

The war was not only a turning point in the economic and political lives of Americans, but it also brought substantial social changes. New opportunities opened up for women, African Americans, and Mexican Americans. Some left their homes to seek new ones where they could take advantage of these opportunities. Asian-Americans were also drafted, and some fought in Europe.

Women Welcome New Opportunities Before the war, some American women campaigned for women's suffrage. They won the vote in several western states and still hoped to gain the franchise nationally. Many feared that the war would draw

A CERTAIN CURE FOR THE
GERMAN MEASLES.

Mix some Woolwich Powders with Tinct. of Iron or Essence of lead, and administer in pills (or shells). Have ready a little British Army (a little goes a long way) some Brussels Sprouts and French Mustard. Add a little Canadian Cheese and Australian Lamb and season with the best Indian Curry. Set it on a Kitchener and keep stirring until quite hot.

If this does not make the Patient perspire freely, rub the best Russian Bears' Grease on his chest and wrap in Berlin Wool.

Dr. Cannon's Prescrip.

P.S. The patient must on no account have any Peace-Soup until the swelling in the head has quite disappeared.

No 147

>> Unlike this humorous postcard with a "cure" for German measles, other anti-German sentiment was often more strident.

attention away from their efforts. In fact, the war gave women new chances and won them more support for the right to vote.

As men entered the armed forces, many women moved into the workforce for the first time. Women filled jobs that were vacated by men who had gone to fight.

They worked in munitions factories, on the railroads, as telegraph operators and trolley conductors, and in other jobs that were previously open only to men. Others labored on farms. Some joined the Red Cross or the American Women's Hospital Service and went overseas. They worked as doctors, nurses, ambulance drivers, and clerks. Thousands enlisted when the Army Corps of Nurses was created in 1918. Women proved that they could succeed in any type of job, regardless of difficulty or risk.

By their efforts and sacrifices during the war, women convinced President Wilson to support their suffrage demands. He contended that granting the vote to women was "vital to winning the war." If women could do the work of men, they certainly deserved the same voting privileges as men. Finally, in 1919, Congress passed the Nineteenth Amendment giving the vote to women. The required two thirds of states ratified the amendment in the summer of 1920, a victory more than 70 years in the making.

African Americans and the Great Migration The war similarly presented new opportunities to African Americans.

From the outset, most African American leaders supported the war. "If this is our country, then this is our war," wrote African American leader W.E.B. Du Bois. He viewed the struggle as an excellent opportunity to show all Americans the loyalty and patriotism of African Americans. Thousands of them enlisted or were drafted into the army and sailed for the battlefields of France. On the battlefield, they fought in segregated units under the command of white officers. Altogether, 367,000 African Americans served in the military. Hundreds died for their country.

Despite their sacrifice, many African American soldiers in Europe were subject to the same racism and disrespect that they suffered at home. White soldiers refused to salute black officers; African American soldiers often received substandard clothing.

Meanwhile, a great movement of African Americans from the rural South to the industrial North was taking place. This movement to the "Land of Hope," as many African Americans referred to the North at that time, is called the **Great Migration**.

A migration is a movement of a group people to a new place. Migrations are often described as being caused by "push-pull" factors: people migrate because some factors "push" them away from where they have been living while other factors "pull" them toward their destination.

For African Americans during the Great Migration, factors that "pushed" them out of the South included Jim Crow segregation laws, lynching and other racial violence, and few economic opportunities other than as servants, sharecroppers, or tenant farmers. Many raised cotton, and the arrival in 1910 of an insect pest called the boll weevil ruined their crops, providing yet another push out of the South.

At the same time, the North "pulled" them with the chance of economic opportunities to be found in prosperous cities and wartime factories. As more African Americans moved North, they themselves became pull factors for family and friends back in the South. Newspapers in the North, such as the Chicago *Defender*, an African American newspaper that was widely read in the South, encouraged the migration:

> I beg you, my brother, to leave the benighted land. . . .Get out of the South. . . . Come north then, all

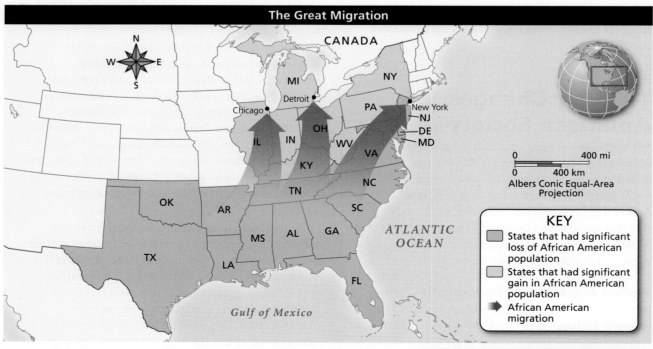

The Great Migration

>> **Analyze Maps** How did World War I help create this demographic shift?

Bounce to Activate Chart

you folks, both good and bad. . . .The *Defender* says come.

—*Chicago Defender*

African Americans moved to Chicago, as the *Defender* encouraged, where they found work in meatpacking plants. They migrated to Detroit, where they obtained jobs in auto factories. They traveled to smaller industrial towns in the Midwest and to the giant cities of the Northeast. Between 1910 and 1930, more than 1.2 million African Americans moved to the North. Millions more eventually made the journey. Although they did not entirely escape discrimination in the North, many did find more opportunity. The Great Migration was one of the most dramatic demographic, or population, shifts in American history.

The effects of this change in demographic pattern are still with us today. For example, in 1910, about one percent of Detroit's population was African American. In 2010, 83 percent of the residents were African American. Similarly, other large cities across the North—Chicago, Philadelphia, New York—have high concentrations of African Americans as a direct result of the Great Migration.

Mexicans Move North Some of the same factors that pushed African Americans out of the South and pulled them to the North caused Mexicans to cross the border into the United States. Because of the ongoing Mexican Revolution, many Mexicans faced violence and desperate poverty. They also wanted better economic opportunities. Most immigrated to the American West, where they sought work on large ranches and farms in Texas and along the Pacific Coast. Increased wartime demands for food and a decrease in American farmworkers (since many were serving in the army) created jobs that Mexican migrants filled.

Some of the Mexican migration was seasonal. Many workers crossed the border to harvest fruits or grains or to pick cotton while each crop was in season, then crossed back into Mexico. But others stayed and made the United States their home. Some Mexican workers migrated first to the Southwest and then to the northern states in search of factory jobs, but a large population stayed in California. They formed *barrios* (BAHR ee ohz), or Hispanic neighborhoods, in Los Angeles and in smaller cities in California's Imperial Valley, a farming region just north of the Mexican border. California had always had a rich Hispanic heritage, but these

>> As Mexican immigrants came to the United States they sought to create new economic opportunities for themselves and their children in the American West.

new immigrants added an important economic dimension to that heritage.

☑ **DRAW CONCLUSIONS** What do you think was the most significant motivation behind the Great Migration?

☑ ASSESSMENT

1. **Generate Explanations** Explain how the role of the federal government changed during World War I.

2. **Draw Conclusions** Discuss the purposes and effects of the Committee on Public Information.

3. **Evaluate Arguments** Discuss the constitutional issues raised by the government's response to antiwar sentiments.

4. **Make Generalizations** How did wartime patriotism affect German Americans?

5. **Identify Cause and Effect** Discuss women's roles in the war effort, and explain how the war influenced the women's suffrage movement.

>> The energy and enthusiasm that American forces brought to the battlefield gave a tremendous boost to the Allied war effort.

 Bounce to Activate Flipped Video

4.3 When the United States entered World War I in the spring of 1917, the conflict had become a deadly, bloody stalemate. The war would be won or lost on the Western Front in France. Since 1914, both sides had tried desperately to break the stalemate there—and failed. The American entry into the war would play a key role in the Allied victory.

>> Objectives

Understand the contributions of the American Expeditionary Force to the Allied victory in World War I.

Describe the issues raised by President Wilson's Fourteen Points.

Analyze the decisions made at the Paris Peace Conference and included in the Treaty of Versailles.

Evaluate the pros and cons of U.S. participation in the League of Nations.

Explain why the U.S. Senate did not ratify the Treaty of Versailles.

>> Key Terms

Vladimir Lenin
John J. Pershing
Fourteen Points
self-determination
League of Nations
Henry Cabot Lodge
irreconcilables
reservationists

American Expeditionary Forces (AEF)

The End of World War I

America Joins the Fighting

To European leaders, the United States was a great unknown. Ethnic divisions in the United States raised questions about how committed American troops would be in combat. Some doubted that the United States could raise, train, equip, and transport an army fast enough to influence the outcome of the war. Desperate German military leaders renewed unrestricted submarine warfare, hoping to end the conflict before the Americans could make a difference.

The Convoy System The Allies immediately felt the impact of the renewed unrestricted submarine warfare. German U-boats sank merchant ships in alarming numbers, faster than replacements could be built. As one merchant ship after another sank to the bottom of the sea, the Allies lost crucial supplies.

Together, the Allies addressed the problem of submarine warfare by adopting an old naval tactic: convoying. In a **convoy**, groups of merchant ships sailed together, protected by warships. The arrangement was designed to provide mutual safety at sea. Convoys made up of British and American ships proved to be an instant success. Shipping losses from U-boat attacks fell as sharply as they had risen. Germany's gamble had failed.

The War Ends on the Eastern Front Meanwhile, the situation on land began to swing in favor of the Central Powers. The Allies were exhausted by years of combat. Russia was torn by revolutions. In March 1917, a moderate, democratic revolution overthrew Czar Nicholas II but kept Russia in the war. In November 1917, radical communists led by **Vladimir Lenin** (LEHN ihn) staged a revolution and gained control of Russia.

Russia stopped fighting in mid-December, and on March 3, 1918, the Treaty of Brest-Litovsk ended the war between Russia (soon to become the Soviet Union) and Germany. The end of the war on the Eastern Front allowed Germany to send more soldiers to the Western Front.

General John J. Pershing and the AEF In the spring of 1918, Germany launched an all-out offensive on the Western Front. A series of five offensives threatened to break through Allied defenses and open a path to Paris. The hard-pressed Allies organized a joint command under French General Ferdinand Foch (fawsh).

General **John J. Pershing**, the commander of U.S. forces in Europe, arrived in France with a small force in mid-1917. However, it was not until early 1918 that U.S. troops began arriving in larger numbers. The forces under Pershing's command were called the **American Expeditionary Forces (AEF)**. By the end of the war, more than two million men would serve overseas in the AEF. Although the Allies wanted to use U.S. soldiers to replenish their armies, Pershing was adamant about keeping U.S. forces independent.

At about the time of Pershing's arrival, the first German offensive began to stall. By the end of March 1918, Allied counterattacks and German exhaustion ended the first great German offensive. Germany had gained miles rather than yards of land but failed to end the war before American troops could arrive in force. Both sides lost hundreds of thousands of men, but the Allied forces were being bolstered by American troops.

More fighting followed, and with each passing week, American troops made more and more contributions on the battlefield, driven forward by Pershing's leadership. Germany launched several more offensives. Allied defenses buckled and stretched but did not break. Each failed offensive weakened Germany more and raised Allied hopes. A British volunteer nurse working near the front described the arrival of new American troops:

I pressed forward with the others
to watch the United States physically

>> A church in Ypres (EE-pruh), Belgium, lies in ruins. The use of powerful new military technologies by both the Allied and Central powers left many parts of Europe devastated.

>> American vessels crossed the Atlantic Ocean in convoys to help defend themselves against German U-boat attacks. **Identify Cause and Effect** Why was it so important to find a solution to the U-boat threat?

entering the War, so god-like, so magnificent, so splendidly unimpaired in comparison with the tired, nerve-wracked men of the British Army. So these were our deliverers at last, marching up the road to Camiers in the spring sunshine!

—Vera Brittain, *Testament of Youth*

American Troops in Battle American troops, called "doughboys," saw significant action in the late spring and summer of 1918. Americans fought on the defensive along with the French at the Second Battle of the Marne and on the offensive at the Battle of Cantigny (kahn tee NYEE), where they dislodged a large German force from fortified positions. They battled valiantly at Château-Thierry (sha TOH tir EE) and Belleau (beh LOH) Wood, Meuse-Argonne (myooz ahr GAHN) and Saint-Mihiel (mee YEHL). Although it took some time, American troops learned quickly and fought bravely.

One of America's greatest war heroes was Alvin York of Tennessee. On October 8, 1918, York was one of thousands of Americans fighting in the Meuse-Argonne region of northeastern France. Trapped behind enemy lines, York and 16 other Americans took cover from blistering machine-gun fire. As half

of the American force fell to German bullets, York took aim with his rifle and silenced a nearby German machine-gun nest. He then dodged a flurry of bullets to attack several other machine gunners and even charged one German position with only a pistol! When the firefight died down, York and the surviving Americans had taken the German position against amazing odds. York's battlefield heroics earned him a Congressional Medal of Honor.

Alvin York was only one of thousands of heroes, many of whom died and most of whom were never recognized for their deeds. They followed orders, fought bravely, and made great sacrifices. Although African American soldiers often faced discrimination in the United States Army, they demonstrated their patriotism in dozens of engagements. For example, an entire African American unit, the 369th Infantry Regiment, received the *Croix de Guerre*, a French award for bravery, for its members' actions in the Meuse-Argonne region.

The fighting in the Meuse-Argonne region is also called the Meuse-Argonne campaign. The campaign was a widespread attack along the Western Front launched in September of 1918. The AEF under General Pershing were tasked with advancing through the thick, tangled Argonne Forest. The dense trees and rocky ridges gave the advantage to the German defenses, but the Americans persisted. After weeks of heavy fighting, they had driven the Germans from the forest. The American victory in

Key Battles Involving Americans in World War I

KEY
- Allies, 1918
- Central Powers, 1918
- Neutral countries, 1918
- Allied front line, July 1918
- Armistice line, November 1918
- Battle, 1918

>> **Analyze Maps** Why did Germany ask for peace while they still controlled most of Belgium and northeast France?

Bounce to Activate Map

the Battle of the Argonne Forest was a devastating defeat for Germany that hastened the end of the war.

Germany Surrenders The American troops, added to those of France, Britain, and Italy, gave the Allies a military advantage. By the fall of 1918, the German front was collapsing. Both the German and Austro-Hungarian armies had had enough. Some men deserted, others mutinied, and many refused to fight. Their leaders faced little choice but to surrender. On November 11, 1918, Germany surrendered to the Allies in a railway car in Compiegne (kohn PYEHN), France. The war was over.

Of the millions of soldiers who mobilized to fight, almost 5 million Allied and 8 million Central Power troops were dead. Nearly 6.5 million civilians were also dead, victims of the terrible conflict. Of the 2 million U.S. soldiers sent to Europe, about 1.4 million served on the front. More than 50,000 lost their lives, and about 230,000 were wounded. It was left to the peacemakers to determine whether the results would justify the costs.

☑ **GENERATE EXPLANATIONS** What contributions did the U.S. military make to World War I?

>> Alvin York, a conscientious objector before the war, earned the Medal of Honor after helping Allied forces defeat the Germans at the Battle of Argonne Forest.

Wilson Wants "Peace Without Victory"

Vladimir Lenin, leader of the communist revolution in Russia, maintained that the entire war was nothing more than an imperialistic land-grab. Once in power, he exposed secret treaties that Russia had made with the other Allies in which they agreed to divide among themselves the empires of their enemies. These revelations undercut the morality of the Allied cause in the war.

For President Woodrow Wilson, however, the war was not about acquisitions and imperialism—it was about peace and freedom. In January 1917, Wilson had introduced the idea of a "peace without victory" in an address to Congress:

Only a tranquil Europe can be a stable Europe. . . .[There] must be a peace without victory . . . .Victory would mean peace forced upon the loser, a victor's terms imposed upon the vanquished. It would be accepted in humiliation...and would leave a sting, a resentment, a bitter memory

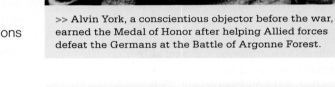

>> President Wilson asks Congress to declare war in April, 1917.

upon which terms of peace would rest, not permanently, but only as upon quicksand.

—Woodrow Wilson, "Peace Without Victory" speech, January 22, 1917

The Fourteen Points In another address to Congress in January 1918, Wilson answered Lenin's charges about the nature of the conflict by outlining America's war aims in what became known as the **Fourteen Points**. At the heart of the Fourteen Points was his idea of "peace without victory." Wilson proposed a peace inspired by noble ideals, not greed and vengeance.

The Fourteen Points raised some major issues. They sought to fundamentally change the world by promoting openness, encouraging independence, and supporting freedom. Critical of all secret treaties, Wilson called for open diplomacy. He insisted on freedom of the seas, free trade, a move toward ending colonialism, and a general reduction of armaments.

He also championed national **self-determination**, or the right of people to choose their own form of government. This would lead to the creation of several new, independent states but also raised many questions of which populations would achieve statehood and under what circumstances. Finally, he asked for a **League of Nations** to secure "mutual guarantees of political independence and territorial integrity to great and small states alike."

Wilson Travels to Paris In early 1919, the victorious Allies held a peace conference in Versailles (ver sı̄), a suburb of Paris, in the former palace of Louis XIV. President Wilson believed that the peace conference was too important to be left to career diplomats and lesser politicians, so he crossed the Atlantic Ocean himself to represent the United States at the conference, something no president had ever done.

Wilson did not invite any leading Republicans to join him in his peace delegation. Wilson's decision angered Republicans, who had won control of Congress in the 1918 elections.

Senator **Henry Cabot Lodge**, a leading Republican foreign policy expert, was especially angry. Wilson left Lodge behind because Wilson disliked him intensely, but the feeling was mutual. Lodge and Wilson had fundamentally different views about America's place on the world stage. Lodge was suspicious of Wilson's progressivism and idealism, which he viewed as dangerously naive. Whereas Wilson spoke of "peace without victory" and "mutual guarantees," Lodge, keen to move the United States into the position of a world power, spoke unabashedly about putting American interests first:

Wilson's Fourteen Points, 1918

1. Make no secret diplomatic agreements.	**6.** Evacuate and restore Russian territories seized during the war.	**11.** Redraw boundaries of Balkan states based on nationalities and historical allegiances.
2. Allow freedom of the seas in peace and war.	**7.** Restore and protect Belgium's sovereignty.	**12.** Separate the Ottoman Empire into independent countries according to nationality; guarantee all nations access to the Dardanelles.
3. Remove as many economic trade barriers as possible between countries.	**8.** Restore French territory and settle the debate over Alsace-Lorraine.	
4. Reduce stockpiles of military armaments to lowest point needed for domestic safety.	**9.** Adjust Italy's boundaries according to the nationalities of populations living there.	**13.** Restore and protect Poland as a sovereign state with access to the sea.
5. Adjust colonial claims, giving more weight to the views of the colonized peoples.	**10.** Allow the peoples of the former Austro-Hungarian Empire to choose their own governments.	**14.** Establish an association of nations to provide collective security and to ensure peace.

>> **Analyze Charts** How did Wilson's Fourteen Points aim to reduce the potential for future wars to develop?

> "I can never be anything else but an American, and I must think of the United States first, and when I think of the United States first . . . I am thinking of what is best for the world, for if the United States fails, the best hopes of mankind fail with it."

—Henry Cabot Lodge, letter to President Woodrow Wilson, 1919

The decision to leave Lodge behind would come back to haunt Wilson.

However, when the American president arrived in France, adoring crowds greeted him. "Never has a king, never has an emperor received such a welcome," wrote one journalist.

☑ **IDENTIFY CENTRAL IDEAS** What was the central idea behind Wilson's "peace without victory" proposal?

The Paris Peace Conference

Wilson's idealism did not inspire the other Allied leaders at the peace conference. They blamed Germany for starting the war, reminded Wilson that they had suffered more in the war than the United States, and insisted that Germany make **reparations,** or payment for war damages. They wanted to weaken Germany so that it would never threaten Europe again.

Allied Leaders Reject Wilson's Ideas British prime minister David Lloyd-George and French premier Georges Clemenceau (klay mahn SOH) knew that the citizens of their countries expected both peace and victory. Lloyd-George insisted on protecting the existing colonial status quo and punishing Germany. Clemenceau wanted to make Germany pay dearly for what it had done to France. In addition to reparations, he demanded the return of Alsace-Lorraine and several key German colonies. Besides Britain and France, other Allies also had goals of their own and were skeptical of Wilson's grand vision.

Once the Versailles conference began, Clemenceau, Lloyd-George, Italian Premier Vittorio Orlando, and other Allied leaders started to chip away at Wilson's Fourteen Points. Onto the scrap heap of failed proposals they piled freedom of the seas, free trade, the liberation of colonial empires, a general disarmament, and several other ideas.

>> Woodrow Wilson joined French Prime Minister Georges Clemenceau on the left, and British Prime Minister David Lloyd George, on the right, at Versailles in 1919.

>> Senator Henry Cabot Lodge disagreed with Wilson over the proposed League of Nations, arguing that entangling the United States in European affairs would weaken U.S. sovereignty.

>> The League of Nations' first session took place in Geneva, Switzerland, in November 1920.

>> The spread of the influenza pandemic from 1918 to 1919 left millions dead worldwide, creating a sense of dread among peoples of all nations. Pictured are soldiers at an army hospital in Kansas.

The League of Nations Wilson lost a number of battles but kept fighting to salvage a League of Nations, a world organization where countries could gather and peacefully resolve their quarrels. On this point, Wilson refused to compromise. The other delegates finally voted to make the League of Nations part of the treaty.

Problems With the Peace In the end, the various peace treaties created almost as many major issues as they solved. The changes in political boundaries that resulted from the international conflict were not always driven by self-determination or the best interests of the people living there. In the new map that emerged from the Paris Peace Conference, national self-determination was violated almost as often as it was confirmed. In Europe, several populations of Germans found themselves attached to non-German nations. The same was true of several Austrian populations.

Furthermore, in the Middle East, the breakup of the Ottoman Empire led to new political boundaries in which ethnic groups were clustered together randomly. To form Iraq, for example, the Versailles peacemakers threw together three provinces of the defeated Ottoman Empire—Basra, Baghdad, and Mosul. But Basra had natural links to the Persian Gulf and India, Baghdad to Persia, and Mosul to Turkey and Syria. The various regions had no sense of Iraqi nationalism. In addition, Iraq, like other holdings in the Middle East, Asia, and Africa, was not allowed to practice self-determination. It was attached to Britain as a mandate, or territory overseen by another nation.

☑ **DRAW CONCLUSIONS** Why did the Allies reject Wilson's ideas for peace?

America Rejects the Treaty of Versailles

When Wilson left Versailles to return to the United States, he knew the treaty was not perfect. But he believed that over time the League could correct its problems. He still thought that a lasting peace could emerge.

The Flu Pandemic The movement from war to peace would have been difficult even in the best of times. But the end of 1918 and 1919 were not the best of times. In September 1918, an unusually deadly form of the **influenza**, or flu, virus appeared. Research in recent years shows that the 1918

Comparing Irreconcilables, Reservationists, and Wilson Democrats

IRRECONCILABLES	RESERVATIONISTS	WILSON DEMOCRATS
• Opposed the treaty in any form • Convinced that the idea of a League of Nations was idealistic and unrealistic • Suspicious of the actions and intents of the other countries in the League of Nations • Wished to maintain American isolationism	• Would accept the treaty if it were modified • Believed the League of Nations removed congressional power to declare war, making it unconstitutional • Opposed Article 10 of the League Covenant, which required the U.S. to defend other members of the League under certain circumstances	• Most supported the treaty • Believed no changes to the treaty were necessary • Wanted U.S. to be part of the League of Nations

>> **Analyze Charts** What was the primary difference between reservationists and irreconcilables?

influenza virus was originally a bird flu that mutated to spread to humans. Many historians now believe that the virus originated in the United States, then traveled around the world, thus becoming a pandemic.

As many as 50 million people died—among them, about 675,000 Americans. The Great Influenza pandemic, also called the Great Pandemic or the Flu Pandemic of 1918, coming on the heels of the Great War, gave a sense of doom and dread to people around the globe.

The pandemic may have even reached Wilson at the Paris Peace Conference. He fell seriously ill, and his temperature reached 103 degrees. Wilson's physician diagnosed the president as suffering from the flu. Although there is some doubt that it was actually the flu, there is no doubt that Wilson's sickness kept him from participating in many meetings. His illness may have been factor in Wilson not achieving all he had hoped to.

Wilson Faces Opposition at Home Much as Wilson faced opposition to his ideas at the Paris Peace Conference, he faced opposition in the United States to the Treaty of Versailles he had negotiated—but for different reasons. German Americans thought the treaty was too harsh toward Germany, especially the "war guilt clause" that suggested that Germany had caused the war. Irish Americans criticized the failure to create an independent Ireland.

Most important, however, the treaty would need to be submitted to the Republican-controlled Senate Foreign Relations Committee and then ratified, or

approved, by the Republic-controlled Senate. In both bodies, as well as in his own Democratic Party, Wilson faced stiff opposition.

A handful of senators believed that the United States should not get entangled in world politics or involved in world organizations at all. Known as **"irreconcilables,"** these isolationist senators opposed any treaty that had a League of Nations folded into it. They particularly disliked Article 10 of the League covenant. Article 10 called for mutual defense by the signers of the treaty, a pledge that each nation would "respect and preserve . . . the territorial integrity and existing political independence of all the Members of the League."

A larger group of senators, led by Henry Cabot Lodge and known as **"reservationists,"** were opposed to the treaty as it was written. Some wanted only small changes, while others demanded larger ones.

For example, many felt Article 10 could lead the United States into a war without the consent of Congress, which was unconstitutional. Reservationists believed that the language of the article was too vague and demanded that it not contradict the power of Congress to declare war. But with some changes, the reservationists were prepared to vote for the Treaty of Versailles. They knew that polls indicated that the American people favored the League of Nations.

Wilson had compromised in Versailles, but he was not ready to compromise in Washington, D.C. When the Senate delayed its ratification vote, Wilson took his case directly to the people. The

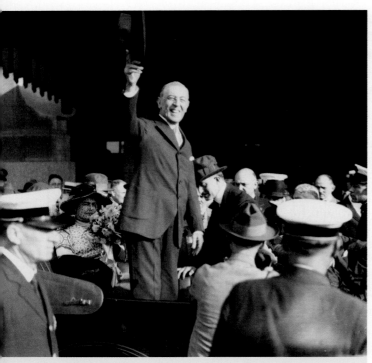

>> As part of his speaking tour to promote the League of Nations, President Wilson makes a stop in St. Louis, Missouri.

Bounce to Activate Chart

League of Nations had become his personal crusade, and convincing the American people of its worth would test his leadership. The qualities of effective leadership, for a president of the United States, include the ability to appeal to a wide variety of people and persuade them that certain ideas are in the best interest of the country. Even though he was ill and weak, he set himself the grueling task of crossing the country and giving 32 addresses in 33 days. But his health failed on September 25, 1919, in Pueblo, Colorado. He was rushed back to Washington, D.C., but suffered a debilitating stroke a few days later. As the Senate prepared to vote on the treaty, Wilson lay close to death, barely able to speak.

The United States Fails to Approve Treaty of Versailles In November 1919, one year after the war ended, a treaty revised to eliminate the complaints of the reservationists reached the Senate for a vote. Wilson would not compromise and told his Democratic supporters to vote with the irreconcilables against it. They did, and it was defeated. Next, the Senate voted on the treaty without any changes. The Democrats voted for it, but the combined strength of the irreconcilables and reservationists defeated it. Once more it was voted on, this time with only modest changes. Again, Wilson told his followers to vote against it. Although

some Democrats voted for it, the combination of Wilson Democrats and irreconcilables defeated the treaty.

The problem was not that most of the Senate was isolationist. Except for the irreconcilables, most senators wanted the United States to participate in world affairs. They differed slightly on what form that participation would take.

However, at a moment that demanded compromise, Wilson and his opponents refused to put aside personal and political differences for the good of the country. The tragedy of the failed votes was that without full American support, the League of Nations would prove unable to maintain peace among nations.

It was the League of Nations that U.S. opponents of the Treaty of Versailles most objected to. In evaluating the pros and cons of U.S. participation in the international organization and treaty, opponents judged that the cons outweighed the pros. They were especially concerned that the League would entangle the United States in conflicts that would not advance U.S. interests. Supporters, in contrast, thought the pros outweighed the cons. They thought the United States would benefit by being part of an international organization in which other countries could come to the aid of the United States. They also wanted the United States to have a voice in international politics—before a huge conflict broke out.

☑ **DRAW CONCLUSIONS** What was the principal argument of the irreconcilables against the Treaty of Versailles?

☑ ASSESSMENT

1. **Evaluate Arguments** Explain the reasoning behind President Wilson's concept of "peace without victory." Do you think it was a viable idea? Explain why or why not.

2. **Apply Concepts** What opposition did President Wilson's ideas face among Allied nations as well as within the United States?

3. **Generate Explanations** Explain how European and Middle Eastern nations adjusted to peace after the Paris Peace Conference.

4. **Describe** the impact of the Great Influenza pandemic after World War I.

5. **Identify Cause and Effect** Explain why the United States failed to approve the Treaty of Versailles, and discuss how this impacted the future of world relations.

The Fourteen Points: Woodrow Wilson

In a speech to Congress on January 8, 1918, President Wilson laid out America's war aims and his vision for peace after the war. His speech included fourteen key points upon which he believed the peace following the war must be based. However, not all of Wilson's ideas were adopted at the Paris Peace Conference.

>> Woodrow Wilson (center foreground) in Paris

We entered this war because violations of right had occurred which touched us to the quick and made the life of our own people impossible unless they were corrected and the world secure once for all against their recurrence. What we demand in this war, therefore, is nothing peculiar [unique] to ourselves. It is that the world be made fit and safe to live in; and particularly that it be made safe for every peace-loving nation which, like our own, wishes to live its own life, [and] determine its own institutions, [choose its own government] be assured of justice and fair dealing by the other peoples of the world as against force and selfish aggression. All the peoples of the world are in effect partners in this interest, and for our own part we see very clearly that unless justice be done to others it will not be done to us. The program of the world's peace, therefore, is our only program; and that program, the only possible program as we see it, is this:

☑ **DISTINGUISH AMONG FACT, OPINION, AND REASONED JUDGMENT** When Wilson says, "The program of the world's peace, therefore, is our only program, the only possible program as we see it, is this," is this a fact, an opinion, or a reasoned judgment? Explain your answer.

1. Open covenants [formal agreements] of peace, openly arrived at, after which there shall be no private international understandings of any kind but [instead] diplomacy shall proceed always frankly [openly and honestly] and in the public view.

☑ **EXPLAIN AN ARGUMENT** Why might Wilson think that prohibiting secret agreements between nations is necessary in order to avoid war?

2. Absolute freedom of navigation upon the seas, outside territorial waters, alike in peace and in war, except as the seas may be closed in whole or in part by international action for the enforcement of international covenants.

☑ **PARAPHRASE** Restate Point 2 in your own words.

3. The removal, so far as possible, of all economic barriers and the establishment of an equality of trade conditions among all the nations consenting to the peace and associating themselves for its maintenance.

4. Adequate guarantees given and taken that national armaments will be reduced to the lowest point consistent with domestic safety.

☑ **ANALYZE WORD CHOICES** What two things does Wilson leave unspecified in Point 4?

5. A free, open-minded, and absolutely impartial adjustment of all colonial claims, based upon a strict observance of the principle that in determining all such questions of sovereignty the interests of the populations concerned must have equal weight with the equitable claims of the government whose title is to be determined....

8. All French territory should be freed and the invaded portions restored, and the wrong done to France by Prussia in 1871 in the matter of Alsace-Lorraine, which has unsettled the peace of the world for nearly fifty years, should be righted, in order that peace may once more be made secure in the interest of all.

9. A readjustment of the frontiers of Italy should be effected along clearly recognizable lines of nationality.

10. The peoples of Austria-Hungary, whose place among the nations we wish to see safeguarded and assured, should be accorded the freest opportunity to autonomous development.

11. Rumania, Serbia, and Montenegro should be evacuated; occupied territories restored; Serbia accorded free and secure access to the sea; and the relations of the several Balkan states to one another determined by friendly counsel along historically established lines of allegiance and nationality; and international guarantees of the political and economic independence and territorial integrity of the several Balkan states should be entered into.

12. The Turkish portion of the present Ottoman Empire should be assured a secure sovereignty, but the other nationalities which are now under Turkish rule should be assured an undoubted security of life and an absolutely unmolested opportunity of autonomous development, and the Dardanelles should be permanently opened as a free passage to the ships and commerce of all nations under international guarantees.

13. An independent Polish state should be erected which should include the territories inhabited by indisputably Polish populations, which should be assured a free and secure access to the sea, and whose political and economic independence and territorial integrity should be guaranteed by international covenant.

14. A general association [organization] of nations must be formed under specific covenants for the purpose of affording mutual guarantees of political independence and territorial integrity to great and small states alike.

INTEGRATE INFORMATION FROM DIVERSE SOURCES Does an association of nations as mentioned in point 14 exist today? If so, what is it?

ASSESSMENT

1. **Compare and Contrast** Points 8–13 deal with specific territorial issues, such as breaking up the Ottoman and Austro-Hungarian Empires and restoring sovereignty to Belgium and Poland. To an American in 1918, how would those points be different from points 1–5 and 14?

2. **Draw Conclusions** Preventing war seems like an admirable goal. Why might a country reject some or all of Wilson's points?

3. **Integrate Information From Diverse Sources** Why might isolationists oppose some or all of Wilson's Fourteen Points?

4. **Draw Inferences** What political impact do you think Wilson's Fourteen Points had?

November 11, 1918, was a day celebrated around the world. World War I—known then as the Great War—had ended with the armistice. The greatest war in human history to date had ended. Every year, the United States celebrates Veteran's Day on November 11 to commemorate the service of Americans in the armed forces in any war. With the war's end, the United States faced a painful adjustment period, then a decade of amazing economic growth and prosperity.

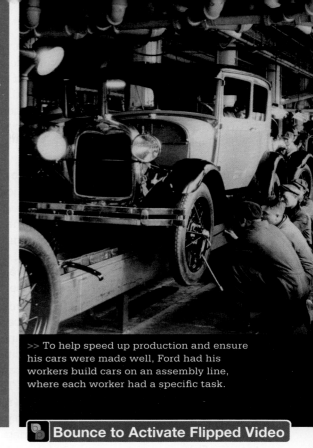

>> To help speed up production and ensure his cars were made well, Ford had his workers build cars on an assembly line, where each worker had a specific task.

Bounce to Activate Flipped Video

The Postwar Economy Booms

Postwar Issues

But in 1918, the victory was bittersweet. The flu pandemic still raged, and it would end up killing far more Americans than had died in the war.

> [The Year]1918 has gone: a year momentous as the termination of the most cruel war in the annals of the human race; a year which marked the end, at least for a time, of man's destruction of man; unfortunately a year in which developed a most fatal infectious disease causing the death of hundreds of thousands of human beings.
>
> —Journal of the American Medical Association, December 28, 1918

The flu faded out in 1919. The next year, an American public tired of world affairs and problems at home, elected a new president. Republican Warren G. Harding easily defeated the Democratic nominee, Governor James M. Cox of Ohio. Harding's campaign

>> Objectives

Describe the economic problems America faced after World War I.

Explain the economic growth and prosperity of the 1920s, including how Henry Ford and the automobile industry helped spark the boom.

Analyze the consumer revolution and the bull market of the 1920s.

Compare the different effects of the economic boom on urban, suburban, and rural America.

>> Key Terms

Henry Ford
mass production
Model T
scientific
  management
assembly lines
consumer revolution
installment buying
buying on margin
inflation
creditor nation

slogan captured perfectly the national mood: "Return to Normalcy," meaning a return to normal life as it was in prewar times. Yet the election itself was not "normal." For the first time, women voted in a presidential election. For the first time, election returns were reported by radio. A return to "normalcy" in a rapidly changing world would prove elusive.

Women and African Americans Confront New Realities
Women and African Americans had made significant advances during the war. However, the end of the war also spelled the end of wartime economic opportunities for both groups. A postwar recession, or economic slowdown, created a competitive job market. By 1920, there were fewer women in the workforce than there had been in 1910.

In northern industrial cities, African American workers vied with returning soldiers for jobs and housing, causing tense race relations. During the hot summer of 1919, race riots erupted in cities throughout the country. The worst, in Chicago, went on for 13 days. In 1921, violence erupted in Tulsa, Oklahoma, when armed African American men—many of them returning veterans—tried to protect a young African American man from lynching. By the time the Tulsa race riots were over, at least 10 whites and 26 African Americans were dead. In one African American neighborhood, white rioters burned 35 city blocks to the ground.

>> Rioters burned the homes of African Americans in Tulsa, Oklahoma, during race riots in 1921.

Inflation and Labor Unrest
During the war, **inflation**, or rising prices, had been held in check. After the conflict, Americans rushed to buy consumer goods rather than war bonds. The scarcity of these goods, coupled with widespread demand, caused inflation. On the other hand, during the war, the price of corn, wheat, cotton, cattle, and other agricultural goods had risen, with help from Hoover's policies. After the war, prices fell sharply, making it difficult for farmers to pay their mortgages or buy what they needed for the next growing season. This began a long period of tough times for farmers.

Another economic effect of the postwar inflation was felt by industrial workers when their wages did not buy as much as they had during the war. In 1919, more than 4 million workers, or 20 percent of the workforce, went on strike at one time or another. Demanding rewards for their wartime patriotism, workers struck for higher wages and shorter workdays. In Boston, even the police force struck.

The workers won some of the strikes, but they lost far more. When some strikes turned violent, the pro-management press blamed the presence of radicals among the strike leaders.

The United States Grows as a World Power
Despite Harding's election and some Americans' desire to return to what life was like before the war, the United States did not plan to totally withdraw from world affairs. By 1920, even with postwar economic problems, the United States was an economic giant. It was the richest, most industrialized country in the world. Even before the war, America led all other nations in industrial output. The war was a turning point for the nation economically. Now, British and French demands for American goods created an immense trade imbalance. Europeans had to borrow money from American bankers and obtain lines of credit with American business firms to pay for the goods.

This situation fundamentally changed America's economic standing in the world. The United States was now the largest **creditor nation** in the world, meaning that other countries owed the United States more money than the United States owed them. World War I shifted the economic center of the world from London to New York City. The United States embraced its new role as a quiet giant. A world without America playing a major economic role had become simply impossible to conceive.

☑ **RECALL** What was a significant cause of inflation after the war?

The Impact of Henry Ford and the Automobile

In the decade after World War I, the American economy experienced tremendous growth. Using revolutionary mass production techniques, American workers produced more goods in less time than ever before. The boom fundamentally changed the lives of millions of people and helped create the modern consumer economy.

The decade got off to a rocky start, however. There was a mild recession in 1918 to 1919 and a more serious one in 1920 to 1921. These were partly due to converting wartime production back to domestic production and the return of soldiers into the workforce. Once the economy did take off, the prosperity was not shared by everyone. Still, there is no doubt that the U.S. economy in the 1920s roared.

Rarely, if ever, has the nation enjoyed such an economic boom as it did during this decade. The recession that had followed World War I quickly ended. All signs pointed to economic growth. Stock prices rose rapidly. Factories produced more and more goods and, with wages on the rise, more and more people could afford to buy them.

Much of this explosive growth was sparked by a single business: the automobile industry. Carmaker **Henry Ford** introduced a series of technological and management innvoations to his fledgling automobile business. Ford's methods and ideas revolutionized production, wages, working conditions, and daily life.

Ford, Mass Production, and the Model T Ford did not originate the idea of **mass production**, the rapid manufacture of large numbers of identical products. It had been used, for example, to make sewing machines and typewriters. But such products involved only hundreds of parts—not the thousands that go into the production of cars. Ford brought mass production to new heights.

Early in the century, only wealthy city dwellers could afford cars. The automobile was often seen as a symbol of the class divisions in the country. City drivers who ventured out onto country roads frightened horses and cows, coated crops with dust, and rutted dirt roads. "To the countryman," said Woodrow Wilson in 1906, cars "are a picture of the arrogance of wealth."

Ransom Olds had introduced a less expensive car, the Oldsmobile, in 1901. But it was Henry Ford who truly brought the automobile to the people. In 1908, he introduced the **Model T**, a reliable car the average American could afford. The first Model T

>> Entrepreneurs like Henry Ford, pictured with his son Edsel, ushered in the age of the automobile and helped create an economic boom after the war.

Bounce to Activate Illustration

sold for $850. Soon after, Ford opened a new plant on the Detroit River. The Detroit location gave Ford easy access to steel, glass, oil, and rubber manufactured in Pennsylvania, Ohio, Indiana, and Illinois.

Ford hired **scientific management** experts to improve his mass-production techniques. Scientific management was a relatively new method of improving efficiency, in which experts looked at every step of a manufacturing process to find ways to reduce time, effort, and expense. Studying a process to minimize the time it takes to do a task is called time-study analysis. Studying a process to minimize the motion it takes to do a task is called motion-study analysis. Together, they are often known as "time and motion study." The idea was pioneered by Frederick Winslow Taylor in his book, *The Principles of Scientific Management*. Scientific management is sometimes called Taylorism.

Ford also studied the techniques of Chicago meatpacking houses, where beef carcasses were moved on chains past a series of meat cutters, each of whom cut off a specific part of the carcass. Ford reversed the process. He put his cars on moving **assembly lines**. At each step, a worker added something to construct the automobile. In two years, the application of assembly line techniques showed huge productivity enhancements, reducing the time it took to manufacture a Model T from more than 12 hours to just 90 minutes.

The efficiency of the assembly line allowed Ford to keep dropping the sale price. The cost of a Model T fell to $350 by 1916 and to $290 by 1927. It was slow, dull, and available only in black. But the Model T was the first car that ordinary people could afford. In 1919, only 10 percent of American families owned an automobile. By 1927, 56 percent did.

When it came to managing the men who made up his labor force, Ford also proved that he was not afraid of innovation. In 1914, he more than doubled the wages of a large number of his workers, from $2.35 to $5 a day. He also reduced their workday from 9 hours to 8 hours. In 1926, he became the first major industrialist to give his workers Saturday and Sunday off. Before Ford, the idea of a "weekend" hardly existed. Ford shrewdly realized that if workers made more money and had more leisure time, they would become potential customers for his automobiles. The combination of the Model T and the "five-dollar day, forty-hour week" made Ford not only a very rich man but also one of the shapers of the modern world.

The Automobile Changes America The boom in the automotive industry, caused in part by Ford's production efficiencies, caused economic growth in other industries related to car manufacture or use.

The steel, glass, rubber, asphalt, wood, petroleum, insurance, and road-construction industries all benefited. For example, one seventh of all steel output was used to make automobiles. The need for gasoline prompted a nationwide search for petroleum deposits. Oil discoveries in California, Texas, New Mexico, and Oklahoma brought vast numbers workers and money to the Southwest. Petroleum-based industries boomed, increasing employment and tax revenues. Thus, energy in the form of gasoline had a major impact on the American way of life.

Road construction also boomed, especially when the federal government introduced the system of numbered highways in 1926. The millions of cars on American roads led to the rapid appearance of thousands of service stations, diners, and motor hotels (a term later shortened to *motels*). The growth in all these industries created new and often better-paying jobs, spurring national prosperity.

The automobile caused additional economic effects. Other forms of ground transportation, such as railroads and trolleys, suffered a decline in use. With cars, people could go where they wanted, when they wanted. They did not have to travel along set tracks on set schedules.

The automobile prompted a new sense of freedom and prosperity. Never had Americans been so mobile. Entire families crowded into their cars for

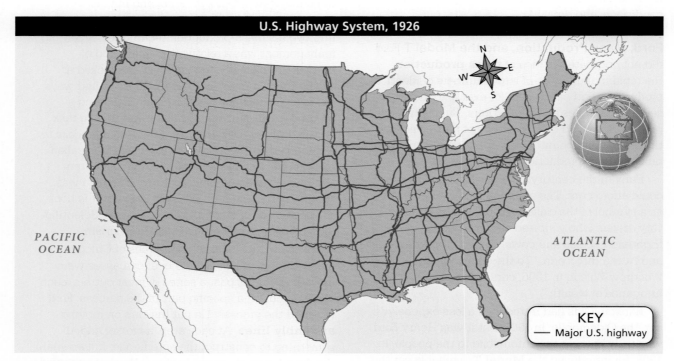

U.S. Highway System, 1926

PACIFIC OCEAN

ATLANTIC OCEAN

KEY
— Major U.S. highway

>> **Analyze Maps** How did the creation of an affordable car affect the development of roads in the United States?

cross-country vacations or Sunday drives. Ownership of an automobile came to symbolize participation in the American dream of success and high standard of living.

Finally, automobiles altered residential patterns. The ability to drive to work permitted people to live farther from their places of employment. This led to the development of suburban communities linked to cities by arteries of highways and roads. Los Angeles, one of the first cities whose growth was influenced by the automobile, developed in a sprawling, haphazard fashion. It became, according to one observer, "a series of suburbs in search of a city."

☑ **IDENTIFY SUPPORTING DETAILS** What effect did increased automobile production have on other industries?

Economic Growth in the 1920s

The 1920s saw what has been called a **consumer revolution**, in which a flood of new, affordable goods became available to the public. The widespread availability of electrical power supported the consumer revolution. Electric washing machines, vacuum cleaners, and irons made housekeeping easier and less time-consuming. Accessible electricity also contributed to radio and refrigerator sales.

Advertising and Installment Buying The growing advertising industry also played its part. Using new "scientific" techniques and psychological research, advertisers were able to sell more products to more Americans than ever before. Magazine and newspaper ads often focused on the desires and fears of Americans more than on what people really needed.

Finally, new ways of buying fueled the consumer revolution. People who did not have enough ready cash could buy what they wanted on credit. **Installment buying**, in which a consumer would make a small down payment and then pay off the rest of the debt in regular monthly payments, allowed Americans to own products they might otherwise have had to save up for years in order to buy.

The Bull Market Consumers were not the only Americans buying and selling in a big way. During the 1920s, the stock market enjoyed a dizzying **bull market**, a period of rising stock prices. More and

>> With the U.S. economy growing again, companies began to use advertisements to target consumers based on their desires rather than their needs.

more Americans put their money into stocks in an effort to get rich quick. By 1929, around 4 million Americans owned stocks.

The desire to strike it rich often led investors to ignore financial risks. As the market soared, people began **buying on margin**—another form of buying on credit. By purchasing stock on margin, a buyer paid as little as 10 percent of the stock price upfront to a broker. The buyer then paid the broker for the rest of the stock over a period of months. The stock served as collateral, or security, for the broker's loan. As long as the price of the stock rose, the buyer had no trouble paying off the loan and making a profit. But if the price fell, the buyer still had to pay off the loan. Buyers gambled that they would be able to sell the stock at a profit long before the loan came due. Buying stocks on the hope that their price will rise is called stock market speculation.

In truth, this big bull market stood on very shaky ground. But most people ignored the dangers. By the middle of 1929, economic authorities proclaimed that America and the stock market had entered a "new era." Stock prices would continue their march upward, they said, while boom-and-bust economics would become a thing of the past.

Science, Technology, and the Free Enterprise System

Science, technology, and the free enterprise system combined to boost the economic development of the United States in the 1920s. The science was not just in scientific management, but in the growing knowledge of many aspects of the world. Scientists conducted research on everything from rubber plants to electronics. This scientific knowledge enabled engineers to create the technologies—automobiles, for example, or radios—that were useful to people.

These new technologies would not have been widespread without the free enterprise system. The profit motive gave business owners a reason to turn technology into products to sell. Competitive markets encouraged innovation. The free enterprise system also created the jobs that provided workers with the money to purchase the many new products that came to market. Thus, the prosperity of the 1920s was boosted by a mix scientific advances, inventive technologies, and the free enterprise system.

☑ **DEFINE** How would you define *installment buying*?

Urban, Suburban, and Rural Areas

The economic boom did not affect all parts of the nation equally. While urban and suburban areas prospered, rural Americans faced hardships.

People Migrate to Cities In the 1920s, the movement of people was toward cities. Immigrants settled in cities. Farmers left their fields for cities. The direction of the African American Great Migration was toward northern cities. Many Mexicans crossing the border relocated to southwestern cities.

As in the late nineteenth century, cities grew and changed shape. In addition, the adoption of skyscraper technology caused cities to stretch skyward. Steel-framed skyscrapers with light coverings of masonry and glass began to dominate the skylines of the nation's cities. New York's Empire State Building, finished in 1931, symbolized the power and majesty of the United States.

Suburbs Expand Improved mass transportation and the widespread use of automobiles caused cities to expand outward. More urban workers moved to the suburbs. Western and southern cities, developed after the automobile revolution, encompassed

>> The economic prosperity Americans experienced during the 1920s prompted large investments in urban construction. Here riveters worked on New York City's Empire State Building in 1931.

>> Rapidly rising stock prices created a daily frenzy of activity in the New York Stock Exchange, where the majority of U.S. stocks were traded.

suburban areas as well as inner cities. Suburbs mushroomed, growing much faster than inner cities.

Slowly at first, but more rapidly as the century progressed, suburbs drained people and resources from the cities, causing the demographic patterns of both types of places to change. Catering to middle- and upper-class residents, suburbs tended to be more conservative and Republican. Meanwhile, one effect of this migration was that the inner cities at the heart of older urban areas began a slow but steady decline.

Many Americans Face Challenges In the cities and suburbs, Americans enjoyed prosperity and the fruits of growth. They participated in the consumer economy and in the joys of automobile ownership. The wealthiest urban residents—owners and managers of businesses—reaped fabulous rewards, which they often pumped back into the bull market. But there were problems looming ahead. America's wealth was poorly distributed. Industrial wages rose at a much slower rate than corporate salaries.

Even worse, farm incomes declined during the decade. Many people living in the country did not participate in the consumer benefits and economic gains of the decade. They formed part of another America—poorer and outside the economic boom. In particular, farmers suffered from growing debt and falling farm prices. A protest song of 1928 expressed their frustration:

> 'Leven-cent cotton, forty-cent meat,
>
> How in the world can a poor man eat?
>
> Mule's in the barn, no crop's laid by,
>
> Corncrib empty and the cow's gone dry.
>
> —Bob Miller and Emma Dermer, "Eleven Cent Cotton"

If the wealthy believed that the country had entered an age of permanent prosperity, the "other Americans" saw things differently.

☑ **IDENTIFY SUPPORTING DETAILS** What general migration patterns existed in the 1920s?

>> As more families could afford automobiles, they moved away from the city to nearby suburbs. **Hypothesize** Why would many Americans want to move from cities to suburbs?

🅑 **Bounce to Activate Gallery**

☑ **ASSESSMENT**

1. **Identify Cause and Effect** Explain how women and African Americans were affected by the postwar economy.

2. **Generate Explanations** Explain how the U.S. position as a world power changed after World War I.

3. **Identify Central Issues** Discuss the innovations and techniques that Henry Ford used in order to make automobiles more affordable.

4. **Identify Patterns** Discuss the impact of the automobile industry on residential patterns.

5. **Draw Conclusions** Describe important changes that affected the consumer experience during the 1920s, and discuss their impact.

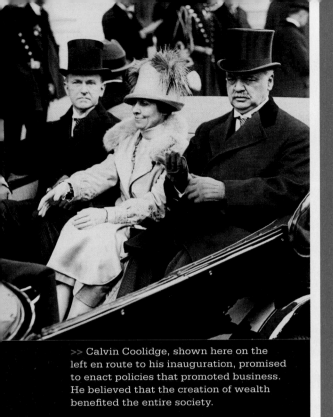

>> Calvin Coolidge, shown here on the left en route to his inauguration, promised to enact policies that promoted business. He believed that the creation of wealth benefited the entire society.

Bounce to Activate Flipped Video

4.5 Woodrow Wilson hoped that the presidential election of 1920 would prove that Americans supported both the League of Nations and his vision of the role the United States should play in the world. He suggested that electing Democratic presidential candidate James M. Cox of Ohio would show support for the League. However, the election of Republican candidate Warren G. Harding of Ohio would serve as a final rejection of U.S. support for the League.

>> Objectives

Analyze how the policies of Presidents Harding and Coolidge encouraged economic growth and prosperity in the 1920s.

Discuss the effects of political scandals, including Teapot Dome, on Harding's presidency.

Explain the role that the United States played in the world during the 1920s.

>> Key Terms

Andrew Mellon
Herbert Hoover
Teapot Dome
 scandal
Calvin Coolidge
Washington Naval
 Disarmament
 Conference
Kellogg-Briand Pact
Dawes Plan
Warren G. Harding

Government in the 1920s

The Harding Administration

Harding had a different view of the presidential race. He knew that national elections seldom turned on a single issue. Harding campaigned for a rejection of Wilsonian idealism. He was tired of Progressive reforms and foreign crusades, and he was betting the American public was, too. Harding won in a landslide, and Republicans won control of Congress, as well. Americans had decisively rejected Wilson's ideas.

What exactly did Harding's election signal? Some interpret it as Americans' desire to retreat from involvement in world affairs, others as a rejection of Progressive reform efforts or a swing back to laissez-faire economics. No matter how it was interpreted, however, it was clear that Harding and his successor, Calvin Coolidge, favored conservative policies that aided the growth of business rather than pursuing reform as the Progressives had done. This pattern—a period of activism followed by a more laissez-faire approach—would repeat itself in the 1950s and 1980s.

Harding's Economic Policies Encourage Growth Harding signaled the economic direction of his administration by naming

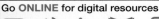

wealthy banker **Andrew Mellon** Secretary of the Treasury. Mellon believed that prudent economic policy meant supporting legislation that advanced business interests. He disliked the relatively new income tax, favoring instead low taxes on individuals and corporations. Mellon also cut the fat from the budget. By 1925, Congress had reduced spending from a wartime high of $18 billion to $3 billion. Instead of sinking deeper into debt, the Treasury actually showed a surplus.

Harding signed a bill raising protective tariff rates by about 25 percent. The tax on imports made it easier for American producers to sell goods at home. However, in retaliation, European nations also hiked tariffs, making American goods harder to sell overseas. This tariff war weakened the world economy and would have ramifications in the 1930s.

Under the Progressive leadership of Roosevelt and Wilson, the federal government had passed laws to break up monopolies, protect workers, and restrict the absolute freedom of business leaders. By contrast, Harding favored a return to a more traditional laissez-faire approach. He and Mellon worked to reduce government regulation of business. Harding's Return to Normalcy, including reducing taxes and reducing government regulation, helped to cause the economic growth and prosperity of the 1920s.

Still, the Harding administration did not abandon social goals. Harding's thoughtful and energetic Secretary of Commerce, **Herbert Hoover** worked with business and labor leaders to achieve voluntary advancements.

What the Progressives hoped to achieve through legislation, Hoover attempted to attain with the cooperation of interest groups. He enjoyed great successes at getting people to work together instead of battling one another.

Some Officials Betray the Public Trust Harding was a kind, likable man, but he was not especially intelligent. Perhaps no President was friendlier, and few had less sense of what was expected of a President. Faced with a tax issue, Harding lamented, "I listen to one side and they seem right . . . I talk to the other side, and they seem just as right, and here I am where I started. . . . What a job!"

Rather than struggle to master the complexities of the job, Harding trusted others to make decisions. Many were his close friends, men he enjoyed relaxing and gambling with at late-night poker games. Known as the Ohio Gang, they were not honest public servants like Mellon and Hoover. They were mostly greedy, small-minded men who saw government service as a chance to get rich at the expense of the very citizens they were supposed to serve.

Charles Forbes, head of the Veterans' Bureau, practiced graft on an immense scale and wasted hundreds of millions of taxpayers' dollars. For example, his department bought $70,000 worth of floor cleaner—enough to last 100 years—at more than 24 times the fair price. Another Harding pal,

Leaders of Business Deregulation

PRESIDENT WARREN G. HARDING AND VICE PRESIDENT CALVIN COOLIDGE	SECRETARY OF THE TREASURY ANDREW MELLON
• Wanted a conservative government that benefited business	• Wanted a conservative government that benefited business
• Promoted the policy of laissez faire for business	• Promoted the policy of laissez faire for business
• Named commissioners who favored government deregulation of business	• Sponsored the Mellon Plan, which reduced taxes for businesses
• Assigned business leaders to government positions	• Lowered taxes for the wealthy (often business owners)
• Turned the Federal Reserve Board and Interstate Commerce Commission into pro-business agencies	

>> **Analyze Charts** How were Harding and Coolidge's plans to stimulate economic production similar to Mellon's plans? How were they different?

Attorney General Harry Daugherty, used his position to accept money from criminals.

The Teapot Dome Scandal Comes to Light

The worst scandal involved Secretary of the Interior Albert Fall. In 1921, Fall arranged to transfer oil reserves in Elk Hills, California, and Teapot Dome, Wyoming, from the Navy Department to the Interior Department. The oil reserves were intended for the navy's use in times of emergency. Harding signed the transfer.

Once Fall had control of the oil, he forgot about the needs of the navy. He leased the properties to private oilmen in return for "loans"—which were actually bribes. Rumors of the deal led to a Senate investigation, and, by 1924, the entire sordid affair was revealed to the public. Later, the oil reserves were returned to the government. Fall was sentenced to a year in prison, but those accused of bribing him were acquitted.

Harding himself never saw the full extent of the **Teapot Dome scandal**. In fact, he only had a growing suspicion that his friends were up to no good. But that was enough, as he said, to keep him "walking the floor nights." In July 1923, he visited Alaska during a speaking tour. On his return voyage,

he suffered a heart attack and died on August 2. Americans mourned Harding as they had mourned no other President since Lincoln. When the full extent of the scandals emerged, however, the public formed a different opinion of him. The Teapot Dome scandal hurt U.S. citizens' trust in the federal government and its leaders, especially the Executive Branch. But the calm and assured manner in which Harding's successor, Calvin Coolidge, eliminated corrupt elements from the government restored most Americans' faith. Coolidge was reelected in a landslide the next year.

☑ **RECALL** What policies did Andrew Mellon pursue when he became Secretary of the Treasury?

Economic Prosperity Under Coolidge

News of Harding's death reached Vice President **Calvin Coolidge** during a visit to his father's Vermont farm. Almost immediately, the elder Coolidge, a justice of the peace, used the family Bible to swear in his son as President.

In personality, Coolidge was far different from the outgoing, back-slapping Harding. Known as Silent Cal, he was quiet, honest, and frugal—a man who measured his words carefully. He placed his trust in business and put his administration in the hands of men who held to the simple virtues of an older America. Political sharpies out to make a quick buck had no place in the Coolidge administration. Neither did Progressives who believed in an activist government bent on sweeping reforms.

Business Leaders Have the Support of the White House

Coolidge admired productive business leaders. "The man who builds a factory," Coolidge once said, "builds a temple." He believed that the creation of wealth benefited the nation as a whole. In 1925, he expressed this view in his best-known speech:

> The chief business of the American people is business. They are profoundly concerned with producing, buying, selling, investing, and prospering in the world. . . .We make no concealment of the fact that we want wealth, but there are many other things that we want very much

>> Secretary of the Interior, Albert Fall, sits on a rock, sipping tea. **Analyze Political Cartoons** What does this cartoon suggest about Fall's role during the Teapot Dome scandal?

🅑 **Bounce to Activate Cartoon**

INCOME TAX RATES IN THE 1920s

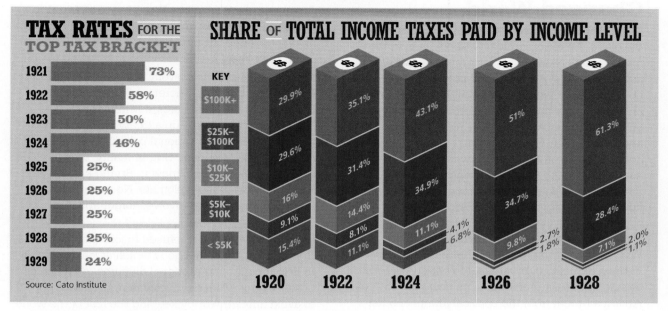

TAX RATES FOR THE TOP TAX BRACKET

Year	Rate
1921	73%
1922	58%
1923	50%
1924	46%
1925	25%
1926	25%
1927	25%
1928	25%
1929	24%

Source: Cato Institute

SHARE OF TOTAL INCOME TAXES PAID BY INCOME LEVEL

KEY: $100K+, $25K–$100K, $10K–$25K, $5K–$10K, < $5K

1920: 29.9%, 29.6%, 16%, 9.1%, 15.4%
1922: 35.1%, 31.4%, 14.4%, 8.1%, 11.1%
1924: 43.1%, 34.9%, 11.1%, 6.8%, 4.1%
1926: 51%, 34.7%, 9.8%, 1.8%, 2.7%
1928: 61.3%, 28.4%, 7.1%, 1.1%, 2.0%

>> **Analyze Charts** How did tax rates change for top earners in the 1920s? How did the share of taxes paid by the top income earners change?

more. We want peace and honor, and that charity which is so strong an element of all civilization. The chief ideal of the American people is idealism.

—Calvin Coolidge, speech to the American Society of Newspaper Editors

Coolidge's statement of values and principles has often been oversimplified as "the business of America is business." However, in his approach to the economy, Coolidge continued to follow the goals of Secretary of the Treasury Mellon by reducing the national debt, trimming the federal budget, and lowering taxes to give incentives for businesses. Collectively referred to as the "Mellon Income Tax Cuts," the Revenue Acts of 1921, 1924, and 1926 successively lowered marginal tax rates on individuals and corporations. Although tax rates on high-income earners were significantly reduced, the total amount paid by those earners increased as incomes rose. In response to the Revenue Acts as well as other factors, the unemployment rate fell from over 6 percent to approximately 3 percent between 1922 and 1929, benefiting workers in all income brackets.

Coolidge thus oversaw increasing tax revenues and a spectacular boom in the national economy. For almost six years, the economy soared, generating industrial profits, spectacular growth in the stock market, and general prosperity, especially for urban Americans.

Some Problems Remain Yet, there were grave problems breeding in the nation. Farmers struggled to keep their land as the prices of their goods fell.

Labor unions demanded higher wages and better working conditions. African Americans faced severe discrimination, especially in the South, where Jim Crow laws made enforced segregation a way of life. African American leaders urged Congress to pass an anti-lynching law. In the Southwest, Mexican Americans confronted shamefully low wages and efforts to force them to return to Mexico.

To all of these concerns, Silent Cal remained silent. Like Harding, he mistrusted the use of legislation to achieve social change. Unlike Progressive Presidents, he believed that it was beyond the federal government's role to help create an ideal nation.

☑ **DESCRIBE** What was the purpose of the Revenue Acts of 1921, 1924, and 1926?

America's Place in a Changed World

World War I had caused sweeping changes around the globe. An old order five hundred years in the making had collapsed in just a few years. It was as if the world's compass was out of whack and no one knew where to turn for directions. German and Russian monarchies toppled, and new forms of government were created. The Austro-Hungarian and Ottoman empires ceased to exist. Britain and France emerged from the war victorious but economically and politically weakened. In contrast, the victorious United States came out of the war strong, confident, and prosperous.

Seeking Stability After World War I While World War I was a turning point for the United States in the realm of foreign affairs, the nation was still unsure of the requirements of its new status. Could America retreat from the political affairs of other countries yet continue to expand its economic reach across the globe? Under both Harding and Coolidge, America continued to play an increasingly important role in world business and trade. Beyond economic interests, U.S. foreign policy was largely shaped by reaction to World War I. No previous war had been as deadly. Citizens of all nations agreed: It must never happen again. But how could this goal be achieved?

One solution was to avoid another arms race, such as the naval rivalry between Germany and Britain that had contributed to the outbreak of the war. In 1921 and 1922, diplomats gathered in Washington, D.C., to halt another naval arms race before it got out of control. World leaders agreed to limit construction of large warships and hammered out a settlement on several problems between Japan and the West. This **Washington Naval Disarmament Conference** did not end the world's naval problems, but it raised hopes that nations could solve disagreements without resorting to war.

A later attempt to prevent war was the **Kellogg-Briand Pact** of 1928. Secretary of State Frank B. Kellogg and French Foreign Minister Aristide Briand (bree AHN) drew up a treaty to "outlaw" war "as an instrument of national policy." Eventually, 62 nations ratified the pact. But, in reality, the pact was unenforceable. Kellogg knew it, Briand knew it, and so did the rest of the diplomats. No sooner was the ink dry than everyone involved forgot about it.

Although Congress applauded the useless Kellogg-Briand Pact, it refused to join the World Court, an international body which at least promised to help mediate international disputes. As much as possible, most American leaders in the 1920s hoped to avoid another war by keeping the rest of the world at arm's length.

Collecting Reparations After the War Money issues were another matter. The United States insisted that Britain and France repay their huge war debts to the United States. For this to happen, though, Germany had to make the reparation payments to Britain and France imposed by the Treaty of Versailles. The complex financial issue threatened to undermine the international economy. Some statesmen suggested reducing or even canceling both war debts and reparations. But the frugal Coolidge insisted that a debt was a debt and had to be paid.

Washington Naval Disarmament Conference, 1921

FOUR-POWER PACT	FIVE-POWER NAVAL LIMITATION TREATY	NINE-POWER PACT
United States, Britain, France, and Japan	**United States, Britain, France, Japan, and Italy**	**United States, China, Britain, France, Japan, Italy, Belgium, the Netherlands, and Portugal**
Any disagreement between two countries regarding territorial possessions in the Pacific would be discussed by all four countries before any action was to be taken.	These countries hoped to reduce the number of warships in their possession by placing tonnage limits on ships.	China was to open its doors equally to all countries wishing to do business there, and all other countries were to recognize China's independence and territorial integrity.

>> **Analyze Charts** How did the Washington Naval Disarmament Conference try to reduce the potential for major wars?

The United States in International Affairs, 1920–1929

DEVELOPMENT	GOAL	U.S. ACTION
League of Nations, 1920	To prevent war and settle disputes between nations	U.S. membership favored by Wilson; rejected by Senate
World Court, 1920	To make judgments in international disputes	U.S. participation favored by Harding; rejected by Senate
Dawes Plan, 1924	To arrange Germany's reparations payments following World War I	U.S. headed a committee to oversee the collection of war debts.
Kellogg-Briand Pact, 1928	To "outlaw war . . . as an instrument of national policy"	U.S. agreed with many other nations to renounce war as a means of settling international disputes.
Policy of Non-Recognition, 1917–1933	To undermine the growing power of the Soviet Union	U.S. refused to recognize the Soviet government.
Nicaragua, 1927–1932	To restore peace and protect American citizens	U.S. sent marines to Nicaragua to crush the rebellion.

>> **Analyze Charts** What international organizations or agreements did the United States take part in? Which did it pass on? Why do you think U.S. leaders chose not to take part in those organizations or agreements?

In 1924, an agreement known as the **Dawes Plan** arranged U.S. loans to Germany. By enabling Germany to make reparation payments to Britain and France, the Dawes Plan helped Britain and France to repay their debts to the United States. Of course, the entire scheme was financed by U.S. money.

After the stock market crash of 1929, however, the well of U.S. money went dry. Germany stopped reparation payments, and Britain and France ended war-debt payments to the United States.

In the end, the war-debt situation damaged America's reputation in the eyes of the world. People from Britain and France thought that it was heartless for American bankers and politicians to insist on repayment of debts and not to take into account the human costs of the war. In the next war, the United States would take a more flexible approach to war loans.

☑ **CHECK UNDERSTANDING** What was the purpose of the Dawes Plan?

☑ ASSESSMENT

1. **Generate Explanations** Discuss the corruption that existed within the Harding administration, and explain how it impacted the American public.

2. **Identify Central Issues** Summarize the main components of President Coolidge's economic philosophy.

3. **Describe** the social and economic problems that existed during the Coolidge administration, and explain why President Coolidge did not address them.

4. **Draw Conclusions** Discuss the international attempts that were made to prevent another world war, and consider why they were unsuccessful.

5. **Classify** Explain the importance of the United States' role in the international collection of reparations after World War I.

>> The temperance movement partially achieved its mission with the ratification of the Eighteenth Amendment in 1919. When Prohibition began, federal agents like these destroyed millions of gallons of alcohol.

In the 1920s, while many city dwellers enjoyed a rising standard of living, most farmers suffered through hard times. Conflicting visions of what the nation should be heightened the urban-rural division. Some of these issues, such as immigration policy and teaching the theory of evolution, still divide Americans today.

Bounce to Activate Flipped Video

>> **Objectives**

Compare economic and cultural life in rural America to that in urban America.

Analyze how foreign events after World War I and nativism contributed to the first Red Scare.

Analyze the causes and effects of changes in U.S. immigration policy in the 1920s.

Describe the goals and motives of the Ku Klux Klan in the 1920s.

Analyze the intended and unintended effects of Prohibition.

>> **Key Terms**

modernism	Red Scare
fundamentalism	Palmer Raids
Scopes Trial	Bartolomeo Vanzetti
Clarence Darrow	William Jennings
Ku Klux Klan	Bryan
Prohibition	Nicola Sacco
Eighteenth	
Amendment	
Volstead Act	

An Unsettled Society

Americans Debate New Ideas and Values

The 1920 census reported that, for the first time in American history, more people lived in urban areas than in rural regions. This simple fact had profound consequences. The nation had been divided before, but usually along north-south or east-west lines. In the 1920s, however, the split was between urban America and rural America. On virtually every important social and cultural issue, the two groups differed.

Urban Americans enjoyed new consumer products and a wide array of leisure activities. They generally showed an openness toward social change and the new discoveries of science. The growing trend to emphasize science and secular values over traditional religious beliefs became known as **modernism**.

By contrast, rural Americans did not participate fully in the consumer bonanzas, and they missed out on many of the new forms of leisure. People in the country generally embraced a more traditional view of religion, science, and culture.

An Evolving Job Market Emphasizes Education

Rural and urban Americans differed in their attitudes toward formal education. In rural America, prolonged formal education had not seemed vital. Farmers expected their children to master the "Three R's"—reading, writing, and arithmetic. But beyond that, having a formal education was not vital to the many farm tasks that needed to be done. Muscle, endurance, and knowledge of crops and animals seemed more important to farmers than abstract knowledge learned from books.

Formal education took on more importance in urban America. Mental ability, not muscular fitness, was seen as the essential ingredient for success. Mastery of mathematics and language could spell the difference between a low-paying, unskilled job and a higher-paying position as an office worker. By 1930, more American teens were graduating from high school, and more Americans than ever before went to college.

Some Embrace Religious Fundamentalism

In the 1920s, many devout Americans believed that Christianity was under siege throughout the world. They pointed to Soviet communist attacks on the Orthodox Church in Russia and to revolutionary assaults on the Roman Catholic Church in Mexico.

At home, a growing number of Christians were upset by what they saw as secular trends in religion and culture. They reaffirmed their belief in the fundamental, or basic, truths of their religion. This approach, often called **fundamentalism** emphasized Protestant teachings and the belief that every word in the Christian Bible was literal truth. Fundamentalists believed that the answer to every moral and scientific question could be found in the Bible. Their ideas took root all over the country but were especially strong in rural America, where revivalists like Billy Sunday inspired the faithful.

Bryan and Darrow Clash Over Evolution

Fundamentalism and modernism clashed head-on in the **Scopes Trial** of 1925. At issue was the theory of evolution, developed by English scientist Charles Darwin. Darwin believed that complex forms of life, such as human beings, had developed gradually from simpler forms of life. According to fundamentalists, this theory clashed with the description of creation in their Bible.

In 1925, Tennessee passed a law making it illegal to teach Darwin's theory in the state's public schools. The American Civil Liberties Union convinced John Scopes, a high school biology teacher in Dayton, Tennessee, to challenge the law.

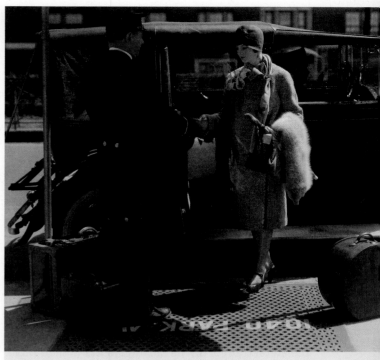

>> The rise of modernism, with its emphasis on urbanism, intellectualism, and individualism, threatened traditionalists who believed America's social foundations were deteriorating.

>> Clarence Darrow (left) and William Jennings Bryan have a conversation during the Scopes Trial.

When Scopes taught evolution in his classroom, he was promptly arrested.

The Scopes Trial drew nationwide attention. Journalists flocked to Dayton to cover the emotionally charged event, which many dubbed the "Monkey Trial" because of the mistaken belief that Darwin claimed that human beings descended from monkeys.

Clarence Darrow, the most celebrated defense attorney in America, traveled from his home in Chicago to defend Scopes. Darrow was well-known for defending labor union leaders like Eugene V. Debs and William Haywood, in addition to other famous cases. A talented speaker, he did not always win his cases, but he often revealed key issues to the public during the well-publicized trials. Three-time presidential candidate **William Jennings Bryan**, a long-time defender of rural values, served as an expert for the prosecution. Bryan, considered one of the greatest orators of his day, was charged with defending what many fundamentalists thought of as the literal truth of divine creation found in their Bible.

Both men had a significant impact on the trial by drawing national attention to it. The highlight of the trial came when Darrow called Bryan to the stand as an expert on the Bible. Bryan affirmed that the Bible stated the literal truth. He testified that he believed that God created Adam and Eve and that Joshua made the sun stand still. Darrow tried to use science to cast doubt on such beliefs, but Bryan firmly stated, "I accept the Bible absolutely."

Scopes was found guilty of breaking the law—a fact that was never in question—and fined $100. The public, however, was paying closer attention to a more essential issue. The trial was a public confrontation between fundamentalism and modernity, between a literal and a liberal interpretation of scripture. While the Scopes Trial showcased a major cultural and religious division, it did not heal the conflict or answer its central questions. When the trial was over, each side still believed in the truth of its position. The conflict over evolution continues today.

☑ **RECALL** How does modernism contrast with more traditional ideas about religion?

The Red Scare

As Americans continued to grapple with the ideas of modernity, the emergence of the Soviet Union as a communist nation challenged other essential U.S ideals. In contrast to capitalism and the free enterprise systems, which emphasized the right to own private property, communist ideology called for public ownership of property and an international workers' revolution as a prelude to the death of capitalism. To this end, Soviet leader Vladimir Lenin encouraged and supported revolutions outside of his country. In Central and Eastern Europe, a series of communist revolts did break out, making it seem like the worldwide revolution was starting.

Fear of a Potential Revolution This revolutionary activity abroad, coupled with labor strikes across the United States following the end of World War I, caused the first American **Red Scare**, a wave of widespread fear of suspected communists and radicals thought to be plotting revolution within the United States. Real revolutionary activity inside

The Scopes Trial: How Did They Differ?

THE PROSECUTION: WILLIAM JENNINGS BRYAN	THE DEFENSE: DUDLEY FIELD MALONE (WITNESS CALLED BY DEFENSE ATTORNEY, CLARENCE DARROW)
"It is high time for the people who believe in religion to make their protest against the teaching of irreligion in the public schools under the guise of science and philosophy."	"We are ready to tell the truth as we understand it and we do not fear all the truth that they can present as facts."

>> **Analyze Charts** Based on the quotes given in the chart, how did the Scopes trial reveal divisions within U.S. society?

America gave substance to the scare. Authorities discovered bombs mailed to important industrialists and government officials, including Attorney General A. Mitchell Palmer. Suspected anarchists, members of a radical political movement, exploded bombs in cities across America, including one that killed about 40 people on Wall Street in 1920.

As the leading law-enforcement official, Palmer mounted a broad offensive against radicals in the United States in 1919 and 1920. In a series of raids in early 1920, known as the **Palmer Raids**, police arrested thousands of people, some who were radicals and some who were simply immigrants from southern or Eastern Europe. Most were never charged or tried for a crime. The government then deported hundreds of radicals or suspected radicals.

To many, these actions seemed to have the effect of attacking the liberties that Americans held most dear. A group of people in New York City formed the American Civil Liberties Union (ACLU) in 1920 to protect these liberties. The ACLU tried to do this by becoming involved in important court cases. To this end, the ACLU became involved in one of America's most controversial court cases: the trial of Nicola Sacco and Bartolomeo Vanzetti.

A Questionable Conviction Nicola Sacco (SAH koh) and **Bartolomeo Vanzetti**(van ZEHT ee) were Italian immigrants and known anarchists. They were charged with shooting and killing two men during a holdup at a shoe factory in a town near Boston. Eyewitnesses of the event said the robbers "looked Italian." Sacco and Vanzetti were arrested and charged with the crime. Even though the ACLU provided defense counsel, the two men were found guilty in a swift and decisive trial, despite the fact that there was little hard evidence against them. Some prominent legal scholars, intellectuals, and liberal politicians charged that the convictions were based more on Sacco and Vanzetti's ethnicity and political beliefs than on the facts of the crime. Nevertheless, on August 23, 1927, the two men were put to death in the electric chair.

At its worst, hysteria accompanied by violence characterized the Red Scare. Mobs attacked suspected radicals, abused immigrants, and committed crimes in the name of justice. By the summer of 1920, the height of the Red Scare had ended. Americans saw that democracy and capitalism were more powerful in the United States than Lenin's call for worldwide revolution. But, as shown by the Sacco and Vanzetti trial, the effects of the great fear would linger throughout the 1920s in negative feelings towards immigrants, labor

>> Lenin's support for revolutions of working class people everywhere against the system of capitalism led leaders to fear just such an uprising within the United States.

>> In New York City, thousands of people protested against the verdict in the Sacco and Vanzetti trial. Many felt government prosecutors were unjustly targeting immigrants without sufficient evidence.

unions, and, to some extent, the reforms pushed by Progressives before World War I.

☑ **RECALL** What was the Red Scare?

Immigration in the 1920s

As the trial of Italian immigrants Sacco and Vanzetti came to a close, another social issue involved the ongoing boom in immigration continued. As in the past, nativists, or those who preferred native-born Americans to immigrants, argued that the new arrivals took jobs away from native-born workers and threatened American religious, political, and cultural traditions.

Eugenics and Social Darwinism Influence the Perception of Immigrants Although nativist politicians had been able to restrict immigration from China in 1882, they had failed to push through laws to restrict immigration from southern and eastern Europe. On the eve of U.S. entry into World War I, however, Congress did pass a law requiring immigrants to take a literacy test.

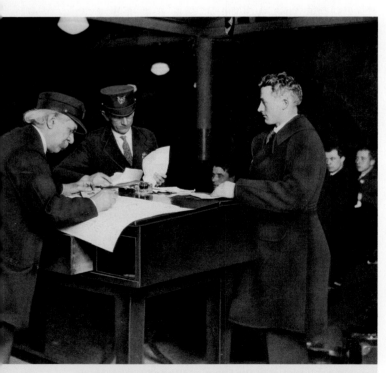

>> The rise of nativism within the United States led to increased restrictions on immigration, such as the rejection of immigrants who could not read and write in their own language.

Immigrants who could not read or write their own language were prohibited from entering the United States. President Wilson vetoed the law, but Congress overrode Wilson's veto. Immigration dropped during the war, worsening labor shortage problems during the war.

During the postwar Red Scare, fear that communists and socialists from eastern Europe were traveling to the United States with their revolutionary doctrines caused the debate to heat up once again. On one side were nativists who disagreed with traditional immigration policy. On the other side were many Americans who viewed the immigration experience as part of what made an American an American. Nearly all Americans who could trace their ancestry back far enough discovered foreign origins.

Nativists were concerned that immigrants would diminish America's political and economic power. They believed that many immigrants had undesirable physical and social traits and would therefore be unproductive members of society.

These views were partly based on **eugenics**, the since-discredited idea that intelligence and other favorable social traits were inheritable characteristics passed on by one's parents and more frequently found in some races than others. Eugenics was related to Social Darwinism, the idea that life was a competition in which only the fittest survive. The rise of both Social Darwinism and eugenics was caused in part by Charles Darwin's theory of natural selection. Both were also motivated by ethnic or racial prejudice to some degree. Those who believed in both theories wanted the United States to be that fittest nation that survived, and to ensure that it was, sought to exclude those they thought of as weaker and undesirable.

Many nativists who believed in eugenics thought the human race could be improved by controlling which people had children. Therefore, they thought it best to restrict immigration to those whom they deemed to have desirable traits that would in turn be passed on to future generations of Americans.

Congressional Legislation Restricts Immigration In addition to eugenics and Social Darwinism, other events such as World War I, the Russian Revolution, and the Red Scare strengthened the nativist position and affected congressional legislation. Two subsequent laws— the Emergency Quota Act of 1921 and the National Origins Act of 1924— established a **quota system** to govern immigration from specific countries.

Effects of Quotas on Immigration

Number of immigrants (y-axis): 0 to 1,100,000
Years (x-axis): 1820–1950

Immigration drops to 420,000 following the Emergency Quota Act of 1921

Immigration drops to 340,000 following the National Origins Act of 1924

SOURCE: *Historical Statistics of the United States*

>> **Analyze Charts** What effect did the Emergency Quota Act of 1921 and the National Origins Act of 1924 have on immigration to the United States?

Bounce to Activate Timeline

The National Origins Act set up a simple formula: The number of immigrants of a given nationality each year could not exceed 2 percent of the number of people of that nationality living in the United States in 1890. The year 1890 was chosen because it was before the great wave of immigration from southern and eastern Europe. For example, the act permitted about 65,721 immigrants from England and Northern Ireland to come to America every year, but it allowed only about 5,802 immigrants from Italy. The act also continued to exclude most Asian immigrants. The effect of eugenics, Social Darwinism, and nativist sentiment in general was that America closed its "golden door" to many of the people trying to enter.

More Mexicans Arrive for Economic Opportunity The quota system did not apply to Mexico, which was still reeling from the 1910 revolution. Settling in sparsely populated regions of the Southwest, Mexican immigrants made significant contributions to local economies. Many found work harvesting crops in California and Texas. A smaller number sought jobs in the factories and farms of the North or Midwest.

Many Mexican immigrants faced discrimination and hostility in their new homes. They often competed with native-born Americans for jobs and were frequently subjected to brutality and violence.

☑ **RECALL** What was the purpose of the National Origins Act?

The Ku Klux Klan in the Early 1900s

Immigration restriction was an attempt to turn back the clock to what many saw as a simpler, better time. Many lashed out against symbols of change. Some even turned to organizations that supported doctrines of hate and employed violence and terror to achieve their ends.

The Klan Reorganizes In 1915, on Stone Mountain in Georgia, a revived **Ku Klux Klan** was formally organized. The original Klan had been formed in the South during Reconstruction largely to terrorize African Americans who sought to vote. Although the new Klan continued to promote hatred of African Americans, it was also aimed at the new America taking shape in the cities. It targeted Jews, Catholics, and immigrants. In the wake of postwar labor unrest, the Klan opposed labor unions—especially because many union members were immigrants or political radicals. The Klan also claimed to stand against lawbreaking and immorality.

At its height, the Klan's "Invisible Empire" had perhaps 4 to 5 million members. Most were in the South, but there were also branches in the Midwest, Northeast, and West—in both rural areas and in small industrial cities. One center of Klan strength was Indiana, where Klan leader David Stephenson ruled with an iron fist and controlled numerous politicians. There were special women's branches of the Klan as well. However, some male Klan leaders were strongly opposed to women taking an active role in politics.

Klan members boycotted businesses owned by anyone who was Jewish, Catholic, or African American. The Klan terrorized citizens in the night, often by burning crosses outside their homes. Klansmen usually wore masks to conceal their identities, met to wave flags and preach hate, and followed leaders with such titles as Grand Dragon and Imperial Wizard. But behind the Klan's confident facade were Americans fearful of change.

Many Americans Oppose the Klan's Values

Organizations such as the NAACP and the Jewish Anti-Defamation League, battled against the Klan and its values. The NAACP continued its anti-lynching crusade, supporting legislation in 1922 that passed in the House of Representatives but not in the Senate. The Anti-Defamation League worked to reduce anti-Semitic slurs in newspapers and break down barriers in higher education and the job market. Individuals also embraced the idea of racial, ethnic, religious, and cultural diversity. For them, the notion of the "melting pot" was as old as America itself. Journalist William Allen White noted:

> To make a case against a birthplace, a religion, or a race is wickedly un-American and cowardly. The whole trouble with the Ku Klux Klan is that it is based upon such deep foolishness that it is bound to be a menace to good government in any community.
>
> —William Allen White, letter to the editor of the *New York World*, 1921

The Klan itself became thoroughly corrupt. Its leaders bribed politicians, stole from its members' dues, and lied to its members. Stephenson ended up going to prison for assault and second-degree murder. By the late 1920s, the Klan stood exposed. Although the organization never disappeared, it became less significant.

☑ What actions did Klan members take to accomplish their goals?

Prohibition Divides Americans

Another divisive issue was **Prohibition**, the banning of alcohol use. Since the early 1800s, temperance reformers had crusaded against alcohol. Temperance was a cause held dear by many Progressives. By 1917, some 75 percent of Americans lived in "dry" counties that had banned liquor. World War I increased support for temperance. It seemed unpatriotic to use corn, wheat, and barley to make alcohol when soldiers overseas needed bread.

The Eighteenth Amendment Bans Alcohol

In 1919, the states ratified the **Eighteenth Amendment** to the Constitution. It forbade the manufacture, distribution, and sale of alcohol anywhere in the United States. The amendment had been passed largely on the strength of rural votes. Many Progressives felt that its passage was one of

>> A group photo of the twentieth annual session of the NAACP in Cleveland, Ohio in 1929.

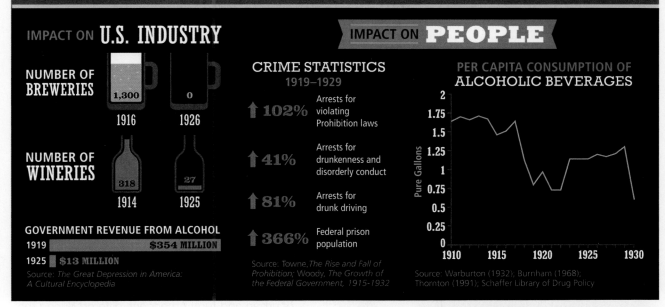

THE IMPACT OF PROHIBITION

IMPACT ON U.S. INDUSTRY

NUMBER OF BREWERIES
1,300 — 1916
0 — 1926

NUMBER OF WINERIES
318 — 1914
27 — 1925

GOVERNMENT REVENUE FROM ALCOHOL
1919 — $354 MILLION
1925 — $13 MILLION

Source: *The Great Depression in America: A Cultural Encyclopedia*

IMPACT ON PEOPLE

CRIME STATISTICS
1919–1929

↑ 102% Arrests for violating Prohibition laws

↑ 41% Arrests for drunkenness and disorderly conduct

↑ 81% Arrests for drunk driving

↑ 366% Federal prison population

Source: Towne, *The Rise and Fall of Prohibition*; Woody, *The Growth of the Federal Government, 1915-1932*

PER CAPITA CONSUMPTION OF ALCOHOLIC BEVERAGES

(y-axis: Pure Gallons, 0 to 2; x-axis: 1910, 1915, 1920, 1925, 1930)

Source: Warburton (1932); Burnham (1968); Thornton (1991); Schaffer Library of Drug Policy

>> **Analyze Charts** Summarize the effects of Prohibition on American society.

Bounce to Activate Gallery

the greatest impacts of the whole Progressive reform movement. Congress then passed the **Volstead Act**, a law that officially enforced the amendment.

Advocates of Prohibition, known as "drys," called it a "noble experiment." They argued that the impact of Prohibition would be improved individuals, strengthened families, and better societies. In fact, drinking—as well as alcoholism and liver disease caused by drinking—did decline during the first years of Prohibition but soon rose again to near pre-Prohibition levels.

Opponents of Prohibition, dubbed "wets," countered that the ban on alcohol did not stop people from drinking. Instead, they argued, Prohibition's impact was to help create an atmosphere of hypocrisy and increased organized crime.

Many Americans Ignore the Volstead Act

As the wets noted, the Volstead Act did not stop Americans from drinking, but it did prevent them from purchasing drinks legally. The gap between the law and individual desires was filled by a large illegal network. People made alcohol in homemade stills or smuggled it in from other countries.

Bootleggers sold illegal alcohol to consumers. In cities, secret drinking establishments, known as speakeasies, attracted eager customers. In South Florida, "rum-runners" smuggled in rum and other spirits from across the Florida Straits.

Government agents worked tirelessly to stop the flow of illegal liquor. However, they were short-handed, and the demand for alcohol was too great. There were millions of dollars to be made by both organized and unorganized criminals. Particularly in cities, policemen and politicians tended to look the other way when liquor was involved. They rationalized their actions by saying that if people wanted to drink, they would drink.

Al Capone, a Chicago gang leader, was the most famous criminal of the Prohibition era. He defended his illegal actions:

> I make my money from supplying a public demand. If I break the law, my customers, who number hundreds of the best people in Chicago, are as guilty as I am. The only difference between us is that I sell and they buy. Everybody calls me a racketeer. I call myself a businessman.

—Al Capone, quoted in *Era of Excess* (Sinclair)

The problem was that under the guise of providing a glass of beer or scotch, organized crime spread into other areas of society. Capone's other "businesses" included prostitution, drugs, robbery,

>> Protesters in 1932 were led by New York City Mayor Jimmy Walker. **Draw Conclusions** Looking at the banners, what reason were the marchers using to advocate the repeal of Prohibition?

like immigration and evolution, the debate over Prohibition became part of a battle over the future of America.

In the culturally divided 1920s, Americans could not reach a satisfactory settlement on the issue. However, illegal economies that thrived on the production and distribution of alcohol continued to thrive and legal enforcement of Prohibition was oftentimes lax. As popular dissatisfaction with the Eighteenth Amendment grew, Congress finally repealed Prohibition with the passage of the Twenty-First Amendment in 1933. It was ratified by the states later that same year.

☑ **IDENTIFY MAIN IDEAS** Why was the Volstead Act passed?

and murder. Thus, one effect of Prohibition was to contribute to the growth of organized crime in America.

The Constitution Is Amended Again By the mid-1920s, most city politicians clamored for the repeal of the Eighteenth Amendment. But to many rural Americans, liquor and crime were tied to other divisive cultural issues of the day. Thus,

☑ **ASSESSMENT**

1. **Make Generalizations** Explain how the lifestyles of urban and rural Americans differed during the 1920s.

2. **Generate Explanations** Explain how the Scopes Trial illustrated the conflict between modernism and fundamentalism.

3. **Apply Concepts** Identify the flaws of the trial of Nicola Sacco and Bartolomeo Vanzetti.

4. **Distinguish Between Fact and Opinion** Discuss the main ideas of eugenics, and explain why it is no longer a prominent belief in the United States.

5. **Identify Cause and Effect** Explain how Prohibition contributed to the growth of organized crime in the United States.

The automobile reshaped American culture, creating new forms of recreation and making it easier for people to travel. Other factors also contributed to changing ways of daily life. Americans listened to the radio, went to the movies, and followed the exploits of sports heroes. In the process, a new mass culture emerged—one whose shape and character closely resemble our own.

>> Charles Lindbergh's successful flight across the Atlantic Ocean gave the fledgling airline industry a boost and encouraged the development of passenger airlines.

Bounce to Activate Flipped Video

The Roaring Twenties

Popular American Culture in the 1920s

The 1920s was in many respects the first decade of our modern era. Even as cultural issues divided Americans from different regions or economic levels, technology was beginning to break down other barriers. Nowhere is this more evident than in the leisure interests of the American people.

Americans Enjoy More Leisure Time The growth of cities changed leisure patterns. On farms, people worked from dawn to dusk, with little time to spare. In the evenings, a farm family might play games, read, or sing together around the piano. Occasionally, they joined other farm families and townsfolk for picnics or a game of baseball. They did not have the time or the money for more extensive leisure pursuits.

City life was different. The average workweek in all industries fell from 70 hours in 1850 to 55 in 1910 to 45 by 1930. The workweek itself also changed from seven days a week to six and at last to five. At the same time, salaries and wages were on the rise.

>> **Objectives**

Describe how increased leisure time and technological innovations led to a widespread shared popular culture in the 1920s.

Analyze the changing role of women in the 1920s.

Describe how the concept of modernism shown in art and literature reflected postwar disillusionment.

>> **Key Terms**

Charlie Chaplin
The Jazz Singer
Babe Ruth
Charles Lindbergh
flapper
Sigmund Freud
"Lost Generation"
F. Scott Fitzgerald
Ernest Hemingway
Sigmund Freud

Innovation in the Motion Picture Industry

With more free time and disposable income, urban and suburban Americans looked to new sources of entertainment. Motion pictures helped supply that demand.

The technology to make motion pictures had been around for a generation, but the movie industry rose to new heights in the 1920s. A handful of huge studios in Hollywood, California, established monopolies that controlled the production, distribution, and exhibition of movies. During the 1920s, from 60 to 100 million Americans went to the movies each week. Ornate movie palaces or small local theaters became America's cultural classrooms.

For most of the decade, the studios made silent pictures. They were an ideal entertainment at a time when millions of immigrants spoke little English. Motion pictures transcended languages and even literacy, treating universal themes in familiar ways that allowed any viewer to follow the stories. Motion pictures became America's democratic art. Unlike theatrical productions or classical concerts, movies were available to anyone with a few cents to spare. In addition, the fact that movies were silent made it easier for them to cut across geographical boundaries. Hollywood's biggest movies and stars became nearly as popular in far corners of the globe as they were at home. By 1926, Hollywood movies accounted for a majority of the British and French film markets. Film was one of the first mediums to diffuse popular American culture to the rest of the world.

Many stars of the silent era portrayed ordinary folks, and films often portrayed the social issues and characteristics of the time in which they were made. Comedian **Charlie Chaplin**, the most popular silent film star, played the Little Tramp in many films. In *The Immigrant*, Chaplin played a penniless immigrant on a voyage across the Atlantic to the United States. Although the film belonged to the genre of comedy, it depicted some of the challenges and uncertainties that many immigrants of the time faced as they made their own way to America's shores. Chaplin's character was equal parts hobo, dreamer, and poet but an eternal optimist in his ability to charm his audience and continually reinvent himself. Other stars played more romantic types. Adorable Mary Pickford was known as "America's Sweetheart" for her girlish roles in light romances. Douglas Fairbanks played handsome, athletic adventurers. In the western genre, William S. Hart was a steely-eyed cowboy who came into town to restore law and order.

In 1927, film history changed, suddenly and forever, with the release of ***The Jazz Singer***, the first movie with sound synchronized to the action. Audiences were amazed when Al Jolson said—not pantomimed—"You ain't heard nothin' yet" and then

INNOVATIONS CHANGE HOW PEOPLE LIVE

HOUSEHOLDS WITH RADIO SETS (THOUSANDS)

Year	Value
1922	60
1923	400
1924	1,250
1925	2,750
1926	4,000
1927	6,750
1928	8,000
1929	10,250
1930	13,000
1931	16,700
1932	18,450
1933	19,250
1934	20,400

Source: *Gold Eagle*

AVERAGE WEEKLY MOVIE ATTENDANCE (PER 100 PEOPLE)

1910	1920	1930	1940
28	36	73	61

Source: *Blockbusting*

HOUSEHOLD EXPENDITURES ON TECHNOLOGY

— MOTOR VEHICLES
— MUSIC, RADIO & TV
— ELECTRICITY

Source: *Historical Statistics of the United States*

By the mid-1920s, 50% of U.S. households had **ELECTRICITY.**

By the mid-1930s, 50% of U.S. households had **AN ELECTRIC STOVE.**

By the mid-1940s, 50% of U.S. households had **A REFRIGERATOR & A TELEPHONE.**

Source: *The Atlantic*

>> **Analyze Graphs** Why do you think there was a significant increase in movie attendance in 1930?

Bounce to Activate Illustration

launched into a song. Silent pictures quickly faded out, replaced by "talkies." But whether silent or with sound, movies spoke directly to the desires, needs, fears, and fantasies of millions of people in the United States and around the world.

The Radio Impacts American Society Like the movies, the phonograph and the radio also became powerful instruments of mass popular culture. Each was the result of both technological advances and business enterprise. Millions of radios and phonographs (as well as phonograph records) were marketed in the 1920s. On a deeper level, the phonograph and radio helped produce a standardized culture. Americans in the East and West and North and South listened to the same songs, learned the same dances, and shared the same popular culture as they never had before.

The radio, or wireless, was developed in the 1890s by Italian inventor Guglielmo Marconi. Before the 1920s, the radio was an innovation used by a small group of military technicians, telephone operators, and amateur "wireless" operators. Then, in 1920, an executive of the Westinghouse company started radio station KDKA in Pittsburgh, Pennsylvania. It was an immediate success. Within three years, there were almost 600 licensed stations broadcasting to more than 600,000 radio sets. Americans listened to music, educational lectures and religious sermons, and news and weather reports. They also heard commercials for a wide variety of consumer products.

Radios brought distant events into millions of homes in a way unmatched by newspapers or magazines. In 1927, much of America listened to a championship boxing match between Gene Tunney and Jack Dempsey. That night, theaters and movie houses played to empty seats as Americans huddled next to their sets. Even the men on death row at Sing Sing prison listened to the broadcast. Before the 1920s, such coverage of an event had been impossible. Although radio programs and music occasionally broadcast racial or cultural stereotypes as well, such as the radio show *Amos 'n Andy* in the 1920s, the radio allowed Americans to keep up with current events around the country as they occurred.

Americans Share Music With the Phonograph
The phonograph allowed people to listen to the same music they heard on the radio, but whenever they wanted. Early phonographs employed difficult-to-use wax cylinders and suffered from poor sound quality. In the 1920s, grooved disc recordings and superior sound reproduction improved the sound of the earlier

>> Before "talkies," or movies with synchronized sound, Americans went to the movies to see silent pictures. Charlie Chaplin was perhaps the most famous of all silent film actors.

>> The invention of the phonograph and grooved disc record stimulated the growth of the music industry. By the 1920s, records had one song on each side and rotated at 78 revolutions per minute (rpm).

machines, and production of phonographs rose to approximately five million in 1929. There was also a corresponding rise in record sales. The first country-western album to sell over one million copies was produced in 1924.

As the popularity of country-western music rose, one positive impact was that the uniquely American symbol of the cowboy and life on the the western frontier was mythologized throughout the country. A negative impact was that stereotypes of westerners and country-dwellers sometimes also spread. Recordings helped bring country and western music from the South and West to the North and East, while pop tunes from New York City's Tin Pan Alley traveled in the other direction, creating national markets for different genres of music. As they listened to the same songs, Americans also learned the same fashionable dances, from the fox trot to the Charleston.

☑ **IDENTIFY MAIN IDEAS** How did films like *The Immigrant* reflect the social issues of the time?

>> With the help of increased newspaper readership and radio coverage, sports figures like Babe Ruth became national heroes and symbols of American culture.

American Role Models

Hollywood's chief rivals for the creation of heroes were the nation's baseball parks, football fields, and boxing rings. Before the 1920s, there were relatively few nationally famous athletes, such as boxer John L. Sullivan and all-around athlete Jim Thorpe. Most sports stars were local heroes. This changed by the 1920s, often called the Golden Age of Sports.

Media Coverage Creates Sports Heroes Thanks to increased newspaper readership and the rise of radio coverage, every major sport boasted nationally famous performers. Perhaps the leading sports hero was baseball home-run king **Babe Ruth**. Others included Red Grange in football, Jack Dempsey in boxing, Bobby Jones in golf, and Bill Tilden in tennis. Women athletes, too, contributed to the hero culture, from tennis player Helen Wills to Gertrude Ederle, the first woman to swim the English Channel.

Why did athletes reach such heights of popularity? Part of the answer is that the Golden Age of Sports was also the Golden Age of the Sportswriter. Such journalists as Damon Runyon and Grantland Rice captured the excitement of sports events in their colorful prose. Turning the finest athletes into seemingly immortal gods, the sportswriters nicknamed Babe Ruth the Sultan of Swat and dubbed Notre Dame's football backfield the Four Horsemen.

The other part of the answer is that the decade needed heroes. World War I had shattered many Americans' faith in progress, making the world seem cheap and flawed. Athletic heroes reassured Americans that people were capable of great feats and lofty dreams. If in our heroes we see our idealized selves, the sports heroes of the 1920s gave Americans a sense of hope.

A Transatlantic Flight Even the biggest sports stars could not match the adoration given to aviators. In the 1920s, the airline industry was in its infancy. Flying aces had played a role in World War I, and a few small domestic airlines carried mail and passengers. But airplanes were still a novel sight to most Americans. The pilot became a new breed of hero, a romantic daredevil who risked death with every flight.

As aviation technology improved by leaps and bounds in the early twentieth century, many dreamed of flying across the Atlantic Ocean. These dreams were made possible by innovators such as Glenn Curtiss, who designed an aircraft engine capable of just such a flight. As flight crews were successfully flying longer distances across the

Atlantic, daring aviators wondered if they could accomplish the same feat alone.

Then aviator **Charles Lindbergh** attempted the long journey alone. In May 1927, he took off from Long Island, New York, in his tiny single-engine plane, the *Spirit of St. Louis*, and headed east— to Paris, France. Other pilots had flown across the Atlantic Ocean before, but Lindbergh was the first to do it solo and non-stop. The flight took more than 33 hours, and the lone pilot had to stay awake the entire time. He also recalled, "In the daytime I knew where I was going, but in the evening and at night it was largely a matter of guesswork."

When Lindbergh landed in Paris, he became an instant media celebrity, dubbed Lucky Lindy and the Lone Eagle. The radio reported on his landing, and movie newsreels showed his triumphant return home. The modest young man from the Midwest made an impact as the greatest hero of his time.

☑ **IDENTIFY** For what accomplishment was Charles Lindbergh known?

The Role of Women Changes

In a 1931 book, *Only Yesterday*, journalist Frederick Lewis Allen attempted to make sense of the fads, heroes, and problems of the 1920s. Featured prominently was the New Woman. During the decade, many women challenged political, economic, social, and educational boundaries to prove that their role was as vital outside the home as inside it. Women's roles began to change in many ways, caused by the overall changes that society was undergoing, as well as the passage of the Nineteenth Amendment in 1920. The effect of these changes was that women made more and more contributions to shape American culture.

Flappers Push Back Against Expectations

During the Victorian Age of the late 1800s and early 1900s, middle-class women had been expected to center their lives on the home and family. The New Woman of the 1920s, noted Allen, was more liberated. She wore dresses with shorter hemlines, put on more makeup, danced to the latest crazes, and generally assumed that she had the same political and social rights as any man.

Popular magazines, sociological studies, novels, and movies all echoed Allen's observations. The rejection of Victorian morality seemed so total and the New Woman so novel that the change amounted

>> The individualism and modernism of the early 1920s prompted many women to see themselves as equals to men, deserving the same political and social rights.

to a "revolution in manners and morals." The symbol of all these changes was the **flapper**, a young woman with short skirts and rouged cheeks who had her hair cropped close in a style known as a bob.

There was only a germ of truth in the various observations. The Victorian code of separate spheres for men and women was disappearing but not as rapidly or as completely as Allen indicated. The flapper was undoubtedly more publicized than imitated. Still, the image of the flapper underscores an important aspect of the decade. Not all women aspired to be flappers, but many wanted more control over their lives—and got it.

Women's Political Rights The great fight for suffrage had been won with the passage of the Nineteenth Amendment. Soon women looked for a way to use their political rights to make an impact. But what was the next step? Some groups, such as the National American Woman Suffrage Association, called on women to work in reform movements, run for office, or fight for laws to protect women and children in the workplace. Some women had success in public life. In 1925, Nellie Tayloe Ross of Wyoming and Miriam Ferguson of Texas became the first women to take office as elected state governors.

The National Women's Party took a more militant position, demanding complete economic, social, and political equality with men. Their primary goal was the passage of an Equal Rights Amendment. Many women, though, believed that a new constitutional amendment was premature. They set more achievable goals and made significant strides in employment. The efforts of these political organizations and women elected to public office redefined the role of women in American culture and opened doors through which others would walk in the decades to come. Although most working women continued to toil in domestic service and manufacturing, others moved into clerical, sales, and management positions. Women also won jobs in journalism, aviation, banking, and the legal and medical professions.

Life at Home Changes Perhaps the most widespread revolution taking place in women's lives was a quiet one. During the decade, women tended to live longer, marry later, and have fewer children, freeing their time to pursue other interests. Some entered the workforce, others devoted more time to charitable work, and still others joined clubs that discussed books and ideas. All these pursuits enlarged the intellectual world of women.

The consumer economy of the 1920s benefited women. Electric vacuum cleaners and irons took some of the labor and drudgery out of household chores. Of course, not all women shared in the blessings of technology. Many homes in rural America had no access to electricity. For women in these regions, household labor continued to involve intense, even painful, work. They drew and carried water from wells, heated irons on stoves, and washed clothes by hand. Here again, the split between urban and rural Americans was distinct.

☑ **RECALL** Why would many who advocated for women's political equality have thought 1925 was a significant year?

Social Issues Are Reflected in Art and Literature

No area of American life, however, reflected the impact of World War I more than literature and the arts. The war altered the way writers and artists viewed the world, changed the way they approached their craft, and inspired them to experiment with new forms and fresh ideas.

Postwar Uncertainty During the Victorian era, most poets and novelists had expressed a belief in progress, placing boundless faith in human potential. But World War I called the notion of progress into question.

How could a society ruled by the idea of progress embark on a war that killed millions of people, destroyed monuments of civilization, and left survivors hungry, homeless, and hopeless? This was not an action of a rational people, a new generation of writers argued, but the irrational exploits of civilization without a sense of direction.

This pessimistic, skeptical worldview sparked an artistic movement known as modernism. Modernism in both art and literature to some extent also reflected some of the issues and characteristics of American society in the 1920s, from the renewed interest in new technology to the uncertainty of many in a rapidly changing world.

The theories of Jewish-Austrian psychologist **Sigmund Freud** (SIHG muhnd froid) also contributed to literary and artistic modernism. Freud argued that much of human behavior is driven not by

>> Modernist painters like Edward Hopper expressed their reservations about the progress of civilization. **Evaluate Sources** What themes does Hopper's 1927 painting "Automat" express?

🅑🅑 **Bounce to Activate Chart**

rational thought but by unconscious desires. To live in society, people learn to suppress these desires. But the tension between outward behavior and the subconscious, said Freud, could lead to mental and even physical illness. Freud's theories led writers and artists to explore the subconscious mind.

Modern Art Moves in New Directions

Modernism clashed head-on with traditionalism most dramatically in the field of modern art. Since the late 1800s, European painters had led the way in seeking a fresh visual idiom, or language. They moved away from art that copied reality and experimented with more abstract styles.

Most Americans got their first real glimpse of the new European approach at a major art show at New York's 69th Infantry Regimental Armory in 1913. Traditionalists were outraged by the Armory Show, and Theodore Roosevelt said that most of it represented the "lunatic fringe" of the art world. But many American painters and sculptors were inspired by the bold new styles. They began their own search for artistic honesty in abstract patterns. In the 1920s, paintings by Edward Hopper, Man Ray, Joseph Stella, and Georgia O'Keeffe demonstrated the richness and varied styles of American artists. At the same time, the works of artists such as Archibald Motley and William H. Johnson portrayed African American perspectives on modern life.

Postwar American Literature Flowers

American writers of the 1920s are often referred to as the **"Lost Generation"** because they no longer had faith in the cultural guideposts of the Victorian era. But many were inspired by their "lost" condition to search for new truths and fresh ways of expressing those truths. Never in American history had one decade seen the emergence of so many great literary talents. A list of writers who rose to distinction in the 1920s includes F. Scott Fitzgerald, Ernest Hemingway, Edith Wharton, Sinclair Lewis, William Faulkner, Gertrude Stein, Eugene O'Neill, and T. S. Eliot. Each of these writers remains today on any list of distinguished American authors.

Novelist **F. Scott Fitzgerald** explored the reality of the American dream of wealth, success, and emotional fulfillment. In *This Side of Paradise*, he wrote that his generation had "grown up to find all Gods dead, all wars fought, and all faiths in man shaken." In *The Great Gatsby* (1925), his most accomplished work, Fitzgerald showed the American dream ending in nightmare.

In the novel, through hard work and careful planning, James Gatz re-creates himself as Jay

>> American writers F. Scott Fitzgerald and his wife Zelda, visited the French Riviera often in the 1920s. In many ways, their turbulent life together mirrored Fitzgerald's stories of striving and tragedy.

Gatsby, a successful tycoon. Gatsby fills his home with wild parties, dancing, and bootleg liquor:

> In the main hall a bar with a real brass rail was set up, and stocked with gins and liquors and with cordials so long forgotten that most of his female guests were too young to know one from another. By seven o'clock the orchestra had arrived, no thin five-piece affair, but a whole pitful of oboes and trombones and saxophones. . . .People were not invited—they went there. They got into automobiles which bore them out to Long Island, and somehow they ended up at Gatsby's door.
>
> —F. Scott Fitzgerald, *The Great Gatsby*

But in the end, Gatsby is destroyed by the very things he hoped to achieve. His lofty dreams end in a violent, meaningless death.

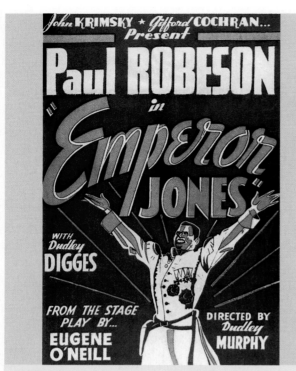

>> *The Emperor Jones* was Eugene O'Neill's initial attempt at expressionism. Starring Paul Robeson, it was the first play on Broadway with a racially integrated cast.

Ernest Hemingway explored similar themes but in a new idiom. Hemingway felt betrayed, not only by the American dream, but also by literary language itself. In *A Farewell to Arms*, his 1929 novel about World War I, Hemingway's narrator says:

> I was always embarrassed by the words sacred, glorious, and sacrifice. . . .I had seen nothing sacred, and the things that were glorious had no glory and the sacrifices were like the stockyards at Chicago if nothing was done with the meat except to bury it. . . .Abstract words such as glory, honor, courage, or hallow were obscene beside the concrete names of villages, the numbers of roads, the names of rivers, the numbers of regiments and the dates.
>
> —Ernest Hemingway, *A Farewell to Arms*

In his short stories and novels, Hemingway worked to develop a writing style that reflected his insights. He wrote in unadorned sentences, stripped of vague adjectives and adverbs.

Influenced by Freud, other writers explored the subconscious mind. Playwright Eugene O'Neill experimented with techniques that put the subconscious right on stage. In *The Emperor Jones*, the title character gets lost in a jungle and is attacked by imaginary beings called Little Formless Fears. In *Strange Interlude*, characters turn away from their conversations with other people on stage and speak their thoughts directly to the audience.

Gay Subculture Becomes More Visible

Prohibition criminalized alcohol-based night life, forcing many people to break the law. In the illegal activities of the speakeasies many "straight" Americans came into contact with openly gay men and lesbians, whose meeting places had been subject to police raids for decades. During the social experimentation of the 1920s, increasing numbers of films, books, and popular songs referenced homosexuality, while in the cities gay men and lesbians also became bolder and more visible. In this rebellious decade, some defied laws against cross-dressing, and in New York City drag balls began attracting thousands, growing larger every year. Yet despite this greater visibility, gay men and lesbians still lived in fear of anti-gay laws. They were still subject to arrest, imprisonment, blackmail, the loss of jobs, and rejection by family for behavior that society considered immoral and criminal.

☑ **CHECK UNDERSTANDING** What themes did F. Scott Fitzgerald include in many of his stories?

☑ ASSESSMENT

1. **Draw Conclusions** Explain why silent pictures were an ideal form of entertainment during the 1920s.

2. **Make Generalizations** Explain why sports heroes became popular during the 1920s.

3. **Identify Central Issues** Explain how modernist literature related to the prominent issues and ideas of the 1920s.

4. **Identify Cause and Effect** Explain how World War I led to the rise of modernism.

5. **Draw Conclusions** Explain how the flapper related to the lives of most American women.

4.8 As a result of World War I and the Great Migration, millions of African Americans relocated from the rural South to the urban North. This mass migration continued through the 1920s and contributed to a flowering of music and literature. Jazz and the Harlem Renaissance made a lasting impact, not only on African Americans but on the culture all Americans share.

>> Louis Armstrong's raspy voice and trumpet playing helped promote the popularity of jazz around the world.

Bounce to Activate Flipped Video

The Harlem Renaissance

Support for Black Nationalism in Urban Areas

Like the immigrants who traveled from Europe and Asia, African Americans who left the South dreamed of a better future. They had heard stories of economic opportunity, social advancement, and greater political rights. The South, they reasoned, was a dead end. Locked into low-paying rural jobs, barred from decent schools, faced with the reality of Jim Crow oppression and the threat of lynching, they pointed their compasses north.

Migration Creates Opportunities and Challenges Most African American migrants to the north probably found a better life. Wages in a Detroit auto plant or a Pittsburgh steel mill were far better than what a sharecropper earned in the South. In such cities as New York, Chicago, Pittsburgh, and Cleveland, African Americans had a growing political voice. In those towns, there also existed black middle and upper classes. African American ministers, physicians, lawyers, teachers, and journalists practiced their professions and served as role models to the younger generation.

>> **Objectives**

Analyze how the Great Migration and the philosophies of Marcus Garvey affected African Americans in the 1920s.

Trace the development of jazz and its impact on American society and the rest of the world.

Discuss the themes explored by writers and artists of the Harlem Renaissance.

>> **Key Terms**

Marcus Garvey
jazz
Louis Armstrong
Bessie Smith
Harlem Renaissance
Claude McKay
Langston Hughes
Zora Neale Hurston

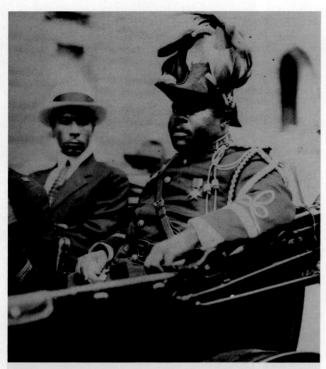

>> Marcus Garvey, an African American nationalist, promoted the idea that African Americans should separate themselves from whites and support their own communities.

Bounce to Activate Timeline

>> The African American population of Harlem, New York continued to grow after World War I and in the 1920s.

But in coming North, African Americans had certainly not escaped racism and oppression. On average, they were forced to live in the worst housing and labor in the lowest paying jobs. In addition, as the race riots of the summer of 1919 demonstrated, violence was a threat to African Americans north as well as south of the Mason-Dixon line. After World War I, African Americans increased their demand for a real solution to the country's racial problems.

New York City's Harlem became the focal point for the aspirations of hundreds of thousands of African Americans. Some 200,000 blacks settled in Harlem. Migrants from the South mixed with recently arrived immigrants from Caribbean islands, such as Jamaica. This dynamic blend of different cultures and traditions bred new ideas.

The Impact of Marcus Garvey The most prominent new African American leader to emerge in the 1920s was **Marcus Garvey**. Born in Jamaica, Garvey traveled widely before immigrating to Harlem in 1916. From his travels, Garvey drew one important conclusion: Blacks were exploited everywhere. To combat the problem, he promoted the idea of universal black nationalism and organized a "Back to Africa" movement. Unlike Booker T. Washington or W.E.B. Du Bois, Garvey did not call for blacks and whites to work together to improve America. Instead, Garvey advocated the separation of the races.

Garvey's message found willing converts in American cities. By the mid-1920s, his Universal Negro Improvement Association boasted almost 2.5 million members and sympathizers. His advocacy of black pride and black support of black-run businesses won considerable support.

Garvey's movement fell apart in the second half of the decade. The federal government sent him to prison for mail fraud and then deported him to Jamaica. Without his powerful leadership, the Universal Negro Improvement Association lost its focus and appeal.

Although Garvey's movement died, his ideas did not fade. The nationalist and separatist aspects of the Nation of Islam and the Black Power movement in the 1960s borrowed from Garvey's ideas. So, too, did later appeals to black pride, self-reliance, and cultural ties to Africa. Harlem's major newspaper, the *Amsterdam News*, later wrote, "In a world where black is despised, he taught [African Americans] to admire and praise black things and black people."

☑ **DESCRIBE** What challenges did many African American migrants face as they moved north?

The Evolution of Jazz

West African and European traditional music

→ Ragtime

→ Southern Dixie

→ Blues

→ JAZZ

→ Fusion

Rap

The European

International Music

Hip-Hop

Acid Jazz

Smooth Jazz

SOURCE: ALLYOURJAZZ.com

>> **Analyze Charts** How is the development of jazz related to modern musical genres such as hip-hop and rap?

The Jazz Age

It was F. Scott Fitzgerald who called the 1920s the "Jazz Age." However, it was African Americans who contributed the jazz. A truly indigenous American musical form, **jazz** is based on improvisation. Jazz musicians creatively recombine different forms of music, including African American blues and ragtime, and European-based popular music. Jazz music was fast, free, loud, rebellious, and fun—a perfect soundtrack for the 1920s.

A Unique Musical Style Jazz emerged in the South and Midwest, particularly New Orleans, where different cultures and traditions fused. Early jazz artists won fame playing in Storyville, a section of New Orleans known for its night life. From the South, it spread north with the Great Migration of African Americans.

Trumpet player **Louis Armstrong** became the unofficial ambassador of jazz. After playing with King Oliver's band in New Orleans and Chicago and with Fletcher Henderson's orchestra in New York, Armstrong began to organize his own groups. His ability to play the trumpet and his subtle sense of improvisation made him a legend and influenced the development of jazz. After Armstrong, all jazz bands featured soloists. Many also began to feature vocal soloists, such as **Bessie Smith**, the "Empress of the Blues."

Jazz Wins Worldwide Popularity Jazz became the sound of the Roaring Twenties. It was part of the Prohibition era, played in speakeasies and nightspots in New York, Chicago, St. Louis, and Los Angeles. It was the sound of the Cotton Club, one of Harlem's most famous attractions, where African Americans played African American music to all-white audiences. Phonograph records and radio spread the influence of jazz across the country and beyond. By the end of the decade, the popularity of jazz had spread to Europe as well.

Many musicians, such as Armstrong, introduced rhythms and themes with clear African roots into their music to better convey the African American cultural experience. Gerald Early, a modern scholar of English and African American studies, predicted that, in the future, America will be best remembered for three great contributions—the Constitution, baseball, and jazz. All three enriched lives, opened windows to new possibilities, and lifted the human spirit. Jazz announced that the United States was a land of shared cultures and traditions.

The jazz movement was then a reflection of an evolving African American identity born of shared historical experience, including the contemporary

>> Duke Ellington's music integrated "big-band" and jazz sounds and increased the popularity of jazz orchestras.

>> African American music legends, including Duke Ellington and Cab Calloway, played regularly at Harlem's many nightclubs.

experiences of the Great Migration and continuing troubled race relations.

Jazz quickly bridged the races. Trumpeter Bix Beiderbecke (Bì der behk) became the first white musician to contribute to the styles and popularity of jazz. Jazz sounds influenced such white songwriters and composers as Cole Porter, Irving Berlin, and George Gershwin, whose jazz-inspired orchestral work *Rhapsody in Blue* premiered in 1924. The title of a song by African American bandleader Duke Ellington best captures how jazz changed popular music: "It Don't Mean a Thing If It Ain't Got That Swing."

☑ **IDENTIFY SUPPORTING DETAILS** What effect did the Great Migration have on the popularity of jazz?

The Harlem Renaissance

Jazz and blues were expressions of the African American experience. The pain of the African American experience can be heard in the blues, and the joy of that experience in the soaring notes of jazz. The range of such African American musicians as Duke Ellington and Cab Calloway speaks to the varieties of African American life. But in the 1920s, there were other expressions of African American culture. Novelists, poets, and artists celebrated their culture and explored questions of race in America. This flowering of African American culture became known as the **Harlem Renaissance**. The Harlem Renaissance helped give a new vocabulary and dynamic to race relations in the United States.

Cultural Movements in Literature and Art In the 1920s, the term the "New Negro" entered the American vocabulary. It suggested a radical break with the past. No longer would African Americans silently endure the old ways of exploitation and discrimination. The new mood was most vividly expressed in Harlem, which attracted African American artists and writers from all over the country and beyond. In their work, these artists and writers explored the pains and joys of being black in America, leaving a legacy that spoke to all Americans of all times.

Artists such as Aaron Douglas created paintings with stylized art that reflected African Americans' racial pride and collective historical experience, while other artists such as Jacob Lawrence and Archibald J. Motley, Jr., expressed similar sentiment in their colorful paintings of urban life.

Many writers communicated the same themes. Jean Toomer's *Cane* (1923) set the literary tone for the Harlem Renaissance. A collection of short stories, poems, and sketches, *Cane* presented African American life and folk culture in all its richness.

Soon, other African American writers joined Toomer at the forefront of the Harlem Renaissance. Jamaican immigrant **Claude McKay** was the most militant of these writers. In his novels and poems, McKay showed ordinary African Americans struggling for dignity and advancement in the face of discrimination and economic hardships. A poem that McKay wrote after Chicago was stricken by violent race riots captured his sense of anger and militancy:

> If we must die—let it not be like hogs,
>
> hunted and penned in an inglorious spot.
>
> While round us bark the mad and hungry dogs,
>
> Making their mock at our accursed lot.
>
> What though before us lies the open grave?
>
> Like men we will face the murderous, cowardly pack,
>
> Pressed to the wall, dying but fighting back!
>
> —Claude McKay, "If We Must Die"

McKay represented the political and ideological left wing of the Harlem Renaissance. More in the center was **Langston Hughes**, probably the most powerful African American literary voice of his time. In more than 50 works of fiction, poetry, journalism, and criticism, he captured the remarkable diversity of everyday African American life.

Another powerful voice was **Zora Neale Hurston**. Hurston traveled the rural back roads of her native Florida, collecting folk tales in books such as *Mules and Men*. But Hurston also looked to the future. Her 1937 novel *Their Eyes Were Watching God* expressed the new longing for independence felt by many women, black and white.

Crossing Boundaries in Harlem The dazzling and glamorous nightlife of 1920s Harlem became world famous. In its nightclubs, speakeasies, and private parties Harlem offered a startling new kind of experience, where audiences could enjoy

>> The writer Jean Toomer's works appealed to African Americans to remember their pasts. **Infer** Why would Toomer emphasize this theme in his works?

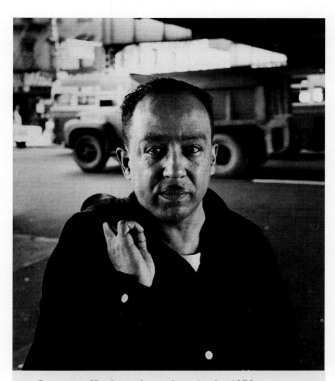

>> Langston Hughes, shown here in the 1950s, emphasized the celebration of the unique aspects of African American culture and history and promoted his vision of a racially integrated, but just, society.

Bounce to Activate Gallery

>> In her work, writer Zora Neale Hurston gave voice to the desire of many women, both African American and white, for greater independence. Hurston's work also explored the rich cultural heritage of African Americans.

A great deal has been accomplished in this decade of 'renaissance'. . . .Today, one may see undesirable stories, but one may also read stories about Negro singers, Negro actors, Negro authors, Negro poets. The connotations of the very word *Negro* have changed. A generation ago many Negroes were half or wholly ashamed of the term.

Today, they have every reason to be proud of it.

—James Weldon Johnson, article in *Harper's Magazine*, 1928

The movement was not, however, without its critics. Some, such as Langston Hughes, expressed a degree of disillusionment with the movement's inability to improve the political status and economic opportunities of African Americans. However, the artistic forms and cultural debates associated with the Harlem Renaissance continue even today.

Although the Harlem Renaissance came to a close as the nation fell into economic difficulty in the late 1920s, the sense of group identity and African American solidarity that it created would become part of the bedrock on which the later civil rights movement would be constructed.

☑ **IDENTIFY** What themes did Langston Hughes and Zora Neale Hurston explore?

☑ **ASSESSMENT**

1. **Compare** Describe how the ways in which African Americans migrated during the Great Migration were similar to the immigrants who arrived from other countries in the early 1900s.

2. **Summarize** Discuss the benefits and the downfalls of African American life in the North.

3. **Draw Conclusions** Discuss the collapse of the Universal Negro Improvement Association and describe its lasting legacy in American culture.

4. **Generate Explanations** Explain why the "Jazz Age" represented an important transition for American society.

5. **Apply Concepts** Analyze the importance of Langston Hughes's writing during the Harlem Renaissance.

cutting-edge musical styles and greater contact between the races was possible. In this more tolerant environment, gay people also became more visible. The annual Hamilton Lodge Ball was the largest drag ball in the city, attracting an interracial, cross-dressing crowd of thousands. In the clubs, performers like Ma Rainey and Gladys Bentley teased audiences with daring references to bisexuality.

However, the leading writers and artists of the Renaissance, such as Langston Hughes, remained more discreet. Taboos against homosexuality, along with society's emphasis on marriage, led public figures like philosopher Alain Locke and poet Countee Cullen to conceal their same-sex desires. The leaders of the Harlem Renaissance kept the focus on African American culture and identity and away from other aspects of their lives.

The Lasting Impact of the Harlem Renaissance
The Harlem Renaissance gave a voice to African American culture. It altered the way many white Americans viewed African American culture and even the way African Americans viewed themselves. James Weldon Johnson, poet and secretary of the NAACP, noted:

Poems: Langston Hughes

Langston Hughes wrote about how it felt to be African American, describing a range of emotions from the pain of racial prejudice to his deep pride in his culture and heritage. The poems below are among his most famous.

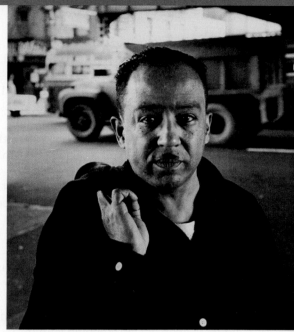

>> Langston Hughes

The Negro Speaks of Rivers

I've known rivers:
I've known rivers ancient as the world and older than the flow of human blood in human veins.

My soul has grown deep like the rivers.

I bathed in the Euphrates [river in the Middle East] when dawns were young.
I built my hut near the Congo [river in Central Africa] and it lulled me to sleep.
I looked upon the Nile [river in Egypt] and raised the pyramids above it.

I heard the singing of the Mississippi when Abe Lincoln went down to New Orleans, and I've seen its muddy bosom turn all golden in the sunset.

I've known rivers:
Ancient, dusky [dark] rivers.

My soul has grown deep like the rivers.

☑ **DETERMINE CENTRAL IDEAS** What point do you think Hughes is making when he names four different rivers around the world, at four different periods in history?

My People

The night is beautiful,
So the faces of my people.

The stars are beautiful,
So the eyes of my people.

Beautiful, also, is the sun.
Beautiful, also, are the souls of my people.

☑ **COMPARE AND CONTRAST** Why does this poem compare "his people" to the night, the stars, and the sun?

The Negro Mother

Children, I come back today
To tell you a story of the long dark way
That I had to climb, that I had to know
In order that the race might live and grow.
Look at my face—dark as the night—
Yet shining like the sun with love's true light.
I am the child they stole from the sand
Three hundred years ago in Africa's land.
I am the dark girl who crossed the wide sea
Carrying in my body the seed of the free.

I am the woman who worked in the field
Bringing the cotton and the corn to yield.
I am the one who labored as a slave,
Beaten and mistreated for the work that I gave—
Children sold away from me, husband sold, too.
No safety, no love, no respect was I due.
Three hundred years in the deepest South:
But God put a song and a prayer in my mouth.
God put a dream like steel in my soul.
Now, through my children, I'm reaching the goal.
Now, through my children, young and free,
I realize the blessings denied to me.
I couldn't read then. I couldn't write.
I had nothing, back there in the night.
Sometimes, the valley was filled with tears,
But I kept trudging on through the lonely years.
Sometimes, the road was hot with sun,
But I had to keep on till my work was done:
I had to keep on! No stopping for me—
I was the seed of the coming Free.
I nourished the dream that nothing could smother
Deep in my breast—the Negro mother.
I had only hope then, but now through you,
Dark ones of today, my dreams must come true:
All you dark children in the world out there,
Remember my sweat, my pain, my despair.
Remember my years, heavy with sorrow—
And make of those years a torch for tomorrow.
Make of my past a road to the light
Out of the darkness, the ignorance, the night.
Lift high my banner out of the dust.
Stand like free men supporting my trust.
Believe in the right, let none push you back.
Remember the whip and the slaver's track.
Remember how the strong in struggle and strife
Still bar you the way, and deny you life—
But march ever forward, breaking down bars.
Look ever upward at the sun and the stars.
Oh, my dark children, may my dreams and my prayers
Impel you forever up the great stairs—
For I will be with you till no white brother
Dares keep down the children of the Negro mother.

☑ **SUMMARIZE** How would you summarize the message of this poem?

Harlem

What happens to a dream deferred?
    Does it dry up
    like a raisin in the sun?
    Or fester like a sore—
    And then run?
    Does it stink like rotten meat?
    Or crust and sugar over—
    like a syrupy sweet?

    Maybe it just sags
    like a heavy load.

    Or does it explode?

☑ **DETERMINE MEANING** What is the meaning of the phrase "a dream deferred"?

☑ ASSESSMENT

1. **Analyze Style and Rhetoric** In the first two poems, Hughes repeats words and sentence structures. What effect does this technique create?

2. **Identify Author's Point of View** What is the speaker's attitude toward his identity as an African American?

3. **Identify Cause and Effect** Hughes was one of the important writers of the Harlem Renaissance, a 1920s creative movement of African American artists and writers. What effect you think Hughes's poems might have had on other African Americans at this time?

4. **Determine Meaning** What is the political message of "Harlem"?

5. **Draw Inferences** Many of Hughes's poems reference women or mothers. How does this connect these poems to the social changes unfolding in the 1920s?

Go online to PearsonSchool.com/CASS and use the texts, quizzes, interactivities, Interactive Reading Notepads, Flipped Videos, and other resources from this Topic to prepare for the Topic Test.

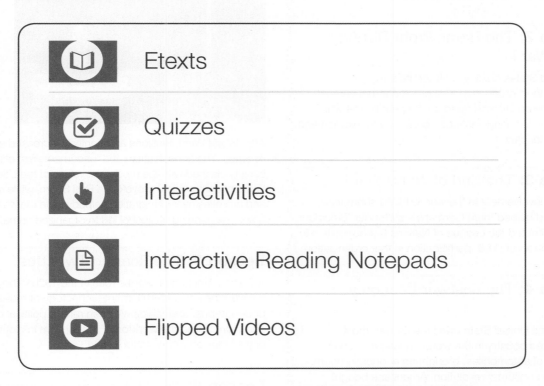

Etexts

Quizzes

Interactivities

Interactive Reading Notepads

Flipped Videos

While online you can also check the progress you've made learning the topic and course content by viewing your grades, test scores, and assignment status.

LESSON SUMMARIES

Use these Lesson Summaries, and the longer versions available online, to review the key ideas for each lesson in this Topic.

Lesson 1: America Enters World War I

In Europe a political assassination, an arms race, nationalism, and a system of alliances helped set off World War I in 1914. The United States tried to remain neutral but entered the war on the side of the Allies in 1917.

Lesson 2: The Home Front During World War I

The United States quickly enlarged its army and increased food production. Congress banned certain publications and limited freedom of speech. The war brought social change as jobs opened up for women and African Americans.

Lesson 3: The End of World War I

America's involvement in the war reduced submarine attacks and helped force Germany's surrender. President Wilson promoted the League of Nations but opposition in Congress stopped U.S. participation in that organization.

Lesson 4: The Postwar Economy Booms

By 1920, the United States was the richest, most industrialized country in the world. Mass production, especially of automobiles, brought an economic boom. During the consumer revolution, Americans bought goods and stocks on credit. The suburbs grew as more people used their cars to commute.

Lesson 5: Government in the 1920s

President Warren Harding, elected in 1920, reduced regulations on business. His administration was rocked by bribery scandals. After Harding's death, President Calvin Coolidge established a more honest administration that also favored big business.

Lesson 6: An Unsettled Society

After World War I, tensions and conflicts increased across America. The conservatism and fundamentalism of rural society clashed with the modernist values of the cities. Fears of communism provoked a Red Scare, while racism and anxieties over immigration helped revive the Ku Klux Klan. The banning of alcohol led to organized crime.

Lesson 7: The Roaring Twenties

As urban Americans' wages rose in the 1920s, they enjoyed the new entertainment technology of movies, phonographs, and radios. Women ran for political office and more joined the workforce. Modernism in clothing, psychology and the arts took hold.

Lesson 8: The Harlem Renaissance

Millions of African Americans left the South to find jobs in northern cities, where they developed middle class communities and a growing political voice. Harlem in New York City became the center of a creative community producing influential music, literature and art.

VISUAL REVIEW

Use these graphics to review some of the key terms, people, and ideas from this Topic.

Causes and Effects of America's Entry into World War I

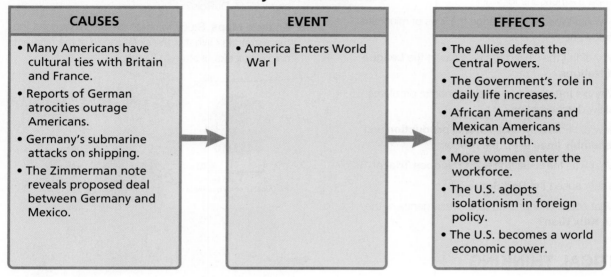

CAUSES	EVENT	EFFECTS
• Many Americans have cultural ties with Britain and France. • Reports of German atrocities outrage Americans. • Germany's submarine attacks on shipping. • The Zimmerman note reveals proposed deal between Germany and Mexico.	• America Enters World War I	• The Allies defeat the Central Powers. • The Government's role in daily life increases. • African Americans and Mexican Americans migrate north. • More women enter the workforce. • The U.S. adopts isolationism in foreign policy. • The U.S. becomes a world economic power.

New Cultural Trends

Mass Culture	Radio and movies influence people of different regions.
Prohibition	Crime rises as Americans defy the ban on alcohol.
Modernism	The arts reflect the rapid changes in attitudes and values underway in industrial societies.
Fundamentalism	Many Christians promote a literal interpretation of the Bible and return to "traditional values".
Jazz	New musical genre blends African American and European styles.
Harlem Renaissance	Literature and art express pride and aspirations of African Americans.

Postwar Economic Boom

Bull market in the stock market

Growth of the advertising industry

U.S. ECONOMY IN THE 1920S

Newly available technology

Buying on credit and installment buying

KEY TERMS AND IDEAS

1. Why did the **Zimmerman note** outrage American public opinion?

2. What measures did the U.S. government take to prepare Americans for war?

3. How did World War I change the lives of minorities and women?

4. Why didn't the United States support the **League of Nations**?

5. Why did **inflation** and other economic problems follow demobilization?

6. How did Ford's system of **mass production** and **assembly lines** affect the economy?

7. What was the issue behind the **Scopes Trial** of 1925?

8. What caused the **Red Scare**?

9. What social changes led to the resurgence of the **Ku Klux Klan**?

CRITICAL THINKING

10. **Make Generalizations** What long-term trends led to the outbreak of World War I?

11. **Make Inferences** How did the technologies of the second Industrial Revolution shape the strategies and course of World War I?

12. **Identify Cause and Effect** (a.) Evaluate how the economic boom of the 1920s changed consumers, businesses, manufacturing, and marketing practices. (b.) How might some of these practices have led to economic problems?

13. **Summarize** How did the war affect America's international economic standing?

14. **Draw Conclusions** What was the relationship between modernism and the Fundamentalist movement?

15. **Compare and Contrast** How did Marcus Garvey's views differ from the views of Booker T. Washington and W.E.B. DuBois?

16. **Analyze Maps** Study the map below. What does the map illustrate? What is the significance of the different colored blocks of states?

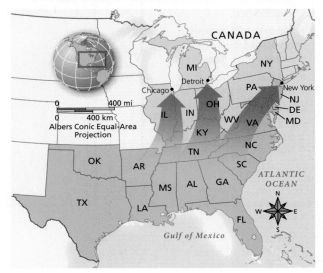

17. **Writing Activity: Use Primary Sources** Analyze this excerpt from a letter from Henry Cabot Lodge to President Woodrow Wilson. Consider how Lodge's view of America's place in the world differs from Wilson's.

> I can never be anything else but an American, and I must think of the United States first, and when I think of the United States first . . . I am thinking of what is best for the world, for if the United States fails, the best hopes of mankind fail with it.
>
> —Henry Cabot Lodge, letter to President Woodrow Wilson, 1919

DOCUMENT-BASED QUESTIONS

During World War I, open debate and political dissent were discouraged and sometimes punished. Read the documents below, then answer the questions that follow.

DOCUMENT A

These excerpts are from laws that Congress passed to support America's war effort during World War I.

> . . . and whoever, when the United States is at war, shall willfully cause or attempt to cause insubordination, disloyalty, mutiny, refusal of duty, in the military or naval forces of the United States, or shall willfully obstruct the recruiting or enlistment service of the United States, to the injury of the service of the United States, shall be punished by a fine of not more than $10,000 or imprisonment for not more than twenty years, or both.
>
> —*Espionage Act, 1917*

> Whoever, when the United States is at war . . . shall willfully utter, print, write, or publish any disloyal, profane, scurrilous, or abusive language about the form of government of the United States, or the Constitution of the United States. . . shall be punished by a fine of not more than $10,000 or imprisonment for not more than 20 years, or both. . .
>
> —*Sedition Act, 1918*

DOCUMENT B

DOCUMENT C

This excerpt is from the trial of Eugene Debs.

> If the law under which I have been convicted is a good law, then there is no reason why sentence should not be pronounced upon me. I listened to all that was said in this court in support and justification of this prosecution, but my mind remains unchanged. I look upon the Espionage Law as a despotic enactment in flagrant conflict with democratic principles and with the spirit of free institutions. . . .
>
> —*Eugene V. Debs, Statement to the Court, 1918*

DOCUMENT D

This is an excerpt from the Supreme Court's decision in *Schenck* v. *United States*, which tested the constitutionality of the 1917 Espionage Act.

> . . . The question in every case is whether the words used are used in such circumstances and are of such a nature as to create a clear and present danger that they will bring about the substantive evils that Congress has a right to prevent. It is a question of proximity and degree. When a nation is at war many things that might be said in time of peace are such a hindrance to its effort that their utterance will not be endured so long as men fight and that no Court could regard them as protected by any constitutional right.
>
> —*Schenck v. United States, 1919*

18. The laws appearing in Document A had the effect of
    A. restricting religious freedom.
    B. ending the right to bear arms.
    C. suspending the right to jury trial.
    D. restricting freedom of speech.

19. **Analyze Images** What point of view is represented by the demonstrators shown in Document B?

20. In Document C, the person being tried clearly believes that the Espionage Act
    A. protects freedom of expression.
    B. is an attack on democratic freedoms.
    C. undermines religious freedom.
    D. would end freedom of assembly.

21. In Document D, the Supreme Court confirms that in times of "clear and present danger" the government may
    A. institute a draft to enlarge the army.
    B. imprison all dissenters.
    C. take control of industrial output.
    D. determine what speech is dangerous.

22. **Writing Activity: Primary Source** Write a paragraph explaining whether you think the government was justified in curtailing freedom of speech after the U.S. entered World War I. Use the sources as well as additional information you have learned about this issue.

End-of-Topic Practice

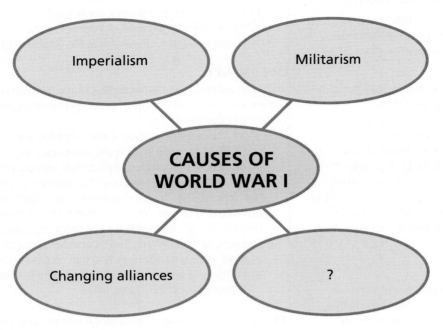

1 What option below best completes the concept web above?

A nationalism

B U.S. involvement

C economic sanctions

D technological advances

---

2 Why might Henry Ford be considered both a successful businessman and a social reformer?

F Ford's use of time and motion studies revolutionized not only the industrial workplace but the family farm as well.

G He was able to maximize profits while improving the lives of his workers.

H Higher wages and a shorter work week gave Ford's employees more money to spend and more leisure time in which to spend it.

I The growth of Ford's advertising department employed many professional writers and artists, leading to a growth of creative job opportunities.

3 As far as the U.S. Congress was concerned, the most controversial political issue raised by the Treaty of Versailles after World War I involved whether—

A ethnic populations across the globe had the right to establish their own national boundaries

B participation in international organizations would draw the United States into unnecessary conflict

C the President of the United States had the right to negotiate a treaty to end an international conflict

D Democrats and Republicans were willing to compromise in order to reach the optimum agreement for all

4 Which statement best describes the effect of the Teapot Dome scandal on the American public as illustrated by this political cartoon?

F Citizens began to realize that petroleum reserves for the military were of extreme importance.

G Citizens recognized the importance of strong government regulation to control the petroleum industry.

H Citizens became aware of the interrelationships among industries including petroleum and agricultural products.

I Citizens lost trust in the executive branch of government due to corrupt and inappropriate use of petroleum reserves.

If you have trouble with...				
Question	1	2	3	4
See Lesson	4.1	4.4	4.3	4.5

CAUSE	EVENTS	EFFECT
Soviet leader Vladimir Lenin encourages worldwide communist revolutions, and some communist revolts break out in Central and Eastern Europe, causing a "Red Scare" in the United States.	Anarchist groups within the United States explode bombs in public places and mail bombs to industrialists and government officials.	Police and law enforcement agencies begin deporting hundreds of immigrants as possible radicals, more on the basis of their countries of origin than their political ideas.

5 How might one interpret the process which led to the establishment of the American Civil Liberties Union?

A The public response to the anarchist threat encouraged Congress to pass strict laws against public protests of any kind.

B The unnecessary deportation of innocent immigrants caused Congress to establish more lenient immigration policies that are still in force.

C The quick growth of communist sentiment among Eastern Europeans caused Congress to prohibit any additional immigration from that region.

D The government's reaction during the Red Scare provoked a counter-reaction to protect civil rights.

6 In what ways did 1920s Harlem embody Marcus Garvey's political vision?

F It was an African American neighborhood with prosperous businesses and a middle class.

G Harlem attracted white audiences to hear African American music.

H It became a haven for African American migrants from the South.

I In Harlem, Garvey established the "Back to Africa" movement to counter the effects of the Great Migration.

> "We claim for ourselves every single right that belongs to a freeborn American . . . and until we get these rights we will never cease to protest . . . How shall we get them? By voting where we may vote, by persistent, unceasing agitation, by hammering at the truth, by sacrifice and work."

7 With which movement, organization, or author might the above quotation be associated?

A the Progressive Movement

B the Anti-Defamation League

C Booker T. Washington

D the Niagara Movement

---

8 In what way might the U.S. approach to trade have been more acceptable to the Chinese than the approach of the other imperial powers?

F The United States funded scholarships for Chinese students to study in America.

G The United States was opposed to spheres of influence and wanted to establish free trade.

H The United States did not ask China to pay an indemnity after the Boxer Rebellion.

I The United States simply wanted Chinese exports.

If you have trouble with...				
Question	5	6	7	8
See Lesson	4.4	4.8	3.3	3.7

[ESSENTIAL QUESTION] What should governments do?

(5) **The Great Depression and the New Deal**

>> Dorothea Lange's photo "Migrant Mother"

Enduring Understandings

- The crash of the stock market, debt of farmers, uneven distribution of wealth, and easy credit all contributed to the Great Depression.

- Unemployment, poverty, and hunger were widespread during the Great Depression.

- The Dust Bowl in the Great Plains destroyed crops and livestock, forcing many to leave the region.

- President Franklin D. Roosevelt sponsored many new programs in response to the Great Depression.

- The New Deal programs greatly increased the size of the federal government.

- The 1930s were a golden age of American culture, reflecting and providing escape from the conditions of the time.

Learn about the impact of Dorothea Lange's photography

Bounce to Activate My Story Video

In this Topic you'll learn about the events of the Great Depression and the New Deal. Look at the lesson outline and explore the timeline. As you study this Topic, you'll complete the Quest team project.

LESSON OUTLINE

5.1 Cases of the Depression
HSS 11.6, HSS 11.6.2

5.2 Americans Suffer
HSS 11.6, HSS 11.6.1, HSS 11.6.2,
HSS 11.6.3, HSS 11.9.7;
Analysis CST.4

5.3 Two Presidents Respond
HSS 11.3.3, HSS 11.6, HSS 11.6.2,
HSS 11.6.4

5.4 The New Deal Expands
HSS 11.6, HSS 11.6.2, HSS 11.6.4,
HSS 11.6.5

5.5 Effects of the New Deal
HSS 11.1.3, HSS 11.6, HSS 11.6.2,
HSS 11.6.4, HSS 11.8.5, HSS 11.11.5

5.6 Culture During the Depression
HSS 11.5.6, HSS 11.6, HSS 11.6.2,
HSS 11.8.8

Key Events of the Great Depression and the New Deal

1929 Stock market crashes; Great Depression begins

1932 Franklin D. Roosevelt elected President

1935 Social Security Act is passed

1938 Fair Labor Standards Act allows workers more rights

1939 The movie *Gone With the Wind* is released

1940 Roosevelt wins third term as President

1925   1930   1935   1940

QUEST!

TEAM PROJECT

Understanding Opposition to the New Deal

As the government took drastic measures to deal with the Great Depression, why did so many oppose these "New Deal" programs? In this Quest you'll investigate this question and then write an essay explaining the reasons for this opposition.

STEP 1

Watch a video about a New Deal public works project. Then discuss it in class or with a partner.

STEP 2

Examine six sources related to New Deal programs and answer the questions attached to each. Prepare to write an essay in which you explain why some Americans opposed the New Deal.

STEP 3

In your essay, explain the problems caused by the Depression and the solutions discussed in the documents. Consider the advantages and disadvantages of each solution.

STEP 4

Reflect on the process of analyzing the documents and writing the essay. Then complete the Self-Assessment.

PEARSON
realize™
PearsonSchool.com/CASS

Go **ONLINE** for complete Quest materials

VIDEO   ETEXT   WRITING   RUBRIC   PDF   ASSESSMENT

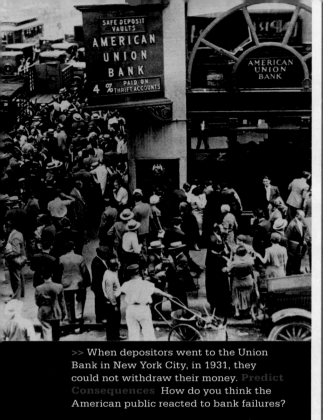

>> When depositors went to the Union Bank in New York City, in 1931, they could not withdraw their money. Predict Consequences How do you think the American public reacted to bank failures?

Bounce to Activate Flipped Video

5.1

During the Roaring Twenties, many Americans enjoyed what seemed like limitless prosperity. Then, in October 1929, the mighty bull market crashed. As production fell and unemployment rose, the U.S. economy lurched into a period of dramatic decline.

>> Objectives

Identify how weaknesses in the economy in the 1920s caused the Great Depression.

Explain why the stock market crashed in 1929 and the crash's effect on the economy.

Describe how the Great Depression deepened in the United States and spread overseas.

Identify the causes of the Great Depression and discuss how historians' differ about them.

>> Key Terms

Herbert Hoover
speculation
Black Tuesday
Great Depression
Hawley-Smoot Tariff
business cycle

Causes of the Depression

Hidden Economic Problems in the Roaring Twenties

At first, some Americans saw this contraction as a regular contraction of the nation's **business cycle**, which explains the periodic growth and contraction of the economy. It most certainly was not regular. Production, employment, and income will normally expand, contract, and expand again over time in a cyclical way. However, a number of factors combined in the 1920s to turn the normal, cyclical expansions and contractions of the nation's economy into an economic collapse in the 1930s. Millions of Americans suffered hardships and despair as a result.

For most of the 1920s, however, Republican leaders exuded confidence about both their party and their country. The Roaring Twenties had been a Republican decade. In 1920, Americans sent Warren G. Harding to the White House, and four years after that, they sent Calvin Coolidge. Neither election had been close.

Once in office, both Presidents watched the country grow increasingly prosperous. Consumption went up, the gross national product went up, and the stock market went up.

No matter what index an economist chose to consult, the conclusion was always the same: Times were good in America—and they were getting better. Republicans took credit for the bullish economy, and most Americans heartily agreed.

Hoover Sweeps to Victory When the Republicans met at their 1928 nominating convention, they chose **Herbert Hoover**—an accomplished public servant—to run for the White House. Born in Iowa, Hoover was orphaned as a child. But he overcame this personal tragedy and eventually graduated from Stanford University with a degree in geology. He became a mining engineer and worked all over the world. By 1914, after amassing a vast fortune, he retired from engineering and devoted himself to public service.

Herbert Hoover came to the attention of Americans during World War I, first as the brilliant coordinator of the Belgium relief program and then as head of the Food Administration. During the Harding and Coolidge administrations, Hoover served as Secretary of Commerce. His philosophy was simple but effective.

He stressed the importance of competition, but he also believed in voluntary cooperation between labor and management. American greatness showed itself, Hoover maintained, when owners, workers, and government officials converged on common goals.

With a solid record of accomplishments behind him and seemingly endless prosperity in front of him, Hoover was a formidable presidential candidate in 1928. While his campaign ads noted how Republicans had "put the proverbial 'chicken in every pot,'" Hoover spoke glowingly of ending poverty in America:

> By adherence to the principles of decentralized self-government, ordered liberty, equal opportunity, and freedom to the individual, our American experiment in human welfare has yielded a degree of well-being unparalleled in all the world. It has come nearer to the abolition of poverty, to the abolition of fear of want, than humanity has ever reached before.

—Herbert Hoover, campaign speech, 1928

>> An affluent middle-class family poses for a portrait in 1924. Many families bought their first automobile and radio during the 1920s as mass-produced consumer products became more affordable.

>> During his 1928 campaign, Herbert Hoover emphasized his belief that competition was vital to ensure robust economic growth.

>> Mechanized farm equipment became more common during the 1920s, but many farmers still used basic equipment such as this horse-drawn plow.

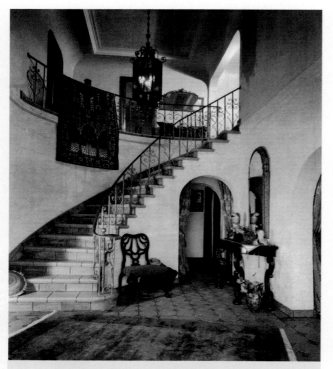

>> The gap between rich and poor widened in the 1920s; the wealthy built large homes and began to fill them with lavish furnishings.

Hoover's contest with Democratic nominee Alfred E. Smith of New York was, in the end, no contest at all. Americans voted overwhelmingly for Hoover, prosperity, and the continuation of Republican government. When the new President took office in March 1929, America was awash in a sea of confidence. Few imagined that an economic disaster lay just seven months in the future.

But even as Hoover delivered his victory speeches, economic troubles were beginning to worry some Americans. The prosperity of the 1920s was not as deep or as sturdy as Hoover claimed. Throughout the U.S. economy, there were troubling signs.

Farmers Face Challenges After World War I

American farmers faced difficult times during the 1920s. Farmers made up one fourth of the American workforce during the decade.

To meet the unprecedented crop demands created by World War I, they had increased harvest yields and bought more land to put under the plow. They also bought costly tractors and other mechanized farm equipment to help them meet demand. Farmers amassed huge debts doing this, and the additional mortgage payments followed them into the 1920s.

After the war, the demand for American crops fell sharply. Despite this drop, postwar production remained high because of increasingly mechanized farm equipment and more intensive farming methods. Farms were getting bigger and yielding bumper crops at harvest. However, farmers were failing to sell off their huge crop surpluses and to pay the debts they owed banks and other institutions.

The result was a rural depression that affected millions of Americans. Hard-pressed to pay their debts, forced to sell their goods in a glutted and competitive world market, and confronted by several natural disasters, farmers did not share in the boom times of the 1920s. They did not have the cash to buy the new consumer goods produced by American industries.

They lived largely on credit from month to month, often teetering on the brink of financial ruin. Any downward slide in the economy was likely to hit America's struggling farmers first and hardest.

A Significant Gap Between the Rich and the Poor

Unlike farmers, industrial workers participated in the great national success story. During the 1920s, their wages rose steadily, as did their disposable income. Many purchased Model T Fords along with a variety of other consumer products. Though they were certainly not wealthy, industrial laborers were

Income Distribution, 1929

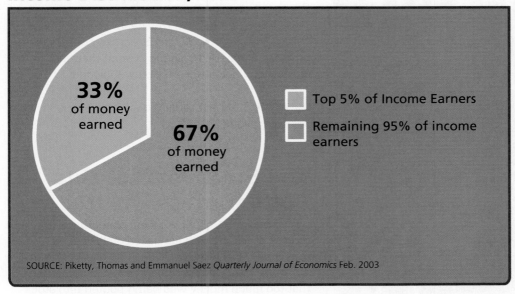

33%
of money
earned

67%
of money
earned

Top 5% of Income Earners

Remaining 95% of income
earners

SOURCE: Piketty, Thomas and Emmanuel Saez *Quarterly Journal of Economics* Feb. 2003

>> **Analyze Graphs** Based on the information in the pie chart, what share of total income earned in 1929 did the top 5 percent of income earners account for?

in a better financial position than their fathers had been a generation before.

But the problem was that while wages rose gradually, worker productivity increased astronomically. Between 1923 and 1929, output per person-hour jumped 32 percent, but workers' wages inched up only 8 percent. During that same period, corporate profits from worker output skyrocketed 65 percent. All these figures pointed to the fact that during the 1920s, the rich became much, much richer, while industrial workers simply became less poor.

In few periods of the country's history have so small a number of rich Americans dominated such a large percentage of the country's total wealth. In 1929, for example, the wealthiest 1 percent of the population earned about the same amount of money as the bottom 42 percent.

Uneven Distribution of Wealth Creates Problems
This uneven distribution of the nation's wealth created economic problems. More than 60 percent of all American families had yearly incomes of less than $2,000 per year. In contrast, 24,000 of the country's wealthiest families enjoyed annual incomes of more than $100,000, which was 50 times more than what most families were earning. But these wealthy families did not eat 50 times more food than lower-income families. The wealthiest households did not purchase 50 times more

automobiles or radios or ovens. The rich undoubtedly spent a lot on consumer products. The problem was that the wealthiest few could not buy enough to keep the economy booming.

A healthy economy needs more people to buy more products, which in turn creates even more wealth. In this way, a healthy economy avoids underconsumption that can limit economic growth. The uneven distribution of wealth in the 1920s pointed to an uncertain future for the American economy.

From the overproduction of the struggling farmer to the underconsumption of the lower-income industrial worker, deep-seated problems created economic instability. Too many Americans did not have enough money to buy what they needed or wanted.

Americans Rely on Credit For a time, the expansion of credit partially hid this problem. Americans bought automobiles, appliances, radios, and other goods on credit. Using the installment plan, they paid a small percentage down and the rest over a period of months or years. By the end of the decade, 80 percent of radios and 60 percent of cars were purchased on installment credit. Americans even bought stock on credit, making such stock purchases on margin. Every year, Americans accumulated more debt. In the past, they had feared

>> Dazed investors gathered outside the New York Stock Exchange as the stock market crashed on October 29, 1929.

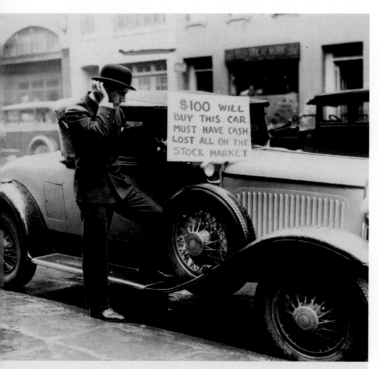

$100 WILL
BUY THIS CAR
MUST HAVE CASH
LOST ALL ON THE
STOCK MARKET

>> Despair gripped many Americans following the stock market crash. Some people who were hardest hit by the crash had to sell their belongings just to pay their bills.

debt and put off buying goods until they had all of the cash to pay for those items.

Easy credit changed this behavior during the 1920s. But the growing credit burden could mask the problem of Americans living beyond their means for only so long before the economy imploded.

☑ **RECALL** What problem did farmers face following World War I?

The Stock Market Hits Bottom

By 1929, some economists were observing that soaring stock prices were based on little more than confidence. The prices had no basis in reality. Although other experts disagreed, it became clear that too much money was being poured into stock **speculation**, as investors gambled (often with money they did not even have) on high-risk stocks in hopes of turning a quick profit. If the market's upward climb suddenly reversed course, many investors would face economic devastation.

On September 3, 1929, the stock market began to sputter and fall. Prices peaked and then slid downward in an uneven way. At the end of October, however, the slide gave way to a free fall.

After the Dow Jones average dropped 21 points in one hour on October 23, many investors concluded that the boom was over. They had lost confidence—the very thing that had kept the market up for so long.

The next day, October 24, came to be known as Black Thursday. With confidence in the stock market failing, nervous investors started to sell. Stock in General Electric that once sold at $400 a share plunged to $283. Across the United States, investors raced to pull their money out of the stock market. On October 29, **Black Tuesday**, the bottom fell out. More than 16 million shares were sold as the stock market collapsed in the Great Crash. Billions of dollars were lost. Whole fortunes were wiped out in hours. Many speculators who had bought stock on margin lost everything they had. President Hoover tried to soothe Americans by insisting that the "business of the country is on a sound and prosperous basis." But by November 13, the Dow Jones average had dropped like a brick from its September high of 381 to 198.7. The Great Crash represented a rare extreme in the nation's business cycle and a turning point for the American economy.

☑ **IDENTIFY** What is stock speculation?

ECONOMIC TRENDS & THE GREAT DEPRESSION

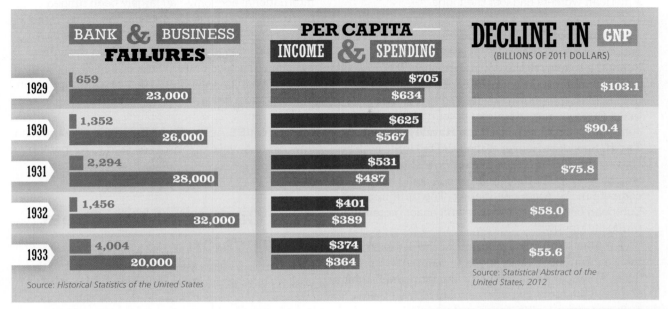

	BANK & BUSINESS FAILURES		PER CAPITA INCOME & SPENDING		DECLINE IN GNP (BILLIONS OF 2011 DOLLARS)
1929	659	23,000	$705	$634	$103.1
1930	1,352	26,000	$625	$567	$90.4
1931	2,294	28,000	$531	$487	$75.8
1932	1,456	32,000	$401	$389	$58.0
1933	4,004	20,000	$374	$364	$55.6

Source: *Historical Statistics of the United States*

Source: *Statistical Abstract of the United States, 2012*

>> **Analyze Graphs** According to the Per Capita Income and Spending graph were Americans as a whole going into debt during the depression, or were they "just getting by"?

Bounce to Activate Chart

The Great Depression Begins

The stock market crash marked the beginning of the **Great Depression**, a period lasting from 1929 to 1941 in which the economy faltered and unemployment soared. Though it did not start the depression by itself, the crash sparked a chain of events that quickened the collapse of the U.S. economy.

Bank Failures Occur Across the Nation One of the first institutions to feel the effects of the stock market crash was the country's banking system. The crisis in confidence continued as frightened depositors feared for their money and tried to withdraw it from their banks. Few banks could survive a sustained "run" of requests by depositors for their money. In 1929, some 641 commercial banks failed. A year later, 1,350 failed. And a year after that, 1,700 went under. By 1932, many Americans feared that no banks would be left standing.

Another cause of many bank failures was misguided monetary policy by the Federal Reserve. During the 1920s, the Federal Reserve, which regulates the amount of money in circulation, cut interest rates to stimulate economic growth. But in 1929, worried about investors speculating too much with borrowed money, the "Fed" limited the money supply to discourage lending. As a result, there was too little money in circulation to help the economy after the stock market crash. When plummeting stock prices sent investors to the banks to secure whatever hard money they had left, the banks were cleaned out of currency and forced to close.

Decreasing Demand Proves Challenging for Businesses Banks were not the only institutions to face the harsh financial realities of the depression. The collapse of stock prices, combined with reduced consumer spending, spelled trouble for American business. Business leaders believed that the survival of their companies depended on production cutbacks, to maintain price levels, and layoffs, to reduce payroll. While their stocks were still falling, companies began closing plants and forcing workers onto the growing ranks of the unemployed. In August 1931, Henry Ford closed several of his Detroit automobile factories, putting nearly 75,000 people out of work.

Like a snowball rolling downhill, the problem of production cuts kept getting bigger and bigger. As businesses closed plants and fired workers to save money, consumers spent less. So businesses cut production even more, closing more plants and firing more workers. By 1933, nearly 25 percent of all American workers had lost their jobs.

The Impact of Tariffs New tariffs compounded the nation's woes and helped to spread the depression. Intending to reverse the downward slide, the government moved to protect American products from foreign competition by raising tariffs, the taxes on goods imported from other countries. In June 1930, Congress passed the **Hawley-Smoot Tariff**. President Hoover signed the bill into law. The Hawley-Smoot Tariff raised taxes on foreign imports to such a level that the foreign goods could not compete in the American market. The tariff inspired European countries to retaliate and enact protective tariffs of their own.

Far from solving the problems of the depression, the Hawley-Smoot Tariff added to them. At a time when American manufacturers and farms had a glut of unsold products, the international move toward high protective tariffs closed markets. This closure was not just harmful to American producers. It was equally disastrous to the global economy. The ripple effect caused by the Hawley-Smoot Tariff helped to damage international trade.

Other Nations Endure Economic Hardship
The Hawley-Smoot Tariff was one of the causes of a depression spreading across the globe. As we saw earlier, the European problems of reparation payments, war debt payments, and international imbalance of trade had already created a shaky economic structure. In the early 1930s, the structure collapsed. Germany ceased their reparation

>> The *Brooklyn Daily Eagle* ran a front-page headline that described the fear and panic that spread immediately after the stock market crashed in late 1929.

Bounce to Activate Chart

payments, and the United States agreed to suspend France and Britain's war debt payments. The international economy had largely been funded by American loans to Europe, but the crisis in the United States drastically curtailed those loans. As a result, European nations experienced the same cycle of business failures, bank collapses, and high unemployment as the United States. The depression had become a global nightmare.

☑ **DESCRIBE** As the Great Depression progressed, how did one wave of job losses lead to further job losses?

The Causes of the Great Depression

Historians and economists struggle to identify the exact causes of the Great Depression. Some have stressed a single root cause in their explanations of the financial crisis. The economist Milton Friedman believed that the depression resulted from the contraction in the money supply. The twin events of the stock market crash in 1929 and the run of bank failures in 1930, added to the Federal Reserve's monetary policy decisions, left too little money in circulation for the nation's economic needs.

John Maynard Keynes was one of the most influential economists of the depression. He argued that the lack of government interference in the economy led to the depression. Critical problems in money supply, distribution of wealth, stock speculation, consumer spending, productivity, and employment could have been controlled, he said, by proactive government policies.

Keynes's work points to a fundamental difference between many economists regarding the depression. While Keynes recommended that governments spend more money to keep people employed when the economy slows, other noted economists like Ludwig von Mises and Friedrich von Hayek criticized centralized economic planning and management.

There will never be a fully accepted answer to the question of what caused the Great Depression. But clearly, problems in consumption contributed heavily to it. Economic hardships before 1929 in Europe and rural America, coupled with an uneven distribution of wealth and over-speculation in the stock market, created dangerous economic conditions. When this was combined with poor or misinformed economic decisions by Congress and President Hoover, the Great Depression resulted.

☑ **CHECK UNDERSTANDING** What factors contributed to the Great Depression?

☑ **ASSESSMENT**

1. **Summarize** the philosophies that led Herbert Hoover to a presidential victory in 1928.

2. **Contrast** the experiences of farmers with those of urban workers during the economic boom of the 1920s.

3. **Generate Explanations** Explain how an uneven distribution of wealth weakened the U.S. economy.

4. **Apply Concepts** Identify the role of confidence in both the boom and the crash of the U.S. economy.

5. **Check Understanding** Explain how the Great Depression extended beyond the United States and became an international problem.

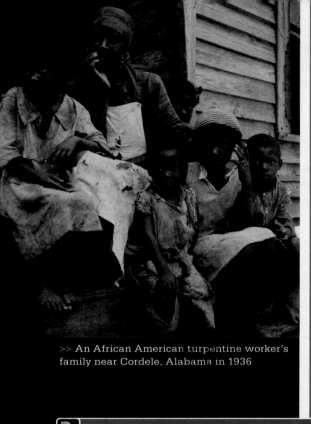

>> An African American turpentine worker's family near Cordele, Alabama in 1936

Bounce to Activate Flipped Video

5.2 The stock market crash signaled the end of boom times and the beginning of hard times. As investors mourned their losses, Americans watched the economy stagger into the Great Depression. In the cities and on the farms, desperate poverty gripped the nation. Even after prosperity returned, those who lived through the crisis would remember the pain and worries of the depression. Tested by extreme hardship, this generation of Americans forged a character and will strong enough to overcome economic ruin and restore prosperity.

>> **Objectives**

Examine the spread of unemployment in America's cities.

Analyze the effects of the Great Depression on farmers.

Analyze the impact of human and geographical factors that created the Dust Bowl.

Describe how the Great Depression affected family life and the lives of African Americans and Mexican Americans.

>> **Key Terms**

bread line
Hooverville
tenant farmer
Dust Bowl
Okies
repatriation

Americans Suffer

Economic Hardship Shakes the Cities

The Great Depression had a deep and lasting impact on the lives of the people who lived through it.

Few Americans grasped the underlying problems of the 1920s economy or the subtle reasons for the stock market crash. Fewer still comprehended how the crash led to the Great Depression. But they did understand the *effects* of the economic crisis. Workers understood having a job one day and being unemployed the next. Whole families knew the fear and shame of losing their homes.

The Great Depression touched most Americans because many Americans either experienced or knew someone who experienced the hardships and loss caused by the economic catastrophe. For many, their lives were never the same again.

Unemployment Leaves Families Struggling The threat of widespread unemployment and destitution effected workers in cities and towns across the United States. Between 1921 and 1929, annual average unemployment rates had never risen above 3.7 percent. But then the depression hit, and the rate shot up. By 1933, it had climbed to a shocking 24.9 percent.

Despite this high rate, millions of workers were able to keep their jobs. However, most had their wages or hours cut. Many workers brought home paychecks that were 10, 20, sometimes 30 percent less than their pre-depression checks.

Yet statistics tell only part of the story. The human drama of unemployment unfolded over and over again, in city after city across the nation. For a man employed as a factory worker, the 1920s had promised a chance at upward economic mobility. He had been able to provide for his family, enjoy a decent standard of living, and save something for retirement. Then the depression hit. The man saw his hours cut and his workweek shortened. Eventually, he was laid off. Looking for another job, he trudged from one factory to the next. "No help wanted here" or "We don't need nobody" greeted him at every turn. The man's clothes began to look worn. His collars and cuffs became frayed, and his pants became shiny at the knees. He said less, stared more, and moved slower.

Maybe his wife was able to find work washing and ironing clothes or laboring as a maid. But those jobs were hard to find, too. At home, children ate smaller meals. Water replaced milk. Meat disappeared from the table.

Hunger lurked about the home like an unwanted guest. Sometimes the parents and children received free meals in public soup kitchens. Often the only place for the family to get a free scrap of food was in a **bread line**, where people lined up for handouts from charities or public agencies.

Poverty Becomes a Reality for Many Men like the factory worker just described moved from unemployed to unemployable. Whole families descended into hunger and homelessness. Their dreams of success and prosperity turned into nightmares of failure and poverty.

The Challenges of Homelessness As Americans lost their jobs and ran through their savings, they had to scrounge wherever they could to keep from going hungry. They sold furniture, pawned jewelry, and moved to cheaper lodgings—anything to keep their pantries stocked and rents paid. In many cities, they ran out of money, were evicted from their homes, and ended up on the streets.

Homeless people slept on park benches, in empty railway cars, or in cardboard boxes. Many grouped together in **Hoovervilles**, makeshift shantytowns of tents and shacks built on public land or vacant lots. Homeless people, some of whom had worked as skilled carpenters before the crisis, cobbled houses

>> Unemployed men gathered outside a busy New York City unemployment office during the 1930s. New York police officers stood guard. **Draw Conclusions** Why do you think this unemployment office required guarding?

>> Struggling Americans built temporary shelters called "Hoovervilles" like this in one Washington, D.C. This encampment was home to war veterans, who were lobbying the government for help.

together out of lumber scraps, tar paper, tin, and glass. One of the largest Hoovervilles in the country sprang up in the middle of Central Park in New York City. There, the homeless covered themselves with newspapers, called Hoover blankets, to stay warm at night. They walked around looking for jobs with their empty pants pockets turned inside out, a sign of poverty known as Hoover flags.

Despite the difficulties of life during the depression, many Americans did what they could to boost morale and help their neighbors. During a New York City newspaper strike, Mayor Fiorello LaGuardia read comic strips to children over the radio. In Reading, Pennsylvania, members of the Taxpayers Protection League staged nonviolent protests to thwart evictions. Nevertheless, thousands of other Americans found no such escapes from their misery.

☑ **IDENTIFY** What was a Hooverville?

Rural America Struggles with Poverty

In cities and towns across the nation, Americans faced a terrible plight. The numbers of the unemployed, homeless, and hopeless increased like a casualty list in some great war. In rural America, people fared no better. In fact, sometimes their condition was even worse. Farmers had been suffering even before the Great Depression. Falling commodity prices and accumulating debt had made it a struggle for farmers to keep their heads above water. Many failed to stay afloat and sank so deep that they lost their farms.

Crop Prices Fall But then the bottom fell out of the economy and the depression added more woes. Crop prices fell even further, and new debts were added to old debts. To make matters even worse, the Great Plains was suffering through a choking drought, an ecological disaster that lasted for years. As a result, many more farmers lost their farms and moved. They traveled about the country, looking for work and fighting for survival.

The basic reality of farm life was the low prices paid to farmers for crops they grew for market. In 1919, a bushel of wheat sold for $2.16; in 1932, it sold for 38 cents. A pound of cotton fetched 35.34 cents in 1919; the same pound fetched 6.52 cents in 1932. The sharp fall in prices was evident with other farm products—corn and beans, cattle and hogs. The income farmers generated was not enough to allow them to continue farming. They could not pay their debts, purchase more seed, repair equipment, and buy what their families needed to survive.

Commodity Price Levels, 1919-1932

SOURCE: St. Louis Federal Reserve Bank

>> **Draw Conclusions** Why did commodity prices fall after 1919, even though the Great Depression was years away?

Overburdened by the diminishing returns for their labor, some farmers buckled under the stress.

In Sioux City, Iowa, in 1932, the Sioux City Milk Producers Association threatened to strike if its members did not see higher profits for their milk. When the association's threats were ignored by local storeowners, farmers dumped 1,000 gallons of milk on a road outside the city. Despite such a drastic—and for many Americans unthinkable—action, farmers everywhere feared losing everything.

Losing the Family Farm Between 1930 and 1934, nearly one million farmers failed to pay their mortgages and lost their farms. Banks foreclosed on their lands and houses and repossessed their farming equipment. The bankers sold what they could at public auctions. Some farmers remained on the land as **tenant farmers**, working for bigger landowners rather than for themselves. But another effect was that many people drifted away from their rural communities, and migrated to cities to look for some other kind of work.

Cesar Chavez, who later became a well-known labor organizer, recalled the troubles his proud father had during the depression. A California bank repossessed his father's small ranch, and the family was evicted from their house. Chavez remembered how it felt to lose his home:

> We had been poor, but we knew every night there was a bed *there*, and *this* was our room. . . . But that all of a sudden changed. When you're small, you can't figure these things out. You know something's not right and you don't like it, but you don't . . . let that get you down.
>
> You sort of just continue to move.
>
> —Cesar Chavez

Like the Chavez family, other farmers moved on after their losses. But for those who remained, Mother Nature dealt a cruel blow to already cruel times.

The Dust Bowl Farmers who survived the tumble in prices were still not safe. Through the mid-1930s, a drought in the Great Plains added to their problems. Water was a constant problem in the region. Normal rainfall seldom exceeded the 20 inches a year that traditional American agricultural practices

>> Dairy farmers poured out their milk as part of a 1932 protest. **Infer** What can you infer about the price farmers received for milk in 1932?

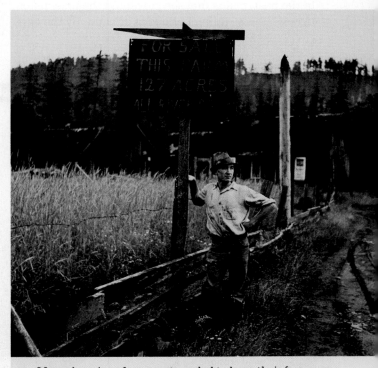

>> Many American farmers struggled to keep their farms during the Great Depression. In time, falling prices and rising debt forced many, like this Oregon farmer, to sell or abandon their farms.

demanded. As a result, droughts on the Great Plains were often more devastating than those in the East and Midwest. In the years before America's western rivers were dammed and irrigation practices became widespread, there were few answers to the drought threat.

New farming methods made drought conditions worse. Intensive farming came to prominence throughout the region in the late nineteenth and early twentieth centuries.

Farmers then had moved onto the plains and plowed under much of the natural grasses in order to plant oceans of winter wheat. And after 1909, there were many more farmers, too. In that year, the federal government expanded the acreage allotted in the Homestead Act to 320 acres per settler. So a new wave of transplants decided to try farming on the often marginal lands that were still available on the Great Plains. All this intensive farming reduced the amount of grassland available to graze livestock, causing overgrazing on what was left. In addition, new tractor-pulled disk plows pulverized the soil, making it more vulnerable to wind erosion. Population growth and shifts in population distribution, along with new methods of farming, tipped the ecological balance of the region. In the past, plains grasses prevented the topsoil from blowing away during periods of drought. By the early 1930s, that dwindling grassy safety net could no longer do the job.

In 1932, the combination of the human geographic factor of loose topsoil caused by overfarming and grazing and the physical geographic factors of drought and high winds resulted in disaster on the Great Plains. The winds kicked up towering dust storms that began to blow east.

These gigantic clouds of dust and dirt could rise from ground level to a height of 8,000 feet. The dust storms moved as fast as 100 miles per hour and blotted out the sun, plunging daylight into darkness.

Most of the dust storms started in the southern Great Plains, especially the high plains regions of Texas, Oklahoma, Kansas, New Mexico, and Colorado. This swath of parched earth became known as the **Dust Bowl**. For people living in these hardest hit regions, depression and dust storms defined the misery of the "dirty thirties."

Those unfortunate enough to be caught in a dust storm were temporarily choked and blinded by the swirling dirt. The storms killed cattle and birds, blanketed rivers, and suffocated fish. Dirt seeped into houses, covering everything with a thick coat of grime. Some dust clouds blew east as far as the Atlantic coast, dumping acres of dirt on Boston, New York, and Washington, D.C. Altogether, dust storms

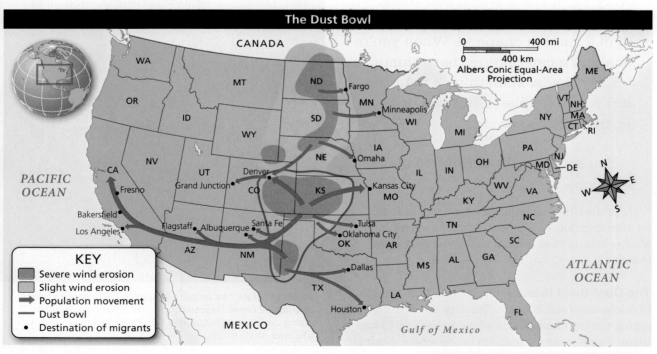

The Dust Bowl

>> **Analyze Maps** Which two states appear to have been hardest hit by erosion? What is unusual about California's location compared to other destinations?

🅱️ **Bounce to Activate Gallery**

displaced twice as much dirt as Americans had scooped out to build the Panama Canal.

Moving Wherever Work Can Be Found Many farm families trapped in the Dust Bowl had little choice but to leave the region. They had lost their farms to the banks and had nowhere to live. Dust storms had destroyed most remaining opportunities in their locale. Although only some came from Oklahoma, Dust Bowl refugees were generally referred to as **Okies**, regardless of their states of origin.

Okie families packed onto rickety trucks and headed toward California or Oregon or Washington, any place where a job might be found. Before the pace slowed, 800,000 people migrated out of Missouri, Arkansas, Oklahoma, and Texas alone.

The collapse of agriculture and the Great Plains Dust Bowl caused millions of other Americans to leave the midwestern and southern regions where they were born. Many migrated to California, lured by the promise of jobs, but were crushed when that promise too often proved empty. In reality, the migrants faced fierce competition from Mexican American, Filipino, and other farm laborers who were also seeking work. Many of them gave up farming and headed for nearby cities such as Los Angeles, San Francisco, and San Diego, hoping to find factory work or to join the military.

In California, the social and economic impact of these migrants was immense. The increased numbers of workers drove wages down. Migrants had to move constantly to follow harvests and formed huge camps that created public health problems.

Other farm families headed north or east to the cities of the Northeast and Midwest, again looking for jobs, shelter, and relief. One of the irreversible effects of this massive migration—some 2.5 million people left the Plains states alone—was that rural states lost population while states with large cities gained population. It was one of the largest migrations in the nation's history, once again changing the nation's demographic patterns.

The Dust Bowl had other effects as well. The farmers best able to survive the Great Depression were the ones with the biggest operations. They often bought repossessed land at rock-bottom prices and expanded their holdings into large commercial farms. The Dust Bowl also motivated the government to help Great Plains farmers. After the initial crisis, immense federal projects dammed western rivers. Dams eventually provided irrigation that made farm profits possible on the Great Plains.

☑ **CHECK UNDERSTANDING** How did some farmers become tenant farmers?

>> Large clouds of dust engulfed farmhouses like these in Stratford, Texas, in 1935. The intensity of Dust Bowl storms caused many to lose their farms to the banks and forced families to migrate.

>> A Missouri family headed west to look for work in 1937. **Make Predictions** What types of opportunities were available to farmers forced to migrate westward?

Hard Times Hit Most Americans

One of the ironies of the depression was the word itself. In the nineteenth and early twentieth centuries, an economic slump was called a "panic" or a "crisis." President Hoover used the word *depression* to describe the state of affairs because he thought it sounded less severe than the other terms. But before long, Hoover's "depression" gave way to the "Depression" and then the "Great Depression." The term described not only a state of mind, but also an economic reality. It showed a despondent America, filled with people overwhelmed by seemingly inescapable poverty. Not only did the depression make victims of the men and women who lost jobs, it also was an economic and emotional crisis that profoundly affected U.S. society.

Families Suffer During the Depression For millions of Americans, the depression was an intensely personal affair. Men who lost their jobs and could not find other work often felt that they had betrayed their families. They had been the "breadwinners," the providers, the ones whose paychecks fed and clothed the family and kept a roof over everyone's head. The loss of a job meant a reduction in status. Different men reacted differently to unemployment. Many labored tirelessly to find a new job, while others sank into shame and despair. Some even deserted their families.

The unemployed were not the only ones who suffered. Men lucky enough to have jobs lived in constant fear that the next paycheck would be their last. They often felt guilty for being employed while so many of their relatives and friends were suffering. Few Americans were spared from the crisis.

Wives and children experienced the pain of their husbands and fathers. Birthrates plummeted to the lowest levels in American history—a sure sign of family distress. Mothers worked constantly to stretch meager family incomes.

They sewed clothes, searched for odd jobs, and valiantly tried to meet their families' needs. With both parents preoccupied with making something out of nothing, family discipline often declined. Some children quit school. Others ran away from home. Families coped with the depression as best they could. Some huddled together, working to survive the hard times. Others broke apart, making those times even harder and lonelier.

Poor Minorities Suffer Disproportionately The depression affected everyone, but it did not affect them equally. Americans on the bottom rung of the economic ladder—the poorest of the poor, often minorities with no financial resources—felt the sting of the depression the keenest. A Howard University sociologist noted early in the crisis that African Americans were "the last to be hired and the first to be fired." In the South, landowners threw African American sharecroppers off the plots they had been farming. Many of these workers migrated to northern cities, but there were no jobs waiting there. Only more poverty greeted them. In 1932, unemployment among African Americans hovered around 50 percent, nearly double the national rate.

However, African Americans had long stood firm against the challenges of poverty. They relied on the emotional resources of family and religion to cope with grim times. During his interview with a depression historian, an African American man explained what the depression meant to African Americans:

> The Negro was born in depression. It didn't mean too much to him, The Great American Depression, as you call it. There was no such thing.

>> Mothers like this one struggled during the Great Depression to find ways to earn additional income, while trying to ensure their children had enough to eat.

🔊 Bounce to Activate Gallery

The best he could be was a janitor or a porter or shoeshine boy. It only became official when it hit the white man.

—Clifford Burke, quoted in *Hard Times*, 1970

Hard times came upon Mexican Americans and others as well. As more Okies headed west out of the Dust Bowl, the competition for jobs between those migrants and Mexican American and Asian American farmworkers in states like California heated up. A flood tide of workers struggled to find and keep farm jobs. Often, Mexican Americans and Asian Americans faced the additional burden of discrimination when competing with white farmhands for those jobs.

In the Southwest, many white Americans clamored for Asian American and Mexican American **repatriation**. Repatriation involved efforts by local, state, and federal governments to encourage or coerce immigrants and their naturalized children to return to their country of origin. Hundreds of thousands of people of Mexican ancestry—many of them U.S. citizens—were pushed out of the United States. Some were deported, others pressured to leave voluntarily. Even so, many more remained. By the end of the 1930s, Mexican Americans were working in most economic sectors of the Southwest, including farming, ranching, and industry.

Compared to the exit of Mexican Americans, the number of Europeans departing was small. Still, nearly 200,000 European immigrants left the United States between 1931 and 1934, the peak years of repatriation. How many of these departures were involuntary is impossible to know.

What is known, however, is that the United States severely restricted all immigration during the depression. Tragically, this policy included denying entrance to thousands of German Jews who were fleeing Nazi persecution in their homeland.

☑ **CHECK UNDERSTANDING** Why did the Great Depression affect minority groups more severely?

☑ **ASSESSMENT**

1. **Generate Explanations** Explain how urban society changed as a result of job loss during the Great Depression.

2. **Describe** the ways in which farmers dealt with the hardships of the Great Depression.

3. **Identify Cause and Effect** Explain how the invention of new farming methods contributed to the Dust Bowl.

4. **Identify Patterns** Discuss the migrations that occurred during the Dust Bowl.

5. **Compare and Contrast** Compare the experiences of African Americans with those of white Americans during the Great Depression.

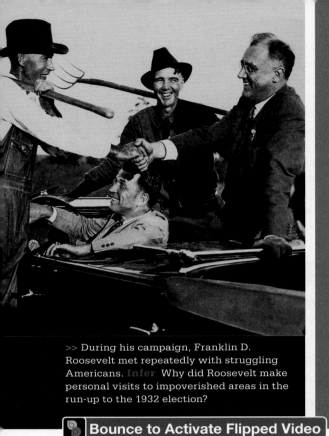

>> During his campaign, Franklin D. Roosevelt met repeatedly with struggling Americans. **Infer** Why did Roosevelt make personal visits to impoverished areas in the run-up to the 1932 election?

Bounce to Activate Flipped Video

From big cities to farms and small towns, the Great Depression spread misery far and wide across America. The unemployed and the homeless crowded into shantytowns. Giant dust storms swallowed the Great Plains. As the crisis deepened, Herbert Hoover struggled to respond to the nation's problems. In 1932, as a result of Hoover's cautious and failed response, Americans would turn to a new leader who called for increased government intervention to try to stop the depression.

>> Objectives

Evaluate Hoover's approaches to resolving the Great Depression and how Americans reacted to them.

Contrast Hoover's approach to the economic crisis with Franklin D. Roosevelt's approach.

Describe the programs that were part of the first New Deal and their immediate effect on Americans' lives.

Identify the New Deal's opponents and their major criticisms.

>> Key Terms

Reconstruction
  Finance
  Corporation (RFC)
Hoover Dam
Bonus Army
Douglas MacArthur
Franklin D.
  Roosevelt
Eleanor Roosevelt
New Deal

Civilian Conservation
  Corps (CCC)
Huey Long

Two Presidents Respond

Hoover's Response Fails

Hoover did not cause the Great Depression. But Americans looked to him as their President to solve the crisis. He tried. Hoover was an intelligent man, familiar with business methods and economic theory. He labored long hours, consulted a wide range of experts, and tried to marshal the resources of the country to solve the problems of the depression. As the effects of the Great Depression on the U.S. economy worsened, he tried several different approaches. In the end, although he failed to discover the right formula, it was not because of a lack of effort.

At the start of the economic downturn, Hoover followed a hands-off policy. Like most economists of the day, Hoover viewed the upswings and downswings of business cycles as natural occurrences. He felt that government should not interfere with such events. Periodic depressions were like storms. They could not be avoided, but strong businesses could weather them without the support of the government.

Relying on Volunteerism A policy of doing nothing, however, was no policy at all. Hoover soon recognized this fact and turned to a policy he had used in the past. As Secretary of Commerce during the 1920s, Hoover had encouraged business and labor to voluntarily work toward common goals. To address the current crisis, he asked business and industrial leaders to keep employment, wages, and prices at current levels. He simultaneously called for the government to reduce taxes, lower interest rates, and create public-works programs. The plan was to put more money into the hands of businesses and individuals to encourage more production and consumption. This, Hoover said, would reverse the cycle that led to the depression.

Lastly, Hoover requested that wealthier individuals give more money to charity. Millions of Americans did give money, clothing, and food to private and religious charities, which then distributed the goods to those in need. The idea was for all Americans to voluntarily join forces to combat the depression.

Voluntary Cooperation Fails Although the plan was well-intentioned, Hoover's program relied too much on voluntary cooperation. The President believed he could persuade Americans to act in the best interests of the country as a whole, rather than in their own best interests. He took care to encourage, not legislate, America's recovery. But volunteerism did not work. Businesses cut wages and laid off workers because business owners thought they had to do so to keep their businesses afloat. Farmers boosted production because they thought that producing more crops would help them keep their family farms. Most Americans followed individual, not cooperative, courses.

Hoover had also asked state and local governments to provide more jobs and relief measures. He had faith in **localism**, the policy whereby problems could best be solved at local and state levels. However, in this severe situation, towns and states simply did not have the financial or human resources to successfully combat the crisis. Making matters worse, the President strongly resisted using federal resources to provide direct relief to individuals. Believing it to be unconstitutional, Hoover opposed public assistance and instead favored "rugged individualism" which allowed people to better themselves through their own efforts. Yet as the months wore on, unemployment increased, charities ran low on money, and local and state governments could no longer plug the leaks in the economy. Some critics began to argue that the crisis demanded decisive federal action.

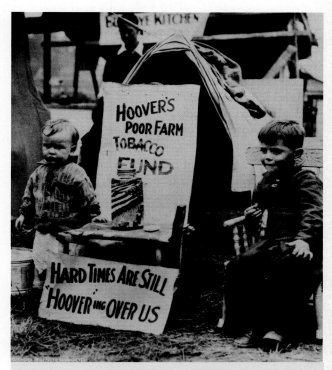

>> Two young residents of a shantytown in Washington, D.C. **Determine Point of View** What do the signs in the photo tell you about how the poor perceived the government's role in the economic crisis?

"IT SEEMS THERE WASN'T ANY DEPRESSION AT ALL!"

>> **Analyze Political Cartoons** What does this cartoon say about the difference between President Hoover's perception of the depression and the reality many Americans faced?

Hoover Reverses Course With Hoovervilles and homelessness on the rise, it became evident that the President's policies were not working. Poor Americans called trucks pulled by horse or mule "Hoover wagons," campfires "Hoover heaters," and cardboard boxes "Hoover houses." The association of the President's name with suffering and want indicated Americans' negative feelings about their leader and his failed policies.

Faced with growing and increasingly harsh criticism, Hoover finally decided to reverse course and use federal resources to battle the depression. Believing the economy suffered from a lack of credit, he urged Congress to create the **Reconstruction Finance Corporation (RFC)**. Created by Congress in early 1932, the RFC gave more than a billion dollars of government loans to railroads and large businesses. The agency also lent money to banks so that they could extend more loans to struggling businesses. Hoover believed that if the government lent money to bankers, they would lend it in turn to businesses. Companies would then hire workers, production and consumption would increase, and the depression would end. This theory, known as **trickle-down economics**, held that money poured into the top of the economic pyramid will trickle down to the base.

Although the RFC put the federal government at the center of economic life, it did not work well under Hoover's guidance. The RFC lent out billions, but all too often bankers did not increase their loans to businesses. Additionally, businesses often did not use the loans they received to hire more workers. In the end, the money did not trickle down to the people who needed it the most.

Despite the failings of the RFC, Hoover succeeded with one project that made a difference. During the 1920s, Secretary of Commerce Hoover had called for the construction of a dam on the Colorado River. By the time Hoover became President in 1929, Congress had approved the project as part of a massive public-works program. Workers broke ground on Boulder Dam (later renamed **Hoover Dam**) in 1930. Construction brought much-needed employment to the Southwest during the early 1930s.

☑ **CHECK UNDERSTANDING** Why was Hoover's faith in localism as a response to the depression misplaced?

Supply-Side or Trickle-Down Economics

↓

Businesses and top earners (the wealthy) receive tax breaks.

↓

Tax breaks allow businesses and top earners to increase investment.

↓

New investment stimulates economic growth, providing new jobs.

↓

Increase in employment raises consumer spending, further stimulating economic growth.

SOURCE: Harvard Kennedy School

>> **Analyze Charts** Supply-side or "trickle-down" economics is a theory that plays out differently based on economic circumstances. In theory, how would "trickle-down economics" generate economic growth?

Challenging Economic Times Lead to Protest

From the Oval Office, Hoover worked hard to end the depression. But to many out-of-work Americans, the President became a symbol of failure. Some people blamed capitalism, while others questioned the responsiveness of democracy. Many believed the American system was due for an overhaul.

Calls for Radical Change Some Americans thought the answer to the country's problems was the rejection of capitalism and the acceptance of socialism or communism. They argued that capitalism created great inequities of wealth and an unhealthy atmosphere of competition in society. In fact, they saw the depression as a sign that capitalism was about to collapse. Looking at the Soviet Union, they maintained that a state-run economy was the only avenue out of the depression. However, even during the worst of the crisis, most Americans were unmoved by communist calls for revolution. Communism's appeal proved no match for Americans' guarantees of individual freedom and dreams of progress and opportunity.

Fascist appeals from the political right also failed to hold any attraction. Economic troubles in Europe contributed to the rise to power of fascist leaders like Benito Mussolini in Italy and Adolf Hitler in Germany. Despite this political shift abroad, fascists failed to gain power in the United States. Although some questioned the ability of America's capitalistic and democratic institutions to overcome the crisis, most Americans never lost faith in their country.

The Bonus Army Marches on Washington Although most Americans did not want a revolution, many did desire substantial changes. In 1932, thousands of World War I veterans marched on Washington, D.C., demanding a solution to their particular problem. They became known as the **Bonus Army**.

In 1924, Congress had passed the Adjusted Compensation Act, which provided for a lump-sum payment to veterans of World War I in 1945. But in 1931, many veteran groups began to call for an early payment of the bonus, arguing that out-of-work vets needed the money to support their families. In May and June of 1932, almost twenty thousand veterans arrived in the capital, setting up camps and occupying empty government buildings. The House of Representatives agreed with their aims and passed a bill to provide early payment of the

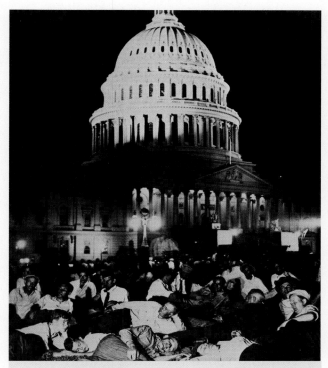

>> Over 2,000 veterans held a vigil on the U.S. Capitol lawn after Congress failed to approve a bill to provide veterans with early bonus pay for their past services.

bonuses. However, the bill was defeated in the Senate in mid-June.

Some of the Bonus Army marchers left, discouraged. Others stayed to continue to lobby for the bill. A riot broke out in July when police tried to evict the marchers from government buildings.

The Protests End Badly Although President Hoover sympathized with the marchers, he called for General **Douglas MacArthur** and federal troops to "[s]urround the affected area and clear it without delay." MacArthur exceeded his order, deciding to move the marchers out of the city altogether. He ordered his troops to ready tear gas and fix bayonets.

The Army force that pushed the marchers out included not only MacArthur but also the future World War II generals Dwight Eisenhower and George Patton. While Eisenhower regretted the use of the Army to solve a political problem, Patton ordered his troops to brandish their sabers in a show of force. Force was exactly what MacArthur used. More than one thousand marchers were tear-gassed, and many were injured, some very badly.

After the removal, MacArthur said that the marchers were a gang of revolutionaries bent on taking over the government:

They had come to the conclusion, beyond a shadow of a doubt, that they were about to take over . . . direct control of the government. . . . It is my opinion that had the President let it go on another week the institutions of our government would have been very severely threatened.

—Douglas MacArthur, 1932

Hoover had not ordered the use of such force against the veterans. Nevertheless, photographs of American troops marching with fixed bayonets against ragged veterans shocked the nation. Evalyn McLean, a Washington, D.C., resident, remembered the army's actions:

I saw in a news reel the tanks, the cavalry, and the gas-bomb throwers running those wretched Americans out of our capital. I was so raging mad. . . .

—Evalyn McLean, Washington, D.C., resident in the summer of 1932

>> General Douglas MacArthur (left) confers with Colonel Dwight Eisenhower (right) as they prepare to clear out the Bonus Army marchers in Washington, D.C.

Any chance that Hoover had for winning reelection in November ended after the summer of 1932.

☑ **RECALL** What argument was made by some in favor of turning to socialism or communism in the face of the depression?

Americans Turn to Roosevelt

In 1928, Herbert Hoover had almost no chance of losing his bid for the presidency. In 1932 however, he had almost no chance of winning reelection. With unemployment nearing 25 percent, people's savings wiped out by bank failures, long lines at soup kitchens, stomachs grumbling from hunger, and the number of homeless increasing every day, the depression had taken its toll. Most Americans felt that their President had failed completely, and they were ready for a change. In July of 1932, the governor of New York, **Franklin D. Roosevelt** accepted the Democratic Party's nomination for President.

Political Success and Personal Challenge
Strangely enough, Democrats had chosen a presidential candidate who had never known economic hardship. As a child, Franklin Delano Roosevelt had enjoyed all the privileges of an upper-class upbringing, including education at elite schools and colleges. From his parents and teachers, FDR gained a great deal of self-confidence and a belief that public service was a noble calling.

In 1905, Franklin married his distant cousin **Eleanor Roosevelt**. President Theodore Roosevelt, Eleanor's uncle and Franklin's fifth cousin gave the bride away. In time, Eleanor would also become deeply involved in public affairs.

Like Teddy Roosevelt, Franklin rose quickly through the political ranks. After election to the New York State Senate, he served as Woodrow Wilson's Assistant Secretary of the Navy. In 1920, Roosevelt was the Democratic Party's vice presidential candidate. Although the Democrats lost the election, many considered him the rising star of the party. Then, in the summer of 1921, tragedy struck.

While vacationing, FDR slipped off his boat into the chilly waters of the North Atlantic. That evening, he awoke with a high fever and severe pains in his back and legs. Two weeks later, Roosevelt was diagnosed with polio, a dreaded disease that at the time had no treatment. He never fully recovered the use of his legs.

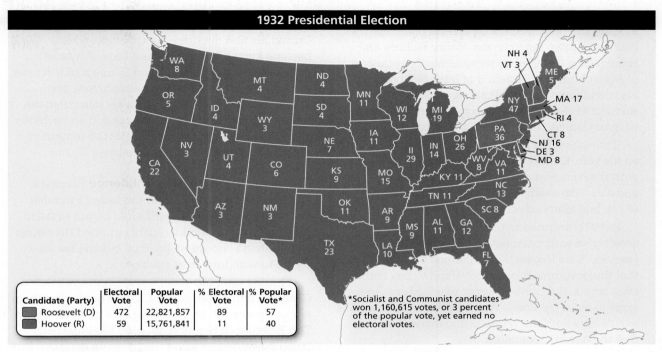

1932 Presidential Election

Candidate (Party)	Electoral Vote	Popular Vote	% Electoral Vote	% Popular Vote*
Roosevelt (D)	472	22,821,857	89	57
Hoover (R)	59	15,761,841	11	40

*Socialist and Communist candidates won 1,160,615 votes, or 3 percent of the popular vote, yet earned no electoral votes.

>> **Analyze Maps** Why is an election such as the 1932 Presidential election referred to as a "landslide victory"?

FDR did not allow his physical disability to break his spirit. With Eleanor's encouragement, he made a political comeback. In 1928, he was elected governor of New York and earned a reputation as a reformer. In 1932, he became the Democrats' presidential candidate, pledging "a new deal for the American people."

Roosevelt Becomes President When FDR pledged a **"New Deal,"** he had only a vague idea of how he intended to combat the depression. Believing that the federal government needed to play an active role in promoting recovery and providing relief to Americans, he experimented with different approaches to see which ones worked best.

> The country needs, and, unless I mistake its temper, the country demands, bold, persistent experimentation. It is common sense to take a method and to try it.
>
> If it fails, admit it frankly and try another. But above all, try something!
>
> —Franklin D. Roosevelt, speech at Oglethorpe University, May 22, 1932

The 1932 election campaign pitted Roosevelt against President Hoover. The two men advocated very different approaches to the problems of the Great Depression. Hoover believed that depression relief should come from state and local governments and private agencies. Roosevelt believed that the depression required strong action and leadership by the federal government. As Hoover correctly noted, "This campaign is more than a contest between two men. . . . It is a contest between two philosophies of government."

Hoover's popularity declined as the Great Depression worsened. Even longtime Republicans deserted him. FDR—with the support of those who embraced his ideas as well as those who opposed Hoover's approach—won a landslide victory, winning the electoral votes of all but six states.

Americans had to wait four long months between Roosevelt's election, in November 1932, and his inauguration, in March 1933. Meanwhile, they watched helplessly as thousands of banks collapsed and unemployment soared. What would Roosevelt do to combat the depression? Even the experts did not know what to expect.

Forming the Brain Trust To help him plan the New Deal, FDR sought the advice of a diverse group of men and women. Among the most influential was a group of professionals and academics whom the press nicknamed the "Brain Trust." Roosevelt, a Democrat, displayed his bipartisan openness by nominating two Republicans, Henry Wallace and Harold Ickes (IHK uhs), to serve as his Secretary of Agriculture and Secretary of Interior. Roosevelt also nominated Frances Perkins, a social worker, to serve as his Secretary of Labor. She became the first woman Cabinet member in U.S. history.

Throughout his presidency, FDR depended heavily on his wife, Eleanor. She traveled widely, interacting with the American people and serving as FDR's "eyes and ears." For example, in 1933, the Bonus Army, which had marched on Washington, D.C.,

in 1932, returned to the capital, once again seeking an early payment of its bonus for World War I service. Like Hoover, FDR informed the marchers that the government could not afford to pay them their bonus. But unlike Hoover, who had sent the army to evict the Bonus Army, FDR sent Eleanor. She sang songs with the veterans and made them feel that the government cared.

☑ **CHECK UNDERSTANDING** In your own words, explain what Hoover meant when he said the 1932 presidential election was "a contest between two philosophies of government."

>> President Roosevelt talked directly to the American public through his "fireside" radio broadcasts. He used these broadcasts as an opportunity to calm the fears of the American people.

 Bounce to Activate Timeline

The New Deal Begins

During his first hundred days in office, which became known as the Hundred Days, Roosevelt proposed and Congress passed 15 major bills. These measures had three goals: relief, recovery, and reform. Roosevelt wanted to provide relief from the immediate hardships of the depression and achieve a long-term economic recovery. He also instituted reforms to prevent future depressions.

Restoring the Nation's Confidence Roosevelt wasted no time dealing with the nation's number one crisis. Late in 1932, banks had begun to fail in great numbers. A banking panic gripped the nation as frightened depositors lined up outside banks, trying to withdraw their savings.

The day after his inauguration, Roosevelt called Congress into a special session and convinced them to pass laws to shore up the nation's banking system. The Emergency Banking Bill gave the President broad powers—including the power to declare a four-day bank "holiday." Banks all over the country were ordered to close. The closings gave banks time to get their accounts in order before they reopened for business.

Eight days after becoming President, Roosevelt delivered an informal radio speech to the American people. This was the first of many presidential **fireside chats**. They became an important way for Roosevelt to communicate with the American people. In the first fireside chat, FDR explained the measures he had taken to stem the run on banks. His calming words reassured the American people. When the bank holiday ended, Americans did not rush to their banks to withdraw their funds. Roosevelt had convinced them that the banks were a safe place to keep their money.

Reforming the Financial System A number of Roosevelt's proposals sought to reform the nation's financial institutions.

One act created the **Federal Deposit Insurance Corporation (FDIC)**, which insured bank deposits up to $5,000. In the following year, Congress established the Securities and Exchange Commission (SEC) to regulate the stock market and make it a safer place for investments.

These financial reforms helped restore confidence in the economy. Runs on banks ended, largely because Americans now had confidence that they would not lose their lifetime savings if a bank failed. Therefore, more Americans trusted their money to a bank, where it could be lended out to individuals and businesses, helping to ensure an adequate

>> Analyze Maps Use the map and the text to describe specifically the number and nature of TVA projects, what states benefited, and how they benefited.

Bounce to Activate Gallery

money supply. The stock markets also stabilized as regulated trading practices reassured investors. Today, both organizations continue to affect the lives of U.S. citizens. The FDIC continues to insure bank deposits so Americans can trust their money to banks. The SEC continues to regulate trading practices so Americans feel comfortable investing in the stock market.

To further solve the banking crisis, FDR took action to combat the currency shortage. In April 1933, Roosevelt ordered individuals and businesses to turn in any gold they owned worth more than $100 to the Federal Reserve and stopped U.S. banks from exporting and redeeming gold. The Federal Reserve began to accumulate and hold on to gold reserves, which it pegged to a certain value. Then in June 1933, a joint resolution of Congress cut the tie between gold and paper money. Americans could no longer redeem their paper money for its value in gold. With these actions, FDR's administration took another step in the shifting trend from a gold standard to fiat money, or money that is not backed by gold or silver, only a government decree. The move had the advantage of making the money supply more flexible and controllable. However, many experts, even some of Roosevelt's advisers, believed that devaluing the dollar was risky and dangerous and would have long-term negative effects.

Reforming Agriculture A number of New Deal programs were aimed at easing the desperate plight of American farmers. For years, the supply of crops grown by American farmers had far exceeded demand. Prices dropped to the point where it was no longer profitable to grow some crops. To counter this, Congress passed the Agricultural Adjustment Act (AAA), which sought to end overproduction and raise crop prices. To accomplish these goals, the AAA provided financial aid, paying farmers subsidies to cut production and forego planting on some of their land. Some farmers plowed under crops and killed off excess livestock. Many Americans believed it was immoral to kill livestock or destroy crops while people went hungry. By 1934, however, farm prices began to rise.

These governmental actions to help farmers proved a mixed blessing for the nation, however. Some farmers didn't qualify for the program.

The increase in farm prices also raised the price of food. In addition, the AAA left many tenant farmers unemployed when large landowners took the land they were farming out of production.

Creating the TVA Americans living in the Tennessee River valley of the rural South were among the poorest in the nation. Few had electricity, running water, or proper sewage systems. In 1933,

Congress responded by creating a government agency called the **Tennessee Valley Authority (TVA)**. The TVA built a series of dams in the Tennessee River valley to control floods and to generate electric power. The agency also replanted forests and built fertilizer plants. These projects created jobs and attracted industry with the promise of cheap power.

Despite its accomplishments, the TVA attracted a host of critics. Some labeled it "socialist," because it gave government direct control of an industry. Private power companies complained that they could not compete with the TVA, because the agency paid no taxes. However, the TVA's successes in improving life in the Tennessee Valley have ensured its survival to the present.

Relief and Recovery During the Hundred Days, Roosevelt proposed and Congress enacted numerous other relief measures. To counter the depression's devastating impact on young men, FDR created the **Civilian Conservation Corps (CCC)**. The CCC provided jobs for more than 2 million young men. They replanted forests, built trails, dug irrigation ditches, and fought forest fires. As time went on, programs such as the CCC became more inclusive, extending work and training to Mexican American

and other minority youth, as well as to whites. FDR called the CCC his favorite New Deal program.

Congress passed a number of other relief acts. The Federal Emergency Relief Act (FERA) granted federal funds to state and local agencies to help the unemployed. The short-lived Civil Works Administration (CWA) provided jobs on public-works projects. On another front, Congress created the Home Owners Loan Corporation (HOLC), which loaned money at low interest rates to homeowners who could not meet mortgage payments. The Federal Housing Administration (FHA) insured bank loans used for building and repairing homes.

These New Deal measures marked a clear break from the policies of the Hoover administration, which had avoided direct relief to individuals. The $500 million appropriated for FERA represented the largest peacetime expenditure by the federal government to that time.

The centerpiece of the early New Deal's recovery program was the National Industrial Recovery Act, which established the **National Recovery Administration (NRA)**. Roosevelt called the NRA "the most important and far-reaching legislation ever enacted by the American Congress." Working with business and labor leaders, the NRA developed codes of fair competition to govern whole industries. These codes established minimum wages for workers and minimum prices for the goods that businesses sold. The idea behind these codes was to increase the wages of workers so they could buy more goods and raise prices so companies could make a profit.

Another major piece of New Deal legislation was the **Public Works Administration (PWA)**, which built bridges, dams, power plants, and government buildings. The PWA was responsible for building many important structures that are still in use today, such as New York City's Triborough Bridge, the Overseas Highway linking Miami and Key West, Florida, and the Bonneville Dam on the Columbia River in the Pacific Northwest. These public-works projects improved the nation's infrastructure and created millions of new jobs for workers.

☑ **RECALL** What was the purpose of FDR's fireside chats?

Critics of the New Deal

While Roosevelt had little difficulty gaining support from Congress for his proposals, a minority of Americans expressed their opposition to the New

>> **Analyze Political Cartoons** Cite evidence from the cartoon that supports the conclusion that New Deal programs had negative effects on the American public.

Deal. Critics on the political right thought the changes the New Deal brought were too radical. Critics on the left thought that they were not radical enough. Several of FDR's critics attracted mass followings and made plans to challenge him for the presidency in 1936.

Too Much or Not Enough? The chief complaint of conservatives against the New Deal was that it made the federal government too powerful. Critics contended that the government was telling business how to operate, spending large sums of money, and piling up a huge national debt.

To many conservatives, the New Deal was destroying free enterprise and undermining individualism. In a 1934 book entitled *The Challenge to Liberty*, former President Herbert Hoover described the New Deal as "the most stupendous invasion of the whole spirit of liberty" in the nation's history. Robert Taft, the son of former President William Howard Taft and a leading Republican in Congress, believed that Roosevelt's programs threatened individual freedom.

In 1934, these critics formed the American Liberty League. Supporters included prominent business leaders, such as Alfred Sloan and William Knudsen of General Motors. Leading Democrats, such as John W. Davis, the Democrats' presidential nominee in 1924, and Al Smith, the nominee in 1928, joined the Liberty League because they felt Roosevelt had deserted the Democratic Party's principles of a limited federal government.

While conservatives accused FDR of supporting socialism, some leading socialists charged that the New Deal did not do enough to end the depression. Norman Thomas, the Socialist Party's presidential candidate, claimed that FDR's only concern was saving the banking system and ensuring profits for big business. The American Communist Party described the New Deal as a "capitalist ruse."

Populist Critics Gain a Following The most significant criticism of FDR came from a cluster of figures whose roots were in the Populist movement. They saw themselves as spokesmen for poor Americans, challenging the power of the elite. Roosevelt's strongest and most popular critics were Francis Townsend, Father Charles Coughlin, and Huey Long.

Townsend, a doctor from California, had a simple approach to resolving the economic effects of the Great Depression. It called for the federal government to provide $200 a month to all citizens over the age of 60. These funds, he argued, would filter out to the

>> Louisiana Senator Huey Long drew attention for his sharp criticism of New Deal programs and his belief that income should be redistributed from the wealthy to the poor through taxes.

rest of society and produce an economic recovery. To promote this plan, he established "Townsend Clubs" and held meetings that resembled old-time church revivals.

Father **Charles Coughlin** presented an even bigger challenge to FDR. Coughlin, a Roman Catholic priest, had attracted millions of listeners to his weekly radio show.

At first, Coughlin supported the New Deal, but in time he broke with FDR, accusing him of not doing enough to fight the depression. Coughlin said that Roosevelt had "out-Hoovered Hoover" and called the New Deal "the raw deal."

Coughlin mixed calls for the nationalization of industry with anti-Semitic remarks and attacks on "communists" who, he charged, were running the country. By the early 1940s, Coughlin's views became so extreme that Roman Catholic officials forced him to end his broadcasts.

Canadian by birth, Coughlin could not run against FDR in the 1936 election. However, he threatened to throw his support behind an even more popular New Deal critic, Senator **Huey Long** of Louisiana. Long was an expert performer whose folksy speeches delighted audiences. Long's approach to solving the depression was his "Share

Our Wealth" program that proposed high taxes on the wealthy and large corporations, and the redistribution of their income to poor Americans.

> God invited us all to come and eat and drink all we wanted. He smiled on our land and we grew crops of plenty to eat and wear. . . . [But then] Rockefeller, Morgan, and their crowd stepped up and took enough for 120,000,000 people and left only enough for 5,000,000 for all the other 125,000,000 to eat. And so the millions must go hungry and without those good things God gave us unless we call on them to put some of it back.
>
> —Huey Long radio broadcast, 1934

Roosevelt viewed Long as a serious political threat. Indeed, a poll taken in 1935 estimated that, under the right circumstances, Long could have attracted up to 4 million votes in the 1936 presidential election. Although not enough votes to win the election, his candidacy could have drawn votes from Roosevelt, damaging the President's chances. But Long never got that opportunity.

For years he had ruled Louisiana as if he owned the state, wresting control of nearly every facet of governance from local and other state officials. On his way to achieving this dominance, he made many enemies. In 1935, a political enemy assassinated Long, ending the most serious threat to Roosevelt's presidency.

☑ **IDENTIFY MAIN IDEAS** Why were many conservatives opposed to New Deal programs?

☑ ASSESSMENT

1. **Generate Explanations** Explain why Herbert Hoover had no chance of winning reelection in 1932.

2. **Compare and Contrast** the political philosophies of Herbert Hoover and Franklin D. Roosevelt regarding economic relief during the Great Depression.

3. **Draw Conclusions** Explain how changing power structures in Europe influenced U.S. politics during the Great Depression.

4. **Compare Points of View** Explain why the Tennessee Valley Authority received support from some Americans and criticism from others.

5. **Identify Central Ideas** Discuss the significance of the Hundred Days.

FDR's goals for the first phases of the New Deal were relief, recovery, and reform. Progress had been made, but there still was a long way to go. Beginning in early 1935, Roosevelt launched an aggressive campaign to find solutions to the ongoing problems caused by the Great Depression. This campaign, sometimes known as the Second New Deal, created Social Security and other programs that continue to have a profound impact on the everyday lives of Americans.

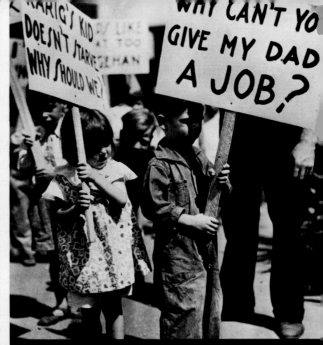

>> Children called attention to the fact that New Deal programs had failed to lift many out of poverty and unemployment by carrying picket signs in support of the Workers Alliance.

Bounce to Activate Flipped Video

The New Deal Expands

Expanding New Deal Programs

In his fireside chats, press conferences, and major addresses, Roosevelt explained the challenges facing the nation. He said that the complexities of the modern world compelled the federal government to "promote the general welfare" and to intervene to protect citizens' rights. Roosevelt used legislation passed during the second phase of the New Deal to try to accomplish these goals. This second wave of legislation addressed the problems of the elderly, the poor, and the unemployed; created new public-works projects; helped farmers; and enacted measures to protect workers' rights. It still focused on relief, recovery, and reform, but with more of a longer-term focus. It was during this period that the first serious challenges to the New Deal emerged.

New Jobs Programs In the spring of 1935, Congress appropriated $5 billion for new jobs and created the **Works Progress Administration (WPA)** to administer the program. Roosevelt placed his longtime associate, Harry Hopkins, in charge. The WPA built or improved a good part of the nation's highways, dredged rivers and harbors, and promoted soil and water conservation.

>> **Objectives**

Analyze ways that the New Deal promoted social and economic reform and its long-term effects.

Explain how New Deal legislation affected the growth of organized labor.

Evaluate the impact of Roosevelt's plan to increase the number of U.S. Supreme Court justices on the course of the New Deal.

>> **Key Terms**

Works Progress
  Administration
  (WPA)
John Maynard
  Keynes
pump priming
Social Security Act
Wagner Act
collective bargaining

Fair Labor
  Standards Act
Congress of
  Industrial
  Organizations
  (CIO)
sit-down strike
court packing

Go **ONLINE** for digital resources

VIDEO   AUDIO   ACTIVITY   ETEXT   WRITING   ASSESSMENT

The WPA even provided programs in the arts for displaced artists, writers, and actors. As Hopkins explained, artists "have to eat just like other people."

By 1943, the WPA had employed more than 8 million people and spent about $11 billion. Its workers built more than 650,000 miles of highways and 125,000 public buildings. Among the most famous projects funded by the WPA were the San Antonio River Walk and parts of the Appalachian Trail.

All of these programs were expensive, and the government paid for them by spending money it did not have. The federal deficit—$461 million in 1932— grew to $4.4 billion in 1936. The enormous expenditures and growing debt led many to criticize the government's public-works projects as wasteful. Some economists disagreed. British economist **John Maynard Keynes** argued that deficit spending was needed to end the depression. According to Keynes, putting people to work on public projects put money into the hands of consumers who would buy more goods, stimulating the economy.

Keynes called this theory **pump priming**. Critics also argued that FDR was using the program to build voter loyalty to the Democratic party.

>> Social Security was established to help retirees. Retired bookkeeper Ida Fuller of Ludlow, Vermont, displayed her monthly check here. It was for $41.30.

Aiding Older Americans The United States was one of the few industrialized nations in the world that did not have some form of pension system for the elderly. During the depression, many elderly people had lost their homes and their life savings and were living in poverty. On January 17, 1935, President Roosevelt unveiled his plans for Social Security.

The **Social Security Act**, passed by Congress in 1935, established a pension system for retirees. It also established unemployment insurance for workers who lost their jobs. In addition, the law created insurance for victims of work-related accidents and provided aid for poverty-stricken mothers and children, the blind, and the disabled. It was funded by a payroll tax on employers and workers.

The Social Security Act had many flaws. At first, it did not apply to domestic workers or farmworkers. Since African Americans were disproportionately employed in these fields, they were not eligible for many of the benefits of Social Security. Widows received smaller benefits than widowers, because people presumed that elderly women could manage on less money than elderly men. Despite these shortcomings, Social Security proved the most popular and significant of the New Deal programs.

Social Security continues today to provide basic economic security to millions of Americans. Its programs act as a safety net for senior citizens, the poor, and others in financial need. Popular support for Social Security continues, although concern mounts over the program's long-term funding and ability to keep making payments.

Supporting American Farms Another New Deal program that passed in 1935 included further help for farmers. When the depression began, only 10 percent of all farms had electricity, largely because utility companies did not find it profitable to run electric lines to communities with small populations. To bring farmers into the light, Congress established the Rural Electrification Administration (REA). The REA loaned money to electric utilities to build power lines, bringing electricity to isolated rural areas. This program had a tremendous, beneficial effect on rural communities. The REA was so successful that by 1950, about 80 percent of American farms had electricity.

New Deal programs changed the relationship of the federal government to the American farmer. The government was now committed to providing price supports, or subsidies, for agriculture. Critics attacked price supports for undermining the free market. Others observed that large farms, not small

AGRICULTURE & THE NEW DEAL

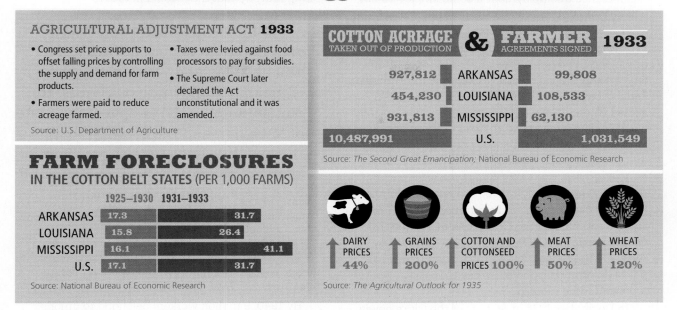

AGRICULTURAL ADJUSTMENT ACT 1933

- Congress set price supports to offset falling prices by controlling the supply and demand for farm products.
- Farmers were paid to reduce acreage farmed.
- Taxes were levied against food processors to pay for subsidies.
- The Supreme Court later declared the Act unconstitutional and it was amended.

Source: U.S. Department of Agriculture

COTTON ACREAGE TAKEN OUT OF PRODUCTION **& FARMER** AGREEMENTS SIGNED **1933**

927,812	ARKANSAS	99,808
454,230	LOUISIANA	108,533
931,813	MISSISSIPPI	62,130
10,487,991	U.S.	1,031,549

Source: *The Second Great Emancipation*; National Bureau of Economic Research

FARM FORECLOSURES
IN THE COTTON BELT STATES (PER 1,000 FARMS)

	1925–1930	1931–1933
ARKANSAS	17.3	31.7
LOUISIANA	15.8	26.4
MISSISSIPPI	16.1	41.1
U.S.	17.1	31.7

Source: National Bureau of Economic Research

DAIRY PRICES	GRAINS PRICES	COTTON AND COTTONSEED PRICES	MEAT PRICES	WHEAT PRICES
44%	200%	100%	50%	120%

Source: *The Agricultural Outlook for 1935*

>> **Analyze Data** How do the data on farm foreclosures point to a need for the Agricultural Adjustment Act of 1933? Did the reduction of cotton acreage have its desired effect on prices?

farmers, benefited most from federal farm programs. Even during the 1930s, many noticed that tenant farmers and sharecroppers, often African Americans, did not fully share in the federal programs. Yet farm prices stabilized, and agriculture remained a productive sector of the economy.

Water for an Expanding West Many of the New Deal public-works water projects had an enormous impact on the development of the American West. The government funded the complex Central Valley irrigation system in California. The massive Bonneville Dam in the Pacific Northwest controlled flooding and provided electricity to a vast number of citizens.

☑ **DESCRIBE** Why was it necessary to establish the Rural Electrification Administration in order to bring electricity to farmers?

Labor Unions Thrive

Even before the Great Depression, most industrial workers labored long hours for little pay. Few belonged to labor unions. During the Great Depression, however, there was an upsurge in union activity. New unions enlisted millions of workers from the mining and automobile industries.

A New Relationship Between Workers and Business Owners Roosevelt believed that the success of the New Deal depended on raising the standard of living for American industrial workers. This, he believed, would improve the entire economy. The National Labor Relations Act was the most important piece of New Deal labor legislation.

Also called the **Wagner Act**, it recognized the right of employees to join labor unions and gave workers the right to **collective bargaining**. Collective bargaining meant that employers had to negotiate with unions about hours, wages, and other working conditions. The law created the National Labor Relations Board (NLRB) to look into workers' complaints.

The **Fair Labor Standards Act** of 1938 provided workers with additional rights. It established a minimum wage, initially at 25 cents per hour, and a maximum workweek of 44 hours. It also outlawed child labor. The minimum wage remains one of the New Deal's most controversial legacies. In the years ahead, the minimum wage would be gradually raised. Today, whenever a raise in the minimum wage is proposed, economists and political leaders debate the wisdom of such an increase. Supporters say such raises are necessary for low-paid workers to keep pace with the rising cost of living. Opponents counter that some producers will pass the wage increases on to consumers in the form of higher prices. They also fear that minimum wage increases will increase unemployment if some employers cut jobs to keep their labor costs the same.

Workers Organize for Gains The upsurge in union activity came at the same time as a bitter feud within the major labor federation, the American Federation of Labor (AFL). The AFL represented skilled workers—such as plumbers, carpenters, and electricians—who joined trade or craft unions. Few workers in the major industries belonged to the AFL, and the AFL made little effort to organize them.

Fed up with the AFL's reluctance to organize these workers, John L. Lewis, the president of the United Mine Workers, and a number of other labor leaders established the **Congress of Industrial Organizations (CIO)**. The workers targeted by the CIO-organizing campaigns tended to be lower paid and ethnically more diverse than those workers represented by the AFL.

In December 1936, members of the CIO's newly formed United Automobile Workers (UAW) union staged a **sit-down strike**, occupying one of General Motors's most important plants in Flint, Michigan. In a sit-down strike, workers refuse to leave the workplace until a settlement is reached. When the police and state militia threatened to remove them by force, the workers informed Michigan governor Frank Murphy that they would not leave.

> We fully expect that if a violent effort is made to oust us many of us will be killed and we take this means of making it known to our wives, to our children, to the people of the State of Michigan and the country, that if this result follows from the attempt to eject us, you are the one who must be held responsible for our deaths!
>
> —Auto workers sit-down committee, Flint, Michigan, January 1936

The strike lasted for 44 days until General Motors, then the largest company in the world, agreed to recognize the UAW. This union success led to others.

By 1940, 9 million workers belonged to unions, twice the number of members in 1930. Just as important, union members gained better wages and working conditions.

☑ **CHECK UNDERSTANDING** Why did workers such as miners and automobile workers feel the need to split away from the AFL and start the CIO?

Minimum Wage, 1938–2013

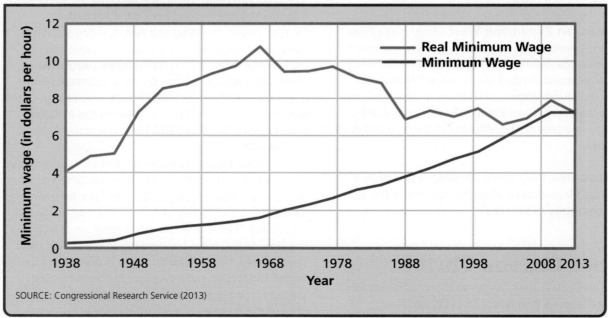

SOURCE: Congressional Research Service (2013)

>> **Analyze Data** The real minimum wage is the constant dollar value of the minimum wage, adjusted for inflation. Using the graph, describe how the real minimum wage has changed since 1938.

Labor Union Membership, 1920–1960

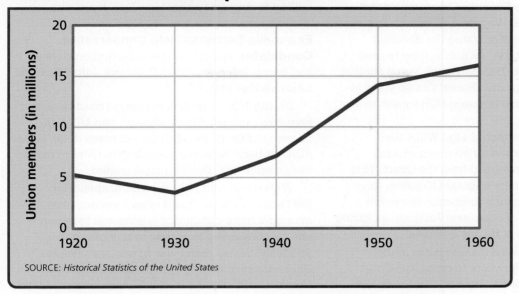

SOURCE: *Historical Statistics of the United States*

>> **Analyze Graphs** What explains the increase in union membership after 1930?

Opposition to the New Deal

Franklin Roosevelt won an overwhelming victory in the presidential election of 1936. He received 61 percent of the vote, compared to just 37 percent for his Republican challenger, Alfred M. Landon. Roosevelt carried every state but Maine and Vermont. FDR entered his second term determined to challenge the group that he considered the main enemy of the New Deal—a Supreme Court that had struck down many of his programs.

Some New Deal Policies Face Judicial Scrutiny A year before the 1936 election, the Supreme Court had overturned one of the key laws of Roosevelt's first hundred days. In the case of *Schechter Poultry v. United States*, the Supreme Court unanimously ruled that since the President has no power to regulate interstate commerce, the National Industrial Recovery Act was unconstitutional. The power to regulate interstate commerce rests with Congress and cannot be delegated to the Executive branch.

One pro–New Deal newspaper captured the mood of many Democrats: "AMERICA STUNNED; ROOSEVELT'S TWO YEARS' WORK KILLED IN TWENTY MINUTES."

Not long afterward, the Court ruled a key part of the Agricultural Adjustment Act unconstitutional. Roosevelt charged that the Court had taken the nation back to "horse-and-buggy" days. He expected the Court to strike down other New Deal measures, limiting his ability to enact new reforms.

Roosevelt's Court-Packing Scheme On February 5, 1937, in a special address to Congress, FDR unveiled a plan that would dilute the power of the sitting Justices of the Supreme Court. He called for adding up to six new Justices to the nine-member Court. He justified his proposal by noting that the Constitution did not specify the number of judges on the Court. He added that many of the Justices were elderly and overworked. Critics, recognizing that Roosevelt's new appointees would most likely be New Deal supporters, called his plan **court packing**. They accused him of trying to increase presidential power and upsetting the delicate balance between the three branches of the federal government.

Some critics urged Americans to speak out.

> If the American people accept this last audacity of the President without letting out a yell to high heaven, they have ceased to be jealous of their liberties and are ripe for ruin.
>
> —Dorothy Thompson, newspaper columnist, 1937

Given Roosevelt's enormous popularity, he might have convinced Congress to enact his plan but he did not have to because the Court began to turn his way. On March 29, 1937, the Court ruled 5 to 4 in favor of a minimum wage law. Two weeks later, again by a vote of 5 to 4, the Supreme Court upheld the constitutionality of the Wagner Act. In both cases, Justice Owen J. Roberts provided the deciding vote. Pundits called it the "switch in time to save nine," because Roberts had previously voted against several New Deal programs. Roberts's two votes in support of the New Deal removed FDR's main reason for packing the Court.

Shortly after this switch, Judge Willis Van Devanter, who had helped strike down several New Deal programs, resigned from the Court. This enabled FDR to nominate a Justice friendlier to the New Deal. With more retirements, Roosevelt nominated a number of other new Justices, including Felix Frankfurter, one of his top advisers.

Indeed, 1937 marked a turning point in the history of the Court. For years to come, the Court more willingly accepted a larger role for the federal government. Yet the court-packing incident had the impact of weakening FDR politically. Before the court-packing plan, FDR's popularity prevented critics from challenging him. FDR's attempt to force a change to the relationship among the executive and judicial branches of government was off-putting to many Americans, even those who had supported him since 1932. Now that Roosevelt had lost momentum, critics felt free to take him on. And even though after 1937 the Court did not strike down

any more laws, Roosevelt found the public much less willing to support further New Deal legislation.

Economic Setbacks Help Conservative Candidates The turmoil over the Supreme Court had barely faded when the Roosevelt administration faced another crisis.

During 1935 and 1936, economic conditions had begun to improve. Unemployment had fallen 10 percent in four years. With the economy doing better, FDR cut back on federal spending in order to reduce the rising deficit. But he miscalculated.

While Roosevelt reduced federal spending, the Federal Reserve Board raised interest rates, making it more difficult for businesses to expand and for consumers to borrow to buy new goods. Suddenly, the economy was in another tailspin. Unemployment soared to more than 20 percent. Nearly all of the gains in employment and production were wiped out.

Largely because of the downturn, the Democrats suffered a setback in the 1938 congressional elections. Republicans picked up 7 Senate and 75 House seats. Although Democrats still maintained a majority in both houses of Congress, Roosevelt's power base was seriously weakened because many southern Democrats already were only lukewarm supporters of the New Deal. Needing their support for his foreign policies, FDR chose not to try to force any more reforms through Congress. In addition,

Unemployment, 1933–1941

SOURCE: *Historical Statistics of the United States*

>> **Analyze Graphs** How did Roosevelt's cutback on federal spending in 1937 affect the unemployment rate?

Bounce to Activate Timeline

the President's attention was increasingly drawn to events in Europe and Asia that would in 1939 lead to the outbreak of World War II.

☑ **CHECK UNDERSTANDING** Why did Roosevelt's critics see his attempt to expand the Supreme Court as a challenge to the balance of power in U.S. government?

☑ ASSESSMENT

1. **Compare and Contrast** Discuss the similarities and differences between the first phase of the New Deal and the second phase.

2. **Identify Cause and Effect** Explain how the second phase of the New Deal affected farmers and changed their relationship with the federal government.

3. **Describe** the New Deal's impact on the American West.

4. **Evaluate Arguments** Discuss the effectiveness of strategies used by the United Automobile Workers' Union to protest General Motors.

5. **Generate Explanations** Explain how the passage of labor reform legislation in 1937 marked a turning point in the history of the Supreme Court.

>> **Analyze Political Cartoons** In this cartoon, what does the artist suggest is the relationship of the new Supreme Court Justices to President Roosevelt? What does Uncle Sam's reaction suggest?

 Bounce to Activate Chart

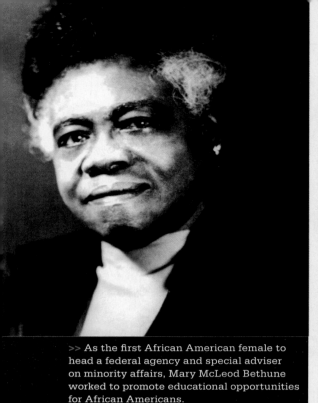

The New Deal provided desperately needed relief from the depression and enacted reforms that guarded against economic catastrophe. It did not end the depression. World War II, with its massive military spending, would do that. Yet, the New Deal mattered enormously because it brought fundamental changes to the nation. It changed the role of the federal government in the economy, the power of the presidency, and the relationship of the American people to their government.

>> As the first African American female to head a federal agency and special adviser on minority affairs, Mary McLeod Bethune worked to promote educational opportunities for African Americans.

Bounce to Activate Flipped Video

>> Objectives

Identify the social and political contributions of Eleanor Roosevelt, Frances Perkins, and other women involved in New Deal programs.

Explain how the New Deal expanded economic opportunities for racial and ethnic minorities.

Analyze how the New Deal changed the shape of American party politics and lessened ethnic and social divisions within American society.

Evaluate the effect of the New Deal on the historical role of the federal government and Franklin D. Roosevelt on the presidency.

>> Key Terms

Black Cabinet
Mary McLeod
   Bethune
Indian New Deal
New Deal coalition
welfare state

Effects of the New Deal

Women Play Increasingly Significant Political Roles

The New Deal provided some women with the opportunity to increase their political influence and to promote women's rights. Foremost among them was Eleanor Roosevelt, who transformed the office of First Lady from a largely ceremonial role to a position of active involvement in the political process. In fact, her more prominent role would set a precedent of increasing involvement in social and political affairs that many subsequent First Ladies would follow. Eleanor Roosevelt made numerous political, social, and economic contributions to American society. Representing the President, she toured the nation. She visited farms and Indian reservations and traveled deep into a coal mine. She helped FDR on his campaigns and offered advice on policy issues. In her newspaper column, "My Day," she called on Americans to live up to the ideal of equal justice for all.

"Eleanor Roosevelt is the First Lady of Main Street," explained magazine writer Margaret Marshall. "She occupies the highest social position in the land. Yet she makes friends on a plane or a train even as you and I." Mrs. Roosevelt's causes included advancing public health and education, promoting the arts in rural areas, and even addressing flood control. She exhibited boundless energy, traveling more than 60,000 miles in two years.

Molly Dewson, head of the Women's Division of the Democratic Party, observed that Eleanor Roosevelt provided women with an unprecedented access to the President. "When I wanted help on some definite point, Mrs. Roosevelt gave [me] the opportunity to sit by the President at dinner and the matter was settled before we finished our soup."

The Roosevelt Administration included the first female Cabinet member, Secretary of Labor Frances Perkins. She played a leading role in establishing Social Security. Perkins also helped win approval of the Fair Labor Standards Act, which ended child labor and established a minimum wage.

However, the New Deal did not fight to end gender discrimination in the workplace. Indeed, some historians have argued that a number of New Deal programs reinforced traditional gender differences. The WPA and other relief programs employed women but made a much greater effort to provide work to men first. For example, women were not eligible to work for the CCC. Domestic workers, a category of jobs held primarily by women, were exempted from Social Security and the Fair Labor Standards Act.

☑ **DESCRIBE** What role did Eleanor Roosevelt play during her husband's presidency?

A Stronger Political Voice for African Americans

When the depression hit, African American workers were often the first to lose their jobs. By 1934, the unemployment rate for African Americans was almost 50 percent, more than twice the national average. Eleanor Roosevelt and others urged the President to improve the situation of African Americans.

As the New Deal progressed, Eleanor Roosevelt increasingly used her position to protest against racial discrimination. At a meeting held by the Southern Conference on Human Welfare, a biracial group that sought to promote racial reforms, the First Lady sat with the black delegates—a daring move in segregated Birmingham, Alabama. When a white police officer told her that she was violating local segregation laws, Mrs. Roosevelt moved her chair to

>> Eleanor Roosevelt visited an Ohio coal mine in one of her many trips around the country. Her outreach changed the role of First Lady, After Eleanor, First Ladies were often expected to be deeply involved in the nation's affairs.

>> Secretary of Labor Frances Perkins, here shaking hands with steel workers, helped secure the passage of key programs that ended child labor and established a minimum wage.

the space between the black and white sides. She then delivered a rousing and provocative keynote address in favor of racial reform.

> We are the leading democracy of the world and as such must prove to the world that democracy is possible and capable of living up to the principles upon which it was founded. The eyes of the world are upon us, and often we find they are not too friendly eyes.
>
> —Eleanor Roosevelt, November 22; 1938

The President invited many African American leaders to advise him. These unofficial advisers became known as the **Black Cabinet**. They included Robert Weaver and William Hastie, Harvard University graduates who rose to high positions within the Department of the Interior. Hastie later served as a federal judge, and Weaver became the first African American Cabinet member in the 1960s.

Mary McLeod Bethune was another member of the Black Cabinet. The founder of what came to be known as Bethune Cookman College in Florida,

she was a powerful champion of racial equality. In her view, the New Deal had created a "new day" for African Americans. She noted that African Americans gained unprecedented access to the White House and positions within the government during Roosevelt's presidency.

Nevertheless, Roosevelt did not always follow the advice of his Black Cabinet. Racial discrimination and injustice continued to plague African Americans. When the NAACP launched an energetic campaign in favor of a federal antilynching law, the President refused to support it. FDR told black leaders that he could not support an antilynching law, because if he did, southern Democrats "would block every bill I ask Congress to pass." Hence, no civil rights reforms became law during the 1930s.

Several New Deal measures also unintentionally hurt African Americans. Federal payments to farmers to produce fewer crops led white landowners to evict unneeded black sharecroppers from their farms. Even though they benefited from the WPA and other relief measures, African Americans often did not receive equal wages. Social Security and the Fair Labor Standards Act exempted domestic workers and farm laborers, two occupations in which African Americans were employed in great numbers.

☑ **RECALL** What role did the Black Cabinet play in the Roosevelt Administration?

New Deal Legislation for Native Americans

Attempting to improve the lives of Native Americans, the Roosevelt administration made major changes in long-standing policies. The 1887 Dawes Act had divided tribal lands into smaller plots. By the early 1930s, it was clear that the act had worsened the condition of the people it was designed to help. Of the original 138 million acres American Indians had owned in 1887, only 48 million remained in American Indian hands, and much of it was too arid to farm. John Collier, the New Deal's Commissioner of Indian Affairs, warned that the Dawes Act was resulting in "total landlessness for the Indians."

To prevent further loss of land and improve living conditions for Native Americans, Collier developed the **Indian New Deal**, a program that gave Indians economic assistance and greater control over their own affairs. Collier got funding from New Deal agencies for the construction of new schools and hospitals and to create an Indian Civilian Conservation Corps. In addition, the Bureau of Indian

>> The New Deal benefited Native Americans as well as other minority groups. It provided funds for the Navajo to open a new hospital in Fort Defiance, Arizona in 1938.

The African American Vote by Party Affiliation, 1932–2012

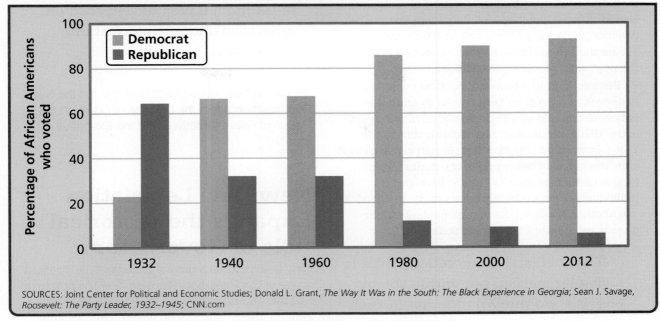

SOURCES: Joint Center for Political and Economic Studies; Donald L. Grant, *The Way It Was in the South: The Black Experience in Georgia*; Sean J. Savage, *Roosevelt: The Party Leader, 1932–1945*; CNN.com

>> **Analyze Graphs** How would you describe the changes in African American voting behavior from 1932 to 2012?

Affairs, in a reversal of previous policies, encouraged the practice of Indian religions, native languages, and traditional customs. Collier also convinced Congress to pass the Indian Reorganization Act of 1934, considered the centerpiece of the Indian New Deal. This law restored tribal control over Native American land.

Although it did not immediately improve their standard of living, the Indian Reorganization Act gave Native Americans greater control over their destiny. But some New Deal measures actually hurt Native Americans. For example, federal authorities determined that large herds of sheep tended by the Navajos were causing soil erosion on the Colorado Plateau.

As a result, the federal government enacted a Navajo Livestock Reduction program, which mandated that the Navajo sell or kill thousands of sheep. The Navajo deeply resented this act. They did not believe that their sheep threatened the soil and they did not trust the motives of government agents.

☑ **IDENTIFY SUPPORTING DETAILS** What was the purpose of the Indian Reorganization Act of 1934?

A New Political Coalition Emerges

By the time he died in 1945, Roosevelt had been elected to four terms as President. His legendary political skills had united an unlikely alliance of Americans into a strong political force called the **New Deal coalition**. This coalition brought together southern whites, northern blue-collar workers—especially those with immigrant roots—poor midwestern farmers, and African Americans.

African American voting patterns show the importance of the New Deal coalition. Before the New Deal, most African Americans voted Republican, the party of Abraham Lincoln. Responding to the efforts of Franklin and Eleanor Roosevelt, African Americans began to vote Democratic during the 1930s. This trend was strongest in the West and the North. For example, in 1934, Arthur W. Mitchell, an African American Democrat, defeated Oscar De Priest, an African American Republican, to represent the largely black south side of Chicago. Mitchell became the first African American Democrat elected to Congress.

The New Deal coalition gave the Democratic Party a sizable majority in both houses of Congress. Before FDR's election, the Democrats had been the minority party in the House of Representatives for all but eight years since 1895. But from 1932 to 1995, the Democrats controlled the majority of seats in the House of Representatives for all but four years. The coalition that elected Roosevelt in 1932 went on to secure the White House for the Democrats in six of the next eight presidential elections.

Besides forging a powerful political coalition, Roosevelt and the New Deal helped to unify the nation. Social and ethnic divisions, so much a part of the 1920s, diminished significantly during the 1930s. Immigrant communities, in particular, gained a greater sense of belonging to the mainstream. Programs such as the CCC and WPA allowed individuals of varied backgrounds to get to know one another, breaking down regional and ethnic prejudices. As one CCC worker observed:

> The Civilian Conservation Corps is a smaller melting pot within the big one. We are thrown together in such a way that we have to get acquainted whether or not we want to. . . . Different races and nationalities look each other in the face, work and eat together for the first time. And it is a safe bet, we think, that this process many times results in the elimination of traditional prejudices based on ignorance and misinformation.
>
> —C. W. Kirkpatrick, CCC worker

☑ **CHECK UNDERSTANDING** How did the New Deal coalition affect the balance of power in the House of Representatives and the Executive branch?

New Deal Legislation Expands the Historical Role of Government

New Deal programs greatly increased the size and scope of the federal government. "For the first time for many Americans," writes historian William Leuchtenburg, "the federal government became an institution that was directly experienced. More than the state and local governments, it came to be *the* government." Moreover, the government began to do things it had never done before, from withdrawing taxes directly from workers' paychecks to distributing benefits to the elderly.

New Deal Legislation Passed After 1935

PROGRAM	EFFECTS
Social Security Act (SSA) 1935	Created a "safety net" in the form of a pension system and unemployment insurance; provided payments to workers injured on the job, the poor, the elderly, and people with disabilities
Works Progress Administration (WPA) 1935	Employed millions of people on government projects ranging from highway construction to arts programs
Rural Electrification Administration (REA) 1935	Provided loans to electric companies to build power lines, bringing electricity to isolated rural areas
National Labor Relations Act (Wagner Act) 1935	Outlawed unfair labor practices; granted workers the right to organize unions and to bargain collectively; created the National Labor Relations Board
National Youth Administration (NYA) 1935	Provided young Americans between 16 and 25 with jobs and counseling; tied to the WPA
Banking Act of 1935 United States Housing	Finalized the creation of the FDIC and made insurance for bank deposits permanent; created a board to regulate the nation's money supply and interest rates on loans
Authority (USHA) 1937	Remedied ineffectual early efforts by the federal government to provide housing for lower income families by assisting individual homebuyers; led to the 1937 passing of the United States Housing Act, which subsidized construction of low-cost public housing by providing federal loans
Fair Labor Standards Act 1938	Expanded the federal government's reach by establishing nationwide compulsory regulation of wages and hours; banned child labor, established a minimum wage of 25 cents per hour, and set the workweek at 44 hours
Food, Drug, and Cosmetic Act 1938	Prohibited the mislabeling of food, drugs, and cosmetics, and ensured the safety and purity of these products

>> **Analyze Charts** The New Deal is considered by some to be a reform movement. Explain whether or not this view can be justified, using specific examples from the chart.

Though the New Deal did not end the depression, it did help restore the American economy. It created the foundation for sustained and stable growth. According to Pulitzer Prize-winning historian David Kennedy, "the unparalleled economic vitality of the post-1940 decades was attributable to many factors. But the [economic expansion] . . . owed much to the New Deal."

An Increasingly Significant Role Promoting Economic Growth With the New Deal, the federal government broke from the tradition of laissez-faire, or leaving the economy alone, which had characterized most of American history. This changed the relationship between government and private business. Instead of being hands-off, now the federal government accepted responsibility for spurring economic growth, or pump priming. For the first time, the government had acted as an employer of the unemployed and a sponsor of work projects. FDR accepted the idea that the federal government had to do something to get the economy going again, and Democrats and many Republicans agreed.

FDR's rejection of laissez-faire policies led a number of New Deal critics to accuse him of promoting socialism. However, many New Deal measures actually strengthened capitalism and helped make possible the economic boom of the post-World War II era.

The FDIC and SEC restored Americans' trust in banks and the stock market, and the significant gap between the rich and the poor remained relatively lower for several decades. The Federal Housing Authority (FHA) provided low-interest loans, increasing home ownership.

The New Deal affected millions of individual workers and their families. The Wagner Act boosted union membership, which continued to grow after World War II. Minimum wage increases improved the purchasing power of minorities and those at the bottom rung of the economic ladder. New Deal legislation created child labor laws, workers' compensation laws, and unemployment insurance, programs that had important and enduring impacts on the U.S. economy.

The New Deal had a great impact on rural Americans. Regional public-works projects, such as the TVA and Bonneville Dam, reduced flooding and provided water for irrigation. Along with the Rural Electrification Administration, these dams brought electricity to farmers in the Southeast and the Northwest. Rose Dudley Scearce of Shelby, Kentucky, recalled what the REA meant to her farm family:

>> Men working on the Arkansas River flood control project funded by the Works Progress Administration (WPA).

🅑 **Bounce to Activate Map**

The first benefit we received from the REA was light, and aren't lights grand? My little boy expressed my sentiments when he said, 'Mother, I didn't realize how dark our house was until we got electric lights.' . . . Like the rest of the people, we changed our storage-battery radio into an electric radio. . . . Next we bought an electric refrigerator. . . . The next benefit we received from the current was our electric stove. . . . Now with a vacuum cleaner, I can even dust the furniture before I clean the carpet, the carpet gets clean, and I stay in good humor.

—Rose Dudley Scearce, "What the REA Service Means to Our Farm House"

In California, the Central Valley Project provided irrigation for the Central Valley by transporting it from reservoirs in the wetter, northern region of the state. The system also produced electricity.

A Federal Safety Net for Those in Need "We are going to make a country in which no one is left out," Franklin Roosevelt once told Frances Perkins. The many programs he enacted to realize this goal led to the rise of a **welfare state** in the United States, a government that assumes responsibility for providing for the welfare of children and the poor, elderly, sick, disabled, and unemployed.

The creation of the American welfare state was a major change in government policy. With the exception of military veterans, most Americans had never received any direct benefits from the federal government. State and local governments, private charities, and families had long served as the safety net for needy Americans. However, New Deal legislation changed the historical roles of state and federal governments. It established the principle that the federal government, not state or local government, was responsible for the welfare of all Americans. In the latter half of the twentieth century, the reach of federal government programs would grow greatly.

New Deal reforms sparked debate over the proper role of the federal government in the private lives of Americans. It energized liberals who would push for an even greater role for the federal government. But it troubled conservatives who argued that the expansion of the federal government limited American rights. For example, many argued that New Deal legislation increasing the strength of unions and raising the minimum wage infringed on the rights of business owners and limited job creation and economic growth. Many also did not support federal welfare programs, because they felt that the federal government was assuming responsibilities that were otherwise granted to the states by the Tenth Amendment. Indeed, this very debate over the role of the federal government in the lives of its citizens divides liberals and conservatives to this day.

Conservation Efforts Produce Mixed Results
Reared in New York State's beautiful Hudson River valley, Franklin Roosevelt had a great love of nature. As a child, FDR also loved outdoor sports and became an expert swimmer and sailor. A number of his New Deal programs, such as the CCC, aimed at restoring forests and preserving the environment.

Other federal agencies started soil conservation efforts. Perhaps most visibly, New Dealers worked hard to end the Dust Bowl, a symbol of the degraded state of the land at the beginning of the depression.

Franklin Roosevelt also continued the conservation work of his cousin, President Theodore Roosevelt. The government set aside about 12 million acres of land for new national parks, including Shenandoah National Park in Virginia, Kings Canyon National Park in California, and Olympic National Park in Washington State.

However, not all New Deal programs helped the environment. Several of the large public-works projects, such as the Central Valley Project, the TVA and the string of dams along the Columbia River, had a mixed impact. The dams controlled floods, generated electric power, and provided irrigation, but they also upset the natural habitats of some aquatic

FDR'S EFFECT ON THE PRESIDENCY

- Increased power of the President and the executive branch
- Made mass media, such as radio, an essential tool in advertising and promoting policies
- Expanded role of the President in managing the economy
- Expanded role of the President in developing social policy
- Won third and fourth terms, leading to passage of Twenty-second Amendment, which limited Presidents to two consecutive terms
- Expanded White House staff to include experts and advisers on domestic and foreign policy
- Shaped the President's image as caretaker of the American people
- Increased the power and involvement of the federal government in American life

>> **Analyze Charts** How did FDR's policies affect the role of the executive branch?

life. Massive reservoirs created by these projects also displaced some people and destroyed some traditional Native American burial, hunting, and fishing grounds.

An Expansion of Executive Power In no area did FDR have a greater impact than on the office of the President itself. The expanding role of the government, including the creation of many new federal agencies, gave the executive branch much more power. New Deal administrators, such as Harry Hopkins, head of the WPA, commanded large bureaucracies with massive budgets and little supervision by Congress. Their authority increased Roosevelt's influence. Indeed, some commentators even began to speak of the rise of an imperial presidency, an unflattering comparison to the power exercised in the past by rulers of great empires.

FDR also affected the style of the presidency. His mastery of the radio captivated Americans. His close relations with the press assured a generally popular response to his projects from the major media. Because he served for such a long time and was such an outstanding communicator, FDR set a standard that future Presidents had a hard time fulfilling.

Later, during World War II, FDR's presidential power grew even greater. As commander in chief of the nation's armed forces, he exercised enormous authority over many aspects of life.

Most Americans accepted the President's increased authority as a necessary condition of wartime. But after the war, they sought to protect the delicate balance between the different branches of government and between the federal and state governments. The debate over the increasing power of the Executive branch relative to other branches is another New Deal legacy that lives on today.

One way that Americans sought to guard against the growing power of the President was by amending the Constitution. When Roosevelt ran for an unprecedented third term in 1940, he knew that he had broken an unwritten rule, established by George Washington, that Presidents should serve only two terms. He won that election and then ran and won again in 1944. But after Roosevelt's death in 1945, there was a growing call for limiting a President's term in office. In 1951, the Twenty-second Amendment was ratified, limiting the President to two consecutive terms.

>> President Roosevelt, here having lunch with CCC recruits, set the standard for all future presidential hopefuls with his ability to relate to and communicate with the American public and press.

Bounce to Activate Chart

☑ **DEFINE** How would you define a welfare state?

☑ ASSESSMENT

1. **Support a Point of View with Evidence** Explain why some people argue that the New Deal reinforced traditional gender differences.

2. **Identify Central Issues** Explain how Franklin and Eleanor Roosevelt affected the civil rights of African Americans.

3. **Generate Explanations** Explain how the New Deal helped to unify people within United States.

4. **Describe** major changes in government policy that occurred during Roosevelt's presidency.

5. **Identify Cause and Effect** Discuss the environmental impact of New Deal programs.

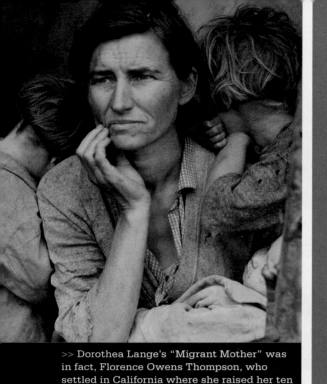

>> Dorothea Lange's "Migrant Mother" was in fact, Florence Owens Thompson, who settled in California where she raised her ten children and passed away in 1983.

Bounce to Activate Flipped Video

5.6 Mass entertainment flourished during the New Deal years as Americans sought escape from the worries of the depression. And, for the first time, the government played an active role in the arts, creating programs that put artists to work. It was a golden age for entertainment, and the movies, music, and works of literature produced during this era hold a unique place in American culture.

>> Objectives

Trace the growth of radio and the movies in the 1930s and how both mediums reflected the characteristics and issues of their time.

Explain the relationship between the New Deal and the arts.

Describe the major themes of literature in the Depression era.

>> Key Terms

Frank Capra
Federal Art Project
mural
Dorothea Lange
John Steinbeck
Lillian Hellman

Culture During the Depression

A New Age in American Entertainment

Entertainment became big business during the 1930s. Large radio networks, such as NBC and CBS, were broadcasting giants while a cluster of film companies—including MGM, Warner Brothers, Twentieth Century Fox, and Paramount—dominated the silver screen. By 1935, two in three homes owned a radio; by the end of the decade, about nine in ten did. In 1939, nearly two thirds of all Americans attended at least one movie a week. Stars in both industries made fortunes and attracted loyal followings. Glossy fan magazines tracked the stars' personal and professional lives.

Temporary Relief From the Challenges of the Depression
Above all, when Americans went to the movies during the Great Depression, they did so as a means of escapism. They sought relief from their concerns through a good laugh, a good cry, a lyrical song, or by seeing good triumph over evil. *The Wizard of Oz*, one of the most memorable depression-era films, delivered all four. It promised weary audiences that their dreams really would come true.

The big movie studios churned out the popular genres of musicals, romantic comedies, and gangster films. Children marveled at the colorful animation of Walt Disney's *Snow White and the Seven Dwarfs*. For a good scare, teens and young adults flocked to *Frankenstein*. Adults watched dancers Fred Astaire and Ginger Rogers glide effortlessly across the ballroom floor in *Top Hat*. And millions wept as they watched the stormy love affair between characters played by Clark Gable and Vivien Leigh in the Civil War epic *Gone With the Wind*.

Depression-Era Films Reflect Social Issues

In the early 1930s, many films reflected the public's distrust of big business and government. Gangster movies, such as *Public Enemy* starring James Cagney, were very popular. These films showed a declining faith in government and law enforcement, with characters turning to crime to survive the depression. But as the New Deal restored confidence, the government regained its glow, and movies began portraying government officials as heroes. In 1935, Cagney portrayed an FBI agent who captured the bad guys in *G-Men*.

Other films reflected the struggle against hardship that many Americans were waging by focusing on the strength of average Americans. Director **Frank Capra** was a leader of this genre. The characters in his films were everyday people struggling with the hardships of the time. In Capra's *Mr. Smith Goes to Washington*, actor James Stewart plays a junior senator who fights against the greed and corruption he finds in the nation's capital. Depression-era audiences cheered Capra's films, which celebrate American idealism and the triumph of the common man over the forces of adversity.

Radio's Increasing Popularity The success of the movie industry was matched by that of radio. The national radio networks broadcast popular shows starring comedians such as Bob Hope and Jack Benny. Americans avidly followed soap operas, variety shows, and humorists, such as Will Rogers. Dramatic shows were also popular. *The Lone Ranger* started its run in 1933 and ran for more than 20 years. The detective serial *The Shadow* began each thrilling episode with the haunting line, "Who knows what evil lurks in the hearts of men?"

In addition to providing entertainment, the family radio provided information. FDR used his fireside chats to explain and promote his New Deal programs. Newscasters delivered the daily news and political commentary.

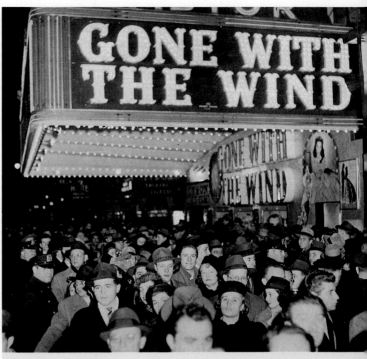

>> Even as the depression continued, Americans flocked to the movies. Adjusted for inflation, the 1939 epic *Gone With the Wind* is the largest grossing movie of all time.

Bounce to Activate Gallery

>> The advent of radio was not simply a way for Americans to listen to music. As the film industry exploded, so did radio shows, such as comedian Bob Hope's variety show.

On at least one occasion, radio listeners had a hard time recognizing the difference between news and entertainment. It happened on the night of October 30, 1938, when millions of Americans tuned in to a drama called *War of the Worlds*, directed by Orson Welles. The Mercury Theatre broadcast was so realistic that many people believed that Martians were actually invading. Panic gripped areas of the country until announcers insisted that it was all make-believe.

The Sounds of an Era Like films and radio shows, various genres of music provided a diversion from hard times. Whether listening to the radio at home or dancing in nightclubs, Americans enjoyed the popular music of the day. "Swing" music played by "big bands" topped the charts. Duke Ellington, Benny Goodman, Artie Shaw, Glenn Miller, and Jimmy and Tommy Dorsey were some of the top swing musicians, a term probably derived from Ellington's tune "It Don't Mean a Thing If It Ain't Got That Swing." The most popular vocalist of the era was Bing Crosby.

Latin music was very popular. The rhythms of the rumba and the samba had a special appeal for dancers, and Latin bands were prominently featured in films and on the radio.

>> Not all popular music in the 1930s described happier days. American blues musician Huddie Ledbetter, better known as "Leadbelly," played music that reflected the harsh experiences of African Americans.

Some genres of music were more somber, reflecting the issues of the time, including folk and ethnic music. Black singers focused on the harsh conditions faced by African Americans.

Huddie Ledbetter, a folk singer known as "Leadbelly," described experiences of African Americans with the songs "Cotton Fields" and "The Midnight Special." Folk singer Woody Guthrie wrote ballads about the Okies, farmers who fled Dust Bowl states and headed to California. Guthrie's song "Dust Bowl Refugee" helped listeners understand the Okies's plight.

☑ **CHECK UNDERSTANDING** Why were many of Frank Capra's films so popular with many Americans?

Increased Funding for the Arts

During the New Deal, the federal government provided funding for the arts for the first time in American history. Recognizing that many artists and writers faced dire circumstances, WPA administrator Harry Hopkins established a special branch of the WPA to provide artists with work. Programs such as the **Federal Art Project**, the Federal Writers' Project, and the Federal Theatre Project offered a variety of job opportunities to artists.

In federally funded theaters, musicians and actors staged performances that were often free to the public. In a series of new state guidebooks, WPA writers recorded the history and folklore of the nation.

Artists painted huge, dramatic **murals** on public buildings across the nation. These paintings celebrated the accomplishments of the workers who helped build the nation. Many of the murals can still be seen in public buildings today.

Photographers also benefited from federal arts programs. The Resettlement and Farm Security Administration (FSA) sought to document the plight of America's farmers. Roosevelt's top aide, Rexford Tugwell, told the head of the FSA, "Show the city people what it's like to live on the farm." Walker Evans and **Dorothea Lange** were among the FSA photographers who created powerful images of impoverished farmers and migrant workers, including Lange's famous photo "Migrant Mother."

When Dorothea took that picture that was the ultimate. She never surpassed it. . . . She has all the suffering of mankind in her but all the perseverance too. A restraint and a strange courage.

—Roy Stryker, FSA, on Dorothea Lange's "Migrant Mother"

Some members of Congress warned of negative impacts of the Federal Art, Writers' and Theatre programs, fearing that they promoted radical values. Congressman J. Parnell Thomas described the Federal Writers' and Theatre projects as "a hotbed for Communists." Eleanor Roosevelt and others defended the programs on the grounds that they did not "believe in censoring anything." Nonetheless, congressional support for the programs declined. Although the Federal Art, Writers' and Theatre programs ceased to exist in the late 1930s and early 1940s, they set a precedent for further federal funding of the arts and humanities in the 1960s.

☑ **DESCRIBE** What was the purpose of the Federal Art Project?

>> The Federal Art Project employed artists to create colorful murals—such as this one at the Coit Tower, in San Francisco, California—in buildings throughout the nation.

🅑 **Bounce to Activate Gallery**

The Depression Era Reflected in Literature

The literature of the 1920s, from authors such as F. Scott Fitzgerald and Ernest Hemingway, sometimes overshadows the literature of the 1930s. Still, the depression era produced some memorable works in multiple genres of literature that reflected some of the issues and characteristics of their unique time.

American Society Under the Microscope

During the depression, many writers drifted to the left and crafted novels featuring working-class heroes. They believed that the American economic system no longer worked and they blamed this failure on political and business leaders. Many artists of the 1930s saw "ordinary Americans" as the best hope for a better day.

The most famous novel of the 1930s was **John Steinbeck's** *The Grapes of Wrath*. Steinbeck follows the fictional Joad family from their home in Oklahoma, which has been ravaged by Dust Bowl conditions, to California, where they hope to build a better life. But instead of the Promised Land, the Joads encounter exploitation, disease, hunger, and political corruption.

>> Like many other authors of the 1930s, John Steinbeck, author of *The Grapes of Wrath* and *Of Mice and Men*, wrote works that focused on the struggles of America's poor and working class.

>> Although comic books were not new, the 1930s saw the birth of the "superhero" comic. The exploits of Superman thrilled comic-book fans in the 1930s.

African American writers captured the special plight of blacks, facing both the depression and continuing prejudice. Richard Wright's *Native Son* explored racial prejudice in a northern urban setting. Wright was an outspoken critic of racial discrimination.

Playwrights Champion Women and the Working Class In New York, some important playwrights had their first successes during the New Deal period. **Lillian Hellman**, a New Orleans native, wrote several plays featuring strong roles for women. Hellman's plays *The Children's Hour, The Little Foxes*, and *Watch on the Rhine* are also notable

for their socially conscious subject matter that reflected some controversial issues of the time.

Clifford Odets was another dramatist who achieved prominence in the 1930s. His plays *Waiting for Lefty* and *Awake and Sing!* chronicle the struggles of the working class during the Great Depression.

Comics Entertain and Inspire On a lighter note, many Americans devoured comic strips and comic books during the 1930s. Among the most popular comic strips were *Flash Gordon*, a science-fiction saga; *Dick Tracy*, a detective story; and *Superman*, the first great "superhero" comic. The success of *Superman*, which began in 1938, quickly led to a radio show and later to a popular television series and several feature films. *Superman* reassured Americans that ordinary citizens, like mild-mannered Clark Kent, could overcome evil.

☑ **RECALL** What were some themes common to Depression-era literature?

☑ ASSESSMENT

1. **Generate Explanations** Explain how music helped to unify people during the Great Depression.

2. **Apply Concepts** Discuss the relationship between escapism and American entertainment during the 1930s.

3. **Compare Points of View** Explain why some people criticized the New Deal's federal arts programs while others defended them.

4. **Draw Conclusions** Explain how the U.S. entertainment industry changed during the 1930s.

5. **Make Generalizations** Explain why John Steinbeck's *The Grapes of Wrath* achieved so much success during the 1930s.

Go online to PearsonSchool.com/CASS and use
the texts, quizzes, interactivities, Interactive Reading Notepads,
Flipped Videos, and other resources from this Topic to prepare
for the Topic Test.

Etexts

Quizzes

Interactivities

Interactive Reading Notepads

Flipped Videos

While online you can also
check the progress you've
made learning the topic and
course content by viewing
your grades, test scores,
and assignment status.

LESSON SUMMARIES

Use these Lesson Summaries, and the longer versions available online, to review the key ideas for each lesson in this Topic.

Lesson 1: Causes of the Depression

The prosperity of the 1920s masked deep economic problems. Although some people had become very rich, they could not buy enough goods to keep the economy strong. In addition, too much money was poured into buying stocks. The stock market crash of 1929 marked the beginning of the Great Depression, which lasted until 1941.

Lesson 2: Americans Suffer

Unemployment rose dramatically during the Great Depression. Americans lost their homes and were forced to migrate in search of work. African Americans in the South moved north. For many, the Great Depression was a time of despair.

Lesson 3: Two Presidents Respond

President Hoover's policies in response to the Great Depression were deeply unpopular. In 1932 Franklin D. Roosevelt was elected President. Roosevelt introduced the first New Deal, which put millions back to work building bridges, dams, and government buildings, providing electricity, and planting forests.

Lesson 4: The New Deal Expands

Roosevelt expanded the New Deal by providing jobs and introducing Social Security. New laws expanded workers' rights, established a minimum wage, and outlawed child labor. The Supreme Court resisted some key laws of the New Deal, but began to accept a larger role for the federal government.

Lesson 5: Effects of the New Deal

The New Deal brought more women and African Americans to positions of political influence. American Indians gained new schools and hospitals as well as control over their lands. New Deal programs increased the size of the government and introduced elements of a welfare state by providing for the poor, elderly, sick, and unemployed.

Lesson 6: Culture During the Depression

Entertainment became big business during the 1930s. Americans went to the movies to escape their worries, while radios brought entertainment and Roosevelt's broadcasts into the home. Swing music and the blues flourished. The federal government funded the arts. Photographers and writers drew attention to social problems.

VISUAL REVIEW

Use these graphics to review some of the key terms, people, and ideas from this Topic.

Major Causes of the Great Depression

Crop surpluses and debts for farmers

Stock speculation

THE GREAT DEPRESSION

Uneven distribution of wealth

Overreliance on credit

Opposition to the New Deal

CRITICISM FROM THE LEFT	CRITICISM FROM THE RIGHT
• New Deal does not do enough to end the Great Depression. • FDR's only concern is saving banks and big business. • New Deal does not address redistribution of wealth.	• New Deal makes government too powerful. • Increased government role in economy equals socialism. • New Deal destroys free enterprise and individual freedom. • New Deal creates huge national debt.

Opposition to the New Deal

Immediate Effects

- Banking system is stabilized.
- Federal payments help farmers.
- Work-relief programs provide jobs.
- Social Security provides safety net.
- New Deal helps unify the nation.

Long-term Effects

- Power of the presidency increases.
- Government takes active role in economy.
- New Deal coalition is powerful political force.
- Wagner Act protects workers and raises standard of living.
- Minorities and women gain positions in government.

KEY TERMS, PEOPLE, AND IDEAS

1. How did the stock market crash contribute to the **Great Depression**?

2. What created the **Dust Bowl**?

3. Why did President Hoover believe in **trickle-down economics**?

4. What policies were adopted during the **"New Deal"**?

5. What is the economic theory behind **pump priming**?

6. How did **Mary McLeod Bethune** help advance the rights of African Americans?

7. What groups made up the **New Deal coalition**?

8. What characterizes a welfare state?

9. Why did some members of Congress oppose the **Federal Arts Project**?

CRITICAL THINKING

10. **Identify Cause and Effect** What economic problems were developing in the 1920s?

11. **Cite Evidence** (a.) Why were farmers hit so badly during the depression? (b.) How did they cope with the situation?

12. **Explain an Argument** Why was the establishment of a minimum wage so controversial?

13. **Draw Conclusions** In what ways did the New Deal change the relationship between the federal government and state government?

14. **Summarize** (a.) How did the arts of the 1930s reflect the social and political realities of the time? (b.) What sort of subject matter attracted artists and writers in the 1930s?

15. **Make Inferences** Why were conservatives so troubled by the policies of the New Deal?

16. **Analyze Graphs** The graph below shows the parties that African Americans voted for between 1932 and 1940. (a.) What kind of change does the graph show? (b.) Why do you think there was such a dramatic shift in 8 years?

The African American Vote by Party Affiliation, 1932–1940

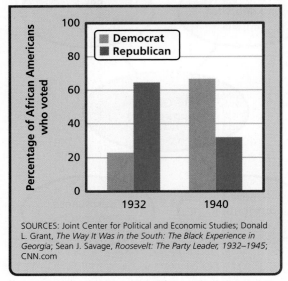

SOURCES: Joint Center for Political and Economic Studies; Donald L. Grant, *The Way It Was in the South: The Black Experience in Georgia*; Sean J. Savage, *Roosevelt: The Party Leader, 1932–1945*; CNN.com

17. **Writing Activity: Use Primary Sources** Evaluate how labor relations changed during the New Deal. Use the excerpt below and your knowledge of the period.

> We feel it proper to recall to you the assurances that you have given many times publicly that you would not permit force or violence to be used in ousting us from the plants. . . . Governor, we have decided to stay in the plant. We have no illusions about the sacrifices which this will entail. We fully expect that if a violent effort is made to oust us many of us will be killed and we take this means of making it known to our wives, to our children, to the people of the State of Michigan and the country, that if this result follows from the attempt to eject us, you are the one who must be held responsible for our deaths.
>
> —*Auto workers sit-down committee, Flint, Michigan, January 1936*

DOCUMENT-BASED QUESTIONS

New Deal programs attracted critics and supporters from across the political spectrum. Read the documents below, then answer the questions that follow.

DOCUMENT A

This excerpt is from a radio speech by the New Deal critic, Huey Long of Louisiana.

> . . . So now, ladies and gentlemen, we come to that plan of mine for which I have been so roundly denounced and condemned by . . . spellers and speakers and spoilers of the Roosevelt administration. It is for the redistribution of wealth and for guaranteeing comforts and conveniences to all humanity out of this abundance in our country. I hope none will be horror-stricken when they hear me say that we must limit the size of the big man's fortune in order to guarantee a minimum of fortune, life and comfort to the little man; . . .
> —*Huey Long, Radio Speech 1935*

DOCUMENT B

This political cartoon was inspired by the economic term "pump priming".

DOCUMENT C

This excerpt is from a speech by Herbert Hoover.

> But their illegal invasions of the Constitution are but the minor artillery with which this New Deal philosophy of government is being forced upon us. They are now using a more subtle and far more effective method of substituting personal power and centralized government for the institutions of free men. It is not by violation of the Constitution that they are making headway today. It is through taking vast sums of the people's money and then manipulating its spending to build up personal power. By this route relief has been centralized in their hands. . . By this route government has entered into business in competition with the citizen. In this way a score of new instruments of public power have been created.
> —*Herbert Hoover, 1936*

DOCUMENT D

This excerpt is from an interview with Claude Pepper, a Florida Senator during the New Deal.

> So, I guess that I came probably under the spell of Roosevelt more than anything else . . . well, my first speech in the Senate, June 17, 1937 . . . was a liberal speech. One of the things that I pointed out was that in every period of the past, whenever there were problems to be met, there was somebody raising the red flag of danger and saying, "you can't afford to do that." Or, "we mustn't do that." And I said, "But the progress of humanity has been achieved by those who have said, 'let's go ahead.'"
> —*Claude Pepper, 1974*

18. In Document A, Huey Long criticizes the New Deal for

   A. its socialist elements.

   B. being too ambitious.

   C. favoring right-wing programs.

   D. not addressing economic injustice.

19. Analyze Political Cartoons Based on Document B, what were some arguments against the New Deal?

20. In Document C, Herbert Hoover is criticizing the New Deal for

   A. increasing government power.

   B. undermining religious freedom

   C. tampering with the Supreme Court

   D. using the arts to promote its propaganda.

21. Document D describes Florida Senator Pepper's

   A. opposition to the New Deal.

   B. support for the New Deal.

   C. fear of new social programs.

   D. warning against government expansion.

22. Writing Activity: Primary Source Write a paragraph explaining whether you think the long-term effects of the New Deal have been bad or good. Use the sources as well as additional information you have learned.

End-of-Topic Practice

1 What role did human emotion play in bringing about the Great Depression?

   A Investors were confident that their stocks would keep rising.

   B Ameriicans bought stock on credit.

   C Americans feared debt and did not buy goods until they had the cash to pay for them.

   D People lost confidence and withdrew their money from banks.

2 During the Great Depression, farmers in the Midwest also suffered from an environmental disaster. What statement below best describes what lay behind the practices that caused the Dust Bowl?

   F Irrigation systems failed during the Great Depression, leaving the land dry and subject to heavy topsoil erosion during windstorms.

   G Unusually high winds pulled up prairie grasses on unfarmed land and blew the soil beneath them in clouds across the level lands of the Great Plains.

   H Because of the economic situation, farmers refused to plant winter wheat, and this left the topsoil exposed to harsh winds from the Rocky Mountains.

   I People did not understand the principles of ecological balance in the region.

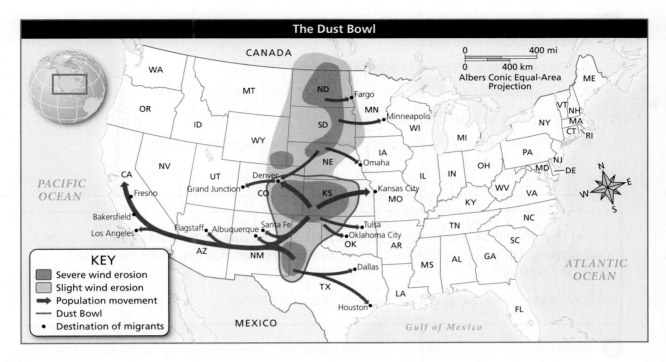

The Dust Bowl

CANADA

WA

MT

ND
Fargo

OR

MN
Minneapolis
WI

ID

SD

WY

NE

IA
Omaha

MI

NY

PACIFIC
OCEAN

NV

UT

Denver
Grand Junction

CO

KS

IL

IN

OH

PA

NJ

MD
DE

CA
Fresno

Kansas City
MO

KY

WV

VA

Bakersfield
Los Angeles

Flagstaff
Albuquerque
Santa Fe

Tulsa
Oklahoma City

TN

NC

AZ

NM

OK

AR

SC

Dallas

MS

AL

GA

ATLANTIC
OCEAN

TX

LA

Houston

FL

MEXICO

Gulf of Mexico

0   400 mi
0   400 km
Albers Conic Equal-Area
Projection

ME

VT
NH
MA
CT
RI

KEY
■ Severe wind erosion
■ Slight wind erosion
➡ Population movement
— Dust Bowl
• Destination of migrants

3 What is the main purpose of this map?

A to show the physical consequences of the farming recession

B to show the limitations of the effects of the Great Depression

C to show the major regions that gained population in the 1930s

D to show the extent of migration from areas affected by erosion

4 Which statement describes a continuing effect of the Social Security Act of 1935?

F A pension system provides economic support to retired workers.

G Payroll taxes are decreased for certain employers and their workers.

H Widows with families receive larger benefits than widowers with families.

I Farm workers and domestic workers have to secure their own insurance.

If you have trouble with...				
Question	1	2	3	4
See Lesson	5.1	5.2	5.2	5.4

5 In what way was Eleanor Roosevelt's approach to her role as First Lady most significant to American society as a whole?

   A She helped make the First Lady role more ceremonial.

   B She established a link between the public and the President.

   C Her actions helped to promote the political influence of women.

   D She made some of the decisions formerly reserved for the President.

> *When Dorothea took that picture that was the ultimate. She never surpassed it. . . . She has all the suffering of mankind in her but all the perseverance too. A restraint and a strange courage.*
>
> *—Roy Stryker, FSA, on Dorothea Lange's "Migrant Mother"*

6 Based on the quotation above, how did Dorothea Lange's photography reassure Americans during the Great Depression?

   F It allowed artists to celebrate the success of Depression recovery programs.

   G It showed a current event that newspapers and radio reports had ignored.

   H It showed the strength of the American people in the midst of their suffering.

   I It allowed the government to paint a rosy picture of economic recovery.

7 What event intensified the Great Migration of African Americans in the decade between 1910 and 1920?

A Many African Americans became disillusioned with conditions in northern factories and moved to the south where they established large farms.

B The war effort recruited workers from northern factories and drew African Americans north to fill their jobs.

C Many African Americans lost their livelihoods in the south when the boll weevil ruined the cotton crop, so they moved north to farm corn and wheat.

D Many African Americans migrated west to California to become farmers in the Imperial Valley, but many later moved to Los Angeles to work in factories.

IRRECONCILABLES	RESERVATIONISTS	WILSON DEMOCRATS
• Opposed the treaty in any form • Convinced that the idea of a League of Nations was idealistic and unrealistic • Suspicious of the actions and intents of the other countries in the League of Nations • Wished to maintain American isolationism	• Would accept the treaty if it were modified • Believed the League of Nations removed congressional power to declare war • Opposed Article 10 of the League Covenant, which required the U.S. to defend other members of the League	• Most supported the treaty • Believed no changes to the treaty were necessary • Wanted U.S. to be part of the League of Nations

8 What were the fears of those who were opposed to the Treaty of Versailles?

F It would create an international organization that would maintain the peace.

G It would give Germany too much economic and political power in the postwar world.

H It would drag the United States into wars and interfere with the government's decisions.

I It would jeopardize British sovereignty and lead to an independent Ireland.

If you have trouble with...				
Question	5	6	7	8
See Lesson	5.5	5.6	4.2	4.3

[ESSENTIAL QUESTION] When is war justified?

⑥ World War II

Enduring Understandings

- World War II began when aggressive dictators tried to expand their empires.

- The United States hesitated to become involved, but the attack on Pearl Harbor drew the country into the war.

- The United States played a crucial role in winning the war, both through its military contributions and its great production capacity.

- Millions were killed during the war, including 6 million Jews and 5 million others murdered by the Nazis in the Holocaust.

- World War II ended the Great Depression in the United States and increased the nation's importance as a player on the world stage.

Hear about one American's experience in World War II.

Bounce to Activate My Story Video

>> American troops in Burma, 1944.

California Topic 6 Overview

In this Topic, you will learn about the events of World War II. Look at the lesson outline and explore the timeline. As you study this Topic, you'll complete the Quest team project.

LESSON OUTLINE

6.1 Rise of Aggressive Dictators
HSS 11.7, HSS 11.7.1

6.2 America Debates Involvement
HSS 11.7, HSS 11.7.1, HSS 11.7.4

6.3 America Enters World War II
HSS 11.7, HSS 11.7.1, HSS 11.7.2, HSS 11.7.6

6.4 A War on Two Fronts
HSS 11.7, HSS 11.7.2, HSS 11.7.6

6.5 The Home Front
HSS 11.7, HSS 11.7.2, HSS 11.7.3, HSS 11.7.5, HSS 11.8.2, HSS 11.9.7, HSS 11.10.1; Analysis CST.4

6.6 The Allies Win World War II
HSS 11.7, HSS 11.7.2, HSS 11.7.7

6.7 The Holocaust
HSS 11.7, HSS 11.7.5

6.8 Impact of World War II
HSS 11.4, HSS 11.4.6, HSS 11.7, HSS 11.8.5, HSS 11.9.1, HSS 11.10.1

Key Events of World War II

1933 Hitler becomes chancellor of Germany

1940 Roosevelt wins third term

1942 Nazis leaders plan a "Final Solution" for Europe's Jews

1944 D-Day landing in France

1930 — 1935 — 1940 — 1945

1939 Germany invades Poland, beginning World War II

June 1941 Germany invades the Soviet Union

December 1941 Japan attacks Pearl Harbor, United States enters World War II

1945 World War II ends

QUEST!

TEAM PROJECT

Building a "Memories of World War II" Website

What was it like to hear about the bombing of Pearl Harbor, to serve in the Army in Europe or the Navy in the Pacific? In this Quest you'll explore life during World War II and document three people's experiences on a website that you'll create.

STEP 1

With your team, make a list of questions you want to answer about how the war affected people, then identify three individuals whose lives were deeply affected by the war.

STEP 2

Research those three people to learn more about their experiences during the war.

STEP 3

Tell the stories of these three people on your website as a tribute to the sacrifices they made during the war.

STEP 4

Share your website with your classmates and community! Reflect on what you've learned about war, human resilience, and teamwork.

PearsonSchool.com/CASS

Go ONLINE for complete Quest materials

 VIDEO   ETEXT   WRITING   RUBRIC   PDF ASSESSMENT

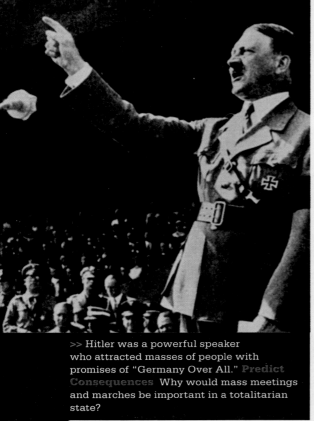

>> Hitler was a powerful speaker who attracted masses of people with promises of "Germany Over All." **Predict Consequences** Why would mass meetings and marches be important in a totalitarian state?

The effects of World War I and the Great Depression touched almost every corner of the world. In some countries, these upheavals led to the rise of a new kind of brutal dictatorship—the totalitarian state. These states were led by absolute dictators, leaders willing to use acts of aggression to invade other nations in order to enhance their own power. Their actions would destroy the peace established after World War I and spark a new, even deadlier, global conflict.

 Bounce to Activate Flipped Video

>> **Objectives**

Explain the rise of dictatorships in the Soviet Union, Italy, Germany, and Japan in the 1930s.

Summarize acts of aggression by Italy, Germany, and Japan.

Analyze the responses of Britain, France, and the United States to the aggressive regimes.

>> **Key Terms**

aggression
totalitarianism
Joseph Stalin
Benito Mussolini
Spanish Civil War
General Francisco
  Franco
appeasement
Franklin D.
  Roosevelt
Anschluss

Neville Chamberlain
Munich Pact
fascism
Adolf Hitler
anti-Semitic

Rise of Aggressive Dictators

Peace Dissolves

In November 1918, World War I ended when Germany surrendered to the Allies. In 1919, delegates from 27 nations met in Versailles to hammer out a peace agreement, but only Britain, France, and the United States had a real say in most of the important decisions. Germany and Russia were not even present. From the first, many Germans resented the resulting Treaty of Versailles. Other nations also grumbled over the peace settlements.

Italy and Japan, both World War I Allies, had expected far more land for their sacrifices. The war that American President Woodrow Wilson had called "a war to end all wars" had left behind a mountain of bitterness, anger, frustration, and despair, often capped by a burning desire for revenge.

During the 1920s many nations, new and old, moved steadily toward democracy and freedom. Others, however, took the opposite direction, embracing repressive dictatorships and **totalitarianism**, a government in which a single party or leader controls the economic, social, and cultural lives of its people. Throughout history there have been dictatorships, countries ruled by one person or small groups of people. But totalitarianism, emerging as a twentieth-century phenomenon, controls all aspects of life. It is more extreme than a simple dictatorship. At the head of the government is a strong, charismatic leader who uses terror, spies, and police force to impose the will of the state upon the citizens. Unlike democracies, people living in totalitarian states have no individual rights. The government controls the media and uses propaganda to indoctrinate people. Schools and youth organizations foster the state ideology. The government crushes opposition and censors any political rivals or divergent ideas.

Why did totalitarian regimes take hold in the years leading up to World War II? Historians lay much of the blame on the destruction and bitterness left behind by World War I and the desperation caused by the Great Depression.

☑ **PREDICT CONSEQUENCES** How do you think totalitarian regimes will affect the peace following World War I?

Strict Regimes in the Soviet Union and Italy

The 1917 communist revolution in Russia inaugurated the first totalitarian state. The communist leader Vladimir Lenin created the beginnings of a totalitarian system of control to maintain power. His programs resulted in civil war, starvation, famine, and the death of millions of Russians.

Stalin Rules the Soviet Union After Lenin's death in 1924, **Joseph Stalin** took Lenin's place as the head of the Communist Party. In Russian, Stalin means "man of steel," and it is an apt description of the dictator's personality. Stalin was suspicious, cruel, ruthless, and tyrannical. He did not think twice about killing rivals or sentencing innocent people to death. His efforts to transform the Soviet Union into an industrial power and form state-run collective farms resulted in the deaths of at least 10 million people.

In what became known as the Great Terror, Stalin purged the Communist Party of real or suspected traitors in the 1930s, ordering the deaths or imprisonment of up to a million people. The purge also included most of the higher officers of the Red Army, among many others. Political prisoners and criminals were sent to dreaded forced labor camps, known as the Gulag.

>> The Paris Peace Conference met at the Palace of Versailles and lasted a year. The crowds of delegates from participating nations wrote a series of treaties.

>> Displaying the totalitarian traits of discipline and militarism, Japanese students march past representatives of Japan, Germany, and Italy.

Bounce to Activate Gallery

>> Shown in a typical pose, Mussolini often spoke of restoring Italian pride. His arrogant stance matched his message.

>> In this staged photo, a fatherly Stalin poses with a young girl. Years later, his government sent her to the Gulag. **Apply Concepts** How is this photo an example of propaganda?

A combination of fear and massive propaganda kept Stalin in power. Publicity about Stalin was designed to create an idol, encouraging a cult of personality in which he was credited for all good things. In newspapers, billboards, and schools, the public was fed a constant diet of communist success. Soviet art was censored; only positive images of Stalin and soviet life were permitted. Images showing Stalin as a kindly father figure masked the reality of labor camps and the consequences of any resistance to his rule.

Mussolini Establishes an Italian Dictatorship

Italian totalitarianism was in many ways a direct result of World War I and the peace treaties that ended it.

Although Italy was on the winning side, it did not get the land along the Adriatic coast it had hoped to obtain from the division of Austria-Hungary. Added to this frustration, the postwar economic depression made it difficult for returning veterans to find jobs. The country began to tumble into chaos. The communist movement grew. Peasants began seizing land and workers went on strike or took over control of factories. Trade declined and taxes increased. New immigration laws limited immigration to the United States. Law and order broke down as competing groups fought each other in the streets. The government, weak and inept, was unable to restore stability.

It was during this period that **Benito Mussolini** entered the world stage. In 1919, Mussolini founded the Fasci di Combattimento (FAH shee dee kohm ba tee MEHN toh), or Fascist Party, a right-wing organization that promised to restore efficiency and order and make Italy great again. **Fascism** appealed to many looking for strong leadership and restored national pride. Followers of Mussolini, known as Black Shirts, fought in the streets against socialists and communists.

Fearing revolution, in 1922 Italian King Victor Emmanuel III asked Mussolini to form a government. Calling himself Il Duce (ihl DOO chay), or "the leader," Mussolini consolidated his control over the government and the army within a few years. He outlawed political parties, took over the press, created a secret police, organized youth groups to indoctrinate the young, and suppressed strikes. He opposed liberalism and socialism. Still, his hold over Italy was never as powerful as Stalin's grip on the Soviet Union.

☑ **COMPARE AND CONTRAST** What did Stalin and Mussolini have in common? In what ways did they differ?

Germany and Japan Change Leadership

After World War I, Germany became a democracy. The Weimar (vī mahr) Republic (named after the town of Weimar where the government was created) struggled throughout the 1920s to establish a functional democracy. However, Germany was beset by severe economic troubles in the 1920s, including runaway inflation. Anger over the Treaty of Versailles and internal disunity also plagued the young government. The Weimar Republic's ship of state was slowly sinking.

Emergence of Nazis In the early 1930s, the worldwide Great Depression hit the Weimar Republic hard, worsening the problems that already existed. Increasingly, antidemocratic parties on the right, especially the National Socialist German Workers' Party, or Nazi (NAHT see) Party, threatened the republic.

Regardless of the party's name, Nazis were not socialists. They bitterly opposed socialism, communism, or any other ism that promoted class interests or workers' rights above German ethnic solidarity. **Adolf Hitler** led the Nazi Party. The son of a minor Austrian civil servant, Hitler was a failed artist, a wounded and decorated World War I soldier, and a person who teetered on the brink of madness.

Hitler joined the small Nazi Party after the war and soon gained control of it. While in prison after the party attempted a rebellion, Hitler dictated the book *Mein Kampf* ("My Struggle"), in which he stated his explanations for the problems facing Germany. He criticized many people, political programs, and ideologies, but his sharpest assaults were against communists and Jews. Hitler was violently **anti-Semitic**, or prejudiced against Jewish people.

Anti-Semitism had troubled Europe for centuries, mainly motivated by religious intolerance and economic resentment. In the late nineteenth century, new pseudo-scientific theories about Jews as a race, along with the rise of nationalism, caused Jews to be marginalized as ethnic outsiders. Hitler believed and spread this type of thinking. He preached that the greatest threat confronting Germany was the Jewish people who lived there. In *Mein Kampf*, which quickly became a national bestseller, Hitler presented a blueprint of his hatreds and plans for world domination.

Hitler Rules a German Dictatorship The shattered German economy—with its widespread unemployment, homelessness, and hunger—

>> Inflation ruined the Weimar Republic. Presses ran day and night printing paper money. By 1923, one dollar was equal to one trillion Marks. Here children play with stacks of worthless money.

>> Both civilians and military personnel welcomed Hitler to a rally in Nuremberg, 1933. Rallies were held yearly as grand propaganda events lasting several days.

Bounce to Activate Gallery

played into the Nazis' hands as they promised that Germany would rise again from the quagmire of reparations and the economic depression. Recognizing the power of Hitler's party, in January 1933 the president of the Weimar Republic appointed Hitler chancellor of Germany. Over the next two years, Hitler became president as well as chancellor, consolidated his power, and ruled unchecked by the Reichstag (RĪKS tahg), or the German parliament.

By 1935, the democratic institutions of the Weimar Republic were silenced, and Hitler spoke alone as the voice of Germany. Like Stalin and Mussolini, Hitler was the symbol of his totalitarian regime. Aided by a secret police that crushed all opposition, a state-controlled press that praised his accomplishments, and a state-controlled educational system that indoctrinated the young, Hitler assumed a godlike aura.

By the late 1930s, Hitler's economic policies, including rearmament and massive public-works projects, had ended the depression in Germany. Many Germans followed his lead and cheered for him at Nazi rallies. For many, his promises came true. "Once Hitler came to power, it was wonderful. Everybody had a job and there weren't any more unemployed people," remembered one German citizen.

However, Hitler's leadership had dark undertones of oppression, based on extreme anti-Semitism and the rejection of democracy. Hitler maintained his power by alternately brainwashing the public with lies and propaganda drives or terrifying them into silence through ruthless violence.

He openly attacked Jewish people, communists, and socialists. Hitler rejected freedom for the people and defined his rule like so in a speech in 1937:

> For everyone has to obey orders. We have obeyed orders. . . . And I must demand this of every German: You, too, must be able to obey orders, . . . We shall educate our People to do this and ignore the obstinacy or stupidity of individuals. Bend or break—one or the other. We cannot permit this authority, the authority of the German People, to be challenged...
>
> —Adolf Hitler, May 1, 1937

Militarism Gains Support in Japan In Japan, as in Germany, the 1920s was a period of increased democracy and peaceful change. The Japanese government reduced the power of the military, passed laws to give all men the right to vote, legalized trade unions, and allowed several diverse political parties to be established. This period ended when the Great Depression discredited Japan's civilian leaders in the 1930s.

Reasserting their traditional powers, military leaders argued that expansion throughout Asia would gain natural resources and new markets. This would solve Japan's economic troubles and guarantee future security. Throughout the 1930s, the military played a significant role in shaping Japanese civilian and military policy. Japan, however, did not become a true totalitarian dictatorship. No charismatic leader like Stalin or Hitler emerged. Japan continued as a nominal constitutional monarchy headed by a mainly aloof emperor, but with the military high command assuming dictatorship-like powers over the masses. As with Germany and Italy, Japanese military leaders had strong control over the life of the people and ended many democratic freedoms. Opposition was suppressed, media was censored, and schools instilled obedience to the nation.

>> Girls experienced military life by marching in formation. Students were taught obedience and self-sacrifice for the good of the nation.

Aggression and Appeasement

AGGRESSIVE ACTION	DATE	WORLD REACTION
Japan invades Manchuria.	1931	League of Nations condemns the action; Japan withdraws from League.
Italy invades Ethiopia.	1935	League of Nations endorses sanctions against Italy but does not enforce them.
Germany sends troops into Rhineland.	1936	League of Nations denounces the move as a violation of the Treaty of Versailles, but takes no action.
Germany and Italy support fascists in Spanish Civil War.	1936–1939	France, Great Britain, and United States refuse to get involved or to provide weapons to democratic Republican forces. League of Nations remains neutral.
Japan invades China.	1937	Japan is criticized for violating peace treaty, but no action taken to stop aggression.
Germany annexes Austria.	1938	World powers take no action to stop violation of the Treaty of Versailles.
Germany demands Sudetenland.	1938	Munich Pact is signed and Germany gains the Czech territory.

>> **Analyze Charts** What was the world reaction to these aggressive actions? What was the effect of this reaction on the aggressors?

 Bounce to Activate Map

The Japanese Empire Expands As the power shifted toward military control, Japan started on a course of aggressive military expansion. Extreme nationalists encouraged Japanese domination of the region. In 1931, Japan attacked Manchuria (man CHUR ee uh), a region in northeastern China, and established a puppet state. The new nation was named Manchukuo (man choo kwoh). Japan controlled its domestic and foreign policies, as well as its abundant natural resources. In 1937, Japan moved against China, gaining control over major Chinese railroad links and coastal areas. In the then capital city of Nanjing, Japanese soldiers acted with such brutality—murdering more than 200,000 residents and burning a large section of the city— that the incident became known as the "Rape of Nanjing."

☑ **IDENTIFY CAUSE AND EFFECT** How did the Great Depression affect political life in Germany and Japan?

Dictators Move to Gain Territory

In the 1930s, the Italian and German dictatorships resorted to acts of aggression similar to those of Japan in Asia. Throughout the decade, neither the League of Nations nor democratic nations succeeded in stopping the aggression. It was a time that recalled a line from Irish poet William Butler Yeats: "The best lack all conviction and the worst are full of passionate intensity."

Weakness of the League of Nations In many ways, the League of Nations never recovered from America's refusal to join it. The League was also handicapped by its own charter.

It had no standing army and no real power to enforce its decrees. It was only as strong as its members' resolve, and during the worldwide depression of the 1930s, those members lacked resolve. When aggressive nations began to test the League, they discovered that the organization was long on words and short on action.

Hitler and Mussolini Challenge the Peace From the first, Hitler focused on restoring Germany's strength and nullifying the provisions of the Treaty of Versailles. From 1933 to 1936, he rebuilt the German economy and dramatically enlarged the army, navy, and air force in direct defiance of the Treaty of Versailles. In the mid-1930s, Hitler began to move toward his goal of reunifying all Germanic people into one Reich, or state. He spoke often of the need for Germany to expand to gain *Lebensraum* (LAY buhns rowm), or living space, for its people. In

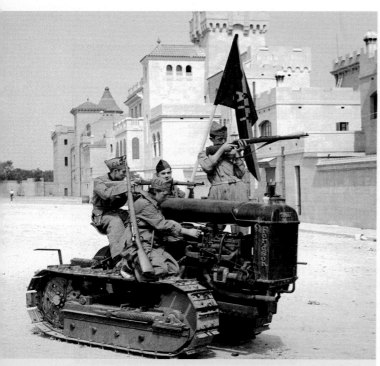

>> Spanish government troops fought fascist-supported rebels.

>> **Analyze Political Cartoon** Who do the small men represent? What point do you think the cartoon was making with this image?

1935, he reclaimed the Saar (sahr) region from French control.

In 1936, in another direct challenge to the League, Hitler sent German troops into the Rhineland. This region was part of western Germany and under German political control.

However, under the terms of the Treaty of Versailles, it was demilitarized; Germany was forbidden to have troops in the region. Reoccupation was a test. Would France or the League defend the terms of the Treaty? The answer was no. To all these actions, the League failed to respond.

Meanwhile, Mussolini commenced his own imperial plans. In 1935, Italy invaded Ethiopia, an independent country in east Africa. Its emperor, Haile Selassie (Hì luh suh lah SEE), appealed to the League of Nations for support. The organization did almost nothing, and Ethiopia fell.

Dictators Support War in Spain Fascists were also victorious in a bloody conflict that raged from 1936 until 1939, know as the **Spanish Civil War**. The Nationalists, who had fascist tendencies, rebelled against Spain's democratic Republican government.

Both Hitler and Mussolini sent military and economic aid to the Nationalist leader, **General Francisco Franco**, using the conflict to test some of their new military technology. Though the Soviet Union provided some support for the Republican side, France, Britain, and the United States remained largely on the sidelines, deploring the bloodshed but refusing to provide weapons to the Republican forces.

☑ **EXPRESS PROBLEMS CLEARLY** Why did the League of Nations fail to halt German and Italian aggression?

Aggression Meets Appeasement

The policy that France and Britain pursued against aggressive nations during the 1930s is known as **appeasement**. It is a policy of granting concessions to a potential enemy in the hope that peace can be maintained. Unfortunately, appeasement only spurred the fascist leaders to become more bold, adventurous, and aggressive.

Why did France and Britain appease the fascist powers? There were a number of reasons. World War I was so horrible that some leaders vowed never to allow another such war to break out. Other leaders believed that the Soviet Union posed a greater threat than Nazi Germany. They maintained that a strong Germany would provide a buffer against the Soviet menace. Still other leaders questioned the resolve of their own people and their allies—particularly the United States.

The United States played an important role in this appeasement policy. Worried about the rise of dictatorships in Europe and Asia, **Franklin D. Roosevelt** wanted to mend fences with America's neighbors. In the 1930s, he pursued a Good Neighbor policy with Latin American nations. The program emphasized trade and cooperation, not military force, as the basis for a stable relationship with Latin American nations. The United States withdrew troops from several nations. It agreed not to intervene in Latin America and to consult with other nations if faced with danger. Roosevelt also improved relations with the Soviet Union by restoring diplomatic relations with the Soviet government, although he remained wary about allying too closely with the communist nation. However, he did not take a forceful line against German aggression. Instead, the country concerned itself with its own economic troubles and embraced a policy of isolationism.

Hitler took advantage of the lack of commitment and unity among France, Britain, and the United States. In the spring of 1938, he brought Austria into his Reich.

Austria was given little choice but to accept this union, called the **Anschluss** (AHN shloos). In the fall, Hitler turned toward the Sudetenland, a portion of western Czechoslovakia that was largely populated by ethnic Germans.

Many people expected the conflict over the Sudetenland to lead to a general war. But once again, Britain and France appeased Germany. At the Munich Conference with Hitler, British prime minister **Neville Chamberlain** and French premier Edouard Daladier sacrificed the Sudetenland to preserve the peace. On his return to London, Chamberlain told a cheering crowd that the **Munich Pact** (MYOO nihk), the agreement reached at the conference, had preserved "peace for our time." He was wrong. It merely postponed the war for 11 months.

☑ **IDENTIFY EFFECTS** Did the appeasement policy of Britain, France, and the United States have the intended effect? Explain your answer.

>> Returning with the signed Munich Pact, Chamberlain announced confidently that it would maintain peace. Instead it was a turning point in the path to war and later became a symbol of failure.

☑ ASSESSMENT

1. **Identify Central Issues** What economic conditions led to the rise of totalitarianism in Europe and Asia?

2. **Generate Explanations** How Hitler and Mussolini use the Spanish Civil war to their advantage?

3. **Support Ideas with Examples** Was the policy of appeasement successful against Hitler and Germany? Explain your answer.

4. **Identify Patterns** What was Franklin Roosevelt's Good Neighbor policy?

5. **Identify Central Issues** In what way did the Anschluss present a challenge to the United States and its allies?

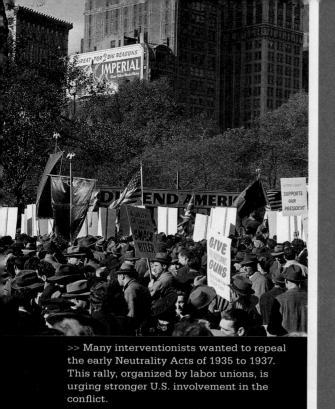

>> Many interventionists wanted to repeal the early Neutrality Acts of 1935 to 1937. This rally, organized by labor unions, is urging stronger U.S. involvement in the conflict.

Bounce to Activate Flipped Video

While Britain and France appeased the dictator in Germany at Munich, American President Franklin Roosevelt condemned aggression in Asia but did little to stop it. As war exploded in Europe, it became increasingly difficult for the United States to maintain its neutrality. Once again, Americans would have to decide what role they were willing to play in shaping world events.

>> Objectives

Understand the course of the early years of World War II in Europe.

Describe Franklin Roosevelt's foreign policy in the mid-1930s and the great debate between interventionists and isolationists.

Explain how the United States became more involved in the conflict.

>> Key Terms

blitzkrieg
Axis Powers
Allies
Winston Churchill
Neutrality Act of 1939
Tripartite Pact
President Franklin Roosevelt
Charles Lindbergh
Lend-Lease Act
Atlantic Charter

America Debates Involvement

Roosevelt Criticizes Acts of War

The unrestrained violence of the 1937 Japanese attack on China shocked Americans, even before the notorious Rape of Nanjing in December 1937. Japan attacked without a declaration of war. Its planes rained terror on Chinese cities, especially Shanghai and Nanjing. The Japanese had even killed three American sailors when Japanese warplanes sank the United States gunboat *Panay* on the Chang River.

In the midst of these bloody events, President Franklin Roosevelt criticized Japan's aggression in a speech in Chicago on October 5,1937. He lamented the "reign of terror and international lawlessness," the bombing of civilian populations, and the horrible acts of cruelty. Speaking in a city where American isolationist sentiments were strong, Roosevelt suggested that no part of the world was truly isolated from the rest of the world. He warned:

When an epidemic of physical disease starts to spread, the community approves and joins in a quarantine of the patients in order to protect the health of the community against the spread of the disease. . . . War is a contagion, whether it be declared or undeclared. It can engulf states and peoples remote from the original scene of hostilities. We are determined to keep out of war, yet we cannot insure ourselves against the disastrous effects of war and the dangers of involvement.

—President Franklin Roosevelt, Quarantine speech, October 5, 1937

Roosevelt's solution for stopping aggression involved an informal alliance of the peace-loving nations, but he did not suggest what steps the peaceful nations should take in quarantining the aggressive ones. Americans, unhappy with the failure of World War I to make the "world safe for democracy," were not ready for another attempt at peacekeeping in Europe.

Roosevelt's speech was widely criticized, and for a time, the President backed away from his more interventionist stance. "It's a terrible thing to look over your shoulder when you are trying to lead—and find no one there." Roosevelt remarked to a speechwriter. The speech did, however, alert some Americans to the threat Japan posed to the United States.

☑ **INTERPRET** Why do you think Roosevelt compared war to a disease in his Quarantine speech?

War Breaks Out in Europe

Roosevelt's words failed to prevent Japan from extending its control over much of China. Similarly, France and Britain's efforts to appease Hitler in Europe failed to limit the dictator's expansionist plans. By the end of 1938, even the leaders of France and Britain realized that Hitler's armed aggression could only be halted by a firm, armed defense. The urgency of the situation grew in the spring of 1939 when Hitler violated the Munich Pact by absorbing the remainder of Czechoslovakia into his German Reich.

Hitler was open about his view of war and conquest. He believed that there was no morality in war, only victory and defeat. Just one month before the attack on Poland, he instructed his generals

>> Japanese planes frequently bombed China during the invasion in 1937. The Chinese army lacked the equipment and training needed to defend the country.

>> President Roosevelt addressed the nation about the world political situation, which he said had "been growing progressively worse." He did not specifically mention the aggressor states, but they were known to be Germany, Italy, and Japan.

to be ruthless and merciless. "When starting and waging a war it is not right that matters, but victory. Close your hearts to pity. Act brutally. Eighty million people [Germans] must obtain what is their right. . . . The stronger man is right."

Poland Falls to German Blitzkrieg Finally, British and French leaders saw the need to take action. They vowed not to let Hitler take over another country without consequences. Poland seemed the next likely target for Hitler, so Britain and France signed an alliance with Poland, guaranteeing aid to the Poles if Hitler attacked.

Hitler, however, was more concerned about war with the Soviet Union than with Britain and France. Not wanting to fight a war on two fronts, Germany signed the Nazi-Soviet Nonaggression Pact with the Soviets on August 23, 1939. The two former rivals publicly promised not to attack one another. Secretly, they agreed to invade and divide Poland and recognize each other's territorial ambitions. The public agreement alone shocked the West and guaranteed a German offensive against Poland.

A new world war that would be a turning point in world history came to Europe in the early hours of September 1, 1939, when a massive German **blitzkrieg** (BLIHTS kreeg), or sudden attack, hit Poland by surprise from three directions. Blitzkrieg means "lightning war."

It was a relatively new style of warfare that emphasized the use of speed and firepower to penetrate deep into the enemy's territory. The newest military technologies made it devastatingly effective. Using a coordinated assault by tanks and planes, followed by motorized vehicles and infantry, Germany broke through Poland's defenses and destroyed its air force.

The situation became even more hopeless on September 17 when the Soviet Union invaded Poland from the east, taking control of the Baltic nations of Estonia, Latvia, and Lithuania soon after. Although France and Britain declared war against Germany, they did nothing to help save Poland. By the end of the month, a devastated Poland fell in defeat.

Axis Powers Overwhelm Western Europe
Europe was at war, just as it had been 21 years earlier. The **Axis Powers** eventually included Germany, Italy, Japan, and several other nations. The **Allies** included Britain, France, and eventually many other nations, including the Soviet Union, the United States, and China.

But after the Polish campaign, the war entered an eight-month period of relative quiet, known in Britain as the "phony war." Things would not remain quiet for long, however.

The next storm erupted with raging fury in the spring of 1940. Germany's nonaggression pact with

Military Expenditures

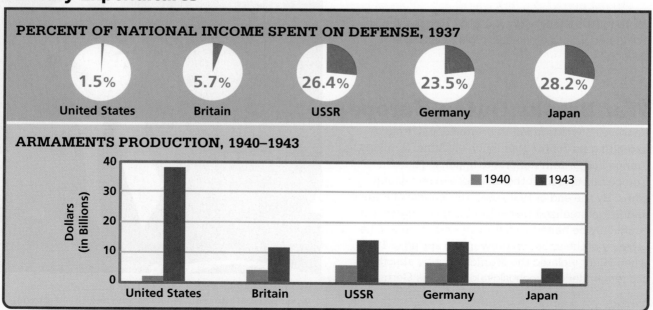

>> In the 1930s, dictators built their power on nationalism and militarism. **Analyze Charts** Which nations were most likely preparing for war in 1937? Why did military spending for the United States and Britain increase so much more than for the Soviet Union between 1940 and 1943?

the Soviet Union freed Hitler to send his army west. On April 9, 1940, Germany attacked Denmark and Norway. The two countries fell almost immediately. On May 10, he sent his blitzkrieg forces into the Netherlands, Belgium, and Luxembourg. The small nations fell like tumbling dominoes. Hitler seemed invincible; his army unstoppable.

France Falls Hitler next set his sights on France. France had prepared for Germany's invasion by constructing an interconnected series of fortresses known as the Maginot Line along its border with Germany. Additionally, France had stationed its finest armies along its border with Belgium—the route that Germany had used to attack France in 1914. In between the Maginot Line and Belgium lay the Ardennes, a hilly, forested area that military experts considered invasion proof.

But once again the military experts were wrong. In early May 1940, German tanks rolled through the Ardennes, ripped a hole in the thin French line there, and raced north toward the English Channel. The German plan involved attacking the French and British forces from the front and the rear and trapping them against the channel. It almost worked. Only a few tactical German mistakes gave Britain enough time to evacuate its forces from the French port of Dunkirk. Some 338,000 British and French troops escaped to Britain. Had they not escaped, it is doubtful if Britain, with 70 percent of its troops at Dunkirk, could have remained in the war.

The Miracle of Dunkirk was a proud moment for Britain, but as the new prime minister **Winston Churchill** cautioned Parliament, "wars are not won by evacuations." Although the British army escaped, the Germans took Paris and forced the French to surrender in the same railway car that the French had used for the German surrender in 1918. France was then divided into two sections: a larger northern section controlled by the Germans and known as Occupied France, and a smaller southern section administered by the French and known as Unoccupied France, or Vichy France, after its capital city. Although Vichy France was officially neutral, it collaborated with the Nazis.

Air Forces Fight Battle of Britain France had fallen to Hitler in just 35 days. Hitler next turned his fury on Britain. After the evacuation at Dunkirk, Churchill made it clear that he had no intention of continuing the policy of appeasement. He told his nation:

>> Speed and massive power contributed to the success of the blitzkrieg.

Bounce to Activate Map

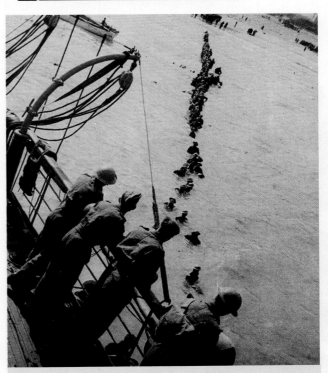

>> British and French troops maintained a disciplined and orderly retreat, even under enemy attack. An assortment of private and military vessels rescued soldiers who would go on to fight again.

>> Winston Churchill succeeded Neville Chamberlain as prime minister in May 1940. He toured London even during intense bombings, inspiring the British to continue the fight.

>> German bombers attacked Britain nightly for months, hoping to break British morale. The planes first attacked airfields and military factories, but then switched to bombing cities and civilians. Londoners took refuge in the city's subways, which were used as air raid shelters.

Bounce to Activate Gallery

We shall go on to the end. We shall fight in France, we shall fight on the seas and oceans, we shall fight with growing confidence and growing strength in the air, we shall defend our island, whatever the cost may be, we shall fight on the beaches, we shall fight on the landing grounds, we shall fight in the fields and in the streets, we shall fight in the hills; we shall never surrender.

—Winston Churchill, June 4, 1940

Churchill's words stirred his nation as the British readied themselves for battle.

Hitler's plan to invade Britain, codenamed Operation Sea Lion, depended upon Germany's Luftwaffe, or air force, destroying the British Royal Air Force and gaining control over the skies above the English Channel. The Battle of Britain, then, was an air battle, fought over the English Channel and Great Britain. It began in July 1940. The British lost nearly 1,000 planes, the Germans more than 1,700. Germany bombed civilian as well as military targets, destroying houses, factories, and churches and conducted a months-long bombing campaign against London itself, known as "the blitz." But the British held on and, sensing failure, Hitler made a tactical decision to postpone the invasion of Britain indefinitely.

☑ **SUMMARIZE** Which side seemed to be winning the war at the end of 1940?

American Reaction Is Divided

Winston Churchill referred to the United States in many of his speeches during the crisis in France and the Battle of Britain. The fight against Hitler, Churchill implied, was more than simply a European struggle. Nazi aggression threatened the freedoms and rights cherished by democratic nations everywhere. The contest was between ideologies as well as nations.

Public Opinion Supports Isolation President Roosevelt shared Churchill's concerns, but at the beginning of the war in Europe he understood that the majority of Americans opposed U.S. intervention.

The severe economic crisis of the Great Depression had served to pin the nation's attention firmly on domestic affairs throughout the 1930s. In addition, many believed that U.S. involvement in World War I had been a deadly, expensive mistake. The rise of fascism in Europe made the sacrifices of World War I seem even more pointless.

In the 1930s, numerous books and articles presented a new theory about why the United States had become involved in World War I that disturbed many Americans. The theory held that big business had conspired to enter the war in order to make huge fortunes selling weapons. In 1934, a senate committee chaired by Gerald Nye of South Dakota looked into the question. Although the Nye Committee discovered little hard evidence, its findings suggested that "merchants of death"— American bankers and arms manufacturers—had indeed pulled the United States into World War I. The committee's findings further reinforced isolationist sentiments.

In order to avoid making the "mistakes" that had led to U.S. involvement in World War I, Congress passed the Neutrality Acts of 1935, 1936, and 1937. The acts imposed certain restrictions on Americans during times of war. For example, Americans were prohibited from sailing on ships owned by belligerents or nations at war. The acts also prevented Americans from making loans to belligerents or selling them arms and munitions. The acts did not distinguish between aggressors like Germany and Italy and victims like Poland, or their allies, France and Britain.

Interventionists Press for Aid to Allies Once war began in Europe, Roosevelt felt confined by the limitations of the Neutrality Acts. Though he issued a proclamation of American neutrality, he was firmly anti-Nazi and wanted to aid the democracies of Europe. In the end, Congress agreed and passed the **Neutrality Act of 1939**, which included a cash-and-carry provision. This provision allowed belligerent nations to buy goods and arms in the United States if they paid cash and carried the merchandise on their own ships. Since the British navy controlled the seas, cash-and-carry in effect aided the Allies.

Many Americans disagreed with Roosevelt's openly pro-Allies position. They argued that FDR's policies violated American neutrality and threatened to push the United States into the war. Between early 1940 and late 1941, a great debate raged in America between isolationists and interventionists. The debate became particularly heated after the fall

THE TUG OF WAR

>> **Analyze Political Cartoons** Do you think this cartoon is arguing for a policy of isolation or intervention? Explain your answer.

of France left Britain standing by itself in Europe against Germany. Interventionist organizations such as the Committee to Defend America by Aiding the Allies claimed that Britain was fighting for free countries everywhere. Sending aid to Britain was a way for America to stay out of the conflict.

Isolationists Plead to Remain Neutral
Isolationists countered by claiming that giving aid to the Allies was automatically harming the Axis and would culminate with the United States entering the conflict. They argued that the only way to keep America safe was to follow a policy of complete neutrality. The America First Committee, an isolationist group, held rallies and sponsored speeches that criticized Roosevelt's openly pro-British policies. **Charles Lindbergh** became the leading isolationist voice.

Lindbergh believed that the real threats to America were the Soviet Union and Japan, and he did not want to see his country weaken itself fighting in Western Europe to save Britain. "We must band together to prevent the loss of more American lives in these internal struggles of Europe. . . . Our safety does not lie in fighting European wars. It lies in our own internal strength, in the character of the

>> With the fall of France, more Americans began to accept the inevitability of U.S. involvement in the war. There was little public resistance to the first peacetime draft.

SAVE FREEDOM OF SPEECH

BUY WAR BONDS

>> Inspired by Roosevelt's speech, the illustrator Norman Rockwell created four paintings, each illustrating one of the Four Freedoms. In *Freedom of Speech*, Rockwell shows a man speaking at a town meeting.

Bounce to Activate Gallery

American people and of American institutions." Lindbergh's addresses were measured and clear. He appealed to Americans' minds but not their hearts.

Roosevelt Shifts Closer to Involvement Events in Europe shocked Americans out of strict neutrality. Reports by Edward R. Murrow, a CBS reporter stationed in London, during the blitz brought the war into American living rooms. His frequent live radio reports, which began with the words "This is London," emphasized that the Germans were bombing not armies or military sites but civilians— grandparents, parents, and children.

These reports and the turn of events in Europe against the Allies convinced many Americans that the United States needed to at least prepare to defend itself.

Shortly after the fall of France in September 1940, Germany, Italy, and Japan signed the **Tripartite Pact** and became allies. In that same month, after a heated debate between isolationists and interventionists, Congress passed a Selective Service Act—a peacetime draft—providing for the military training of 1.2 million troops and 800,000 reserve troops each year.

At the same time, President Roosevelt took an additional step to strengthen Britain. He gave Britain fifty World War I-era destroyers in exchange for eight British defense bases. Britain needed the ships to convoy goods across the Atlantic. Believing the act to be an emergency measure, Roosevelt made the transfer without the consent of Congress.

The American people evaluated FDR's leadership the next month in the presidential election. Roosevelt ran for an unprecedented third term against Republican nominee Wendell L. Willkie of Indiana. Willkie was critical of FDR's handling of both the economy and foreign affairs but not of the President's basic positions on either.

Given such little differences between candidates, Americans voted overwhelmingly not to change leaders in the middle of a crisis.

☑ **IDENTIFY CENTRAL ISSUES** What were the main arguments in the debate between isolationists and interventionists?

America Moves Closer Toward War

Once safely reelected, President Roosevelt increased his support of Britain. When Britain began to run short on funds to purchase cash-and-carry goods

Lend-Lease Aid Given by the United States

YEAR	TO BRITISH EMPIRE	TO SOVIET UNION
1941 (March-December)	$ 1.1 billion	$20.0 million
1942	$ 4.8 billion	$ 1.4 billion
1943	$ 9.0 billion	$ 2.4 billion
1944	$10.8 billion	$ 4.1 billion
1945 (January-August)	$ 4.4 billion	$ 2.8 billion
TOTAL	$30.1 billion	$10.7 billion

SOURCE: *British War Economy,* W.K. Hancock and M.M. Gowing

>> **Analyze Charts** How much Lend-Lease aid did the United States give the Allies by the end of 1941? Why did the United States give more aid to the British Empire than to the Soviet Union?

in the United States, FDR took the opportunity to address Congress. On January 6, 1941, he spoke about "four freedoms"—freedom of speech, freedom of worship, freedom from want, and freedom from fear—that were threatened by Nazi and Japanese militarism. Roosevelt believed that the best way to stay out of the conflict with Germany was to aid Britain.

The United States Helps the Allies With the Lend-Lease Act
Roosevelt compared America's situation to the scenario of a fire in a neighbor's home. If a neighbor asked to borrow your fire hose to put out the fire, you would not debate the issue or try to sell the hose. Extending help was both being a good neighbor and acting to keep the fire from spreading to your own home.

Britain, Roosevelt said, needed American aid, and it had run out of money to pay for it. The President called for America to become "the great arsenal for democracy." Once again, America answered Britain's plea for help. In March 1941, Congress approved the **Lend-Lease Act**, symbolically numbered 1776, after another heated debate between isolationists and interventionists.

The act authorized Roosevelt to "sell, transfer title to, exchange, lease, lend, or otherwise dispose of, to any such government any defense article" whenever he thought it was "necessary in the interests of the defense of the United States." By 1945, the United States had sent more than $40 billion of Lend-Lease aid to the Allies, including the Soviet Union. The Lend-Lease Act was nothing less than an economic declaration of war against Germany and the Axis Powers.

The Atlantic Charter Outlines Mutual Goals
In August 1941, President Roosevelt and Prime Minister Churchill met secretly on a warship off the misty coast of Newfoundland.

They discussed their mutual war aims, the first being strategy: Their priority was the defeat of Germany, then Japan. They talked not only about Britain's problems in the war but also about their hopes for the world after Hitler's defeat. There would be no conquests made in subjugated territories. On board the ship they signed the **Atlantic Charter**, a document that endorsed national self-determination and an international system of "general security."

The signing of the Atlantic Charter signaled the deepening alliance between the two nations and the full moral support of United States to Britain. The meeting with Churchill and the Atlantic Charter showed Roosevelt's international leadership in coordinating the U.S. relationship with its allies. The charter also cast the conflict in moral terms with the Allies dedicated to freedom in contrast to domination by totalitarian dictatorships.

>> In this photo, German Admiral Doenitz reviewed sailors standing aboard passing U-boats. The U-boats attacked merchant ships, preventing supplies from reaching Britain. By 1940, they were traveling in "wolf packs."

U.S. Navy Battles German U-Boats Hitler was not blind to America's actions in support of the Allies. Nor did he fail to notice the fact that the United States had begun to escort arms shipments to Iceland, where the British picked them up and transported them to England.

In the fall of 1941, he ordered his German U-boats, or submarines, to attack American ships. The U-boats shot at the USS *Greer*, hit the USS *Kearny*, and sunk the USS *Reuben James*, killing more than a hundred sailors. The attacks shocked and angered Americans, moving them closer to declaring war on Germany. Though the United States was still officially a neutral nation, Roosevelt gave orders to the navy to attack German U-boats on sight. In June 1941, Germany had gone to war against the Soviet Union, and by November, war against the United States seemed inevitable.

☑ **CATEGORIZE** Would you categorize President Roosevelt as an isolationist or an interventionist? Give two reasons for your answer.

☑ ASSESSMENT

1. **Draw Conclusions** Did most Americans support President Roosevelt when he condemned Japanese aggression in Asia?

2. **Generate Explanations** Why did Germany sign a non-aggression pact with the Soviet Union?

3. **Describe** Describe Germany's successes at the beginning of World War II.

4. **Identify Patterns** Why did most Americans support isolationism at the beginning of the war?

5. **Support Ideas with Examples** After war began in Europe did Roosevelt follow an interventionist or isolationist policy? Support your answer with examples.

Four Freedoms: Franklin D. Roosevelt

In his State of the Union address to Congress on January 6, 1941, President Franklin D. Roosevelt stressed the danger that aggressive dictatorships presented to the United States. He urged the American people to support "those who are resisting aggression and are thereby keeping war away from our Hemisphere"—namely the Allies. At the end of his speech, Roosevelt sets out the ideals that he believed Americans should fight for: the Four Freedoms.

SAVE FREEDOM OF SPEECH

BUY WAR BONDS

>> Poster showing *Freedom of Speech* by Norman Rockwell

I address you, the Members of the Seventy-seventh Congress, at a moment unprecedented in the history of the Union. I use the word "unprecedented," because at no previous time has American security been as seriously threatened from without as it is today. . . .

. . . I suppose that every realist knows that the democratic way of life is at this moment being directly assailed in every part of the world—assailed either by arms, or by secret spreading of poisonous propaganda by those who seek to destroy unity and promote discord in nations that are still at peace.

During sixteen long months this assault has blotted out the whole pattern of democratic life in an appalling number of independent nations, great and small. And the assailants are still on the march, threatening other nations, great and small.

☑ **DETERMINE MEANING** Who was threatening democracy when Roosevelt gave this speech?

Therefore, as your President, performing my constitutional duty to "give to the Congress information of the state of the Union," I find it, unhappily, necessary to report that the future and the safety of our country and of our democracy are overwhelmingly involved in events far beyond our borders. . . .

. . . In the future days, which we seek to make secure, we look forward to a world founded upon four essential human freedoms.

☑ **DETERMINE MEANING** Roosevelt explains that he is describing "essential human freedoms." How do the words *essential* and *human* help define his meaning of freedom?

The first is freedom of speech and expression—everywhere in the world.

The second is freedom of every person to worship God in his own way—everywhere in the world.

☑ **ASSESS AN ARGUMENT** In his description of the first and second freedoms, Roosevelt refers to the First Amendment in the Constitution. **a.** Why do you think Roosevelt refers to the Constitution? **b.** Do you think that the reference strengthens or weakens his argument? Explain.

The third is freedom from want—which, translated into world terms, means economic understandings which will secure to every nation a healthy peacetime life for its inhabitants—everywhere in the world.

☑ **DRAW INFERENCES** The third freedom is not mentioned in the First Amendment. Roosevelt introduces it here. The word *want* as it is used here means lacking things that are necessary to survive, such as food and shelter. Recall that this speech was given in early 1941. Think about what happened in the United States in the 1930s. What reaction do you think the idea of "freedom from want" would have caused in Roosevelt's listeners?

The fourth is freedom from fear—which, translated into world terms, means a world-wide reduction of armaments [weapons] to such a point and in such a thorough fashion that no nation will be in a position to commit an act of physical aggression against any neighbor—anywhere in the world. . . .

☑ **DETERMINE AUTHOR'S POINT OF VIEW** The fourth freedom is "freedom from fear." What is Roosevelt's interpretation of "freedom from fear"?

That is no vision of a distant millennium [thousand years]. It is a definite basis for a kind of world attainable in our own time and generation. That kind of world is the very antithesis of the so-called new order of tyranny which the dictators seek to create with the crash of a bomb.

To that new order we oppose the greater conception—the moral order. A good society is able to face schemes of world domination and foreign revolutions alike without fear.

☑ **USE CONTEXT CLUES** After outlining the four freedoms, Roosevelt speaks about his vision and what is happening in Axis-controlled countries. **a.** Use context clues to determine the meaning of *antithesis*. **b.** Find a word in the text that is the antithesis of Roosevelt's vision of freedom.

Since the beginning of our American history, we have been engaged in change—in a perpetual [continuous, lasting] peaceful revolution—a revolution which goes on steadily, quietly adjusting itself to changing conditions—without the concentration camp or the quick-lime in the ditch. The world order which we seek is the cooperation of free countries, working together in a friendly, civilized society.

☑ **DETERMINE CENTRAL IDEAS** Describe the "revolution" Roosevelt refers to.

This nation has placed its destiny in the hands and heads and hearts of its millions of free men and women; and its faith in freedom under the guidance of God. Freedom means the supremacy of human rights everywhere. Our support goes to those who struggle to gain those rights or keep them. Our strength is our unity of purpose. To that high concept there can be no end save victory.

☑ **DETERMINE MEANING** What victory is Roosevelt referring to?

☑ ASSESSMENT

1. **Draw Inferences** What does Roosevelt believe America's role in the world should be?

2. **Analyze Structure** How does Roosevelt develop the concept of freedom over the course of his speech?

3. **Compare Points of View** How do you think an isolationist would respond to Roosevelt's speech?

4. **Determine Author's Purpose** Do you think Roosevelt highlighted the "Four Freedoms" during his 1941 State of the Union address to prepare the nation for war? Why or why not? Cite specific passages from his speech to support your answer.

In the beginning of December 1941, the United States had engaged in warlike activity but had yet to commit itself to fighting with either side. A surprise attack on Pearl Harbor, an American naval base in Hawaii, ended all debate and brought the United States into the war. The participation of the United States in this war, as in World War I, would decide the struggle's conclusion.

>> The USS *West Virginia* burned for hours after being hit by several torpedoes during the Japanese attack on Pearl Harbor. In the foreground, sailors on a small boat rescue a survivor in the water.

 Bounce to Activate Flipped Video

The United States Enters World War II

Japan Attacks the United States

Although Japan and the United States had been allies in World War I, conflict over power in Asia and the Pacific had been brewing between the two nations for decades prior to 1941. Japan, as the area's industrial and economic leader, resented any threats to its authority in the region. The presence of the United States in Guam and the Philippines posed such a threat. The United States also supported China in its ongoing struggle with Japan by sending aid and providing military advice. Still Japan relied on trade with the United States to supply much-needed natural resources.

U.S. Involvement in the Pacific Grows As war broke out in Europe, the Japanese Empire continued to grow in China and began to move into Indochina. In July of 1940, President Roosevelt tried to stop this expansion by placing an embargo on important naval and aviation supplies to Japan, such as oil, iron ore, fuel, steel, and rubber.

After Japan signed the Tripartite Pact in September of 1940 with Germany and Italy, FDR instituted a more extensive

>> **Objectives**

Explain why Japan decided to attack Pearl Harbor, and describe the attack itself.

Outline how the United States mobilized for war after the attack on Pearl Harbor.

Summarize the course of the war in the Pacific through the summer of 1942.

>> **Key Terms**

Hideki Tojo
Pearl Harbor
George Marshall
Women's Army
  Corps (WAC)
Douglas MacArthur
Bataan Death March
Battle of Coral Sea

> "
I saw more planes coming in, passing over Battleship Row dropping bombs. I remember very clearly what looked like a dive-bomber coming in over the *Arizona* and dropping a bomb. I saw that bomb go down through what looked like a stack, and almost instantly it cracked the bottom of the *Arizona*, blowing the whole bow loose. It rose out of the water and settled. I could see flames, fire, and smoke coming out of that ship, and I saw two men flying through the air and the fire, screaming as they went.

—Corpsman James F. Anderson, aboard the hospital ship USS *Solace* in Pearl Harbor

>> The USS *Arizona* sank during the attack. Nearly 1,200 sailors and marines died aboard this ship, which still lies at the bottom of the harbor.

Bounce to Activate Map

embargo. The embargo slowed, but did not stop, Japanese expansion as the Japanese were able to secure the resources they needed within their new possessions.

In 1941, General **Hideki Tojo** (hì DEHK ee TOH joh) became the Japanese prime minister. Known as "the Razor" for his sharp mind, he focused intently on military expansion but sought to keep the United States neutral. Throughout the summer of 1941, Japan and the United States attempted to negotiate an end to their disagreement, but with little success. Japan was bent on further expansion, and the United States was firmly against it. Finally, in late November 1941, Cordell Hull, the U.S. Secretary of State, rejected Japan's latest demands.

Diplomatic relations continued for the next week, but Tojo had given up on peace. By early December he had made the decision to deliver a decisive first blow against the United States.

The Attack on Pearl Harbor As Japanese diplomats wrangled in the U.S. capital, Japan's navy sailed for **Pearl Harbor**, Hawaii, the site of the United States Navy's main Pacific base. The forces that Tojo sent from Japan under the command of Vice Admiral Chuichi Nagumo (joo EE chee nah GOO moh) included 6 aircraft carriers, 360 airplanes, an assortment of battleships and cruisers, and a number of submarines. Their mission was to eradicate the American naval and air presence in the Pacific with a surprise attack. Such a blow would prevent Americans from mounting a strong resistance to Japanese expansion.

The attackers struck with devastating power, taking the American forces completely by surprise.

The Aftermath of the Attack The Americans suffered heavy losses: nearly 2,500 people killed, 8 battleships severely damaged, 3 destroyers left unusable, 3 light cruisers damaged, and 160 aircraft destroyed and 128 more damaged. The U.S. battle fleet was out of commission for nearly six months, allowing the Japanese to access the raw materials of their newly- conquered territories, just as they had planned.

Despite these losses, the situation was not as bad as it could have been. The most important ships—aircraft carriers—were out at sea at the time of the attack and survived untouched. In addition, seven heavy cruisers were also out at sea. Of the battleships in Pearl Harbor, only three—the USS *Arizona*, the USS *Oklahoma*, and the USS *Utah* — suffered irreparable damage. American submarine bases also survived the morning, as did important fuel supplies and maintenance facilities.

In the final analysis, Nagumo proved too conservative. He canceled a third wave of bombers and refused to seek out the aircraft carriers. The American Pacific Fleet survived.

Roosevelt Declares War The attack on Pearl Harbor was a turning point for the United States. The Japanese dictatorship's aggression, culminating in the attack on Pearl Harbor, was a compelling reason for the United States to enter the war.

As the news spread across the nation and FDR prepared to address Congress, Americans rallied together. Many did not know what to expect, but they anticipated monumental changes. Journalist Marquis Child recalled thinking, "Nothing will ever be the same," and added, "it never was the same."

The smoke rising from Pearl Harbor left little doubt in anyone's mind about the necessity of declaring war on Japan. Earlier in 1941, further qualms about supporting the Allies had risen when Stalin's Soviet Union joined their ranks. The Soviet Union became one of the Allies when Germany went back on the Nazi-Soviet Nonaggression Pact and invaded the Soviet Union in June 1941. Although the alliance with the Soviet Union would continue to be an uneasy one, Pearl Harbor finally ended the political divisions between isolationists and interventionists.

On December 8, President Roosevelt gave a speech to Congress asking for a declaration of war:

Yesterday, December 7, 1941—a date which will live in infamy— the United States of America was suddenly and deliberately attacked by naval and air forces of the Empire of Japan. . . . The facts of yesterday speak for themselves. The people of the United States have already formed their opinions and well understand

>> In late 1941, the prime minister of Japan, Hideki Tojo, planned a surprise attack on American forces.

>> Japanese planes are readied for the attack aboard the Japanese aircraft carrier *Hiryu*. **Determine Point of View** Who do you think took this picture? Why would that person have wanted to document this event?

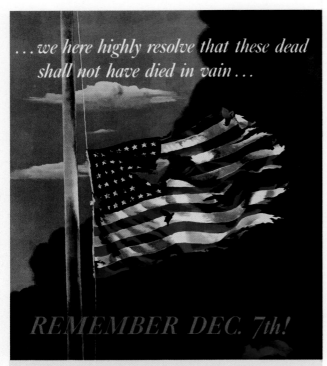

...we here highly resolve that these dead shall not have died in vain ...

REMEMBER DEC. 7th!

>> To inspire the war effort, this poster shows a battered American flag and a quote from Lincoln's Gettysburg Address. **Connect** Why did the poster's creator recall the Gettysburg Address?

the implications to the very life and safety of our nation. . . . No matter how long it may take us to overcome this premeditated invasion, the American people in their righteous might will win through to absolute victory.

—President Franklin Roosevelt, *Message Asking for War Against Japan, December 8, 1941*

After President Roosevelt's speech, the House voted 388 to 1 to declare war against Japan, and the Senate joined them unanimously. True to their military commitments with Japan, Germany and Italy declared war on the United States. Congress in turn declared war on Germany and Italy.

The United States became a full ally with Britain, France, and the Soviet Union against the Axis Powers. Democrats and Republicans put aside their political differences to unify the nation as it faced the task of winning a war on multiple fronts.

☑ **IDENTIFY CAUSE AND EFFECT** How did Pearl Harbor change American opinion about the war?

Patriotism Inspires Rapid Mobilization

Following the Japanese attack, a spirit of patriotism and service swept across the country, inspiring exceptional actions by military personnel and civilians alike. Americans searched for ways to contribute to the war effort. They joined the military, volunteered with the Red Cross and other organizations, and moved into new jobs to help.

High Levels of Enlistment in the Military
The military draft was already in place under the Selective Training and Service Act of 1940. After Pearl Harbor, however, men rushed to volunteer for the various branches of the armed forces. In all, 38.8 percent of those who served in the military volunteered, with the remaining 61.2 percent responding to the draft.

Organizing and prioritizing the needs of the military was a massive job. As army chief of staff, General **George Marshall** directed the military buildup, from coordinating and training troops to overseeing the manufacturing and delivery of all the necessary supplies.

During the course of the war, more than 16 million Americans served in the military. From 1941

>> Young men waited in line to volunteer for the United States Navy on December 8, 1941. The draft was already in place, but many young men volunteered before being drafted.

Bounce to Activate Gallery

to 1942 alone, the army grew from about 1.4 million to more than 3 million, the navy increased from under 300,000 to more than 600,000, and the marines expanded from about 54,000 to almost 150,000.

Americans from all ethnic and racial backgrounds joined the fight. Approximately 300,000 Mexican Americans and 25,000 Native Americans served in integrated units. More than 250,000 Filipinos joined up. Nearly one million African Americans also joined the military. At first, they were limited to supporting roles. However, about 50,000 African Americans eventually served in combat units. In addition, many of those in service and support units played vital, dangerous roles in military operations such as the D-Day invasion and the Battle of the Bulge. A small number of African Americans eventually served in integrated units, but the military was not officially desegregated until after the war. Despite the obstacles facing them, African Americans served patriotically and with distinction.

Gay Men and Lesbians Face Official Hostility

One minority, however, faced a unique kind of hostility as they signed up—homosexuals endured an unprecedented effort to screen them out and reject them from the war effort. During the 1930s, psychiatrists had begun to define homosexuality as a mental illness, a diagnosis that influenced the policies of the U.S. military. Although gay men and lesbians still served in the armed forces in significant numbers, they were forced to conceal their identity, risking imprisonment or dishonorable discharge if their sexual orientation was revealed. However, the mass enlistment of the war drew gay men and lesbians out of small towns and into the larger cities and bases, where they began meeting one another. Ironically, the wartime persecution of homosexuals helped forge a sense of gay identity and set the stage for an increasingly organized resistance and the beginnings of the gay rights movement.

Women Join the Fight

Over 350,000 women also responded to the call. In 1941, Congresswoman Edith Nourse Rogers introduced a bill to establish a Women's Army Auxiliary Corps. This group became the **Women's Army Corps (WAC)** in 1943. The WAC was part of the regular army, not an auxiliary attachment, and women who served in it received the same benefits as men. More than 150,000 women volunteered for the service.

The WACs fulfilled important functions as clerical workers, truck drivers, instructors, and lab technicians for the United States Army. Over the course of the war, 15,000 WACs served abroad and over 600 received medals for their service. Around

>> Mexican Americans served in integrated units during World War II. Some units, like this one, were mostly Mexican American because they were recruited from Mexican American communities.

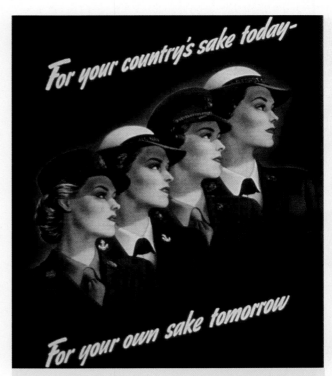

>> This poster shows (left to right) women in the Marines, Navy, Army, and Coast Guard. **Interpret** What strikes you about their appearance? Why did the artist portray them like that?

>> The Liberty Ship *Robert E. Peary* was built in four days. Kaiser's shipyards welded rather than riveted prefabricated parts, cutting the time it took to make these cargo ships by one third.

>> Workers at Chrysler's Detroit Tank Arsenal assemble M-3 Medium tanks. Nicknamed the "General Grant," these tanks arrived just in time to help the British hold North Africa.

100,000 American women joined the navy's female corps and tens of thousands more joined similar marine and Coast Guard groups. More than 57,000 nurses served in the Army Nurse Corps, putting themselves in danger to care for the wounded.

FDR Leads Domestic Industry's Rapid Mobilization From the start, Roosevelt and the other Allied leaders knew that American production would play a key role in helping the Allies win the war. Although America's industry had started to mobilize in response to the Lend-Lease Act, American production still needed to churn out war materials faster. In January 1942, FDR created the War Production Board (WPB) to oversee the conversion of peacetime industry to war industry.

The WPB called for factories to convert to airplane, tank, or bomb production. Conversions started immediately, although the competing demands of different industries and agencies for scarce resources caused much confusion.

Next, FDR and Congress created a host of other agencies that worked together to organize the production effort. Together, the agencies allocated scarce materials into the proper industries, regulated the production of civilian goods, established production contracts, negotiated with organized labor, and controlled inflation. The Office of War Mobilization (OWM) supervised all of these efforts.

FDR also reached out to business leaders, who as a group had often opposed his New Deal programs, to get their expertise at leading or advising several of these agencies. Called "Dollar-a-Year-Men," many executives were paid little or nothing to come to Washington to help in the war effort.

The Production Miracle Under government direction, Americans created a "production miracle." The massive defense spending finally ended the Great Depression. The unemployment rate fell from 19 percent in 1938 to just 1.2 percent in 1944. For the first time in more than a decade there was a job for almost every worker. Each year of the war, the United States raised and met its production goals for military materials.

The Ford Motor Company poured its resources into war production, building over 8,000 B-24 Liberator bombers. Using an innovative assembly process, Henry J. Kaiser's shipyards produced large merchant "Liberty Ships" in as little as three and a half days. In 1944, American production levels were double those of all the Axis nations put together. The success of American domestic industry's rapid

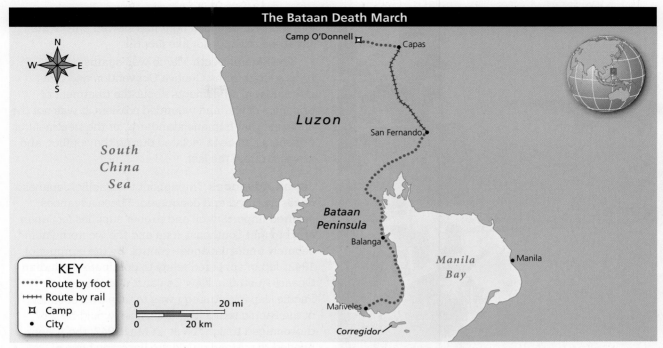

The Bataan Death March

Camp O'Donnell
Capas
Luzon
San Fernando
South China Sea
Bataan Peninsula
Balanga
Manila Bay
Manila
Mariveles
Corregidor

KEY
····· Route by foot
+++++ Route by rail
⌂ Camp
• City

0   20 mi
0   20 km

>> The march from Bataan is notorious for the inhumane way the Allied prisoners of war were treated. **Analyze Maps** Which parts of the march were by foot? Which parts were by rail?

mobilization gave the Allies a crucial advantage. In a toast at a wartime conference, Allied leader Joseph Stalin praised American production: "To American production, without which the war would have been lost."

California played a huge role in America's war effort as the number of military bases in the state increased from 16 to 41. By the end of the war, California would be the nation's fastest growing state, and the experience of war would transform the state demographically, economically, socially, and politically.

☑ **CLASSIFY** Which was more important, military or industrial mobilization?

The Early War in the Pacific

After Pearl Harbor, the Japanese knew they had to move fast to gain footholds in Asia and the Pacific. Although Japan's population was smaller than that of the United States, the Japanese did have military advantages, including advanced weapons and a well-trained and highly motivated military. At the start of the Pacific war, the outlook was grim for America.

Losses in the Philippines In December 1941, General **Douglas MacArthur**, commander of United States Army forces in East Asia, struggled to hold the U.S. positions in the Philippines with little support. The task grew even more daunting when the Japanese destroyed half of the army's fighter planes in the region and rapidly took Guam (gwahm), Wake Island, and Hong Kong. The main land attack came on December 22.

With Japanese forces advancing on two sides, MacArthur and his troops fell back from Manila to the Bataan (buh TAN) Peninsula and a fortification on Corregidor (kuh REHG uh dor) Island, where they dug in for a long siege. Trapped, the Allies suffered greatly, lacking necessary supplies and rations.

Realizing that it was only a matter of time before the Allies were forced to surrender, Roosevelt ordered MacArthur to leave to take command of the army in the Southwest Pacific. After MacArthur left on March 11, the remaining Allied forces held out on the Bataan Peninsula until early April, when about 70,000 troops surrendered.

Japanese troops forced the sick and malnourished prisoners of war to march more than 60 miles inland. More than 7,000 American and Filipino troops died on the grueling journey, which is known as the **Bataan Death March**. In early May 1942, the Allies

>> A B-25 bomber plane takes off from the aircraft carrier USS *Hornet* on April 18, 1942. This plane and its five crewmembers, along with 15 other planes, made a daring raid on Tokyo.

>> Pilots from the famous Flying Tigers flew planes painted with their trademark tiger shark faces.

lost the Philippines when the citadel on Corregidor surrendered. The long fight had slowed part of the Japanese advance for five months.

The Bataan Death March was against the rules set out in the Geneva Convention and other international agreements about the treatment of prisoners of war and wounded soldiers. It was not the first time that humane standards for the treatment of prisoners had been violated during the conflict, and it was far from the last.

Japan Advances Throughout the Pacific, Japanese forces attacked and conquered. These advances secured important oil and rubber supplies for Japan and brought Southeast Asia and the western Pacific securely under Japanese control. By the summer of 1942, Japan appeared ready to dominate the Indian Ocean, Australia, New Zealand, and the central Pacific. Japan's strategy was to take over so much of the Pacific region that the Allies would be too discouraged to fight back. In May 1942, the Allies needed to regroup quickly to have any hope of victory in the Pacific.

The United States Strikes Back After Pearl Harbor, FDR wanted the United States to retaliate against Japan. American military leaders devised a plan for a nighttime bombing raid from the deck of the aircraft carrier USS *Hornet*, led by Colonel James Doolittle. While still 800 miles away from mainland Japan, the *Hornet* was detected, so rather than wait for night, Doolittle led a force of 16 B-25 bombers against Tokyo. They delivered their payload on the Japanese capital just after noon.

The raid killed 50 Japanese people and damaged 100 buildings. The pilots then flew to China, where they crash-landed. Doolittle's Raid proved a minimal military gain, but it bolstered American morale for the long fight ahead.

Another group that contributed bravely to the American cause was the American Volunteer Group, known as the Flying Tigers. Led by retired army captain Claire Chennault, the pilots volunteered to fight the Japanese in the Pacific in 1941, flying their missions out of Burma. Between December 1941 and July 1942, the Flying Tigers destroyed 296 Japanese aircraft in China and Burma.

The Battle of Coral Sea Halts the Advance The **Battle of Coral Sea** also helped to kindle hope for the American military in the Pacific. In early May 1942, the Japanese moved to take Port Moresby in

Japanese Aggression, December 1941–June 1942

Legend:
- Extent of Japanese control, Dec 1941
- Extent of Japanese control, June 1942
- Areas under Japanese control, 1942
- Japanese advance, December 1941
- Japanese advance, January–May 1942
- Battle

>> By mid-1942, the Japanese controlled much of Southeast Asia and the Pacific. **Analyze Maps** Summarize the position of the Allies in the Pacific in June 1942.

Bounce to Activate Map

New Guinea. From that position they could threaten Australia and protect their important military bases at Rabaul (also in New Guinea). To counter Japan's move, the United States sent two aircraft carriers, the USS *Lexington* and USS *Yorktown*, along with support vessels. On May 7 and 8, in the middle of a Pacific storm, Japanese and U.S. aircraft carriers engaged in battle. It was the first sea fight in which enemy warships never sighted one another. Instead, U.S. airplanes attacked Japanese ships and vice versa.

Although technically the Battle of Coral Sea proved a draw, strategically it was a victory for the United States because it forced the Japanese to call off their attack on New Guinea. It marked a shift in momentum toward the Americans. From that day on, the Pacific theater of battle would be won or lost on the strength of aircraft carriers and planes. Here the productive capacity of the United States gave Americans a marked advantage over their adversaries. The war would last three more years, but the dark days of early 1942 were over.

☑ **SEQUENCE EVENTS** What happened in the Pacific theater from December 1941 through May 1942?

☑ ASSESSMENT

1. **Identify Central Issues** Why did having the Soviet Union as an ally contradict one of the reasons for United States involvement in the war?

2. **Compare and Contrast** the contributions of Generals George Marshall and Douglas MacArthur during the first months of the war.

3. **Support Ideas with Examples** What actions did Americans take to show their patriotism after Pearl Harbor?

4. **Identify Patterns** What about the nature of warfare during World War II made the ability to produce war material so important?

5. **Make Predictions** What did the Bataan Death March foreshadow about the war in the Pacific?

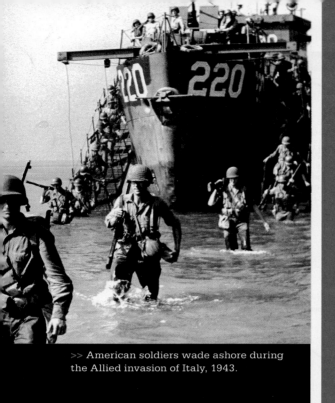

>> American soldiers wade ashore during the Allied invasion of Italy, 1943.

Bounce to Activate Flipped Video

6.4 The attack on Pearl Harbor brought America into World War II on the Allied side. By June 1942, the Allies were battered but still fighting. British pilots had fought off a Nazi invasion of their island, while at the Battle of Coral Sea, the U.S. Navy had frustrated Japanese plans to extend their domination in the Pacific. Though years of fighting lay ahead, the Allies spied signs of hope.

>> Objectives

Analyze the reasons for and impact of the Allies' "Europe First" strategy.

Explain why the battles of Stalingrad and Midway were major turning points in the war.

Discuss how the Allies put increasing pressure on the Axis in North Africa and Europe.

>> Key Terms

Dwight Eisenhower
George S. Patton, Jr.
unconditional surrender
saturation bombing
strategic bombing
Tuskegee Airmen
Chester Nimitz
Battle of Midway
Omar Bradley

A War on Two Fronts

Allied Strategy

The Axis Powers never had a coordinated strategy to defeat the Allies. Germany, Italy, and Japan shared common enemies but had strategies that reflected their individual political and military goals. Hitler wanted to dominate Europe and eliminate "inferior" peoples. Mussolini had dreams of an Italian empire stretching from the eastern Adriatic to East Africa. Tojo sought Japanese control of the Western Pacific and Asia.

The Allies shared more unified goals, although they did not completely trust one another. Roosevelt and Churchill feared that Stalin wanted to dominate Europe.

Stalin believed that the West wanted to destroy communism. None of the Allies wanted to risk a breakdown in their alliance, however. Roosevelt worked closely with Churchill to manage the relationship with their powerful but problematic ally, Stalin.

Roosevelt, Churchill, and Stalin considered Germany the most dangerous enemy. None felt Japan or Italy posed a serious long-term threat. Only Germany had the resources to simultaneously bomb Britain, fight U.S. and British navies on the Atlantic, and invade the Soviet Union across a 1,200-mile front. Thus, although their ultimate goal was to fight and win a two-front war, Roosevelt and the other Allied leaders agreed to pursue a "Europe First" strategy.

They would focus on finishing the war in Europe before trying to end the war in Asia.

☑ **INFER** Why do you think Churchill and Stalin favored a Europe First strategy?

The European Front

The first blow America struck against the Axis was by fulfilling Roosevelt's promise to be the "arsenal of democracy." American factories turned out millions of tons of guns, tanks, and other supplies—enough to keep the Soviets and British battling Germany for years. The problem was delivering the weapons, food, and medical supplies that fueled the Allied war machine.

War in the Atlantic Hitler was determined to cut the supply lines between the United States and Europe before American aid could make a difference. German U-boats patrolled the Atlantic and Caribbean, sinking more than 3,500 merchant ships and killing tens of thousands of Allied seamen. "The only thing that ever really frightened me during the war was the U-boat peril," Churchill wrote.

Finally, in mid-1943, the Allies began to win the war in the North Atlantic. As in World War I, convoys of escort carriers protected Allied shipping.

A new invention, radar, helped Allied vessels locate U-boats on the surface at night. Bombers and underwater depth charges allowed Allied forces to sink U-boats faster than Germany could manufacture them.

Soviets and Nazis Battle for Stalingrad
Germany had attacked the Soviet Union in June 1941, sending one army north toward Leningrad, a second east toward Moscow, and a third south toward Stalingrad. Although Hitler's forces pushed deep into Soviet territory, killing or capturing millions of soldiers and civilians, they did not achieve their main objective of conquering the Soviet Union. Soviet resistance and brutal winter weather stopped the German advance.

In 1942, Hitler narrowed his sights and concentrated his armies in the southern Soviet Union. His goal this time was to control the rich Caucasus oil fields. To achieve this objective, he would have to capture the city of Stalingrad.

The struggle for Stalingrad was especially ferocious. German troops advanced slowly, fighting bitter block-by-block, house-by-house battles in the bombed-out buildings and rubble.

>> German troops march through Berlin, Germany, to mark the surrender of France in 1940. **Interpret** What does this photo suggest about the power of the Axis armies during the early years of the war?

>> American sailors watch as Allied bombers attack a German U-boat, 1944. A few minutes after this photo was taken, the U-boat was sunk.

 Bounce to Activate Gallery

>> Soviet troops fought in the ruins of buildings in Stalingrad in 1942.

>> Airplanes played a key role during the war in North Africa, bombing enemy troops and carrying supplies to war zones. Here, a U.S. cargo plane flies over pyramids in Egypt.

Bounce to Activate Gallery

Soviet troops then counterattacked, trapping the German forces. Yet Hitler refused to allow his army to retreat. Starving, sick, and suffering from frostbite, the surviving German troops finally surrendered on January 31, 1943.

The battle of Stalingrad was the true turning point of the war in Europe, ending any realistic plans Hitler had of dominating the entire continent. Nazi armies were forced to retreat westward back toward Germany. Instead, it was the Soviet Union that now went on the offensive.

War in North Africa Meanwhile, another important campaign was taking place in the deserts and mountains of North Africa, where the British had been fighting the Germans and Italians since 1940. Several goals motivated the Allied campaign in North Africa. Stalin had wanted America and Britain to open a second front against Germany in Western Europe, which would help relieve German pressure on the Soviet Union.

Roosevelt and Churchill felt they did not have the resources to prepare for an invasion of mainland Europe. An invasion of North Africa, however, required less planning and fewer supplies. In addition, forcing Germany out of North Africa would pave the way for an Allied invasion of Italy.

Allied soldiers had to fight in many different types of terrain during the war. But the Sahara of North Africa—the world's largest desert—presented special challenges. In hot, dry weather, sandstorms choked and blinded troops. Tanks kicked up enormous dust clouds that were visible miles away, making it difficult for troops to move without being seen. Furthermore, most supplies for Allied troops in North Africa had to be brought in by sea, where transport ships faced German attacks.

In November 1942, the British won a major victory at El Alamein (ehl al uh MAYN) in Egypt and began to push westward. The victory prevented Germany from gaining access to the Suez Canal and oil fields in the Middle East.

About the same time, Allied troops landed in Morocco and Algeria and began to move east toward key German positions. An energetic American officer, General **Dwight Eisenhower** —known as Ike—commanded the Allied invasion of North Africa.

In February 1943, German general Erwin Rommel (known as the Desert Fox) led his Afrika Korps against the Americans at the Kasserine Pass in Tunisia. Rommel broke through the American lines in an attempt to reach the Allied supply base at Tebessa in Algeria. Finally, American soldiers stopped the assault. Lack of supplies then forced Rommel to retreat.

Allies Take Over North Africa The fighting at the Kasserine Pass taught American leaders valuable lessons. They needed aggressive officers and troops better trained for desert fighting. To that end, Eisenhower put American forces in North Africa under the command of **George S. Patton, Jr.**, an innovative tank commander.

A single-minded general known as Blood and Guts, Patton told his junior officers:

> You usually will know where the front is by the sound of gunfire, and that's the direction you should proceed. Now, suppose you lose a hand or an ear is shot off, or perhaps a piece of your nose, and you think you should walk back to get first aid. If I see you, it will be the last . . . walk you'll ever take.
> —George S. Patton, Jr., 1943

>> General George Patton was one of the most famous American military leaders during World War II. He led American troops to victory in North Africa.

Serving under Patton was another able general, **Omar Bradley,** who took command of Patton's group in March 1943 when Patton moved on to plan the next Allied move. American forces advanced east toward Tunisia with increasing confidence. Simultaneously, the British pressed westward from Egypt, trapping Axis forces in a continually shrinking pocket in Tunisia. Rommel escaped, but his army did not. In May 1943, the remaining German and Italian forces in North Africa—some 240,000 troops—surrendered.

☑ **IDENTIFY CAUSE AND EFFECT** How did geographic factors affect the war on the North Atlantic, at Stalingrad, and in North Africa?

Axis Powers on the Defensive

Germany was now on the defensive, and the Allies planned to keep it that way. In January 1943, Roosevelt and Churchill met in Casablanca, Morocco, to plan their next move. The conference resulted in two important decisions. First, the Allies decided to increase bombing of Germany and invade Italy. Second, Roosevelt announced that the Allies would accept only **unconditional surrender**, or giving up completely without any concessions. Hitler, Mussolini, and Tojo could not hope to stay in power through a peace agreement.

Italy Surrenders The Allies next eyed Italy. The island of Sicily was the obvious target for an invasion, as it was situated across the Mediterranean from Tunisia and only two miles from the Italian mainland. The Allies could invade Sicily without great risk from U-boats and under the protection of Allied aircraft. In July 1943, British and American armies made separate landings in Sicily and began to advance across the island before joining forces in the north. Once again, Eisenhower commanded the joint American-British forces, with Patton and Bradley both leading significant American forces.

Eisenhower hoped to trap Axis forces on Sicily, but they escaped to the Italian mainland. Still, the 38-day campaign achieved important results: It gave the Allies complete control of the western Mediterranean, paved the way for an invasion of Italy, and ended the rule of Benito Mussolini. On September 3, 1943, Italy surrendered to the Allies and five weeks later declared war on Germany.

But Hitler was not through with Italy. After a small German airborne force rescued Mussolini from a mountaintop fortress, Hitler installed him as head of a puppet state in northern Italy. In the south, German military forces continued the fight against the Allies.

The invasion of Italy was a slow, grinding slog. Italy was crisscrossed with mountains and rivers. Heavy rains and mountain snows made combat difficult. Soldiers fought in ankle-deep mud. In the mountains, where tanks and heavy artillery were useless, Allied forces depended on mules to haul supplies up slippery and steep roads. To make matters worse, the Germans occupied the best defensive positions. Fighting continued into 1945. The Allies won battles, but none were important enough to end the war in Italy.

Allied Bombers Attack Germany Stalin continued his demand that Roosevelt and Churchill open a second front in France. While the Allies did not launch a massive invasion of France until 1944, they did open a second front of another kind in early 1942. From bases in England, Allied bombers launched nonstop attacks against Germany.

Flying by night in order to avoid being shot down in large numbers, British planes dropped massive amounts of bombs on German cities, including civilian targets. The goal of this **saturation bombing** was to inflict maximum damage.

By day, American bombers targeted Germany's key political and industrial centers. The goal of this campaign of **strategic bombing** was to destroy Germany's capacity to make war. A Nazi official later commented that "the fleets of bombers might appear at any time over any large German city or important factory."

The bravery and contributions of an African American fighter squadron known as the **Tuskegee Airmen** played a key role in the campaign, escorting bombers and protecting them from enemy fighter pilots. In more than 1,500 missions over enemy territory in Europe, the Tuskegee Airmen did not lose a single bomber.

Overall, though, the bombing missions cost the Allies dearly. Bomber crews suffered an incredibly high 20 percent casualty rate. But they successfully carried the war into Germany, day after day and night after night. This second front in the sky did indeed relieve some of the pressure on the Soviet armies on the Eastern Front and helped pave the way for an all-out Allied offensive.

☑ **PARAPHRASE** What was the situation in Italy after September 1943?

>> The B-24 *Liberator*, shown here in a cross-section, was the king of American bombers during the war, faster than previous planes and able to fly on longer missions while carrying more bombs.

Bounce to Activate 3D Model

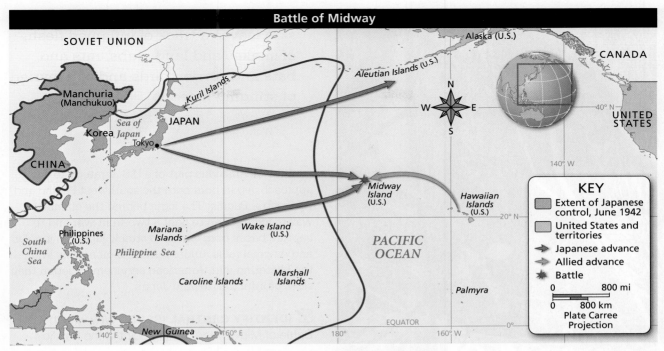

Battle of Midway

>> **Analyze Maps** Why was the location of Midway Island so significant? **Make Predictions** What impact would a Japanese victory at Midway have on the war in the Pacific?

Turning Points in the Pacific

While the Allies pursued their "Europe First" strategy, they did not ignore the Pacific. Through May 1942, Japanese forces continued to advance with seemingly unstoppable momentum. They had attacked American, British, and Dutch colonies, winning control of the Philippines, Malaya, Dutch East Indies, Hong Kong, Wake Island, Guam, and Burma. Then, the United States struck back. The American success at the Battle of Coral Sea in May 1942 served as a warning that the war in the Pacific was about to change.

Americans Triumph at Midway Admiral Yamamoto, commander of Japanese forces in the Pacific, knew that the United States Navy was a powerful threat. Before the Americans could retaliate for Pearl Harbor, Yamamoto sought to destroy American aircraft carriers in the Pacific. He turned his attention to Midway, an American naval base in the Central Pacific that was vital to the defense of Hawaii. Losing Midway would force American defenses back to the California coast. Yamamoto's ambitious plan entailed taking Midway and establishing a military presence in the Aleutians, a string of islands off the coast of Alaska.

What Yamamoto did not realize was that Admiral **Chester Nimitz**, commander of the United States Navy in the Pacific, knew the Japanese plans. U.S. Navy code breakers had intercepted Japanese messages. To meet the expected assault, Nimitz sent his only available aircraft carriers to Midway. The Japanese navy was stretched out across more than a thousand miles, from the Aleutians to well west of Midway. American forces were all concentrated near Midway.

The Japanese began their attack on June 4, 1942. In the **Battle of Midway**, the most important naval battle of World War II, the United States dealt Japan a decisive defeat. American torpedo planes and dive bombers sank four Japanese aircraft carriers, along with all 250 aircraft on board and many of Japan's most experienced pilots. America lost only one aircraft carrier.

Midway was the turning point of the war in the Pacific, ending the seemingly unstoppable Japanese advance. Japan still had a powerful navy, committed troops, and fortified positions. But Japanese forces would never again threaten Hawaii or dominate the Pacific. Japan was now on the defensive.

Americans Take the Offensive The first American offensive in the Pacific took place in August 1942,

>> U.S. soldiers in the jungles of Guadalcanal, 1942. **Express Problems Clearly** How might conditions like this affect the U.S. advance through the Pacific toward Japan?

whose foul scurrying across human skin leaves a track of inflamed flesh, of snakes and land crabs, rats and bats and carrion birds and of a myriad of stinging insects.

—Robert Leckie, *Delivered From Evil: The Saga of World War II*

Guadalcanal was part of a U.S. strategy to approach Japan from both the southwest Pacific and the central Pacific. The logic behind the offensives was to force Japan to fight a two-front war and to capture bases from which to attack Japan. In jungles and on coral reefs, under torrential monsoons and the blistering sun, American servicemen began their slow, painful trek toward Japan.

☑ **IDENTIFY CENTRAL ISSUES** Why was the Battle of Midway the turning point in the Pacific?

with an assault on the island of Guadalcanal. One marine described fighting on Guadalcanal:

It was beautiful, but beneath the loveliness . . . Guadalcanal was a mass of slops and stinks and pestilence; of scum-crusted lagoons and vile swamps inhabited by giant crocodiles . . . of ants that bite like fire, of tree leeches that fall, fasten and suck; of scorpions, of centipedes

☑ ASSESSMENT

1. **Identify Central Issues** Why did Roosevelt support a "Europe First" strategy even though it had been Japan that had first attacked the United States?

2. **Draw Conclusions** Why was the Battle of Stalingrad a turning point in the European war?

3. **Describe** What was Germany's response to Italy's surrender to the Allies?

4. **Compare and Contrast** British and American bombing strategies in Europe.

5. **Apply Concepts** How does the Battle of Midway illustrate the importance of intelligence gathering and espionage in modern warfare?

While fathers, sons, husbands, and brothers served overseas, their families served on the home front. Every American, regardless of age or background, was expected to help boost morale and make sacrifices to shoulder the cost of the war. The war effort stirred patriotism and caused ordinary citizens to take exceptional actions.

>> During World War II, women gained well-paying factory jobs. **Cite Evidence** Look at the photo. What details can you find that make the work seem pleasant or unpleasant?

Bounce to Activate Flipped Video

The Home Front

Patriotism on the Home Front

The war also promoted economic recovery and spurred a massive movement of people around the country. And, while wartime fears and tensions tested civil liberties, new opportunities for women and minorities would spur stronger efforts to ensure equal rights after the war was over.

The Financial Cost of the War The war eventually cost Americans $330 billion, which was double the total amount of federal expenditures since the founding of the nation. In six years, the national debt skyrocketed from $42 billion to $269 billion. To help raise funds, Congress levied a 5 percent tax on all working Americans.

In addition, millions of Americans bought war bonds. In a **war bond**, citizens lend the government money in order to help fund the war. They bought the bonds at face value, say $25, and then received a certain amount of interest after ten years. The bonds allowed Americans both to save income and invest in the war effort. The government reminded Americans that every dollar spent on war bonds meant another bullet or bomb and another step closer to victory.

>> **Objectives**

Examine how the need to support the war effort changed American lives.

Analyze the effects of the war on civil liberties for Japanese Americans and others.

Explain how World War II increased opportunities for women and minorities.

Describe how World War II caused migration within the United States and the effects of that migration.

>> **Key Terms**

A. Philip Randolph
Executive Order 8802
bracero program
internment
442nd Regimental Combat Team
rationing
Office of War Information (OWI)
war bond
Demographics

Controlling Shortages With factories converting to make goods needed for the war, consumer products soon became scarce. As shortages led to price increases, many feared that inflation would run wild. To manage this problem, FDR created the Office of Price Administration, which had the authority to control wages and set maximum prices.

Another form of economic control was **rationing**. Americans were issued coupon books that limited the amount of certain goods that they could buy. Rationing ensured that raw materials such as rubber and gasoline found their way into war production. Also, rationing of food items ensured that fighting troops would have enough food.

Rationing of food and raw materials created shortages. To help with these shortages, people carpooled to work, recycled tires, and grew their own food in "victory gardens" planted in vacant lots or in their backyards. By 1943, more than 20 million victory gardens had been planted, from tiny household plots to public areas like Copley Square in Boston. Although most Americans accepted the need for wartime controls, others resented the restrictions. Unscrupulous profiteers manipulated the ration coupon system to create a "black market," an illegal underground network for the sale of restricted goods.

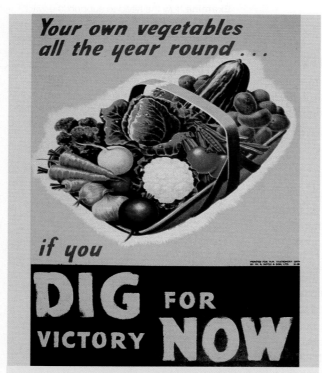

>> In this poster, people on the home front are urged to grow vegetables for victory. **Determine Point of View** Why would the idea of a victory garden have appealed to Americans?

Labor Unrest The government also restricted job mobility to ensure constant production. In some places, wages lagged behind rising prices and profits, and working conditions were less than ideal. Some workers also opposed sharing the workplace with women and African Americans. In 1940 and 1941, strikes were common throughout the country. The nation's labor unions worked with the National War Labor Board to resolve most issues, however, and the strikes never seriously impacted production.

Raising Morale The federal **Office of War Information (OWI)** worked closely with the media to encourage support of the war effort. The OWI tried to spotlight common needs, minimize racial and economic divisions, and downplay problems of poverty and crime. Under the OWI's guidance, the radio, print, and film industries reminded Americans that they were in a struggle between dictatorship and democracy.

Hollywood proved a capable and willing ally in this cause. Documentaries like Frank Capra's *Why We Fight* series highlighted the need to defeat fascism. Fiction films showed patriotic Americans pitching in overseas or on the home front. Movie stars and popular singers volunteered their time to sell war bonds and entertain the troops. Through the United Service Organizations (USO), volunteers boosted the morale of those who were fighting the war.

Encouraged by government and media, Americans voluntarily contributed to the war effort in dozens of large and small ways. They took new jobs and worked overtime at them. Retired citizens went back to work to help out. Americans bought war bonds and paid higher taxes. They volunteered for the Red Cross, manning blood banks, rolling bandages, and sending millions of care packages to soldiers overseas. They collected paper, scrap metal, and cooking fat to recycle for the effort. Instead of buying new, many people followed the motto "Use it up, wear it out, make it do, or do without."

☑ **SUMMARIZE** How did the federal government control resources needed for the war effort?

Japanese Internment During World War II

Not all Americans were included in the spirit of unity. The attack on Pearl Harbor also spread fear across America. The federal government began drafting policies aimed toward immigrants and aliens from the Axis nations. Aliens are foreign citizens living in the United States. All resident "enemy aliens" were required to register with the government, submit to fingerprinting, and list their organizational affiliations.

Executive Order 9066 Originally, laws made no distinction among nationalities. German, Italian, and Japanese aliens were subject to arrest or deportation if deemed dangerous to national security. Some 11,000 German immigrants and hundreds of Italian immigrants were held in camps; others faced curfews or travel restrictions. Federal orders also forced all three groups to vacate the West Coast temporarily in the winter of 1942. Once public fears subsided, FDR removed Germans and Italians from the enemy aliens list.

Japanese aliens and Japanese American citizens received no such respite. Believing people of Japanese ancestry to be inherently disloyal, West Coast leaders pressed FDR to address the "threat." In February 1942, the President issued Executive Order 9066, designating certain areas as war zones from which anyone might be removed for any reason.

By September, the government evacuated more than 100,000 Japanese Americans on the West Coast. Evacuees—including both Issei, Japanese immigrants, and Nisei, native-born American citizens of Japanese descent—were forced to sell their property at a loss and allowed to take only necessary items.

Why did Japanese Americans generally face harsher treatment than Italian or German Americans? Several factors help explain the difference: racism, the smaller numbers of Japanese Americans, their lack of political clout, and their relative isolation from other Americans. In Hawaii, where Japanese Americans comprised one third of a multiracial society, they escaped a similar fate.

Japanese Americans Are Interned The first orders stipulated only that Japanese Americans must leave designated military zones, but leaders in interior states objected. The governor of Arizona insisted his state did not want to become a "dumping ground for enemy aliens." The War Department then initiated a policy of **internment**,

>> All German, Italian, and Japanese citizens in the United States had to register with the U.S. government. **Identify Supporting Details** Why was this notice printed in four languages?

>> This family from Washington state was sent to an internment camp in California. **Express Problems Clearly** What constitutional issues were raised by these evacuations?

>> The Japanese American owner of this store had to sell his goods quickly and at a loss before he relocated. Few Japanese Americans were able to recover their property after the war.

or temporary imprisonment of members of a specific group. Japanese American men, women, and children were transported to camps in isolated locations such as Poston, Arizona, and Jerome, Arkansas. With few exceptions, Nisei and Issei remained in the camps for the duration of the war.

Families huddled into stark one-room shacks, while single people were herded into drafty bunkhouses. Camp schools were hopelessly underfunded. Internees often suffered from food shortages and substandard medical care. The psychological effects could be just as severe.

> The resettlement center is actually a jail—armed guards in towers with spotlights and deadly tommy guns, fifteen feet of barbed-wire fences, everyone confined to quarters at nine. . . .
>
> What really hurts [is being called] 'Japs.' 'Japs' are the guys we are fighting.
> —Ted Nakashima, *The New Republic*, June 5, 1942

Japanese Americans Fight for Rights Since many of those interned in the camps were American citizens, the federal government's policy of internment raised constitutional issues. Some Japanese Americans went to court to seek their rights. In two cases, *Hirabayashi* v. *United States* (1943) and *Korematsu* v. *United States* (1944), the Supreme Court upheld the government's wartime internment policy. Not until 1988 did the government offer an apology and $20,000 payments to surviving internees.

Japanese Americans also faced another form of discrimination. At first, they were not accepted into the armed forces. But after the government lifted the ban in early 1943, many eagerly enlisted. The all-Nisei **442nd Regimental Combat Team** fought in the Italian campaign and became the most decorated military unit in American history.

The 442nd helped counter the notion that Japanese Americans were not loyal citizens.

☑ **CONSTRUCT** Why were Japanese Americans interned during World War II?

>> Veterans of the 442nd Regimental Combat Team gather in Honolulu for the seventieth anniversary of Pearl Harbor. The group had been awarded the Congressional Gold Medal the month before.

Increased Opportunities in Employment

All over the United States, American industry quickly converted to war production to meet the nation's military needs. As the economic effects of World War II brought the Great Depression to an end, the millions of unemployed men who had been such a common sight during the 1930s seemed to vanish overnight. They either joined the military, worked to produce food for the world on the nation's rich farms, or labored in factories producing war materiel. Soon, factories needed to hire workers outside of their usual pool of mostly white men. To keep production going, more women and more African Americans found opportunity in defense industries, although they still faced significant obstacles to gaining and succeeding in those jobs.

Women Work in Defense Industries Government and industry launched an all-out publicity campaign urging women to do their part to meet wartime production quotas. The image of a strong, determined female worker, hair tucked under a kerchief, graced countless magazines and posters. The name "Rosie the Riveter" was first used in a 1942 song, and several real-life Rosies won national publicity. But "Rosie" was really a symbol for an army of women who made artillery shells, sewed uniforms, and welded planes.

Years later, one of them spoke about the contribution that women had made:

> Our war effort . . . it was a good success and a good thing that we did it. It's a good thing that the women went in. It's a good thing that they showed the world that they can do things too. 'Oh, it's dirty work.' Well, making a pie can be dirty work.

—Meda Montana Hallyburton Brendall, Veterans History Project, Library of Congress

Despite the government's encouragement, there were still obstacles to women working in war industry. They were generally paid less than men for the same or similar work. Some new workers also faced hostility in their new workplaces. Still, by the end of the war, women made up more than one third of the wartime workforce.

A woman working outside the home was nothing new, but wartime pressures created two sharp breaks from the past. Many women found jobs,

>> Posters like this one sought to motivate women to take jobs in the defense industry. **Evaluate Sources** How does the artist convey the message that women should work for the war effort?

especially in heavy industry, that fell outside the traditional realm of women's work. The need for labor also weakened the common practice that a woman quit her job once she married. Three fourths of women working in war industries were married, and 60 percent were older than 35 years.

Wartime Work Changes Women's Lives
Although the image of Rosie the Riveter working in a factory was widespread, women labored in both blue-collar and white-collar jobs. Most factory owners expected women to step aside once men returned home at war's end. In white-collar settings, however, the war accelerated long-term trends toward increased employment. During the 1940s, the number of women employed in secretarial and clerical work increased fivefold.

With fathers in the military and mothers in the workplace, children's lives began to change. The federal government spent $50 million building day-care centers for children of working mothers. Still, only about 130,000 kids ended up in day-care centers and most were not filled to capacity. Many parents preferred to leave their children in the care of neighbors or relatives.

>> A. Philip Randolph was a leader in the campaign for civil rights for African Americans for decades. He was one of the key voices behind the influential March on Washington in 1963.

"NATIONAL WAR AGENCIES, ARMY AND NAVY DEPARTMENTS URGE MORE EXTENSIVE USE OF NEGRO WORKERS IN WAR INDUSTRIES".... NEWS ITEM

HE'S WILLING HE'S CAPABLE AND WE NEED HIM — USE HIM !!"

>> This cartoon is from 1943, two years after Executive Order 8802. **Analyze Political Cartoons** Who is the figure in the middle? Why do you think this cartoon was necessary in 1943?

Wartime work helped women move closer to achieving the American Dream, gaining success through hard work and initiative. They benefited from the experience in several ways. They earned paychecks, some for the first time, formed new and different relationships, and gained organizational experience. "I decided that if I could learn to weld like a man," noted one laborer, "I could do anything it took to make a living." The confidence and knowledge women developed enriched their postwar experiences and helped create opportunities for their daughters in the years ahead.

African Americans Seek Employment Opportunities Many African American leaders hoped that the war might provide jobs and alleviate their dismal economic situations. However, few found meaningful employment with national defense employers before Pearl Harbor. Out of 100,000 Americans working in the aircraft industry in 1940, for example, only 240 were African Americans. Even jobs provided by the government and military remained segregated.

African American leaders stressed the need for a "Double V" campaign—victory against fascism abroad and victory against discrimination at home. The charismatic and savvy labor leader **A. Philip Randolph** asserted that African Americans would no longer accept second-class citizenship. "We loyal Negro American citizens demand the right to work and fight for our country," he proclaimed.

In June 1941, Randolph presented President Roosevelt a list of demands, including the end of discriminatory practices in government-funded training, employment, and the armed services. He also took steps to organize a massive protest march on Washington, D.C.

Roosevelt Issues Executive Order 8802 FDR had hoped to put civil rights reform on the back burner while war raged in Europe and Asia. But Randolph persisted in his plans. With the United States nearing involvement in the war, Roosevelt feared that the sight of a huge protest march on the nation's capital would undermine unity and fuel enemy propaganda. So, under pressure, he issued **Executive Order 8802**. This measure assured fair hiring practices in any job funded with government money and established the Fair Employment Practices Committee to enforce these requirements. By 1944, nearly 2 million African Americans worked in defense industries, although racist practices were still common.

Such victories encouraged African Americans to join organizations dedicated to promoting equal rights. The NAACP grew to 500,000 members. In 1942, civil rights leaders founded the Congress of Racial Equality (CORE), an organization that sought to apply nonviolent protest as a means of fighting segregation. Although segregation still prevailed in the military, the South, and other parts of the nation, wartime developments helped set the agenda for the civil rights struggles of the coming decades.

☑ **COMPARE AND CONTRAST** How were the employment experiences for women and African Americans the same? How did they differ?

Migration During World War II

Wartime needs encouraged migration. People from rural areas, whites and African Americans, moved north to industrial cities and west to California. They sought jobs in wartime industries or near military bases. Farmers looked for creative ways to keep their farms producing necessary food. The moving population and new jobs invigorated Americans but the effects of changing demographics also led to strain and unrest in some areas.

Workers on the Move During World War II, California alone gained 2 million new residents seeking work in shipyards and other industries related to the war. The South lost residents in its rural areas, but grew by a million new people as a whole. Older industrial cities in the North, such as Detroit and Chicago, also boomed. Movement of people fostered long-term changes in the country's demographic patterns.

Demographics are statistics that show human characteristics of a population. After receiving billions of dollars to fund industry and build military bases, the South and Southwest became a growing economic and political force.

Population shifts affected Native Americans, too. As Native Americans left reservations to work in defense industries, they had the opportunity to learn new skills and had greater contacts with non-Indians. Many of these people, as well as Native American veterans, never returned to the reservations after the war.

Migration Changes Farming Meanwhile, American farmers faced a challenge. They needed to produce more food than ever before to power both

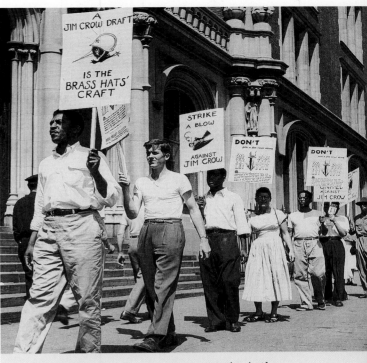

>> In this photo, a group protests segregation in the military in early 1948. **Identify Cause and Effect** How might wartime experiences have strengthened the will to fight a Jim Crow military?

🅑 **Bounce to Activate Gallery**

>> This Mexican family heads to the United States to help fill jobs under the bracero program, which continued into the 1960s.

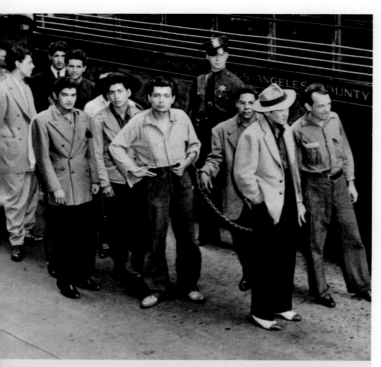

>> Los Angeles police arrest a group of young Mexican Americans in 1943. Some of them, like the second prisoner from the right, wear the flashy zoot suits that gave the incident its name.

Conflict Springs From Migration In the summer of 1943, migration led to racial violence in some cities. The worst occurred in Detroit, where conflict rose over the construction of housing for black workers drawn north to defense plants. Some 100,000 whites and blacks broke into scattered fights at a city park. By the next morning, full-scale riots erupted in which 34 people were killed. Federal troops ended the violence, but the city's problems were never resolved. Mexican Americans had long dealt with similar obstacles.

Few had mastered the English language, and many languished in slums while struggling to find work. A violent incident highlighted the problems. In the Los Angeles area, many Mexican and Mexican American youths dressed in stylish "zoot suits" with baggy pants and long jackets. In June 1943, mobs of off-duty sailors roamed through the Mexican sections of Los Angeles, attacking "zooters." When the fighting ended, police arrested the zoot-suited victims, not their attackers.

After the riots, an indignant Governor Earl Warren formed a committee to investigate the causes of the outbreak and demanded that the guilty parties be punished. Although the committee blamed the lack of sufficient recreation for the violence, long-brewing racial tensions acted as the true spark.

☑ **DEFINE** What was the bracero program?

the American war effort and send to Allies abroad. However, more and more people left farms for the military or jobs in the cities. Farmers developed new farming methods, including more efficient machinery and better fertilizers, to improve yields with fewer workers.

They also found several solutions to alleviate the rural population drain. First, teenagers too young to enlist helped out more.

Also, tens of thousands of Axis prisoners of war were paid to work on farms, which was allowed under the Geneva Convention. Finally, the United States partnered with Mexico to operate the **bracero program**, bringing laborers from Mexico to work on American farms especially in the West. During the war years, several hundred thousand braceros embraced this opportunity and migrated to the United States. In the long term, the bracero program initiated decades of migratory labor in the West.

☑ ASSESSMENT

1. **Identify Central Issues** What were some positive effects of the war on the U.S. economy?

2. **Predict Consequences** Predict two possible consequences for wartime women factory workers when men began to return from overseas after the war.

3. **Synthesize** How did the war affect American farming?

4. **Compare** How were the causes of the Detroit race riots and the Los Angeles Zoot Suit Riots similar?

5. **Make Predications** How did the U.S. government deal with Japanese Americans during the war? How did they respond?

6.6 In 1942 and 1943, the Allies turned back the Axis advances. In the last two years of the war, 1944 and 1945, they delivered the final, crushing blow. They attacked Germany from the west and east, and the United States advanced across the Pacific to the doorstep of Japan. In the process, Americans created a new form of weapon that would change both warfare and global politics.

>> American troops prepare for an attack during the Battle of the Bulge, January 4, 1945. **Express Problems Clearly** How might weather conditions like this affect soldiers?

Bounce to Activate Flipped Video

The Allies Win the War

Planning Germany's Defeat

Opening a Second Front Throughout 1943, Franklin Roosevelt, Winston Churchill, and Joseph Stalin argued over when they would start a second front in France. Up to that point, Soviet troops had done most of the fighting in Europe. Stalin insisted that Britain and the United States carry more of the military burden by attacking Germany in the west, thereby forcing Germany to divide its troops.

Roosevelt sympathized with Stalin's position, but Churchill hesitated and delayed. Recalling the slaughter of British troops on the Western Front in World War I, he was not anxious to see history repeat itself. He argued that the German U-boat presence was too great in the English Channel and that the Allies needed more equipment, more landing craft, and better-trained soldiers.

The Big Three Meet In November 1943, Roosevelt and Churchill traveled to Teheran, Iran, for their first face-to-face meeting with Stalin. Churchill continued to voice concerns about an invasion of France, but Roosevelt sided with Stalin. Reluctantly, Churchill

>> Objectives

Analyze the planning and impact of the invasion of Normandy.

Understand how the Allies achieved final victory in Europe.

Explore the reasons President Truman decided to use the atomic bomb against Japan.

>> Key Terms

Battle of the Bulge
Harry S. Truman
island-hopping
kamikaze
Albert Einstein
Manhattan Project
J. Robert
   Oppenheimer

agreed. After years of war, British and American soldiers would invade France and begin their march toward Germany. At the end of the Teheran Conference, the Big Three issued a joint statement that gave no hint of their earlier disagreements:

> We have reached complete agreement as to the scope and timing of the operations to be undertaken from the east, west and south. The common understanding which we have here reached guarantees that victory will be ours. . . . No power on earth can prevent our destroying the German armies by land, their U Boats by sea, and their war planes from the air.
>
> —Declaration of the Three Powers, December 1, 1943

Six months after the Teheran Conference, the plan to open a second front in France became reality. The massive Allied invasion of France was given the code name Operation Overlord.

☑ **IDENTIFY SUPPORTING DETAILS** Why did Roosevelt and Churchill not agree to open a second front in France until late 1943?

The Invasion of Normandy

Operation Overlord involved the most experienced Allied officers in Europe. American General Dwight D. Eisenhower again served as Supreme Commander. British General Bernard Montgomery served as commander of the ground forces, while General Omar Bradley led the American troops who would participate in the invasion.

Eisenhower Plans the Invasion U.S. Army chief of staff George Marshall had long pushed for an Allied invasion of France, believing that the British strategy of invading North Africa and Italy would not contribute to Germany's defeat. Although he was the obvious choice to lead the invasion of Normandy once the Allies had finally agreed to do so, Roosevelt decided that he was too valuable to remove from his current position. Instead, Roosevelt looked to Eisenhower.

Eisenhower had been given command of all American forces in Europe in 1942—even though

>> Joseph Stalin, Franklin Roosevelt, and Winston Churchill (left to right) at the Teheran Conference, November 1943

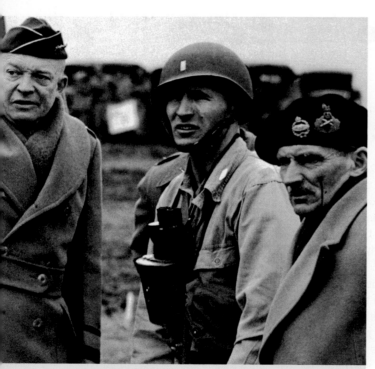

>> General Dwight Eisenhower (left) and British General Bernard Montgomery (right) led the Allied invasion of Normandy.

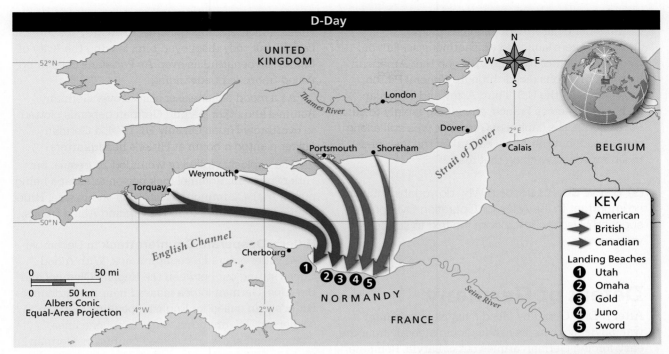

D-Day

>> **Analyze Maps** Summarize the Allied invasion of Normandy. Support your answer with evidence from the map.

Bounce to Activate Gallery

more than 350 other generals had more seniority. After strong performances in North Africa and Italy, he was made Supreme Commander of Allied Forces. In this role, he planned Operation Overlord.

Overlord involved landing 21 American divisions and 26 British, Canadian, and Polish divisions on a 50-mile stretch of beaches in Normandy. The fleet was the largest ever assembled, comprising more than 4,400 ships and landing crafts.

The plan involved striking five Normandy beaches (code-named Utah, Omaha, Gold, Juno, and Sword), but it also included an elaborate deception: the creation of a fictional Allied army under American General George S. Patton. The Allies set up fake headquarters in southeast England across the English Channel from Calais, France, equipped with wood and cardboard tanks, useless ships, and radio messages. The Allies hoped to convince the Germans that the Allied attack would come at Calais, not farther west in Normandy. In the end, the deception worked. Hitler ordered his top tank division to Calais.

Allies Storm the Beaches On June 6, 1944—known as D-Day—the Allies launched the invasion. More than 11,000 planes prepared the way, attempting to destroy German communication and

transportation networks and soften Nazi beach defenses. At 6:30 A.M., after a rough crossing of the English Channel, the first Allied troops landed.

On four beaches, the landings were lightly opposed and casualties were low. But at Omaha, one of the two beaches assigned to American forces, the Germans offered strong opposition.

Germans Defend Normandy On the cliffs overlooking the beach, the Germans had dug trenches and built small concrete pillbox structures from which heavy artillery could be fired. They had the beach covered with a wide variety of deadly guns. They had also heavily mined the beaches. When the first American soldiers arrived, they stepped out of their landing crafts into a rainstorm of German bullets and shells. Some crafts dumped their occupants too far from the beach; soldiers, weighted down by heavy packs and weapons, drowned.

One writer called D-Day "the longest day." For many American soldiers, it was a very short day—and their last day on Earth. Some fought bravely and died. Others fought bravely and survived. By the end of the day, the Allies had gained a toehold in France. Within a month, more than one million Allied troops had landed at Normandy—but there they were held by German defenses.

In mid-July, under General Bradley—the commander of all American forces in France—Allied bombers launched an enormous assault on the German lines, opening up a gap that American armored divisions raced through. General Patton took charge of the U.S. Third Army and began an all-out drive across France, advancing rapidly toward Paris. Berlin, the capital of Germany, was still a long road ahead, but the Allies had taken the first, and most important, step on that road.

☑ **DRAW CONCLUSIONS** Why do you think it was so important to the Allies for Operation Overlord to succeed? Use evidence from the text to support your answer.

Defeat of Germany

After D-Day, Germany faced a hopeless two-front war. Soviet soldiers were advancing steadily from the east, forcing German armies out of Latvia, Romania, Slovakia, and Hungary. Mile by mile, Germany lost the lands it had once dominated and the natural resources it had once plundered.

Allies on the Move Allied armies were also on the move in the west. British and Canadian troops had finally broken through the German lines in northern France and moved south to join Patton's American

>> An American soldier waves from his tank as the Allies enter Paris in August 1944.

forces. In August 1944, the Allies liberated Paris. Hitler had ordered his generals to destroy the French capital, but they disobeyed him, leaving the "City of Lights" as beautiful as ever. As Parisians celebrated, Allied troops kept advancing.

As a mood of hopelessness fell over Germany, Rommel and other leading German generals plotted to overthrow Hitler. On July 20, 1944, a German officer planted a bomb at Hitler's headquarters.

The explosion killed or wounded 20 people, but Hitler survived. Rommel took poison to escape being put on trial. Claiming that fate was on his side, Hitler refused to surrender to the advancing Allied troops.

Hitler's Desperate Counterattack In December 1944, Hitler ordered a counterattack. With Allied troops strung out between the English Channel and the Alps, German forces massed near the Ardennes. Hitler's plan called for English-speaking German soldiers in U.S. uniforms to cut telephone lines, change road signs, and spread confusion. German tanks would then secure communication and transportation hubs.

The counterattack, known as the **Battle of the Bulge**, almost succeeded. The Germans caught the Allies by surprise, created a bulge in the American line, and captured several key towns. Snowy, cloudy skies prevented the Allies from exploiting their air superiority. But at the Belgian town of Bastogne (bas TOHN), American forces led by Eisenhower and Patton held despite frostbite and brutal German assaults. Then, on December 23, the skies cleared and Allied bombers attacked German positions.

After reinforcements arrived, the Allies went back on the offensive, steadily pushing the Germans out of France. The Battle of the Bulge was a desperate attempt to drive a wedge between American and British forces. Instead, the battle crippled Germany by forcing it to use its reserve troops and supplies. Ultimately, it shortened the time Hitler had left.

Winston Churchill gave U.S. forces full credit for the Allied victory at the Battle of the Bulge:

The United States troops have done almost all the fighting and have suffered almost all the losses. They have suffered losses almost equal to those of both sides at the Battle of Gettysburg. . . . [The Battle of the Bulge] will, I believe, be regarded as an ever-famous American victory.

—Winston Churchill, Address to the House of Commons, January 18, 1945

World War II in Europe, 1942–1945

KEY
- Greatest extent of Axis control, 1942
- Allied territory, 1942
- Neutral nations, 1942
- Allied advance
- Major battle

>> **Analyze Maps** Use the information on the map to summarize the course of World War II in Europe from 1942 through 1945. Support your answer with evidence from the map.

Bounce to Activate Map

Courage Under Fire The sacrifices made by American troops in battles such as the Battle of the Bulge were significant—as was the courage these young soldiers showed in combat. In fact, some 40 percent of the Congressional Medals of Honor—the highest military award given by the United States—awarded since 1900 were given for service in World War II. Of the 464 Medals of Honor awarded for World War II, 266 were given posthumously.

Audie Murphy was one recipient of the Medal of Honor. In fact, he received more medals than any other American in World War II. In January 1945, his squad was set upon by German troops. Ordering his men to withdraw, Murphy climbed atop a burning tank that was in danger of exploding. For an hour, he used the tank's machine gun to hold off the enemy:

Germans reached as close as 10 yards, only to be mowed down by his fire. He received a leg wound, but ignored it and continued the single-handed fight until his ammunition was exhausted. He then made his way to his company, refused medical attention, and organized the company in a counterattack.

—Medal of Honor Citation for Audie Murphy

Germany Surrenders By January 1945, the Soviet Army had reached the Oder River outside Berlin. The Allies also advanced northward in Italy. In April, Benito Mussolini tried to flee but was captured and executed. By this time, American and British troops had crossed the Rhine River into Germany, and a U.S. force soon reached the Elbe River, 50 miles west of Berlin. Allied forces were now in position for an all-out assault against Hitler's capital.

Hitler was by now a physical wreck: shaken by tremors, paranoid from drugs, and kept alive by mad dreams of a final victory. He gave orders that no one followed and planned campaigns that no one would ever fight. Finally, on April 30, he and a few of his closest associates committed suicide. His "Thousand Year Reich" had lasted only a dozen years.

On May 7, in a little French schoolhouse that had served as Eisenhower's headquarters, Germany surrendered. Americans celebrated V-E (Victory in Europe) Day. Sadly, President Roosevelt did not see the momentous day. He had died a few weeks earlier.

It would be up to the new President, **Harry S. Truman**, to see the nation through to final victory.

☑ **IDENTIFY SUPPORTING DETAILS** Why do you think the authors write that "Germany faced a hopeless two-front war" after D-Day? Use evidence from the text to support your answer.

Americans Advance Toward Japan

While war still raged in Europe, American forces in the Pacific had been advancing in giant leaps. Under the leadership of General Douglas MacArthur, they followed an **island-hopping** strategy, capturing some Japanese-held islands and ignoring others in a steady path toward Japan.

Navajo troops played a vital role in the Pacific island-hopping campaign. The Navajo language has no written alphabet, and at the start of the war only a small number of non-Navajo people could understand it—none of them Japanese. Navajo radio operators developed and memorized a secret code using the language, and they used it to send critical messages from island to island. The code was never broken by the Japanese.

Struggle in the Pacific From Tarawa and Makin in the Gilbert Islands, American forces jumped ahead to Eniwetok and Kwajalein in the Marshall Islands. Then, they took another leap to Saipan, Tinian, and Guam in the Mariana Islands. By 1944, the United States Navy, under Admiral Nimitz, was blockading Japan, and in October General MacArthur began the fight to retake the Philippines.

American forces took each island only after a difficult struggle. Time and again, Japanese defenders fought virtually to the last man. Rather than surrender, many Japanese troops readily killed themselves. At the same time, Japanese **kamikaze** (kah muh KAH zee) pilots deliberately crashed their planes into American ships. By the end of the war, more than 3,000 Japanese pilots had died in kamikaze missions. Their deaths, however, did not prevent MacArthur from retaking the Philippines—as he had promised when he left the islands in 1942—or the U.S. Navy from sinking Japanese ships.

American Forces Near Japan One of the fiercest battles in the island-hopping campaign took place in February and March 1945.

On Iwo Jima (EE woh JEE muh), a 5-mile-long island 650 miles southeast of Tokyo, the capital of Japan, United States Marines faced a dug-in,

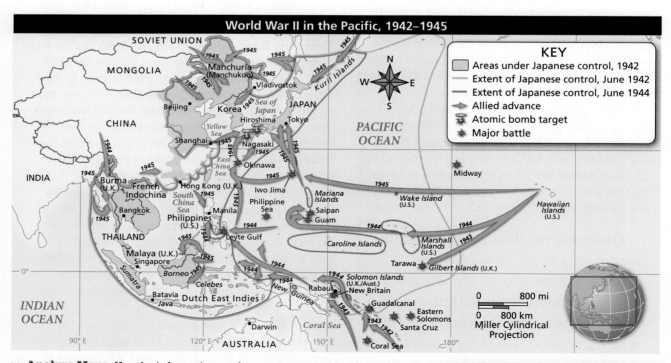

>> **Analyze Maps** Use the information on the map to summarize the course of World War II in the Pacific from 1942 through 1945. Support your answer with evidence from the map.

🅟 **Bounce to Activate Map**

determined enemy. In 36 days of fighting, more than 23,000 marines became casualties. But in the end, the Allies took the island.

The fight for Okinawa (oh kuh NAH wuh) in April 1945 was even deadlier than Iwo Jima. Only 340 miles from Japan, Okinawa contained a vital air base, necessary for the planned invasion of Japan. Taking Okinawa was the most complex and costly operation in the Pacific campaign, involving half a million troops and 1,213 warships. U.S. forces finally took Okinawa but at a cost of roughly 50,000 casualties.

Americans Bombers Attack Japan From Okinawa and other Pacific bases, American pilots could bomb the Japanese home islands. Short on pilots and aircraft, low on fuel and ammunition, Japan was virtually defenseless. American bombers hit factories, military bases, and cities. In a single night in March 1945, B-29 bombers destroyed 16 square miles of Tokyo. The raid killed over 83,000 Japanese—more than either of the later atomic bombs—and injured 100,000 more.

☑ **USE VISUAL INFORMATION** Look at the image of destruction in Tokyo. How might American bombing like this affect the war in the Pacific?

The War Comes to an End

Advances in technology helped determine the outcome of World War II. Allied and Axis scientists labored to make planes faster, bombs deadlier, and weapons more accurate. As always in warfare, specific military needs resulted in scientific discoveries and technological innovations.

Science and Technology Help Win the War
Scientists and engineers on both sides of the war worked on the development of conventional weapons at a rapid pace, creating and improving many wartime technologies. They developed fast and powerful aircraft, ships, and weapons, as well as radar and sonar to detect enemy aircraft and ships. To treat sick and wounded soldiers, they developed a way to mass-produce penicillin, an antibiotic, and to more easily transport and store blood plasma.

To supply military needs, they invented synthetic materials such as nylon, used to make parachutes and vehicle tires. But the most crucial scientific development of all was the atomic bomb.

Scientists Develop the Atomic Bomb In the early 1930s, scientists learned how to split the nuclei

>> A two-man team of Navajo code talkers transmit secret orders over their radio. **Summarize** How did code talkers contribute to the American war effort?

>> In 1945, U.S. bombers launched devastating attacks on Tokyo, killing tens of thousands of people and destroying large areas of the city.

Bounce to Activate Gallery

>> The world's first atomic bomb, code-named Trinity, was detonated in the New Mexico desert on July 16, 1945. **Hypothesize** Why do you think it was important to the Allies that they successfully develop an atomic bomb before the Axis?

>> President Harry Truman decided to use the atomic bomb against Japan in an effort to end the war and limit American casualties.

of certain elements. They also discovered that this process of nuclear fission released tremendous energy. Over the next decade, they learned more about the nature of the atom, the effect of a chain reaction, and the military uses of uranium.

Early in the war, **Albert Einstein**, the world's most famous scientist, signed a letter that alerted President Roosevelt about the need to proceed with development of atomic weapons. In 1942, Roosevelt gave the highest national priority to the development of an atomic bomb. The program, code-named the **Manhattan Project**, cost several billion dollars and employed tens of thousands of people.

The two primary leaders of the project were General Leslie Groves and physicist **J. Robert Oppenheimer**. Groves was responsible for building facilities, acquiring materials, recruiting scientists, and providing security. Oppenheimer ran the scientific aspect of the project from Los Alamos, New Mexico. Scientists working on the top-secret project included many refugees from Europe, including Enrico Fermi, developer of the first atomic reactor.

On the morning of July 16, 1945, in a barren area outside of Alamogordo, New Mexico, the first atomic bomb was tested. The flash of light was clearly visible 180 miles away, and the sound was heard at a distance of 100 miles. Watching the blast, Oppenheimer recalled the following line from a Hindu poem: "Now I am become Death, the destroyer of Worlds."

The general's thoughts were less poetic. Turning to an aide, Groves said, "The war's over. One or two of those things and Japan will be finished."

Truman Decides to Use the Bomb The decision to use the bomb fell directly on the shoulders of Harry Truman.

The new President fully understood the ethical issues presented by using the bomb, especially against civilians. At the same time, he also knew that the Axis Powers had nuclear scientists, and there was no way to tell how close they were to developing their own bomb. Ultimately, Truman's chief priority was to save American lives. His military advisers predicted that, in light of the ferocious defense waged by Japanese soldiers during the island-hopping campaign, an invasion of Japan might cost as many as 1,000,000 American casualties.

In truth, Truman did not agonize over the decision to use the atomic bomb against Japan. For the President, abstract ethical issues did not outweigh very real American lives and an opportunity to end the war. Later, some critics would condemn Truman's decision. But in the late summer of 1945, no one close to him did so.

Hiroshima and Nagasaki Are Destroyed On August 6, 1945, U.S. pilots dropped an atomic bomb on Hiroshima. It exploded at 8:15 A.M. One survivor of the blast later recalled the first moments:

> After I noticed the flash, white clouds spread over the blue sky. It was amazing. It was as if blue morning-glories had suddenly bloomed up in the sky. . . . Then came the heat wave. It was very, very hot. Even though there was a window glass in front of me, I felt really hot. It was as if I was looking directly into a kitchen oven.

—Isao Kita, *Hiroshima Witness*

Within two minutes, more than 60,000 of Hiroshima's 344,000 residents were dead or missing.

Over the next three days, Japanese leaders debated whether to surrender or continue to fight. Then, on August 9, two events rocked Japan. First, the Soviet Union declared war against Japan and invaded Japanese-held Manchuria. Next, the United States dropped a second atomic bomb on Nagasaki, killing 35,000 residents.

Japan Surrenders Debate continued at the highest levels of Japanese government. Finally, Emperor Hirohito made the decision to surrender.

On August 15, the Allies celebrated V-J (Victory in Japan) Day. Japan officially surrendered on September 2 aboard the USS *Missouri.*

But even as the Allies celebrated victory, the horrifying costs of the war began to become clear. As many as 60 million people, mostly civilians, had died in the conflict. Cities, factories, farms, and roads lay in ruins in large parts of Europe and Asia, and millions of refugees were homeless. More than 400,000 Americans had lost their lives. Winning the war had been an enormous effort for the Allies. Peace would bring new challenges.

☑ **SUMMARIZE** How did scientific discoveries and technological innovations affect the war?

>> Americans celebrate the surrender of Japan in August 1945, New York City. At long last, World War II was over.

☑ **ASSESSMENT**

1. **Draw Conclusions** Which Ally bore the brunt of Germany's assault during the first years of the war?

2. **Draw Conclusions** On what issues did Stalin, Roosevelt, and Churchill disagree?

3. **Draw Conclusions** Where and when did the Allies open a second front in Europe? What was the result?

4. **Synthesize** How did the Allies go about pushing the Japanese back in the Pacific?

5. **Make Predications** What were the consequences of the decision to bomb Hiroshima and Nagasaki?

>> In this photograph, Nazi troops remove Jewish residents from the Warsaw ghetto after a failed uprising in 1943. This has become one of the most famous images associated with the Holocaust.

Bounce to Activate Flipped Video

6.7 From the time he came to power, Adolf Hitler had targeted Jews for persecution. By the end of the war, the Nazis had murdered 6 million Jews and 5 million other people they considered inferior. In 1945, there was no word for Hitler's murderous plan of extermination. Today, it is called the Holocaust. We continue to remember this tragedy and seek ways to prevent anything like it from ever happening again.

The Holocaust

Roots of the Holocaust

The mass murders of Jews, as well as other "undesirables," were a direct result of a racist Nazi ideology that considered Aryans (white gentiles, especially those of Germanic, Nordic, and Anglo-Saxon blood) superior to other people. Among the groups that the Nazis considered inferior were the Slavic peoples of Russia and Eastern Europe.

From the start, the Nazi movement trafficked in **anti-Semitism**. Hitler blamed Jews for all the ills of Germany, from communism to inflation to abstract painting—and, especially, for the defeat of Germany in World War I. Other extremists influenced Hitler's ideas and shared his prejudices. In the 1920s, his was just another angry voice in the Weimar Republic, advancing simplistic answers for the nation's grave economic, political, and social troubles. In 1933, however, Hitler became chancellor of Germany.

Hitler's Campaign Against the Jews Hitler's persecution of the Jews began as soon as he came to power. At first, his focus was economic. He urged Germans to boycott Jewish-owned businesses, and he barred Jews from jobs in civil service, banking, the stock exchange, law, journalism, and medicine. In 1935, Hitler moved to a broader legal persecution. The Nuremberg

>> Objectives

Trace the roots and progress of Hitler's campaign against the Jews.

Explain the goals of Hitler's "final solution" and the nature of Nazi death camps.

Examine how the United States responded to the Holocaust.

>> Key Terms

Holocaust
anti-Semitism
Nazism
Kristallnacht
genocide
concentration
   camps
death camps
War Refugee Board

Laws, named for the city that served as the spiritual center of **Nazism**. They denied German citizenship to Jews, banned marriage between Jews and non-Jews, and segregated Jews at every level of society. Yet even these measures were not enough for Hitler. He hinted that, in the future, there might be what he called the "Final Solution to the Jewish question."

Hitler employed the full power of the state in his anti-Semitic campaigns. Newspapers printed scandalous attacks against Jews. Children in schools and the Hitler Youth movement were taught that Jews were "polluting" German society and culture. Comic books contained vile caricatures of Jews.

The Violence of Kristallnacht Acts of violence against Jews were common. The most serious attack on German Jews took place on November 9, 1938. It became known as **Kristallnacht** (KRIHS tahl nahkt), or the "Night of the Broken Glass." After a Jewish refugee killed a German diplomat in Paris, Nazi officials ordered attacks on Jews in Germany, Austria, and the Sudetenland. Secret police and military units destroyed more than 1,500 synagogues and 7,500 Jewish-owned businesses, killed more than 200 Jews, and injured more than 600 others. The Nazis arrested thousands of Jews.

Refugees Try to Escape Between 1933 and 1937, about 129,000 Jews fled Germany and Nazi-controlled Austria. They included some of the most notable figures in the scientific and artistic world, including physicist Albert Einstein.

More Jews would have left, but they were not generally welcomed into other countries. During the Great Depression, with jobs scarce, the United States and other countries barred their doors to many Jews. In 1939, the ocean liner *St. Louis* departed Germany for Cuba with more than 900 Jewish refugees on board. Only 22 of the passengers received permission to stay in Cuba. U.S. officials refused to accept any of the refugees. The ship returned to Germany. Almost 600 of the Jews aboard the *St. Louis* later died in Nazi concentration camps.

☑ **IDENTIFY STEPS IN A PROCESS** How did Hitler and the Nazis gradually deprive Jewish people of their rights?

Hitler's "Final Solution"

Since 1933, the Nazis had denied Jews the rights of citizenship and committed acts of brutality against them. These acts of persecution were steps toward Hitler's "Final Solution to the Jewish question":

>> This propaganda poster from 1935 glorifies the image of what the Nazis saw as the ideal Aryan youth. At the same time, posters and comic books viciously caricatured people the Nazis considered "inferior."

>> Hitler is greeted by children in Poland. The white shirts and ties worn by the girls were part of the uniform of the female branch of the Hitler Youth movement.

nothing short of the systematic extermination of all Jews living in the regions controlled by the Third Reich. Today, we use the word **genocide** to describe such willful annihilation of a racial, political, or cultural group.

The First Concentration Camps In 1933, the year he became chancellor, Hitler opened the first Nazi **concentration camps**, areas where members of specially designated groups were confined. The earliest camps included Dachau, Sachsenhausen, and Buchenwald. Later, Ravensbruck, not far from Berlin, was opened for female prisoners.

In theory, the camps were designed not to kill prisoners, but to turn them into "useful members" of the Third Reich. The Nazis imprisoned political opponents such as labor leaders, socialists, and communists, as well as anyone—journalists or novelists, ministers or priests—who spoke out against Hitler. Many Jews as well as Aryans who had intimate relations with Jews were sent to camps. Other groups targeted as "undesirable" included Gypsies, Jehovah's Witnesses, homosexuals, beggars, drunkards, conscientious objectors, the physically disabled, and people with mental illness.

Camp administrators tattooed numbers on the arms of prisoners and dressed them in vertically striped uniforms with triangular insignias. For example, political prisoners wore red insignias, homosexuals pink, Jews yellow, and Jehovah's Witnesses purple. Inside the walls of the concentration camps, there were no real restraints on sadistic guards. They tortured and even killed prisoners with no fear of reprisals from their superiors.

Death by starvation and disease was an everyday occurrence. In addition, doctors at camps such as Dachau conducted horrible medical experiments that either killed inmates or left them deformed. Prisoners were made subjects of bogus experiments on oxygen deprivation, hypothermia, and the effects of altitude. Bodies were mutilated without anesthesia. Thousands of prisoners died in agonizing pain, including some 5,000 mentally or physically disabled children.

The Nazis Build Death Camps When Germany invaded Poland and the Soviet Union, the Nazis gained control of large territories that were home to millions of Jews. Under Nazi rule, Jews in Warsaw, Lodz, and other Polish cities were forced to live in crowded, walled ghettos. Nazis also constructed additional concentration camps in Poland and Eastern Europe.

At first, the murder of Jews and other prisoners tended to be more arbitrary than systematic. But

Concentration Camps in Europe

KEY
- ■ Death camp
- ■ Major concentration or forced-labor camp

>> **Analyze Maps** How did the locations of death camps differ from the location of concentration camps?

Bounce to Activate Gallery

Color-Coding of Prisoners at Dachau

Jew

Jehovah's Witness

Political prisoner

Homosexual

Immigrant

Criminal

"Antisocial"

>> Prisoners in Nazi concentration camps were identified by triangular color-coded patches. Some prisoners might be forced to wear combinations of patches.

at the Wannsee Conference in January 1942, Nazi leaders made the decision to move toward Hitler's "Final Solution." Reinhard Heydrich, an SS leader known as "the man with an iron heart," outlined a plan to exterminate about 11,000,000 Jews. Although the minutes of the meeting do not use the word "kill," everyone there understood that killing was their goal.

Many concentration camps, especially in Poland, were designated as **death camps**, camps where prisoners were systematically exterminated. The largest death camp was Auschwitz in southern Poland. Others included Treblinka, Maidenek, Sobibor, Belsec, and Chelmno. Prisoners from various parts of the Reich were transported by trains to the death camps and murdered. Nazis forced prisoners into death chambers and pumped in carbon monoxide or crammed the prisoners into shower-like facilities and released the insecticide Zyklon B.

Some concentration camps that the Nazis converted into death camps did not have gassing equipment. In these camps, Nazi guards shot hundreds of thousands of prisoners. Nazi "Action Groups" that followed the army into Eastern Europe also shot several million Jews and buried them in ditches.

In fully functioning death camps, the bodies of murdered prisoners were further desecrated. Human fat was turned into soap; human hair was woven into wigs, slippers, and mattresses; cash, gold fillings, wedding rings, and other valuables were stripped off the victims. After the Nazis had taken what they wanted, they burned the bodies in crematoriums.

By 1945, about 6 million European Jews had been murdered. But Jews were not the only victims. As many as 5 million others lay dead, including nearly 2 million non-Jewish Poles. While many survivors lived with constant nightmares of the experience, or with the sorrow and guilt of being the last members of their families, many others determined to rebuild their lives and families in the United States, Israel, or elsewhere and continue to be productive citizens.

☑ **SUMMARIZE** What actions did the Nazis take to carry out Hitler's "Final Solution?"

Allied Response to the Holocaust

Could the Holocaust have been prevented? Could western democracies—especially Britain, France, and the United States—have intervened to stop the slaughter of millions of innocent people? There are no simple answers. However, many people today believe that the West could have done more than it did.

Early Inaction Before the war, the United States and other countries could have accepted more Jewish refugees from Germany and Austria. However, the U.S. State Department at first made a conscious effort to block Jewish immigration. Later commentators have blamed this failure on several factors: anti-Semitism, apathy, preoccupation with the Great Depression, and a tendency to underestimate Hitler's genocidal plans.

The United States Takes Limited Action Once the war started, news of the mass killings filtered to the West.

By the end of 1942, the Allies acknowledged that Jews were being taken to Poland and killed. In April 1943, British and American officials hosted the Bermuda Conference to discuss rescuing surviving Jewish refugees from Europe. However, no concrete action was taken.

By early 1944, however, FDR began to respond to the reports. He established the **War Refugee Board**, a government agency that worked with the Red Cross to save thousands of Eastern European Jews, especially in Romania and Hungary.

Tragically, too few were saved. Of the Allies, the Soviet Union was closest to the death camps, but

>> These Jewish children from Austria were among those who eventually found homes with adoptive families in the United States.

Stalin showed no concern. Britain and the United States expressed sympathy, but their resources and strategy were focused on defeating Hitler not on stopping his genocidal campaign. They might have bombed railway lines to the death camps, but the camps were not military targets.

A War Department official told the Refugee Board that bombing the railway lines "could be executed only by the diversion of considerable air support essential to the success of our forces now engaged in decisive operations elsewhere." The Allies also refused to pressure countries within the Nazi sphere of influence to stop the transportation of Jews to Germany.

The Liberation of the Concentration Camps
As they pushed toward Germany from the east and west, Soviet and American troops liberated the camps one by one. For most Americans, the enormity of the Nazi crime became real only when the camp liberators began to report back on what they found. When they saw it all—the piles of dead bodies, the warehouses full of human hair and jewelry, the ashes in crematoriums, the half-dead emaciated survivors—they realized as never before that evil was more than an abstraction.

Hardened by war, accustomed to the sight and smell of death, the liberators were nevertheless unprepared for what they saw. Major Richard Winters was stunned almost beyond belief:

> The memory of starved, dazed men, who dropped their eyes and heads when we looked at them through the chain-link fence, in the same manner that a beaten, mistreated dog would cringe, leaves feelings that cannot be described and will never be forgotten. The impact of seeing those people behind that fence left me saying, only to myself, 'Now I know why I'm here.'
>
> —Richard Winters, quoted in *Band of Brothers* (Ambrose)

The liberation of the camps led to an outpouring of American sympathy and sincere longing to aid the victims. Many survivors found temporary or permanent homes in the United States.

The revelation of the Holocaust also increased demand and support for an independent Jewish homeland. In 1948, when the Jewish community in Palestine proclaimed the State of Israel, President

Truman immediately recognized the new nation. Since then, the United States has continued to offer strong support to Israel.

Today, people in the United States and around the world are working to make sure that the Holocaust is not forgotten. In 1993, the United States Holocaust Memorial Museum opened in Washington, D.C. Holocaust memorials can also be found in many states, including Texas, California, Florida, Indiana, and Virginia. In 1994, movie director Steven Spielberg founded an institute that recorded nearly 52,000 interviews with survivors and witnesses of the Holocaust.

☑ **CLASSIFY** Do you think the U.S. military made the right decision or the wrong decision when they decided not to bomb railway lines leading to the death camps?

☑ ASSESSMENT

1. **Generate Explanations** How were Hitler's racial ideas and policies connected to his concept of extreme nationalism?

2. **Describe** How did Hitler enforce anti-Semitism as chancellor of Germany?

3. **Define** What was the "Final Solution"?

4. **Interpret** How did the U.S. government respond to the German campaign against European Jews?

5. **Connect** How are the Holocaust and the creation of Israel connected?

>> In April 1945, former prisoners of Dachau gather as their American liberators raise the American flag over the camp.

Bounce to Activate Chart

>> This Holocaust museum in Texas is one of many museums and memorials across the United States. **Draw Conclusions** Why do Americans believe it is important to remember the Holocaust?

The Diary of a Young Girl: Anne Frank

In 1933, Adolf Hitler was elected Chancellor of Germany. During World War II, his Nazi Party rounded up European Jews, many of whom were transported to death camps. Anne Frank was a young Jewish girl who hid with her family in small, concealed rooms in her father's office. Frank kept a diary from June 12, 1942 to August 1, 1944, when her family's hiding place was discovered. She died in a concentration camp in 1945. Frank's father survived and published her diary to share Anne's story with the world.

>> Anne Frank

Saturday, June 20, 1942

My father was thirty-six when he married my mother, who was then twenty-five. My sister Margot was born in 1926 in Frankfort-on-Main. I followed on June 12, 1929, and, as we are Jewish, we emigrated to Holland in 1933, where my father was appointed Managing Director of Travies N.V. This firm is in close relationship with the firm of Kolen & Co. in the same building, of which my father is a partner.

The rest of our family, however, felt the full impact of Hitler's anti-Jewish laws, so life was filled with anxiety. In 1938 after the pogroms [organized killing and other persecution of Jews], my two uncles (my mother's brothers) escaped to the U.S.A. My old grandmother came to us, she was then seventy-three. After May 1940 good times rapidly fled: first the war, then the capitulation [surrender]; followed by the arrival of the Germans, which is when the sufferings of us Jews really began.

☑ **IDENTIFY SUPPORTING DETAILS** What details from the passage above show that Frank and her family were concerned about the Nazis?

Anti-Jewish decrees followed each other in quick succession. Jews must wear a yellow star. Jews must hand in their bicycles. Jews are banned from trains and are forbidden to drive. Jews are only allowed to do their shopping between three and five o'clock and then only in shops which bear the placard [sign] "Jewish shop." Jews must be indoors by eight o'clock and cannot even sit in their own gardens after that hour. Jews are forbidden to visit theaters, cinemas, and other places of entertainment. Jews may not take part in public sports. Swimming baths, tennis courts, hockey fields, and other sports grounds are all prohibited to them. Jews may not visit Christians. Jews must go to Jewish schools, and many more restrictions of a similar kind.

So we could not do this and were forbidden to do that. But life went on in spite of it all. Jopie [Jacqueline van Mearsen, Anne's best friend] used to say to me, "You're scared to do anything, because it may be forbidden." Our freedom was strictly limited. Yet things were still bearable.

☑ **DETERMINE MEANING** What does Jopie mean when she says, "You're scared to do anything, because it may be forbidden"?

Thursday, November 19, 1942

Countless friends and acquaintances have gone to a terrible fate. Evening after evening the green and gray army lorries [trucks] trundle [roll] past.

The Germans ring at every front door to inquire if there are any Jews living in the house. If there are, then the whole family has to go at once. If they don't find any, they go on to the next house. No one has a chance of evading [avoiding] them unless one goes into hiding. Often they go around us with lists, and only ring when they know they can get a good haul. Sometimes they let them off for cash—so much per head, it seems like the slave hunts of olden times. But it's certainly no joke; it's much too tragic for that. In the evenings when it's dark, I often see rows of good, innocent people accompanied by crying children, walking on and on, in charge of a couple of these chaps, bullied and knocked about until they almost drop. No one is spared—old people, babies, expectant mothers, the sick—each and all join in the march of death.

How fortunate we are here, so well cared for and undisturbed. We wouldn't have to worry about all this misery were it not that we are so anxious about all those dear to us whom we can no longer help. I feel wicked sleeping in a warm bed, while my dearest friends have been knocked down or have fallen into a gutter somewhere out in the cold night. I get frightened when I think of close friends who have now been delivered into the hands of the cruelest brutes that walk the earth. And all because they are Jews!

☑ **ASSESS AN ARGUMENT** Why does Frank say she is "fortunate" to have a hiding place? Do you agree? Explain and support your response.

Wednesday, May 3, 1944

Why all this destruction? The question is very understandable, but no one has found a satisfactory answer to it so far. Yes, why do they make still more gigantic planes, still heavier bombs and, at the same time, prefabricated [mass-produced] houses for reconstruction? Why should millions be spent daily on the war and yet there's not a penny available for medical services, artists, or for poor people?

Why do some people have to starve, while there are surpluses [extra amounts] rotting in other parts of the world? Oh, why are people so crazy?

Saturday, July 15, 1944

In spite of everything I still believe that people are really good at heart. I simply can't build up my hopes on a foundation consisting of confusion, misery, and death. I see the world gradually being turned into a wilderness, I hear the ever approaching thunder, which will destroy us too, I can feel the sufferings of millions and yet, if I look up into the heavens, I think that it will all come right, that this cruelty too will end, and that peace and tranquility [calm] will return again.

☑ **EXPLAIN AN ARGUMENT** Why does Frank describe people as "crazy"? What problems does she observe?

☑ **ASSESSMENT**

1. **Draw Inferences** What was the purpose of the restrictions the Nazis imposed on Jews? What were the effects of these laws?

2. **Analyze Style and Rhetoric** How would you describe the tone of Frank's diary? How does she relate to her subject matter?

3. **Determine Central Ideas** How does reading Frank's diary differ from reading a secondary source about the Holocaust? What might her diary teach readers today that other sources cannot?

>> The Potsdam Conference was the only time Harry Truman and Joseph Stalin met face to face. Though they seem friendly in this photo, their mutual distrust helped shape the postwar world.

 Bounce to Activate Flipped Video

6.8 World War II (1939-1945) was a turning point that changed the nation and the world in profound ways. Many Americans came home determined to extend the ideals of democracy and freedom at home as well as abroad. In addition, the United States emerged from the war prepared to take on the complex and vital role in world affairs that it still holds today.

>> Objectives

Evaluate the goals that Allied leaders set for the postwar world.

Describe the steps that United States and other nations took toward international cooperation.

Explain the impact of World War II on the postwar United States.

>> Key Terms

Yalta Conference
superpowers
General Agreement
  on Tariffs and
  Trade (GATT)
United Nations (UN)
Universal
  Declaration of
  Human Rights
Geneva Convention
Nuremberg Trials

Impact of World War II

Planning the Postwar World

World War II differed from World War I in several ways. One major difference was that it was fought to the bitter end.

In 1918, the Kaiser surrendered before the Allies could invade Germany. By contrast, in World War II, Japan and Germany kept fighting long after their defeat was certain. In the last year of the war, they lost battle after battle, retreated from the lands they had conquered, and saw the slow destruction of their military forces. Allied bombing devastated their cities and industries. Yet Germany fought on until Hitler committed suicide, and Japan refused to surrender until after the bombing of Hiroshima and Nagasaki.

The Yalta Conference The protracted fighting gave the Allies time to make plans for a postwar world. Roosevelt, Churchill, and Stalin met at Yalta on the Black Sea in February 1945 to discuss final strategy and crucial questions concerning postwar Germany, Eastern Europe, and Asia. At the **Yalta Conference**, the Big Three agreed that Poland, Bulgaria, and Romania would hold free elections. However, Stalin later reneged on this promise.

Roosevelt and Churchill were not in a good position to press Stalin too hard. The Red Army already occupied much of Eastern Europe, and Roosevelt wanted Soviet help in the war against Japan. Vague promises were about as much as Stalin would give.

The Potsdam Conference A dramatically altered Big Three met in July 1945 in the Berlin suburb of Potsdam. Although Stalin remained in power in the Soviet Union, Harry S. Truman had become U.S. President in April upon the death of FDR. After the start of the conference, Clement Atlee replaced Churchill as prime minister of Britain.

At Potsdam, Truman took the reins of international leadership and began to reshape the relationship of the United States with its Allies. While in Potsdam, Truman learned of the successful test of the atomic bomb. But he was more focused on Europe and the Soviet Union than on Asia. Truman was more distrustful of Stalin than Roosevelt had been. Fearing Soviet domination of Eastern Europe, Truman continued to press for free elections after the war.

At the meeting, the Big Three formalized the decision to divide Germany into four zones of occupation: Soviet, American, British, and French. They agreed to new borders and free elections for Poland, and they recognized the Soviets' right to claim reparations for war damages from the German sector they controlled. Stalin also reaffirmed his Yalta pledge to enter the war against Japan.

☑ **COMPARE AND CONTRAST** How did the leaders and decisions made at the Potsdam Conference differ from those at the Yalta Conference?

International Impact of the War

After the war ended in August 1945, plans for the postwar world had to be turned into realities. However, the changes that took place were often not what the Allies had envisioned at Yalta and Potsdam.

Worldwide Political Changes World War II changed political boundaries in many parts of the world. The borders of Poland, for example, shifted slightly to the west. In time, as you will learn, differences between the Soviet Union and its former Allies led to the division of Germany into two countries: communist East Germany and

noncommunist West Germany. Nearly all the nations of Eastern Europe became communist states under Soviet control.

Other countries experienced profound political changes. Communist and noncommunist interests clashed in Eastern Europe. In China, a long-standing civil war between Nationalists and communists resumed.

In Japan, General Douglas MacArthur headed an American military occupation and supervised the writing of a new constitution. It abolished the armed forces except for purposes of defense, gave women the right to vote, enacted democratic reforms, and established the groundwork for full economic recovery. In 1951, Japan and the United States signed a peace treaty that formally ended World War II and disbanded what was left of Japan's colonial empire.

The War Weakens Imperialism The war also marked the end of Western European domination of the world. Since the 1500s, nations such as Britain, France, and Spain had exerted paramount influence on global developments. They colonized much of Africa, the Middle East, Asia, and the Americas. They controlled world trade and finance, led the

>> This photograph shows (left to right) Churchill, Roosevelt, and Stalin at the Yalta Conference. Roosevelt died only a few months after this picture was taken.

🅑 **Bounce to Activate Map**

industrial revolution, and stood at the forefront of world military power.

The aggressive acquisition of territories by Japan and Germany underscored the abuses of imperialism. After World War II, colonial peoples renewed their drive for independence from European powers. Freed from Japanese domination, the East Indies had no interest in returning to Dutch colonial status.

Nor did Indochina want to see the return of French rule. India, Burma, colonies in the Middle East and Africa—all had their sights set on independence.

By the end of the war, it was clear that the Age of Imperialism was in the twilight of its existence. The British Empire, the predominant power of the nineteenth century, came out of the war suffering severe economic shortages and, within decades, would see the loss of most of its colonies.

New Superpowers Emerge Into the power vacuum stepped the United States and the Soviet Union. They had played the most decisive roles in defeating the Axis Powers, and they emerged from the war confident and strong. Indeed, they so dominated the postwar world that they became known as **superpowers**.

>> Red Army troops proudly parade through Prague, Czechoslovakia, in 1945. **Connect** How does this photograph illustrate two advantages the Soviet Union enjoyed in the postwar world?

Of the two superpowers, the United States was clearly the stronger. Except for the attack on Pearl Harbor, no major battle had been fought on U.S. soil. In addition, American industry had boomed during the war. By 1945, America was wealthy, militarily powerful, and confident. By contrast, much of the war had been fought on Soviet soil. Its industries, cities, and peoples had suffered terribly.

Still, the Red Army controlled most of Eastern Europe and threatened to move farther west. Militarily, although the Americans had the atomic bomb, the Soviets had the Red Army, the world's largest military force.

☑ **IDENTIFY EFFECTS** What impact did World War II have on the relative roles of the United States and Britain in the world?

International Organizations and Treaties

Americans were quick to recognize that their nation had taken on a new position in the world. After World War I, the Senate had rejected the Treaty of Versailles and refused to join the League of Nations. Many Americans now viewed these decisions as mistakes that contributed to the rise of fascism and the outbreak of another war. As World War II drew to a close, Americans were ready to embrace the idea of world organizations.

Economic Effects of World War II World War II paved the way for a restructuring of the world economy. The United States took on major responsibilities in shaping the postwar world economy.

After meeting in 1944 with the Allies in Bretton Woods, New Hampshire, the U.S. government pushed for establishment of the International Monetary Fund and the World Bank. The United States provided most of the working capital for these new organizations, which worked to foster global economic and financial stability. The agreements made at Bretton Woods also represented another step in the shifting trend from the gold standard to fiat money. The international currency system was pegged to the U.S. dollar, with the United States agreeing to keep the price of gold at a certain level, effectively making the dollar the new standard.

In 1947, the United States signed the **General Agreement on Tariffs and Trade (GATT)**, a treaty designed to expand world trade by reducing tariffs. It went into effect on January 1, 1948. Between its signing and 1993, average tarrifs dropped from 40 percent to 5 percent. Losing protective tariffs has caused some industries in the United States to suffer from competition with foreign goods but the lower tariffs encouraged world trade in general. GATT was replaced by the World Trade Organization (WTO) in 1995.

The United Nations Even more importantly, the United States led the charge for the establishment of the **United Nations (UN)**, an organization that many hoped would succeed where the League of Nations had failed. In April 1945, delegates from 50 nations met in San Francisco to write the charter for the UN. The Senate overwhelmingly ratified the charter, and the UN later set up its permanent home in New York City. A major goal of the UN was to prevent further world wars or events such as the Holocaust.

The United Nations was organized on the basis of cooperation between the Great Powers, not on the absolute equality of all nations. All member nations sat on the General Assembly. However, the five major World War II Allies—the United States, the Soviet Union, Britain, France, and China—were assigned permanent seats on the most powerful arm of the UN, the Security Council.

President Truman named former First Lady Eleanor Roosevelt to represent the United States at the UN. Mary McLeod Bethune was appointed consultant on interracial affairs at the UN's charter conference.

As elected chair of the Commission on Human Rights, she guided the drafting of the **Universal Declaration of Human Rights**, a 1948 document that defined rights that belonged to all people in the world. It states:

> Recognition of the inherent dignity and of the equal and inalienable rights of all members of the human family is the foundation of freedom, justice and peace in the world. . . . All human beings are born free and equal in dignity and rights. They are endowed with reason and conscience and should act toward one another in a spirit of brotherhood.

—Universal Declaration of Human Rights

>> American, British, and Soviet delegates vote at a United Nations meeting. The three Allies held permanent seats on the Security Council, but wartime cooperation soon turned to conflict.

>> This statue of Eleanor Roosevelt stands at the Franklin D. Roosevelt Memorial in Washington, D.C. Behind her is the insignia of the UN.

The Declaration condemns slavery and torture, upholds freedom of speech and religion, and affirms that "everyone has the right to a standard of living adequate for the health and well-being of himself and his family." Though the document sets lofty goals it has proved difficult to enforce.

Over the next decades, the UN set up a refugee agency to help people displaced by the war.

It also aided the move away from colonialism, helped to create the Jewish state of Israel, mediated regional conflicts, and provided food and other aid to much of the world.

Not all Americans support participation in the United Nations and other international bodies. Some argue that giving decision-making authority to global organizations undermines U.S. sovereignty.

War Crimes Trials In the effort to create a better world, the Allies did not forget to punish the people who had caused so much destruction and death. During the war, the Axis Powers had repeatedly violated the **Geneva Convention**, an international agreement governing the humane treatment of wounded soldiers and prisoners of war.

The Allies tried more than a thousand Japanese citizens for committing atrocities in China, Korea, and Southeast Asia and brutally mistreating prisoners of war. Hundreds were condemned to death, including Prime Minister Hideki Tojo and the general responsible for the Bataan Death March.

Americans more closely followed the **Nuremberg Trials**, in which the Allies prosecuted Nazis for war crimes. The trials turned a glaring spotlight on the evils of the Third Reich. The first of the Nuremberg Trials involved key leaders of Nazi Germany, such as Hermann Goring. Day by day, prosecutors described their crimes, detailing especially the horrors of the Holocaust. Most of the defendants pleaded that they were just following orders, that Hitler was the source of all the crimes. But Robert Jackson, the American prosecutor, pointed out the importance of holding former Nazi officials responsible for their actions:

No half-century ever witnessed slaughter on such a scale, such cruelties and inhumanities. . . . If we cannot eliminate the causes and prevent the repetition of these barbaric events, it is not an irresponsible prophecy to say that this twentieth century may yet succeed in bringing the doom of civilization.

—Robert Jackson, closing speech, Nuremberg War Crimes Trials, 1946

Some of the Nazis were hanged; others received long prison terms. The evidence presented at the trials increased world support for the establishment of Israel as a Jewish homeland.

In the following decades, Allied or Israeli authorities captured and tried such other Nazis as Adolf Eichmann, a leading architect of the "Final Solution," and Klaus Barbie, a Gestapo officer convicted of torturing and murdering Jews and resistance fighters in Lyon, France. The periodic trials kept alive the memory of the Nazi crimes against humanity.

☑ **IDENTIFY STEPS IN A PROCESS** What steps did the United States take to increase its role in the postwar world?

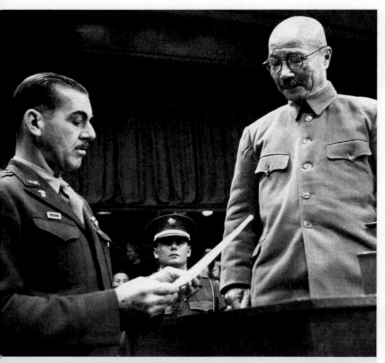

>> A 1948 war crimes tribunal found Tojo guilty of waging wars of aggression and allowing inhumane treatment of prisoners of war. Tojo accepted full responsibility and was condemned to death.

Bounce to Activate Gallery

Domestic Impact of the War

A new American identity rose from World War II. Americans regarded the Nazis as totalitarian, racist, and warlike. During the war, U.S. leaders and American popular culture had emphasized that the Allies were fighting a "people's war" for tolerance, freedom, democracy, and peace. Although many Americans felt that their country had not always lived up to that ideal, they hoped that the postwar period would usher in significant changes.

A Leader on the Global Stage Millions of Americans had spent several years closely following the war. They had attached world maps to their walls and traced the paths of U.S. troops in the deserts of North Africa, the forests of Europe, and the coral islands of the Pacific. For this generation of Americans, the world had somehow become a smaller, more interconnected place. They had learned to think in global terms.

Few Americans called for a return to a policy of isolationism or retreat from their global responsibilities. They recognized that what happened in the far reaches of the globe affected them, that America's national security was linked to world security.

Impact on the Economy and Government World War II ended the Great Depression and ushered in decades of economic growth. Expansion in world trade, spurred by GATT and other treaties, also contributed to postwar economic prosperity.

The war also redistributed wealth across the country. Defense industries and military bases in the South and West spurred people to move to these regions, which in turn created more wealth and encouraged further migration. Wartime factory work also created new and higher-paying job opportunities for women, African Americans, and other minorities, raising their expectations of what they should be able to achieve.

Like other wars, World War II led to a greater governmental influence in economic affairs. From the collection of raw materials to attempts to control inflation, the government had made the important decisions to guide the economy. In the process, it established the expanded economic role that government would play in postwar America.

The war also increased the power of the U.S. presidency. The War Powers Acts of 1941 and 1942 gave the President broad powers to conduct the war. Backed by these laws, FDR issued Executive Orders to take actions he felt necessary to win

1778   1943

AMERICANS
will always fight for liberty

>> This 1943 poster emphasizes America as a defender of liberty. After the war, the United States continued to take on the role of leader of the Free World in opposition to the Soviet Union.

Bounce to Activate Gallery

the war. These included orders that established a Censorship Board and banned hiring discrimination in government-funded defense industries. The War Powers Acts raised constitutional issues in that some felt that the greater powers of the Executive branch threatened the traditional separation of powers laid out in the Constitution. The increased use of Executive Orders as a presidential tool remains controversial today.

Demanding Equal Rights African American soldiers in World War II had clearly believed they were fighting two foes: dictatorship overseas and racism in the United States. Less than two months after Pearl Harbor, one of the nation's leading black newspapers published a letter from a young man in Wichita, Kansas:

Being an American of dark complexion and some 26 years, these questions flash through my mind: 'Should I sacrifice my life to live half American?' 'Will things be better for the next generation in the peace to follow?' . . .

> I suggest that while we keep defense and victory in the forefront that we don't lose sight of our fight for true democracy at home.

—James G. Thompson, letter to the *Pittsburgh Courier*, January 31, 1942

World War II gave renewed vigor to the fight for civil rights. In this battle, African Americans were not alone. A growing number of white Americans also called for the nation to fully live up to its promise as a beacon of freedom, democracy, and justice.

Impact on California The defense-related industries became particularly important to California's economy, helping drive other kinds of development, such as the manufacturing sector and the science-technology establishment. These jobs drew enormous numbers of migrants from other parts of the country and eventually spurred the creation of suburbs, highways, and shopping complexes. Meanwhile, immigration continued, especially to California, which depended on agricultural labor provided by immigrants, particularly Mexicans, who came through the Bracero Program that continued until 1964.

☑ **MAKE PREDICTIONS** How do you think World War II will change the way Americans view America's role in the world in the following decades?

☑ ASSESSMENT

1. **Predict Consequences** Predict at least one postwar issue that the former Allies will disagree about following the war.

2. **Compare** In what way were the Universal Declaration of Human Rights and the postwar push for civil rights both reactions to the war?

3. **Analyze Context** Why did Americans agree to participate in the UN after World War II when many had rejected participation in the League of Nations after World War I?

4. **Identify Patterns** How did World War II impact the American economy? Did the war have the same impact on the British economy?

5. **Categorize** In your opinion, what was the most important effect of World War II on the United States? Support your answer with evidence.

Charter of the United Nations

In 1945, representatives of 50 countries met in San Francisco to sign a charter creating the United Nations, a new peacekeeping organization. Here are the preamble and first two articles of that charter.

>> Delegates vote at UN meeting

WE THE PEOPLES OF THE UNITED NATIONS DETERMINED

- to save succeeding [later] generations from the scourge of war, which twice in our lifetime has brought untold sorrow to mankind, and
- to reaffirm faith in fundamental human rights, in the dignity and worth of the human person, in the equal rights of men and women and of nations large and small, and
- to establish conditions under which justice and respect for the obligations arising from treaties and other sources of international law can be maintained, and
- to promote social progress and better standards of life in larger freedom,

AND FOR THESE ENDS

- to practice tolerance and live together in peace with one another as good neighbours, and
- to unite our strength to maintain international peace and security, and
- to ensure, by the acceptance of principles and the institution of methods, that armed force shall not be used, save in the common interest, and
- to employ international machinery for the promotion of the economic and social advancement of all peoples,

HAVE RESOLVED TO COMBINE OUR EFFORTS TO ACCOMPLISH THESE AIMS

Accordingly, our respective Governments, through representatives assembled in the city of San Francisco, who have exhibited their full powers found to be in good and due form, have agreed to the present Charter of the United Nations and do hereby establish an international organization to be known as the United Nations.

☑ **DRAW INFERENCES** The preamble mentions "the scourge of war, which twice in our lifetime has brought untold sorrow to mankind." To what events is the preamble referring in this excerpt?

CHAPTER I: PURPOSES AND PRINCIPLES

Article 1

The Purposes of the United Nations are:
  1. To maintain international peace and security, and to that end: to take effective collective measures for the prevention and removal of

threats to the peace, and for the suppression of acts of aggression or other breaches of the peace, and to bring about by peaceful means, and in conformity with the principles of justice and international law, adjustment or settlement of international disputes or situations which might lead to a breach of the peace;

2. To develop friendly relations among nations based on respect for the principle of equal rights and self-determination of peoples, and to take other appropriate measures to strengthen universal peace;

3. To achieve international co-operation in solving international problems of an economic, social, cultural, or humanitarian character, and in promoting and encouraging respect for human rights and for fundamental freedoms for all without distinction as to race, sex, language, or religion; and

4. To be a centre for harmonizing the actions of nations in the attainment of these common ends.

Article 2

The Organization and its Members, in pursuit of the Purposes stated in Article 1, shall act in accordance with the following Principles.

1. The Organization is based on the principle of the sovereign equality of all its Members.

2. All Members, in order to ensure to all of them the rights and benefits resulting from membership, shall fulfill in good faith the obligations assumed by them in accordance with the present Charter.

3. All Members shall settle their international disputes by peaceful means in such a manner that international peace and security, and justice, are not endangered.

4. All Members shall refrain in their international relations from the threat or use of force against the territorial integrity or political independence of any state, or in any other manner inconsistent with the Purposes of the United Nations.

5. All Members shall give the United Nations every assistance in any action it takes in accordance with the present Charter, and shall refrain from giving assistance to any state against which the United Nations is taking preventive or enforcement action.

6. The Organization shall ensure that states which are not Members of the United Nations act in accordance with these Principles so far as may be necessary for the maintenance of international peace and security.

7. Nothing contained in the present Charter shall authorize the United Nations to intervene in matters which are essentially within the domestic jurisdiction of any state or shall require the Members to submit such matters to settlement under the present Charter; but this principle shall not prejudice the application of enforcement measures under Chapter VII.

☑ **DETERMINE MEANING** In Article 2, Principle 1, what does *sovereign* mean?

☑ ASSESSMENT

1. **Cite Evidence** If one country's governing party is inflicting terrible human rights abuses on members of the opposition party, can the United Nations intervene? Cite the part(s) of the charter that support your opinion.

2. **Explain an Argument** Consider this scenario: several years of drought in western Asia have led to widespread famine. The UN arranges to bring convoys of food to starving people. One country, a member of the UN, does not want to let relief workers cross its borders. Does any part of the charter cited here support or rebut the country's position? Explain your answer.

3. **Draw Conclusions** Has the United Nations been successful in its mission "to save succeeding generations from the scourge of war"? Explain your answer.

Go online to PearsonSchool.com/CASS and use the texts, quizzes, interactivities, Interactive Reading Notepads, Flipped Videos, and other resources from this Topic to prepare for the Topic Test.

Etexts

Quizzes

Interactivities

Interactive Reading Notepads

Flipped Videos

While online you can also check the progress you've made learning the topic and course content by viewing your grades, test scores, and assignment status.

LESSON SUMMARIES

Use these Lesson Summaries, and the longer versions available online, to review the key ideas for each lesson in this Topic.

Lesson 1: Rise of Aggressive Dictators

Throughout the 1930s, the rise of dictatorships in the Soviet Union, Germany, Italy, and Japan challenged world peace. Seeking to preserve the peace, Western democracies responded to acts of aggression with appeasement policies.

Lesson 2: America Debates Involvement

As the war raged in Europe, the United States maintained an isolationist position, which became increasingly difficult as its allies fell under German occupation.

Lesson 3: The United States Enters World War II

American neutrality ends when Japan orders a surprise attack on Pearl Harbor in 1941. The United States declares war on Japan. Germany and Italy declare war on the United States.

Lesson 4: A War on Two Fronts

In June 1942, American forces won the Battle of Midway, ending Japanese expansion in the Pacific. The following year, the Russians turned back the German invasion of the Soviet Union, while American forces defeated German and Italian troops in North Africa before invading and defeating Italy. By the end of 1943, both Germany and Japan were on the defensive.

Lesson 5: The Home Front

In the United States, the civilian population helped the war effort in various ways: jobs opened up for women and minorities, people moved to work in defense industries, and the government brought Mexican laborers to work on farms. After the attack on Pearl Harbor, the government moved Japanese Americans to isolated camps, where they were held for the duration of the war.

Lesson 6: The Allies Win World War II

On June 6, 1944, known as D-Day, British and American forces invaded France. In 1945, the advance of the Soviet Army from the east, and the United States Army from the west forced Germany to surrender on May 7. In the Pacific, American forces slowly advanced on Japan. In August, 1945, U.S. pilots dropped atomic bombs on Hiroshima and Nagasaki, forcing Japan to surrender.

Lesson 7: The Holocaust

When Allied soldiers began to liberate Nazi concentration camps, they uncovered the horrors of the Holocaust. After the war, President Truman immediately recognized the new nation of Israel when it was established by Jews in Palestine.

Lesson 8: Impact of World War II

As World War II ended, Allied leaders met to discuss the postwar world and divided Germany into four zones. After the war, the United States led the move to establish the United Nations and the U.S. and Soviet Union became world superpowers.

VISUAL REVIEW

Use these graphics to review some of the key terms, people, and ideas from this Topic.

Allied Leaders, World War II

WORLD POLITICAL	U.S. MILITARY
• Winston Churchill, Britain • Joseph Stalin, Soviet Union • Franklin D. Roosevelt, United States • Harry S. Truman, United States	**In Europe** • Dwight Eisenhower • George S. Patton • Omar Bradley **In the Pacific** • Douglas MacArthur • Chester Nimitz

Five Turning Points of World War II

1942	**Battle of Midway** halts Japanese expansion in the Pacific.
1942	**Battle of El Alamein** begins Allied offensive against Axis Powers in North Africa.
1942–1943	**Battle of Stalingrad** ends Nazi advances in Europe.
1944	**D-Day** invasion opens second front in Europe, paving way for final defeat of Germany.
1945	**Manhattan Project** develops atomic bomb, used to end war in the Pacific.

World War II Home Front

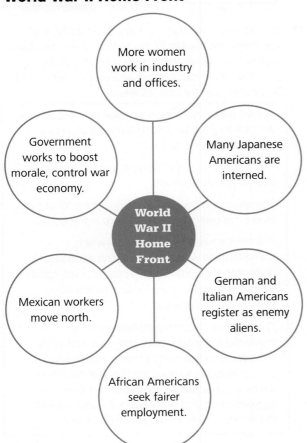

World War II Deaths, Selected Nations

COUNTRY	MILITARY DEATHS	CIVILIAN DEATHS
AXIS		
Germany	3,500,000	780,000
Italy	242,000	153,000
Japan	1,300,000	672,000
ALLIES		
France	213,000	350,000
Britain	264,000	93,000
China	1,310,000	1,000,000
Soviet Union	7,500,000	15,000,000
United States	292,000	6,000

California Topic 6 Assessment

KEY TERMS, PEOPLE, AND IDEAS

1. How did **Adolf Hitler** contribute to the outbreak of World War II?

2. How did the Allies turn the tide against the Axis?

3. What Americans were subject to **internment** during the war?

4. How did the Allies defeat the Axis powers?

5. How did **anti-Semitism** lead to the **Holocaust**?

6. Why did **Franklin D. Roosevelt** sponsor the **Lend-Lease Act**?

7. How did the war change America at home?

8. How did the Holocaust develop and what were its results?

9. What were the major immediate and long-term effects of World War II?

CRITICAL THINKING

10. **Find the Main Idea** Identify three key events in the U.S. transition from isolationism to involvement in the early years of World War II.

11. **Summarize** (a) What was the chief goal of Allied leaders during World War II? (b) What strategy did they evolve to meet this goal?

12. **Make Generalizations** Make a generalization about how American women contributed to the war effort, both on the home front and in combat. Give two examples to support your generalization.

13. **Evaluate Information** (a) Why did Stalin want Roosevelt and Churchill to open a second front in Europe? (b) What action did the Allies take to accomplish this goal? (c) Evaluate its success.

14. **Draw Conclusions** Explain the significance of World War II as a turning point in history. Consider the following as you frame your answer: the roles of the United States and the Soviet Union in the postwar years and the introduction of nuclear warfare as a result of the war.

15. **Make Generalizations** Describe how American involvement in World War II had economic effects on the home front.

16. **Analyze Maps** Look at the map below. (a) What event does the map illustrate? (b) Describe this event. (c) Why do you think the people responsible were tried as war criminals after the war?

17. **Writing Activity: Use Primary Sources** Evaluate how President Franklin D. Roosevelt's Four Freedoms speech changed America's relationship with its allies. Use the excerpt below and your knowledge of Roosevelt's international leadership.

> In the future days, which we seek to make secure, we look forward to a world founded upon four essential human freedoms.
>
> The first is freedom of speech and expression—everywhere in the world.
>
> The second is freedom of every person to worship God in his own way—everywhere in the world.
>
> The third is freedom from want—which, translated into world terms, means economic understandings which will secure to every nation a healthy peace time life for its inhabitants—everywhere in the world.
>
> The fourth is freedom from fear—which, translated into world terms means a worldwide reduction of armaments to such a point and in such a fashion thorough fashion that no nation will be in a position to commit an act of physical aggression against any neighbor—anywhere in the world. … —*Franklin Delano Roosevelt*

DOCUMENT-BASED QUESTIONS

President Truman's decision to use the atomic bomb against Japan continues to stir controversy. Read the documents below, then answer the questions that follow.

DOCUMENT A

This excerpt is from a petition signed by 154 of the scientists who developed the atomic bomb.

> The war has to be brought speedily to a successful conclusion and attacks by atomic bombs may very well be an effective method of warfare. We feel, however, that such attacks on Japan could not be justified, at least not unless the terms which will be imposed after the war on Japan were made public in detail and Japan were given an opportunity to surrender. …
>
> The development of atomic power will provide the nations with new means of destruction. The atomic bombs at our disposal represent only the first step in this direction, and there is almost no limit to the destructive power which will become available in the course of their future development.
>
> —*Leó Szilárd, Petition to the President of the United States, July 17, 1945*

DOCUMENT B

This photograph shows Hiroshima after the bombing on August 6, 1945. The single bomb destroyed 4.7 square miles of Hiroshima and some 68% of its buildings. Between 70,000 and 80,000 people were killed by the explosion or its aftereffects.

DOCUMENT C

This excerpt is from a letter written by Truman.

> When the message came to Potsdam that a successful atomic explosion had taken place in New Mexico, there was much excitement and conversation about the effect on the war then in progress with Japan. … I asked Gen. Marshall what it would cost in lives to land on the Tokyo plain and other places in Japan. It was his opinion that 1/4 million casualties would be the minimum cost as well as an equal number of the enemy.
>
> We sent an ultimatum to Japan. It was ignored. …
>
> Dropping the bombs ended the war, saved lives and gave the free nations a chance to face the facts.
>
> —*Harry Truman, January 12, 1953*

DOCUMENT D

This excerpt is from a book written by a onetime historian for the Nuclear Regulatory Commission.

> The use of atomic bombs was decisive in ending the war. After Hiroshima, the emperor for the first time came out unequivocally for surrender, and he soon intervened directly to persuade the cabinet to accept the Potsdam Declaration. …
>
> Even without use of the atomic bombs, the war would probably have ended before an American invasion of Kyushu [one of Japan's main islands] became necessary. Conditions in Japan were steadily deteriorating before the atomic attacks and would have continued to worsen as the war dragged on. The destruction of cities from B-29 raids, diminishing food supplies, and decreasing public morale fostered enough discontent to worry the emperors and his advisers. …
>
> —*J. Samuel Walker, Prompt and Utter Destruction, 1997*

18. The scientists who signed the petition believed that atomic weapons

   A. would not help bring the war to a quick end.

   B. should be used immediately to end the war.

   C. might be used if there was no other option.

   D. were too dangerous to use for any reason.

19. **Analyze Photographs** Based on Document B, what effect do you think the bombing might have had on those who witnessed it?

20. According to Truman, his main goal in deciding to use the atomic bomb was to

   A. save American and Japanese lives.

   B. punish Japan for carrying on the war.

   C. demonstrate the power of nuclear weapons.

   D. destroy the nation of Japan.

21. **Writing Activity: Primary Source** Write a paragraph explaining whether you think Truman's decision to use the atomic bomb on Hiroshima and Nagasaki was justified. Use the sources as well as additional information you have learned about the bombings.

End-of-Topic Practice

March 1941	August 1941	September 1941
Lend-Lease Act authorizes the United States to sell, lease, lend or otherwise provide arms to other governments in defense of the United States.	Atlantic Charter plots mutual American and British war strategies against the Axis powers.	After German U-boats attack U.S. naval ships escorting arms shipments to the Allies, President Roosevelt issues an order to the navy to shoot U-boats on sight.

1 Based on the time line, what were President Roosevelt's intentions in the months leading up to American participation in World War II?

A He was attempting to provoke Germany into declaring war on the United States.

B He was determined to keep the United States out of the war at all costs.

C He was trying to secretly help defeat Germany by destroying the U-boat "wolf packs" that patrolled the Atlantic.

D He was leading the nation closer to entering the war, even though the United States' official stance was one of neutrality.

2 Why did Japan wait until 1941 to attack Pearl Harbor?

F Japan was waiting to see if Germany would declare war on the United States first.

G Japan was waiting until its expanding empire gave it access to the resources it needed to fight.

H Japan was trying to bring the United States into the war as an ally.

I Japan was hoping that most American troops on Pacific bases would be transferred to Europe.

3 Roosevelt signed a fair employment executive order in 1941, partly because he was afraid that a large protest march in Washington D.C. would fuel enemy propaganda. How might the enemy have used this as propaganda?

A to show that many Americans did not support the war effort

B to show that many Americans supported the Axis powers

C to show that democracy was also based on racial discrimination

D to prove that the United States was still a segregated society

SCIENCE AND TECHNOLOGY OF WORLD WAR II

THE U.S. GOVERNMENT CONVERTED OVER **10 MILLION** PINTS OF BLOOD INTO DRIED **BLOOD PLASMA** TO TREAT WOUNDED SOLDIERS.

THE ALLIES USED **NYLON** —AN ARTIFICIALLY-MADE FABRIC— TO MAKE PARACHUTES. ONE PARACHUTE FACTORY PRODUCED NEARLY **1,500 PARACHUTES** PER WEEK

BY THE END OF THE WAR, THE UNITED STATES WAS PRODUCING NEARLY **650 BILLION** UNITS OF **PENICILLIN** —AN ANTIBIOTIC USED TO KILL HARMFUL BACTERIA— EACH MONTH.

FAST, POWERFUL **JET ENGINES** WERE DEVELOPED BY SEVERAL COUNTRIES AT THE SAME TIME.

SEVERAL NATIONS DEVELOPED **RADAR** SECRETLY TO DETECT ENEMY AIRCRAFT AND SHIPS.

ALLIED CODEBREAKERS USED EARLY **CALCULATING MACHINES** TO HELP SOLVE GERMAN CODED MESSAGES.

4 Based on this graphic, what technology did the United States perfect to keep diseases from spreading among American forces?

F The use of radar for laser surgery

G Methods of drying blood plasma

H The mass production of penicillin

I The mass production of nylon for bandages

If you have trouble with...				
Question	1	2	3	4
See Lesson	6.2	6.3	6.5	6.6

5 What lessons does the Holocaust offer to modern nations?

A The persecution of minorities only happens under totalitarian regimes.

B No one is safe when governments disregard civil rights.

C Only democracies can protect minorities from persecution.

D Nationalism inevitably leads to racial discrimination.

INTERNATIONAL ECONOMIC ORGANIZATIONS AND AGREEMENTS

	WORLD BANK	INTERNATIONAL MONETARY FUND (IMF)	GENERAL AGREEMENT ON TARIFFS AND TRADE (GATT)
CREATED	1944	1945	1948
GOAL	to reduce poverty and finance world economic development	to stabilize finances of nations and encourage economic growth	to expand world trade
ACTIONS	offers loans and technical advice to developing nations	stabilizes exchange rates between countries; lends money to countries in financial crisis	reduced tariffs and other trade barriers between nations. Replaced in 1995 by World Trade Organization (WTO)

6 Based on this chart, how did the GATT differ from the World Bank and the IMF?

F It stabilized the finances of war-torn nations by increasing tariffs to pay the cost of rebuilding.

G It encouraged trade among nations by loaning money to impoverished nations to grow their businesses.

H In addition to providing technical advice to developing nations, it removed obstacles to international trade.

I Instead of providing loans and other financial aid to nations, it encouraged trade among nations by lowering tariffs.

> *This campaign is more than a contest between two men. . . . It is a contest between two philosophies of government.*
>
> —*Herbert Hoover, 1932*

7 What contrast did President Herbert Hoover refer to in this statement?

A His concern for enacting laws to control and regulate economic disasters, contrasted to Roosevelt's laissez-faire philosophy.

B His belief that state and local governments could solve economic issues, contrasted to Roosevelt's focus on federal aid programs.

C His approach to creating a modern expansionist foreign policy, contrasted to the isolationist policy of Roosevelt.

D His ideal that private agencies should control government, contrasted to Roosevelt's ideal that government should maintain control over private agencies.

---

8 How did Frank Capra's film *Mr. Smith Goes to Washington* reflect the issues of its time?

F It emphasized the importance of being politically active.

G It reinforced the public's declining faith in law enforcement.

H It celebrated the strength and determination of the common man.

I It portrayed a government with only the best interests of the public in mind.

If you have trouble with...				
Question	5	6	7	8
See Lesson	6.7	6.8	5.3	5.6

In the 1930s, the policies of isolationism and appeasement did nothing to stop the rise of dictatorships and the outbreak of global war. After World War II, U.S. leaders viewed these past policies as mistakes. They sought new ways to keep the United States safe as well as to protect its interests around the world.

>> The United States and Great Britain supplied goods to West Berlin by plane during the Berlin Airlift.

Bounce to Activate Flipped Video

>> Objectives

Trace the reasons that the wartime alliance between the United States and the Soviet Union unraveled.

Explain how President Truman responded to Soviet aggression in Eastern Europe.

Describe the causes and results of Stalin's blockade of Berlin.

>> Key Terms

satellite state
Cold War
Truman Doctrine
George F. Kennan
containment
Marshall Plan
Berlin airlift
North Atlantic Treaty
   Organization
   (NATO)
Warsaw Pact
iron curtain

The Beginning of the Cold War

Background of the Cold War

When Franklin Roosevelt died in April 1945, the nation was at a critical point. The United States was still at war. In addition, relations with the Soviet Union—one of the most important wartime allies—were beginning to break down.

Soviet Aggression Against Its Citizens The United States and the Soviet Union had been united only in their opposition to Nazi Germany. Beyond that, they had little in common. The United States was a capitalist democracy. Its citizens believed in free elections, economic and religious freedom, private property, and respect for individual differences. The Soviet Union was a dictatorship.

Under Joseph Stalin, the Communist Party made all key economic, political, and military decisions. The Soviet people could not worship as they pleased, own private property, or express their views freely. Those who opposed or questioned Stalin risked imprisonment and death.

> *This campaign is more than a contest between two men. . . . It is a contest between two philosophies of government.*
>
> —*Herbert Hoover, 1932*

7 What contrast did President Herbert Hoover refer to in this statement?

A His concern for enacting laws to control and regulate economic disasters, contrasted to Roosevelt's laissez-faire philosophy.

B His belief that state and local governments could solve economic issues, contrasted to Roosevelt's focus on federal aid programs.

C His approach to creating a modern expansionist foreign policy, contrasted to the isolationist policy of Roosevelt.

D His ideal that private agencies should control government, contrasted to Roosevelt's ideal that government should maintain control over private agencies.

---

8 How did Frank Capra's film *Mr. Smith Goes to Washington* reflect the issues of its time?

F It emphasized the importance of being politically active.

G It reinforced the public's declining faith in law enforcement.

H It celebrated the strength and determination of the common man.

I It portrayed a government with only the best interests of the public in mind.

If you have trouble with...				
Question	5	6	7	8
See Lesson	6.7	6.8	5.3	5.6

[**ESSENTIAL QUESTION**] What is America's role in the world?

⑦ Postwar America

Enduring Understandings

- After World War II, a "Cold War" rivalry developed between the United States and the Soviet Union.

- The Cold War exploded into armed conflict in Korea, ending in an uneasy truce and a growing concern about the communist threat to the free world.

- Domestic spy cases increased fear of communist influence in the U.S. government, leading to a new Red Scare.

- The U.S. economy boomed in the 1950s.

- During the postwar population shift, many moved from the cities to the suburbs and the Sunbelt.

- Despite postwar prosperity, discontent grew among minorities and the young.

Learn how Senator Margaret Chase Smith responded to events in postwar America.

Bounce to Activate My Story Video

>> A school air-raid drill in 1952

California Topic 7 Overview

In this Topic, you'll learn about America in the years after World War II. Look at the lesson outline and explore the timeline. As you study this Topic, you'll complete the Quest team project.

LESSON OUTLINE

7.1 The Beginning of the Cold War
HSS 11.4.6, HSS 11.7, HSS 11.7.8, HSS 11.8, HSS 11.9, HSS 11.9.2, HSS 11.9.3

7.2 The Korean War
HSS 11.4.6, HSS 11.9, HSS 11.9.2, HSS 11.9.3

7.3 The Cold War Intensifies
HSS 11.4.6, HSS 11.8, HSS 11.9, HSS 11.9.3

7.4 Cold War Fears at Home
HSS 11.8, HSS 11.9.3, HSS 11.9.4

7.5 Postwar Prosperity
HSS 11.8, HSS 11.8.1, HSS 11.8.3, HSS 11.8.4, HSS 11.8.5, HSS 11.8.7, HSS 11.10.1, HSS 11.11.2, HSS 11.11.7; Analysis CST.4

7.6 Mass Culture in the 1950s
HSS 11.8, HSS 11.8.4, HSS 11.8.7, HSS 11.8.8, HSS 11.10.2, HSS 11.11.3, HSS 11.11.7; Analysis CST.4

7.7 Social Issues of the 1950s
HSS 11.2.3, HSS 11.8, HSS 11.8.2, HSS 11.8.8, HSS 11.9.7; Analysis CST.4

Key Events of Postwar America

1945
World War II ends; Soviets occupy Eastern Europe

1948
Congress approves Marshall Plan

1949
NATO is formed

1950
Korean War begins; McCarthy begins anti-communist campaign

1951
Suburb of Levittown is built

1953
The Rosenbergs are executed

1956
Interstate Highway Act expands highway construction

1945   1950   1955   1960

SEN. McCARTHY

 QUEST! **TEAM PROJECT**

Understanding McCarthyism in the 1950s

How did Senator Joseph McCarthy become so powerful during the Red Scare of the 1950s? Why did McCarthyism have such an impact on domestic United States policy? In this Quest you'll explore this question before writing an essay to present your answer.

STEP 1

Watch the video and discuss it in class or with a partner. Consider the questions it raises about the Red Scare and McCarthyism.

STEP 2

Examine the source documents relating to McCarthyism and answer the questions attached to each document. Then review the relevant skills tutorials.

STEP 3

Consider all the evidence and draw your own conclusions. Write an essay to answer the question: Why did McCarthyism have such a powerful effect on American life in the 1950s?

STEP 4

Reflect on the process of analyzing the documents and writing the essay and then complete the Self-Assessment.

PEARSON realize™
PearsonSchool.com/CASS

Go ONLINE for complete Quest materials

 VIDEO   ETEXT   WRITING RUBRIC PDF   ASSESSMENT

In the 1930s, the policies of isolationism and appeasement did nothing to stop the rise of dictatorships and the outbreak of global war. After World War II, U.S. leaders viewed these past policies as mistakes. They sought new ways to keep the United States safe as well as to protect its interests around the world.

>> The United States and Great Britain supplied goods to West Berlin by plane during the Berlin Airlift.

 Bounce to Activate Flipped Video

>> **Objectives**

Trace the reasons that the wartime alliance between the United States and the Soviet Union unraveled.

Explain how President Truman responded to Soviet aggression in Eastern Europe.

Describe the causes and results of Stalin's blockade of Berlin.

>> **Key Terms**

satellite state
Cold War
Truman Doctrine
George F. Kennan
containment
Marshall Plan
Berlin airlift
North Atlantic Treaty
  Organization
  (NATO)
Warsaw Pact
iron curtain

The Beginning of the Cold War

Background of the Cold War

When Franklin Roosevelt died in April 1945, the nation was at a critical point. The United States was still at war. In addition, relations with the Soviet Union—one of the most important wartime allies—were beginning to break down.

Soviet Aggression Against Its Citizens The United States and the Soviet Union had been united only in their opposition to Nazi Germany. Beyond that, they had little in common. The United States was a capitalist democracy. Its citizens believed in free elections, economic and religious freedom, private property, and respect for individual differences. The Soviet Union was a dictatorship.

Under Joseph Stalin, the Communist Party made all key economic, political, and military decisions. The Soviet people could not worship as they pleased, own private property, or express their views freely. Those who opposed or questioned Stalin risked imprisonment and death.

Soviets Control Eastern Europe By the time Roosevelt, Stalin, and Churchill met at Yalta in February 1945, it was clear that the Allies would defeat Germany. But it was unclear how Germany and the nations of Eastern Europe would be governed after the war. Soviet troops already occupied much of Eastern Europe and parts of Germany.

Stalin wanted to keep Germany weak and divided. He also wanted Eastern Europe to remain under the control of the Soviet Union. The United States and Great Britain sought a stronger, united Germany and independent nations in Eastern Europe. At the conference, Stalin agreed to establish "broadly representative" governments and free elections in Eastern Europe and to divide Germany only temporarily into zones of occupation.

Despite Stalin's promises, nearly all of the lands occupied by the Soviet Red Army in the spring of 1945 remained under Soviet control after the war. The Eastern European countries of Poland, Czechoslovakia, Hungary, Romania, and Bulgaria, as well as the eastern portion of Germany, became **satellite states** controlled by the Soviet Union.

Wartime Alliance Unravels By the time Soviet, British, and U.S. leaders met at Potsdam in the summer of 1945, Harry Truman had succeeded Roosevelt as President. Truman and Clement Attlee, the new British prime minister, hoped that Stalin would confirm the decisions made at Yalta. However, Stalin refused to make a commitment to allow free elections in Eastern Europe.

Truman left Potsdam believing that the Soviet Union was "planning world conquest" and that the alliance with the Soviet Union was falling apart. With the Soviet Red Army at his command, Stalin seemed to present a real threat. Thus, the stage was set for a worldwide rivalry between the United States and the Soviet Union. The 46-year struggle became known as the **Cold War** because the two superpowers never faced each other directly in a "hot" military conflict.

☑ **CONTRAST** How did the goals of U.S. and Soviet foreign policy differ after World War II?

Responding to the Soviet Challenge

President Truman was not the only world leader who believed that Stalin had aspirations toward world domination. Winston Churchill also spoke

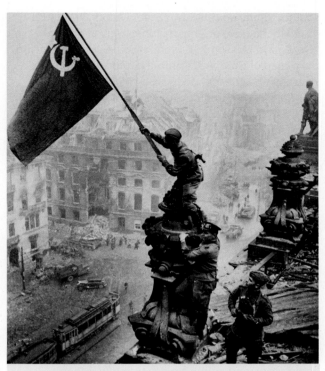

>> Russian soldier raising the Soviet flag over Berlin, Germany, in April, 1945.

>> Winston Churchill delivers his "Iron Curtain" speech. This descriptive phrase became a lasting symbol of the brutal division that communism had created in Western Europe.

Bounce to Activate Timeline

out forcefully against the Soviet Union. On March 5, 1946, he gave an important speech at Fulton College in Missouri, Truman's home state. Referring to a map of Europe, Churchill noted that "an **iron curtain** has descended across the Continent."

East of that iron curtain, the Soviet Union was gaining more control by installing communist governments and police states and by crushing political and religious dissent. In addition, Churchill feared, the Soviets were attempting to spread communism to Western Europe and East Asia. The only solution, Churchill said, was for the United States and other democratic countries to stand firm.

Truman Faces Soviet Aggression in Eastern Europe

Truman shared Churchill's beliefs. Born in a small town in Missouri, Truman had been too poor to attend college. He was the only president in the twentieth century with no college education. Instead, he worked the family farm, fought in France during World War I, and eventually began a political career. His life was a testament to honesty, integrity, hard work, and a willingness to make difficult decisions. "The buck stops here," was his motto as President. It meant that the person sitting in the Oval Office had the obligation to face problems head on and make hard decisions.

In 1947, no issue was more weighty than the growing crisis between the United States and the Soviet Union. After the war, a number of European and Asian countries were struggling against communist movements supported by the Soviets. In particular, the governments of Greece and Turkey were battling communist forces seeking to gain control. Greece and Turkey needed aid, and in 1947 the United States was the only country with the resources to help them.

The Truman Doctrine Opposes Soviet Aggression

On March 12, 1947, President Truman addressed both houses of Congress. With emotion in his voice, Truman described the plight of the Greek and Turkish people. The fight they were waging, he said, was the fight that all free people had to confront. Truman requested money from Congress "to support free peoples who are resisting attempted subjugation [conquest] by armed minorities or by outside pressures." If the United States retreated into isolationism, he warned, the peace of the world and the welfare of the nation would be in danger. The fall of a nation to communism, Truman argued, could lead its neighbors into communism as well.

> I believe that it must be the policy of the United States to support free peoples who are resisting attempted subjugation by armed minorities or by outside pressures. I believe that we must assist free peoples to work out their own destinies in their own way. I believe that our help should be primarily through economic and financial aid which is essential to economic stability and orderly political processes.
>
> —President Harry S. Truman, Address Before a Joint Session of Congress, March 12, 1947

Congress responded by voting to give $400 million in aid for Greece and Turkey. President Truman's promise to aid nations struggling against communist movements became known as the

>> Greek soldiers bring in possible guerrilla operatives for questioning. The anticommunist struggle in Greece and Turkey led President Truman to formulate the Truman Doctrine.

Truman Doctrine, and it set a new course for American foreign policy.

☑ **IDENTIFY CAUSE AND EFFECT** What events caused President Truman to propose what became known as the Truman Doctrine?

The United States Contains Soviet Expansion

In the July 1947 issue of the magazine *Foreign Affairs,* a writer who called himself "X" published an article titled "The Sources of Soviet Conduct." The author was really **George F. Kennan**, an American diplomat and a leading authority on the Soviet Union. His article presented a blueprint for the American policy that became known as **containment** because its goal was to keep communism contained within its existing borders.

Kennan Urges a Policy of Containment Kennan contended that while Stalin was determined to expand the Soviet empire, he would not risk the security of the Soviet Union for expansion. In Kennan's view, the Soviet Union would only expand when it could do so without serious risks. Stalin would certainly not chance war with the United States—a war that might destroy his power in the Soviet Union—just to spread communism.

Kennan cautioned his readers that there would be no quick, easy solution to the Soviet threat. Containment would require a full commitment of American economic, political, and military power:

We are going to continue for a long time to find the Russians difficult to deal with. It does not mean that they should be considered as embarked upon a do-or-die program to overthrow our society by a given date. . . . In these circumstances, it is clear that the main element of any United States policy toward the Soviet Union must be that of long-term, patient but firm and vigilant containment of Russian expansive tendencies.

—George Kennan, "The Sources of Soviet Conduct"

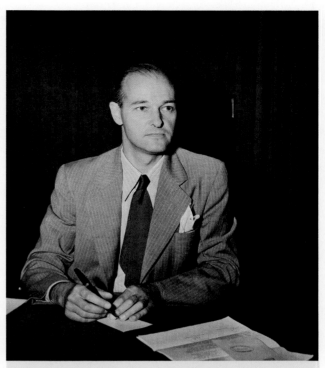

>> George Kennan, an expert on Russian history and culture, was the driving force behind American policy toward the Soviet Union in the early years of the Cold War.

>> German workers reconstruct a Berlin concert hall. The Marshall Plan helped Germany rebuild all aspects of its society, improving Germans' quality of life in the difficult postwar years.

United States Responds with Marshall Plan

The containment policy's first great success was in Western Europe. After World War II, people there confronted severe shortages of food, fuel, and medical supplies, as well as brutally cold winters.

In this environment of desperate need, Secretary of State George C. Marshall unveiled a recovery plan for Europe. In a speech at Harvard University, he warned that without economic health, "there can be no political stability and no assured peace."

In early 1948, Congress approved the **Marshall Plan**. Over the next four years, the United States gave about $13 billion in grants and loans to nations in Western Europe. The program provided food to reduce famine, fuel to heat houses and factories, and money to jump-start economic growth. Aid was also offered to the Soviet satellite states in Eastern Europe, but Stalin refused to let them accept it.

The Marshall Plan provided a vivid example of how U.S. aid could serve the ends of both economic and foreign policy. The aid helped countries that desperately needed assistance. The prosperity it stimulated then helped the American economy by increasing trade. Finally, the good relationships that the aid created worked against the expansion of communism.

☑ **IDENTIFY MAIN IDEAS** Why did George Kennan think that containment would work against Soviet expansion?

Soviet Aggression Drives Cold War

The front lines of the Cold War were located in Germany. The zones that were controlled by France, Britain, and the United States were combined to form West Germany. West Germany was bordered on the east by the Soviet-controlled East Germany. The Allies also controlled the western part of Berlin, a city tucked deep inside communist East Germany.

United States and Britain Respond with Berlin Airlift West Berlin was, as one Soviet leader later described it, "a bone in the throat" of the Soviet Union. Its relative prosperity and freedom stood in contrast to the bleak life of East Berliners. Stalin was determined to capture West Berlin or win other concessions from the Western allies. In June 1948, he stopped all highway, railway, and waterway traffic from western Germany into West Berlin. Without any means of receiving aid, West Berlin would fall to the communists.

Stalin was able to close roads, stop barges, and block railways, but he could not blockade the sky. As a result, the United States and Britain supplied West Berlin through a massive airlift that lasted nearly one year. Food, fuel, medical supplies, clothing, toys—everything the residents of West Berlin needed was flown into the city.

Even through rain and snow, goods arrived regularly. The **Berlin airlift** demonstrated to West Berlin, the Soviet Union, and the world how far the United States would go to protect noncommunist parts of Europe and contain communism.

The North Atlantic Treaty Organization
In May 1949, Stalin was forced to acknowledge that his attempt to blockade Berlin had failed. The Berlin airlift was a proud moment for Americans and Berliners and a major success for the policy of containment. One Berlin resident later recalled her feelings when the blockade was finally lifted:

Sheer joy—nothing else. Nothing else. Joy, and [the feeling that], 'We

Shipments Financed by the Marshall Plan, 1948–1951

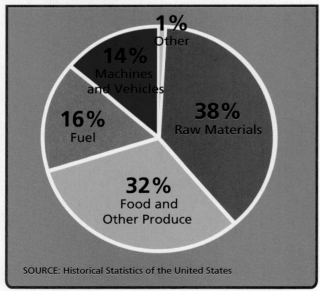

- 1% Other
- 14% Machines and Vehicles
- 16% Fuel
- 38% Raw Materials
- 32% Food and Other Produce

SOURCE: Historical Statistics of the United States

>> **Analyze Graphs** This graph shows the shipments financed by the Marshall Plan. Based on the chart, why would Food and Other Produce take up such a large percentage of the shipments?

🅱 **Bounce to Activate Gallery**

Cold War Alliances, 1955

NATO		WARSAW PACT
Belgium	Netherlands	Albania
Canada	Norway	Bulgaria
Denmark	Portugal	Czechoslovakia
France	Turkey	East Germany
Greece	United Kingdom	Hungary
Iceland	United States	Poland
Italy	West Germany	Romania
Luxembourg		Soviet Union

>> **Analyze Tables** Which NATO countries were not located in Europe?

have done it! And it works!' . . . That was so very important. The West has won! I say this quite deliberately in such a crass way because you wanted to know how I felt emotionally. The West—well, we have succeeded. And the West has won and the others have not!

—Ella Barowsky, CNN interview, 1996

The Berlin airlift demonstrated that Stalin could be contained if Western nations were prepared to take forceful action. The **North Atlantic Treaty Organization (NATO)**, formed in 1949, provided the military alliance to counter Soviet expansion. Twelve Western European and North American nations agreed to act together in the defense of Western Europe. Member nations agreed that "an armed attack against one or more of them . . . shall be considered an attack against all of them." This principle of mutual military assistance is called collective security.

In 1955, West Germany became a member of NATO. In response, the Soviet Union and its satellite states formed a rival military alliance, called the **Warsaw Pact**. All the communist states of Eastern Europe except Yugoslavia were members.

Like members of NATO, nations of the Warsaw Pact pledged to defend one another if attacked.

Although members agreed on paper not to interfere in one another's internal affairs, the Soviet Union continued to exert firm control over its Warsaw Pact allies.

☑ **EXPLAIN** How did the United States and its allies respond to Soviet aggression in Europe?

☑ ASSESSMENT

1. **Distinguish** between the political systems of the United States and the Soviet Union during the Cold War.

2. **Identify Cause and Effect** Describe the factors that led to the creation of the Truman Doctrine, as well as how the doctrine affected U.S. foreign policy.

3. **Evaluate Arguments** Describe George F. Kennan's argument in favor of the containment policy, and explain why he thought it would be successful.

4. **Generate Explanations** How did the concept of collective security lead to the creation of the North Atlantic Treaty Organization (NATO)?

5. **Summarize** the effects of the Marshall Plan on the United States and Western European countries.

>> A U.S. soldier aims a missile while his fellow soldiers take cover during a Korean War battle. For President Truman, supporting South Korea in the Korean War was about stopping the spread of communism.

Bounce to Activate Flipped Video

7.2 Europe had been the first focus of the Cold War. But in the early 1950s, U.S. involvement in the Korean War made East Asia the prime battleground in the long, hard Cold War struggle. The division between North and South Korea remains a source of international tension today.

>> Objectives

Explain how Mao Zedong and the communists gained power in China.

Describe the causes and the reasons for U.S. involvement in the Korean War.

Identify the long-term effects and outcomes of the Korean War.

>> Key Terms

Jiang Jieshi
Mao Zedong
38th parallel
Douglas MacArthur
limited war
Southeast
 Asia Treaty
 Organization
 (SEATO)

The Korean War

China Turns Communist

Since the time of the Russian Revolution in 1917, the Soviets had hoped to spread communism to every corner of the world, training foreigners in Marxist theory and revolutionary strategy. The Soviets were confident that communism would reach worldwide influence. In 1949, events in China seemed to justify their confidence.

U.S. Policy During China's Civil War Before Japan invaded China in 1937, Nationalist leader **Jiang Jieshi** (zhee AHNG zhì SHEE), known in the United States as Chiang Kai-shek, had been fighting a civil war against communists led by **Mao Zedong** (mow zeh DUHNG). Although Jiang and Mao temporarily joined forces in an uneasy alliance to fight Japan, the civil war resumed with a new fury after the war ended.

The Soviet Union supported Mao, while the United States sent several billion dollars in aid to Jiang. American leaders feared that Jiang's defeat would create a communist superpower spanning most of Asia.

Jiang's regime proved unequal to the task. Nationalist generals were reluctant to fight. And, while masses of Chinese people faced starvation, corrupt officials diverted U.S. aid dollars into their own pockets. By promising to feed the people, Mao won increased support.

China Falls to Communism In 1948, Mao's forces dominated the war. Jiang appealed for American military intervention. However, the U.S. government had no intention of sending American troops to support the corrupt Jiang. In 1949, Jiang fled the Chinese mainland, taking control of the large offshore island of Taiwan. Mao's communists then took control of the world's most populous country, renaming it the People's Republic of China.

Mao's victory was an immense shock to Americans. Not only was China under the control of sworn enemies of the United States, but communist regimes now controlled about one fourth of the world's landmass and one third of its population. "Who lost China?" Americans asked. Many critics blamed the Truman administration, saying that the United States had failed to give enough support to Jiang. But Secretary of State Dean Acheson argued:

> The unfortunate but inescapable fact is that the ominous result of the civil war in China was beyond the control of the government of the United States. Nothing that this country did or could have done within the reasonable limits of its capabilities could have changed the result.
>
> —Secretary of State Dean Acheson, "White Paper on China," August 1949

☑ **CHECK UNDERSTANDING** Why were the communists able to win the Chinese Civil War?

U.S. Involvement in Korea

The focus of attention turned to the peninsula of Korea, separated from northeast China by the Yalu River. Once controlled by Japan, Korea had been divided into two independent countries by the United States and the Soviet Union after World War II. The dividing line was set at the **38th parallel**. The Soviets installed a communist government and equipped the armed forces in North Korea. The United States provided smaller amounts of aid to noncommunist South Korea.

>> Jiang Jieshi, shown with his U.S.-educated wife Soong May-ling, led a nationalist Chinese government that attracted Western support.

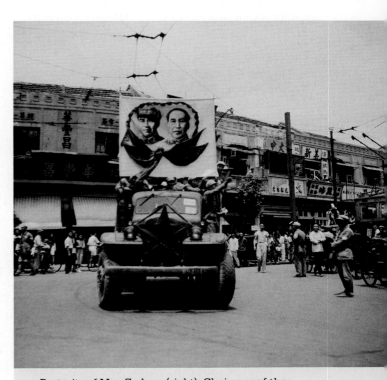

>> Portraits of Mao Zedong (right), Chairman of the People's Government, and Zhu De (left), leader of the People's Liberation Army, adorn a truck during a celebration of the founding of the People's Republic of China.

North Korea Invades South Korea American occupation troops remained in South Korea until June 1949. Their departure coincided with the communist victory in China. Soon after, North Korea began a major military buildup.

On June 25, 1950, North Korean forces attacked across the 38th parallel. The 90,000 North Korean troops were armed with powerful tanks and other Soviet weapons. Within days, the northerners overtook the South Korean capital city of Seoul and set out in pursuit of the retreating South Korean army.

Reasons for U.S. Involvement President Truman remembered how the policy of appeasement had failed to check the German aggression that sparked World War II. This knowledge, coupled with the U.S. policy of containment, caused Truman to announce that the United States would aid South Korea.

Within days, the UN Security Council unanimously voted to follow Truman's lead, recommending that "the Members of the United Nations furnish such assistance to the Republic of Korea as may be necessary to repel the armed attack and to restore international peace and security in the area." Undoubtedly, the Soviet Union would have used its veto power to block the UN resolution if it

had been present for the vote. However, it had been boycotting Security Council sessions because the UN had refused to seat Mao's People's Republic of China.

Truman did not ask Congress for a formal declaration of war, as required by the Constitution. However, supported by the UN resolution, Truman ordered American troops who were stationed in Japan to move to South Korea. The soldiers were mainly occupation troops who had not been trained for forced marches in monsoon rains or heavy combat in rice paddies, nor did they have the military equipment needed to stop the invasion. Soon, they joined their South Korean allies in retreating to the southeast corner of the peninsula near the city of Pusan. There, the allies held fast. As fresh supplies and troops arrived from Japan, soldiers from other UN countries joined the American and South Korean forces.

The U.S. and Its Allies Counterattack By September 1950, the UN forces were ready to counterattack. General **Douglas MacArthur**, the World War II hero, had a bold plan to drive the invaders from South Korea. He suspected that the rapid advance of North Korean troops had left North Korea with limited supply lines. He decided to strike at this weakness by launching a surprise attack on the port city of Inchon, well behind enemy lines. Because Inchon was such a poor landing site, with swift currents and treacherous tides, MacArthur knew that the enemy would not expect an attack there.

MacArthur's bold gamble paid off. On the morning of September 15, 1950, U.S. Marines landed at Inchon and launched an attack on the rear guard of the North Koreans. Communist forces in South Korea began fleeing back to North Korea. By October 1950, the North Koreans had been driven north of the 38th parallel.

With the retreat of North Korean forces, U.S. officials had to decide what to do next. Should they declare their UN mandate accomplished and end the war? Or should they send their forces north of the 38th parallel and punish the communists for the invasion? Truman was concerned about the action China would take if the United States carried the war into North Korea. Chinese leaders publicly warned the Americans not to advance near its borders. But MacArthur did not take this warning seriously. He assured Truman that China would not intervene in the war. Based on this advice, the United States pushed a resolution through the UN,

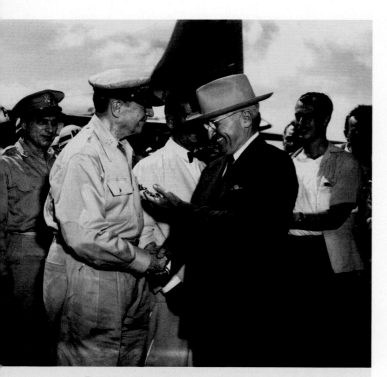

>> President Truman pins a medal on General Douglas MacArthur, who commanded the coalition of American-led United Nations forces in Korea.

EFFECTS OF THE KOREAN WAR

AMERICAN CASUALTIES

37,000 KILLED IN ACTION

103,000 WOUNDED IN ACTION

4,817 STILL LISTED AS MISSING IN ACTION

ADDITIONAL KILLED OR MISSING

SOUTH KOREAN MILITARY 217,000

NORTH KOREAN MILITARY 406,000

CHINESE MILITARY 600,000

KOREAN CIVILIANS 1,600,000

U.S. NATIONAL DEFENSE OUTLAYS
(BILLIONS)

$13 BEFORE THE WAR — 1947

$26 DURING THE WAR — 1952

$45 AFTER THE WAR — 1957

Source: The White House Office of Budget and Management

After the Korean War, the United States engaged in more **military actions without Congressional approval.**

1964–1973 Vietnam
1965 Dominican Republic
1983 Grenada
Panama 1989
Somalia 1993
Bosnia 1995
1994 Haiti
Kosovo 1999
1998 Afghanistan, Sudan
Libya 2011

>> **Analyze Data** After the Korean War how much more did the U.S spend on defense than before the war?

Bounce to Activate Map

---

calling for a "unified, independent, and democratic" Korea.

Truman and MacArthur Disagree on Military Goals Highly confident, MacArthur attacked north of the 38th parallel. Despite mountainous terrain and freezing temperatures, by Thanksgiving the Allied advance had reached the Chinese border at the Yalu River. Then, on November 25, 1950, some 300,000 Chinese soldiers attacked South Korean and U.S. positions. Badly outnumbered, the UN troops were forced back.

With China now in the war, the United States confronted a major land war in Asia. It was possible that this war could not be won without huge commitments of troops and even atomic weapons. Truman steadfastly ruled out both of these options. MacArthur, who favored an invasion of China, was enraged. He distrusted Truman's policy of a **limited war** fought to achieve only specific goals. As a soldier, MacArthur favored total victory.

Unable to sway Truman, the general sent a letter to the House Republican leader attacking the President's policies. After the letter became public, Truman fired MacArthur for insubordination.

There was a huge outcry in the United States, and MacArthur returned home a national hero.

☑ **RECALL** How did President Truman react to the North Korean invasion of South Korea?

Outcomes of the Korean War

By the spring of 1951, Allied forces had regrouped and stabilized their position near the 38th parallel. The stalemate lasted until 1953. During that time, the two sides fought small, bloody battles with limited results. At the same time, diplomats tried to devise an acceptable peace agreement.

Short-Term Outcomes of the Korean War The stalemate was a key issue in the presidential election of 1952. Republican candidate Dwight D. Eisenhower promised that if elected he would end the war. Upon his election, he visited Korea, spoke with the troops, and studied the enemy's fortifications.

Eisenhower became president in January 1953. The former general was convinced that only strong action would break the stalemate. When peace talks threatened to fail, he hinted that he might introduce nuclear weapons into the conflict. That warning,

>> Ongoing military exercises between U.S. and South Korean forces, such as these on the Namhan River, emphasize the U.S. commitment to the safety and security of the South Korean people.

along with the death of Joseph Stalin, convinced the communists to settle the conflict. On July 27, 1953, after slightly more than three years of fighting, the two sides signed a cease-fire. That cease-fire is still in effect today.

Long-Term Outcomes of the Korean War There was no victory in the Korean War. North Korea remained a communist country allied to China and the Soviet Union, and South Korea stayed a noncommunist country allied to the United States and the major democracies. The two Koreas remained divided at about the 38th parallel.

Yet the war had important long-term outcomes. Truman had committed U.S. troops to battle without a congressional declaration of war. This set a precedent that future Presidents would follow. The Korean War also seemed to support the growing belief among policymakers that the fall of one nation to communism could have a ripple effect throughout the region. The Korean War also led to increased military spending. By 1960, military spending accounted for nearly half of the federal budget. More than a million U.S. soldiers were stationed around the world.

A new alliance underscored U.S. interest in Asia. Like NATO, the **Southeast Asia Treaty Organization (SEATO)** was a defensive alliance aimed at preventing the spread of communism. Its members included Pakistan, Thailand, the Philippines, Australia, New Zealand, France, Britain, and the United States.

☑ **IDENTIFY CAUSE AND EFFECT** What were the most important outcomes of U.S. participation in the Korean War?

☑ ASSESSMENT

1. **Generate Explanations** Why did the United States send financial aid to Jiang Jieshi at the beginning of the Chinese civil war, but later refuse his request for military aid?

2. **Identify Patterns** Explain how President Truman's knowledge of previous historical events influenced him to initiate U.S. involvement in Korea.

3. **Summarize** General Douglas MacArthur's plan for a counterattack against North Korea.

4. **Contrast** the opinions of President Truman and General MacArthur regarding U.S. military action in Korea after China became involved.

5. **Identify Cause and Effect** What long-term impact did the result of the Korean War have on the United States' foreign and military policy?

By 1950, the United States and the Soviet Union were, by far, the two most powerful nations in the world. The conflicting ideologies and goals of these rival nations led to a worldwide struggle for influence. The policies followed by the two superpowers would help shape the history of the twentieth century for much of the world, from Latin America to the Middle East.

>> **Analyze Political Cartoons** A vise squeezes the world between the two superpowers' weapons. What does this cartoon have to say about efforts to build up nuclear arms?

Bounce to Activate Flipped Video

The Cold War Intensifies

The Arms Race Intensifies Tensions

A change in the balance of world power is usually gradual, taking place over decades or even centuries. But sometimes, the shift happens in a blink of an eye. Such a major shift in the balance of power in the Cold War took place on September 2, 1949. Instruments in an American B-29 aircraft flying over Alaska detected unusual atmospheric radiation. The radiation cloud was drifting eastward from the direction of Siberia.

American nuclear scientists analyzed the data that the aircraft had gathered. They then reached an inescapable conclusion: The Soviet Union had set off an atomic bomb.

Cold War Worries Rise The news shook U.S. leaders. They had believed that the Soviet Union was years away from developing an atomic bomb. Now, the Americans no longer had a monopoly on atomic weaponry.

The news that the Soviets had the bomb was followed the next month by news of the communist takeover of China. In a very

>> **Objectives**

Describe how Cold War tensions were intensified by the arms race between the United States and the Soviet Union.

Explain how Eisenhower's response to communism differed from that of Truman.

Analyze the impact on the United States of significant international Cold War conflicts.

Describe how Cold War tensions were intensified by the space race.

>> **Key Terms**

mutually assured
  destruction
John Foster Dulles
massive retaliation
brinkmanship
Nikita Khrushchev
nationalize
Suez crisis
Eisenhower Doctrine

Central Intelligence
  Agency (CIA)
National Aeronautics
  and Space
  Administration
  (NASA)

short time, Americans sensed that the world was a much more dangerous and threatening place.

The Arms Race Speeds Up During the Cold War, specific needs resulted in scientific discoveries and technological innovations in the military. Three months after news that the Soviets had developed an atomic bomb, Truman ordered the Atomic Energy Commission to produce a hydrogen bomb. Developers predicted that the H-Bomb would be 1,000 times as powerful as an atomic bomb. They hoped it would restore the United States' military advantage over the Soviets.

Some scientists, such as J. Robert Oppenheimer and Albert Einstein, opposed developing the H-Bomb, claiming it would only lead to a perpetual arms race. Others argued that Stalin would continue to develop more powerful weapons no matter what the United States did.

In 1952, the United States tested the first hydrogen bomb. The next year, the Soviets tested one of their own. More bombs and tests followed. Most of these tests were conducted above ground, spewing radioactive waste into the atmosphere. Atomic testing in the American west, at sites such as the Nevada desert, led to increased atmospheric

radiation and long-range health problems for people living downwind of the test sites.

During the next four decades, the United States and the Soviet Union developed and stockpiled increasingly powerful nuclear weapons. They armed planes, submarines, and missiles with nuclear warheads powerful enough to destroy each country many times over. Both sides hoped that this program of **mutually assured destruction** would prevent either country from actually using a nuclear device against the other. Still, the threat of nuclear destruction seemed to hang over the world like a dark cloud.

☑ **RECALL** Why did the United States government decide to build a hydrogen bomb?

Eisenhower's Response to Soviet Aggression

President Dwight Eisenhower knew firsthand the horrors of war and the need to defend democracy. He had led the World War II Allied invasions of North Africa, Italy, and Normandy. Having worked with top military and political leaders during the war, he was capable of speaking the language of both.

Eisenhower accepted much of Truman's foreign policy. He believed strongly in a policy to actively contain communist aggression. Eisenhower's secretary of state, **John Foster Dulles**, was an experienced diplomat who had helped organize the United Nations after World War II. Dulles endorsed the President's vision of the role the United States should play in the world and had stood firmly behind U.S.

efforts to contain communism through involvement in Korea. Containment, Dulles believed, could prevent the possibility of a "domino effect" throughout Southeast Asia with one country after another falling under communist rule.

In their approach toward foreign policy, Eisenhower and Dulles differed significantly from both Truman and his Secretary of State, Dean Acheson. Both teams of men considered the spread of communism the greatest threat to the free world. But Eisenhower believed that Truman's approach to foreign policy had dragged the United States into an endless series of conflicts begun by the Soviet Union. These limited, regional conflicts threatened to drain the country's resources.

>> Like Truman, President Eisenhower (left) and his Secretary of State, John Foster Dulles (right), believed that the containment of communism was essential to U.S. foreign policy.

Eisenhower's Policies toward Communism
Eisenhower opposed spending billions of dollars on

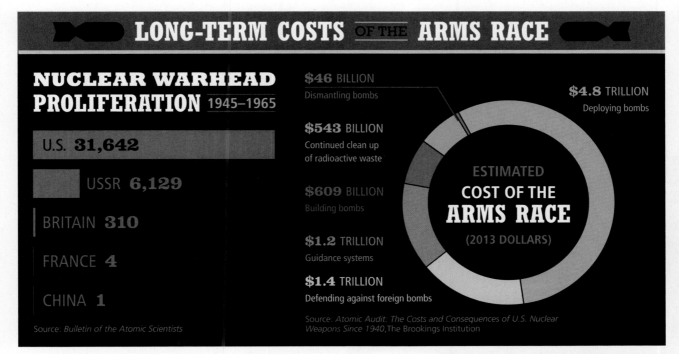

LONG-TERM COSTS OF THE ARMS RACE

NUCLEAR WARHEAD PROLIFERATION 1945–1965

U.S. **31,642**

USSR **6,129**

BRITAIN **310**

FRANCE **4**

CHINA **1**

Source: *Bulletin of the Atomic Scientists*

$46 BILLION
Dismantling bombs

$543 BILLION
Continued clean up
of radioactive waste

$609 BILLION
Building bombs

$1.2 TRILLION
Guidance systems

$1.4 TRILLION
Defending against foreign bombs

$4.8 TRILLION
Deploying bombs

ESTIMATED
COST OF THE
ARMS RACE
(2013 DOLLARS)

Source: *Atomic Audit: The Costs and Consequences of U.S. Nuclear Weapons Since 1940,* The Brookings Institution

>> **Analyze Data** How does the data shown in the infographic illustrate Eisenhower's approach to defense spending?

Bounce to Activate Chart

conventional forces, such as troops, ships, tanks, and artillery. Instead, he focused on stockpiling nuclear weapons and building the planes, missiles, and submarines needed to deliver them. He assumed that if there were a major war, it would be nuclear.

Eisenhower's new policy drew some criticism: conservatives felt that downgrading conventional forces would weaken American defense, while liberals feared that preparing for nuclear war made such a war more likely. Still, Eisenhower's approach did save money by providing a "bigger bang for the buck." In 1953, the defense budget was $50.5 billion; in 1955, it dropped down to $35.8 billion.

In 1954, Dulles announced the policy of **massive retaliation**. The United States would respond to communist threats to its allies by threatening to use crushing, overwhelming force, perhaps even nuclear weapons.

A potential aggressor must know that he cannot always prescribe battle conditions to suit him. . . . The way to deter aggression is for the free community to be willing and able to respond vigorously at places and with means of his choosing.

—John Foster Dulles, 1954

Dulles further believed that only by going to the brink of war could the United States protect its allies, discourage communist aggression, and prevent war. "You have to take some chances for peace, just as you must take chances in war," he said in 1956. Dulles's approach became known as **brinkmanship**.

Stalin's Death Eases Tensions On March 5, 1953, Soviet dictator Joseph Stalin died, setting off a short power struggle. **Nikita Khrushchev** soon emerged as the new head of the Soviet Union. Although a communist and a determined opponent of the United States, Khrushchev was not as suspicious or as cruel as Stalin. He condemned the excesses of the Stalin regime and inched toward more peaceful relations with the democratic West.

In July 1955, Khrushchev met with Eisenhower at a conference in Geneva, Switzerland. Although the meeting yielded few significant results, it did seem

>> In 1956, Poland revolted against Soviet rule. Here, the crowd carries a Polish flag during an anti-communist demonstration.

>> Hungarian nationalists in 1956 burn a portrait of Hungarian communist party leader Matyas Rakosi. Unlike the protests in Poland, the uprising in Hungary was violently put down by the Soviet military.

to be a small move toward "peaceful coexistence" of the two powers.

☑ CONTRAST How was Eisenhower's approach to foreign affairs different from that of Truman's?

International Cold War Conflicts

Peaceful co-existence was easier to imagine than it was to practice. The United States and the Soviet Union remained deeply divided. The Soviet Union would not allow free elections in the areas it controlled, and it continued to attempt to spread communism around the world. Dulles talked about "rolling back" communism and liberating the countries under Soviet rule.

Uprisings Behind the Iron Curtain: Poland and Hungary American talk of "rolling back" communist borders and Khrushchev's talk of "peaceful co-existence" were taken seriously by people in Soviet-dominated countries behind the iron curtain. People in Poland, Hungary, and Czechoslovakia resented the control exerted by the Soviet Union. Many hungered for more political and economic freedom.

In 1956, two uprisings shook Eastern Europe. First, workers in Poland rioted against Soviet rule and won greater control of their government. Since the Polish government did not attempt to leave the Warsaw Pact, Soviet leaders permitted the actions.

Then, encouraged by Khrushchev's words and Poland's example, Hungarian students and workers organized huge demonstrations. They demanded that pro-Soviet Hungarian officials be replaced, that Soviet troops be withdrawn, and that noncommunist political parties be organized. Khrushchev responded brutally, sending Soviet soldiers and tanks to crush the Hungarian revolution. The Soviets executed many of the revolution's leaders, killed hundreds of other Hungarians, and restored hard-line communists to power.

Americans could only watch these events in horror. Eisenhower's massive retaliation approach was powerless. The United States would not use nuclear weapons—or any other weapons—to guarantee Hungarian independence from the Soviet Union.

The Hungarian revolt added a new level of hostility to international relations. At the 1956 Olympic Games, held that November in Melbourne, Australia, the bitter feelings surfaced. A water-polo match between the Soviet Union and Hungary

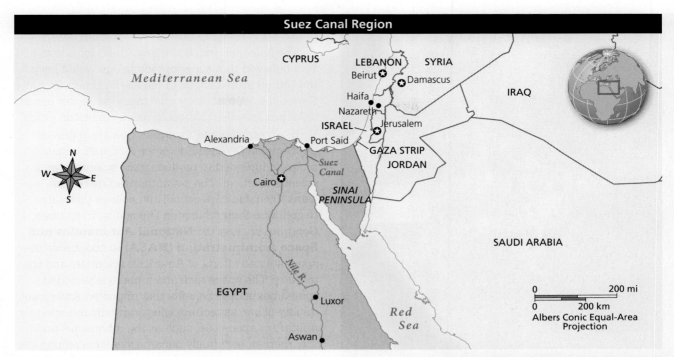

Suez Canal Region

CYPRUS
LEBANON SYRIA
Beirut ⊛ ◉ Damascus
IRAQ

Mediterranean Sea

Haifa
Nazareth
ISRAEL ◉ Jerusalem
Alexandria Port Said
GAZA STRIP
JORDAN
Suez Canal
Cairo ⊛
SINAI PENINSULA
SAUDI ARABIA

Nile R.

EGYPT
Luxor
Red Sea
Aswan

| 0 | 200 mi |
| 0 | 200 km |

Albers Conic Equal-Area Projection

>> **Analyze Maps** The Suez Canal connects the Mediterranean Sea and the Red Sea. Why was the canal so strategically important?

Bounce to Activate Map

turned violent. Sportswriters called it the "blood in the water" match.

The Suez Crisis The United States found itself involved in another Cold War conflict, this time in the Middle East. As Cold War tensions intensified, Egypt's president Gamal Abdel Nasser tried to use the U.S.–Soviet rivalry to his advantage.

Nasser wanted to construct a dam on the Nile River at Aswan. The United States and Britain initially offered to fund the project, but when Nasser recognized the communist People's Republic of China and opened talks with the Soviet Union, the Eisenhower administration withdrew its offer. In response, Nasser **nationalized** the Suez Canal, placing it under government control. The canal, which connects the Mediterranean Sea and the Red Sea, had originally been managed by a British-French company and was protected by British armed forces.

Nasser's action threatened the flow of Middle Eastern oil to Europe. Without consulting with Eisenhower, Britain and France plotted to get the canal back into Western hands. They joined forces with Israel, a young nation that had long suffered from raids along its border with Egypt. Britain and France used the **Suez crisis** as an excuse to seize control of the Suez Canal. Israel viewed

Egypt's nationalization of the canal as a violation of international law and wanted to preserve freedom for Israeli shipping.

President Eisenhower was outraged by these actions. Rather than support his Western allies, Eisenhower criticized them and refused to supply them with U.S. oil. The three nations had counted on Eisenhower's support, and when it did not come, they were forced to withdraw their troops from Egypt.

The Eisenhower Doctrine Eisenhower's response to the attempted seizure of the Suez Canal did not mean that he was unconcerned with communist influence in the Middle East. In response to Soviet influence there and elsewhere, the President made a statement in January 1957 that became known as the **Eisenhower Doctrine**. Eisenhower announced that the United States would use force to help any Middle Eastern nation threatened by communism. Eisenhower used his doctrine in 1958 to justify sending troops to Lebanon to put down a revolt against its pro-American government.

The Eisenhower administration also used the **Central Intelligence Agency (CIA)** in its struggle against communism. Congress had created the CIA in 1947 as an intelligence-gathering organization. Eisenhower gave it a new task. He approved covert,

>> In the years immediately following the Soviets' launch of *Sputnik 1*, the United States responded by developing many more satellites, such as this one in 1960.

🅱 **Bounce to Activate Gallery**

or secret, CIA operations to protect American interests. In 1953, the CIA aided a coup that installed a new government in Iran. In 1954, it accomplished a similar mission in Guatemala. While both operations helped to place anticommunist leaders in power, they also created long-term resentment against the United States.

The Space Race Increases Tensions Although the United States successfully contained the spread of communism on the ground, it did suffer a setback in space. On October 4, 1957, the Soviet Union launched a 184-pound steel ball containing a small transmitter into an orbit of Earth. The Soviets named the tiny satellite *Sputnik 1*. The following month they launched a much larger satellite. It carried a dog, named Laika, to see how a living creature would react to space travel. Since there was no way to return the satellite to Earth, Laika died in orbit.

The launches shocked many Americans, who had long believed that superior technology would keep the United States ahead of the Soviet Union. Would Soviet space technology give them the rocket power to launch missiles that could reach American cities?

In a state of crisis, Congress quickly approved the National Defense Education Act, a $1 billion program intended to produce more scientists and science teachers. The act authorized money for loans to enable high school and college graduates to continue their education in science. In addition, Congress created the **National Aeronautics and Space Administration (NASA)** to coordinate the space-related efforts of American scientists and the military. The space race and arms race provided some unexpected benefits that improved Americans' quality of life, as technologies originally intended for military or space use, such as the microwave and the internet, eventually became available among the wider population.

☑ **IDENTIFY CENTRAL ISSUES** How did the Hungarian and Suez crises of 1956 intensify Cold War tensions?

☑ **ASSESSMENT**

1. **Generate Explanations** Explain how the concept of mutually assured destruction influenced the course of the Cold War.

2. **Compare and Contrast** the foreign policies of Eisenhower and Truman.

3. **Generate Explanations** Explain the logic behind John Foster Dulles' concept of brinkmanship.

4. **Identify Cause and Effect** Discuss how Stalin's death affected tensions between the Soviet Union and the United States.

5. **Identify Patterns** Explain how the Eisenhower administration used the CIA to fight the spread of communism in various countries.

Americans have often faced the difficult task of balancing the need to provide national security with the need to protect people's rights and freedoms. In times of crisis, rights have sometimes been limited. Beginning in the late 1940s, the Cold War dominated American life. For some of those years, the nation was in the grip of a new Red Scare. The hunt for communists netted some spies, but it also disrupted the lives of thousands of innocent Americans.

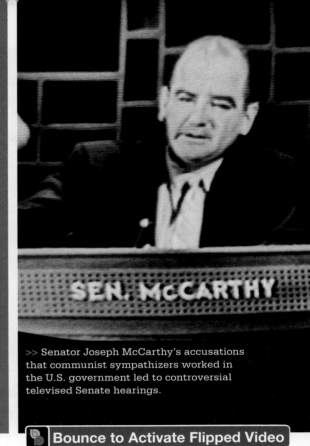

>> Senator Joseph McCarthy's accusations that communist sympathizers worked in the U.S. government led to controversial televised Senate hearings.

Bounce to Activate Flipped Video

Cold War Fears at Home

Cold War Tensions Rise at Home

The Cold War influenced many aspects of American life. American soldiers fought and died in Korea. Industries hummed with activity, turning out weapons and supplies. Americans read newspaper articles about who "lost" China or who was winning the "space race." Popular culture reflected an us-versus-them attitude—democrats versus totalitarians, capitalists versus communists, the West versus the East. In the end, the Cold War was turning out to be every bit as global and as encompassing as World War II had been.

The Second Red Scare The fear that communists both outside and inside America were working to destroy American life created a reaction known as a **Red Scare**. This fear was not unique to the late 1940s and 1950s. The 1917 Russian Revolution and the communists' call for worldwide revolution had led to a similar Red Scare in 1919 and 1920. However, the Red Scare that followed World War II went deeper and wider—and lasted far longer—than the earlier one. Truman's Attorney General, J.

>> **Objectives**

Describe the efforts of President Truman and the House Un-American Activities Committee to fight communism at home.

Explain how domestic spy cases intensified fears of communist influence in the U.S. government.

Analyze the rise and fall of Senator Joseph McCarthy and the methods of McCarthyism.

>> **Key Terms**

Red Scare
Smith Act
House Un-American
  Activities
  Committee
  (HUAC)
Hollywood Ten
blacklist
Alger Hiss
Julius and Ethel
  Rosenberg
Venona Papers

McCarthyism
Joseph R. McCarthy

Go ONLINE for digital resources
VIDEO   AUDIO   ACTIVITY   ETEXT   WRITING   ASSESSMENT

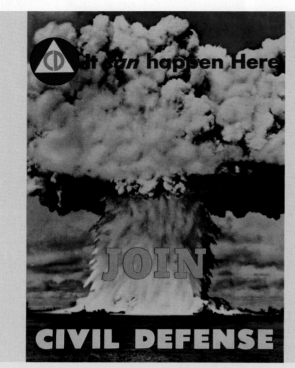

>> Civil Defense posters warned Americans to remain on high alert for a nuclear attack.

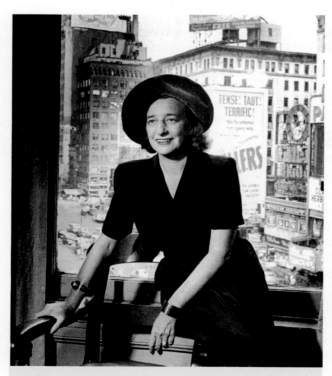

>> Playwright and screenwriter Lillian Hellman was blacklisted after telling HUAC, "I am not willing...to bring bad trouble to people who, in my past association with them, were completely innocent of any talk or any action that was disloyal or subversive."

Howard McGrath, expressed the widespread fear of communist influence when he warned that communists "are everywhere—in factories, offices, butcher stores, on street corners, and private businesses. And each carries in himself the death of our society."

The spread of communism into Eastern Europe and Asia raised concerns that American communists, some in influential government positions, were working for the enemy. In truth, some American communists were agents of the Soviet Union, and a handful of them held high-ranking positions in government. However, overwhelmingly, government officials were loyal to the United States.

Recognizing public concern about domestic communism, President Truman used an executive order to create a Federal Employee Loyalty Program in March 1947. The order permitted the FBI and other government security agencies to screen federal employees for signs of political disloyalty. About 3,000 federal employees either were dismissed or resigned after the investigation.

The order also empowered the Attorney General to compile a list of "totalitarian, fascist, or subversive organizations" in the United States. Americans who belonged to or supported organizations on the Attorney General's list were singled out for more intense scrutiny. Many were labeled "security risks" and dismissed from their jobs.

The Truman administration also used the 1940 **Smith Act** to cripple the Communist Party in the United States. This act made it unlawful to teach or advocate the violent overthrow of the U.S. government. In 1949, a New York jury found 11 communists guilty of violating the Smith Act and sent them to prison.

The House Un-American Activities Committee
Congress joined in the search for communists. In 1938, the House of Representatives had created the **House Un-American Activities Committee (HUAC)** to investigate possible subversive activities by fascists, Nazis, or communists. After the war, the committee conducted several highly publicized hearings on communist activities in the United States. Cold War fears were intensified by HUAC investigators, who probed the government, armed forces, unions, education, science, newspapers, and other aspects of American life.

The best-known HUAC hearings targeted the movie industry in 1947. The HUAC investigations uncovered people who were, or had been, communists during the 1930s and 1940s. A group of left-wing writers, directors, and producers known as the **Hollywood Ten** refused to answer questions, asserting their Fifth Amendment rights against self-incrimination. The hearings turned into a war of attacks and counterattacks as committee members and witnesses yelled at each other and pointed accusatory fingers.

After the hearings, the Hollywood Ten were cited for contempt of Congress and were tried, convicted, and sent to prison. Movie executives circulated a **blacklist** of entertainment figures who should not be hired because of their suspected communist ties. The careers of those on the list were shattered. Not until the case of *Watkins* v. *United States* (1957) did the Supreme Court decide that witnesses before HUAC could not be forced to name radicals they knew.

The HUAC investigation had a powerful impact on filmmaking. In the past, Hollywood had been willing to make movies about controversial subjects such as racism and anti-Semitism. Now, most producers concentrated only on entertainment and avoided addressing sensitive social issues.

Red Scare Intensifies Cold War Fears The case of the Hollywood Ten demonstrated that in the mood of fear created by Soviet aggression, freedom of speech was not guaranteed. Americans lost their jobs because they had belonged to or contributed to an organization on the Attorney General's list. Others were fired for associating with people who were known communists or for making remarks that were considered disloyal. Teachers and librarians, mail carriers and longshoremen, electricians and construction workers—people from all walks of life— might be accused and dismissed from their jobs.

The effort to root out communist influence from American life cut across many levels of society. Communists were exposed and blacklisted in the country's academic institutions, labor unions, scientific laboratories, and city halls. No one was above suspicion. The case of J. Robert Oppenheimer illustrates the difficulty of distinguishing loyalty from disloyalty. During World War II, Oppenheimer had led the Manhattan Project, which developed the atomic bomb. After the war, he became chairman of the General Advisory Committee of the U.S. Atomic Energy Commission (AEC). However, Oppenheimer had ties to people who belonged to the Communist Party, including his wife and brother.

In 1954, the AEC denied Oppenheimer access to classified information. Although the AEC had no evidence that Oppenheimer himself had ever been disloyal to the United States, it questioned whether

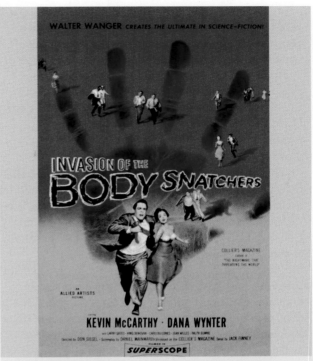

>> The 1956 film *Invasion of the Body Snatchers* expressed Americans' fears of invasion and infiltration during the era of the Red Scare.

Bounce to Activate Gallery

his communist ties disqualified him from holding this position.

☑ **SUMMARIZE** What steps did Truman and Congress take to investigate communist influence in the United States?

Domestic Spy Cases Increase Fears

Two sensational spy trials drew the nation's attention to the threat posed by communist agents working to subvert the United States. The accused in the two cases could not have been more different. **Alger Hiss** had been educated at Johns Hopkins University and Harvard Law School. **Julius and Ethel Rosenberg** were from the poor, lower east side of Manhattan. Although Hiss and the Rosenbergs never met, their crimes and their trials have linked them in the public's imagination.

HUAC Investigates Alger Hiss Until 1948, Alger Hiss's career seemed flawless. A seemingly dedicated government servant, Hiss had worked on several important New Deal agencies and helped to organize the United Nations. But a man named Whittaker Chambers disputed Hiss's image. As a young man, Chambers had become a communist espionage agent. But Chambers later turned against communism because of the brutality of Stalin's rule. Chambers began writing compellingly about the evils of communism. In 1948, he testified before HUAC about his communist past and named Alger Hiss as one of his contacts in the federal government.

Hiss soon appeared before HUAC. He denied that he was a communist and an espionage agent, and he denied that he even knew Whittaker Chambers. But Richard Nixon, a young member of Congress from California, convinced the other committee members to press the case. Slowly, Hiss's story began to unravel. Chambers proved that he did know Hiss and that Hiss had given him confidential government documents. Chambers had even kept a microfilm copy of some of those documents, storing them in a hollowed-out pumpkin on his Maryland farm.

Hiss was tried for perjury. The first trial ended in a hung jury. At his second trial, he was found guilty and sentenced to five years in prison. Even after his conviction, many Americans continued to believe that Hiss was innocent. However, as years

passed, the evidence grew overwhelmingly against him. The fact that someone as influential as Hiss was a communist agent raised serious concerns. The Hiss case had another unexpected effect. The congressional hearings thrust Richard Nixon into the national spotlight. In 1952, he was named Eisenhower's running mate and would later become President.

The Rosenbergs and the Venona Papers

Nothing created more concern about internal security than the charge that some Americans had helped the Soviets build an atomic bomb. The case began when a scientist named Klaus Fuchs was charged with sending atomic secrets to the Soviet Union. The investigation against Fuchs ultimately led to the arrest of Ethel and Julius Rosenberg in 1950. The Rosenbergs were charged with conspiring to pass secret information about nuclear science to Soviet agents.

The trial of the Rosenbergs generated intense controversy in America and around the world. The case against them was based largely on the word of one confessed spy. Pleading innocent, the Rosenbergs claimed that they were being persecuted for being Jewish and for holding unpopular beliefs. In the end, both were found guilty and sentenced to death. Many believed that the harsh sentence was intended as a lever to force them to identify other members of the alleged spy ring. But the Rosenbergs claimed they had no such information. After 26 months on death row, the Rosenbergs were electrocuted in 1953.

Years of debate followed the executions. Some insisted that anti-Semitic sentiment led to the Rosenbergs' conviction and death. However, in 1995, the U.S. National Security Agency released secret Soviet messages that the United States had intercepted in the 1940s, known as the **Venona Papers**. The papers revealed the names of many Americans who spied for the Soviet Union. These documents confirmed the guilt of some of those investigated by HUAC, including the Rosenbergs and Alger Hiss.

☑ **EXPLAIN** Why did the Rosenberg case attract nationwide attention and controversy?

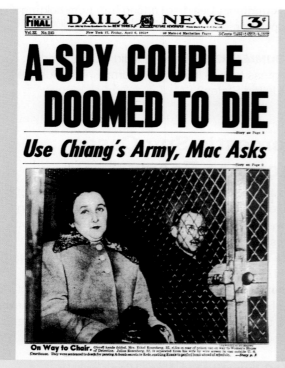

>> A jury found Julius and Ethel Rosenberg guilty of passing atomic secrets to the Soviet Union, and sentenced them to death for espionage.

▶ **Bounce to Activate Timeline**

McCarthyism

The early Cold War years saw one ominous event after another. The fall of China, Soviet nuclear bombs, and the exposure of Soviet agents in the United States all undermined American confidence.

At that time, as Americans worried about the nation's security, a clever and unscrupulous man began to take advantage of this sense of fear and helplessness. He suggested that these setbacks were really caused by the work of traitors inside the United States.

The Rise of Senator Joe McCarthy In February 1950, a little-known senator from Wisconsin made a speech in Wheeling, West Virginia. The senator, **Joseph R. McCarthy**, charged that the State Department was infested with communist agents. He waved a piece of paper, which, he said, contained the names of State Department employees who were secretly communists.

> The reason why we find ourselves in a position of [weakness] is not because the enemy has sent men to invade our shores, but rather because of the traitorous actions of those who have had all the benefits that the wealthiest nation on earth has had to offer—the finest homes, the finest college educations, and the finest jobs in Government we can give. . . . I have here in my hand a list of 205 [individuals] that were known to the Secretary of State as being members of the Communist Party and who nevertheless are still working and shaping the policy of the State Department.
>
> —Joseph McCarthy, February 9, 1950

The charge provoked a furor. When challenged to give specific names, McCarthy said he had meant that there were "205 bad security risks" in the department. Then he claimed that 57 employees were communists. Over the next months, the numbers on his list changed. McCarthy never did produce the list of communists. Still, with the outbreak of the Korean War in June 1950, McCarthy's accusations grabbed the attention of the American public.

At the time of the above speech, McCarthy was finishing his first term in the Senate. He had accomplished very little in that term and was looking for a popular issue on which to focus his 1952 reelection campaign. Anticommunism seemed to be

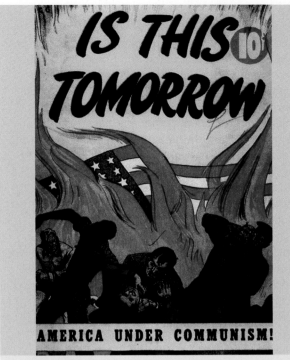

>> The charges from McCarthy and others that communists were working from within to overthrow the American government helped spread panic through popular culture.

just the issue. McCarthy was easily reelected to a second term.

The Methods of McCarthyism In the following four years, McCarthy put forward his own brand of anticommunism—so much so that the term **McCarthyism** became a catchword for extreme, reckless charges. By making irresponsible allegations, McCarthy did more to discredit legitimate concerns about domestic communism than any other single American. Between 1950 and 1954, McCarthy was perhaps the most powerful politician in the United States. Piling baseless accusations on top of charges that could not be proved, McCarthy became chairman of an investigations subcommittee. Merely being accused by McCarthy caused people to lose their jobs and destroyed their reputations. He attacked ruthlessly. When caught in a lie, he told another.

When one case faded, he introduced a new one. Confident because of his increasing power, McCarthy took on larger targets. He attacked former Secretary of State George Marshall, a national hero and author of the Marshall Plan. Even other senators came to fear McCarthy. They worried that he would brand them as communist sympathizers.

The "Lavender Scare" Hysteria over national security also targeted homosexuals, who were considered vulnerable to blackmail and thus likely to reveal national secrets. The Red Scare of the 1950s overlapped with a homophobic Lavender Scare. Congress held closed-door as well as open public hearings on the threat posed by homosexuals in sensitive government positions. The systematic investigation, interrogation, and firing of thousands of suspected gay men and lesbians from federal government positions soon extended further—into surveillance and persecution of suspected lesbians and gay men in state and local government, education, and private industry.

McCarthy Loses Support In 1954, McCarthy went after the United States Army, claiming that it, too, was full of communists. Army leaders responded that McCarthy's attacks were personally motivated.

Finally, the Senate decided to hold televised hearings to sort out the allegations. For weeks, Americans were riveted to their television sets. Most were horrified by McCarthy's bullying tactics. For the first time, the public saw McCarthy badger witnesses, twist the truth, and snicker at the suffering of others. It was an upsetting sight for many Americans.

By the time the hearings ended in mid-June, the senator had lost many of his strongest supporters. The Senate formally censured, or condemned, him for his reckless accusations. Although McCarthy continued to serve in the Senate, he had lost virtually all of his power and influence.

McCarthy's downfall in 1954 signaled the decline of the Red Scare, although in some places, McCarthy-style investigations continued. The nation had been damaged by the suppression of free speech and by the lack of open, honest debate. However, Americans had come to realize how important their democratic institutions were and how critical it was to preserve them.

☑ **IDENTIFY CAUSE AND EFFECT** What events led to Senator McCarthy being censured by the U.S. Senate?

☑ ASSESSMENT

1. **Support Ideas with Examples** In what ways did McCarthyism intensify tensions within the United States during the Cold War?

2. **Summarize** Explain the purpose of the House Un-American Activities Committee, or HUAC, and the effect the committee had on the American public.

3. **Use Context Clues** Discuss how U.S. involvement in the Korean War contributed to the fears Americans had about the communist threat during the Cold War.

4. **Generate Explanations** Why did the televising of the Senate hearings help end McCarthyism?

5. **Compare Points of View** Explain the debate on the convictions of Julius and Ethel Rosenberg, and how this debate changed when the Venona Papers were revealed.

7.5 After World War II, many Americans worried that the war's end would bring renewed economic depression. Numerous economists shared this pessimistic view of the future, predicting that the American economy could not produce enough jobs to employ all those who were returning from the military. Yet instead of a depression, Americans experienced the longest period of economic growth in American history, a boom that enabled millions of Americans to enter the middle class. This era of sustained growth fostered a widespread sense of optimism about the nation's future.

>> President Dwight D. Eisenhower led the United States during a time of exuberant growth and prosperity.

Bounce to Activate Flipped Video

Postwar Prosperity

Causes and Effects of Prosperity in the 1950s

At the end of the war in August 1945, more than 12 million Americans were in the military. Thousands of American factories were churning out ships, planes, tanks, and all the materials required to help fight the war in the Pacific. Virtually overnight, both the need for such a huge military machine and the focus on war production came to an end. Orders went out from Washington, D.C., canceling defense contracts, causing millions of defense workers to lose their jobs. Wartime industries had to be converted to meet peacetime needs.

As Americans set about enjoying the fruits of peace, President Harry Truman responded to calls to "bring the boys home for Christmas" by starting the **demobilization**, or sending home members of the army. By July 1946, only 3 million remained in the military.

Americans were happy that the war was over, but they retained some sense of unease about the future. One poll taken in the fall of 1945 showed that 60 percent of Americans expected their earnings to fall with the return of a peacetime economy. "The American soldier is . . . worried sick about postwar joblessness," *Fortune* magazine observed.

>> **Objectives**

Describe how the Unites States made the transformation to a booming peacetime economy.

Discuss the growth of the Sunbelt and the effects of migration.

Describe changes in the U.S. economy in the postwar period.

Discuss the accomplishments and leadership qualities of Presidents Harry Truman and Dwight Eisenhower.

>> **Key Terms**

demobilization
GI Bill of Rights
baby boom
productivity
Taft-Hartley Act
Fair Deal
Sunbelt
service sector
information industry

franchise business
multinational
   corporation
AFL-CIO
Estee Lauder
Sam Walton

Impact of the GI Bill To help deal with this anxiety, the federal government enacted the Servicemen's Readjustment Act of 1944, also popularly known as the **GI Bill of Rights**. It granted veterans a variety of benefits. It provided a year of unemployment payments to veterans who were unable to find work. Those who attended college after the war received financial aid. The act also entitled veterans to government loans for building homes and starting businesses.

The GI bill had an enormous impact on American society. Home loans to veterans fueled an upsurge in home construction, which led to explosive growth in suburban areas. Perhaps the greatest contribution of the GI bill came in education. The average soldier was inducted into the armed forces at the time when he or she would have been finishing high school.

The bill encouraged veterans to enter or return to college. Each veteran was eligible to receive $500 a year for college tuition. The bill also provided $50 a month for living expenses and $75 a month for married veterans. Eight million veterans eventually took advantage of the education benefits.

A Baby Boom Increases Consumption Upon their return, soldiers quickly made up for lost time by marrying and having children. Americans had put off having children because of the depression and war. Now, confident that the bad times were behind them, many married couples started families.

This led to what population experts termed a **baby boom**. In 1957, at the peak of the baby boom, one American baby was born every 7 seconds, a grand total of 4.3 million for the year. One newspaper columnist commented, "Just imagine how much these extra people . . . will absorb—in food, in clothing, in gadgets, in housing, in services. . . ." Between 1940 and 1955, the U.S. population experienced its greatest increase, growing 27 percent from about 130 to about 165 million.

Postwar Inflation Fortunately, unemployment did not materialize, nor did a depression return. However, Americans experienced some serious economic problems. The most painful was skyrocketing prices. With war's end, the federal government ended rationing and price controls, both of which had helped keep inflation in check during the war. A postwar rush to buy goods created severe inflationary pressures. There was just too much money to spend on too few goods. Overall, prices rose about 18 percent in 1946. The price of some products, such as beef, nearly doubled within a year.

Free Enterprise Improves U.S. Standard of Living During the depression, Americans could not buy the goods they desired. The economy improved during the war, but wartime restrictions kept spending down and limited economic growth.

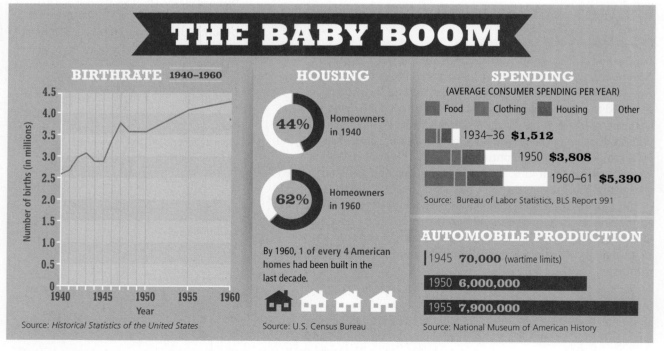

THE BABY BOOM

BIRTHRATE 1940–1960

Number of births (in millions)

Source: *Historical Statistics of the United States*

HOUSING

44% Homeowners in 1940

62% Homeowners in 1960

By 1960, 1 of every 4 American homes had been built in the last decade.

Source: U.S. Census Bureau

SPENDING
(AVERAGE CONSUMER SPENDING PER YEAR)

Food Clothing Housing Other

1934–36 **$1,512**
1950 **$3,808**
1960–61 **$5,390**

Source: Bureau of Labor Statistics, BLS Report 991

AUTOMOBILE PRODUCTION

1945 **70,000** (wartime limits)
1950 **6,000,000**
1955 **7,900,000**

Source: National Museum of American History

>> **Analyze Data** In your opinion, which is more important to the U.S. economy, home ownership or automobile ownership? Why?

The end of wartime restrictions finally opened the floodgates to consumer purchases. As demand soared, businesses employed more people to produce goods. This created a cycle in which people bought new goods, leading businesses to hire more workers, who in turn bought more goods.

At the end of World War II, the United States was the only developed nation largely untouched by the devastation. Although it had only 6 percent of the world's population, the United States produced about 50 percent of the world's total output. Americans at this time enjoyed a higher standard of living than any other nation in the world.

Technological Progress Enhances Productivity

The American economy benefited from numerous technological advances during the postwar period. Some developments, such as the use of atomic energy, were the result of war research. The use of computers increased, and businesses gradually began to depend on them. Farms benefited from improved machinery and chemicals, allowing farmers to grow more crops with fewer laborers. Worker **productivity**—the rate at which goods are produced or services performed—continued to improve, largely because of new technology.

Military Spending Supports Growth Increased government spending boosted the economy, too. The Cold War had a number of economic effects. With the outbreak of the Korean War and the escalating Cold War with communist nations in Europe and Asia, the United States once again committed a significant part of its budget to defense spending. This was an expense that led President Eisenhower to warn about the rise of a "military-industrial complex" that would endanger democracy. Military spending led to the development of new technologies and new materials, such as plastics and new light metal alloys, that found widespread use outside the military. Other large federal spending programs, such as the Marshall Plan, initiated foreign demand for goods made in the United States.

☑ **IDENTIFY CAUSE AND EFFECT** How did the baby boom help cause increased economic prosperity during the 1950s?

Americans Migrate to the Sunbelt

Another crucial trend of the postwar era was the growth of the **Sunbelt**, the name given to the southern and western states. By the mid-1960s,

>> The end of the war and the nation's newfound prosperity prompted many young Americans to start families. The result was a "baby boom" that increased the population by 27 percent.

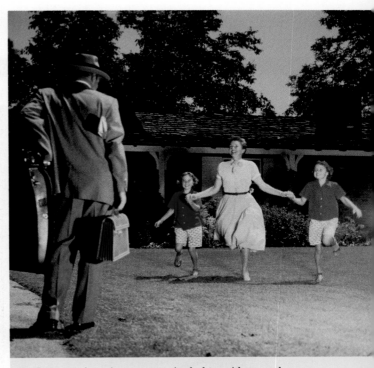

>> Postwar American prosperity led to widespread depictions in the media of an idealized suburban society.

California passed New York as the state with the largest population. The migration to Sunbelt cities, such as Houston, Texas, and Los Angeles, California, continued for the rest of the twentieth century.

Causes of Migration Many factors played a role in attracting people to the Sunbelt. A warm, sunny climate drew some Americans. A booming industrial economy and rapidly growing cities attracted people to Texas, which added more than 3 million new residents in the 1940s and 1950s. The explosive growth of the aerospace and electronics industries also attracted newcomers to the Sunbelt.

The development of air conditioning also played a major role. Invented in 1902, air conditioners were at first used only in public buildings, such as movie theaters and courthouses. But after World War II, the development of window units made it possible to cool homes. Northerners who had visited states like Florida, Texas, or Arizona only in winter could now live in hotter climates all year round.

Latinos contributed to the growth of the Sunbelt. In the late 1950s and early 1960s, many Cubans, who were escaping the new regime of Fidel Castro, made Miami, Florida, their new home. Prior to World War II, most Mexican Americans lived in rural areas. However, by the 1960s, the majority of them migrated to urban areas, such as Los Angeles, El Paso, and Phoenix.

Effects of Migration on Society and the Environment As people moved to the suburbs and the Sunbelt, their political power went with them. Thus, suburbs and the Sunbelt gained representation. Urbanites in the Northeast and Midwest lost political power.

Urban and suburban growth created environmental concerns, ranging from traffic jams and smog to water shortages. To meet growing populations, communities utilized once valuable open lands for housing, schools, roads, new businesses, and parking lots. In the 1960s and 1970s, environmental groups would begin to grapple with some of the byproducts of this growth.

☑ **CHECK UNDERSTANDING** What motivated so many Americans to migrate to the Sunbelt?

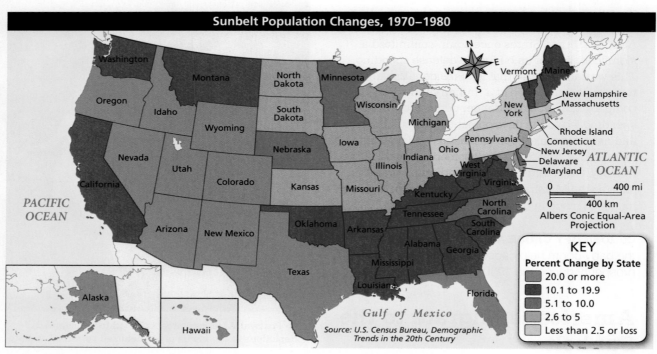

>> **Analyze Maps** Several states in the Sunbelt saw significant growth in their populations. Based on the map, which states had the most growth? Which states lost population?

Innovations and Economic Development

The important postwar population shifts were matched by equally groundbreaking structural changes in the American economy. For the first time in American history, more people found employment in the **service sector**—businesses that provide services, such as healthcare, law, retail, banking, or insurance—than in the manufacturing sector. These shifts led some to describe the United States as a postindustrial society.

Innovative Computers Drive Economic Growth

Between 1947 and 1957, the percentage of the American workforce employed in industrial or blue-collar jobs declined 4 percent. During the same time period, employment in the service sector, or white-collar jobs, rapidly grew.

The new workforce included many who worked in **information industries**, including those who built or operated the first computers. These computers were enormous. One of the first, named ENIAC, short for Electronic Numerical Integrator and Computer, took up roughly 18,000 square feet, or the size of three basketball courts! Despite its size, it was less powerful than today's desktop computer.

Still, ENIAC was a remarkable advance. By the 1960s, the government and private industry had found many uses for the computer. Hotels used computers to help make reservations, and banks used them to keep track of accounts. Industries started using computers to automate work or perform jobs once done by people. All these technological innovations clearly revealed that the free enterprise system was improving the standard of living in the United States.

Changes in the Labor Force

Meanwhile, the number of women in the labor force continued to grow, doubling between 1940 and 1960. Many of these women worked part time. Few pursued long-term careers and most remained underpaid. Yet without their paychecks, their families would have found it difficult to remain in the middle class.

While the service sector grew rapidly, both the number and the percentage of Americans who made a living by farming continued to decline. In 1935, one fourth of the nation's families lived on farms. By 1960, less than one in ten families did. At the same time, improvements in technology, ranging from

>> During the 1950s, many Americans moved to the warm and sunny South and West, the so-called "Sunbelt." Huge developments, like Lakeland Park in California, met their need for housing.

mechanical cotton pickers to chemical pesticides, made agriculture much more productive. This allowed fewer workers to grow even more food. New irrigation systems helped transform much of the land in the Southwest from arid to fertile fields.

The Role of Entrepreneurs

At home, the postwar era saw the rise of **franchise businesses**. A franchise business allows a company to distribute its products or services through retail outlets owned by independent operators.

Franchises were attractive to consumers because they stressed quality and sameness, no matter where one was in the United States. The Holiday Inn franchise came into existence following a trip that home builder Kemmons Wilson took to Washington, D.C., with his family of five children. Frustrated, Wilson found hotels difficult to locate, overpriced, and lacking adequate parking facilities. As he traveled, according to author David Halberstam, "Wilson became more irritated until he turned to his wife and announced that he was going into the hotel business. Everyone in this country, he thought, had a car and a family, and sooner or later everyone had to go somewhere." Today, there are tens of thousands of Holiday Inn hotels all over the world.

Many postwar critics lamented the growth of franchise businesses. For them, the franchises represented a growing lack of originality, evidence that the United States was becoming a "bland" nation in which people ate bland food, lived in bland look-a-like houses, and watched bland television shows that followed the same plot line.

Entrepreneurs Lead Management Innovations

The transition from an industry-based to a service-based economy created opportunities for entrepreneurs. For example, Californians Richard and Maurice McDonald opened their new restaurant in 1948. The brothers emphasized efficiency, low prices, high volume, and quick service. They did away with anything that slowed down the process, including plates, glasses, dishwashing, and tipping. In 1955, Ray Kroc began to franchise McDonald's system and name. By the end of the century, McDonald's had become the most successful food service organization in history, and the name McDonald's came to stand for low-priced, standardized-quality food.

>> The original McDonald's restaurant in San Benardino, California featured 15 cent hamburgers.

Bounce to Activate Gallery

Other entrepreneurs' names also came to represent their businesses. For example, Wal-Mart, a discount merchandising business founded by **Sam Walton**, became one of the most successful businesses in the late twentieth century. Another entrepreneur, **Estee Lauder**, founded a cosmetics company that specialized in skin care and protection products.

Lauder's focus on selling her products only in high-end department stores created a $100 million dollar business by the 1970s. Walton and Lauder are just two of the millions of small business entrepreneurs whose businesses grew, allowing them to achieve the American dream.

American Corporations Go Multinational As the postwar economy expanded, so did **multinational corporations**, companies that produced and sold their goods and services all over the world and established branches abroad. General Motors, General Electric, and IBM produced a larger and larger share of all of the goods sold. Changing business strategies and management innovations allowed many of these corporations to earn large portions of their profits abroad. Coca Cola, for instance, sold its soft drinks all over the globe. Hollywood movies found eager audiences in Tokyo, Mexico City, and Germany.

Effects of Prosperity on Labor The prosperity of the 1950s was reflected in generally good times for the labor movement. In 1955, the AFL and the CIO, which had split in the mid-1930s, united to form the **AFL-CIO**. The new organization enjoyed a good deal of political clout, especially within the Democratic Party. Yet trade unions also lost some momentum during the late 1940s and early 1950s. Most of the new white-collar workers did not join unions, and labor's image was tarnished by a corruption scandal involving the Teamsters Union. Government investigators accused the Teamsters, who represented truck drivers, of illegally using their members' funds.

☑ **EXPLAIN** In what ways did American business change during the postwar period?

Truman's Postwar Leadership

As the postwar economy evolved and new demographic patterns changed society, American leaders faced rapidly shifting domestic and foreign political landscapes. On April 12, 1945, when Franklin Roosevelt died, Harry S. Truman had been Vice President for only 4 months. When Eleanor Roosevelt told him that her husband had died, Truman responded, "Is there anything I can do for you?" She replied, "Is there anything we can do for you? For you are the one in trouble now."

Eleanor Roosevelt's remark captured Harry Truman's predicament. He had to preside over one of the more difficult times in American history. The postwar years saw the beginning of the Cold War and communist takeovers in Europe and Asia. At home, there was inflation and labor unrest. Communist advances and a troubled domestic economy created a sense of deep unrest in the American public during the Truman years.

Relationships with Congress and Labor From the first days of his presidency, Truman faced a double-barreled challenge: a restless labor movement and a combative Republican Party. Trade unionists demanded pay increases to keep up with inflation. When employers refused to meet labor's demands, millions of steel, coal, railroad, and automotive workers went on strike.

The wave of strikes was one of the largest in American history. It prompted Congress to enact the **Taft-Hartley Act**, a law that outlawed the closed shop—a workplace in which only union members can be hired. Taft-Hartley rolled back some of the rights that labor unions had gained during the New Deal. Although Truman vetoed the Taft-Hartley Act, Congress overrode his veto.

Support for Civil Rights Unlike FDR, who feared challenging the power of white southern senators and representatives, Truman refused to remain passive, insisting that "we must correct the remaining imperfections in our practice of democracy." He established a special committee on civil rights to investigate race relations. The committee made several recommendations for civil rights reforms.

However, Congress did not pass any meaningful civil rights reforms until the late 1950s. Truman also issued an executive order desegregating the military. This was more successful. By 1951, most units had been integrated.

Truman Defeats Dewey By the spring of 1948, Truman's standing had sunk so low that he faced challenges from both the right and the left in his own Democratic Party. Southern Democrats, angry at Truman's support for civil rights, left the party and

>> Unmet demands for pay raises in the face of inflation led to labor unrest, such as this strike at a Pittsburgh steel mill, during the Truman administration.

established the States' Rights Party. They named South Carolina governor Strom Thurmond as their candidate for President. At the other end of the political spectrum, Henry Wallace, who had been Vice President during FDR's third term, broke with Truman over foreign policy issues. Wallace became the candidate of a new Progressive Party.

The breakaway of two large blocs of Democrats was accompanied by the Republican Party's nomination of Thomas Dewey, the governor of New York, for President. Few people thought that Truman had any chance of winning the 1948 election. Truman, however, did not see it that way.

He staged an energetic "whistle stop" train tour of the nation, delivering over 300 speeches and traveling 31,000 miles in a matter of weeks. At train stops in small towns, Truman attacked the current Congress as "do nothing" and the worst in history. "Give 'em hell, Harry!" some in the crowd would cry out during his speeches. Although every political poll predicted that Dewey would win easily, Truman won by a narrow victory. He had managed the political upset of the century.

Consequences of Truman's Presidency Shortly after the election, Truman announced a far-ranging legislative program, which he called the **Fair Deal**. The Fair Deal, he explained, would strengthen existing New Deal reforms and establish new programs, such as national health insurance. But

>> Americans enjoyed peace and prosperity under the Eisenhower administration. For many, it was a time for new homes, new cars, and family vacations.

 Bounce to Activate Chart

Congress was not in a reforming mood, and Truman failed to win approval for most of his Fair Deal proposals.

Legislative failure and a stalled war in Korea contributed to Truman's loss of popularity. He chose not to seek the 1952 Democratic nomination. His reputation, however, has improved through the years. Today, many historians applaud him for his common-sense approach, as the first President to challenge public discrimination and as a determined opponent of communist expansion.

☑ **RECALL** Why was Truman's victory in 1948 so surprising?

Eisenhower Leads a Thriving Nation

The 1952 election was hardly a contest. The Republican candidate, Dwight Eisenhower, was so popular that both the Democratic and Republican parties had wanted him as their presidential candidate. Eisenhower, whose nickname was

Ike, charmed the public with his friendly smile, reassuring personality, and record of service and honesty. The Democratic candidate, Adlai Stevenson, a senator from Illinois, failed to catch the popular imagination the way Eisenhower did.

Dwight Eisenhower had spent nearly his entire adult life in the military and had never held a political office before 1952. Thus, Americans could not know for certain which way he would guide the nation upon taking office. However, most Americans believed that Eisenhower's calm personality mirrored his political views and that he would keep to the "middle road," achieving a balance between liberal and conservative positions.

Eisenhower charted a middle course as President. While he shared the conservative view that the federal government had grown too strong, he did not repeal existing New Deal programs, such as Social Security and the minimum wage. Federal spending actually increased during his presidency. Eisenhower even introduced several large new programs. For example, he created an interstate highway system and began to spend federal dollars for education, specifically to train more scientists.

One reason for Eisenhower's popularity was the strength of the American economy during the 1950s. His presidency was one of the most prosperous, peaceful, and politically tranquil in the twentieth century.

☑ **IDENTIFY SUPPORTING DETAILS** Why did federal spending increase during Eisenhower's presidency?

☑ ASSESSMENT

1. **Summarize** the reasons for American prosperity at the end of World War II.

2. **Evaluate Arguments** Discuss the different viewpoints on franchise businesses.

3. **Infer** Why did so many veterans choose to enter or return to college after the war?

4. **Support Ideas with Examples** What effects did technology have on the agricultural sector in the postwar years?

5. **Generate Explanations** What effects did the baby boom have on the economy between 1940 and 1955?

7.6 The 1950s marked a period of changing national population distribution. Between 1940 and 1960, more than 40 million Americans moved to the suburbs, one of the largest mass migrations in history. Rural regions suffered the most dramatic decline in population, but people also came by the thousands from older industrial cities, seeking, as one father put it, a place where "a kid could grow up with grass stains on his pants." During the same time period, many older industrial cities lost population.

>> Americans' yearning for a better life after World War II, coupled with innovations in home building, led to an explosion of growth in suburban areas.

Bounce to Activate Flipped Video

Mass Culture in the 1950s

Suburban Migration

Causes and Effects of Suburban Growth People flocked to the suburbs in part because the nation suffered from a severe shortage of urban housing. During the depression and World War II, new housing construction had come to a near standstill. At war's end, as Americans married and formed families, they went in search of a place they could call their own.

Fortunately, at this time of peak demand, developers figured out how to build affordable housing in a hurry. William Levitt became a leader in mass producing suburban homes. Entire rows of houses in Levittown, a suburb of New York City on Long Island, were built using the same plan. This method enabled workers to build houses in weeks rather than in months. On the installment plan, buyers could pay $58 a month toward the cost of a home. Demand for the homes was so great that Levitt built two other Levittowns—one outside Philadelphia, Pennsylvania, and the other in New Jersey. These houses were ideal for young couples starting out because they were affordable and comfortable. Other

>> **Objectives**

Examine the rise of the suburbs and the growth of the interstate highway system.

Explain the causes and effects of prosperity in the 1950s on consumers.

Discuss postwar changes in family life.

Describe changes in education in the postwar period.

Describe the rise of new forms of mass culture.

>> **Key Terms**

consumerism
median family
   income
nuclear family
Benjamin Spock
Interstate Highway
   Act
California Master
   Plan
Billy Graham

developers adopted Levitt's innovative techniques, and suburbs were soon springing up across the country.

Suburban development benefited from investment by the government. State and federal governments constructed thousands of miles of highways that linked the suburbs to cities. New home buyers also benefited from the GI bill and the Federal Housing Administration (FHA), which provided low-interest loans. FHA-backed loans allowed home buyers to pay as little as 5 to 10 percent of the purchase price and to pay off their mortgages over 30 years. However, these suburban communities remained predominantly white, because of discriminatory practices by real estate agents, landlords, and property owners.

Residents of new suburbs faced the challenge of establishing new towns with churches, synagogues, schools, and police and fire departments. Through these institutions, the suburbanites forged a sense of community. During the 1950s, the suburbs became increasingly self-contained. While suburban residents of earlier generations had depended on the city for entertainment and shopping, the postwar suburban dweller could find a vast array of goods and services in nearby shopping centers.

>> President Eisenhower authorized funding of the massive new interstate highway system. One outcome was that new suburbanites could more easily commute by car to jobs in major cities.

 Bounce to Activate Illustration

Interstates Support Migration and Prosperity

Free enterprise was supported by government policy to improve the quality of life in suburban communities. Committed to the idea of easing automobile travel, President Eisenhower authorized the first funding of the interstate system in 1953. Further legislation passed by Congress in 1956 resulted in the **Interstate Highway Act**, which authorized funds to build 41,000 miles of highway consisting of multilane expressways that would connect the nation's major cities.

Such expressways, Eisenhower argued, would safely carry the nation's growing automobile traffic, boost economic prosperity, and provide a valuable transportation network to strengthen national defense. This represented the biggest expenditure on public works in history, bigger by far than any project undertaken during the New Deal. In 1990, further recognition of President Eisenhower's role in establishing the massive highway system led to a renaming of the highways. It became the Dwight D. Eisenhower System of Interstate and Defense Highways.

Besides easing commutes from suburbs to cities, highways boosted the travel and vacation industries. Vacationers drove to national parks, to beaches, and to new destinations, such as Las Vegas. With more money and more children, families sought leisure activity. Walt Disney met this demand by building an extraordinary amusement park in California. Disneyland excited the imagination with visions of the future, including make-believe rides in space.

Technological Innovations Lead to the "Car Culture" During the 1920s, automobile ownership had soared in the United States. With the explosion of suburban growth in the 1950s, Americans grew even more dependent upon their cars. The number of registered automobiles jumped from 26 million in 1945 to 60 million in 1960.

These new automobiles tended to have big engines and enormous horsepower. They came with the newest technology, such as power steering and brakes and automatic transmissions. Harley Earl of the Ford Motor Company captured the mood of the 1950s by designing cars with lots of chrome that reminded people of jet planes.

While some suburbanites rode the train or other forms of mass transportation, Americans increasingly depended upon their cars to commute to work. Suburbanites also needed their cars to shop at suburban shopping malls. Entrepreneurs opened fast-food restaurants and drive-in movie theaters, both of which catered to the car culture. While these

Median Family Income, 1947 and 1970

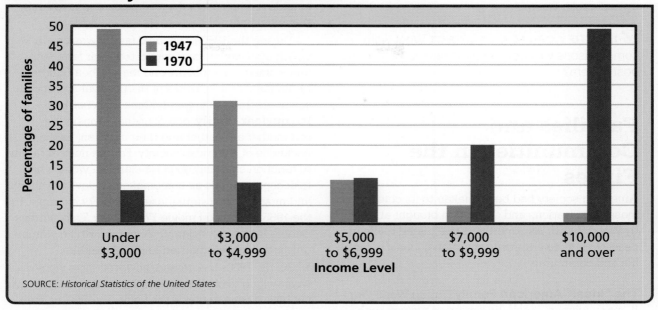

SOURCE: *Historical Statistics of the United States*

>> **Analyze Data** How did the percentage change in the top two income brackets shown affect U.S. consumer culture?

businesses flourished, many older businesses, often located in older city neighborhoods, struggled to survive.

☑ **CHECK UNDERSTANDING** How did suburban free enterprise benefit from the "car culture"?

Increased Consumption and Consumerism

For much of our history, Americans had been taught to save their money. "A penny saved is a penny earned," advised Benjamin Franklin. However, as the U.S. economy began to boom in the postwar era, Americans were caught up in a wave of **consumerism**, buying as much as they could, much of it on credit. What accounted for this spending spree?

Free Enterprise System Improves Standards of Living One reason Americans spent more was that they had more money to spend. During the 1950s, **median family income**, or average family income, rose from $3,319 to $5,417.

The average American family now had twice as much real income as the average family had during the prosperous years of the 1920s. Consumer-oriented companies found new and innovative ways to encourage buying on credit. For example, General Motors advertised its cars with the slogan "Buy Now, Pay Later." The Diner's Club introduced the first credit card.

Technological Innovations Drive New Conveniences Embracing the free-enterprise system, American businesses developed technological and purchasing innovations that improved the standard of living. Home appliances topped the list of the goods that Americans bought. Families purchased electric washing machines and dryers, refrigerators and ranges. These labor-saving appliances helped transform housework, lessening the physical demands of everything from washing clothes to preserving foods.

With money to spend, easy credit, and new goods to buy, shopping became a new pastime for Americans. Supermarkets, where customers could buy everything from milk to mops, appeared. Shopping centers sprouted all over suburbia.

One product that Americans bought in record numbers was a television. In 1946, manufacturers produced fewer than 6,000 TV sets. Seven years later, Americans purchased 7 million sets, and by the end of the decade, 90 percent of all households owned a television.

☑ **IDENTIFY CAUSE AND EFFECT** What were some reasons why consumption skyrocketed in the postwar era?

Families and Communities in the Fifties

American society had been shaken to its core by the mass mobilizations and disruption brought about by World War II. As Americans readjusted to life in peacetime, they embraced traditional ideals of family life and community.

The "Ideal" American Family During World War II, many women—including married women with children — had gone off to work in factories. In 1943, women made up 25 percent of the workers in the wartime auto industry. With the war's end, however, most of the women who had entered the workforce returned to being homemakers. Now, a more traditional image of the family took hold, one in which women stayed home and men served

>> Women in the 1950s were encouraged to return to traditional family roles by staying home to raise families.

as "breadwinners." Women who wanted a career outside the home faced social pressures to rethink their decisions.

During the 1950s, the ideal family was one in which men worked and supported their families and women stayed home and reared their children. In the popular magazines of the postwar era, social scientists and other opinion makers described the **nuclear family**, or a household consisting of a mother and father and their children, as the backbone of American society. For the nuclear family to function smoothly, experts claimed, women had to accept their role as homemakers. Television shows and movies made similar assertions. For example, in the 1955 Hollywood movie *The Tender Trap*, actress Debbie Reynolds declared, "A woman isn't a woman unless she's been married and had children."

As the 1950s progressed, however, more women were willing to challenge the view that a woman could not have a career outside the home. By 1960, women held one third of the nation's jobs. Approximately half of these women workers were married.

Challenges to the Postwar Ideal As television and movies were reinforcing the postwar ideal of heterosexual family life and rigid gender roles, a series of highly publicized events seemed to challenge those very ideals. In 1948 and 1953 Alfred Kinsey, a biologist and zoologist, along with his team of researchers, published reports on male and female sexuality. The reports outraged many people due to their startling conclusions and discussion of taboo subjects. Among his other findings, Kinsey revealed that homosexuality was far more widespread than ever suspected. The sheer number of "normal" people who admitted to homosexual feelings challenged the assumption that homosexuality was sick or pathological. Around the same time, a former U.S. soldier underwent sex reassignment surgery (currently referred to as "gender confirmation surgery") to become a woman—Christine Jorgensen. In the early 1950s, the media turned Jorgensen into a celebrity, and she used her fame and wit to speak out in defense of transgender people (at that time referred to as "transsexuals").

Baby Boom Increases Focus on Children More so than in the past, family life revolved around children. Not surprisingly, the best-selling book of the era was **Dr. Benjamin Spock's** *Common Sense Book of Baby and Child Care*. Parents bought and read his book because they wanted expert advice on how to raise their children. Spock emphasized the importance of nurturing children, from their earliest days as infants through their teen years. Mothers,

Spock suggested, should not worry about spoiling their children because children could not get too much comfort and love. Some criticized Spock for promoting what they called "a permissive culture." Nevertheless, Spock's book remained extremely popular for several decades.

As baby boomers became teens, their impact on the economy and American culture became even more noticeable. While as children they received toys, such as Davy Crockett caps and Barbie dolls, as teens they purchased very expensive items. As *LIFE* magazine observed:

> The time is past when a boy's chief possession was his bike and a girl's party wardrobe consisted of a fancy dress worn with a string of dime-store pearls. . . . Today's teenagers surround themselves with a fantastic array of garish and often expensive baubles and amusements. They own 10 million phonographs, over a million TV sets, 13 million cameras.
>
> —*LIFE*, August 31, 1959

Billy Graham Contributes to a Religious Revival

The 1950s also witnessed a revival of religion in the United States. Organized religious groups became more powerful and more houses of worship were built. Regular church attendance rose from about 50 million in 1940 to about 80 million in 1958. The evangelist **Billy Graham** attracted millions to religious revivals that he held around the nation.

During the 1950s, Congress added the words "In God We Trust" to the dollar bill and "under God," to the Pledge of Allegiance. These additions were aimed at making clear the contrast between the centrality of religion in American society and the atheist basis of communist societies.

Specific Needs Lead to Medical Innovations

During the 1950s, American families benefited from numerous advances in medicine. By 1952, Dr. Jonas Salk was refining a vaccine against polio, the disease that had struck down Franklin Roosevelt and that, in 1952 alone, had crippled tens of thousands and killed 1,400, mostly children. By 1960, the widespread distribution of Salk's new vaccine and an oral vaccine developed by Albert Sabin had nearly eliminated the disease.

>> In 1954, Dr. Jonas Salk created a polio vaccine. The vaccine was ordered for all American children and was eventually used around the globe to virtually eradicate polio.

Bounce to Activate Gallery

At the same time, antibiotics, such as penicillin, came into widespread use. The antibiotics helped control numerous infectious diseases caused by bacteria, such as whooping cough and tuberculosis. As a result of these medical advances and a better understanding of the importance of diet, children born after 1946 had a longer life expectancy than those born before 1946.

The year 1946 also saw the founding of the Communicable Disease Center, which later became the Centers for Disease Control and Prevention (CDC), in order to influence health promotion and prevent disease.

☑ **CONNECT** How did the focus on children and teenagers help develop prosperity during the 1950s?

Educational Opportunities and Priorities

As the economy grew, so too did opportunities for Americans to attain higher education. A more educated work force boosted economic productivity. In 1940, only about 15 percent of college-age

Americans attended college. By the early 1960s, however, close to 40 percent did. The percentage of Americans who completed high school also rose sharply. "The astonishing growth of education in the late 1940s (and thereafter)," wrote historian James Patterson, "seemed yet another sign that the American Dream was well and alive."

Defense Spending Shapes Education Priorities

New priorities meant that students had expanded opportunities. In Texas, for example, the state legislature passed laws guaranteeing young people the chance to attend public school through the twelfth grade. Large sums of money were needed to meet the education needs of the baby-boom generation. Most of the funding for education came from local and state governments, but after the Soviet Union launched Sputnik 1 in 1957, many Americans called for more federal funds for education.

In a mood of crisis, Congress quickly approved the National Defense Education Act. Its $1 billion program was aimed at producing more scientists and science teachers. The act authorized money for loans to high school and college graduates to continue their scientific education.

Education Becomes More Accessible The postwar era saw the stirrings of a movement to make education more accessible. Many states poured funds into their public universities, making it easier for ordinary Americans to attend college. California, for example, established a **California Master Plan**,

>> Television gained such popularity during the 1950s that many families got into the habit of watching their favorite shows even while eating dinner.

which called for three tiers of higher education: research universities, state colleges, and community colleges. All of them were to be accessible to all of the state's citizens. Other states also built or expanded their college systems.

On another front, in 1954, the Supreme Court ruled in *Brown* v. *Board of Education of Topeka* that segregated schools were unconstitutional. However, it would be years before many schools were actually integrated.

☑ **EXPLAIN** How did American educational priorities change in the years following World War II?

Television Shapes American Culture

In 1938, when television was still just a curiosity, E. B. White, author of *Charlotte's Web*, wrote that it "is going to be the test of the modern world. . . . We shall stand or fall by the television." While White's view may have been exaggerated, clearly television has had an enormous impact on American society.

Between 1945 and 1960, Americans purchased television sets at a faster pace than they had bought either radios or cars during the 1920s. The popularity of this new technology threatened the movie industry because families stayed home to watch TV rather than go out to watch movies at the theater.

Although television attracted viewers of all ages, it had a special influence on children. Baby-boom children rushed home from school to watch the *Howdy Doody Show* or the *Mickey Mouse Club*. Children also watched hours of cartoons and shows featuring their favorite superheroes, such as the Lone Ranger. Westerns were especially popular during the 1950s and early 1960s.

Among the most memorable shows were sitcoms about families. Fifty million Americans tuned in each week to watch the *I Love Lucy* show, starring the comedic actress Lucille Ball. Other popular family sitcoms included *Leave It to Beaver*, *The Adventures of Ozzie and Harriet*, and *Father Knows Best*.

These shows reflected and reinforced the ideal of the 1950s family. None of the family sitcoms had important African American characters. None of the major characters got divorced. Major real-life problems, such as mental illness, alcoholism, and personal depression, rarely, if ever, appeared. Writes David Halberstam, "No family problem was so great that it could not be cleared up within the allotted twenty-two minutes."

Even before television emerged in the 1950s, a mass national culture had begun to develop in the United States. Nationally broadcast radio programs, Hollywood films, and other forms of popular culture had helped erode distinct regional and ethnic cultures. Television sped up and reinforced this process. Americans in every region of the country watched the same shows and bought the same goods they saw advertised.

Television changed political campaigns. During the 1952 presidential campaign, Americans could see the candidates in action. Usually, candidates with more money could buy more advertising time. The impact of television on elections continues today.

☑ **SUMMARIZE** How did television reflect and reinforce the ideal of the nuclear family in the postwar period?

☑ ASSESSMENT

1. **Identify Cause and Effect** Discuss how the religious revival during the 1950s was linked to America's response to communism.

2. **Support Ideas with Evidence** Describe the role television played for children during the 1950s.

3. **Support a Point of View with Evidence** "The astonishing growth of education in the late 1940s (and thereafter) seemed yet another sign that the American Dream was well and alive." —historian James Patterson explains how the increase in the number of Americans finishing high school and attending college supports Patterson's statement.

4. **Summarize** Explain the connection between the prosperity of the 1950s and increased consumerism.

5. **Generate Explanations** Explain the effect that the car culture had on businesses in older inner-city neighborhoods.

>> Not everyone experienced prosperity during this time. Stubborn areas of long-term poverty, such as this part of rural West Virginia, saw little benefit from the boom times.

Bounce to Activate Flipped Video

7.7 Despite the prosperity of the 1950s, not all people benefited. Some felt left out of the era's prosperity. Others, who had obtained more wealth, wondered whether all of the material things they acquired had actually led to a better life. The discontents of the 1950s would manifest the first signs of the dissent that would dominate the 1960s.

>> **Objectives**

Summarize the arguments made by critics who rejected the culture of the fifties.

Describe the causes and effects of urban and rural poverty.

Explain the problems that many minority groups faced in the postwar era.

>> **Key Terms**

beatniks
urban renewal
termination policy
rock-and-roll
Elvis Presley

Social Issues of the 1950s

Critics and Rebels Emerge

The failure to provide equal opportunities to minorities was one source of postwar discontent. Another was the belief that despite material abundance the *quality* of life had not improved. Many intellectuals and artists did not consider suburban homes, shopping centers, and a supply of new products as representing a better life.

Cultural Movements Against Conformity Many social critics complained about an emphasis on conformity. In a book called *The Lonely Crowd*, sociologists David Riesman and Nathan Glazer lamented that Americans had sacrificed their individualism in order to fit into the larger community. They also criticized the power of advertising to mold public tastes. The theme of alienation, or not fitting in, dominated a number of popular novels of the era. The bestseller *The Man in the Gray Flannel Suit*, by Sloan Wilson, followed a World War II veteran who could not find real meaning in life after the war. Holden Caulfield, the main character in J. D. Salinger's *Catcher in the Rye*, a favorite among many teens, mocked the phoniness of adult society.

The Impact of the Beat Generation on American Society

An additional critique of American society came from a small group of writers and artists called **beatniks**, or the beats. The beats refused to conform to accepted ways of behavior. Conformity, they insisted, stifled individualism. They displayed their dislike of American society by careless dress and colorful jargon.

In their poems, such as Allen Ginsberg's "Howl," and novels, such as Jack Kerouac's *On the Road*, the beats lambasted what they saw as the crass materialism and conformity of the American middle class. Many Americans, in turn, were outraged by their behavior and believed that Beatnik values would have a negative impact on society.

Hollywood captured this rebellious spirit and youthful defiance in several influential films in the 1950s. In *Rebel Without a Cause*, James Dean portrayed a tormented teenager who rejects the values of the establishment while trying to fit in with his peers.

Actor Marlon Brando became a symbol of rebellion for his role as the leader of a motorcycle gang in the film *The Wild One*. These characters—and ultimately, Dean and Brando themselves—became role models for disenchanted youth.

The LGBT Community Organizes in California

Meanwhile, other rebellions were stirring. In the 1950s, anti-gay laws continued to criminalize homosexuality. Government purges, bar raids, and police entrapments sent thousands to prison or mental institutions every year. Faced with this repression, lesbian, gay, bisexual, and transgender (LGBT) people began organizing to defend their rights. In Los Angeles in 1950, Harry Hay founded the Mattachine Society, one of the first post World War II gay rights organizations. While Mattachine focused on the rights of gay men, another organization, the Daughters of Bilitis, was founded in San Francisco by Del Martin and Phyllis Lyon in 1955 to advocate for lesbian civil rights. In 1958 Mattachine won a legal victory when the Supreme Court ruled that Mattachine's magazine *One* was not obscene—a decision that opened the way for freedom of speech for LGBT publications.

A New Style of Music

In the summer of 1951, a relatively unknown white disc jockey named Alan Freed began broadcasting what commonly had been called "race" music to listeners across the Midwest. Renaming the music **rock-and-roll**, Freed planted the seed for a cultural revolution that would blossom in the mid-1950s.

>> Some popular entertainment of the 1950s, including movies such as *Rebel Without a Cause*, questioned the values of the middle class.

>> Chuck Berry was one of the most popular musicians of early rock-and-roll. This new musical genre blurred the racial divisions of 1950s society.

Rock music originated in the rhythm and blues traditions of African Americans. As African Americans began to move north, they brought their musical traditions with them. Independent recording companies began recording rhythm and blues (R&B) music. Rock-and-roll borrowed heavily from rhythm and blues. As Chuck Berry, known as the pioneer of rock-and-roll, put it, "It used to be called boogie-woogie, it used to be called blues, used to be called rhythm and blues. . . . It's called rock now."

Live performances of rhythm and blues music had long been kept separate from whites by Jim Crow laws in the South or by more subtle forms of segregation in the North. But now, through the radio, it began to attract a wider white audience in the postwar era. For example, a young **Elvis Presley** listened to a Memphis radio station that played African American gospel tunes. He began to integrate those tunes into the music he played. Meanwhile, in the early 1950s, Sam Phillips set up a recording studio in Memphis to record and play the music of some of Memphis's best African American blues performers, such as B. B. King. One day Phillips heard Presley and almost immediately recognized that he had found the person he had been looking for.

Presley's arrival set off the new rock craze. His first hit, "Heartbreak Hotel," sold in the millions, and his success sparked popularity for rock music. Presley, along with African American performers such as Chuck Berry, Fats Domino, Little Richard, and Ray Charles, had profound influence on popular music throughout the world.

Yet at first, not everyone liked Elvis or the new rock craze, which many saw as having a very negative impact on culture. When Ed Sullivan, the host of a famous TV variety show, invited Elvis to sing on his show, he directed cameramen to show Elvis only from the waist up, because many parents objected to Elvis's gyrating hips and tight pants. Ministers complained about the passions that rock music seemed to unleash among so many youngsters. Congress held hearings on the subversive nature of rock music.

☑ **INFER** Why would Elvis Presley have achieved greater success than African American musicians in the 1950s?

Poverty in the Cities and Rural Areas

Behind the new household appliances, the spreading suburbs, the burgeoning shopping malls, and the ribbons of highways was a very different United States. It was a nation of urban slums, desperate rural poverty, and discrimination. People who were poor and dispossessed were well hidden.

In an influential 1962 book entitled *The Other America*, Michael Harrington shocked many Americans by arguing that poverty was widespread in the United States. Harrington claimed that 50 million Americans, one fourth of the nation, lived in poverty. Despite American affluence, Harrington said, poverty plagued African Americans in the inner cities, rural whites in areas such as Appalachia, and Hispanics in migrant farm labor camps and urban barrios. Harrington argued that Americans could not afford to ignore the existence of the poor:

> The poor live in a culture of poverty. [They] get sick more than anyone else in the society. . . . Because they are sick more often and longer than anyone else, they lose wages and work and find it difficult to hold a steady job. And because of

>> Rock-and-roll singer Elvis Presley became extremely popular with young people, but some Americans worried that his hip-shaking performances were subversive or immoral.

▶ **Bounce to Activate Gallery**

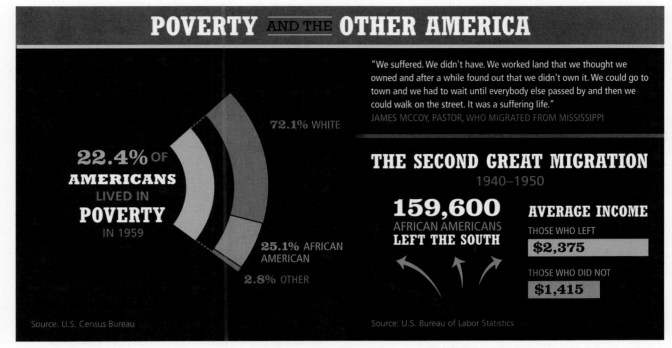

POVERTY AND THE OTHER AMERICA

22.4% OF AMERICANS LIVED IN POVERTY IN 1959

72.1% WHITE

25.1% AFRICAN AMERICAN

2.8% OTHER

Source: U.S. Census Bureau

"We suffered. We didn't have. We worked land that we thought we owned and after a while found out that we didn't own it. We could go to town and we had to wait until everybody else passed by and then we could walk on the street. It was a suffering life."
JAMES MCCOY, PASTOR, WHO MIGRATED FROM MISSISSIPPI

THE SECOND GREAT MIGRATION
1940–1950

159,600 AFRICAN AMERICANS LEFT THE SOUTH

AVERAGE INCOME

THOSE WHO LEFT
$2,375

THOSE WHO DID NOT
$1,415

Source: U.S. Bureau of Labor Statistics

>> **Analyze Data** What push and pull factors might have affected Americans in the South during this period?

this, . . . their prospect is to move to an even lower level . . . toward even more suffering.

—Michael Harrington, *The Other America*, 1962

Effects of Migration on Cities During the decades that followed World War II, African Americans and other nonwhite minorities moved in great numbers from rural areas to cities in search of better economic opportunities. In the same period, however, American cities were suffering a severe decline as middle-class white families moved to the suburbs.

The loss of the middle class hurt cities economically because the middle class paid a large share of the taxes. It hurt them politically, as well, because as the suburbs gained population, they also gained representation in state legislatures and the national government. This combination of declining economic and political power put a serious strain on cities, leading to a deterioration of services, such as garbage removal and street repair. In turn, as the conditions worsened and crime increased in what was now called the inner city, more of the middle class decided to move to the suburbs.

Federal, state, and local governments tried to reverse the downward trend in American cities by developing **urban renewal** projects. With these

projects, the government cleared large tracts of older housing and built freeways and developments that, it was hoped, would "revitalize" downtown areas. Unfortunately, the projects often backfired. Urban renewal drove people from their homes to make room for the new projects and highways. The poor were forced to seek housing in neighborhoods that were already overcrowded and overburdened. One resident of East Harlem, New York, who lost his home to an urban renewal project, observed:

Middle-class flight only worsened inner-city problems, such as inadequate services and schools.

Nobody cared what we wanted when they built this place. They threw our houses down and pushed us there and pushed our friends somewhere else. We don't have a place around here to get a cup of coffee or a newspaper even, or borrow fifty cents.

—*America's History Since 1865*

The federal government tried to ease the shortage of affordable housing by constructing public housing. At the time, these housing projects seemed a godsend to those who lived there. Rent was cheap and the residents often enjoyed certain services, like hot running water, for the first time in their lives. Yet, since the public housing was often built in poor neighborhoods, the projects led to an even greater concentration of poverty. This, in turn led to other problems, such as crime.

Migration from Rural Areas The plight of the rural poor was just as bad if not worse than that of the urban poor. Mississippi Delta sharecroppers, coal miners in Appalachia, and farmers in remote areas were left behind as others prospered, and often their economic situation got worse as time passed. A major transformation in farming was taking place. Corporations and large-farm owners came to dominate farm production. Many independent small-farm owners found it difficult to compete with the large farms and slipped into poverty.

Many farmers responded by leaving their rural communities behind, joining the waves of the poor who relocated to the city. Others remained behind, wondering if they would ever get to enjoy the benefits of the new economy.

☑ **RECALL** How did the federal government respond to the decline of American cities?

Struggles of Minorities

During the postwar years, the battle for civil rights in the South began to gain headlines. Yet, in the same time period, African Americans and other minorities also fought for equality in the urban north and west. Central to their struggles were efforts to overcome housing and employment discrimination.

Discrimination against Puerto Ricans Latinos from Puerto Rico and Mexico and Native Americans faced many of the same problems that African Americans encountered in the years following World War II. Puerto Rican migrants to New York City, for example, often found themselves clustered together in many of the poorest inner city neighborhoods with employment opportunities limited by both formal and informal forms of discrimination. As newcomers whose native language was not English, they enjoyed little political power. Thus, they received little help from city governments in getting better services, education, or an end to discriminatory practices.

Labor Conditions and Mexicans Both Mexicans and Mexican Americans faced a similar situation in the United States. During World War II, the U.S. government had established the bracero program as a means of addressing the shortage of agricultural workers. *Braceros* was a term for Mexican migrant farmworkers in the United States. The program gave temporary visas to Mexican immigrants. By

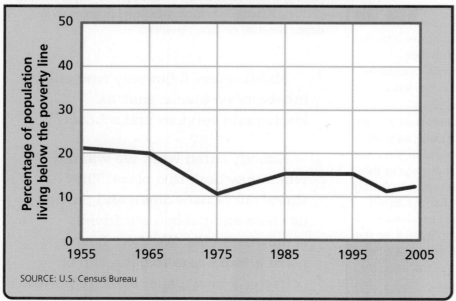

Poverty Levels in the United States, 1955–2005

SOURCE: U.S. Census Bureau

>> **Analyze Graphs** This graph shows how poverty levels changed from 1955–2005. Overall, what was the poverty trend in this period?

1964, 3 million Mexicans had worked in the United States under the program, most of them as farm laborers. Many were exploited and cheated by their employers. Mexican workers followed crops from state to state. Often, children worked alongside their parents. The migrants had little power to oppose the exploitation, for if they complained about conditions, employers threatened to deport them back to Mexico. One U.S. Department of Labor official called the program "legalized slavery."

One champion of the rights of Mexican migrant workers, Ernesto Galarza, joined the effort to organize unions for Mexican farm laborers.

Americanization of Native Americans In 1953, the federal government enacted the **termination policy**, a major change in the rules governing Native Americans. The law sought to end tribal government and to relocate Native Americans to the nation's cities. It also terminated federal responsibility for the health and welfare of Native Americans. Proponents of the policy argued that it would free American Indians to assimilate, or merge, into American society. While some Native Americans praised the intent of the program, most came to agree with Senator Mark Hatfield of Oregon who argued that it made things worse for them. "[T]he social and economic devastation which these policies have wrought upon many groups has been tremendous. . . . While these problems were already severe among Indian societies generally, they have become epidemic among terminated Indians."

☑ **EXPLAIN** What were some of the problems that minorities had to overcome in the postwar era?

☑ **ASSESSMENT**

1. **Make Generalizations** Describe the impact beatniks had on society and culture in the 1950s.

2. **Support Ideas with Evidence** Describe the struggles and discrimination minorities faced in post–World War II America.

3. **Draw Conclusions** Explain the significance of Alan Freed renaming race music as rock-and-roll music.

4. **Support Ideas with Examples** Describe the causes for the feelings of discontent that came to the surface during the 1950s.

5. **Identify Central Issues** Describe the impact that the migration of middle-class families to suburbs had on the economic stability of the nation's cities.

>> Puerto Ricans, like previous waves of immigrants, formed communities in specific urban neighborhoods.

Bounce to Activate Map

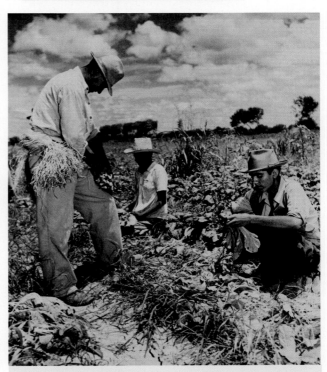
>> The sheer difficulty of the work undertaken by migrant farmworkers, coupled with the low wages, led directly to activism and, eventually, positive changes.

LESSON SUMMARIES

Use these Lesson Summaries, and the longer versions available online, to review the key ideas for each lesson in this Topic.

Lesson 1: The Beginning of the Cold War

After the defeat of Nazi Germany, the Soviet Union set up communist governments in Eastern Europe. The U.S. resisted Soviet power through a policy of containment and by providing economic aid to Europe. Stalin's blockade of West Berlin ended with a humanitarian victory for the West.

Lesson 2: The Korean War

In 1950, a year after the communist Mao Zedong took control of China, troops from communist North Korea invaded South Korea. American and United Nations forces battled North Korea until a cease-fire was declared in 1953.

Lesson 3: The Cold War Intensifies

An arms race between the United States and the Soviet Union began in 1949. During the 1950s a series of world crises threatened to bring the superpowers into direct confrontation. As tensions grew, President Eisenhower declared that the U.S. would use force to help any nation threatened by communism.

Lesson 4: Cold War Fears at Home

During the Red Scare of the late 1940s, an anti-communist panic spread in the United States. 3000 federal employees lost their jobs, and a blacklist destroyed the careers of entertainers. Spy trials took place in the early 1950s while Senator McCarthy was leading a campaign of accusations against suspected communists.

Lesson 5: Postwar Prosperity

After World War II, the GI Bill of Rights helped veterans start careers. Veterans also started families and a baby boom followed. The nation was now in the longest period of economic growth in its history. Populations shifted, the service sector grew, and President Eisenhower helped create the highway system.

Lesson 6: Mass Culture in the 1950s

American culture was transformed in the 1950s, as millions moved to the suburbs. Family income rose as did consumer spending. Women were encouraged to stay at home rather than start careers. Televisions became widely available, and educational opportunities expanded.

Lesson 7: Social Issues of the 1950s

Discontent with postwar American suburban life soon emerged among artists, writers, and the young. Many began calling attention to urban slums, rural poverty, and racial discrimination. A youth culture of revolt found expression in the new musical genre of rock-and-roll.

VISUAL REVIEW

Use these graphics to review some of the key terms, people, and ideas from this Topic.

America's Postwar Boom

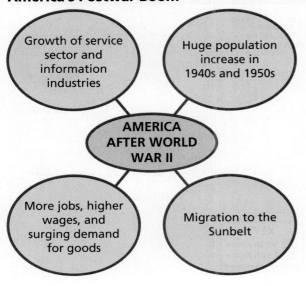

- Growth of service sector and information industries
- Huge population increase in 1940s and 1950s
- **AMERICA AFTER WORLD WAR II**
- More jobs, higher wages, and surging demand for goods
- Migration to the Sunbelt

Early Cold War Flashpoints

FLASHPOINT	ACTION AND REACTION
Poland	• U.S. urges democratic elections. • USSR installs communist government.
Turkey	• USSR demands territory from Turkey; communist rebels threaten Greece. • U.S. adopts Truman doctrine to aid Turkey, Greece, and other states resisting communism
Berlin	• USSR blockades West Berlin. • U.S. and Britain airlift supplies to the city.
Korea	• North Korea invades South Korea. • U.S. and UN enter war on South Korean site. • China enters war on North Korean side.
Europe	• U.S. forms NATO for mutual defense. • USSR forms Warsaw Pact for mutual defense.

Cold War Alliances, 1955

NATO	WARSAW PACT
Belgium, Netherlands, Canada, Norway, Denmark, Portugal, France, Turkey, Greece, United Kingdom, Iceland, United States, Italy, West Germany, Luxembourg	Albania, Bulgaria, Czechoslovakia, East Germany, Hungary, Poland, Romania, Soviet Union

The Cold War at Home

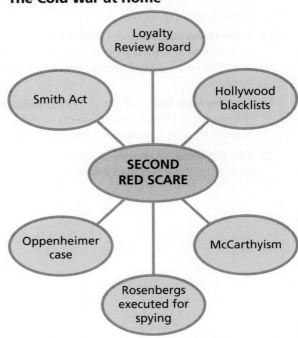

- Loyalty Review Board
- Smith Act
- Hollywood blacklists
- **SECOND RED SCARE**
- Oppenheimer case
- McCarthyism
- Rosenbergs executed for spying

KEY TERMS, PEOPLE, AND IDEAS

1. What political developments led to the beginning of the **Cold War**?

2. How did the **Marshall Plan** serve both economic and foreign policy?

3. Why were **NATO** and the **Warsaw Pact** formed?

4. How did the **Truman Doctrine** shape U.S. foreign policy?

5. How did the U.S. policy of containment shape the Korean War?

6. How did President Eisenhower and **John Foster Dulles** change the tone of the arms race?

7. Why was the postwar United States described as a postindustrial society?

8. How did the **Interstate Highway Act** transform American communities?

9. How did the baby boom affect the U.S. economy?

CRITICAL THINKING

10. **Determine Central Ideas** (a) Why was the Berlin airlift considered such a moral victory for the West? (b) How was the airlift related to the policy of containment?

11. **Identify Cause and Effect** What factors contributed to American postwar prosperity?

12. **Draw Inferences** (a) How did postwar prosperity increase social divisions? (b) How did this prosperity increase ethnic divisions?

13. **Make Generalizations** (a.) How did women's roles change in the years immediately following World War II? (b.) How did this contrast with their roles during the war?

14. **Find the Main Idea** (a.) Why did HUAC investigate Hollywood? (b.) What were the effects of these investigations on filmmaking and scriptwriting?

15. **Cite Evidence** What signs of rebellion and discontent emerged in the arts of the 1950s?

16. **Analyze Maps** Look at the map below. (a.) What role did the 38th parallel play in the Korean War? (b.) How did the truce reflect the U.S. foreign policy of containment?

17. **Writing Activity: Use Primary Sources** Evaluate how George Kennan's advice determined U.S. foreign policy. Use the excerpt below and your knowledge of foreign policy events.

> We are going to continue for a long time to find the Russians difficult to deal with. It does not mean that they should be considered as embarked upon a do-or-die program to overthrow our society by a given date. . . . In these circumstances, it is clear that the main element of any United States policy toward the Soviet Union must be that of long-term, patient but firm and vigilant containment of Russian expansive tendencies.
>
> —*George Kennan, "The Sources of Soviet Conduct"*

DOCUMENT-BASED QUESTIONS

The Cold War helped create a Red Scare. Read the documents below, then answer the questions that follow.

DOCUMENT A

This excerpt is from a famous speech by Senator Joseph McCarthy.

> In my opinion the State Department, which is one of the most important government departments, is thoroughly infested with communists. I have in my hand 57 cases of individuals who would appear to be either card-carrying members or certainly loyal to the Communist Party, but who nevertheless are still helping to shape our foreign policy. One thing to remember in discussing the communists in our government is that we are not dealing with spies who get 30 pieces of sliver to steal the blueprints of new weapons. We are dealing with a far more sinister type of activity because it permits the enemy to guide and shape our policy.
> —*Senator Joseph McCarthy, February 1950*

DOCUMENT B

This cover is from a propaganda comic book published in 1947.

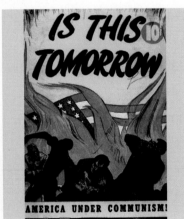

DOCUMENT C

This excerpt is from a secondary source on Joseph McCarthy.

> [He] was in many ways the most gifted demagogue ever bred on these shores. No bolder seditionist ever moved among us—nor any politician with a surer, swifter access to the dark places of the American mind. The major phase of McCarthy's career was mercifully short. It began in 1950, three years after he had taken his seat in the Senate, where he had seemed a dim and inconsiderable figure. . . . If he was anything at all in the realm of ideas, principles, doctrines, he was a species of nihilist; he was an essentially destructive force, a revolutionist without any revolutionary vision, a rebel without a cause.
> —*Richard H. Rovere, Senator Joe McCarthy*

DOCUMENT D

This excerpt is from a secondary source.

> Emotions ran very, very high about how to conduct the Cold War, about how to deal with the threat of Stalinism, both abroad but also at home. You had American soldiers dying in Korea. The Korean War formed the vivid backdrop for all of McCarthy's career. There was a bitter, bitter partisan battle in which people were prepared to say almost anything to blacken the reputations and to smear their political opponents. McCarthy did it, and his Republican allies did it. You also have to remember that the Democrats were quite prepared to do the same thing, and often did against McCarthy, calling him a Nazi sympathizer, talking about his investigations as posing a threat to American democracy and so on, charges which really don't, in the light of historical evidence and historical perspective, hold any kind of water.
> —*Arthur Herman, The Rise and Fall of Joseph McCarthy*

18. In Document A, McCarthy's accusation is that
    A. foreign spies are stealing documents.
    B. communists are shaping government policy.
    C. communists are working in state governments.
    D. the military is full of communist sympathizers.

19. **Analyze Images** How do you think images like the one in Document B prepared the ground for the Red Scare?

20. In Document C, the author depicts McCarthy as
    A. bold and perceptive.
    B. unworthy of notice.
    C. sinister and powerful.
    D. principled and honorable.

21. Document D, the historian's view of McCarthy is that
    A. his tactics posed no threat to democracy.
    B. he nearly destroyed democracy in the 1950s.
    C. his campaign was completely unjustified.
    D. he was out of touch with world events.

22. **Writing Activity: Primary Source** Write a paragraph explaining what effects the Red Scare had on domestic policy and politics. Use the sources as well as additional information you have learned.

1 Why was the outcome of the Berlin Airlift such a propaganda victory for the West?

A The United States established Radio Free Europe to counter Soviet propaganda.

B The success of the Berlin Airlift showed that the West could defeat the Soviet Union militarily.

C Western powers proved that they were better organized than Soviet forces.

D The West was seen as protecting a city from starvation at the hands of the Soviet Union.

2 In the controversy surrounding the proliferation of nuclear weapons, why did some American scientists oppose developing the hydrogen bomb?

F It was not as strong as the atomic bomb.

G They feared that this would lead to an arms race.

H The Soviet Union had launched the Sputnik satellite.

I The Soviets were about to develop a hydrogen bomb.

3 Why did the House Un-American Activities Committee hearings have such a chilling effect on filmmakers' freedom of speech?

    A Filmmakers stopped making movies altogether for a few months.

    B Filmmakers began making science-fiction films about alien invasions.

    C Filmmakers were afraid to make movies about controversial social topics.

    D Filmmakers had to show movies to the committee before they could be screened in theaters.

The GI Bill of Rights

• Veterans were granted a year of unemployment benefits.

• Veterans were granted financial aid to attend college.

• ?

---

4 What statement below replaces the question mark to explain how the GI Bill of Rights increased prosperity in the United States after World War II?

    F Veterans were granted guaranteed factory jobs.

    G Veterans were granted extended military pension plans.

    H Veterans were granted family leave to help raise their children.

    I Veterans were granted access to low-cost home and business loans.

If you have trouble with...				
Question	1	2	3	4
See Lesson	7.1	7.3	7.4	7.5

5 What social disruptions of the wartime period may have brought about the desire to return to family life and traditional gender roles in the 1950s?

A The war effort had encouraged migrations of workers within the country.

B Television reinforced traditional gender roles of the husband as breadwinner and the wife as homemaker.

C The war had divided families and brought women to fill men's jobs in the factories.

D A religious revival in the 1950s made organized faith-based groups more powerful.

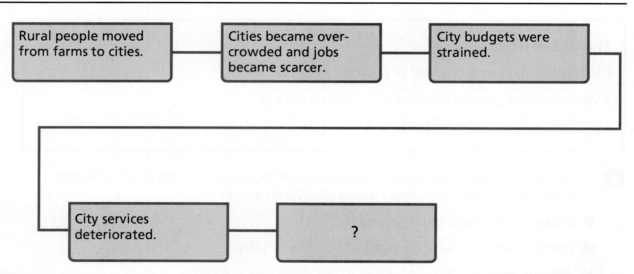

6 What option below best replaces the question mark to explain the effects of migration into and out of urban areas in the graphic above?

F Schools were built in inner cities.

G Rates of crime decreased in cities.

H More houses were needed in inner cities.

I More middle class people moved to the suburbs.

7 Why did people in various countries support dictatorships in the 1930s?

A Monarchs appointed dictators because they feared the prospect of revolution.

B Voters elected parties that promised to destroy democracy.

C Economic distress drove people to support angry men who promised easy solutions.

D Voters everywhere felt humiliated and wanted to restore a sense of national pride.

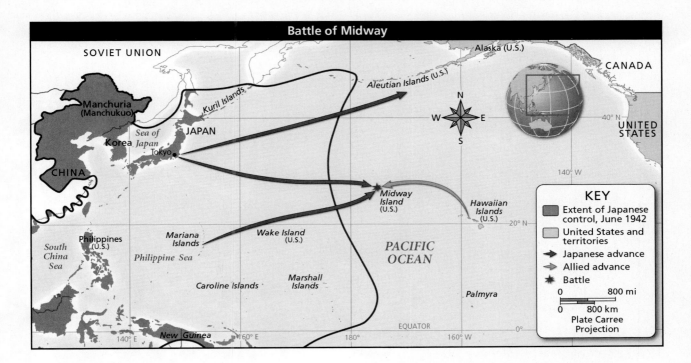

Battle of Midway

8 Based on the extent of Japanese control in the Pacific as shown on this map, why was the Allied victory at the battle of Midway a World War II turning point?

F The victory caused Japan to surrender Wake Island and the Mariana Islands.

G The victory allowed Admiral Nimitz to claim the Aleutian Islands for the Allies.

H The victory halted the Japanese advance across the Pacific and put Japan on the defensive.

I The victory forced Japan to attempt an attack on Hawaii from the Marshall Islands rather than from Midway Island.

If you have trouble with...

Question	5	6	7	8
See Lesson	7.6	7.7	6.1	6.4

[**ESSENTIAL QUESTION**] How can we ensure equality for all?

(8) **Civil Rights and Reform in the 1960s**

Enduring Understandings

- After World War II, a growing civil rights movement challenged discrimination in America.

- Martin Luther King, Jr. led the civil rights movement, encouraging nonviolent protest.

- The movement faced resistance in Congress and violence in the streets.

- In the late 1960s, some African Americans grew militant, as frustration erupted into urban violence.

- Under the Kennedy and Johnson administrations, laws were enacted to protect voting rights and civil rights.

- President Johnson's "Great Society" programs tried to improve the quality of life in America.

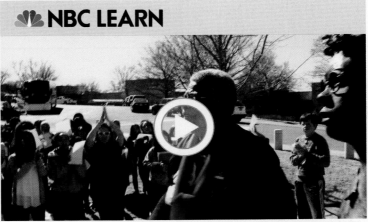

Learn more about how teenager Minnijean Brown-Trickey helped advance the cause of civil rights.

Bounce to Activate My Story Video

>> Dr. Martin Luther King Jr. during the March on Washington in 1963.

California Topic 8 Overview

In this Topic, you'll learn about the civil rights movement and the reforms of the 1960s. Look at the lesson outline and explore the timeline. As you study this Topic, you'll complete the Quest team project.

LESSON OUTLINE

8.1 The Civil Rights Movement Strengthens
HSS 11.3, HSS 11.3.1, HSS 11.10, HSS 11.10.1, HSS 11.10.4, HSS 11.10.5, HSS 11.11.2; Analysis CST.4

8.2 The Movement Surges Forward
HSS 11.10, HSS 11.10.3, HSS 11.10.4, HSS 11.10.5, HSS 11.10.6; Analysis CST.4

8.3 Successes and Setbacks
HSS 11.10, HSS 11.10.2, HSS 11.10.4, HSS 11.10.5, HSS 11.10.6, HSS 11.11.7; Analysis CST.3, CST.4

8.4 Kennedy's Reforms
HSS 11.11.2

8.5 Reform Under Johnson
HSS 11.3, HSS 11.3.5, HSS 11.11.1, HSS 11.11.2, HSS 11.11.6

Civil Rights and Reform

1948
President Truman desegregates the military

1954
Brown v. Board of Education

1957
Desegregation of Central High in Little Rock, Arkansas

1962
James Meredith enrolls at the University of Mississippi

1963
March on Washington

1964
Civil Rights Act is passed

1968
Dr. Martin Luther King is assassinated

1945   1955   1965   1975

QUEST!

Creating an Interactive Timeline on Civil Rights

How much have the lives of African Americans changed since the Civil Rights movement of the 1960s? Has the nation achieved the promise of full equality for its people? In this Quest you'll explore these questions and then create a timeline that displays your findings.

STEP

With your team, discuss questions you have about how the lives of African Americans have changed and what you might show on your timeline.

STEP

Identify 10 events of the civil rights movement and choose charts, maps, and other graphics that might appear on your timeline.

STEP

Create the timeline and chart your progress in the Project Tracker. Publish your timeline on the web.

STEP

Present your timeline to a live audience and explain your conclusions. Allow your audience to react and discuss their observations. Reflect on what you have learned.

PEARSON realize™
PearsonSchool.com/CASS

Go **ONLINE** for complete Quest materials

 VIDEO   ETEXT   WRITING   RUBRIC   PDF ASSESSMENT

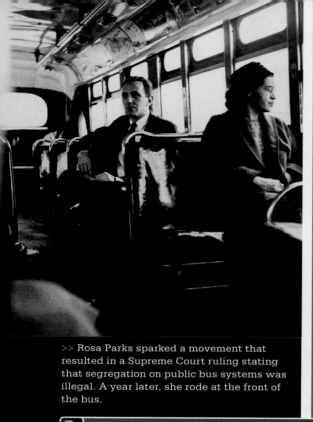

>> Rosa Parks sparked a movement that resulted in a Supreme Court ruling stating that segregation on public bus systems was illegal. A year later, she rode at the front of the bus.

Bounce to Activate Flipped Video

8.1 The postwar period brought prosperity to many, but most African Americans were still treated as second-class citizens. The civil rights movement, a broad and diverse effort to attain racial equality, compelled the nation to live up to its ideal that all are created equal. The movement also demonstrated that ordinary men and women could perform extraordinary acts of courage and sacrifice to achieve social justice, a lesson that continues to inspire people around the world today.

>> Objectives

Describe efforts to end segregation in the 1940s and 1950s.

Explain the importance of the landmark case of Brown v. Board of Education.

Describe the controversy over school desegregation in Little Rock, Arkansas.

Discuss the Montgomery bus boycott and its impact.

>> Key Terms

de jure segregation
de facto segregation
Thurgood Marshall
Earl Warren
Civil Rights Act of
   1957
Martin Luther King,
   Jr.
Rosa Parks
Orval Faubus

The Civil Rights Movement Strengthens

Segregation Limits Equality

African Americans had a long history of fighting for their rights. After World War II, the struggle intensified, as African Americans grew increasingly dissatisfied with their second-class status.

Separate but Not Equal In the South, Jim Crow laws enforced strict separation of the races. Segregation that is imposed by law is known as **de jure segregation**. In 1896, in *Plessy* v. *Ferguson*, the Supreme Court had ruled that such segregation was constitutional as long as the facilities for blacks and whites were "separate but equal." But this was seldom the case. The facilities for African Americans were rarely, if ever, equal.

In the South and elsewhere, segregation extended to most areas of public life. Officials enforced segregation of schools, hospitals, transportation, restaurants, cemeteries, and beaches. One city even forbade blacks and whites from playing checkers together.

Discrimination Throughout the Country In the North, too, African Americans faced segregation and discrimination. Even where there were no explicit laws, **de facto segregation**, or segregation by unwritten custom or tradition, was a fact of life. African Americans in the North were denied housing in many neighborhoods. They faced discrimination in employment and often could get only low-paying jobs.

Jim Crow laws and more subtle forms of discrimination had a widespread and severe impact on African Americans. Black Americans occupied the bottom rungs of the economic ladder. Compared to white Americans, they had significantly higher rates of poverty and illiteracy, as well as lower rates of homeownership and life expectancy. Although African Americans living in the North could vote, most who lived in the South could not. Very few African Americans held public office.

In the West and Southwest, Asian Americans and Mexican Americans, too, faced de facto segregation and, in some cases, legal restrictions.

Civil Rights Advance Slowly in the 1940s In many ways, World War II set the stage for the rise of the modern civil rights movement. President Roosevelt banned discrimination in defense industries in 1941. Gunnar Myrdal's publication in 1944 of *An American Dilemma* brought the issue of American prejudice to the forefront of public consciousness. Lastly, after risking their lives defending freedom abroad, African Americans were unwilling to accept discrimination at home.

In the 1940s, new organizations arose to try to bring an end to racial injustice and expand participation in the democratic process. James Farmer and several others founded the Congress of Racial Equality (CORE) with the goal of ending discriminatory policies and improving relations between races. Its members were deeply influenced by the teachings of Henry David Thoreau and Mohandas Gandhi about the use of nonviolent protest to confront injustice. They became convinced that African Americans could apply similar nonviolent methods to gain civil rights. CORE organized nonviolent protests such as sit-ins against segregation in public facilities in Chicago, Detroit, Denver, and other northern cities.

Success was limited, but one highly visible break in the wall of segregation did take place in 1947. Jackie Robinson joined the Brooklyn Dodgers, becoming the first African American to play major league baseball. Robinson braved death threats and rough treatment, but throughout his career he won the hearts of millions and paved the way for integration of other sports.

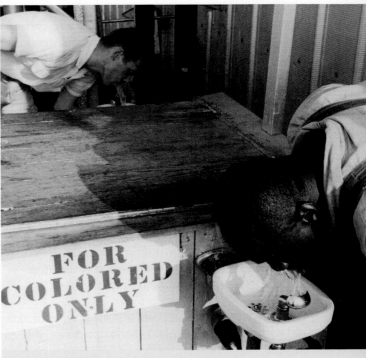

>> Segregated drinking fountains in the South were a stark reminder that the ideals of equality described in the Declaration of Independence had yet to be attained.

Bounce to Activate Gallery

>> On February 26, 1946, racial tensions led to mass arrests of African Americans in Columbia, Tennessee. A young attorney named Thurgood Marshall helped with their legal defense.

Bounce to Activate Gallery

Nevertheless, African Americans continued to face discrimination and felt that racial equality was long overdue. However, the vast majority of white Americans took the opposite view. Racial violence erupted in the South, sometimes against African American veterans who were just trying to register to vote.

In the wake of this violence, President Truman appointed a Committee on Civil Rights to investigate race relations. In its report, the committee recommended a number of measures to ensure equal opportunity for all Americans, including an antilynching law and federal protection of voting rights. Unfortunately, Truman was unable to win congressional support for these initiatives. However, in 1948, he did use his executive power to order the desegregation of the military. Over time, the U.S. armed forces would become one of the most integrated institutions in the United States.

☑ **IDENTIFY SUPPORTING DETAILS** What tactics did some civil rights organizations use during the 1940s?

A Landmark Supreme Court Decision

Although the civil rights movement had made some gains in the 1940s, it stalled in the early 1950s. One of its greatest disappointments was the NAACP's failure, after decades of lobbying Congress, to make the lynching of African Americans a federal crime. Feeling that the executive and legislative branches of government were unwilling to promote additional reforms, the NAACP decided to turn to litigation in the federal courts to attain its political goals.

The NAACP Turns to Litigation in the Courts
Thurgood Marshall

In 1950, the NAACP won a number of key court cases. In *Sweatt* v. *Painter,* the Supreme Court ruled that the state of Texas had violated the Fourteenth Amendment by establishing a separate, but unequal, all-black law school. Similarly, in the *McLaurin* v. *Oklahoma State Regents*, the Court ruled that the state of Oklahoma had violated George McLaurin's constitutional rights. Even though McLaurin had been admitted to the graduate school of the University of Oklahoma, he was denied equal access to the library, dining hall, and classrooms. According to the Supreme Court, a truly equal education involved more than simply admitting African Americans to previously all-white universities.

The Supreme Court Issues a Broad Decision

Not long after it won these cases, the NAACP mounted a much broader challenge to segregated public education at all grade levels. This challenge became known as *Brown* v. *Board of Education*. In the *Sweatt* and *McLaurin* cases, the NAACP

>> In 1954, each state had its own laws governing segregation in public schools.
Analyze Maps What states required segregation in 1954?

EFFECTS OF BROWN v. BOARD OF EDUCATION

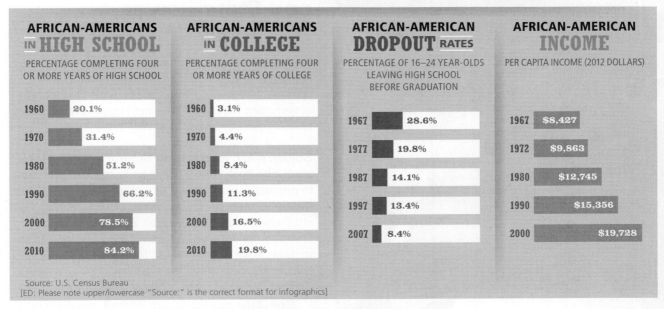

AFRICAN-AMERICANS IN HIGH SCHOOL	AFRICAN-AMERICANS IN COLLEGE	AFRICAN-AMERICAN DROPOUT RATES	AFRICAN-AMERICAN INCOME
PERCENTAGE COMPLETING FOUR OR MORE YEARS OF HIGH SCHOOL	PERCENTAGE COMPLETING FOUR OR MORE YEARS OF COLLEGE	PERCENTAGE OF 16–24 YEAR-OLDS LEAVING HIGH SCHOOL BEFORE GRADUATION	PER CAPITA INCOME (2012 DOLLARS)
1960 — 20.1%	1960 — 3.1%	1967 — 28.6%	1967 — $8,427
1970 — 31.4%	1970 — 4.4%	1977 — 19.8%	1972 — $9,863
1980 — 51.2%	1980 — 8.4%	1987 — 14.1%	1980 — $12,745
1990 — 66.2%	1990 — 11.3%	1997 — 13.4%	1990 — $15,356
2000 — 78.5%	2000 — 16.5%	2007 — 8.4%	2000 — $19,728
2010 — 84.2%	2010 — 19.8%		

Source: U.S. Census Bureau
[ED: Please note upper/lowercase "Source:" is the correct format for infographics]

>> In what ways are these graphs related? **Analyze Data** Cite evidence to support the claim that school desegregation improved the lives of minorities living in the United States.

asserted that Texas and Oklahoma had failed to provide equal educational experiences. In the *Brown* case, however, the NAACP challenged the "separate but equal" principle itself, which had been established in the 1896 *Plessy* v. *Ferguson* case.

The Supreme Court agreed with the NAACP's argument that segregated public education violated the U.S. Constitution. All nine of the Court's Justices supported the *Brown* decision, which was written by newly appointed Chief Justice **Earl Warren**. "Does segregation of children in public schools solely on the basis of race . . . deprive the children of the minority group equal education opportunities?" Warren asked in his decision. "We believe that it does." The Chief Justice and the Court declared, "in the field of public education the doctrine of 'separate but equal' has no place."

In the same month as the *Brown* decision, the Supreme Court decided another civil rights case, this time involving Mexican Americans. In *Hernandez* v. *Texas*, the Court ended the exclusion of Mexican Americans from trial juries. The *Hernandez* decision was the first Supreme Court ruling against discrimination targeting a group other than African Americans.

The Public Response The *Brown* decision was one of the most significant and controversial in

American history. Because public education touched so many Americans, it had a much greater impact than cases involving only professional and graduate schools. Moreover, by overturning the principle of "separate but equal," the Court lent its support to the views of many civil rights advocates that all forms of segregation are wrong.

In a separate ruling, known as *Brown II*, the Court called for the implementation of its decision "with all deliberate speed" across the nation. However, most southerners had no intention of desegregating their schools without a fight. In 1956, about 100 southern members of Congress endorsed "The Southern Manifesto." They pledged to oppose the *Brown* ruling through all "lawful means," on the grounds that the Court had misinterpreted the Constitution.

More ominously, the Ku Klux Klan staged a revival. Many prominent white southerners and businessmen organized "White Citizens Councils" that declared that the South would not be integrated. The Citizens Councils imposed economic and political pressure against those who favored compliance with the Supreme Court's decision.

☑ **CHECK UNDERSTANDING** How did earlier legal decisions differ from *Brown* v. *Board of Education*?

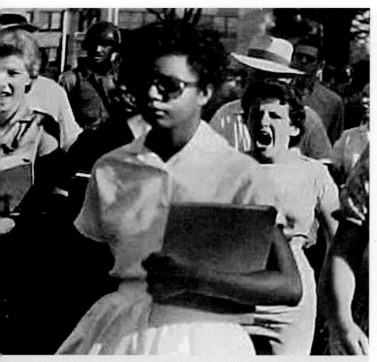

>> Elizabeth Eckford, one of nine students chosen to integrate Little Rock High School in Little Rock, Arkansas, walked past an angry crowd as officers from the National Guard stood by.

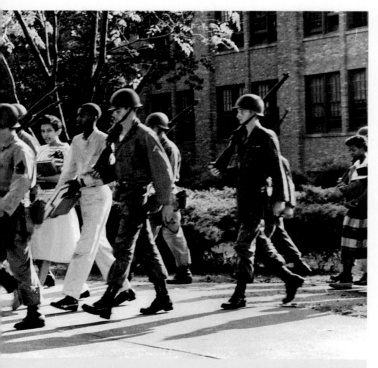

>> President Eisenhower ordered troops from the National Guard to protect African American students as they entered Little Rock High School in Little Rock, Arkansas.

Conflict Between Federal and State Power

Historically, education had been a state matter. States and local school boards ran the schools, and the federal government had little involvement. Local and state officials resisted the *Brown* decision's order to desegregate, and clashes with the federal government resulted. The most famous battle took place in 1957 in Little Rock, Arkansas.

Soldiers Arrive at a High School in Little Rock
The Little Rock school board had established a plan to gradually desegregate its schools, beginning with Central High School. Nine young African American students volunteered to enroll. But Arkansas Governor **Orval Faubus** announced his opposition to integration and called out the Arkansas state National Guard. When the nine students arrived at Central High, the soldiers blocked their way.

One of the nine, Elizabeth Eckford, has described the scene. An angry white mob began to approach her, with some screaming, "Lynch her! Lynch her!" Eckford sought out a friendly face, someone who might help. "I looked into the face of an old woman and it seemed a kind face," she recalled, "but when I looked at her again she spat on me." Fortunately, another white woman whisked Eckford away on a public bus before the mob could have its way. None of the Little Rock Nine gained entrance to the school that day.

Up until the Little Rock crisis, President Eisenhower had provided little leadership on the civil rights front. Following the *Brown* decision, he did not urge the nation to rapidly desegregate its schools. Privately, he expressed his misgivings about the ruling. But when Governor Faubus resisted the will of the federal courts, Eisenhower realized he had to act. He sent federal troops to Little Rock to protect the students and to enforce the Court's decision. Eisenhower explained this action in a nationally televised address:

It is important that the reasons for my action be understood by all our citizens. . . . A foundation of our American way of life is our national respect for law. . . .

If resistance to the federal court orders ceases at once, the further presence of federal troops will be unnecessary and the City of Little Rock will return to its normal habits of peace and order and a blot upon the fair name and high honor of our nation in the world will be removed.

—President Dwight D. Eisenhower, "Address on Little Rock," 1957

For the entire school year, federal troops stayed in Little Rock, escorting the nine students to and from Central High and guarding them on the school grounds. On the last day of class, Ernest Green, the one senior of the nine, became the first African American to graduate from Central High School. The showdown demonstrated that the President would not tolerate open defiance of the law. Still, most southern states found ways to resist full compliance with the Court's decision. Many years would pass before black and white children went to school together.

Political Lobbying Leads to a New Civil Rights Act While organizations like CORE continued to nonviolently protest discrimination in public places in the North, the political lobbying efforts of civil rights forces yielded a small victory when Congress voted to pass the **Civil Rights Act of 1957**. President Eisenhower signed the bill into law, which established the United States Civil Rights Commission and gave it the power to investigate violations of civil rights. It empowered the U.S. Attorney General to bring lawsuits to address civil rights violations. The law also gave the Attorney General greater power to protect the voting rights of African Americans. But overall, it lacked teeth. CORE leader Bayard Rustin noted, however, that it had symbolic importance as the first civil rights law passed by Congress since Reconstruction.

☑ **IDENTIFY MAIN IDEAS** How did the crisis in Little Rock spark a conflict between state and federal government?

The Montgomery Bus Boycott

In addition to legal efforts during this era, some civil rights activists took direct action to end segregation. On December 1, 1955, **Rosa Parks**, an African American seamstress, did just that. She boarded a bus in Montgomery, Alabama, and sat down in an empty seat. Several stops later, the bus driver requested that she give up her seat to a white passenger. Montgomery law required African American passengers to give up their seats to whites. After Rosa Parks refused to obey the law, she

>> For years, public buses in many states segregated riders along racial lines.

was arrested. "The [policemen] asked if the driver had asked me to stand up, and I said yes, and they wanted to know why I didn't," Parks later recalled. "I told them I didn't think I should have to stand up. After I had paid my fare and occupied a seat, I didn't think I should have to give it up."

Rosa Parks's Act Transforms a Movement
Parks's action set in motion a chain of events that transformed the civil rights movement. Over the next few days, a core of civil rights activists in Montgomery organized a one-day bus boycott. They called upon the black community to refuse to ride the buses as a way to express their opposition to Parks's arrest, in particular, and segregation, in general. Meanwhile, during the Montgomery bus boycott, the NAACP began preparing a legal challenge.

For a long while, many people thought that Parks had refused to give up her seat simply because she was tired after a long day of work. In reality, Parks had a record of fighting for civil rights. She had been active in the Montgomery chapter of the NAACP for years. This does not mean that she set out to get arrested and spark a movement. However, her choice to not give up her seat was an effective form of nonviolent protest and an influential moment in the civil rights movement's struggle for the equality of political rights.

>> Dr. Martin Luther King, Jr., became known for his powerful speeches calling for desegregation and racial equality.

Bounce to Activate Gallery

Martin Luther King Calls for Nonviolent Protest On the evening following the boycott, the Montgomery Improvement Association (MIA), the organization that sponsored the bus boycott, held a meeting. Dr. **Martin Luther King, Jr.**, a Baptist minister, addressed the group. Though he had little time to prepare, King delivered an inspirational speech that brought the audience to its feet. Noting that African Americans were tired of segregation and oppression, King declared that there was no alternative but to protest. However, he called for the protest to be nonviolent. He urged them not to become resentful, which would lead to hatred toward whites, but rather to follow Christian doctrine and love them.

After King spoke, the MIA vowed to continue the boycott and chose King as its leader. For more than a year, African Americans in Montgomery maintained their boycott of the buses. They did so despite economic pressures from their employers and threats of violence by the Ku Klux Klan. King himself survived a bombing of his house. Fortunately, his wife and baby daughter were not home at the time.

Finally, in 1956, the Supreme Court ruled that the Montgomery city law that segregated buses was unconstitutional. After more than a year, the MIA ended its boycott, and African Americans began to ride the buses again.

Ministers Inspire the Movement The bus boycott represented a tremendous victory for African Americans in Montgomery and across the nation. The boycott revealed the power that African Americans could have if they joined together. The protest also elevated King and his philosophy of nonviolence into a prominent position within the civil rights movement.

After the boycott, King and another Montgomery minister, Ralph Abernathy, established the Southern Christian Leadership Conference (SCLC) to continue the struggle for civil rights. Made up largely of southern African American ministers, the SCLC advocated nonviolent resistance to fight injustice. The SCLC went on to organize a series of protests, including a Prayer Pilgrimage in Washington, D.C., in 1957, which helped convince Congress to pass civil rights legislation. Still, discrimination and segregation remained widespread.

☑ **CHECK UNDERSTANDING** Why did the Montgomery Improvement Association ask African Americans to boycott Montgomery's bus system?

☑ ASSESSMENT

1. **Generate Explanations** Explain how events during World War II set the stage for the rise of the modern civil rights movement.

2. **Compare Points of View** Explain how President Eisenhower's position on civil rights changed after Governor Orval Faubus brought the Arkansas National Guard to Little Rock.

3. **Summarize** the effect that Dr. Martin Luther King, Jr. had on the Montgomery bus boycott.

4. **Contrast** Explain how the Brown v. Board of Education case differed from previous Supreme Court cases.

5. **Distinguish** between de jure segregation and de facto segregation.

8.2 Despite the *Brown* decision and other civil rights victories, little changed in the everyday lives of most African Americans. Nonetheless, activists continued to struggle for civil rights. In the early 1960s, the movement experienced a groundswell of support. This surge produced a dramatic shift in race relations, led to the passage of landmark civil rights legislation in 1964, and set the stage for future reforms.

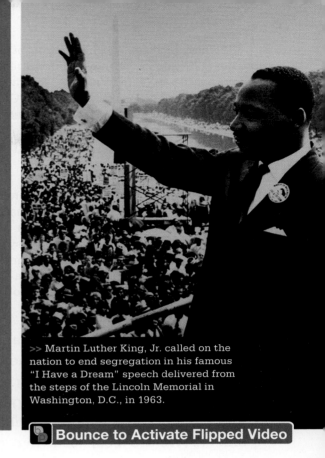

>> Martin Luther King, Jr. called on the nation to end segregation in his famous "I Have a Dream" speech delivered from the steps of the Lincoln Memorial in Washington, D.C., in 1963.

Bounce to Activate Flipped Video

The Movement Surges Forward

Student Activists Promote Civil Rights

After the *Brown* decision, many black youths expected that their schools would integrate quickly and that other racial reforms would follow. Change was not quick to come, however. Disappointed by the lack of progress, young African Americans began to challenge segregation with new vigor and determination.

Nonviolent Protests Challenge Segregation On February 1, 1960, four African American college students ordered doughnuts and coffee at a Woolworth's lunch counter in Greensboro, North Carolina. As they expected, the white waitress refused to serve them. In the South, nearly all restaurants that served whites refused to serve blacks. To protest this discrimination, the four students sat down on the stools at the lunch counter, where they stayed until closing time.

Word of the Greensboro **sit-in** spread rapidly, sparking a wave of similar protests across the nation. In Nashville, Tennessee, for instance, students led by the Reverend James Lawson staged sit-ins and, later, marches to protest racial inequality.

>> **Objectives**

Describe the sit-ins, freedom ride, and the actions of James Meredith in the early 1960s.

Explain how the protests at Birmingham and the March on Washington were linked to the Civil Rights Act of 1964.

Describe how the Civil Rights Act of 1964 addressed minority rights in the United States.

>> **Key Terms**

sit-in
Student Nonviolent
   Coordinating
   Committee
"freedom ride"
James Meredith
Medgar Evers
George Wallace
March on
   Washington
filibuster
Civil Rights Act of
   1964

Elsewhere, protesters held "wade-ins" at public beaches and "read-ins" at public libraries, refusing to leave beaches or libraries reserved for whites only. African Americans boycotted buses. Groups of demonstrators knelt in prayer. Other activists carried picket signs in demonstrations and wrote letters to newspapers and government officials to express their support of the protests in the South.

Political Organizations Encourage Nonviolent Protest The sit-ins marked the birth of a new militancy, especially among young African Americans. To build on the momentum they had gained, about 175 students from 30 states met at Shaw University, in Raleigh, North Carolina. There, on Easter weekend in 1960, they listened to James Lawson deliver an inspiring address:

> We who are demonstrators are trying to raise what we call the 'moral issue.' That is, we are pointing to the viciousness of racial segregation and prejudice and calling it evil or sin. . . . [We are also] asserting, 'get moving.' The pace of change is too slow. At this rate it will be another generation before the major forms of segregation disappear. . . . Most of us will be grandparents before we can live normal human lives.
>
> —James Lawson, "From a Lunch Counter Stool," 1960

Ella Baker, a veteran of the struggle for civil rights, had organized the meeting. The granddaughter of enslaved African Americans, Baker had been active in the National Association for the Advancement of Colored People (NAACP) and the Southern Christian Leadership Conference (SCLC). She helped the young activists to establish a new civil rights organization, the **Student Nonviolent Coordinating Committee**, or SNCC. Its goal was to create a grass-roots movement that involved all classes of African Americans in the struggle to defeat white racism and to obtain equality.

☑ **RECALL** How did students and other young people energize the civil rights movement in the 1960s?

Freedom Rides Begin Throughout the South

The next battleground was interstate transportation. Political activists targeted this industry because they knew that travel between states was subject to federal rather than state regulation. In fact, the Supreme Court had recently ruled in *Boynton v. Virginia* (1960) that segregation on interstate buses and in waiting rooms was illegal. Civil rights activists were now going to test the federal government's willingness to enforce the law.

Freedom Riders Risk Physical Harm In the spring of 1961, CORE staged a **"freedom ride"** through the Deep South. Riders set off in two separate buses from Washington, D.C., bound for New Orleans. En route, they defied segregationist codes. African Americans sat in the front of the bus and used "white" restrooms in bus stations.

In Alabama, the trip took a dangerous turn. After departing from Anniston, segregationists firebombed one of the buses. When the second bus arrived in Birmingham, a white mob attacked the riders.

>> In 1960, students at the University of Michigan joined the call for civil rights and equality for all Americans.

Bounce to Activate Gallery

The President Intervenes Photographs of the bombed-out bus and the injured riders appeared in newspapers and on television screens around the world, prodding President John F. Kennedy to intervene. Kennedy had intervened before. The previous year, when he was running for the presidency, Kennedy had helped to win Martin Luther King's release from a Georgia prison after state officials had sentenced King to six months in jail for a traffic violation. King was freed and Kennedy, with the help of African American voters, went on to win the presidential election of 1960.

Kennedy now took action to stem the violence against the freedom riders. His administration worked out a deal with Mississippi's leaders. Police and state troopers agreed to protect the riders. The Federal Transportation Commission also issued an order mandating the desegregation of interstate transportation.

In exchange, the Kennedy administration agreed not to intervene when Mississippi authorities arrested the activists and sentenced them to jail for disturbing the peace.

The freedom riders achieved their immediate goal. They compelled a reluctant federal government to act. By refusing to allow violent mobs to deter them, the riders also displayed that intimidation would not defeat the movement.

☑ **DESCRIBE** What did the freedom rides accomplish?

Public Institutions Open Doors to Minorities

In the fall of 1962 and spring of 1963, protests against racial discrimination intensified. The protesters put pressure on the federal government to help break down legal, or *de jure*, segregation. Meanwhile, violent resistance against the civil rights movement continued to grow, with many white Southerners opposing what they regarded as an overly-intrusive federal government interfering with race relations.

Litigation Against the University of Mississippi
One struggle that gained international attention involved **James Meredith**. Meredith was an Air Force veteran who sought to enroll at the all-white University of Mississippi, known as "Ole Miss." He was aided by the NAACP, a political organization that had been using litigation to challenge the legality of segregation in the courts. In September 1962, with the support of the NAACP, Meredith won a federal court case that ordered the university to

>> Senator John F. Kennedy campaigns in 1960. Martin Luther King's endorsement of Kennedy helped Kennedy win the African American vote.

🔲 **Bounce to Activate Gallery**

>> James Meredith, shown here with a federal escort, became the first African American student to integrate the University of Mississippi after winning a federal case guaranteeing his right to do so in 1962.

desegregate. Civil rights activist **Medgar Evers** was instrumental in this effort.

Mississippi governor Ross Barnett was determined to prevent the integration of the university. The issue became a standoff between the governor and the federal government.

On September 30, rumors of Meredith's arrival on the university's campus began to spread. Federal marshals had been assigned to protect him. Over the course of the night, a full-scale riot erupted, with federal marshals battling white protesters intent on scaring Meredith away.

As the rioting took place, President Kennedy addressed the nation on television. "Americans are free . . . to disagree with the law but not to disobey it," he declared. "For any government of laws . . . , no man, however prominent and powerful . . . is entitled to defy a court of law." The rioting went on throughout the night. By the time it ended, 160 people had been injured and 2 men had been killed.

The following morning, Meredith registered as a student and took his first class. He graduated from Ole Miss in 1963 and went on to obtain his law degree from Columbia University in New York City. Tragically, Medgar Evers was assassinated, on his front doorstep, in June 1963. Three years later,

>> Scenes of young protesters being attacked with high-pressure hoses and dogs shocked Americans, prompting a cry for federal action.

Meredith was shot and nearly killed. Both shootings stand as historical reminders of the high costs of fighting racial discrimination.

A Letter from Birmingham Jail In the spring of 1963, Martin Luther King, Jr., and the SCLC targeted Birmingham, Alabama, for a major civil rights campaign. They chose Birmingham because of its reputation as the most segregated city in the South.

The campaign began nonviolently at first with protest marches and sit-ins. City officials got a court order prohibiting the demonstrations. On Good Friday, April 12, 1963, King decided to violate the order and join the demonstration personally, even though he knew it would lead to his arrest.

From his jail cell, King wrote a letter explaining why he and other civil rights activists were tired of waiting for reform: "For years now I have heard the word 'wait!' It rings in the ear of every Negro with piercing familiarity. This 'Wait!' has almost always meant 'Never.'"

One of the most poignant passages of the letter describes King's concern about the impact of discrimination on his children:

Perhaps it is easy for those who have never felt the stinging darts of segregation to say, 'Wait.' But . . . when you suddenly find your tongue twisted and your speech stammering as you seek to explain to your six-year-old daughter why she can't go to the public amusement park that has just been advertised on television, and see tears welling up in her eyes when she is told that Funtown is closed to colored children. . . . Then you will understand why we find it difficult to wait.

—Martin Luther King, Jr., "Letter from Birmingham Jail," 1963

The SCLC gave King's letter to the press, and it soon appeared in newspapers across the nation. The letter provided Americans with a clear explanation of King's philosophy of nonviolence and his use of direct action. Its powerful message and eloquence also stirred many white moderates to support the civil rights movement.

After King was released from jail, the SCLC increased the frequency of the demonstrations. For the first time, schoolchildren joined the "freedom marches." Eventually, Birmingham's Public Safety Commissioner, T. Eugene "Bull" Connor used police dogs and fire hoses on the protesters. Many Americans were shocked by media coverage of nonviolent protesters set upon by dogs and overwhelmed by the powerful jets of water. They sent telegrams and letters by the thousands to the White House, calling on the President to act.

Kennedy Addresses Minority Rights In Alabama, Governor **George Wallace** made it clear where he stood on civil rights: "I say segregation now! Segregation tomorrow! Segregation forever!" In response to the impending entrance of two African American students, Vivian Malone and James Hood, to the University of Alabama, Wallace vowed to stand "in the schoolhouse door" and personally block any attempt to integrate Alabama schools. Faced with this showdown, President Kennedy became convinced that he had to take a more active role in promoting civil rights.

On June 11, 1963, in order to facilitate the registration of Malone and Hood, Kennedy ordered the secretary of defense to call up the Alabama National Guard. Faced with the authority of the federal government, Governor George Wallace backed down.

He stepped aside and allowed the two students to enter the University of Alabama—only after proclaiming the rights of states to control their own schools. Later, reflecting on the showdown with Wallace, Vivian Moore stated, "I didn't feel I should sneak in. I didn't feel I should go around the back door. If [Wallace] were standing in the door, I had every right to face him and go to school."

That evening, as a result of the events in Alabama, President Kennedy delivered a moving televised address. Calling civil rights a "moral issue," he declared that the nation had an obligation to "fulfill its promise" of giving all Americans "equal rights and equal opportunities." President Kennedy sent to Congress a proposal for sweeping civil rights legislation. His brother, Attorney General Robert F. Kennedy, led the charge for passage of the bill. The president also helped form a group of African American and white lawyers who would collaborate to fight segregation.

☑ **EXPLAIN** How did James Meredith and Martin Luther King, Jr. prompt President Kennedy to promote civil rights?

>> Alabama Governor George Wallace, a staunch advocate of segregationist policies, attempted to block the integration of the University of Alabama in 1963.

Thousands Gather in the Nation's Capital

To put pressure on Congress to pass the new civil rights bill and to improve economic opportunities for blacks, supporters made plans for a massive nonviolent protest in Washington, D.C. The event brought together the major political organizations promoting civil rights—including the NAACP, SCLC, and SNCC—as well as labor unions and religious groups.

The **March on Washington** took place on August 28, 1963. Organizers had hoped for 100,000 demonstrators. More than double that number showed up. They were a diverse group—young and old and from many different classes and religious backgrounds. More than a quarter of the marchers were white. Bayard Rustin, the chief organizer of the march, was one of the many gay supporters who participated.

Before the march, there had been some concern about maintaining order at such a huge demonstration. Yet despite the massive numbers, the day was peaceful and even festive, as famous entertainers performed. Celebrities and entertainers were on hand to perform for the crowd.

The Washington Monument was the starting point for the day's events. Prominent singers performed songs, including the civil rights movement's unofficial anthem, "We Shall Overcome." Then the throng marched to the Lincoln Memorial. The main rally took place in front of the Lincoln Memorial, where a distinguished roster of speakers addressed the crowd. A. Philip Randolph, the elder statesman of the civil rights movement, gave the opening remarks. He was followed by representatives of various religious and labor groups.

The highlight of the day came when the final speaker, Martin Luther King, Jr., took the podium. King held the audience spellbound as he described his dream of a colorblind society "when all of God's children" would be free and equal. Millions more watched King's address live on television. This powerful and eloquent speech has come to be known as the "I Have a Dream" speech.

Behind the scenes, there was some tension between the organizations that had planned the March. SNCC, in particular, had wanted to stage a more militant protest to show its dissatisfaction with the pace of change. Yet for the public at large and for most who took part, the March on Washington represented a magical moment in American history.

The March on Washington was one of the largest political demonstrations in U.S. history. Widely covered in the media, the March increased awareness of the movement and built momentum for the passage of civil rights legislation.

Despite the huge numbers and the emotional intensity of the day, the March remained orderly and is considered a model for peaceful protest. The March on Washington has come to symbolize the civil rights movement.

☑ **IDENTIFY** Why did Martin Luther King, Jr.'s speech during the March on Washington have such a profound effect on the nation?

A Significant Congressional Vote Addresses Minority Rights

On September 15, 1963, less than three weeks after the march, a bomb exploded in the Sixteenth Street Baptist Church in Birmingham. The church had been the SCLC's headquarters earlier that spring. Four young African American girls, all dressed in their Sunday best, were killed in the bombing.

Two months later, on November 22, 1963, President John F. Kennedy was assassinated in Dallas, Texas. Vice President Lyndon B. Johnson assumed the presidency.

Johnson was a southerner with an undistinguished record on racial matters. However, he surprised many Americans by immediately throwing his support behind the cause of civil rights. "No eulogy could more eloquently honor President Kennedy's memory," Johnson told Congress and the nation, "[than the] earliest passage of the civil rights bill for which he fought so long."

The civil rights bill faced strong opposition in Congress, but Johnson put his considerable political skills to work for its passage. The bill passed in the House of Representatives, but it faced a more difficult fight in the Senate, where a group of southern Democratic senators attempted to block it by means of a **filibuster**. This is a tactic by which senators give long speeches to hold up legislative business. The filibuster went on for more than 80 days until supporters finally put together enough votes to overcome it. In the end, the measure passed in the Senate, and President Johnson signed the **Civil Rights Act of 1964** into law in July.

IN MEMORY OF

...ISE McNAIR CYNTHIA WESLEY ADDIE MAE COLLINS CAROL ROBERTSON

THEIR LIVES WERE TAKEN BY UNKNOWN PARTIES ON SEPTEMBER 15, 1963 WHEN THE SIXTEENTH STREET BAPTIST CHURCH WAS BOMBED.

"MAY MEN LEARN TO REPLACE BITTERNESS AND VIOLENCE WITH LOVE AND UNDERSTANDING"

>> A plaque outside the Sixteenth Street Baptist Church in Birmingham, Alabama, honors the four girls who died there. Three local Ku Klux Klansmen were eventually convicted of this crime.

The act banned segregation in public accommodations and gave the federal government the ability to compel state and local school boards to desegregate their schools. The act also allowed the Justice Department to prosecute individuals who violated people's civil rights and outlawed discrimination in employment on account of race, color, sex, or national origin. It also established the Equal Employment Opportunity Commission (EEOC), which is responsible for enforcing these provisions and investigating charges of job discrimination.

☑ **IDENTIFY SUPPORTING DETAILS** How did the Civil Rights Act of 1964 try to end discrimination?

☑ ASSESSMENT

1. **Draw Conclusions** What link do you see between the mass protests of the early 1960s and the Montgomery bus boycott of 1955?

2. **Contrast** Explain how the Student Nonviolent Coordinating Committee differed from other civil rights organizations.

3. **Analyze Information** What were some outcomes of the freedom rides?

4. **Summarize** the main points of Martin Luther King Jr.'s argument in "Letter from Birmingham Jail."

5. **Generate Explanations** Explain why the Student Nonviolent Coordinating Committee was dissatisfied after the March on Washington.

Letter from Birmingham Jail: Martin Luther King, Jr.

These two excerpts are both from Dr. Martin Luther King, Jr. The first excerpt, "Letter from Birmingham Jail" was written in 1963, when King was jailed for disobeying a court order to stop leading a campaign of nonviolent protest against segregation and discrimination in Birmingham, Alabama. The letter was written in response to white Alabama clergymen who opposed the tactics of the protesters. The second excerpt is from King's closing address at the March on Washington— one of the most powerful speeches ever made.

>> Dr. Martin Luther King Jr. during the March on Washington

My Dear Fellow Clergymen, While confined here in the Birmingham City Jail, I came across your recent statement calling our present activities "unwise and untimely." . . .

We have waited for more than 340 years for our constitutional and God-given rights. The nations of Asia and Africa are moving with jetlike speed toward the goal of political independence, and we still creep at horse and buggy pace toward the gaining of a cup of coffee at a lunch counter.

☑ **COMPARE AND CONTRAST** What point is King making when he compares America's civil rights progress with that of nations in Asia and Africa?

I guess it is easy for those who have never felt the stinging darts of segregation to say wait. But when you have seen vicious mobs lynch your mothers and fathers at will and drown your sisters and brothers at whim; when you have seen hate-filled policemen curse, kick, brutalize, and even kill your black brothers and sisters with impunity [without punishment]; when you see the vast majority of your 20 million Negro brothers smothering in an airtight cage of poverty in the midst of an affluent society; when you suddenly find your tongue twisted and your speech stammering as you seek to explain to your six-year-old daughter why she can't go to the public amusement park that has just been advertised on television, and see the tears welling up in her little eyes when she is told that Funtown is closed to colored children, . . . then you will understand why we find it difficult to wait. . . .

☑ **ANALYZE STYLE AND RHETORIC** In this passage, how does King's imagery discredit the arguments of those urging civil rights activists to be patient and wait for change?

You express a great deal of anxiety over our willingness to break laws. . . . The answer is found in the fact that there are two types of laws: There are just and there are unjust laws. I would agree with Saint Augustine that "An unjust law is no law at all." . . .

All segregation statutes are unjust because segregation distorts the soul and damages the personality. It gives the segregator a false sense of superiority, and the segregated a false sense of inferiority. . . .

☑ **IDENTIFY CAUSE AND EFFECT** What does King say are the effects of segregation?

Let us all hope that the dark clouds of racial prejudice will soon pass away and the deep fog of misunderstanding will be lifted from our fear-drenched communities and in some not too distant tomorrow the radiant stars of love and brotherhood will shine over our great nation with all their scintillating beauty.

Yours for the cause of Peace and Brotherhood, Martin Luther King, Jr.

"I Have a Dream": Martin Luther King, Jr.

. . . And so even though we face the difficulties of today and tomorrow, I still have a dream. It is a dream deeply rooted in the American dream.

I have a dream that one day this nation will rise up and live out the true meaning of its creed [set of fundamental beliefs or principles]: "We hold these truths to be self-evident; that all men are created equal."

I have a dream that one day on the red hills of Georgia, the sons of former slaves and the sons of former slave owners will be able to sit down together at the table of brotherhood.

I have a dream that one day even the state of Mississippi . . . will be transformed into an oasis of freedom and justice.

I have a dream that my four little children will one day live in a nation where they will not be judged by the color of their skin but by the content of their character.

I have a *dream* today.

I have a dream that one day, down in Alabama, . . . one day right there in Alabama little black boys and black girls will be able to join hands with little white boys and white girls as sister and brothers.

This is our hope and this is the faith with which I return to the South.

With this faith we will be able to hew [chop, cut, shape] out of the mountain of despair a stone of hope. With this faith we will be able to transform the jangling discords of our nation into a beautiful symphony of brotherhood . . . .

—this will be the day when all of God's children will be able to sing with new meaning:

"My country 'tis of thee, sweet land of liberty, of thee I sing.

Land where my father died, land of the Pilgrims' pride,

From every mountainside, let freedom ring.". . .

When we allow freedom to ring—when we let it ring from every village and every hamlet [small village], from every state and every city, we will be able to speed up that day when *all* of God's children, black men and white men, Jews and Gentiles [non-Jews], Protestants and Catholics, will be able to join hands and sing in the words of the old Negro spiritual: "Free at last! Free at last!

Thank God Almighty, we are free at last!"

☑ **ANALYZE WORD CHOICES** Why does King envision people of all races and religions to one day be "free at last"? What would they be free from?

☑ ASSESSMENT

1. **Analyze Style and Rhetoric** In his letter from Birmingham Jail, how does King use rhetorical devices to support his argument against racial segregation? Cite specific examples from the text.

2. **Identify Supporting Details** In the letter, what details does King offer to support his main point that racial segregation is unjust?

3. **Analyze Style and Rhetoric** Cite three metaphors in King's speech.

4. **Draw Inferences** Why do you think King singles out three states in his speech? What effect does this have on his overall purpose?

5. **Analyze Style and Rhetoric** Like many powerful phrases, "the American dream" is open to interpretation. Why did King construct his speech around this well-known phrase?

>> African Americans vote in the 1964 presidential election in New York City. In the South, however, it was much more difficult for African Americans to vote.

Bounce to Activate Flipped Video

8.3 During the 1950s and 1960s, the civil rights movement made great strides forward. Yet racial injustice was not fully eradicated. Frustration with this situation led some African Americans to turn to more radical and sometimes violent methods. African Americans achieved further successes, but for some the radicalism of the times left a bitter legacy.

>> **Objectives**

Explain the significance of Freedom Summer, the march on Selma, and why violence erupted in some American cities in the 1960s.

Compare and contrast the goals and approaches taken by African American leaders to expand political rights and economic opportunities.

Describe the social and economic situation of African Americans by 1975.

>> **Key Terms**

Freedom Summer
Voting Rights Act
Twenty-fourth
 Amendment
Kerner Commission
Malcolm X
Nation of Islam
black power
Black Panthers
Lester Maddox
affirmative action

Successes and Setbacks

Increasing Participation in the Political Process

None of the federal court decisions or civil rights measures passed through 1964 fundamentally affected the right to vote. The problem was a southern political system that used literacy tests, poll taxes, and intimidation to keep blacks from voting.

In Mississippi, in 1964, for instance, not a single African American person was registered to vote in five counties that had African American majorities. All of the major civil rights organizations sought to overcome these political injustices.

SNCC and Political Rights SNCC had spent several years organizing voter education projects in Mississippi. It met with little success and a great deal of violent opposition. But in 1964, it decided to get more directly involved in the political process. It called for a major campaign, known as **Freedom Summer**. About 1,000 volunteers, mostly black and white students, were to flood Mississippi to register African Americans to vote. They also formed the Mississippi Freedom Democratic Party (MFDP), an alternative to Mississippi's all-white regular Democratic Party, to give African Americans a voice in state politics. Fannie Lou Hamer, who had helped organize the Freedom Summer campaign, was elected vice-chair of the party.

Even before most of the Freedom Summer volunteers had arrived, three civil rights workers—Michael Schwerner, James Chaney, and Andrew Goodman—disappeared. SNCC claimed that they were murdered; state authorities denied these charges.

President Johnson ordered a massive search for the three, which ended when their bodies were found buried in an earthen dam. All had been shot at point-blank range. Yet, despite the obvious dangers, almost all of the other volunteers remained in the state.

Work of Political Organizations After Freedom Summer ended in August 1964, an MFDP delegation traveled to the Democratic Convention in New Jersey, seeking to be recognized as Mississippi's only Democratic Party. At the convention, Fannie Lou Hamer, one of the MFDP's leaders, gave powerful testimony. She described how she and other activists had been beaten, fired from their jobs, and displaced from their homes all because, as she put it, they wanted "to register" and "live as decent human beings."

Despite Hamer's testimony, the Democrats refused to seat the MFDP. Instead, party officials offered a compromise: they would seat two MFDP members as "at-large delegates" and reform the nomination rules to guarantee greater minority representation in the future. The MFDP rejected this offer. Ironically, Mississippi's regular Democratic delegation left the convention in protest because the national party had made the offer to the MFDP.

Martin Luther King, Jr., Leads the March on Selma Early in 1965, Martin Luther King, Jr., and the SCLC organized a major campaign in Selma, Alabama, to pressure the federal government to enact voting rights legislation. The protests climaxed in a series of confrontations on the Edmund Pettus Bridge, on the main route from Selma to Montgomery. The first of these confrontations took place on March 7, 1965, a day that became known as "Bloody Sunday." Heavily armed state troopers and other authorities attacked the marchers as they tried to cross the bridge. Sheyann Webb, a six-year-old girl at the time, recalled the scene:

> I heard all of this screaming and . . . somebody yelled, 'Oh God, they're killing us!' . . . And I looked and I saw the troopers charging us . . . swinging their arms and throwing canisters of tear gas. . . . Some of them had clubs

Civil Rights Organizations

ORGANIZATION AND DATE FOUNDED	KEY PEOPLE	KEY FEATURES
National Association for the Advancement of Colored People (NAACP) 1909	Thurgood Marshall	Focused on legal cases to end segregation and gain legal equality
Nation of Islam 1930	Elijah Muhammad Malcolm X	Advocated separation of the races
Congress of Racial Equality (CORE) 1942	James Farmer	Organized peaceful protests to gain civil rights
Southern Christian Leadership Conference (SCLC) 1957	Martin Luther King, Jr. Ralph Abernathy	Church-based group dedicated to nonviolent resistance; organized demonstrations and protest campaigns
Student Nonviolent Coordinating Committee (SNCC) 1960	James Lawson Ella Baker Stokely Carmichael	Grass-roots movement of young activists; organized voter education projects in the South
Black Panther Party 1966	Huey Newton Bobby Seale	Militant group advocating armed confrontation; organized antipoverty campaigns

>> **Analyze Charts** What do you think are the strengths and weaknesses of each organization's approach to gaining civil rights for African Americans?

and others had ropes and whips. . . . It was like a nightmare. . . . I just knew then that I was going to die.

—Sheyann Webb, *Selma, Lord, Selma*, 1980

Webb survived, but the rampage continued. Television coverage of the violence outraged the nation. On March 15, President Johnson went on national television and called for a strong federal voting rights law. Historically, regulation of voting rights had been left to the states, but Johnson argued that "it is wrong to deny any of your fellow citizens the right to vote." He added, "Their cause is our cause too, because it is not just Negroes, but really it is all of us, who must overcome the crippling legacy of bigotry and injustice. And *we shall overcome.*"

Voting Rights Act of 1965 Spurred by the actions of protesters, lobbying by the Washington bureau of the NAACP, and the words of the President, Congress passed the **Voting Rights Act** of 1965. The act banned literacy tests and empowered the federal government to oversee voting registration and elections in states that had discriminated against minorities. In 1975, Congress extended coverage to Hispanic voters in the Southwest.

Some legislation laid the groundwork for the Voting Rights Act. One such legal landmark was the **Twenty-fourth Amendment** to the Constitution, ratified in 1964. It banned the poll tax, which had been used to keep poor African Americans from voting. Also, in response to litigation, the federal courts handed down several important decisions that expanded the right to participate in the democratic process. *Baker* v. *Carr* and *Reynolds* v. *Simms* limited racial gerrymandering, the practice of drawing election districts in such a way as to dilute the African American vote, and established the legal principle of "one man, one vote." In 1973, the Supreme Court further challenged racial gerrymandering in *White* v. *Regester*.

These laws and decisions had a profound impact. Particularly in the Deep South, African American participation in politics skyrocketed. In Mississippi, the percentage of African Americans registered to vote jumped from just under 7 percent in 1964 to about 70 percent in 1986. Nationwide, the number of African American elected officials rose from fewer than 100 to more than 6,000 by the mid-1980s.

☑ **IDENTIFY CAUSE AND EFFECT** What impact did the protests in Selma, Alabama, have on the nation?

>> **Analyze Data** In which state did African Americans make the most gains in voter registration? Do you believe it's more important for African Americans to increase their representation in Congress, or in state government?

Violence Troubles Civil Rights Efforts

Many celebrated the passage of the Voting Rights Act of 1965. Yet for some African Americans, things had not changed much. In many urban areas, there was anger and frustration over continuing discrimination and poverty. That anger exploded into violence in several cities.

Disorder in the Cities Less than a week after Johnson signed the Voting Rights Act, one of the worst race riots in American history erupted in the predominantly African American neighborhood of Watts in Los Angeles. Violence, looting, and arson spread for several days before National Guard troops restored order.

Watts was one of many race riots that erupted in the 1960s. The worst violence occurred in Newark, New Jersey, and Detroit, Michigan, in the summer of 1967. In Detroit, 43 people died, and property damage reached $50 million. The outbursts frightened many white Americans.

In most previous race riots, whites had used violence to keep African Americans "in their place." But now, blacks were using violence against police and white business owners in black neighborhoods.

Investigating the Race Riots To determine the causes of the riots, President Johnson established the National Advisory Commission on Civil Disorders, known as the **Kerner Commission**. It concluded that long-term racial discrimination stood as the single most important cause of violence. The commission also recommended establishing and expanding federal programs aimed at overcoming the problems of America's urban ghettos.

> Our nation is moving toward two societies, one black, one white, separate and unequal. . . . Segregation and poverty have created the racial ghetto and a destructive environment totally unknown to most Americans.

—National Advisory Commission on Civil Disorders, *Report*, 1967

The Kerner Commission's findings proved highly controversial. A number of conservative commentators argued against expanding federal spending.

>> During the 1960s, race riots, like this one in Detroit, often left significant parts of largely African American neighborhoods burned out or otherwise destroyed.

Bounce to Activate Map

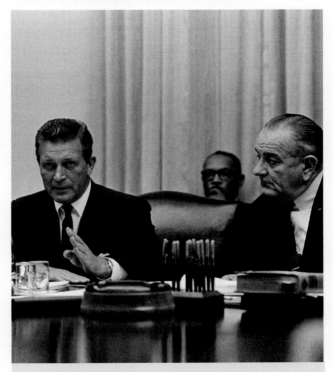

>> Conservative critics argued that the Kerner Commission did not satisfactorily explain why the riots occurred.

>> Malcolm X speaks to a crowd at the Unity Rally in Harlem, New York City, on June 29, 1963. He drew criticism from many civil rights activists for his belief that the races should be separated.

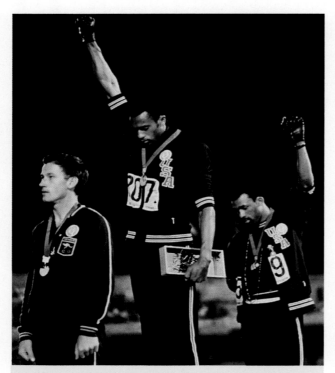

>> At the 1968 Summer Olympic Games, U.S. athletes Tommie Smith, center, and John Carlos, right, raise their gloved fists to show their support for the black-power movement.

They said that this amounted to rewarding the rioters. Others noted that the black-white split that the report described ignored other minorities.

President Johnson did not follow up on the commission's recommendations, largely because the Vietnam War was consuming enormous sums of federal money. The riots also fueled a white backlash. Many whites opposed further reforms. However, the private sector stepped in to create economic opportunities for citizens. In 1967, the life insurance industry formed an Urban Problems Committee of CEOs who created a "Billion Dollar Urban Investment Program" to provide investments for low- and moderate- income housing and job-creating enterprises in poor urban areas.

☑ **RECALL** Why was the Kerner Commission formed?

New Civil Rights Groups

The racial rioting of the mid-1960s coincided with the radicalization of many African Americans, particularly young urban African Americans. Rather than advocating nonviolence and integration, they called for another approach.

Malcolm X Offers a Different Vision The most well-known African American radical was **Malcolm X**, who was born Malcolm Little in Omaha, Nebraska, in 1925. He adopted the X to represent his lost African name. Little, he argued, was his slave name. Malcolm had a difficult childhood. In his teens, he moved to Boston and then to New York City, where he became involved in drugs and crime and landed in prison on burglary charges at age 21.

While in prison, Malcolm became a convert to the **Nation of Islam**, a religious sect headed by Elijah Muhammad. The group prescribed strict rules of behavior, including no drugs or alcohol, and demanded a separation of the races.

After his release from prison, Malcolm became the Nation of Islam's most prominent minister. In this role, he preached a message of self-reliance and self-protection. He called for black pride and spread the idea of black nationalism, a belief in the separate identity and racial unity of the African American community. Malcolm was a "charismatic speaker who could play an audience as great musicians play instruments." His dynamic speeches won many adherents to his cause.

In 1964, Malcolm X broke away from the Nation of Islam and formed his own organization. He then made a pilgrimage to Mecca, the holy city of Islam, afterward adopting the religious name el-Hajj Malik el-Shabazz. Returning to the United States, he seemed willing to consider limited acceptance of whites. In February 1965, however, Malcolm X was shot and killed. Three members of the Nation of Islam were convicted of the murder.

The "Black Power" Movement Many young African Americans saw themselves as heirs of the radical Malcolm X. They began to move away from the principle of nonviolence. They also began to question the goal of integration. As SNCC leader Stokely Carmichael put it:

> Integration . . . has been based on complete acceptance of the fact that in order to have a decent house or education, blacks must move into a white neighborhood or send their children to a white school. This reinforces the notion . . . that 'white' is automatically better and 'black' is by definition inferior.

—Stokely Carmichael, "What We Want," 1966

Carmichael first used the term **"black power"** in 1966. In that year, James Meredith had set off on a "March Against Fear" across the state of Mississippi to encourage African Americans to register and vote. Meredith traveled only 20 miles before he was shot and left for dead by a white supremacist. SNCC, CORE, and SCLC members vowed to continue the march.

When they reached Greenwood, Mississippi, Carmichael and some other marchers were arrested. After his release, Carmichael told a crowd that African Americans needed "black power."

He later said that black power meant African Americans should collectively use their economic and political muscle to gain equality. Yet many white Americans felt threatened. They believed that black power meant black violence.

The Black Panthers' Approach Not long after Carmichael's "black power" speech, Huey Newton and Bobby Seale formed the Black Panther Party in Oakland, California. Almost overnight, the **Black Panthers** became the symbol of young militant African Americans. The Black Panthers organized armed patrols of urban neighborhoods to protect people from police abuse. They also created antipoverty programs, such as free breakfasts for

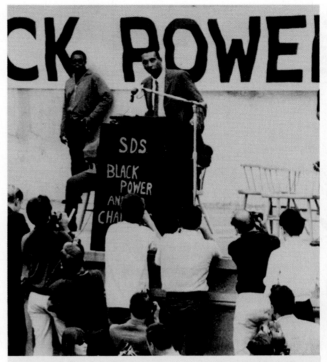

>> At the University of California at Berkeley, Stokely Carmichael advocated combining the economic, social, and political power of African Americans to achieve civil rights.

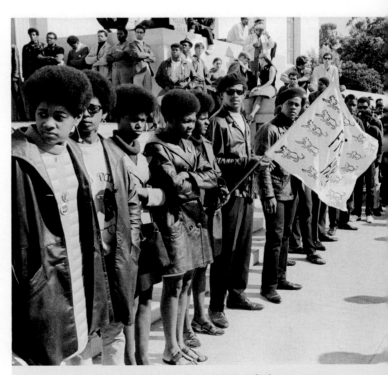

>> Members and sympathizers demonstrate their support for Black Panther leader Huey Newton as he stands trial for the murder of an Oakland police officer in Alameda County, California.

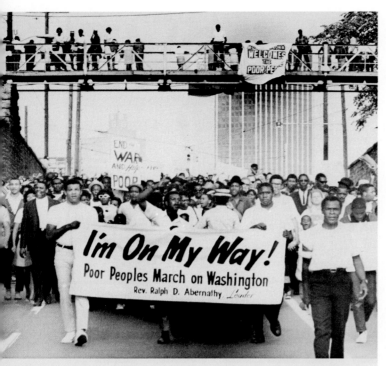

>> Poor People's Campaign members march through Atlanta on May 10, 1968, to promote economic justice. **Draw Conclusions** How did the goal of this march differ from previous civil rights demonstrations?

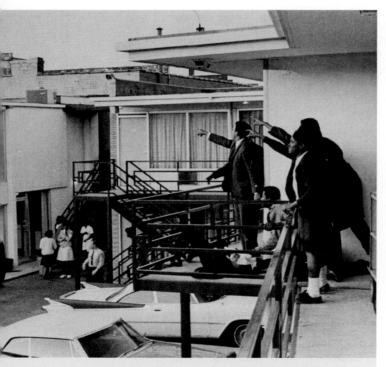

>> Civil rights activists at the Lorraine Motel in Memphis point toward the sniper's position moments after Dr. Martin Luther King, Jr., was shot by an assassin.

poor African American children. The Black Panthers gained national attention when they entered the state capitol in Sacramento carrying shotguns and wearing black leather jackets and berets to protest attempts to restrict their right to bear arms.

The Panthers' style appealed to many young African Americans, who began to wear their hair in "Afros" and to refer to themselves as "black" rather than "Negro" or "colored."

Some, following the lead of Malcolm X, changed their name and celebrated their African heritage. At the same time, the Panthers' militancy often led to violent confrontations with police. Each side accused the other of instigating the violence.

☑ **EXPLAIN** What effect did Malcom X have on the civil rights movement?

King Expands His Dream

Martin Luther King understood the anger and frustration of many urban African Americans whose lives had changed little despite the civil rights reforms of the 1960s. However, he disagreed with the call for "black power" and sought a nonviolent alternative to combat economic injustice.

After spending about a year in Chicago's slums to protest conditions there, King made plans for a massive "Poor People's Campaign." The campaign's goal was to broaden civil rights' goals to address economic inequality in America.

King's Assassination: A Turning Point As part of this effort, King journeyed to Memphis, Tennessee, in early April 1968. There, he offered his assistance to sanitation workers who were striking for better wages and working conditions.

On April 3, King addressed his followers. He referred to threats that had been made against his life. "Like anybody, I would like to live a long life," King declared. "But I'm not concerned about that now. I just want to do God's will."

The following day, as King stood on the balcony outside his motel room, he was struck by a shot from a high-powered rifle. He died at a hospital shortly afterward, at the age of 39. James Earl Ray, a white ex-convict, was later charged with King's murder.

King's assassination marked an important turning point. His efforts had increased minority participation in the political process and encouraged racial integration. Yet much racist hostility persisted. For example, **Lester Maddox**, a restaurant owner in Atlanta, Georgia, gained national attention when

Civil Rights Legislation

Civil Rights Act of 1964	• Banned segregation in public accommodations • Increased federal authority to enforce school desegregation • Outlawed discrimination in employment on basis of race, color, and sex
Twenty-fourth Amendment (1964)	• Eliminated poll tax as voting requirement
Voting Rights Act of 1965	• Banned literacy tests as voting requirement • Empowered the federal government to supervise voter registration and elections
Fair Housing Act of 1968	• Banned discrimination in housing

>> **Analyze Information** Based on the information in the chart, which legislation dealt specifically with voting rights?

he closed his business rather than comply with 1964 Civil Rights Act that banned discrimination against African Americans. Hoping to maintain the status quo, Maddox then ran for and was elected governor of Georgia. After King's assassination, Governor Maddox would not even allow the civil rights leader's body to lie in state in the Georgia state capitol building.

The protests for black freedom and racial equality that began in the mid-1950s crested in the late 1960s around the time of King's death. By then, the civil rights movement had made significant gains. Yet the impact of King's legacy would continue to grow. His messages of political equality and economic opportunity for all continue to define political discourse to this day.

Robert F. Kennedy Responds Robert F. Kennedy was campaigning for the presidency in Indianapolis when he heard of King's death. RFK stopped his campaign speech to give the audience the sad news. He reminded them that he had lost his own brother to an assassin's bullet. Kennedy asked those assembled to honor King's memory by replacing their anger and desire for revenge "with an effort to understand with compassion and love." Despite Kennedy's plea, riots broke out in hundreds of cities after King's assassination. Two months later, Robert Kennedy's life, too, was cut short by an assassin.

☑ **CHECK UNDERSTANDING** Why did King go to Memphis in 1968?

Results of the Civil Rights Movement

The civil rights movement of the 1950s and 1960s succeeded in eliminating legal, or de jure, segregation and knocking down barriers to African American voting and participation in the political process. During the same period, African American poverty rates fell and the median income of African American men and women rose rapidly, as did the number of African Americans who graduated from high school.

One symbol of the progress that had been made was the appointment of Thurgood Marshall as the first African American Supreme Court Justice in 1967. The following year, in the wake of King's murder, Congress passed one final civil rights measure, the Fair Housing Act, which banned discrimination in housing. Yet, in spite of these efforts to create economic opportunity, the social and economic gap between many blacks and whites remained. New measures aimed at closing this gap tended to provoke more controversy than consensus in America.

Controversies over Busing and Affirmative Action Attempts to increase economic opportunities for African Americans and to integrate neighborhoods and schools encountered great difficulties. To achieve desegregated schools, the federal courts had ordered the use of forced busing. Richard Nixon, who succeeded Lyndon Johnson as

>> African American poll watchers observe voters in Tuskegee, Alabama, on May 31, 1966. **Hypothesize** Why were poll watchers present during voting?

president, criticized busing as a means of attaining racial balance.

At the same time, the Nixon administration formally established **affirmative action** as a means of closing the economic gap between blacks and whites. In a short period of time, colleges and universities, businesses, and local and state governments followed the federal government's lead and implemented their own affirmative action plans to increase African American representation in schools and the workforce. In 1978, the Supreme Court, in its University of *California* v. *Bakke* decision, ruled that race could be taken into account when admitting students to college. However, the court also ruled that specific racial quotas were not allowed.

Affirmative action proved controversial almost from the start. Some whites argued that it constituted reverse discrimination and violated the goal of creating a colorblind society. Justice Thurgood Marshall disagreed. "Three hundred and fifty years ago, the Negro was dragged to this country in chains to be sold into slavery," Marshall wrote. "The position of the Negro today in America is the tragic but inevitable consequence of centuries of unequal treatment." Until the nation addressed the legacy of this unequal treatment, Marshall asserted,

it would not fulfill its promise of providing equal rights and opportunities to all.

Affirmative action remains divisive. Critics—and even some supporters—contend that the practice has had unintended consequences, sometimes hurting the very people it is intended to help. For example, some studies show that minority students accepted through affirmative action at the nation's most selective universities do not have as high a graduation rate as minority students accepted through the regular admissions process at less selective institutions.

Changes to the Voting Rights Act The Voting Rights Act of 1965 continues to encourage minority participation in the democratic process. Congress has renewed the law four times. Recently, however, the Supreme Court has redefined the scope of the Act's provisions. In 1993, the Court ruled that the first district in North Carolina to elect an African American to Congress was shaped in a way that violated the rights of white voters. In 2013, the Court severely weakened the heart of the act, Section 5, which empowered the federal government to oversee election practices in states where voting rights are at risk. In a 5-4 decision, the Court released nine states, seven of them in the South, from federal supervision. The ruling cited the gains those states had made since 1965 in black voter registration as rationale for the decision.

☑ **LIST** What gains had the civil rights movement made by the early 1970s?

☑ ASSESSMENT

1. **Generate Explanations** Explain how Martin Luther King, Jr.'s assassination marked a turning point for the civil rights movement.

2. **Compare Points of View** Discuss the reasoning behind affirmative action, and compare it with criticisms of the policy.

3. **Sequence Events** Describe the events that led to President Johnson's call for federal voting legislation in 1965.

4. **Compare and Contrast** the efforts of Martin Luther King, Jr., and the Black Panthers to reform economic injustice.

5. **Draw Conclusions** Discuss the conclusions of the Kerner Commission, and explain why many people found it controversial.

The civil rights movement had begun gaining momentum in the 1950s, when President Dwight Eisenhower was presiding over a time of peace and prosperity. But even during this optimistic Eisenhower era, there were a number of issues that caused Americans grave concern. The launch of *Sputnik 1* showed that the rivalry between the United States and the Soviet Union was still intense. The U-2 spy plane incident demonstrated that the Cold War might heat up at a moment's notice. Deep, unsettled problems remained—problems for a new decade and a new generation of political leadership.

>> President Kennedy and First Lady Jacqueline Kennedy brought youthful energy and glamour to the White House.

 Bounce to Activate Flipped Video

Kennedy's Reforms

The Torch is Passed to a New Generation

Kennedy Versus Nixon In the presidential election of 1960, Democrat **John F. Kennedy** and Republican **Richard M. Nixon** were quite similar in a variety of ways. For the first time in U.S. history, both candidates had been born in the twentieth century, Nixon in 1913 and Kennedy in 1917. Both had served in the navy during World War II. Both had been elected to Congress in 1946 and to the Senate in the early 1950s. Both were passionate about foreign affairs and supported the Cold War fight against communism. Young and energetic, intelligent and hardworking, both wanted to be the first of their generation to lead the country.

Their differences, however, were as significant as their similarities. Kennedy was the son of a wealthy Boston businessman. His grandfather had been a state senator, and his father had served as the ambassador to Great Britain. Kennedy attended Harvard University. Although he was a Catholic and his religion was an issue in the election, he insisted that what church he attended should not be a factor.

Nixon, born in California, did not enjoy the advantages of a wealthy upbringing. His father struggled to make a living. As a

>> Objectives

Discuss the election of 1960.

Evaluate Kennedy's domestic policies.

Assess the impact of Kennedy's assassination.

>> Key Terms

New Frontier
Equal Pay Act
deficit spending
space race
Warren Commission
John F. Kennedy
Richard M. Nixon

young man, Nixon had to balance his time between his school studies and work to help support the family. Many voters, however, respected him for his experiences as Vice President under Eisenhower.

Television Influences Voter Opinion The 1960 election highlighted the growing power and influence of television. The candidates agreed to four televised debates. During the campaign, Nixon was hospitalized with a knee infection. After getting out of the hospital, he committed himself to a grueling schedule of public appearances.

By the time of the first debate, held in late September in Chicago and watched by about 70 million people, Nixon looked pale and exhausted. He arrived at the television studio an hour early, but he refused the offer to have makeup applied to hide his newly growing beard. By contrast, Kennedy, tanned from open-air campaigning in California, looked healthy and confident. His relaxed manner, easy charm, and quick sense of humor added to his appeal.

In many ways, the debate boiled down to how the candidates looked and spoke, rather than what they said. Most Americans who listened to the debate on radio believed that Nixon had won. But the larger audience who watched the debate on television concluded that Kennedy was the clear victor. Although Nixon tried to change his image in the later debates, he was unable to significantly alter the country's initial impression of him. Kennedy's "victory" in Chicago proved crucial in the election.

Kennedy Wins a Close Election Kennedy not only looked better on television, but he also demonstrated an ability to react more quickly to unexpected events. For example, several weeks before the election, civil rights leader Martin Luther King. Jr., and a group of African American students were jailed during a protest in Atlanta, Georgia. Nixon said nothing publicly about the episode. Kennedy, however, telephoned King's wife, Coretta Scott King, to voice his concern. He also worked behind the scenes to obtain King's release on bail. Kennedy's actions attracted the strong support of African Americans in the election.

The election of 1960 was the tightest presidential election since 1888. In an election that witnessed the largest voter turnout in the country's history, Kennedy won by less than 120,000 of the 68 million votes cast. His electoral victory was more convincing. He carried enough states to give him 303 electoral votes to Nixon's 219. However, had a few thousand people voted differently in Illinois and Texas, the electoral vote and the election would have gone to Nixon.

☑ **RECALL** How did Kennedy attract strong support among African American voters?

A President's Unique Charisma

Kennedy's determination to change life at home resulted in his domestic agenda, called the New Frontier. Faced with a conservative Congress, Kennedy met with opposition as he fought to turn his vision into a reality. Still, he had some success in making changes in Social Security benefits, dealing with poverty and racial discrimination, and spurring new interest and expectations for the space program.

As John Kennedy showed in his 1960 campaign and in his Inaugural Address, he had a special charm—or charisma—that separated him from other politicians. With his exquisitely tailored clothes, quick smile, and sense of humor, he seemed closer

The Presidential Election of 1960

CANDIDATE	POPULAR VOTE	% POPULAR VOTE	ELECTORAL VOTE	% ELECTORAL VOTE
John Kennedy (Democrat)	34,227,096	49.7	303	56.4
Richard Nixon (Republican)	34,107,646	49.6	219	40.8

>> **Analyze Data** How do the percentages of the electoral vote compare to those of the popular vote?

Bounce to Activate Gallery

to a movie star than to a run-of-the-mill politician. Although he suffered many health problems, he projected youthful health and energy.

He surrounded himself with other distinguished men. Reporters dubbed them "the best and the brightest." They came from some of the country's most prestigious businesses and universities. Robert McNamara, president of Ford Motor Company, agreed to serve as Secretary of Defense. Dean Rusk, president of the Rockefeller Foundation, signed on as Secretary of State. Arthur Schlesinger, Jr., a Pulitzer Prize-winning historian, worked at the White House as a spokesperson for liberal causes and was a source of ideas for the President.

President Kennedy promised Americans that his administration would blaze a "**New Frontier**." The term described Kennedy's proposals to improve the economy, education, healthcare, and civil rights. He also hoped to jump-start the space program. In his nomination acceptance speech on July 15, 1960, in Los Angeles, California, Kennedy said,

> I stand tonight facing west on what was once the last frontier. . . . From the lands that stretch three thousand miles behind me, the pioneers of old gave up their safety, their comforts and sometimes their lives to build a new world here in the West. . . .
>
> But the problems are not all solved and the battles are not all won, and we stand today on the edge of a new frontier—the frontier of the 1960s— the frontier of unknown opportunities and perils—a frontier of unfulfilled hopes and threats.
>
> —John F. Kennedy, July 15, 1960

☑ **IDENTIFY CENTRAL IDEAS** Why did many feel that Kennedy was a different kind of politician?

Domestic Priorities

Early in his presidency, occupied by events in Cuba and Berlin, Kennedy devoted most of his attention to foreign affairs. But by 1963 he had become more concerned about pressing problems at home.

>> President John F. Kennedy discusses the upcoming disarmament talks at Geneva with his top cabinet-level advisers in the White House on March 9, 1962.

>> During the early 1960s, studies found that millions of women working in skilled and technical jobs across the country received lower pay than men doing the same work.

Kennedy was troubled by the high levels of poverty in the United States. *The Other America*, Michael Harrington's bestselling and influential 1962 exposé of poverty in America, shocked Kennedy and many other Americans.

While Kennedy failed to get Congress to accept his more ambitious social programs, he did push through an increase in the minimum wage, an extension in Social Security benefits, and improvements in the welfare system.

In addition, in 1962 Kennedy established the President's Commission on the Status of Women, a blue-ribbon panel that studied how poverty and discrimination affected women. The difference in wages received by men and women for the same work was an especially glaring problem. And as Kennedy pointed out, working women with children "bear the heaviest burden of any group in our Nation." The **Equal Pay Act** (1963) required equal wages for "equal work" in industries engaged in commerce or producing goods for commerce. Although it contained various loopholes, the law was a crucial step on the road to fair and equal employment practices. The next year Congress would prohibit discrimination by employers on the basis of race, color, religion, national origin, or sex.

One Approach to Economic Stimulus Kennedy believed that increased prosperity would help to eliminate some of the nation's social problems. When he became President, the country was suffering from a high unemployment rate and a sluggish economy. To help the economy, Kennedy proposed tax credits to spur business investment in new factory equipment. At the same time, increased military spending created new jobs and boosted the economy.

In addition, Kennedy accepted the "new economics" of theorist John Maynard Keynes that advocated **deficit spending** to stimulate the economy. Deficit spending is the government practice of borrowing money in order to spend more than is received from taxes. In 1963, Kennedy called for dramatic tax cuts for middle-class Americans as a way to put more money in the pockets of more people. At the same time, he increased the tax burden on wealthier citizens. Kennedy's economic initiatives jump-started the tremendous economic growth of the late 1960s.

Cautious Steps toward Civil Rights Kennedy pursued a timid approach toward civil rights. He had narrowly won the 1960 election, and he had little real influence in Congress or even complete partisan support. He did not want to anger conservative, white southern members of Congress in his own party. They stood ready to block any civil rights legislation.

While Kennedy remained largely passive on civil rights issues, African Americans and their white allies challenged segregation in the South. In 1961,

Wage Disparity by Gender, 1960–2010

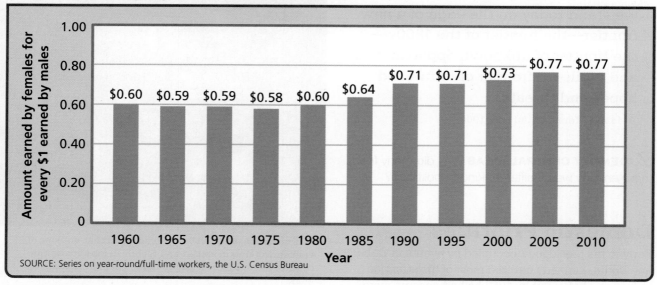

SOURCE: Series on year-round/full-time workers, the U.S. Census Bureau

>> **Analyze Data** Based on the data in the table, how many years did it take for the Equal Pay Act of 1963 to make a significant impact on women's rate of pay as compared to men's?

Key Events in the American Space Program

February 1962
John Glenn is the first American to orbit Earth.

October 1958
NASA is created.

July 1969
Apollo 11 astronauts land on the moon.

January 1986
The *Challenger* space shuttle explodes 73 seconds after takeoff, killing 7 astronauts.

November 2000
The first crew occupies the *International Space Station*.

November 1998
Construction begins on the *International Space Station*.

1950   1960   1970   1980   1990   2000

May 1961
Alan Shepard is the first American to fly in space.

June 1976
Viking 1 transmits images of Mars.

April 1990
Hubble Space Telescope is launched.

January 1967
During training, a space capsule fire kills astronauts Roger Chaffee, Virgil Grissom, and Edward White.

April 1997
Pathfinder lands on Mars.

>> **Analyze Information** Based on the events in the timeline, how did the goals of the space program change over time?

they took "freedom rides" to desegregate interstate bus travel.

In 1963, Martin Luther King, Jr., took the civil rights struggle to Birmingham, Alabama. Such actions took courage and were met by angry, oftentimes violent, responses by white southerners.

In early 1963, Kennedy introduced a civil rights bill that demanded prosecution for voting-rights violations and federal money to aid school desegregation. Further violence in the South prompted Kennedy to introduce stronger civil rights legislation.

First to the Moon The launching of the satellite *Sputnik 1* by the Soviet Union in 1957 called into question American technological superiority. Although Congress created the National Aeronautics and Space Administration (NASA) in 1958, the Soviets' space program remained several steps ahead of the American program. In April 1961, for example, the Soviet cosmonaut Yuri Gagarin became the first human to orbit Earth.

Kennedy recognized that the United States and the Soviet Union were locked in a "**space race**," a competition between the Soviet Union and the United States to develop technology to land on the moon. In May 1961, NASA put astronaut Alan Shepard into a suborbital space flight aboard

the Project Mercury space capsule Freedom 7. Encouraged by the success of Project Mercury, Kennedy committed the United States to landing a man on the moon by 1970.

America's quest to reach the moon was punctuated by enormous successes and heartbreaking failures. Astronaut John Glenn became the first American to orbit Earth in February 1962. But astronauts Virgil Grissom, Edward White, and Roger Chaffee burned to death when their docked capsule exploded in fire during a routine test. Finally, in July 1969, astronaut Neil Armstrong left his spacecraft *Columbia's* landing vehicle and became the first man to step on the moon. The mission was a successful completion of Kennedy's bold dream.

The moon landing in 1969 was a turning point in the space race. Never again would the Soviet Union rival the United States for supremacy in space. In addition, the space program's many innovations improved Americans' quality of life. For example, materials developed for the visors on the moon astronauts' helmets allowed eyeglass manufacturers to replace glass lenses with lighter, scratch-resistant ones. Today's cordless tools use the same technology that astronauts used on the moon. Manufacturers of athletic shoes applied high-tech features found in the astronauts' boots. Memory foam, enriched baby food, and freeze-drying technology are also among

>> President Kennedy and his wife ride with Texas Governor John Connally and his wife in the presidential motorcade through Dallas, Texas, just prior to the President's assassination on November 22, 1963.

maturity was his ability to inspire Americans to dream noble dreams and work toward lofty ends.

In November 1963, Kennedy traveled to Dallas, Texas, to mend political fences for his 1964 reelection bid. He never lived to see 1964. While his motorcade moved through the city, assassin Lee Harvey Oswald, perched by a window on the sixth floor of the Texas School Book Depository, fired three shots at the President. The third shot hit Kennedy in the back of his head. A half hour later, doctors at Parkland Memorial Hospital pronounced him dead.

Texan Lyndon B. Johnson, Kennedy's Vice President, was sworn in as the new President. Although many people would later question whether Oswald acted alone, the **Warren Commission**, which conducted the official investigation of the assassination, described Oswald as the "lone killer."

The senseless murder deeply saddened Americans across the nation. Millions of people watched Kennedy's funeral procession on television, and many reacted as if they had lost a family member. It seemed as if part of America's innocence had died with him.

☑ **DESCRIBE** What was the purpose of the Warren Commission?

the hundreds of ways that space exploration has benefited society and improved the quality of life.

☑ **CHECK UNDERSTANDING** Why did Kennedy change his approach to civil rights issues?

Kennedy Is Assassinated

During his first two and a half years in office, Kennedy made the transition from politician to national leader. In foreign affairs he confronted Soviet challenges, made hard decisions, and won the respect of Soviet leaders and American citizens. He also spoke eloquently about the need to move toward a peaceful future. In domestic affairs he finally came to the conclusion that the federal government had to lead the struggle for civil rights. Added to his new

☑ ASSESSMENT

1. **Compare and Contrast** the backgrounds and political beliefs of John F. Kennedy and Richard M. Nixon.

2. **Generate Explanations** Explain how television influenced the presidential election of 1960.

3. **Summarize** Discuss the accomplishments of the "New Frontier," President Kennedy's domestic policy plan.

4. **Identify Cause and Effect** Discuss the impact that the moon landing of 1969 had on American standards of living and on American foreign relations.

5. **Draw Conclusions** Explain how the United States' economy changed during President Kennedy's term.

Inaugural Address: John F. Kennedy

On January 20, 1961, President John F. Kennedy delivered his inaugural address. Kennedy projected youth and determination in his address. The speech was a call to action for all Americans

>> President Kennedy and First Lady Jacqueline Kennedy

. . . Let the word go forth from this time and place, to friend and foe alike, that the torch has been passed to a new generation of Americans—born in this century, tempered [toughened; strengthened] by war, disciplined by a hard and bitter peace, proud of our ancient heritage—and unwilling to witness or permit the slow undoing of those human rights to which this Nation has always been committed, and to which we are committed today at home and around the world.

☑ **DETERMINE MEANING** Why does Kennedy characterize the post-war period as "a hard and bitter peace"?

Let every nation know, whether it wishes us well or ill, that we shall pay any price, bear any burden, meet any hardship, support any friend, oppose any foe, in order to assure the survival and the success of liberty. . . .

To that world assembly of sovereign states, the United Nations, our last best hope in an age where the instruments of war have far outpaced the instruments of peace, we renew our pledge of support—to prevent it from becoming merely a forum for invective—to strengthen its shield of the new and the weak—and to enlarge the area in which its writ may run.

Finally, to those nations who would make themselves our adversary, we offer not a pledge but a request: that both sides begin anew the quest for peace, before the dark powers of destruction unleashed by science engulf all humanity in planned or accidental self-destruction.

We dare not tempt them with weakness. For only when our arms are sufficient beyond doubt can we be certain beyond doubt that they will never be employed.

But neither can two great and powerful groups of nations take comfort from our present course--both sides overburdened by the cost of modern weapons, both rightly alarmed by the steady spread of the deadly atom, yet both racing to alter that uncertain balance of terror that stays the hand of mankind's final war.

☑ **DETERMINE CENTRAL IDEAS** To what "two great and powerful groups of nations" is Kennedy referring?

So let us begin anew—remembering on both sides that civility is not a sign of weakness, and sincerity is always subject to proof. Let us never negotiate out of fear. But let us never fear to negotiate.

Let both sides explore what problems unite us instead of belaboring those problems which divide us.

Let both sides, for the first time, formulate serious and precise proposals for the inspection and control of arms—and bring the absolute power to destroy other nations under the absolute control of all nations.

Let both sides seek to invoke the wonders of science instead of its terrors. Together let us explore the stars, conquer the deserts, eradicate disease, tap the ocean depths and encourage the arts and commerce.

Let both sides unite to heed in all corners of the earth the command of Isaiah—to "undo the heavy burdens . . . (and) let the oppressed go free."

And if a beach-head of cooperation may push back the jungle of suspicion, let both sides join in creating a new endeavor, not a new balance of power, but a new world of law, where the strong are just and the weak secure and the peace preserved.

All this will not be finished in the first one hundred days. Nor will it be finished in the first one thousand days, nor in the life of this Administration, nor even perhaps in our lifetime on this planet. But let us begin.

In your hands, my fellow citizens, more than mine, will rest the final success or failure of our course. Since this country was founded, each generation of Americans has been summoned to give testimony to its national loyalty. The graves of young Americans who answered the call to service surround the globe.

Now the trumpet summons us again—not as a call to bear arms, though arms we need; not as a call to battle, though embattled we are—but a call to bear the burden of a long twilight struggle, year in and year out, "rejoicing in hope, patient in tribulation [an experience that causes distress or suffering]"—a struggle against the common enemies of man: tyranny, poverty, disease, and war itself. . . .

☑ **CITE EVIDENCE** One phrase in this passage of the speech is quoted from the Bible. Identify the phrase. Why do you think Kennedy included it?

In the long history of the world, only a few generations have been granted the role of defending freedom in its hour of maximum danger. I do not shrink from this responsibility—I welcome it. . . .

And so, my fellow Americans: ask not what your country can do for you—ask what you can do for your country.

My fellow citizens of the world: ask not what America will do for you, but what together we can do for the freedom of man. . . .

☑ **DETERMINE MEANING** What does *shrink* mean in the sense that Kennedy uses it? What is he saying in that sentence?

. . . unwilling to witness or permit the slow undoing of those human rights to which this Nation has always been committed, and to which we are committed today at home and around the world.

☑ **DRAW INFERENCES** What does Kennedy believe is responsible for the undoing of those human rights?

☑ ASSESSMENT

1. **Compare and Contrast** How does Kennedy address America's allies as compared to America's enemies? Cite examples from the speech to support your answer.

2. **Analyze Style and Rhetoric** What phrases from this address have you heard before? Why are they so memorable?

8.5 Lyndon B. Johnson, who became President after Kennedy's assassination, shared the same goals as his predecessor. These goals shaped the purpose of Johnson's Great Society program. A seasoned politician, Johnson successfully pushed through significant domestic legislation that he hoped would become the first step to achieving the quality of life he thought all Americans should enjoy.

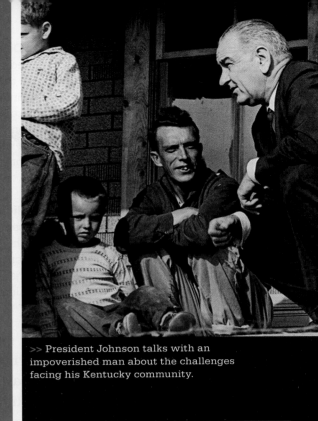

>> President Johnson talks with an impoverished man about the challenges facing his Kentucky community.

Bounce to Activate Flipped Video

Reform Under Johnson

Johnson's Path to the Presidency

Born in Stonewall, Texas, Lyndon B. Johnson was raised in the Hill Country town of Johnson City. He attended Southwest Texas State College and then taught for several years in Cotulla, Texas. There, at a tiny segregated school for Mexican Americans, he confronted firsthand the challenges faced by poverty-stricken minority students, and the lessons he learned remained with him for the rest of his life.

An Influential Legislator After teaching for several years, Johnson entered politics—first as a Texas congressman's secretary and then as the head of the Texas National Youth Administration.

In 1937, Johnson was elected to Congress, and during the next several decades he became the most powerful person on Capitol Hill. Elected to the Senate in 1948, Johnson proved himself a master of party politics and rose to the position of Senate majority leader in 1955. In the Senate, he was adept at avoiding conflict, building political coalitions, and working out compromises. His skill was instrumental in pushing the 1957 Civil Rights Act through Congress.

>> **Objectives**

Evaluate Johnson's policies up to his victory in the 1964 presidential election.

Analyze Johnson's goals and actions as seen in his Great Society programs.

Assess the achievements of the Great Society in creating economic opportunities for citizens.

Analyze the effects of U.S. Supreme Court decisions.

>> **Key Terms**

Civil Rights Act
War on Poverty
Economic
  Opportunity Act
Great Society
Medicare
Medicaid
Immigration and
  Nationality Act of
  1965
Warren Court
Barry Goldwater
Tinker v. Des Moines
  School District
judicial interpretation

In 1960, he hoped to be chosen by the Democratic Party to run for President, but when Kennedy got the nomination Johnson agreed to join him on the ticket as the vice presidential nominee. A New Englander and a Catholic, Kennedy needed Johnson to help carry the heavily Protestant South. Johnson was also popular both with Mexican American voters and in the Southwest. He was an important part of Kennedy's victory in 1960.

Continuing Kennedy's Civil Rights Policies On becoming President after Kennedy's assassination, Johnson radiated reassurance and strength. His every action indicated that he was ready for the job and that the government was in good hands. Less than a week after the assassination, Johnson addressed a joint session of Congress.

> . . . [N]o memorial oration or eulogy could more eloquently honor President Kennedy's memory than the earliest possible passage of the Civil Rights Bill for which he fought so long.

—President Johnson, Speech before a Joint Session of Congress, 1963

With Johnson's ability to build consensus, or agreement on an issue by a group, the **Civil Rights Act** became law in the summer of 1964. It outlawed discrimination in voting, education, and public accommodations. The act demanded an end to discrimination in hospitals, restaurants, theaters, and other places open to the public. It also created the Equal Employment Opportunity Commission to fight discrimination in hiring.

African Americans and Mexican Americans who faced almost daily discrimination benefited immeasurably from the legislation. Finally, Title VII of the 1964 Civil Rights Act prohibited discrimination on the basis of sex.

The Fight to Expand Economic Opportunity Johnson made his intentions clear in his first State of the Union address when he said it was time to "declare an unconditional war on poverty." The new President planned to fuse his own dreams for America onto Kennedy's legislative agenda. Although Kennedy had failed to get Congress to approve his tax bill calling for dramatic tax cuts for middle-class Americans, Johnson was able to maneuver it through. In addition, he had added a billion-dollar **War on Poverty** to the bill.

Johnson's War on Poverty introduced measures to train the jobless, educate the uneducated, and

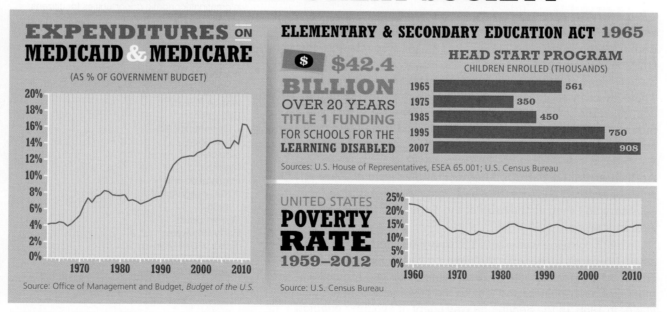

LEGACY OF THE GREAT SOCIETY

EXPENDITURES ON MEDICAID & MEDICARE
(AS % OF GOVERNMENT BUDGET)

Source: Office of Management and Budget, *Budget of the U.S.*

ELEMENTARY & SECONDARY EDUCATION ACT 1965

$ $42.4 BILLION OVER 20 YEARS TITLE 1 FUNDING FOR SCHOOLS FOR THE **LEARNING DISABLED**

HEAD START PROGRAM
CHILDREN ENROLLED (THOUSANDS)

Year	Children (thousands)
1965	561
1975	350
1985	450
1995	750
2007	908

Sources: U.S. House of Representatives, ESEA 65.001; U.S. Census Bureau

UNITED STATES POVERTY RATE 1959–2012

Source: U.S. Census Bureau

>> **Analyze Information** Use information from the chart to evaluate the effects of the Great Society on U.S. poverty levels over time. Do you think the programs were a success? Why or why not?

Bounce to Activate Chart

provide healthcare for those in need. The 1964 **Economic Opportunity Act** created the Job Corps to train young men and women between the ages of 16 and 21 in the work skills they needed to acquire better jobs and move out of poverty.

The act also established Volunteers in Service to America, or VISTA, patterned after Kennedy's Peace Corps, which sent American volunteers into poverty-stricken American communities in an effort to solve the country's pressing economic, educational, and medical problems. The volunteers served in inner city schools and on Indian reservations. They worked in rural health clinics and urban hospitals.

Perhaps the most successful element of the Economic Opportunity Act was the Head Start program. Funds were provided for play groups, day care, and activities designed to help underprivileged children get ready for elementary school. Head Start enjoyed bipartisan support for decades.

Johnson Defeats a Conservative Challenger

If Johnson was to continue his War on Poverty and other social goals, he needed to win the 1964 presidential election. In that year, the Republicans nominated Arizona senator **Barry Goldwater**, whose economic and social views were directly opposed to Johnson's.

Whereas Johnson believed the federal government could best regulate the economy and promote social justice, Goldwater maintained that the federal government was the problem, not the solution. According to Goldwater, social and economic issues, such as racism and poverty, should not be addressed by the federal government.

Goldwater promised to rein in the federal government by reducing its size and restricting its activities. He favored significant tax cuts and right-to-work laws, and he opposed social welfare legislation and government spending on educational, public housing, and urban renewal programs.

In 1964, most Americans were not ready for Goldwater's conservative message. In addition, Johnson's campaign portrayed Goldwater as an extremist, suggesting that his election would ensure the repeal of civil rights legislation and economic ruin.

Johnson had prosperity on his side, as well as his own impressive legislative record and the legacy of Kennedy. In the November election, he won a landslide victory, capturing more than 60 percent of the popular vote and carrying all but six states.

Goldwater carried only Arizona and five southern states— Louisiana, Mississippi, Alabama, Georgia, and South Carolina. Furthermore, the outcome of

>> Barry Goldwater, the Republican nominee for President in 1964, strongly opposed the use of federal resources to address social issues.

the election was significant. The South was no longer solidly Democrat. Not only had Johnson won a ringing victory, but Democrats had captured both houses of Congress.

Although Goldwater suffered a crushing political defeat in 1964, his conservative ideas resonated with many. Support for Goldwater's message remained strong in parts of California, propelling Ronald Reagan to the governor's office in 1966. When a conservative tide swept Reagan into the White House in 1981, Goldwater regained some influence and continued to be a strong voice on behalf of modern American conservatives.

☑ **RECALL** How did Johnson continue Kennedy's plan to eliminate poverty in the United States?

Creating the Great Society

In the spring of 1964, in a speech at the University of Michigan, Johnson outlined his vision for America, calling it the **Great Society**. He said that during the past hundred years, Americans had spread across the continent, developed industrially, and created great wealth. But the work of America was not complete. He added,

> The challenge of the next half century is whether we have the wisdom to use that wealth to enrich and elevate our national life, and to advance the quality of our American civilization. . . .
>
> [W]e have the opportunity to move not only toward the rich society and the powerful society, but upward to the Great Society.

—President Johnson, University of Michigan, May 22, 1964

For Johnson, the Great Society demanded "an end to poverty and racial injustice" and opportunity for every child.

Increasing Access to Healthcare In the first half of 1965, Congress passed parts of Johnson's Great Society legislation. Kennedy had supported similar legislation that failed to win congressional support.

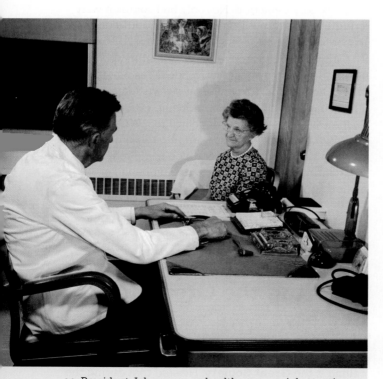

>> President Johnson gave healthcare special attention. With Medicare and Medicaid, more Americans would be able to receive basic healthcare.

Johnson's agenda amended the Social Security Act by adding the Medical Care for the Aged Program, or **Medicare**, as it was more popularly called. Medicare provided basic health insurance for Americans in the Social Security system who were age 65 and older. It was funded by a new tax on workers' earnings and by payments from the Social Security benefits of retirees.

The new law also included a **Medicaid** feature that provided basic medical services to poor and disabled Americans who were not part of the Social Security system. Johnson signed the bill into law in Independence, Missouri, home of former President Harry Truman, who had called for a national health insurance program almost 20 years earlier.

When the Social Security Act was amended, few questions were raised about how programs like Medicare and Medicaid would be paid for in the years to come. Medicare has become increasingly expensive as medical costs have risen, the percent of retirees in the population relative to workers has increased, and because people live longer now than they did in 1965.

Investing in Public Education Along with health, education was one of the centerpieces of the Great Society program. Improved healthcare and education were necessary steps toward the goal of ending poverty.

The 1965 Elementary and Secondary Education Act was designed to aid schools in poorer communities. It provided federal funds to improve school libraries, learning centers, language laboratories, and services in impoverished school districts. The act dramatically increased funding for Indian, inner city, and Mexican American schools.

Environmental and Consumer Protection The Great Society program extended to improving the overall quality of American life. In the early 1960s, several best-selling books raised Americans' awareness about environmental and consumer problems. Rachel Carson's *Silent Spring* (1962) detailed how chemical fertilizers and pesticides were damaging the fragile ecosystem. Ralph Nader's *Unsafe at Any Speed* (1965) attacked the automotive industry for its lack of concern for passenger safety.

Both these books helped to foster environmental and consumer activity and led to several important pieces of legislation. The National Traffic and Motor Vehicle Safety Act (1966) established safety standards for automotive vehicles and created the National Highway Traffic Safety Administration to administer them. The Water Quality Act (1965),

U.S. Immigration and the Immigration and Nationality Act of 1965

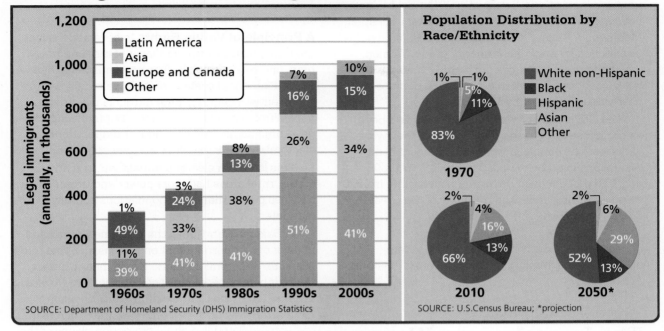

SOURCE: Department of Homeland Security (DHS) Immigration Statistics

SOURCE: U.S.Census Bureau; *projection

>> **Analyze Charts** Based on the data in the pie charts, which ethnic group is projected to grow the most by 2050?

the Clean Water Restoration Act (1966), and the Air Quality Act (1967) aimed at improving water and air standards in the country. The U.S. Public Health Service was empowered to enforce air quality standards, but dealing with water pollution was largely left to the states. Not until the Environmental Protection Agency was created in 1970 did the federal government gain significant regulatory power to protect the environment.

Less Restrictive Immigration Policies

Meanwhile, the civil rights movement was raising questions about America's long-standing immigration policy. The National Origins Acts of 1921 and 1924 had established a quota system that favored Western European immigrants and limited immigrants from other parts of the world. Such a discriminatory policy was clearly out of touch with the mood of the country in the early 1960s.

The **Immigration and Nationality Act of 1965** altered the quota system. Nearly 170,000 immigrants from the Eastern Hemisphere were allowed into the country. Nearly 120,000 immigrants from the Western Hemisphere were welcomed. Although family reunification was emphasized, same-sex partners of U.S. citizens were rejected. Immigrants from Latin America, Central America, the Caribbean, and Asia soon began to pour into the

United States, providing the country with a pool of ideas, talent, and skills.

The doors of America were once again open to immigrants from around the world. During the 1960s and 1970s, millions of immigrants would arrive on American shores. Like earlier immigrants, many came seeking economic opportunity. Others were fleeing war or social unrest or were in search of political or religious freedom. As in the late nineteenth and early twentieth centuries, New York and the urban East and West coasts attracted many of the country's newest immigrants.

The Legacy of the Great Society Although critics said that Great Society programs did not work, many point out that these programs have improved the lives of millions of individual Americans. Poverty and infant mortality rates declined. Medicare and Medicaid delivered needed healthcare to millions of elderly and poor Americans. Head Start and other antipoverty programs provided the educational tools many underprivileged Americans needed to escape poverty. Congress also provided artists and scholars with assistance through the National Endowment for the Arts and Humanities, created in 1965.

The better future that the Great Society envisioned inspired many Americans, including women and minorities, to take action to expand their economic opportunities. Latino farm workers formed a union and organized national boycotts of farm products to win better wages. Latino students boycotted their schools to demand better education. Meanwhile, Asian Americans made economic gains unmatched by any other minority group. Women, too, made great advances during this time. By 1970 the percentage of women with college degrees was nearly double what it had been in 1950.

The Great Society victories may not have been as grandiose as Johnson predicted, but they were victories. The simple fact that 22.2 percent of all Americans lived below the poverty line in 1960 and 12.6 percent lived below the poverty line in 1970 says something about the triumphs of the Great Society.

☑ **IDENTIFY** Which immigrant groups were affected by the Immigration and Nationality Reform Act of 1965?

The Impact of the Warren Court

During the 1960s, the Supreme Court demonstrated a willingness to take the lead on controversial social, religious, and political issues. Led by Chief Justice Earl Warren, the Supreme Court at this time—often called the **Warren Court**—became the most liberal in American history. Its decisions supported civil

rights, civil liberties, voting rights, and personal privacy.

A Principle of Voting Rights In several decisions the Supreme Court ruled in favor of the "one man, one vote" principle. The problem was one of apportionment of seats in state legislatures. During the twentieth century, large numbers of voters moved from rural to urban areas, but many state governments had not changed, or reapportioned, electoral districts to reflect the new conditions.

This led to an electoral imbalance. In many states, rural areas had more power and urban areas had less power than their populations actually mandated.

In *Baker* v. *Carr* (1962), the Supreme Court ruled in favor of reapportionment on the basis of "one man, one vote." Electoral districts, it said, had to reflect the numbers of people in those districts. In *Reynolds* v. *Sims* (1964), the Court reaffirmed its decision, adding that any arrangement other than "one man, one vote" violated the equal protection clause of the Fourteenth Amendment.

Redefining Civil Rights and Liberties In several decisions, the Warren Court expanded the definition of what constitutes free speech. For example, in **Tinker v. Des Moines School District** (1969), the Court ruled that wearing black armbands in school to protest the Vietnam War was protected as "symbolic" speech. The decision also made it clear that students do not give up all of their rights to free speech while in school.

In the *Tinker* decision, critics complained that the Court interpreted the Constitution too loosely, taking their judicial interpretation of the Constitution too far. The Court applied what critics have called **judicial interpretation** to the Constitution. That is, the Justices expanded the Constitution's meaning beyond the framers' original intent. In this case, the Court expanded the definition of free speech to include more than the spoken word. A narrow, or strict, construction of the First Amendment would have protected only actual speech.

The Warren Court also showed a heightened concern for the constitutional rights of accused lawbreakers. In four landmark cases, the Court broadened the individual rights of accused criminals and narrowed those of federal, state, and local government officials. In *Mapp* v. *Ohio* (1961), the Court ruled that evidence obtained illegally violated the Fourth Amendment and had to be excluded from federal and state trials. In *Gideon* v. *Wainwright* (1963), the Court decided that all accused criminals

>> The Warren Court issued many landmark rulings in the areas of civil rights, criminal justice, the First Amendment, and legislative districting.

Bounce to Activate Gallery

had the right to a lawyer whether or not they could pay for one.

In *Escobedo* v. *Illinois* (1964), the Warren Court expanded on *Gideon* v. *Wainwright* by adding that every accused lawbreaker had to be offered access to a lawyer before questioning, and all evidence obtained from a suspect who had not been informed of his or her right to a lawyer could not be used in court. Finally, in *Miranda* v. *Arizona* (1966), the Court ruled that an accused criminal had to be informed of his or her Fifth and Sixth Amendment rights before being questioned.

Critics of these decisions argued that the Warren Court had tipped the balance of justice in favor of the rights of accused criminals. Today, many conservative justices still side with this opinion. The majority of the members of the Warren Court, however, countered that the rights of individuals had to be protected, especially when freedom hung in the balance.

Expanding Marriage Rights In 1967, the Warren Court ruled against laws forbidding interracial marriages. In *Loving* v. *Virginia*, the court ruled in favor of Mildred Loving, a black woman, and Richard Loving, a white man, who had both been sentenced to prison for violating Virginia's anti-miscegenation laws by marrying each other. The ruling led to an increase in interracial marriages and eventually helped the legal case in favor of same-sex marriage.

Church and State in the Public Sphere The Warren Court addressed the separation of church and state in the case of *Engel* v. *Vitale* (1962). The case involved whether or not a public school could require students to recite a state-sanctioned prayer. The Court ruled that school prayer was a violation of the First Amendment and an attempt by a governmental body to promote religion. The next year, the Court ruled in *Abington* v. *Schempp* that Bible reading in public schools also violated the First Amendment. The two decisions divided religious groups and the American people. Some welcomed the rulings, saying the government should have no say in personal religious matters. Others insisted the decisions were hostile to religion. The two decisions ignited, and continue to ignite, controversy. For more than 40 years, various religious groups have railed against these decisions.

☑ **IDENTIFY** What major court ruling gave a person accused of a crime the right to have a lawyer?

>> In the years following the *Miranda* v. *Arizona* decision, the reading of a suspect's "Miranda rights" became part of standard police procedure.

☑ ASSESSMENT

1. **Define** What is a strict construction of the Constitution?

2. **Summarize** the policies that President Johnson implemented in order to "declare an unconditional war on poverty."

3. **Compare** President Johnson's success in the civil rights movement with President Kennedy's civil rights achievements.

4. **Generate Explanations** Explain why Lyndon B. Johnson defeated Barry Goldwater in the 1964 presidential election.

5. **Draw Conclusions** Describe the impact that the Warren Court had on the separation of church and state in the United States.

LESSON SUMMARIES

Use these Lesson Summaries, and the longer versions available online, to review the key ideas for each lesson in this Topic.

Lesson 1: The Civil Rights Movement Strengthens

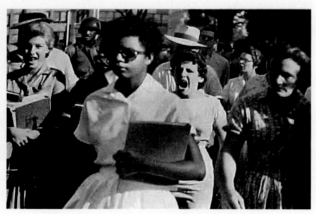

Civil Rights activism strengthened in the 1950s. In Montgomery, Alabama during a bus boycott against segregation, Dr. Martin Luther King called for nonviolent resistance. In Little Rock, Arkansas, federal troops arrived to protect African American students and enforce a Supreme Court decision challenging segregated public education.

Lesson 2: The Movement Surges Forward

Young people launched a surge of civil rights protest in the early 1960s. Sit-ins, freedom rides, and other nonviolent protests swept the nation. A lawsuit helped desegregate the University of Mississippi. In Birmingham Alabama, the police attacked demonstrators. A massive demonstration in Washington D.C. helped pass the Civil Rights Act of 1964.

Lesson 3: Successes and Setbacks

With African Americans prevented from voting in the South, a massive campaign to register voters took place in 1964. In Selma, Alabama, marchers were attacked by state troopers. The nonviolence of the early civil rights movement gave way to more violent protests. Martin Luther King was assassinated, and Congress banned discrimination in housing.

Lesson 4: Kennedy's Reforms

The 1960 presidential election was won by John F. Kennedy, who increased the minimum wage and tried to gain equal pay for women. Kennedy also helped aid school desegregation and strengthened the space program. President Kennedy was assassinated in 1963.

Lesson 5: Reform Under Johnson

Lyndon Johnson, who became President after Kennedy's assassination, continued Kennedy's policies. The Civil Rights Act was passed along with other "Great Society" legislation designed to end poverty and racial injustice. Medicare and Medicaid were created, and the Supreme Court became more liberal in its decisions.

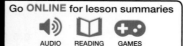

VISUAL REVIEW

Use these graphics to review some of the key terms, people, and ideas from this Topic.

Key Civil Rights Dates

May 1954
Brown v. Board of Education of Topeka case is decided.

Feb. 1960
Greensboro, North Carolina, sit-in.

May 1961
Freedom Rides begin.

Aug. 1963
March on Washington, D.C.

1954 | 1955 | 1956 | 1957 | 1958 | 1959 | 1960 | 1961 | 1962 | 1963 | 1964 | 1965

Dec. 1955
Montgomery Bus Boycott begins.

Sept. 1957
Little Rock Central High School is integrated.

Sept. 1962
James Meredith attempts to enroll at Ole Miss.

July 1964
Civil Rights Act signed into law.

Civil Rights Legislation

Civil Rights Act of 1964	• banned segregation in public accommodations. • increased federal authority to enforce school desegregation. • outlawed discrimination in employment on basis of race, color, and sex.
Twenty-fourth Amendment (1964)	• eliminated poll tax as voting requirement.
Voting Rights Act of 1965	• banned literacy tests as voting requirement. • empowered the federal government to supervise voter registration and elections.
Fair Housing Act of 1968	• banned discrimination in housing.

KEY TERMS, PEOPLE, AND IDEAS

1. What is the difference between **de jure** and **de facto segregation**?

2. What role did **Rosa Parks** play in the civil rights movement?

3. What was the relationship between the **freedom rides** and *Boynton* v. *Virginia*?

4. What recent changes have been made to the **Voting Rights Act** of 1965?

5. What was President Nixon's position on busing and **affirmative action**?

6. How did *Miranda* v. *Arizona* affect the rights of the accused?

7. What measures did President Kennedy take to improve women's rights?

8. What immigration policies were changed in the 1960s?

9. How did President Johnson fund **Medicare**?

CRITICAL THINKING

10. **Draw Inferences** (a.) Why were the nonviolent tactics of Dr. Martin Luther King and the SCLC so effective in influencing public opinion? (b.) What role might television have played in gaining support for the movement?

11. **Draw Conclusions** (a.) Why were young people of all races so active in the protests of the civil rights movement? (b.) Evaluate the success of this kind of coalition.

12. **Find the Main Idea** Why was school desegregation such an important goal for the civil rights movement?

13. **Evaluate Information** (a.) What was the purpose of the Civil Rights Act of 1964? (b.) In what ways did the Act strengthen *Brown* v. *Board of Education*?

14. **Compare and Contrast** How did the Black Panther movement differ from the earlier civil rights movement?

15. **Summarize** What was the relationship between the Great Society and the New Deal?

16. **Analyze Graphs** Study the graphs at the top of the next column. How do they relate to *Brown* v. *Board of Education*?

EFFECTS OF **BROWN v. BOARD OF EDUCATION**

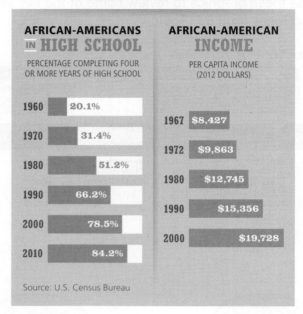

AFRICAN-AMERICANS IN HIGH SCHOOL
PERCENTAGE COMPLETING FOUR OR MORE YEARS OF HIGH SCHOOL

1960	20.1%
1970	31.4%
1980	51.2%
1990	66.2%
2000	78.5%
2010	84.2%

AFRICAN-AMERICAN INCOME
PER CAPITA INCOME (2012 DOLLARS)

1967	$8,427
1972	$9,863
1980	$12,745
1990	$15,356
2000	$19,728

Source: U.S. Census Bureau

17. **Writing Activity: Use Primary Sources** Evaluate why Dr. Martin Luther King called for nonviolent direct action. Use the excerpt below and your knowledge of the civil rights movement.

> Oppressed people cannot remain oppressed forever. The yearning for freedom eventually manifests itself, and that is what has happened to the American Negro. . . . If one recognizes this vital urge that has engulfed the Negro community, one should readily understand why public demonstrations are taking place. The Negro has many pent-up resentments and latent frustrations, and he must release them. So let him march; let him make prayer pilgrimages to the city hall; let him go on freedom rides—and try to understand why he must do so. If his repressed emotions are not released in nonviolent ways, they will seek expression through violence; this is not a threat but a fact of history. So I have not said to my people: "Get rid of your discontent." Rather, I have tried to say that this normal and healthy discontent can be channeled into the creative outlet of nonviolent direct action.
>
> —*Dr. Martin Luther King, Jr., "Letter From Birmingham Jail," 1963*

DOCUMENT-BASED QUESTIONS

Great Society programs were as controversial as the New Deal had been in the 1930s. Read the documents below, then answer the questions that follow.

DOCUMENT A

In this excerpt from a speech, President Johnson describes the "Great Society" he hopes to create.

> The Great Society rests on abundance and liberty for all. It demands an end to poverty and racial injustice, to which we are totally committed in our time. But that is just the beginning.
>
> The Great Society is a place where every child can find knowledge to enrich his mind and to enlarge his talents. It is a place where leisure is a welcome chance to build and reflect, not a feared cause of boredom and restlessness. It is a place where the city of man serves not only the needs of the body and the demands of commerce but the desire for beauty and the hunger for community.
>
> —*President Lyndon Johnson, 1964*

DOCUMENT B

Study the photograph and answer the related question in the assessment section.

DOCUMENT C

This excerpt is from an article in the *Washington Post*.

> The backlash against the Great Society has been as enduring as its successes.
>
> Virtually every political battle that rages today has roots in the federal expansion and experimentation that began in the 1960s. It set terms of engagement for ideological warfare over how to grapple with income inequality, whether to encourage a common curriculum in schools, affirmative action, immigration. . .
>
> Many Great Society programs are now so popular it is hard to imagine the country as we know it without them. Others—including some of its more grandiose urban renewal efforts—are generally regarded as failures. Poverty remains with us, with the two parties in deep disagreement over whether government has alleviated it or made it harder to escape.
>
> —*Karen Tumulty, The Washington Post, May 17, 2014*

DOCUMENT D

This is an excerpt from the introduction to the memoir of Senator Everett Dirksen.

> On many domestic issues, Dirksen continued the balancing act so central to his effectiveness . . . He took issue with Medicare, for example: "I would be eligible," he said indignantly. "Why should I be allowed to use dollars the government is taking from some young factory worker in Cleveland in the promise of providing for his old age?" The accumulation of Great Society spending programs appalled Dirksen. The taxpayers would have to come up with nearly $160 billion to fund them. Moreover, the programs brought with them an expanding federal bureaucracy and increasing centralization. To Dirksen, the Great Society was a misguided attempt at creating an immediate, utopian "blueprint for paradise."
>
> —*The Education of a Senator, Frank H. Mackaman, 1998*

18. In Document A, Johnson imagines the Great Society
    A. as an unattainable and unrealistic goal.
    B. as a society that undervalues commerce.
    C. as a place of self-gratification.
    D. as a society without poverty or injustice.

19. **Analyze Photographs** Based on Document B, what Great Society programs might relate to this scene.

20. In Document C, the writer argues that the Great Society programs
    A. are no longer relevant.
    B. were destructive and useless.
    C. ended in the 1970s.
    D. have shaped modern America.

21. Document D, the writer describes Senator Dirksen as
    A. supportive of Johnson's programs.
    B. an opponent of the Great Society.
    C. in favor of Medicare.
    D. idealistic and visionary.

22. **Writing Activity: Primary Source** Write a paragraph discussing the successes and failures of Johnson's Great Society programs in promoting social and economic stability. Use the sources as well as additional information you have learned.

1 What decision resulted from the Brown v. Board of Education case?

A Separate-but-equal schools are not equal, and so they are a violation of the U.S. Constitution.

B Segregated schools must be within five miles of each other in order to assure equal physical access.

C Segregated schools within the same school district must be controlled by the same Board of Education.

D Separate-but-equal schools must file a report with the government showing that they are providing a high-level of education.

2 Study this photo of Dr. King speaking at a civil rights meeting. Why did King's approach strike such a chord during the Montgomery Bus Boycott?

F People were inspired to take their frustrations to the street, which resulted in rioting and arrests.

G Protestors became angry listening to Dr. King, which resulted in them getting involved in politics that opposed Dr. King.

H Dr. King's activist, nonviolent approach appealed to Americans who were frustrated with the lack of progress in gaining civil rights.

I People realized that actions like the bus boycott were ineffective or took too long to have an effect.

3 What recurring conflict in U.S. history reemerged in the battles over integration?

   A workers vs. management

   B state vs. federal power

   C northern states vs. southern states

   D free trade vs. protectionism

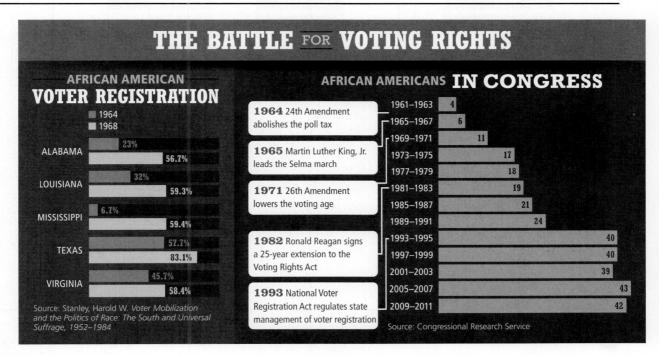

THE BATTLE FOR VOTING RIGHTS

AFRICAN AMERICAN VOTER REGISTRATION

■ 1964
■ 1968

ALABAMA — 23% / 56.7%

LOUISIANA — 32% / 59.3%

MISSISSIPPI — 6.7% / 59.4%

TEXAS — 57.7% / 83.1%

VIRGINIA — 45.7% / 58.4%

Source: Stanley, Harold W. *Voter Mobilization and the Politics of Race: The South and Universal Suffrage, 1952–1984*

AFRICAN AMERICANS IN CONGRESS

1964 24th Amendment abolishes the poll tax

1965 Martin Luther King, Jr. leads the Selma march

1971 26th Amendment lowers the voting age

1982 Ronald Reagan signs a 25-year extension to the Voting Rights Act

1993 National Voter Registration Act regulates state management of voter registration

1961–1963   4
1965–1967   6
1969–1971   11
1973–1975   17
1977–1979   18
1981–1983   19
1985–1987   21
1989–1991   24
1993–1995   40
1997–1999   40
2001–2003   39
2005–2007   43
2009–2011   42

Source: Congressional Research Service

4 What does the chart reveal about the effects of the Voting Rights Act of 1965?

   F It increased political participation among southern African Americans, but the percentage of voters was still low.

   G It was not embraced by the state of Mississippi as much as by the other four states included on the chart.

   H It was a national success which resulted in getting most African Americans to the voting booths immediately.

   I It prevented increases in the African American vote until large numbers of African Americans were seated in Congress.

If you have trouble with...				
Question	1	2	3	4
See Lesson	8.1	8.1	8.2	8.3

February 1962
John Glenn is the first American to orbit Earth.

January 1986
The *Challenger* space shuttle explodes 73 seconds after takeoff, killing 7 astronauts.

November 2000
The first crew occupies the *International Space Station*.

October 1958
NASA is created.

July 1969
Apollo 11 astronauts land on the moon.

November 1998
Construction begins on the *International Space Station*.

1950　1960　1970　1980　1990　2000

May 1961
Alan Shepard is the first American to fly in space.

June 1976
Viking 1 transmits images of Mars.

April 1990
Hubble Space Telescope is launched.

January 1967
During training, a space capsule fire kills astronauts Roger Chaffee, Virgil Grissom, and Edward White.

April 1997
Pathfinder lands on Mars.

5 Apart from demonstrating technological superiority, what other advantage would winning the space race have given America?

A economic advantage

B educational advantage

C military advantage

D cultural advantage

---

6 The U.S. immigration laws from the 1920s favored Western European immigrants. The changes in the 1965 law welcomed many immigrants from other parts of the world. What "push" factors might have been most important after 1965?

F flight from racism

G flight from religious persecution only

H flight from conflict and persecution

I the promise of better jobs

1949	1949	1952	1957
The Soviet Union sets off an atomic bomb.	Communists take over the government of mainland China.	The United States develops and tests a hydrogen bomb.	?

7 Which turning point in the Cold War best replaces the question mark on the time line?

A The Soviet Union develops microwave technology.

B The Soviet Union launches Sputnik I and ignites the space race.

C The United States ignites the space race with the first international space station.

D The United States installs a new government in Iran to prevent a communist takeover.

8 What effect did computers have on the economic development of the United States in the 1950s?

F Computers accounted for growth in white-collar jobs.

G Computers helped drive up the number of unemployed Americans.

H Computer entrepreneurs were encouraged to franchise their research.

I Computers allowed people more free time to develop entrepreneurial businesses.

If you have trouble with...				
Question	5	6	7	8
See Lesson	8.4	8.5	7.3	7.5

[**ESSENTIAL QUESTION**] What is America's role in the world?

⑨ **The Vietnam War Era**

Enduring Understandings

- The United States responded to Soviet aggression worldwide and supported anticommunist forces in Vietnam.

- U.S. involvement in Vietnam moved from an advisory to a combat role.

- The Vietnam War drained U.S. troops, money, and morale.

- Lack of progress and a rising death toll reduced public support for the war.

- Although President Nixon expanded the war into Cambodia, all parties signed the Paris Peace Accords in January 1973.

- The Vietnam War had a long-lasting effect on politics and attitudes in the United States.

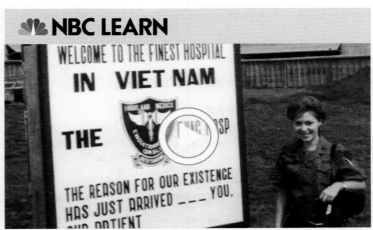

Learn more about the experiences of Edie Meeks, a Vietnam War nurse

Bounce to Activate My Story Video

>> U.S. soldiers near their base in Vietnam, 1966.

In this Topic, you'll learn about the events of the Vietnam War era. Look at the lesson outline and explore the timeline. As you study this Topic, you'll complete the Quest team project.

LESSON OUTLINE

9.1 The Cold War and Vietnam
HSS 11.8.5, HSS 11.9, HSS 11.9.2, HSS 11.9.3

9.2 America's Role Escalates
HSS 11.9, HSS 11.9.3

9.3 The Antiwar Movement
HSS 11.9, HSS 11.9.3, HSS 11.9.4; Analysis HI.2

9.4 The War's End and Effects
HSS 11.8.5, HSS 11.9, HSS 11.9.3, HSS 11.9.4

Key Events of the Vietnam War Era

1954 Vietnam is divided into two countries

1962 Cuban missile crisis

1964 Gulf of Tonkin Resolution

1968 Riots outside the Chicago Democratic Convention

1959 Cubans fleeing communism settle in Florida

1963 Kennedy is assassinated; Johnson becomes president

1965 Heavy U.S. bombing of Vietnam begins

1973 Paris Peace Accords

1975 Saigon falls to the North Vietnamese

1950   1960   1970   1980

QUEST! TEAM PROJECT

Analyzing the Reasons Behind the Antiwar Movement

Why did so many Americans oppose the Vietnam War? What were the anti-war movement's causes and consequences? In this Quest you'll explore the reasons why so many Americans were against the war and then write an essay explaining your findings.

STEP 1

Watch the video and discuss it in class or with a partner. Think about how and why the movement against the war gained momentum as the war progressed.

STEP 2

Examine sources relating to the Vietnam War and opposition to it. Answer the questions attached to each document.

STEP 3

Use the documents and your knowledge of history to write an essay that answers the question "Why did an antiwar movement develop in response to the Vietnam War?"

STEP 4

Reflect on the process of analyzing the documents and writing the essay and then complete the Self-Assessment.

PearsonSchool.com/CASS

Go **ONLINE** for complete Quest materials

 VIDEO ETEXT WRITING RUBRIC PDF ASSESSMENT

>> During a May Day rally in Havana, Cuban Prime Minister Fidel Castro stokes public distrust of the United States, accusing it of preparing to attack Cuba through nearby Latin American countries.

Bounce to Activate Flipped Video

9.1 John Kennedy's 1960 campaign stressed the need for the United States to move forward with vigor and determination. Kennedy argued that during the Eisenhower years America had lost ground in the Cold War struggle against communism. He pointed to the new communist regime under Fidel Castro in Cuba and charged that there was now a "missile gap" that left the U.S. nuclear missile force inferior to that of the Soviet Union. The first goal of the Kennedy administration would be to build up the nation's armed forces.

>> Objectives

Explain the steps Kennedy took to change American foreign policy.

Analyze the causes and effects of the Bay of Pigs invasion and the Cuban Missile Crisis.

Assess the outcome of the Berlin Crisis and other foreign-policy events of the 1960s.

Describe the reasons that the United States helped the French fight the Vietnamese.

Identify ways in which the United States opposed communism in Southeast Asia.

Analyze how the United States increased its involvement in Vietnam.

>> Key Terms

John Kennedy
Fidel Castro
Peace Corps
Bay of Pigs invasion
Cuban missile crisis
Nikita Khrushchev
Nuclear Test Ban
   Treaty
Berlin Wall
Ho Chi Minh
domino theory
Vietcong
Gulf of Tonkin
   Resolution

The Cold War and Vietnam

Kennedy Strives to Win the Cold War

Nowhere was the difference between Eisenhower and Kennedy more evident than in two important 1961 addresses. In his farewell address, Eisenhower counseled caution in foreign affairs. "The potential for the disastrous rise of misplaced power exists and will persist," he said.

As the first President born in the twentieth century, Kennedy proclaimed that a "new generation of Americans" was ready to meet any challenge. In his inaugural address, Kennedy warned his country's enemies:

> Let every nation know, whether it wishes us well or ill, that we shall pay any price, bear any burden, meet any hardship, support any friend, oppose any foe, in order to assure the survival and the success of liberty.

—John F. Kennedy, Inaugural Address, January 20, 1961

As the Cold War continued into the 1960s, Kennedy took office facing the spread of communism abroad and the threat of nuclear war. Determined to succeed where he felt Eisenhower had failed, Kennedy's enthusiasm and commitment to change offered the hope that with hard work and persistence the United States could win the Cold War. Kennedy issued a challenge to Americans: "Ask not what your country can do for you; ask what you can do for your country."

Significant National Decisions Impact the Cold War Eisenhower's defense policy of "massive retaliation" had emphasized the construction of nuclear weapons. Although Kennedy did not ignore the possibility of a nuclear war, he wanted to make sure that the United States was prepared to fight both conventional wars and conflicts against guerrilla forces. Kennedy therefore gave increased funding to conventional U.S. Army and Navy forces as well as to Army Special Forces, such as the Green Berets. He wanted a "**flexible response**" defense policy, one that prepared the United States to fight any type of conflict.

Important International Decisions Shape the Cold War The "Third World," as it was known at the time, was made up of the developing nations in Africa, Asia, and Latin America that did not align themselves with the United States or the Soviet Union. According to Soviet propaganda, Western capitalism created poverty and inequalities in the Third World, whereas communism promoted equality.

Like previous American leaders, Kennedy believed that democracy combined with prosperity would contain or limit the spread of communism. Therefore, he initiated programs to economically and politically strengthen the nations of the Third World. The **Peace Corps**, created in 1961, sent American volunteers around the world on "missions of freedom" to assist developing countries. They worked to provide technical, educational, and health services. The first Peace Corps volunteers arrived in Ghana, Africa, in 1961, to work as teachers. By the end of the year, the Peace Corps had volunteers working in two other countries in Africa—Nigeria and Tanzania. The program celebrated its 50th anniversary in 2011 and had 8,073 volunteers in 76 countries in 2012.

Other programs stressed purely economic development. One such project, the **Alliance for Progress** promised to resurrect America's Good Neighbor policy toward Latin America. During the 1950s, many Latin Americans had grown increasingly resentful of the United States, claiming

>> President-elect Kennedy meets President Eisenhower at the White House in December, 1960. After he took office, Kennedy increased defense spending by $6 billion.

>> By 1963, the Peace Corps had over 7,300 volunteers serving in over 40 countries, including Togo. President Kennedy appointed his brother-in-law, Sargent Shriver, as the Peace Corps's first director.

that it had too much influence in their region. Kennedy hoped the Alliance for Progress would change that view.

At its start in 1961, the program pledged $20 billion to help 22 Latin American nations raise their per capita income, distribute income more equitably, and improve industry, agriculture, health, and welfare. Unlike the Peace Corps, however, the Alliance for Progress was not successful.

☑ **CONTRAST** How did the message of Kennedy's inaugural address differ from that of Eisenhower's farewell address?

Kennedy Responds to Communism in Cuba

In 1959, Cuban revolutionary Fidel Castro succeeded in overthrowing the regime of Fulgencio Batista. Initially, the United States attempted to cultivate good relations with Castro. However, it soon became clear that the Cuban leader was determined to nationalize land held by U.S. citizens, enforce radical reform measures, and accept Soviet economic and military aid. Thousands of wealthy and middle-class Cubans fled their country, many settling in Miami and southern Florida. Proud of their heritage and deeply anticommunist, they made new lives for themselves and their families in the United States.

Bay of Pigs Invasion After breaking diplomatic relations with Cuba in 1961, the Eisenhower administration authorized the Central Intelligence Agency (CIA) to plan an invasion of Cuba to overthrow Castro. The CIA recruited Cuban exiles and trained them in Guatemala. But when Eisenhower left office, the invasion plan was still that—an unexecuted plan.

Pressured by members of the CIA and his own aides, Kennedy decided to implement the plan. On April 17, 1961, a CIA-led force of Cuban exiles attacked Cuba in the **Bay of Pigs invasion**. The invasion was greatly mismanaged. The poorly equipped forces landed at the site with no protective cover. All but 300 of the 1,400 invaders were killed or captured. Not only did the Bay of Pigs invasion fail, it probably strengthened Castro's position in Cuba. It also turned many Cuban Americans against Kennedy.

Kennedy took personal responsibility for the failed invasion. He emphasized, however, that the United States would continue to resist "communist penetration" in the Western Hemisphere.

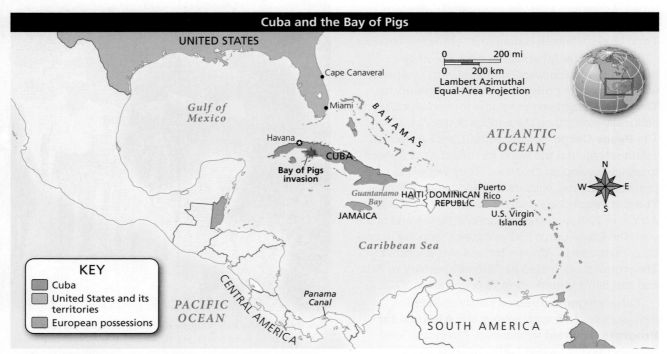

Cuba and the Bay of Pigs

>> **Analyze Maps** Based on the information in the map, what factors might have influenced President Kennedy's decision to launch the Bay of Pigs invasion of Cuba, in 1961?

Bounce to Activate Timeline

Kennedy's Role in the Cuban Missile Crisis

Kennedy's efforts to contain communism were severely threatened during the **Cuban missile crisis**. In August and September of 1962 U.S. intelligence discovered that the Soviets were building nuclear missile sites in Cuba, apparently to protect Castro from another American invasion. When the sites were completed, major East Coast cities and the Panama Canal would be in range of the missiles.

In response to this Soviet aggression, Kennedy demanded the removal of the missiles. In a dramatic television address on October 22, 1962, he blamed **Nikita Khrushchev**, the Soviet premier, for causing a "reckless and provocative threat to world peace." He also announced that he had approved a naval quarantine (blockade) of Cuba to prevent the Soviets from completing the bases. Behind the scenes, however, Kennedy worked toward a diplomatic settlement. He indicated that he would remove U.S. missiles in Turkey and Italy if the Soviets removed their missiles in Cuba.

After six tense days during which nuclear war seemed a real possibility, Khrushchev agreed to honor the blockade and remove the missiles. As Secretary of State Dean Rusk later told a reporter, "Remember, when you report this, that, eyeball to eyeball, they blinked first."

The Impact of the Crisis During the Cuban missile crisis, Kennedy and Khrushchev stood on the edge of a nuclear war and then slowly backed away. In the Soviet Union, Khrushchev lost prestige and more hard-line leaders chipped away at his power. In the United States, Kennedy emerged as a more mature and thoughtful leader, one who had faced a frightening test and had remained calm and resolute. The crisis prompted both leaders to move toward détente—a relaxing of tension between rivals. They installed a "**hot line**" telephone system between Moscow and Washington, D.C., to improve communication. In 1963, the year after the crisis, the United States, Great Britain, and the Soviet Union signed the **Nuclear Test Ban Treaty**, the first nuclear-weapons agreement, which ended aboveground nuclear tests. Thirty-six other nations soon signed the agreement.

☑ **IDENTIFY SUPPORTING DETAILS** What diplomatic enticement did Kennedy offer the Soviets to help solve the Cuban Missile Crisis?

>> Kennedy and Khrushchev smile for the cameras, but their June 1961 summit in Vienna, less than 2 months after the Bay of Pigs, was tense and combative.

>> In 1961, workers build part of the Berlin Wall. The ninety-six-mile-long wall would divide Soviet controlled East Berlin from democratic West Berlin.

The Causes and Outcomes of the Berlin Crisis

Since 1958, Khrushchev wanted to sign a peace treaty that would put the western zones of Berlin under control of East Germany. His actions were motivated by the steady flow of skilled East German workers into West Berlin. Desiring to show his strength, Kennedy stood firm on America's commitment to defending the rights of West Berliners and West Germans. At a conference in Vienna in June 1961, Kennedy and Khrushchev focused on Berlin as the key issue. Khrushchev called the present situation "intolerable."

He demanded that the United States recognize the formal division of Germany and end its military presence in West Berlin. Kennedy refused. He did not want to give up occupation rights he considered critical to defending Western Europe. In a tense atmosphere, Khrushchev said, "I want peace, but if you want war, that is your problem." Kennedy answered, "It is you, not I who wants to force a change." The meeting ended abruptly. The conference, meant to relax Cold War tensions, only increased them.

After returning home, both world leaders made moves that threatened the peace. Kennedy asked Congress to dramatically increase military spending. Khrushchev ordered the construction of a wall between East and West Berlin. The **Berlin Wall** became a visible symbol of the reality of the two Germanys and the gulf between the communist East and the democratic West. Kennedy responded by sending 1,500 U.S. troops to West Berlin. For a time, Russian and American tanks moved within sight of each other. Yet, neither side could fully claim a victory.

☑ **HYPOTHESIZE** For what reason might the Soviets have wanted to gain control of West Berlin?

Reasons for U.S. Involvement in Indochina

Presidents Kennedy and Johnson shared a vision for a better America in the 1960s. They also shared a vision for a better world in which America would emerge victorious from its Cold War struggle against global communism. As part of this strategic and ideological battle, the United States established a new line of defense against communism in Vietnam. The conflict in Southeast Asia would grow to be one of the most costly wars in American history.

Situated far away in Southeast Asia, Vietnam did not attract significant American attention until the 1960s. Television news shows rarely mentioned it, and many Americans could not locate it on a

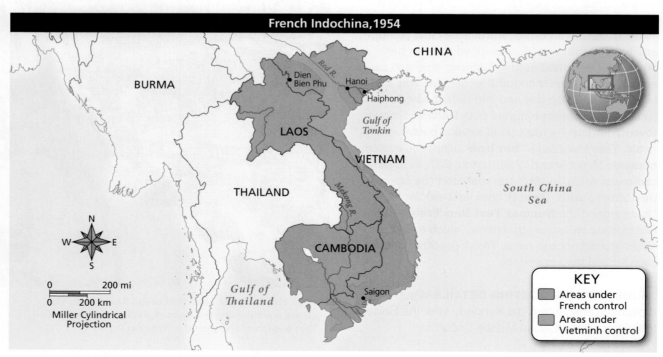

French Indochina, 1954

KEY
- Areas under French control
- Areas under Vietminh control

>> **Analyze Maps** Based on the information in this map, which regions of present-day Vietnam were particularly dangerous for French forces?

map. But over a span of more than ten years, the United States sent several million soldiers to fight in Vietnam. America's involvement in Vietnam had roots in European colonialism, Cold War politics, and Vietnamese calls for national independence.

French Control of Indochina in Southeast Asia

In the 1800s, French military forces established control over Indochina, a peninsula in Southeast Asia that includes the modern countries of Vietnam, Cambodia, and Laos. Slightly larger than the state of Texas, Indochina included almost 27 million people by the end of World War II. French colonial officials ruled Vietnam with an iron fist. They transplanted French laws into Vietnam and imposed high taxes. French business people acquired large rice and rubber plantations and controlled the mineral wealth of the country. Some Vietnamese, especially wealthier members of society, benefited from western culture and technology. Many others, however, were impoverished by colonialism.

Some Vietnamese rebelled against France's exploitative rule. **Ho Chi Minh** became the most important voice demanding independence for Vietnam. Born in 1890, Ho became involved in anti-French organizations as a young man and fled Vietnam in 1912.

He traveled the world, visiting American ports and living periodically in London, Paris, and Moscow. During his 30-year absence, Ho constantly thought and wrote about Vietnam, and he searched for westerners who would support his plans for Vietnamese independence. Ho embraced communism, and eventually Soviet communists rallied to his cause.

The French Fight Nationalism and Communism

During World War II, Japan had undermined French control over Vietnam. But when the conflict ended, France reasserted its colonial claims there. France's problem, however, was that colonialism was a dying institution. World War II had strengthened nationalist movements while weakening the economic and military positions of traditional European powers. In Vietnam, Ho Chi Minh clamored for independence as France struggled to maintain its dwindling global power.

Meanwhile, the United States faced a difficult decision. On the one hand, it supported decolonization. On the other hand, America wanted France as an ally in its Cold War effort to contain the Soviet Union.

President Harry S. Truman believed that if he supported Vietnamese independence, he would

>> Ho Chi Minh was a revolutionary leader who fought against French occupation. Later, he became the prime minister, then president of the Democratic Republic of Vietnam (North Vietnam).

weaken anticommunist forces in France. So, to ensure a strong, anticommunist Western Europe, Truman sacrificed his own anticolonial sentiments.

Vietnam thus became a pawn in Cold War politics. To ensure French support in the Cold War, Truman agreed to aid France's efforts to regain control over Vietnam. After communist forces won the civil war in China in 1949, America increased its aid to the French in Vietnam. Truman did not want to see another communist victory in Asia. Between 1950 and 1954, the United States contributed $2.6 billion to France's war efforts. Containing Ho Chi Minh's communist Vietminh—an abbreviation of the League for the Independence of Vietnam— became a national priority.

The Domino Theory Spurs U.S. Involvement in Vietnam

When President Dwight D. Eisenhower took office in early 1953, he continued Truman's policies toward Vietnam. He sent monetary aid to the French, arguing that by battling Ho Chi Minh, they were containing the spread of communism.

Eisenhower told a journalist that the fight in Vietnam involved more than the future of just one country:

You have a row of dominoes set up, you knock over the first one, and what will happen to the last one is the certainty that it will go over very quickly. So you could have a beginning of a disintegration that would have the most profound influences.

—Dwight D. Eisenhower, Arpil 7, 1954

The **domino theory** was the idea that if Vietnam fell to communism, its closest neighbors would follow. This in turn would threaten Japan, the Philippines, and Australia. In short, stopping the communists in Vietnam was important to the protection of the entire region.

In 1954, however, the French lost their eight-year struggle to regain Vietnam. The Vietminh trapped a large French garrison at Dien Bien Phu, a military base in northwest Vietnam, and laid siege to it for 55 days. During the siege, which one Frenchman described as "hell in a very small place," Vietminh troops destroyed the French airstrip, cut French supply lines, and dug trenches to attack key French positions. Finally, on May 7, 1954, after suffering some 15,000 casualties, the French surrendered.

The very next day at an international peace conference in Geneva, Switzerland, France sued for peace. According to the Geneva Accords, France granted independence to Vietnam, Laos, and Cambodia. The accords also divided Vietnam at the seventeenth parallel into two countries, North Vietnam and South Vietnam. Ho Chi Minh's communist forces ruled in North Vietnam, and an anticommunist government, supported by the United States, assumed power in South Vietnam. The accords also called for free elections in 1956 to unify Vietnam.

☑ **CHECK UNDERSTANDING** Why was supporting the French in Indochina problematic for President Truman?

The United States Responds to Communism in Vietnam

During the Battle of Dien Bien Phu, France appealed to the United States for military support. President Eisenhower was willing to supply money but not soldiers. Ike would not commit American troops to defend colonialism in Asia. Nevertheless, the President firmly supported the new anticommunist government of South Vietnam.

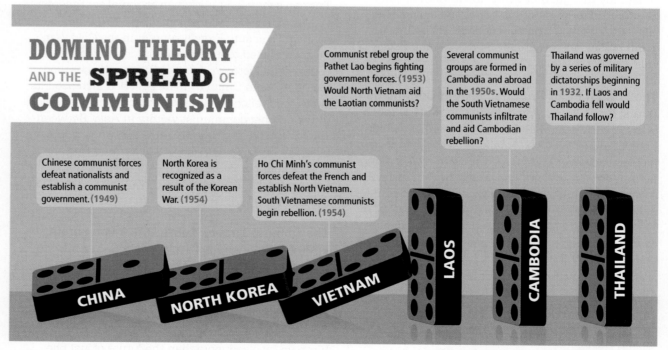

DOMINO THEORY AND THE SPREAD OF COMMUNISM

Chinese communist forces defeat nationalists and establish a communist government. (1949)

North Korea is recognized as a result of the Korean War. (1954)

Ho Chi Minh's communist forces defeat the French and establish North Vietnam. South Vietnamese communists begin rebellion. (1954)

Communist rebel group the Pathet Lao begins fighting government forces. (1953) Would North Vietnam aid the Laotian communists?

Several communist groups are formed in Cambodia and abroad in the 1950s. Would the South Vietnamese communists infiltrate and aid Cambodian rebellion?

Thailand was governed by a series of military dictatorships beginning in 1932. If Laos and Cambodia fell would Thailand follow?

CHINA   NORTH KOREA   VIETNAM   LAOS   CAMBODIA   THAILAND

>> **Support a Point of View with Evidence** The graphic shows the international chain reaction that American strategists of the 1950s most feared. Were these strategists justified in their concern about the spread of communism? Explain.

Bounce to Activate Gallery

The U.S. Escalates Involvement in South Vietnam

America channeled aid to South Vietnam in different ways. In 1954, the United States and seven other countries formed the **Southeast Asia Treaty Organization (SEATO)**. Similar to NATO's goal in Europe, SEATO's goal was to contain the spread of communism in Southeast Asia.

The United States provided economic and military aid to the South Vietnamese government led by Ngo Dinh Diem. Diem was an ardent nationalist and anticommunist. Although he lacked popular appeal, his anticommunism guaranteed American support. When it came time for the 1956 unification elections, American intelligence analysts predicted that Diem would lose to the more popular Ho Chi Minh. Rather than risk losing, Diem refused to participate in the elections, a move made with the support of the U.S. government.

Impact of the Communist Insurgency

By 1957, a communist rebel group in the South, known as the National Liberation Front (NLF), had committed itself to undermining the Diem government and uniting Vietnam under a communist flag. NLF guerrilla fighters, called **Vietcong**, launched an insurgency in which they assassinated government officials and destroyed roads and bridges. Supplied by communists in North Vietnam, the Vietcong employed surprise hit-and-run tactics to weaken Diem's hold on South Vietnam.

Diem's own policies also weakened his position in South Vietnam. A devout Roman Catholic in an overwhelmingly Buddhist nation, Diem did little to build a broad political base. Instead, he signed anti-Buddhist legislation and refused to enact significant land reforms. His lack of popular support hurt him in the civil war against North Vietnam. Only the support of the United States kept the unpopular leader in power.

Kennedy Sends U.S. Troops to Vietnam

After his election in 1960, President John F. Kennedy took a more aggressive stand against the communists in Vietnam. Beginning in 1961, he sent Special Forces troops to South Vietnam to advise the Army of the Republic of Vietnam (ARVN) on more effective ways to fight the communist forces. By 1963, more than 15,000 American military personnel were fighting in Vietnam.

Although U.S. military personnel fought bravely and achieved some success, Diem continued to alienate South Vietnamese citizens. By late 1963, his regime was in shambles. Buddhists protested his restrictive policies, occasionally by setting

>> French soldiers march Vietminh prisoners captured during fighting near Dien Bien Phu.

>> Viet Cong guerillas patrol the Saigon River in South Vietnam.

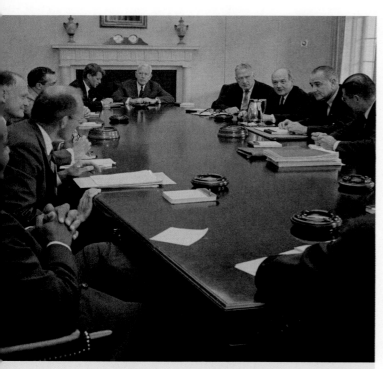

>> President Johnson meets with his cabinet to discuss the Gulf of Tonkin incident. **Predict Consequences** How might the Gulf of Tonkin incident affect U.S. policy in Vietnam?

themselves on fire. The Kennedy administration eventually concluded that South Vietnam needed new leadership. Working behind the scenes, Americans plotted with anti-Diem generals to overthrow Diem's government. On November 1, 1963, Diem was removed from power; he was assassinated the following day.

Johnson Leads the Nation into the Vietnam War

Three weeks after Diem's fall, an assassin's bullet struck down President Kennedy. Vice President Lyndon B. Johnson was sworn in as the new President. Johnson was a Cold War traditionalist who held a monolithic view of communism. For this "Cold Warrior," communism in the Soviet Union, China, and Vietnam were all the same. He did not recognize subtle differences. He also knew that the American people expected victory in Vietnam.

Reasons for Escalating Conflict

In 1964, President Johnson faced his first crisis in Vietnam. On August 2, North Vietnamese torpedo boats fired on the American destroyer USS *Maddox* as it patrolled the Gulf of Tonkin off the coast of North Vietnam. The *Maddox* was not hit, and it returned fire on the North Vietnamese boat. Johnson promptly responded to the attack and to other North Vietnamese provocations. He announced that "aggression by terror against peaceful villages of South Vietnam has now been joined by open aggression on the high seas against the United States of America." Troubled by increasing strikes against an American ally, Johnson ordered an airstrike against North Vietnam.

Congress Gives Johnson Broad Military Powers

The President next asked Congress to authorize the use of force to defend American troops. With little debate and only two senators voting against it, Congress agreed to Johnson's request and passed the **Gulf of Tonkin Resolution**. The resolution authorized the President "to take all necessary measures to repel any armed attack against the forces of the United States and to prevent further aggression." The resolution gave Johnson tremendous war powers. It allowed him to commit U.S. troops to South Vietnam and fight a war against North Vietnam without ever going back to Congress to ask for a declaration of war. By authorizing the resolution, Congress had handed its war powers as expressed in the Constitution to the executive branch. This raised questions about the relationship between the legislative and executive branches of government. Presidents Johnson and Nixon used the resolution as the legal basis for their military policies in Vietnam.

☑ **DESCRIBE** What role did religious issues play in Diem's troubles as leader of South Vietnam?

☑ ASSESSMENT

1. **Contrast** the foreign policies of Eisenhower and Kennedy during the Cold War.

2. **Generate Explanations** Explain how Kennedy's response to the Cuban Missile Crisis mixed diplomacy and force.

3. **Identify Cause and Effect** Explain how World War II affected French colonial power in Vietnam.

4. **Draw Conclusions** Discuss reasons why the United States supported Ngo Dinh Diem, and explain how this changed in later years.

5. **Determine Point of View** Discuss President Truman's decision to support French efforts in Vietnam during the Cold War.

After the Gulf of Tonkin Resolution, President Johnson began to shift U.S. military efforts in Vietnam into high gear. But America's leaders and soldiers soon found themselves stuck in a deadly quagmire with no quick victory in sight. The war began to weaken the economy, divide the American people, and erode the nation's morale.

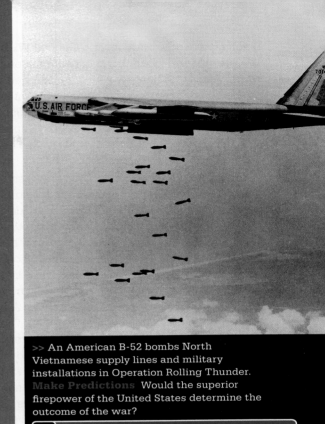

>> An American B-52 bombs North Vietnamese supply lines and military installations in Operation Rolling Thunder. **Make Predictions** Would the superior firepower of the United States determine the outcome of the war?

Bounce to Activate Flipped Video

America's Role Escalates

Escalation of Forces in Vietnam

In February 1965, President Johnson dramatically altered the U.S. role in the Vietnam War. In response to a Vietcong attack that killed American troops at Pleiku, Johnson ordered the start of Operation Rolling Thunder, the first sustained bombing campaign against North Vietnam. Johnson hoped that this new strategy of intensive bombing would convince North Vietnam to stop reinforcing the Vietcong in South Vietnam.

The bombs caused widespread destruction, but they failed to convince North Vietnam to make peace. As the communist forces continued to fight, the United States committed more troops to battle them on the ground. American soldiers moved beyond their advisory roles and assumed greater combat responsibilities, while South Vietnamese troops accepted a secondary, more limited role in the war. U.S. military and civilian leaders hoped that American airstrikes, along with the troops on the ground, would eventually force the communists to the peace table.

Johnson Changes Strategies Johnson's change in strategy in 1965 stemmed primarily from the counsel of Secretary of

>> **Objectives**

Analyze the major issues and events that caused President Johnson to increase American troop strength in Vietnam.

Assess the nature of the war in Vietnam and the difficulties faced by each side.

Evaluate the effects of low morale on American troops and on the home front.

>> **Key Terms**

William Westmoreland
napalm
hawk
dove

Defense Robert McNamara and General **William Westmoreland**, the American commander in South Vietnam. These two advisors believed that the United States needed to increase its military presence in Vietnam and do more of the fighting in order to win the war. Operation Rolling Thunder and increased troop commitments fulfilled this need to "Americanize" the war effort.

Beginning in March 1965, U.S. airstrikes hammered North Vietnam and Vietcong strong points in South Vietnam. Meanwhile, a secret bombing campaign against communist forces was also underway in Laos. Between 1965 and 1973, American pilots dropped more than 6 million tons of bombs on enemy positions—almost three times the tonnage dropped by all the combatants during World War II. In addition to conventional bombs, American pilots dropped napalm and sprayed Agent Orange. **Napalm** is a jellied gasoline which was dropped in large canisters that exploded on impact, covering large areas in flames. It clung to anything it touched and was difficult to extinguish. Agent Orange is an herbicide meant to kill plant life. U.S. forces used it to defoliate forest areas that might conceal enemy fighters and to disrupt the enemy's food supply. Almost half of South Vietnam's forested areas were sprayed at least once, and the ecological impact was devastating. There also may have been a hidden human cost, as many scientists believe that Agent Orange causes cancers and other physical problems.

As airstrikes intensified, American ground troops landed in South Vietnam. On March 8, 1965, U.S. Marines arrived to defend the airbase at Da Nang. They were soon followed by other troops. The soldiers accepted a wide range of missions. Some guarded bases. Others conducted search-and-destroy missions to kill as many Vietcong guerrillas as they could. Helicopters ferried commandos to and from remote locations for quick strikes against enemy positions.

Vietcong Tactics and Strategies Large-scale battles against Vietcong or North Vietnamese Army units were not typical of America's strategy in Vietnam. American soldiers generally fought lightly armed Vietcong guerrillas in small engagements.

Ho Chi Minh's military doctrine hinged on fighting only when victory was assured, which meant never fighting on his opponents' terms. He compared his troops to a tiger, while the Americans were like an elephant. If the tiger stands still, the elephant will crush it. But if the tiger keeps moving and occasionally jumps on the elephant to take a bite out of it, the elephant will slowly bleed to death.

During the war, the Vietcong behaved like Ho's tiger. They traveled light, often carrying just a rifle and a few handfuls of rice. They hid in tunnels during the day and emerged at night to ambush American patrols. They infiltrated American bases and set off explosives. They set booby traps that

>> **Analyze Maps** Based on the information in the map, what advantage did the Ho Chi Minh Trail give the Vietcong?

Bounce to Activate Chart

VIETNAM EFFECTS OF ESCALATION

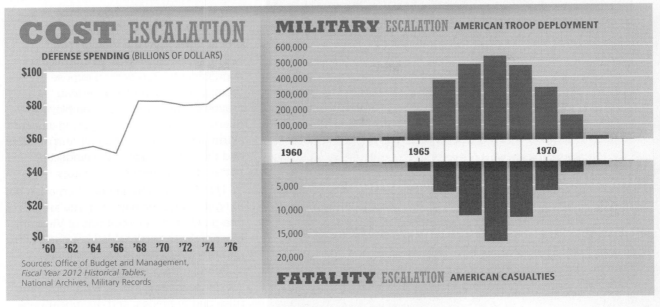

COST ESCALATION

DEFENSE SPENDING (BILLIONS OF DOLLARS)

$100
$80
$60
$40
$20
$0

'60 '62 '64 '66 '68 '70 '72 '74 '76

Sources: Office of Budget and Management,
Fiscal Year 2012 Historical Tables;
National Archives, Military Records

MILITARY ESCALATION AMERICAN TROOP DEPLOYMENT

600,000
500,000
400,000
300,000
200,000
100,000

1960   1965   1970

5,000
10,000
15,000
20,000

FATALITY ESCALATION AMERICAN CASUALTIES

>> **Analyze Data** What does the data reveal about the war during the years 1965 to 1968?

maimed and crippled American troops. Their strategy was to wear the Americans down. The leaders of North Vietnam and the Vietcong remained convinced that if they could just avoid losing the war, the Americans would eventually leave.

American Casualties Escalate American strategy during this stage of the war yielded limited results. U.S. bombers did disrupt North Vietnamese industry and slow the movement of supplies to the Vietcong. But when the communists did not sue for peace, American troop commitments and battlefield deaths escalated rapidly. By the end of 1965, there were 184,300 U.S. troops in Vietnam, and only 636 American soldiers had died in the war. Three years later, there were more than 500,000 U.S. troops in Vietnam, and the number of American dead had risen to more than 30,000.

Each year, the war claimed more American lives and cost more American dollars. But at the end of each year, the United States seemed no closer to success. America's mission was to help South Vietnam build a stable noncommunist nation and thereby win the "hearts and minds" of its citizens. But corruption plagued the South Vietnamese administrative structure. Outside of the major cities, the government enjoyed little support. Although American forces won most of the larger battles, they did not achieve a successful end to the war. By 1967,

the war had devolved into a stalemate. Some U.S. critics of the war compared it to a quagmire—muddy terrain that sinks underfoot and is difficult to exit.

☑ **INFER** Why did General Westmoreland and Secretary of Defense McNamara want to "Americanize" the war?

Patriotism, Heroism, and Sinking Morale

For American soldiers in the field, the Vietnam War presented difficult challenges that demanded courage and patience. Unlike World War II, the Vietnam War did not emphasize territorial acquisition. The United States and its allies did not invade North Vietnam, march on Ho Chi Minh's capital of Hanoi, or attempt to destroy the communist regime. As in the Korean War, the United States was wary of triggering both Chinese and Soviet entry into the conflict. Instead, U.S. forces supported the survival and development of South Vietnam, which was besieged by the Vietcong and their North Vietnamese allies. In this fight, U.S. troops could never fully tell their friends from their enemies. Yet from the outset, they faced the dangers of Vietnam's battlefields with dedication and bravery.

> "I volunteered. . . . Ever since the American Revolution my family had people in all the different wars, and that was always the thing—when your country needs you, you go. You don't ask a lot of questions. . . ."
>
> —David Ross, United States Army medic

>> Lieutenant Commander Dorothy Ryan, a Navy Nurse aboard the hospital ship USS *Repose,* was one of about 10,000 American women who bravely served in Vietnam.

New Battlefield Dangers and Guerrilla Warfare Although American troops won numerous battles, they could not win the war outright. The problem was that the Vietcong and North Vietnamese avoided significant engagements. Rather than expose themselves to superior American firepower, the communists employed guerrilla warfare tactics, fighting smaller skirmishes where their small-unit abilities and their knowledge of the landscape bettered their chances for victory.

U.S. forces often had no alternative but to fight indecisive battles in the jungles, rice paddies, and mountains of Vietnam. Most of these battlefields abounded with natural cover. Clad in black clothing, Vietcong gunmen would spring out of the dense foliage, attack with automatic rifles and grenades, and disappear back into the landscape. Much of this fighting took place at night, which reduced the effectiveness of American planes, artillery, and troop tactics.

American Soldiers Fulfill Their Duty Despite the trials of war, American soldiers adapted to adverse conditions in Vietnam and fought with the same intensity that U.S. forces had shown in World Wars I and II. Many fought to prevent the spread of communism. Some fought to protect villagers in South Vietnam and win their trust and respect. Others fought because their country was at war, and they felt it was their duty. A medic in the First Infantry Division explained his reason for going to Vietnam:

> I volunteered. . . . Ever since the American Revolution my family had people in all the different wars, and that was always the thing— when your country needs you, you go. You don't ask a lot of questions. . . .
>
> —David Ross, United States Army medic

Later, many did ask questions about America's involvement in the war, but overwhelmingly while they were in Vietnam, the soldiers met their duties with courage. More than 58,000 of them gave their lives for their country.

Impact of the War on the U.S. Economy, 1968

INFLATION	Reached 4%
TAXES	Income tax increased by 10%
GDP (GROSS DOMESTIC PRODUCT)	Reached a high of 9.5% devoted to the war effort
GREAT SOCIETY INITIATIVES	President Lyndon B. Johnson's reform programs weakened by rising costs of the war: $94.3 billion spent on the war, $14.9 billion spent on welfare
EDUCATION	Out of the $277 billion spent by the U.S., 16% was directed toward education, 34% toward the war effort

>> **Analyze Data** In your opinion, which two effects had the most negative impact and why?

Women also displayed courage and valor. About 10,000 American military women served in Vietnam during the war. Most female military personnel were nurses.

Not only did they face danger working close to the front, but they also had to cope with the emotional toll of constantly working with injured and dying soldiers and civilians.

Lynda Van Devanter volunteered to go to Vietnam and spent a year there as a nurse. Like other nurses, she confronted war and death on a daily basis. However, on one occasion she had to deliver a baby. She later recalled:

It was creation of life in the midst of all that destruction. And creation of life restored your sanity. . . . Those were the things that kept you going. That there was life coming. There was still hope.

—Lynda Van Devanter, United States Army nurse

Questioning the Cause As the war lengthened, many Americans began to question U.S. involvement. The earliest soldiers in Vietnam had been volunteers, men committed to the fight against communism. But by the end of 1965, most American soldiers in Vietnam had been drafted into military service, and they were not as certain that preserving the government in South Vietnam was crucial to American interests. They sensed that many South Vietnamese people were indifferent—if not openly hostile—to their own nation. Increasingly, it seemed that Americans were dying to defend a nation whose people were unwilling to die to defend themselves.

☑ **DESCRIBE** What relatively successful tactic did North Vietnamese and Vietcong fighters employ against U.S. forces?

Doubt Grows on the Home Front

The lack of progress toward victory in Vietnam also led to doubt in the United States. When President Johnson had begun to send troops to war, Americans had expected a relatively quick victory. After all, the United States was a militarily powerful, technologically advanced country, and North Vietnam was a poor country with comparatively little technology. Over the next few years, the Johnson administration kept asserting that an American victory was close at hand. But when that did not come, many began to question the President's foreign policy.

Impact of Defense Spending on the Economy
The war strained government finances. President Johnson's Great Society plan called for enormous domestic spending to eliminate poverty, improve

education and medical care, and fight racial discrimination. The costs of fighting a war on the other side of the world were just as mammoth. Although massive government spending lowered the unemployment rate, it also led to rising prices and inflation. The combination of heavy government spending, rising prices, and inflation forced Johnson to raise taxes. Ultimately, Johnson had to cut back on his Great Society reform initiatives to help pay for the war.

An Antiwar Movement Emerges As long as America's involvement in Vietnam had been small and relatively inexpensive, few politicians voiced serious opposition. Congress offered bipartisan support for the Vietnam policies of Johnson's predecessors. Soon after the Gulf of Tonkin Resolution, however, Congressional support began to waver over the President's escalation of the war.

Beginning in 1967, Congress—and eventually most of the nation—divided into two camps: hawks and doves. The mostly conservative **hawks** supported Johnson's war policy. Believing strongly in the containment of communism and the domino theory, they accepted rising troop levels, escalating costs, and increasing numbers of battlefield deaths. For the hawks, Vietnam was a crucial front in the Cold War. **Doves**, however, broke with Johnson's war policy. A diverse group that included liberal politicians, pacifists, student radicals, and civil rights leaders, doves questioned the war on both moral and strategic grounds. For them, the conflict was a localized civil war, not a vital Cold War battleground.

Senator J. William Fulbright, chairman of the Senate Foreign Relations Committee, emerged as the early leader of the doves in Congress. A Democrat who had supported the Gulf of Tonkin Resolution, Fulbright soon came to believe that the war in Vietnam was a national civil war, not a Cold War conflict directed from Moscow or Beijing. In 1967 and 1968, Fulbright held public hearings on the war, providing a platform for critics of the conflict.

☑ **RECALL** How did the growing belief that the Vietnam War was not a vital, Cold War conflict affect American society?

☑ ASSESSMENT

1. **Distinguish** Discuss the relationship between U.S. troops and South Vietnamese troops during the Vietnam War.

2. **Identify Cause and Effect** Explain how Operation Rolling Thunder represented a change in the U.S. war strategy.

3. **Compare and Contrast** Explain the advantages that North Vietnamese and Vietcong soldiers had over U.S. soldiers during the war.

4. **Generate Explanations** Explain the respective goals of the United States and North Vietnam during the Vietnam War.

5. **Determine Point of View** Discuss reasons that some Americans opposed the Vietnam War.

President Johnson sent more American troops to Vietnam in order to win the war. But with each passing year, casualty lists got longer and victory seemed further away. As soldiers died abroad and hawks and doves argued at home, the Vietnam War opened up a deep emotional rift in American society. After the war ended, it would take years for the country to heal itself.

>> Antiwar students at the University of South Carolina protest the U.S. invasion of Cambodia, in May 1970.

Bounce to Activate Flipped Video

The Antiwar Movement

Antiwar Sentiment Grows

The war in Vietnam divided Americans more deeply than any conflict since the Civil War. Although most Americans initially supported President Johnson's bombings and troop deployments, by 1966 critics began speaking out. Senator Fulbright's opposition to the war hurt Johnson in Congress, and the senator was soon joined by like-minded activists who believed that American soldiers were dying in a war that had little to do with American interests.

Protesting the Draft By 1965, most of the troops sent to Vietnam were no longer volunteers who had enlisted in the army. Instead, they were **draftees**—young men drafted into military service—who had been assigned a tour in Vietnam. In accordance with the Selective Service Act of 1948, the government drafted more than 1.5 million men into military service during the Vietnam War. All males had to register for the draft when they turned 18, and the Selective Service System called up draftees based on projected military needs.

Critics of the Selective Service System argued that the draft was not fair. The system gave local draft boards considerable

>> **Objectives**

Describe the divisions within American society over the Vietnam War.

Analyze the Tet Offensive and the American reaction to it.

Summarize the factors that influenced the outcome of the 1968 presidential election.

>> **Key Terms**

draftee
Students for a
  Democratic
  Society (SDS)
"credibility gap"
Tet Offensive
Eugene McCarthy
Robert Kennedy

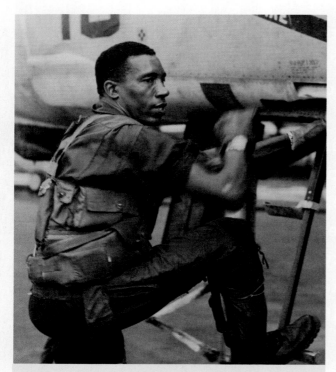

>> Frank E. Petersen, who later became the first African American Marine Corps general, prepares for combat in Vietnam.

influence in selecting men for service, and it also granted deferments to college students and men who worked in certain designated occupations. Most of the 2.5 million men who served in Vietnam came from working-class and poor backgrounds.

During the Johnson presidency, the number of African American troops fighting and dying in Vietnam was also disproportionately high. At the beginning of the war, African Americans suffered more than 20 percent of the total combat deaths, roughly twice the percentage of the U.S. population. Additionally, African American soldiers were more likely to serve in combat positions and less likely to become commissioned officers.

Civil rights leader Martin Luther King Jr., spoke out against the added war burden shouldered by African American soldiers. Speaking at a New York church in 1967, King said that the war was hurting both poor blacks and whites. Vietnam was drawing human and economic resources away from America's other wars on poverty and discrimination. He added that it hindered poor Americans in other more direct ways:

It was sending their sons and their brothers and their husbands to fight and to die in extraordinary high proportions relative to the rest of the population. . . . [W]e have been repeatedly faced with the cruel irony of watching Negro and white boys on TV screens as they kill and die together for a nation that has been unable to seat them together in the same schools.

—Martin Luther King, Jr., 1967

Perceived inequities in the draft led to widespread resistance. Antiwar advocates sponsored Stop the Draft Week in October 1967, and some draft-eligible males burned their draft cards in protest. Finally, in 1969, the Selective Service System adopted a lottery that was designed to eliminate deferment abuses and create a more diverse army of draftees.

Protests on College Campuses Across America, college campuses became centers of antiwar sentiment. Professors and students criticized the war for a variety of reasons, ranging from pacifism and the war's effects on the economy to a personal desire to avoid military service. Antiwar activity on college

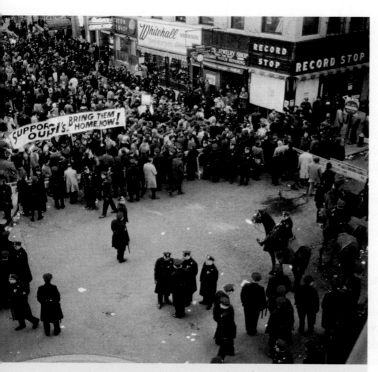

>> Over 4,000 protestors marched near the Armed Forces Induction Center in New York City to voice their opposition to the draft during Stop-the-Draft week in October 1967.

Bounce to Activate Chart

campuses did not, however, reflect the attitudes of all Americans.

In fact, many professors remained vocal in their defense of the war effort during lectures and at protest rallies. For the most part, though, colleges and universities were focal points of the strongest antiwar opinion.

Antiwar activities were part of more significant changes taking place on college campuses. Never before the 1960s had so many Americans entered colleges and universities. Between 1946 and 1970, the number of students enrolled in institutions of higher education increased from 2 million to 8 million. Many college students became a class unto themselves—segregated from the workforce, free from many adult responsibilities, and encouraged by their professors to think critically. Many of the students who embraced the antiwar cause came from middle-class families. Students from working-class families were less likely to protest against the war.

The University of Michigan and the University of California at Berkeley became important hubs of the antiwar movement. The **Students for a Democratic Society (SDS)** was founded in 1960 at the University of Michigan. Originally formed to campaign against racism and poverty, the SDS soon began campaigning to end the war in Vietnam. By 1964, SDS had organized campus "teach-ins" and demonstrations against the war and encouraged draft-age males to sign "We Won't Go" petitions.

The 26th Amendment Although today people take for granted that 18- to 20-year-olds can vote, this was not the case until 1971. The drive to gain voting rights for young adults was yet another instance of people during this era demanding equality of political rights. In addition, since the issue concerned rights for young people, student activism played a key role in getting out the movement's key message: "old enough to fight, old enough to vote."

This idea was not exactly new. President Eisenhower, the former Supreme Commander of Allied Forces in WWII, backed the idea in his 1954 State of the Union message. In it, he said that since 18- to 20-year-old citizens were again and again summoned to risk their lives for our nation, "they should participate in the political process that produces this fateful summons."

But it was not until the issue was pressed by young people whose lives might soon be on the line in Vietnam that support for this area of voting rights gained steam. Once the proposed constitutional amendment won congressional support on March

>> Journalist Mike Wallace reports from the front lines. New broadcast technology meant that television viewers in the U.S. got an intimate glimpse of events in the war zone.

Bounce to Activate Gallery

23, 1971, it was quickly ratified by the states. By July 7, 1971, once the ratification was certified, the 26th Amendment was in place.

The Role of the Media and the "Credibility Gap" Outside college campuses, other Americans soon enlisted in the antiwar cause. Hawks and doves drifted farther apart. More groups organized against the war, their names corresponding with whom they represented—Vietnam Veterans Against the War, Catholic Peace Fellowship, Another Mother for Peace, and so on.

Antiwar sentiment was to some degree the result of the news media's extensive coverage of the war. A large majority of American households now had television sets. Most Americans learned the news of the war by watching TV news reports. Thus, the war in Vietnam became the first "living-room war." Americans watched its progress—or lack of it—in their living rooms on nightly newscasts.

For the first time, the brutal reality of war was broadcast into Americans' homes. They saw what the TV cameramen saw: death, destruction, horrible injuries, civilian casualties, and chaos. Horrific images also filled newspapers and news magazines. War correspondents issued reports, not of a string of great American victories leading to a clear goal, but of a messy conflict that seemed to lack a clear objective. As early as 1962, the printed the following gloomy forecast: "The United States seems inextricably committed to a long, inconclusive war."

Yet television and print journalists also broadcast and reported on government officials issuing optimistic statement after optimistic statement. Soon, a **"credibility gap"** emerged between what the Johnson administration said about the war and what many journalists reported about it. This gap referred to the American public's growing distrust of the statements made by the government.

☑ **ANALYZE INFORMATION** Before changes were made in 1969, why was the Selective Service System the subject of criticism?

The Tet Offensive

In November 1967, President Johnson brought General Westmoreland home from Vietnam to address the nation's concerns about the war. Westmoreland said that the Vietcong were declining in strength and could no longer mount a major offensive. As Westmoreland made his claims, however, the North Vietnamese and Vietcong were planning just such an attack.

Widespread Attacks In early 1968, U.S. officials anticipated a communist offensive. As expected, on January 21, the North Vietnamese Army hit Khe Sanh in northwest South Vietnam. However, ten days later, the communists expanded their attack by hitting U.S. and ARVN positions throughout South Vietnam. The **Tet Offensive**—named after the Vietnamese lunar new year—was a coordinated assault on 36 provincial capitals and 5 major cities, as well as the U.S. embassy in Saigon.

The communists planned to take and hold the cities until the urban population took up arms in their support. They thought the Tet Offensive had a good chance of ending the war.

The fighting was fierce, but in the end, American and South Vietnamese forces repelled the offensive, and there was no popular uprising against the government of South Vietnam. Although U.S. forces won a tactical victory by preventing the Vietcong and North Vietnamese Army from achieving their primary objectives, the Tet Offensive was a strategic blow to the Americans. It demonstrated that the communists had not lost the will or the ability to fight on.

Shifting Policy from Victory to Peace After the Tet Offensive, American military leaders seemed less confident of a quick end to the war. When Westmoreland requested more troops, President

>> **Analyze Maps** Identify two regions of South Vietnam that were hard-hit by the Tet Offensive.

Johnson asked his new Secretary of Defense, Clark Clifford, to take an objective look at the military and political situation in Vietnam. The deeper Clifford delved into the matter, the more pessimistic he became. Sending more troops would inevitably require raising taxes, increasing draft rolls, and calling up reserves. It would lead to increased casualties in the field and dissent at home. And it still might not lead to victory. Clifford, calling the war "a bottomless pit," concluded that the President should radically shift U.S. policy from one that pursued victory to one that pursued a negotiated peace.

Johnson Refuses to Seek Reelection While Clifford deliberated, many Americans began to turn dramatically against the war. Some marched in protest and engaged in antiwar activities. Others registered their disapproval at the polls. In early 1968, Minnesota senator **Eugene McCarthy**, the antiwar candidate for the Democratic Party nomination, made a surprisingly strong showing in the New Hampshire primary. Sensing that Johnson was in a politically weakened position, New York's Democratic senator **Robert Kennedy** announced his candidacy for the presidency. Both McCarthy and Kennedy believed that the war had divided America and drained resources away from the fights against poverty and discrimination. What Johnson feared most was happening: The war was undermining his presidency.

On March 31, 1968, two months after the Tet Offensive, the President addressed the nation on television. He announced that America would limit its bombing of North Vietnam and seek a negotiated settlement to the war. Johnson then shocked the nation by announcing that he would not run for another term as President. The speech marked another turning point in the war. The fight for victory was over. Peace was now the official government policy.

☑ **DETERMINE RELEVANCE** What was the relevance of the Tet Offensive for U.S. policy makers?

The 1968 Presidential Race

Johnson's decision not to seek reelection in 1968 threw the presidential race wide open. Many Americans believed it provided an opportunity to enact fundamental political and social changes.

>> An American tank patrols among the ruins in Saigon following the Tet Offensive in 1968. American forces were unprepared due to a cease-fire supposedly in effect during the celebration of Tet.

>> The assassination of presidential candidate Robert Kennedy in June 1968 shocked the nation and the world.

They argued that the future of the country was at stake. It was a time of new ideas and new plans. But the optimism and high hopes of the early campaign would soon die amidst political infighting, violence, and assassination.

King and Kennedy Assassinated In the spring and summer of the campaign season, bullets struck down two Americans who spoke out eloquently for peace in Vietnam and peaceful change in American society. Martin Luther King Jr., the most prominent leader of the civil rights movement, had publicly turned against the war in 1967. He contributed compelling social and moral reasons to the argument for peace. But his voice was tragically silenced on April 4, 1968, when a racist assassin shot and killed him in Memphis, Tennessee.

Robert Kennedy was the next leader to fall. He had based his campaign for the presidency on compassion and idealism, and millions of Americans rallied to his camp. On June 5, 1968, at a rally celebrating his victory in the California primary, Kennedy asserted that "we are a great country, an unselfish country, a compassionate country," and that he intended "to make that the basis of my running." Minutes later, a Palestinian immigrant named Sirhan Sirhan shot Kennedy in the head,

killing him instantly. Sirhan may have wanted revenge for America's support for Israel in that country's war with Egypt the year before.

The Chicago Democratic Convention The murders of King and Kennedy cast a dark shadow over the election campaigns. In August 1968, the Democrats convened in Chicago to choose a presidential candidate to represent their party in the November election. As the delegates arrived, so too did antiwar protesters. Chicago's mayor deployed police and members of the National Guard to prevent any outbreaks of violence.

Inside the convention, the Democrats angrily debated placing an antiwar plank in the party platform. They chose Hubert Humphrey, Johnson's Vice President, over Eugene McCarthy, who had garnered support from many antiwar groups. As the delegates cast their votes, violence between police and protesters erupted outside the convention. After police beat activists with nightsticks, some protesters retaliated by throwing rocks and bottles at the onrushing tide of police.

The television coverage of the fierce fighting in the streets and the bitter arguments on the convention floor shocked Americans. Chaos and civil disorder appeared to have replaced civil debate in the political arena. The divisions and violence in Chicago mirrored the deep divisions in American politics and the heartbreaking violence on the front lines in Vietnam.

Richard Nixon Wins the Presidency At a much more peaceful convention in Miami, Republicans nominated Richard M. Nixon, who promised if elected he would deliver "peace with honor." He wanted the United States out of Vietnam, but he also demanded honorable peace terms.

He promised to listen to "the great, quiet forgotten majority—the nonshouters and the nondemonstrators." This large group of Americans, described by one commentator as "the unyoung, the unblack, and the unpoor," was dubbed the "silent majority." Throughout his campaign, Nixon used a "Southern strategy" of courting more conservative Southern voters with appeals to law and order, striving to pull them away from their traditional support of the Democratic Party.

Alabama governor George Wallace also ran for the presidency on a third-party ticket. A lifelong Democrat prior to his entry into the race, Wallace said that neither of the traditional political parties represented Southern voters who were unsettled by the cultural and social changes in the country.

>> Chaos ensued as police clashed with protestors outside the 1968 Democratic National Convention, held in Chicago.

He had no sympathy for the demands of antiwar radicals, counterculture hippies, or African American militants. He represented the "white backlash" against the civil rights movement and the desire to press forward to victory in Vietnam.

The combination of Nixon's "Southern strategy" and Wallace's third-party candidacy siphoned traditionally Democratic votes away from Humphrey. In a close election, Nixon captured victory by winning 43.6 percent of the popular vote and 301 electoral votes. Humphrey received 42.5 percent of the popular vote and Wallace 13.6 percent. The election marked the end of the Democratic "Solid South" and signaled significant changes in the nation's political landscape. Richard Nixon's ascendancy marked a new Republican domination of the American presidency.

☑ **EXPRESS IDEAS CLEARLY** In your own words, who were the so-called "Silent Majority" and why did Nixon call them that?

☑ ASSESSMENT

1. **Determine Point of View** Discuss the reasons that many Americans criticized the draft system during the Vietnam War.

2. **Make Generalizations** Discuss the role of college students in the antiwar movement.

3. **Generate Explanations** Explain why the Vietnam War became known as the first "living-room war."

4. **Apply Concepts** Discuss the factors that influenced Richard Nixon's victory in the 1968 presidential election.

5. **Analyze Information** Explain how the Tet Offensive affected U.S. confidence in the Vietnam War.

>> Fourteen-year-old Mary Ann Vecchio kneels over the body of Kent State student Jeffrey Miller, age 20. Also killed were Allison Krause, 19; William Schroeder, 19; and Sandra Scheuer, 20.

Bounce to Activate Flipped Video

As a presidential candidate, Richard Nixon promised "peace with honor" and an end to a war that had fractured American society. Nixon did indeed withdraw American troops, and the Vietnam War finally ended. But the impact of the war endured. As the nation recovered from war, Americans reexamined the struggle against communism, the power of the presidency, and America's role in the world.

>> **Objectives**

Assess Nixon's new approach to the war, and explain why protests continued.

Explain what led to the Paris Peace Accords and why South Vietnam eventually fell to the communists.

Evaluate the impact of the Vietnam War on the United States.

>> **Key Terms**

Vietnamization
My Lai
Pentagon Papers
Paris Peace Accords
War Powers Act
Roy P. Benavidez

The War's End and Effects

Attempts to Withdraw from Vietnam

Nixon's defenders argued that he was a hard-working patriot with a new vision for America. His critics charged that he was a deceitful politician bent on acquiring power and punishing his enemies. There were elements of truth to both views. But defenders and critics alike agreed that Richard Nixon was a determined man with abundant political talent. From his first day in office, the new President realized that ending the Vietnam War was the key to everything else he hoped to achieve.

Peace Talks Stall Though formal peace talks between the warring parties had begun in May 1968, the talks bogged down from the outset due to disagreements and a lack of compromise. When Richard Nixon took office in January 1969, his peace delegation firmly believed they could break the impasse. The Americans and South Vietnamese wanted all communist troops out of South Vietnam.

They also wanted prisoners of war (POWs) returned. Meanwhile, the North Vietnamese demanded an immediate

American withdrawal from Vietnam and the formation of a coalition government in South Vietnam that would include representatives from the Vietcong. Still hoping to win the war in the field, North Vietnam refused to budge from its initial position. And South Vietnam refused to sign any agreement that compromised its security.

Vietnamization President Nixon refused to accept the North Vietnamese peace terms. He was committed to a policy of "peace with honor" and believed that there were still military options.

He continued a gradual pullout of American troops, and expressed faith in the ability of the Army of the Republic of Vietnam (ARVN) to assume the burden of war. He called his approach **Vietnamization**—U.S. forces would withdraw as ARVN troops assumed more combat duties. The hope was that with continued American aid behind the front lines, the ARVN would fight its own battles to secure South Vietnam.

To reduce the flow of communist supplies to the Vietcong, Nixon ordered the secret bombing of the Ho Chi Minh Trail in Cambodia. This was a controversial move because it widened the scope of the war and helped to undermine the neutral government in Cambodia. In the end, neither Vietnamization nor secret bombings dramatically improved South Vietnam's chances of winning a war against the communists.

☑ **GENERATE EXPLANATIONS** Explain why you think the bombings in Cambodia were kept secret.

Events Intensify the Antiwar Movement

Nixon inherited two things from Lyndon Johnson: an unpopular war and a vocal American opposition to it. The new President wanted "peace with honor," security for America's ally South Vietnam, and international respect for U.S. foreign policy. Antiwar activists wanted the war ended and American troops out of Vietnam—on any terms. Nixon found it increasingly difficult to achieve his goals and satisfy the snowballing antiwar movement.

The War Widens into Cambodia More than a year into office, Nixon had grown impatient with the snail's pace of the peace negotiations. In 1970, he attempted to break the stalemate by ordering a ground attack on North Vietnamese Army and Vietcong bases in Cambodia. Nixon also hoped to

>> President Nixon meets with his defense team in January 1971.

🅱 **Bounce to Activate Timeline**

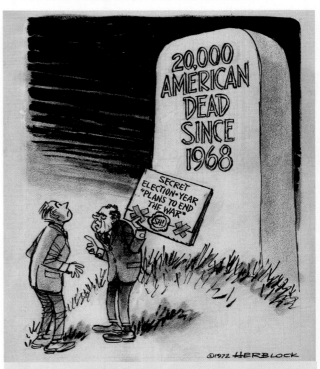

>> **Analyze Political Cartoons** What is the cartoon saying about the consequences of Nixon's lack of follow-through on a 1968 campaign promise?

aid the pro-American Cambodian government in its fight against the Khmer Rouge, a communist movement supported by North Vietnam.

On the evening of April 30, Nixon addressed the American people, informing them of his decision to carry the war into Cambodia. He stressed that the war had become a measure of how committed the United States was to preserving freedom around the world:

> If, when the chips are down, the world's most powerful nation, the United States of America, acts like a pitiful, helpless giant, the forces of totalitarianism and anarchy will threaten free nations . . . throughout the world.
>
> —President Richard Nixon, 1970

The next morning, U.S. and ARVN forces crossed the border into Cambodia. These soldiers captured large stockpiles of weapons and supplies, but they did not break the stalemate. North Vietnam remained determined to have peace on its terms or no peace at all.

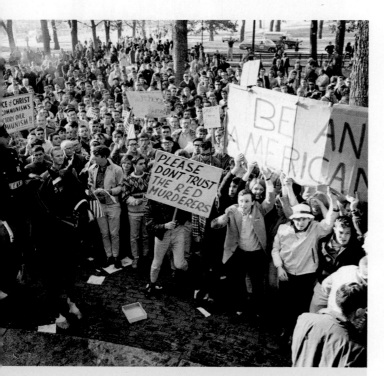

>> Students protesting American involvement in Vietnam are heckled by opposing students, many of whom carry anti-communist signs.

The Kent State Killings The Cambodian incursion had a profound impact on the peace movement at home. It stirred antiwar activists, who argued that Nixon had widened the war and made the world a more dangerous place. Throughout the country, college campuses erupted with protests. Several demonstrations prompted the police and National Guard to step in to preserve order.

On two campuses, confrontations between students and armed authorities led to deaths. Four days after Nixon's speech, demonstrators at Kent State University in Ohio threw rocks and bottles at members of the National Guard. When one guardsman thought he heard a sniper's shot, he fired his rifle. The shot prompted other National Guardsmen to discharge a volley of gunfire into a group of protesters, killing four youths. The Kent State killings led to demonstrations on other campuses. At Jackson State University, a historically African American college in Mississippi, a confrontation between students and police ended with two students dead.

College demonstrations against the war sometimes prompted counterprotests by Americans who supported the President. In response to a May 8, 1970, antiwar rally in downtown New York City, construction workers staged a counter-demonstration, carrying American flags and chanting "All the Way USA."

Believing that some anti-war demonstrators had spit on the American flag, they pushed into the crowd and started hitting the antiwar protesters. The clash drew national attention. Days later, thousands of construction workers, businessmen, secretaries, and housewives marched peacefully through Manhattan's streets in support of Nixon and the war effort. One man expressed his feelings about the march:

> I'm very proud to be an American, and I know my boy that was killed in Vietnam would be here today if he was alive, marching with us. . . . I know he died for the right cause, because in his letters he wrote to me he knew what he was fighting for: to keep America free. . . .
>
> —Robert Geary, May 20, 1970

As the fighting continued in Vietnam, the American home front became its own physical and emotional battlefield.

The My Lai Massacre In 1971, two events increased the pressure on Nixon to pull U.S. troops out of Vietnam. The first event had roots in a U.S. action in South Vietnam three years earlier.

On March 16, 1968, American forces searching for enemy troops in an area with a strong Vietcong presence came upon the village of **My Lai**. By this point in the war, many American troops had been injured and killed by Vietcong fighters posing as civilians. It was a recipe for disaster at My Lai, where Lieutenant William Calley's unit began shooting and killing unarmed civilians. During the assault, U.S. soldiers killed between four and five hundred Vietnamese.

Lt. Calley later maintained that he was following orders, but many of the soldiers present did not participate in the massacre. At least one risked his own life to stop it. The tragedy was made even worse by an inadequate military investigation of the incident. *Life* magazine eventually published disturbing photos taken during the event, and in March 1971, a military court convicted Lt. Calley of his participation in the attack. News of the My Lai massacre, the coverup, and Calley's trial shocked many Americans and added fuel to the burning antiwar fire.

The Pentagon Papers On the heels of My Lai came the 1971 publication of the **Pentagon Papers** in *The New York Times*. The papers were a classified government history of America's involvement in Vietnam. The study was leaked to *The Times* by one of its coauthors, Daniel Ellsberg. Nixon tried to block the full publication, but in *New York Times* v. *United States,* the Supreme Court ruled against the administration. The study revealed that American leaders involved the United States in Vietnam without fully informing the American people and occasionally even lied to Congress. Along with the invasion of Cambodia, the killings on college campuses, and the My Lai Massacre, the Pentagon Papers turned even more Americans against the war.

☑ **CHECK UNDERSTANDING** Why did the Nixon administration try to stop publication of the Pentagon Papers?

The Vietnam War Ends

The failings of Vietnamization and growing dissent at home forced President Nixon to search for some final way out of the conflict. A 1971 public-opinion poll revealed that two thirds of Americans favored withdrawing American troops, even if it meant a

>> A photographer captured the terrible scene in the village of My Lai where American troops killed civilians.

>> U.S. troops wait to return home after completing their tours in Vietnam. **Hypothesize** What difficulties might be faced by soldiers returning from duty?

ⓑ **Bounce to Activate Gallery**

communist takeover of South Vietnam. Sensitive to the public mood, Congress pressed Nixon to bring the troops home. Many believed that to win reelection in 1972, he had to end the war.

American Troops Withdraw from Vietnam In October 1972, the United States and North Vietnam came to terms on a peace settlement. One month later, with lasting peace almost at hand, Nixon easily defeated the antiwar Democrat George McGovern for reelection. But Nixon's triumph was short-lived. The Vietnamese peace fell apart when North Vietnam refused to sign the agreement. Talks broke off, but renewed American bombing in North Vietnam finally induced the North Vietnamese to resume negotiations.

At last, in January 1973, the United States, South Vietnam, North Vietnam, and the Vietcong signed the **Paris Peace Accords.** The parties agreed to a cease-fire and a U.S. troop withdrawal from South Vietnam. POWs would be exchanged, but North Vietnamese troops would remain in South Vietnam. The National Liberation Front (Vietcong) would become a legitimate political party in South Vietnam, and South Vietnam's noncommunist government would remain in power pending a political settlement. With the war ended, the last American troops came home. Among the returning soldiers were more than 550 POWs, most of whom were pilots shot down during the war.

The Fall of Saigon For the United States, the war in Vietnam was over. For the Vietnamese, however, it continued. Neither North nor South Vietnam honored the cease-fire or worked toward a diplomatic settlement of their differences. In the spring of 1975, minor fighting escalated when North Vietnam launched an offensive against the South.

Without American aid and ground support, the ARVN was no match for the Soviet-supplied North Vietnamese Army. By the end of April, the communists had taken Saigon. After decades of fighting and millions of deaths, Vietnam was unified under one flag.

☑ **RECALL** Did the Paris Peace Accords bring an end to fighting in Vietnam? Explain.

Effects of the Vietnam War

More than 58,000 American soldiers gave their lives serving their country in Vietnam; another 300,000 were wounded. Although figures are not exact, the Vietnamese death toll most likely exceeded 2 million.

HUMAN COST OF THE VIETNAM WAR

SERVICE UNIT
38,224 ARMY
14,844 MARINE CORPS
2,586 AIR FORCE
2,559 NAVY
7 COAST GUARD

58,220 AMERICANS KILLED OR MISSING

FATALITY CATEGORY
40,934 KILLED IN ACTION
9,107 ACCIDENTAL
5,299 FROM WOUNDS
2,880 OTHER

Source: National Archives Military Records

VIETNAM WAR DEATHS (THOUSANDS)
AMERICAN SOLDIERS 58,220
SOUTH VIETNAMESE SOLDIERS 200,000–250,000
NORTH VIETNAMESE SOLDIERS 900,000
VIETNAMESE CIVILIANS 1,000,000–2,000,000
CAMBODIAN CIVILIANS 500,000
LAOTIAN CIVILIANS 200,000

>> **Analyze Data** Compare the total number of civilian casualties to the number of military casualties. What do the totals tell you about the effects of modern warfare on civilian populations?

Peace, however, did not mean the end of pain and hardship. The end of the war created other problems in Southeast Asia. The war also affected American attitudes toward world affairs.

Southeast Asia After the War Many foreign-policy experts in the United States had predicted that if North Vietnam won the Vietnamese civil war, communism would spread to other nations in Southeast Asia. In a limited sense, they were right. Communist regimes eventually came to power in both Laos and Cambodia. In Cambodia, the ruling Khmer Rouge unleashed a genocide on the populace, killing everyone who had ties to the West or previous Cambodian governments. Between 1975 and 1979, upwards of 2 million Cambodians were executed or died in labor camps.

In an expanded sense, however, many American foreign-policy strategists misjudged the spread of communism. They concluded it was a monolithic global movement controlled by Moscow and Beijing. However, as the war's aftermath would attest, communist movements in Southeast Asia were nationalistic and intolerant of outside influences. In 1978, Vietnam invaded Cambodia and installed a pro-Vietnamese government. China supported the ousted Khmer Rouge. For more than ten years that followed, the U.S. supported a coalition of anti-communist Cambodian opposition groups that included the Khmer Rouge.

American Veterans Return Home The war and the peace divided Americans. Some argued that the United States should never have entered the war and that their leaders had lied to them. Others countered that the war was part of an ongoing struggle against communism and that in the end, the United States betrayed South Vietnam. An unfortunate result of the controversy was that the nation never fully expressed its appreciation to the returning veterans.

Overwhelmingly, the 2.5 million enlisted men who served in Vietnam did so with honor and distinction. Yet, unlike the soldiers that returned to the United States after World Wars I and II—the famed Doughboys and G.I. Joes—few Vietnam vets enjoyed the warmth and adulation of victory parades. In addition to the indifference that some veterans encountered, some also suffered from physical and psychological ailments for years when they returned home.

Not until almost a decade after the end of the war did Americans begin to fully honor the courage and sacrifice of these veterans. The Vietnam Veterans Memorial, dedicated in Washington, D.C., in 1982,

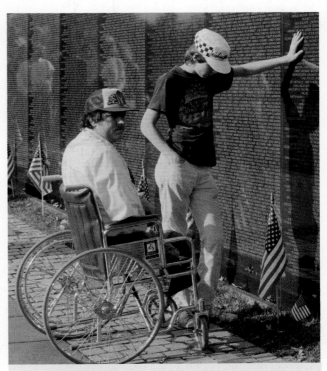

>> A veteran and his son visit the Vietnam Memorial in Washington, D.C. On this wall are the names of all military personnel who lost their lives in the war.

stands as an eloquent testament to the men and women who served and died in Vietnam.

Individuals of all races and genders served their country during the Vietnam War. There were countless actions of heroism and sacrifice, some of which were singled out for the Congressional Medal of Honor. For example, Army Sergeant Peter C. Lemon fought off numerous enemy assaults even after being seriously wounded three times. Marine Sergeant Rodney M. Davis was one of an astounding number of soldiers who gave his life to save the lives of others by diving on a live grenade and absorbing the explosion. Green Beret Sergeant **Roy P. Benavidez** was also decorated for his bravery in combat. Despite terrible injuries, he rescued the lives of at least eight men. For his outstanding gallantry, he was awarded the nation's highest military award: the Congressional Medal of Honor.

Sergeant Benavidez' gallant choice to join voluntarily his comrades who were in critical straits, to expose himself constantly to withering enemy fire, and his refusal to be stopped despite numerous severe wounds, saved the lives of at least eight men. His fearless personal leadership, tenacious devotion to duty, and extremely valorous actions in the face of overwhelming odds were in keeping with the highest traditions of the military service, and reflect the utmost credit on him and the United States Army.

—Citation, Congressional Medal of Honor, Sergeant Roy P. Benavidez

The Impact on U.S. Domestic and Foreign Policies The war was costly both monetarily and in the human toll of shattered lives. The war also altered American domestic and foreign policies. Lyndon Johnson's Great Society campaign against poverty and racism fell victim to the conflict. Increasingly, between 1964 and 1968, Johnson could not pay for both the Vietnam War and the Great Society. Paying for more guns left less money to pay for textbooks, school lunches, and prenatal care.

Additionally, the war undermined Americans' trust in their leaders and fragmented the Cold War

>> The voting age was reduced from 21 to 18 in 1971. **Draw Conclusions** Why did the war focus attention on the voting age?

consensus on foreign affairs. In 1973, Congress passed the **War Powers Act**. The act restricted the President's war-making powers by requiring him to consult with Congress within 48 hours of committing American forces to a foreign conflict. The act was a congressional attempt to check the unilateral formation of American foreign policy and stop the growth of the "imperial presidency."

Thus, the Vietnam War had an important impact on the relationship between the legislative and executive branches of government. With the Gulf of Tonkin Resolution, Congress had years earlier granted the President a great deal of power to conduct war using "all necessary measures" without further legislative approval.

The War Powers Act was an attempt to regain some of that power from the executive branch and return it to the legislative branch. Ultimately, the question of where war-making power lies is a constitutional issue. On one hand, the Constitution gives the power to declare war to Congress. On the other, it makes the President commander in chief of the armed forces.

The Vietnam War had an impact on America foreign policy, as well. The deaths and costs and ultimate failure of the war left many Americans with "war fatigue." Even those who had not been personally touched by the war had grown weary of the conflict. This weariness of war became a social factor that would be reflected in the U.S. role in the world from the 1970s through 1990. Throughout this time, American citizens would cite the Vietnam War as a cautionary tale whenever the country considered using force abroad. Many Americans would view conflicts in Central America, Africa, the Balkans, and the Middle East through a lens tinted by the fear of "another Vietnam."

The Impact on the American Economy The United States spent about $738 billion (in 2011 dollars) to fight the Vietnam War. Since that time, the government has spent an additional $270 billion on benefits for veterans and their families. These payments continue, costing the federal government more than $20 billion every year. Therefore, the Vietnam War can be said to have cost the country more than $1 trillion—and the price keeps going up.

This is a staggering amount of money, and it has had an enormous impact on the American economy. Many economists view the spending on the Vietnam War as marking the end of the prosperity of post–World War II America. War spending meant war production, and so American factories made military goods instead of consumer goods, warping

Economic Problems of the mid-1970s

UNEMPLOYMENT	Unemployment in the U.S. rose from 4 percent in 1970 to 9.5 percent by 1975.
INFLATION	Inflation reached 10 percent in the mid-1970s, the highest it had been in the twentieth century up to that point.
ENERGY CRISIS	An oil embargo in 1973 caused a severe shortage of gas, and prices soared from 40 cents per gallon in 1973 to $1.20 by 1980.
GOVERNMENT SPENDING	In 1970, total government spending was $321.8 billion; by 1975, spending had risen to $550.5 billion.

>> **Analyze Information** What economic problems affected the greatest number of Americans? Explain.

American industry. Although the relationships are complex, war spending was a factor in federal budget deficits, inflation, higher interest rates, and a weaker dollar.

Interestingly, this greatly increased amount of defense spending did not cut into the amount of money the nation spent on education. By one estimate, public school expenditures actually increased by 58 percent in the 1960s and 27 percent in the 1970s. Federal aid outlays to college students also increased between 1965 and 1975. All in all, however, the American economy in the 1970s was marked by crises, which many attribute to the economic effects of the Vietnam War.

☑ **ANALYZE INFORMATION** What effect did the quagmire in Vietnam have on U.S. foreign policy through 1990?

☑ **ASSESSMENT**

1. **Identify Central Issues** Discuss the measures that President Nixon took in order to withdraw U.S. troops from the Vietnam War.

2. **Sequence Events** Explain the events leading up to the Kent State killings.

3. **Identify Cause and Effect** Discuss the economic effects of the Vietnam War, and explain how its costs are still affecting the United States today.

4. **Generate Explanations** Discuss the "war fatigue" that many Americans felt after the Vietnam War, and explain how it affected U.S. foreign policy.

5. **Generate Explanations** Explain how the spread of communism after the Vietnam War differed from U.S. strategists' expectations.

LESSON SUMMARIES

Use these Lesson Summaries, and the longer versions available online, to review the key ideas for each lesson in this Topic.

Lesson 1: The Cold War and Vietnam

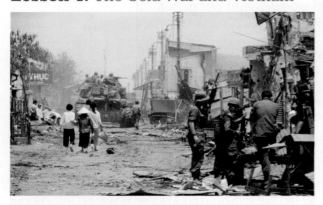

A failed U.S. invasion of Cuba was followed by another crisis as President Kennedy forced the Soviets to remove nuclear missiles from that island. The Soviets build a wall between communist East Berlin and free West Berlin. The U.S. helped the French as they lost control of Vietnam, then committed more troops to that country.

Lesson 2: America's Role Escalates

In 1965, President Johnson launched a bombing campaign in Vietnam but was unable to gain a military advantage against the guerrilla tactics of the Vietcong. By 1968 the war had become a stalemate, with tens of thousands of Americans dead. Meanwhile, the financial costs of the war deepened political division at home.

Lesson 3: The Antiwar Movement

Optimistic U.S. government reports about the progress of the war were contradicted by events on the ground and led many Americans to doubt official statements. A communist offensive in 1968 showed that the enemy was strong enough to fight a long war. Opposition to the war and the draft grew, leading to violent disorder at home.

Lesson 4: The War's End and Effects

Although President Nixon began withdrawing U.S. troops from Vietnam, his decision to launch attacks in Cambodia revived the antiwar movement. In 1973 an agreement allowed U.S. troops to withdraw, but fighting continued until South Vietnam was defeated by the communists.

VISUAL REVIEW

Use these graphics to review some of the key terms, people, and ideas from this Topic.

Kennedy's Foreign Policy

FOREIGN POLICY EVENT	OUTCOME
1959 Castro takes control of Cuba; thousands flee to Miami and southern Florida.	1961 In Bay of Pigs invasion of Cuba, Kennedy launches Eisenhower's plan to overthrow Castro but fails.
1961 Soviets build Berlin Wall.	Kennedy sends troops to West Berlin.
1962 Cuban missile crisis	Kennedy forces Soviets to withdraw missiles from Cuba.

Roots of U.S. Involvement in Vietnam

FRANCE LOSES CONTROL OF VIETNAM	
BEFORE	AFTER
French-Indochina War: French forces battle Vietnamese communists under Ho Chi Minh.	**Geneva Accords:** France grants independence to former colonies; Vietnam divided.
Cold War: Truman helps France in order to maintain Cold War alliance against the Soviets.	**SEATO:** U.S. assembles coalition to oppose spread of communism in Southeast Asia.
Domino Theory: Eisenhower continues aid to French to prevent communist victory.	**U.S. Intervention:** U.S. supports anticommunist Diem regime and sends troops to Vietnam.

The Antiwar Movement

- Civil Rights leaders speak out against the war.
- Loss of confidence in domino theory.
- The draft system is perceived as unjust.
- **OPPOSITION TO VIETNAM WAR**
- Belief that war was not a vital Cold War battleground.
- Some oppose for economic reasons.
- Pacifists oppose warfare.

Long-term Consequences of Vietnam War

U.S. Foreign Policy	• Congress passes War Powers Act to restrict President's war powers. • Post-World War II consensus on foreign affairs fragments. • U.S. grows wary of involvement in foreign conflicts.
U.S. Domestic Policy	• Trust in government is undermined. • Costs of war weaken Great Society programs. • Veterans' benefits continue to rise.

KEY TERMS, PEOPLE, AND IDEAS

1. What was the philosophy behind Kennedy's creation of the **Peace Corps** and the **Alliance for Progress**?

2. What role did **Nikita Khrushchev** play in the **Cuban missile crisis**?

3. How did Castro's revolution affect the United States?

4. How did the **domino theory** shape U.S. policy in Vietnam?

5. How did the **Tet Offensive** affect U.S. policy and public support for the war?

6. Why did Nixon expand the war into Cambodia?

7. How did the **Pentagon Papers** increase Americans' opposition to the war?

8. Why did Congress pass the **War Powers Act**?

9. What happened in Vietnam in the years after the **Paris Peace Accords** were signed?

CRITICAL THINKING

10. **Compare and Contrast** (a.) What was Kennedy's flexible response defense policy? (b.) How did it differ from Eisenhower's policy?

11. **Cite Evidence** What were some successes and failures of Kennedy's foreign policy?

12. **Identify Cause and Effect** What factors caused the American involvement in the Vietnam War?

13. **Draw Inferences** (a.) How did the Gulf of Tonkin Resolution expand the President's power? (b.) How did the resolution affect the relationship between the legislative and executive branches of government?

14. **Draw Conclusions** (a.) What military advantages did the communist forces have in Vietnam? (b.) How did these advantages undermine the strength of U.S. forces?

15. **Make Generalizations** What were the consequences of the Vietnam War?

16. **Analyze Maps** Look at the map below. Why did the United States feel increasingly threatened by Castro's regime after the failed Bay of Pigs invasion?

17. **Writing Activity: Use Primary Sources** Walter Cronkite was the most influential broadcast journalist of the 1960s. Use the excerpt below and your knowledge of the Vietnam War to evaluate how the media shaped public opinion about the war.

> To say that we are closer to victory today is to believe, in the face of the evidence, the optimists who have been wrong in the past. To suggest we are on the edge of defeat is to yield to unreasonable pessimism. To say that we are mired in stalemate seems the only realistic, yet unsatisfactory, conclusion. . . . But it is increasingly clear . . . that the only rational way out then will be to negotiate, not as victors, but as an honorable people who lived up to their pledge to defend democracy, and did the best they could.
>
> This is Walter Cronkite. Good night.
>
> —*Walter Cronkite, February 27, 1968*

DOCUMENT-BASED QUESTIONS

The Vietnam War transformed American politics, especially in the 1968 presidential race. Read the documents below, then answer the questions that follow.

DOCUMENT A

This excerpt is from a secondary source about Lyndon Johnson and Robert Kennedy.

> The feud that helped define the public lives of LBJ and RFK also helped shape the two greatest national undertakings of their times—the war on poverty and the war in Vietnam. Consumed by contempt for Kennedy, Johnson transformed a potential ally into an archenemy. . . . As Johnson and Kennedy became ever more bitter enemies, they divided constituencies they once shared, weakening their party by forcing its members to choose between them. They exposed and exacerbated the growing divide within the Democratic Party and American politics in general.
>
> —*Jeff Shesol, Mutual Contempt*

DOCUMENT B

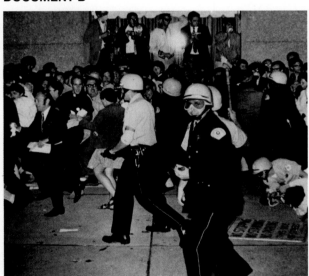

DOCUMENT C

This excerpt is from President Johnson's announcement on March 31, 1968.

> It is true that a house divided against itself by the spirit of faction, of party, of region, of religion, of race, is a house that cannot stand. There is division in the American house now. . . . I should not permit the Presidency to become involved in the partisan divisions that are developing in this political year. With America's sons in the fields far away, with America's future under challenge right here at home, with our hopes and the world's hopes for peace in the balance every day, I do not believe that I should devote an hour or a day of my time to any personal partisan causes or to any duties other than the awesome duties of this office—the Presidency of your country. Accordingly, I shall not seek, and I will not accept, the nomination of my party for another term as your President.
>
> —*President Lyndon B. Johnson, March 31, 1968*

DOCUMENT D

This excerpt is from a speech by Richard Nixon.

> For four years America's fighting men have set a record for courage and sacrifice unsurpassed in our history. . . . Never has so much military and economic and diplomatic power been used so ineffectively. . . . I say the time has come for the American people to turn to new leadership not tied to the mistakes and policies of the past. That is what we offer to America. And I pledge to you tonight that the first priority foreign policy objective of our next Administration will be to bring an honorable end to the war in Vietnam.
>
> —*Republican Presidential Nominee Richard M. Nixon, August 8, 1968*

18. In Document A, the relationship between President Johnson and Robert Kennedy is described as
  A. strengthening the Democratic Party.
  B. dividing the Republicans from the Democrats.
  C. a feud destroying the Democrats from within.
  D. caused by disagreement over Vietnam.

19. Analyze Photographs What does Document B reveal about the Democratic National Convention of 1968?

20. In Document C, Johnson explains that he will not run for a second term as president because
  A. he is afraid of losing the election.
  B. his Democratic support would be too weak.
  C. he fears splitting the Democratic Party.
  D. the Vietnam conflict is consuming his attention.

21. Document D, Nixon is implying that
  A. the war has been mismanaged.
  B. the war is dividing the nation.
  C. his administration would seek peace immediately.
  D. the domino theory was bad foreign policy.

22. Writing Activity: Primary Source Write a paragraph explaining the political divisions that split the nation and the Democratic Party in 1968. Use the sources as well as additional information you have learned.

End-of-Topic Practice

1 How did U.S. involvement in postwar Germany contribute to the construction of the Berlin Wall?

A The East Germans built the wall to keep American soldiers from invading East Berlin.

B The United States was forced to build the wall to contain the communist regime of East Berlin.

C The Soviets built the wall after the United States refused to give up its occupation of West Berlin.

D The Soviets built the wall to stop U.S. soldiers from crossing the border into East Berlin without permission.

---

2 What constitutional questions did Congress raise by passing the Gulf of Tonkin Resolution?

F Congress ceded many of its war powers to the executive branch.

G Congress affirmed its powers to declare war under the Constitution.

H Congress handed all its legislative powers to the President.

I A conflict was created between federal and state power.

3 Growing numbers of Americans came to believe that the Vietnam War was a civil war. What effect did this have on Cold War assumptions?

A It challenged the idea of an international communist conspiracy.

B It undermined the idea that the U.S. had to take sides in every foreign conflict.

C It demonstrated that the doctrine of containment was ineffective.

D It showed that some communist groups were not getting Russian or Chinese support.

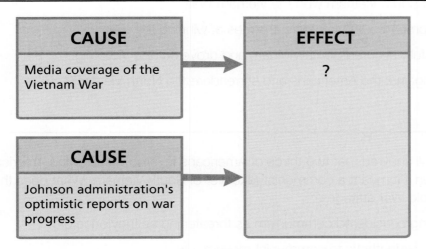

CAUSE

Media coverage of the Vietnam War

EFFECT

?

CAUSE

Johnson administration's optimistic reports on war progress

4 What phrase best replaces the question mark in the graphic organizer above?

F A credibility gap for the American public

G An increase in public support for the war

H A willingness in Congress to cut war funding

I The censorship of news reports from Vietnam

If you have trouble with...				
Question	1	2	3	4
See Lesson	9.1	9.1	9.2	9.3

End-of-Topic Practice

Vietnamization

- Gradual pullout of American troops

- Assumption of more combat duties by South Vietnamese troops (ARVN)

- American aid behind the front lines as opposed to on the battlefield

---

5 What was the result of the policy of Vietnamization?

A The United States and South Vietnam won the Vietnam War.

B The policy failed to improve South Vietnam's chances of winning the war.

C ARVN troops successfully secured South Vietnam and drove out the Vietcong.

D ARVN troops turned against the Americans and surrendered to North Vietnam.

---

6 A 1971 public-opinion poll showed that two thirds of Americans favored withdrawing American troops from Vietnam, even if it meant a communist takeover of South Vietnam. What does this reveal about changing Cold War attitudes?

F Most Americans no long considered communism as threatening as they once did.

G Americans were more sympathetic to communist movements.

H Most Americans had turned against South Vietnam.

I Americans thought that their country was the aggressor in the conflict.

7 What did some of the tactics of nonviolent civil rights protesting aim to accomplish?

    A to force state legislatures to pass civil rights laws

    B to refuse to interact with people who did not support civil rights

    C to provoke others to commit violence

    D to test state-level compliance with Supreme Court decisions

LEGACY OF THE GREAT SOCIETY

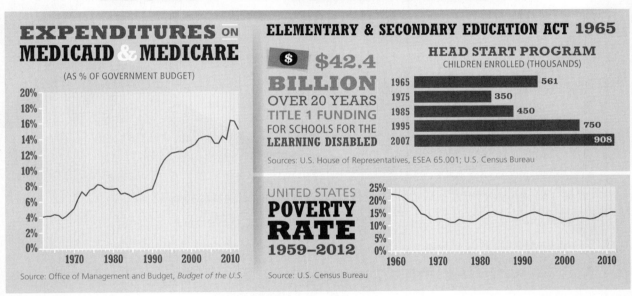

EXPENDITURES ON MEDICAID & MEDICARE
(AS % OF GOVERNMENT BUDGET)

Source: Office of Management and Budget, *Budget of the U.S.*

ELEMENTARY & SECONDARY EDUCATION ACT 1965

$ $42.4 BILLION OVER 20 YEARS TITLE 1 FUNDING FOR SCHOOLS FOR THE **LEARNING DISABLED**

HEAD START PROGRAM
CHILDREN ENROLLED (THOUSANDS)

Year	Enrolled
1965	561
1975	350
1985	450
1995	750
2007	908

Sources: U.S. House of Representatives, ESEA 65.001; U.S. Census Bureau

UNITED STATES POVERTY RATE 1959–2012

Source: U.S. Census Bureau

8 Based on the information from the lessons and in the chart, which statement most clearly represents a positive result of the Great Society initiatives?

    F The poverty rate decreased between 1960 and 2010.

    G Fewer children were enrolled in Head Start in 1985 than in 1965.

    H More than 40 billion tax dollars have been spent on Title 1 funding.

    I Government spending for Medicaid and Medicare has increased over the last 30 years.

If you have trouble with...				
Question	5	6	7	8
See Lesson	9.4	9.4	8.1	8.5

[**ESSENTIAL QUESTION**] What are the challenges of diversity?

(10) **An Era of Change**

STOCK
ART FAIR

ents

N

ARIAN

SITION

AKE, N.Y.*

>> 1969 Poster for the famous music festival at Woodstock, New York

Enduring Understandings

- The United States experienced a period of rapid social and cultural change in the 1960s and 1970s.

- Movements for equal rights for women and minorities emerged in the 1960s.

- Economic problems at home and political problems abroad characterized the 1970s.

- The political turbulence of the 1960s provoked a conservative reaction in the 1970s.

NBC LEARN

Learn more about Betty Friedan, the feminist activist.

Bounce to Activate My Story Video

In this Topic, you'll learn about events during an era of great change that began in 1960. Look at the lesson outline and explore the timeline. As you study this Topic, you'll complete the Quest team project.

LESSON OUTLINE

10.1 The Counterculture of the 1960s
HSS 11.8.8

10.2 The Women's Rights Movement
HSS 11.10.7, HSS 11.11.3

10.3 Expanding the Push for Equality
HSS 11.6.5, HSS 11.10.5; Analysis CST.4

10.4 The Environmental Movement
HSS 11.8.6, HSS 11.11.5; Analysis HI.5

10.5 The Two Sides of the Nixon Presidency
HSS 11.9, HSS 11.11.2, HSS 11.11.4

10.6 Ford and Carter Struggle
HSS 11.3, HSS 11.9, HSS 11.9.3

An Era of Change (1960–1980)

1962 Rachel Carson's *Silent Spring* is published

1967 Hippies converge on San Francisco

1973 Oil embargo causes U.S. energy prices to soar

1974 Nixon resigns; Ford becomes president

1966 United Farm Workers union is formed

1969 Huge countercultural festival held at Woodstock, NY

1979 Protesters seize U.S. embassy hostages in Tehran, Iran

1960　　1965　　1970　　1975　　1980

QUEST!

TEAM PROJECT

Analyzing the Leadership Qualities of Nixon, Ford, and Carter

What effects did the leadership styles of Nixon, Ford and Carter have on the nation? How can we evaluate the success of these presidents' foreign and domestic policies? In this Quest you'll learn about presidential leadership and write an essay on the subject.

STEP ①

Watch a video about Watergate. Then discuss the video in class or with a partner. Write down questions you might have about Nixon's leadership.

STEP ②

Examine six sources relating to the leadership styles of Nixon, Ford, and Carter. Answer the questions attached to each document.

STEP ③

Draw your own conclusions based on all the evidence and viewpoints. Remember to read and revise your essay before submitting it to your teacher.

STEP ④

Reflect on what you have learned about the subject and about the process of writing your essay.

PEARSON
realize™
PearsonSchool.com/CASS

Go ONLINE for complete Quest materials

 VIDEO   ETEXT   WRITING   RUBRIC   PDF   ASSESSMENT

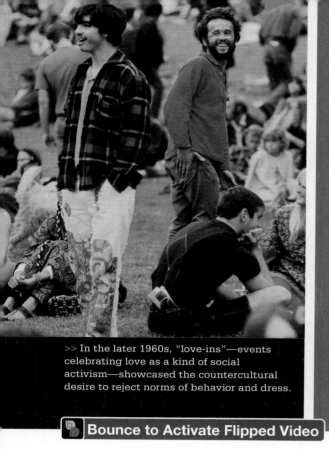

>> In the later 1960s, "love-ins"—events celebrating love as a kind of social activism—showcased the countercultural desire to reject norms of behavior and dress.

Bounce to Activate Flipped Video

Many of the generation born after the challenging times of the Great Depression and World War II embraced a different worldview than that of their parents—a worldview that found dramatic expression in the counterculture movement that arose in the 1960s. Members of the counterculture adopted values that ran counter to mainstream culture. They rebelled against long-standing customs in dress, music, and personal behavior. The counterculture both challenged the values of mainstream American society and provoked a countermovement to reassert traditional values.

>> Objectives

Describe the rise of the counterculture.

List the major characteristics of the counterculture.

Evaluate the positive and negative impacts of the counterculture movement on American society.

>> Key Terms

counterculture
generation gap
Beatles
communes
counterculture

The Counterculture of the 1960s

A Counterculture Emerges

Countercultural Values The counterculture was rooted in the events of the preceding decade. In the 1950s, the Beat movement had rejected materialism and emphasized the importance of personal experience. The civil rights movement introduced the idea of social and political protest, which intensified the Vietnam antiwar movement. Both movements prompted many to challenge a range of traditional social behavior, from restrictions on rights to cultural norms in dress or hairstyles. The counterculture also heightened distrust of authority, leading some young people to warn their peers, "Don't trust anyone over 30."

Members of the counterculture valued youth, spontaneity, and freedom of expression. In the mid-1960s a subculture known as the hippies emerged. These young people claimed to value peace, love, and freedom. They experimented with new styles of dress and music, freer sexual relationships, and the recreational use of drugs. Their values were so different from traditional ones that many social analysts described America as experiencing a **generation gap**, in which there was a lack of understanding and communication between the old and young. Jerry Rubin, a political activist, described how young people's fashion for long hair divided parents from their children:

> Young kids identify short hair with authority, discipline. . . . Wherever we go, our hair tells people where we stand on Vietnam, Wallace, campus disruption, dope. . . . Yesterday I was walking down the street. A car passed by, parents in the front seat and a young kid, about eight, in the back seat. The kid flashed me the clenched fist sign. [Meaning: He identified with Rubin's long hair.]
>
> —Jerry Rubin, *America in the Sixties*

The baby boom that followed World War II resulted in a huge student population in the 1960s. Through their numbers alone, the baby boomers became a force for social change. The music industry rushed to produce the music they liked; clothing designers copied the styles they introduced; universities were forced to change college courses and rules to accommodate them.

The Generation Gap The large population of baby boomers and their emerging influence emphasized the growing divide between the younger and older generations. In the 1960s and 1970s, many parents and their children had little in common apart from their genes. Parents of boomer children were heavily influenced by the two major events of their own childhoods, the Depression and World War II. Boomers' parents had learned to live frugally through years of rationing during the Depression and war.

As teens, they had listened to big-band music. They generally valued loyalty and authority, and respected the military and veterans. Many also married at a young age, choosing to take on the responsibilties of a family. As a result, many in this so-called "silent generation," sought stability by conforming.

Their baby-boomer children on the other hand rejected tradition and authority in favor of individuality. "Do your own thing!" became the catchphrase of the young. Boomers did not want to fit in; they wanted to stand out. With the economic difficulties of the 1930s and 40s a distant memory, boomers grew up in a time of prosperity for much of the nation. Many embraced political activism and opposed the Vietnam War. The boomer generation

>> The generation gap in dress: Ed Sullivan, the reserved TV host born in 1901, thanks the Rolling Stones' Mick Jagger after the Stones' performance on Sullivan's show in 1969.

Bounce to Activate Gallery

>> Members of the counterculture movement came together to promote what they felt was missing from mainstream culture; an emphasis on personal experience, love, and freedom.

also expressed a distrust of tradition and authority, which was expressed in popular magazines like *MAD*. Rock-and-roll music shaped their worldview and set them apart from their parents, who had grown up in a very different world.

☑ **IDENTIFY SUPPORTING DETAILS** What accounts for the generational differences between baby boomers and their parents?

The Counterculture Shapes a Generation

Many people have used the so-called trinity of the counterculture—sex, drugs, and rock-and-roll—to define the youth generation. But the counterculture was also marked by an interest in spirituality.

A Cultural Revolution in the Arts By the 1960s, rock-and-roll had become a defining characteristic of the baby-boom generation. When the **Beatles** made a triumphant visit to the United States in 1964, more than 70 million Americans watched the English rock band perform on Ed Sullivan's television show. The Beatles also had an impact on folk musicians like Bob Dylan, whose protest songs highlighted the civil rights and peace movements.

As radical poet and activist John Sinclair put it, rock became "a weapon of cultural revolution," that urged listeners to reject conventions and, in many cases, the political policies of the government. Even after the counterculture had declined in significance, rock music remained popular among baby-boomers as well as their children.

The art and literature of the 1960s and 1970s also displayed a rebellious side. Andy Warhol's realistic paintings of ordinary grocery items, such as Campbell's soup cans, questioned traditional ideas of art and mocked the values of consumerism. In literature, the novels of Tom Wolfe and Hunter S. Thompson blurred the lines between reporting and political activism.

Experiments in Living and the Sexual Revolution Members of the counterculture rejected many traditional restrictions on sexual behavior in what became known as the "sexual revolution." They called for the enjoyment of sex for its own sake and often advocated new living patterns. For example, many hippies lived together in **communes**, or small communities in which the people have common interests and share resources.

The sexual revolution was one of the strongest indicators of the generation gap. One poll showed that nearly two-thirds of all Americans over the age

>> The Beatles, a rock band that emerged from the British counterculture, transformed American popular music and fashion in the 1960s.

>> This concert poster for the rock band The Grateful Dead shows the kind of "psychedelic" art that emerged from San Francisco in the 1960s.

of 30 opposed premarital sex, whereas a majority of those under age 29 did not. Eventually, however, the sexual revolution led to a more open discussion of sex in the mainstream media.

Impact of the Hippie Culture in San Francisco

In 1967, as many as 2,000 people flocked to the Haight-Ashbury district of San Francisco, a center of the counterculture. Hippies there experimented with drugs, wore unconventional clothing, and listened to rock music and speeches by political radicals such as Timothy Leary, a one-time Harvard researcher. He preached that drugs could free the mind, and he encouraged American youths to "tune in," "turn on" to drugs, and "drop out" of mainstream society. The hippies of San Francisco attracted a great deal of media attention, much of it critical of the lifestyles they advocated. Life in Haight-Ashbury did lead to negative consequences. As in other enclaves of hippie culture, it experienced high rates of drug abuse that led to increased crime.

Seeking New Forms of Spirituality Some members of the counterculture sought spiritual enlightenment outside of the Judeo-Christian traditions in which they had been raised. Many explored Buddhism and other Eastern religions, while others sought spirituality by living in harmony with nature. Particularly in the late 1960s and early 1970s, some hippies established rural communes, seeking to live off the land as Native Americans had in the past. These beliefs had a lasting impact on the budding environmental movement.

Positive and Negative Effects of the Counterculture By the end of the 1960s, many people, even those within the counterculture, had become disillusioned with some of its excesses. The utopian urge to discover a more authentic way of living had an unfortunate underside. Drug addictions and deaths from overdoses rose. The hedonism and violence of rock-and-roll seemed to be having a negative effect, as a number of rock musicians, most famously Jimi Hendrix and Janis Joplin, died of drug overdoses while only in their twenties. The downward spiral continued in 1969 with a tragedy at a music festival in Altamont, California.

While the Rolling Stones played, members of the Hells Angels, a motorcycle gang that had been hired to provide security, stabbed to death a black man who had approached the stage. The ugly violence contradicted the values of "peace and love" that many hippies embraced.

At the same time, the movement's values were becoming increasingly shallow and self-centered.

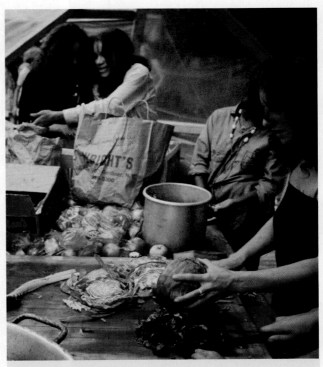

>> Members of the Hog Farm commune gather to prepare a meal. Living off the land, they created a community of like-minded people.

Bounce to Activate Gallery

When the counterculture fell apart, most hippies abandoned their social experiments and melted right back into the mainstream. Still, the seeds of protest they had planted would influence the growing "rights revolution."

☑ **IDENTIFY SUPPORTING DETAILS** In what ways was the music of artists like Bob Dylan relevant to the time?

☑ ASSESSMENT

1. **Contrast** the values of the baby boomers with those of the "silent generation."

2. **Describe** the defining characteristics of the counterculture movement.

3. **Generate Explanations** Explain how earlier social and political movements influenced the counterculture movement of the 1960s.

4. **Identify Cause and Effect** Discuss significant events that led to the decline of the counterculture movement.

5. **Draw Conclusions** Discuss the lasting effects of the counterculture movement.

>> Coretta Scott King, widow of Martin Luther King Jr., addresses a group of feminists at a National Women's Conference in support of minority women's rights.

Bounce to Activate Flipped Video

10.2 In the 1960s and 1970s, American women launched a broad-based movement to expand economic opportunities and attain equal rights. The women's movement fundamentally changed many aspects of American life— from family and education to careers and political issues. Today, the contributions of people of various gender groups continue to shape American culture.

>> Objectives

Analyze why a movement to expand women's political rights arose in the 1960s.

Identify the goals and methods that political organizations used to promote women's rights.

Assess the impact of the women's movement on American society.

>> Key Terms

feminism
Betty Friedan
National
  Organization for
  Women (NOW)
Equal Rights
  Amendment (ERA)
Gloria Steinem
Phyllis Schlafly

The Women's Rights Movement

A New Feminist Movement Pushes for Equality

Historians often refer to the women's movement of the 1960s and 1970s as the second wave of **feminism**, or the theory of political, social, and economic equality of men and women. The struggle for women's rights in the United States has had a long history, going back at least to the 1840s, when women drafted the Declaration of Sentiments at Seneca Falls, New York.

The phrase *second wave of feminism* also reminds us that the first wave, which culminated with women winning the right to vote in 1920, ended well before the nation addressed the call for full equality. In the decades that followed, women made little legal or social headway in the battle for equal rights. In fact, after World War II, most women gave up their jobs to returning servicemen and went back to their homes to take care of their families. During the 1950s, social analysts and popular culture portrayed women, especially suburban housewives, as the personification of America's achievement of the good life. By the 1960s, attitudes like these had begun to change.

Seeking to Redefine Traditional Roles Several factors influenced the rebirth of the women's movement in the 1960s and 1970s. The civil rights struggle prompted women to look at the ways in which society judged and discriminated against them as a group. As Casey Hayden and Mary King, two veterans of that movement, put it: "Sex and caste. There seem to be many parallels that can be drawn between the treatment of Negroes and the treatment of women in society as a whole." Hayden and King used the phrase "Jane Crow" to emphasize a link between racial and gender discrimination.

The civil rights movement both inspired women to demand gender equality and taught them how to achieve it. It also brought black and white women together, strengthening their shared cause.

Women also wanted to redefine how they were viewed. Many women objected to the inaccuracy of the housewife stereotype. Some needed to work to support themselves or their families. Others wanted more opportunities outside the home. **Betty Friedan** powerfully articulated this message in her groundbreaking book *The Feminine Mystique*.

> The problem lay buried, unspoken, for many years in the minds of American women. It was a strange stirring, a sense of dissatisfaction. . . . Each suburban wife struggled with it alone. As she made the beds, shopped for groceries, matched slipcover material, ate peanut butter sandwiches with her children, chauffeured Cub Scouts and Brownies, lay beside her husband at night— she was afraid to ask even of herself the silent question—'Is this all?'
>
> —Betty Friedan, *The Feminine Mystique*, 1963

Fighting Workplace Discrimination Despite the stereotypes, the number of women in the workforce grew throughout the 1950s and 1960s. Yet working women often found themselves in dead-end jobs. Regardless of the quality of their work, women found it difficult to advance or even retain their positions. Pregnancy, for example, was all too often seen as grounds for dismissal or demotion. In many cases, pregnant women were routinely denied leave or forced to take unpaid leave.

Even women with advanced training and education had their access to careers or advancement blocked, in many cases, by blatantly discriminatory employers. Sandra Day O'Connor, who ultimately became the first female Supreme

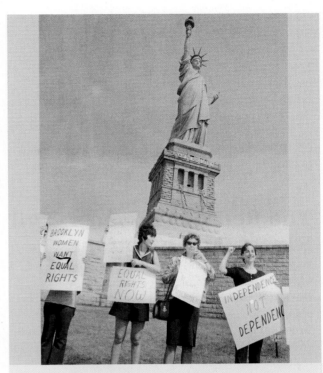

>> The 1960s and 1970s witnessed a broad-based struggle for equal rights among women in the United States.

>> Betty Friedan, president of the National Organization for Women (NOW), claimed that it was not simply men, but society in general, that kept women unequal.

Court Justice, graduated near the top of her class at Stanford Law School in the early 1950s.

Yet while she found few employment opportunities upon graduation, her male counterparts won job offers at prestigious law firms. Facing such restrictions, women increasingly demanded equal treatment in the workplace.

☑ **IDENTIFY MAIN IDEAS** What was an essential goal of the feminist movement?

The Role of Women's Civil Rights Organizations

Several years after she wrote *The Feminine Mystique*, Betty Friedan helped establish the **National Organization for Women (NOW)**. The organization—which dedicated itself to winning "true equality for all women" and to attaining a "full and equal partnership of the sexes"—galvanized the women's movement.

NOW Works to Expand Rights Through Lobbying NOW was formed to compel the federal government to enforce the part of the Civil Rights Act of 1964 that outlawed sex discrimination in

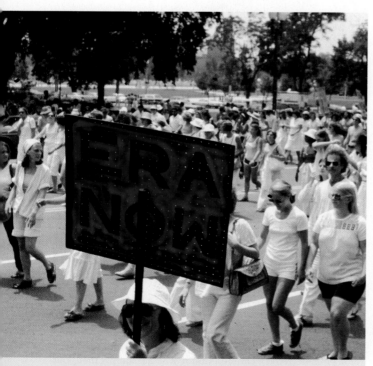

>> In 1978, over 100,000 women marched in Washington, D.C., to demand that Congress extend the deadline for ratification of the Equal Rights Amendment.

Bounce to Activate Timeline

employment. The organization set out to break down barriers of discrimination in the workplace and in education. It attacked stereotypes of women in the media and called for more balance in roles in marriages. Its major goal in the 1970s was to bring about passage of the **Equal Rights Amendment (ERA)**, an amendment to the Constitution that would guarantee gender equality under the law. The ERA initially had been proposed in the early 1920s but had never passed. NOW also wanted to protect reproductive rights, especially the right to an abortion. NOW worked within the existing political system, lobbying for political reforms and readying court cases to compel the government to enforce existing legislation that banned discrimination. For some women, NOW seemed too extreme; for others, it was not extreme enough. Still, NOW served as a rallying point to promote equality for all women.

Feminists Raise Society's Awareness Through Different Methods Finding NOW too tame, radical feminists sought a more fundamental restructuring of society. Rather than seeking legislative change, these protesters sought to show the way society trapped women into adopting restrictive roles. Like the civil rights campaigners, they adopted a variety of nonviolent methods. In addition to public protests of the Miss America Pageant, radical feminists engaged in small-scale consciousness-raising efforts. Other feminists sought to raise public awareness by making personal issues political. Charlotte Bunch, for example, wrote that "there is no private domain of a person's life that is not political and there is no political issue that is not ultimately personal."

Some feminists, like **Gloria Steinem**, tried to change awareness through the mass media. After graduating from college, Steinem worked as a freelance writer, including a stint of undercover work at a club run by *Playboy* magazine. While society tended to view Playboy bunnies in glamorous terms, Steinem revealed how much humiliation they had to endure to make a living. In 1972, she helped co-found *Ms.*, a feminist magazine. Its title was meant to protest the social custom of identifying women by their marital status rather than as individuals.

Phyllis Schlafly and Conservatives Oppose the Women's Movement Some Americans—both men and women—openly challenged the women's movement. **Phyllis Schlafly**, for example, is a conservative political activist who denounced women's liberation as "a total assault on the family, on marriage, and on children." She worked hard to defeat the ERA, arguing that the act would compel women to fight in the military, end sex-segregated bathrooms, and hurt the family. Her argument resonated with many conservatives. Due to conservative opposition, the ERA fell three states short of becoming a constitutional amendment.

☑ **RECALL** What was the purpose of the proposed Equal Rights Amendment?

The Impact of the Women's Movement

The women's movement affected all aspects of American society. Women's roles and opportunities expanded. Women gained legal rights that had been denied them. And feminists sparked an important debate about equality that continues today. Yet the issues they raised continue to divide Americans. Some say that women haven't made enough gains. Others fear that the movement has actually harmed society.

Achieving Equality of Political Rights Through Litigation Before the 1960s, there were no federal laws prohibiting gender discrimination. The Civil Rights Act of 1964, however, gave feminists a legal tool. It included a clause, called Title VII, that outlawed discrimination on the basis of sex. The clause was actually inserted by civil rights opponents, who thought it was so outlandish that it would make the entire bill look ridiculous.

When the bill actually passed, however, women used Title VII to challenge discrimination. The bill also set up the Equal Employment Opportunity Commission (EEOC) to enforce the federal prohibition on job discrimination.

Enforcing Title VII, even with the EEOC, was often difficult. Still, NOW and other feminist organizations tirelessly filed suits against employers who refused to hire women or to pay them fairly, compelling the federal government to act. President Kennedy established the Commission on the Status of Women in 1961 to examine workplace discrimination. Title IX of the Higher Education Act of 1972 banned discrimination in education. The Equal Credit Opportunity Act, passed in 1974, made it illegal to deny credit to a woman just because of her gender.

Title IX applied to many facets of educational opportunities but had an especially profound impact on collegiate athletics. In effect, Title IX said that

>> The battle for women's rights took place in many venues. In 1973, tennis player Billie Jean King demonstrated women's equality with men by defeating Bobby Riggs in The Battle of the Sexes.

>> As a result of Title IX, women's athletics increased dramatically in the 1980s. Many, like the Women's USA Basketball Team, now dominate international competitions.

the ratio of women to men participating in collegiate athletics had to mirror the ratio of women to men enrolled in the school.

Participation by women in college athletics has increased dramatically since 1972. Since then, however, the number of women coaches has decreased significantly. As women's sports gained in popularity and became revenue-generating sports, male coaches were drawn to these higher-profile positions. In 1972, the number of women coaching collegiate women's sports was over 90 percent. By 2010, that number was down to approximately 42 percent. This is one of the ways in which Title IX created unintended consequences that have been difficult to counteract.

Some feminists considered their most important legal victory to be the 1973 Supreme Court decision in *Roe* v. *Wade*, which assured women the right to legal abortions. Prior to *Roe*, most states outlawed or severely restricted abortion. Some women turned to illegal and often dangerous ways to end their pregnancies. The case and its decision were highly controversial at the time and still are today.

Expanding Economic and Employment Opportunities The women's movement fostered a shift in attitudes among both men and women, and the American workplace today reflects this change. The percentage of women in the workforce has grown, from about 30 percent in 1950 to more than 60 percent in 2000. So, too, has the number of married female workers. Fields long closed or severely limited to women—such as medicine, law, and accounting—have opened up as well. The general shift in attitudes symbolized by these changes has created a world of possibilities for many young women who never knew a time when women were not allowed to do these things.

Despite these gains, the average woman still earns less than the average man, partly because many women continue to work in fields that pay less. Some people have referred to this situation as a "pink-collar ghetto." Whether this is because of discrimination, or because women who shoulder family responsibilities often have limited job choices, remains a matter of debate. Many studies suggest that a "glass ceiling" exists, limiting the advancement of even the most highly educated and skilled women workers.

Most troubling, the United States has witnessed a feminization of poverty over the past 30 years. This means that the majority of the nation's poor people are single women. These are the women in the lowest-paying jobs, with the fewest benefits. Many of these poor women are single mothers, who must bear the costs and responsibilities of raising children alone while also working.

☑ **IDENTIFY** What was the purpose of Title IX of the Higher Education Act of 1972?

THE LEGACY OF TITLE IX FOR WOMEN

EDUCATIONAL PROFILE OF WOMEN IN THE WORKFORCE

— SOME HIGH SCHOOL
— HIGH SCHOOL DIPLOMA
— SOME COLLEGE
— COLLEGE GRADUATE

Source: U.S. Bureau of Labor Statistics

$ WAGE EQUALITY (MEDIAN WEEKLY EARNINGS, 2013)

Occupation	Women	Men
MANAGEMENT, PROFESSIONAL, AND RELATED OCCUPATIONS	$962	$1,345
SERVICE OCCUPATIONS	$461	$534
SALES AND OFFICE OCCUPATIONS	$615	$750
OFFICE AND ADMINISTRATIVE SUPPORT OCCUPATIONS	$632	$658
NATURAL RESOURCES, CONSTRUCTION, AND MAINTENANCE OCCUPATIONS	$565	$766
PRODUCTION, TRANSPORTATION, AND MATERIAL MOVING OCCUPATIONS	$498	$657

Source: U.S. Bureau of Labor Statistics

>> **Analyze Data** What data support the conclusion that the women's rights reform movement affected women's opportunities outside the home environment? Bounce to Activate Chart

1. **Compare and Contrast** Identify similarities and differences between the first and second waves of feminism.

2. **Generate Explanations** Explain how the civil rights movement influenced the women's rights movement of the 1960s.

3. **Compare Points of View** Discuss both the support and criticism that the National Organization for Women received in the 1960s.

4. **Identify Central Issues** Discuss the achievements of Title IX, as well as its unintended consequences.

5. **Describe** the feminization of poverty that has occurred in recent decades.

>> Cesar Chavez, leader of United Farm Workers, helped to improve working conditions that migrants faced on the fruit and vegetable farms where they worked.

Bounce to Activate Flipped Video

(10.3) Successes in the civil rights and women's movements signaled a growing rights revolution in the United States. Latinos, Native Americans, and Asian Americans engaged in their own struggles for equality during the 1960s and 1970s, fighting to influence laws and government. Meanwhile, activists worked to expand rights for two broad groups: consumers and people with disabilities.

>> Objectives

Analyze the causes of the growth of the Latino population after World War II.

Evaluate significant leaders and the methods they used to achieve equality in political rights for Latinos.

Evaluate the means by which Native Americans sought to expand their rights.

Describe the expansion of rights for consumers and the disabled.

>> Key Terms

Cesar Chavez
migrant farmworker
United Farm
   Workers (UFW)
Chicano movement
American Indian
   Movement (AIM)
Japanese American
   Citizens League
Ralph Nader
Hector P. Garcia
Dolores Huerta

Expanding the Push for Equality

Latino Immigration Surges

After World War I, the United States passed legislation limiting European immigration. Yet during and after World War II, the country faced a growing demand for cheap labor. At the same time, the populations of Mexico and other Latin American nations grew steadily while job opportunities there declined. The combination of these factors created a steady stream of new immigrants to the United States. Some immigrants came legally, but others crossed the border illegally.

Latinos in the United States People whose family origins are in Spanish-speaking Latin America are called Latinos or Hispanics. They come from many different places, but they share the same language and some elements of culture. Spanish-speaking people lived in many parts of western North America before settlers from the United States arrived, and their numbers have grown steadily. Mexican Americans, known as Chicanos, have always made up the largest group of U.S. Latinos.

Legal and Illegal Immigration Beginning in 1942, Mexican immigrants came to the United States under the *bracero*, or farmhand, program. This program granted Mexican migrants temporary guest worker status, and over a period of 25 years, more than 4 million entered the United States. The *braceros* played a crucial role in sustaining agriculture during and after World War II.

Along with Mexicans who had migrated to the United States illegally in search of work, *braceros* who had outstayed their permits were targeted for deportation in the 1950s. In 1965, however, the government passed the Immigration and Nationality Act Amendments, eliminating national-origin quotas for immigrants. In the decades that followed, the number of legal Mexican and Asian immigrants surged. More than 400,000 Mexicans arrived during the 1960s, another 630,000 in the 1970s, and more than 1.5 million in the 1980s.

Latino Communities on the East Coast After World War II, large numbers of Puerto Ricans, Dominicans, and Cubans migrated to the United States. As citizens of a United States territory, Puerto Ricans came legally, leaving their homeland in search of better-paying jobs. In contrast, most Cuban and Dominican immigrants came to America as political refugees, fleeing their countries to escape the harsh rule of dictators. Most Puerto Rican, Cuban, and Dominican immigrants settled in urban areas, especially in New York City and Miami, Florida, which had notable effects on the demographic patterns in these cities.

☑ **DESCRIBE** How did the farmhand program encourage Mexicans to legally migrate to the U.S.?

Latino Organizations Fight for Rights

Like other minorities, Latinos had long faced discrimination. After World War II, Latino veterans began agitating for equal treatment. Veteran **Hector P. Garcia**, for example, formed the American G.I. Forum to battle discrimination. In the 1960s and 1970s, influenced by the growing civil rights movement, Latinos increasingly fought for equal rights. They demanded better working conditions, salaries, and educational opportunities. Like African Americans, they sought federal protection of their right to vote and campaigned to elect politicians who represented their interests.

United States Latino Population

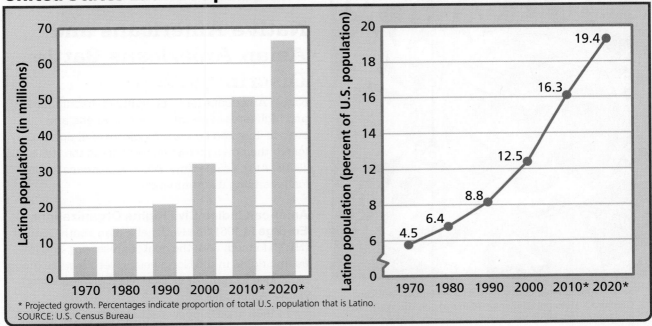

* Projected growth. Percentages indicate proportion of total U.S. population that is Latino.
SOURCE: U.S. Census Bureau

>> **Analyze Data** Based on the information in the chart, how much did the Latino population increase in the United States between 1970 and 2010?

The Role of Cesar Chavez in Organizing Farmworkers Immigrants, including Latino Americans and Filipino Americans, played a central role in the farm labor movement. The most influential Latino activist was **Cesar Chavez**. Chavez fought for rights for farm laborers, who were among the most exploited workers in the nation. Because they migrated from farm to farm—and often from state to state—to pick fruits and vegetables, they were known as **migrant farmworkers**. They labored for long hours in deplorable conditions, with no benefits.

Dolores Huerta was another activist who shared Cesar Chavez's concerns about migrant farmworkers. Huerta worked as a leader of a community service organization in Stockton, California. She founded the Agricultural Workers Association, which organized voter registration drives and worked to improve Hispanic neighborhoods. In 1962, Chavez and Huerta organized a farmworkers' union in Delano, California. In the late 1960s, Chavez and Huerta merged the union with a union of Filipino farm laborers to form what became the **United Farm Workers (UFW)**.

Committed to nonviolent tactics, the UFW implemented a workers' strike and consumer boycott of table grapes. With the help of Huerta, Chavez's top aide, the UFW urged people across the nation to boycott California grapes in order to win recognition from the growers. In 1975, California passed a law requiring collective bargaining between growers and union representatives. Farmworkers finally had a legal basis to ask for better working conditions.

Actions Taken to Improve Opportunities While Chavez focused on farmworkers' rights, a broader Mexican American social and political effort grew, which came to be known as the **Chicano movement**. Part of it was dedicated to increasing Latinos' awareness of their history and culture. The Chicano Mural Movement, in which Mexican-American culture was celebrated in large, outdoor paintings, sprang up at this time. At California colleges and high schools, and in other states with a Mexican American population, Chicano students demanded that educators teach more about their heritage. Others in the movement focused on quality-of-life issues. For example, the National Council of La Raza was founded in 1968 with the goal of reducing poverty and discrimination and providing better opportunities for Latinos.

Much of the movement's energy was concentrated on attaining political strength for Latinos, or what some called "brown power." By 1980, six Hispanics sat in Congress, representing districts from New York to California. Moreover, Hispanics gained greater representation in state, county, and city governments.

☑ **IDENTIFY CENTRAL IDEAS** Why was the United Farm Workers (UFW) formed in the 1960s?

Native Americans and Asian Americans Battle Discrimination

Native Americans had long suffered discrimination and high rates of poverty, unemployment, and suicide. Inspired by the struggle for civil rights, they forged their own protest movements in the 1960s and 1970s. At the same time, Asian Americans fought long-standing discrimination.

American Indian Civil Rights Organizations Emerge In 1961, the National Indian Youth Council (NIYC) formed, with the goal of preserving native fishing rights in the Northwest. Over time, the group expanded its aims to include broad civil rights for Native Americans.

In 1968, the Chippewa activists Dennis Banks and George Mitchell helped found the **American Indian Movement (AIM)**. At first, AIM focused on helping Indians living in urban ghettos. Before long,

>> To celebrate aspects of Mexican-American culture, Chicano artists painted colorful murals on the walls of city buildings, churches, housing projects, and schools throughout the Southwest.

ⓑ Bounce to Activate Gallery

however, AIM was addressing all civil rights issues, particularly the securing of land, legal rights, and self-government for Native Americans.

Activism Leads to Confrontation In late 1969, a group of American Indians occupied the island of Alcatraz, the site of a federal prison in San Francisco Bay that had closed in 1963. Members of the Sioux tribe asserted that the island belonged to them under a treaty provision granting them unused federal land. About 100 American Indians representing 50 tribes joined the occupation. In spite of efforts by the Coast Guard and other federal authorities to evict them, the Indians controled the island until mid-1971.

The 1970s saw another series of confrontations. In 1972, led by Dennis Banks and Russell Means, AIM orchestrated a "long march" from San Francisco to Washington, D.C. Upon arriving in the capital, they took control of the Bureau of Indian Affairs building.

Tragedy Returns to Wounded Knee In 1970, Dee Brown published *Bury My Heart at Wounded Knee,* which includes a chapter about the 1890 massacre of Sioux at Wounded Knee, South Dakota. Brown noted that in all the history of the American West,

> Only occasionally was the voice of an Indian heard, and then more often than not it was recorded by the pen of a white man. The Indian was the dark menace of the myths, and even if he had known how to write in English, where would he have found a printer or a publisher?

The best-selling book raised public consciousness about the historic mistreatment of Native Americans. Building on this momentum, AIM planned a dramatic confrontation at Wounded Knee.

In late February of 1973, AIM took over the village and refused to leave until the government agreed to investigate the condition of reservation Indians. Federal authorities put Wounded Knee under siege, and two AIM members died in the resulting gunfire. The standoff ended in May when the government pledged to reexamine native treaty rights.

Fighting Discrimination Through Litigation
Several landmark cases in the 1940s paved the way for Native Americans to fight discrimination through

>> Russell Means (center), and Dennis Banks (right), early leaders of the American Indian Movement (AIM), brought the struggle for Native Americans' rights to the public's attention.

Bounce to Activate Gallery

litigation. In 1947, the Ninth Circuit Court of Appeals upheld the decision in *Mendez* v. *Westminster*, ruling that the segregation of Mexican American students in schools in California was unconstitutional. The 1948 decision in *Delgado* v. *Bastrop I.S.D.* ended segregation in the Texas public school system. The ruling stated that the segregation of children of Mexican descent in Texas was illegal.

Native American activism spurred the passage of several laws in the 1970s. The Indian Self-Determination Act of 1975, for instance, granted tribes greater control over resources and education on reservations. Native Americans also continued to win legal battles to regain land, mineral, and water rights. While politicians debated how the government should treat Native Americans, the Indians themselves continued to suffer from disproportionately high rates of unemployment and other social ills.

Asian Americans Fight Discrimination
Prejudice against people of Japanese and Chinese ancestry had long been a problem. The **Japanese American Citizens League**, founded in 1929 to protect Japanese Americans' civil rights, worked for decades to receive compensation for property lost by

Japanese Americans interned in camps during World War II.

During the expanding rights revolution of the 1960s and 1970s, many other groups formed to combat discrimination and protect the rights of all Asian Americans. The Immigration and Nationality Act Amendments (1965) also aided Asian immigrants.

☑ **DESCRIBE** What was the significance of the *Mendez* v. *Westminster* court decision?

Rights for Consumers and the Disabled

During these years of reform many worked to protect the rights of consumers and Americans with disabilities.

A New Movement for Consumer Rights During the Progressive Era, reformers had pushed for measures to protect consumers, ranging from the Pure Food and Drug Act to the Meat Inspection Act. The consumer rights movement reemerged during the 1960s and 1970s. It was led by **Ralph Nader**, a lawyer who investigated whether flawed car designs led to increased traffic accidents. His book, *Unsafe at Any Speed* (1965), attacked automakers whose thirst for profits produced unsafe vehicles.

Nader's best-selling book prompted Congress to pass the National Traffic and Motor Vehicle Safety Act in 1966. The act made safety belts

standard equipment in all cars. Nader went on to form several consumer advocacy groups. Under his influence, consumer advocacy adopted many of the practices that shape it today, including research and government lobbying. Advocacy for workers began to gain more prominence as well. The Nixon administration proposed the idea for the Occupational Safety and Health Administration (OSHA), which mandated workplace safety regulations.

Historically, the nation had treated people with disabilities as defective. FDR hid the fact that he could not walk because he did not want society to assume he was incapable of serving as President. Yet by the 1970s, Americans with disabilities were expanding their rights. Disabled veterans from the Korean and Vietnam wars took part in this activism. The Kennedy administration called for change by establishing the Panel on Mental Retardation in 1961 to explore ways for the government to help people with intellectual disabilities.

The next year, Eunice Shriver, President Kennedy's sister, began an athletic camp for young people with disabilities that eventually became the Special Olympics. Over the next few years, the government passed a number of Congressional acts guaranteeing equal access to education for people with disabilities.

☑ **IDENTIFY SUPPORTING DETAILS** What effects did the publication of the book *Unsafe at Any Speed* have on public safety?

Rights-Expanding Legislation

LEGISLATION OR PANEL	PLANNED OR ACTUAL EFFECT
Equal Rights Amendment (ERA) (First proposed 1921; never passed)	Proposed constitutional amendment to guarantee gender equality
Panel on Mental Retardation (1961)	Explored ways the government could help people with disabilities
Title VII of the Civil Rights Act (1964)	Outlawed sex-based discrimination
Immigration and Nationality Act (1965)	Eased restrictions, making immigration easier for Latinos and Asians
National Traffic and Motor Vehicle Safety Act (1966)	Mandated safety equipment in cars
Indian Self-Determination Act (1975)	Gave Native Americans control over resources on reservations

>> **Analyze Charts** How did legislation enacted during the 1960s lead to the expansion of rights for minorities?

The Gay Rights Movement Advances

In the 1950s, the early gay-rights organizations were secretive and cautious in their approach. Then, as the political and cultural climate changed in the early 1960s, gay activists became bolder.

California Activists Organize In San Francisco, José Sarria ran for a seat on the city's board of supervisors in 1961—the first openly gay person to run for public office. In 1964, a turning point came when gay activists in San Francisco allied with religious leaders and the press to denounce a police raid on a fund-raising ball. Police raids stopped; the gay community had become a political force. In 1966, an attempt to arrest transgender patrons of Compton's Cafeteria in San Francisco led to a riot in which the patrons fought back—a major turning point in the gay rights movement.

Direct Action in Washington, D.C. After Franklin Kameny was fired from a government job because of his homosexuality, he began organizing direct-action protests influenced by the strategies of the civil rights movement. In 1965, he and others of what was known as the Homophile movement organized picketers at the White House to protest the government's anti-gay hiring policy. More public demonstrations targeting a range of homophobic laws and policies soon followed.

The Stonewall Riots In New York City, protests over entrapment and police raids on gay bars had been intensifying in the late 1960s. Then, in the early morning of June 28, 1969, patrons of the Stonewall Inn in Greenwich Village rioted in response to a routine police raid. The riots continued for several days as news of the event attracted more LGBT supporters. The Stonewall Riots ignited a new militant phase in the gay-rights movement as people, such as the transgender activist Sylvia Rivera, channeled the political skills they had gained in the civil rights and anti-war movements into gay activism.

Almost overnight, new organizations such as the Gay Liberation Front and the Gay Activists alliance sprang up, calling on all LGBT people to "come out" of hiding and declare their sexual identity to their friends, families, and co-workers. Adopting this tactic, LGBT people worldwide began organizing annual Gay Pride marches every summer, to commemorate the Stonewall Inn uprising of 1969, to increase visibility and to agitate for change in attitudes and laws. By the mid-1970s, mobilization led to successes: the American Psychiatric Association

>> The first Gay Pride Parade, held in 1970 to commemorate the Stonewall Riots of 1969, takes place in New York City.

stopped classifying homosexuality as a mental illness in 1973; 17 states had repealed laws criminalizing gay sexual behavior; 36 cities had passed laws banning anti-gay discrimination; and gay-identified neighborhoods had emerged in major cities.

☑ **RECALL** How did the LGBT movement change after Stonewall?

☑ ASSESSMENT

1. **Generate Explanations** Explain why the United States experienced a new wave of immigration after World War II.

2. **Summarize** Discuss the role of the United Farm Workers in securing civil rights for Mexican Americans.

3. **Identify Central Issues** Describe the American Indian activism that occurred during the 1960s and 1970s, and explain why this activism often led to confrontations with the U.S. government.

4. **Identify Steps in a Process** Discuss changes that altered the treatment of disabled people during the 1960s and 1970s.

5. **Describe** Ralph Nader's contributions to the consumer rights movement.

>> Many people hoped nuclear energy would provide a safe alternative to fossil fuels, but the accident at Three Mile Island, in 1979, created resistance to nuclear energy production.

Bounce to Activate Flipped Video

10.4 The "rights revolution" of the 1960s and 1970s eventually influenced all aspects of American life—including people's right to a clean and safe environment. In 1962 a book called *Silent Spring* by biologist Rachel Carson pointed out that human actions were harming not only the environment but people themselves. Public awareness of environmental issues prompted an important debate about the government's role in environmental regulations.

>> **Objectives**

Assess the causes and effects of the environmental movement.

Analyze why environmental protection became a controversial issue.

>> **Key Terms**

Rachel Carson
toxic waste
Earth Day
Environmental
  Protection Agency
  (EPA)
Clean Air Act
Clean Water Act
Endangered
  Species Act

The Environmental Movement

Environmental Activists Sound the Alarm

In the 1920s, Progressives had worked to conserve public lands and parks. But few worried much about the ill effects of industrialization. In 1952, however, a blanket of deadly smog, caused by coal fires, engulfed the city of London, killing some 12,000 people. Ten years after London's Great Smog, a book sparked the modern environmental movement.

***Silent Spring* Launches a Movement** Coal smog is just one kind of **toxic waste**, or poisonous byproduct of human activity. Another is acid rain, or moisture in the air caused by the mixing of water with chemicals produced by the burning of fossil fuels. Toxic wastes are also produced when nuclear power is generated. Throughout the 1960s and 1970s, scientists learned more about toxic wastes and other environmental threats.

Rachel Carson's book *Silent Spring* described the deadly impact that pesticides were having on birds and other animals. Her book caused a sensation. Though the chemical industry fought back, the public was convinced by her argument. Carson did more than point to the dangers of chemicals and toxic waste. She also insisted that human activity drastically altered the environment and that humans had a responsibility to protect it. Her work eventually compelled Congress to restrict the use of the pesticide DDT. It also spurred widespread environmental activism among Americans.

When a fire erupted on the Cuyahoga River in Cleveland, Ohio, in 1969, activists instantly spoke out. The fire occurred when a spark ignited floating oil and debris—byproducts of industrialization—on the river's surface. *Time* magazine reported that the river "oozes, rather than flows." Even more luridly, the magazine remarked that in the Cuyahoga, a person "does not drown but decays."

A Grassroots Movement Creates Earth Day

Events like the Cuyahoga River fire seemed to confirm the dire predictions of *Silent Spring*. One response to growing environmental concerns was a nationwide protest called **Earth Day**. Wisconsin senator Gaylord Nelson, who played the leading role in organizing the protest, wanted "to shake up the political establishment and force this issue [the environment] onto the national agenda." On April 22, 1970, close to 20 million Americans took part in

Earth Day events across the nation. The yearly event attracted the support of many of the same people who had advocated civil and women's rights. It was also backed by a number of grassroots groups, including the Sierra Club, founded by John Muir in 1892, and the Wilderness Society, established in 1935. Historically, these groups had focused on conservation. With the rise of the environmental movement, however, they called for broader environmental protections.

Nixon Creates Government Entities to Manage the Environment

In 1969, President Nixon declared that the 1970s "must be the years when America pays its debts to the past by reclaiming the purity of its air, its water and our living environment." Nixon had not come into office as an environmental activist. But the public's increasing concern with protecting the environment convinced him to support environmental reforms.

Under Nixon's leadership, Congress created the **Environmental Protection Agency (EPA)** in 1970. This federal agency's mission was to protect the "entire ecological chain." In addition to cleaning up and protecting the environment, the EPA sought to limit or to eliminate pollutants that posed a risk to the public's health, such as toxic substances that cause cancer. Nixon also signed a number of environmental laws.

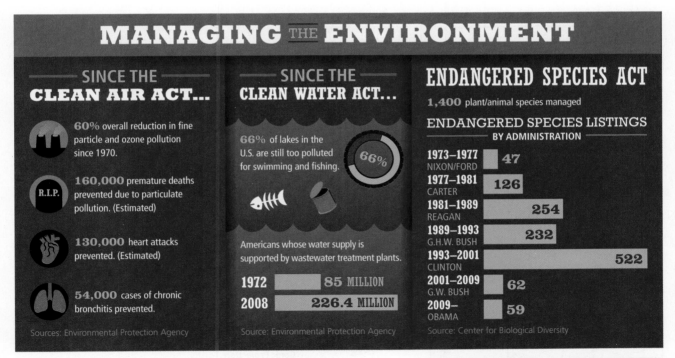

MANAGING THE ENVIRONMENT

SINCE THE CLEAN AIR ACT...

- **60%** overall reduction in fine particle and ozone pollution since 1970.
- **160,000** premature deaths prevented due to particulate pollution. (Estimated)
- **130,000** heart attacks prevented. (Estimated)
- **54,000** cases of chronic bronchitis prevented.

Sources: Environmental Protection Agency

SINCE THE CLEAN WATER ACT...

66% of lakes in the U.S. are still too polluted for swimming and fishing.

66%

Americans whose water supply is supported by wastewater treatment plants.

1972	85 MILLION
2008	226.4 MILLION

Source: Environmental Protection Agency

ENDANGERED SPECIES ACT

1,400 plant/animal species managed

ENDANGERED SPECIES LISTINGS
BY ADMINISTRATION

Administration	Listings
1973–1977 NIXON/FORD	47
1977–1981 CARTER	126
1981–1989 REAGAN	254
1989–1993 G.H.W. BUSH	232
1993–2001 CLINTON	522
2001–2009 G.W. BUSH	62
2009– OBAMA	59

Source: Center for Biological Diversity

>> **Analyze Data** Use the tables to determine whether 1970s environmental legislation had a positive, neutral, or negative effect on the environment and the American public.

Bounce to Activate Chart

The **Clean Air Act** (1970) combated air pollution by, among other things, limiting the emissions from factories and automobiles. The **Clean Water Act** (1973) sought to limit the pollution of water by industry and agriculture. This law built on the Water Quality Act enacted by President Johnson. The **Endangered Species Act** (1973) promoted the protection of endangered plants and animals.

President Gerald Ford continued in Nixon's footsteps. In 1974, he created the Nuclear Regulatory Commission to make sure nuclear materials would be handled safely without harmful impacts on people or the environment.

☑ **EXPLAIN** How did the modern environmental movement develop?

Impact of Environmental Regulations

As the 1970s drew to a close, a series of environmental crises made the headlines. They reinforced the public's concern about the environment and produced calls for even more far-reaching actions. Yet, at the same time, a number of people began to wonder if the government had enacted too many regulations and was threatening property rights. Rather than calling for more federal actions, they tried to limit the government's role in environmental protection.

The EPA Investigates Love Canal In 1978, a resident of Love Canal, a community near Niagara Falls in upstate New York, hung a sign from his home that read: "Give me Liberty. I've Already Got Death."

This sign referred to the fact that residents of the community had exceptionally high rates of birth defects and cancer. Newspaper reporters and EPA investigators determined that these illnesses were caused by thousands of tons of toxic chemicals, which industries had been dumping in the ground for decades. One EPA administrator recalled the scene he witnessed following a heavy rain that sent toxic chemicals percolating up through the ground.

I visited the canal area at that time. Corroding waste disposal drums could be seen breaking up through the grounds of backyards. Trees and gardens were turning black and dying. . . . Puddles of noxious substances were pointed out to me by the residents. Some of these puddles were in their yards, some were in their basements, others yet were

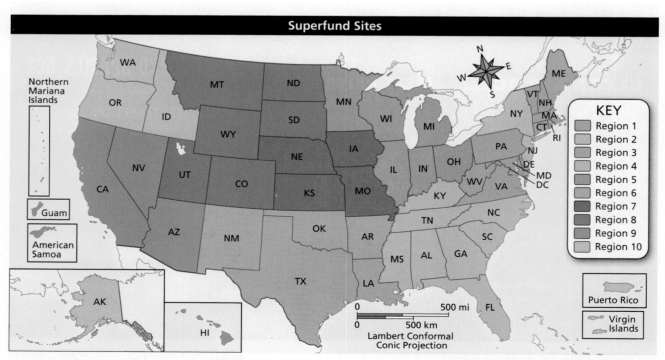

Superfund Sites

KEY
Region 1
Region 2
Region 3
Region 4
Region 5
Region 6
Region 7
Region 8
Region 9
Region 10

>> **Analyze Maps** This is how the EPA organizes its work by region. In what ways might hazardous waste vary by region?

Bounce to Activate Map

on the school grounds. Everywhere the air had a faint, choking smell. Children returned from play with burns on their hands and faces.

—Eckhardt Beck, *EPA Journal*, 1979

The Love Canal contamination, along with other events involving hazardous waste, prompted Congress to establish Superfund in 1980.

Meltdown at Three Mile Island Alters Public Opinion Shortly after the investigation at Love Canal, an accident occurred in the nuclear energy industry. On March 28, 1979, the core of the nuclear reactor at Three Mile Island outside Harrisburg, Pennsylvania, began to melt after the reactor malfunctioned. When the plant threatened to release radioactive gas, the governor declared a state of emergency and shut it down. To reassure the public that plant managers had contained the accident, President Jimmy Carter and his wife traveled to Three Mile Island and toured the reactor.

Even though the incident was contained and there proved to be no health risks, it had profound effects on America's energy policy. In the wake of the accident, public opinion shifted against nuclear energy, as Americans became fearful of possible disasters. The government temporarily stopped building new nuclear power plants. Even though it later lifted the ban, no new American nuclear plants were ordered for more than a quarter of a century. In the 2000s, with the nation threatened by energy shortages, many Americans began to call for building new nuclear plants.

Governmental Actions Challenge Fifth Amendment Rights As more environmental regulations were passed, opposition to them grew. Based on an understanding of the Fifth Amendment, which holds that citizens shall not be deprived of property without due process of law, many complained that environmental regulations stripped individuals, the businesses they owned, and the communities they lived in of their property rights by restricting what they could or could not do with their land. Some argued that private property owners would do a better job of protecting the environment than the government because the owners had an interest in preserving the profitability of their land. Many people—and especially industry leaders—also worried that too much environmental regulation would hamper business and jobs by diverting funds to cleaning up the air and water. Therefore, as the 1970s came to a close—and, indeed, to this day—

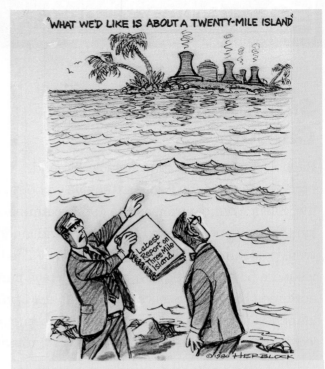

"WHAT WE'D LIKE IS ABOUT A TWENTY-MILE ISLAND"

>> **Analyze Political Cartoons** What do you think the palm trees on the island suggest about the release of radiation at Three Mile Island?

Americans remained divided about what role the government should play in regulating industry and protecting the environment.

☑ **EXPLAIN** What arguments were raised against the environmental movement?

☑ ASSESSMENT

1. **Describe** the environmental disasters of the 1960s and 1970s that strengthened environmental activism in the United States.

2. **Identify Patterns** Explain how the written word helped the environmental movement to gain momentum during the 1960s and 1970s.

3. **Compare and Contrast** Discuss the relationship between the environmental movement and other campaigns such as civil and women's rights movements.

4. **Identify Cause and Effect** Determine the causes of the Love Canal contamination, and explain its effects on the American public.

5. **Determine Point of View** Explain why some opposed the environmental movement.

Silent Spring: Rachel Carson

Rachel Carson was a marine biologist and conservationist who wrote extensively about ocean life. *Silent Spring*, published in 1962, examined how synthetic pesticides used by farmers and landowners were poisoning people and wildlife alike. The book issued a pointed critique against the ways human activities harmed the natural world. *Silent Spring* help launched a movement of concerned consumers, which led to the creation of the Environmental Protection Agency and a ban on a number of pollutants.

>> Rachel Carson

There once was a town in the heart of America where all life seemed to live in harmony with its surroundings. The town lay in the midst of a checkerboard of prosperous farms, with fields of grain and hillsides of orchards, where, in spring, white clouds of bloom drifted above the green fields. In autumn, oak and maple and birch set up a blaze of color that flamed and flickered across a backdrop of pines. Then foxes barked in the hills and deer silently crossed the fields, half hidden in the mists of the fall mornings.

Along the roads, laurel, viburnum and alder, great ferns and wildflowers delighted the traveler's eye through much of the year. Even in winter the roadsides were places of beauty, where countless birds came to feed on the berries and on the seed heads of the dried weeds rising above the snow. The countryside was, in fact, famous for the abundance and variety of its bird life, and when the flood of migrants was pouring through in spring and fall people traveled from great distances to observe them. Others came to fish the streams, which flowed clear and cold out of the hills and contained shady pools where trout lay. So it had been from the days many years ago when the first settlers raised their houses, sank their wells, and built their barns.

☑ **ANALYZE STYLE AND RHETORIC** What phrases help create an image of life lived "in harmony with its surroundings"?

Then a strange blight [plant disease] crept over the area and everything began to change. Some evil spell had settled on the community: mysterious maladies [illnesses] swept the flocks of chickens; the cattle and sheep sickened and died. Everywhere was a shadow of death. The farmers spoke of much illness among their families. In the town the doctors had become more and more puzzled by new kinds of sickness appearing among their patients. There had been several sudden and unexplained deaths, not only among adults but even among children, who would be stricken suddenly while at play and die within a few hours.

There was a strange stillness. The birds, for example—where had they gone? Many people spoke of them, puzzled and disturbed. The feeding stations in the backyards were deserted. The few birds seen anywhere were moribund; they trembled violently and could not fly. It was a spring without voices. On the mornings that had once throbbed with the dawn chorus of robins, catbirds, doves, jays, wrens, and scores of other bird voices there was now no sound; only silence lay over the fields and woods and marsh.

On the farms the hens brooded, but no chicks hatched. The farmers complained that they were unable to raise any pigs—the litters were small and the young survived only a few days. The apple trees were coming into bloom but no bees droned among the blossoms, so there was no pollination and there would be no fruit. The roadsides, once so attractive, were now lined with browned and withered vegetation as though swept by fire. These, too were silent, deserted by all living things. Even the streams were now lifeless. Anglers no longer visited them, for all the fish had died.

☑ **COMPARE AND CONTRAST** How do the events and the imagery of these paragraphs compare to the descriptions in the first paragraphs?

. . . No witchcraft, no enemy action had silenced the rebirth of new life in this stricken [distressed] world. The people had done it to themselves.

. . . This town does not actually exist, but it might easily have a thousands counterparts in America or elsewhere in the world. I know of no community that has experienced all the misfortunes I describe. Yet every one of these disasters has actually happened somewhere, and many real communities have already suffered a substantial number of them. A grim specter has crept upon us almost unnoticed, and this imagined tragedy may easily become a stark reality we all shall know. What has already silenced the voices of spring in countless towns in America? This book is an attempt to explain.

☑ **SUMMARIZE** What is the world like that Carson describes in this passage, and why does she begin her book with this description?

. . . Only within the moment of time represented by the present century has one species—man—acquired significant power to alter the nature of his world.

During the past quarter century this power has not only increased to one of disturbing magnitude [great size] but it has changed in character. The most alarming of all man's assaults upon the environment is the contamination of air, earth, rivers, and sea with dangerous and even lethal [enough to cause death] materials. This pollution is for the most part irrecoverable [unable to be recovered]; the chain of evil it initiates not only in the world that must support life but in living tissues is for the most part irreversible. In this now universal contamination of the environment, chemicals . . . [are] changing the very nature of the world—the very nature of its life.

☑ **IDENTIFY CAUSE AND EFFECT** According to Carson, why has nature begun to noticeably change in recent times?

☑ ASSESSMENT

1. **Identify Cause and Effect** According to Carson, how are chemicals affecting life on Earth?

2. **Draw Inferences** Why do you think Carson chose to write this book? What changes do you think she hoped to instigate?

3. **Analyze Style and Rhetoric** How would you describe Carson's writing style in this passage, and how do you think this style advances her argument?

>> President Richard Nixon meets with Chairman Mao Zedong in Beijing in 1972. **Summarize** How did Nixon's meeting with Mao Zedong reflect a shift in the foreign policy of the United States?

Bounce to Activate Flipped Video

10.5

In the 1970s, President Nixon introduced many environmental reforms. Along with his leadership on environmental issues, Nixon took the nation in a new direction in foreign affairs. As a presidential candidate, Nixon had promised to end U.S. military involvement in the Vietnam War. Recognizing the potency of Soviet power and the increasing unwillingness of many Americans to pay the costs of containing communism everywhere, Nixon developed a new approach to the Cold War. His bold program redefined America's relations with the two titans of global communism, China and the Soviet Union.

>> Objectives

Describe Richard Nixon's leadership in foreign policy.

Define Nixon's foreign policy toward China and the Soviet Union.

Describe Richard Nixon's attitude toward "big" government.

Analyze Nixon's southern strategy.

Describe the effects of the Watergate political scandal.

>> Key Terms

Henry Kissinger
realpolitik
Zhou Enlai
Strategic Arms
  Limitation Treaty
  (SALT I)
détente
silent majority
Organization
  of Petroleum
  Exporting
  Countries (OPEC)
southern strategy
affirmative action
Watergate
Twenty-fifth
  Amendment
executive privilege

The Two Sides of the Nixon Presidency

Nixon's New Approach to Foreign Policy

Nixon's Cold War Foreign Policy During his years in office, Richard Nixon fundamentally reshaped the way the United States approached the world. Before Nixon took office, most American leaders shared a common Cold War ideology.

They stressed that a basic conflict existed between democratic, capitalist countries and totalitarian, communist ones. They divided the world into "us" and "them," and they established policies based on an assumption commonly held that "the enemy of my enemy is my friend." Therefore, a country opposed to communism was, by this definition, a friend of the United States. In a number of ways, Nixon and **Henry Kissinger**, his leading advisor on national security and international affairs, altered this Cold War policy approach.

At first glance, Richard Nixon's partnership with Henry Kissinger seemed improbable. Nixon was a conservative California Republican, suspicious of the more liberal East Coast Republicans and exhausted with the political and strategic theories of Ivy League intellectuals. Kissinger was a Harvard-educated Jewish émigré from Germany and a prominent figure in East Coast intellectual circles. In several prior presidential campaigns, Kissinger had actually worked against Nixon. However, both men were outsiders, equipped with an outsider's readiness to question accepted orthodoxy.

Kissinger and Realpolitik In foreign affairs, Nixon and Kissinger embraced the idea of **realpolitik**, a German word meaning "real politics." According to realpolitik, political goals should be defined by concrete national interests instead of abstract ideologies. The two statesmen argued that if Americans would put aside their Cold War biases and look at the world with fresh eyes, U.S. global interests could be surveyed not in black and white but in shades of gray. For example, China and the Soviet Union—America's ideological enemies—had the potential to become excellent trading partners. At the same time, West Germany and Japan—America's ideological friends—were fast developing into economic rivals.

Nixon and Kissinger also questioned some lingering Cold War assumptions. For instance, they concluded that there was no united worldwide communist movement, as Lyndon Johnson and other Presidents had believed. There were important differences between the unique ideologies of the Soviet Union and China and other communist countries, such as Yugoslavia, North Korea, and North Vietnam, which often behaved quite independently. As President, Nixon insisted on a flexible, pragmatic foreign policy that avoided ideological absolutes.

☑ **EXPLAIN** How did Nixon and Kissinger reshape America's approach to foreign affairs?

Opening Relations With China

From his first days in office, Nixon seemed determined to leave his mark on the nation's international affairs. Lyndon Johnson focused primarily on domestic affairs—the nuts and bolts of legislation and political deal-making. Nixon was more a man of the world, fascinated by global politics and shifting alliances. Johnson believed his Great Society would solidify his reputation as a great President. In stark contrast, Nixon thought his reorientation of American foreign policy would cement his legacy in the annals of U.S. history.

>> As head of the National Security Council (1969–1975) and as secretary of state (1973–1977), Henry Kissinger had a massive influence on American foreign policy.

🅑 **Bounce to Activate Map**

>> In 1969, a parade in Beijing's Tiananmen Square celebrated the 20th anniversary of the founding of the People's Republic of China.

Reaching Out to China "You're not going to believe this," a Nixon aide told a journalist in 1969, "but Nixon wants to recognize China." It was an odd, almost unbelievable, statement. At the time, the communist People's Republic of China was the most populous country in the world, but it was not officially recognized by the United States. Nor had it been admitted to the United Nations. The China that the United States recognized as the official representative body of the Chinese people was the Nationalist Chinese government exiled on the island of Taiwan. Nixon built his impressive career as a hard-line "Cold Warrior," a vigilant opponent of communism. He was the last politician Americans could imagine to extend the olive branch of recognition—and thus peace—to the communists.

Ever the political realist, however, Nixon knew that the People's Republic of China could not be ignored forever. He recognized that establishing diplomatic relations with the Chinese communists would benefit the United States. From an economic standpoint, improved relations would bring significant trade agreements, especially benefiting California and the Pacific Coast. Politically, U.S. normalization would drive a wedge between China and the Soviet Union, who had strayed from their traditional alliance and become rivals for territory and diplomatic influence. Finally, if the United States forged stronger relations with the Chinese, they might pressure North Vietnam to accept a negotiated peace to end the conflict still raging at the time.

Normalizing U.S.-China Relations With so much to gain and so little to lose, Nixon quietly pushed ahead with his plans. In public, the Chinese made symbolic overtures toward a meeting. In April 1971, China invited an American table-tennis team to play against its athletes. This small action demonstrated China's willingness to talk. Henry Kissinger worked behind the scenes, talking with Chinese leaders and ironing out sensitive issues with Premier **Zhou Enlai**. Then, in July 1971, Nixon announced that he would make an official state visit to China.

In February 1972, the President made the trip and toured the Great Wall, the Imperial Palace, and other historic sites. Nixon sat down for lengthy talks with Zhou Enlai and Communist Party Chairman Mao Zedong. He even learned enough Chinese to make a toast in the language of his host country. The visit was a great success and an important step toward normalizing diplomatic relations with China.

The following year, American tourists started visiting and American companies set up a thriving trade with China. Nixon's China trip was the high point of his presidency. It bridged, as Zhou Enlai said, "the vastest ocean in the world, twenty-five years of no communication." In 1979, the United States and China established full diplomatic relations.

☑ **LIST** Why did Nixon reach out to China?

Nixon's Policy of Détente

Nixon's trip to the People's Republic of China prompted an immediate reaction from the Soviet Union, which had strained relations with both countries. Soviet leader Leonid Brezhnev feared that improved U.S.-Chinese relations would isolate Russia. Therefore, he invited Nixon to visit Moscow.

Establishing a Relationship with China

Pros	Cons
• Created a stronger front against the Soviet threat	• Upset anti-communist American allies
• Strengthened economic ties between both countries	• Increased tensions temporarily between the United States and the Soviet Union
• Lifted the 22-year ban on travel to China	• Eventually created a rift between the United States and China over the political status of Taiwan
• Formed stronger bond between East and West and greater cultural exchange	

>> **Analyze Charts** Based on the information in the chart, why was Nixon's policy toward China likely to be supported by American businesses?

Key Points of the SALT I Treaty, 1972

OFFENSIVE WEAPONS	DEFENSIVE WEAPONS
• Froze the number of intercontinental ballistic missiles (ICBMs) • Limited nuclear warheads to 5,700 each • Limited nuclear submarines to 42 each	• Prevented further development of antiballistic missiles (ABMs) • Limited ABMs to 200 each • Limited the ABM deployment area to 1 each • Limited the sites protected by ABMs to 2 each

>> **Analyze Charts** Based on the information in the chart, what was the purpose of the Salt I treaty?

Nixon made the trip in May 1972. Afterward, the President reported to Congress that he and Brezhnev had reached agreements in a wide variety of areas:

> Recognizing the responsibility of the advanced industrial nations to set an example in combating mankind's common enemies, the United States and the Soviet Union have agreed to cooperate in efforts to reduce pollution and enhance environmental quality. We have agreed to work together in the . . . conquest of cancer and heart disease.

—Richard Nixon, speech to Congress, June 1, 1972

Nixon also announced plans to conduct a joint U.S.-Soviet space mission. However, by far the high point of the summit was the signing of the first **Strategic Arms Limitation Treaty**. Otherwise known as SALT I, the treaty froze the deployment of intercontinental ballistic missiles (ICBMs) and placed limits on antiballistic missiles (ABMs), but it did not alter the stockpiling of the more dangerous multiple independent reentry vehicles (MIRVs). SALT I did not end the arms race between the United States and the Soviet Union. But it was a giant step in the right direction.

The importance of SALT I stemmed first and foremost from U.S. and Soviet efforts to reduce tensions between them. A policy aimed at easing Cold War tensions, **détente**, had replaced previous diplomatic efforts based on suspicion and distrust. With his visits to China and the Soviet Union coming within six months of each other, Richard Nixon dramatically altered America's global strategy. He relaxed the nation's inflexible stance toward communism and applied a more pragmatic approach to foreign policy. In the short term, the new relationships he forged helped the United States to end the Vietnam War. In the long term, Nixon's foreign-policy breakthroughs moved the world a step closer to the end of the Cold War.

☑ **EXPLAIN** How did SALT I support Nixon's new policy for dealing with the Soviet Union?

Nixon's Domestic Policy

Having eased tensions with the nation's two great Cold War adversaries, Richard Nixon stood at the summit of his long government career when he was reelected President in a landslide in November 1972. Yet, less than two years later, Nixon left office in disgrace—the first time a President of the United States had resigned. The Watergate scandal gripped the nation and shaped the values and attitudes toward government that many Americans hold today.

Nixon's Long Political Career Richard Nixon's political career had more ups and downs than a roller coaster ride. Brought up in hard times, he worked his way through college and law school. After service in the navy during World War II, Nixon was elected to the House of Representatives in 1946 and then to the Senate in 1950. As Dwight Eisenhower's running mate in 1952, he became Vice President with Eisenhower's victory. Nixon was not yet 40 years old.

Then came the defeats. In 1960, Nixon narrowly lost to John F. Kennedy in the race for the White House. Two years later, Nixon's career hit bottom when he lost an election to become governor of California. In 1968, however, Nixon made a dramatic comeback. Calling himself "the new Nixon," he narrowly defeated Democrat Hubert Humphrey to win the presidency.

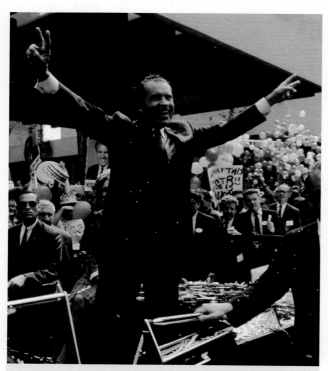

>> A 1972 re-election campaign poster of President Nixon suggests that the country urgently needs his leadership.

>> Richard Nixon displays his signature victory signal to supporters during a 1968 rally. After he took office, he proposed to establish "new federalism," that would restructure American government.

Nixon's "New Federalism" During the campaign for President, Nixon cast himself as the spokesperson for those he called Middle Americans, or the **silent majority**. As Nixon put it at the 1968 Republican convention, he sought to speak for the "non-shouters, the non-demonstrators," the men and women who "work in America's factories . . . run America's businesses . . . serve in the Government . . . provide most of the soldiers . . . [and] give life to the American dream."

Winning the support of Middle America proved a tricky task. Nixon believed that Americans had tired of the "big" government of Lyndon Johnson's Great Society. However, he also believed that the American people still wanted the government to address various social ills, ranging from crime to pollution.

Nixon's solution was to call for the establishment of a "new federalism." As he explained in his 1971 State of the Union address, the nation needed "to reverse the flow of power and resources from the States and communities to Washington and start power and resources flowing back from Washington to the States and communities." Nixon proposed revenue sharing with the states. Under revenue sharing, the federal government gave the states the money to fund social programs. The states then controlled the operations of these programs.

Increasing the Size and Role of Government However, while returning power and money to the states, Nixon also sponsored many programs that increased the size and role of the federal government. During his presidency, a number of powerful new federal agencies and laws came into existence. The Occupational Safety and Health Administration (OSHA) regulates workplaces to make them safer for workers. The DEA, or Drug Enforcement Administration, administers the federal war against illegal drugs. The Environmental Protection Agency (EPA) enforces federal environmental standards. The Clean Air Act, signed into law in 1970, gives the EPA the power to set air quality standards.

Nixon's welfare policies also reflected his complicated domestic strategy. To decrease the power of the federal government, Nixon began to dismantle the Office of Economic Opportunity, the cornerstone of Lyndon Johnson's "war on poverty." Yet, Nixon also proposed creating a Family Assistance Plan (FAP), which called for providing a guaranteed or minimum income to every American family. Although the FAP did not become law, federal spending on other social programs, such as Social Security, Medicare, and public housing, grew steadily.

Federal Agencies Established Under Nixon

AGENCY	PURPOSE
Minority Business Development Agency (1969)	The MBDA fosters minority business enterprise. In 2012, the MBDA helped create and maintain 16,730 jobs.
Environmental Protection Agency (1970)	The EPA establishes federal standards to protect the environment. Today, the EPA continues working toward reducing water and air pollution and promoting human health. In 2009, the EPA made the first official finding regarding greenhouse gases and their detrimental effects on human health and the environment.
Occupational Safety and Health Administration (1971)	OSHA's goal is to protect citizens from death, illness, and injury sustained on the job. Between 1970 and 2013, employment in the United States has doubled; meanwhile, workplace fatalities have fallen more than 65 percent and on-the-job injuries and illnesses have been reduced by 67 percent.
Drug Enforcement Administration (1973)	The DEA provides a unified front against the global war on drugs. At its inception, the DEA had a budget of $75 million with 1,470 special agents. Today, these figures have risen to $2.02 billion and 5,000 special agents.

>> **Analyze Charts** Based on the information in the table, how did the creation of OSHA affect American workers?

A 1970 reform added yearly cost-of-living increases to the checks of Social Security recipients. In 1972, Nixon signed legislation that increased the Social Security benefits of widows and widowers of retirees. He also signed the largest expansion of Medicare in the program's history. The legislation extended Medicare coverage to nearly 2 million Americans under age 65 who were receiving Social Security disability payments. The costs of these programs continues to rise, prompting many to voice their concerns about the long-term solvency of Social Security and Medicare.

The Struggling Economy As his presidency progressed, Nixon grappled with an increasingly troublesome economy. After decades of strong growth and low inflation, the U.S. economy experienced both recession and inflation at the same time. These symptoms began during the Johnson administration, but they grew stronger during the Nixon years, thanks partly to Vietnam War defense spending under both administrations. The combination of recession and inflation baffled economists and led them to coin a new term, **stagflation**, to describe the dual conditions of a stagnating economy and inflationary pressures.

Stagflation had several causes. Expanding federal budget deficits caused by spending for the Vietnam War produced inflation. Another cause was rising foreign competition, which cost thousands of

Americans their jobs. Heavy industries such as steel and auto production, which had enjoyed a dominant position since World War II, proved especially vulnerable to foreign competition. Yet the factor that caused most Americans pain was the rapid increase in the price of oil.

In 1973, the **Organization of Petroleum Exporting Countries (OPEC)**, a multinational organization that sells oil to other nations and cooperates to regulate the price and supply of oil, raised oil prices by 70 percent. Then, in October, in response to the United States' support of Israel during the 1973 Arab war against Israel, OPEC's Arab members, who had formed OAPEC (Organization of Arab Petroleum Exporting Countries), placed an embargo on Israel's allies, including the United States. Dependent on imports for nearly one third of their energy, Americans soon felt the sting of this embargo as oil prices skyrocketed 400 percent in a single year. The embargo lasted until the spring of 1974 and resulted in gas lines at the pumps that stretched for blocks. With the end of the embargo, gas prices remained high.

Nixon fought stagflation in a variety of ways. In August 1971, he ended the Bretton Woods system of monetary management, in which other countries' currencies were pegged to the U.S. dollar, which in turn was pegged to a set amount of gold. Because this system was increasingly difficult to maintain and was unbalancing the U.S. economy, Nixon ended the convertibility between dollars and gold, meaning that dollars were no longer tied to gold prices. To fight stagflation, Nixon also placed a 90-day freeze on all wages and prices. The controls worked for a short time, causing a spurt of economic growth. However, price controls do not work well in a free economy, and the economy went into a tailspin in the mid-1970s.

☑ **IDENTIFY** What was the goal of President Nixon's "new federalism"?

Nixon's "Southern Strategy"

Having narrowly won the presidency in 1968, Richard Nixon set out to expand his base of support. He targeted blue-collar workers and southern whites, both of whom had traditionally voted for Democrats. Even before the election, he nominated Spiro Agnew, a relatively unknown Governor from Maryland, to serve as his running mate, in order to attract southern voters. By winning the support of southern whites, Nixon hoped to make the Republican Party a powerful force in the South. Commentators called this Nixon's **southern strategy**.

As part of his southern strategy, Nixon tried to place a number of conservative southerners as judges in federal courts. Most prominently, he nominated Clement Haynsworth and G. Harrold Carswell to serve on the U.S. Supreme Court. Both men failed to win Senate confirmation, in part because both had supported segregation in the past.

The School Busing Controversy Criticizing court-ordered busing of children to schools outside their neighborhood was another way Nixon reached out to southern whites and urban blue-collar workers. For years, many school districts in both the South and the North had resisted desegregation. In 1971, federal courts ordered school districts to bus students to achieve greater racial balance. Recognizing the unpopularity of busing, Nixon made a nationally televised address in which he called for a moratorium, or freeze, on court-ordered busing. By speaking forcefully, Nixon won the support of many busing opponents.

New Civil Rights Initiatives Yet, as with much else that he did, Nixon's stance on civil rights was mixed. In 1969, the Nixon administration initiated the Philadelphia Plan, a program that required labor unions and federal contractors to submit goals and timetables for the hiring of minorities. It was a type of **affirmative action**, a policy that gives special consideration to women and minorities in the fields of education and employment, in order to make up for past discrimination.

>> **Analyze Graphs** How did the 1973 oil embargo affect the price of gasoline in the United States?

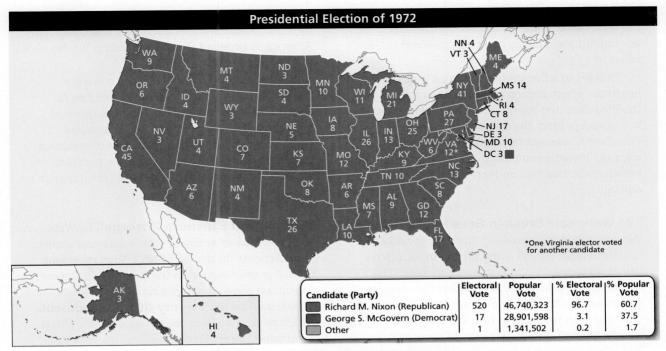

Candidate (Party)	Electoral Vote	Popular Vote	% Electoral Vote	% Popular Vote
Richard M. Nixon (Republican)	520	46,740,323	96.7	60.7
George S. McGovern (Democrat)	17	28,901,598	3.1	37.5
Other	1	1,341,502	0.2	1.7

*One Virginia elector voted for another candidate

>> In 1972, a majority of voters in the American South were Democrats. **Analyze Maps** Based on the information in the map, what was significant about the presidential election of 1972?

Nixon's Assistant Secretary of Labor, Arthur Fletcher, who designed the Philadelphia Plan, argued:

> The Federal Government has an obligation to see that every citizen has an equal chance at the most basic freedom of all—the right to succeed. . . . Segregation didn't occur naturally— it was imposed. . . . The gap . . . between black and white . . . was growing wider and wider. . . . Visible, measurable goals to correct [these] imbalances are essential.

—Arthur Fletcher, Assistant Secretary of Labor, speech on affirmative action, 1969

Nixon's Strategy Succeeds By the 1972 election, Nixon enjoyed high approval ratings. Some of this popularity was based on his trips to the Soviet Union and China. Some was based on his domestic policies.

Nixon ran a masterful political campaign in 1972, positioning himself as a moderate. He portrayed his opponents—George McGovern, an antiwar senator

from South Dakota, and Alabama governor George Wallace—as extremists.

(Wallace's campaign was cut short when he was shot and left paralyzed by a would-be assassin.) Nixon and his Vice President, Spiro Agnew, successfully cast themselves as spokespersons for the silent majority. On election day, Nixon won almost 61 percent of the popular vote and nearly all of the electoral votes. He became the first Republican presidential candidate to sweep the entire South.

☑ **EXPLAIN** In what ways did Nixon appear to send mixed messages about civil rights?

The Watergate Scandal Brings Nixon Down

As a triumphant Richard Nixon stood before the cameras on election night 1972, he had no idea that the seeds of his downfall had already begun to sprout. The botched burglary of Democratic Party headquarters at the Watergate complex in June 1972 received little attention at first. But as investigators began to unravel the connections between the burglars and the White House, **Watergate**, as the scandal become known, came to dominate the national news.

The Watergate burglars were tried in 1973. After the trial, one of them, James McCord, charged that administration officials had been involved in the break-in.

This led to a Senate investigation and to televised hearings, where numerous witnesses charged that the President and his top aides had taken part in a coverup. From the first news of the break-in, President Nixon denied any wrongdoing. Yet, as time went on, investigators discovered important links between the burglars and top Nixon administration officials.

The Watergate Break-in Goes Public Two young *Washington Post* journalists, Bob Woodward and Carl Bernstein, played a crucial role in lifting the veil of secrecy from the Watergate scandal. The two reporters followed tips provided by a secret government informant known as "Deep Throat," who was later revealed to be a top official of the FBI. Woodward and Bernstein reported that the men who had attempted to burglarize the Watergate hotel had close ties to Nixon's reelection committee.

Nixon repeatedly proclaimed his innocence. For example, in November 1973, long after evidence had implicated his top aides and forced them to resign, Nixon declared, "I am not a crook." Yet the polls

>> Watergate Committee Chair Senator Sam Ervin sits with other members of the committee as they listen to testimony at the 1973 Watergate hearings.

Bounce to Activate Chart

indicated that the public disagreed. One poll, taken the next month, showed that fewer than one in five Americans believed that he was being honest about the Watergate affair.

The Watergate scandal created a crisis in the relationship among the three branches of government. How far would Congress go to investigate the President? Would the courts demand that the President turn over information that might implicate him? And if the courts sided with Congress, would the President comply with its decisions?

The Limits of Executive Privilege The Watergate scandal came to a climax with a dizzying array of developments. In the fall of 1973, Vice President Spiro Agnew resigned in the face of an unrelated corruption scandal. According to the procedures established by the **Twenty-fifth Amendment**, which deals with presidential succession, Nixon nominated Gerald Ford to become his new Vice President.

Nixon's troubles multiplied when, in the summer of 1973, it was revealed that he had been secretly taping Oval Office conversations for many years. Many commentators speculated that these tapes would show that the President had played a leading role in trying to cover up the break-in.

Nixon refused to turn over these tapes to the special prosecutor investigating the scandal. The President justified withholding the tapes by claiming **executive privilege**. Executive privilege is the principle that the President has the right to keep certain information confidential. It took almost a year for the courts to sort out the matter. On July 24, 1974, in the case of *United States* v. *Nixon,* the Supreme Court disagreed that the tapes fell under the principle of executive privilege and ordered Nixon to turn them over. Chief Justice Warren Burger made it clear that the Court rejected Nixon's claim of executive privilege in this instance:

The expectation of a President to the confidentiality of his conversations and correspondence . . . has all the values to which we accord deference for the privacy of all citizens. . . . But this presumptive privilege must be considered in light of our historic commitment to the rule of law [the principle that all citizens are bound by the same laws]. . . .

> The very integrity of the judicial system and public confidence in the system depend on full disclosure of all the facts, within the framework of the rules of evidence.
>
> —U.S. Supreme Court, *United States* v. *Nixon*, 1974

Nixon Resigns When investigators listened to the tapes, they found that crucial parts of the conversations were missing. Nixon claimed his secretary had mistakenly erased them. Still, the tapes provided enough evidence of Nixon's involvement in the coverup to lead the Judiciary Committee of the House of Representatives to vote to impeach the President. The committee charged Nixon with obstructing justice in the coverup of the Watergate break-in, misuse of power, and refusing to comply with House subpoenas. A number of Republican committee members joined the Democrats in voting for impeachment.

Recognizing that the full House of Representatives would vote in favor of impeachment and that many Republicans would vote to convict him in a trial in the Senate, Nixon decided to resign. In a speech to the American public on August 8, 1974, Nixon informed the nation that he would step down the following day in the hope that he "will have hastened the start of that process of healing which is so desperately needed in America." The long ordeal of Watergate had finally come to an end. With it, Nixon became the first and only President to resign the presidency.

Historians disagree about whether Nixon knew beforehand of the decision to burglarize Democratic Party headquarters. Few doubt, however that he took part in the coverup. Testimony by his top aides, the Watergate tapes, and evidence gathered in the prosecution of the burglars all show that Nixon sought to quash the investigation.

Moreover, investigations revealed that Nixon had committed other abuses of presidential power. His reelection team had engaged in dirty tricks to secure his election. He had developed an "enemies list" and used federal agencies to go after his enemies. The President had ordered the FBI to place wiretaps on the telephones of those government employees and reporters he suspected of leaking information unfavorable to the administration.

Watergate's Lasting Impact In pursuit of personal power, Richard Nixon damaged the reputation of the presidency and shook the public's confidence

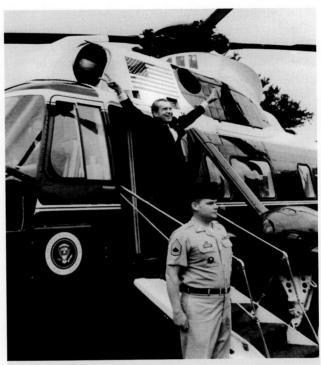

>> On August 9, 1974, Richard Nixon waved farewell as he prepared to leave the grounds of the White House, after resigning as President of the United States.

in government. One conservative commentator, formerly a supporter of Nixon, echoed the disillusionment of many Americans:

> The lies, the lies, the lies! . . . What a pity, what a pity! Here was a President who got us out of Vietnam, ended the draft . . . and by his bold overtures to Red China opened new avenues toward world peace. Now the good vanishes in the wreckage of the bad. The swearing-in of Gerald Ford can't come one hour too soon.
>
> —James J. Kilpatrick, *National Review*, August 30, 1974

Polls revealed that from the late 1950s to the mid-1970s, the percentage of Americans who believed in the truth of government statements plummeted from 80 percent to 33 percent.

In the wake of Watergate, Congress enacted numerous reforms to try to restore the public's confidence in government and to prevent abuses of power in the future. It established a procedure for naming an independent counsel to investigate charges against the White House. The Federal Election Campaign Act of 1974 sought to limit the amount of money that individuals could give candidates, in order to prevent the corruption of the political process.

Yet, the Watergate affair also demonstrated that the nation could weather such a crisis. It showed the strength of the system of checks and balances. Both Congress and the Supreme Court had successfully checked the power of the President. According to *Time* magazine, Nixon's resignation represented an "extraordinary triumph of the American system." Watergate demonstrated that no person, not even a President, is above the law. As Gerald Ford said when he became President: "Our great republic is a government of laws and not of men."

☑ **DESCRIBE** What role did Richard Nixon and his top aides play in the Watergate scandal?

☑ ASSESSMENT

1. **Compare and Contrast** the backgrounds and beliefs of Richard Nixon and Henry Kissinger.

2. **Generate Explanations** Explain why President Nixon decided to recognize China.

3. **Identify Cause and Effect** Explain why gas prices skyrocketed during Nixon's presidency.

4. **Describe** President Nixon's position on civil rights.

5. **Make Generalizations** Discuss the lasting effects of the Watergate scandal.

10.6 The Watergate scandal of the early 1970s took place during a decade that witnessed significant social, economic, and cultural changes. These changes contributed to a growing sense among Americans that something had gone wrong, that the nation had gotten off the right track. This sense of disquiet is even now a part of the nation's political dialogue.

>> Despite repeated efforts to reach an agreement, President Carter failed to secure the release of American hostages in Iran, who were taken prisoner during the Iranian Revolution.

Bounce to Activate Flipped Video

Ford and Carter Struggle

Ford Governs Through Difficult Times

Gerald Ford had been Nixon's Vice President and became President when Nixon resigned. Although only recently appointed as Vice President following the resignation of Nixon's two-term Vice President, Spiro Agnew, Ford brought a long record of public service to the presidency. A star football player at the University of Michigan, Ford enlisted in the United States Navy and fought in World War II. Following the war, Ford successfully ran for a seat in the U.S. Congress, where he served for 25 years, rising to the position of House Minority Leader in 1965. Democrats as well as Republicans supported Ford's nomination for Vice President because he had a reputation for hard work, integrity, and dependability.

Ford stepped into a delicate situation when he became President after Richard Nixon's resignation. Watergate had scarred the public's faith in government. Furthermore, the nation struggled with the most severe economic problems it had faced since the Depression. Ford wrestled with these problems but not

>> **Objectives**

Evaluate the presidency of Gerald Ford.

Evaluate Ford's foreign policies.

Assess the domestic policies of Jimmy Carter.

Discuss changing U.S. foreign policy in the developing world.

Analyze how American society changed in the 1970s.

>> **Key Terms**

Gerald Ford
pardon
Jimmy Carter
Christian fundamentalist
amnesty
televangelist
Helsinki Accords
human rights
SALT II
boat people
sanctions
developing world
Camp David Accords
Community Reinvestment Act
Ayatollah Lahore Khomeini
Wisconsin v. Yoder

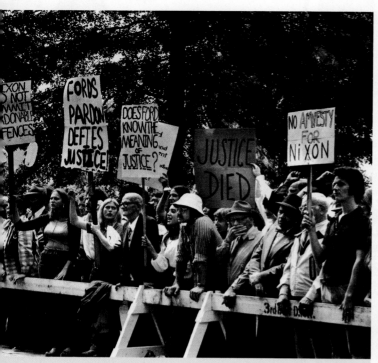

>> President Ford pardoned Richard Nixon on September 8, 1974. **Identify Cause and Effect** Why did this act reduce public support for Ford as President?

>> President Ford's "WIN," or Whip Inflation Now, strategy called for a combination of personal saving and discipline coupled with government action to stabilize the economy.

very successfully. He left office with the economy still suffering and the public's distrust of government still high.

Pardoning Nixon Ford moved quickly to try to restore confidence in government. He selected Nelson Rockefeller, a former governor of New York State, to serve as his Vice President. He also promised to continue the foreign policy approaches of the Nixon administration.

Whatever support he gained from these steps was lost when Ford announced that he had **pardoned**, or officially forgiven, Richard Nixon for any crimes he may have committed as President. Though the pardon was meant to heal the nation's wounds, in some ways it achieved just the opposite. Ford's critics accused him of having made a secret deal, promising Nixon the pardon in exchange for the vice presidential nomination. Though Ford strongly denied this, his popularity declined dramatically.

The congressional election results of 1974 indicated the public's disapproval of the pardon and the impact of Watergate in general. The Republicans lost 48 seats in the House of Representatives, including Ford's longtime district in Grand Rapids, Michigan.

Stagflation Continues President Ford might have overcome this backlash if not for the troubled economy. The stagflation that plagued the nation during Nixon's presidency continued under Ford. Inflation hit double digits in 1974 and early 1975. To fight skyrocketing prices, Ford promoted a mostly voluntary plan known as WIN, or Whip Inflation Now. Unfortunately, WIN was a clear failure. Instead of improving, the economy took a turn for the worse. Factories closed down, consumer demand for goods dropped sharply, and the rate of unemployment rose steadily. Ford's popularity plummeted.

☑ **EXPLAIN** How did President Ford's WIN program try to address inflation?

Ford Continues Nixon's Foreign Policies

The ordeal of the Vietnam War led many to question the direction of American foreign policy. They asked: Why was the United States so concerned with fighting communism that it ended up supporting oppressive anticommunist governments? Should the United States continue to pursue détente with the Soviets? Or should it instead demand that the

Soviet government grant its people more freedoms? Although the Soviet Union no longer exists, similar debates over the relationship between foreign policy and human rights continue to be heard today.

Relations with the Soviet Union remained central to U.S. foreign policy during the Ford administration. Upon assuming the presidency, Gerald Ford made clear that his foreign policy would differ little from that of Richard Nixon's. He retained Henry Kissinger as his Secretary of State and continued to pursue détente with the Soviet Union and China.

Continuing to Pursue Détente Ford and Soviet leader Leonid Brezhnev met in late 1974 and again the next year, when the two leaders endorsed the **Helsinki Accords**. This document put the nations of Europe on record in favor of **human rights**, or the basic rights that every human being is entitled to have. Some thought that President Ford would try to compel the Soviet Union to allow more political freedoms, but Ford decided to put arms control ahead of human rights. At his direction, the United States continued disarmament talks with the Soviets. These talks eventually led to an agreement known as **SALT II**, in which the two nations pledged to limit nuclear arms production. However, the U.S. Senate never ratified the treaty.

Trouble in Southeast Asia Under Ford, the United States sought to forget turmoil of the Vietnam War. When the communist Khmer Rouge government of Cambodia began a genocidal slaughter of civilians, killing about 1.5 million people between 1975 and 1979, the United States did not intervene.

The main exception to this policy of noninvolvement came in May 1975, when the Khmer Rouge seized an American merchant ship, the *Mayaguez*, which had been steaming just outside Cambodian waters. Ford responded by sending in some United States Marines, who freed the ship.

South Vietnam fell to North Vietnam during Ford's presidency. As the communists took over, hundreds of thousands of Vietnamese, many of whom had worked with the United States, tried to escape. Many refugees took to the seas in rickety, unseaworthy boats. These **boat people** represented the largest mass migration of humanity by sea in modern history. Over a 20-year period, more than one million men, women, and children braved storms, pirates, and starvation in search of refuge abroad. Their immediate destinations were in other nations of Southeast Asia, but many eventually found refuge in the United States and Canada.

☑ **DESCRIBE** How did Ford deal with foreign policy challenges during his presidency?

>> The Soviet Union continued to limit its people's freedoms. Alexander Solzhenitsyn was expelled from the Soviet Union in 1974 for writing novels that exposed the harsh conditions in Soviet labor camps.

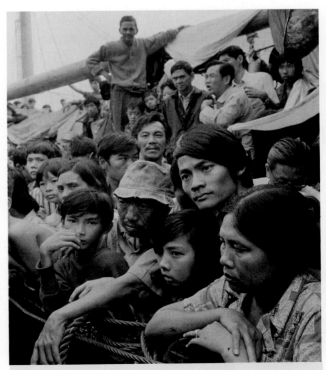

>> Hundreds of Vietnamese refugees were stranded for months on the freighter Tung An, waiting for a country to give them permission to disembark.

A New President Faces Challenges

Prior to the mid-1970s, few Americans outside Georgia had ever heard of **Jimmy Carter**, a one-time governor of that state. But on election day 1976, Americans elected Carter President of the United States. He won a slim popular majority, receiving slightly more than 50 percent of the vote to Ford's 48 percent. In the electoral college, Carter won 297 votes compared to 240 for Ford.

Carter's rise was the result of several factors. Most important was the turmoil of the 1960s and Watergate, which created a backlash against professional politicians. Carter seized this opportunity by casting himself as a fresh face, a "Washington outsider" with no ties to Washington, D.C. A born-again Christian who taught Sunday school, Carter won the support of many **Christian fundamentalists**, people who believe in a strict, literal interpretation of the Bible as the foundation of the Christian faith. This group became increasingly involved in politics in the 1970s.

The Cost of Inexperience From the beginning of his presidency, Jimmy Carter sought to portray himself as a "citizens' President." He became the first President since William Henry Harrison to walk all the way from the Capitol to the White House during the inaugural parade. He held town meetings, wore casual clothes, and carried his own suitcase.

However, Carter's inexperience, which helped him get elected, hurt him during the early days of his presidency. As an outsider, he did not have close ties with the Democratic leadership in Congress. He also surrounded himself with aides whose experience in Washington was limited. Carter submitted numerous bills to Congress, but few of them passed without major changes by his own party.

Just one day after his inauguration, Carter fulfilled one of his campaign pledges by granting **amnesty**, or political pardons, to Americans who had evaded the draft during the Vietnam War. Carter hoped this act would help the nation move beyond the divisions caused by that war.

Yet the war remained an emotional issue, and many criticized the President for forgiving those who had refused to fight. Republican senator Barry Goldwater called the amnesty "the most disgraceful thing that a President has ever done."

Economic Problems Sap Confidence Like Ford, Carter contended with the energy crisis and severe inflation. Inflation ate away at people's savings, raised prices, and made American goods more costly abroad. The U.S. automobile industry, long a symbol of the nation's economic power, became a symbol of its ills. Japanese car companies vastly expanded their sales in the United States by selling better-built and more fuel-efficient cars at reasonable prices. The situation grew so bad that Chrysler, one of the three major American automobile companies, needed a federal loan to survive.

At the center of the nation's economic ills lay the ongoing energy crisis. In 1973, a gallon of gas cost about 40 cents. By the end of the decade, it cost close to $1.20. To make matters worse, the winter of 1976–1977 was an especially bitter one in parts of the United States, increasing the need for heating oil. Fuel shortages caused factory closings and business losses. The 1979 Oil Crisis caused another spike in gas prices and inflation.

Carter responded to the oil crisis by calling on Americans to conserve and by asking Congress to raise taxes on crude oil, which he hoped would encourage conservation. However, the bill that finally passed in the Senate had few of the President's ideas in it. Critics saw this as one more example of Carter's poor leadership skills.

>> Both during and after his presidency, Jimmy Carter, shown here with his mother, portrayed himself as an average American and political "outsider" who could help "clean up" Washington.

Carter's Sanctions Against the Soviet Union, 1979–1980

RESPONSES TO THE SOVIET INVASION OF AFGHANISTAN
Asked the U.S. Senate not to ratify SALT II
Imposed a grain embargo on the Soviet Union in 1980
Called for a boycott of the 1980 Summer Olympics in Moscow
Revoked export licenses for high-technology items
Recalled the U.S. ambassador to the Soviet Union
Increased aid to Afghan resistance fighters

>> **Analyze Charts** What can you infer about the United States' relationship with the Soviet Union during the Carter administration?

Carter did implement several domestic policies that his successors would build on during the 1980s. To fight inflation, Carter nominated Paul Volcker to head the Federal Reserve Board. Under Volcker's lead, the Federal Reserve began raising interest rates. In the long term, this policy helped to end the inflation that had plagued the nation for so long.

The **Community Reinvestment Act** which Congress passed and Carter signed into law in 1977, also helped address the nation's economic woes. In order to create economic opportunity for citizens, this law required banks to make loans in the same neighborhoods where they took deposits. This requirement enabled many low- to moderate-income Americans, especially ethnic minorities, to become homeowners. The law remains in effect today. Whether it has had unintended consequences, possibly contributing to the mortgage crisis that triggered the Great Recession of 2007 to 2011 is an issue hotly debated in the business community.

LGBT Politicians Are Elected The growth of the lesbian, gay, bisexual, and transgender rights movement led to the pioneering role of gay politicians such as Elaine Noble, who was elected to the Massachusetts House of Representatives in 1974, and Harvey Milk, elected in 1977 to the San Francisco Board of Supervisors. Tragically, Harvey Milk was assassinated a year later. His death was deeply mourned by the LGBT community who regarded him as a martyr to the cause of gay rights. In 2009 he was awarded the Presidential Medal of Freedom.

☑ **LIST** What challenges did President Carter face?

Foreign Policy Changes Under Carter

Early in his presidency, Jimmy Carter proclaimed that as much as possible, American foreign policy would be guided by a concern for human rights. Carter hoped to make his foreign policy into a tool to end acts of political repression such as torture, murder, and imprisonment without trial. This policy helped reaffirm the position of the United States as a nation of freedom and justice. However, it undercut the goal of better relations with the Soviet Union.

Soviet-American Relations Cool At first, Carter continued Nixon's and Ford's policies toward the Soviet Union. He continued efforts at arms control, meeting with Leonid Brezhnev in June 1979 and signing the SALT II treaty.

However, relations between the two superpowers soon took a decidedly frosty turn. The SALT II treaty was bitterly debated in the United States Senate, where its opponents argued that it put the national security of the United States in jeopardy. Then, in December 1979, the Soviet Union invaded Afghanistan to prop up a tottering communist government. Carter responded by withdrawing the SALT II treaty from Senate consideration and by imposing **sanctions**, or penalties, on the Soviets. The sanctions included a U.S. boycott of the 1980 Summer Olympic Games held in Moscow as well as a suspension of grain sales to the Soviet Union.

Attempts to Protect Human Rights Since the end of World War II, American Presidents had tended to see the **developing world**—the less developed nations of Asia, Africa, and Latin America—as

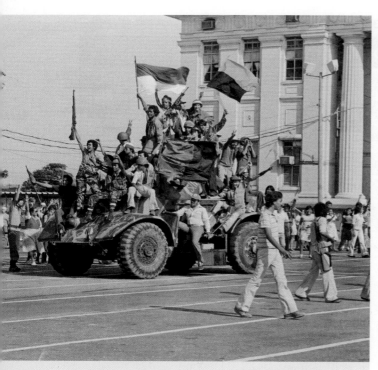

>> Sandinistas celebrate on the streets of Managua, Nicaragua's capital, after their defeat of the dictator Anastasio Somoza and his troops in July 1979.

>> President Carter helped to ease tensions in the Middle East by inviting Israeli Prime Minister Menachem Begin and Egyptian President Anwar Sadat to Camp David for peace talks in 1978.

another stage for the Cold War. Carter broke with that approach and insisted that U.S. relations with foreign countries should be determined by how a country treated its citizens.

Carter's emphasis on human rights led him to alter the U.S. relationship with a number of dictators. In Nicaragua, the Somoza family had ruled the country with an iron grip since the mid-1930s, most of the time with the support of the United States. In 1978, a leftist group known as the Sandinistas began a rebellion against the country's ruler, General Anastasio Somoza. His brutal response to the rebellion helped convince Carter to withdraw U.S. support. Without U.S. aid, General Somoza had to flee Nicaragua, and the Sandinistas came to power.

Other Foreign Policy Initiatives in Latin America The Carter administration briefly sought to improve relations with communist Cuba, ruled by Fidel Castro since 1959. U.S.-Cuban relations soured in 1980, however, when Castro announced that any Cuban could leave the island from the port of Mariel for the United States. However, Castro insisted that any boats headed to the United States would also have to take criminals from Cuba's prisons.

Because of this requirement, the Mariel boatlift developed a bad reputation in the eyes of many Americans. Fewer than 20 percent of the people transported had spent time in prison, and many of those were political prisoners. Still, Americans were repelled by Castro's lack of concern for the welfare of the emigrants and by the idea that he would send criminals to the United States.

Carter's most controversial foreign policy move involved his decision to return the Panama Canal Zone to Panama. You will recall that in 1903, Panama had given the United States control of a wide strip of land across the middle of the country that later became the site of the Panama Canal. In 1977, Carter negotiated a set of treaties to return the Canal Zone to Panama by 1999. Many Americans worried that the loss of control over the canal would threaten American shipping and security. Nonetheless, the United States Senate narrowly ratified the treaties in 1978, and all control of the canal was ultimately turned over to Panama.

☑ **IDENTIFY** In what way did President Carter's policies differ from those of Ford?

Success and Setback in the Middle East

Carter's greatest achievement in foreign policy came in the region that also saw his greatest setback. He helped negotiate a historic peace agreement between Israel and Egypt, but he failed to win the release of Americans held hostage by Iranian radicals.

The Camp David Accords Egypt had opposed Israel's existence since Israel's founding in 1948. As recently as 1973, Egypt and Syria had attacked Israel. By 1977, eager to improve relations, Egyptian President Anwar el-Sadat and Israeli Prime Minister Menachem Begin met in Jerusalem to negotiate a peace agreement.

To help continue the negotiations, Carter invited the two leaders to Camp David, the presidential retreat. For nearly two weeks, the three leaders carried on the difficult negotiations that produced what is known as the **Camp David Accords**. These agreements provided the framework for a peace treaty in which Egypt formally recognized the nation of Israel, becoming the first Arab nation to do so. In return, Israel withdrew its troops from the Sinai Peninsula, which it had controlled since the 1967 war. The preamble to the Accords states:

> After four wars during 30 years, despite intensive human efforts, the Middle East, which is the cradle of civilization and the birthplace of three great religions, does not enjoy the blessings of peace. . . . [Israel and Egypt] recognize that for peace to endure, it must involve all those who have been most deeply affected by the conflict. They therefore agree that this framework, as appropriate, is intended by them to constitute a basis for peace not only between Egypt and Israel, but also between Israel and each of its other neighbors. . . .

—Camp David Accords, September 19, 1978

The Iran Hostage Crisis Carter hoped that the Camp David Accords would usher in a new era of cooperation in the Middle East. Yet, events in Iran showed that troubles in the region were far

>> Ayatollah Khomeini is shown here in exile in France in 1978. A leader of the Iranian Revolution, he became the Supreme Ruler of Iran after the Shah was overthrown.

Bounce to Activate Timeline

from over. Since the 1950s, the United States had supported the anticommunist rule of the Shah, or emperor, of Iran. In the 1970s, however, opposition to the Shah began to grow within Iran. Anger toward the nation that had long propped up the Shah's repressive regime—the United States— would soon boil over as well.

Dying of cancer, the Shah fled Iran in January 1979. Fundamentalist Islamic clerics, led by the Ayatollah Khomeini (i yuh TOH luh koh MAYN ee), took power. Carter allowed the Shah to enter the United States to seek medical treatment. Enraged radical Iranian students invaded the U.S. Embassy and took 66 Americans as hostages. The Khomeini government took control of both the embassy and the hostages to defy the United States.

The hostage crisis consumed Carter's attention during the last year of his presidency. To many Americans, his failure to win the hostages' release was evidence of American weakness. As Peter Bourne put it in his biography of Jimmy Carter, "Because people felt that Carter had not been tough enough in foreign policy . . . some bunch of students could seize American diplomatic officials and hold them prisoner and thumb their nose at the United States."

The hostage crisis began to change the way Americans viewed the world outside their borders. Nuclear war between the two superpowers was no longer the only threat to the United States. Although the Cold War still concerned Americans, the threats posed by conflicts in the Middle East threatened to become the greatest foreign policy challenge of the United States.

☑ **DESCRIBE** How did the seizure of the U.S. Embassy by Iranian students affect Americans' view of the world?

Unease Over Changing Values

Social and cultural changes that had begun in the 1950s and 1960s continued unabated in the 1970s. As a result, by the end of the decade, the United States was a very different society from the one it had been a generation earlier. These differences gave rise to an ongoing debate about the nation's values.

Migration, Immigration, and Politics After World War II, there had been a demographic shift as American moved to the southern and western states, in search of jobs and a better climate. The migration

of Americans to the Sunbelt and the continued growth of the suburbs, both of which had begun in the post–World War II years, continued during the 1970s. As northern industries suffered, many blue-collar workers and their families moved from the Rust Belt states of the Northeast and Midwest to the Sunbelt of the South and West.

They sought work in the oil fields of Texas and Oklahoma and in the defense plants of southern California, the Southwest, and the Northwest. These changing demographic patterns changed the face of the United States.

The elections of Richard Nixon and Jimmy Carter demonstrated the growing political power of the Sunbelt. Earlier in the century, Presidents tended to come from the large northern industrial states, such as New York and Ohio. In the latter decades of the twentieth century, Presidents tended to come from the Sunbelt.

The influx of immigrants from Latin America and Asia represented a different kind of demographic change. Even before the 1970s, hundreds of thousands of Cubans, Puerto Ricans, and Mexicans had migrated to the United States in search of work and a better life. This migration, both legal and illegal, especially from Mexico and other Latin American countries, showed continued strength in the 1970s. The growing power of the Latino vote did

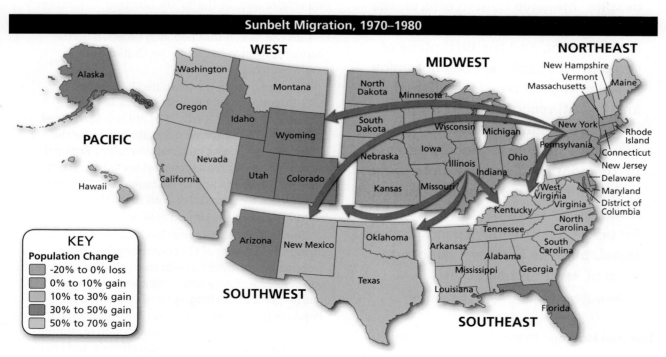

Sunbelt Migration, 1970–1980

KEY
Population Change
-20% to 0% loss
0% to 10% gain
10% to 30% gain
30% to 50% gain
50% to 70% gain

>> **Analyze Maps** Which regions of the United States most likely suffered economically as a result of population loss during the 1970s and 1980s?

not escape the notice of politicians. Richard Nixon was the first presidential candidate to seriously court the Spanish-speaking vote.

Countercultural Styles Spread in the "Me Decade" During the 1960s, radicals had challenged many of society's traditional values. They questioned restrictions on premarital sex and drug use. They sported casual clothing and long hairstyles that many of their parents' generation found improper. Yet the counterculture remained a relatively isolated phenomenon during the 1960s. By the end of the 1970s, in contrast, these behaviors had become more widespread. Nationwide, the divorce rate had more than doubled between 1965 and 1979, and twice as many children were born out of wedlock. To some Americans, the new ways were a sign of troubled times.

Some critics called the 1970s the "me decade" because many Americans appeared to be absorbed with improving themselves. This trend was reflected in the rise of movements like Transcendental Meditation (TM), a practice based in Eastern religious ideas. Those who practiced TM sought to find inner relaxation and vitality by chanting their personal mantras for about half an hour twice a day.

The seventies also witnessed an increasing interest in personal fitness and health. Millions began to jog for exercise and to eat natural, or less processed, foods. In 1970, just over 100 men and women ran in the New York City Marathon. Ten years later, more than 14,000 ran in the race. Body building took off, too, largely due to the influence of Arnold Schwarzenegger. A charismatic personality, Schwarzenegger went on to become one of Hollywood's most popular actors and, later, governor of California.

Conservatives Call for a Return to Traditional Values The 1970s witnessed a resurgence of fundamentalist Christianity, partly as a response to the shift in values. To some commentators, it seemed as if the nation was experiencing another Great Awakening, like the great religious movements of the eighteenth and nineteenth centuries. Although the total number of Americans who attended church on a regular basis did not change much, the number of men and women who belonged to evangelical churches rose rapidly. One in five Americans considered himself or herself a religious fundamentalist by 1980.

Religious conservatives firmly opposed many of the social changes begun in the 1960s that had gone mainstream in the 1970s. They opposed the Supreme

>> Televangelists, such as Reverend Jerry Falwell, were opposed to social changes that began in the 1960s and took root in the 1970s. They felt America was deviating from its moral path.

Bounce to Activate Chart

Court's rulings that legalized abortion and restricted prayer in school. Religious conservatives saw the latter as an unfair curtailment of religious freedom. In 1972, however, the Court upheld religious freedom in **Wisconsin v. Yoder** when it ruled that the state could not compel Amish children to attend school beyond the eighth grade because doing so violated Amish religious principles.

In opposing some Supreme Court rulings and what they believed were the negative effects of social change, evangelical ministers used the media to gain a broader following. Those who preached on television, such as Jerry Falwell, Oral Roberts, and Marion "Pat" Robertson, became known as **televangelists**. These preachers reached millions of television viewers. Falwell's weekly television show, for example, was broadcast to 1.5 million viewers.

In 1979, Falwell formed a prominent Christian conservative organization known as the Moral Majority. He voiced the concerns of many fundamentalists:

We must reverse the trend America finds herself in today. Young people . . . have been born and reared in a different world than Americans of past worlds. . . . They have learned to disrespect the family as God has established it. . . . They have been taught that the Bible is just another book of literature. . . . They have been introduced to the drug culture.

—Reverend Jerry Falwell, *Listen America*, 1980

During the 1970s, religious conservatives began forming alliances with other conservatives. They worked with economic conservatives, who sought to cut taxes and government spending, as well as with supporters of a stronger foreign policy, who favored increasing defense spending. Together, they began forging a new political majority. By 1980, Ronald Reagan, another political outsider, would use this alliance to win election to the White House.

☑ **LIST** In what ways did the United States change socially and culturally during the 1970s?

1. **Generate Explanations** Explain why President Ford faced significant disapproval from the American public.

2. **Summarize** Discuss President Ford's efforts to pursue détente with the Soviet Union.

3. **Describe** the crises that occurred in Southeast Asia during Ford's presidency, and discuss the role of United States in these events.

4. **Draw Conclusions** Explain how President Carter's support for human rights influenced his foreign policy.

5. **Identify Cause and Effect** Discuss some of the factors that influenced a resurgence of Christian fundamentalism during the 1970s.

Go online to PearsonSchool.com/CASS and use the texts, quizzes, interactivities, Interactive Reading Notepads, Flipped Videos, and other resources from this Topic to prepare for the Topic Test.

Etexts

Quizzes

Interactivities

Interactive Reading Notepads

Flipped Videos

While online you can also check the progress you've made learning the topic and course content by viewing your grades, test scores, and assignment status.

LESSON SUMMARIES

Use these Lesson Summaries, and the longer versions available online, to review the key ideas for each lesson in this Topic.

Lesson 1: The Counterculture of the 1960s

During the 1960s, the generation born after World War II created a rebellious counterculture that brought about dramatic changes in fashion, music, and sexual behavior.

Lesson 2: The Women's Rights Movement

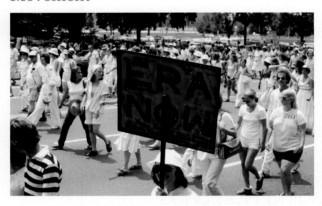

Inspired by the success of the civil rights movement, the women's rights movement gained strength in the 1960s. Although women won new legal rights, the Equal Rights Amendment was defeated.

Lesson 3: Expanding the Push for Equality

The civil rights movement also inspired other minorities such as Latinos, Native Americans, and Americans with disabilities to fight for their rights. A consumer rights movement prompted Congress to pass laws protecting the public.

Lesson 4: The Environmental Movement

The political activism of the 1960s also helped start the environmental movement. Public outcry over industrial pollution persuaded Congress to create the Environmental Protection Agency. New laws were passed to clean and protect the environment, although many feared that such laws would harm business.

Lesson 5: The Two Sides of the Nixon Presidency

President Nixon refocused American foreign policy toward economic benefits rather than ideology and reestablished a relationship with China. Negotiations were also opened with the Soviets. At home, however, Nixon faced economic problems and a political scandal that forced him to resign as President.

Lesson 6: Ford and Carter Struggle

Economic problems troubled Presidents Ford and Carter. Both Ford and Carter continued arms control negotiations with the Soviet Union, but Carter's foreign policy emphasized human rights. Although Carter succeeded in brokering peace between Egypt and Israel, he faced a crisis when Americans were taken hostage in the U.S. embassy in Iran. Meanwhile, fundamentalist Christians became more politically active.

VISUAL REVIEW

Use these graphics to review some of the key terms, people, and ideas from this Topic.

Values and Interests of the Counterculture

racial equality

spirituality and eastern religions

communal living

personal freedom

environmentalism and health foods

THE COUNTERCULTURE OF THE 1960s

distrust of authority

sexual freedom

folk music and rock-and-roll

opposition to Vietnam War

recreational drug use

Influence of the Civil Rights Movement

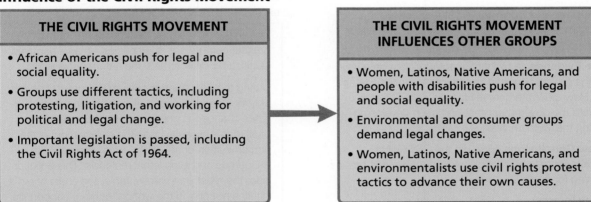

THE CIVIL RIGHTS MOVEMENT

- African Americans push for legal and social equality.
- Groups use different tactics, including protesting, litigation, and working for political and legal change.
- Important legislation is passed, including the Civil Rights Act of 1964.

THE CIVIL RIGHTS MOVEMENT INFLUENCES OTHER GROUPS

- Women, Latinos, Native Americans, and people with disabilities push for legal and social equality.
- Environmental and consumer groups demand legal changes.
- Women, Latinos, Native Americans, and environmentalists use civil rights protest tactics to advance their own causes.

America's Foreign Policy Before and After Vietnam

PRESIDENTS	POLICIES
Truman Eisenhower Kennedy Johnson	Cold War Consensus: Belief that the U.S. faced a unified worldwide communist movement.
Vietnam War and its aftermath raise doubts about the worldwide unity of communism.	
Nixon	More pragmatic approach Opens dialogue with China and détente with USSR
Ford	Continues Nixon's policies
Carter	Emphasis on human rights

KEY TERMS, PEOPLE, AND IDEAS

1. Why did a **generation gap** develop in the 1960s?

2. Why is the decision in *Roe* v. *Wade* so controversial?

3. What was the **Equal Rights Amendment (ERA)** intended to achieve?

4. By 1980, what were some signs that Latinos were gaining political power across the nation?

5. What problems did the **American Indian Movement (AIM)** intend to address?

6. Why was the **Environmental Protection Agency (EPA)** founded?

7. In what ways did **Henry Kissinger** and **Richard Nixon** change U.S. foreign policy?

8. How did Nixon's **southern strategy** change the political landscape?

9. How did the Iran Hostage Crisis affect Carter's presidency?

CRITICAL THINKING

10. **Compare and Contrast** What features did the social movements of the 1960s and 1970s have in common?

11. **Cite Evidence** (a.) What impact did Watergate have on the government and people of the United States? (b.) How did Watergate reinforce public attitudes toward the government that had been developing during the Vietnam War?

12. **Draw Conclusions** How did the Civil Rights movement help build coalitions among various groups fighting for rights?

13. **Draw Inferences** (a.) How did Nixon's domestic programs reflect his complex attitude to government power? (b.) Give example of some of Nixon's domestic programs.

14. **Evaluate** How successfully did government health policies and regulations promote public health and disease prevention in the 1970s?

15. **Identify Cause and Effect** How did President Carter's concern for human rights guide his foreign policy?

16. **Analyze Graphs** Study the graph below. Describe the impact of the oil embargo on the United States.

AVERAGE U.S. CRUDE OIL PRICES (PRICE PER BARREL)

OCTOBER 1973
Embargo on oil exports to U.S. begins

27% Amount of U.S. oil imports to meet demand in 1973

$1.80 (1970) $2.24 (1971) $2.48 (1972) $3.29 (1973) $11.58 (1974) $11.53 (1975) $12.80 (1976) $13.92 (1977) $14.02 (1978) $31.61 (1979) $36.83 (1980)

Source: British Petroleum

17. **Writing Activity: Use Primary Sources** Evaluate the impact that passages like this from Rachel Carson's *Silent Spring* had on environmental legislation. Use the excerpt below and your knowledge of this issue.

> Only in the moment of the time represented by the present century has one species—man—acquired significant power to alter the nature of his world.
>
> During the past quarter century this power has not only increased to one of disturbing magnitude but it has changed in character. The most alarming of all man's assaults upon the environment is the contamination of air, earth, rivers, and sea with dangerous and even lethal materials. This pollution is for the most part irrecoverable; the chain of evil it initiates not only in the world that must support life but in living tissues is for the most part irreversible. In this now universal contamination of the environment, chemicals . . . [are] changing the very nature of the world—the very nature of its life.
>
> —Rachel Carson, *Silent Spring*

DOCUMENT-BASED QUESTIONS

The Watergate scandal has had a long-lasting impact on Americans' attitude to government. Read the documents below, then answer the questions that follow.

DOCUMENT A

This excerpt is from a famous television interview with President Nixon.

> If the president, for example, approves something because of the national security, or in this case because of a threat to internal peace and order of significant magnitude, then the president's decision in that instance is one that enable those who carry it out, to carry it out without violating a law. . . . in war time, a president does have certain extraordinary powers which would make acts that would otherwise be unlawful, lawful if undertaken for the purpose of preserving the nation and the Constitution, which is essential for the rights we're all talking about.
>
> —*President Nixon, from an interview with British TV host, David Frost, May 19, 1977*

DOCUMENT B

This photograph, taken on August 9, 1974, shows Richard Nixon after resigning as president.

DOCUMENT C

This excerpt is from a speech made by Barbara Jordan in Congress during the impeachment of Richard Nixon.

> . . . the president has counseled his aides to commit perjury, willfully disregard the secrecy of grand jury proceedings, conceal surreptitious entry, attempt to compromise a federal judge, while publicly displaying his cooperation with the processes of criminal justice. . . . Has the president committed offenses, and planned and directed, and acquiesced in a course of conduct which the Constitution will not tolerate? That's the question.
>
> —*Barbara Jordan, statement at the U.S. House Judiciary Committee Impeachment Hearings, Washington, D.C., July 25, 1974*

DOCUMENT D

This excerpt is from the website of the *Washington Post*, the newspaper that investigated the Watergate break-in.

> The Watergate affair was over, but its influence was not. The interlinked scandals generated a new and enduring skepticism about the federal government in American public opinion. The lingo of the scandal—"to cover-up," to "stonewall," and "to leak"—became part of the American political vocabulary. The newly assertive Congress passed campaign finance reform legislation and probed abuses of power at the CIA and other national security agencies. . . . Before long, the appointment of special prosecutors to investigate allegations of presidential wrongdoing became the norm in Washington. Watergate had changed American politics permanently and profoundly.
>
> —*The Washington Post Website*

18. In Document A, Nixon appears to be arguing that
    A. only war time justifies certain acts.
    B. everyone is equal in a court of law.
    C. violating the law is never acceptable.
    D. the President is above the law.

19. **Analyze Photographs** What does Document B reveal about Nixon's attitude as he left office?

20. In Document C, Barbara Jordan is
    A. defending the actions of the President.
    B. establishing the grounds for impeachment.
    C. clarifying Congress's role in the Watergate scandal.
    D. explaining that the Constitution allows the President's conduct.

21. Document D, the writer points out that Watergate
    A. shaped public attitudes and legislation.
    B. led to greater public trust in government.
    C. polarized the American public.
    D. destroyed political careers.

22. **Writing Activity: Primary Source** Write a paragraph explaining whether you think the Watergate scandal revealed strengths or weaknesses in the political system. Use the sources as well as additional information you have learned.

1 What phenomenon of the 1960s does this photograph illustrate?

A the younger generation's respect for the status quo

B the generation gap between younger and older people

C the older generation's values of individuality and activism

D the importance of fashion to both the older and younger generations

---

Strategies for Expanding Women's Rights

• Lobbying the government

• Using mass media, such as magazines, to educate the public

• ?

2 What option best replaces the question mark in the list above?

F Staging public protests

G Writing letters to business leaders

H Circulating petitions to local governments

I Canvassing door-to-door to build awareness

3 In the 1960s and 1970s, Latinos sought federal protection for the right to vote. What does that reveal about America during those decades?

   A American Latino citizens had always had the right to vote.

   B The right of all races to vote was protected at the state level.

   C Many believed that only the states would be able to protect the right to vote.

   D Some were trying to block Latinos from voting.

ENVIRONMENTAL REGULATIONS

hamper business by diverting funds to clean up air and water	don't trust land owners to protect and preserve their own land	?

4 This graphic lists the reasons why many were opposed to environmental regulations. What option below best fits in the flowchart to explain additional opposition to environmental regulations based on Fifth Amendment rights?

   F strip individuals of full property rights by restricting land use

   G take private land away from individuals to create national parks

   H compel an individual to use his or her land for government projects

   I pay individuals to use land in ways dictated by the Environmental Protection Agency

If you have trouble with...				
Question	1	2	3	4
See Lesson	10.1	10.2	10.3	10.4

Establishing a Relationship with China

Pros

- Created a stronger front against the Soviet threat
- Strengthened economic ties between both countries
- Lifted the 22-year ban on travel to China
- Formed stronger bond between East and West and greater cultural exchange

Cons

- Upset anti-communist American allies
- Increased tensions temporarily between the United States and the Soviet Union
- Eventually created a rift between the United States and China over the political status of Taiwan

5 Based on the chart above, how would you characterize President Nixon's foreign policy?

A shaped by pragmatism and economic considerations

B full of Cold War anti-communist rhetoric

C governed by a concern for human rights

D inspired by a program of imperialist expansion

6 In the 1970s, what realization began to shape the debate over foreign policy?

F the fact that communism was spreading and threatening government stability

G the fact that radical Islamists were threatening governments in the Middle East

H the fact that some anticommunist allies were oppressing their people

I the fact that the Khmer Rouge was conducting a genocidal slaughter of Cambodians

7 In what ways did the Vietnam War undermine American confidence?

   A It helped build support for Republican candidates.

   B It forced patriotic Americans to speak out in support of the war effort.

   C It shook trust in government and the military, challenged Cold War assumptions, and weakened the Democrats.

   D It weakened funding for President Johnson's welfare programs.

Economic Problems of the mid-1970s

UNEMPLOYMENT	Unemployment in the U.S. rose from 4 percent in 1970 to 9.5 percent by 1975.
INFLATION	Inflation reached 10 percent in the mid-1970s, the highest it had been in the twentieth century up to that point.
ENERGY CRISIS	An oil embargo in 1973 caused a severe shortage of gas, and prices soared from 40 cents per gallon in 1973 to $1.20 by 1980.
GOVERNMENT SPENDING	In 1970, total government spending was $321.8 billion; by 1975, spending had risen to $550.5 billion.

8 What factor partly explains government spending in the early 1970s?

   F a surplus in tax revenues

   G more children in elementary schools

   H lower unemployment

   I the costs of fighting the Vietnam War

If you have trouble with...				
Question	5	6	7	8
See Lesson	10.5	10.6	9.3	9.4

[ESSENTIAL QUESTION] What makes a government successful?

⑪ **America in the 1980s and 1990s**

Enduring Understandings

- In the 1970s, a conservative movement strengthened, leading to the election of Ronald Reagan as President in 1980.

- "Supply-side economics" aimed to improve the economy by cutting taxes.

- Reagan's policy of Peace Through Strength helped end the Cold War.

- During the 1980s and 1990s, the U.S. acted as a peacekeeper worldwide.

- Republicans announced their "Contract with America," calling for a reduction of government and a balanced budget.

- President Clinton was impeached, but not convicted, for perjury and obstruction of justice.

NBC LEARN

Learn more about the experiences of Irene Zoppi, a Gulf War veteran.

Bounce to Activate My Story Video

>> President Ronald Reagan at a reelection campaign rally.

In this Topic, you'll learn about America in the 1980s and 1990s. Look at the lesson outline and explore the timeline. As you study this Topic, you'll complete the Quest team project.

LESSON OUTLINE

11.1 The Conservative Movement Surges
HSS 11.3, HSS 11.3.2, HSS 11.11.2, HSS 11.11.6; Analysis CST.4

11.2 The Reagan Era
HSS 11.6.5

11.3 The Cold War Ends
HSS 11.9.3, HSS 11.9.4, HSS 11.9.5, HSS 11.9.6

11.4 A New Era in Foreign Policy
HSS 11.9, HSS 11.9.6

11.5 Clinton and the 1990s
HSS 11.8.7, HSS 11.9

An Era of Change

1980
Ronald Reagan wins the presidency

1983
Economy starts to recover from recession

1986
Space shuttle Challenger explodes after launch

1989
Berlin Wall falls

1991
Soviet Union breaks up; Cold War ends; Persian Gulf War

1993
Al Qaeda explodes bomb under World Trade Center

1998
President Clinton is impeached

1980   1985   1990   1995   2000

QUEST! TEAM PROJECT

Civic Discussion: Laissez-Faire?

Should government intervene to help the economy, or is it better for government not to interfere with the economy at all? In this Quest you'll discuss the question: Would laissez faire be the best economic policy for the United States?

STEP ❶
Read the Discussion Launch and take notes about the major points. Discuss the points with the other members of your group.

STEP ❷
Examine several sources that will provide different perspectives on the main question. As you read and analyze each source, fill in Step 2 of the Information Organizer.

STEP ❸
After your group has been assigned a YES or NO position on the main question, prepare the most compelling arguments in support of your position. Present your arguments and then switch sides.

STEP ❹
Discuss the main question from your own point of view. Reflect on what you've read and heard about the question and how different perspectives have broadened your understanding of the issues involved.

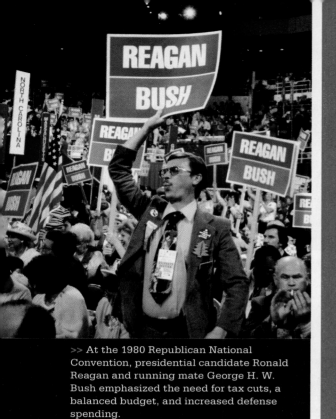

>> At the 1980 Republican National Convention, presidential candidate Ronald Reagan and running mate George H. W. Bush emphasized the need for tax cuts, a balanced budget, and increased defense spending.

Bounce to Activate Flipped Video

(11.1) The two major political parties in the United States in the late twentieth century were the Democrats, many of whom were "liberals," and the Republicans, who were often labeled "conservatives." Liberals generally favored government intervention to help the needy, whereas conservatives generally favored allowing the free market, private organizations, and individuals to do that. Although the two parties did agree on many basic issues, including core American values such as freedom and equality, they diverged on many others. In addition, individual members within both parties did not always conform to the views of their party's majority.

>> Objectives

Describe the differences between liberal and conservative viewpoints.

Analyze the causes behind the conservative resurgence in the early 1980s.

Explain why Ronald Reagan won the presidency in 1980.

>> Key Terms

liberal
conservative
New Right
unfunded mandate
Moral Majority
Ronald Reagan

The Conservative Movement Surges

Liberals and Conservatives Diverge

In order to understand the Republican party of the late twentieth century, one has to revisit the 1964 election, which marked a low point for conservatives. Republican Barry Goldwater, a favorite of the conservative movement, lost the election in a landslide to liberal Democrat Lyndon Johnson. Nonetheless, conservatives were not discouraged by this loss at the polls. On the contrary, they set out to build an organization and to put forth a clear vision of their goals and values that would enable them to win in the future.

Meanwhile, Goldwater returned to the Senate, where he continued to be the voice of conservatism and to forcefully advocate for conservative views. Goldwater found a supporter in California Governor Ronald Reagan, who was emerging as a conservative leader. By 1980, the conservatives' efforts had paid off. Their new standard bearer, Ronald Reagan, was elected president. The modern conservative movement that Reagan spearheaded shaped the nation's policies for decades.

Liberalism's Ideas and Goals In the late 1970s, liberals tended to believe that the federal government should play a significant role in improving the lives of all Americans. They valued social programs that helped the poor, unemployed, elderly, and others. They also sponsored laws that protected the rights of minorities and women, especially in the post–World War II period. They supported greater government regulation of industry. In the foreign policy realm, liberals tended to favor cooperating with international organizations like the United Nations.

Conservatism's Ideas and Goals In contrast, some conservatives felt that a large central government endangered economic growth and individual choice. They felt the liberal policies of the 1960s and 1970s left a legacy of rising inflation and enormous waste. Furthermore, some conservatives criticized the liberal solution of "throwing money" at social problems. They sought to reduce taxes and limit government regulation of industry in order to promote economic growth.

As conservative economist Milton Friedman and his wife Rose Friedman wrote in their book *Free to Choose*, "The story of the United States is the story of an economic miracle. . . . What produced this miracle? Clearly not central direction by government."

Other conservatives, neoconservatives or traditionalists, warned about the dangers posed to society by abandoning traditional values in favor of the new freedoms exemplified by the counterculture and advertised by the mass media. This concern with social issues, such as the perceived degeneration of modern youth, dovetailed with many conservatives' religious beliefs.

Anticommunism formed the third leg of modern conservatism. Most anticommunists focused on the dangers posed to the United States by the Soviet Union. They questioned the wisdom of the détente policy followed by Republican presidents Nixon and Ford, and by Democrat Jimmy Carter. They also fought against the SALT II treaty in the Senate.

☑ **IDENTIFY** According to conservatives, what is the best way to promote economic growth?

The Increasing Popularity of the New Right

During the 1940s and 1950s, the lines separating Republicans and Democrats had blurred. The two parties had developed a bipartisan foreign policy aimed at containing communism. Both favored a relatively significant role for the government in domestic affairs. However, during the 1960s and 1970s, many Republicans became increasingly critical of the liberal policies of the Democrats. They advanced a new conservative agenda. The differences between the two major parties grew more pronounced. The **New Right**, as the resurgent

Liberal Viewpoints in the 1980s

ISSUE	VIEWPOINT
Role of government in the economy	Favored more government involvement to lessen extreme economic inequalities through • social programs (often leading to higher taxes) • government regulation of industry
Foreign policy	Favored international diplomacy to combat communism in other countries
Healthcare	Favored government regulation of healthcare and believed everyone had a right to healthcare
Energy	Favored exploring alternatives to oil and believed the government should regulate the gas and electric industries

SOURCE: *The road from here: Liberalism and realities in the 1980s*

>> **Analyze Information** In the 1980s, what might a liberal have believed about government involvement in the economy?

 Bounce to Activate Chart

conservative movement was called, grew rapidly and was a coalition of several different groups with varying ideas and goals. This movement built part of its base through evangelical churches, televangelism, and other media outlets. Its leaders formed their ideology through organizations like the Young Americans for Freedom and went on to found a variety of think tanks and lobbying organizations.

The Decline of Liberalism One reason for the revival of the Republican Party was the unraveling of the Democratic Party. The Vietnam War and urban riots of the 1960s divided the same people who had rallied around President Johnson's vision of the Great Society.

The rise of the counterculture alienated many midwestern Americans and white conservative Christians in the South. Feminist advances were opposed by social leaders like Phyllis Schlafly. Watergate, the oil crises of the 1970s, and the Iran hostage crisis further weakened the public's faith in the federal government.

Just as importantly, the shifts in the economy of the 1970s, including the decline in northern industries, dampened America's optimism about the future. America had supported the Great Society, in part, because Johnson had suggested that the war on poverty and other new programs would not demand higher taxes. When the economy stagnated, liberal ideas lost their pull and conservative beliefs became more attractive.

Criticizing Liberal Programs Many conservatives believed that liberal policies were responsible for stagflation and other economic problems of the late 1970s. They believed that the government taxed citizens and businesses too heavily and spent too much on the wrong programs. They complained about **unfunded mandates**, programs required but not paid for by the federal government.

Some conservatives also criticized federal welfare programs, arguing that they rewarded lack of effort. Furthermore, they thought that Great Society programs did not work and that these programs had made the problem of poverty worse, not better. They pointed to other unintended consequences of such programs. For example, they charged that welfare contributed to the rise in the number of children born out of wedlock and therefore encouraged the decline of the traditional family—consisting of a married father and mother and their children. They also felt that affirmative action programs went too far and contributed to reverse discrimination.

Another group that supported the conservative platform was the "sagebrush rebels." Sagebrush rebels were activists who believed that the federal government controlled too much land in Western states. They thought the federal government should give control of this land to the states, to be used to their best economic advantage. Most environmentalists opposed the movement, because they did not want to expose preserved lands to possible development.

U.S. Inflation, 1978–1980

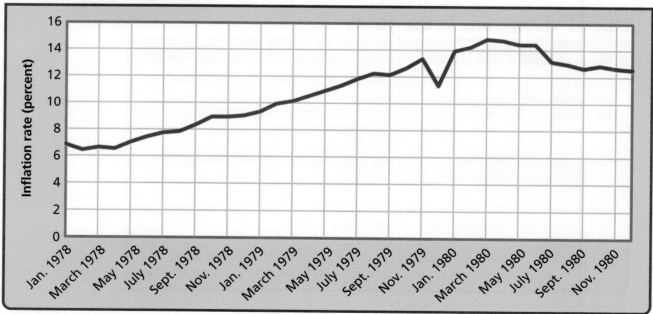

SOURCE: Bureau of Labor Statistics

>> **Analyze Data** During which years did the inflation rate rise steadily?

The Religious Right Emerges At the same time, concern with cultural change caused more religious groups to become actively involved in politics. The **Moral Majority**, founded by Reverend Jerry Falwell in 1979, was a political organization working to fulfill religious goals. It also worried about the decline of the traditional family. The Moral Majority opposed the 1962 Supreme Court decision *Engel* v. *Vitale*, which forbade government-written prayers in public schools, as well as the historic 1973 *Roe* v. *Wade* decision, which legalized abortion. It also condemned the Equal Rights Amendment and the gay rights movement, which had begun to suffer defeats nationally after Anita Bryant launched her successful 1977 campaign to repeal a local anti-discrimination ordinance in Dade County, Florida.

The Moral Majority boosted the Republican Party's chances of winning the presidency by reaching out to Americans who had traditionally not participated in the political process. With other groups like it, the Moral Majority registered at least 2 million new voters before the 1980 presidential election. One of their tactics was to distribute Moral Majority "report cards" on candidates, which almost always favored Republicans.

Changing Demographic Patterns Boost Conservatism Demographic, or population, trends also strengthened the conservative movement. Historically, northern cities stood as strongholds of liberal Democrats. When an increasing number of Americans moved to the suburbs, their attachment to liberalism waned as they struggled financially during the tough economic days of the late 1970s. At the same time, Republicans emphasized issues that they believed would convince moderate liberals to switch their party allegiance. For instance, Republicans attacked school busing as a form of social engineering that threatened the long-cherished ideal of neighborhood schools.

Republicans benefited from the migration of Americans from the Rust Belt to the Sunbelt. This demographic shift, which began in the 1950s and continued through the 1970s, had many causes, including the sunny climate and opportunities for jobs in aerospace, technology, and other growing industries. Republicans also benefited from a historical realignment of white voters in the Deep South. Since the Civil War, most white southerners had voted for the Democratic Party.

Following the enactment of civil rights legislation in the mid-1960s, however, many white southerners began to shift their party allegiance. The effect of these shifts in demographics and voter loyalties was

>> Ronald Reagan, shown here in a 1951 Hollywood studio shot, originally supported New Deal policies. He later became a conservative, believing that Americans should oppose the expansion of the federal government.

that by the 1980s, the Republicans had become the dominant political party in the South.

☑ **RECALL** Why did the Moral Majority oppose the 1962 Supreme Court *Engel* v. *Vitale* decision?

A Conservative Wins the White House

The growing conservative movement swept the Republican presidential candidate **Ronald Reagan**, to victory in the 1980 election. Much more charismatic and polished than Goldwater, Reagan made clear his opposition to big government, his support for a strong military, and his faith in traditional values. Just as importantly, he radiated optimism, convincing Americans that he would usher in a new era of prosperity and patriotism.

Reagan's Path to the Presidency Born in Tampico, Illinois, in 1911, Reagan suffered the hardships of the Great Depression as a young adult before landing a job in Hollywood as a movie actor. Never a big star, Reagan appeared in many "B" or low-budget films. His most famous starring role was in *Knute Rockne*, a film based on the life of Notre Dame's legendary football coach.

When his acting career began to wane, Reagan became a spokesperson for General Electric and toured the nation giving speeches. Although once a staunch New Dealer, Reagan had become a Goldwater conservative. In these speeches he began to criticize big government and high taxes and warned of the dangers of communism. In 1964, near the end of Goldwater's presidential campaign, Reagan delivered a nationally televised address in which he spelled out these views:

> "This is the issue of this election, whether we believe in our capacity for self-government or whether we abandon the American Revolution and confess that a little intellectual elite in a far-distant capital can plan our lives for us better than we can plan them ourselves."
>
> —Ronald Reagan, "A Time for Choosing," 1964

While the speech failed to bolster Goldwater's campaign, it won the admiration of many conservatives. Two years later, Reagan won the governorship of California. He served for two terms as governor and nearly won the Republican presidential nomination in 1976. In 1980, he won the nomination by a landslide. His opponent was Jimmy Carter, the Democratic incumbent.

The 1980 Election As the 1980 presidential election approached, Carter looked like a lame duck. Persistent inflation, the Iran hostage crisis, and the Soviet invasion of Afghanistan made it easy for Reagan to cast the Carter presidency in a negative light. "Are you better off than you were four years ago?" Reagan asked audiences on the campaign trail, knowing that most Americans would answer, "No."

The race remained relatively close until about one week before the election, when Reagan and Carter held their only presidential debate. In this debate, Reagan's gifts as a communicator shone. He appeared friendly and even-tempered and calmed fears that he did not have enough experience to serve as president. On Election Day, Reagan won 50.7 percent of the popular vote. Because most states award electoral votes on a "winner-takes-all" basis, Reagan won an overwhelming majority of electoral college votes despite the narrow margin by which he won the popular vote. Even though the Democrats maintained control of the House of Representatives,

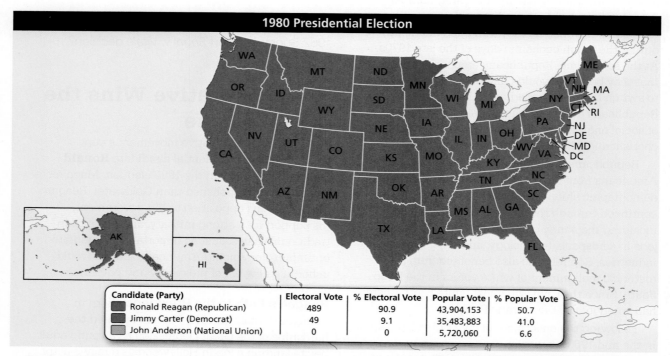

1980 Presidential Election

Candidate (Party)	Electoral Vote	% Electoral Vote	Popular Vote	% Popular Vote
Ronald Reagan (Republican)	489	90.9	43,904,153	50.7
Jimmy Carter (Democrat)	49	9.1	35,483,883	41.0
John Anderson (National Union)	0	0	5,720,060	6.6

>> **Analyze Information** Some describe the 1980 presidential election as a close contest. In what way was this true? In what way was it not true?

Bounce to Activate Timeline

Republicans captured the U.S. Senate for the first time since 1955. The conservatives were back.

☑ **IDENTIFY CENTRAL IDEAS** What policies made Ronald Reagan attractive to conservative voters?

☑ ASSESSMENT

1. **Compare and Contrast** the beliefs of liberals and conservatives in the late twentieth century.

2. **Describe** the factors that contributed to the decline of liberalism in the late 1970s.

3. **Apply Concepts** Discuss the emergence of the Moral Majority and explain its connection to the Republican Party.

4. **Generate Explanations** Explain how Ronald Reagan rose to prominence within the Republican Party.

5. **Identify Patterns** Explain how changing demographics contributed to the rise of conservatism in the 1970s.

>> President Reagan and First Lady Nancy Reagan celebrate his reelection at an inaugural ball in January 1985. A rebounding economy helped Reagan win election to his second term in office.

Bounce to Activate Flipped Video

11.2 Conservatives celebrated Ronald Reagan's election as the fulfillment of their dreams. Some even referred to his coming to power as the "Reagan Revolution." The Reagan Revolution would bring a significant shift in the political direction of the nation.

>> Objectives

Analyze Reagan's economic policies as President.

Examine Reagan's leadership and how he strengthened the conservative movement.

Evaluate the steps taken to address various issues in the 1980s and early 1990s.

>> Key Terms

supply-side economics
deregulation
budget deficit
national debt
Savings and Loan crisis
voucher
Acquired Immunodeficiency Syndrome (AIDS)
Sandra Day O'Connor

The Reagan Era

A New Direction for the American Economy

Tax Cuts and Deregulation Reagan and his advisors based their economic policies on the theory of "supply-side economics," sometimes called "Reaganomics." The theory of **supply-side economics** rests on the assumption that if taxes are reduced, the wealthy would invest more and thus create jobs.

The new jobs would give people more money to spend, causing the economy to grow. The government will then collect more in taxes. To cut taxes while still balancing the federal budget, however, Reagan also needed to reduce federal spending on programs favored by both Democrats and Republicans.

Congress approved most of Reagan's plan to institute supply-side economics by passing the Economic Recovery Act of 1981, which reduced taxes by 23 percent over three years. The richest Americans received the largest tax cuts. Reagan justified this move by saying that the wealthy would use the money they saved to invest in new businesses, which would help everyone. Reagan also convinced Congress to cut about $40 billion from the federal budget, mostly by cutting spending for social programs.

In addition to cutting taxes, Reagan also reduced the government's role in the economy by calling for **deregulation**, or the removal of government control over industry. By the mid-1980s, Congress had deregulated the airline, telecommunications, and banking industries. The Reagan administration also cut funding for federal agencies that oversaw many other industries.

Significant Societal Issues Shortly after Reagan took office, the economy experienced a severe recession from 1980 to 1982. Unemployment rose to more than 10 percent in 1982. The recession hit blue-collar workers particularly hard. Many farmers, facing overseas competition, lost their farms. The policies that Paul Volcker, as head of the Federal Reserve Board, had introduced to tame the great inflation of the 1970s contributed to the recession in the early 1980s. Beginning in early 1983, however, the economy began to turn around. Inflation fell dramatically. The Gross National Product, or the annual income earned by Americans and American businesses, expanded at a healthy pace. America's economy seemed revitalized.

Despite this, the number of poor people, including the working poor, actually increased. In addition, immigrants from Latin America and Asia, attracted by employment prospects and political freedom, continued to pour into the United States. Among the Asian immigrants were the Sikhs, a religious group that originated in the Punjab, a region in Pakistan and northern India. In the 1980s, more than 7.3 million legal immigrants and hundreds of thousands of undocumented immigrants entered the country. Many of these newcomers worked in low-paying jobs and struggled to make ends meet. Meanwhile, the richest Americans grew richer.

In Texas, tensions from this economic disparity reached a head in 1984 when a poor, largely Mexican American school system sued the state commissioner of education over inequalities in the education of minorities. After a nearly 10-year struggle, the case, *Edgewood I.S.D.* v. *Kirby*, led to a school funding system where some tax money from more affluent, largely white school districts was transferred to less affluent, largely minority districts to help these poor districts provide better education to their students.

Problems With Deficits Reagan increased defense spending but failed to win the huge cuts in government spending that he wanted in other areas. These were some of the factors, along with a recession, that caused the federal **budget deficit**, or the shortfall between the amount of money spent and the amount taken in by the government, to

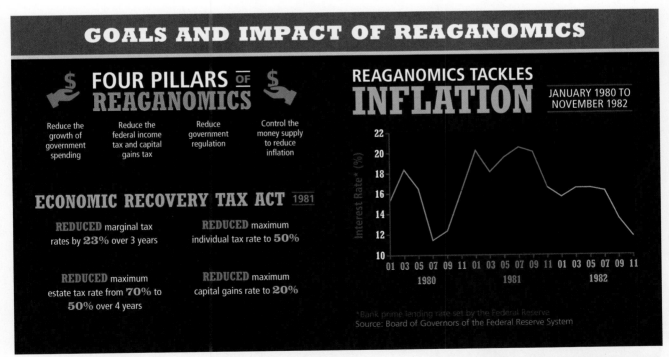

GOALS AND IMPACT OF REAGANOMICS

FOUR PILLARS OF REAGANOMICS

Reduce the growth of government spending

Reduce the federal income tax and capital gains tax

Reduce government regulation

Control the money supply to reduce inflation

ECONOMIC RECOVERY TAX ACT 1981

REDUCED marginal tax rates by **23%** over 3 years

REDUCED maximum individual tax rate to **50%**

REDUCED maximum estate tax rate from **70%** to **50%** over 4 years

REDUCED maximum capital gains rate to **20%**

REAGANOMICS TACKLES INFLATION JANUARY 1980 TO NOVEMBER 1982

*Bank prime lending rate set by the Federal Reserve
Source: Board of Governors of the Federal Reserve System

>> Ronald Reagan had to find a way to deal with inflation and stimulate the economy. **Analyze Data** How effective were Reaganomics in tackling inflation?

Bounce to Activate Chart

skyrocket from about $79 billion in 1981 to more than $221 billion in 1986. The **national debt**, the amount of money the federal government owes to owners of government bonds, rose to $2.5 trillion.

In response to persistent budget deficits, Congress passed the Gramm Rudman-Hollings Act in 1985. The act sought to balance the budget by 1990 by requiring automatic cuts in federal spending if the deficit exceeded a certain amount. The federal budget deficit set new records, however, into the early 1990s.

The **Savings and Loan crisis** (also called the S&L crisis) in 1989 exacerbated deficit problems. In the late 1980s, about 1,000 Savings and Loan banks failed, some because of fraudulent behavior and others because they made too many risky loans. Critics blamed Reagan's deregulation policies for encouraging the banks to invest in riskier propositions. To prevent a broader panic, the federal government spent upwards of $200 billion to bail out depositors at the failed banks.

In the 1980s, the rising cost of Social Security also caused concern. As the number of elderly people in America grew, the Social Security system began to collect less money than it paid out. In 1983, Reagan signed the Social Security Reform Act, which raised the minimum retirement age and increased payroll taxes for Social Security. It provided a temporary fix but did not solve the long-term problems of the Social Security program.

Trade Imbalance With Japan Another deficit that alarmed Americans was the nation's growing imbalance in world trade. American exports had been falling steadily since the 1970s due to a decline in domestic automobile, electronics, and other manufacturing industries.

Japan began to dominate the American market in televisions, automobiles, and other consumer products. At the same time, Japan's markets remained closed to many American-made goods.

When Japan refused to ease its restrictions on American imports, Reagan placed a tariff on Japanese electronics that doubled their price in American stores. Japanese trade restrictions eased in a deal to get this tariff removed. However, the United States continued to import many more Japanese products than American companies were able to sell in Japan.

Reagan and Organized Labor In 1981 when thousands of air-traffic controllers went on strike, Reagan refused to negotiate with the Professional Air Traffic Controllers Organization (PATCO) and fired the striking workers because they were violating a law forbidding federal employees from striking. Many Americans admired Reagan's strong, decisive stance. Some union supporters, however, claimed that Reagan's action represented an assault on the labor movement.

U.S. Trade Deficit with Japan, 1980–1990

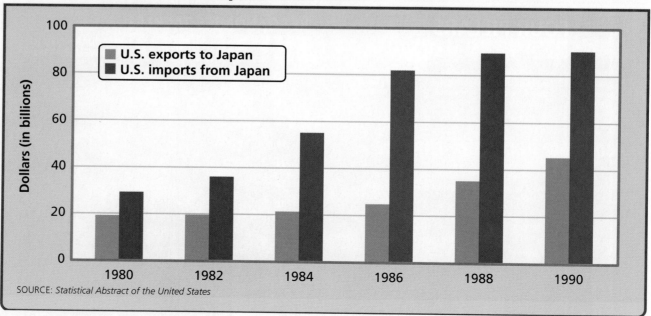

SOURCE: *Statistical Abstract of the United States*

>> **Analyze Data** What happened to the trade deficit with Japan between 1980 and 1990?

The PATCO strike marked a turning point for organized labor. As the nation became more conservative, anti-union feelings grew. By 1980, the labor movement was already shrinking from its high levels of memberhip in the 1950s and 1960s. After the PATCO strike's highly visible failure, however, the decline became more rapid. Reagan's actions also signaled that it was acceptable for businesses to get tough with unions.

The Private Sector Creates Economic Opportunities Reagan believed that volunteerism and private initiative could create economic opportunities for citizens. In 1981, he praised an organization called the Clearinghouse on Corporate Social Responsibility for their work in improving Americans' quality of life. The Clearinghouse had evolved from the committee of insurance company CEOs who had first met in response to the urban riots of the late 1960s. One of the unintended consequences of this meeting was that by 1981, the organization had expanded to include life and health insurance trade associations. It actively supported community projects, employment of women and minorities, environment and energy conservation, and socially responsible investments. In 1982 it changed its name to the Center for Corporate Public Involvement.

☑ **IDENTIFY MAIN IDEAS** What is the central theory of Reaganomics, or supply-side economics?

Conservative Momentum Continues

Despite budget and debt problems, the economic recovery improved the national mood and helped Ronald Reagan's popularity. Reagan used his time in office to strengthen the conservative cause. Private conservative educational and research groups, such as Washington D.C.'s Heritage Foundation, supported Reagan and lobbied Congress on behalf of his programs.

Winning a Second Term During his 1984 campaign for reelection, President Reagan used the phrase "It is morning in America" as a campaign slogan:

"It's morning again in America. In a town not too far from where you live, a young family has just moved into a new home. . . . Right down the

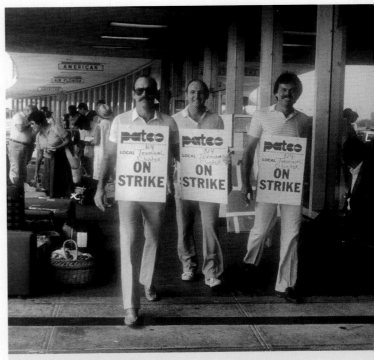

>> Members of the air traffic controllers union, PATCO, picket at New York's LaGuardia Airport in August 1981.

street, one of the neighbors has just bought himself a new car with all the options. The factory down the river is working again. . . . Life is better, America is back. And people have a sense of pride they never felt they'd feel again."

—Campaign commercial for the reelection of Ronald Reagan, 1984

This theme dovetailed nicely with Reagan's upbeat spirit, which he displayed even in his darkest moments. For example, on March 30, 1981, a disturbed man named John Hinckley, Jr., tried to assassinate the president. One bullet from Hinckley's gun lodged in Reagan's chest. According to one account, Reagan joked to his doctors, "I hope you are all Republicans."

Americans voted overwhelmingly to reelect Reagan in 1984. He easily defeated Walter Mondale, the Democratic presidential nominee, and his running mate, Geraldine Ferraro, the first woman to be nominated for vice president by a major political party. However, Reagan's momentum did not lead to a total triumph for conservatives, as Democrats retained control of the House of Representatives.

>> In 1981 Sandra Day O'Connor became the first woman on the Supreme Court. To offset what he saw as liberal bias, President Reagan appointed three conservative judges to the Court during his presidency.

>> In 1988 after serving for eight years as Vice President, George H.W. Bush ran for President against Democrat Michael Dukakis.

Creating Conservative Courts During his two terms, Reagan appointed judges who he hoped would reverse the liberal drift of the federal courts. He appointed three new Justices — Sandra Day O'Connor, Antonin Scalia, and Anthony Kennedy—to the Supreme Court and elevated William Rehnquist, a well-known conservative, to the position of Chief Justice in 1986. **Sandra Day O'Connor**, nominated in 1981, was the first female Justice and a moderate conservative. Although she voted with other conservatives on many issues, she consistently voted to uphold *Roe* v. *Wade*, which Reagan opposed.

Near the end of Reagan's first term, Congress passed the Equal Access Act. This act required public secondary schools to allow any group equal access to school facilities. Conservative Christian groups supported the act's passage because many public schools did not allow religious groups to meet on school property. The Supreme Court confirmed the constitutionality of the Equal Access Act in 1990 in *Board of Education of Westside Community Schools* v. *Mergens*.

George H.W. Bush Becomes President Reagan used his personal popularity to promote George H.W. Bush, his Vice President for eight years, as Bush campaigned for the presidency against Massachusetts governor Michael Dukakis in 1988. Bush had enjoyed a long and distinguished political career. He had served the nation in many ways: as a member of Congress from Texas, ambassador to the United Nations under Nixon, American envoy to China under Ford, and head of the Central Intelligence Agency (CIA). Despite these impressive credentials, Bush lacked the support of conservatives in the Republican Party, who questioned his commitment to their cause.

Although Bush called for a "kinder, gentler nation" in his campaign, both candidates attacked each other in negative campaign ads. Bush cemented his support among conservatives by promising not to raise taxes and by casting himself as a defender of traditional values. Although Bush defeated Dukakis in the presidential election, Democrats won a majority of seats in both houses of Congress.

President Bush sought to control federal spending by encouraging Americans to volunteer. Government, he asserted, could take a smaller role in daily life if, "like a thousand points of light," community organizations and volunteers provided more help to the disabled, illiterate, and poor.

When Congress passed the Americans With Disabilities Act (ADA) in July 1990, Bush signed it into law. The act ensured that persons with disabilities would receive the same opportunities in employment as well as access to public places and transportation that other Americans took for granted. It benefited more than 43 million people and represented another step in the quest to protect the rights of all Americans.

☑ **CHECK UNDERSTANDING** Did President Reagan's appointees to the Supreme Court follow his conservative agenda in full? Explain.

Culture, Challenge, and Change

Despite Reagan's vision of "morning in America" and Bush's "thousand points of light," in truth a great cultural and economic divide existed in 1980s society—a division partially defined by race, ethnicity, and gender. The economic recovery of the mid-1980s did not affect all segments of society equally. As the number of poor increased, so did violence and drug use in the nation's inner cities. At the same time, a culture of acquisition intensified among Americans.

Material Culture in the 1980s "I am a material girl," sang Madonna in her 1985 hit. For many Americans, her anthem to acquiring things characterized the decade.

Material acquisition especially defined a segment of society that came to be known as young urban professionals, or "yuppies"—Americans born in the baby boom that followed World War II and who made $40,000 a year or more in the 1980s. Because there were so many people in this demographic, their spending habits were noticed and often criticized by the media. Yuppies were characterized by their attachment to flashy cars and other possessions and for their obsession with making and spending money.

Another trend of the 1980s was a new obsession with physical fitness. Being "fit," however, meant more than just being healthy. It also meant looking good. Americans spent more than ever before on diet drinks and vitamins, sportswear, health club memberships, and home fitness videos and equipment. Some large companies, recognizing that healthy employees were more productive, opened in-house fitness facilities. They also sponsored programs and provided other incentives to help their employees get healthier. By the mid-1980s, nearly half of Americans exercised daily, compared to just 24 percent 20 years earlier. Critics observed

>> President Bush signs the Americans With Disabilities Act on the South Lawn of the White House in 1990. Signing ceremonies often include key participants involved with the legislation.

>> A young urban professional, or yuppie, speaks on an early model of a cell phone in 1983.

that these trends embodied the materialistic values of the 1980s. They complained that instead of trying to improve society, Americans were focused on improving themselves both physically and financially.

The Space Program in the 1980s The National Aeronautics and Space Administration (NASA) added a new type of spacecraft to its fleet in 1981. Unlike rockets that fell to earth and were discarded after a single use, the new space shuttle looked and landed like an airplane. It could take off again and again to complete multiple missions.

The promising shuttle program suffered a disastrous setback in January 1986, however, when the space shuttle *Challenger* exploded in midair less than 2 minutes after takeoff from Cape Canaveral in Florida. Its entire crew of seven astronauts was killed. The crew included New Hampshire schoolteacher Christa McAuliffe, the first private citizen to go into space. The explosion halted NASA's shuttle program for two years while scientists worked to eliminate technical problems. Nevertheless, space program technology continued to inspire many products—such as improved radial tires, the portable cordless vacuum cleaner, and

>> On January 28, 1986, millions of Americans watched on television as the space shuttle *Challenger* exploded minutes after takeoff. The tragedy shocked the nation, but the U.S. space program continued.

Bounce to Activate 3D Model

better firefighting gear—that improved Americans' quality of life.

Cold War Culture in the 1980s The ongoing Cold War also shaped the 1980s culture in the United States. The Olympic Games were held in Los Angeles in 1984. It was the first time the summer Olympics had come to this country in nearly 50 years. The festive opening ceremonies typified the Reagan era's emphasis on the renewal of America's greatness and patriotism.

The Olympics became a tool in the nation's Cold War rivalry with the Soviet Union. Along with most other communist countries, the Soviet Union boycotted the Los Angeles games. The Soviet-led boycott was in retaliation for President Carter's boycott of the 1980 games in Moscow to protest the Soviet invasion of Afghanistan. The United States won an unusually high number of medals at the Los Angeles games, an outcome that contributed to the Reagan era's sense of a revival in American strength and patriotism.

Confronting Challenging Issues at Home One of the most troubling problems the nation faced in the 1980s was a dramatic increase in the use of illegal drugs. The main culprit in this increasing drug use was the spread of cocaine. Once a problem largely confined to crime-infested areas of the nation's inner cities, cocaine use became much more widespread among other classes of American society during this time.

Reformers called for stopping the seemingly unrestricted flow of drugs into the United States and for harsher penalties for drug dealers. President Reagan responded by enlisting the Army and Navy to help stop the cocaine smuggling route into south Florida. The effort was successful. But by 1985, drug smugglers had shifted their operations to the U.S. border with Mexico. In 1986, Congress made the possession of drugs for sale an offense punishable by a minimum of 10 years in prison.

Many Americans also worried about the state of America's public education system. In 1983, the Department of Education issued *A Nation at Risk*. This study showed that students were consistently scoring lower on standardized tests as time passed. The report argued that America's schools failed to prepare students adequately to compete with students around the globe.

Even before the report appeared, conservatives called for providing **vouchers**, or government checks, that could be used by parents to pay tuition at private schools. Conservatives argued that vouchers would force public schools to improve in order to attract and retain students. Liberals in Congress argued that vouchers would take much-needed money away from public schools.

In addition, the nation faced the threat of a new disease, **Acquired Immunodeficiency Syndrome (AIDS)**, which first came to doctors' attention in 1981. AIDS is the last stage of the Human Immunodeficiency Virus (HIV), which attacks the immune system of its victims. There is no known cure. When AIDS first reached the United States, it spread mainly among homosexual men and intravenous drug users. Later, the virus began infecting various other groups of people. By 1994, AIDS had killed more than 250,000 Americans.

President Reagan was criticized for the government's lack of response to the AIDS epidemic. Congress consistently felt that Reagan's requests for funds to battle the epidemic were too low and nearly doubled the money earmarked for AIDS research and education.

Meanwhile, AIDS activist groups such as ACT UP (AIDS Coalition to Unleash Power) demonstrated throughout the country, protesting governmental and societal indifference to the epidemic. ACT UP demanded a coordinated government policy to fight the disease and protested the high cost of AIDS treatments. In Washington, D.C., activists unveiled a memorial quilt, conceived by the LGBT activist Cleve Jones, containing the names of some 2000 people who had died of AIDS. But not until George H.W. Bush's presidency did funding for research on the disease rise substantially.

The attempt on Reagan's life in a 1981 shooting and the serious wounding of his aide, James Brady, renewed calls for stronger controls on handguns. These efforts were opposed by the National Rifle Association (NRA), led by Harlon Carter, which casted itself as the defender of Americans' Second Amendment right to keep and bear arms. In spite of the efforts of this powerful conservative group, attempts in the 1980s to ban armor-piercing bullets and plastic handguns that could get by airport metal detectors were eventually passed by Congress.

☑ **DESCRIBE** How did the 1984 summer Olympics in Los Angeles help to bolster confidence during the Reagan era?

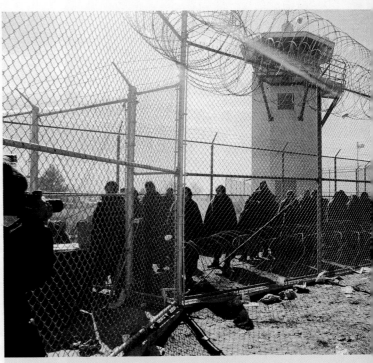

>> Prison inmates were guarded outdoors at the New Mexico State Penitentiary, where rioting due to overcrowding left the prison buildings destroyed.

☑ **ASSESSMENT**

1. **Identify Cause and Effect** Describe the causes and effects of the economic recession that occurred from 1980–1982.

2. **Describe** the significant cultural changes that emerged during the 1980s.

3. **Draw Conclusions** Discuss the significance of President Reagan's use of the phrase "It is morning in America."

4. **Identify Central Issues** Discuss the significance of the 1984 summer Olympics in relation to the Cold War.

5. **Generate Explanations** Explain why President Reagan received criticism for his administration's response to the AIDS epidemic.

>> This famous handshake between Reagan and Gorbachev at the 1988 Moscow Summit Conference symbolized the growing cooperation between the United States and the Soviet Union.

Bounce to Activate Flipped Video

11.3 President Ronald Reagan believed that the United States had lost its way in the wake of the Vietnam War. Rather than détente, he felt the United States should seek to roll back Soviet rule in Eastern Europe and elsewhere. Reagan believed that peace would come through strength. Although Reagan's foreign policies initially increased tension between the two superpowers, they contributed to the end of the Cold War.

>> Objectives

Analyze the ways that Ronald Reagan challenged communism and the Soviet Union.

Explain the end of the Cold War.

Describe other foreign policy challenges that faced the United States in the 1980s.

>> Key Terms

Strategic Defense
 Initiative (SDI)
Contras
Mikhail Gorbachev
glasnost
perestroika
Iran-Contra affair

The Cold War Ends

Reagan Leads with "Peace Through Strength"

President Reagan believed that the United States needed to weaken communism by challenging it as much as possible without provoking war. To this end, he devised policies aimed at toppling communist nations, ranging from building new nuclear missile systems to funding covert operations against Soviet troops and allies around the globe.

Reagan Decides on U.S. Military Buildup Under Reagan, the United States committed itself to the largest peacetime military buildup in its history. Reagan dedicated billions of dollars to the development and production of B-1 and B-2 bombers, MX missile systems, and other projects. In spite of massive protests by the nuclear freeze movement in the United States and abroad, the Reagan administration placed a new generation of nuclear missiles in Europe.

Reagan supported this massive military buildup, in part, because he did not believe that the Soviet Union could afford to spend as much on defense as the United States could. Reagan felt this applied particularly to the **Strategic Defense Initiative (SDI)**, a proposed program in which land and space-based lasers would destroy any missiles aimed at the United States before they could reach their targets. Some dubbed the missile program "Star Wars," after the popular science-fiction movie trilogy, and claimed that it was unrealistic.

Reagan Involves the U.S. in the Middle East and Central America
Reagan also sought to weaken the Soviet Union by supporting anticommunist rebellions around the globe. To this end, the United States funded and trained the mujahadeen (moo jah huh DEEN), anti-Soviet rebels in Afghanistan. Reagan's advisors believed that with U.S. help, these guerrillas could drive the Soviets out of Afghanistan. In 1988, Soviet forces finally began to withdraw after years of fierce Afghan resistance.

Closer to home, Secretary of State Alexander Haig feared that the newly formed Sandinista government in Nicaragua provided the Soviets with a "safe house" in America's backyard. To counter this threat, the administration backed a group of anticommunist counterrevolutionaries, known as the **Contras**. At the same time, the United States supported a right-wing government in El Salvador that was battling leftist rebels.

Many human rights activists strongly objected to this policy; even U.S. Ambassador Robert White described the legal system in El Salvador as "rotten" and called for the United States to suspend aid to the nation. Instead, Congress made funding for El Salvador's government dependent on the nation making progress on human rights.

In 1983, Reagan acted to counter another perceived threat in the Western Hemisphere. Members of a radical leftist movement, with some help from Cuba, had violently ousted the Grenadian prime minister. On October 25, 1983, U.S. troops invaded Grenada to prevent the island nation from becoming a communist outpost and to protect the lives of American medical students. Even though the legal grounds for this invasion proved questionable, most Americans approved of Reagan's decision.

Economic Pressures Force Gorbachev to Pursue Reforms
In 1985, **Mikhail Gorbachev** (mee kah EEL GOR buh chawf) became the president of the Soviet Union. Gorbachev ushered in a new Soviet era by pursuing the twin policies of *glasnost* and *perestroika*. **Glasnost** means "a new openness," and **perestroika** refers to reforming the Soviet system—for instance, by moving away from a socialist, or state-controlled, economy. Gorbachev's reforms created an opening for a shift in relations between the two superpowers. Gorbachev started these reforms mostly because the Soviet Union's economy had fundamentally failed. The nation

>> **Analyze Data** Based on the information in the graphic, summarize Reagan's "peace through strength" approach to national defense.

faced regular shortages of food. Its factories and workers could not compete with their Western counterparts. A huge chunk of the Soviet economy's money went toward paying for the military. The war in Afghanistan had drained Soviet resources. Gorbachev realized that his nation could not match the military buildup initiated by the Reagan administration.

Reagan and Gorbachev Reevaluate Their Positions Gorbachev's policies and personality helped soften the Soviet Union's international image. Reagan responded to this change by moderating his own stance toward the Soviet Union. While the two nations had held no summits during Reagan's first four years in office, their leaders met four times between 1985 and 1989.

During their final meeting in Moscow, Reagan and Gorbachev toasted each other at a state dinner, toured the sights like old friends, and held a joint press conference. At the press conference, a reporter asked Reagan about his description of the Soviet Union as an "evil empire." Reagan responded, "I was talking about another era." Then, Gorbachev allowed President Reagan to address students at Moscow State University on the benefits of the free-enterprise system and democracy:

"Your generation is living in one of the most exciting times in Soviet history. It is a time when the first breath of freedom stirs the air and the heart beats to the accelerated rhythm of hope, when the accumulated spiritual energies of a long silence yearn to break free. . . . We do not know what the conclusion of this journey will be, but we're hopeful that the promise of reform will be fulfilled . . . leading to a new world of reconciliation, friendship, and peace."

—Ronald Reagan, May 31, 1988

Even before this summit, the two nations had signed a historic nuclear arms pact and had begun negotiations on the START I Treaty, which would reduce the number of nuclear weapons in the world.

☑ **CHECK UNDERSTANDING** Aside from his overall idea of "peace through strength," what other motivation did Reagan have for his massive military spending?

Impact of the End of the Cold War

1991 was a turning point in American and world history. In a little over three years' time after Reagan's speech in Moscow, the Cold War had come to an end. The Berlin Wall came down; Poland, Czechoslovakia, and Hungary held democratic elections; and the Soviet Union disintegrated into numerous separate republics. *Time* magazine observed: "It was one of those rare times when the tectonic plates of history shift beneath men's feet, and nothing after is quite the same."

Communist Governments Fall in Eastern Europe More so than any other event, the fall of the Berlin Wall symbolized the end of communism in Europe. For decades, the wall had blocked travel from communist East Berlin to democratic West Berlin. Guards shot those who attempted to escape over the wall to West Berlin. Then, in November 1989, following the fall of East Germany's communist government, East German authorities opened the wall's gates.

>> President Reagan meets for the first time with Soviet leader Mikhail Gorbachev in Geneva, Switzerland, in 1985.

Bounce to Activate Chart

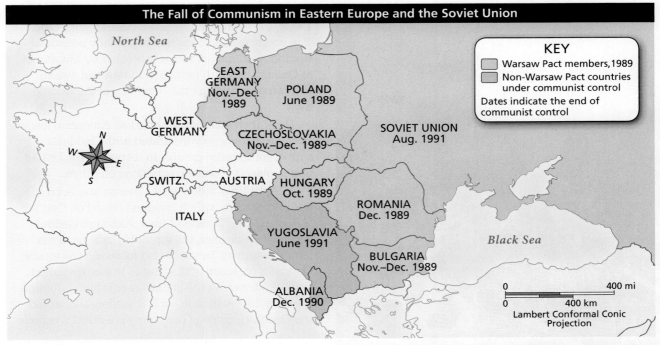

KEY

Warsaw Pact members, 1989

Non-Warsaw Pact countries under communist control

Dates indicate the end of communist control

EAST GERMANY Nov.–Dec. 1989

POLAND June 1989

WEST GERMANY

CZECHOSLOVAKIA Nov.–Dec. 1989

SOVIET UNION Aug. 1991

SWITZ. AUSTRIA HUNGARY Oct. 1989

ITALY

ROMANIA Dec. 1989

YUGOSLAVIA June 1991

BULGARIA Nov.–Dec. 1989

ALBANIA Dec. 1990

North Sea

Black Sea

0   400 mi
0   400 km
Lambert Conformal Conic Projection

>> **Analyze Maps** Compare this map to a current map of eastern Europe. What has happened to these former communist countries since 1991?

Bounce to Activate Gallery

Thousands climbed atop the wall; some even took sledgehammers and chipped away at the barricade. Within a year, East and West Germany would reunite as one single nation. Communists also lost power in Poland, Hungary, Czechoslovakia, Bulgaria, and Romania in 1989; in Albania in 1990; and in Yugoslavia in 1991.

The Soviet Union Disintegrates In August 1991, hard-liners in the Soviet Union attempted to stage a coup in a last-gasp attempt to maintain communist rule. But when millions of Russians, led by Boris Yeltsin, rallied in the streets of Moscow in support of Gorbachev, the coup fell apart. Not long afterward, the Communist Party lost power, and the Soviet Union separated into 15 independent republics. Boris Yeltsin became the new leader of the largest new republic, the Russian Federation.

Historians do not totally agree on what caused the Soviet Union to collapse. Most acknowledge that Gorbachev's policy of *glasnost* opened the floodgates to rebellions against Soviet domination of Eastern Europe. Likewise, they note that his policy of *perestroika* fostered a challenge to communist rule within the Soviet Union.

Yet, a number of scholars give Reagan credit for bringing an end to the Cold War. By dedicating America to a massive arms buildup, they argue, he

hastened the collapse of the Soviet economy. In turn, this compelled Gorbachev to promote reform at home and relinquish control of Eastern Europe.

The key rival, competitor, and enemy of the United States for so many years had suddenly disappeared. President George H.W. Bush met and signed agreements with first Gorbachev and then Yeltsin to scale down and even eliminate certain types of nuclear weapons. Bush and Yeltsin issued a joint statement in 1992 pledging friendship and cooperation. The long Cold War, which had absorbed so much of the energy and resources of the Soviet Union and the United States since 1945, was finally over.

☑ **DESCRIBE** What happened to the Soviet Union in the immediate aftermath of its breakup?

U.S. Involvement in the Middle East and the Iran-Contra Affair

Conflicts in the Middle East in the 1980s tested political relationships throughout the world. The Iran-Iraq War from 1980–1988 and increasing incidents of terrorism brought the United States into direct confrontation with several countries in the region.

>> The explosion at the U.S. Marine barracks in Beirut, Lebanon, in 1983 resulted in more than 240 casualties, including over 200 marines—the most killed in a single day since the Battle of Iwo Jima in 1945.

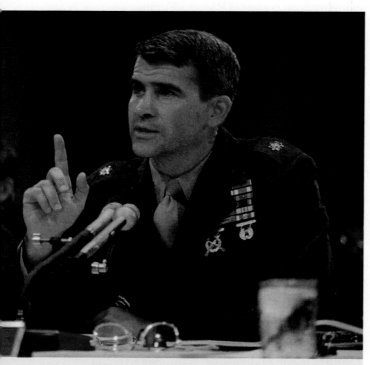

>> Colonel Oliver North testifies to Congress about the Iran-Contra affair in 1987. He was responding to allegations that the Reagan administration had illegally funded anticommunist Nicaraguan rebels.

The U.S. Retaliates Against Libya

During the 1980s, the United States often clashed with Libya. The countries had once had a mutually beneficial trading relationship. Libya was ruled by Muammar al-Qaddafi (MOO uh mahr al kuh DAH fee), whom Reagan described as the "mad dog of the Middle East."

U.S.-Libya relations fell apart as American leaders became increasingly frustrated with Qaddafi's support of terrorist groups. In response, the United States placed economic sanctions on Libya.

In April 1986, following a terrorist attack on a Berlin nightclub, which Reagan blamed on Qaddafi, U.S. warplanes bombed Libya. Although Qaddafi survived unharmed, the air raid killed one of his family members. In the period following the attack, Qaddafi's criticism of the United States dwindled. Tensions between the countries continued through the early 1990s, though, as U.S. leaders suspected the Qaddafi regime of producing chemical weapons.

Reagan Sends Marines Into Lebanon

Even as the Soviet Union collapsed and conflicts with Libya ignited, the United States faced additional problems in the Middle East. In 1982, Reagan sent a group of 800 United States Marines to Lebanon as part of an international force trying to bring peace to that nation, which was torn by civil war.

On October 23, 1983, a truck loaded with thousands of pounds of explosives smashed through barriers at the headquarters of the United States Marines in Beirut (bay ROOT), Lebanon's capital, and into a four-story building that housed hundreds of military personnel. The explosion killed 241 marines. Reagan withdrew the remaining marines in February 1984. The incident illustrated, once again, the complicated and dangerous nature of Middle Eastern politics.

The Iran-Contra Affair Shakes the Presidency

Reagan's presidency started with a breakthrough in the Middle East. Twenty minutes after he took the oath of office on January 20, 1981, Iran released all 52 Americans it had held hostage since 1979. But during his second term, the Iran-Contra affair tarnished Reagan's reputation.

The **Iran-Contra affair** began when the United States sold weapons to Iran in 1985 in exchange for Iran's promise to pressure terrorist groups in Lebanon to release some American hostages. The plan didn't work, and it contradicted the administration's policy of refusing to negotiate with terrorists.

Then, the administration used the money from the sale to fund the Contras in Nicaragua, despite the fact that in 1983 Congress had banned sending funds to the Contras. News of these deals became public in 1986. Although President Reagan accepted responsibility for the actions of his administration, he never admitted to ordering his aides to support the Contras. Ultimately, several leading administration officials and a top aide, Oliver North, were convicted on charges stemming from the scandal, although many of the convictions were later overturned on technical grounds. In spite of this, Reagan left office with high approval ratings.

☑ **RECALL** Why did the Iran-Contra affair threaten the credibility of the Reagan administration?

☑ ASSESSMENT

1. **Identify Cause and Effect** Discuss the components of President Reagan's "peace through strength" policy, and identify its effects.

2. **Identify Central Issues** Describe reasons for and responses to U.S. involvement in Central America during the 1980s.

3. **Generate Explanations** Explain how economic hardships and changing political relationships gave rise to a new era for the Soviet Union during the 1980s.

4. **Describe** events that altered the relationship between Libya and the United States during the 1980s.

5. **Sequence Events** Discuss the events that occurred during the Iran-Contra affair and explain how they affected Reagan's presidency.

"Tear Down This Wall": Ronald Reagan

On June 12, 1987, President Reagan spoke in West Berlin, in front of the Brandenburg Gate at the Berlin Wall. His speech acknowledged the new Soviet leader Mikhail Gorbachev's efforts at reform in the Soviet Union. However, Reagan was not satisfied with Gorbachev's limited measures. He challenged the Soviet leader to show a real commitment to reform by tearing down the Berlin Wall that had stood between East and West Berlin since 1961. This wall symbolized the division between communism and democracy.

>> President Reagan in Berlin

Chancellor Kohl, Governing Mayor Diepgen, ladies and gentlemen: Twenty-four years ago, President John F. Kennedy visited Berlin, speaking to the people of this city and the world at the City Hall. Well, since then two other presidents have come, each in his turn, to Berlin. And today I, myself, make my second visit to your city.

We come to Berlin, we American presidents, because it's our duty to speak, in this place, of freedom. But I must confess, we're drawn here by other things as well: by the feeling of history in this city, more than 500 years older than our own nation; by the beauty of the Grunewald and the Tiergarten; most of all, by your courage and determination. . . .

. . . Our gathering today is being broadcast throughout Western Europe and North America. I understand that it is being seen and heard as well in the East. To those listening throughout Eastern Europe, a special word: Although I cannot be with you, I address my remarks to you just as surely as to those standing here before me. For I join you, as I join your fellow countrymen in the West, in this firm, this unalterable belief: Es gibt nur ein Berlin. [There is only one Berlin.]

☑ **DETERMINE AUTHOR'S PURPOSE** Was this speech meant for one or multiple audiences? What was the intent behind this speech?

Behind me stands a wall that encircles the free sectors of this city, part of a vast system of barriers that divides the entire continent of Europe. From the Baltic, south, those barriers cut across Germany in a gash of barbed wire, concrete, dog runs, and guard towers. Farther south, there may be no visible, no obvious wall. But there remain armed guards and checkpoints all the same—still a restriction on the right to travel, still an instrument to impose upon ordinary men and women the will of a totalitarian state. Yet it is here in Berlin where the wall emerges most clearly; here, cutting across your city, where the news photo and the television screen have imprinted this brutal division of a continent upon the mind of the world. Standing before the Brandenburg Gate, every man is a German, separated from his fellow men. Every man is a Berliner, forced to look upon a scar. . . .

☑ **DETERMINE CENTRAL IDEAS** What was the significance of the Berlin Wall during the Cold War?

President von Weizsacker has said, "The German question is open as long as the Brandenburg Gate is closed." Today I say: As long as the gate is closed, as long as this scar of a wall is permitted to stand, it is not the German question alone that remains open, but the question of freedom for all mankind.

Yet I do not come here to lament. For I find in Berlin a message of hope, even in the shadow of this wall, a message of triumph. . . .

. . . In the 1950s, Khrushchev predicted: "We will bury you." But in the West today, we see a free world that has achieved a level of prosperity and well-being unprecedented [never having happened or existed before] in all human history. In the Communist world, we see failure, technological backwardness, declining standards of health, even want of the most basic kind—too little food. Even today, the Soviet Union still cannot feed itself. After these four decades, then, there stands before the entire world one great and inescapable conclusion: Freedom leads to prosperity. Freedom replaces the ancient hatreds among the nations with comity [courtesy] and peace. Freedom is the victor [winner].

☑ **CITE EVIDENCE** What do you think Reagan thought about Khrushchev's prediction? Cite evidence from the speech to support your answer.

And now the Soviets themselves may, in a limited way, be coming to understand the importance of freedom. We hear much from Moscow about a new policy of reform and openness. Some political prisoners have been released. Certain foreign news broadcasts are no longer being jammed. Some economic enterprises have been permitted to operate with greater freedom from state control.

☑ **IDENTIFY SUPPORTING DETAILS** What evidence does Reagan give that the Soviet Union may be becoming freer?

Are these the beginnings of profound changes in the Soviet state? Or are they token gestures, intended to raise false hopes in the West, or to strengthen the Soviet system without changing it? We welcome change and openness; for we believe that freedom and security go together, that the advance of human liberty can only strengthen the cause of world peace. There is one sign the Soviets can make that would be unmistakable, that would advance dramatically the cause of freedom and peace.

General Secretary Gorbachev, if you seek peace, if you seek prosperity for the Soviet Union and Eastern Europe, if you seek liberalization: Come here to this gate! Mr. Gorbachev, open this gate! Mr. Gorbachev, tear down this wall!

☑ **DETERMINE CENTRAL IDEAS** According to Reagan, why would the tearing down of the Berlin Wall be a logical outcome of Gorbachev's policies?

☑ ASSESSMENT

1. **Distinguish Among Fact, Opinion, and Reasoned Judgment** When Reagan says, "freedom is the victor," is that a fact, an opinion, or a reasoned judgment? Cite evidence from the speech to support your answer.

2. **Draw Conclusions** Why was Reagan's speech at the Berlin Wall such an important moment in his presidency?

3. **Analyze Style and Rhetoric** The greatest speeches rely on simple imagery that inspires strong emotions. What is so powerful about the image of a wall and its destruction?

When the Cold War came to an end, many Americans hoped that a new era of peace would dawn. Yet, America's foreign policy during the Bush years demonstrated that the end of the Cold War would not lead to a new era of peace, but instead to a dangerous era of regional conflicts.

>> Democratic presidential candidate Bill Clinton and his wife Hillary speak to supporters during the 1992 presidential campaign.

 Bounce to Activate Flipped Video

>> Objectives

Analyze why George H.W. Bush decided to use force in some foreign disputes and not in others.

Summarize the Persian Gulf War and its results.

Explain why Bill Clinton won the presidency in 1992.

Assess the foreign policy goals and actions of the Clinton administration.

Describe U.S. relations with various Middle Eastern countries and groups.

>> Key Terms

Manuel Noriega.
Tiananmen Square
apartheid
Nelson Mandela
divest
Operation Desert
 Storm
William Jefferson
 Clinton
H. Ross Perot
ethnic cleansing
al Qaeda

A New Era in Foreign Policy

Bush Forges a New Role in the World

When the Soviet Union collapsed, the United States became an unopposed superpower—poised to take a leading role in world affairs under the leadership of President George H.W. Bush. Few leaders entered the White House with as much foreign policy experience as Bush. A graduate of Yale and a veteran of World War II, Bush had served as the U.S. Ambassador to the United Nations, as director of the CIA, and as Ronald Reagan's vice president. His experience would be put to the test as the United States faced a series of international crises during the late 1980s and early 1990s.

Political Changes and the War on Drugs in Latin America

In the late 1980s and early 1990s, Latin America experienced a wave of democracy. In Central America, a peace plan devised by Costa Rican leader Oscar Arias (AH ree uhs) brought free elections in Nicaragua and the end of a long civil war in El Salvador. In Chile, the notorious military dictator Augusto Pinochet (ah GOO stoh pee noh SHAY) gave up power.

Not all developments in Latin America, however, pleased the Bush administration. Since the Nixon administration, the government had been waging a "war on drugs," or an attempt to stop illegal drug use by going after both sellers and users. Groups of racketeers in Latin America supplied a significant amount of the illegal drugs in the United States. The Bush administration arrested and tried several international drug figures, including Eduardo Martinez Romero, the reputed financier of a Colombian drug cartel. Even more spectacularly, in December 1989, Bush sent more than 12,000 U.S. troops to invade Panama and arrest Panama's military strongman **Manuel Noriega**.

Brought to the United States for trial, Noriega was convicted of several charges of drug trafficking and sentenced to 40 years in prison.

China Resists Calls for Democracy Meanwhile, in the spring of 1989, Chinese students captured the world's attention by staging pro-democracy protests in **Tiananmen Square** in the heart of Beijing. Many Americans hoped that these protests might result in the fall of communism in China. Instead, on June 4, Chinese tanks rolled into Beijing, killed hundreds of protesters, crushed the demonstrations, and imprisoned many pro-democracy activists.

The Bush administration condemned this action and suspended arms sales to China. However, Bush did not believe that stiffer penalties would influence Chinese leaders. He made the pragmatic choice to remain engaged with China economically and diplomatically, rather than cut off ties with the country.

Pressures Force Changes in South Africa
While China resisted changes, long overdue ones were taking place in South Africa. For years, the South African government, controlled by whites, had maintained an oppressive system of rigid segregation known as **apartheid**. The leader of the antiapartheid movement, **Nelson Mandela** (man DEHL uh), had been imprisoned since 1962. In the late 1980s, protests against apartheid within South Africa and around the globe grew. In the United States, many private firms **divested**, or withdrew investments, from South Africa. Congress imposed economic sanctions instead of fully divesting, not wanting to destabilize the struggling nation. President Bush met with Mandela after his release from jail in 1990 and endorsed the drive to bring democracy to South Africa. Soon after, apartheid began to be dismantled, and in 1994, South Africans elected Mandela as their leader in their first free elections.

>> President Bush and First Lady Barbara Bush visit American troops in Saudi Arabia in 1990.

 Bounce to Activate Map

>> In 1990, President Bush welcomed Nelson Mandela to the White House to discuss ways to bring an end to apartheid in South Africa.

U.S. Works for Peace and Human Rights

With the fall of communism in 1991, the nation of Yugoslavia disintegrated into a bloody civil war. During this new crisis in the Balkans, Bush chose not to send troops because he feared that the tangled conflict could embroil the United States in another Vietnam. Not until 1992, however, did he back a modest UN plan to restore peace in Bosnia, one of the new republics carved out of Yugoslavia. By then, more than 150,000 civilians had died.

The Bush administration acted more swiftly to protect human rights in Somalia. As part of "Operation Restore Hope," United States Marines landed in this East African nation in December 1992 to help establish a cease-fire between rival warlords and to deliver food to hundreds of thousands of starving people. The American humanitarian mission reinforced UN efforts at peacekeeping and relief. Even some of Bush's most persistent critics applauded his decision to intervene in Somalia.

☑ **EXPRESS IDEAS CLEARLY** Explain the Bush administration's reaction to the Chinese government's crackdown on prodemocracy protests in Tiananmen Square.

>> **Hypothesize** Why was Iraq's invasion of Kuwait in 1990 considered such a threat by so many nations?

The Persian Gulf War

The most important foreign-policy challenge faced by the Bush administration took place in the Persian Gulf. On August 2, 1990, Iraq invaded its tiny neighbor Kuwait. Nearly 150,000 Iraqi troops quickly overran Kuwaiti forces.

A Dictator's Thirst for Power Leads to War

Saddam Hussein, Iraq's ruthless dictator, had run the Middle Eastern nation with an iron fist since 1979. By invading Kuwait, Hussein sought to take over Kuwait's rich oil deposits. With Kuwait in his power, Hussein would control nearly 20 percent of the oil produced around the world. The United States feared how Hussein would use the influence that controlling such a large amount of oil would give him. In addition, nearby Saudi Arabia possessed even greater oil reserves. The United States did not want Hussein to seek to gain control of those reserves next. Oil drove much of the world's economies, including America's. In 1970, the United States consumed around 14 million barrels of oil each day. By 1990, that number had increased to 17 million barrels a day.

President Bush made it clear that he would not tolerate Iraq's aggression against its neighbor. He worked to build an international coalition and backed a UN resolution demanding that Iraqi troops withdraw.

U.S. Spearheads Operation Desert Storm By late fall, about 700,000 troops had assembled in Saudi Arabia, including nearly 500,000 American forces. Britain, France, Egypt, and Saudi Arabia, among others, also sent troops. Other nations, for example Japan, agreed to help pay for the costs of the operation. Initially, Bush hoped that the presence of these troops, along with the economic sanctions against Iraq, would convince Hussein to withdraw his soldiers. At the same time, the president asked for and received from Congress the authority to use force, if necessary, to back up the UN's resolution that Iraq leave Kuwait.

Operation Desert Storm, the name given to the American-led attack on Iraqi forces, began on January 16, 1991. General Colin Powell, the Chairman of the Joint Chiefs of Staff, and General Norman Schwarzkopf devised and executed a strategy that began with five weeks of devastating aerial bombardment on Iraqi forces. Iraq countered by launching Scud missiles on both coalition forces and Israel. Although these missiles did little serious damage, they struck terror in the hearts of many who feared they were armed with chemical warheads.

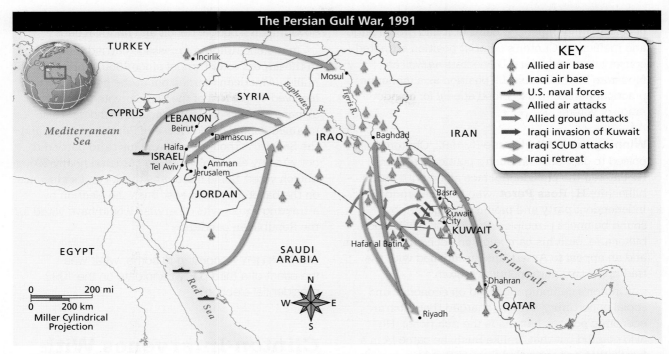

KEY
- Allied air base
- Iraqi air base
- U.S. naval forces
- Allied air attacks
- Allied ground attacks
- Iraqi invasion of Kuwait
- Iraqi SCUD attacks
- Iraqi retreat

TURKEY · Incirlik
Mosul
SYRIA
CYPRUS
LEBANON
Beirut
Damascus
Haifa
ISRAEL
Tel Aviv
Amman
Jerusalem
JORDAN
IRAQ
Baghdad
IRAN
Basra
Kuwait City
KUWAIT
Hafar al Batin
Persian Gulf
SAUDI ARABIA
Dhahran
QATAR
Riyadh
EGYPT
Red Sea
Mediterranean Sea
Euphrates R.
Tigris R.

0 — 200 mi
0 — 200 km
Miller Cylindrical Projection

N W E S

>> **Analyze Maps** What nations did Saddam Hussein retaliate against during the Persian Gulf War?

Bounce to Activate Gallery

Lasting Effects of the War On February 24, coalition troops stormed into Kuwait. Completely overwhelmed, Iraqi troops surrendered or fled, setting fire to Kuwaiti oil rigs along the way. Less than five days after the ground war began, Iraq agreed to a UN-brokered cease-fire. It had lost an estimated 25,000 soldiers. American deaths totaled 148. "We've kicked the Vietnam syndrome once and for all," proclaimed Bush. He then chose to limit American actions to enforcing the UN resolution. The coalition's forces would compel Iraq to leave Kuwait but would not continue on to Baghdad, Iraq's capital, to topple Saddam Hussein. As a result, Hussein and his regime survived the war. Bush's public approval rating skyrocketed.

The United States remained in the region to help Iraqi refugees, establishing no-fly zones over northern and southern Iraq. However, Saddam Hussein and his supporters resented the U.S. presence. During Operation Desert Storm, similar resentment toward U.S. forces also grew in Saudi Arabia, where many troops were stationed. This resentment may have helped attract new recruits to the anti-American propaganda of the terrorist organization al Qaeda.

☑ **DRAW CONCLUSIONS** Why did Saddam Hussein's regime survive the war?

Clinton Wins the 1992 Election

After the 1991 Persian Gulf War ended, President George H.W. Bush's approval rating reached 91 percent. In less than one year, however, public opinion had changed. Saddam Hussein had stayed in power, continuing to threaten peace in the Middle East. The American economy had gone into recession and the federal deficit had risen. People were angered by Bush's betrayal of his 1988 campaign pledge not to raise taxes. Bush's sinking popularity opened up the way for the Democratic challenge.

"New Democrats" Emerge The Democrats nominated **William Jefferson Clinton**, governor of Arkansas, as their presidential candidate. Clinton was born in 1946 into a humble home and had worked his way through college and law school before being elected governor of Arkansas in 1978. To widen his appeal and distance himself from the stereotype of "tax and spend" liberals, Clinton promoted himself as a "New Democrat." New Democrats were centrists who sought to reconcile liberal and conservative ideals. They believed in strong national defense, tough stands on crime, free trade, welfare reform, and closer ties with corporations. They believed that government was necessary and important but that it had grown large and inefficient. Clinton's centrist position attracted conservative and liberal Democrats as well as moderate Republicans. His position as a moderate, practical Democrat had broad appeal for a wide range of voters.

Winning the White House By 1992, Clinton was poised to capitalize on Bush's political problems. He entered the presidential race along with Texas billionaire **H. Ross Perot**, who led a self-funded independent party and promised to govern by sound business principles. Ross Perot, a self-made billionaire, built his campaign on economic populism and an appeal to Americans dissatisfied with the traditional two-party political system.

Clinton's campaign focused on economic and social opportunity. Clinton charged that Bush's economic policies had made the rich richer. He also pointed out that, unlike Bush, he came from a family that had struggled through hard times and knew what it was like to worry about paying bills. Bush responded by attacking Clinton's character. Republicans accused the governor of draft-dodging, marital infidelity, and other moral laxities. Bush also suggested that Clinton and his vice presidential candidate, Al Gore, were too inexperienced to lead the nation. Unlike his opponents, Perot opposed free-trade agreements with Mexico and Canada

and stressed the importance of eliminating the U.S. government's budget deficit and national debt.

In the end, Clinton's message carried the election. In the largest voter turnout since 1960, more than 100 million Americans turned out at the polls. Clinton received 43 percent of the popular vote to Bush's 37 percent and Perot's 19 percent. Democrats also retained control of the House of Representatives and the Senate. Although Perot and his third party did not win any electoral votes, he garnered nearly 20 million votes. Some historians think Perot's presence on the ballot may have cost Bush the election by attracting voters who otherwise would have voted for the Republican candidate.

☑ **IDENTIFY** According to some, what was the effect of a third party candidate on the 1992 presidential election?

Clinton Intervenes With Mixed Success

When Bill Clinton became president, the more than 40-year-old American foreign policy of fighting communism had just ended. The United States needed to develop a role for itself in the post–Cold War world. Americans were willing to provide economic aid, as they did to nations of the former Soviet Union. But many of them questioned military

★ 1992 PRESIDENTIAL ELECTION ★

Bill Clinton
Democrat
44,909,889
(43.01%)

George H.W. Bush
Republican
39,104,545
(37.05%)

1992 ELECTION **POPULAR VOTE**

Ross Perot
Independent
19,742,267
(18.91%)

Source: Federal Election Commission

Bill Clinton
Democrat
370
(68.8%)

George H.W. Bush
Republican
168
(31.2%)

1992 **ELECTORAL VOTE**

Ross Perot
Independent
0

★ THE LEGACY OF ★
ROSS PEROT
— IN 1992 —

Source: *The Polling Report, January 30, 2012*

- Used the economy as the main campaign issue

- First **third-party candidate** to gain a significant share of votes since 1912

- Perot won **30%** of independent voters, **17%** of Republican voters, and **13%** of Democratic voters

>> **Analyze Information** What was Ross Perot's impact on the 1992 election?

Breakup of Yugoslavia

>> **Analyze Maps** From the map, which republic appears to have the potential to be the strongest? Consider not only size, but location of the former capital of Yugoslavia.

intervention abroad, fearing a costly commitment like the Vietnam War. With violence surging in regional conflicts throughout the world, however, Clinton found it necessary to intervene. He did so with mixed success.

U.S. Intervention in Somalia and Haiti In the late 1980s, civil war broke out in Somalia. By 1991, the government had disintegrated and the fighting had caused widespread famine. In 1992, the United States led a multinational force, later joined by the UN, to bring about peace and distribute food.

The coalition fell apart in 1994 when several countries, including the United States, suffered steep casualty rates and withdrew their troops. Eventually, the UN also withdrew, and civil war dragged on for several more years in the devastated country.

Meanwhile, conflict was simmering in Haiti. In 1990, Haitians brought Jean Bertrand Aristide to the presidency, in the nation's first free elections. Less than a year later, a military coup overthrew Aristide, plunging the country into turmoil. Thousands of Haitians left the country by boat to immigrate to the United States as political refugees. Many were sent back by American immigration officials, causing a public outcry. In 1994, Clinton sent American troops to Haiti to restore Aristide to power. Although American action improved the situation, within a

decade Haiti faced a sinking economy and rising rates of disease and crime.

U.S. Involvement in the Balkans Crisis In the Balkans, the collapse of communism broke up the country of Yugoslavia. For decades, the communist leader Josip Broz Tito had contained ethnic and religious strife.

But his death in 1980, and the collapse of communism in 1989, left the country with no unifying forces. Soon, four of Yugoslavia's six major republics broke away and became independent nations, and long-suppressed ethnic and religious hostilities came boiling to the surface.

In newly independent Bosnia and Herzegovina, ethnic and religious rivalries among Eastern Orthodox Serbs, Catholic Croats, and Bosnian Muslims eventually led to civil war. Serbs, with the help of Serbia-dominated Yugoslavia, attacked Bosnians and Croats. In many cases, they forcibly removed Bosnians and Croats from their homes and later murdered them. This state-sanctioned mass murder, violence, and rape, known as **ethnic cleansing**, shocked the world. The UN intervened with humanitarian aid. Yet atrocities continued on all sides of the struggle, and years went by before the world community intervened to stop the slaughter.

Clinton Galvanizes NATO Forces Finally in the late summer of 1995, Clinton encouraged NATO to bomb Serbian strongholds. This was the first time the organization had gone into combat, and its use of force quickly brought about a cease-fire. In December 1995, the Dayton Accords established a federated, multinational Bosnia. Although the ethnic cleansing had ended, the enforced peace had not solved the problems of the region. In 1998, violence flared up anew—this time in Kosovo, a province in southern Serbia that borders on Albania. The fighting once again involved ethnic cleansing and also spread to the neighboring countries of Macedonia and Albania. NATO forced Serbs to withdraw from Kosovo.

The Rwanda Genocide As ethnic hatred led to atrocities in the Balkans, mass murder was also underway far to the south in the African nation of Rwanda. Between April and July of 1994, Rwanda's majority Hutu population committed genocide as they exterminated more than 800,000 members of the Tutsi population. The bloodbath in turn forced 2,000,000 people to flee Rwanda, creating a major humanitarian crisis. The UN was unable to bring about a cease-fire, and President Clinton and other world leaders were criticized for their silence on this tragedy. Eventually, Tutsi-led forces gained ground

and established a government of national unity, bringing the genocide to an end.

✅ **CHECK UNDERSTANDING** What happened to Yugoslavia soon after the death of its long-time communist leader?

America and the Middle East in the 1990s

In the 1990s, Israel's military responded to attacks by Palestinians. The level of violence grew increasingly fierce. Meanwhile, instability had increased in the region as a whole. As Clinton worked to address it, violence originating in the region spread outward, with the United States increasingly a target.

Small Steps Toward Peace in Israel In 1993, Palestinians and Israelis conducted secret negotiations in Oslo, Norway. The resulting Declaration of Principles promised Palestinian self-rule in Jericho and the Gaza Strip, as well as security for the Israelis. The declaration did not adequately address the issues of Israeli settlements in the West Bank, nor did it placate extremists on either side, who had no interest in compromise.

Israel and the Palestinian Territories, 2011

KEY
- Israeli Territory
- Palestinian Territory

>> **Analyze Maps** What city is located on the border between Israeli and Palestinian territory?

Chronic violence continued even though Israel withdrew from much of the West Bank, and later from Gaza. Israeli Prime Minister Yitzhak Rabin, who had agreed to the declaration, fell victim to the fury in 1995 when an Israeli religious extremist assassinated him.

In 2000, Clinton invited Palestinian leader Yasir Arafat and Israeli prime minister Ehud Barak to Camp David to work on a peace agreement. They came close to signing one, but Arafat was not satisfied with any of the proposals. Back in Israel, Barak was replaced as prime minister by Ariel Sharon, a "hawk" who once opposed any concessions to the Palestinians. In 2005, however, Sharon withdrew all Israeli settlers from Gaza. Nonetheless, Palestinian suicide bombings increased, and with them so did crackdowns by the Israeli military.

Terrorists Hit U.S. Targets In 1993, an Islamist terrorist group called **al Qaeda** exploded a truck bomb in the parking garage beneath the World Trade Center in New York City, killing six people and injuring more than one thousand others. Al Qaeda was led by a wealthy man from Saudi Arabia named Osama bin Laden.

Bin Laden had fought in Afghanistan in the 1980s on the side of Islamists who sought to expel the Soviet Union. By the late 1990s, he had formed al Qaeda with the purpose of ending American involvement in Muslim countries.

Five years after the 1993 bombing at the World Trade Center, al Qaeda set off car bombs within minutes of each other at American embassies in Nairobi, Kenya, and in Dar es Salaam, Tanzania. The blasts killed 225 people and injured more than 5,500 others. In 2000, al Qaeda bombed the USS *Cole* an American warship anchored off the coast of Yemen, killing 17 American sailors. In spite of these attacks, most Americans remained much more focused on domestic issues than on the threat of international terrorism. No one fully understood the threat that al Qaeda posed to American interests and world peace.

☑ **RECALL** Where did Osama bin Laden establish his credentials as an Islamic fundamentalist fighter in the 1980s?

>> In 1993, Islamist terrorists detonated a bomb in the parking garage of the World Trade Center in New York City, intending to destroy the buildings.

☑ **ASSESSMENT**

1. **Describe** the political changes that occurred in Latin America during the 1980s and 1990s.

2. **Generate Explanations** Explain how U.S. policies influenced the fall of apartheid in South Africa.

3. **Identify Cause and Effect** Describe the events that led to Operation Desert Storm, and discuss the campaign's lasting effects.

4. **Generate Explanations** Explain why President Bush's popularity declined after the Persian Gulf War, and determine how this influenced President Clinton's election.

5. **Express Problems Clearly** Explain why Yugoslavia collapsed after the Cold War, and describe the problems that occurred as a result.

"Glory and Hope": Nelson Mandela

Nelson Mandela delivered this speech after having been elected president in South Africa's first multiracial election in 1994. Knowing that the injustices of apartheid would be hard to overcome, Mandela asked the people to work together for peace and justice.

>> Nelson Mandela and President George H.W. Bush

Your majesties, your royal highnesses, distinguished guests, comrades and friends:

Today, all of us do, by our presence here, and by our celebrations in other parts of our country and the world, confer [give] glory and hope to newborn liberty.

Out of the experience of an extraordinary human disaster that lasted too long must be born a society of which all humanity will be proud.

Our daily deeds as ordinary South Africans must produce an actual South African reality that will reinforce humanity's belief in justice, strengthen its confidence in the nobility of the human soul and sustain all our hopes for a glorious life for all. . . .

☑ **DETERMINE MEANING** What does Mandela mean by "an actual South African reality"?

To my compatriots, I have no hesitation in saying that each one of us is as intimately attached to the soil of this beautiful country as are the famous jacaranda trees of Pretoria and the mimosa trees of the bushveld.

Each time one of us touches the soil of this land, we feel a sense of personal renewal. The national mood changes as the seasons change.

We are moved by a sense of joy and exhilaration when the grass turns green and the flowers bloom.

That spiritual and physical oneness we all share with this common homeland explains the depth of the pain we all carried in our hearts as we saw our country tear itself apart in terrible conflict, and as we saw it spurned, outlawed and isolated by the peoples of the world, precisely because it has become the universal base of the pernicious ideology and practice of racism and racial oppression. . . .

We, the people of South Africa, feel fulfilled that humanity has taken us back into its bosom, that we, who were outlaws not so long ago, have today been given the rare privilege to be host to the nations of the world on our own soil.

We thank all our distinguished international guests for having come to take possession with the people of our country of what is, after all, a common victory for justice, for peace, for human dignity.

We trust that you will continue to stand by us as we tackle the challenges of building peace, prosperity, nonsexism, nonracialism and democracy. . . .

The time for the healing of the wounds has come.

The moment to bridge the chasms that divide us has come.

The time to build is upon us.

We have, at last, achieved our political emancipation [freedom from bondage or control by others]. We pledge ourselves to liberate all our people from the continuing bondage [slavery] of poverty, deprivation [lack of materials necessary for survival], suffering, gender and other discrimination. . . .

We have triumphed in the effort to implant [insert] hope in the breasts of the millions of our people. We enter into a covenant [binding agreement] that we shall build the society in which all South Africans, both black and white, will be able to walk tall, without any fear in their hearts, assured of their inalienable right to human dignity—a rainbow nation at peace with itself and the world.

☑ **SUMMARIZE** What freedoms does Mandela call for in this passage?

As a token of its commitment to the renewal of our country, the new Interim Government of National Unity will, as a matter of urgency, address the issue of amnesty for various categories of our people who are currently serving terms of imprisonment.

We dedicate this day to all the heroes and heroines in this country and the rest of the world who sacrificed in many ways and surrendered their lives so that we could be free.

Their dreams have become reality. Freedom is their reward.

We are both humbled and elevated by the honor and privilege that you, the people of South Africa, have bestowed on us, as the first President of a united, democratic, nonracial and nonsexist South Africa, to lead our country out of the valley of darkness.

☑ **DETERMINE CENTRAL IDEAS** What are the civic ideals of the new South Africa?

We understand it still that there is no easy road to freedom.

We know it well that none of us acting alone can achieve success.

We must therefore act together as a united people, for national reconciliation [a settling of differences that results in harmony], for nation building, for the birth of a new world.

Let there be justice for all. Let there be peace for all. Let there be work, bread, water, and salt for all.

Let each know that for each the body, the mind and the soul have been freed to fulfill themselves.

Never, never, and never again shall it be that this beautiful land will again experience the oppression of one by another and suffer the indignity of being the skunk of the world.

The sun shall never set on so glorious a human achievement!

Let freedom reign. God bless Africa!

☑ **PARAPHRASE** In one or two sentences, write in your own words how Mandela concludes his speech.

☑ ASSESSMENT

1. **Explain an Argument** When apartheid ended, there was a danger of a backlash by blacks against whites who supported apartheid. How does Mandela's speech respond to that danger?

2. **Determine Author's Point of View** How would you describe the tone of Mandela's speech? How does this tone reflect Mandela's view of his country and its future?

3. **Determine Author's Purpose** Why do you think Mandela talks about building a new world, not just a new South Africa?

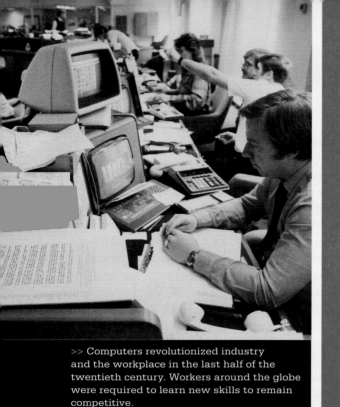

>> Computers revolutionized industry and the workplace in the last half of the twentieth century. Workers around the globe were required to learn new skills to remain competitive.

Bounce to Activate Flipped Video

11.5 When Bill Clinton took the presidential oath of office on January 20, 1993, he faced a great challenge. Since 1968, Americans had chosen Republican presidents in five out of six elections. The Republican argument that government needed to be smaller and less intrusive resonated with many Americans. Clinton therefore needed to chart a middle course between the limited role for government advocated by Republicans and the traditional Democratic reliance on government programs to address social problems.

>> **Objectives**

Assess the success of Clinton's domestic policies.

Describe the Contract With America and its impact.

Analyze the Clinton impeachment.

Evaluate the changes that new technological innovations brought to the economy and daily life in the 1990s.

>> **Key Terms**

Family Medical
   Leave Act
Brady Bill
Newt Gingrich
Contract With
   America
Kenneth Starr
impeachment
personal computer
biotechnology
satellite
Internet
Robert Johnson

Clinton and the 1990s

Clinton Enacts New Domestic Policies

Family Medical Leave Act Becomes Law Early in his presidency, Clinton signed the **Family Medical Leave Act**, which had been vetoed by President Bush. The act guaranteed most full-time employees 12 workweeks of unpaid leave each year for the birth and care of a newborn child, to recover from a serious illness, or to care for an close family member. The Clinton administration also raised the minimum wage, increased access to college loans, and expanded tax credits for higher education.

An Uphill Battle on Healthcare Reform Healthcare reform headed Clinton's list of priorities. The United States was the only developed country without national healthcare. Though Clinton did not advocate socialized medicine, he wanted a program that would guarantee care for all Americans. His wife, Hillary Clinton, was appointed to head a healthcare task force to investigate the issue. The task force conducted highly publicized hearings and produced a long, detailed proposal that attracted immediate criticism from diverse interest groups. The bill never won congressional support and was ultimately dropped after about a year of debate.

Clinton had miscalculated Americans' faith in the federal government to solve the country's social problems. Many Americans simply did not feel that enlarging the federal bureaucracy and allowing the government to run healthcare was a good idea.

Fighting Crime and Violence Clinton also tried to address the issue of violence in American society. In 1993, he signed the **Brady Bill**, a gun-control act named for presidential aide James Brady, who had been wounded in the 1981 assassination attempt on Ronald Reagan. Under Clinton, Congress also passed a $30 billion anticrime bill that increased funding for police and banned several kinds of assault weapons.

Still, violence continued to haunt the nation. In 1995, Americans were horrified by the bombing of a government building in Oklahoma City that killed 168 people and injured more than 800 others. The mass murder was not committed by foreign terrorists, but rather by homegrown anti-government extremists.

To ward off similar terrorist attacks, federal buildings in major cities were surrounded with barriers. New laws were passed to deter terrorism and impose stiffer penalties.

In 1999, yet another act of senseless violence stirred nationwide debate. At Colorado's Columbine High School, two heavily armed students killed 12 fellow students and a teacher, as well as wounding 24 others, before taking their own lives. In the aftermath of this tragedy, many schools across the nation installed metal detectors and other security measures. Still other schools instituted new anti-bully policies and "zero tolerance" approaches to school violence.

☑ **DESCRIBE** Describe what the Clintons' healthcare reform package sought to supply for Americans.

Republicans Lead a Conservative Resurgence

After two years in office, Clinton had achieved a few lasting legislative victories. Yet the failure of his healthcare initiative signaled that his popularity, and his control of Congress, was waning. With the 1994 midterm elections approaching, congressional Republicans seized the opportunity to advance their own ideas.

>> In April 1995, domestic terrorist Timothy McVeigh detonated a bomb in front of the Alfred P. Murrah Federal Building in Oklahoma City. The attack killed more than 160 people and injured several hundred others.

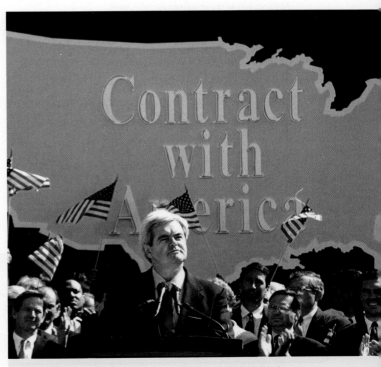

>> In 1994, Congressman Newt Gingrich organized Republican opposition to Democratic policies around his Contract With America campaign.

Bounce to Activate Gallery

Gingrich's Contract With America Georgia congressman **Newt Gingrich** led the opposition to Clinton. Gingrich was bold and aggressive and not interested in compromising with the Democrats: "We will cooperate, but we won't compromise." Many people thought that Gingrich's goal of the Republicans gaining control of the House of Representatives in 1994 was a nearly impossible task. After all, the Democrats had controlled the House for 58 of the previous 62 years.

Gingrich, however, galvanized Republicans around his **Contract With America**, a plan that attacked big government and emphasized patriotism and traditional values. The Contract With America called for congressional term limits, reduction of the federal bureaucracy, a balanced budget amendment to the Constitution, and large tax cuts, as well as increased defense spending, significant welfare reform, and tough anti-crime legislation. The idea was to capture the votes of Americans who felt the federal government was too big, too wasteful, and too liberal.

Republicans Sweep the 1994 Elections
Although most eligible voters did not vote in 1994, there was a strong turnout among Republicans. For the first time in 40 years, the Republicans won control of the House. They also captured the Senate and most of the governorships.

Newsweek magazine observed:

"Last week in one of the most profound electoral routs in American history, Republicans won the right to occupy the Capitol and mount what their . . . commanders think of as a counterrevolution: a full-scale attack on the notion that a central government should play a central role in the life of the nation."

Once in office, Republicans in the House passed most of Gingrich's program. Getting the program through the Senate and signed by Clinton was not as successful, with only a handful of contract points becoming law. In addition, Republican attempts to slash Medicare and other government programs proved unpopular. Many Americans were also upset when the government shut down in 1995 because Congress would not pass Clinton's budget. Meanwhile, Clinton incorporated some of the conservative agenda into his own 1996 reelection bid. He signed a bill to reform welfare, passed legislation that appropriated more money for law enforcement, and called for stiffer sentencing for criminals. Finally, he made balancing the budget and reducing the federal deficit a priority.

A Strong Economy Lifts Clinton to Reelection
Beginning in the mid-1990s, the American economy broke out of recession and began to soar, starting the longest period of sustained growth in the country's history. Americans benefited from low unemployment, low inflation levels, and the government's efforts to balance the budget and reduce the deficit. In 1994, Clinton's disapproval rating had exceeded 60 percent, and few expected him to win a second term. As the 1996 election approached, however, the booming economy meant that few Americans had a compelling reason to change leadership.

The Republicans nominated Senate Majority Leader Robert Dole, a World War II hero and a moderate Republican. H. Ross Perot entered the race as the Reform Party candidate. Clinton skillfully captured the middle ground, labeling Dole as out-of-touch and Perot as a political quack. On election

"Republican Revolution" of 1994

PARTY AFFILIATION	HOUSE OF REPRESENTATIVES	CHANGE	SENATE	CHANGE
REPUBLICANS	230	+54	52	+9
DEMOCRATS	204	−54	48	−9

SOURCES: U.S. House of Representatives; *The Washington Post*

>> **Analyze Charts** How did the Republican Revolution affect the balance of power between Democrats and Republicans in the federal government?

Federal Budget, 1990–2000

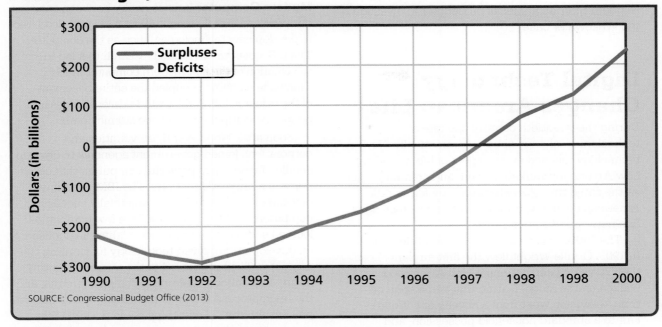

SOURCE: Congressional Budget Office (2013)

>> **Analyze Charts** What effect did President Clinton's economic policies have on the federal budget between 1993 and 2000?

day, Americans chose Clinton by a wide margin. The House of Representatives and Senate, however, retained their Republican majorities.

☑ **RECALL** Why did large numbers of Americans vote for Republican congressional candidates who supported the Contract With America?

Scandals, Impeachment, and Trial

President Clinton had dodged scandals from his first days in office. One, a sexual harassment suit, had stemmed from his years as governor of Arkansas. Another concerned investments that Bill and Hillary Clinton had made in the Whitewater Development Corporation, an Arkansas real estate company, in the 1970s and 1980s.

Investigating Clinton Leads to New Scandal A special prosecutor appointed by Attorney General Janet Reno investigated the Whitewater investment case and recommended that no criminal charges be filed. However, in July, Congress passed a new law requiring that special prosecutors be selected by a three-judge panel from the U.S. Court of Appeals. As a result, in August of 1994, special prosecutor **Kenneth Starr** was appointed to investigate the case again.

In seven years of investigation, Starr failed to uncover any conclusive evidence of the Clintons' guilt, though some of their associates were convicted.

In the process of prosecuting Whitewater, Starr began investigating Clinton's relationship with a White House intern. Clinton had denied under oath that the two had an affair. Eventually, Clinton admitted that he had lied. In 1998, Starr recommended **impeachment** proceedings on a number of counts, all related to the intern scandal rather than to Whitewater.

Impeaching and Acquitting the President
Most Americans condemned Clinton's actions but opposed impeachment. Congressional Democrats, similarly, did not believe his behavior met the standard of "Treason, Bribery, or other high Crimes and Misdemeanors" required by the Constitution for the impeachment and removal of a president. Nevertheless, the House of Representatives, led by the Republican majority, impeached Clinton on the charges of perjury and obstruction of justice.

In January 1999, the Senate tried the president. The removal of a president requires a two-thirds majority of senators, but Clinton's opposition did not have the necessary votes. The president was acquitted on both counts on February 12. However, the political scandal undermined confidence in the federal government and its leaders.

☑ **IDENTIFY** What led to the appointment of Kenneth Starr as a special prosecutor to investigate the Whitewater case?

Digital Technology Changes American Life

During the twentieth century, the rate of technological change sped up dramatically. New technology touched every aspect of life, including how Americans worked, played, and communicated. At the same time, globalization transformed the American economy, bringing both new challenges and new opportunities.

The 1900s was a century of unparalleled change. In 1903, Orville Wright flew the first airplane. Less than 70 years later, astronaut Neil Armstrong walked on the moon. During that same span of time, television went from a novelty at a World's Fair to a standard household possession, and sophisticated microscopes and telescopes unveiled previously hidden worlds. One of the most important innovations was the development of the computer.

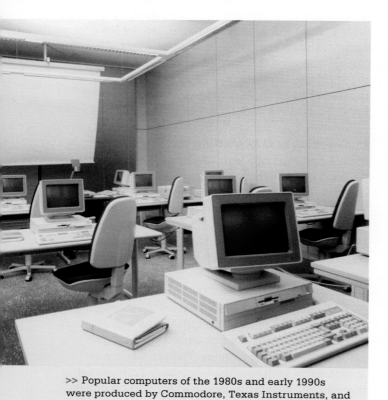

>> Popular computers of the 1980s and early 1990s were produced by Commodore, Texas Instruments, and Coleco.

Microchips and Microprocessors Lead to the Modern Computer Intense rivalry between enemies during World War II brought about a life-and-death race to develop new technologies, such as the computer. The U.S. government funded research that led to the creation of the first modern computer in 1946. This huge machine occupied the entire basement of the research lab. It calculated artillery ranges and performed computations for the atomic bomb.

Soon after World War II, universities and corporations joined government agencies to develop smaller, faster, more powerful computers that could perform a range of functions. The IBM company developed one of the first commercially successful computers in 1954. In the 1960s, a few companies located south of San Francisco, California, focused on developing improved technology for running the computer. Their efforts led to the microchip, a tiny fragment of silicon containing complex circuits, and the microprocessor, a silicon chip that held a central processing unit. These chips made possible the development of small computers, called **personal computers**.

Transforming Business and Industry At first, personal computers were a novelty item, used mainly by hobbyists. But by the 1980s, computers were transforming industries, research labs, and businesses. Personal computers could perform many different tasks but were small and simple enough for the average person to use. The technology that created them eventually spread to many other industries. Video games, cellular telephones, and other electronics all depended on microchips and microprocessors. Entrepreneurs played a large role in accelerating the use of personal computers. Steve Jobs's Apple Computers and Bill Gates's Microsoft made computers and software affordable for millions of Americans. Jeff Bezos's Amazon.com ushered in buying and selling products by computer. Like Andrew Carnegie and John D. Rockefeller a century before, these entrepreneurs amassed great fortunes by pioneering new technologies.

The great demand for newer, faster, and more versatile digital devices—coupled with the potential fortunes awaiting those who successfully delivered them—motivated a new breed of inventors and entrepreneurs. Improvements in technology and manufacturing helped develop faster-working and smaller components that drove down costs, allowing a great number of people to use these new technologies.

The Rise of Technology

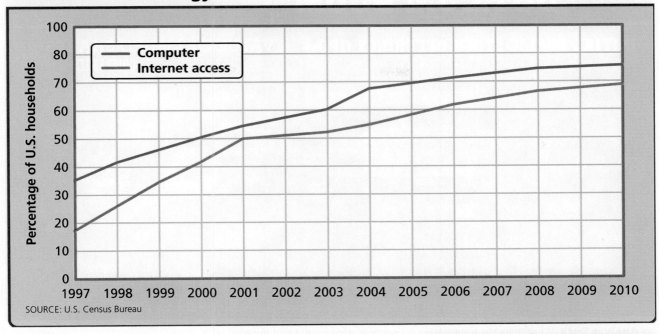

SOURCE: U.S. Census Bureau

>> **Analyze Data** Which indicator changed more rapidly—the number of households with Internet access or those with computers?

Bounce to Activate Chart

Science and Agriculture Innovations Medical science also moved ahead by gigantic leaps in the late twentieth century, often aided by computer technology. Scientists developed drugs that extended patients' lives, reduced pain, and battled a huge number of diseases. They made artificial hearts and learned how to successfully transplant body organs. Such advancements, along with **biotechnology**, or the use of living organisms in the development of new products, produced a level of healthcare far above that known to any previous generation. Many of the advances in the biological sciences were spurred by federal research grants, such as those from the National Institute of Health and the National Science Foundation.

Advances in agricultural technology, including improved machinery, irrigation techniques, and growing methods, have brought profound changes to American society. While farms have grown larger and more productive, fewer people are needed to work them. In 1900, 50 percent of the labor force worked on farms. At the end of the century, only 2 percent did.

Satellite Technology Transforms Communication and Navigation Satellite technology increased the speed of global communications. **Satellites** are mechanical

devices that orbit Earth in space, receiving and sending information-filled signals that are then relayed to televisions, telephones, and computers. Originally developed for military purposes during the Cold War, satellite technology was used in the 1970s by businessman Ted Turner to run the first "superstation." In 1980, **Robert Johnson** launched BET (Black Entertainment Television) using technology to broadcast into cable-equipped households across the country. Also in 1980, Turner began the 24-hour-per-day, all-news Cable News Network (CNN). Cellular telephones used similar satellite technology, allowing people to communicate away from their homes.

Scientists and engineers in the U.S. Department of Defense also applied satellite technology to develop the first Global Positioning System (GPS). They developed the system for use in the American military, but nonmilitary use later became widespread.

In GPS, a receiver on Earth measures how long radio signals from multiple satellites take to arrive at its location. Using this information, the receiver performs the necessary calculations to determine the user's latitude, longitude, or even altitude. Since its inception, the accuracy of GPS (and the fact that its signals are available for free) has caused a massive change in navigation for industrial and everyday users.

DOT.COM BOOM CHANGES THE ECONOMY

INITIAL PUBLIC STOCK OFFERINGS (IPOs)
FOR SOME TECHNOLOGY COMPANIES 1998–2000

VA LINUX OPEN $30.00 — CLOSE $239.25 — GAIN **697.5%**

FOUNDRY NETWORKS* OPEN $25.00 — CLOSE $156.25 — GAIN **525%**

WEBMETHODS* OPEN $35.00 — CLOSE $212.62 — GAIN **507.5%**

NON-TECH IPOs

CONOCO OPEN $23.00 — CLOSE $24.88 — GAIN **8%**

METLIFE OPEN $14.25 — CLOSE $14.75 — GAIN **3.5%**

KRISPY KREME OPEN $32.00 — CLOSE $37.00 — GAIN **16%**

Source: University of Florida   *No longer trading or acquired

VALUE OF ISSUED SHARES FOR TECHNOLOGY & NON-TECH COMPANIES 1998

- MICROSOFT $156
- INTEL $115
- IBM $102
- HEWLETT PACKARD $65
- CISCO $56
- GENERAL ELECTRIC $103
- PROCTOR & GAMBLE $94
- MCDONALD'S $79
- BOEING $56
- THE GAP $37

Source: National Bureau of Economic Research

>> **Analyze Data** What does the information on net operating profits and initial public stock offering suggest about investment in technology companies in the late 1990s?

Creating the Internet In the 1970s, various branches of the U.S. government along with groups in several American universities led efforts to link computer systems together via cables and satellites. By the 1980s, the **Internet**, or World Wide Web, had been born, reaching the general public in the 1990s.

The Web made communication and access to information almost instantaneous. This breakthrough completely and profoundly transformed commerce, education, research, and entertainment. Email provided great advantages over the delays of postal mail and the expense of telephones. The impact has been especially great on people living in rural areas. The Internet's immense storage capacity also changed the world of research. In the 1980s, scientists and scholars primarily used the Internet to share information. By the early 1990s, they were using it as a research tool and an online database.

The Tech Boom Fuels Economic Growth In many ways, the free enterprise system drives technological innovation and has filled the marketplace with inexpensive personal computers, global positioning products, and cell phones. Such technological innovations have improved the standard of living in the United States. Fueled in part by the high-tech boom, the U.S. economy in the 1990s flourished. The strong economy produced the lowest unemployment rate in 30 years and high home-ownership rates. In addition, the federal government operated on the first balanced budget since the late 1960s and held the largest budget surplus in U.S. history. The era became America's longest peacetime expansion.

☑ **DESCRIBE** What was the original inspiration for the development of the Internet?

☑ ASSESSMENT

1. **Generate Explanations** Explain how the passage of new legislation reformed employment and education during Bill Clinton's presidency.

2. **Describe** the major acts of terrorist violence that occurred in the United States in the 1990s.

3. **Draw Conclusions** Discuss the impact of the conservative resurgence and determine its effect on the 1996 presidential election.

4. **Identify Cause and Effect** Discuss the causes and effects of President Clinton's impeachment.

5. **Generate Explanations** Explain how changes in technology affected the U.S. economy during the twentieth century.

Bush and Clinton Speeches
"A Thousand Points of Light"
George H.W. Bush

By tradition, after a president has been inaugurated, or sworn in, to a four-year term of office, he has given a speech known as an inaugural address. President George H.W. Bush gave his inaugural address on January 20, 1989.

>> Presidents George H.W. Bush and Bill Clinton

… No President, no government can teach us to remember what is best in what we are. But if the man you have chosen to lead this government can help make a difference; if he can celebrate the quieter, deeper successes that are made not of gold and silk but of better hearts and finer souls; if he can do these things, then he must.

☑ **EXAMINE SYMBOLISM** What is Bush using gold and silk to represent?

America is never wholly herself unless she is engaged in high moral principle. We as a people have such a purpose today. It is to make kinder the face of the Nation and gentler the face of the world. … We have a deficit to bring down. We have more will than wallet, but will is what we need. … For not only leadership is passed from generation to generation but so is stewardship [the careful, responsible management of something]. And the generation born after the Second World War has come of age.

I have spoken of a Thousand Points of Light, of all the community organizations that are spread like stars throughout the Nation, doing good. We will work hand in hand, encouraging, sometimes leading, sometimes being led, rewarding. We will work on this in the White House, in the Cabinet agencies. I will go to the people and the programs that are the brighter points of light, and I'll ask every member of my government to become involved. The old ideas are new again because they're not old,

they are timeless: duty, sacrifice, commitment, and a patriotism that finds its expression in taking part and pitching in.

☑ **DETERMINE MEANING** What is Bush referring to when he mentions "a thousand points of light"?

… To my friends, and, yes, I do mean friends — in the loyal opposition and, yes, I mean loyal — I put out my hand. I am putting out my hand to you, Mr. Speaker. I am putting out my hand to you, Mr. Majority Leader. For this is the thing: This is the age of the offered hand. And we can't turn back clocks, and I don't want to. But when our fathers were young, Mr. Speaker, our differences ended at the water's edge. And we don't wish to turn back time, but when our mothers were young, Mr. Majority Leader, the Congress and the Executive were capable of working together to produce a budget on which this nation could live. Let us negotiate soon and hard. But in the end, let us produce. The American people await action. They didn't send us here to bicker. They ask us to rise above the merely partisan. "In crucial things, unity" — and this, my friends, is crucial.

☑ **DRAW INFERENCES** President Bush was a Republican. Were the Senate Majority Leader and the Speaker of the House Republicans or Democrats? Explain your reasoning.

Sixth State of the Union Address: Bill Clinton

Article II, Section 3 of the Constitution says, in part, that the President "shall from time to time give to the Congress Information of the State of the Union, and recommend to their Consideration such Measures as he shall judge necessary and expedient." These speeches to joint sessions of Congress were formally known as Annual Messages until 1946. In 1947, the term that had been used informally, the State of the Union Address, became the official name. President Bill Clinton gave this State of the Union Address on January 27, 1998.

The information age is, first and foremost [most importantly], an education age, in which education must start at birth and continue throughout a lifetime. Last year, from this podium, I said that education has to be our highest priority. I laid out a 10-point plan to move us forward and urged all of us to let politics stop at the schoolhouse door. Since then, this Congress—across party lines— and the American people have responded, in the most important year for education in a generation, expanding public school choice, opening the way to 3,000 new charter schools, working to connect every classroom in the country to the information superhighway [internet], committing to expand Head Start [a government agency that promotes early childhood education, nutrition, and health]to a million children, launching America Reads, sending literally thousands of college students into our elementary schools to make sure all our 8-year-olds can read.

... If I've got the math right, more teachers teaching smaller classes requires more classrooms. So I also propose a school construction tax cut to help communities modernize or build 5,000 schools.

☑ **DETERMINE AUTHOR'S PURPOSE** What math is required to determine that smaller classes require more classrooms? Why do you think Clinton included the phrase "If I've got the math right"?

We must also demand greater accountability. When we promote a child from grade to grade who hasn't mastered the work, we don't do that child any favors. It is time to end social promotion in America's schools. Last year, in Chicago, they made that decision—not to hold our children back but to lift them up. Chicago stopped social promotion and started mandatory summer school to help students who are behind to catch up. I propose to help other communities follow Chicago's lead. Let's say to them: Stop promoting children who don't learn, and we will give you the tools to make sure they do.

☑ **DRAW INFERENCES** What do you think "social promotion" is?

I also ask this Congress to support our efforts to enlist colleges and universities to reach out to disadvantaged children, starting in the sixth grade, so that they can get the guidance and hope they need so they can know that they, too, will be able to go on to college. As we enter the 21st century, the global economy requires us to seek opportunity not just at home but in all the markets of the world. We must shape this global economy, not shrink from it. In the last five years, we have led the way in opening new markets, with 240 trade agreements that remove foreign barriers to products bearing the proud stamp "Made in the USA." Today, record high exports account for fully one-third of our economic growth. I want to keep them going, because that's the way to keep America growing and to advance a safer, more stable world.

☑ ASSESSMENT

1. **Compare and Contrast** How are the tones of the two speeches similar? How are they different?

2. **Determine Central Ideas** How do Bush's stated plans for improving Americans' lives different from Clinton's?

3. **Draw Conclusions** Do you think the fact that Bush's speech was an inaugural address and Clinton's a State of the Union Address might account for some or all of the difference you noted in the previous question? Why or why not?

Go online to PearsonSchool.com/CASS and use the texts, quizzes, interactivities, Interactive Reading Notepads, Flipped Videos, and other resources from this Topic to prepare for the Topic Test.

Etexts

Quizzes

Interactivities

Interactive Reading Notepads

Flipped Videos

While online you can also check the progress you've made learning the topic and course content by viewing your grades, test scores, and assignment status.

LESSON SUMMARIES
Use these Lesson Summaries, and the longer versions available online, to review the key ideas for each lesson in this Topic.

Lesson 1: The Conservative Movement Surges

In the 1970s the conservative movement of the New Right grew rapidly. Conservatives opposed the counterculture and blamed liberal policies for economic problems. Some conservatives believed that religion should play a greater part in politics. The conservative movement helped Ronald Reagan defeat Jimmy Carter in the 1980 presidential election.

Lesson 2: The Reagan Era

President Reagan reduced taxes and removed government control over industries. He also appointed conservative judges to federal courts and increased defense spending. While some grew rich, the number of poor increased and the national debt rose. Reagan remained popular and was reelected overwhelmingly in 1984.

Lesson 3: The Cold War Ends

Under President Reagan, the United States worked to weaken communism. Relations between the superpowers improved. The Cold War ended as communists lost power across Eastern Europe, and the Soviet Union fragmented. Reagan's second term was tarnished by a scandal involving weapons sales to Iran.

Lesson 4: A New Era in Foreign Policy

Under President George H.W. Bush, U.S. troops invaded Panama and arrested its dictator for drug trafficking. In the Middle East, U.S. forces went to war against Iraq after Iraq invaded Kuwait. In 1992, William Jefferson Clinton was elected President. Clinton intervened in conflicts in Somalia and Haiti and persuaded NATO to act militarily in the former Yugoslavia. The terrorist group al Qaeda attacked U.S. targets in New York City and around the world.

Lesson 5: Clinton and the 1990s

President Clinton was opposed by Newt Gingrich, who helped Republicans win sweeping victories in the 1994 midterm election. A scandal over Clinton's relationship with a young intern brought the President to trial, during which he was acquitted. The 1980s and 1990s also saw rapid technological change that began transforming modern life.

PEARSON realize™ PearsonSchool.com/CASS
Go ONLINE for lesson summaries
 AUDIO READING GAMES

VISUAL REVIEW

Use these graphics to review some of the key terms, people, and ideas from this Topic.

Key Dates in the Conservative Resurgence

1964	President Johnson signs Civil Rights Act; Southern Democrats begin defecting to Republican Party.
1968	In this presidential election year, disagreement over the Vietnam War splits and weakens the Democratic Party.
1973	*Roe* v. *Wade* legalizes abortion.
1977	In Dade County, Florida, Anita Bryant launches anti-gay campaign, focusing conservative attention on the growing gay-rights movement.
1979	Reverend Jerry Falwell founds the Moral Majority; opposes *Engel* v. *Vitale*, *Roe* v. *Wade*, the ERA, and gay rights.
1980	Moral Majority mobilizes millions of voters to help elect Ronald Reagan.
1983	In Orlando, Florida, President Ronald Reagan denounces the Soviet Union as an "Evil Empire".

Liberal and Conservative Positions in the 1980s

LIBERAL POSITION	CONSERVATIVE POSITION
• Federal Government can improve lives through social programs. • The law should protect rights of minorities and women. • Industry should be regulated. • Encourage international diplomacy to combat communism; support détente.	• Large federal government endangers economic growth and personal freedom. • Policies of 1960s and 1970s are wasteful. • Reduce taxes to spur growth. • Limit regulation of industry. • Strengthen traditional values; oppose the counterculture. • Confront communism abroad.

President Reagan's Foreign Policy

Middle East	• Helps Anti-Soviet rebels in Afghanistan • Sends U.S. Marines to Lebanon but withdraws them after a terrorist bombing there
Latin America	• In Nicaragua, helps anticommunist Contras fight the Sandanista government • In El Salvador, supports the right-wing government against leftist rebels
The Caribbean	• U.S. troops invade Grenada to oppose communist forces.
Africa	• U.S. planes bomb Libya in retaliation for a terrorist attack in Berlin.

New Technology in the Late Twentieth Century

KEY TERMS, PEOPLE, AND IDEAS

1. What kinds of groups made up the coalition of the **New Right**?

2. What policies did **Ronald Reagan** promote during the 1980 election?

3. What is the theory behind **supply-side economics**?

4. What was the goal of the Gramm Rudman-Hollings Act?

5. What events ended the Cold War in 1991?

6. What contradiction in the Reagan administration's foreign policy came to light in the **Iran-Contra affair**?

7. What events led to **Operation Desert Storm**?

8. How did schools across the country react to the tragedy at Columbine High School in Colorado?

9. What changes did the **Internet** bring about?

CRITICAL THINKING

10. **Identify Cause and Effect** (a.) What economic developments contributed to the conservative resurgence? (b.) What solutions to America's economic problems did conservatives support?

11. **Make Inferences** What caused the realignment of white voters in the Deep South?

12. **Cite Evidence** What effect did Reagan have on the labor movement?

13. **Make Inferences** What are the political aims of terrorist organizations like al Qaeda?

14. **Draw Conclusions** What elements of the Conservative agenda did President Clinton incorporate into his 1996 election bid?

15. **Summarize** What industries helped power economic growth in the 1990s?

16. **Analyze Maps** Study the map below. (a.) What former communist nation broke up into the new nations shown here? (b.) Why did this event lead to an international crisis?

17. **Writing Activity: Use Primary Sources** Use the excerpt below and your knowledge of history to evaluate how the debate over federal spending influenced politics of the 1990s.

> Federal borrowing has both advantages and disadvantages. . . . Borrowing, in lieu of higher taxes or lower government spending, may be viewed as appropriate during times of economic recessions, war, and other temporary challenges. . . . Federal borrowing might also be viewed as appropriate for federal investment, such as building roads, training workers, and conducting scientific research, contributing to the nation's capital stock and productivity. . . . In concept, federal spending that is well chosen . . . could ultimately contribute to producing a larger economy from which to pay the interest and principal on the borrowed funds. However, in practice, [the Congressional Budget Office] concluded that many federal investments might not significantly increase economic growth because some are selected for political or other noneconomic reasons and others displace more productive investments by the private sector or state and local governments.
>
> —from *Federal Debt: Answers to Frequently Asked Questions*, U.S. Government Accountability Office, 2004

DOCUMENT-BASED QUESTIONS

In the early 1980s, President Reagan's foreign policy was highly controversial. Read the documents below, then answer the questions that follow.

DOCUMENT A

This excerpt is from President Ronald Reagan's famous "Evil Empire" speech in Orlando, Florida.

> The truth is that a freeze now would be a very dangerous fraud, for that is merely the illusion of peace. The reality is that we must find peace through strength.
>
> I would agree to a freeze if only we could freeze the Soviets' global desires. A freeze at current levels of weapons would remove any incentive for the Soviets to negotiate seriously in Geneva. . .
>
> So, in your discussions of the nuclear freeze proposals, I urge you to beware the temptation of pride—the temptation of blithely declaring yourselves above it all and label both sides equally at fault, to ignore the facts of history and the aggressive impulses of an evil empire, to simply call the arms race a giant misunderstanding and thereby remove yourself from the struggle between right and wrong and good and evil.
>
> —*Ronald Reagan, address to the National Association of Evangelicals in Orlando, Florida*

DOCUMENT B

This photograph shows Soviet leader Mikhail Gorbachev and President Ronald Reagan at the 1988 Moscow Summit Conference.

DOCUMENT C

The excerpt concerning U.S.-Soviet relations at the top of the next column is from a government website.

> Although formal nuclear arms control talks resumed, the relationship between Washington and Moscow remained tense throughout Reagan's first term. The President spoke of leaving "Marxism-Leninism on the ash-heap of history;" labeled the Soviet Union an "evil empire;" and introduced the Strategic Defense Initiative ("Star Wars"), which Soviet leaders found highly threatening.
>
> —*U.S. Department of State Office of the Historian*

DOCUMENT D

This excerpt is from a *Washington Post* article about Ronald Reagan and the Cold War.

> Less than a year after Reagan left office, the Berlin Wall fell, and the Cold War ended in 1991. The Soviet collapse was the result of many things, including shocks such as the Chernobyl disaster, rebellion in the Baltic republics and the rising expectations of consumers in a socialist system that could not produce a decent pair of jeans.
>
> But one of the major shocks was Reagan.
>
> —*David E. Hoffman, "Hastening an End to the Cold War," The Washington Post, June 6, 2004*

18. In Document A, Reagan argues that a freeze would
   A. allow the forces of good to triumph.
   B. limit U.S. bargaining power.
   C. force the Soviets to disarm.
   D. end religious liberty.

19. Analyze Photographs Based on Document B, what progress was made in nuclear negotiations with the Soviets under Reagan?

20. Document C describes Reagan's foreign policy speeches as
   A. alarming the Soviets.
   B. highly religious in tone.
   C. reassuring to the Soviets.
   D. cautious and calculating.

21. In Document D, the writer says that the Soviet Union collapsed
   A. despite Reagan's efforts.
   B. because Reagan forced the Soviets to compete.
   C. because its economy was weak.
   D. for many reasons, including Reagan's policies.

22. Writing Activity: Primary Source Write a paragraph explaining the role that Ronald Reagan played in the end of the Cold War. Use the sources as well as additional information you have learned.

1 In the 1970s, what domestic concerns began to distinguish the two parties?

   A communism, spies, and loyalty oaths

   B economic growth, welfare, and the size of government

   C religious affiliation and class status

   D climate change

Comparing Supply-Side and Keynesian Economics

Problem: Economic Recession
Consumer demand for goods and services decreases, and the nation's factories and businesses reduce their output, resulting in an overall slowing of the economy.

Keynesian government response
The government itself increases spending on goods and services in order to increase demand and encourage economic output by factories and businesses.

Supply-side government response
The government cuts taxes in order to encourage consumer spending as well as consumer saving and investment. Savings and investments are borrowed by creative entrepreneurs to grow their companies by creating new products and services.

Goal: Economic Recovery
Employment increases, consumer demand for goods and services increases, and economic output rises, resulting in an overall recovery of the economy.

SOURCE: Pearson (2013)

2 What do Keynesian and Supply-Side economics, also called "Reaganomics," have in common?

   F They both favor cutting taxes.

   G They have nothing in common.

   H They both have the goal of economic recovery.

   I They both favor increased government spending.

3 What social issue arose in the 1980s and led these citizens to protest government inaction and indifference?

A drug abuse

B a new disease

C unemployment

D illegal immigration

4 Which of the following is an example of President Reagan's "Peace Through Strength" policy?

F *Glasnost*

G *Perestroika*

H Iran-Contra Affair

I Strategic Defense Initiative

If you have trouble with...				
Question	1	2	3	4
See Lesson	11.1	11.2	11.3	11.4

5 In what ways did Republicans affect the policies of Clinton and the New Democrats?

A The New Democrats defined themselves by opposing every Republican policy.

B Popular support for the Republicans caused the New Democrats to shift further to the left.

C Clinton and the New Democrats adopted many Republican policies.

D The Democrats adopted many of the Republicans' anti-free trade policies.

6 What was the Republicans' metaphor of a contract meant to suggest?

F a document that would shrink or contract the size of government

G a work agreement that would guarantee full employment

H a set of promises that would be legally binding

I a treaty that would reconcile the two warring parties

7 Which goal of the women's movement of the 1960s proved hardest to implement?

   A secure women the right to vote, thereby expanding political opportunities

   B end workplace discrimination based on gender, thereby expanding economic opportunities

   C persuade white and black women to work together, thereby expanding social opportunities

   D increase women's access to higher education, thereby increasing the influence of women on college administrations

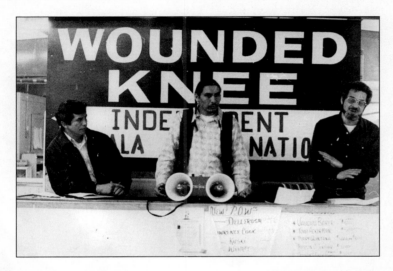

8 Why did the American Indian Movement (AIM) choose the village of Wounded Knee as a protest site?

   F AIM used the village as a place to rest during the "long march" from San Francisco, CA to Washington, DC.

   G The village's name drew attention to the cultural wounds of Native Americans.

   H AIM recorded the experiences of Native American residents of the village and played a tape of the anecdotes to a large audience.

   I It wanted to stir memories of an earlier injustice.

If you have trouble with...				
Question	5	6	7	8
See Lesson	11.4	11.5	10.2	10.3

[**ESSENTIAL QUESTION**] What are the benefits and costs of technology?

(12) America in the Twenty-First Century

Enduring Understandings

- A revolution in technology continues to transform American business, industry, health, science, and lifestyles.

- Globalization has changed the national economy and tied America more closely to the world.

- The attacks of September 11, 2001 shaped domestic security and foreign policy in the early 2000s.

- The United States faces challenges and opportunities in the 21st century.

Learn more about Leslie Bradshaw, a technology entrepreneur.

Bounce to Activate My Story Video

>> Woman using Google Earth application on a tablet computer

In this Topic, you'll learn about America in the Twenty-first century. Look at the lesson outline and explore the timeline. As you study this Topic, you'll complete the Quest team project.

LESSON OUTLINE

12.1 America and the World Economy
HSS 11.6.5, HSS 11.8.7, HSS 11.9.1,
HSS 11.9.7, HSS 11.11, HSS 11.11.6

12.2 The George W. Bush Presidency
HSS 11.9, HSS 11.9.6, HSS 11.11

12.3 The Barack Obama Presidency
HSS 11.3.4, HSS 11.5.6, HSS 11.8.6,
HSS 11.8.7, HSS 11.9, HSS 11.11,
HSS 11.11.1, HSS 11.11.3, HSS 11.11.7;
Analysis CST.4

12.4 Americans Look to the Future
HSS 11.9.6, HSS 11.11.1; Analysis HRE.4

America in the Twenty-First Century

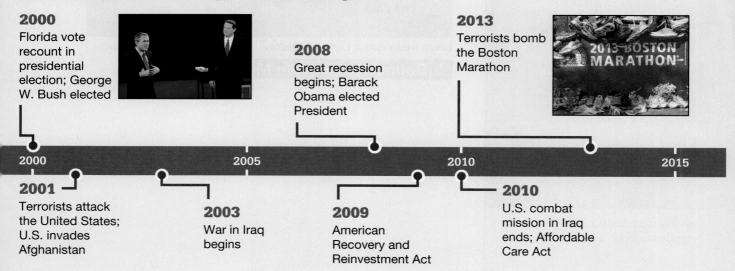

2000
Florida vote recount in presidential election; George W. Bush elected

2008
Great recession begins; Barack Obama elected President

2013
Terrorists bomb the Boston Marathon

2000 — 2005 — 2010 — 2015

2001
Terrorists attack the United States; U.S. invades Afghanistan

2003
War in Iraq begins

2009
American Recovery and Reinvestment Act

2010
U.S. combat mission in Iraq ends; Affordable Care Act

QUEST!

TEAM PROJECT

Creating a U.S. Citizenship Course

What is your definition of a good citizen? What are some things that all U.S. citizens should know? In this Quest you'll learn more about American values and the duties and responsibilities of citizenship as you create a course for prospective U.S. citizens.

STEP

Read the project launch and select quotes from the recommended source to include on your timeline.

STEP

Divide American history into distinct historical eras and write test questions relating to each of these eras.

STEP

With your team, create a multimedia course using maps, charts, and other graphics to show how certain American values developed over time.

STEP 4

Present your course to an audience of your classmates or to a group of prospective citizens. Hold a team meeting to reflect on what you have learned.

>> Workers at a Philippine manufacturing plant make Blu-ray components, many of which will end up in products imported into the United States.

12.1 With the end of the Cold War, the United States emerged as the sole superpower in a dramatically changing world. No longer defined by its role as the leading opponent of communism, the United States had to carve out new roles for itself in a world of globalization and increasing regional conflict. President Clinton, the nation's first baby-boomer President, ushered in this new period of American soul-searching. The free trade agreements made during his presidency showed how clearly he understood the impact of government policies on the economy. These policies will continue to shape the American economy in the twenty-first century.

Bounce to Activate Flipped Video

>> Objectives

Understand how the United States is affected by emerging economic issues such as changes in the global economy.

Explain how globalization and the rise of the service sector affects the American economy.

Understand the productivity enhancements resulting from management innovations.

Understand the global economic challenges facing the United States.

>> Key Terms

globalization
multinational corporations
service economy
European Union (EU)
The North American Free Trade Agreement (NAFTA)
General Agreement on Tariffs and Trade (GATT)
World Trade Organization (WTO)

America and the World Economy

Free Trade and Treaties

In the 1990s, the United States was both an important promoter of global trade and an example for newly industrializing nations. As more nations participated in economic globalization, the United States adjusted its own policies to ensure it would remain an economic powerhouse.

U.S. International Trade Policies and the Role of Free Trade As an economic leader and champion of the free enterprise system, America has had a major role in globalization. Free trade—the guiding principle of globalization—has been hotly debated in American politics. Americans want the lower costs that free trade creates but worry about the loss of American jobs to other countries. Generally, Republicans have supported the interests of business and free trade agreements. Democrats have been more sympathetic to labor interests and have often opposed legislation that would cost American workers' jobs. Depending on which party has been in power, free trade has either been encouraged or opposed by social and political advocacy organizations across the political spectrum.

Bill Clinton challenged the traditional Democratic thinking by supporting free trade blocs, which in theory would increase the economic prosperity of particular regions. Europe is an example of a region in which such a bloc was set up. In 1993, a number of European nations established the **European Union (EU)** to coordinate monetary and economic policies. By the end of the century, the EU had adopted a single currency, the euro, to promote economic efficiency. The EU's combined resources both encouraged trade among its members and challenged the economic leadership of the United States. North American free trade proponents believed a similar bloc would stimulate their own region.

The United States Joins NAFTA The North **American Free Trade Agreement (NAFTA)**, a direct response to the EU, was originally proposed during the Bush administration. President Bush and leaders of the other nations signed the agreement in 1992, but Congress blocked it. It called for a gradual removal of trade restrictions among the United States, Canada, and Mexico. NAFTA's supporters maintained that creating a free trade zone in North America would promote economic growth, reduce prices, increase exports, and encourage economic investment. Most labor leaders, environmentalists, and liberal Democrats argued that NAFTA would force American

manufacturers to relocate to Mexico, where wages were lower and environmental controls were less rigid. They feared that hundreds of thousands of American jobs would be lost. President Clinton embraced NAFTA and pushed it through Congress. It went into effect in 1994, and since then the three countries have also signed agreements covering environmental protection, safety standards, and workers' rights. Fourteen years later, with the removal of remaining trade restrictions between the United States and Mexico, the final provisions of NAFTA went into effect in January 2008. However, tensions remain, and President Trump, who condemned NAFTA repeatedly during the 2016 presidential campaign, may try to renegotiate the treaty.

Expanding Global Trade Through the Free Enterprise System President Clinton signed a total of 270 free trade agreements, including the revision of the **General Agreement on Tariffs and Trade (GATT)** in 1994 and the accords of the **World Trade Organization (WTO)** in 1995. GATT's goal was to reduce tariffs to promote free trade. The WTO replaced GATT, expanding the organization's authority to negotiate trade agreements, settle disputes, and enforce compliance with them. Clinton also continued the strong U.S. support of the World Bank.

Critics complain that the WTO and World Bank favor business interests over environmental concerns

The European Union

>> **Analyze Maps** In which part of Europe has EU membership expanded in the 21st century?

Bounce to Activate Gallery

and workers' rights. At the 1999 WTO meeting in Seattle, protesters filled the streets, disrupting the proceedings.

Yet most people agree that economic globalization has had a number of positive effects, such as exposing people to new ideas, technologies, and communications. Another positive effect is that nations involved in free trade have often become more democratic. Normalizing trade—engaging in free trade with countries rather than imposing sanctions based on disagreements—can also tend to strengthen economic ties. For example, normalizing trade with China has encouraged that country to adopt free market reforms.

☑ **EXPLAIN** why labor leaders, environmentalists, and liberal Democrats opposed NAFTA.

Technological and Management Innovations in the American Economy

Today, technological changes continue to have a dramatic effect on the American economy, raising the standard of living. New technology influences how and where people do their jobs. In this changing economy, one sector—the service industry—has grown rapidly. A lower percentage of Americans than ever before work on assembly lines or on farms. Instead, they provide services.

The Impact of Multinational Corporations on the 21st Century Economy New communications infrastructures—especially satellites and computers—have made it easier for companies to do global business. This has increased **globalization**, or the process by which national economies, politics, cultures, and societies become integrated with those of other nations around the world. **Multinational corporations** are one example of a globalized business.

Such a corporation might have its financial headquarters in one country and manufacturing plants in several others and may obtain its raw materials from many different places. The company then sells the products it makes to a worldwide market. When properly implemented, these innovations in how business operations are managed can lead to greater productivity both for individual workers within the corporation and for the corporation as a whole.

Globalization has made more products and services available to greater numbers of people, often at lower prices. It has hastened the development of

THE UNITED STATES & GLOBAL BUSINESS

1 IN 5 U.S. WORKERS IN THE PRIVATE SECTOR WORKS FOR A U.S. **MULTINATIONAL CORPORATION**

Source: Bureau of Labor Statistics

WORLD'S **TOP 25 PUBLIC COMPANIES** BY INDUSTRY

BANKING **36%**

OIL AND GAS **32%**

OTHER **32%** Semiconductors, telecommunications, insurance, retail, technology hardware, investment services

Source: *Forbes Global 2000 Leading Companies, 2013*

U.S. MULTINATIONAL CORPORATIONS
DOMESTIC VS. **FOREIGN SALES** 2010

	Domestic	Foreign
WAL-MART	$311 BILLION	$109 BILLION
EXXON-MOBIL	$188 BILLION	$154 BILLION
GENERAL ELECTRIC	$69 BILLION	$80 BILLION
FORD	$63 BILLION	$66 BILLION
IBM	$36 BILLION	$64 BILLION
DOW CHEMICAL	$18 BILLION	$36 BILLION
INTEL	$7 BILLION	$37 BILLION
AMAZON	$19 BILLION	$15 BILLION
MCDONALD'S	$8 BILLION	$16 BILLION
NIKE	$10 BILLION	$11 BILLION

Source: U.S. News and World Report

>> **Analyze Data** If you combine domestic and foreign sales, which is the largest multinational company in the U.S.?

Bounce to Activate Chart

some nations. But it has also had some drawbacks. Industrial nations have seen their manufacturing jobs flow out to less developed nations. Steel that was once manufactured in Pittsburgh, for example, might now be made in South Korea. In less developed nations, workers often do not enjoy the protections that workers have in industrial nations. Finally, the interconnection of world economies almost guarantees that economic problems in one region will be felt in others.

Technology Transforms Workplaces Computer technology has also changed the nature of the American economy. Many workers have found that they need computer skills to get jobs. Banking, stockbroking, programming, and the many other occupations dependent on information and computers have added millions of jobs to the service economy.

Many white-collar workers in the information economy have seen their jobs radically change. Professional workers are linked by a network of computers, fax machines, television screens, and cellphones. They often telecommunicate, holding meetings that involve participants sitting in offices around the world.

Computers have had a huge impact on American industry. Computer-driven industrial robots perform tasks such as welding, loading, packaging, and assembling cars and electronics. Because they can deliver high quality work around the clock, they have enhanced productivity, allowing many businesses to become more competitive. Computers also allow managers to accurately forecast demand for their goods. Applying just-in-time inventory strategies, producers can receive goods as they are needed, increasing efficiency by reducing their inventory costs and waste.

The Service Sector Expands With the production of services increasing faster than the production of goods, some economists say that America now has a **service economy**. Jobs in the service sector vary widely. Lawyers, teachers, doctors, research analysts, police officers, professional athletes, and movie stars are all service workers, as are salespeople and the people behind fast-food counters. Service workers are among the lowest paid and the highest paid people in the United States.

The transition from an industry-based economy to a service-based one has created opportunities for small business entrepreneurs to achieve the American dream. Sergey Brin and Larry Page launched Google in 1998 to help Internet users locate

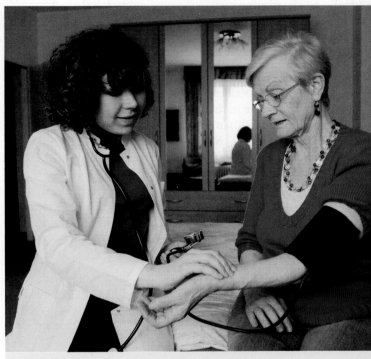

>> In the first decade of the twenty-first century, manufacturing was still an important source of employment, but an increasing proportion of U.S. jobs became available in service industries such as healthcare and education.

information as efficiently as possible. The success of Google has made both men billionaires. Mark Zuckerberg and several college roommates launched Facebook while still students at Harvard University. Facebook enables its users to build networks among people with similar interests, activities, and backgrounds. The world's interest in social media made Zuckerberg one of the wealthiest people in America.

Individuals like Zuckerberg continue to have an impact on the twenty-first century economy. Computer and mobile communication technology continues to push small entrepreneurs to develop innovative products and services.

The Decline of Organized Labor The rise of the service economy and the decline in American coal mining, steelmaking, and automobile manufacturing has had a strong impact on organized labor. When union membership was at its peak in 1945, about 35 percent of all American workers belonged to unions. In 2013, less than 12 percent of workers did. Blue-collar jobs, once the mainstay of American labor, declined dramatically in the second half of the twentieth century. As a result, the political power of labor unions, as well as farm organizations, has fallen. At the same time, workers' average wages—especially those of nonprofessional workers—have fallen.

The stagnant or decreasing wealth of working- and middle-class Americans has been compounded by changes in tax structures and safety-net programs. It has also been amplified by higher costs for education, child care, and housing. In recent years, a growing populist movement has sought to bring attention to the income gap.

☑ **IDENTIFY CAUSE AND EFFECT** What effect has the development of robotics had on American businesses and why?

The Role of the United States in the Future Economy

Since the 1920s, the United States has had the world's largest national economy. The reasons are many and varied, but include political stability, abundant natural resources, high worker productivity, favorable immigration policies, and a culture that emphasizes hard work, free enterprise, education, and innovation. All of these advantages have almost guaranteed America's economic success. Today, however, the United States faces new challenges in a rapidly changing world economy.

New Economies Rise During the past decade, strong new economic competitors have emerged in China, India, and Brazil—large, populous nations with abundant natural resources and developing industrial bases. The United States has formed economic ties with these growing economies, while engaging in healthy competition with them. Of these three major competitors, China is the nation that causes the greatest concern. Because unlike Western European nations and Japan, which have democratic systems similar to that of the United States, China's government is communist, with harsh restrictions on freedom of expression. However, China has been moving rapidly toward a modified free market. Although there has been friction between the United States and China over issues such as patents and intellectual property, as well as industrial spying and computer hacking, the two powerful nations have forged mutually profitable trade agreements.

Competing in a Global Economy For more than a century, successful competition in the global economy has depended on three factors: producing better, less expensive goods; staying on the cutting

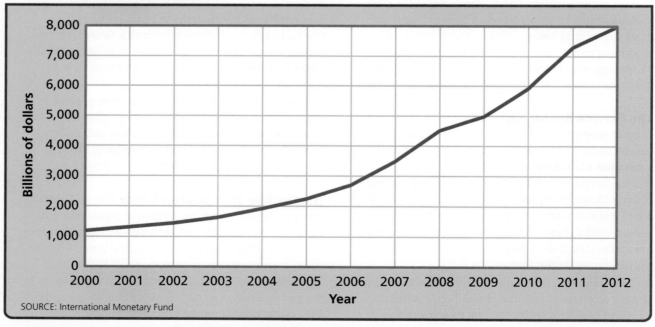

China's GDP, 2000–2012

SOURCE: International Monetary Fund

>> The U.S. GDP increased from $9.9 trillion in 2000 to $15.7 trillion in 2012. **Analyze Data** Predict China's GDP relative to the U.S. GDP in 25 years.

edge of research and development; and educating and preparing students for work in high-tech industries. Ultimately competitions among nations are won by people of intelligence and strong work ethics who are encouraged by governments that value progress and innovation.

Since the passage of NAFTA and GATT in the 1990s, economic borders have become more flexible. The outsourcing of jobs and the growth of multinational corporations have changed the nature of economic nationalism. However, in 2016, several international events suggested that free trade and globalization were under threat. In that year, citizens of the United Kingdom voted to leave the European Union. This British exit, or "Brexit," encouraged other anti-EU politicians across Europe to promise to take their countries out of the EU. Meanwhile, in the United States, Donald Trump led a campaign against free trade and international treaties like NAFTA, which he accused of destroying American jobs. In Europe and the United States at least, the tide seemed to be turning against globalization and free trade.

☑ **IDENTIFY** the three factors that contribute to success in the global marketplace.

1. **Compare Points of View** Discuss the positions of Democrats and Republicans with regard to free trade.

2. **Describe** President Clinton's position on free trade, and explain how this challenged traditional expectations.

3. **Identify Cause and Effect** Describe the positive and negative effects of the World Trade Organization (WTO).

4. **Generate Explanations** Explain why the United States experienced a shift from an industry-based economy to a service-based economy.

5. **Draw Conclusions** Discuss the new economic competitors emerging in the world today, and explain how they affect the United States.

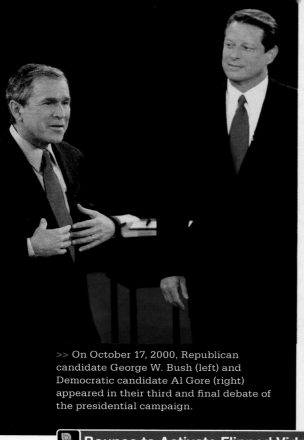

The year 2000 brought an end to Clinton's two terms as President. Clinton's legacy of a strong economy coupled with personal scandal polarized voters. As candidates geared up for the 2000 presidential race, it promised to be a close election.

>> On October 17, 2000, Republican candidate George W. Bush (left) and Democratic candidate Al Gore (right) appeared in their third and final debate of the presidential campaign.

 Bounce to Activate Flipped Video

>> **Objectives**

Assess the outcome of the 2000 presidential election.

Explain the goals and achievements of George W. Bush's domestic policy.

Explain the significance of terrorist attacks on the United States and U.S. involvement in world affairs.

Summarize the important issues of Bush's second term.

Understand the causes and effects of the 2008 financial crisis and economic recession.

>> **Key Terms**

George W. Bush
No Child Left Behind
   Act
Taliban
USA PATRIOT Act
Department of
   Homeland
   Security
weapons of mass
   destruction (WMD)
habeas corpus
Lionel Sosa

The George W. Bush Presidency

Controversy in the 2000 Election

The Candidates Clinton's Vice President, Al Gore, Jr., of Tennessee, ran for the Democrats. Gore selected Connecticut Senator Joseph Lieberman as his Vice President. Lieberman was the first Jewish person to be on the ticket of a major party.

The Republicans chose **George W. Bush** as their candidate. A son of George H.W. Bush and a former governor of Texas, Bush was popular with conservatives. As governor, Bush had worked with Democrats as well as Republicans. He struck many Americans as sincere.

Ralph Nader, a third-party candidate from the left-of-center Green Party, also joined the presidential race in 2000. Many Democrats urged Nader to withdraw from the race, pointing out that any vote for him would likely be a vote taken away from Gore. Nader's candidacy would end up having a profound impact on the election.

A Close Vote The campaigns focused mainly on how to spend the federal budget surplus. Bush favored tax cuts. Gore proposed strengthening Social Security and paying down the national debt. On election night, Americans voted mainly by party affiliation.

The vote margin in the Electoral College was razor thin. Although Gore received a half million more votes than Bush, both fell short of winning the 270 electoral votes needed to capture the presidency. The issue was Florida's 25 electoral votes. The popular vote in Florida was so close that a state law mandated an automatic statewide recount. Bush led by a margin of 537 popular votes. He was awarded 271 electoral votes, one more than was needed to win the election. Ralph Nader received more than 97,000 votes in the state of Florida. If, as many Democrats believe, the vast majority of votes for Nader would have otherwise gone to Gore, then Gore would have garnered Florida's 25 electoral votes and won the presidency.

The Supreme Court Steps In Given the extreme closeness of the votes, Democrats demanded a hand recount in several Florida counties. Republicans countered by suing in a Miami court to prevent the recount.

For more than a month, confusion reigned. The election was now affecting the relationships among the legislative, executive, and judicial branches of government.

Finally, the Supreme Court ruled on the issue. In the case of *Bush* v. *Gore*, the court ended the re-recounting by a 5-to-4 decision. On December 12, 2000, Gore conceded defeat, and Bush delivered a conciliatory victory speech.

The election showed an interesting geographical pattern. The Democrats captured votes in their traditional strongholds: the two coasts and large cities. Republicans won a large bloc of voters in the Midwest and the South.

☑ **CHECK UNDERSTANDING** Why was a Supreme Court decision necessary to determine the winner of the 2000 election?

The Bush Domestic Agenda

Once in office, Bush turned his attention to domestic issues. Like most Republicans, Bush believed that tax cuts would stimulate the economy and create new jobs. In 2001, Bush pushed a highly controversial $1.3 trillion tax cut through Congress. The tax cut put more money in the hands of consumers. But most of the benefits of the tax cut went to the wealthiest Americans. As a result, the federal budget deficit increased.

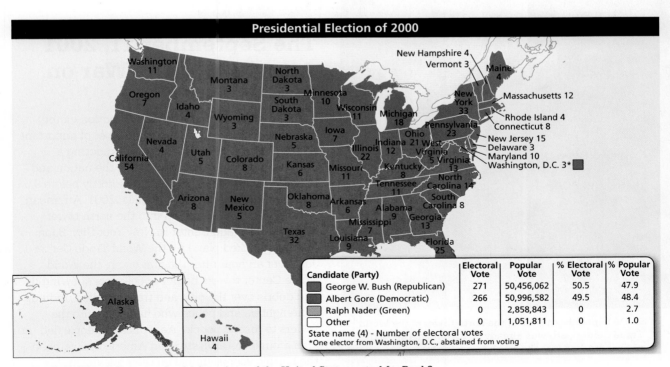

Presidential Election of 2000

Candidate (Party)	Electoral Vote	Popular Vote	% Electoral Vote	% Popular Vote
George W. Bush (Republican)	271	50,456,062	50.5	47.9
Albert Gore (Democratic)	266	50,996,582	49.5	48.4
Ralph Nader (Green)	0	2,858,843	0	2.7
Other	0	1,051,811	0	1.0

State name (4) - Number of electoral votes
*One elector from Washington, D.C., abstained from voting

>> **Analyze Maps** In general, which regions of the United States voted for Bush? Which voted for Gore?

>> In 2002, President Bush signed the No Child Left Behind Act, fulfilling his campaign promise to pursue a domestic agenda that improved educational opportunities for America's children.

>> On September 11, 2001, the north tower of the World Trade Center (left) was already on fire when a second airliner crashed into the south tower (right).

Focus on Education Bush's other domestic priority was education. He supported legislation that tied the federal funding of schools to academic achievement. The 2002 **No Child Left Behind Act** penalized schools that did not reach federal performance standards. It also called for improving teacher quality and other reforms.

Bush also addressed the concerns of older Americans who faced rising costs for prescription drugs. In 2003, Congress extended Medicare to cover prescription drugs for senior citizens. The measure was controversial. It was expensive, and many seniors found its provisions confusing and its coverage inadequate.

Reforming Entitlements In his inauguration address, Bush promised to reform Social Security and Medicare, the government-run health plan for senior citizens. Together these programs account for about one third of the federal budget. Bush was concerned that because of a rapidly aging U.S. population and the rising cost of Medicare, these government programs would eventually become insolvent unless changes were made. Bush was able to make some progress on Medicare with the Medicare Act of 2003. But Democratic opposition to Social Security reform thwarted Bush's efforts.

☑ **RECALL** What two benefits did Bush claim his tax cut would provide?

The September 11, 2001 Attacks and the War on Terror

As the first anniversary of Bush's election victory approached, the nation faced a number of important but typical problems. No one was expecting a devastating attack that would stun the nation and usher in a new era in U.S. history. Shortly before 9 A.M Eastern time on September 11, 2001, American Airlines Flight 11 slammed into the north tower of the World Trade Center in New York City. Soon another hijacked plane hit the World Trade Center. Just over an hour after the first crash, the World Trade Center towers began to collapse, spewing dust and debris over the city, and trapping the hundreds of firefighters and police who had gone into the towers to rescue people. As panicked people fled the area around the site, stunned Americans watched the horrific scenes unfold on their televisions. These two crashes were not accidents, but part of a carefully planned assault on the United States

At 9:40 A.M. a third airliner that had been hijacked after leaving Washington, D.C., crashed into the Pentagon. Meanwhile, passengers on a fourth hijacked plane learned of the earlier crashes on their cellphones. They bravely stormed the cockpit, refusing to allow the hijackers to target another building. At 10:03 A.M., this fourth airliner crashed in a field near Pittsburgh. That same day, it was confirmed that the al Qaeda Islamist terrorist group had spearheaded the attacks. In time, Americans also learned that nearly 3,000 people had died as a result of the attacks on 9/11.

Al Qaeda's Campaign of Terrorism The suddenness, surprise, and cruelty of the 9/11 attacks against thousands of defenseless people was unprecedented in American history. However, Americans soon began to realize that the 9/11 attacks were the most destructive in a series of attacks that al Qaeda had launched against the United States. Al Qaeda, led by Osama bin Laden, the son of a wealthy businessman from Saudi Arabia, was a terrorist group committed to an extreme form of Islam. One of its goals was to end all American involvement in Muslim countries.

Throughout the 1990s, al Qaeda had been targeting Americans at home and abroad, and in fact, it had attempted to blow up the World Trade Center once before. In 1993 it exploded a bomb at the site, killing six people and injuring more than a thousand. In 1998, the organization set off car bombs at American embassies in Nairobi, Kenya, and Dar es Salaam, Tanzania, killing 225 people and injuring more than 5,500. In 2000, al Qaeda bombed the , an American ship anchored off the coast of Yemen, killing 17 American sailors. In 2001, al Qaeda chose to attack the World Trade Center and the Pentagon because these buildings represented American economic and military power.

Americans responded to the 9/11 attacks as a unified, determined people. On the day of the attacks, President Bush addressed the nation:

"Today, our fellow citizens, our way of life, and our very freedom came under attack in a series of deliberate and deadly terrorist acts. . . . Thousands of lives were suddenly ended by evil, despicable acts of terror. . . . These acts of mass murder were intended to frighten our nation into chaos and retreat. But they

>> In addition to the September 11 attacks in New York City, hijackers crashed a plane into the Pentagon in northern Virginia, taking the lives of more than one hundred government employees.

>> Osama bin Laden was a member of a wealthy Saudi Arabian family and a founder of the al Qaeda terrorist network.

Bounce to Activate Gallery

have failed. . . . Terrorist attacks can shake the foundations of our biggest buildings, but they cannot touch the foundation of America. These acts shatter steel, but they cannot dent the steel of American resolve."

—President George W. Bush, September 11, 2001

Americans Unite in Troubling Times Americans were shocked by the 9/11 attacks, but they rallied to defend their nation. Millions of Americans rushed to donate money, supplies, services, and their own blood. Throughout the country, Americans put up flags to show their patriotism and determination. Many held candlelight vigils and prayer services for the dead and bereaved. Continued fears of more terrorist attacks, however, kept the nation on edge. In October 2001, a newspaper editor in Florida died from an anthrax infection. Anthrax is a type of bacteria that has been used by several countries to create biological weapons. Traces of anthrax then appeared in news offices in New York City and in the office of a U.S. senator in Washington. Two postal

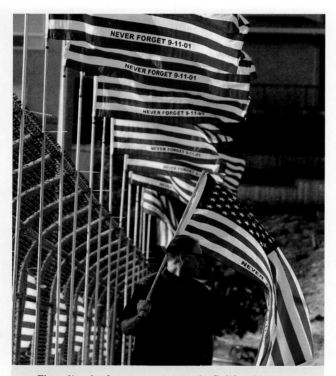

>> Flags lined a freeway overpass in California on September 11, 2006, the fifth anniversary of the attacks. **Identify Cause and Effect** How does this photograph express the continuing impact of the September 11 attacks on American society?

workers who had handled materials containing anthrax died. Although the FBI investigated, no terrorists were caught.

The Legacy of 9/11 September 11, 2001, became a watershed in modern American history, when Americans' confidence in their nation's security was deeply shaken. Americans came together to grieve, rebuild, and decide how to deal with the threat of terrorism. The name "9/11" quickly entered the national lexicon, with people viewing historical events and even ideas as "before 9/11" or "after 9/11."

The 9/11 attacks also had great impact on the nation's economy. Despite increased airport security, some Americans remained wary of air travel, which hurt the airline and travel industries. Businesses and households entered a period of uncertainty during which spending decreased. Estimates indicate that the attacks cost the economy one million jobs and reduced the country's output by three percent.

The War on Terror and the Invasion of Afghanistan President Bush had been in office less than a year when these attacks occurred. The al Qaeda terrorist attack against the nation challenged the new President in unforeseen ways and led to a major shift in American foreign policy. In the wake of September 11, Bush and his advisers agreed that the most important priority should be finding and prosecuting the people behind 9/11. This would be just the first step in what Bush called the "war on terror." American government officials had determined that Osama bin Laden's al Qaeda network had been behind the attacks. Bin Laden opposed the presence of American troops in Saudi Arabia, the U.S. economic boycott against Iraq, and U.S. support for Israel. Bin Laden and other al Qaeda leaders were in Afghanistan, where the Islamist **Taliban** government allowed them to operate training camps for terrorists.

Bush believed that any government that sponsored terrorism should be held accountable. He demanded that the Taliban turn bin Laden over to U.S. custody. When the Taliban refused, American forces, joined by Great Britain, invaded Afghanistan. Allied forces quickly overthrew the Taliban. Although American troops captured several of al Qaeda's leaders, Osama bin Laden escaped.

Ensuring National Security Bush moved quickly to prevent future terrorist attacks. Soon after September 11, Congress passed the **USA PATRIOT Act** to give law enforcement broader powers to monitor suspected terrorists. Critics claimed that the

USA PATRIOT Act violated civil liberties. But many Americans were willing to give up some freedoms in return for improved security. Congress also approved Bush's call for the creation of a new Cabinet-level **Department of Homeland Security** to coordinate security matters among federal, state, and local agencies.

The Bush administration exercised broad powers fighting the war on terror. The U.S. operations in Afghanistan led to the capture of alleged members of the Taliban and others fighting against the United States. These prisoners were sent to a U.S. base located at Guantanamo Bay, Cuba. Many of these prisoners were held for years without formal charges brought against them.

Controversy surrounded the holding of the prisoners, mostly on the grounds that their detentions violated the writ of **habeas corpus**. Because of the constitutional issues raised by federal government policy changes, the Supreme Court heard a series of cases dealing with this issue and the Bush administration's use of military tribunals rather than civilian courts to prosecute enemy combatants. In *Hamdan* v. *Rumsfeld*, the Court ruled that the Bush administration's use of military courts violated the Geneva Conventions and U.S. federal law, including the U.S. Uniform Code of Military Justice.

War on Terror Moves to Iraq Bush next contemplated invading Iraq as part of his wider war on terrorism. Many people believed that Iraqi president Saddam Hussein was building nuclear, biological, and chemical **weapons of mass destruction (WMD)**. Despite many Americans' belief that UN weapons inspectors should be allowed to continue their search for Iraqi WMD, Congress authorized Bush to use military force against Iraq. On March 19, 2003, American and British military forces invaded Iraq in Operation Iraqi Freedom.

Saddam's forces collapsed almost immediately. As the Iraqi capital of Baghdad fell, Saddam and other Iraqi leaders went into hiding.

☑ **RECALL** Why did the fourth hijacked plane not reach its target on 9/11?

Bush's Second Term

The Iraq war, terrorism, and the federal budget deficit weighed heavily on Americans' minds as they voted in the 2004 presidential election. Bush campaigned as a "war president," saying he had proved his competency as commander-in-chief. Bush

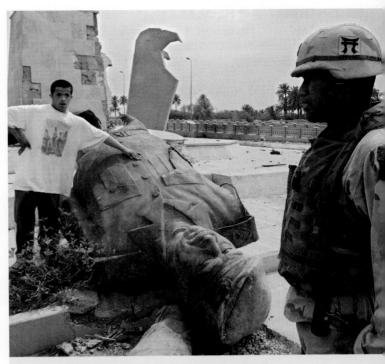

>> In Baghdad, Iraq's capital city, Saddam Hussein's statue was torn down following the U.S. invasion in 2003.

Bounce to Activate Map

defeated the Democratic candidate for president, Massachusetts senator John Kerry, by a comfortable margin.

Among those casting ballots for Bush in 2004 were the nation's Latino voters. The Bush campaign turned to a Texas advertising agency run by **Lionel Sosa**. With Sosa's help, Bush captured an estimated 40 percent of Latino voters in 2004. Just 8 years earlier, Republican candidate Bob Dole could attract only 21 percent of Latino voters.

Problems Surface in Iraq Iraq remained a major focus of Bush's second term as the war raged on. However, by late 2005, Iraq had a new constitution and the beginnings of a democracy. The following year, Saddam Hussein was tried and executed. Saddam's brutal rule had kept fighting in check among Iraq's three major groups: Sunnis, Shi'a, and Kurds. Now these groups fought bitterly for power. An American troop surge in 2007 lessened the violence. However, Iraq's democracy remained fragile.

In 2008, a Senate Intelligence Committee report determined that there was no credible evidence to support claims that Iraq was developing WMD or had ties to terrorist groups. Some accused the Bush administration of deliberately misleading Congress and the American people to win support for the war.

Troubles at Home Meanwhile, Bush faced domestic challenges. In August 2005, Hurricane Katrina hit the Gulf Coast. Katrina caused much destruction in New Orleans. As fierce as the winds and rains of Katrina had been, New Orleans suffered even more after the storm passed. Rising waters soon breached levees protecting the low-lying city. Citizens were forced onto rooftops to await rescue and thousands of others sought shelter at the Superdome stadium. The government's slow response to the damage was widely criticized. National discontent was reflected in the 2006 elections. For the first time in 12 years, Democrats won control of the House and the Senate.

Bush Reaffirms American Sovereignty In February 2005, the Kyoto Protocol went into effect around the world. The treaty signed by 140 nations is aimed at controlling global warming linked to carbon dioxide and other greenhouse gases. Negotiations took place in Kyoto, Japan, in 1997, with the help of the United States. Just months after assuming the presidency in 2001, George W. Bush announced that the United States would not abide by the treaty. The Bush administration argued that the treaty did not place emission limits on developing countries and that it could harm the U.S. economy.

Many considered the Kyoto Protocol as yet another example of an international treaty undermining U.S. sovereignty.

☑ **EXPLAIN** how discontent with the government's response to Hurricane Katrina was reflected in the 2006 elections.

The Financial Crisis of 2008

During the autumn of 2008, Americans faced a potentially disastrous economic crisis centered on the financial industry. The crisis stemmed in part from "subprime" home mortgage loans that banks had made to less-qualified, low-income borrowers. The higher interest rates on these loans made them more profitable for banks. The loans were then sold as mortgage-backed securities to investors.

The U.S. Slides into Recession After the U.S. economy slid into a recession in late 2007, unemployed Americans could no longer pay their mortgages. Foreclosures—seizures of property from borrowers who are unable to repay their loans—increased.

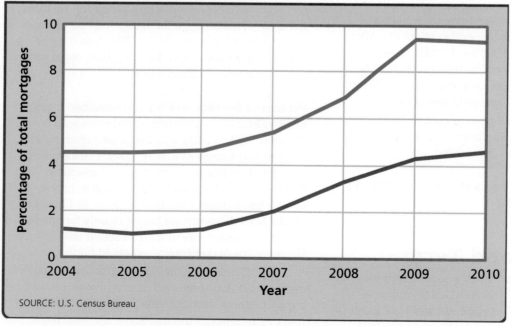

Housing Bubble Collapse, 2004–2010

SOURCE: U.S. Census Bureau

>> **Analyze Data** The blue line shows the foreclosure rate, while the purple line shows the delinquency rate. In what year did trouble begin in the housing market?

The First Years of Recession, 2007–2008

2007	2008
• **January 25** – Home sales reach their lowest point since the late 1980s.	• **January 21–22** – Global stock markets collapse.
• **February 21** – The rising default rate hits the subprime mortgage industry.	• **June 26** – Crude oil hits a peak of $140 per barrel.
• **August 10** – The Federal Reserve pumps $38 billion into the banking system.	• **September 7** – The federal government takes over Fannie Mae and Freddie Mac.
• **November 12** – A $75 billion superfund is approved to help build confidence in the credit markets.	• **October 6** – The federal government lends banks $900 billion.
• **November 15** – The House passes the Mortgage Reform and Anti-Predatory Act of 2007.	• **November 4** – Barack Obama wins the presidential election.
• **December 12** – The Federal Reserve pumps $40 billion into the U.S. financial system.	

SOURCE: California Department of Finance

>> **Analyze Information** Based on the timeline, how did the federal government respond to the initial rise in default rates on home mortgages?

 Bounce to Activate Chart

As a result, housing prices fell and mortgage-related investments lost their value. Several large banking and investment firms collapsed or were sold.

Too Big to Fail—The Financial Industry Bailout
In September 2008, the stock market plunged. The country faced its worst economic crisis since the Great Depression. Treasury Secretary Henry Paulson and Federal Reserve chairman Ben Bernanke proposed a $700 billion bailout of the banks that had engaged in risky lending practices. The Troubled Asset Relief Program (TARP) was supported by Bush and approved by Congress.

TARP funds were used to make multibillion-dollar loans to at-risk banks. Public outrage over the taxpayer-funded bailout grew after executives at some of these companies received multimillion-dollar bonuses. However, many credit the bailout with preventing a financial meltdown.

☑ **RECALL** What was the source of public outrage at the taxpayer-funded bailout of the financial industry?

☑ ASSESSMENT

1. **Compare and Contrast** the 2000 presidential campaigns of George W. Bush and Al Gore.

2. **Describe** the key components of President Bush's domestic agenda, and explain why some of these initiatives were controversial.

3. **Support a Point of View with Evidence** Explain why the United States opposed the Taliban.

4. **Compare Points of View** Describe the purpose of Operation Iraqi Freedom, and explain why it was controversial among Americans.

5. **Generate Explanations** Discuss the intentions of the Kyoto Protocol, and explain why President Bush refused to abide by the treaty.

>> Barack Obama takes the oath of office as his wife Michelle holds the Bible and daughters Malia (left) and Sasha (right) look on.

Bounce to Activate Flipped Video

The 2008 election broke new ground in American politics. Democratic senator Barack Obama of Illinois became the first African American to be nominated for president by a major party. Arizona senator John McCain, the Republican nominee for president, chose Governor Sarah Palin of Alaska to be his running mate. Palin was only the second woman to be selected as a vice-presidential nominee. The first, Geraldine Ferraro, ran with Walter Mondale in 1984.

>> Objectives

Assess the outcome of the 2008 presidential election.

Explain the goals of Barack Obama's economic and healthcare policy.

Describe Barack Obama's involvement in world affairs.

Summarize Obama's Second Term.

>> Key Terms

Barack Obama
Tea Party Movement
Hillary Clinton

The Barack Obama Presidency

The 2008 Election

Contrasting Candidates John McCain, the son and grandson of navy admirals, served as a pilot in the Vietnam War. He endured six years as a prisoner of war after his plane was shot down. He won election to the House of Representatives in 1982. McCain was elected to the United States Senate in 1986.

A graduate of Columbia University and Harvard Law School, Barack Obama had been a community organizer in Chicago. The son of a white woman from Kansas and a black man from Kenya, Obama served in the Illinois state legislature before being elected to the United States Senate.

A Historic Moment On January 20, 2009, Barack Obama became the 44th U.S. President and the first African American to hold the office. At a huge victory rally in Chicago in November, his words captured the historic moment: "If there is anyone out there who still doubts that America is a place where all things are possible, who still wonders if the dream of our founders is alive in our time, who still questions the power of our democracy, tonight is your answer."

The election drew a large voter turnout, with 62 percent of voters citing the economy as their main concern. Bush's low approval ratings, combined with McCain's missteps, made a Republican victory seem almost impossible. In Congress, Democrats expanded their majority.

☑ **RECALL** Describe Barack Obama's background before he assumed the presidency in 2008.

President Obama Takes Action

Before taking office, President Obama had developed an economic stimulus package to pump money into the sinking economy. The $787 billion bill, the American Recovery and Reinvestment Act, was approved by Congress in February 2009. The stimulus package included tax cuts, aid to state and local governments, and funds for infrastructure projects.

Obama's Appointments Elected with the help of a coalition of minority voters, women, and young voters, President Obama sought to reflect the country's diversity in his cabinet appointments.

Perhaps his most prominent appointment was that of **Hillary Clinton**, his former Democratic primary opponent. Clinton, the wife of President Bill Clinton and a senator from New York, served as Secretary of State during Obama's first term in office.

President Obama's first Supreme Court nomination added diversity to the Court. He nominated Sonia Sotomayor, the daughter of Puerto Rican parents. Sotomayor grew up in a public housing project in the Bronx and had overcome a difficult childhood. A federal judge since 1992, Sotomayor was confirmed in 2009, becoming the first Hispanic to serve as a Supreme Court justice. In 2010, Obama nominated Elena Kagan to fill a vacancy in the Court. Kagan was known for working with both conservatives and liberals and had built a reputation as a passionate advocate of civil rights, including gay rights.

Healthcare Reform In 2008, more than 46 million Americans had no health insurance. During the campaign, Obama had pledged to create a national health plan to provide affordable coverage. He assigned Congress the job of fixing the healthcare system.

In November 2009, the House approved an overhaul of the nation's healthcare system. The

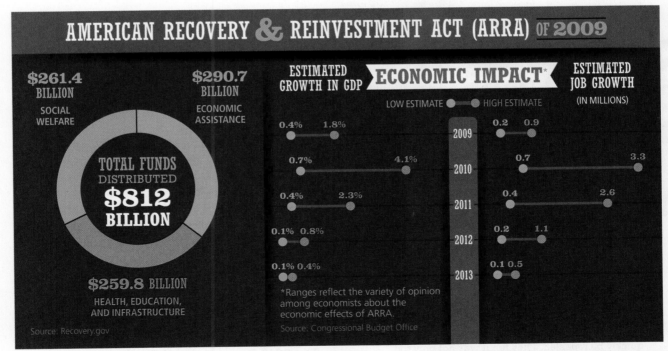

AMERICAN RECOVERY & REINVESTMENT ACT (ARRA) OF 2009

$261.4 BILLION SOCIAL WELFARE

$290.7 BILLION ECONOMIC ASSISTANCE

TOTAL FUNDS DISTRIBUTED **$812 BILLION**

$259.8 BILLION HEALTH, EDUCATION, AND INFRASTRUCTURE

Source: Recovery.gov

ESTIMATED GROWTH IN GDP — **ECONOMIC IMPACT** — ESTIMATED JOB GROWTH (IN MILLIONS)

LOW ESTIMATE ●━━○ HIGH ESTIMATE

	ESTIMATED GROWTH IN GDP		ESTIMATED JOB GROWTH (IN MILLIONS)
2009	0.4%	1.8%	0.2 0.9
2010	0.7%	4.1%	0.7 3.3
2011	0.4%	2.3%	0.4 2.6
2012	0.1% 0.8%		0.2 1.1
2013	0.1% 0.4%		0.1 0.5

*Ranges reflect the variety of opinion among economists about the economic effects of ARRA.
Source: Congressional Budget Office

>> Unemployment benefits are classified as social welfare. **Analyze Data** Based on the information in the pie chart, what inference can you make about the unemployment rate in 2009?

Bounce to Activate Chart

Senate passed its own healthcare bill in December. However, after Democrats lost their filibuster-proof majority in the Senate, healthcare reform was in jeopardy. President Obama campaigned for the bill and won the support of wavering Democrats. In March 2010, in a dramatic vote, the House approved the Senate's healthcare bill. Despite unanimous Republican opposition in the House and Senate, it was the most significant federal healthcare legislation since Medicare was passed in 1965.

The bill, the Patient Protection and Affordable Care Act, quickly became known as "Obamacare."

It extends coverage to the uninsured, prevents insurance companies from denying coverage to patients with pre-existing medical conditions, and provides subsidies to help low-income earners buy insurance. Still, many Americans opposed the new plan. They argued that it cost too much, put too great a burden on small businesses, and gave the federal government too much power.

Iraq, Afghanistan, and Libya In August 2010, Obama announced, "The American combat mission in Iraq has ended." When the final pull-out took place in late 2011, more than 4,000 Americans had been killed and more than 31,000 wounded. During the American troop surge, Iraq was significantly more stable, although acts of terrorism continued. About 50,000 American troops remained behind in support roles.

At the same time, Obama increased the American military presence in Afghanistan. American and allied troops had gone into Afghanistan shortly after the 9/11 terrorist attacks, but they had never rid the country of the Taliban forces that had protected Osama bin Laden. Now, Obama asserted, American forces would focus on the Taliban in Afghanistan and their allies in Pakistan.

In May 2011, President Obama announced the death of al Qaeda leader Osama bin Laden. In a secret operation lasting less than an hour, Navy SEALS raided a compound in Pakistan and killed bin Laden, the mastermind behind the 9/11 terrorist attacks. However, Americans were well aware that the death of bin Laden did not end the threat of terrorism. Intelligence officers examined computer files and other evidence seized at bin Laden's compound in the hopes that such materials would aid the continuing war on terrorism.

During the spring and summer of 2011, the United States also participated in an international coalition aiding the rebels who were fighting to overthrow the Libyan dictator Muammar al-Qaddafi. Qaddafi had long supported terrorist groups, and was finally overthrown and executed by rebel fighters.

Economic Issues and Reforms America's economic problems continued. Unemployment had risen throughout 2009, peaking at 10.2 percent. Although the economy had stabilized by the spring of 2010, sluggish economic growth and a high unemployment rate left many Americans fearful about the future.

In July 2010, Obama signed into law a sweeping financial reform bill aimed at changing the Wall Street practices that had contributed to the 2008 financial crisis. The new law increased federal oversight of banks, hedge funds, and other financial institutions. It also created a consumer protection agency to oversee credit card rates, bank fees, mortgages, and car loans. Critics argued, however, that the 2,300-page bill was too complex and too confusing to yield significant results. They said it would tighten credit and lead to further economic woes.

The 2010 Congressional Elections As the 2010 congressional elections approached, the nation seemed increasingly divided. While many

>> Some Americans hoped that "Obamacare" would quickly be repealed. They felt it was not only too expensive but that its provisions went beyond the powers given to the government by the Constitution.

▶▶ Bounce to Activate Chart

House of Representatives, 112th Congress

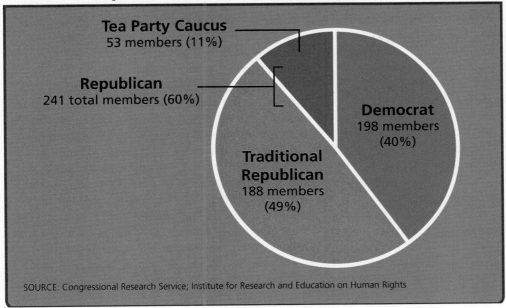

Tea Party Caucus
53 members (11%)

Republican
241 total members (60%)

Traditional Republican
188 members (49%)

Democrat
198 members (40%)

SOURCE: Congressional Research Service; Institute for Research and Education on Human Rights

>> **Infer** Based on the pie chart, what can you infer about the political power of the Tea Party?

Americans supported President Obama, others were angered by his actions. The strongest challenge came from the **Tea Party Movement** which emerged during Obama's first year in office. The movement took its name from the Boston Tea Party, a colonial protest against British taxes. The Tea Party Movement was made up of many local groups, united by a common desire to reduce the size and scope of the federal government.

Although they ran as Republicans, they were not traditional party candidates. They criticized many other Republicans as big spenders and urged a phase-out of programs such as Social Security and Medicare. In the 2010 elections, more than 40 candidates endorsed by the Tea Party were elected to the House and Senate.

Republicans won back control of the House of Representatives in the 2010 mid-term elections. Leaders of the new Republican-controlled House announced that their first priority would be to repeal Obama's healthcare bill. Meanwhile, in the final months of 2010, Congress passed a number of important measures, including extensions of the Bush tax cuts and an arms-control treaty with Russia.

☑ **IDENTIFY** What did the different Tea Party groups across the country have in common?

Obama's Second Term

As the 2012 presidential election approached, the nation's economy remained a major concern. Continued economic worries led to political polarization, and the established political parties were criticized by activists on the left and right. On the right, the Tea Party Movement urged Republicans to reduce taxation and the power of the federal government. On the left, critics from the Occupy Movement claimed that democracy was threatened by the accumulation of wealth and power in the hands of 1 percent of the population. For several months in late 2011 and early 2012, the mainly young people of the Occupy Movement set up tented encampments in American cities to draw attention to their cause.

Although the economic situation did not seem to be improving, the Obama administration received good news on another front. In June 2012, the Supreme Court, in *National Federation of Independent Business* v. *Sebelius*, granted Obama a judicial victory by ruling that it was within Congress's power to introduce most provisions of the Affordable Care Act. The ruling surprised many observers who were convinced that the Act was unconstitutional.

The Election of 2012 The Democrats used the issue of income inequality in President Obama's

2012 election campaign against the Republican candidate Mitt Romney, whom they portrayed as out of touch with ordinary people. After a deeply divisive campaign, Romney was defeated by Obama, who received 51.1 percent of the popular vote and 332 electoral votes. Exit polls offered an insight into America's changing demographics: Obama's victory rested partly on a coalition of minority voters and the young. With surveys showing a shrinking white population, some suggested that the Republican party would have to broaden its appeal to minority voters and young people in order to win future elections.

Obama began his second term amidst a continuing economic recession at home and lingering military problems abroad, his power weakened by a divided electorate. Many conservative voters still questioned the wisdom of his universal healthcare act and leadership in the war against terrorism.

Continuing Economic Problems With an unemployment rate of just under eight percent, and job creation lagging behind presidential expectations, Obama faced a difficult task. The problems were significant. America imported more than it exported, creating an unfavorable balance of trade. In addition there were charges, and some evidence, that the country's economic competitors were guilty of unfavorable trade practices. Slow economic growth and failure to significantly reduce spending added to the woes.

Although the stock market moved steadily upward, so did gas prices, home prices, and overall consumer debt. Yet Democrats and Republicans in Congress showed little incentive to negotiate in order to pass effective legislation. In the autumn of 2013, negotiations to raise the borrowing limit for the government stalled as Republicans demanded a number of political concessions that Democrats refused to give. Among these Republican demands were a postponement of the Affordable Care Act, tax reform, and energy deregulation. As the parties could not agree on a budget bill to fund the government, certain government services were forced to shut down temporarily.

Foreign Policy During Obama's Second Term
Revolutions and civil wars in the Middle East continued to challenge American policy. Although the scheduled pull-out of American troops from Iraq was completed in 2011, the country remains politically unstable and wracked by sectarian violence. In Afghanistan, U.S. combat troops began withdrawing, although some U.S. forces remained. Meanwhile, as civil war raged in Syria, the Obama administration found itself in a difficult position, wary of sending arms that might find their way into the hands of terrorists and reluctant to become involved in another war in the Middle East. Tensions also remained high over Iran's nuclear program, which many observers believe is intended to produce weapons rather than domestic energy. In November 2013, President Obama and other Western leaders persuaded Iran to accept an interim agreement to halt elements of its nuclear program and agree to weapons inspections in exchange for Western nations lifting some sanctions against that country.

The Boston Marathon Bombings The issue of America's involvement in the Middle East was cited as the motive behind a horrific terrorist attack in Boston. On April 15, 2013, two pressure cooker bombs exploded near the finish line of the Boston Marathon.

The explosions transformed a day of celebration into grief, as Americans mourned the three people who were killed and the 264 who were injured. Authorities soon identified the bombers as two

>> Donald Trump is sworn in as the 45th President in 2017.

brothers, Islamist extremists upset by America's wars in Iraq and Afghanistan. One of the brothers died as he fled from authorities. Police captured the other, who was an American citizen. The attack traumatized and stunned millions of American citizens who followed the events on the news and social media.

☑ **IDENTIFY SUPPORTING DETAILS** What foreign policy challenges did President Obama face in his second term?

The Road to the 2016 Presidential Election

During the final two years of Obama's presidency, concerns over new technologies, globalization, terrorism, and immigration, fueled a growing sense of anxiety about the future.

Republicans Control Congress The mid-term elections of 2014 created a Republican majority in the Senate. With Republicans controlling both houses, Obama broke the gridlock by issuing executive orders on a range of issues from civil rights to environmental protection.

ISIS Spreads Fear By December 2015, a terrorist organization sometimes known as the Islamic State of Iraq and Syria (ISIS), had set up a so-called "Islamic State" over territory in the Middle East. From this base, ISIS recruited young people online and encouraged them to kill civilians in Western countries that opposed them militarily. In the United States, a series of ISIS-inspired attacks included the murder of forty-nine people at a gay nightclub in Orlando, Florida in June 2016, by a shooter who declared allegiance to ISIS. It was the worst terror attack on U.S. soil since 9/11.

Globalization and the Rustbelt Decades of free trade and globalization had moved manufacturing into poorer nations as corporations cut production costs. Both Republican and Democratic administrations encouraged this trend, which had helped create "rustbelts"—once prosperous manufacturing areas that now suffered from unemployment and depopulation. In most of the rustbelt and rural areas, the post-2008 economic recovery under President Obama never took hold. The lack of jobs increased resentment of illegal immigrants and led to calls for greater border controls.

"Obamacare" Divides Opinion Although President Obama's healthcare program expanded health insurance to 20 million more Americans,

premium hikes and the penalties for those who did not buy insurance drew criticism. With Republicans demanding repeal, the future of the Patient Protection and Affordable Care Act became a major issue in the 2016 election.

The 2016 Election During an unpredictable campaign, the Republican nominee Donald Trump, a property tycoon and television celebrity, ran against the Democratic nominee Hillary Clinton, a former Secretary of State and First Lady. Clinton was the first female presidential nominee of a major party, while Trump was the first presidential nominee since Eisenhower without political experience. Trump's call to "Make America Great Again" reflected some Americans' fears of economic decline and anxiety over jobs, trade, terrorism, and immigration. Clinton stressed how her political experience better qualified her for the job, while Trump presented himself as an anti-establishment candidate.

During the campaign, outrage over Trump's comments on immigrants, Muslims, women, and minorities provoked violent protests at Trump rallies. Many were also angered by Clinton's use of a private email server instead of an official server while she was Secretary of State.

Although Clinton won the popular vote by almost 3 million votes, Trump won the electoral college, in a victory that surprised all those following the polls and the press.

☑ **EXPLAIN** What was an important economic issue in the election?

☑ **ASSESSMENT**

1. **Check Understanding** Discuss the goals and beliefs of the Tea Party Movement.

2. **Describe** the economic concerns and political actions of the Occupy Movement.

3. **Generate Explanations** Explain how changing demographics led to President Obama's reelection in 2012.

4. **Draw Conclusions** Explain how U.S. involvement in the Middle East led to violence in the United States during President Obama's second term.

5. **Identify Central Issues** Explain how the issue of income inequality influenced the 2012 presidential election.

>> America's civic unity and ethnic diversity continue to be a source of strength as young Americans look to the future.

12.4 As the twenty-first century dawned, American society looked very different from the way it had during the previous century. It also faced different challenges. As the nation entered the new millennium, it sought ways to preserve its heritage while at the same time adapting to rapid social, political, and technological change.

Bounce to Activate Flipped Video

>> Objectives

Analyze the causes and effects of immigration on American society.

Summarize the causes and effects of changing demographics.

Discuss the environmental issues facing Americans.

Explain the effects of communications technology on the economy.

Understand the issues Americans face in the 21st century.

>> Key Terms

Immigration Act of
   1990
bilingual education
Immigration Reform
   and Control Act of
   1986
affirmative action
Violence Against
   Women Act
privatizing
Oprah Winfrey

Americans Look to the Future

Immigration Changes American Society

It is often said that the United States is a nation of immigrants. Over the centuries, American protection of religious and personal freedom, along with opportunities for social and economic mobility, has attracted huge numbers of immigrants, both legal and illegal. Such a steady flow of immigrants has ensured that American demographics are in a state of constant change. Over time, however, the nature of immigration has changed.

Expanding Immigration For years, the government limited immigration to mainly northern and western Europeans. In the 1960s, however, laws began to relax immigration limitations. The **Immigration Act of 1990** increased quotas by 40 percent and eased most remaining restrictions. As a result, the period from the 1990s to the 2000s saw the largest numbers of immigrants in the country's history. During that time, almost one million immigrants arrived in America each year from all over the globe, representing a wide variety of cultures and religions. Today, immigrants account for more than 10 percent of the total American population. This large-scale immigration during the twentieth century has helped expand religious pluralism in the United States and California.

Latinos Exert Their Influence Most of the new immigrants were Latinos. In 2000, 27 percent of the total immigrant population were Mexicans, with people from the Caribbean and Central America making up almost 17 percent. Mexicans and Central Americans settled largely in the South and Southwest. Caribbean immigrants, many of them Cubans, settled in Florida. The census of 2000 showed that a third or more of the residents of Texas, New Mexico, Arizona, and California were Latinos.

Like all immigrants, Latinos have varying educational and employment backgrounds. Often they are forced to take lower-paying jobs with no benefits. However, Latino immigrants have had a profound social, cultural, and political impact. By 2001, Latinos held about 5,000 political offices and 4 percent of the seats in Congress, primarily as Democrats. Cuban Americans in Florida, generally Republican, have had an enormous influence on American political policy concerning Cuba.

The Growing Asian Population Asians make up the second-largest source of the new immigration. In 2000, they were nearly 23 percent of the total immigrant population, with the largest numbers coming from China, the Philippines, and India. The majority of Asian immigrants have settled in California, adding to the large Asian population in that state.

Overall, Asian immigrants have the highest level of education. Some came to America with college degrees and marketable skills and found professional jobs. Others came from war-torn countries, with very little education.

Effects of Immigration on American Society Immigration has long been debated in this country. People who would restrict it worry that immigrants take jobs and social services away from native-born Americans. They generally oppose **bilingual education**, in which students are taught in their native languages as well as in English, as they believe that immigrants should learn English in order to assimilate into American society. Proponents point out that immigrants contribute to the economy, often by taking jobs no one else wants. They also argue that with the U.S. birthrate falling, immigrants help the country by maintaining its population.

Sources of Immigration, 2000–2010

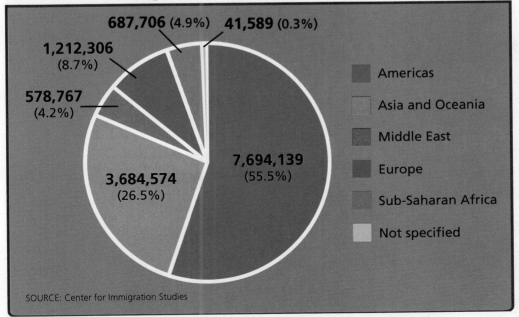

SOURCE: Center for Immigration Studies

>> **Analyze Graphs** Given what you've learned about immigration during the early 20th Century, how have the sources of immigration to the U.S. changed over the last 100 years?

Much of the debate concerns illegal immigrants. A large number of immigrants to the United States, especially Latinos, have come illegally. They labor in low-paying jobs, such as migrant farmwork, and receive no benefits. The goal of the **Immigration Reform and Control Act of 1986** was to stop the flow of immigrants who were entering the country illegally by penalizing employers who hired them and by granting resident status to those living in the United States since 1982. But immigrants still regularly cross U.S. borders illegally. How to treat these unauthorized workers is an ongoing debate. In 2008, the Bush administration proposed changes that would make it easier for farm employers to legally hire immigrant workers. Bush also proposed a process by which immigrants who entered illegally or whose visitation documents expired could eventually gain citizenship.

Immigration reform became a significant political issue again in 2013. A new comprehensive immigration reform bill brought before Congress provided a conditional path to citizenship for many of the estimated 11 million undocumented immigrants already living in the country.

It also provided money to secure the borders against future illegal immigration as well as strategies for fixing various aspects of visa programs. But while the bill passed in the Senate, the House of Representatives declined to vote on it. House Republicans were not in favor of the bill.

Activism in California By the 2000s, the status of Mexican-Americans and Mexican immigration became a national political discussion. In California Latino/as became the largest ethnic group in 2010, and Latino/a children comprised more than 51 percent of public school students. It was within this context that the Latino/a community became increasingly politically active.

☑ **GENERATE EXPLANATIONS** Why do some Americans oppose bilingual education?

American Demographics in Transition

At the beginning of 2000, Americans were on the move more than ever. Coastal cities as well as the Sunbelt, or the region of warm southern and southwestern states, saw rapid population and economic growth as people left the cold Northeast and the Rust Belt. Meanwhile, the family itself was changing.

New and Diverse Families In 1960, more than 70 percent of American households were headed by a

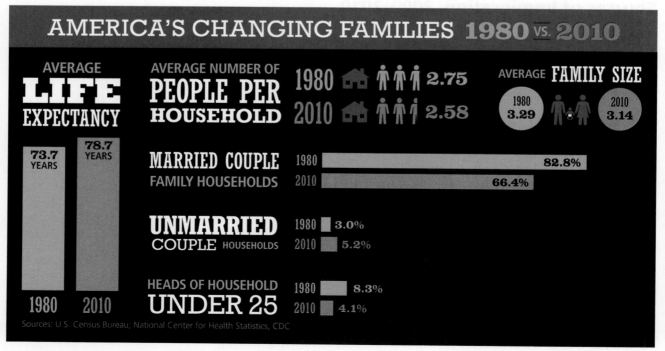

AMERICA'S CHANGING FAMILIES 1980 vs. 2010

AVERAGE **LIFE** EXPECTANCY

73.7 YEARS — 1980
78.7 YEARS — 2010

AVERAGE NUMBER OF **PEOPLE PER HOUSEHOLD**

1980 — 2.75
2010 — 2.58

AVERAGE **FAMILY SIZE**
1980 — 3.29
2010 — 3.14

MARRIED COUPLE FAMILY HOUSEHOLDS
1980 — 82.8%
2010 — 66.4%

UNMARRIED COUPLE HOUSEHOLDS
1980 — 3.0%
2010 — 5.2%

HEADS OF HOUSEHOLD **UNDER 25**
1980 — 8.3%
2010 — 4.1%

Sources: U.S. Census Bureau; National Center for Health Statistics, CDC

>> **Analyze Data** Using the information in the graphs, describe how the American family has changed over the past several decades.

working father and a nonworking mother, neither of whom had ever been divorced. By 2000, fewer than 15 percent of households fit this model.

In 2000, one out of every two marriages ended in divorce, and in a high percentage of households both parents worked outside the home. Single-parent households were far more common, with a quarter of all children growing up in a single-parent household. The number of children born to unmarried mothers also rose. In 1960, only 5 percent of children were born out of wedlock. In 2011, one out of every four white babies, one out of every three Latino babies, and two out of every three African American babies were born to unmarried mothers.

Debating and Challenging Affirmative Action In the 1960s, President Johnson introduced the idea of **affirmative action**, or improving opportunities for women and minorities by giving preference to them in school admissions and job applications. Since that time, affirmative action has been hotly debated. Proponents argue that without such initiatives, minorities cannot overcome discrimination. Opponents say that the policy is unfair and that one of its unintended consequences is that it discriminates against nonminorities. In California Proposition 209 of 1996, Californians voted to end affirmative action in state hiring and education.

That same year, a federal court struck down an affirmative action admissions program at the University of Texas. In 2003, however, the Supreme Court decided in two cases involving the University of Michigan that while race could not be the deciding factor in admissions, it could be one of several factors. One of these cases was *Grutter* v. *Bollinger*, in which it was decided that such considerations did not constitute a quota system.

In 2013, the Supreme Court allowed affirmative action to survive in college admissions *Fisher* v. *University of Texas* but imposed a tough legal standard, ruling that schools must prove that "available, workable race-neutral alternatives" are failing before race can be taken into account in admission decisions. The case was sent back to a federal appeals court for review.

During this same session, the Court heard a case that tests whether voters can ban affirmative action programs through a referendum. The successful referendum at issue in this case was passed in Michigan in 2006, and it was a backlash to the University of Michigan rulings in 2003.

Expanding and Protecting the Rights of All Americans Social advocacy groups such as the

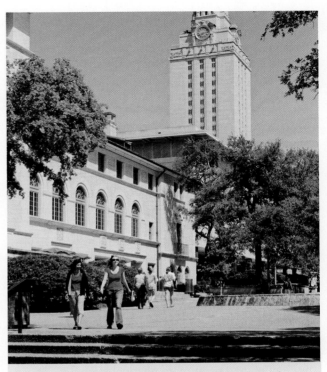

>> Supreme Court cases involving the University of Michigan and the University of Texas continue to explore the role race plays in college admission policies.

National Association for the Advancement of Colored People (NAACP) and the National Organization for Women (NOW) continued the fight to ensure African Americans and women continued to make social and political gains. By 2002, 33 percent of African American families enjoyed incomes of at least $50,000, placing them in the middle class. Also in 2002, 17 percent of African Americans over the age of 25 held bachelor's degrees. At the same time, legislation to enforce equal pay for equal work, address child-care needs for working women, and end sexual harassment in the workplace has improved the lives of working women. Outside of the world of work, women have also achieved victories. Issues such as spouse abuse and date rape are now widely discussed. Incidents of violence against women are more often reported and more often punished than ever before. The 1994 **Violence Against Women Act** increased federal resources to apprehend and prosecute men guilty of violent acts against women.

Civil rights are also expanding for members of the Lesbian, Gay, Bisexual, and Transgender Community (LGBT), helped by social and political advocacy organizations such as the Human Rights Campaign, the National Gay and Lesbian Task Force and Lambda Legal. In 2011, the ban against openly gay service members in the U.S. military was lifted. An increasing number of states and towns have passed laws against anti-gay discrimination. In 2013 a major supreme court case, the *United States* v. *Windsor*, resulted in the Supreme Court striking down part of a law that banned federal recognition of same-sex marriages. Soon after this, another Supreme Court ruling (*Obergefell* v. *Hodges*) made same-sex marriage legal throughout the nation. These rulings mean that married same-sex couples are now entitled to the same rights enjoyed by heterosexual married couples. These rights include Social Security benefits, hospital visitation rights, healthcare benefits, and military family benefits. However, despite these advances, LGBT people still have no federal law to protect them from discrimination in housing or employment.

An Aging Population While the life expectancy of an American born in 1900 was less than 50 years, an American born in 2011 can expect to live to age 79. By 2000, older Americans tended to retire earlier, live longer, and exert more political influence. These factors have strained the country's social welfare system, especially Social Security and Medicare. In 1960, the federal government spent less than $100 billion on social welfare. By 2013, the amount had increased to $1.9 trillion.

With the large baby-boom generation reaching retirement age, the issue of elder care has become critical. Falling birthrates over the past two decades have meant that when the huge population of baby boomers retires, there will not be enough workers to cover their Social Security benefits. Politicians have been debating this impending reality.

In his second term, President Bush called for **privatizing** Social Security by allowing younger workers to invest some of their earnings in individual retirement accounts. Critics defeated the measure, saying that it would put younger workers at the mercy of fluctuating stock market returns without addressing the shortfall of funds. Today the debate continues.

☑ **DESCRIBE** why politicians have been debating the issue of Social Security.

Energy and the Environment

On June 25, 2013, President Obama addressed an audience at Georgetown University on the subject of the environment. Briefly mentioning that the twelve warmest years in recorded history had occurred over the course of the previous fifteen years, he focused on the problems of global warming:

> Last year, temperatures in some areas of the ocean reached record highs, and ice in the Arctic shrank to its smallest size on record—faster than most models had predicted it would. These are facts.

—President Obama, Georgetown University, June 25, 2013

President Obama's Climate Action Plan

EPA REGULATORY GOALS	
• Speed up the process of implementing regulations on greenhouse gas emissions	• Work with foreign, state, and local governments to solve issues
• Issue flexible regulations to individual states to help reduce emissions	• Improve the EPA's internal management and workforce
• Replace use of hydrofluorcarbons (HFCs) in the United States with alternatives	• Empower communities to advance the cause of environmental protection
• Promote scientific research and development	• Support the Presidential Council for an Advanced Energy Economy

SOURCE: Presidential Climate Action Project

>> **Analyze Information** How would President Obama's Climate Action Plan lower carbon-based emissions?

Coastal areas of the United States will be under threat if, as many scientists predict, the warming of the atmosphere leads to a rise in sea levels. In low-lying areas of Florida, high tides are already leading to periodic flooding, especially in cities such as Miami. With Florida heavily dependent on tourism, an increase in sea levels could seriously affect the state's economy. In Hawaii, there is concern that sea levels, which have been rising for the last 100 years, may accelerate, threatening urban areas.

But global warming has implications far beyond rising seas. The Environmental Protection Agency reports that in Alaska, where the increase in warming temperatures is more than twice the warming in the rest of the United States, forest wildfires are increasing, while sea ice is decreasing. Lakes are changing size, and permafrost is thawing. This melting permafrost, which may lead to ground subsidence, is a direct threat to transportation networks and buildings.

Legislating to Protect the Environment In recent years, environmental issues have aroused political controversy. Some deny that our planet is experiencing a period of warming temperatures. Others, while accepting global warming as fact, deny that such warming is the product of human activity. Those who believe that human activity is the cause of global warming have urged the federal government to move forcefully to pass environmental legislation. But given the variety of opinion on environmental matters, it is not surprising that government regulations have attracted plenty of opposition. The main argument against environmental legislation is that it hurts the economy and the nation's industries.

During the Obama administration, regulations were passed to control emissions from power plants, prompting many coal industry officials to condemn the administration for waging a "war on coal." Many Republicans also criticized Obama's efforts to support renewable energy. When Donald Trump became president, he attempted to roll back Obama's environmental efforts, signing an executive order limiting the government's enforcement of climate regulations. Trump claimed that this would help protect American jobs.

The Environment and Local Economies

Environmental issues have become controversial largely because the environment is closely tied to local economies. The continental United States can be divided into four main environmental regions: the West, the South, the Northeast, and the Midwest. In the West, water is an important environmental and

>> Wind farms, like this one near Palm Springs, California, can produce electricity without releasing harmful carbon-based emissions, although some claim such farms are dangerous to wildlife.**Check Understanding** Are there any negative aspects of wind power?

Bounce to Activate Gallery

economic issue because it is so scarce. Population growth and drought put pressure on this important resource, which must be shared by private homes and businesses. Recent periods of drought in California, which supplies produce to the nation, have had a dramatic effect on the state's farming economy.

The West is also a region with vast tracts of land owned by the federal government. The government's management of this land touches issues of mining, logging, grazing and other development. In recent years the opening up of oil and gas development on public land has become a controversial issue.

Other regions face different environmental issues. The 2010 Deepwater Horizon spill in the Gulf of Mexico created environmental problems along the coast of many Southern states. In the Midwest, the Keystone XL pipeline project has attracted protesters and litigation to stop it. This pipeline, which would transport crude oil from Canada to the oil refineries of the Gulf of Mexico, was opposed by President Obama but approved by President Trump. Critics have condemned this project for its possible damage to the environment, while the project's supporters promise that it will bring jobs and a reliable oil supply.

Recycling and Green Architecture The environmental movement has achieved victories at a local level. These have often focused on the strategy of "reduce, reuse, recycle" to conserve resources and decrease the amount of waste going into landfills. State and local governments drive recycling efforts. Several states have a deposit policy on recyclable cans and glass bottles to encourage recycling.

The 2000s also saw increased interest in "green architecture," or architecture that integrates technology with environmental concerns to lessen the human impact on the environment. Green buildings might feature recycled materials, increased insulation to reduce heating and cooling energy use, and alternative sources of energy, such as solar or wind power.

As buildings become more energy-efficient, environmental groups are working to make cities healthier places to live. After decades of urban decline, American cities have become safer and more prosperous, attracting new residents and businesses. Larger concentrations of population means less dependence on cars, as more commuters walk or use public transportation. Parks are being restored and waterways cleaned. In many places,

>> Crops are grown on the top of this "green" building in the Brooklyn Navy Yards in New York City. The produce is sold to local restaurants and grocers and at farmers' markets.

Bounce to Activate 3D Model

urban agriculture is taking off, providing local residents with fresh produce.

☑ **EXPLAIN** What is "green architecture"?

President Trump Changes Course

During the 2016 election campaign, Donald Trump promised to set the nation on a very different course. The first months of Mr. Trump's presidency were marked by a host of executive orders and attempts to repeal and replace the Affordable Care Act.

Immigration and Refugees In January 2017, President Trump issued executive orders expanding the use of detention, limiting access to asylum, increasing enforcement along the U.S.-Mexico border, and authorizing the building of a wall along that border. Trump also limited the number of refugees entering the U.S. and tried to suspend the issuance of visas to nationals from several Muslim-majority countries. Courts across the country have forced adjustments to this "travel ban."

Supreme Court Success Despite resistance from Democrats, Neil Gorsuch, President Trump's nominee to the Supreme Court, took over the seat vacated by the late conservative justice Antonin Scalia.

Attack on Regulations Claiming that environmental regulations stifled economic growth, President Trump issued an executive order that allowed coal mining on federal lands and revoked Obama-era orders meant to curb climate change. Trump permitted work to proceed on the Keystone XL pipeline, which would transport crude oil from Canada to oil refineries near the Gulf of Mexico. On June 1, 2017, Trump announced that the U.S. would withdraw from the Paris climate agreement.

Trump also attacked Obama-era financial regulations, ordering the heads of regulatory agencies to come up with ideas for changing regulations in order to foster growth.

New Trade Policies Trump issued an executive order withdrawing U.S. participation in the TPP (Trans-Pacific Partnership) and threatened to pull out of NAFTA, the free trade deal with Canada and Mexico. Such policies are designed to bring back jobs by encouraging a rebirth of U.S. manufacturing.

Healthcare Reform Although disagreements among Republican factions in Congress doomed the first attempt to repeal and replace the Affordable Care Act, The Republican party succeeded in getting a new version of its healthcare bill (called the American Health Care Act) approved by the House of Representatives. However, this bill failed to gain enough votes in the Senate.

Resistance Grows The combination of Trump's electoral victory and Republican control of Congress triggered huge political opposition on the left. Even before Mr. Trump took office, civil rights organizations were reporting a surge in financial donations. On the day after the inauguration, millions of demonstrators swamped cities nationwide to support women's rights and oppose the president's agenda. Grassroots activism continued in the months after the inauguration, and a number of "sanctuary cities" promised to resist efforts to deport immigrants. With both the executive and the legislative branches of the government in Republican hands, Democrats saw the judiciary as the only branch of government to act as a check on the administration's plans.

☑ **DESCRIBE** How did President Trump's agenda differ from that of President Obama?

Technology Transforms Life

Digital technology in the form of cellphones, laptops, and tablet devices have all brought about rapid change in our way of life and have improved our standard of living. The microchips that were developed for computers have become essential components of modern televisions, CD players, VCRs, fax machines, dishwashers, refrigerators, washing machines, and hundreds of other appliances. This technology helps to regulate traffic, entertain millions of people, and facilitate shopping through home shopping sites.

Computers, telephone and satellite communications have shaped the economic development of the United States. Technological innovation has also created new industries and employment opportunities at home, while increasing the competitiveness of American products in world markets. Various technological and management innovations such as robotics and computer management allow American companies to produce high-tech exports including computers,

>> Manufacturing increasingly relies on robotics to produce goods.

pharmaceuticals, electrical machinery, and scientific instruments, as well as products for the aerospace industry. In the years to come, America's renewable-energy industry may surpass China's. The United States is now profiting from its solar, wind, and smart-grid technology exports. That's good news for the American economy and for the planet!

Mobile Technology Connects America and the World A revolution in information technology is underway as technology transforms the ways we obtain information. More and more people are getting their news online rather than through traditional print media. This has led to major disruptions and transformations in the media industry. The information revolution is not only limited to world news. We can now access social media sites for information about friends or celebrities. Never in human history has so much information been so easily obtained.

Meanwhile, technology is also changing the way we gain access to entertainment. Music, movies, and television shows can be retrieved in seconds on a personal computer linked to the Internet or with a smart phone. At times it seems as if streaming videos and podcasts are helping the Internet replace television as our main entertainment machine. But the Internet is also spreading that entertainment wider than television ever could, by making

American culture accessible to much of the world's population. Through films and videos, American freedoms and economic opportunities are being broadcast to a growing audience worldwide. This trend is not without its dangers, as it has provoked violent reactions from radical groups who fear that local culture and traditions are being overwhelmed by American political and social ideals.

The American civic values of religious tolerance, respect for diversity, and freedom of speech are particularly threatening to extremists worldwide. Many foreign governments are also alarmed by this diffusion of American culture. But the open nature of the Internet has made it difficult for authoritarian regimes to block the flow of information.

Advances in Science The application of scientific discoveries and technological innovations by the free enterprise system continues to improve the standard of living in the United States. Just as American high-tech research has made the country the leader in computer and other digital technology, American research and development laboratories have ensured that the country remains on the cutting-edge of medical and scientific innovation. No country spends more on medical research, and none has introduced more advances in the field. In particular, new research in genetics is opening up promising new possibilities for the treatment of cancer and other ailments. Genetic research will lead to safer pharmaceutical drugs.

Today, Americans have a wider range of medical options than ever before. From heart, kidney, and other organ transplants to microsurgery using micro video and fiber-optic cameras, American advanced medical treatment is the envy of the world. In addition, such American companies as Johnson & Johnson, Merck, Eli Lilly, and Pfizer have ensured that the United States leads the world in pharmaceutical innovation.

Concerns and Hopes Americans today are concerned about jobs and the solvency of long-term entitlement programs such as Social Security and Medicare, In addition, the nation is passing through a confusing time of rapid technological change. The revolution in digital and information technologies is comparable to the earlier industrial revolutions of the eighteenth and nineteenth centuries. These eras of change were characterized by disruption, anxiety, and fears but also by hopes and opportunities. Americans today are particularly worried about changing patterns of employment, and the growing strength of economic competitors. But the shifting

ground is also providing new perspectives and opportunities for innovation and entrepreneurship, activities that have always stood the nation in good stead. Throughout the country's history, America's resourcefulness and initiative have always been one of its greatest strengths.

The American ethos, or character, is made up of many other strengths that will continue to guarantee success in these changing times. U.S. citizens, whatever their origins or ancestry, hold a common bond in standing for certain self-evident truths. In a world torn apart by sectarian strife, America's great advantage lies in its religious and ethnic diversity and tolerance, and in its concept of a nation based not on a single, monolithic religious or ethnic identity but on civic virtues and ideals. These virtues and ideals are the foundation of the republic. In contrast to many other countries, whose governments retain power through brutal political repression, the American political system provides a unique advantage. American representative democracy allows great flexibility—to decide what policies to adopt or when to change political course. Unlike more authoritarian political systems, where only one party or group remains in control, America is open to diversity of thought and action and to peaceful political change. "We, the people" have the civic and patriotic responsibility to participate in this democratic process, and the commitment to political education and voting is a reflection of this patriotism.

In a very real sense, Americans work together to make a "more perfect union." These are the civic ideals that will continue to ensure success in a changing world.

☑ **EXPLAIN** Why has the role of print media in daily life diminished in the 21st century?

☑ ASSESSMENT

1. **Generate Explanations** Explain how immigration has affected American society in recent decades.

2. **Describe** how the American family has changed.

3. **Identify Central Issues** Discuss new civil rights initiatives that have affected the United States.

4. **Compare Points of View** Compare and contrast opinions about environmental issues.

5. **Identify Cause and Effect** Explain how changes in technology have affected American culture.

Go online to PearsonSchool.com/CASS and use the texts, quizzes, interactivities, Interactive Reading Notepads, Flipped Videos, and other resources from this Topic to prepare for the Topic Test.

Etexts

Quizzes

Interactivities

Interactive Reading Notepads

Flipped Videos

While online you can also check the progress you've made learning the topic and course content by viewing your grades, test scores, and assignment status.

LESSON SUMMARIES

Use these Lesson Summaries, and the longer versions available online, to review the key ideas for each lesson in this Topic.

Lesson 1: America and the World Economy

In the 1990s, the United States was the world's sole superpower. The U.S. created a free trade zone in North America. Technological advances transformed working life and accelerated globalization. America continued shifting to a service economy as manufacturing industries declined. Labor unions grew weaker and wages continued to fall.

Lesson 2: The George W. Bush Presidency

The results of the 2000 presidential election were disputed. In Florida the vote was very close. The Supreme Court intervened and George W. Bush won. Bush attempted to improve education but Democrats resisted his attempts to reform Social Security. On September 11, 2001, terrorists from the group al Qaeda attacked the United States. Bush declared a war on terrorism, and the U.S. invaded first Afghanistan and then Iraq. In 2008 a major financial crisis began.

Lesson 3: The Barack Obama Presidency

In 2008, Barack Obama was elected as the first African American President. Obama ended the U.S. military mission in Iraq and introduced national health care reform. Although the American economy remained sluggish, Obama won reelection in 2010.

Lesson 4: Americans Look to the Future

At the beginning of the twenty-first century, immigration continues to change American society and remains a controversial issue. Civil rights are expanding for many Americans. Environmental concerns remain an important political issue, while technology continues its transformation of all aspects of life.

VISUAL REVIEW

Use these graphics to review some of the key terms, people, and ideas from this Topic.

Events in the Clinton and George W. Bush Presidencies

PRESIDENT	EVENT
Bill Clinton	• 1992 Signed NAFTA; sent forces into Somalia • 1993 Signed Brady Bill; helped negotiate Declaration of Principles • 1994 Sent troops to Haiti • 1995 Sent forces into Bosnia as part of NATO • 1996 Signed bill to reform welfare • 1999 Impeached; cleared of charges
George W. Bush	• 2001 Pushed for major tax cuts; sent troops to war in Afghanistan; signed Patriot Act • 2002 Signed No Child Left Behind Act • 2003 Sent troops to war in Iraq • 2004 Bush reelected

Issues of Concern for Americans in the 2000s

Technology	Computers, satellites, and advances in agriculture raise productivity and efficiency, but challenge many workers and industries.
Globalization	Globalization brings consumers more choices and opportunities, but can result in the loss of American jobs.
Terrorism	As terrorist attacks increase worldwide, government must work to make America more secure.
Immigration	Although immigrants enrich American society and fuel its economy, their increasing numbers spark debate.
Demographics	Federal and local governments must find ways to support older Americans, Americans on the move, and nontraditional families.

Environmental Concerns and Debates

- global warming
- destruction of natural habitat
- rising population straining resources
- oil spills
- fracking
- environmental legislation hurting economy and industry

KEY TERMS, PEOPLE, AND IDEAS

1. How has technology increased **globalization**?

2. What role do **multinational corporations** play in the global economy?

3. Why wasn't the Electoral College vote able to determine the outcome of the 2000 Presidential election?

4. What effect did the al Qaeda attacks of September 11, 2001 have on the American people and economy?

5. Why did American forces overthrow the **Taliban** in Afghanistan?

6. Why did the Bush administration invade Iraq?

7. What were the goals of the **Tea Party Movement**?

8. How did the **Immigration Act of 1990** change U.S. demographics?

9. Why are there growing concerns about Social Security benefits?

CRITICAL THINKING

10. **Identify Cause and Effect** (a.) Why has the nature of the American economy changed? (b.) What kinds of jobs are available to American workers?

11. **Cite Evidence** How did the "war on terror" affect domestic security?

12. **Summarize** (a.) What issues were addressed by *Hamdan* v. *Rumsfeld*? (b.) How did the Supreme Court rule in this case?

13. **Evaluate Information** (a.) Why did President Obama introduce the Patient Protection and Affordable Care Act? (b.) Why did many oppose it?

14. **Draw Inferences** What areas of the United States are most threatened by climate change?

15. **Make Generalizations** Why are some environmental issues so controversial?

16. **Analyze Graphs** Study the Graph below. (a.) Identify the largest source of immigration. (b.) Explain why so many have come from this region.

Sources of Immigration, 2000–2010

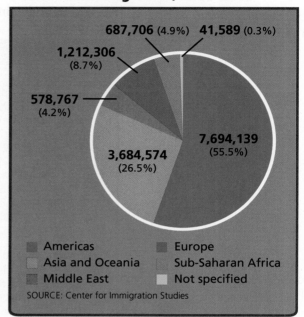

687,706 (4.9%)   41,589 (0.3%)

1,212,306 (8.7%)

578,767 (4.2%)

7,694,139 (55.5%)

3,684,574 (26.5%)

- Americas
- Asia and Oceania
- Middle East
- Europe
- Sub-Saharan Africa
- Not specified

SOURCE: Center for Immigration Studies

17. **Writing Activity: Use Primary Sources** Evaluate how this excerpt from President Barack Obama's second inaugural address outlines his political views. Use the excerpt below and your knowledge of Obama's programs and policies.

> But we have always understood that when times change, so must we; that fidelity to our founding principles requires new responses to new challenges; that preserving our individual freedoms ultimately requires collective action. For the American people can no more meet the demands of today's world by acting alone than American soldiers could have met the forces of fascism or communism with muskets and militias. No single person can train all the math and science teachers we'll need to equip our children for the future, or build the roads and networks and research labs that will bring new jobs and businesses to our shores. Now, more than ever, we must do these things together, as one nation and one people.
>
> —*Barack Obama, January 21, 2013*

DOCUMENT-BASED QUESTIONS

The War in Iraq was a controversial event both nationally and internationally. Read the documents below, then answer the questions that follow.

DOCUMENT A

This excerpt is from a contemporary newspaper editorial.

> Mr. Bush's "Plan for Victory" speech was, of course, the usual unadulterated nonsense. Its overarching theme—"We will never accept anything less than complete victory"—was being contradicted even as he spoke by rampant reports of Pentagon plans for stepped-up troop withdrawals. . . . The specifics were phony, too. Once again inflating the readiness of Iraqi troops, Mr. Bush claimed that the recent assault on Tal Afar "was primarily led by Iraqi security forces"—a fairy tale immediately unmasked by Michael Ware, a Time reporter embedded in the battle's front lines, as "completely wrong."
>
> —Frank Rich, The New York Times, December 11, 2005

DOCUMENT B

The photograph shows a toppled statue in Iraq after the U.S.-led invasion.

DOCUMENT C

This excerpt is from an address by Donald Rumsfeld, Secretary of Defense under Bush.

> It's a strange time:
> - . . . when a senior editor at Newsweek, disparagingly refers to the brave volunteers in our armed forces . . . as a "mercenary army;"
> - When the former head of CNN accuses the American military of deliberately targeting journalists. . . .
>
> Those who know the truth need to speak out against these kinds of myths and distortions that are being told about our troops and about our country.

America is not what's wrong with the world.
> —Donald Rumsfeld, Address at the American Legion National Convention, August 29, 2006

DOCUMENT D

In this excerpt from a lecture, Amy Goodman, a journalist, examines media coverage of the war.

> Fairness and Accuracy in Reporting did a study. In the week leading up to General Colin Powell going to the Security Council to make his case for the invasions and the week afterwards—this was the period where more than half of the people in this country were opposed to an invasion—they did a study of . . . the four major newscasts. Two weeks. Three hundred and ninety-three interviews on war. Three were anti-war voices. Three of almost four hundred, and that included PBS. . . . [T]hey have to provide the diversity of opinion that fully expresses the debate and the anguish and the discussions that are going on all over this country. That is media serving a democratic society.
>
> —Amy Goodman, "Independent Media in a Time of War," April 21, 2003

18. In Document A, the writer claims that Bush's statements about the Iraq War are
   A. too optimistic to be true.
   B. the result of misinformation.
   C. a reliable source of information about the war.
   D. not revealing the truth about the situation.

19. **Analyze Photographs** Discuss the significance of the photograph shown in Document B.

20. In Document C, the media is characterized as
   A. biased in favor of the war.
   B. biased against the military.
   C. supportive of the enemy.
   D. influenced by foreign media.

21. In Document D, the speaker believes the media
   A. was too supportive of the administration.
   B. should have been supporting the war effort.
   C. was gagged by the Bush administration.
   D. was too favorable to the enemy.

22. **Writing Activity: Primary Source** Write a paragraph explaining why you think the Iraq War remains so controversial. Use the sources as well as additional information you have learned about this conflict.

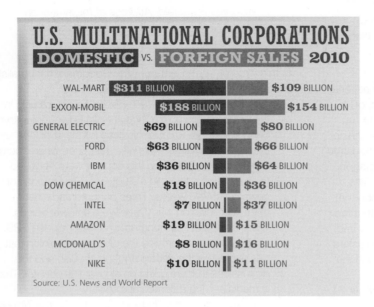

U.S. MULTINATIONAL CORPORATIONS
DOMESTIC vs. FOREIGN SALES 2010

	DOMESTIC	FOREIGN
WAL-MART	$311 BILLION	$109 BILLION
EXXON-MOBIL	$188 BILLION	$154 BILLION
GENERAL ELECTRIC	$69 BILLION	$80 BILLION
FORD	$63 BILLION	$66 BILLION
IBM	$36 BILLION	$64 BILLION
DOW CHEMICAL	$18 BILLION	$36 BILLION
INTEL	$7 BILLION	$37 BILLION
AMAZON	$19 BILLION	$15 BILLION
MCDONALD'S	$8 BILLION	$16 BILLION
NIKE	$10 BILLION	$11 BILLION

Source: U.S. News and World Report

1 Based on this graph, what statement below best describes the impact of U.S. multinational corporations on the 21st century economy?

A Manufacturing and selling goods worldwide is a better idea for electronics companies than it is for retail outlets.

B Manufacturing and selling goods worldwide has benefited the American automobile industry, but not the oil and gas industry.

C Manufacturing and selling goods worldwide has increased productivity and sales, sometimes more internationally than nationally.

D Manufacturing and selling goods worldwide has led to a decrease in retail and gas sales, but has increased domestic sales of food and athletic equipment.

2 Why did Ralph Nader's run as a candidate for the Green Party affect the 2000 presidential election in the United States?

F Nader wanted to deprive the Democrats of votes.

G The Green Party wanted him to win votes that would otherwise have gone to the Republican candidate.

H The Green Party wanted to make a point by attracting votes from both parties.

I Green Party concerns were not being addressed by either of the major parties.

Signed by 140 nations

Did not place emission limits on developing nations

KYOTO PROTOCOL

Went into effect 2005

Aimed to control global warming linked to greenhouse gases

3 Despite its important goal and worldwide support, why did President George W. Bush refuse to honor the Kyoto Protocol treaty?

A Because the treaty put undue emphasis on the United States and Europe, it undermined the economy of the free world.

B He did not believe the United States had a problem with greenhouse gases, and limiting them would harm U.S. manufacturers.

C The treaty was negotiated and signed by Bush's predecessor in office, and Bush wanted to bring his own views on climate control to the table.

D Because it did not place emission limits on all countries, he believed it could hurt the U.S. economy and undermine the sovereignty of the United States.

> *If there is anyone out there who still doubts that America is a place where all things are possible, who still wonders if the dream of our founders is alive in our time, who still questions the power of our democracy, tonight is your answer.*
>
> —*Barack Obama, November 2008*

4 How might many Americans have interpreted this statement?

F Americans elected Barack Obama, the youngest president ever to serve.

G The Republicans named Sarah Palin as the first female vice-presidential candidate.

H Americans elected Barack Obama, the United States' first African American president.

I Congress passed the Dream Act, allowing rights to the children of undocumented immigrants.

If you have trouble with...				
Question	1	2	3	4
See Lesson	12.1	12.2	12.2	12.3

5 How has recent immigration affected the demographics of the United States?

A Latino immigrants now hold more than ten percent of Congressional seats.

B Most Asian immigrants are now choosing to live in Midwestern cities and suburbs.

C Immigration to the United States has declined lately due to the troubled economy.

D Immigrants now account for more than ten percent of the population of the United States.

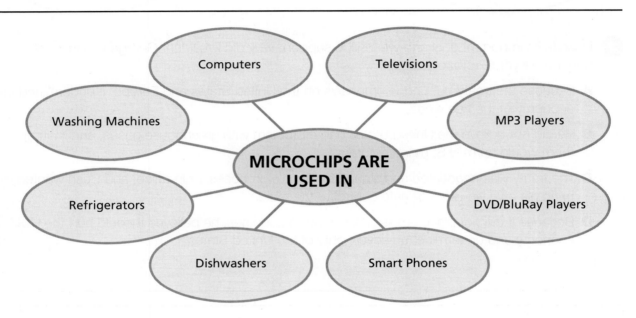

6 How does this concept web support the idea that free enterprise drives technological innovations?

F Computers have made it easier to develop new technology without the expense of building scale models and running lengthy tests.

G As the price of computer chips dropped, the companies that make the appliances that use them can collect higher profits from their sale.

H The U.S. government has pledged to subsidize computer-related research to add more high-profile manufacturing jobs to the economy.

I Profit motives have inspired entrepreneurs, inventors, and researchers to compete to develop new technology and find new uses for existing technology.

7 Which of the following might represent a liberal point of view?

A Government should support a free, unregulated market.

B Government intervention is necessary to help the needy.

C Citizens should solve their own problems through individual effort.

D Private organizations should take responsibility for solving social problems.

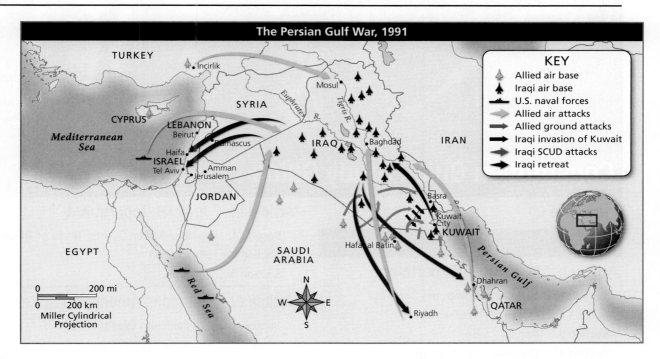

The Persian Gulf War, 1991

KEY
- Allied air base
- Iraqi air base
- U.S. naval forces
- Allied air attacks
- Allied ground attacks
- Iraqi invasion of Kuwait
- Iraqi SCUD attacks
- Iraqi retreat

8 During the Persian Gulf War, what explains the location of most Allied air bases?

F to avoid travel through Iranian air space

G to protect Turkey and Israel

H to provide cover for advancing Allied troops

I to shorten flying times and protect Saudi Arabia

If you have trouble with...				
Question	5	6	7	8
See Lesson	12.4	12.4	11.1	11.4

Stock Connection Blue/Alamy

Constitution Quick Study Guide

Preamble

Articles

The Preamble states the broad purposes the Constitution is intended to serve—to establish a government that provides for greater cooperation among the States, ensures justice and peace, provides for defense against foreign enemies, promotes the general well-being of the people, and secures liberty now and in the future. The phrase We the People emphasizes the twin concepts of popular sovereignty and of representative government.

Legislative Department

Section 1. Legislative power; Congress

Congress, the nation's lawmaking body, is bicameral in form; that is, it is composed of two houses: the Senate and the House of Representatives. The Framers of the Constitution purposely separated the lawmaking power from the power to enforce the laws (Article II, the Executive Branch) and the power to interpret them (Article III, the Judicial Branch). This system of separation of powers is supplemented by a system of checks and balances; that is, in several provisions the Constitution gives to each of the three branches various powers with which it may restrain the actions of the other two branches.

Section 2. House of Representatives

▶ **Clause 1. Election** Electors means voters. Members of the House of Representatives are elected every two years. Each State must permit the same persons to vote for United States representatives as it permits to vote for the members of the larger house of its own legislature. The 17th Amendment (1913) extends this requirement to the qualification of voters for United States senators.

▶ **Clause 2. Qualifications** A member of the House of Representatives must be at least 25 years old, an American citizen for seven years, and a resident of the State he or she represents. In addition, political custom requires that a representative also reside in the district from which he or she is elected.

▶ **Clause 3. Apportionment** The number of representatives each State is entitled to is based on its population, which is counted every 10 years in the census. Congress reapportions the seats among the States after each census. In the Reapportionment Act of 1929, Congress fixed the permanent size of the House at 435 members with each State having at least one representative. Today there is one House seat for approximately every 700,000 persons in the population.

The words "three-fifths of all other persons" referred to slaves and reflected the Three-Fifths Compromise reached by the Framers at Philadelphia in 1787; the phrase was made obsolete, was in effect repealed, by the 13th Amendment in 1865.

---

* The gray words indicate portions of the Constitution altered by subsequent amendments to the document.

▶ **Clause 4. Vacancies** The executive authority refers to the governor of a State. If a member leaves office or dies before the expiration of his or her term, the governor is to call a special election to fill the vacancy.

United States Constitution

PREAMBLE

We the People of the United States, in Order to form a more perfect Union, establish Justice, insure domestic Tranquility, provide for the common defence, promote the general Welfare, and secure the Blessings of Liberty to ourselves and our Posterity, do ordain and establish this Constitution for the United States of America.

Article I.

Section 1.

All legislative Powers herein granted shall be vested in a Congress of the United States, which shall consist of a Senate and House of Representatives.

Section 2.

▶ 1. The House of Representatives shall be composed of Members chosen every second Year by the People of the several States, and the Electors in each State shall have the Qualifications requisite for Electors of the most numerous Branch of the State Legislature.

▶ 2. No Person shall be a Representative who shall not have attained to the age of twenty-five Years, and been seven Years a Citizen of the United States, and who shall not, when elected, be an Inhabitant of that State in which he shall be chosen.

▶ 3. Representatives and direct Taxes* shall be apportioned among the several States which may be included within this Union, according to their respective Numbers, which shall be determined by adding to the whole Number of free Persons, including those bound to Service for a Term of Years and excluding Indians not taxed, three fifths of all other Persons. The actual Enumeration shall be made within three Years after the first Meeting of the Congress of the United States, and within every subsequent term of ten Years, in such Manner as they shall by Law direct. The Number of Representatives shall not exceed one for every thirty Thousand, but each State shall have at Least one Representative; and, until such enumeration shall be made, the State of New Hampshire shall be entitled to choose three, Massachusetts eight, Rhode Island and Providence Plantations one, Connecticut five, New York six, New Jersey four, Pennsylvania eight, Delaware one, Maryland six, Virginia ten, North Carolina five, South Carolina five, and Georgia three.

▶ 4. When vacancies happen in the Representation from any State, the Executive Authority thereof shall issue Writs of Election to fill such Vacancies.

5. The House of Representatives shall choose their Speaker and other Officers; and shall have the sole Power of Impeachment.

Section 3.

1. The Senate of the United States shall be composed of two Senators from each State chosen by the Legislature thereof for six Years; and each Senator shall have one Vote.

2. Immediately after they shall be assembled in Consequences of the first Election, they shall be divided, as equally as may be, into three Classes. The Seats of the Senators of the first Class shall be vacated at the Expiration of the second Year; of the second Class, at the Expiration of the fourth Year; and of the third Class, at the Expiration of the sixth Year; so that one-third may be chosen every second Year; and if Vacancies happen by Resignation, or otherwise, during the Recess of the Legislature of any State, the Executive thereof may make temporary Appointments until the next Meeting of the Legislature, which shall then fill such Vacancies.

3. No Person shall be a Senator who shall not have attained to the Age of thirty Years, and been nine Years a Citizen of the United States, and who shall not, when elected, be an Inhabitant of that State for which he shall be chosen.

4. The Vice President of the United States shall be President of the Senate but shall have no Vote, unless they be equally divided.

5. The Senate shall choose their other Officers, and also a President pro tempore, in the Absence of the Vice President, or when he shall exercise the Office of President of the United States.

6. The Senate shall have the sole Power to try all Impeachments. When sitting for that Purpose, they shall be on Oath or Affirmation. When the President of the United States is tried, the Chief Justice shall preside: And no Person shall be convicted without the Concurrence of two thirds of the Members present.

7. Judgment in Cases of Impeachment shall not extend further than to removal from Office, and disqualification to hold and enjoy any Office of honor, Trust, or Profit under the United States: but the Party convicted shall nevertheless be liable and subject to Indictment, Trial, Judgment and Punishment, according to Law.

▶ **Clause 5. Officers; impeachment** The House elects a Speaker, customarily chosen from the majority party in the House. Impeachment means accusation. The House has the exclusive power to impeach, or accuse, civil officers; the Senate (Article I, Section 3, Clause 6) has the exclusive power to try those impeached by the House.

Section 3. Senate

▶ **Clause 1. Composition, election, term** Each State has two senators. Each serves for six years and has one vote. Originally, senators were not elected directly by the people, but by each State's legislature. The 17th Amendment, added in 1913, provides for the popular election of senators.

▶ **Clause 2. Classification** The senators elected in 1788 were divided into three groups so that the Senate could become a "continuing body." One-third of the Senate's seats are up for election every two years.

The 17th Amendment provides that a Senate vacancy is to be filled at a special election called by the governor; State law may also permit the governor to appoint a successor to serve until that election is held.

▶ **Clause 3. Qualifications** A senator must be at least 30 years old, a citizen for at least nine years, and must live in the State from which elected.

▶ **Clause 4. Presiding officer** The Vice President presides over the Senate, but may vote only to break a tie.

▶ **Clause 5. Other officers** The Senate chooses its own officers, including a president pro tempore to preside when the Vice President is not there.

▶ **Clause 6. Impeachment trials** The Senate conducts the trials of those officials impeached by the House. The Vice President presides unless the President is on trial, in which case the Chief Justice of the United States does so. A conviction requires the votes of two-thirds of the senators present.

No President has ever been convicted. In 1868 the House voted eleven articles of impeachment against President Andrew Johnson, but the Senate fell one vote short of convicting him. In 1974 President Richard M. Nixon resigned the presidency in the face of almost certain impeachment by the House. The House brought two articles of impeachment against President Bill Clinton in late 1998. Neither charge was supported by even a simple majority vote in the Senate, on February 12, 1999.

▶ **Clause 7. Penalty on conviction** The punishment of an official convicted in an impeachment case has always been removal from office. The Senate can also bar a convicted person from ever holding any federal office, but it is not required to do so. A convicted person can also be tried and punished in a regular court for any crime involved in the impeachment case.

Section 4. Elections and Meetings

▶ **Clause 1.** **Election In 1842** Congress required that representatives be elected from districts within each State with more than one seat in the House. The districts in each State are drawn by that State's legislature. Seven States now have only one seat in the House: Alaska, Delaware, Montana, North Dakota, South Dakota, Vermont, and Wyoming. The 1842 law also directed that representatives be elected in each State on the same day: the Tuesday after the first Monday in November of every even-numbered year. In 1914 Congress also set that same date for the election of senators.

▶ **Clause 2.** **Sessions Congress** must meet at least once a year. The 20th Amendment (1933) changed the opening date to January 3.

Section 5. Legislative Proceedings

▶ **Clause 1.** **Admission of members; quorum** In 1969 the Supreme Court held that the House cannot exclude any member-elect who satisfies the qualifications set out in Article I, Section 2, Clause 2.

A majority in the House (218 members) or Senate (51) constitutes a quorum. In practice, both houses often proceed with less than a quorum present. However, any member may raise a point of order (demand a "quorum call"). If a roll call then reveals less than a majority of the members present, that chamber must either adjourn or the sergeant at arms must be ordered to round up absent members.

▶ **Clause 2.** **Rules** Each house has adopted detailed rules to guide its proceedings. Each house may discipline members for unacceptable conduct; expulsion requires a two-thirds vote.

▶ **Clause 3.** **Record** Each house must keep and publish a record of its meetings. The Congressional Record is published for every day that either house of Congress is in session, and provides a written record of all that is said and done on the floor of each house each session.

▶ **Clause 4.** **Adjournment** Once in session, neither house may suspend (recess) its work for more than three days without the approval of the other house. Both houses must always meet in the same location.

Section 4.

▶ 1. The Times, Places and Manner of holding Elections for Senators and Representatives, shall be prescribed in each State by the Legislature thereof; but the Congress may at any time by law make or alter such Regulations, except as to the Places of choosing Senators.

▶ 2. The Congress shall assemble at least once in every Year, and such Meeting shall be on the first Monday in December, unless they shall by Law appoint a different Day.

Section 5.

▶ 1. Each House shall be the Judge of the Elections, Returns and Qualifications of its own Members, and a Majority of each shall constitute a Quorum to do Business; but a smaller Number may adjourn from day to day, and may be authorized to compel the Attendance of absent Members, in such Manner, and under such Penalties, as each House may provide.

▶ 2. Each House may determine the Rules of its Proceedings, punish its Members for disorderly Behavior, and, with the Concurrence of two thirds, expel a Member.

▶ 3. Each House shall keep a Journal of its Proceedings, and from time to time publish the same, excepting such Parts as may in their Judgment require Secrecy; and the Yeas and Nays of the Members of either House on any question shall, at the Desire of one fifth of those Present, be entered on the Journal.

▶ 4. Neither House, during the Session of Congress, shall, without the Consent of the other, adjourn for more than three days, nor to any other Place than that in which the two Houses shall be sitting.

Section 6.

▶ 1. The Senators and Representatives shall receive a Compensation for their Services, to be ascertained by Law, and paid out of the Treasury of the United States. They shall in all Cases, except Treason, Felony, and Breach of the Peace, be privileged from Arrest during their Attendance at the Session of their respective Houses, and in going to and returning from the same; and for any Speech or Debate in either House, they shall not be questioned in any other Place.

▶ 2. No Senator or Representative shall, during the Time for which he was elected, be appointed to any civil Office under the Authority of the United States, which shall have been created, or the Emoluments whereof shall have been increased during such time; and no Person holding any Office under the United States, shall be a Member of either House during his Continuance in Office.

Section 7.

▶ 1. All Bills for raising Revenue shall originate in the House of Representatives; but the Senate may propose or concur with amendments as on other Bills.

▶ 2. Every Bill which shall have passed the House of Representatives and the Senate, shall, before it become a law, be presented to the President of the United States: If he approve, he shall sign it, but if not he shall return it, with his Objections to that House in which it shall have originated, who shall enter the Objections at large on their Journal, and proceed to reconsider it. If after such Reconsideration two thirds of the House shall agree to pass the Bill, it shall be sent, together with the Objections, to the other House, by which it shall likewise be reconsidered, and if approved by two thirds of that House, it shall become a Law. But in all such Cases the Votes of both Houses shall be determined by Yeas and Nays, and the Names of the Persons voting for and against the Bill shall be entered on the Journal of each House respectively. If any Bill shall not be returned by the President within ten Days (Sunday excepted) after it shall have been presented to him, the Same shall be a law, in like Manner as if he had signed it, unless the Congress by their Adjournment, prevent its Return, in which Case it shall not be a Law.

▶ 3. Every Order, Resolution, or Vote to which the Concurrence of the Senate and House of Representatives may be necessary (except on a question of adjournment) shall be presented to the President of the United States; and before the Same shall take Effect, shall be approved by him, or, being disapproved by him, shall be repassed by two thirds of the Senate and House of Representatives, according to the Rules and Limitations prescribed in the Case of a Bill.

Section 6. Compensation, Immunities, and Disabilities of Members

▶ **Clause 1. Salaries; immunities** Each house sets its members' salaries, paid by the United States; the 27th Amendment (1992) modified this pay-setting power. This provision establishes "legislative immunity." The purpose of this immunity is to allow members to speak and debate freely in Congress itself. Treason is strictly defined in Article III, Section 3. A felony is any serious crime. A breach of the peace is any indictable offense less than treason or a felony; this exemption from arrest is of little real importance today.

▶ **Clause 2. Restrictions on office holding** No sitting member of either house may be appointed to an office in the executive or in the judicial branch if that position was created or its salary was increased during that member's current elected term. The second part of this clause—forbidding any person serving in either the executive or the judicial branch from also serving in Congress—reinforces the principle of separation of powers.

Section 7. Revenue Bills, President's Veto

▶ **Clause 1. Revenue bills** All bills that raise money must originate in the House. However, the Senate has the power to amend any revenue bill sent to it from the lower house.

▶ **Clause 2. Enactment of laws; veto** Once both houses have passed a bill, it must be sent to the President. The President may (1) sign the bill, thus making it law; (2) veto the bill, whereupon it must be returned to the house in which it originated; or (3) allow the bill to become law without signature, by not acting upon it within 10 days of its receipt from Congress, not counting Sundays. The President has a fourth option at the end of a congressional session: If he does not act on a measure within 10 days, and Congress adjourns during that period, the bill dies; the "pocket veto" has been applied to it. A presidential veto may be overridden by a two-thirds vote in each house.

▶ **Clause 3. Other measures** This clause refers to joint resolutions, measures Congress often passes to deal with unusual, temporary, or ceremonial matters. A joint resolution passed by Congress and signed by the President has the force of law, just as a bill does. As a matter of custom, a joint resolution proposing an amendment to the Constitution is not submitted to the President for signature or veto. Concurrent and simple resolutions do not have the force of law and, therefore, are not submitted to the President.

Section 8. Powers of Congress

▶ **Clause 1.** The 18 separate clauses in this section set out 27 of the many expressed powers the Constitution grants to Congress. In this clause Congress is given the power to levy and provide for the collection of various kinds of taxes, in order to finance the operations of the government. All federal taxes must be levied at the same rates throughout the country.

▶ **Clause 2.** Congress has power to borrow money to help finance the government. Federal borrowing is most often done through the sale of bonds on which interest is paid. The Constitution does not limit the amount the government may borrow.

▶ **Clause 3.** This clause, the Commerce Clause, gives Congress the power to regulate both foreign and interstate trade. Much of what Congress does, it does on the basis of its commerce power.

▶ **Clause 4.** Congress has the exclusive power to determine how aliens may become citizens of the United States. Congress may also pass laws relating to bankruptcy.

▶ **Clause 5.** has the power to establish and require the use of uniform gauges of time, distance, weight, volume, area, and the like.

▶ **Clause 6.** Congress has the power to make it a federal crime to falsify the coins, paper money, bonds, stamps, and the like of the United States.

▶ **Clause 7.** Congress has the power to provide for and regulate the transportation and delivery of mail; "post offices" are those buildings and other places where mail is deposited for dispatch; "post roads" include all routes over or upon which mail is carried.

▶ **Clause 8.** Congress has the power to provide for copyrights and patents. A copyright gives an author or composer the exclusive right to control the reproduction, publication, and sale of literary, musical, or other creative work. A patent gives a person the exclusive right to control the manufacture or sale of his or her invention.

▶ **Clause 9.** Congress has the power to create the lower federal courts, all of the several federal courts that function beneath the Supreme Court.

▶ **Clause 10.** Congress has the power to prohibit, as a federal crime: (1) certain acts committed outside the territorial jurisdiction of the United States, and (2) the commission within the United States of any wrong against any nation with which we are at peace.

Section 8.

The Congress shall have Power

▶ 1. To lay and collect Taxes, Duties, Imposts and Excises to pay the Debts and provide for the common Defence and general Welfare of the United States; but all Duties, Imposts and Excises, shall be uniform throughout the United States;

▶ 2. To borrow Money on the credit of the United States;

▶ 3. To regulate Commerce with foreign Nations, and among the several States, and with the Indian Tribes;

▶ 4. To establish an uniform Rule of Naturalization, and uniform Laws on the subject of Bankruptcies throughout the United States;

▶ 5. To coin Money, regulate the Value thereof, and of foreign Coin, and fix the Standard of Weights and Measures;

▶ 6. To provide for the Punishment of counterfeiting the Securities and current Coin of the United States;

▶ 7. To establish Post Offices and post Roads;

▶ 8. To promote the Progress of Science and useful Arts, by securing, for limited Times to Authors and Inventors the exclusive Right to their respective Writings and Discoveries;

▶ 9. To constitute Tribunals inferior to the supreme Court;

▶ 10. To define and punish Piracies and Felonies committed on the high Seas, and Offences against the Law of nations;

▶ 11. To declare War, grant Letters of Marque and Reprisal, and make Rules concerning Captures on Land and Water;

▶ 12. To raise and support Armies; but no Appropriation of Money to that Use shall be for a longer Term than two Years;

▶ 13. To provide and maintain a Navy;

▶ 14. To make Rules for the Government and Regulation of the land and naval Forces;

▶ 15. To provide for calling forth the Militia to execute the Laws of the Union, suppress Insurrections and repel Invasions;

▶ 16. To provide for organizing, arming, and disciplining the Militia, and for governing such Part of them as may be employed in the Service of the United States, reserving to the States respectively the Appointment of the Officers, and the Authority of training the Militia according to the discipline prescribed by Congress;

▶ 17. To exercise exclusive Legislation in all Cases whatsoever, over such District (not exceeding ten Miles square) as may, by Cession of Particular States, and the Acceptance of Congress, become the Seat of the Government of the United States, and to exercise like Authority over all Places purchased by the Consent of the Legislature of the State in which the Same shall be, for the Erection of Forts, Magazines, Arsenals, Dockyards and other needful Buildings;— And

▶ 18. To make all Laws which shall be necessary and proper for carrying into Execution the foregoing Powers and all other Powers vested by this Constitution in the Government of the United States, or in any Department or Officer thereof.

Section 9.

▶ 1. The Migration or Importation of such Persons as any of the States now existing shall think proper to admit, shall not be prohibited by the Congress prior to the Year one thousand eight hundred and eight, but a Tax or duty may be imposed on such Importation, not exceeding ten dollars for each Person.

▶ **Clause 11.** Only Congress can declare war. However, the President, as commander in chief of the armed forces (Article II, Section 2, Clause 1), can make war without such a formal declaration. Letters of marque and reprisal are commissions authorizing private persons to outfit vessels (privateers) to capture and destroy enemy ships in time of war; they were forbidden in international law by the Declaration of Paris of 1856, and the United States has honored the ban since the Civil War.

▶ **Clauses 12 and 13.** Congress has the power to provide for and maintain the nation's armed forces. It established the air force as an independent element of the armed forces in 1947, an exercise of its inherent powers in foreign relations and national defense. The two-year limit on spending for the army insures civilian control of the military.

▶ **Clause 14.** Today these rules are set out in three principle statutes: the Uniform Code of Military Justice, passed by Congress in 1950, and the Military Justice Acts of 1958 and 1983.

▶ **Clauses 15 and 16.** In the National Defense Act of 1916, Congress made each State's militia (volunteer army) a part of the National Guard. Today, Congress and the States cooperate in its maintenance. Ordinarily, each State's National Guard is under the command of that State's governor; but Congress has given the President the power to call any or all of those units into federal service when necessary.

▶ **Clause 17.** In 1791 Congress accepted land grants from Maryland and Virginia and established the District of Columbia for the nation's capital. Assuming Virginia's grant would never be needed, Congress returned it in 1846. Today, the elected government of the District's 69 square miles operates under the authority of Congress. Congress also has the power to acquire other lands from the States for various federal purposes.

▶ **Clause 18.** This is the Necessary and Proper Clause, also often called the Elastic Clause. It is the constitutional basis for the many and far-reaching implied powers of the Federal Government.

Section 9. Powers Denied to Congress

▶ **Clause 1.** The phrase "such persons" referred to slaves. This provision was part of the Commerce Compromise, one of the bargains struck in the writing of the Constitution. Congress outlawed the slave trade in 1808.

Clause 2. A writ of habeas corpus, the "great writ of liberty," is a court order directing a sheriff, warden, or other public officer, or a private person, who is detaining another to "produce the body" of the one being held in order that the legality of the detention may be determined by the court.

Clause 3. A bill of attainder is a legislative act that inflicts punishment without a judicial trial. See Article I, Section 10, and Article III, Section 3, Clause 2. An ex post facto law is any criminal law that operates retroactively to the disadvantage of the accused. See Article I, Section 10.

Clause 4. A capitation tax is literally a "head tax," a tax levied on each person in the population. A direct tax is one paid directly to the government by the taxpayer—for example, an income or a property tax; an indirect tax is one paid to another private party who then pays it to the government—for example, a sales tax. This provision was modified by the 16th Amendment (1913), giving Congress the power to levy "taxes on incomes, from whatever source derived."

Clause 5. This provision was a part of the Commerce Compromise made by the Framers in 1787. Congress has the power to tax imported goods, however.

Clause 6. All ports within the United States must be treated alike by Congress as it exercises its taxing and commerce powers. Congress cannot tax goods sent by water from one State to another, nor may it give the ports of one State any legal advantage over those of another.

Clause 7. This clause gives Congress its vastly important "power of the purse," a major check on presidential power. Federal money can be spent only in those amounts and for those purposes expressly authorized by an act of Congress. All federal income and spending must be accounted for, regularly and publicly.

Clause 8. This provision, preventing the establishment of a nobility, reflects the principle that "all men are created equal." It was also intended to discourage foreign attempts to bribe or otherwise corrupt officers of the government.

Section 10. Powers Denied to the States

Clause 1. The States are not sovereign governments and so cannot make agreements or otherwise negotiate with foreign states; the power to conduct foreign relations is an exclusive power of the National Government. The power to coin money is also an exclusive power of the National Government. Several powers forbidden to the National Government are here also forbidden to the States.

Clause 2. This provision relates to foreign, not interstate, commerce. Only Congress, not the States, can tax imports; and the States are, like Congress, forbidden the power to tax exports.

2. The Privilege of the Writ of Habeas Corpus shall not be suspended, unless when in Cases of Rebellion or Invasion the public safety may require it.

3. No Bill of Attainder or ex post facto Law shall be passed.

4. No Capitation, or other direct, Tax shall be laid, unless in Proportion to the Census of Enumeration hereinbefore directed to be taken.

5. No Tax or Duty shall be laid on Articles exported from any State.

6. No Preference shall be given by any Regulation of Commerce or Revenue to the Ports of one State over those of another: nor shall Vessels bound to, or from, one State, be obliged to enter, clear or pay Duties in another.

7. No Money shall be drawn from the Treasury, but in Consequence of Appropriations made by Law; and a regular Statement and Account of the Receipts and Expenditures of all public Money shall be published from time to time.

8. No Title of Nobility shall be granted by the United States: And no Person holding any Office of Profit or Trust under them, shall, without the Consent of the Congress, accept of any present, Emolument, Office, or Title, of any kind whatever, from any King, Prince, or foreign State.

Section 10.

1. No State shall enter into any Treaty, Alliance, or Confederation; grant Letters of Marque and Reprisal; coin Money; emit Bills of Credit; make any Thing but gold and silver Coin a Tender in Payment of Debts; pass any Bill of Attainder, ex post facto Law, or Law impairing the Obligation of Contracts, or grant any Title of Nobility.

2. No State shall, without the Consent of the Congress, lay any Imposts or Duties on Imports or Exports, except what may be absolutely necessary for executing its inspection Laws; and the net Produce of all Duties and Imposts, laid by any State on Imports or Exports, shall be for the Use of the Treasury of the United States; and all such Laws shall be subject to the Revision and Control of the Congress.

3. No State shall, without the Consent of Congress, lay any Duty of Tonnage, keep Troops, or Ships of War in time of Peace, enter into any Agreement or Compact with another State, or with a foreign Power, or engage in War, unless actually invaded, or in such imminent Danger as will not admit of delay.

Article II
Section 1.

▶ 1. The executive Power shall be vested in a President of the United States of America. He shall hold his Office during the Term of four Years, and, together with the Vice President, chosen for the same Term, be elected as follows:

▶ 2. Each State shall appoint, in such Manner as the Legislature thereof may direct, a Number of Electors, equal to the whole Number of Senators and Representatives to which the State may be entitled in the Congress: but no Senator or Representative, or Person holding an Office of Trust or Profit, under the United States, shall be appointed an Elector.

▶ 3. The Electors shall meet in their respective States, and vote by Ballot for two Persons, of whom one at least shall not be an Inhabitant of the same State with themselves. And they shall make a List of all the Persons voted for, and of the Number of Votes for each; which List they shall sign and certify, and transmit sealed to the Seat of the Government of the United States, directed to the President of the Senate. The President of the Senate shall, in the Presence of the Senate and House of Representatives, open all the Certificates, and the Votes shall then be counted. The Person having the greatest Number of Votes shall be the President, if such Number be a majority of the whole Number of Electors appointed; and if there be more than one who have such Majority, and have an equal Number of Votes, then, the House of Representatives shall immediately choose by Ballot one of them for President; and if no Person have a Majority, then from the five highest on the List the said House shall in like Manner choose the President. But in choosing the President, the Votes shall be taken by States, the Representatives from each State having one Vote; a quorum for this Purpose shall consist of a Member or Members from two thirds of the States, and a Majority of all the States shall be necessary to a Choice. In every Case, after the Choice of the President, the Person having the greatest Number of Votes of the Electors shall be the Vice President. But if there should remain two or more who have equal Votes, the Senate shall choose from them by Ballot the Vice President.

▶ **Clause 3.** A duty of tonnage is a tax laid on ships according to their cargo capacity. Each State has a constitutional right to provide for and maintain a militia; but no State may keep a standing army or navy. The several restrictions here prevent the States from assuming powers that the Constitution elsewhere grants to the National Government.

Executive Department
Section 1. President and Vice President

▶ **Clause 1. Executive power, term** This clause gives to the President the very broad "executive power," the power to enforce the laws and otherwise administer the public policies of the United States. It also sets the length of the presidential (and vice-presidential) term of office; see the 22nd Amendment (1951), which places a limit on presidential (but not vice-presidential) tenure.

▶ **Clause 2. Electoral college** This clause establishes the "electoral college," although the Constitution does not use that term. It is a body of presidential electors chosen in each State, and it selects the President and Vice President every four years. The number of electors chosen in each State equals the number of senators and representatives that State has in Congress.

▶ **Clause 3. Election of President and Vice President** This clause was replaced by the 12th Amendment in 1804.

Clause 4. Date Congress has set the date for the choosing of electors as the Tuesday after the first Monday in November every fourth year, and for the casting of electoral votes as the Monday after the second Wednesday in December of that year.

Clause 5. Qualifications The President must have been born a citizen of the United States, be at least 35 years old, and have been a resident of the United States for at least 14 years.

Clause 6. Vacancy This clause was modified by the 25th Amendment (1967), which provides expressly for the succession of the Vice President, for the filling of a vacancy in the Vice Presidency, and for the determination of presidential inability.

Clause 7. Compensation The President now receives a salary of $400,000 and a taxable expense account of $50,000 a year. Those amounts cannot be changed during a presidential term; thus, Congress cannot use the President's compensation as a bargaining tool to influence executive decisions. The phrase "any other emolument" means, in effect, any valuable gift; it does not mean that the President cannot be provided with such benefits of office as the White House, extensive staff assistance, and much else.

Clause 8. Oath of office The Chief Justice of the United States regularly administers this oath or affirmation, but any judicial officer may do so. Thus, Calvin Coolidge was sworn into office in 1923 by his father, a justice of the peace in Vermont.

Section 2. President's Powers and Duties

Clause 1. Military, civil powers The President, a civilian, heads the nation's armed forces, a key element in the Constitution's insistence on civilian control of the military. The President's power to "require the opinion, in writing" provides the constitutional basis for the Cabinet. The President's power to grant reprieves and pardons, the power of clemency, extends only to federal cases.

▶4. The Congress may determine the Time of choosing the Electors, and the Day on which they shall give their Votes; which Day shall be the same throughout the United States.

▶5. No Person except a natural born Citizen, or a Citizen of the United States, at the time of the Adoption of this Constitution, shall be eligible to the Office of President; neither shall any person be eligible to that Office who shall not have attained to the Age of thirty-five Years, and been fourteen Years a Resident within the United States.

▶6. In Case of the Removal of the President from Office, or of his Death, Resignation, or Inability to discharge the Powers and Duties of the said Office, the Same shall devolve on the Vice President, and the Congress may by Law provide for the Case of Removal, Death, Resignation or Inability, both of the President and Vice President, declaring what Officer shall then act as President, and such Officer shall act accordingly, until the Disability be removed, or a President shall be elected.

▶7. The President shall, at stated Times, receive for his Services, a Compensation, which shall neither be increased nor diminished during the Period for which he shall have been elected, and he shall not receive within that Period any other Emolument from the United States, or any of them.

▶8. Before he enter on the Execution of his Office, he shall take the following Oath or Affirmation:
"I do solemnly swear (or affirm) that I will faithfully execute the Office of President of the United States, and will to the best of my Ability, preserve, protect and defend the Constitution of the United States."

Section 2.

▶1. The President shall be Commander in Chief of the Army and Navy of the United States, and of the Militia of the several States, when called into the actual Service of the United States; he may require the Opinion, in writing, of the principal Officer in each of the executive Departments, upon any Subject relating to the Duties of their respective Offices, and he shall have Power to Grant Reprieves and Pardons for Offences against the United States, except in Cases of Impeachment.

2. He shall have Power, by and with the Advice and Consent of the Senate, to make Treaties, provided two thirds of the Senators present concur; and he shall nominate, and by and with the Advice and Consent of the Senate, shall appoint Ambassadors, other public Ministers and Consuls, Judges of the supreme Court, and all other Officers of the United States, whose Appointments are not herein otherwise provided for, and which shall be established by Law: but the Congress may by Law vest the Appointment of such inferior Officers, as they think proper, in the President alone, in the Courts of Law, or in the Heads of Departments.

3. The President shall have Power to fill up all Vacancies that may happen during the Recess of the Senate, by granting Commissions which shall expire at the End of their next Session.

Section 3.

He shall from time to time give to the Congress Information of the State of the Union, and recommend to their Consideration such Measures as he shall judge necessary and expedient; he may, on extraordinary Occasions, convene both Houses, or either of them, and in Case of Disagreement between them, with Respect to the Time of Adjournment, he may adjourn them to such Time as he shall think proper; he shall receive Ambassadors and other public Ministers; he shall take Care that the Laws be faithfully executed, and shall Commission all the Officers of the United States.

Section 4.

The President, Vice President and all Civil Officers of the United States, shall be removed from Office on Impeachment for and Conviction of, Treason, Bribery, or other high Crimes and Misdemeanors.

Article III

Section 1.

The judicial Power of the United States, shall be vested in one supreme Court, and in such inferior Courts as the Congress may from time to time ordain and establish. The Judges, both of the supreme and inferior Courts, shall hold their Offices during good Behaviour, and shall, at stated Times, receive for their Services, a Compensation, which shall not be diminished during their Continuance in Office.

▶ **Clause 2. Treaties, appointments** The President has the sole power to make treaties; to become effective, a treaty must be approved by a two-thirds vote in the Senate. In practice, the President can also make executive agreements with foreign governments; these pacts, which are frequently made and usually deal with routine matters, do not require Senate consent. The President appoints the principal officers of the executive branch and all federal judges; the "inferior officers" are those who hold lesser posts.

▶ **Clause 3. Recess appointments** When the Senate is not in session, appointments that require Senate consent can be made by the President on a temporary basis, as "recess appointments." Recess appointments are valid only to the end of the congressional term in which they are made.

Section 3. President's Powers and Duties

The President delivers a State of the Union Message to Congress soon after that body convenes each year. That message is delivered to the nation's lawmakers and, importantly, to the American people, as well. It is shortly followed by the proposed federal budget and an economic report; and the President may send special messages to Congress at any time. In all of these communications, Congress is urged to take those actions the Chief Executive finds to be in the national interest. The President also has the power: to call special sessions of Congress; to adjourn Congress if its two houses cannot agree for that purpose; to receive the diplomatic representatives of other governments; to insure the proper execution of all federal laws; and to empower federal officers to hold their posts and perform their duties.

Section 4. Impeachment

The Constitution outlines the impeachment process in Article I, Section 2, Clause 5 and in Section 3, Clauses 6 and 7.

Judicial Department

Section 1. Judicial Power, Courts, Terms of Office

The judicial power conferred here is the power of federal courts to hear and decide cases, disputes between the government and individuals and between private persons (parties). The Constitution creates only the Supreme Court of the United States; it gives to Congress the power to establish other, lower federal courts (Article I, Section 8, Clause 9) and to fix the size of the Supreme Court. The words "during good Behaviour" mean, in effect, for life.

Section 2. Jurisdiction

▶ **Clause 1.** **Cases to be heard** This clause sets out the jurisdiction of the federal courts; that is, it identifies those cases that may be tried in those courts. The federal courts can hear and decide—have jurisdiction over—a case depending on either the subject matter or the parties involved in that case. The jurisdiction of the federal courts in cases involving States was substantially restricted by the 11th Amendment in 1795.

▶ **Clause 2.** **Supreme Court jurisdiction** Original jurisdiction refers to the power of a court to hear a case in the first instance, not on appeal from a lower court. Appellate jurisdiction refers to a court's power to hear a case on appeal from a lower court, from the court in which the case was originally tried. This clause gives the Supreme Court both original and appellate jurisdiction. However, nearly all of the cases the High Court hears are brought to it on appeal from the lower federal courts and the highest State courts.

▶ **Clause 3.** **Jury trial in criminal cases** A person accused of a federal crime is guaranteed the right to trial by jury in a federal court in the State where the crime was committed; see the 5th and 6th amendments. The right to trial by jury in serious criminal cases in the State courts is guaranteed by the 6th and 14th amendments.

Section 3. Treason

▶ **Clause 1.** **Definition** Treason is the only crime defined in the Constitution. The Framers intended the very specific definition here to prevent the loose use of the charge of treason—for example, against persons who criticize the government. Treason can be committed only in time of war and only by a citizen or a resident alien.

▶ **Clause 2.** **Punishment** Congress has provided that the punishment that a federal court may impose on a convicted traitor may range from a minimum of five years in prison and/or a $10,000 fine to a maximum of death; no person convicted of treason has ever been executed by the United States. No legal punishment can be imposed on the family or descendants of a convicted traitor. Congress has also made it a crime for any person (in either peace or wartime) to commit espionage or sabotage, to attempt to overthrow the government by force, or to conspire to do any of these things.

Section 2.

▶ 1. The judicial Power shall extend to all Cases, in Law and Equity, arising under this Constitution, the Laws of the United States, and Treaties made, or which shall be made, under their Authority;— to all Cases affecting Ambassadors, other public ministers, and Consuls;— to all Cases of Admiralty and maritime Jurisdiction;— to Controversies to which the United States shall be a Party;— to Controversies between two or more States;— between a State and Citizens of another State;— between Citizens of different States;— between Citizens of the same State claiming Lands under Grants of different States, and between a State, or the Citizens thereof, and foreign States, Citizens, or Subjects.

▶ 2. In all Cases affecting Ambassadors, other public Ministers and Consuls, and those in which a State shall be a Party, the supreme Court shall have original Jurisdiction. In all the other Cases before mentioned, the supreme Court shall have appellate Jurisdiction, both as to Law and Fact, with such Exceptions, and under such Regulations as the Congress shall make.

▶ 3. The trial of all Crimes, except in Cases of Impeachment, shall be by Jury; and such Trial shall be held in the State where the said Crimes shall have been committed; but when not committed within any State, the Trial shall be at such Place or Places as the Congress may by Law have directed.

Section 3.

▶ 1. Treason against the United States shall consist only in levying War against them, or in adhering to their Enemies, giving them Aid and Comfort. No Person shall be convicted of Treason unless on the Testimony of two Witnesses to the same overt Act, or on Confession in open Court.

▶ 2. The Congress shall have Power to declare the Punishment of Treason, but no Attainder of Treason shall work Corruption of Blood, or Forfeiture except during the Life of the Person attainted.

Article IV

Section 1.

Full Faith and Credit shall be given in each State to the public Acts, Records, and judicial Proceedings of every other State. And the Congress may by general Laws prescribe the Manner in which such Acts, Records and Proceedings shall be proved, and the Effect thereof.

Section 2.

▶ 1. The Citizens of each State shall be entitled to all Privileges and Immunities of Citizens in the several States.

▶ 2. A Person charged in any State with Treason, Felony, or other Crime, who shall flee from justice, and be found in another State, shall on Demand of the executive Authority of the State from which he fled, be delivered up, to be removed to the State having Jurisdiction of the Crime.

▶ 3. No Person held to Service or Labor in one State, under the Laws thereof, escaping into another, shall, in Consequence of any Law or Regulation therein, be discharged from Service or Labor, but shall be delivered up on Claim of the Party to whom such Service or Labor may be due.

Section 3.

▶ 1. New States may be admitted by the Congress into this Union; but no new State shall be formed or erected within the Jurisdiction of any other State; nor any State be formed by the Junction of two or more States, or Parts of States, without the Consent of the Legislatures of the States concerned as well as of the Congress.

▶ 2. The Congress shall have Power to dispose of and make all needful Rules and Regulations respecting the Territory or other Property belonging to the United States; and nothing in this Constitution shall be so construed as to Prejudice any Claims of the United States, or of any particular State.

Section 4.

The United States shall guarantee to every State in this Union a Republican Form of Government, and shall protect each of them against Invasion; and on Application of the Legislature, or of the Executive (when the Legislature cannot be convened) against domestic Violence.

Relations Among States

Section 1. Full Faith and Credit

Each State must recognize the validity of the laws, public records, and court decisions of every other State.

Section 2. Privileges and Immunities of Citizens

▶ **Clause 1. Residents of other States** In effect, this clause means that no State may discriminate against the residents of other States; that is, a State's laws cannot draw unreasonable distinctions between its own residents and those of any of the other States. See Section 1 of the 14th Amendment.

▶ **Clause 2. Extradition** The process of returning a fugitive to another State is known as "interstate rendition" or, more commonly, "extradition." Usually, that process works routinely; some extradition requests are contested however—especially in cases with racial or political overtones. A governor may refuse to extradite a fugitive; but the federal courts can compel an unwilling governor to obey this constitutional command.

▶ **Clause 3. Fugitive slaves** This clause was nullified by the 13th Amendment, which abolished slavery in 1865.

Section 3. New States; Territories

▶ **Clause 1. New States** Only Congress can admit new States to the Union. A new State may not be created by taking territory from an existing State without the consent of that State's legislature. Congress has admitted 37 States since the original 13 formed the Union. Five States—Vermont, Kentucky, Tennessee, Maine, and West Virginia—were created from parts of existing States. Texas was an independent republic before admission. California was admitted after being ceded to the United States by Mexico. Each of the other 30 States entered the Union only after a period of time as an organized territory of the United States.

▶ **Clause 2. Territory, property** Congress has the power to make laws concerning the territories, other public lands, and all other property of the United States.

Section 4. Protection Afforded to States by the Nation

The Constitution does not define "a republican form of government," but the phrase is generally understood to mean a representative government. The Federal Government must also defend each State against attacks from outside its border and, at the request of a State's legislature or its governor, aid its efforts to put down internal disorders.

Provisions for Amendment

This section provides for the methods by which formal changes can be made in the Constitution. An amendment may be proposed in one of two ways: by a two-thirds vote in each house of Congress, or by a national convention called by Congress at the request of two-thirds of the State legislatures. A proposed amendment may be ratified in one of two ways: by three-fourths of the State legislatures, or by three-fourths of the States in conventions called for that purpose. Congress has the power to determine the method by which a proposed amendment may be ratified. The amendment process cannot be used to deny any State its equal representation in the United States Senate. To this point, 27 amendments have been adopted. To date, all of the amendments except the 21st Amendment were proposed by Congress and ratified by the State legislatures. Only the 21st Amendment was ratified by the convention method.

National Debts, Supremacy of National Law, Oath

Section 1. Validity of Debts

Congress had borrowed large sums of money during the Revolution and later during the Critical Period of the 1780s. This provision, a pledge that the new government would honor those debts, did much to create confidence in that government.

Section 2. Supremacy of National Law

This section sets out the Supremacy Clause, a specific declaration of the supremacy of federal law over any and all forms of State law. No State, including its local governments, may make or enforce any law that conflicts with any provision in the Constitution, an act of Congress, a treaty, or an order, rule, or regulation properly issued by the President or his subordinates in the executive branch.

Section 3. Oaths of Office

This provision reinforces the Supremacy Clause; all public officers, at every level in the United States, owe their first allegiance to the Constitution of the United States. No religious qualification can be imposed as a condition for holding any public office.

Ratification of Constitution

The proposed Constitution was signed by George Washington and 37 of his fellow Framers on September 17, 1787. (George Read of Delaware signed for himself and also for his absent colleague, John Dickinson.)

Article V

The Congress, whenever two thirds of both Houses shall deem it necessary, shall propose Amendments to this Constitution, or, on the Application of the Legislatures of two thirds of the several States, shall call a Convention for proposing Amendments, which, in either Case, shall be valid to all Intents and Purposes, as Part of this Constitution, when ratified by the Legislatures of three fourths of the several States, or by Conventions in three fourths thereof, as the one or the other Mode of Ratification may be proposed by the Congress; Provided that no Amendment which may be made prior to the Year One thousand eight hundred and eight shall in any Manner affect the first and fourth Clauses in the Ninth section of the first Article; and that no State, without its Consent, shall be deprived of its equal Suffrage in the Senate.

Article VI

Section 1.

All Debts contracted and Engagements entered into, before the Adoption of this Constitution, shall be as valid against the United States under this Constitution, as under the Confederation.

Section 2.

This Constitution, and the Laws of the United States which shall be made in Pursuance thereof; and all Treaties made, or which shall be made, under the Authority of the United States, shall be the supreme Law of the Land; and the Judges in every State shall be bound thereby, anything in the constitution or Laws of any State to the Contrary notwithstanding.

Section 3.

The Senators and Representatives before mentioned, and the Members of the several State legislatures, and all executive and judicial Officers, both of the United States and of the several States, shall be bound by Oath or Affirmation, to support this Constitution; but no religious Test shall ever be required as a Qualification to any Office or public Trust under the United States.

Article VII

The ratification of the Conventions of nine States, shall be sufficient for the Establishment of this Constitution between the States so ratifying the same.

Done in Convention by the Unanimous Consent of the States present the Seventeenth Day of September in the Year of our Lord one thousand seven hundred and Eighty-seven and of the Independence of the United States of America the twelfth. In witness whereof We have hereunto subscribed our Names.

Attest:
William Jackson,
Secretary
George Washington,
*President and Deputy
from Virginia*

New Hampshire
John Langdon
Nicholas Gilman

Massachusetts
Nathaniel Gorham
Rufus King

Connecticut
William Samuel Johnson
Roger Sherman

New York
Alexander Hamilton

New Jersey
William Livingston
David Brearley
William Paterson
Jonathan Dayton

Pennsylvania
Benjamin Franklin
Thomas Mifflin
Robert Morris
George Clymer
Thomas Fitzsimons
Jared Ingersoll
James Wilson
Gouverneur Morris

Delaware
George Read
Gunning Bedford, Jr.
John Dickinson
Richard Bassett
Jacob Broom

Maryland
James McHenry
Daniel of St. Thomas
Jenifer
Daniel Carroll

Virginia
John Blair
James Madison, Jr.

North Carolina
William Blount
Richard Dobbs Spaight
Hugh Williamson

South Carolina
John Rutledge
Charles Cotesworth
Pinckney
Charles Pinckney
Pierce Butler

Georgia
William Few
Abraham Baldwin

The first 10 amendments, the Bill of Rights, were each proposed by Congress on September 25, 1789, and ratified by the necessary three-fourths of the States on December 15, 1791. These amendments were originally intended to restrict the National Government—not the States. However, the Supreme Court has several times held that most of their provisions also apply to the States, through the 14th Amendment's Due Process Clause.

1st Amendment. Freedom of Religion, Speech, Press, Assembly, and Petition

The 1st Amendment sets out five basic liberties: The guarantee of freedom of religion is both a protection of religious thought and practice and a command of separation of church and state. The guarantees of freedom of speech and press assure to all persons a right to speak, publish, and otherwise express their views. The guarantees of the rights of assembly and petition protect the right to join with others in public meetings, political parties, interest groups, and other associations to discuss public affairs and influence public policy. None of these rights is guaranteed in absolute terms, however; like all other civil rights guarantees, each of them may be exercised only with regard to the rights of all other persons.

2nd Amendment. Bearing Arms

The right of the people to keep and bear arms was insured by the 2nd Amendment.

3rd Amendment. Quartering of Troops

This amendment was intended to prevent what had been common British practice in the colonial period; see the Declaration of Independence. This provision is of virtually no importance today.

4th Amendment. Searches and Seizures

The basic rule laid down by the 4th Amendment is this: Police officers have no general right to search for or seize evidence or seize (arrest) persons. Except in particular circumstances, they must have a proper warrant (a court order) obtained with probable cause (on reasonable grounds). This guarantee is reinforced by the exclusionary rule, developed by the Supreme Court: Evidence gained as the result of an unlawful search or seizure cannot be used at the court trial of the person from whom it was seized.

5th Amendment. Criminal Proceedings; Due Process; Eminent Domain

A person can be tried for a serious federal crime only if he or she has been indicted (charged, accused of that crime) by a grand jury. No one may be subjected to double jeopardy—that is, tried twice for the same crime. All persons are protected against self-incrimination; no person can be legally compelled to answer any question in any governmental proceeding if that answer could lead to that person's prosecution. The 5th Amendment's Due Process Clause prohibits unfair, arbitrary actions by the Federal Government; a like prohibition is set out against the States in the 14th Amendment. Government may take private property for a legitimate public purpose; but when it exercises that power of eminent domain, it must pay a fair price for the property seized.

1st Amendment

Congress shall make no law respecting an establishment of religion, or prohibiting the free exercise thereof, or abridging the freedom of speech, or of the press; or the right of the people peaceably to assemble, and to petition the Government for a redress of grievances.

2nd Amendment

A well-regulated Militia being necessary to the security of a free State, the right of the people to keep and bear Arms, shall not be infringed.

3rd Amendment.

No Soldier shall, in time of peace be quartered in any house, without the consent of the Owner, nor, in time of war, but in a manner to be prescribed by law.

4th Amendment.

The right of the people to be secure in their persons, houses, papers, and effects, against unreasonable searches and seizures, shall not be violated, and no Warrants shall issue, but upon probable cause, supported by Oath or affirmation, and particularly describing the place to be searched, and the persons or things to be seized.

5th Amendment.

No person shall be held to answer for a capital, or otherwise infamous crime, unless on a presentment or indictment of a Grand Jury, except in cases arising in the land or naval forces, or in the Militia, when in actual service in time of War, or public danger; nor shall any person be subject for the same offence to be twice put in jeopardy of life or limb; nor shall be compelled in any criminal case to be a witness against himself, nor be deprived of life, liberty, or property, without due process of law; nor shall private property be taken for public use, without just compensation.

6th Amendment

In all criminal prosecutions, the accused shall enjoy the right to a speedy and public trial, by an impartial jury of the State and district wherein the crime shall have been committed, which district shall have been previously ascertained by law, and to be informed of the nature and cause of the accusation; to be confronted with the witnesses against him; to have compulsory process for obtaining witnesses in his favor, and to have the Assistance of Counsel for his defence.

7th Amendment

In Suits at common law, where the value in controversy shall exceed twenty dollars, the right of trial by jury shall be preserved, and no fact tried by a jury, shall be otherwise re-examined in any Court of the United States, than according to the rules of the common law.

8th Amendment

Excessive bail shall not be required, nor excessive fines imposed, nor cruel and unusual punishment inflicted.

9th Amendment

The enumeration in the Constitution, of certain rights, shall not be construed to deny or disparage others retained by the people.

10th Amendment

The powers not delegated to the United States by the Constitution, nor prohibited by it to the States, are reserved to the States respectively, or to the people.

6th Amendment. Criminal Proceedings

A person accused of crime has the right to be tried in court without undue delay and by an impartial jury; see Article III, Section 2, Clause 3. The defendant must be informed of the charge upon which he or she is to be tried, has the right to cross-examine hostile witnesses, and has the right to require the testimony of favorable witnesses. The defendant also has the right to be represented by an attorney at every stage in the criminal process.

7th Amendment. Civil Trials

This amendment applies only to civil cases heard in federal courts. A civil case does not involve criminal matters; it is a dispute between private parties or between the government and a private party. The right to trial by jury is guaranteed in any civil case in a federal court if the amount of money involved in that case exceeds $20 (most cases today involve a much larger sum); that right may be waived (relinquished, put aside) if both parties agree to a bench trial (a trial by a judge, without a jury).

8th Amendment. Punishment for Crimes

Bail is the sum of money that a person accused of crime may be required to post (deposit with the court) as a guarantee that he or she will appear in court at the proper time. The amount of bail required and/or a fine imposed as punishment must bear a reasonable relationship to the seriousness of the crime involved in the case. The prohibition of cruel and unusual punishment forbids any punishment judged to be too harsh, too severe for the crime for which it is imposed.

9th Amendment. Unenumerated Rights

The fact that the Constitution sets out many civil rights guarantees, expressly provides for many protections against government, does not mean that there are not other rights also held by the people.

10th Amendment. Powers Reserved to the States

This amendment identifies the area of power that may be exercised by the States. All of those powers the Constitution does not grant to the National Government, and at the same time does not forbid to the States, belong to each of the States, or to the people of each State.

11th Amendment. Suits Against States

Proposed by Congress March 4, 1794; ratified February 7, 1795, but official announcement of the ratification was delayed until January 8, 1798. This amendment repealed part of Article III, Section 2, Clause 1. No State may be sued in a federal court by a resident of another State or of a foreign country; the Supreme Court has long held that this provision also means that a State cannot be sued in a federal court by a foreign country or, more importantly, even by one of its own residents.

12th Amendment. Election of President and Vice President

Proposed by Congress December 9, 1803; ratified June 15, 1804. This amendment replaced Article II, Section 1, Clause 3. Originally, each elector cast two ballots, each for a different person for President. The person with the largest number of electoral votes, provided that number was a majority of the electors, was to become President; the person with the second highest number was to become Vice President. This arrangement produced an electoral vote tie between Thomas Jefferson and Aaron Burr in 1800; the House finally chose Jefferson as President in 1801. The 12th Amendment separated the balloting for President and Vice President; each elector now casts one ballot for someone as President and a second ballot for another person as Vice President. Note that the 20th Amendment changed the date set here (March 4) to January 20, and that the 23rd Amendment (1961) provides for electors from the District of Columbia. This amendment also provides that the Vice President must meet the same qualifications as those set out for the President in Article II, Section 1, Clause 5.

13th Amendment. Slavery and Involuntary Servitude

Proposed by Congress January 31, 1865; ratified December 6, 1865. This amendment forbids slavery in the United States and in any area under its control. It also forbids other forms of forced labor, except punishments for crime; but some forms of compulsory service are not prohibited—for example, service on juries or in the armed forces. Section 2 gives to Congress the power to carry out the provisions of Section 1 of this amendment.

11th Amendment

The Judicial power of the United States shall not be construed to extend to any suit in law or equity, commenced or prosecuted against one of the United States by Citizens of another State, or by Citizens or Subjects of any Foreign State.

12th Amendment

The Electors shall meet in their respective States and vote by ballot for President and Vice President, one of whom, at least, shall not be an inhabitant of the same State with themselves; they shall name in their ballots the person voted for as President, and in distinct ballots the person voted for as Vice President, and they shall make distinct lists of all persons voted for as President, and of all persons voted for as Vice President, and of the number of votes for each, which lists they shall sign and certify, and transmit sealed to the seat of the government of the United States, directed to the President of the Senate;— The President of the Senate shall, in the presence of the Senate and the House of Representatives, open all the certificates and the votes shall then be counted;— the person having the greatest Number of votes for President shall be the President, if such number be a majority of the whole number of Electors appointed; and if no person have such a majority, then, from the persons having the highest numbers not exceeding three on the list of those voted for as President, the House of Representatives shall choose immediately, by ballot, the President. But in choosing the President, the votes shall be taken by States, the representation from each State having one vote; a quorum for this purpose shall consist of a member or members from two thirds of the States, and a majority of all the States shall be necessary to a choice. And if the House of Representatives shall not choose a President whenever the right of choice shall devolve upon them, before the fourth day of March next following, then the Vice President shall act as President, as in case of death or other constitutional disability of the President. The person having the greatest number of votes as Vice President, shall be the Vice President, if such number be a majority of the whole number of Electors appointed, and if no person have a majority, then from the two highest numbers on the list, the Senate shall choose the Vice President; a quorum for the purpose shall consist of two thirds of the whole number of Senators, a majority of the whole number shall be necessary to a choice. But no person constitutionally ineligible to the office of President shall be eligible to that of Vice-President of the United States.

13th Amendment

Section 1. Neither slavery nor involuntary servitude, except as a punishment for crime whereof the party shall have been duly convicted, shall exist within the United States, or any place subject to their jurisdiction.

Section 2. Congress shall have power to enforce this article by appropriate legislation.

14th Amendment

Section 1. All persons born or naturalized in the United States and subject to the jurisdiction thereof, are citizens of the United States and of the State wherein they reside. No State shall make or enforce any law which shall abridge the privileges or immunities of citizens of the United States; nor shall any State deprive any person of life, liberty, or property, without due process of law; nor deny to any person within its jurisdiction the equal protection of the laws.

Section 2. Representatives shall be apportioned among the several States according to their respective numbers, counting the whole number of persons in each State, excluding Indians not taxed. But when the right to vote at any election for the choice of electors for President and Vice President of the United States, Representatives in Congress, the Executive and Judicial officers of a State, or the members of the Legislature thereof, is denied to any of the male inhabitants of such State, being twenty-one years of age and citizens of the United States, or in any way abridged, except for participation in rebellion, or other crime, the basis of representation therein shall be reduced in the proportion which the number of such male citizens shall bear to the whole number of male citizens twenty-one years of age in such State.

Section 3. No person shall be a Senator or Representative in Congress, or elector of President and Vice President, or hold any office, civil or military, under the United States, or under any State, who, having previously taken an oath, as a member of Congress, or as an officer of the United States, or as a member of any State legislature, or as an executive or judicial officer of any State, to support the Constitution of the United States, shall have engaged in insurrection or rebellion against the same, or given aid or comfort to the enemies thereof. But Congress may, by a vote of two thirds of each House, remove such disability.

Section 4. The validity of the public debt of the United States, authorized by law, including debts incurred for payment of pensions and bounties for services in suppressing insurrection or rebellion, shall not be questioned. But neither the United States nor any State shall assume or pay any debt or obligation incurred in aid of insurrection or rebellion against the United States, or any claim for the loss or emancipation of any slave; but all such debts, obligations and claims shall be held illegal and void.

Section 5. The Congress shall have power to enforce, by appropriate legislation, the provisions of this article.

14th Amendment. Rights of Citizens

Proposed by Congress June 13, 1866; ratified July 9, 1868. Section 1 defines citizenship. It provides for the acquisition of United States citizenship by birth or by naturalization. Citizenship at birth is determined according to the principle of jus soli—"the law of the soil," where born; naturalization is the legal process by which one acquires a new citizenship at some time after birth. Under certain circumstances, citizenship can also be gained at birth abroad, according to the principle of jus sanguinis—"the law of the blood," to whom born. This section also contains two major civil rights provisions: the Due Process Clause forbids a State (and its local governments) to act in any unfair or arbitrary way; the Equal Protection Clause forbids a State (and its local governments) to discriminate against, draw unreasonable distinctions between, persons.

Most of the rights set out against the National Government in the first eight amendments have been extended against the States (and their local governments) through Supreme Court decisions involving the 14th Amendment's Due Process Clause.

The first sentence here replaced Article I, Section 2, Clause 3, the Three-Fifths Compromise provision. Essentially, all persons in the United States are counted in each decennial census, the basis for the distribution of House seats. The balance of this section has never been enforced and is generally thought to be obsolete.

This section limited the President's power to pardon those persons who had led the Confederacy during the Civil War. Congress finally removed this disability in 1898.

Section 4 also dealt with matters directly related to the Civil War. It reaffirmed the public debt of the United States; but it invalidated, prohibited payment of, any debt contracted by the Confederate States and also prohibited any compensation of former slave owners.

15th Amendment. Right to Vote— Race, Color, Servitude

Proposed by Congress February 26, 1869; ratified February 3, 1870. The phrase "previous condition of servitude" refers to slavery. Note that this amendment does not guarantee the right to vote to African Americans, or to anyone else. Instead, it forbids the States from discriminating against any person on the grounds of his "race, color, or previous condition of servitude" in the setting of suffrage qualifications.

16th Amendment. Income Tax

Proposed by Congress July 12, 1909; ratified February 3, 1913. This amendment modified two provisions in Article I, Section 2, Clause 3, and Section 9, Clause 4. It gives to Congress the power to levy an income tax, a direct tax, without regard to the populations of any of the States.

17th Amendment. Popular Election of Senators

Proposed by Congress May 13, 1912; ratified April 8, 1913. This amendment repealed those portions of Article I, Section 3, Clauses 1 and 2 relating to the election of senators. Senators are now elected by the voters in each State. If a vacancy occurs, the governor of the State involved must call an election to fill the seat; the governor may appoint a senator to serve until the next election, if the State's legislature has authorized that step.

18th Amendment. Prohibition of Intoxicating Liquors

Proposed by Congress December 18, 1917; ratified January 16, 1919. This amendment outlawed the making, selling, transporting, importing, or exporting of alcoholic beverages in the United States. It was repealed in its entirety by the 21st Amendment in 1933.

19th Amendment. Equal Suffrage—Sex

Proposed by Congress June 4, 1919; ratified August 18, 1920. No person can be denied the right to vote in any election in the United States on account of his or her sex.

15th Amendment

Section 1. The right of citizens of the United States to vote shall not be denied or abridged by the United States or by any State on account of race, color, or previous condition of servitude.

Section 2. The Congress shall have power to enforce this article by appropriate legislation.

16th Amendment

The Congress shall have power to lay and collect taxes on incomes, from whatever source derived, without apportionment among the several States, and without regard to any census or enumeration.

17th Amendment

The Senate of the United States shall be composed of two Senators from each State, elected by the people thereof, for six years; and each Senator shall have one vote. The electors in each State shall have the qualifications requisite for electors of the most numerous branch of the State legislatures.

When vacancies happen in the representation of any State in the Senate, the executive authority of such State shall issue writs of election to fill such vacancies: Provided, That the legislature of any State may empower the executive thereof to make temporary appointments until the people fill the vacancies by election as the legislature may direct.

This amendment shall not be so construed as to affect the election or term of any Senator chosen before it becomes valid as part of the Constitution.

18th Amendment.

Section 1. After one year from the ratification of this article the manufacture, sale, or transportation of intoxicating liquors within, the importation thereof into, or the exportation thereof from the United States and all territory subject to the jurisdiction thereof for beverage purposes is hereby prohibited.

Section 2. The Congress and the several States shall have concurrent power to enforce this article by appropriate legislation.

Section 3. This article shall be inoperative unless it shall have been ratified as an amendment to the Constitution by the legislatures of the several States, as provided in the Constitution, within seven years of the date of the submission hereof to the States by Congress.

19th Amendment

The right of citizens of the United States to vote shall not be denied or abridged by the United States or by any State on account of sex.

Congress shall have power to enforce this article by appropriate legislation.

20th Amendment

Section 1. The terms of the President and Vice President shall end at noon on the 20th day of January, and the terms of Senators and Representatives at noon on the 3d day of January, of the years in which such terms would have ended if this article had not been ratified; and the terms of their successors shall then begin.

Section 2. The Congress shall assemble at least once in every year, and such meeting shall begin at noon on the 3d day of January, unless they shall by law appoint a different day.

Section 3. If, at the time fixed for the beginning of the term of the President, the President elect shall have died, the Vice President elect shall become President. If a President shall not have been chosen before the time fixed for the beginning of his term, or if the President-elect shall have failed to qualify, then the Vice President elect shall act as President until a President shall have qualified; and the Congress may by law provide for the case wherein neither a President elect nor a Vice President elect shall have qualified, declaring who shall then act as President, or the manner in which one who is to act shall be selected, and such person shall act accordingly until a President or Vice President shall have qualified.

Section 4. The Congress may by law provide for the case of the death of any of the persons from whom the House of Representatives may choose a President whenever the right of choice shall have devolved upon them, and for the case of the death of any of the persons from whom the Senate may choose a Vice President whenever the right of choice shall have devolved upon them.

Section 5. Sections 1 and 2 shall take effect on the 15th day of October following the ratification of this article.

Section 6. This article shall be inoperative unless it shall have been ratified as an amendment to the Constitution by the legislatures of three fourths of the several States within seven years from the date of its submission.

21st Amendment

Section 1. The eighteenth article of amendment to the Constitution of the United States is hereby repealed.

Section 2. The transportation or importation into any State, Territory, or possession of the United States for delivery or use therein of intoxicating liquors, in violation of the laws thereof, is hereby prohibited.

Section 3. This article shall be inoperative unless it shall have been ratified as an amendment to the Constitution by conventions in the several States, as provided in the Constitution, within seven years from the date of the submission hereof to the States by the Congress.

20th Amendment. Commencement of Terms; Sessions of Congress; Death or Disqualification of President-Elect

Proposed by Congress March 2, 1932; ratified January 23, 1933. The provisions of Sections 1 and 2 relating to Congress modified Article I, Section 4, Clause 2, and those provisions relating to the President, the 12th Amendment. The date on which the President and Vice President now take office was moved from March 4 to January 20. Similarly, the members of Congress now begin their terms on January 3. The 20th Amendment is sometimes called the "Lame Duck Amendment" because it shortened the period of time a member of Congress who was defeated for reelection (a "lame duck") remains in office.

This section deals with certain possibilities that were not covered by the presidential selection provisions of either Article II or the 12th Amendment. To this point, none of these situations has occurred. Note that there is neither a President-elect nor a Vice President-elect until the electoral votes have been counted by Congress, or, if the electoral college cannot decide the matter, the House has chosen a President or the Senate has chosen a Vice President.

Congress has not in fact ever passed such a law. See Section 2 of the 25th Amendment, regarding a vacancy in the vice presidency; that provision could some day have an impact here.

Section 5 set the date on which this amendment came into force.

Section 6 placed a time limit on the ratification process; note that a similar provision was written into the 18th, 21st, and 22nd amendments.

21st Amendment. Repeal of 18th Amendment

Proposed by Congress February 20, 1933; ratified December 5, 1933. This amendment repealed all of the 18th Amendment. Section 2 modifies the scope of the Federal Government's commerce power set out in Article I, Section 8, Clause 3; it gives to each State the power to regulate the transportation or importation and the distribution or use of intoxicating liquors in ways that would be unconstitutional in the case of any other commodity. The 21st Amendment is the only amendment Congress has thus far submitted to the States for ratification by conventions.

22nd Amendment. Presidential Tenure

Proposed by Congress March 21, 1947; ratified February 27, 1951. This amendment modified Article II, Section I, Clause 1. It stipulates that no President may serve more than two elected terms. But a President who has succeeded to the office beyond the midpoint in a term to which another President was originally elected may serve for more than eight years. In any case, however, a President may not serve more than 10 years. Prior to Franklin Roosevelt, who was elected to four terms, no President had served more than two full terms in office.

23rd Amendment. Presidential Electors for the District of Columbia

Proposed by Congress June 16, 1960; ratified March 29, 1961. This amendment modified Article II, Section I, Clause 2 and the 12th Amendment. It included the voters of the District of Columbia in the presidential electorate; and provides that the District is to have the same number of electors as the least populous State—three electors—but no more than that number.

24th Amendment. Right to Vote in Federal Elections—Tax Payment

Proposed by Congress August 27, 1962; ratified January 23, 1964. This amendment outlawed the payment of any tax as a condition for taking part in the nomination or election of any federal officeholder.

25th Amendment. Presidential Succession, Vice Presidential Vacancy, Presidential Inability

Proposed by Congress July 6, 1965; ratified February 10, 1967. Section 1 revised the imprecise provision on presidential succession in Article II, Section 1, Clause 6. It affirmed the precedent set by Vice President John Tyler, who became President on the death of William Henry Harrison in 1841. Section 2 provides for the filling of a vacancy in the office of Vice President. The office had been vacant on 16 occasions and remained unfilled for the rest of each term involved. When Spiro Agnew resigned the office in 1973, President Nixon selected Gerald Ford per this provision; and, when President Nixon resigned in 1974, Gerald Ford became President and chose Nelson Rockefeller as Vice President.

22nd Amendment

Section 1. No person shall be elected to the office of the President more than twice, and no person who has held the office of President, or acted as President, for more than two years of a term to which some other person was elected President shall be elected to the office of the President more than once. But this Article shall not apply to any person holding the office of President, when this Article was proposed by the Congress, and shall not prevent any person who may be holding the office of President, or acting as President, during the term within which this Article becomes operative from holding the office of President or acting as President during the remainder of such term.

Section 2. This article shall be inoperative unless it shall have been ratified as an amendment to the Constitution by the legislatures of three fourths of the several states within seven years from the date of its submission to the States by the Congress.

23rd Amendment.

Section 1. The District constituting the seat of Government of the United States shall appoint in such manner as the Congress may direct:

A number of electors of President and Vice President equal to the whole number of Senators and Representatives in Congress to which the District would be entitled if it were a State, but in no event more than the least populous State; they shall be in addition to those appointed by the States, they shall be considered, for the purposes of the election of President and Vice President, to be electors appointed by a State; and they shall meet in the District and perform such duties as provided by the twelfth article of amendment.

24th Amendment.

Section 1. The right of citizens of the United States to vote in any primary or other election for President or Vice President, for electors for President or Vice President, or for Senator or Representative in Congress, shall not be denied or abridged by the United States or any State by reason of failure to pay any poll tax or other tax.

Section 2. The Congress shall have power to enforce this article by appropriate legislation.

25th Amendment.

Section 1. In case of the removal of the President from office or of his death or resignation, the Vice President shall become President.

Section 2. Whenever there is a vacancy in the office of the Vice President, the President shall nominate a Vice President who shall take office upon confirmation by a majority vote of both Houses of Congress.

Section 3. Whenever the President transmits to the President pro tempore of the Senate and the Speaker of the House of Representatives his written declaration that he is unable to discharge the powers and duties of his office, and until he transmits to them a written declaration to the contrary, such powers and duties shall be discharged by the Vice President as Acting President.

Section 4. Whenever the Vice President and a majority of either the principal officers of the executive departments or of such other body as Congress may by law provide, transmit to the President pro tempore of the Senate and the Speaker of the House of Representatives their written declaration that the President is unable to discharge the powers and duties of his office, the Vice President shall immediately assume the powers and duties of the office as Acting President.

Thereafter, when the President transmits to the President pro tempore of the Senate and the Speaker of the House of Representatives his written declaration that no inability exists, he shall resume the powers and duties of his office unless the Vice President and a majority of either the principal officers of the executive department or of such other body as Congress may by law provide, transmit within four days to the President pro tempore of the Senate and the Speaker of the House of Representatives their written declaration that the President is unable to discharge the powers and duties of his office. Thereupon Congress shall decide the issue, assembling within forty-eight hours for that purpose if not in session. If the Congress, within twenty-one days after receipt of the latter written declaration, or, if Congress is not in session, within twenty-one days after Congress is required to assemble, determines by two-thirds vote of both Houses that the President is unable to discharge the powers and duties of his office, the Vice President shall continue to discharge the same as Acting President; otherwise, the President shall resume the powers and duties of his office.

This section created a procedure for determining if a President is so incapacitated that he cannot perform the powers and duties of his office.

Section 4 deals with the circumstance in which a President will not be able to determine the fact of incapacity. To this point, Congress has not established the "such other body" referred to here. This section contains the only typographical error in the Constitution; in its second paragraph, the word "department" should in fact read "departments."

26th Amendment.

Section 1. The right of citizens of the United States, who are eighteen years of age or older, to vote shall not be denied or abridged by the United States or by any State on account of age.

Section 2. The Congress shall have the power to enforce this article by appropriate legislation.

27th Amendment.

No law varying the compensation for the services of the Senators and Representatives, shall take effect, until an election of Representatives shall have intervened.

26th Amendment. **Right to Vote—Age**
Proposed by Congress March 23, 1971; ratified July 1, 1971. This amendment provides that the minimum age for voting in any election in the United States cannot be more than 18 years. (A State may set a minimum voting age of less than 18, however.)

27th Amendment. **Congressional Pay**
Proposed by Congress September 25, 1789; ratified May 7, 1992. This amendment modified Article I, Section 6, Clause 1. It limits Congress's power to fix the salaries of its members—by delaying the effectiveness of any increase in that pay until after the next regular congressional election.

Name	Party	State [a]	Entered Office	Age On Taking Office	Vice President(s)
George Washington (1732–1799)	Federalist	Virginia	1789	57	John Adams
John Adams (1735–1826)	Federalist	Massachusetts	1797	61	Thomas Jefferson
Thomas Jefferson (1743–1826)	Dem-Rep[b]	Virginia	1801	57	Aaron Burr/George Clinton
James Madison (1751–1836)	Dem-Rep	Virginia	1809	57	George Clinton/Elbridge Gerry
James Monroe (1758–1831)	Dem-Rep	Virginia	1817	58	Daniel D. Tompkins
John Q. Adams (1767–1848)	Dem-Rep	Massachusetts	1825	57	John C. Calhoun
Andrew Jackson (1767–1845)	Democrat	Tennessee (SC)	1829	61	John C. Calhoun/Martin Van Buren
Martin Van Buren (1782–1862)	Democrat	New York	1837	54	Richard M. Johnson
William H. Harrison (1773–1841)	Whig	Ohio (VA)	1841	68	John Tyler
John Tyler (1790–1862)	Democrat	Virginia	1841	51	none
James K. Polk (1795–1849)	Democrat	Tennessee (NC)	1845	49	George M. Dallas
Zachary Taylor (1784–1850)	Whig	Louisiana (VA)	1849	64	Millard Fillmore
Millard Fillmore (1800–1874)	Whig	New York	1850	50	none
Franklin Pierce (1804–1869)	Democrat	New Hampshire	1853	48	William R. King
James Buchanan (1791–1868)	Democrat	Pennsylvania	1857	65	John C. Breckinridge
Abraham Lincoln (1809–1865)	Republican	Illinois (KY)	1861	52	Hannibal Hamlin/Andrew Johnson[c]
Andrew Johnson (1808–1875)	Democrat	Tennessee (NC)	1865	56	none
Ulysses S. Grant (1822–1885)	Republican	Illinois (OH)	1869	46	Schuyler Colfax/Henry Wilson
Rutherford B. Hayes (1822–1893)	Republican	Ohio	1877	54	William A. Wheeler
James A. Garfield (1831–1881)	Republican	Ohio	1881	49	Chester A. Arthur
Chester A. Arthur (1829–1896)	Republican	New York (VT)	1881	51	none
Grover Cleveland (1837–1908)	Democrat	New York (NJ)	1885	47	Thomas A. Hendricks
Benjamin Harrison (1833–1901)	Republican	Indiana (OH)	1889	55	Levi P. Morton
Grover Cleveland (1837–1908)	Democrat	New York (NJ)	1893	55	Adlai E. Stevenson

Name	Party	State[a]	Entered Office	Age On Taking Office	Vice President(s)
William McKinley (1843–1901)	Republican	Ohio	1897	54	Garret A. Hobart/ Theodore Roosevelt
Theodore Roosevelt (1858–1919)	Republican	New York	1901	42	Charles W. Fairbanks
William H. Taft (1857–1930)	Republican	Ohio	1909	51	James S. Sherman
Woodrow Wilson (1856–1924)	Democrat	New Jersey (VA)	1913	56	Thomas R. Marshall
Warren G. Harding (1865–1923)	Republican	Ohio	1921	55	Calvin Coolidge
Calvin Coolidge (1872–1933)	Republican	Massachusetts (VT)	1923	51	Charles G. Dawes
Herbert Hoover (1874–1964)	Republican	California (IA)	1929	54	Charles Curtis
Franklin Roosevelt (1882–1945)	Democrat	New York	1933	51	John N. Garner/ Henry A. Wallace/Harry S Truman
Harry S Truman (1884–1972)	Democrat	Missouri	1945	60	Alben W. Barkley
Dwight D. Eisenhower (1890–1969)	Republican	New York (TX)	1953	62	Richard M. Nixon
John F. Kennedy (1917–1963)	Democrat	Massachusetts	1961	43	Lyndon B. Johnson
Lyndon B. Johnson (1908–1973)	Democrat	Texas	1963	55	Hubert H. Humphrey
Richard M. Nixon (1913–1994)	Republican	New York (CA)	1969	56	Spiro T. Agnew [d]/Gerald R. Ford [e]
Gerald R. Ford (1913–2006)	Republican	Michigan (NE)	1974	61	Nelson A. Rockefeller [f]
James E. Carter (1924–)	Democrat	Georgia	1977	52	Walter F. Mondale
Ronald W. Reagan (1911–2004)	Republican	California (IL)	1981	69	George H. W. Bush
George H.W. Bush (1924–)	Republican	Texas (MA)	1989	64	J. Danforth Quayle
William J. Clinton (1946–)	Democrat	Arkansas	1993	46	Albert Gore, Jr.
George W. Bush (1946–)	Republican	Texas	2001	54	Richard B. Cheney
Barack Obama (1961–)	Democrat	Illinois (HI)	2009	47	Joseph R. Biden
Donald J. Trump (1946–)	Republican	New York	2017	70	Michael R. Pence

[a] State of residence when elected; if born in another State, that State in parentheses.
[b] Democratic-Republican
[c] Johnson, a War Democrat, was elected Vice President on the coalition Union Party ticket.
[d] Resigned October 10, 1973.
[e] Nominated by Nixon, confirmed by Congress on December 6, 1973.
[f] Nominated by Ford, confirmed by Congress on December 19, 1974.

[Declaration of Independence]

Introduction

By signing the Declaration of Independence, members of the Continental Congress sent a clear message to Britain that the American colonies were free and independent states. Starting with its preamble, the document spells out all the reasons the people of the United States have the right to break away from Britain.

Primary Source

The Unanimous Declaration of the Thirteen United States of America

When in the Course of human events, it becomes necessary for one people to dissolve the political bands which have connected them with another, and to assume among the powers of the earth, the separate and equal station to which the Laws of Nature and of Nature's God entitle them, a decent respect to the opinions of mankind requires that they should declare the causes which impel [force] them to the separation. We hold these truths to be self-evident, that all men are created equal, that they are endowed [gifted] by their Creator with certain unalienable [cannot be taken away] Rights, that among these are Life, Liberty and the pursuit of Happiness. That to secure these rights, Governments are instituted among Men, deriving their just powers from the consent of the governed. That whenever any Form of Government becomes destructive of these ends, it is the Right of the People to alter or to abolish it, and to institute new Government, laying its foundation on such principles and organizing its powers in such form, as to them shall seem most likely to effect their Safety and Happiness. Prudence [cautiousness], indeed, will dictate that Governments long established should not be changed for light and transient causes; and accordingly all experience hath shown that mankind are more disposed to suffer, while evils are sufferable, than to right themselves by abolishing the forms to which they are accustomed. But when a long train of abuses and usurpations [unjust uses of power], pursuing invariably the same Object evinces a design to reduce them under absolute Despotism [rule of absolute power], it is their right, it is their duty, to throw off such Government, and to provide new Guards for their future security.

Such has been the patient sufferance of these Colonies; and such is now the necessity which constrains them to alter their former Systems of Government. The history of the present King of Great Britain is a history of repeated injuries and usurpations, all having in direct object the establishment of an absolute Tyranny over these States. To prove this, let Facts be submitted to a candid world.

He has refused his Assent to Laws, the most wholesome and necessary for the public good.

He has forbidden his Governors to pass Laws of immediate and pressing importance, unless suspended in their operation till his Assent should be obtained; and when so suspended, he has utterly neglected to attend to them.

He has refused to pass other Laws for the accommodation of large districts of people, unless those people would relinquish [give up] the right of Representation in the Legislature, a right inestimable [priceless] to them and formidable to tyrants only.

He has called together legislative bodies at places unusual, uncomfortable, and distant from the depository of their public Records, for the sole purpose of fatiguing them into compliance with his measures.

He has dissolved Representative Houses repeatedly, for opposing with manly firmness his invasions on the rights of the people.

He has refused for a long time, after such dissolutions [closing down], to cause others to be elected; whereby the Legislative powers, incapable of Annihilation, have returned to the People at large for their exercise; the State remaining in the mean time exposed to all the dangers of invasion from without, and convulsions [riots] within.

He has endeavoured to prevent the population of these States; for that purpose obstructing the Laws for Naturalization of Foreigners; refusing to pass others to encourage their migrations hither, and raising the conditions of new Appropriations of Lands.

He has obstructed the Administration of Justice by refusing his Assent to Laws for establishing Judiciary powers.

He has made Judges dependent on his Will alone, for the tenure [term] of their offices, and the amount and payment of their salaries.

He has erected a multitude of New Offices, and sent hither swarms of Officers to harass our people, and eat out their substance.

He has kept among us, in times of peace, Standing Armies without the Consent of our legislatures.

He has affected to render the Military independent of and superior to the Civil power.

He has combined with others to subject us to a jurisdiction foreign to our constitution, and unacknowledged by our laws; giving his Assent to their Acts of pretended Legislation:

For quartering [lodging] large bodies of armed troops among us:

For protecting them, by a mock Trial, from punishment for any Murders which they should commit on the Inhabitants of these States:

For cutting off our Trade with all parts of the world:

For imposing Taxes on us without our Consent:

For depriving us in many cases, of the benefits of Trial by Jury: For transporting us beyond Seas to be tried for pretended offences:

For abolishing the free System of English Laws in a neighbouring Province, establishing therein an Arbitrary government, and enlarging its Boundaries so as to render it at once an example and fit instrument for introducing the same absolute rule into these Colonies:

For taking away our Charters, abolishing our most valuable Laws, and altering fundamentally the Forms of our Governments:

For suspending our own Legislatures, and declaring themselves invested with power to legislate for us in all cases whatsoever.

He has abdicated Government here, by declaring us out of his Protection and waging War against us.

He has plundered our seas, ravaged our Coasts, burnt our towns, and destroyed the lives of our people.

He is at this time transporting large Armies of foreign Mercenaries [soldiers] to complete the works of death, desolation, and tyranny, already begun with circumstances of Cruelty and perfidy [dishonesty] scarcely paralleled in the most barbarous ages, and totally unworthy the Head of a civilized nation.

He has constrained our fellow Citizens taken Captive on the high Seas to bear Arms against their Country, to become the executioners of their friends and Brethren, or to fall themselves by their Hands.

He has excited domestic insurrections amongst us, and has endeavoured to bring on the inhabitants of our frontiers, the merciless Indian Savages whose known rule of warfare, is an undistinguished destruction of all ages, sexes and conditions.

In every stage of these Oppressions We have Petitioned for Redress [correction of wrongs] in the most humble terms: Our repeated Petitions have been answered only by repeated injury. A Prince, whose character is thus marked by every act which may define a Tyrant, is unfit to be the ruler of a free people.

Nor have We been wanting in attentions to our British brethren. We have warned them from time to time of attempts by their legislature to extend an unwarrantable jurisdiction over us. We have reminded them of the circumstances of our emigration and settlement here. We have appealed to their native justice and magnanimity [generosity], and we have conjured [begged] them by the ties of our common kindred, to disavow these usurpations, which would inevitably interrupt our connections and correspondence. They too have been deaf to the voice of justice and of consanguinity [relation by blood]. We must, therefore, acquiesce in the necessity, which denounces our Separation, and hold them, as we hold the rest of mankind, Enemies in War, in Peace Friends.

We, therefore, the Representatives of the United States of America, in General Congress, Assembled, appealing to the Supreme Judge of the world for the rectitude [justness] of our intentions, do, in the Name, and by Authority of the good People of these Colonies, solemnly publish and declare, That these United Colonies are, and of Right ought to be Free and Independent States; that they are Absolved from all Allegiance to the British Crown, and that all political connection between them and the State of Great Britain, is and ought to be totally dissolved; and that as Free and Independent States, they have full Power to levy War, conclude Peace, contract Alliances, establish Commerce, and to do all other Acts and Things which Independent States may of right do. And for the support of this Declaration, with a firm reliance on the protection of Divine Providence, we mutually pledge to each other our Lives, our Fortunes and our sacred Honor.

ASSESSMENT

1. **Identify Cause and Effect** How might the ideas about equality expressed in the Declaration of Independence have influenced later historical movements, such as the abolitionist movement and the women's suffrage movement?
2. **Identify Key Steps in a Process** Why was the Declaration of Independence a necessary document for the founding of the new nation?

3. **Draw Inferences** English philosopher John Locke wrote that government should protect "life, liberty, and estate." How do you think Locke's writing influenced ideas about government put forth in the Declaration of Independence?

4. **Analyze Structure** How does the Declaration organize its key points from beginning to end?

[The Pledge of Allegiance]

Introduction

The Pledge of Allegiance was first written in 1892. It was revised twice before 1954, when the words "under God" were added, and it became the version that is still recited today.

Primary Source

I pledge allegiance [loyalty] to the Flag of the United States of America, and to the Republic for which it stands, one Nation under God, indivisible, with liberty and justice for all.

Sequence

Sequence means "order," and placing things in the correct order is very important. What would happen if you tried to put toppings on a pizza before you put down the dough for the crust? When studying history, you need to analyze the information by sequencing significant events, individuals, and time periods in order to understand them. Practice this skill by using the reading on this page.

> Richard Nixon was elected to the House of Representatives in 1946 and then to the Senate four years later. In 1952, with Dwight Eisenhower's election as President, Nixon became Vice President. However, Nixon lost to John F. Kennedy in the 1960 presidential election, and two years later lost an election for governor of California. However, in 1968, Nixon defeated Hubert Humphrey to win the presidency.

[1.] Identify the topic and the main events that relate to the topic. Quickly skim titles and headings to determine the topic of the passage. As you read the passage, write a list of significant events, individuals, or time periods related to the topic.

[2.] Note any dates and time words such as "before" and "after" that indicate the chronological order of events. Look through your list of events, individuals, or time periods and write down the date for each. This will give you information to apply absolute chronology by sequencing the events, individuals, or time periods. Remember that some events may have taken place over a number of months or years. Is your date the time when the event started or ended? Make sure to note enough details that you can remember the importance of the information. If no date is given, look for words such as "before" or "after" that can tell you where to place this event, time period, or individual compared to others on your list. This will allow you to apply relative chronology by sequencing the events, individuals, or time periods.

[3.] Determine the time range of the events. Place the events in chronological order on a timeline. Look for the earliest and latest events, individuals, or time periods on your list. The span of time between the first and last entries gives you the time range. To apply absolute chronology, sequence the entries by writing the date of the first event on the left side of a piece of paper and the date of the last event on the right side. Draw a line connecting the two events. This will be your timeline. Once you have drawn your timeline, put the events in order by date along the line. Label their dates. To apply relative chronology, sequence the significant individuals, events, or time periods on an undated timeline, in the order that they happened. You now have a clear image of the important events related to this topic. You can organize and interpret information from visuals by analyzing the information and applying absolute or relative chronology to the events. This will help you understand the topic better when you can see how events caused or led to other events. You will also be able to analyze information by developing connections between historical events over time.

Categorize

When you analyze information by categorizing, you create a system that helps you sort items into categories, or groups with shared characteristics, so that you can understand the information. Categorizing helps you see what groups of items have in common. Practice this skill as you study the map on this page.

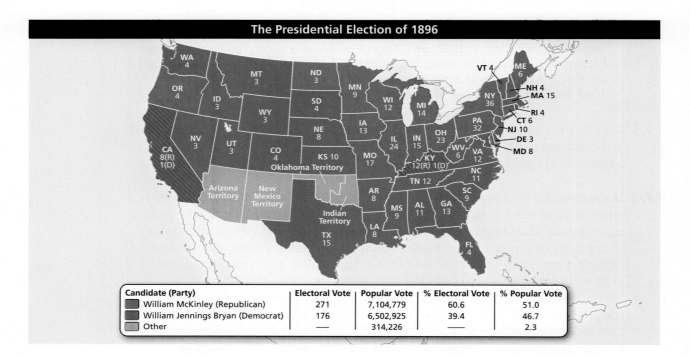

The Presidential Election of 1896

Candidate (Party)	Electoral Vote	Popular Vote	% Electoral Vote	% Popular Vote
William McKinley (Republican)	271	7,104,779	60.6	51.0
William Jennings Bryan (Democrat)	176	6,502,925	39.4	46.7
Other	—	314,226	—	2.3

[**1.**] Identify similarities and differences among items you need to understand. You need to pay careful attention and sometimes do research to find the similarities and differences among the facts, topics, or objects that you need to understand. Scientists find groups, or categories, of related animals by analyzing the details of the animals' bodies. For example, insects with similar wings, legs, and mouthparts probably belong in the same category. Gather similar information about all the things you need to understand. For example, if you know the location of one thing, try to find the locations of all the things you are studying. If you have different types of information about your topics, you will not be able to group them easily.

[**2.**] Create a system to group items with common characteristics. Once you have gathered similar kinds of information on the items you need to understand, look for items that share characteristics or features. Create categories based on a feature shared by all of the facts, topics, or objects you need to understand. For example, if you have gathered information on the population and political systems of several countries, you could categorize them by the size of their population or their type of political system.

[3.] Form the groupings. Put each of the items that you are studying into one of the categories that you have created. If some items do not fit, you may need to make a new category or modify your categories. Label each category for the characteristic shared by its members. Examples of labels for categories might include "Countries with more than 100 million people," "Countries with fewer than 1 million people," "Democracies," or "Dictatorships."

Analyze Cause and Effect

When you analyze information by identifying cause-and-effect relationships, you find how one event leads to the next. It is important to find evidence that one event caused another. If one event happened earlier than another, it did not necessarily cause the later event. Understanding causes and effects can help you solve problems. Practice this skill as you study the cause-and-effect chart on this page.

Agricultural Causes of the Depression of 1893

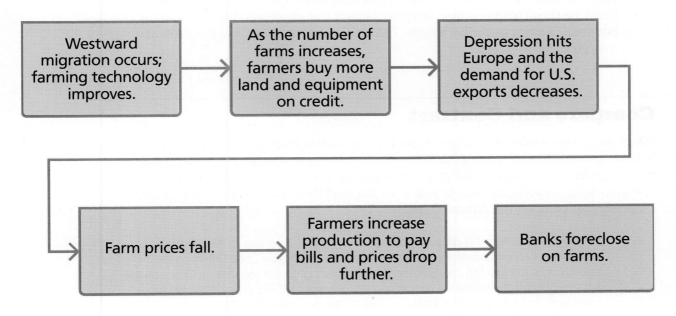

[1.] Choose a starting point of observation. When trying to understand a historical event, choose the time of that event. If you are trying to understand a current event, you can work backward from a starting point in the present.

PearsonSchool.com/CASS
View Video Tutorials and other
21st Century Skills

[**2.**] Consider earlier events to try to find connections to your starting point, including any language that signals causes. Put the evidence together to identify true causes. When reading, look for events that come before your starting point. Analyze whether these earlier events caused later events. Identify words that signal cause, such as "reason," "because," and "led to." Analyze the information by developing connections between historical events. Make sure that there is evidence showing that the earlier events caused the later events and did not just happen earlier.

[**3.**] Consider later events to try to find connections to your starting point, including any language that signals effects. Put the evidence together to determine true effects. Look for events that come after your starting point. Analyze the information in order to determine whether these later events are effects of earlier events. Identify words that signal effect, such as "led to," "so," and "therefore." Make sure that there is evidence showing that these later events were caused by earlier events and did not just happen later.

[**4.**] Summarize the cause-and-effect relationship and draw conclusions. Once you have identified the cause-and-effect relationships between different events, describe these relationships. Draw a diagram that develops the connections between the two historical events. Draw conclusions about any relationships that you see.

Compare and Contrast

When you analyze information by comparing and contrasting two or more things, you look for similarities and differences between them. This skill helps you understand the things that you are comparing and contrasting. It is also a skill that you can use in making choices. Practice this skill as you read the text excerpt on this page. Compare and contrast the critics of the New Deal.

> While Roosevelt had little difficulty gaining support from Congress for his proposals, a minority of Americans expressed their opposition to the New Deal. Critics on the political right thought the changes the New Deal brought were too radical. Critics on the left thought that they were not radical enough. Several of FDR's critics attracted mass followings and made plans to challenge him for the presidency in 1936.

[**1.**] Look for related topics and characteristics that describe them. When you are looking for similarities and differences between two things, it can help to start by identifying relationships between them. What do the two things have in common? If two things have nothing in common, such as a dog and a piece of pie, it will be difficult to find similarities or differences. On the other hand, you can compare and contrast two countries or political systems. Look through the information you have on the things or topics you want to compare and contrast, and identify the characteristics, or features, that describe those things or topics.

[2.] Look for words that signal comparison ("both," "similar to," "also") or contrast ("unlike," "different," "instead"). Look for words that show comparison, or similarity, and those that show contrast, or difference. Take notes on these similarities and differences. This will make it possible to analyze information more quickly.

[3.] Identify similarities and differences in the topics, and draw conclusions about them. Look through your notes and analyze the ways in which your topics are similar and different. Usually, topics have both similarities and differences. Try to find patterns in these similarities and differences. For example, all the similarities between two countries might be related to climate, and all the differences might be related to economics. Draw conclusions based on these patterns. In this example, you might conclude that a country's economy does not depend on its climate. Identifying similarities and differences by comparing and contrasting two topics lets you draw conclusions that help you analyze both topics as well as other topics like them.

Identify Main Ideas and Details

You can analyze information in a selection by finding the main idea. A main idea is the most important point in a selection. Identifying the main idea will help you remember details, such as names, dates, and events, which should support the main idea. Practice this skill by reading the paragraph on this page. Find the main idea of this paragraph and the supporting details.

> During his first hundred days in office, which became known as the Hundred Days, Roosevelt proposed and Congress passed 15 major bills. These measures had three goals: relief, recovery, and reform. Roosevelt wanted to provide relief from the immediate hardships of the depression and achieve a long-term economic recovery. He also instituted reforms to prevent future depressions.

[1.] Scan titles, headings, and visuals before reading to see what the selection is about. Often, important ideas are included in titles, headings, and other special text. Special text may be primary sources, words that are highlighted, or ideas listed with bullet points. Also, take a look at visuals and captions. By analyzing these parts of the text, you should quickly get a sense of the main idea of the article.

[2.] Read the selection and then identify the main point of the selection, the point that the rest of the selection supports: this is the main idea. Read through the selection to identify the main idea. Sometimes, the main idea will be the first or second sentence of one of the first few paragraphs. Sometimes, it will be the last sentence of the first paragraph. Other times, no single sentence will tell you the main idea. You will have to come up with your own sentence answering the question, "What is the main point of this selection?"

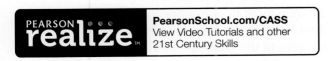

[3.] Find details or statements within the selection that support or build on the main idea. Once you have identified the main idea, look for details that support the main idea. Many or most of the details should be related to the main idea. If you find that many of the details are not related to what you think is the main idea, you may not have identified the main idea correctly. Identify the main idea that the details in the selection support. Analyze the information in the text by finding the main idea and supporting details.

Summarize

When you analyze information by summarizing, you restate the main points of a passage in your own words. Using your own words helps you understand the information. Summarizing will help you understand a text and prepare for tests or assignments based on the text. Practice this skill by follow the steps to summarize the excerpt on this page.

> One of the most terrifying aspects of the Cold War was the arms race that began right after World War II. At first, the United States was the only nuclear power. By 1949, however, the Soviet Union had also developed nuclear weapons.
>
> Critics argued that a nuclear war would destroy both sides. Yet each superpower wanted to be able to deter the other from launching its nuclear weapons. Both sides engaged in a race to match each other's new weapons. The result was a "balance of terror." Mutually assured destruction—in which each side knew that the other side would itself be destroyed if it launched its weapons—discouraged nuclear war. Still, people around the world lived in constant fear of nuclear doom.

[1.] Identify and write down the main point of each paragraph in your own words. You may identify the main idea right at the beginning of each paragraph. In other cases, you will have to figure out the main idea. As you read each paragraph, ask yourself, "What is the point this paragraph makes?" The point the paragraph makes is the main idea. Write this idea down in your own words.

[2.] Use these main points to write a general statement of the overall main idea of the passage in your own words. Once you have written down the main idea for each paragraph, write down the main idea of the passage. Write the main idea in your own words. If you have trouble identifying the main idea of the passage, review the titles and headings in the passage. Often, titles and headings relate to the main idea. Also, the writer may state the main idea in the first paragraph of the passage. The main idea of a passage should answer the question, "What is the point this passage makes?"

[3.] Use this general statement as a topic sentence for your summary. Then, write a paragraph tying together the main points of the passage. Leave out unimportant details. Analyze the information in the passage by summarizing. Use the main idea of the passage as a topic sentence for your summary paragraph. Use the main ideas that you identified for each paragraph of the passage to write sentences supporting the main idea of the passage. Leave out details that are not needed to understand the main idea of the passage. Your summary should be in your own words, and it should be much shorter than the original passage. Once your summary is written, review it to make sure that it contains all the main points of the passage. If any are missing, revise your summary to include them. If the summary includes unimportant details, remove them.

Generalize

One good way to analyze materials about a particular subject is to make generalizations and predictions. What are the patterns and connections that link the different materials? What can you say about the different materials that is true of all them? Practice this skill by reading the following descriptions about the population of California in the 1850s. What generalization can you make about the people who went to California during the Gold Rush?

- Free African Americans ran churches and a newspaper, worked in the mines, and owned businesses that supplied miners.

- The work of Chinese immigrants in construction and services helped build the booming state. They also helped build the railroads that linked California with the rest of the country.

- Women played an important role in the California Gold Rush. Women ran stores, hotels, and provided food for the miners.

[**1.**] Make a list. Listing all of the specific details and facts about a subject will help you find patterns and connections.

[**2.**] Generate a statement. From your list of facts and specific details, decide what most of the items listed have in common. Analyze your information by making generalizations and predictions.

[**3.**] Ensure your generalization is logical and well supported by facts. Generalizations can be valid or invalid. A generalization that is not logical or supported by facts is invalid.

Make Predictions

You can analyze information by making generalizations and predictions. Predictions are educated guesses about the future, based on clues you find in written material and information you already have. When you analyze information by making generalizations and predictions, you are thinking critically about the material you read. Practice this skill by analyzing the definition of spoils system and predicting the possible negative effects of the spoils system if used in a corporation or sports team.

spoils system practice of the political party or group in power giving jobs and appointments to its supporters, rather than to people based on their qualifications.

[**1.**] Review the content. Read your material carefully and research any terms or concepts that are new to you. It's important to understand the material before analyzing the information to make a prediction.

[**2.**] Look for clues. Gathering evidence is an important part of making predictions. Look for important words, statements, and evidence that seem to support the writer's point of view. Ask questions about what you are reading, including who, what, where, when, why, and how. Look for and analyze clues to help you generalize and predict.

[**3.**] Consider what you already know. Use related prior knowledge and/or connect to your own experiences to help you make an informed prediction. If you have experience with the subject matter, you have a much better chance of making an accurate prediction.

[**4.**] Generate a list of predictions. After studying the content, list the clues you've found. Then use these clues, plus your prior knowledge, to form your predictions. List as many possible outcomes as you can based on clues in the material and the questions you have considered.

Draw Inferences

What is the author trying to tell you? To make a determination about the author's message, you analyze information by drawing inferences and conclusions. You consider details and descriptions included in the text, compare and contrast the text to prior knowledge you have about the subject, and then form a conclusion about the author's intent. Practice this skill by analyzing the chart and drawing inferences about conditions in the United States between 1929 and 1933.

U.S. Immigration, 1929–1933

YEAR	IMMIGRANTS ADMITTED	IMMIGRANTS DEPARTED
1929	279,678	69,203
1930	241,700	50,661
1931	97,139	61,882
1932	35,576	103,295
1933	23,068	80,081

SOURCE: *Statistical Abstract of the United States, 1935*

[1.] Study the image or text. Consider all of the details and descriptions included. What is the author trying to tell you? Look for context clues that hint at the topic and subject matter.

[2.] Make a connection. Use related prior knowledge to connect to the text or image. Analyze information by asking questions such as who, what, where, when, and how. Look for cause-and-effect relationships; compare and contrast. This strategy will help you think beyond the available surface details to understand what the author is suggesting or implying.

[3.] Form a conclusion. When you draw an inference, you combine your own ideas with evidence and details you found within the text or image to form a new conclusion. This action leads you to a new understanding of the material.

Draw Conclusions

When you analyze information by drawing inferences and conclusions, you connect the ideas in a text with what you already know in order to understand a topic better. Using this skill, you can "fill in the blanks" to see the implications or larger meaning of the information in a text. Practice this skill by reading the excerpt of text on this page. What conclusions can you draw based on the information in the paragraphs?

Challenging Economic Times

From the Oval Office, Hoover worked hard to end the depression. But to many out-of-work Americans, the President became a symbol of failure. Some people blamed capitalism, while others questioned the responsiveness of democracy. Many believed the American system was due for an overhaul.

Although some questioned the ability of America's capitalistic and democratic institutions to overcome the crisis, most Americans never lost faith in their country.

[1.] Identify the topic, main idea, and supporting details. Before reading, look at the titles and headings within a reading. This should give you a good idea of the topic, or the general subject, of a text. After reading, identify the main idea. The main idea falls within the topic and answers the question, "What is the main point of this text?" Find the details that the author presents to support the main idea.

[2.] Use what you know to make a judgment about the information. Think about what you know about this topic or a similar topic. For example, you may read that the English settlers of Jamestown suffered from starvation because many of them were not farmers and did not know how to grow food. Analyzing the information about their situation and what you know about people, you could draw the conclusion that these settlers must have had little idea, or the wrong idea, about the conditions that they would find in America.

[3.] Check and adjust your judgment until you can draw a well-supported conclusion. Look for details within the reading that support your judgment. Reading a little further, you find that these settlers thought that they would become rich after discovering gold or silver, or through trading with Native Americans for furs. You can use this information to support your conclusion that the settlers were mistaken about the conditions that they would find in America. By analyzing the information further, you might infer that the settlers had inaccurate information about America. To support your conclusions, you could look for reliable sources on what these settlers knew before they left England.

Interpret Sources

Outlines and reports are good sources of information. In order to interpret these sources, though, you'll need to identify the type of document you're reading, identify the main idea, organize the details of information, and evaluate the source for point of view and bias. Practice this skill by finding a newspaper or online report on a bill recently passed by Congress or a decision recently decided by the Supreme Court. What steps will you take to interpret this report?

[1.] Identify the type of document. Is the document a primary or secondary source? Determine when, where, and why it was written.

[2.] Examine the source to identify the main idea. After identifying the main idea, identify details or sections of text that support the main idea. If the source is an outline or report, identify the topic and subtopics; review the supporting details under each subtopic. Organize the information from the outline or report and think about how it connects back to the overall topic listed at the top of the outline or report.

[3.] Evaluate the source for point of view and bias. Primary sources often have a strong point of view or bias; it is important to analyze primary sources critically to determine their validity. Evaluating each source will help you interpret the information they contain.

Create Databases

Databases are organized collections of information which can be analyzed and interpreted. You decide on a topic, organize data, use a spreadsheet, and then pose questions which will help you to analyze and interpret your data. Practice this skill as you create a database of changes in your state's population since 1960. You can find many kinds of state data in the U.S. Census. (census.gov)

[1.] Decide on a topic. Identify the information that you will convert into a table. This information may come from various sources, including textbooks, reference works, and Internet sites.

[2.] Organize the data. Study the information and decide what to include in your table. Only include data that is pertinent and available. Based on the data you choose, organize your information. Identify how many columns there will be and what the column headings will be. Decide the order in which you are going to list the data in the rows.

[3.] Use a spreadsheet. A spreadsheet is a computer software tool that allows you to organize data so that it can be analyzed. Spreadsheets allow you to make calculations as well as input data. Use a spreadsheet to help you create summaries of your data. For instance, you can compute the sum, average, minimum, and maximum values of the data. Use the graphing features of your spreadsheet program to show the data visually.

[4.] Analyze the data. Once all of your data is entered and you have made any calculations you need, you are ready to pose questions to analyze and interpret your data. Organize the information from the database and use it to form conclusions. Be sure to draw conclusions that can be supported by the data available.

Analyze Data and Models

Data and models can provide useful information about geographic distributions and patterns. To make sense of that information, though, you need to pose and answer questions about data and models. What does the data say? What does it mean? What patterns can you find? Practice this skill as you study the graph below.

Immigration from Europe, 1870-1910

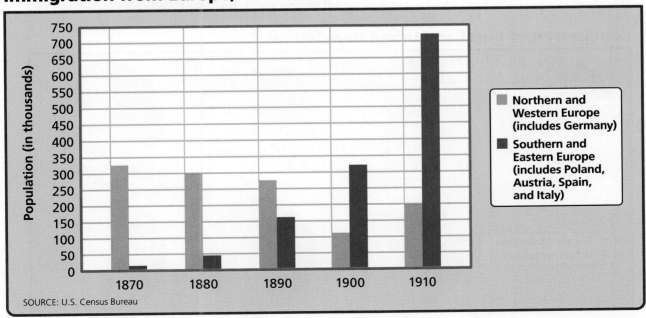

SOURCE: U.S. Census Bureau

[1.] Read the title to learn the geographic distributions represented by the data set, graph, or model.

[2.] Read the data given. When reviewing a graph, read the labels and the key to help you comprehend the data provided. Pose and answer questions to further understand the material. For example, you might ask "Who could use this data?" or "How could this data be used?" or even "Why is this data presented in this particular format?" Thinking critically about the data presented will help you make predictions and comprehend the data.

[3.] Study the numbers, lines, and/or colors to find out what the graphs or data represent. Next, find similarities and differences between multiple models of the same data. Do any additional research to find out more about why the information in the models differs.

[4.] Interpret the graph, data set, or model. Look for interesting geographic distributions and patterns in the data. Look at changes over time or compare information from different categories. Draw conclusions.

Read Charts, Graphs, and Tables

If you pose and answer questions about charts, graphs, or tables you find in books or online, you can find out all sorts of information, such as how many calories are in your favorite foods or what the value of a used car is. If you are trying to solve a math problem that includes a chart, graph, or table, you may need to also use a tool such as a concrete model, a ruler, a protractor, a calculator, a spreadsheet, a computer algebra system, a statistical package, or dynamic geometry software. Analyzing and interpreting the information you find in thematic charts, graphs, and tables can help you make decisions in your life. Practice this skill as you study the graph below.

Comparison of Rural and Urban Populations

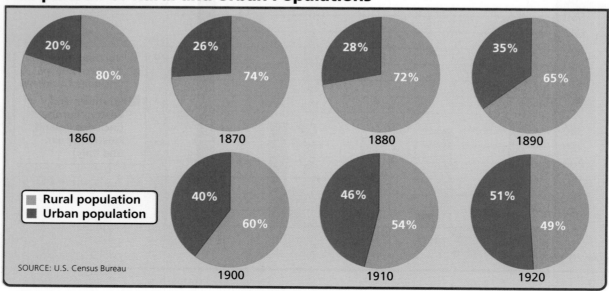

- ■ Rural population
- ■ Urban population

SOURCE: U.S. Census Bureau

1860 — 20% / 80%
1870 — 26% / 74%
1880 — 28% / 72%
1890 — 35% / 65%
1900 — 40% / 60%
1910 — 46% / 54%
1920 — 51% / 49%

[1.] Identify the title and labels of a chart, graph, or table, and read the key, if there is one, to understand the information presented. The title often tells you the topic of the chart, graph, or table, or the type of information you will find. Make sure you understand how the graph shows information. A key or legend often appears in a small box near the edge of the graph or chart. The key will tell you the meaning of lines, colors, or symbols used on the chart or graph. Notice also the column and row headings, and use your reading skills to figure out the meanings of any words you don't know.

[2.] Determine consistencies and inconsistencies, to see whether there is a trend in a graph, chart, or table. Organize information from visuals such as charts and graphs and decide whether or not there is a trend or pattern in the information that you see. Evaluate the data and determine whether the trend is consistent, or steady. Remember that there could be some inconsistencies, or exceptions to the pattern. Try not to miss the overall pattern because of a couple of exceptions.

[3.] Draw conclusions about the data in a chart, graph, or table. Once you understand the information, try to analyze and interpret the information and draw conclusions. If you see a pattern, does the pattern help you to understand the topic or predict future events?

[4.] Create a chart or graph to make the data more understandable or to view the data in a different way. Does the data in the chart or graph help you answer questions you have about the topic or see any causes or effects? For example, you could use your mathematical skills to create circle graphs or bar graphs that visually organize the data in a different way that allows you to interpret the data differently.

[5.] Use the data or information in charts and graphs to understand an issue or make decisions. Use your social studies skills to make inferences, draw conclusions, and take a stand on the issue.

Create Charts and Maps

Thematic charts, graphs, and maps are visual tools for representing information. When you create a thematic chart, graph, or map you will start by selecting the type of data you want to represent. Then you will find appropriate data to include, organize your data, and then create symbols and a key to help others understand your chart, graph, or map. Practice this skill by creating a map of the presidential election of 1952. Use computer software to show how each state voted by party.

[1.] To create a chart or map, first select a region or set of data. Use a map to represent data pertaining to a specific region or location; use a chart to represent trends reflected in a set of data.

PEARSON realize™

PearsonSchool.com/CASS
View Video Tutorials and other
21st Century Skills

[2.] Research and find the data you would like to present in the chart or map. Your choice of data will be based on the theme you wish to explore. For example, a chart or map that explores the theme of changing demographics in New York might include data about the location of different ethnic groups in New York in the nineteenth, twentieth, and twenty-first centuries.

[3.] Organize the data according to the specific format of your chart or map.

[4.] Create symbols, a key (as needed), and a title. Create symbols to represent each piece of data you would like to highlight. Keep each symbol simple and easy to understand. After you have created the symbols, place them in a key. Add a title to your map or chart that summarizes the information presented. Your symbols and key will make it easier for others to interpret your charts and maps.

Analyze Political Cartoons

Political cartoons are visual commentaries about events or people. As you learn to analyze political cartoons, you will learn to identify bias in cartoons and interpret their meaning. You can start by carefully examining the cartoon and considering its possible meanings. Then you can draw conclusions based on your analysis. Practice this skill as you study the political cartoon below.

[1.] Fully examine the cartoon. Identify any symbols in the cartoon, read the text and title, and identify the main character or characters. Analyze the cartoon to identify bias and determine what each image or symbol represents. Conduct research if you need more information to decipher the cartoon.

[2.] Consider the meaning. Think about how the cartoonist uses the images and symbols in the cartoon to express his or her opinion about a subject. Try to interpret the artist's purpose in creating the image.

[3.] Draw conclusions. Use what you have gleaned from the image itself, plus any prior knowledge or research, to analyze, interpret, and form a conclusion about the artist's intentions.

Read Physical Maps

What mountain range is closest to where you live? What major rivers are closest to you? To find out, you would look at a physical map. You can use appropriate reading skills to interpret social studies information such as that found on different kinds of maps. Physical maps show physical features, such as elevation, mountains, valleys, oceans, rivers, deserts, and plains. Practice this skill as you study the map on this page.

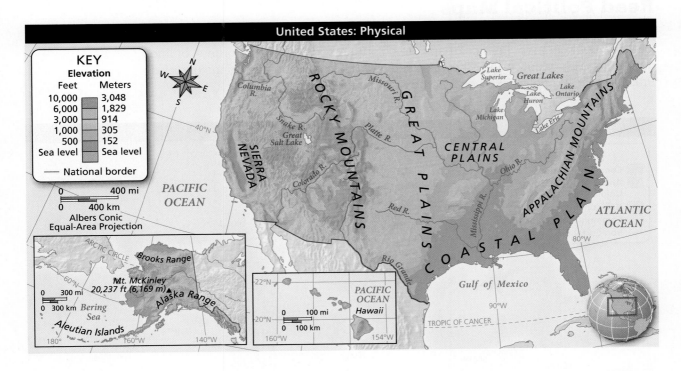

[1.] Identify the title and region shown on a map. A map's title can help you to identify the region covered by the map. The title may also tell you the type of information you will find on the map. If the map has no title, you can identify the region by reading the labels on the map.

[2.] Use the map key to interpret symbols and colors on a map. A key or legend often appears in a small box near the edge of the map. The legend will tell you the meaning of colors, symbols, or other patterns on the map. On a physical map, colors from the key often show elevation, or height above sea level, on the map.

[3.] Identify physical features, such as mountains, valleys, oceans, and rivers. Using labels on the map and colors and symbols from the key, identify the physical features on the map. The information in the key allows you to interpret the information from visuals such as a map. Rivers, oceans, lakes, and other bodies of water are usually colored blue. Colors from the key may indicate higher and lower elevation, or there may be shading on the map that shows mountains.

[4.] Draw conclusions about the region based on natural resources and physical features. Once you understand all the symbols and colors on the map, try to interpret the information from the map. Is it very mountainous or mostly flat? Does it have a coastline? Does the region have lots of lakes and rivers that suggest a good water supply? Pose and answer questions about geographic distributions and patterns shown on the map. Physical maps can give you an idea of lifestyle and economic activities of people in the region.

Read Political Maps

What is the capital of your state? What countries border China? To find out, you could look at a political map. Political maps are colorful maps that show borders, or lines dividing states or countries. They also show capitals and sometimes major cities. Practice reading political maps by studying the map below.

[**1.**] Identify the title of the political map and the region shown. A map's title can help you identify the region covered by the map. The title may also tell you the type of information you will find on the map. If the map has no title, you can identify the region by reading the labels on the map.

[**2.**] Use the map key to interpret symbols and colors on the map. A key or legend often appears in a small box near the edge of the map. The key will help you interpret information from visuals, including maps, by telling you the meaning of colors, symbols, or other patterns on the visual.

[**3.**] Identify boundaries between nations or states. Evaluate government data, such as borders, using the map. It is often easy to see borders, because each state or country will be a different color. If you cannot find the borders, check the key to find the lines used to mark borders on the map.

[**4.**] Locate capital cities. Look at the key to see how capital cities are shown on the map. They are often marked with a special symbol, such as a star.

[**5.**] Draw conclusions about the region based on the map. Once you understand all the symbols and colors on the map, use appropriate reading and mathematical skills to interpret social studies information, such as that shown on the map, in order to draw conclusions about the region. For example, are some countries very large with many cities? These countries are likely to be powerful and influential.

Read Special-Purpose Maps

Some maps show specific kinds of information. These special-purpose maps may show features such as climate zones, ancient trade routes, economic and government data, geographic patterns, or population. Locating and interpreting information from visuals, including special-purpose maps, is an important research skill. Practice this skill as you study the map on this page.

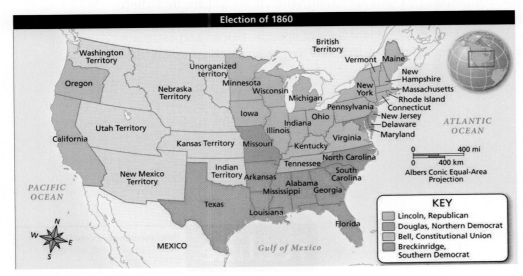

[1.] Identify the title and determine the purpose of a map. A map's title can help you identify the region covered by the map. The title may also tell you the purpose of the map. If the map has no title, see what information the map shows to determine its purpose.

[2.] Use the map key to make sense of symbols and colors on a map. A key or legend often appears in a small box near the edge of the map. The key will tell you the meaning of colors, symbols, or other patterns on the map. Special-purpose maps use these colors and symbols to present information.

[3.] Draw conclusions about the region shown on a map. Once you understand all the symbols and colors on the map, you can use appropriate skills, including reading and mathematical skills, to analyze and interpret social studies information such as maps. You can pose and answer questions about geographic patterns and distributions that are shown on maps. For example, a precipitation or climate map will show you which areas get lots of rainfall and which are very dry. You can evaluate government and economic data using maps. For example, a population map will show you which regions have lots of people and which have small, scattered populations. A historical map will show you the locations of ancient empires or trade routes. Thematic maps focus on a single theme or topic about a region. For example, you can interpret information from a thematic map representing various aspects of Texas during the nineteenth or twentieth century by studying the Great Military Map, which shows forts established in Texas during the nineteenth century, or by studying a map covering Texas during the Great Depression and World War II. By mapping this kind of detailed information, special-purpose maps can help you understand a region's history or geography.

Use Parts of a Map

If you understand how to organize and interpret information from visuals, including maps, you will be able to find the information you are looking for. Understanding how to use the parts of a map will help you find locations of specific places and estimate distances between different places. Practice this skill as you study the map on the Mexican-American War.

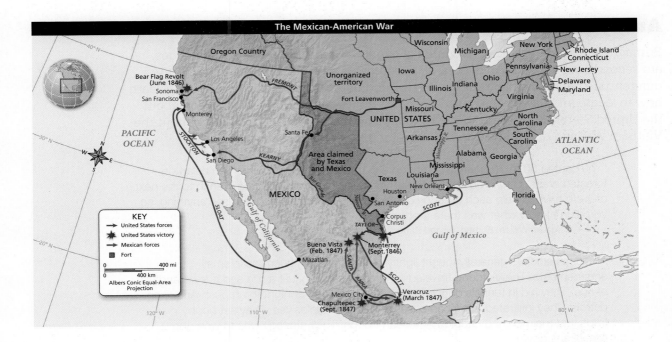

The Mexican-American War

KEY
→ United States forces
★ United States victory
→ Mexican forces
■ Fort

0   400 mi
0   400 km
Albers Conic Equal-Area
Projection

[1.] Identify the title and region of a map. Use appropriate reading skills to interpret social studies information such as map labels. A map's title can help you to identify the region covered by the map. The title may also tell you the type of information you will find on the map. If the map has no title, you can identify the region by reading the labels on the map.

[2.] Use the compass rose to determine direction. Although on most maps north is at the top of the map, you should always double check the compass rose. Often, on the compass rose, the first letter of each direction represents that direction. For example, "N" represents the direction "north." Some compass roses are as simple as an arrow pointing north.

[3.] Use the scale to estimate the distance between places. Use appropriate mathematical skills to interpret social studies information such as a map scale. The scale on a map shows how a measurement on the map compares to the distance on the ground. For example, if one inch on the map represents a mile, the number of inches between two places on the map is the distance in miles.

[4.] Use the key or legend on a map to find information about colors or symbols on a map. A key or legend often appears in a small box near the edge of the map. The legend will tell you the meaning of colors, symbols, or other patterns on the map.

[5.] Use the latitude and longitude grid to determine absolute locations. An absolute location is an exact description of a location on Earth's surface based on latitude and longitude. You can use the latitude and longitude lines on a map to find the absolute location of a place.

Analyze Primary and Secondary Sources

Primary sources are firsthand accounts of events. By contrast, secondary sources are secondhand accounts of events. Both sources are useful, but it is important to differentiate between valid primary and secondary sources. In this lesson, you'll learn how to locate and use primary and secondary sources to acquire information about the United States. Practice this skill by analyzing the two selections below about the Vietnam War and distinguishing between the primary and secondary source.

> "You carried 50 to 70 pounds of equipment, and it was tough going, particularly in forested areas. Often you'd have to pull yourself along from one tree branch to the next, or we'd have to help each other by gripping hands. And you couldn't see anything, so you didn't know what was there around you."
> —Sergeant William Ehrhart, United States Marines

American soldiers generally fought lightly armed Vietcong guerrillas in small engagements. The Vietcong traveled light, often carrying just a rifle and a few handfuls of rice. They hid in tunnels during the day and emerged at night to ambush American patrols. They infiltrated American bases and set off explosives. They set booby traps that maimed and crippled American troops. Their strategy was to wear the Americans down.

[1.] Determine who created the source as well as when and why it was created. Determine whether it is a primary or secondary source. Identify the author of the document. Next, look for the date the document was written or the date when the document was first published. Most primary sources are written close to the date of the events described. Secondary sources are often written well after the events described. Firsthand observers or participants in an event create primary sources. People who did not witness an event create secondary sources. Primary sources record an event. Secondary sources analyze or draw conclusions about events. Secondary sources rely on both primary and secondary sources. Good research requires you to analyze and evaluate the validity of information, arguments, and counterarguments from a primary or secondary source for frame of reference.

[2.] Identify the main idea and supporting details, and determine whether they are facts or opinions. Read the text carefully and ask yourself, "What point is this text making?" This point is the main idea. Then reread the text and list details that support this main idea. Decide whether these details are facts or opinions. If the details are facts, it should be possible to confirm them in other sources. If the author uses emotional language that shows feelings, the supporting details are probably opinions. Carefully analyze and evaluate the validity of information, arguments, and counterarguments from primary and secondary sources for point of view.

[3.] Decide whether the source's information is biased or if it is accurate and credible. Check statements in the text against reliable sources, such as encyclopedias or books written by experts on the topic. If reliable sources agree with the text, it is probably fairly accurate. If most of the text seems to be opinions rather than facts, it is not an accurate source of information. Still, these opinions can teach you about the author's world. A writer who observed an exciting or scary event may use emotional language to describe the event, but the source may still be a reliable account. An important part of research is analyzing and evaluating the validity of the information, arguments, and counterarguments from primary and secondary sources for bias or propaganda.

Compare Viewpoints

When people disagree about a topic, they have different viewpoints. Knowing how to analyze and evaluate the validity of information, arguments, and counterarguments from both primary and secondary sources for point of view can help you to learn more about a topic. Practice this skill by reading the following quotations and comparing the viewpoints on dictatorship.

> "Dictatorship...involves costs which the American people will never pay: The cost of having our children brought up, not as free and dignified human beings, but as pawns..."
> –Franklin Roosevelt, State of the Union Address, January 4, 1939

> "The [Nazi Party] has laid down the directive...we must insist that all organs of education...have to [fulfill] their duty towards the community..."
> –Adolf Hitler, Speech delivered in German Reichstag on January 30, 1937

[1.] Identify the authors of texts presenting different points of view and identify each author's frame of reference. Frame of reference is a term that describes the experiences, values, and ideas that influence a person's opinions and actions. It can also be referred to as *point of view*. First, identify the group or individual that wrote each text. Determine if the source is primary or secondary. As you read, take note of any information about the author's experiences or background. Also, look for any signs of what the author thinks is important. These types of statements can help you analyze and evaluate the validity of information, arguments, and counterarguments from both primary and secondary sources for point of view.

[2.] Recognize any similarities and differences between the authors' frames of reference and identify the opinion of each author. Pay attention to any similarities and differences between the two authors' experiences, values, and ideas. Read carefully to identify the opinion of each author. In an article about a rock band, an author who played guitar in a band for ten years argues that Band A is the best band today because of its great guitarist. In a second article, another author who sang for many years argues that Band B is the best because of its lead singer. Notice how authors' arguments and counterarguments are shaped by their frame of reference, or point of view.

[3.] Draw conclusions about similarities and differences between authors' points of view. With some information about the point of view of each author, you can understand why they have different opinions. This helps you to analyze and evaluate the validity of the information, arguments, and counterarguments. In the example of the two authors writing about rock bands, each author stresses his or her own areas of expertise. You might decide to listen to the band recommended by the singer if you share an interest in vocals. If you are more interested in instrumentals, you might choose the band recommended by the guitarist.

Identify Bias

Being able to analyze and evaluate the validity of information, arguments, and counterarguments for bias helps you to determine whether primary or secondary sources you find online, in books, or in the media are reliable. When you are able to identify bias in written, oral, and visual material, you can see when someone is presenting only one side of an issue or basing an argument on emotion instead of facts. Practice this skill by applying the steps below whenever you read an editorial or an op-ed piece in the news media.

[1.] Identify the author of a source and the author's purpose. First, identify the author of the source. The author may be a group or an organization rather than a single person. The author may state his or her purpose very clearly in the source. If not, the type of source may give you an idea of the purpose. For example, the writer of an encyclopedia aims to summarize information about a subject. The author of a political Web site may want you to vote for a candidate.

[2.] Identify the main idea, and check whether the main idea is supported with facts or opinions. Read the document carefully and ask yourself, "What is the main point of this selection?" Your answer to this question is the main idea. Reread the document and list details that support this main idea. Decide whether these details are facts or opinions. To find out whether they are facts, check whether other reliable sources include the same information. If your source uses statements that shows feelings, those statements are probably opinions.

[3.] Look for the use of emotional language or one-sided opinions. Look for words that can show opinions such as "good" and "bad." Be aware of statements that make you feel angry, scared, or excited. Also, watch out for statements that only express one side of an issue. These are all signs of bias.

[4.] Draw conclusions about the author's bias, if any. Is the author using mostly emotional language with few facts to support his or her ideas? Are there insults or other very negative language in the source? If so, the source is probably biased. Similarly, if you notice that the author is presenting only one side of an issue, the source is probably not reliable. It is important to analyze and evaluate the information, arguments, and counterarguments in both primary and secondary sources for bias.

Evaluate Existing Arguments

When you evaluate existing arguments, you must evaluate and analyze the point of view and biases of your sources and their authors. Who is the author and what is he or she trying to accomplish? How valid are the arguments in your primary and secondary sources? If you master these skills, you will be able to analyze and interpret social studies information such as speeches. Practice this skill as you read and evaluate the excerpt on this page.

> We hold these truths to be self-evident: that all men and women are created equal; that they are endowed by their Creator with certain inalienable rights; that among these are life, liberty, and the pursuit of happiness. . . .
>
> The history of mankind is a history of repeated injuries and usurpations [seizures] on the part of man toward woman, having in direct object the establishment of an absolute tyranny over her. To prove this, let facts be submitted to a candid [fair] world.
>
> He has never permitted her to exercise her inalienable right to the elective franchise.
>
> He has compelled her to submit to law in the formation of which she had no voice. . . .
>
> He has made her, if married, in the eye of the law, civilly dead. He has taken from her all right in property, even to the wages she earns. . . .
>
> Now, in view of this entire disfranchisement of one-half the people of this country, their social and religious degradation, in view of the unjust laws above mentioned, and because women do feel themselves aggrieved, oppressed, and fraudulently deprived of their most sacred rights, we insist that they have immediate admission to all the rights and privileges which belong to them as citizens of the United States.
>
> —*Declaration of Sentiments and Resolutions*, 1848

[1.] Identify the claim or thesis. What is the author or source claiming? The claim or thesis is usually found in the introduction and/or conclusion of a written or spoken argument.

[2.] Identify the reasons (claims to truth or facts) the author offers in support of his or her claim. What evidence does the author or source provide to support their claims? Make a list of the evidence provided to support each claim.

[3.] Evaluate the argument. Analyze and evaluate the validity of the evidence presented to support each claim. Use the appropriate skills to analyze and interpret social studies information, such as speeches. Research each claim to be sure that the author's statements are accurate. Carefully check for evidence of bias or propaganda. Be sure you understand the author's point of view and his or her frame of reference. Finally, check to be sure that the author's conclusions follow logically from the evidence presented. If the evidence is accurate, the author is free from bias, and conclusions follow logically from the evidence, the claims are probably valid.

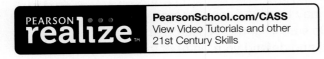

Consider and Counter Opposing Arguments

Before you can effectively counter opposing arguments, you'll need to analyze possible counterarguments for frame of reference, bias, point of view, and propaganda. You'll plan your response ahead of time, collecting research and data. Then, you'll make a point of acknowledging the opposing view before presenting your counterarguments. To practice this skill, suppose you are preparing for a debate about raising the minimum wage in your state. Choose a side of the debate to support. What arguments will you use to support your side of the debate? What counterarguments will you anticipate the other side using? Why is it useful to anticipate the other side's arguments?

[**1.**] Fully understand your argument and the potential counter points. Do research as needed to find out more about other opposing views. Analyze and evaluate the validity of possible counterarguments from primary and secondary sources for frame of reference, bias, point of view, and propaganda.

[**2.**] Make predictions and outline a response to several of the opposing views. Continue researching as needed. Researching, analyzing, and evaluating the validity of opposing arguments will help you support and strengthen your own. Opposing arguments can consist of any reasons, conclusions, or claims that oppose yours. Outline your response to each opposing reason, conclusion, or claim.

[**3.**] To counter an opposing argument, first acknowledge the opposing view. This strategy shows that you have heard the opposing argument and are responding accordingly. Consider using statements such as "I understand your point, but you should also consider the following..." You can also respond by refuting facts, logic, etc. Be sure to respond to each opposing argument. Ignoring or dismissing a counterargument shows that your response is weak and unsupported.

Participate in a Discussion or Debate

When you participate effectively in a collaborative discussion or debate, your goal is to explain, analyze, and defend a point of view—often related to a current political or economic issue. To be a successful debater, you'll do your research, present your position, and defend your point of view in a courteous manner. You'll build on others' ideas and express your own clearly and persuasively. Use the steps below to prepare for a discussion on this question: Do you think the United States should act as a "global policeman?" Why or why not?

[**1.**] Research. Before participating in a discussion or debate, come to discussions prepared. Do research to gain knowledge of your subject so that you may be an informed and prepared participant. Take notes as needed to help you prepare. Jot down main points and any questions you may have. As you research, decide where you might stand on the issue. Be sure to gather research and sources that will allow you to explain, analyze, and defend your point of view.

[2.] Present your position. After you have organized your thoughts and decided where you stand, explain and defend your point of view. Explicitly draw on your preparation by referring to evidence from texts and other research on the topic to stimulate a thoughtful, well-reasoned exchange of ideas. Be sure to stay focused on the topic and your line of argument. Ask questions that challenge the accuracy, logic, or relevance of opposing views.

[3.] During the discussion or debate, be patient and courteous. Work with your classmates to promote civil, democratic discussions. Listen attentively, be respectful and supportive of peers, and speak only when instructed to do so by the moderator. Be sure to allow others to express their views; do not monopolize the debate or discussion. Speak clearly and slowly. Propel conversations by posing and responding to questions that may probe your reasoning and evidence.

Give an Effective Presentation

When you create a written, visual, and oral presentation, you teach, convince, or share information with an audience. Effective presentations use both words and visuals to engage audiences. Delivery is also important. For example, you can use the way you move, speak, and look at the audience to keep people interested. Use the steps below to prepare and deliver a presentation on U.S. President Richard Nixon's visit to China in 1972.

[1.] Identify the purpose of your presentation and your audience. Think about the purpose of your written, visual, and oral presentation. If this is a research report, you will need facts and data to support your points. If you are trying to persuade your audience, look for powerful photos. Keep your audience in mind. Consider their interests and present your topic in a way that will engage them.

[2.] Write the text and find visual aids for your presentation. Look online and in books and magazines for information and images for your presentation. Organize the information and write it up carefully so that it is easy for your audience to understand. Diagrams can show complicated information in a clear way. Visuals also get people interested in the presentation. So choose large, colorful images that people in the back of the audience will be able to see.

[3.] Practice and work to improve your presentation. Keep practicing your oral presentation until you know the material well. Then, practice some more, focusing on improving your delivery.

[**4.**] Use body language, tone of voice, and eye contact to deliver an effective presentation. Answer questions if the audience has them. At the beginning of your oral presentation, take a breath, smile, and stand up tall. Speak more loudly and more clearly than you would in normal conversation. Also, try not to rush through the presentation. Glance at your notes but speak naturally, rather than reading. Look at people in the audience. If people are confused, pause to clarify. Finally, leave time for people in the audience to ask questions.

Write an Essay

There are four steps to writing an essay. You'll start by selecting a topic and research sources, then you'll write an outline and develop a thesis or point of view. After drafting your essay, you'll carefully proofread it to be sure you've used standard grammar, spelling, sentence structure, and punctuation. Finally, you'll revise and polish your work. To practice this skill, select a topic that interests you about the modern U.S. presidency and develop a thesis. Then explain to a partner the steps you will take to write your essay.

[**1.**] Choose your topic and research sources. Check which types of sources you will need. Gather different types of reliable sources that support the argument you will be making.

[**2.**] Write an outline and generate a thesis. First write your topic at the top of the page then list all the points or arguments you want to make about the topic; also list the facts and examples that support these points. Your thesis statement will inform the reader of the point you are making and what question you will be answering about the topic. When writing your thesis, be as specific as possible and address one main idea.

[**3.**] Draft your essay. After finishing your research and outline, begin writing the body of your essay; start with the introduction then write a paragraph for each of your supporting points, followed by a conclusion. As you write, do your best to use standard grammar, spelling, sentence structure, and punctuation. Be sure any terminology is used correctly.

[**4.**] Revise. An important part of the writing process involves checking for areas in which information should be added, removed, or rewritten. Try to imagine that this paper belongs to someone else. Does the paper have a clear thesis? Do all of the ideas relate back to the thesis? Read your paper out loud and listen for awkward pauses and unclear ideas. Lastly, check for mistakes in standard grammar, spelling, sentence structure, punctuation, and usage.

Avoid Plagiarism

When you don't attribute ideas and information to source materials and authors, you are plagiarizing. Plagiarizing—claiming others' ideas and information as your own—is considered unethical. You can avoid plagiarizing by carefully noting down which authors and sources you'll be using, citing those authors and sources in your paper, and listing them in a bibliography. The issue of plagiarism in mass media and digital sources has become an important issue in recent years. As Internet users gain wider access to copyright information, the legal dangers of reusing someone else's work have grown. Practice this skill by following these steps.

[1.] Keep a careful log of your notes. As you read sources to gain background information on your topic, keep track of ideas and information and the sources and authors they come from. Write down the name of each source next to your notes from that particular source so you can remember to cite it later on. Create a separate section in your notes where you keep your own thoughts and ideas so you know which ideas are your own. Using someone else's words or paraphrasing their ideas does not make them yours.

[2.] Cite sources in your paper. You must identify the source materials and authors you use to support your ideas. Whenever you use statistics, facts, direct quotations, or paraphrases of others' views, you need to attribute them to your source. Cite your sources within the body of your paper. Check your assignment to find out how they should be formatted.

[3.] List your sources in a bibliography at the end of your paper. List your source materials and authors cited in alphabetical order by author, using accepted formats. As you work, be sure to check your list of sources from your notes so that none are left out of the bibliography.

Solve Problems

Problem solving is a skill that you use every day. It is a process that requires an open mind, clear thinking, and action. Practice this skill by considering the lack of volunteers for a local project such as a food bank or park clean up and using these steps to solve the problem.

[1.] Understand the problem. Before trying to solve a problem, make sure that you gather as much information as possible in order to identify the problem. What are the causes and effects of the problem? Who is involved? You will want to make sure that you understand different perspectives on the problem. Try not to jump to conclusions or make assumptions. You might end up misunderstanding the problem. If the problem is mathematical, you should start by explaining to yourself the meaning of a problem and look for entry points to its solution.

[2.] Consider possible solutions and choose the best one. Once you have identified the problem and gathered some information, list and consider a number of possible options. Right away, one solution might seem like the right one, but try to think of other solutions. Be sure to consider carefully the advantages and disadvantages of each option. It can help to take notes listing benefits and drawbacks. Look for the solution whose benefits outweigh its drawbacks. After considering each option, choose the solution you think is best. You should analyze givens, constraints, relationships, and goals, making conjectures about the form and meaning of the solution and planning a solution pathway rather than simply jumping into a solution attempt.

[3.] Make and implement a plan. Choose and implement a solution. Make a detailed, step-by-step plan to implement the solution that you choose. Write your plan down and assign yourself a deadline for each step. That will help you to stay on track toward completing your plan. Try to think of any problems that might come up and what you will do to address those problems. Of course, there are many things that you cannot predict. Stay flexible. Evaluate the effectiveness of the solution and adjust your plan as necessary.

Make Decisions

Everyone makes decisions. The trick is to learn how to make good decisions. How can you make good decisions? First, identify a situation that requires a decision and gather information. Then, identify possible options and predict the consequences of each option. Finally, choose the best option and take action to implement a decision. Practice this skill by considering the steps you should take when making a decision about which candidate you should vote for in a local, state, or national election.

[1.] Determine the options between which you must decide. In some cases, like ordering from a menu at a restaurant, your options may be clear. In other cases, you will need to identify a situation that requires a decision, gather information, and identify the options that are available to you. Spend some time thinking about the situation and brainstorm a number of options. If necessary, do a little research to find more options. Make a list of options that you might choose.

[2.] Review the costs and benefits of each option. Carefully predict the consequences of each option. You may want to make a cost-benefit list for each option. To do this, write down the option and then draw two columns underneath it. One column will be the "pro" or benefit list. The other column will be the "con" or cost list. Note the pros and cons for each of your options. Try not to rush through this process. For a very important decision, you may even want to show your list to someone you trust. This person can help you think of costs and benefits that you had not considered.

[3.] Determine the best option and act on it. Look through your cost-benefit lists. Note any especially serious costs. If an option has the possibility of an extremely negative consequence, you might want to cross it off your list right away. Look closely at the options with the most benefits and the fewest costs, and choose the one that you think is best. Once you have made a choice, take action to implement a decision. If necessary, make a detailed plan with clear steps. Set a deadline to complete the steps to keep yourself moving toward your goal.

Being an Informed Citizen

Informed citizens understand the responsibilities, duties, and obligations of citizenship. They are well informed about civic affairs, involved with their communities, and politically active. When it comes to issues they personally care about, they take a stand and reach out to others.

[1.] Learn the issues. A great way to begin to understand the responsibilities of citizenship is to first find topics of interest to you. Next, become well informed about civic affairs in your town, city, or country. Read newspapers, magazines, and articles you find online about events happening in your area or around the world. Analyze the information you read to come to your own conclusions. Radio programs, podcasts, and social media are also great ways to keep up with current events and interact with others about issues.

[2.] Get involved. Attend community events to speak with others who know the issues. Become well informed about how policies are made and changed. Find out who to speak to if you would like to take part in civic affairs and policy creation. There are government websites that can help direct you to the right person. These websites will also provide his or her contact details.

[3.] Take a stand and reach out. Write, call, or meet with your elected officials to become a better informed, more responsible citizen. Do research about candidates who are running for office to be an informed voter. Start your own blog or website to explore issues, interact with others, and be part of the community or national dialogue.

Political Participation

Political participation starts with an understanding of the responsibilities, duties and obligations of citizenship, such as serving the public good. When you understand your role as a political participant, you can get involved through volunteering for a political campaign, running for office, or interacting with others in person or online.

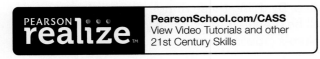

PEARSON realize™

PearsonSchool.com/CASS
View Video Tutorials and other
21st Century Skills

[1.] Volunteer for a political campaign. Political campaigns offer a wide variety of opportunities to help you become involved in the political process and become a responsible citizen by serving the public good. As a political campaign volunteer you may have the opportunity to attend events, make calls to voters, and explore your community while getting to know how other voters think about the responsibilities, duties, and obligations of citizenship.

[2.] Run for office in your school or community. A good way to become involved in your school or community is to run for office. Student council or community positions offer a great opportunity for you to become familiar with the campaign and election process.

[3.] Reach out to others. Start or join an interest group. Interest groups enable people to work together on common goals related to the political process. Write a letter or email a public official. By contacting an elected official from your area, you can either support or oppose laws or policies. You can also ask for help or support regarding certain issues.

[4.] Interact online. Social networking sites and blogs offer a great way for people of all ages to interact and write about political issues. As you connect with others, you'll become more confident in your role as a citizen working for the public good.

Voting

Voting is not only a right. It is also one of the primary responsibilities, duties, and obligations of citizenship. Before you can legally vote, however, you must understand the voter registration process and the criteria for voting in elections. You should also understand the issues and know where different candidates stand on those issues.

[1.] Check eligibility and residency requirements. In order to vote in the United States, you must be a United States citizen who is 18 years or older, and you must be a resident of the place where you plan to vote.

[2.] Register to vote. You cannot vote until you understand the voter registration process. You can register at city or town election offices, or when you get a driver's license. You can also register by mail or online. You may also have the option of registering at the polls on Election Day, but this does not apply in all states. Make sure to find out what you need to do to register in your state, as well as the deadline for registering. You may have the option of declaring a political party when registering.

[3.] Learn the issues. As the election approaches, research the candidates and issues in order to be an informed voter. Watch televised debates, if there are any. You can also review the candidates' websites. By doing these things and thinking critically about what you learn, you will be prepared to exercise your responsibility, duty and obligation as a United States citizen.

[4.] Vote. Make sure to arrive at the correct polling place on Election Day to cast your ballot. Research to find out when the polls will be open. Advance voting, absentee voting, and voting by mail are also options in certain states for those who qualify.

Serving on a Jury

As an American, you need to understand the duties, obligations and responsibilities of citizenship; among these is the expectation that you may be required to serve on a jury. You will receive a written notice when you are summoned to jury duty and you'll receive instruction on the special duties and obligations of a juror. You'll follow the American code of justice which assumes that a person is innocent until proven guilty, and you'll follow instructions about keeping trial information confidential.

[1.] Wait to receive notification. If you are summoned to serve as a juror, you will be first notified by mail. If you are chosen to move on to the jury selection phase, lawyers from both sides will ask you questions as they select the final jury members. It is an honor to serve as a juror, as it is a responsibility offered only to American citizens.

[2.] Follow the law and remain impartial. Your job is to determine whether or not someone broke the law. You may also be asked to sit on the jury for civil cases (as opposed to criminal cases); these cases involve lawsuits filed against individuals or businesses for any perceived wrong doing (such as broken contracts, trespassing, discrimination, etc.). Be sure to follow the law as it is explained to you, regardless of whether you approve of the law or not. Your decision about the trial should not be influenced by any personal bias or views you may have.

[3.] Remember that the defendant is presumed innocent. In a criminal trial, the defendant must be proven guilty "beyond a reasonable doubt" for the verdict to be guilty. If the trial team fails to prove the defendant to be guilty beyond a reasonable doubt, the jury verdict must be "not guilty."

[4.] During the trial, respect the court's right to privacy. As a juror, you have specific duties, obligations, and responsibilities under the law. Do not permit anyone to talk about the case with you or in your presence, except with the court's permission. Avoid media coverage once the trial has begun so as to prevent bias. Keep an open mind and do not form or state any opinions about the case until you have heard all of the evidence, the closing arguments from the lawyers, and the judge's instructions on the applicable law.

PEARSON realize ™

PearsonSchool.com/CASS
View Video Tutorials and other
21st Century Skills

Paying Taxes

Paying taxes is one of the responsibilities of citizenship. How do you go about figuring out how much you've already paid in taxes and how much you still owe? It's your duty and obligation to find out, by determining how much has been deducted from your pay and filing your tax return.

[1.] Find out how taxes are deducted from your pay. In the United States, payroll taxes are imposed on employers and employees, and they are collected and paid by the employers. Check your pay stub to find out how much money was deducted for taxes. Be sure to also save the W-2 tax form your employer sends to you. You will need this form later on when filing your tax paperwork. Also save any interest income statements. All this information will help you fulfill your obligation as an American taxpayer.

[2.] Check the sales taxes in your state. All but five states impose sales and use taxes on retail sale, lease, and rental of many goods, as well as some services. Sales tax is calculated as the purchase price times the appropriate tax rate. Tax rates vary widely from less than one percent to over ten percent. Sales tax is collected by the seller at the time of sale.

[3.] File your tax return. Filing your tax return is more than an obligation: it's also a duty and responsibility of citizenship. You may receive tax forms in the mail, or pick them up at the local Post Office or library. Fill the forms in and then mail or electronically send completed tax forms and any necessary payments to the Internal Revenue Service (IRS) and your state's department of revenue. The IRS provides free resources to help people prepare and electronically file their tax returns; go to IRS.gov to learn more. Note: certain things such as charitable donations and business expenses are tax deductible.

Analyze Images

When analyzing an image, it's important to go beyond your first impressions. Look closely to determine the content of the image, make careful note of details in the image, and consider the context in which the image appears. Using clues you collect through this process, you can identify the purpose of the image shown.

[1.] dentify the content. When reviewing an image, look closely at the features and text, and determine which information is important. Consider the overall message of the image.

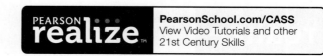

[2.] Note the details. When analyzing images of people, study facial expressions and body positions. Consider the emotions these expressions or positions suggest. Also consider the arrangement (how the objects or people are placed in an image). When considering the arrangement, examine the location (where something is placed) and the scale (the size of the visual components). For example, is one individual placed front and center while another is set far to the side? If so, the central figure is probably the most important.

[3.] Consider context. Where does the image appear? Is it on a billboard? In a textbook? In a magazine? Read all of the captions and credits. If possible, gather information about who created or paid for the image. Understanding the context of an image will help you to better understand its message.

[4.] Identify the purpose. Why did the artist create this image? Images can help illustrate a point, persuade an audience, or sell a product. If it is in an advertisement, chances are its purpose is to sell a product. If it's a political cartoon, it is probably offering commentary on a political situation or event. If it's in a newspaper, it is most likely intended to provide information to support a news story.

Use Context Clues

Using context clues can help you figure out the meaning of an unknown word. You look for context clues in the text surrounding an unfamiliar word. Once you find enough clues to predict a word's meaning, then you can check it by using a dictionary. Sometimes an author will define an unfamiliar word. Notice how James Madison defines the term "faction" in this excerpt from the *Federalist*, No. 10:

> AMONG the numerous advantages promised by a well constructed Union, none deserves to be more accurately developed than its tendency to break and control the violence of faction. . . . By a faction, I understand a number of citizens, whether amounting to a majority or a minority of the whole, who are united and actuated by some common impulse of passion, or of interest, adversed to the rights of other citizens, or to the permanent and aggregate interests of the community. . . .

[1.] Stop and reread the sentence when you find a word you do not know. When you find a word that you do not know, take a minute to reread the sentence. Do your best to understand the general meaning of the sentence even though there is a word that you do not know.

[2.] Identify the topic of the sentence and see if this helps you figure out the unknown word's meaning. After you have reread the sentence, determine its topic. The word that you do not know may be related to the topic of the sentence. This can help you get a sense of the meaning of the word.

[**3.**] Check around the unknown word for phrases or other words that describe it or link to ideas that are familiar to you. If the unknown word is not related to the topic of the sentence, check for other words and phrases that you know. Look to see how the unknown word is related to other words and phrases in the sentence.

[**4.**] Predict the word's meaning and then look up its definition in a dictionary. Try to predict the meaning of the word based on its connection to the topic or to other words in the sentence. Then, check your guess in a dictionary.

Develop a Clear Thesis

A thesis is a statement of your position or perspective on a topic. In order to define and express your thesis, you'll need to review the assignment, research and narrow down your topic, and then determine your position or point of view on the topic.

[**1.**] Review the assignment. First determine what kind of paper you are being asked to write (some examples are persuasive, analytical, narrative, or expository).

[**2.**] Research and narrow your topic. After selecting your topic, do research to find out what others have written about it. Familiarize yourself with the topic and be sure to explore sources that present varying viewpoints. Narrow the topic by focusing on one or two specific areas of interest.

[**3.**] Take a position on the topic. Form your own conclusion about the topic. Be specific and avoid general statements; this conclusion will serve as the thesis you address in your paper. Make sure you can support your thesis with evidence; you may need to make revisions as you move forward in the researching and drafting process. Your thesis statement should answer a specific question. A clear thesis will express one main idea and show your conclusions about a subject.

Distinguish Between Fact and Opinion

When you distinguish between fact and opinion, you separate information that is true from statements showing a person's beliefs or feelings. Separating fact from opinion will help you decide whether to trust the information in a source.

[**1.**] Identify the author of a source and his or her purpose for writing. Consider that purpose as you look for facts and opinions. First, find the author of the source. The author may be a group or an organization rather than a single person. The author may state his or her purpose very clearly in the source. If not, the type of source may give you an idea of the purpose. For example, the writer of an encyclopedia aims to summarize information about a subject. The author of a political Web site may want you to vote for a candidate.

[**2.**] Identify possible facts by looking for information that can be proven true. Do research to find out if the information is actually true. Read through the source and write down statements made by the author. Check other sources on this subject to see if they agree. Try to find reliable sources, such as encyclopedias, your textbook, and books written by experts on the topic. If you discover that reliable sources do not confirm statements in your source, it is not reliable. The statements you have identified are probably not true facts.

[**3.**] Decide if the author is expressing an opinion by looking for language that signals opinions and by looking for statements that are personal beliefs or judgments. Look for words that can show opinions, such as "good," "bad," "should," and "must." Statements such as "I think" and "I believe" also indicate opinions. Be aware of statements that make you feel angry, scared, or excited. The author may be using emotion rather than facts to support his or her ideas. Consider the evidence that the author gives to support his or her ideas and opinions. Sources that are full of opinions with few facts to support them are not reliable. Even if the source contains some facts, be careful if those facts all support the author's opinion. Check other reliable sources to see if the author has left out facts that do not support his or her opinion.

Evaluate Web Sites

Knowing how to evaluate Web sites will help you to understand how reliable a Web site is. Some Web sites are biased toward one point of view. Others may contain inaccurate information. The Internet is full of a confusing variety of sources and content that ranges from the reliable and accurate to the biased and false. Digital sources may also be full of slander and libel, so always check who has produced the content found on the Internet. Finally, many Web sites are out of date.

[**1.**] Identify the author or sponsor of the Web site, assess the reliability of the author, and identify any bias to find out whether the Web site is objective. Finding the author or sponsor of a Web site is not always easy. Check the bottom of the home page or look for a link that says "About Us." Then, try to learn about the author or sponsor. What is the goal of the Web site? Do you see emotional language or other language that suggests that the Web site is biased? Avoid Web sites with a clear bias, as they may not present both sides of a topic.

[2.] Identify when the Web site was last updated and determine whether the information is current. The copyright date or date that the Web site was created or updated can often be found at the bottom of the home page. For online encyclopedias, blogs, and other sites that frequently add new content, be sure to check the date of each entry. Some content may be much more recent than the date when the site was created. Think about your topic and then decide if the site in current. Are you researching something for a history class? In that case, even if the Web site is a number of years old, it may be a good source. On the other hand, if you are looking for information about an ongoing current event, information from a month ago might already be out of date.

[3.] Compare the content of the Web site to other Web sites and sources on the same topic. Once you have decided that a Web site seems reliable and up-to-date, be sure to check the site against other sources. Even the best sites may have mistakes. Read other reliable Web sites or do some more research at the library. Having at least two reliable sources for each piece of information will help to make sure that you have accurate information.

Analyze Media Content

When you analyze media content, you think carefully about who produced the content and why they produced it. You think critically about all aspects of the content. When you think carefully about content in this way, you can draw conclusions about the message and its intended impact. This is particularly important when analyzing content on the Internet, with its confusing variety of sources and content that ranges from the reliable and accurate to the biased and false. Digital sources may also be full of slander and libel, so always check who has produced the content found on the Internet. To practice this skill, research a controversial political topic on the Internet. Take note of the viewpoint of each source and identify the author. Explain how the bias of the author shapes the information that you have found.

[1.] Identify the media source and important information about the author. The source of a piece of media content may be a single writer or a whole organization. The name of the author may appear at the beginning of a book or article. However, for Web sites and some documents, you may need to look carefully for the person or organization that created the content. Try to learn all you can about the source. What experience does the author have? If the source is an organization, who gives money to the organization?

[2.] Determine the economic, social, and political context of the message. The context is the background that helps shape the message. Is the writer responding to a certain problem or situation? Is there an event, such as an upcoming election, that might be important to the writer? These factors may help you figure out the purpose of the writer and whether or not the writer is biased.

[3.] Identify the message, noting what is missing, and determine whether the message relies on stereotypes. Try to figure out the meaning of the message. Is the source leaving out important information? Is the message based on stereotypes or other inaccurate information? If you are not certain, you may want to read more about the topic to understand it better.

[4.] Draw conclusions about the intended impact of the message. Once you have thought about the context and content of the message, try to draw a conclusion about the purpose of the message. What does the writer hope that you will think or do after reading the message?

Organize Your Ideas

Before writing a paper or planning a speech, it's important to organize your ideas. You'll start by thinking about the task for which you're preparing. Next, you'll brainstorm organizational ideas and create an outline.

[1.] Consider the task. Before organizing your ideas, review the project you're working on. Why are you organizing your ideas? Who will be using your organized ideas? Are you planning a project, writing a paper, or getting ready to give a speech?

[2.] Brainstorm. Drawing a brainstorming map might help you see how your thoughts connect to one another, which will help you when you begin organizing your writing. Alternatively, brainstorm by simply listing your ideas. Another strategy is to explain your thinking out loud to someone else; this may help you organize your ideas in a more logical way.

[3.] Create an outline. Outline your main points and jot down the supporting details under each section.

Publish Your Work

Using the Internet, you can share your work by publishing it on Web sites, blogs, or wikis. Blogs are like online personal journals, and wikis are Web sites that many people can write and maintain.

[**1.**] Choose a topic that interests you and write about it in a classroom wiki or blog. Before picking a topic, think about the purpose or theme of the classroom wiki or blog. Choose a topic that fits that purpose. Read reliable sources to learn about your topic. Think about the best way to organize your ideas. After organizing your ideas, write your entry. Be sure to check for spelling and grammar errors before posting to the site. If possible, list your sources on the site.

[**2.**] Upload digital images to your entry in order to enhance the information. Search online for images related to your topic. Be careful to pick images that you have permission to use. In some cases, the person who made a photo or owns a photo does not want the photo to be used by other people. You may be able to find more information about a photo by clicking on it. In addition to photos, you can use maps, charts, graphs, and illustrations.

[**3.**] Ask classmates to build upon your ideas and post their comments. Engage in an online discussion forum with classmates and respond to one another's comments. In a wiki, your classmates may be able to edit your work. If you write a blog post, your classmates can make comments on your work. Try to respond to the comments of your classmates. If a classmate makes a good suggestion, edit your entry to improve it. If you think that your classmate's suggestion might not be correct, write a comment to explain this respectfully to your classmate. It is easy to feel self-conscious if a lot of people are reading your work. Focus on learning from your classmates and seeing your work from a fresh perspective.

Search for Information on the Internet

You can use the Internet for answers to all kinds of questions. The trick is to make sure you are finding reliable sources that provide accurate information. This is particularly important when analyzing content on the Internet, with its confusing variety of sources and content that ranges from the reliable and accurate to the biased and false. Digital sources may also be full of slander and libel, so always check who has produced the content found on the Internet. To practice this skill, research a topic on the Internet by first going to the website of a governmental or educational organization. Then find a website of a private individual and compare the information to the content found on a more reliable source.

[1.] Identify the topic and information you need, and enter key words or phrases about the topic into a search engine. Make a list of key words or phrases related to your topic. These could be names, dates, or other details about the topic. Enter your key words into a search engine. Read the titles of the first 10–20 results. If these results are too general, try adding more specific key words until you get results related to your topic.

[2.] Analyze headings and URLs to find reliable sources. Look for URLs that end in .edu or .gov, or Web sites of well-known newspapers, news magazines, and news broadcasters. Avoid sites that show bias, and try to find sites that give reliable sources for their information. You may get many results from the search engine. Look at the URLs, or Web addresses, to get clues about the source of the Web site. Within the URL, you may see the name of a newspaper, government office, or other reliable source. URLs that end in .edu are usually university Web sites. URLs that end in .gov are government offices. Writers at universities and government offices are often experts in their field and will try to present the facts without bias. Focus on the sites that seem the most reliable.

[3.] Use information from a variety of sites and check the online information against other sources, such as other reliable Web sites, encyclopedias, and newspapers. Be careful not to base your research on a single Web site. Even the best sites may have mistakes. Read other reliable Web sites or do some additional research at the library. Reading multiple sources will give you a better understanding of your topic.

Set a Purpose for Reading

When you set a purpose for reading, you decide what you want to learn from a text and make a plan for getting what you want. First, you get familiar with the text. Next, you identify exactly what you want to learn. Then, you can analyze the information by finding the main idea as you read.

[1.] Preview the text and scan titles, headings, special text, and images to identify the main ideas covered in the topic. Often, main ideas are included in titles, headings, and other special text. Special text may be primary sources, words that are highlighted, or ideas listed with bullet points. Also, take a look at visuals and captions. By previewing these pieces of information, you should quickly get a sense of the main idea of a text.

[2.] Think about the topic and decide *why* you are reading— your purpose, or what you want to learn. Before reading the text in more detail, make sure that you know why you are reading the text. What do you want to learn from this text? What information do you need? Having a clear purpose for your reading will help you to analyze the text, identify the main idea, and find the information that you need more quickly.

[3.] Analyze the text to find information that serves your purpose or tells you what you want to know. Take notes if needed. Read actively with your purpose in mind. Analyze the information in the text by finding the main idea. If the main idea of a paragraph does not seem related to your purpose, read through the paragraph quickly. In a long passage, you may even be able to skip some sections. Spend more time analyzing the sections that are related to your purpose. Make sure that you understand these sections. Take notes as you find the information that you need.

Support Ideas with Evidence

Without supporting evidence, your writing is just a statement of opinion. With evidence, however, it becomes a statement of fact. When you support ideas with evidence, you start by checking your assignment to be sure you know what kind of evidence you need. Next, you'll examine your sources to be sure they are appropriate for your topic. Finally, you'll correctly incorporate your evidence into your essay. If you are using the Internet to find evidence to support your opinion, remember to carefully avoid unreliable websites that might be full of inaccuracies and bias.

[1.] Review the assignment. Before you gather sources, make sure you understand the type of evidence you need to include to support your ideas.

[2.] Examine your sources. Ensure your evidence is related to your overall argument. Ask yourself the following: Why is this information important? Why does it matter? Does this evidence support my thesis? If so, how?

[3.] Incorporate your evidence. There are several different ways to present your evidence in writing. You can use quotes from your sources or include a summary; make sure to cite all of your sources so they can be identified. Other options include graphs, charts, or tables; excerpts from an interview; or photographs or illustrations. Make sure to cite evidence to back up each supporting point.

Write a Journal Entry

Journals are a great place to brainstorm and get creative. The process is simple: just think of a topic, express your ideas, and then review what you wrote. A Journal will allow you to write routinely over a period of time, whether it is months or days.

[**1.**] Think of a topic that interests you.

[**2.**] Be open minded and express your ideas. Use your journal as a forum to explore your own unique thoughts. Journals are great for experimenting with creative writing, problem solving, and brainstorming.

[**3.**] Reread what you have written. Reviewing your journal will help you to remember some of the great ideas you've come up with and may help you in your creative or essay writing. What's more, revisiting past material will help you see how your writing has developed and give you a chance to think of new ideas to explore.

[The United States: Political]

[The United States: Physical]

Elevation

Feet	Meters
Above 10,000	Above 3,000
7,000–10,000	2,000–3,000
3,000–7,000	1,000–2,000
700–3,000	200–1,000
0–700	0–200
Below sea level	Below sea level

Cape Cod
Long Island
Atlantic Ocean
Chesapeake Bay
Cape Hatteras
40°N
70°W

APPALACHIAN MOUNTAINS

ATLANTIC COASTAL PLAIN

L. Ontario
L. Erie
L. Huron
L. Superior
L. Michigan

Tennessee R.
Alabama R.
Ohio R.
Mississippi R.
Mississippi R.
Missouri R.

GULF COASTAL PLAIN

L. Okeechobee
Gulf of Mexico
Tropic of Cancer
80°W
90°W

Conic Projection
0   200   400 mi
0   200   400 km

INTERIOR PLAINS

OZARK PLATEAU
OUACHITA MTS.
Red R.

GREAT   PLAINS

BLACK HILLS
Pikes Peak
Arkansas R.
LLANO ESTACADO
Rio Grande

Mt. Elbert

Platte R.
Missouri R.

ROCKY   MOUNTAINS

Colorado R.
Snake R.
Great Salt Lake
GRAND CANYON

GREAT BASIN

CASCADE RANGE
Mt. Rainier
Columbia R.

SIERRA NEVADA
Mt. Whitney

Pacific Ocean

Hawaii
Mauna Kea
Kauai
Oahu
Molokai
Maui
22°N
Miller Projection
0   75   150 mi
0   75   150 km

Arctic Ocean
BROOKS RANGE
Mt. McKinley
Gulf of Alaska
70°N
140°W
150°W
160°W
170°W
60°N
50°N
Conic Projection
0   300   600 mi
0   300   600 km

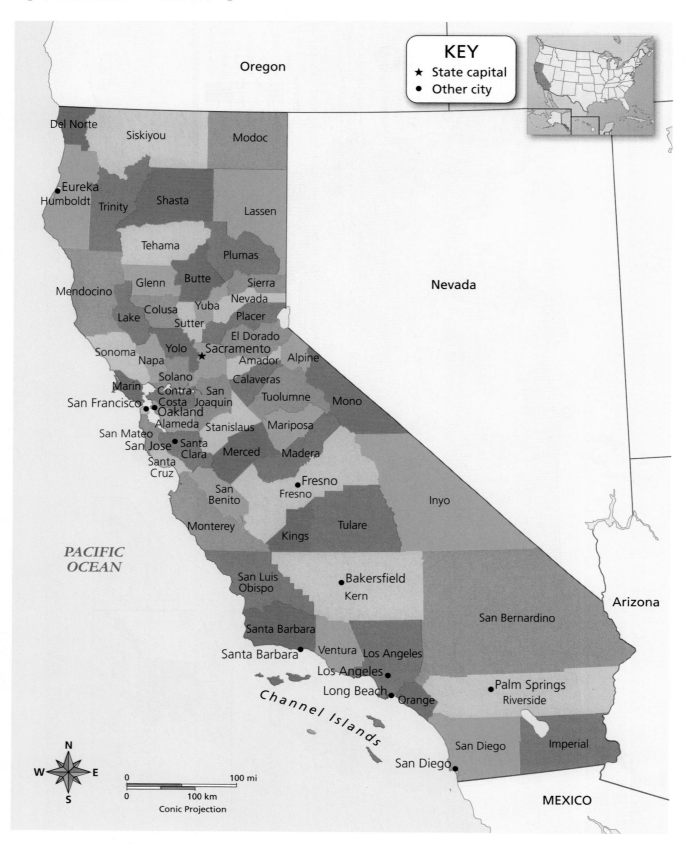

[California: Political]

KEY
★ State capital
● Other city

Oregon

Del Norte
Siskiyou
Modoc

● Eureka
Humboldt
Trinity
Shasta
Lassen

Tehama

Plumas

Mendocino
Glenn
Butte
Sierra

Colusa
Yuba
Nevada

Lake
Sutter
Placer

El Dorado

Sonoma
Yolo
★ Sacramento
Amador
Alpine

Napa

Solano
Calaveras

Marin
Contra
San
Tuolumne
Mono

San Francisco
Costa
Joaquin

● Oakland
Alameda

San Mateo
Stanislaus
Mariposa

San Jose ● Santa
Clara
Merced
Madera

Santa
Cruz

● Fresno
Fresno

San
Benito
Inyo

Monterey

Kings
Tulare

Nevada

PACIFIC
OCEAN

San Luis
Obispo
● Bakersfield
Kern

San Bernardino

Arizona

Santa Barbara

Ventura
Los Angeles

Santa Barbara ●
● Los Angeles

Channel Islands
Long Beach ●
● Orange

● Palm Springs
Riverside

San Diego
Imperial

● San Diego

MEXICO

N
W E
S

0   100 mi
0   100 km
Conic Projection

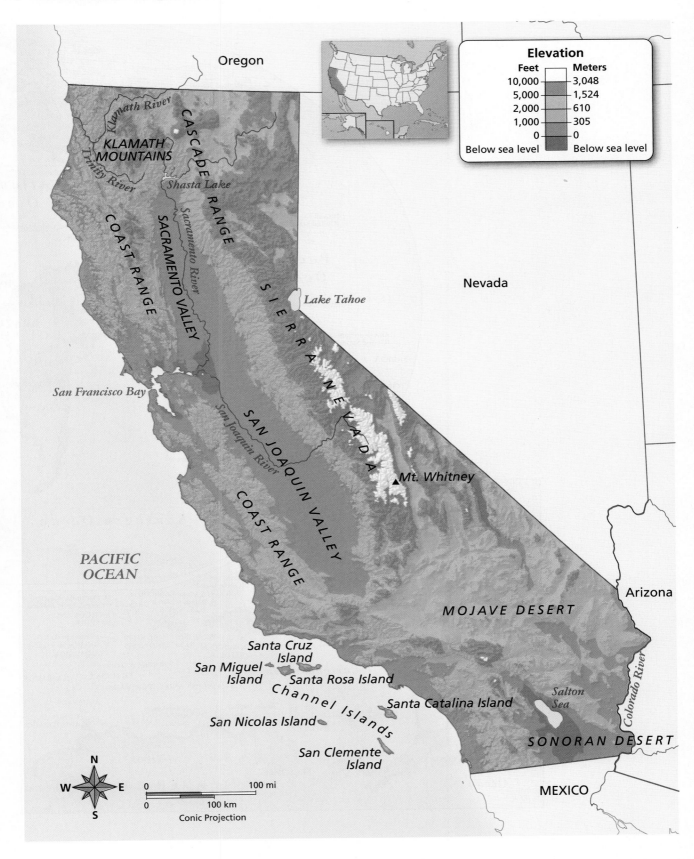

Oregon

Elevation

Feet		Meters
10,000		3,048
5,000		1,524
2,000		610
1,000		305
0		0
Below sea level		Below sea level

Klamath River

CASCADE RANGE

KLAMATH
MOUNTAINS

Trinity River

Shasta Lake

COAST RANGE

SACRAMENTO VALLEY

Sacramento River

Nevada

Lake Tahoe

S I E R R A   N E V A D A

San Francisco Bay

San Joaquin River

SAN JOAQUIN VALLEY

COAST RANGE

▲Mt. Whitney

PACIFIC
OCEAN

Arizona

MOJAVE DESERT

Santa Cruz
Island

San Miguel
Island

Santa Rosa Island

Channel Islands

Santa Catalina Island

*Salton
Sea*

Colorado River

San Nicolas Island

San Clemente
Island

SONORAN DESERT

N
W   E
S

0   100 mi

0   100 km

Conic Projection

MEXICO

Alaska
(United States)

CANADA

NORTH

AMERICA

Toronto
Chicago • • New York

UNITED STATES ⊗ Washington, D.C.

Los Angeles •

Atlantic

Ocean

Hawaii
(United States)

Tropic of Cancer

MEXICO

see inset below

Mexico City ⊗

Pacific

Ocean

0° Equator

Line Islands
(United States)

Galápagos
Islands
(Ecuador)

COLOMBIA ⊗ Bogotá

French Guiana
(France)

SURINAME

ECUADOR

PERU

BRAZIL

SOUTH

AMERICA

American Samoa
(United States)

BOLIVIA

Rio de
Janeiro

SAMOA

PARAGUAY

São Paulo

TONGA

French Polynesia
(France)

Tropic of Capricorn

CHILE

Pitcairn Islands
(U.K.)

ARGENTINA URUGUAY ⊗

⊗ Capital

• Other city

Buenos Aires

160°W   140°W   120°W   100°W   80°W   60°W

Southern Ocean

Antarctic Circle

90°W   85°W   80°W

Gulf of Mexico   UNITED
STATES

B
A
H
A
M
A
S

25°N

Tropic of Cancer

160°W   140°W   120°W   100°W   80°W   60°W

Turks and
Caicos Islands
(U.K.)

St. Martin (St. Maarten)
(France & Neth. Antilles)

CUBA

U.S. Virgin British Virgin
Islands Islands
(U.S.) (U.K.)

Anguilla
(U.K.)

ANTIGUA AND
BARBUDA

20°N

MEXICO

Cayman Islands
(U.K.)

HAITI

Puerto Rico
(U.S.)

ST. KITTS
AND NEVIS

Montserrat (U.K.)
Guadeloupe (France)

JAMAICA

DOMINICA

BELIZE

DOMINICAN
REPUBLIC

Martinique (France)

GUATEMALA

Caribbean Sea

ST. LUCIA

BARBADOS

HONDURAS

15°N

ST. VINCENT AND THE GRENADINES

EL SALVADOR

GRENADA

NICARAGUA

Conic Projection

0   200   400 mi

Aruba (Neth.)

Netherlands
Antilles
(Neth.)

TRINIDAD
AND TOBAGO

0   200   400 km

75°W

60°W

10°N

Caracas ⊗

Pacific

Ocean

COSTA RICA

PANAMA

COLOMBIA

Lake
Maracaibo

VENEZUELA

SOUTH AMERICA

GUYANA

90°W   85°W   80°W

Arctic Ocean

Arctic Circle

ICELAND

Greenland
(Denmark)

EUROPE

RUSSIA

ASIA

KAZAKHSTAN

MONGOLIA

GEORGIA
AZER.
ARMENIA
UZBEK.
TURKMEN.
KYRGYZSTAN
TAJIKISTAN

NORTH
KOREA

Beijing
Seoul
SOUTH
KOREA

JAPAN
Tokyo

Pacific
Ocean

Tehran
IRAQ
IRAN AFGHAN.
CHINA

Shanghai

MOROCCO
ALGERIA
LIBYA
ISRAEL
JORDAN
Cairo
EGYPT
KUWAIT
BAHRAIN
QATAR
PAKISTAN
NEPAL
BHUTAN
New Delhi
Karachi
U.A.E.
OMAN
SAUDI
ARABIA

MYANMAR
(BURMA)
TAIWAN
(Claimed by China)

Hong Kong

CAPE
RDE

AFRICA
CHAD
SUDAN
ERITREA
YEMEN

INDIA
BANGLADESH
LAOS
Mumbai

MARSHALL
ISLANDS

CEN.
AFR.
REP.
SOUTH
SUDAN
DJIBOUTI
Addis Ababa
ETHIOPIA
SOMALIA

CAMEROON

DEM. REP.
OF THE
CONGO
UGANDA
KENYA
RWANDA

SRI
LANKA

THAILAND
Bangkok
CAMBODIA
VIETNAM

PHILIPPINES

KIRIBATI

SÃO TOMÉ
AND PRÍNCIPE
GABON
CONGO
BURUNDI
TANZANIA

MALDIVES

BRUNEI
MALAYSIA
SINGAPORE

FEDERATED STATES
OF MICRONESIA

NAURU
SOLOMON
ISLANDS
TUVALU

see inset below

Atlantic
Ocean

ANGOLA
MALAWI
ZAMBIA

SEYCHELLES

COMOROS

Indian
Ocean

INDONESIA

Jakarta

TIMOR
LESTE

PAPUA NEW
GUINEA

ZIMBABWE
BOTSWANA
MADAGASCAR

MAURITIUS

OCEANIA
VANUATU
FIJI
ISLANDS

NAMIBIA

New
Caledonia
(France)

SWAZILAND
SOUTH AFRICA
LESOTHO

AUSTRALIA

Cape Town

Sydney

NEW
ZEALAND

N
W   E
S

Robinson Projection

0   1,000   2,000 mi

0   1,000   2,000 km

Southern Ocean

Barents
Sea

ANTARCTICA

Western
Sahara
(Morocco)

ALGERIA

N
W   E
S

MAURITANIA

SWEDEN
FINLAND

NORWAY

Conic Projection
0   200   400 mi

0   200 400 km

Moscow

SENEGAL
GAMBIA

MALI

NIGER

IRELAND
UNITED
KINGDOM

North
Sea
DENMARK

ESTONIA
LATVIA
LITHUANIA
RUSSIA

BELARUS

RUSSIA

GUINEA-
BISSAU

GUINEA

BURKINA
FASO

London

NETHERLANDS
GERMANY
Berlin
POLAND

Kiev

Atlantic
Ocean
BELGIUM
LUX.
Paris
CZECH REP.
SLOVAKIA
UKRAINE

SIERRA
LEONE

BENIN
TOGO
GHANA

NIGERIA

Bay of
Biscay
FRANCE
LIECH.
SWITZ.
AUSTRIA
HUNGARY
SLOVENIA
CROATIA

MOLDOVA
ROMANIA

CÔTE
D'IVOIRE

LIBERIA

Lagos

PORTUGAL
ANDORRA
MONACO
ITALY
SAN
MARINO
BOS. AND
HERZ.
SERBIA
AND
MONT.
BULGARIA
Black Sea
Istanbul

Madrid
SPAIN
Corsica
(France)
VATICAN
CITY
Rome
ALBANIA
MAC.
TURKEY

Azimuthal Equidistant
Projection

0   200   400 mi

0   200   400 km

Gulf of Guinea
EQUATORIAL GUINEA

Gibraltar
(U.K.)
Ceuta
(Spain)
Melilla
(Spain)
Sardinia
(Italy)
Balearic Isands
(Spain)
GREECE

Sicily
(Italy)
CYPRUS
SYRIA
LEBANON

MOROCCO
ALGERIA
TUNISIA
MALTA
Mediterranean
Sea
Crete
(Greece)

[Africa: Political]

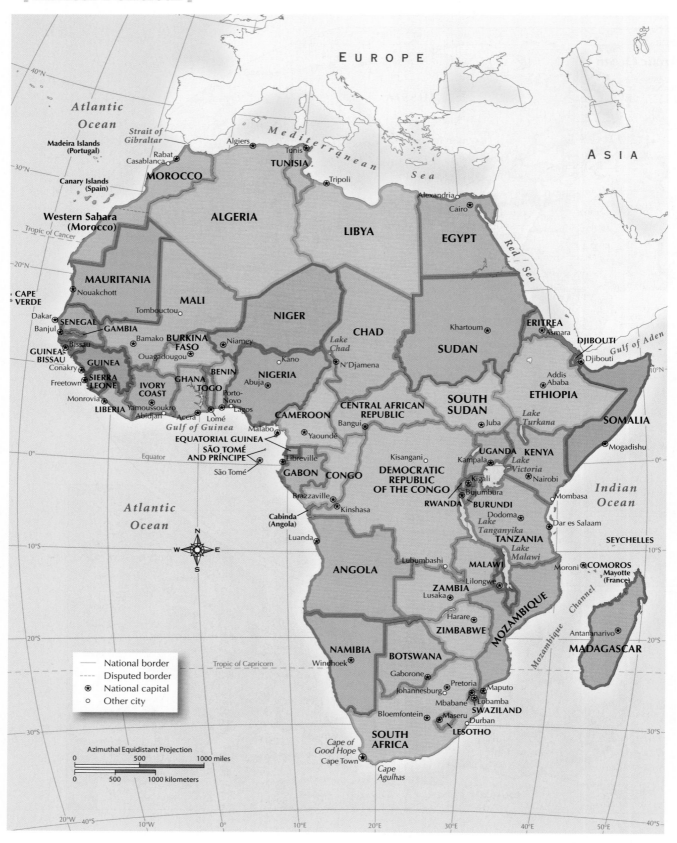

EUROPE

ASIA

Atlantic Ocean

Madeira Islands (Portugal)

Strait of Gibraltar

Canary Islands (Spain)

Western Sahara (Morocco)

Tropic of Cancer

CAPE VERDE

M e d i t e r r a n e a n   S e a

Algiers

Tunis

Rabat

Casablanca

MOROCCO

TUNISIA

Tripoli

ALGERIA

LIBYA

EGYPT

Alexandria

Cairo

Red Sea

MAURITANIA

Nouakchott

MALI

Tombouctou

NIGER

CHAD

Khartoum

SUDAN

ERITREA

Asmara

DJIBOUTI

Gulf of Aden

Dakar

SENEGAL

Banjul

GAMBIA

Bamako

BURKINA FASO

Niamey

Lake Chad

Kano

N'Djamena

Djibouti

Bissau

GUINEA-BISSAU

Ouagadougou

GUINEA

Conakry

SIERRA LEONE

Freetown

IVORY COAST

GHANA

BENIN

TOGO

NIGERIA

Abuja

Porto-Novo

CENTRAL AFRICAN REPUBLIC

SOUTH SUDAN

Addis Ababa

ETHIOPIA

Monrovia

LIBERIA

Yamoussoukro

Abidjan

Accra

Lomé

Lagos

CAMEROON

Bangui

Juba

Lake Turkana

SOMALIA

Gulf of Guinea

Malabo

EQUATORIAL GUINEA

Yaoundé

UGANDA

KENYA

Mogadishu

SÃO TOMÉ AND PRÍNCIPE

Equator

Libreville

São Tomé

GABON

CONGO

Kisangani

Kampala

Lake Victoria

Kigali

Nairobi

Indian Ocean

DEMOCRATIC REPUBLIC OF THE CONGO

RWANDA

Bujumbura

BURUNDI

Dodoma

Atlantic Ocean

Brazzaville

Kinshasa

Mombasa

Cabinda (Angola)

Dar es Salaam

Luanda

TANZANIA

Lake Tanganyika

SEYCHELLES

ANGOLA

Lubumbashi

Lake Malawi

MALAWI

Moroni

COMOROS

Mayotte (France)

Lilongwe

ZAMBIA

Lusaka

Mozambique Channel

Harare

MOZAMBIQUE

Antananarivo

ZIMBABWE

MADAGASCAR

Tropic of Capricorn

NAMIBIA

BOTSWANA

Windhoek

Gaborone

Pretoria

Maputo

Johannesburg

Mbabane

Lobamba

SWAZILAND

Bloemfontein

Maseru

Durban

LESOTHO

Cape of Good Hope

SOUTH AFRICA

Cape Town

Cape Agulhas

Legend

— National border
--- Disputed border
⊛ National capital
○ Other city

N
W · E
S

Azimuthal Equidistant Projection

0   500   1000 miles

0   500   1000 kilometers

EUROPE

ASIA

Atlantic
Ocean

Strait of
Gibraltar

Madeira
Islands

Canary
Islands

Mediterranean
Sea

Suez
Canal

Qattara
Depression

Sinai
Peninsula

ATLAS MOUNTAINS

of Cancer

S A H A R A

Ahaggar
Mountains

Tibesti
Mountains

LIBYAN DESERT

Nile

Arabian Desert

Red Sea

Lake
Nasser

NUBIAN
DESERT

Senegal R.

River

Niger

S A H E L

Fouta
Djallon

Volta R.

Lake
Chad

River

White Nile R.

Blue Nile

Lake Tana

Gulf of Aden

10°N

Lake Volta

Benue River

Adamawa
Highlands

ETHIOPIAN
HIGHLANDS

SUDD

GREAT RIFT VALLEY

Gulf of Guinea

Bioko

Ubangi R.

Congo R.

Lake
Albert

Lake
Turkana

São Tomé

Equator

CONGO
BASIN

Mt. Kilimanjaro
19,341 ft. (5,895 m)

0°

Atlantic
Ocean

N
W E
S

Lake
Victoria

Serengeti
Plain

Lake
Tanganyika

Zanzibar

Indian
Ocean

Lake
Malawi

Comoro
Islands

10°S

Zambezi R.

Mozambique Channel

Madagascar

Okavango
Basin

20°S

NAMIB DESERT

Tropic of Capricorn

KALAHARI
DESERT

Limpopo R.

Orange R.

Drakensberg

30°S

Cape of
Good Hope

Cape
Agulhas

Elevation

Feet	Meters
More than 13,000	More than 3,960
6,500–13,000	1,980–3,960
1,600–6,500	480–1,980
650–1,600	200–480
0–650	0–200
Below sea level	Below sea level

—— National border
----- Disputed border

Azimuthal Equidistant Projection

0   500   1000 miles

0   500   1000 kilometers

20°W   40°S   10°W   0°   10°E   20°E   30°E   40°E   50°E   40°S

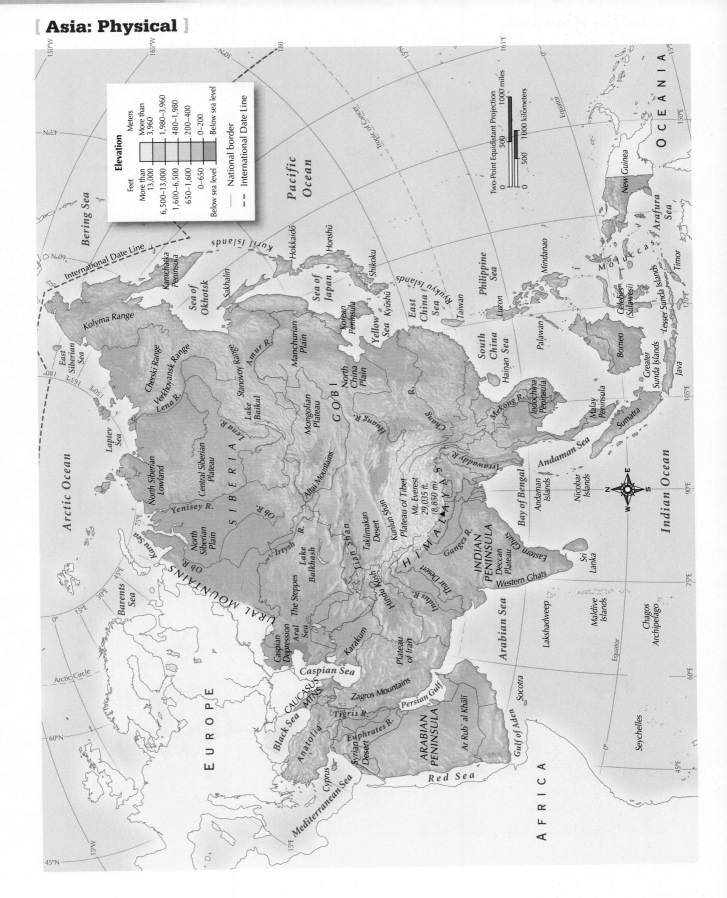

Elevation

Feet	Meters
More than 13,000	More than 3,960
6,500–13,000	1,980–3,960
1,600–6,500	480–1,980
650–1,600	200–400
0–650	0–200
Below sea level	Below sea level

—— National border
----- International Date Line

Two-Point Equidistant Projection

Bering Sea

Pacific Ocean

International Date Line

Kolyma Range

Kamchatka Peninsula

Sea of Okhotsk

Sakhalin

Kuril Islands

Hokkaidō

Honshū

Sea of Japan

Shikoku

Kyūshū

Korean Peninsula

East China Sea

Ryukyu Islands

Taiwan

Philippine Sea

Luzon

Mindanao

New Guinea

OCEANIA

Arafura Sea

Moluccas

Celebes (Sulawesi)

Timor

Lesser Sunda Islands

Borneo

Greater Sunda Islands

Java

Sumatra

Malay Peninsula

Indochina Peninsula

South China Sea

Hainan

Mekong R.

Palawan

East Siberian Sea

Cherski Range

Verkhoyansk Range

Lena R.

Stanovoy Range

Amur R.

Manchurian Plain

North China Plain

Yellow Sea

GOBI

Mongolian Plateau

Huang R.

Chang R.

Laptev Sea

SIBERIA

Lake Baikal

Ob R.

Irrawaddy R.

Andaman Sea

Andaman Islands

Nicobar Islands

Indian Ocean

Arctic Ocean

North Siberian Lowland

Central Siberian Plateau

Yenisey R.

North Siberian Plain

Altai Mountains

Taklimakan Desert

Kunlun Shan

Plateau of Tibet

Mt. Everest 29,035 ft. (8,850 m)

HIMALAYAS

Ganges R.

INDIAN PENINSULA

Deccan Plateau

Eastern Ghats

Bay of Bengal

Sri Lanka

Kara Sea

Irtysh

Lake Balkhash

Tian Shan

Hindu Kush

Indus R.

Thar Desert

Western Ghats

Lakshadweep

Maldive Islands

Chagos Archipelago

URAL MOUNTAINS

Barents Sea

The Steppes

Aral Sea

Karakum

Plateau of Iran

Arabian Sea

Socotra

Seychelles

Equator

Arctic Circle

EUROPE

Caspian Depression

Caspian Sea

Zagros Mountains

Persian Gulf

Ar Rub' al Khālī

CAUCASUS MTNS.

Black Sea

Anatolia

Tigris R.

Euphrates R.

Syrian Desert

ARABIAN PENINSULA

Gulf of Aden

Red Sea

Cyprus

Mediterranean Sea

AFRICA

Elevation

Feet	Meters
More than 13,000	More than 3,960
6,500–13,000	1,980–3,960
1,600–6,500	480–1,980
650–1,600	200–400
0–650	0–200
Below sea level	Below sea level

— National border

URAL MOUNTAINS

Pechora R.
Kama R.
Ural R.
Caspian Sea
Volga R.
Caspian Depression
CAUCASUS MTS.
Mt. Elbrus 18,510 ft. (5,642 m)
Volga Upland
Don R.
Sea of Azov
Black Sea
Sea of Marmara
ASIA
Bosporus
Dardanelles
Aegean Sea
N. Dvina R.
Central Russian Upland
Barents Sea
Kola Peninsula
White Sea
Lake Onega
Lake Ladoga
Dnieper R.
Dniester R.
Danube R.
Crete
NORTH EUROPEAN PLAIN
Gulf of Finland
Gulf of Bothnia
SCANDINAVIAN PENINSULA
Kjölen Mountains
Lake Vänern
Lake Vättern
Gotland
Sjælland
Baltic Sea
Vistula R.
Oder R.
Carpathian Mountains
Transylvanian Alps
Great Hungarian Plain
Balkan Mountains
BALKAN PENINSULA
Pindus Mts.
ARCTIC OCEAN
Arctic Circle
Jan Mayen
Norwegian Sea
Faeroe Islands
Shetland Islands
North Sea
Elbe R.
Jutland
Rhine R.
Danube R.
Dinaric Alps
Adriatic Sea
Ionian Sea
Tyrrhenian Sea
Maltese Islands
Sicily
Mediterranean Sea
Iceland
Denmark Strait
British Isles
Ireland
Great Britain
Thames R.
English Channel
Seine R.
Loire R.
Lake Geneva
Mt. Blanc 15,775 ft. (4,808 m)
ALPS
Massif Central
Garonne R.
Po R.
Apennines
ITALIAN PENINSULA
Corsica
Sardinia
Balearic Islands
Bay of Biscay
Pyrenees
Ebro R.
Douro R.
Meseta
Tagus R.
IBERIAN PENINSULA
Guadalquivir R.
Strait of Gibraltar
ATLANTIC OCEAN
AFRICA

Lambert Conformal Conic
0   200   400 miles
0   200   400 kilometers

[North and South America: Political]

ASIA

EUROPE

Arctic Ocean

Bering Strait

180°

0°

International Date Line

Beaufort Sea

Greenland (Denmark)

Arctic Circle

60°N

Bering Sea

Baffin Bay

Davis Strait

Nuuk

Gulf of Alaska

Alaska (United States)

Great Bear Lake

Great Slave Lake

Hudson Bay

Labrador Sea

45°N

45°N

CANADA

Vancouver

Lake Winnipeg

Great Lakes

Ottawa

Atlantic Ocean

Toronto

Chicago

New York

Washington, D.C.

UNITED STATES

30°N

30°N

Los Angeles

Houston

Tropic of Cancer

Gulf of Mexico

Nassau

DOMINICAN REPUBLIC

MEXICO

Havana

BAHAMAS

Mexico City

CUBA

HAITI

Puerto Rico (United States)

15°N

Belmopan

JAMAICA

Kingston

Port-au-Prince

Santo Domingo

U.S. Virgin Islands (United States)

15°N

BELIZE

Guatemala City

HONDURAS

Guadeloupe (France)

Martinique (France)

GUATEMALA

Tegucigalpa

Caribbean Sea

San Salvador

NICARAGUA

DOMINICA

BARBADOS

EL SALVADOR

Managua

TRINIDAD AND TOBAGO

San José

Caracas

GUYANA

COSTA RICA

Panama

VENEZUELA

Georgetown

Paramaribo

PANAMA

Bogotá

Cayenne

French Guiana (France)

COLOMBIA

SURINAME

Quito

Equator

0°

Galápagos Islands (Ecuador)

ECUADOR

0°

Pacific Ocean

PERU

BRAZIL

Lima

15°S

Lake Titicaca

La Paz

Brasília

15°S

BOLIVIA

Sucre

Tropic of Capricorn

PARAGUAY

Rio de Janiero

Asunción

São Paulo

CHILE

ARGENTINA

Santiago

30°S

URUGUAY

30°S

Buenos Aires

Montevideo

Rio de la Plata

Atlantic Ocean

— National border
- - - International Date Line
⊛ National capital
○ Other city

Lambert Azimuthal Equal-Area Projection

0   1000   2000 miles

0   1000   2000 kilometers

Falkland Islands (U.K.)

45°S

45°S

165°W   150°W   135°W   120°W   105°W   90°W   75°W   60°W   45°W   30°W   15°W

Elevation

Feet	Meters
More than 13,000	More than 3,960
6,500–13,000	1,980–3,960
1,600–6,500	480–1,980
650–1,600	200–400
0–650	0–200
Below sea level	Below sea level

.... National border
– – – International Date Line

Lambert Azimuthal Equal-Area Projection

0   1000   2000 miles
0   1000   2000 kilometers

[Australia, New Zealand, and Oceania: Political-Physical]

Elevation

Feet	Meters	
More than 13,000	More than 3,960	
6,500–13,000	1,980–3,960	
1,600–6,500	480–1,980	
650–1,600	200–480	
0–650	0–200	
Below sea level	Below sea level	

- International Date Line
- National border
- State border
- Reef
- ⊛ National capital
- ★ State capital
- ○ Other city

Sea of Okhotsk
Cherski Range
Kamchatka Peninsula
Kolyma R.
Kolyma Range
International Date Line
Laptev Sea
120°E
90°E
60°E
Kara Sea
Novaya Zemlya
Barents Sea
Kola Peninsula
Lake Ladoga
EUROPE
Gulf of Bothnia
Baltic Sea
SCANDINAVIA
Severnaya Zemlya
Novosibirskiye Ostrova
East Siberian Sea
Franz Josef Land
30°E
Arctic Ocean
Svalbard
Norwegian Sea
North Sea
Wrangel Island
Chukchi Peninsula
180°
North Pole
Greenland Sea
Jan Mayen
Arctic Circle
0°
Shetland Islands
Aleutian Islands
Bering Sea
60°N
Chukchi Sea
80°N
Faeroe Islands
British Isles
Ireland
St. Lawrence Island
Bering Strait
North Magnetic Pole
Denmark Str.
Iceland
Atlantic Ocean
Nunivak Island
Mt. McKinley (Denali) 20,320 ft. (6,194 m) Alaska ▲
Brooks Range
150°W
90°W
Ellesmere Island
Greenland
60°N
Beaufort Sea
120°W
Queen Elizabeth Islands
Alaska Peninsula
Alaska Range
Yukon River
Banks Island
Baffin Bay
Kodiak Island
ROCKY MOUNTAINS
Mackenzie River
Amundsen Gulf
Victoria Island
Baffin Island
Davis Strait
Lambert Azimuthal Equal Area Projection
Pacific Ocean
Gulf of Alaska
Great Bear Lake
NORTH AMERICA
Foxe Basin
60°W
30°W

Lambert Azimuthal Equal Area Projection

| 0 | 400 | 800 miles |

| 0 | 400 | 800 kilometers |

Elevation

Feet		Meters
More than 13,000		More than 3,960
6,500–13,000		1,980–3,960
1,600–6,500		480–1,980
650–1,600		200–400
0–650		0–200
Below sea level		Below sea level

—— National border
– – International Date Line

[Antarctica: Physical]

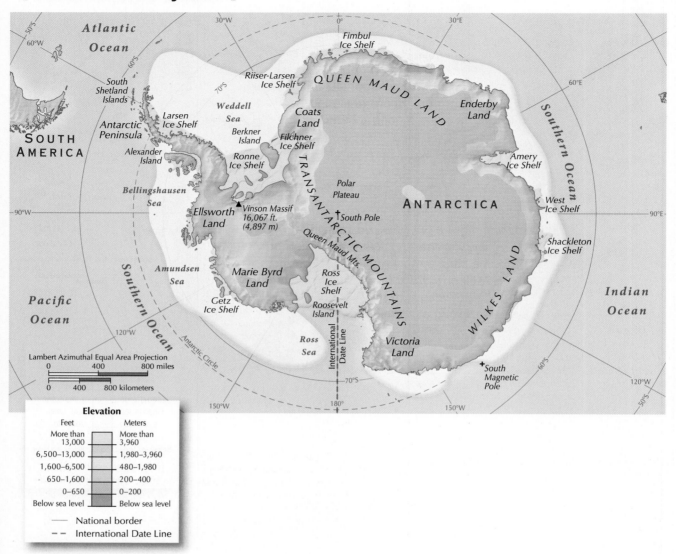

Atlantic Ocean

60°W

50°S

30°W

0°

30°E

60°E

Southern Ocean

South Shetland Islands

South America

Antarctic Peninsula

Alexander Island

Larsen Ice Shelf

Weddell Sea

Berkner Island

Ronne Ice Shelf

Riiser-Larsen Ice Shelf

Coats Land

Filchner Ice Shelf

Fimbul Ice Shelf

QUEEN MAUD LAND

Enderby Land

Amery Ice Shelf

Bellingshausen Sea

Ellsworth Land

Vinson Massif 16,067 ft. (4,897 m)

TRANSANTARCTIC MOUNTAINS

Polar Plateau

South Pole

ANTARCTICA

West Ice Shelf

Southern Ocean

Pacific Ocean

Amundsen Sea

Marie Byrd Land

Getz Ice Shelf

Queen Maud Mts.

Ross Ice Shelf

Roosevelt Island

Shackleton Ice Shelf

WILKES LAND

Indian Ocean

Southern Ocean

Lambert Azimuthal Equal Area Projection
0   400   800 miles
0   400   800 kilometers

Ross Sea

Antarctic Circle

International Date Line

Victoria Land

South Magnetic Pole

90°W

90°E

120°W

120°W

150°W

180°

150°E

70°S

60°S

50°S

60°S

Elevation

Feet		Meters
More than 13,000		More than 3,960
6,500–13,000		1,980–3,960
1,600–6,500		480–1,980
650–1,600		200–400
0–650		0–200
Below sea level		Below sea level

—— National border

- - - International Date Line

A

abolitionists reformers who advocated a complete end to slavery

Acquired Immunodeficiency Syndrome (AIDS) disease that attacks the immune system and has no known cure; it began spreading in the early 1980s and remains a serious global health crisis today

ACT UP Acronym for AIDS Coalition to Unleash Power, a direct action group formed in 1987 to advocate for people with AIDS, to protest discrimination, and to motivate government to respond to the AIDS crisis by introducing medical research, treatment, and legislation

Addams, Jane Jane Addams (1860–1935) cofounded Hull House, a settlement house in Chicago, in 1889. She lived and worked out of Hull House for the rest of her life. A pacifist and determined advocate for women's suffrage, Addams wrote many books and lectured widely. In 1931, she shared the Nobel Peace Prize.

affirmative action policy that gives special consideration to women and minorities to make up for past discrimination

AFL-CIO in 1955, the American Federation of Labor (AFL) and the Congress of Industrial Organization (CIO) labor unions united

aggression hostile actions or unprovoked attacks

Aguinaldo, Emilio Emilio Aguinaldo (1869–1964) was the leader of the Filipino forces that fought for independence against Spain in the 1890s. Disillusioned with the U.S. presence in the Philippines following the war, Aguinaldo helped organize an insurrection against U.S. rule. He was captured by U.S. forces in 1901, effectively ending the Filipino's fight for independence.

al Qaeda terrorist group established by Osama bin Laden to rid Muslim countries of Western influence

Alger, Horatio Horatio Alger (1832–1899) was an American author who sold more than 20 million copies of novels that explored the rags-to-riches theme. Alger created characters who rose to fame and wealth through hard work and determination.

Alliance for Progress President Kennedy's program that gave economic aid to Latin America

Allies group of countries led by Britain, France, the United States, and the Soviet Union that fought the Axis Powers in World War II

Alsace-Lorraine territory lost to Germany by France in 1871

American Expeditionary Forces (AEF) American forces in Europe during World War I

American Federation of Labor (AFL) labor union that organized skilled workers in a specific trade and made specific demands rather than seeking broad changes

American Indian Citizenship Act of 1924 granted citizenship to all Native Americans born within the territorial limits of the United States

American Indian Movement (AIM) group that focused on helping Indians, including the securing of legal rights, land, and self-government for Native Americans

Americanization belief that assimilating immigrants into American society would make them more loyal citizens

amnesty general pardon for certain crimes

Anaconda Plan the Union military strategy for winning the war

Angel Island immigrant processing station that opened in San Francisco Bay in 1910

Anschluss union of Germany and Austria in 1933

Anthony, Susan B. Susan B. Anthony (1820–1906) was a women's rights activist who worked toward gaining the right to vote for women

Anti-Defamation League organization formed in 1913 to defend Jews against physical and verbal attacks and false statements

anti-Semitic displaying prejudice and discrimination against Jewish people

anti-Semitism hatred of and discrimination against Jews

Antifederalists the opponents of ratifying the U.S. Constitution

apartheid political system of strict segregation by race in South Africa

appeasement policy of granting concessions in order to keep peace

Armstrong, Louis Louis Armstrong (1901–1971) was a jazz trumpeter and one of the most influential artists in the jazz history. He was also a bandleader, singer and comedian during his career.

Articles of Confederation the first plan for a national government in the United States; it created a confederation of 13 states

assembly lines arrangement of equipment and workers in which work passes from operation to operation in direct line until the product is assembled

assimilated absorbed into the main culture of a society

Atlantic Charter pact signed by Great Britain and the United States that endorsed certain principles for building a lasting peace and establishing free governments in the world

Axis Powers group of countries led by Germany, Italy, and Japan that fought the Allies in World War II

B

baby boom increase in births between 1945 and 1964

Baruch, Bernard Bernard Baruch (1870–1965) was chairman of the War Industries Board during World War I. Baruch was a financier turned statesman who advised seven American presidents.

Bataan Death March during World War II, the forced march of American and Filipino prisoners of war under brutal conditions led by the Japanese military

Battle of Coral Sea World War II battle that took place between Japanese and American aircraft carriers in May 1942, halting the Japanese advance in the Pacific

Battle of Gettysburg a Civil War battle that took place in southern Pennsylvania; a Union victory, it marked the last major Confederate attempt to invade the North

Battle of Midway turning point of World War II in the Pacific, in which the Japanese advance was stopped

Battle of the Bulge last major German offensive on the Western Front during World War II; it was an unsuccessful attempt to push back the Allies that crippled Germany by forcing it to use more resources than it could afford

Battle of the Little Big Horn 1876 battle in which the Sioux defeated U.S. Army troops

Bay of Pigs invasion failed 1961 invasion of Cuba by a CIA-led force of Cuban exiles

Beatles The Beatles were an English rock-and-roll group featuring John Lennon, Paul McCartney, George Harrison, and Ringo Starr. From 1962 to 1970, the Beatles' songwriting and musical experimentation greatly expanded the scope of rock music.

beatniks small group of writers and artists, in the 1950s and early 1960s, who were critical of American society

Benavidez, Roy P. Roy P. Benavidez (1935–1998) was born in Cuero, Texas, but grew up in El Campo, where he was raised by his aunt and uncle after his parents died. He joined the army at the age of 19 and eventually went to Vietnam in 1965. For his bravery while wounded during a rescue mission in Cambodia in 1968, Benavidez was awarded the Medal of Honor (in 1981).

Berlin airlift program in which U.S. and British pilots flew supplies to West Berlin during a Soviet blockade

Berlin Wall dividing wall built by East Germany in 1961 to isolate West Berlin from communist-controlled East Berlin

Bessemer process method developed in the mid-nineteenth century for making steel more efficiently

Bethune, Mary McLeod Mary McLeod Bethune (1875–1955) was an American educator who served as a special adviser on minority affairs to President Franklin D. Roosevelt, as well as being active in several other reform organizations.

"Big stick" diplomacy Theodore Roosevelt's policy of creating and using, when necessary, a strong military to achieve America's goals

bilingual education system in which students are taught in their native languages as well as in English

bill of rights the protections for personal liberty that limit the power of the government over individuals

biotechnology application of technology to solving problems affecting living organisms

Black Cabinet group of African-American leaders who served as unofficial advisers to Franklin D. Roosevelt

black codes laws that restricted African Americans' rights and opportunities

Black Panthers organization of militant African Americans founded in 1966

black power movement in the 1960s that urged African Americans to use their collective political and economic power to gain equality

Black Tuesday October 29, 1929, when stock prices fell sharply in the Great Crash

blacklist list of persons who were not hired because of suspected communist ties

blitzkrieg "lightning war" that emphasized the use of speed and firepower to penetrate deep into the enemy's territory

boat people refugees who fled nations of Southeast Asia by boat beginning in the 1970s

Bonus Army group of World War I veterans who marched on Washington, D.C., in 1932 to demand early payment of a bonus promised them by Congress

Bootlegger one who sells illegal alcohol

Boxer Rebellion violence started by members of a secret society in China, which prompted the governments of Europe and America to send troops to squash the rebellion

bracero program plan that brought laborers from Mexico to work on American farms

Bradley, Omar Omar Bradley (1893–1981) was a U.S. Army officer who in World War II commanded Allied troops in North Africa, leading them to victory in the campaign. He then led his forces in the invasion of Sicily and helped plan the invasion of Normandy. From the Normandy invasion to the end of the war, Bradley commanded the massive U.S. ground forces attacking Germany from the west, over 1 million troops in all. After World War II, he served as chief of staff of the Army and as the first chairman of the U.S. Joint Chiefs of Staff.

Brady Bill law passed in 1993 requiring a waiting period on sales of handguns, along with a criminal background check on the buyer

bread line line of people waiting for food handouts from charities or public agencies

Breckinridge, John C. John C. Breckinridge (1821–1875) was a Kentucky statesman who served as Vice President under President James Buchanan; he won the presidential nomination of the southern Democratic Party in 1860.

brinkmanship belief that only by going to the brink of war could the United States protect itself against Soviet aggression

Brown, John John Brown (1800–1859) was an abolitionist who led a raid on the federal arsenal at Harpers Ferry hoping to spark a slave rebellion.

Bryan, William Jennings William Jennings Bryan (1860–1925) was a Democratic and Populist leader who ran unsuccessfully three times for the U.S. presidency. During his career as a lawyer, politician, and speaker, he fought for reforms such as the income tax, Prohibition, and women's suffrage.

budget deficit shortfall between the amount of money spent and the amount of money taken in by the federal government

bull market period of rising stock prices

Bush, George W. George W. Bush (1946–) was a businessman and governor of Texas from 1995 to 2000 before being elected the 43rd president of the United States. Bush, a son of President George H.W. Bush, led the United States during the September 11 terrorist attacks in 2001 and the initial years of the wars in Afghanistan and Iraq. Bush was elected to a second term in 2004, finishing his presidency as the world's financial industry was on the verge of collapse in late 2008.

business cycle periodic growth and contraction of the economy

buying on margin system of buying stocks in which a buyer pays a small percentage of the purchase price while the broker advances the rest

C

California Master Plan a plan that called for three tiers of higher education: research universities, state colleges, and community colleges, all of which were to be accessible to all of the state's citizens

Camp David Accords 1978 agreement brokered by President Jimmy Carter between Egyptian and Israeli leaders that made a peace treaty between the two nations possible

Capra, Frank Frank Capra (1897–1991) was an American motion picture director best known for his work during the 1930s and 1940s, for which he won three Academy Awards.

Carnegie, Andrew Andrew Carnegie (1835–1919) was an American industrialist and philanthropist who began Carnegie Steel, a corporation that dominated the American steel industry. He created charitable trust foundations and provided money for cultural and educational institutions.

carpetbagger a negative term for Northerners who moved to the South after the Civil War

Carson, Rachel Rachel Carson (1907–1964) was an American biologist most famous for writing *Silent Spring* and a number of other works on environmental pollution and the history of the oceans. Carson worked as a scientist and writer for the U.S. government before turning to writing full time.

cartel association of producers of a good or service that prices and controls stocks in order to monopolize the market

Carter, Jimmy Jimmy Carter (1924–) was the governor of Georgia from 1970 to 1974. In 1976, he defeated Gerald R. Ford to become President. After losing the presidency to Ronald Reagan in 1980, Carter devoted himself to national and international social concerns, advancing democracy, and human rights.

cash crop crop grown for sale

Castro, Fidel Fidel Castro (1926–) helped to overthrow the Cuban government in 1959, and led the country from then until 2008. His communist government and ties to the Soviet Union were a source of conflict between Cuba and the United States.

casualty a soldier killed, wounded, or missing

Catt, Carrie Chapman Carrie Chapman Catt (1859–1947) was an educator before becoming involved in the women's suffrage movement in 1887. In 1890, she joined the National American Woman Suffrage Association (NAWSA). She became its president in 1900, and headed the organization almost without interruption until her death.

Central Intelligence Agency (CIA) U.S. intelligence-gathering organization

Chamberlain, Neville prime minister of Great Britain from 1937–1940. In an effort to avoid war, he signed the Munich Pact with Germany, giving Hitler control of the Sudetenland, a part of Czechoslovakia. The agreement became an infamous symbol for the failure of appeasement.

Chaplin, Charlie Charlie Chaplin (1889–1977) was a British comedian who produced, wrote, and directed many films throughout his career. Many consider him the greatest comic artist in motion picture history.

Chavez, Cesar Cesar Chavez (1927–1993) spent his childhood toiling, like his parents, as a migrant farmworker. As an adult, he established the National Farm Workers Association (NFWA) in 1962. Chavez led several high-profile non-violent protests that generally ended with better conditions for workers.

checks and balances a set of counteracting influences that regulate a political system so that power is not concentrated in the hands of a single group

Chicano movement movement to promote Mexican American social and political issues and culture

Chinese Exclusion Act 1882 law that prohibited the immigration of Chinese laborers

cholera a severe bacterial infection of the small intestine that causes dehydration, usually caused by drinking contaminated water

Christian fundamentalist a Christian who believes in a strict, literal interpretation of the Bible as the foundation of the Christian faith

Churchill, Winston Prime Minister of Great Britain from 1940 to 1945, Churchill inspired the British during World War II. After the war, he was not re-elected. However, he resumed office again between 1951 to 1955. He strongly opposed the expansion of Soviet communism, referring to nations under communism as being behind the "Iron Curtain."

Civil Rights Act 1964 law that banned discrimination in public places and employment based on race, religion, or national origin

Civil Rights Act of 1866 a law that established federal guarantees of civil rights for all citizens

Civil Rights Act of 1875 a law that banned discrimination in public facilities and transportation

Civil Rights Act of 1957 law that established a federal Civil Rights Commission to investigate violations of civil rights

Civil Rights Act of 1964 outlawed discrimination in public places and employment based on race, religion, or national origin

civil service government departments and their non-elected employees

Civilian Conservation Corps (CCC) New Deal program that provided young men with relief jobs on environmental conservation projects, including reforestation and flood control

Clayton Antitrust Act 1914 law that strengthened the Sherman Antitrust Act

Clean Air Act act passed in 1970 that sought to lessen air pollution by limiting the emissions from factories and automobiles

Clean Water Act 1973 law designed to restrict the pollution of water by industry and agriculture

Clinton, Hillary Hillary Clinton (1947–) was a successful and influential lawyer and advocate for children and families before becoming First Lady of the United States in 1992. She took an active role in Bill Clinton's administration, heading up the Task Force on National Health Care. In 2000, won a U.S. Senate seat for the State of New York. She sought, but failed to win, the Democratic presidential nomination in 2008, but was appointed Secretary of State by President Obama later that year. She resigned from that post in 2013.

Clinton, William Jefferson Bill Clinton (1946–) became the 42nd president of the United States in 1993 at the age of 46—the first "boomer" President. He was reelected to a second term in 1996. Two years later he was impeached by the House of Representatives but was acquitted by the Senate in 1999. Clinton presided over the longest period of peace-time economic expansion in American history, which included a balanced budget and a federal surplus.

Cold War worldwide rivalry between the United States and the Soviet Union

collective bargaining process in which employers negotiate with labor unions about hours, wages, and other working conditions

Committee on Public Information (CPI) federal government agency created during World War I to encourage Americans to support the war

communes small communities where people with common interests live and share resources

Community Reinvestment Act 1977 law that requires banks, and especially those that operate in low- to middle-income minority neighborhoods, to loan a portion of their deposits to the residents of those neighborhoods

company towns communities in which residents rely upon one company for jobs, housing, and buying goods

Compromise of 1850 several acts of Congress that included California's admission to the Union as a free state, passage of the Fugitive Slave Act, and a law allowing territories acquired from Mexico to decide the issue of slavery themselves as they entered the Union

Compromise of 1877 an agreement by which Rutherford B. Hayes won the 1876 presidential election and in exchange agreed to remove all remaining federal troops from the South

concentration camps camps used by the Nazis to imprison "undesirable" members of society

Confederate States of America A government set up in 1861 by seven states that seceded from the United States; four other states later joined them.

confederation an alliance or league of governments pledged to work together

Congress of Industrial Organizations (CIO) labor organization founded in the 1930s that was composed of industrial unions which represented all workers in an industry regardless of their job or skill

conscientious objector person whose moral or religious beliefs forbid him or her to fight in wars

conservative person who tends to support limited government involvement in the economy, community help for the needy, and traditional values

conspicuous consumerism purchasing of goods and services with the purpose of impressing others

consumer revolution flood of new, affordable goods in the decades after World War I

consumerism large-scale buying, much of it on credit

containment policy of keeping communism contained within its existing borders

contraband goods prohibited by law or treaty from being imported or exported

Contract With America Republican plan headed by Newt Gingrich that focused on scaling back the government, balancing the budget, and cutting taxes

Contras anticommunist counterrevolutionaries who opposed the Sandinista government in Nicaragua in the 1980s

convoy group of merchant ships sailing together, protected by warships

Coolidge, Calvin Calvin Coolidge (1872–1933) was President of the United States from 1923 to 1929. He acceded to office after the death of Warren Harding and continued many of the pro-business policies of his predecessor.

corporation company recognized as a legal unit that has rights and liabilities separate from each of its members

cotton gin a machine that reduced the time and cost of separating cotton fiber from its hard shell

Coughlin, Charles Charles Coughlin (1891–1979) served as pastor of a Catholic Church in Michigan from 1926 to 1966. He won a huge audience in the 1930s for his radio broadcasts, first supporting President Roosevelt's New Deal and later opposing it as he adopted ultraconservative views. Coughlin vocally opposed U.S. entrance into World War II and after he began making anti-Semitic remarks, Catholic officials ordered him to stop broadcasting in 1942.

counterculture movement that upheld values different from those of mainstream culture

court packing President Franklin D. Roosevelt's plan to add six new justices to the nine-member Supreme Court after the Court had ruled some New Deal laws to be unconstitutional

Credibility gap American public's growing distrust of statements made by the government during the Vietnam War

creditor nation country which is owed more money by other countries than it owes other countries

Creel, George George Creel (1876–1953) was a journalist who served as chairman of the Committee on Public Information during World War I. He went on to hold other positions in the federal government. Creel was also an author. One of his books was *How We Advertised America*.

Crittenden Compromise a proposed constitutional amendment introduced in 1860 that would have allowed slavery in western territories south of the Missouri Compromise line

Cuban missile crisis 1962 conflict between the United States and the Soviet Union resulting from the Soviet installation of nuclear missiles in Cuba

D

Darrow, Clarence Clarence Darrow (1857–1938) was a lawyer whose work as defense council in many trials secured his place in legal history. He is best known for his defense of John Scopes in 1925.

Davis, Jefferson Jefferson Davis (1808–1889) was a Mississippi statesman who served as the first and only president of the Confederate States of America.

Dawes General Allotment Act 1887 law that divided reservation land into private family plots

Dawes Plan agreement in which the United States loaned money to Germany, allowing Germany to make reparation payments to Britain and France

de facto segregation a separation of the races that exists because of social patterns rather than the enforcement of laws

de jure segregation legal separation of the races

death camps Nazi camp designed for the extermination of prisoners

Debs, Eugene V. Eugene V. Debs (1855–1926) was a labor organizer and social leader who advocated for the rights of railway workers. He ran for president five times between 1900 and 1920 as a candidate for the Socialist Party.

Declaration of Sentiments a document created at the Seneca Fall Convention in 1848 that demanded equal rights for women

deficit spending practice of a nation paying out more money than it is receiving in revenues

demobilization sending home members of the army

Democratic Republican Party an early American political party that supported states' rights and policies that advanced agriculture and the simple lifen part

Demographics statistics that show human characteristics of a population

Department of Homeland Security department created by President Bush to coordinate domestic security efforts

deregulation reduction or removal of government controls over an industry, based on the belief that more freedom leads to greater success and profitability

détente flexible diplomacy adopted by President Richard Nixon to ease tensions between the United States, the Soviet Union, and the People's Republic of China

developing world countries that are less economically advanced than developed countries such as the United States and those of Western Europe

Dewey, George George Dewey (1837–1917) was an American naval officer who commanded the U.S. fleet that defeated the Spanish at the Battle of Manila Bay during the Spanish-American War. In 1899, Congress promoted Dewey to the rank of admiral of the navy, the highest rank ever held by a U.S. naval officer.

direct primary election in which citizens themselves vote to select nominees for upcoming elections

disenfranchise take away a person or group's voting rights

divest to take away or rid oneself of

Dole, Sanford B. Sanford B. Dole (1844–1926) played an important role in the overthrow of the Hawaiian monarchy. After the overthrow, Dole was elected president of the Provisional Government. He petitioned the American government to annex the Hawaiian Islands. In 1898, Hawaii became a United States territory with Dole as its first governor.

Dollar diplomacy President Taft's policy of expanding American investments abroad

domino theory idea that if a nation falls to communism, its closest neighbors will also fall under communist control

Douglass, Frederick Frederick Douglass (1818?–1895) was a former slave who had been taught to read and write before he escaped to the North; he went on to become one of the most important voices in the abolitionist movement.

dove person who opposed U.S. involvement in the Vietnam War

draft law an act of Congress giving the government authority to enlist men in the army without those men's consent

draftee a young American man drafted into military service

Dred Scott v. Sandford an 1857 Supreme Court ruling that declared that slaves had no constitutional rights and that Congress could not decide the issue of slavery for new states

Du Bois, W.E.B. W.E.B. Du Bois (1868–1963) was an African American civil rights activist who advocated steps to create immediate legal, social, and political equality for blacks.

Dulles, John Foster John Foster Dulles (1888–1959) was a diplomat and political thinker. A strong anti-communist, he helped organize the United Nations after World War II and later served as Secretary of State under President Dwight Eisenhower. In this role, he helped formulate the Cold War policies of brinkmanship and "massive retaliation".

Dust Bowl term used for the central and southern Great Plains during the 1930s, when the region suffered from drought and dust storms

E

Earth Day annual event of environmental activism and protest, begun in 1970

Economic Opportunity Act law passed in 1964 creating antipoverty programs

Edison, Thomas Thomas Edison (1847–1931) was an American inventor. He held over 1,000 patents for inventions, including the light bulb, an early movie camera, and an alkaline battery.

egalitarianism the view that people are equal and should be treated the same

Eighteenth Amendment constitutional amendment banning the manufacture, distribution, and sale of alcohol in the United States

Einstein, Albert German-born physicist Albert Einstein (1879–1955) developed the general theory of relativity, which describes the effects of gravity on the universe, and won the Nobel Prize for Physics in 1921. Einstein left Germany in the early 1930s after Nazi attacks on his work and settled in the United States, where he continued to pioneer new developments in the theory of general relativity. He is generally considered to be the most influential physicist of the 20th century.

Eisenhower Doctrine policy of President Eisenhower that stated that the United States would use force to help any nation threatened by communism

Eisenhower, Dwight Dwight D. Eisenhower (1890–1969) was given command of all American forces in Europe in 1942. After strong performances in North Africa and Italy, he was made Supreme Commander of Allied Forces. His skillful handling of the D-Day invasion and the drive to Germany won wide respect. Eisenhower went on to serve two terms as President before retiring.

Ellis Island island in New York Harbor that served as an immigration station for millions of immigrants arriving to the United States

Emancipation Proclamation a presidential order that freed slaves in Union-held territory in states that had seceded from the Union

embargo a restriction on all trade with another country

Endangered Species Act law passed in 1973 with the goal of protecting endangered plants and animals

Enforcement Acts 1870 and 1871 laws, also known as the Ku Klux Klan Acts, that made it a federal offense to interfere with a citizen's right to vote

English Bill of Rights an act of Parliament that limited the rights of the English monarchy and enumerated certain political rights

Enlightenment an intellectual movement in Europe during the seventeenth and eighteenth centuries that emphasized reason and individualism over faith and tradition

entrepreneurs people who build and manage businesses or enterprises in order to make a profit, often risking their own money or livelihoods

Environmental Protection Agency (EPA) government agency committed to cleaning up and protecting the environment

Equal Pay Act 1963 law requiring men and women to receive equal pay for equal work

Equal Rights Amendment (ERA) proposed amendment to the Constitution to guarantee gender equality

Espionage Act act passed by Congress in 1917 enacting severe penalties for anyone engaged in disloyal or treasonable activities

ethnic cleansing systematic effort to purge a society of an ethnic group through murder or deportation

eugenics the idea that the human race can be improved by controlling which people have children

European Union (EU) economic and political union of European nations established in 1993

Evers, Medgar Medgar Evers (1925–1963) became the NAACP's first field secretary in Mississippi in 1954. He traveled the state recruiting members and organized voter-registration drives, demonstrations, and boycotts of companies that practiced discrimination. In 1963, he was assassinated outside of his home in Jackson, Mississippi.

Executive Order 8802 World War II measure that assured fair hiring practices in any job funded by the government

executive privilege principle that the President has the right to keep private certain communications between himself and other members of the executive branch

Exodusters African Americans who migrated from the South to the West after the Civil War

expansionists people who favor territorial growth

extractive economies economy in a colony where the colonizing country removed raw materials and shipped them back home to benefit its own economy

F

Fair Deal President Truman's program to expand New Deal reforms

Fair Labor Standards Act 1938 law that set a minimum wage, a maximum work week of 44 hours, and outlawed child labor

Family Medical Leave Act law guaranteeing most full-time employees 12 workweeks of unpaid leave each year for personal or family health reasons

Farmers' Alliance network of farmers' organizations that worked for political and economic reforms in the late 1800s

fascism a political movement that stressed extreme nationalism and autocratic rule

Faubus, Orval Orval Faubus (1910–1994) was the governor of Arkansas from 1954 to 1967. He is best known for ordering the Arkansas National Guard to block nine African American students from entering Little Rock Central High School in 1957, in defiance of a federal court order that mandated the end of racial segregation in schools. His efforts failed when President Eisenhower sent federal troops to usher the students into the school.

Federal Art Project division of the Works Progress Administration that hired unemployed artists to create artworks for public buildings and sponsored art-education programs and exhibitions

Federal Deposit Insurance Corporation (FDIC) government agency created during the New Deal that insures bank deposits, guaranteeing that depositors' money will be safe

Federal Reserve Act 1913 law that placed national banks under the control of a Federal Reserve Board, which operates regional banks that hold the reserve funds from commercial banks, sets interest rates, and supervises commercial banks

Federal Trade Commission (FTC). government agency established in 1914 to identify monopolistic business practices, false advertising, and dishonest labeling

federalism a system of government that divides power between the national and state governments

Federalist Papers, The a collection of essays written by James Madison, Alexander Hamilton, and John Jay originally published in New York newspapers to persuade voters to ratify the Constitution

Federalist Party an early American political party that supported a strong and active federal government and policies intended to promote industrialization and economic growth

feminism theory that women and men should have political, social, and economic equality

fiat money currency not backed by gold or silver

Fifteenth Amendment the constitutional amendment, ratified in February 1870, which guaranteed voting rights to all males regardless of race

filibuster tactic by which senators give long speeches to hold up legislative business

fireside chats informal radio broadcasts in which President Franklin D. Roosevelt explained his view of issues at hand (including the Great Depression, New Deal programs, and World War II) to average Americans

Fitzgerald, F. Scott F. Scott Fitzgerald (1896–1940) was an American writer known for his depictions of American life in the 1920s, especially *The Great Gatsby,* published in 1925.

flapper young woman from the 1920s who defied traditional rules of conduct and dress

flexible response defense policy allowing for the appropriate action in any type of conflict

Foraker Act law establishing a civil government in Puerto Rico

Ford, Gerald Gerald Ford (1913–2006) was elected to Congress in 1949 and was named Vice President after Spiro T. Agnew resigned in 1973. Ford became President the next year when Nixon resigned. After losing the 1976 election to Jimmy Carter, Ford retired from politics.

Ford, Henry Henry Ford (1863–1947) was the founder of the Ford Motor Company. Ford revolutionized the automobile industry with his assembly line and treatment of workers. Ford's Model T ushered in the age of the automobile in the United States.

Fort Sumter a Union-held fort in South Carolina that was the site of the first battle of the Civil War

442nd Regimental Combat Team World War II unit made up of Japanese American volunteers

Fourteen Points list of terms for resolving World War I and future wars outlined by American President Woodrow Wilson

Fourteenth Amendment the constitutional amendment, ratified in July 1868, which guaranteed full citizenship status and rights to every person born in the United States, protected due process, and guaranteed equal protection of the law

franchise business to allow a company to distribute its products or services through retail outlets owned by independent operators

Francis Ferdinand Francis Ferdinand (1863–1914) was an archduke and heir to the throne of Austria-Hungary. His assassination in Sarajevo was an immediate cause of World War I.

Franco, General Francisco led a successful military revolt against the Spanish democratic government in the Spanish Civil War (1936–1939). He continued to rule Spain as a dictator until his death in 1975.

free enterprise freedom of private business to organize and operate for profit in a competitive system without interference by government beyond regulation necessary to protect public interest and keep the national economy in balance

Free-Soil Party a political party formed in 1848 dedicated to preventing the spread of slavery into the western territories

freedmen former slaves who were now emancipated

Freedmen's Bureau a federal agency created to provide aid for emancipated slaves

Freedom ride 1961 protest by activists who rode buses through southern states to test their compliance with laws banning segregation on interstate buses

Freedom Summer 1964 effort to register African American voters in Mississippi

Freud, Sigmund Sigmund Freud (1856–1939) developed psychological theories of the human psyche and therapies known as psychoanalysis.

Friedan, Betty Betty Friedan (1921–2006) was an American feminist who wrote the influential book *The Feminine Mystique* in 1963 and co-founded the National Organization for Women (NOW) in 1966.

Fugitive Slave Act a law requiring any state, whatever its laws on slavery, to assist in the return of runaway slaves to their owners

fundamentalism movement or attitude stressing strict and literal adherence to a set of basic religious principles

G

Garcia, Hector P. Hector P. Garcia (1914–1996) was an army doctor who served with distinction in World War II, earning the Bronze Star for his service in North Africa and Italy. He was born in Mexico but grew up in Mercedes, Texas. After leaving the army as a major in 1945, Garcia returned to Texas to practice medicine, but he also began his lifelong work as a community leader, civil rights advocate, and political activist. In 1948, he helped to found the American G.I. Forum, an organization that supports Hispanic veterans and their families.

Garvey, Marcus Marcus Garvey (1887–1940) was a charismatic leader who organized a black nationalist movement in Harlem during the 1920s. Garvey promoted economic and cultural independence for African Americans.

General Agreement on Tariffs and Trade (GATT) international agreement first signed in 1947 aimed at lowering trade barriers

generation gap lack of understanding and communication between older and younger members of society

Geneva Convention international agreement governing the humane treatment of wounded soldiers and prisoners of war

genocide willful annihilation of a racial, political, or cultural group

"Gentlemen's Agreement" pact between the United States and Japan to end segregation of Asian children in San Francisco public schools; in return, Japan agreed to limit the emigration of its citizens to the United States

Gettysburg Address a speech given by President Lincoln at the site of the Battle of Gettysburg in which he reaffirmed the ideals for which the Union was fighting

GI Bill of Rights eased the return of World War II veterans by providing education and employment aid

Gilded Age term coined by Mark Twain to describe the post-Reconstruction era as a facade of prosperity

Gingrich, Newt Newt Gingrich (1943–) is an American politician, author, and television commentator best known for serving as speaker of the U.S. House of Representatives from 1995 to 1998. Gingrich led the Republican takeover of the House in the 1994 midterm elections by helping to write the influential Contract With America platform.

glasnost Russian term for "new openness," a policy in the Soviet Union in the 1980s calling for open discussion of national problems

globalization process by which national economies, politics, cultures, and societies mix with those of other nations around the world

gold standard policy of designating monetary units in terms of their value in gold

Goldwater, Barry Barry Goldwater (1909–1998) served nearly 25 years in the U.S. Senate. In 1964, he ran for president and was soundly defeated by Lyndon Johnson. In 1974, Goldwater was instrumental in persuading President Nixon to resign in the aftermath of the Watergate scandal.

Gompers, Samuel Samuel Gompers (1850–1924) was an American labor leader and the first president of the American Federation of Labor. He advocated organized strikes and boycotts to achieve the organization's goals.

Gorbachev, Mikhail Mikhail Gorbachev (1931–) is a Soviet politician who served as the leader of the Soviet Union from 1985 to 1991. Gorbachev is best known for supporting the policies of *glasnost* and *perestroika*, which led to the collapse of the Soviet Union. Gorbachev's role in the rise of democratic government in Eastern Europe earned him the Nobel Peace Prize in 1990.

Gorras Blancas, Las (the White Caps) group of Mexican Americans living in New Mexico who attempted to protect their land and way of life from encroachment by white landowners

Graham, Billy Billy Graham (1918) is an American evangelist who rose to prominence during the religious revival of the 1950s in the United States.

grandfather clause a law to disqualify African American voters by allowing the vote only to men whose fathers and grandfathers had voted before 1866 or 1867

Grange farmers' organization formed after the Civil War

Grant, Ulysses S. Ulysses S. Grant (1822–1885) was a military leader and statesman who served as the final commander of the Union army during the Civil War and later as the 18th President.

Great Awakening a religious movement in the North American colonies that emphasized individual salvation and high standards of personal morality

Great Depression period lasting from 1929 to 1941 in which the U.S. economy faltered and unemployment soared

Great Migration movement of African Americans in the twentieth century from the South to the North

Great Society President Lyndon Johnson's goals in the areas of health care, education, the environment, discrimination, and poverty

Great White Fleet battleships sent by President Theodore Roosevelt in 1907 on a "good will cruise" around the world

guerrilla warfare nontraditional combat methods

Gulf of Tonkin Resolution 1964 congressional resolution that authorized President Johnson to commit U.S. troops to South Vietnam to fight a war against North Vietnam

H

habeas corpus a constitutional guarantee that no one can be held in prison without specific charges filed against them

Hancock, John John Hancock (1737–1793) was a Massachusetts statesman who served as the president of the Second Continental Congress.

Harding, Warren G. Warren G. Harding (1865–1923) served as president of the United States from 1921 to 1923. He promoted a "return to normalcy" following U.S. involvement in World War I. Harding died during his first term in office in 1923.

Harlem Renaissance period during the 1920s in which African American novelists, poets, and artists celebrated their culture

hawk person who supported U.S. involvement in the Vietnam War

Hawley-Smoot Tariff protective tax on imports enacted by Congress in 1930 in an effort to counter the nation's slide into the Great Depression

Hay, Harry Harry Hay (1912–2002) was a leading American gay rights activist who founded the Mattachine Society in 1948, an early gay rights organization. Mattachine Societies spread throughout California during the 1950s, paving the way for the more radical gay activism of the 1960s. Hay became a co-founder of the Los Angeles Gay Liberation Front in 1969 and in 1979 was a co-founder of the Radical Faeries, a gay spiritual movement.

Hay, John John Hay (1838–1905) served as U.S. secretary of state from 1895 to 1905, guiding U.S. diplomacy as the country emerged as a world power. He was instrumental in crafting the Open Door policy toward China.

Hayes, Rutherford B. Rutherford B. Hayes (1822–1893) was the nineteenth president of the United States. His election in 1876 was disputed, and his victory was secured by a Congressional commission and the Compromise of 1877. Hayes oversaw the withdrawal of the remaining federal troops from the South, signaling the end of Reconstruction.

Haymarket Riot 1886 labor-related protest in Chicago which ended in deadly violence

Hearst, William Randolph William Randolph Hearst (1863–1951) was an American newspaper publisher who created the nation's largest newspaper chain. Hearst, along with Joseph Pulitzer, helped popularize investigative reporting and sensationalist journalism.

Hellman, Lillian Lillian Hellman (1905–1984) was an American playwright and screenwriter known for her dramas that focused on social injustice and exploitation.

Helsinki Accords agreement made in 1975 among the nations of Europe, the Soviet Union, the United States, and Canada to respect and support human rights

Hemingway, Ernest Ernest Hemingway (1899–1961) was an American writer who won the Nobel Prize for Literature in 1954. He is known for his adventurous life and novels such as *The Sun Also Rises* and *For Whom the Bell Tolls.*

Hepburn Act 1906 law that gave the Interstate Commerce Commission the authority to set maximum shipping rates for railroads and for ferries, toll bridges, and oil pipelines

Hiss, Alger Alger Hiss (1904–1996) was a former high-ranking State Department official investigated by HUAC as a communist spy and later convicted of perjury, but not espionage. Documents released in the 1990s supported the accusations against him.

Hitler, Adolf leader of the National Socialist (Nazi) party and dictator of Germany from 1933–1945. He rose to power by promoting racist and nationalist views. In 1939, he invaded Poland, which began World War II. He established a system of concentration camps, leading to the Holocaust, a systematic and brutal murder of millions of Jews and others.

Ho Chi Minh Ho Chi Minh (1890–1969) was one of the most influential anticolonial leaders in Asia. Ho led North Vietnam's fight to reunify North and South Vietnam, serving as president of the Democratic Republic of Vietnam (North Vietnam) from 1945 to 1969.

Hollywood Ten group of movie writers, directors, and producers who refused to answer HUAC questions about communist ties

Holocaust the Nazi attempt to kill all Jews under their control

Homestead Act 1862 law that gave 160 acres of land to persons willing to live on and cultivate it for five years

Homestead Strike 1892 strike against Carnegie's steelworks in Homestead, Pennsylvania

Hoover Dam dam on the Colorado River that was built during the Great Depression

Hoover, Herbert Herbert Hoover (1874–1964) served as secretary of Commerce and later as the President of the United States from 1929 to 1933, during the Great Depression. His administration's response to the Great Depression was widely criticized for its ineffectiveness.

Hooverville term used to describe makeshift shantytowns set up by homeless people during the Great Depression

horizontal integration system of consolidating many firms in the same business

hot line direct telephone line between the White House and the Kremlin set up after the Cuban Missile Crisis

House of Burgesses the legislature for the Jamestown colony established by the Virginia Company in 1619; it was the first legislative assembly in North America

House Un-American Activities Committee (HUAC) congressional committee that investigated possible subversive activities within the United States

Houston, Sam Sam Houston (1793–1863) was a Texas military leader and the first president of the Republic of Texas.

Huerta, Dolores Dolores Huerta (1930–) grew up in Stockton, California, eventually becoming an elementary school teacher. After seeing the poverty of her students, many of whom were children of farm workers, she got involved in advocacy work for the workers and their families. In 1962 with Cesar Chavez, Huerta cofounded the farm workers union that would become the United Farm Workers (UFW). While Chavez was the face of the organization, it was Huerta who used her organizational and negotiating skills to help the UFW succeed on behalf of its members.

Hughes, Langston Langston Hughes (1902–1967) was an influential poet and writer who thought of his work as a means to communicate the black experience in the United States.

human rights basic rights held by every human being, including religious freedom, education, and equality

Hurston, Zora Neale Zora Neale Hurston (1891–1960) was a writer associated with the Harlem Renaissance who was trained as an anthropologist and went on to teach for a number of years. One of her more influential works was *Their Eyes Were Watching God,* published in 1935.

I

Immigration Act of 1990 law that increased the number of immigrants allowed in the U.S. per year

Immigration and Nationality Act of 1965 law that changed the national quota system to limits of 170,000 immigrants per year from the Eastern Hemisphere and 120,000 per year from the Western Hemisphere

Immigration Reform and Control Act of 1986 legislation that granted resident status to illegal immigrants residing in the United States since 1982 and penalized employers who hired illegal immigrants

impeach the act of bringing charges against a public official in order to determine whether he or she should be removed from office

impeachment accusation against a public official of wrongdoing in office

imperialism political, military, and economic domination of strong nations over weaker territories

Indian New Deal 1930s legislation that gave Indians greater control over their affairs and provided funding for schools and hospitals

Indian Removal Act act passed by Congress in 1830 that allowed the federal government to negotiate land trades with the Indians in the Southeast

Industrial Revolution a period in the seventeenth and eighteenth centuries when output grew significantly through the use of machines and new methods of production

inflation A general rise in the price of goods and services.

influenza flu virus

information industry business that provide informational services

initiative process in which citizens put a proposed new law directly on the ballot

installment buying method of purchase in which buyer makes a small down payment and then pays off the rest of the debt in regular monthly payments

insurrection rebellion

integration the process of bringing together people of different races, religions, and social classes

Internet computer network that links people around the world, also called World Wide Web

internment temporary imprisonment of members of a specific group

Interstate Commerce Commission (ICC) first federal agency monitoring business operations, created in 1887 to oversee interstate railroad procedures

Interstate Highway Act the 1956 law that authorized the spending of $32 billion to build 41,000 miles of highway

Iran-Contra affair political scandal under President Reagan involving the use of money from secret arms sales to Iran to illegally support the Contras of Nicaragua

iron curtain term coined by Winston Churchill to describe the border between the Soviet satellite states and Western Europe

irreconcilables isolationist senators who oppose any treaty ending World War I that had a League of Nations folded into it

island-hopping World War II strategy that involved seizing selected Japanese-held islands in the Pacific while bypassing others

J

Jackson, Andrew Andrew Jackson (1767–1845) was a Tennessee officer and statesman who became famous during the War of 1812 and later served as the seventh President.

Jacksonian democracy a celebration of majority rule and the dignity of ordinary Americans that resulted in widespread popular participation in politics and an emphasis on the concerns of average citizens

Japanese American Citizens League organization that worked to protect the civil rights of Japanese Americans

jazz American musical form developed by African Americans, based on improvisation and blending blues, ragtime, and European-based popular music

Jazz Singer, The an American musical released in 1927 that was the first feature-length movie with synchronized dialogue

Jefferson, Thomas Thomas Jefferson (1743–1826) was a Virginia statesman who wrote the Declaration of Independence and served as the third President of the United States.

Jiang Jieshi Jiang Jieshi (1887–1975), also known as Chiang Kai-shek, was a Chinese Nationalist leader who opposed Mao Zedong's communist forces during the Chinese civil war. After the fall of mainland China, Jieshi became the leader of a Nationalist government on the island of Taiwan.

Jim Crow laws state laws passed throughout the South to enforce racial segregation of public facilities

jingoism aggressive nationalism; support for warlike foreign policy

Johnson, Andrew Andrew Johnson (1808–1875) was a Tennessee statesman who became the 17th President after the assassination of Abraham Lincoln.

Johnson, Robert Beginning in the mid-1970s, Robert Johnson (1946–) worked in Washington, D.C., for the Corporation for Public Broadcasting and as a lobbyist for the new and growing cable industry. In 1980, he used his experience and connections to start BET, a cable network aimed at the largely underserved African American viewing audience. After many years of growth and success, Johnson and his investment partners sold BET in 1998, for $3 billion. The deal made Johnson the nation's first African American billionaire.

Joseph, Chief Chief Joseph (1840–1904) succeeded his father as chief of the Nez PercŽ in 1871. Six years later he led his followers on an unsuccessful flight to escape confinement on a reservation. First sent to Oklahoma, they were eventually returned to a new reservation in Washington state. However, Joseph was unable to secure their return to their tribal homeland.

judicial interpretation practice by which the courts expand and apply the Constitution's intent beyond the meaning of its written words

judicial review the power for courts to decide the constitutionality of law

K

kamikaze Japanese pilots who deliberately crashed planes into American ships during World War II

Kansas-Nebraska Act an act of Congress allowing Kansas and Nebraska to decide the issue of slavery themselves as they entered the Union

Kelley, Florence Florence Kelley (1859–1932) played a major role at Hull House in calling attention to the working conditions of women and children. In 1899, she headed the newly founded National Consumers League. In 1909 Kelley helped found the NAACP.

Kelley, Oliver H. Oliver H. Kelley (1826–1913) was an employee in the U.S. Department of Agriculture who worked to improve the lives of farmers and the agricultural industry. He recognized the need to bring farmers together to protect their livelihoods. Kelly served as the first secretary of the Grange from 1867 until 1878.

Kellogg-Briand Pact 1928 agreement in which many nations agreed to outlaw war

Kennan, George F. George F. Kennan (1904–2005) was an American diplomat who spent several years serving in Eastern Europe and the Soviet Union. His observations about Soviet political attitudes and actions contributed to the formation of the U.S. policy of containment.

Kennedy, John John F. Kennedy (1917–1963) was elected the 35th President of the United States in 1960. While in office, Kennedy faced several foreign crises, including the Cuban Missile Crisis, and pressed for the safeguarding of human and civil rights in the United States and around the world. He was assassinated in 1963 in Dallas, Texas.

Kennedy, John F. John F. Kennedy (1917–1963) served in both the House of Representatives and the Senate before becoming the 35th President in 1961. He faced a number of foreign crises, especially in Cuba and Berlin, and managed to secure such achievements as the Nuclear Test-Ban Treaty and the Alliance for Progress. He was assassinated in Dallas, Texas.

Kennedy, Robert assassinated antiwar candidate for the 1968 Democratic Party presidential nomination

Kerner Commission group set up to investigate the causes of race riots in American cities in the 1960s

Keynes, John Maynard John Maynard Keynes (1883–1946) was a British economist best known for his advocacy of government intervention to protect the economy from the negative effects of recessions, depressions, and booms. He outlined his ideas in *The General Theory of Employment, Interest, and Money*, published in 1936.

Khomeini, Ayatollah Ruhollah Ayatollah Ruhollah Khomeini (1902–1989) was an influential Iranian scholar and cleric. After leading an unsuccessful rebellion against the Shah of Iran in 1963, he fled to France, where his religious and political ideas became more extreme. After the Shah's overthrow in 1979, Khomeini returned to Iran and, supported by revolutionary forces, seized power, holding it until his death in 1989.

Khrushchev, Nikita Nikita Khrushchev (1894–1971) was a Communist Party leader who served as premier of the Soviet Union from 1958 to 1964. Khrushchev led the Soviet Union during the Cuban Missile Crisis but lost power soon afterwards.

King, Martin Luther, Jr. Martin Luther King, Jr. (1929–1968) advocated nonviolent methods of protest while becoming perhaps the most influential leader of the civil right movement. He led the March on Washington in 1963, where he delivered his famous "I Have a Dream" speech. He was assassinated in 1968.

Kissinger, Henry Henry Kissinger (1923–) served as a foreign policy advisor to Presidents Kennedy and Johnson. President Nixon appointed him National Security Advisor In 1969 and Secretary of State in 1973. Kissinger received the Nobel Peace Prize in 1973 for his role in ending the Vietnam War.

Knights of Labor labor union that sought to organize all workers and focused on broad social reforms

Kristallnacht "Night of the Broken Glass," organized attacks on Jewish communities in Germany on November 9, 1938

Ku Klux Klan a secret society formed in the South with the intention of promoting white supremacy and denying African Americans the exercise of their new rights

L

laissez-faire the absence of government control over personal and economic life

land grants land designated by the federal government for building schools, roads, or railroads

Lange, Dorothea Dorothea Lange (1895–1965) was an American documentary photographer known for her portraits of displaced farmers and others suffering economic hardship during the Great Depression.

Lauder, Estee Estee Lauder (1908?–2004) was an American businesswoman and philanthropist who founded a fragrance and cosmetics empire.

League of Nations world organization established after World War I to promote peaceful cooperation among countries

Lee, Robert E. Robert E. Lee (1807–1870) was a Virginia military leader who commanded the Confederate army during the Civil War.

Lend-Lease Act act passed in 1941 that allowed President Roosevelt to sell or lend war supplies to any country whose defense he considered vital to the safety of the United States

Lenin, Vladimir Vladimir Lenin (1870–1924) founded the Communist Party in Russia and led the Russian Revolution. He became dictator of Soviet Russia and promoted communism wherever he could. Lenin believed that a dedicated party of revolutionaries, as opposed to the population generally, was necessary for successful communist revolutions.

LGBT An initialism that stands for Lesbian, Gay, Bisexual, and Transgender

liberal person who tends to support government intervention to help the needy and favors laws protecting the rights of women and minorities

Liluokalani, Queen Queen Liluokalani (1838–1917) succeeded her brother King Kalakaua in 1891 as the leader of the Hawaiian people. She was the first and only reigning Hawaiian queen and the last Hawaiian sovereign to govern the islands. Although Liluokalani tried to regain control of lands owned by white plantation owners, she was overthrown in 1893, and the U.S. annexed Hawaii in 1898.

limited war war fought to achieve only specific goals

Lincoln, Abraham Abraham Lincoln (1809–1865) was an Illinois statesman who served as the 16th President of the United States; his term of office included the Civil War period.

Lindbergh, Charles Charles Lindbergh (1902–1974) was an American aviator who completed the first non-stop, solo flight across the Atlantic Ocean.

literacy test a reading and writing test formerly used in some southern states to prevent African Americans from voting

localism policy relied on by President Hoover in the early years of the Great Depression, whereby local and state governments act as primary agents of economic relief

Locke, John John Locke (1632–1704) was an English philosopher who wrote *Two Treatises of Government*.

Lodge, Henry Cabot Henry Cabot Lodge (1850–1924) was a leading Republican senator who led the successful fight to keep the United States from joining the League of Nations after World War I. Before becoming a senator, he had served in the House. Earlier, he worked as a magazine editor and historian.

Long, Huey Huey Long (1893–1935) was elected governor of Louisiana in 1928, where he won a wide following by providing reforms to help the poor during the depression. While serving in U.S. Senate (1932–1935), he became a vocal critic of Roosevelt's New Deal and called for a redistribution of the nation's wealth. In 1935, he announced his plan to run for President but was assassinated that same year.

Lost Generation term for American writers of the 1920s marked by disillusion with World War I and a search for a new sense of meaning

Louisiana Purchase the acquisition of the Louisiana Territory, which extended from the Mississippi River to the Rocky Mountains, from France for $15 million

Lusitania British passenger liner sunk by a German U-boat during World War I

M

MacArthur, Douglas Douglas MacArthur (1880–1964) commanded American troops in World War I, where he developed a reputation for bravery. As supreme commander of Allied forces in the Pacific (1942–1945), he accepted Japan's surrender to end World War II. In 1950, he became commander of UN forces in the Korean War. He retired after his controversial removal from command in 1951, following a dispute with President Harry Truman.

Maddox, Lester Lester Maddox (1915–2003) was born in Atlanta, Georgia. A high school dropout, he ran a restaurant in the city from 1947 to 1964, when he closed it because he refused to serve African Americans. Elected governor (1967–1971), he fought against school desegregation.

Madison, James James Madison (1751–1836) was a Virginia statesman who played an important role in the debates at the Constitutional Convention and served as the fourth President of the United States.

Magna Carta a document limiting the power of the king of England and guaranteeing certain rights to Englishmen

Mahan, Alfred T. Alfred T. Mahan (1840–1914) was an American naval officer and historian who urged American leaders to build a stronger navy and to obtain naval bases in Cuba, Hawaii, and the Philippines. Mahan was also an early proponent of building a canal through Central America to allow U.S. naval vessels to move quickly between the Atlantic and Pacific Oceans.

Malcolm X Malcolm X (1925–1965) served as a spokesman and minister for the Nation of Islam. His work helped the Nation of Islam, which had only 400 members when he was released from prison in 1952, grow to 40,000 members by 1960. He broke with the group shortly before his assassination in 1965.

Mandela, Nelson Nelson Mandela (1918–2013), the son of a chief of the African Tembu people, became the first black president of South Africa in 1994. As a lawyer, Mandela began his fight against apartheid in 1952. In 1964 he was sentenced to life imprisonment for his anti-apartheid activism. He was released in 1990. Working with South African President F.W. de Klerk, Mandela helped end the country's apartheid system of racial segregation. He shared the Nobel Prize for Peace in 1993.

Manhattan Project code name of the U.S. government research project that developed the atomic bomb

Manifest Destiny the idea that the United States was destined by God to occupy territory spanning from the Atlantic to Pacific Oceans

Mao Zedong Mao Zedong (1893–1976) was a Chinese leader who successfully led a communist revolution in mainland China. He was chairman of the communist People's Republic of China from 1949 to 1959 and chairman of the country's Communist Party until 1976.

March on Washington 1963 demonstration in which more than 200,000 people rallied for economic equality and civil rights

Marshall Plan foreign policy that offered economic aid to Western Europe after World War II

Marshall, George C. George C. Marshall (1880–1959) became the army's chief of staff in 1939. Marshall used his quiet strength, negotiating skills, and planning genius to build a fighting force as quickly as possible. As Secretary of State after the war, he devised a plan of aid, called the Marshall Plan, to help Western Europe recover. In 1950, he returned as Secretary of Defense at the start of the Korean War and helped to prepare the army one more time.

Marshall, John John Marshall (1755–1835) was a Virginia statesman who served as Chief Justice of the Supreme Court for 35 years, leaving a lasting influence on the role of the Court.

Marshall, Thurgood Thurgood Marshall (1908–1993) became counsel for the NAACP in 1938 and won 29 of the 32 major civil rights cases he argued over the next 23 years. In 1967, he became the first African American to sit on the Supreme Court and held the post until poor health caused him to retire in 1991.

Martí, José José Martí (1853–1895) was an exiled Cuban writer who became the symbol of Cuba's struggle for independence from Spain. Martí helped establish the Cuban Revolutionary Party and was elected its leader in 1892. In 1895 Martí helped launch a war of independence against Spain. He died a month later in battle on the plains of Dos Ríos.

mass culture similar cultural patterns throughout a society as a result of the spread of transportation, communication, and advertising

mass production production of goods in large numbers through the use of machinery and assembly lines

mass transit public transportation systems that carry large numbers of people

massive retaliation policy of threatening to use massive force in response to aggression

Mayflower Compact the governing document for Plymouth Colony that established forms of self-government for the colonists

McCarthy, Eugene Eugene McCarthy (1916–2005) was an antiwar candidate for the 1968 Democratic Party presidential nomination.

McCarthy, Joseph R. Joseph R. McCarthy (1908–1957) was a U.S. Senator who led a series of high-profile investigations into Americans whom he accused of being disloyal to the United States. His tactics, known as McCarthyism, helped define the Red Scare of the 1950s.

McCarthyism negative catchword for extreme, reckless changes of disloyalty

McKay, Claude Claude McKay (1890–1948) was a Jamaican-born poet and novelist whose influential work during and after the Harlem Renaissance sought to define a distinctive black identity.

McKinley, William William McKinley (1843–1901) was the 25th president of the United States, serving from 1897 to 1901. McKinley led the United States during the Spanish-American War in 1898. McKinley's second term as president was cut short by an assassin in 1901.

Meat Inspection Act 1906 law that empowered the federal government to inspect meat sold across state lines and required federal inspection of meat processing plants

median family income a measure of average family income

Medicaid federal program created in 1965 to provide low-cost health insurance to poor Americans of any age

Medicare federal program created in 1965 to provide basic hospital insurance to most Americans over the age of 65

Mellon, Andrew Andrew Mellon (1835–1937) served as secretary of the Treasury from 1921 to 1932. He played a significant role in reforming the U.S. tax structure by lowering marginal tax rates for individuals and businesses.

Melting pot society in which people of different nationalities assimilate to form one culture

Meredith, James James Meredith (1933–) attended an all-black college before becoming the first black student at the University of Mississippi in 1962. After he graduated, he earned a law degree and became involved in Republican Party politics. He was shot in Mississippi while on a protest march in 1966. After he recovered, he continued to be active in the civil rights movement.

migrant farmworker person who travels from farm to farm to pick fruits and vegetables

militarism glorification of the military

Milk, Harvey Harvey Milk (1930–1978) was one of the first openly gay elected officials in the United States. After serving in the U.S. Navy, Milk worked in New York in a succession of jobs including teaching and banking. Milk moved to California, where he was elected to the San Francisco Board of Supervisors in 1977. The gay rights ordinance that was passed under his supervision revealed the growing political power of the gay community. In the following year, however, Milk and Mayor George Moscone of San Francisco were assassinated.

Model T automobile manufactured by Henry Ford to be affordable on the mass market

modernism artistic and literary movement sparked by a break with past conventions

monetary policy control of the money supply by a central authority, including influencing interest rates to promote economic growth and stability

monopoly exclusive control by one company over an entire industry

Monroe Doctrine a declaration in which the United States asserted that the monarchies of Europe had no business meddling with American republics, including those in Latin America

"Moral diplomacy" Woodrow Wilson's statement that the U.S. would not use force to assert influence in the world, but would instead work to promote human rights

Moral Majority political organization established by Reverend Jerry Falwell in 1979 to advance religious goals

Mott, Lucretia Lucretia Mott (1793–1880) was a Quaker social reformer who worked for the abolition of slavery and the expansion of women's rights.

muckraker writer who uncovers and exposes misconduct in government or business

Muir, John John Muir (1838–1914) emigrated with his family from Scotland in 1849. In 1876 he urged the federal government to adopt a forest conservation policy and was later instrumental in the establishment of California's Yosemite and Sequoia national parks. In 1892, Muir founded the Sierra Club, one of today's leading conservationist organizations.

multinational corporation company that produces and sells its goods and services all over the world

multinational corporations companies that produce and sell their goods and services all over the world

Munich Pact agreement made between Germany, Italy, Great Britain, and France in 1938 that sacrificed the Sudetenland to preserve peace

mural large painting applied directly to a wall or a ceiling

Mussolini, Benito fascist leader and dictator of Italy between 1922–1945. He was called Il Duce ("the leader") and established a totalitarian dictatorship that promoted extreme nationalism. During his dictatorship, Italy invaded Ethiopia and partnered with Germany during World War II.

mutualistas organized groups of Mexican Americans that make loans and provide legal assistance to other members of their community

mutually assured destruction policy in which the United States and the Soviet Union hoped to deter nuclear war by building up enough weapons to destroy one another

My Lai village in South Vietnam where in 1968 American forces opened fire on unarmed civilians; U.S. soldiers killed between 400 and 500 Vietnamese

N

Nader, Ralph Ralph Nader (1934–) is an American lawyer and consumer advocate who has been involved in a variety of issues, including car safety, land use, insecticide regulation, and safe meat processing.

napalm jellied gasoline dropped in canisters that explode on impact and cover large areas in flame; dropped by U.S. planes during the Vietnam War

Nation of Islam African American religious organization founded in 1930 that advocated separation of the races

National Aeronautics and Space Administration (NASA) government agency that coordinates U.S. efforts in space

National American Woman Suffrage Association (NAWSA) group founded in 1890 that worked on both the state and national levels to gain women the right to vote

National Association for the Advancement of Colored People (NAACP) interracial organization founded in 1909 to abolish segregation and discrimination and to achieve political and civil rights for African Americans

National Consumers League (NCL) group organized in 1899 to investigate the conditions under which goods were made and sold and to promote safe working conditions and a minimum wage

national debt total amount of money that the federal government owes to the holders of government bonds

National Organization for Women (NOW) organization established by Betty Friedan to combat discrimination against women

National Reclamation Act 1902 law that gave the federal government the power to decide where and how water would be distributed through the building and management of dams and irrigation projects

National Recovery Administration (NRA) New Deal agency that promoted economic recovery by regulating production, prices, and wages

nationalize to place a private resource under government control

nativism inclination to favor native inhabitants as opposed to immigrants

Nazism instituted legal discrimination against Jews

Neutrality Act of 1939 act that allowed nations at war to buy goods and arms in the United States if they paid cash and carried the merchandise on their own ships

New Deal programs and legislation pushed by President Franklin D. Roosevelt during the Great Depression to promote economic recovery and social reform

New Deal coalition political force formed by diverse groups who united to support Franklin D. Roosevelt and his New Deal

New Freedom Woodrow Wilson's program to place government controls on corporations in order to benefit small businesses

New Frontier President Kennedy's plan to improve the economy, fight racial discrimination, and explore space

"New" immigrants Southern and Eastern European immigrants who arrived in the United States in a great wave between 1880 and 1920

New Nationalism President Theodore Roosevelt's plan to restore the government's trustbusting power

New Right political movement supported by reinvigorated conservative groups in the latter half of the twentieth century

Niagara Movement group of African American thinkers founded in 1905 that pushed for immediate racial reforms, particularly in education and voting practices

Nimitz, Chester Chester Nimitz (1885–1966) he took command of the U.S. Pacific Fleet shortly after the attack on Pearl Harbor in 1941. Under his leadership, the U.S. forces won victories at Midway, Tarawa, Marianas, and Iwo Jima, among other places. Nimitz's quiet leadership was key to the American victory in the Pacific during World War II.

Nineteenth Amendment 1920 constitutional amendment that gave women the right to vote

Nixon, Richard M. Richard M. Nixon (1913–1994) served as a Republican member of Congress and of the Senate as well as Vice President under Dwight D. Eisenhower. He ran for President in 1960 and lost to John F. Kennedy but won the office in 1968. His presidency was marked by significant accomplishments in foreign relations. In 1974, he resigned rather than be impeached for covering up illegal activities in the Watergate affair.

No Child Left Behind Act 2002 law aimed at improving the performance of primary and secondary schools particularly through mandated sanctions against schools not reaching federal performance standards

Noriega, Manuel Manuel Noriega (1938–) is a former Panamanian military officer who gained control of the army in 1983, becoming the dominate leader in Panama. Allegations of election fraud, drug trafficking, money laundering, and espionage against the United States led to his capture by U.S. forces. He was found guilty in 1992 and sentenced to 40 years imprisonment.

North American Free Trade Agreement (NAFTA) agreement signed in 1993 calling for the removal of trade restrictions among Canada, Mexico, and the United States

North Atlantic Treaty Organization (NATO) military alliance formed to counter Soviet aggression

Northwest Territory part of the territory ceded to the United States by Great Britain in the Treaty of Paris; it lay north of the Ohio River, east of the Mississippi River, and west of the established boundaries of Pennsylvania

nuclear family an ideal or typical household with a father, mother, and children

Nuclear Test Ban Treaty 1963 nuclear-weapons agreement that banned aboveground nuclear tests

nullification the idea that states could nullify, or void, any federal law they deemed unconstitutional

Nuremberg Trials trials in which Nazi leaders were charged with war crimes

O

Obama, Barack Barack Obama (1961–) was elected the 44th president of the United States in 2008, becoming the first African American to hold the office. Obama served in the Illinois state legislature and the U.S. Senate prior to becoming President. Obama faced the wars in Afghanistan and Iraq, as well as a financial recession upon assuming the presidency. In 2009, Obama was awarded the Nobel Peace Prize.

O'Connor, Sandra Day Sandra Day O'Connor (1930–) received her undergraduate and law degrees from Stanford University, but because she was a woman, could not find work at a law firm. Instead, she found employment as a deputy district attorney in Northern California. After distinguishing herself for years in a number of fields—as an assistant attorney general, a senator, a Superior Court judge, and a judge for the Court of Appeals (all in the state of Arizona)—she became the first female U.S. Supreme Court Justice in 1981.

Office of War Information (OWI) government agency that encouraged support of the war effort during World War II

Okies general term used to describe Dust Bowl refugees

Olmsted, Frederick Law Frederick Law Olmsted (1822–1903) was an influential American landscape architect best known for designing Central Park in New York City. Olmsted also contributed to the preservation of the Yosemite park in California, the park spaces around Niagara Falls, and a large system of public parks in Boston.

Open Door Policy an American statement that the government did not want colonies in China, but favored free trade there

open-range system method of ranching in which the rancher allowed his or her livestock to roam and graze over a vast area of grassland

Operation Desert Storm 1991 American-led attack on Iraqi forces after Iraq refused to withdraw its troops from Kuwait

Oppenheimer, J. Robert American physicist J. Robert Oppenheimer (1904–1967) was the director of the Manhattan Project, the U.S. government research project during World War II that produced the first atomic bombs. After the war, he became head of the Institute for Advanced Study in New Jersey, a center for theoretical research.

Organization of Petroleum Exporting Countries (OPEC) group of countries that sell oil to other nations and cooperate to regulate the price and supply of oil

Otis, Elisha Elisha Otis (1811–1861) was an American who invented the safety elevator in 1852. Otis's "safety hoist" was first designed for freight but was soon adapted for passenger services. The first elevator for passengers was installed in a store in New York City in 1857. Otis also developed a steam-powered elevator that became the basis for the Otis Elevator Company.

P

Palmer Raids the series of raids in the early 1920s initiated by Attorney General A. Mitchell Palmer, against suspected radicals and communists

Panama Canal human-made waterway linking the Atlantic to the Pacific across the Isthmus of Panama

Panic of 1837 the start of a prolonged downturn in the American economy touched off by changes in government policy

pardon official forgiveness of a crime and its punishment

Paris Peace Accords 1973 Peace agreement between the United States, South Vietnam, North Vietnam, and the Vietcong that effectively ended the Vietnam War

Parks, Rosa Rosa Parks (1913–2005) began the Montgomery bus protest in 1955 when she refused to give up her seat to a white passenger. She continued to be active in the civil rights movement while working for a member of Congress and starting a nonprofit organization to help young people.

patent official rights given by the government to an inventor for the exclusive right to develop, use, and sell an invention for a set period of time

Patton, George S., Jr. A colorful personality and a forceful leader greatly admired by troops under his command, George S. Patton (1885–1945) commanded U.S. tanks during World War I and quickly demonstrated his skill at leading mobile fighting units. During World War II, he led U.S. troops in North Africa and Europe, sweeping rapidly across France and Germany in the closing months of the war.

Paul, Alice Alice Paul (1885–1977) joined the leadership of the National American Woman Suffrage Association in 1912 but soon left to found a more militant organization, which became the National Woman's Party in 1917. After the passage of the 19th Amendment, Paul expanded her work for women's rights. In 1923 she introduced the first equal rights amendment into Congress.

Peace Corps American government organization that sends volunteers to provide technical, educational, and medical services to developing countries

Pearl Harbor American military base attacked by the Japanese on December 7, 1941

Pendleton Civil Service Act 1883 law that created a civil service system for the federal government in an attempt to hire employees on a merit system rather than on a spoils system

Pentagon Papers classified U.S. government study that revealed American leaders involved the United States in Vietnam without fully informing the American people; leaked to the *New York Times* in 1971

perestroika policy in the Soviet Union in the late 1980s calling for restructuring of the stagnant Soviet economy

Perot, H. Ross Ross Perot (1930–) is a self-made billionaire who founded Electronic Data Systems in 1962. Perot ran as an independent candidate for U.S. President in 1992, capturing 19 percent of the vote. In 1995 he founded the Reform Party and ran in the presidential election of 1996, but he did not win.

Perry, Matthew Matthew Perry (1794–1858) was a U.S. naval officer who led an American naval fleet in 1853 to 1854 that forced Japan into trade and diplomatic relations with the West after more than two centuries of isolation. Perry's journey opened further American expansion across the Pacific Ocean.

Pershing, John J. John J. Pershing (1860–1948) commanded the American Expeditionary Forces (AEF) in Europe during World War I. Earlier, he had served in the Philippines and in Mexico. After World War I, he served as chief of staff of the U.S. Army.

personal computer small computer intended for individual use

Pinchot, Gifford Gifford Pinchot (1865–1946) was appointed to head the U.S. Forest Service, but was fired in 1910 after a dispute with President Taft's Secretary of the Interior. In 1912, he helped form the Progressive Party that nominated Theodore Roosevelt to run for President. Pinchot continued his conservation work in Pennsylvania, where he was elected governor in 1922.

Platt Amendment set of conditions under which Cuba was granted independence in 1902, including restrictions on rights of Cubans and granting the U.S. the "right to intervene" to preserve order in Cuba

political machines a political party's organization that wins voter loyalty and guarantees power to a small group of leaders, who often abuse it for their own gain

Polk, James K. James K. Polk (1795–1849) was a Tennessee statesman who served as the eleventh President.

poll tax a tax charged on voters

popular sovereignty a doctrine allowing new states to decide the issue of slavery for themselves

populism the widespread participation of regular citizens in the political process and the inclusion of their concerns in political debates

Populist Party People's Party; political party formed in 1891 to advocate a larger money supply and other economic reforms

Powderly, Terence V. Terence V. Powderly (1849–1924) was an American labor leader who led the Knights of Labor for several years in the late nineteenth century with the goal of leading American workers out of what he saw as the bondage of wage labor.

Presley, Elvis Elvis Presley (1935–1977) was an American musician who became known as the "King of Rock-and-Roll." Presley's music combined elements of African American blues, gospel, country songs, and Tin Pan Alley ballads. His flamboyant personality and nonconformist image made Presley a teen idol and an inspiration to future rock-and-roll artists throughout the world.

privatizing to transfer from governmental ownership or control to private interests

productivity the rate at which goods are produced or services performed

Progressive Party political party that emerged from the Taft-Roosevelt battle that split the Republican Party in 1912

Progressivism movement that responded to the pressures of industrialization and urbanization by promoting reforms

Prohibition the forbidding by law of the manufacture, transport, and sale of alcohol

protective tariffs the taxes on imported goods designed to protect domestic industry

Public Works Administration (PWA) New Deal agency that provided millions of jobs constructing public buildings as well as airports, dams, and bridges

Pulitzer, Joseph Joseph Pulitzer (1847–1911) was an influential American newspaper editor and publisher. Pulitzer helped format the modern newspaper and included investigative reporting, sports and fashion coverage, comics, and illustrations in his papers.

Pullman Strike violent 1894 railway workers' strike which began outside of Chicago and spread nationwide

pump priming economic theory that favored public works projects because they put money into the hands of consumers who would buy more goods, stimulating the economy

Pure Food and Drug Act 1906 law that allowed federal inspection of food and medicine and banned the interstate shipment and sale of impure food and the mislabeling of food and drugs

Q

quota system arrangement that limited the number of immigrants who could enter the United States from specific countries

R

Radical Republicans a group of Republican political leaders dedicated to imposing harsh conditions on the states that had seceded from the Union during the Civil War

Randolph, A. Philip A. Philip Randolph (1889–1979) was a strong labor leader and leader of the civil rights movement for decades. In 1925, he became head of the Brotherhood of Sleeping Car Porters. After more than a decade of battling, he got the Pullman Corporation to sign the first contract in history between a major company and a predominantly African American labor union. Next Randolph turned his attention to discrimination in war industries, convincing President Roosevelt to issue Executive Order 8802 in 1941. After the war, he persuaded President Truman to pass another executive order banning discrimination in the military. Randolph was a driving force behind the 1963 March on Washington.

ratify to officially approve the adoption of a document

rationing government-controlled limits on the amount of certain goods that civilians could buy during wartime

Reagan, Ronald Ronald Reagan (1911–2004) got his famous easy communication style from his background as a radio sports announcer, a host for TV shows, and most famously, an actor in movies. Although he was a Democrat as a young man, his views became more conservative, and he switched to the Republican Party. He was elected governor of California in 1966 where he carried out a conservative agenda during his two terms. In 1980, Reagan was elected to the first of his two terms as President.

realpolitik a foreign policy based on concrete national interests instead of abstract ideologies; promoted by Henry Kissinger during the Nixon administration

recall process by which voters can remove elected officials from office before their term ends

Reconstruction the period during which the federal government controlled the states that had seceded from the Union during the Civil War

Reconstruction Finance Corporation (RFC) federal agency set up by Congress in 1932 to provide emergency government credit to banks, railroads, and other large businesses

Red Scare fear that communists were working to destroy the American way of life

Redeemer a term for white southern Democrats who returned to political power after 1870

referendum process that allows citizens to approve or reject a law passed by a legislature

reparations payment for war damages

repatriation process by which government officials return persons to their country of origin

republican government a government in which officials are representatives elected by the people; also known as a representative democracy

reservationists group of U.S. senators who were prepared to vote for the Treaty of Versailles as long as some changes were made to it

reservations public lands where Native Americans were required to live by the federal government

Riis, Jacob Jacob Riis (1849–1914) was a Danish immigrant who became a New York City newspaper reporter in 1873. In 1888, as the crime reporter for the *New York Evening Sun,* he took photos of night life in the slums. Published in his 1890 book, *How the Other Half Lives,* the photos moved New York Police Commissioner Theodore Roosevelt to take up the cause of urban reform.

rock-and-roll popular music that grew out of the gospel and blues traditions of African Americans

Rockefeller, John D. John D. Rockefeller (1839–1937) was an American industrialist and philanthropist. He began the Standard Oil Company and dominated the oil industry with innovative, aggressive business practices. He also contributed money to different causes through the Rockefeller Foundation.

Roosevelt Corollary President Theodore Roosevelt's reassertion of the Monroe Doctrine to keep the Western Hemisphere free from intervention by European powers

Roosevelt, Eleanor Eleanor Roosevelt (1884–1962) was the wife of President Franklin D. Roosevelt. With FDR's election as President in 1932, Eleanor Roosevelt became a public figure in her own right, traveling the country promoting the causes of helping women, children, and the poor. After her husband's death, she served as a U.S. delegate to the United Nations (1945–1951), focusing on human rights and women's issues.

Roosevelt, Franklin D. Franklin D. Roosevelt (1882–1945) served as assistant secretary of the Navy (1913–1920), before running unsuccessfully for Vice President on the Democratic ticket in 1920. Stricken with polio the following year, Roosevelt recovered to resume his political career as governor of New York (1929–1933). Elected President in 1932, he lead the nation through the Great Depression and World War II before dying in office in 1945.

Roosevelt, Theodore Theodore Roosevelt (1858–1919) was governor of New York before becoming Vice President in 1901. Roosevelt became the youngest man to assume the presidency soon after. He was known for his anti-monopoly and conservation policies. He made an unsuccessful bid for another term in 1912 as the candidate of the Progressive Party.

Rosenberg, Julius y Ethel Julius (1918–1953) and Ethel Rosenberg (1915–1953) were two American civilians controversially convicted and executed for espionage during the Red Scare of the 1950s. Later evidence from the Venona Papers confirmed that both did have ties to Soviet espionage.

Rough Riders group of men, consisting of rugged westerners and upper-class easterners who fought during the Spanish-American War

rural-to-urban migrants people who move from an agricultural area to a city

Russo-Japanese War a war between Japan and Russia in 1904 over the presence of Russian troops in Manchuria

Ruth, Babe Babe Ruth (1895–1948) was a professional baseball player known for his showmanship and ability to hit homeruns. He is a member of the Baseball Hall of Fame.

S

Sacco, Nicola Nicola Sacco (1891–1927) was an Italian immigrant convicted of murder and executed in 1927.

SALT II proposed agreement between the United States and the Soviet Union to limit certain types of nuclear arms production; also known as the Strategic Arms Limitation Treaty II, it was never ratified by the United States Senate

sanctions penalties intended to make people obey laws and rules, especially measures taken to force a country to obey international law

Sand Creek Massacre 1864 incident in which Colorado militia attacked a camp of Cheyenne and Arapaho Indians, some of who were under U.S. Army protection

Sanger, Margaret Margaret Sanger (1879–1966) first coined the term "birth control" in a pamphlet she published in 1914. A medical organization she founded, the Birth Control Research Bureau, evolved into Planned Parenthood in 1942.

satellite mechanical device that orbits Earth, receiving and sending communication signals or transmitting scientific data

satellite state independent nation under the control of a more powerful nation

saturation bombing tactic of dropping massive amounts of bombs in order to inflict maximum damage

Savings and Loan crisis 1989 failure of about 1000 savings and loan banks, also known as S&Ls, as a result of risky and sometimes fraudulent business practices

scalawag a negative term for a southern white who supported the Republican Party after the Civil War

Schlafly, Phyllis Phyllis Schlafly (1924–), an American writer and political activist, is a well-known and outspoken defender of the traditional family. She is most famous for opposing the Equal Rights Amendment.

scientific management approach to improving efficiency, in which experts looked at every step of a manufacturing process, trying to find ways to reduce time, effort, and expense

Scopes Trial 1925 trial of a Tennessee school teacher for breaking a law that forbade teaching Darwin's theory of evolution

Second Great Awakening a Protestant movement in the early 1800s that increased membership in evangelical movements

segregation a forced separation, often by race

Selective Service Act act passed by Congress in 1917 authorizing a draft of men for military service

self-determination the right of people to choose their own form of government

Seneca Falls Convention a meeting of both women and men in Seneca Falls, New York, in 1848 which kicked off the women's rights movement in the United States

service economy economic system focused on the buying and selling of services

service sector businesses that provide services rather than manufactured goods

settlement house community center organized at the turn of the twentieth century to provide social services to the urban poor

Seventeenth Amendment 1913 constitutional amendment that allowed for the direct election of U.S. senators by citizens

share-tenancy much like sharecropping, except that the farmer chooses what crop to plant and buys the supplies

sharecropping a system in which a farmer tends to a portion of a planter's land in return for a share of the crop

Shays' Rebellion an armed uprising of Massachusetts farmers led by Daniel Shays intended to shut down the courts and block foreclosures of farms

Sherman Antitrust Act 1890 law banning any trust that restrained interstate trade or commerce

Sherman, William T. William T. Sherman (1820–1891) was a general in the Union army whose "March to the Sea" left a wide path of destruction through the South.

silent majority phrase introduced by President Richard Nixon to refer to a significant number of Americans who supported his policies but chose to not express their views

Sinclair, Upton Upton Sinclair (1878–1968) began writing for newspapers and completed several successful novels soon after he graduated college in 1897. His most famous work, *The Jungle*, was published in 1906. Sinclair continued to write muckraking pieces and in time became active in California politics, running unsuccessfully for governor in 1934. In 1942, he won a Pulitzer Prize for his novel *Dragon's Teeth*.

sit-down strike organized labor action in which workers stop working and occupy the workplace until their demands are met

sit-in form of protest during which participants sit and refuse to move

Sitting Bull Sitting Bull (1831?–1890) was a war chief and important spiritual leader who became the first-ever chief of all the Lakota Sioux bands in the 1860s. After surrendering to the Army in 1881, he lived on a reservation where he was killed by Indian police sent to arrest him.

Sixteenth Amendment 1913 constitutional amendment that gave Congress the authority to levy an income tax

skyscrapers very tall buildings

Smith Act law that made it unlawful to teach or advocate the violent overthrow of the United States government

Smith, Bessie Bessie Smith (1898?–1937) was a blues vocalist widely known as the "Empress of the Blues." Smith sang with some of the great jazz musicians of the time, including Louis Armstrong.

Social Darwinism the belief held by some in the late nineteenth century that certain nations and races were superior to others and therefore destined to rule over them

Social Gospel reform movement that emerged in the late nineteenth century that sought to improve society by applying Christian principles

Social Security Act 1935 law that set up a pension system for retirees, established unemployment insurance, created insurance for victims of work-related accidents, and provided aid for poverty-stricken mothers and children, the blind, and the disabled

socialism system or theory under which the means of production are publicly controlled and regulated rather than owned by individuals

Sosa, Lionel Lionel Sosa (1939–) is an advertising executive who gained success by helping companies market their products to Latino consumers. But he may be most famous for helping Republican candidates reach out to Latino voters. In the 2004 election with Sosa's help, George W. Bush was able to garner an estimated 40% of Latino votes, a huge increase over previous Republican presidential candidates.

Southeast Asia Treaty Organization (SEATO) defensive alliance aimed at preventing communist aggression in Asia

southern strategy tactic of the Republican Party to win presidential elections by securing the electoral vote of southern states

space race competition between the United States and the Soviet Union to successfully land on the moon

Spanish Civil War war in which Nationalist forces led by General Francisco Franco rebelled against the democratic Republican government of Spain

speculation practice of making high-risk investments in hopes of obtaining large profits

spheres of influence a region dominated and controlled by an outside power

Spock, Benjamin Benjamin Spock (1903–1998) was an American pediatrician and author whose 1946 book *Common Sense Book of Baby and Child Care* was one of the most influential books on parenting in the twentieth century. Spock broke from tradition by advising parents to show affection, understanding, and flexibility and to promote and appreciate each child's individuality.

spoils system practice of the political party in power giving jobs and appointments to its supporters rather than to people based on their qualifications

Square Deal President Theodore Roosevelt's program of reforms to keep the wealthy and powerful from taking advantage of small business owners and the poor

stagflation term for the economic condition created in the late 1960s and 1970s by high inflation combined with stagnant economic growth and high unemployment

Stalin, Joseph Joseph Stalin (1879–1953) was leader of communist Union of Soviet Socialist Republics (U.S.S.R.) from 1924 to 1953. His efforts to transform the Soviet Union into an industrial power and form state-run collective farms caused extreme hardship and millions of deaths. A partner with Germany in 1939, Stalin later joined the Allies in World War II. After the war, Stalin became an aggressive participant in the Cold War.

Stanton, Elizabeth Cady Elizabeth Cady Stanton (1815–1902) was a leading figure in the American women's rights movement.

Starr, Kenneth Kenneth Starr (1946–) is an American lawyer who served as the independent counsel in charge of the investigation that led to the impeachment of President Bill Clinton in 1998.

steerage third-class accommodations on a steamship

Steffens, Lincoln Lincoln Steffens (1866–1936) was a reporter and editor for the *New York Post* and, later, the muckraking *McClure's* magazine. Steffens wrote articles and books exposing government corruption at the state and municipal levels.

Steinbeck, John John Steinbeck (1902–1968) was an American novelist who frequently wrote about migratory farmworkers and other laborers during the Great Depression.

Steinem, Gloria Gloria Steinem (1934–) is an American feminist, political activist, and writer-editor, who played an influential role in the Women's Movement in the late twentieth century. In 2013, Steinem was awarded the Presidential Medal of Freedom.

Stonewall Riots A series of violent protests that began in the early morning of June 28, 1969, when police raided an LGBT bar in Greenwich Village, New York City. The riots marked a radical new change of strategy for the gay rights movement and inspired worldwide annual Gay Pride parades to commemorate the event.

Stowe, Harriet Beecher Harriet Beecher Stowe (1811–1896) was an abolitionist author who wrote *Uncle Tom's Cabin* to show the human impact of slavery.

Strategic Arms Limitation Treaty (SALT I) 1972 treaty between the United States and the Soviet Union that froze the deployment of intercontinental ballistic missiles and placed limits on antiballistic missiles

strategic bombing tactic of dropping bombs on key political and industrial targets

Strategic Defense Initiative (SDI) nicknamed "Star Wars," President Reagan's plan to develop innovative defenses to guard the United States against nuclear missile attacks

Student Nonviolent Coordinating Committee grass-roots movement founded in 1960 by young civil rights activists

Students for a Democratic Society (SDS) organization founded in 1960 at the University of Michigan to fight racism and poverty

Suez crisis attempt by France and Great Britain to seize control of the Suez Canal in 1956

suffrage the right to vote

Sunbelt name given to the region of states in the South and the Southwest

superpowers strong nations that dominated the postwar world

supply-side economics economic theory which says that reducing tax rates stimulates economic growth

sweatshops small factories where employees have to work long hours under poor conditions for little pay

T

Taft-Hartley Act a law that restricted the power of labor unions

Taft, William Howard William Howard Taft (1857–1930) was the 27th president of the United States from 1909 to 1913. In 1901, Taft became the first civilian governor of the Philippines. In that post, Taft worked to rebuild the economy and reestablish order. In 1921, President Harding appointed Taft the 10th chief justice of the United States, where he served for 9 years.

Taliban Islamist faction that controlled most of Afghanistan from 1996 to 2001

Taney, Roger Roger Taney (1777–1864) was Chief Justice of the Supreme Court from the 1830s through the 1860s; he wrote the Court's *Dred Scott* ruling.

Tea Party Movement informal movement made up of local groups who want to reduce the size and scope of the federal government

Teapot Dome scandal Harding administration scandal in which the Interior Secretary leased government oil reserves to private oilmen for bribes

temperance movement movement aimed at stopping alcohol abuse and the problems created by it

tenant farming a system in which a farmer paid rent to a landowner for the use of the land

tenements multistory buildings divided into apartments to house as many residents as possible

Tennessee Valley Authority (TVA) government agency created during the New Deal to build dams in the Tennessee River valley to control flooding and generate electric power

termination policy a policy ending all programs monitored by the Bureau of Indian Affairs. It also ended federal responsibility for the health and welfare of Native Americans.

Tet Offensive communist assault on a large number of South Vietnamese cities in early 1968

Thirteenth Amendment a constitutional amendment, ratified in December 1865, that abolished slavery in the United States.

38th parallel dividing line between North and South Korea

Tiananmen Square site in Beijing where Chinese students' prodemocracy protests were put down by the Chinese government in 1989

Tin Pan Alley section on 28th Street in New York City that became the center of the music publishing industry in the late 1800s; genre of popular American music

Tinker v. Des Moines School District 1969 Supreme Court case in which the Court ruled that the right to free speech extended to other types of expression besides the spoken word

Tocqueville, Alexis de Alexis de Tocqueville (1805–1859) was a French aristocrat whose travels in the United States in the 1830s resulted in the publication of *Democracy in America,* an influential analysis of American politics.

Tojo, Hideki Hideki Tojo (1884–1948) became Japan's prime minister in October of 1941 when plans were already underway to attack the United States Navy at Pearl Harbor. He led Japan until July 1944. After the war, he was tried for war crimes and hanged in December 1948.

totalitarianism a theory of government in which a single party or leader controls the economic, social, and cultural lives of its people

Trail of Tears forced march of the Cherokee Indians to move west of the Mississippi in the 1830s

Transcontinental Railroad rail link between the eastern and the western United States

Treaty of Guadalupe Hidalgo the treaty that ended the Mexican-American War; the United States acquired territory in the future states of Arizona, California, Colorado, New Mexico, Nevada, Utah, and Wyoming

Treaty of Paris an agreement signed by the United States and Spain in 1898, which officially ended the Spanish-American War

trickle-down economics economic theory that holds that financial benefits given to banks and large businesses will trickle down to smaller businesses and consumers

Tripartite Pact agreement that created an alliance between Germany, Italy, and Japan during World War II

Truman Doctrine President Truman's promise to help nations struggling against communist movements

Truman, Harry S. Harry S. Truman (1884–1972) was President of the United States from 1945–1953. Truman took office after Franklin Roosevelt's death and led the nation during the final months of World War II, making the decision to use atomic weapons against Japan. In the early years of the Cold War, Truman worked to rebuild Europe and to oppose the spread of communism. When communist North Korea invaded South Korea in 1950, beginning the Korean War, Truman sent American troops into the conflict.

Trump, Donald J. Donald J. Trump was born in New York City in 1946. His father was a wealthy real estate developer. Upon graduation from the University of Pennsylvania in 1968, Trump joined his father's firm. By the 1990s, he owned vast real estate holdings, including the Empire State Building, various hotels, condominiums, apartment buildings, and casinos. He also starred in a reality television show, The Apprentice (later The Celebrity Apprentice). He considered a run for the presidency in 1999, but it was not until 2016 that he officially decided to run. He won the Republican nomination in the summer of 2016 and in November of that year, Donald J. Trump was elected the 45ᵗʰ President of the United States.

trust group of separate companies that are placed under the control of a single managing board in order to form a monopoly

Turner, Frederick Jackson Frederick Jackson Turner (1861–1932) was an American historian whose works greatly influenced future writings about American history. Turner promoted using social sciences in historical writings and stressed the use of concepts such as immigration, urbanization, economic development, and social and cultural history when trying to understand historical events.

Tuskegee Airmen African American squadron that escorted bombers in the air war over Europe during World War II

Twain, Mark Mark Twain (1835–1910) was the pen name for Samuel Langhorne Clemons, an American novelist and humorist who wrote famous works such *as Life on the Mississippi, The Adventures of Tom Sawyer,* and *The Adventures of Huckleberry Finn.* Twain's stories reflected the American experience as he saw it.

Twenty-fifth Amendment constitutional amendment ratified in 1967 that deals with presidential succession, vice presidential vacancy, and presidential disability

Twenty-fourth Amendment constitutional amendment that banned the poll tax as a voting requirement

U

U-boats German submarine

unconditional surrender giving up completely without any concessions

underground railroad a secret network of "conductors" who hid runaway slaves in farm wagons and on riverboats and then moved them to destinations in the North or in Canada and sometimes as far away as England

unfunded mandate program or action required but not paid for by the federal government

United Farm Workers (UFW) labor union of farm workers that used nonviolent tactics, including a workers' strike and consumer boycott of table grapes

United Nations (UN) organization founded in 1945 to promote peace

Universal Declaration of Human Rights document issued by the UN to promote basic human rights and freedoms

Urban League network of churches and clubs that set up employment agencies and relief efforts to help African Americans get settled and find work in cities

urban renewal government programs for redevelopment of urban areas

urbanization expansion of cities and/or an increase in the number of people living in them

USA PATRIOT Act law passed following September 11, 2001, giving law enforcement broader powers in monitoring possible terrorist activities

V

Vanzetti, Bartolomeo Bartolomeo Vanzetti (1888–1927) was an Italian immigrant convicted of murder and executed in 1927.

vaudeville type of show that included dancing, singing, and comedy sketches and became popular in the late nineteenth century

Venona Papers a series of Cold War-era secret Soviet documents intercepted and later released by U.S. intelligence officials

vertical integration system of consolidating firms involved in all steps of a product's manufacture

Vietcong South Vietnamese communist rebels who waged a guerrilla war against the government of South Vietnam throughout the Vietnam War

Vietnamization President Nixon's plan for gradual withdrawal of U.S. forces as South Vietnamese troops assumed more combat duties

vigilantes self-appointed law enforcers

Villa, Francisco "Pancho" Francisco "Pancho" Villa (1878–1923) was a Mexican revolutionary and guerrilla leader. In 1916 Villa's forces killed 18 Americans in New Mexico, which resulted in U.S. General John J. Pershing's unsuccessful expedition into Mexico with 10,000 troops to capture and punish Villa.

Violence Against Women Act law passed in 1994 that increased federal resources to apprehend and prosecute men guilty of violent acts against women

Volstead Act law enacted by Congress to enforce the Eighteenth Amendment

Voting Rights Act law that banned literacy tests and empowered the federal government to oversee voter registration

voucher certificate or other document that can be used in place of money

W

Wade-Davis Bill a law that required a majority of prewar voters in Confederate states to swear loyalty to the Union before restoration could begin

Wagner Act New Deal law that abolished unfair labor practices, recognized the right of employees to organize labor unions, and gave workers the right to collective bargaining

Wallace, George George Wallace (1919–1998) served as governor of Alabama from 1963 to 1967. He ran for president in 1968 on the American Independent Party ticket, championing states rights and winning five southern states in the election. Serving three more terms as governor (1971–1979, 1983–1987), he eventually renounced his segregationist beliefs.

Walton, Sam Sam Walton (1918–1992) was an American retail pioneer who founded Wal-Mart Stores, Inc., which became the largest retail sales chain in the United States.

war bond a bond bought to fund a war effort, redeemable for interest after a certain period of time

War on Poverty President Lyndon Johnson's programs aimed at aiding the country's poor through education, job training, proper health care, and nutrition

War Powers Act 1973 law passed by Congress restricting the President's war-making powers; the law requires the President to consult with Congress before committing American forces to a foreign conflict

War Refugee Board U.S. government agency founded in 1944 to save Eastern European Jews

Warren Commission committee that investigated the assassination of President Kennedy

Warren Court Supreme Court of the 1960s under Chief Justice Earl Warren, whose decisions supported civil rights

Warren, Earl Earl Warren (1891–1974) served three terms as governor of California before serving as Chief Justice of the Supreme Court from 1953 to 1969. Under his leadership, the Court decided several landmark cases that affected civil rights, criminal procedures, voting rights, and separation of church and state.

Warsaw Pact military alliance of the Soviet Union and its satellite states

Washington Naval Disarmament Conference meeting held in 1921 and 1922 where world leaders agreed to limit construction of warships

Washington, Booker T. Booker T. Washington (1856–1915) was an African American activist dedicated to promoting educational and economic advancement for blacks as a road to racial equality.

Washington, George George Washington (1732–1799) was a Virginia officer and statesman who led the Continental Army during the Revolutionary War and served as the first President of the United States.

Watergate political scandal involving illegal activities that led to the resignation of President Richard Nixon in 1974

weapons of mass destruction (WMD) nuclear, biological, and chemical weapons intended to kill or harm on a large scale

welfare state government that assumes responsibility for providing for the welfare of the poor, elderly, sick, and unemployed

Wells, Ida B. Wells Ida B. Wells (1862–1931) was an African American journalist who worked throughout her life to end the practice of lynching in the South. She contributed to several newspapers, including the *Memphis Free Speech,* the *New York Age,* and the *Chicago Conservator.* In 1895, she published a detailed inquiry into lynching, entitled *A Red Record.*

Western Front battle front between the Allies and Central Powers in western Europe during World War I

Westmoreland, William From 1964 to 1968, General William Westmorland (1914–2005) was the commander of U.S. forces in the Vietnam War. Westmorland had previously served in World War II and the Korean War.

Whig Party a short-lived political party that favored a strong federal government to manage and grow the economy

Willard, Frances Frances Willard (1839–1898) was a professor who grew interested in the temperance movement in 1874. She joined the Women's Christian Temperance Union (WCTU), where she clashed with other members by insisting on linking its goals with women's suffrage. By 1879, she had gained enough support to be elected president of the WCTU, a position she held the rest of her life.

William II William II (1859–1941) was the German emperor and king of Prussia until the end of World War I in 1918.

Wilmot Proviso a call for a ban on slavery in any territory that the United States gained from Mexico as a result of the Mexican-American War

Wilson, Woodrow Woodrow Wilson (1856–1924) entered politics in 1910 when he was elected governor of New Jersey. His reforms there brought him national attention and the Democratic presidential nomination in 1912. As President he guided the nation through World War I and negotiated the Versailles Treaty.

Winfrey, Oprah Oprah Winfrey (1954–) worked as a television news reporter and anchor person before working as a morning talk show host. Her Chicago show, *The Oprah Winfrey Show,* began in 1985 and was syndicated nationally the next year. The show was a huge hit and spawned her media and entertainment empire, which includes a magazine and a cable television channel. Winfrey is a mainstay of *Forbes* magazine's list of richest people in America. Her net worth in 2013 was estimated at $2.9 billion.

Wisconsin v. Yoder 1972 Supreme Court decision that extended freedom of religion to allow Amish parents, on religious grounds, to withdraw their children from public school after the eighth grade

Women's Army Corps (WAC) United States Army group established during World War II so that women could serve in non-combat roles

women's rights movement the campaign for equal rights for women

Works Progress Administration (WPA) key New Deal agency that provided work relief through various public works projects

World Trade Organization (WTO) international organization formed in 1995 to encourage the expansion of world trade

Wounded Knee 1890 confrontation between U.S. cavalry and Sioux that marked the end of Indian resistance

Y

Yalta Conference 1945 strategy meeting between Roosevelt, Churchill, and Stalin

Yellow Press newspapers that used sensational headlines and exaggerated stories in order to promote readership

Z

Zhou Enlai Zhou Enlai (1898–1976) lived abroad as a young man before returning to his native China in 1924 to help Mao Zedong lead a communist revolution there. When Mao established People's Republic of China in 1949, Zhou became its prime minister and foreign minister and was later the main architect of China's policy of détente with the United States in 1972.

Zimmermann note telegram written by German Foreign Minister Zimmermann proposing an alliance between Germany and Mexico against the United States during World War I

A

abolitionists > movimiento abolicionista Movimiento del siglo XIX que buscaba suprimir la esclavitud.

Acquired Immunodeficiency Syndrome (AIDS) > Síndrome de Inmunodeficiencia Adquirida (SIDA) Enfermedad que ataca el sistema inmunitario de sus víctimas; empezó a extenderse a principios de la década de 1980 y aún hoy sigue representando una seria crisis de salud mundial puesto que no se conoce cura.

ACT UP > ACT UP siglas en inglés para AIDS Coalition to Unleash Power (Coalición de SIDA para Liberar el Poder), grupo de acción directa formado en 1987 para ayudar a las personas con SIDA, para protestar por la discriminación, y para motivar al gobierno a enfrentar la crisis por el SIDA mediante la intruducción de legislación, tratamiento, e investigación médica

Addams, Jane > Addams, Jane (1860–1935) fue cofundadora de Hull House, una casa de asistencia en Chicago, en 1889. Vivió y trabajó en Hull House por el resto de su vida. Pacifista y determinada defensora del sufragio femenino, Addams escribió numerosos libros e impartió conferencias. En 1931 compartió el Premio Nobel de la Paz.

affirmative action > acción afirmativa Política que da trato especial a las mujeres y minorías para resarcirlas de la discriminación del pasado.

AFL-CIO > Federación Estadounidense del Trabajo-Congreso de Organización Industrial En 1955 dos sindicatos de trabajadores (la Federación Estadounidense del Trabajo y el Congreso de Organización Industrial) se unieron.

aggression > agresión Acción hostil o ataque no provocado.

Aguinaldo, Emilio > Aguinaldo, Emilio (1869–1964) fue el líder del ejército filipino que luchó por su independencia contra España en la década de 1890. Desilusionado con la presencia de los Estados Unidos en Filipinas después de la guerra, Aguinaldo ayudó a organizar una insurrección en contra del gobierno estadounidense. En 1901 fue capturado por el ejército de los Estados Unidos, terminando así la lucha filipina por su independencia.

al Qaeda > al Qaeda Grupo terrorista establecido por Osama bin Laden para eliminar la influencia occidental en los países musulmanes.

Alger, Horatio > Alger, Horatio (1832–1899) fue un escritor estadounidense que vendió más de 20 millones de ejemplares de novelas que exploraban el tema de harapos a riquezas. Alger creó personajes que lograban fama y riqueza mediante el trabajo duro y la determinación.

Alliance for Progress > Alianza para el Progreso Programa del presidente Kennedy que daba asistencia económica a América Latina.

Allies > Aliados Grupo de países encabezado por Gran Bretaña, Francia, los Estados Unidos y la Unión Soviética, que peleó contra los Poderes del Eje en la Segunda Guerra Mundial.

Alsace-Lorraine > Alsacia-Lorena Territorio de Francia perdido ante Alemania en 1871.

American Expeditionary Forces (AEF) > Fuerzas Expedicionarias Estadounidenses Ejército estadounidense durante la Primera Guerra Mundial.

American Federation of Labor (AFL) > Federación Estadounidense del Trabajo Sindicato que organizó a los trabajadores calificados en oficios específicos e hizo pequeñas demandas en lugar de buscar cambios amplios.

American Indian Citizenship Act of 1924 > Ley de Ciudadanía Indígena de 1924 Ciudadanía otorgada a todos los nativos americanos nacidos dentro de los límites territoriales de los Estados Unidos.

American Indian Movement (AIM) > Movimiento de Indígenas Estadounidenses Grupo que se concentró en ayudar a los indígenas, incluyendo velar por sus derechos legales, su tierra y sus derechos de autodeterminación.

Americanization > americanización Creencia que sostenía que la asimilación de los inmigrantes por la sociedad estadounidense los haría ciudadanos más leales.

amnesty > amnistía Perdón general a ciertos delitos.

Anaconda Plan > Plan Anaconda Estrategia del Norte durante la Guerra Civil con la que se pretendía causar la hambruna en el Sur, bloqueando los puertos marítimos y controlando el río Mississippi.

Angel Island > Isla Ángel Estación de procesamiento de inmigrantes que abrió sus puertas en la bahía de San Francisco en 1910.

Anschluss > Anschluss Unión de Alemania y Austria en 1933.

Anthony, Susan B. > Anthony, Susan B. (1820–1906) fue una activista de los derechos de la mujer que trabajó para ganar el derecho al voto de las mujeres.

Anti-Defamation League > Liga Antidifamación Organización formada en 1913 para defender a los judíos contra los ataques físicos y verbales así como las falsas declaraciones.

anti-Semitic > antisemítico Mostrar prejuicio y discriminación contra las personas judías.

anti-Semitism > antisemitismo Odio y discriminación contra las personas judías.

Antifederalists > antifederalistas Aquellos que se oponían a la ratificación de la Constitución.

apartheid > *apartheid* Sistema político de segregación intransigente basada en la raza, en Sudáfrica.

appeasement > apaciguamiento Política de otorgar concesiones a fin de mantener la paz.

Armstrong, Louis > Armstrong, Louis (1901–1971) fue un trompetista y uno de los artistas más influyentes en la historia del jazz. También fue el director de una banda, cantante y comediante.

Articles of Confederation > Artículos de la Confederación Constitución federal original preparada por el Congreso Continental en 1777.

assembly lines > línea de montaje Organización de equipos y trabajadores en la que el trabajo pasa de una operación a otra en una línea directa hasta que el producto queda ensamblado.

assimilated > asimilado Ser absorbido por la cultura dominante de una sociedad.

Atlantic Charter > Carta del Atlántico Acuerdo firmado por Gran Bretaña y los Estados Unidos que respaldaba determinados principios para construir una paz duradera y establecer gobiernos libres en el mundo.

Axis Powers > Poderes del Eje Grupo de países encabezado por Alemania, Italia y Japón que peleó contra los Aliados en la Segunda Guerra Mundial.

B

baby boom > *baby boom* Aumento de nacimientos entre 1945 y 1964.

Baruch, Bernard > Baruch, Bernard (1870–1965) fue director de la Junta de Industrias Bélicas durante la Primera Guerra Mundial. Fue un financiero convertido en estadista que asesoró a siete presidentes estadounidenses.

Bataan Death March > Jornada de la Muerte desde Baatan Durante la Segunda Guerra Mundial, la marcha forzada de prisioneros de guerra estadounidenses y filipinos en condiciones brutales impuestas por los militares japoneses.

Battle of Coral Sea > Batalla del Mar del Coral Batalla entre aviones japoneses y estadounidenses, durante la Segunda Guerra Mundial, ocurrida en mayo de 1942 en el escenario del Pacífico.

Battle of Gettysburg > Gettysburg Lugar de una batalla de la Guerra Civil que tuvo lugar en territorio de la Unión del 1 al 3 de julio de 1863, la cual dio como resultado la victoria de la Unión y obligó a las fuerzas confederadas a retirarse al Sur.

Battle of Midway > Batalla de Midway Momento decisivo de la Segunda Guerra Mundial en el Pacífico, en que se detuvo el avance de los japoneses.

Battle of the Bulge > Campaña de las Ardenas Última ofensiva alemana en el frente occidental durante la Segunda Guerra Mundial; fue un intento infructuoso de hacer retroceder a los Aliados que dañó a Alemania al obligarla a usar más recursos de los que se podía permitir.

Battle of the Little Big Horn > Batalla del Little Big Horn Batalla de 1876 durante la cual los sioux derrotaron a las tropas del Ejército de los Estados Unidos.

Bay of Pigs invasion > Invasión de la Bahía de Cochinos Invasión de 1961 por exilados cubanos encabezados por la CIA que fracasaron al tratar de invadir Cuba.

Beatles > Beatles, los Los Beatles fue un grupo inglés de rock and roll formado por John Lennon, Paul McCartney, George Harrison y Ringo Starr. De 1962 a 1970, la composición y la experimentación musical de los Beatles ampliaron considerablemente el ámbito de la música rock.

beatniks > beatniks Pequeño grupo de escritores y artistas, en la década de 1950 y principios de los 1960, que criticaban a la sociedad estadounidense.

Benavidez, Roy P. > Benavidez, Roy P. (1935–1998) nació en Cuero, Texas, pero creció en El Campo, donde fue criado por sus tíos después de la muerte de sus padres. Se unió al ejército a los 19 años de edad y finalmente fue a Vietnam en 1965. Benavidez fue recompensado con la Medalla de Honor (en 1981) por su valor estando herido durante una misión de rescate en Camboya en 1968.

Berlin airlift > puente aéreo de Berlín Programa en el que pilotos estadounidenses y británicos volaban llevando suministros a Berlín Occidental durante un bloqueo soviético.

Berlin Wall > Muro de Berlín Pared divisoria construida por Alemania Oriental en 1961 para aislar a Berlín Occidental de Berlín Oriental, que era controlado por los comunistas.

Bessemer process > proceso Bessemer Método desarrollado a mediados del siglo XIX para fabricar más eficientemente el acero.

Bethune, Mary McLeod > Bethune, Mary McLeod (1875–1955) fue una educadora estadounidense que sirvió como asesora especial para asuntos de las minorías para el presidente Franklin D. Roosevelt, además de ser activa en otras organizaciones de reformas.

"Big stick" diplomacy > "diplomacia del garrote" Política seguida por Theodore Roosevelt según la cual se organizaría y usaría, cuando fuera necesario, una fuerza militar poderosa para lograr los objetivos de los Estados Unidos.

bilingual education > educación bilingüe Sistema en el que se enseña a los estudiantes en su idioma nativo así como en inglés.

bill of rights > Carta de Derechos Protecciones a la libertad personal que limitan el poder del gobierno sobre los individuos.

biotechnology > biotecnología Aplicación de la tecnología para resolver problemas que afectan a los organismos vivos.

Black Cabinet > Gabinete Negro Grupo de líderes afroamericanos que fungieron como consejeros extraoficiales de Franklin D. Roosevelt.

black codes > códigos negros Leyes que limitaron los derechos y oportunidades de los afroamericanos.

Black Panthers > Panteras Negras Organización de militantes afroamericanos fundada en 1966.

black power > poder negro Movimiento de la década de 1960 que exhortó a los afroamericanos a usar su poder político y económico colectivo para lograr la igualdad.

Black Tuesday > Martes Negro El 29 de octubre de 1929, los precios de las acciones cayeron precipitadamente en la Gran Caída de la Bolsa.

blacklist > lista negra Lista de personas que no fueron contratadas por ser sospechosas de tener vínculos comunistas.

blitzkrieg > blitzkrieg "Guerra relámpago" que enfatizaba el uso de la velocidad y la capacidad bélica para penetrar muy adentro en el territorio enemigo.

boat people > balseros Refugiados que huían de sus naciones del sureste de Asia en botes durante la década de 1970

Bonus Army > Ejército del Bono Grupo de veteranos de la Primera Guerra Mundial que marcharon en Washington, D.C. en 1932, para exigir el pago anticipado de un bono que les prometiera el Congreso por sus servicios militares.

Bootlegger > contrabandista Quien vende alcohol ilegalmente.

Boxer Rebellion > Rebelión Bóxer Actos de violencia iniciados por miembros de una sociedad secreta en China, que provocó que los gobiernos de Europa y los Estados Unidos enviaran tropas para sofocar la rebelión.

bracero program > programa de braceros Plan que trajo trabajadores de México a trabajar en granjas estadounidenses.

Bradley, Omar > Bradley, Omar (1893–1981) fue un oficial del ejército de los Estados Unidos que en la Primera Guerra Mundial dirigió las tropas aliadas en el norte de África, llevándolas a la victoria en la campaña. Luego dirigió a sus ejércitos a la invasión de Sicilia y ayudó a planear la invasión de Normandía. Desde la invasión de Normandía hasta el fin de la guerra, Bradley dirigió a las numerosas fuerzas terrestres de los Estados Unidos en el ataque a Alemania desde el oeste, más de un millón de hombres en total. Después de la Segunda Guerra Mundial, fue jefe de Estado Mayor de las Fuerzas Armadas y el primer presidente del Estado Mayor Conjunto de los Estados Unidos.

Brady Bill > Ley Brady Ley aprobada en 1993 que exige un período de espera para la venta de revólveres, junto con una verificación de los antecedentes delictivos del comprador.

bread line > cola de alimentación Fila de personas que esperan alimentos gratuitos de obras caritativas o agencias públicas.

Breckinridge, John C. > Breckinridge, John C. (1821–1875) fue un estadista de Kentucky que sirvió como Vicepresidente bajo el presidente James Buchanan; ganó la nominación presidencial del Partido Demócrata del sur en 1860.

brinkmanship > brinkmanship Creencia según la cual sólo estando al borde de la guerra los Estados Unidos podían protegerse contra la agresión comunista.

Brown, John > Brown, John (1800–1859) fue un abolicionista que atacó el arsenal federal en Harpers Ferry con la esperanza de comenzar una rebelión de los esclavos.

Bryan, William Jennings > Bryan, William Jennings (1860–1925) fue un líder demócrata y populista que se postuló sin éxito tres veces para la presidencia de los Estados Unidos. Durante su carrera profesional como abogado, político y orador, luchó a favor de las reformas como el impuesto sobre la renta, la prohibición y el sufragio femenino.

budget deficit > déficit presupuestario Faltante entre la cantidad de dinero gastado y la cantidad de dinero captado por el gobierno federal.

bull market > mercado alcista Período durante el cual suben los precios de las acciones.

Bush, George W. > Bush, George W. (1946–) fue un hombre de negocios y gobernador de Texas de 1995 a 2000 antes de ser electo el 43° Presidente de los Estados Unidos. Bush, hijo del presidente George H.W. Bush, dirigió a los Estados Unidos durante los ataques terroristas del 11 de septiembre de 2001 y los primeros años de las guerras en Afganistán e Irak. Bush fue electo para un segundo periodo en 2004, terminando su presidencia cuando la industria financiera mundial estaba al borde del colapso a finales de 2008.

business cycle > ciclo económico Crecimiento y contracción periódicos de la economía.

buying on margin > comprar por margen Sistema de compra de acciones en el que el comprador paga un pequeño porcentaje del precio de compra mientras que el corredor anticipa el resto.

C

California Master Plan > Plan Maestro de California Plan que llamaba a la creación de tres niveles de educación superior: universidades de investigación, universidades estatales y centros educacionales comunitarios, los cuales deberían ser accesibles para todos los ciudadanos del estado.

Camp David Accords > Acuerdos de Camp David Acuerdo de 1978 negociado por el presidente Jimmy Carter entre los lideres de Egipto e Israel, el cual hizo posible un tratado de paz entre ambas naciones.

Capra, Frank > Capra, Frank (1897–1991) fue un director de cine estadounidense mejor conocido por su trabajo durante las décadas de 1930 y 1940, el cual le valió tres Premios de la Academia.

Carnegie, Andrew > Carnegie, Andrew (1835–1919) fue un industrial y filántropo estadounidense que comenzó la Carnegie Steel, una corporación que dominó la industria acerera de los Estados Unidos. Creó organizaciones de beneficiencia y dio dinero a instituciones culturales y educativas.

carpetbagger > *carpetbagger* Sobrenombre despectivo dado a los norteños que se mudaron al Sur después de la Guerra Civil.

Carson, Rachel > Carson, Rachel (1907–1964) fue una bióloga estadounidense mejor conocida por escribir *Silent Spring* y una serie de obras sobre la contaminación ambiental y la historia de los océanos. Carson trabajó como científica y escritora para el gobierno de los Estados Unidos antes de dedicarse todo el tiempo a escribir.

cartel > cártel Asociación de productores de un bien o servicio que coordina los precios y la producción.

Carter, Jimmy > Carter, Jimmy (1924–) fue gobernador de Georgia de 1970 a 1974. En 1976, derrotó a Gerald R. Ford en la lucha por la presidencia. Después de perder la presidencia ante Ronald Reagan en 1980, Carter se dedicó a cuestiones nacionales e internacionales y a la defensa de la democracia y los derechos humanos.

cash crop > cultivo comercial Cosecha cultivada para la venta.

Castro, Fidel > Castro, Fidel (1926–) ayudó a derrocar al gobierno cubano en 1959 y dirigió al país desde entonces hasta 2008. Su gobierno y sus alianzas comunistas con la Unión Soviética fueron una fuente de conflicto entre Cuba y los Estados Unidos.

casualty > baja Soldado muerto, herido o desaparecido.

Catt, Carrie Chapman > Catt, Carrie Chapman (1859–1947) Fue educadora antes de involucrarse en el movimiento sufragista femenino en 1887. En 1890, se unió a la Asociación Nacional Americana para el Sufragio Femenino (NAWSA, por sus siglas en inglés). Llegó a ser su presidenta en 1900 y dirigió la organización casi sin interrupciones hasta su muerte.

Central Intelligence Agency (CIA) > Agencia Central de Inteligencia Organización estadounidense para la recolección de inteligencia.

Chamberlain, Neville > Chamberlain, Neville Primer ministro de Gran Bretaña de 1937 a 1940. En un esfuerzo por evitar la guerra, firmó el Pacto de Munich con Alemania, dando a Hitler el control de los Sudetes, una parte de Checoslovaquia. El acuerdo se convirtió en un símbolo infame del fracaso del apaciguamiento.

Chaplin, Charlie > Chaplin, Charlie (1889–1977) fue un comediante británico que produjo, escribió y dirigió muchas películas durante su carrera. Muchos le consideran el mejor artista cómico en la historia del cine.

Chavez, Cesar > Chávez, César (1927–1993) pasó su niñez trabajando duro como obrero agrícola, igual que sus padres. Ya de adulto, estableció la Asociación Nacional de los Trabajadores Agrícolas (NFWA, por sus siglas en inglés) en 1962. Chávez lideró varias manifestaciones no violentas de alto perfil que generalmente terminaron con mejores condiciones para los trabajadores.

checks and balances > sistema de controles y equilibrios Sistema en que cada poder del gobierno tiene la facultad para vigilar y limitar las acciones de los otros dos.

Chicano movement > Movimiento Chicano Movimiento para promover la cultura y los problemas políticos de los mexicoamericanos.

Chinese Exclusion Act > Ley de Exclusión China Ley de 1882 que prohibía la inmigración de trabajadores chinos.

cholera > cólera Grave infección bacteriana del intestino delgado que causa deshidratación, provocada generalmente por beber agua contaminada.

Glosario

Christian fundamentalist > fundamentalista cristiano Persona cristiana que cree en la interpretación estricta y literal de la Biblia como el fundamento de la fe cristiana.

Churchill, Winston > Churchill, Winston Primer ministro de Gran Bretaña de 1940 a 1945, Churchill inspiró a los británicos durante la Segunda Guerra Mundial. Después de la guerra no fue reelegido. Sin embargo, reasumió el cargo entre 1951 y 1955. Se opuso enérgicamente a la expansión del comunismo soviético, argumentando que todas las naciones bajo el comunismo se encontraban detrás de la "Cortina de Hierro".

Civil Rights Act > Ley de los Derechos Civiles Ley de 1964 que prohibió la discriminación en lugares y empleos públicos con base en la raza, religión o nacionalidad.

Civil Rights Act of 1866 > Ley de los Derechos Civiles de 1866 Ley que estableció las garantías federales a los derechos civiles de todos los ciudadanos.

Civil Rights Act of 1875 > Ley de los Derechos Civiles de 1875 Ley que prohibió la discriminación en lugares y transporte públicos.

Civil Rights Act of 1957 > Ley de los Derechos Civiles de 1957 Ley que estableció una Comisión Federal de Derechos Civiles.

Civil Rights Act of 1964 > Ley de los Derechos Civiles de 1964 Ley que prohibió la discriminación en lugares y empleos públicos con base en la raza, religión o nacionalidad.

civil service > servicio civil Departamentos gubernamentales y sus empleados que no son de elección popular.

Civilian Conservation Corps (CCC) > Cuerpo Civil de Conservación (CCC) Programa del Nuevo Trato que proporcionaba ayuda a los jóvenes con trabajo en proyectos de conservación del medio ambiente, incluyendo reforestación y control de inundaciones.

Clayton Antitrust Act > Ley Clayton Antimonopolio Ley de 1914 que fortalecía la Ley Sherman Antimonopolio.

Clean Air Act > Ley para el Aire Puro Ley aprobada en 1970 que buscaba disminuir la contaminación del aire al limitar las emisiones de fábricas y automóviles.

Clean Water Act > Ley para el Agua Limpia Ley aprobada en 1973 que buscaba restringir la contaminación industrial y agrícola del agua.

Clinton, Hillary > Clinton, Hillary (1947–) fue una exitosa e influyente abogada y defensora de los niños y las familias antes de convertirse en Primera Dama de los Estados Unidos en 1992. Desempeñó un papel activo en la administración de Bill Clinton, liderando un grupo de trabajo para investigar cómo garantizar servicios médicos a todos los estadounidenses. En 2000, ganó un escaño en el Senado para el Estado de Nueva York. Trató de ganar la nominación presidencial demócrata en 2008, pero no lo logró; fue nombrada secretaria de Estado por el presidente Obama ese año. Dimitió del cargo en 2013.

Clinton, William Jefferson > Clinton, William Jefferson (1946–) fue el 42° Presidente de los Estados Unidos en 1993 a la edad de 46 años, el primer presidente *boomer*. Fue reelecto para un segundo mandato en 1996. Dos años más tarde fue desacreditado por la Cámara de Representantes pero fue absuelto por el Senado en 1999. Clinton presidió el periodo más largo de expansión económica en tiempos de paz en la historia de los Estados Unidos, lo que incluía un presupuesto equilibrado y un excedente federal.

Cold War > Guerra Fría Rivalidad mundial entre los Estados Unidos y la Unión Soviética.

collective bargaining > negociación colectiva Proceso en el que los patrones negocian con los sindicatos sobre los horarios, salarios y otras condiciones de trabajo.

Committee on Public Information (CPI) > Comité de Información Pública Organización creada por el gobierno durante la Primera Guerra Mundial para animar al público estadounidense a apoyar la guerra.

communes > comunas Pequeñas comunidades donde personas con intereses comunes viven y comparten los recursos.

Community Reinvestment Act > Ley de Reinversión en la Comunidad Ley de 1977 que requiere que los bancos, y especialmente aquellos que operan en barrios de bajos y medios ingresos, presten una parte de sus depósitos a los residentes de esos barrios.

company towns > pueblos de compañía Comunidades cuyos residentes dependen de una compañía para obtener empleo, vivienda y compras.

Compromise of 1850 > Acuerdo de 1850 Acuerdo político que permitió la admisión de California a la Unión como estado libre al permitir la soberanía popular en los territorios y aplicar una ley más estricta a los esclavos fugitivos.

Compromise of 1877 > Acuerdo de 1877 Acuerdo por el cual Rutherford B. Hayes ganó las elecciones presidenciales de 1876 y a cambio aceptó retirar las tropas federales que permanecían en el Sur.

concentration camps > campos de concentración Campos usados por los nazis para encarcelar a miembros "indeseables" de la sociedad.

Confederate States of America > Estados Confederados de América Gobierno de 11 estados sureños que se separó de los Estados Unidos y peleó contra la Unión en la Guerra Civil.

confederation > confederación Alianza o liga de gobiernos que se comprometen a trabajar juntos.

Congress of Industrial Organizations (CIO) > Congreso de Organización Industrial Organización de trabajadores fundada en la década de 1930 que representó a sindicatos industriales de mano de obra no especializada.

conscientious objector > objetor de conciencia Persona que rehúsa pelear en una guerra por convicciones morales o religiosas.

conservative > conservador Que tiende a apoyar una participación gubernamental limitada en la economía, ayuda comunitaria para los necesitados, y mantiene los valores tradicionales.

conspicuous consumerism > consumismo desenfrenado Compra de bienes y servicios para efectos de impresionar a los demás.

consumer revolution > revolución consumista Flujo de bienes nuevos y asequibles durante las decadas posteriores a la Primera Guerra Mundial.

consumerism > consumismo Compras a gran escala, la mayoría de éstas a crédito.

containment > contención Política de mantener el comunismo contenido dentro de sus fronteras existentes.

contraband > contrabando Mercancías prohibidas por ley o tratado para ser importadas o exportadas; durante la Guerra Civil, el término fue utilizado para referirse a los esclavos afroamericanos que escaparon tras las líneas del Norte antes de la Proclamación de Emancipación.

Contract With America > Contrato con los Estados Unidos Plan republicano encabezado por Newt Gingrich enfocado en la reducción del gobierno, el equilibrio del presupuesto y la reducción de los impuestos.

Contras > Contras Contrarrevolucionarios anticomunistas opuestos al gobierno Sandinista de Nicaragua en la década de 1980.

convoy > convoy Grupo de buques mercantes que navegan juntos bajo la protección de buques de guerra.

Coolidge, Calvin > Coolidge, Calvin (1872–1933) fue Presidente de los Estados Unidos de 1923 a 1929. Accedió al cargo después de la muerte de Warren Harding y continuó muchas de las políticas a favor de las empresas de su predecesor.

corporation > corporación Compañía reconocida como entidad legal con derechos y responsabilidades separados de los de cada uno de sus miembros.

cotton gin > desmotadora de algodón Máquina inventada en 1793 para separar la fibra del algodón de la cáscara.

Coughlin, Charles > Coughlin, Charles (1891–1979) Sirvió como pastor de la Iglesia católica en Michigan de 1926 a 1966. Ganó una enorme audiencia en la década de 1930 por sus programas de radio, primero apoyando el Nuevo Trato del presidente Roosevelt y más tarde oponiéndose a él cuando adoptó puntos de vista ultraconservadores. Coughlin se opuso con ímpetu a la entrada de los Estados Unidos en la Segunda Guerra Mundial y en 1942, después de que comenzara a hacer observaciones antisemitas, las autoridades católicas le ordenaron detener sus emisiones.

counterculture > contracultura Movimiento que mantuvo valores diferentes a los de la cultura tradicional.

court packing > reorganización de la Corte Plan del presidente Franklin D. Roosevelt para agregar seis nuevos magistrados a los nueve miembros de la Corte Suprema luego de que la Corte dictaminó que algunas leyes del Nuevo Trato eran inconstitucionales.

Credibility gap > brecha de credibilidad Creciente desconfianza del público estadounidense ante declaraciones del gobierno durante la Guerra de Vietnam.

creditor nation > país acreedor País al que otros países le deben más dinero del que éste les debe.

Creel, George > Creel, George (1876–1953) Fue un periodista que sirvió como jefe del Comité de Información Pública durante la Primera Guerra Mundial. Ocupó otros cargos en el gobierno federal. También fue escritor. Uno de sus libros fue *How We Advertised America*.

Crittenden Compromise > Resolución de Crittenden Enmienda constitucional propuesta en 1861 para intentar evitar la secesión de los estados del Sur al proponer que se permitiera la esclavitud en todos los territorios al sur de la línea del Acuerdo de Missouri.

Cuban missile crisis > crisis de los misiles de Cuba Conflicto entre los Estados Unidos y la Unión Soviética en 1962 como resultado de la instalación de misiles nucleares en Cuba por parte de los soviéticos.

D

Darrow, Clarence > Darrow, Clarence (1857–1938) fue un abogado cuyo trabajo como consejero de defensa en muchos juicios le aseguraron su lugar en la historia del derecho. Es muy conocido por su defensa de John Scopes en 1925.

Davis, Jefferson > Davis, Jefferson (1808–1889) Fue un hacendado sureño que llegó a ser el presidente de los Estados Confederados de América. Nació en Kentucky y creció en una plantación en Mississippi. Asistió a la Academia Militar de West Point y también sirvió en la Guerra de Halcón Negro y en la Guerra México-Estadounidense. Aunque se oponía a la secesión, renunció a su cargo en el Senado de los Estados Unidos cuando Mississippi se separó. Fue elegido presidente de la Confederación en la Convención Confederada, e inaugurado en el cargo el 18 de febrero de 1861.

Dawes General Allotment Act > Ley de Asignación General Dawes Ley de 1887 que dividió las tierras de las reservaciones en parcelas familiares privadas.

Dawes Plan > Plan Dawes Acuerdo en el que los Estados Unidos prestó dinero a Alemania, permitiéndole a ésta hacer pagos de reparación a Gran Bretaña y Francia.

de facto segregation > segregación de facto Segregación basada en la costumbre o la tradición no escrita.

de jure segregation > segregación de iure Segregación impuesta por la ley.

death camps > campos de la muerte Campos diseñados por los nazis para el exterminio de prisioneros.

Debs, Eugene V. > Debs, Eugene V. (1855–1926) fue un líder organizador y social que defendió los derechos de los trabajadores de los ferrocarriles. Se postuló cinco veces entre 1900 y 1920 como candidato por el Partido Socialista.

Declaration of Sentiments > Declaración de Sentimientos Documento creado en la Convención de Seneca Falls en 1848 que demandaba la igualdad de derechos para las mujeres.

deficit spending > déficit de gastos Práctica gubernamental de gastar más de lo que se recibe a través de los impuestos recaudados.

demobilization > desmovilización Enviar a los miembros del ejército de vuelta a casa.

Democratic Republican Party > Republicanos democráticos Miembros del Partido Republicano Democrático, uno de los primeros partidos políticos de los Estados Unidos, dirigido por Jefferson y Madison. También eran conocidos como los republicanos.

Demographics > Demografía Estadísticas que muestran las características humanas de una población.

Department of Homeland Security > Departamento de Seguridad Nacional Departamento a nivel de gabinete creado por el presidente Bush para coordinar los esfuerzos de seguridad interior.

deregulation > desregulación Reducción o eliminación de los controles gubernamentales en una industria, basada en la creencia de que más libertad conduce a mayor éxito y rentabilidad.

détente > distensión Diplomacia flexible adoptada por el presidente Richard Nixon para aliviar las tensiones entre los Estados Unidos, la Unión Soviética y la República Popular China.

developing world > mundo en vías de desarrollo Países con menor avance económico que los países desarrollados, como los Estados Unidos o los de Europa occidental.

Dewey, George > Dewey, George (1837–1917) fue un oficial de la Marina estadounidense que dirigió la flota que derrotó a los españoles en la batalla de la Bahía de Manila durante la Guerra Hispano-Estadounidense. En 1899, el Congreso promovió a Dewey al rango de admirante de la Marina, el mayor rango al que puede aspirar un oficial de la Marina de los Estados Unidos.

direct primary > elección primaria Elecciones en las que los ciudadanos votan directamente para elegir los candidatos para las siguientes elecciones.

disenfranchise > privación del derecho al voto Acción que consiste en negarle a alguien el derecho a votar.

divest > desposeer Quitarse o librarse de algo.

Dole, Sanford B. > Dole, Sanford B. (1844–1926) desempeñó un papel importante en el derrocamiento de la monarquía hawaiana. Después del derrocamiento, Dole fue electo presidente del Gobierno Provisional. Pidió al gobierno estadounidense que se anexaran las islas de Hawái. En 1898, Hawái pasó a ser territorio de los Estados Unidos siendo Dole su primer gobernador.

Dollar diplomacy > diplomacia del dólar Política del presidente Taft de expandir las inversiones estadounidenses en el exterior.

domino theory > efecto dominó Idea de que si una nación cae en el comunismo, sus vecinos más cercanos también caerán bajo el control comunista.

Douglass, Frederick > Douglass, Frederick (1818?–1895) Nació esclavo en Maryland y escapó al Norte en 1838. En 1841, compartió de manera espontánea sus experiencias como esclavo en una convención contra la esclavitud y pronto se convirtió en el portavoz de la causa abolicionista. Su autobiografía, *Narrative of the Life of Frederick Douglass,* fue publicada por primera vez en 1845, lo que llegó todavía a más personas. Durante la Guerra Civil, Douglass trabajó como asesor del presidente Lincoln. También prestó un fuerte apoyo al movimiento de las mujeres.

dove > paloma Persona opuesta a la participación estadounidense en la Guerra de Vietnam.

draft law > proyecto de ley Ley del Congreso que daba al gobierno la autoridad de alistar a los hombres en el ejército sin su consentimiento.

draftee > recluta Varón estadounidense joven reclutado para el servicio militar.

Dred Scott v. Sandford > Dred Scott contra Sandford Veredicto de 1857 de la Corte Suprema que declaraba que los esclavos no tenían derechos constitucionales y que el Congreso no podía decidir sobre el tema de la esclavitud en los nuevos estados.

Du Bois, W.E.B. > Du Bois, W.E.B. (1868–1963) Fue un educador, reformador y defensor estadounidense de los derechos civiles. Es más conocido por su libro *The Souls of Black Folk* en el cual critica el enfoque más condescendiente de Booker T. Washington y aboga por los plenos derechos civiles para los afroamericanos. Du Bois también fundó la Asociación Nacional para el Progreso de la Gente de Color (NAACP, por sus siglas en inglés).

Dulles, John Foster > Dulles, John Foster (1888–1959) fue un diplomático y pensador político. Convencido anticomunista, ayudó a organizar las Naciones Unidas después de la Segunda Guerra Mundial y más tarde sirvió como secretario de Estado bajo el presidente Dwight Eisenhower. En este cargo, ayudó a formular las políticas arriesgadas y de "represalia masiva" de la Guerra Fría.

Dust Bowl > Dust Bowl Término usado para describir las Grandes Llanuras, durante la década de 1930 cuando la región quedó desolada por la sequía y las tormentas de polvo.

E

Earth Day > Día de la Tierra Evento anual de activismo y protesta ambiental, iniciado en 1970.

Economic Opportunity Act > Ley de Igualdad de Oportunidades Ley aprobada en 1964 que creó programas contra la pobreza.

Edison, Thomas > Edison, Thomas (1847–1931) fue un inventor estadounidense. Registró más de 1,000 patentes por inventos, entre ellos la bombilla eléctrica, una primera cámara de cine y una batería alcalina.

egalitarianism > igualitarismo La visión de que la gente es igual y debería ser tratada igual.

Eighteenth Amendment > Decimoctava Enmienda Enmienda constitucional que prohibió la fabricación, distribución y venta de alcohol en los Estados Unidos.

Einstein, Albert > Einstein, Albert Albert Einstein, físico de origen alemán (1879–1955), desarrolló la teoría general de la relatividad que describe los efectos de la gravedad en el universo y ganó el Premio Nobel de Física en 1921. Einstein abandonó Alemania a principios de la década de 1930, después de que los nazis atacaran su trabajo, y se estableció en los Estados Unidos, donde continuó siendo un pionero en el desarrollo de la teoría general de la relatividad. Por lo general es considerado el físico más influyente del siglo XX.

Eisenhower Doctrine > Doctrina Eisenhower Política del presidente Eisenhower que indicaba que los Estados Unidos usarían la fuerza para ayudar a cualquier nación amenazada por el comunismo.

Eisenhower, Dwight > Eisenhower, Dwight (1890–1969) recibió el mando de todos los ejércitos estadounidenses en Europa en 1942. Después de sus rotundos éxitos en el norte de África e Italia, fue nombrado comandante supremo de las Fuerzas Aliadas. Su hábil manejo de la invasión del Día D y el avance hacia Alemania le hicieron ganar un amplio respeto. Antes de retirarse, Eisenhower fue Presidente durante dos periodos.

Ellis Island > Isla Ellis Isla en el puerto de Nueva York que se usó como puesto de migración para millones de inmigrantes que llegaron a los Estados Unidos.

Emancipation Proclamation > Proclamación de Emancipación Decreto del 1 de enero de 1863 en el que el presidente Lincoln declaraba libres a los esclavos que vivían en los estados y en los territorios confederados aún en rebelión en contra de la Unión.

embargo > embargo Prohibición o restricción oficial del comercio.

Endangered Species Act > Ley de Especies en Peligro de Extinción Ley aprobada en 1973 con el propósito de proteger las plantas y animales en peligro de extinción.

Enforcement Acts > Leyes de Aplicación Leyes de 1870 y 1871, también conocidas como Leyes del Ku Kux Klan, que definían como delito federal la interferencia con el derecho de un ciudadano de emitir su voto.

English Bill of Rights > Declaración de Derechos inglesa Documento firmado en 1689 que garantizaba los derechos de los ciudadanos ingleses.

Enlightenment > Ilustración Movimiento del siglo XVIII inspirado por filósofos europeos que creían que los problemas de la sociedad se podían resolver mediante la razón y la ciencia.

entrepreneurs > empresario Persona que construye y administra negocios o empresas para obtener una ganancia, arriesgando a menudo su propio dinero o subsistencia.

Environmental Protection Agency (EPA) > Agencia de Protección Ambiental Agencia gubernamental comprometida con la limpieza y protección del ambiente.

Equal Pay Act > Ley de Pago Equitativo Ley aprobada en 1963 que exigía que hombres y mujeres recibieran paga igual por un trabajo igual.

Equal Rights Amendment (ERA) > Enmienda de Igualdad de Derechos Enmienda propuesta a la Constitución para garantizar la igualdad entre los sexos.

Espionage Act > Ley de Espionaje Ley aprobada por el Congreso en 1917 que establecía penas severas para cualquiera que participara en actividades desleales o de traición.

ethnic cleansing > limpieza étnica Esfuerzo sistemático para purgar una zona o sociedad de un grupo étnico mediante el asesinato o la deportación.

eugenics > eugenesia La idea de que la raza humana se puede mejorar controlando qué personas tienen hijos.

European Union (EU) > Unión Europea Unión económica y política de las naciones europeas establecida en 1993.

Evers, Medgar > Evers, Medgar (1925–1963) se convirtió en el primer secretario de campo de la Asociación Nacional para el Progreso de la Gente de Color (NAACP, por sus siglas en inglés) en Mississippi en 1954. Viajó por el estado reclutando miembros y organizó campañas de registro de votantes, manifestaciones y boicots a las compañías que practicaban la discriminación. En 1963, fue asesinado fuera de su casa en Jackson, Mississippi.

Executive Order 8802 > Orden Ejecutiva 8802 Medida durante la Segunda Guerra Mundial que garantizaba prácticas justas de empleo en cualquier puesto financiado por el gobierno.

executive privilege > privilegio ejecutivo Principio que indica que el Presidente tiene derecho a mantener en privado ciertas comunicaciones con otros miembros del poder ejecutivo.

Exodusters > Exodusters Grupo de afroamericanos que emigraron del Sur al Oeste después de la Guerra Civil.

expansionists > expansionista Persona que favorece la expansión del territorio o influencia de un país.

extractive economies > economía de extracción Economía de una colonia donde el país colonizador extraía materias primas y las enviaba a la madre patria para beneficiar su propia economía.

F

Fair Deal > Trato Justo Programa del presidente Truman para expandir las reformas del Nuevo Trato.

Fair Labor Standards Act > Ley de Normas Laborales Justas Ley de 1938 que estableció el salario mínimo, una semana laboral de un máximo de 44 horas, y prohibió el trabajo infantil.

Family Medical Leave Act > Ley de Permiso Médico Familiar Ley que garantiza a la mayoría de los empleados de tiempo completo 12 semanas laborales de permiso sin goce de sueldo cada año por razones personales o de salud familiar.

Farmers' Alliance > Alianza de Granjeros Red de organizaciones agrícolas que luchó por alcanzar reformas políticas y económicas a finales del siglo XIX.

fascism > fascismo Movimiento político que hace hincapié en el nacionalismo extremo y el gobierno autocrático.

Faubus, Orval > Faubus, Orval (1910–1994) fue el gobernador de Arkansas de 1954 a 1967. Es mejor conocido por ordenar a la Guardia Nacional de Arkansas que impidieran el paso de nueve estudiantes afroamericanos a la Escuela Secundaria Little Rock Central en 1957, desafiando la sentencia de una corte federal que ordenó el fin de la segregación racial en las escuelas. Sus esfuerzos fallaron cuando el presidente Eisenhower envió tropas federales para escoltar la entrada de los estudiantes a la escuela.

Federal Art Project > Proyecto Federal de Arte División de la Administración de Progreso de Obras que contrató artistas desempleados para crear obras de arte en edificios públicos y patrocinó programas educativos y exhibiciones artísticas.

Federal Deposit Insurance Corporation (FDIC) > Corporación Federal de Seguro de Depósitos Agencia gubernamental creada durante el Nuevo Trato que asegura los depósitos bancarios, garantizando que el dinero de los depositantes estará seguro.

Federal Reserve Act > Ley de Reserva Federal Ley de 1913 que sometió a todos los bancos del país bajo el control de una Junta de Reserva Federal, que opera los bancos regionales que mantienen un fondo de reserva de los bancos comerciales, fija tasa de intereses y supervisa a los bancos comerciales.

Federal Trade Commission (FTC). > Comisión Federal de Comercio Agencia de gobierno establecida en 1914 para identificar las prácticas comerciales monopolistas, falsa propaganda y rótulos deshonestos.

federalism > federalismo Sistema político en el cual el poder se comparte entre el gobierno nacional y los gobiernos estatales.

Federalist Papers, The > *Federalist, The* Serie de 85 ensayos escritos por James Madison, Alexander Hamilton y John Jay que explicaban y defendían la Constitución.

Federalist Party > federalista Partidario de la ratificación de la Constitución.

feminism > feminismo Teoría que las mujeres y los hombres deben tener igualdad política, social y económica.

fiat money > dinero fiduciario Moneda no respaldada por el oro y la plata.

Fifteenth Amendment > Decimoquinta Enmienda Enmienda constitucional de 1870 que garantizó el derecho al sufragio, independientemente de la raza o condición previa de servitud.

filibuster > discurso obstruccionista Táctica empleada por los senadores que consistió en hacer prolongados discursos para detener los asuntos legislativos.

fireside chats > charlas junto a la chimenea Transmisión informal de radio en la que el presidente Franklin D. Roosevelt explicaba su visión de los asuntos y programas del momento (incluyendo la Gran Depresión, los programas del Nuevo Trato y las cuestiones de la Segunda Guerra Mundial) a los estadounidenses promedio.

Fitzgerald, F. Scott > Fitzgerald, F. Scott (1896–1940) fue un escritor estadounidense conocido por sus representaciones de la vida de los Estados Unidos en la década de 1920, especialmente *El gran Gatsby*, publicada en 1925.

flapper > *flapper* Mujer joven de la década de 1920 que desafiaba las reglas tradicionales de conducta y atuendo.

flexible response > respuesta flexible Política de defensa que permite acciones apropiadas en conflictos de cualquier tamaño o tipo.

Foraker Act > Ley Foraker Ley que estableció un gobierno civil en Puerto Rico.

Ford, Gerald > Ford, Gerald (1913–2006) fue elegido para el Congreso en 1949 y nombrado Vicepresidente después de que Spiro T. Agnew renunciara en 1973. Ford fue Presidente al año siguiente de la renuncia de Nixon. Después de perder las elecciones de 1976 ante Jimmy Carter, Ford se retiró de la política.

Ford, Henry > Ford, Henry (1863–1947) Fue el fundador de la Ford Motor Company. Revolucionó la industria automotriz con su línea de montaje y el trato a los trabajadores. Su Modelo T dio lugar a la era del automóvil en los Estados Unidos.

Fort Sumter > Fuerte Sumter Fuerte federal ubicado en Charleston, Carolina del Sur, donde se dispararon las primeras balas de la Guerra Civil.

442nd Regimental Combat Team > Equipo de Combate del Regimiento 442 Unidad de la Segunda Guerra Mundial compuesta por voluntarios estadounidenses de origen japonés.

Fourteen Points > Catorce Puntos Lista de condiciones planteada por el presidente estadounidense Woodrow Wilson para resolver la Primera Guerra Mundial y guerras futuras.

Fourteenth Amendment > Decimocuarta Enmienda Enmienda constitucional ratificada en julio de 1868, que garantizaba la plena ciudadanía y derechos a toda persona nacida en los Estados Unidos, protegía el debido proceso y garantizaba la protección igual por la ley.

franchise business > franquicia comercial Permiso para que una compañía distribuya sus productos o servicios por medio de establecimientos minoristas e independientes.

Francis Ferdinand > Francisco Fernando (1863–1914) fue un archiduque y heredero al trono de Austria-Hungría. Su asesinato en Sarajevo fue una causa inmediata de la Primera Guerra Mundial.

Franco, General Francisco > Franco, General Francisco Dirigió con éxito un alzamiento militar en contra del gobierno democrático español en la Guerra Civil Española (1936–1939). Gobernó España como dictador hasta su muerte en 1975.

free enterprise > libre empresa Libertad de las empresas privadas para organizar y operar con el fin de lograr beneficios en un sistema competitivo sin interferencia del gobierno más allá de la regulación necesaria para proteger el interés público y mantener en equilibrio la economía nacional.

Free-Soil Party > Partido "Free Soil" Partido político antiesclavista de mitad del siglo XIX que promulgaba la libertad de suelo.

freedmen > liberto Esclavo que ha obtenido la libertad.

Freedmen's Bureau > Oficina de Libertos Agencia federal creada para ayudar a los esclavos liberados y a los granjeros blancos pobres del Sur después de la Guerra Civil.

Freedom ride > viaje por la libertad Protesta de activistas que en 1961 viajaron en autobús a través de los estados sureños para probar si acataban la prohibición contra la segregación en los autobuses interestatales.

Freedom Summer > Verano de Libertad Esfuerzo de 1964 por empadronar a votantes afroamericanos en Mississippi.

Freud, Sigmund > Freud, Sigmund (1856–1939) desarrolló teorías psicológicas de la mente humana y terapias conocidas como psicoanálisis.

Friedan, Betty > Friedan, Betty (1921–2006) fue una feminista estadounidense que escribió el influyente libro *The Feminine Mystique* en 1963 y fue cofundadora de la Organización Nacional para Mujeres (NOW, por sus siglas en inglés) en 1966.

Fugitive Slave Act > Ley de Esclavos Fugitivos Ley que obligaba a todos los ciudadanos a apoyar el arresto de los esclavos fugitivos; parte del Acuerdo de 1850.

fundamentalism > fundamentalismo Movimiento o actitud que enfatiza un cumplimiento estricto y literal de un conjunto de principios básicos.

G

Garcia, Hector P. > Garcia, Hector P. (1914–1996) fue un médico del ejército que sirvió con honores en la Segunda Guerra Mundial, ganando la Estrella de Bronce por sus servicios en el norte de África e Italia. Nació en México pero creció en Mercedes, Texas. Después de dejar el ejército como mayor en 1945, García regresó a Texas para practicar medicina, pero también comenzó su trabajo de toda una vida como líder de la comunidad, defensor de los derechos civiles y activista político. En 1948, ayudó a fundar la American G.I. Forum, una organización que apoya a los veteranos hispanos y sus familias.

Garvey, Marcus > Garvey, Marcus (1887–1940) fue un carismático líder que organizó un movimiento nacionalista de las personas de raza negra en Harlem durante la década de 1920. Garvey promovía la independencia cultural y económica para los afroamericanos.

General Agreement on Tariffs and Trade (GATT) > Acuerdo General sobre Aranceles y Comercio Tratado internacional firmado originalmente en 1947 diseñado para disminuir las barreras comerciales.

generation gap > brecha generacional Falta de entendimiento y comunicación entre los miembros más viejos y más jóvenes de la sociedad.

Geneva Convention > Convención de Ginebra Acuerdo internacional que regula el tratamiento humanitario de soldados heridos y prisioneros de guerra.

genocide > genocidio Aniquilación intencional de un grupo racial, político o cultural.

"Gentlemen's Agreement" > "Pacto entre Caballeros" Acuerdo entre los Estados Unidos y Japón para terminar la segregación de niños asiáticos en las escuelas públicas de San Francisco. A cambio, Japón aceptó limitar la migración de sus ciudadanos hacia los Estados Unidos.

Gettysburg Address > Discurso de Gettysburg Discurso del presidente Lincoln durante la inauguración del cementerio nacional en Gettysburg, Pennsylvania, en el que reafirmó las ideas por las que la Unión estaba peleando la Guerra Civil; lo pronunció el 19 de noviembre de 1863.

GI Bill of Rights > Declaración de Derechos de los soldados Ley que facilitó el retorno de los veteranos de la Segunda Guerra Mundial al brindarles educación y empleo.

Gilded Age > Edad Dorada Término usado para describir la era posterior a la Reconstrucción, que se caracterizó por una fachada de prosperidad para el país.

Gingrich, Newt > Gingrich, Newt (1943–) es un político, autor y comentarista de televisión estadounidense, mejor conocido por servir como presidente de la Cámara de Representantes de los Estados Unidos de 1995 a 1998. Gingrich lideró la toma de poder republicana de la Cámara en las elecciones de medio término de la Cámara de 1994 al ayudar a redactar la influyente plataforma Contrato con América.

glasnost > glásnost Palabra rusa que significa "nueva apertura", política de la Unión Soviética de finales de la década de 1980 que hacía un llamado a la apertura y discusión de los problemas nacionales.

globalization > globalización Proceso mediante el cual las economías, políticas, culturas y sociedades de naciones se mezclan con las de las otras naciones de todo el mundo.

gold standard > patrón oro Política de designar las unidades monetarias en términos de su valor en oro.

Goldwater, Barry > Goldwater, Barry (1909–1998) sirvió casi 25 años en el Senado de los Estados Unidos. En 1964, se presentó como candidato a la presidencia pero fue derrotado por mayoría por Lyndon Johnson. En 1974, Goldwater fue un elemento clave para convencer al presidente Nixon de que renunciara como consecuencia del escándalo Watergate.

Gompers, Samuel > Gompers, Samuel (1850–1924) Fue un líder laborista estadounidense y el primer presidente de la Federación Estadounidense del Trabajo. Defendía las huelgas organizadas y los boicots para lograr los objetivos de la organización.

Gorbachev, Mikhail > Gorbachov, Mijail (1931–) Político soviético líder de la Unión Soviética de 1985 a 1991. Gorbachov es más conocido por apoyar las políticas de *glasnost* y *perestroika,* que llevaron al colapso de la Unión Soviética. Por su papel en el surgimiento de gobiernos democráticos en Europa Oriental, le fue otorgado el Premio Nobel de la Paz en 1990.

Gorras Blancas, Las > Gorras Blancas, Las Grupo de estadounidenses de origen mexicano radicados en Nuevo México que intentaron proteger sus tierras y estilo de vida de la expansión de los terratenientes blancos.

Graham, Billy > Graham, Billy (1918) es un evangelista estadounidense que se destacó durante el renacimiento religioso de la década de 1950 en los Estados Unidos.

grandfather clause > cláusula del abuelo Ley para descalificar a los votantes afroamericanos que permitía votar sólo a los hombres cuyos padres y abuelos habían votado antes de 1867.

Grange > Grange Organización de granjeros formada después de la Guerra Civil.

Grant, Ulysses S. > Grant, Ulysses S. (1822–1885) Fue un general de la Unión que más tarde llegó a ser el 18° presidente de los Estados Unidos de 1869 a 1877. Ganó victorias clave en el río Mississippi, entre ellas la Batalla de Shiloh y la Batalla de Vicksburg. En marzo de 1864 fue nombrado comandante de todos los ejércitos de la Unión, y los llevó a la victoria en Appomattox Court House, donde aceptó la derrota del general Lee el 9 de abril de 1865.

Great Awakening > Gran Despertar Movimiento religioso en las colonias inglesas durante las décadas de 1730 y 1740, fuertemente inspirado por los predicadores evangélicos.

Great Depression > Gran Depresión Período entre 1929 y 1941 durante el cual la economía de los Estados Unidos falló y el desempleo creció.

Great Migration > Gran Migración Desplazamiento de afroamericanos durante el siglo XX del Sur al Norte.

Great Society > Gran Sociedad Objetivos del presidente Johnson en las áreas de salud, educación, ambiente, discriminación y pobreza.

Great White Fleet > Gran Flota Blanca Barcos de guerra enviados por el presidente Theodore Roosevelt en 1907 en una "misión de buena voluntad" alrededor del mundo.

guerrilla warfare > guerra de guerrillas Métodos de combate no tradicional.

Gulf of Tonkin Resolution > Resolución del Golfo de Tonkin Resolución del Congreso de 1964 que autorizó al presidente Johnson a enviar tropas estadounidenses a Vietnam del Sur y entrar en guerra contra Vietnam del Norte.

H

habeas corpus > hábeas corpus Garantía constitucional para que nadie permanezca en prisión sin que se hayan presentado cargos en su contra.

Hancock, John > Hancock, John John Hancock (1737–1793) fue un estadista de Massachusetts que fue presidente del Segundo Congreso Continental.

Harding, Warren G. > Harding, Warren G. (1865–1923) sirvió como Presidente de los Estados Unidos de 1921 a 1923. Promovió el "regreso a la normalidad" que continuó con la participación de los Estados Unidos en la Primera Guerra Mundial. Harding murió durante su primer mandato en el cargo en 1923.

Harlem Renaissance > Renacimiento de Harlem Período durante la década de 1920 en el que los novelistas, poetas, y artistas afroamericanos celebraron su cultura.

hawk > halcón Persona que apoyó la participación estadounidense en la Guerra de Vietnam.

Hawley-Smoot Tariff > Arancel Hawley-Smoot Impuesto de importaciones protector aprobado por el Congreso en 1930 en un esfuerzo por contrarrestar la caída de la nación a la Gran Depresión.

Hay, Harry > Hay, Harry (1912–2002) importante activista estadounidense por los derechos de los homosexuales quien fundó la Sociedad Mattachine en 1948, una de las primeras organizaciones en favor de los derechos de los homosexuales. Las Sociedades Mattachine se esparcieron por toda California durante la década de 1950, abriendo el camino para el activismo homosexual más radical de la década de 1960. Hay fue cofundador del Frente de Liberación Gay de Los Ángeles en 1969, y en 1979 fue cofundador de Radical Faeries (Hadas Radicales) un movimiento espiritual gay.

Hay, John > Hay, John (1838–1905) fue secretario de Estado de 1895 a 1905, guiando la diplomacia de los Estados Unidos cuando el país emergía como una potencia mundial. Fue un elemento clave en la organización de la política de puertas abiertas hacia China.

Hayes, Rutherford B. > Hayes, Rutherford B. (1822–1893) Fue el 19° presidente de los Estados Unidos. Su elección en 1876 fue disputada y su victoria fue asegurada por la comisión del Congreso y el Acuerdo de 1877. Supervisó la retirada de las tropas federales que quedaban en el Sur, firmando el fin de la Reconstrucción.

Haymarket Riot > Revuelta de Haymarket Protesta de 1886 de origen laboral ocurrida en Chicago que terminó con muertes violentas.

Hearst, William Randolph > Hearst, William Randolph (1863–1951) fue un editor de periódico que creó la cadena de periódicos más grande de la nación. Hearst, junto con Joseph Pulitzer, ayudó a popularizar el reporte de investigación y la prensa amarillista.

Hellman, Lillian > Hellman, Lillian (1905–1984) fue una autora teatral y guionista conocida por sus dramas que se enfocaban en la injusticia social y la explotación.

Helsinki Accords > Acuerdos de Helsinki Acuerdo realizado en 1975 entre los Estados Unidos, Canadá y las naciones de Europa, incluyendo la Unión Soviética, en la que todos los países acordaron apoyar los derechos humanos.

Hemingway, Ernest > Hemingway, Ernest (1899–1961) fue un escritor estadounidense que ganó el Premio Nobel de Literatura en 1954. Es conocido por su vida aventurera y novelas como *Fiesta* y *Por quién tocan las campanas*.

Hepburn Act > Ley Hepburn Ley de 1906 que otorgó al gobierno la autoridad de fijar y limitar las tarifas ferroviarias y fijar los precios máximos para trasbordadores, peaje de puentes y oleoductos.

Hiss, Alger > Hiss, Alger (1904–1996) fue un funcionario de alto rango del Departamento de Estado investigado por el Comité de la Casa de Representantes de Actividades Anti Estadounidenses (HUAC, por sus siglas en inglés) como espía comunista y más tarde condenado por perjurio, pero no por espionaje. Los documentos liberados en la década de 1990 apoyaron las acusaciones en su contra.

Hitler, Adolf > Hitler, Adolfo Líder del Partido Nacionalsocialista (Nazi) y dictador alemán de 1933 a 1945. Subió al poder promoviendo puntos de vista racistas y nacionalistas. En 1939 invadió Polonia, lo cual comenzó la Segunda Guerra Mundial. Estableció un sistema de campos de concentración que llevó al Holocausto, un asesinato sistemático y brutal de millones de judíos y otros.

Ho Chi Minh > Ho Chi Minh (1890–1969) Fue uno de los líderes anticolonialistas más influyentes de Asia. Ho dirigió la lucha de Vietnam del Norte para reunificar Vietnam del Norte y del Sur, sirviendo como presidente de la República Democrática de Vietnam (Vietnam del Norte) de 1945 a 1969.

Hollywood Ten > diez de Hollywood Grupo de guionistas, directores y productores que se rehusaron a contestar preguntas del HUAC sobre vínculos comunistas.

Holocaust > Holocausto Nombre que se usa actualmente para describir el asesinato sistemático de judíos y otros por los nazis.

Homestead Act > Ley de Repartición de Tierras Ley de 1862 que otorgó 160 acres de terreno a los ciudadanos deseosos de habitarlo y cultivarlo por cinco años.

Homestead Strike > Huelga de Homestead Huelga en 1892 en contra de las plantas siderúrgicas de Carnegie en Homestead, Pennsylvania.

Hoover Dam > Represa Hoover Represa en el río Colorado construida durante la Gran Depresión.

Hoover, Herbert > Hoover, Herbert (1874–1964) Sirvió como secretario de Comercio y más tarde como presidente de los Estados Unidos de 1929 a 1933, durante la Gran Depresión. La respuesta de su administración a la Gran Depresión fue ampliamente criticada por su ineficacia.

Hooverville > Hooverville Término usado para describir las barriadas de casuchas establecidas por los desposeídos durante la Gran Depresión.

horizontal integration > integración horizontal Sistema de consolidación de muchas empresas en el mismo ramo de negocios.

hot line > línea directa Llínea de comunicación telefónica directa entre la Casa Blanca y el Kremlin establecida luego de la crisis de los misiles de Cuba.

House of Burgesses > Cámara de los Burgueses Asamblea de representantes en la Virginia colonial formada en 1619.

House Un-American Activities Committee (HUAC) > Comité de la Cámara de Representantes contra Actividades Antiestadounidenses Comité del Congreso que investigó posibles actividades subversivas dentro de Estados Unidos.

Houston, Sam > Houston, Sam (1793–1863) Fue el único estadounidense en servir como gobernador de dos estados diferentes "primero Tennessee, luego Texas". Entre estos cargos, fue comandante del ejército de Texas, presidente de la República de Texas y senador de los Estados Unidos por Texas. Aunque era dueño de esclavos, Houston se oponía a la expansión de la esclavitud en el Oeste. Fue retirado de la gobernación de Texas después de hablar en contra de la separación de Texas de la Unión.

Huerta, Dolores > Huerta, Dolores (1930–) creció en Stockton, California, y llegó a ser maestra de escuela elemental. Después de ver la pobreza de sus estudiantes, muchos de ellos hijos de agricultores, se involucró en defender el trabajo de los obreros y sus familias. En 1962, fundó junto con César Chávez el sindicato de los trabajadores del campo que se convertiría en Unión de Campesinos (UFW, por sus siglas en inglés). Aunque Chávez era la cara de la organización, fue Huerta quien empleó sus habilidades de organización y negociación para ayudar a que UFW tuviera éxito en nombre de sus miembros.

Hughes, Langston > Hughes, Langston (1902–1967) fue un influyente poeta y escritor que consideraba que su obra era un medio de comunicar la experiencia de las personas de raza negra de los Estados Unidos.

human rights > derechos humanos Derechos básicos que tiene todo ser humano por el hecho de serlo y que incluyen la libertad religiosa, la educación y la igualdad.

Hurston, Zora Neale > Hurston, Zora Neale (1891–1960) fue una escritora asociada con el Renacimiento de Harlem que tenía formación de antropóloga y siguió enseñando durante años. Una de sus obras más influyentes fue *Sus ojos miraban a Dios,* publicada en 1935.

I

Immigration Act of 1990 > Ley de Migración de 1990 Ley que aumenta el número de inmigrantes permitidos en los Estados Unidos cada año.

Immigration and Nationality Act of 1965 > Ley de Migración y Nacionalidad de 1965 Ley que cambió el sistema de cuotas nacionales para limitar a 170,000 por año los inmigrantes del hemisferio oriental y 120,000 por año los del hemisferio occidental.

Immigration Reform and Control Act of 1986 > Ley de Migración y Control de 1986 Legislación que otorgó la condición de residentes a los inmigrantes ilegales que vivían en los Estados Unidos desde 1982 y penaliza a los patrones que contratan inmigrantes ilegales.

impeach > enjuiciar políticamente Acusar a un funcionario público de un delito cometido en el ejercicio de su cargo.

impeachment > juicio político Acción de encausar a un funcionario público para determinar si debe ser retirado del cargo.

imperialism > imperialismo Dominio político, militar y económico de naciones poderosas sobre territorios más débiles.

Indian New Deal > Nuevo Trato Indígena Legislación de 1930 que otorgó mayor control a los indígenas estadounidenses sobre asuntos y financió escuelas y hospitales.

Indian Removal Act > Ley de Expulsión de Indígenas Ley aprobada por el Congreso en 1830 que permitió al gobierno federal negociar intercambios de tierras con los indígenas estadounidenses del Sureste.

Industrial Revolution > Revolución Industrial Cambio del trabajo manual al trabajo mecanizado que empezó en Gran Bretaña durante el siglo XVIII y llegó a los Estados Unidos a principios del siglo XIX.

inflation > inflación Aumento de los precios.

influenza > influenza Virus de la gripe.

information industry > industrias de la información Empresas que brindan servicios de información.

initiative > iniciativa Proceso en el que los ciudadanos proponen directamente una nueva ley en la papeleta de una elección.

installment buying > compras a plazos Método de compra mediante el cual el comprador paga un pequeño enganche y luego paga el resto de la deuda con abonos mensuales regulares.

insurrection > insurrección Rebelión.

integration > integración Proceso de unir personas de diferentes razas, religiones y clases sociales.

Internet > Internet Red de computadoras que enlaza a personas de todo el mundo, también llamada Red Mundial.

internment > reclusión Encarcelamiento temporal para miembros de un grupo específico.

Interstate Commerce Commission (ICC) > Comisión Interestatal de Comercio Primera agencia federal en vigilar las operaciones comerciales, creada en 1887 para supervisar los procedimientos del ferrocarril interestatal.

Interstate Highway Act > Ley de Carreteras Interestatales Ley de 1956 que autorizó el gasto de $32 mil millones para construir 41,000 millas de carreteras.

Iran-Contra affair > asunto Irán-Contra Incidente Irán-Contras escándalo político en la administración del presidente Reagan que involucró el uso de dinero procedente de la venta secreta de armas a Irán para apoyar ilegalmente a los Contras en Nicaragua.

iron curtain > cortina de hierro Término acuñado por Winston Churchill para describir la frontera entre los estados satélites soviéticos y Europa occidental.

irreconcilables > irreconciliables Senadores aislacionistas opuestos a cualquier tratado para finalizar la Primera Guerra Mundial que tuviera alguna conexión con la Liga de las Naciones.

island-hopping > salto entre islas Estrategia aliada durante la Segunda Guerra Mundial de retomar algunas de las islas ocupadas por los japoneses e ignorar y pasar de largo de otras.

J

Jackson, Andrew > Jackson, Andrew (1767–1845) Fue un oficial estadounidense antes de servir en la Cámara de Representantes y en el Senado, y finalmente como el séptimo Presidente de 1829 a 1837. Como general del Ejército de los Estados Unidos durante la Guerra de 1812, Jackson defendió con éxito Nueva Orleans. Como Presidente, vetó la renovación de la carta del Banco de los Estados Unidos, que se oponía al tema de anulación de Carolina del Sur y comenzó un sistema de prebendas.

Jacksonian democracy > Democracia de Jackson Andrew Jackson y los partidarios de su filosofía política se preocuparon de los intereses de la gente común y de limitar las funciones del gobierno federal.

Japanese American Citizens League > Liga de Ciudadanos Japoneses-Americanos Organización que trabajaba para proteger los derechos civiles de los japoneses americanos.

jazz > jazz Forma musical estadounidense creada por los afroamericanos , basada en la improvisación y la mezcla del blues, ragtime y música popular de origen europeo.

Jazz Singer, The > *Jazz Singer, The* Musical estadounidense estrenado en 1927 que fue la primera película de cine de larga duración con diálogo sincronizado.

Jefferson, Thomas > Jefferson, Thomas (1743–1826) Fue un granjero, hacendado, autor, arquitecto, abogado y estadista estadounidense. Se unió a la Cámara de los Burgueses de Virginia en 1768 y en la década de 1770 comenzó a abogar a favor de la independencia de los Estados Unidos. Jefferson representó a Virginia en el Segundo Congreso Continental; durante ese tiempo redactó y revisó la Declaración de Independencia. Sirvió como diplomático en Francia y como primer secretario de estado, segundo vicepresidente y tercer presidente de la nación. También fundó la Universidad de Virginia.

Jiang Jieshi > Jiang Jieshi (1887–1975) También conocido como Chiang Kai-shek, fue un líder nacionalista chino que se opuso al ejército comunista de Mao Zedong durante la guerra civil china. Después de la caída de la China continental, Jieshi se convirtió en el líder del gobierno nacionalista en la isla de Taiwán.

Jim Crow laws > Leyes Jim Crow Leyes segregacionistas implantadas en el Sur después de la Reconstrucción.

jingoism > patrioterismo Nacionalismo agresivo; apoyo a una política exterior belicosa.

Johnson, Andrew > Johnson, Andrew (1808–1875) Fue un sastre de Tennessee que ascendió hasta llegar a ser el 17° presidente de los Estados Unidos. En 1864, Johnson ocupó el cargo de vicepresidente bajo el presidente Lincoln. Menos de un año después, llegó a ser Presidente después del asesinato de Lincoln. Sus disputas con los republicanos radicales sobre La Reconstrucción llevaron a su juicio político en 1868. Después de su presidencia, Johnson regresó a Tennessee. Ocupó el cargo de senador de los Estados Unidos hasta su muerte.

Johnson, Robert > Johnson, Robert Empezando a mediados de la década de 1970, Robert Johnson (1946–) trabajaba en Washington, D.C. para la Corporation for Public Broadcasting y como activista en un grupo de presión para la nueva y creciente industria de la televisión por cable. En 1980, usó su experiencia y conexiones para comenzar BET, una compañía de red por cable dirigida a una amplia audiencia afroamericana marginada. Después de muchos años de crecimiento y éxito, Johnson y los socios de la inversión vendieron BET en 1998, por $3 mil millones de dólares. El trato hizo de Johnson el primer afroamericano multimillonario del país.

Joseph, Chief > Joseph, jefe (1840–1904) El jefe Joseph sucedió a su padre como jefe de los nez percé en 1871. Seis años más tarde dirigió a sus seguidores en una huida sin éxito para escapar de su confinamiento en una reserva. Primero fueron enviados a Oklahoma y finalmente a una nueva reserva en el estado de Washington. Sin embargo, Joseph no pudo asegurar el regreso de su tribu a su tierra natal.

judicial interpretation > interpretación jurídica Práctica por la cual los tribunales desarrollan y aplican el propósito de la Constitución más allá del significado de sus palabras escritas.

judicial review > revisión judicial Poder que le permite a la Corte Suprema decidir si los actos de un Presidente o las leyes aprobadas por el Congreso son constitucionales.

K

kamikaze > kamikaze Pilotos japoneses que deliberadamente chocaban aviones contra buques estadounidenses durante la Segunda Guerra Mundial.

Kansas-Nebraska Act > Ley Kansas-Nebraska Ley de 1854 que dividió el territorio de Nebraska en Kansas y Nebraska, dándole a cada territorio el derecho de decidir si permitiría la esclavitud o no.

Kelley, Florence > Kelley, Florence (1859–1932) desempeñó un papel importante en Hull House al llamar la atención sobre las condiciones de trabajo de las mujeres y los niños. En 1899, encabezó la recién fundada Liga Nacional de Consumidores (NCL, por sus siglas en inglés). En 1909 Kelley ayudó a fundar la Asociación Nacional para el Progreso de la Gente de Color (NAACP, por sus siglas en inglés).

Kelley, Oliver H. > Kelley, Oliver H. (1826–1913) fue un empleado en el Departamento de Agricultura de los Estados Unidos que trabajó para mejorar la vida de los trabajadores y de la industria agrícola. Reconoció la necesidad de unir a los granjeros para proteger su subsistencia. Kelly sirvió como el primer secretario de la Grange de 1867 a 1878.

Kellogg-Briand Pact > Pacto Kellogg-Briand Acuerdo de 1928 en el que los delegados de muchas naciones estuvieron anuentes a prohibir la guerra.

Kennan, George F. > Kennan, George F. (1904–2005) fue un diplomático estadounidense que pasó varios años sirviendo en Europa del este y la Unión Soviética. Sus observaciones sobre las actitudes y acciones políticas soviéticas contribuyeron a la formación de la política de contención de los Estados Unidos.

Kennedy, John > Kennedy, John (1917–1963) fue electo el 35° Presidente de los Estados Unidos en 1960. Mientras estuvo en el cargo, enfrentó varias crisis de política exterior, entre ellas la crisis de los misiles cubanos, así como presión por la salvaguarda de los derechos humanos y civiles en los Estados Unidos y todo el mundo. Fue asesinado en 1963 en Dallas, Texas.

Kennedy, John F. > Kennedy, John F. (1917–1963) sirvió en la Cámara de Representantes y en el Senado antes de convertirse en el 35° Presidente en 1961. Enfrentó una serie de crisis en el extranjero, especialmente en Cuba y Berlín, y logró asegurar logros como el Tratado de Prohibición de Pruebas de Armas Nucleares y la Alianza para el Progreso. Fue asesinado en Dallas, Texas.

Kennedy, Robert > Kennedy, Robert Candidato presidencial antibélico por el Partido Demócrata en 1968 y que fue asesinado.

Kerner Commission > Comisión Kerner Grupo que se formó para investigar las causas de los disturbios raciales en las ciudades estadounidenses en la década de 1960.

Keynes, John Maynard > Keynes, John Maynard (1883–1946) fue un economista británico mejor conocido por su defensa de la intervención del gobierno para proteger la economía de los efectos negativos de las recesiones, depresiones y auges. Esbozó sus ideas en la obra *Teoría general del empleo, el interés y el dinero,* publicada en 1936.

Khomeini, Ayatollah Ruhollah > Jomeini, ayatolá Ruhollah (1902–1989) fue un influyente erudito y clérigo iraní. Después de liderar sin éxito una rebelión en contra del sah de Irán en 1963, huyó a Francia donde sus ideas religiosas y políticas se hicieron más radicales. Después del derrocamiento del sah en 1979, Jomeini regresó a Irán y, apoyado por las fuerzas revolucionarias, se hizo con el poder que mantuvo hasta su muerte en 1989.

Khrushchev, Nikita > Jrushchov, Nikita (1894–1971) fue un líder del Partido Comunista que sirvió como presidente de la Unión Soviética de 1958 a 1964. Khrushchev lideró la Unión Soviética durante la crisis de los misiles cubanos, pero perdió poder poco después.

King, Martin Luther, Jr. > King, Martin Luther, Jr. (1929–1968) defendía los métodos no violentos de protesta mientras se convertía quizá en el líder más influyente del movimiento de los derechos civiles. Dirigió la Marcha a Washington en 1963, donde dio su famoso discurso "Tengo un sueño". Fue asesinado en 1968.

Kissinger, Henry > Kissinger, Henry (1923–) sirvió como asesor de política exterior a los presidentes Kennedy y Johnson. En 1969, el presidente Nixon lo nombró asesor en Seguridad Nacional y secretario de Estado en 1973. Kissinger recibió el Premio Nobel de la Paz en 1973 por su papel en el fin de la Guerra de Vietnam.

Knights of Labor > Caballeros del Trabajo Sindicato de trabajadores que procuró organizar a todos los trabajadores y se enfocó en reformas sociales amplias.

Kristallnacht > *Kristallnacht* "Noche de los cristales rotos", ataques organizados contra comunidades judías en Alemania, el 9 de noviembre de 1938.

Ku Klux Klan > Ku Klux Klan Organización que promueve el odio y la discriminación contra determinados grupos étnicos, raciales y religiosos.

L

laissez-faire > *laissez-faire* Teoría que aboga por una mínima injerencia gubernamental en la economía.

land grants > concesión de tierra Terrenos designados por el gobierno federal para construir escuelas, carreteras o ferrocarriles.

Lange, Dorothea > Lange, Dorothea (1895–1965) fue una fotógrafa documentalista estadounidense conocida por sus retratos de agricultores desplazados y otros que sufrieron las dificultades económicas durante la Gran Depresión.

Lauder, Estee > Lauder, Estée (1908?–2004) fue una mujer de negocios y filántropa estadounidense que fundó un imperio de perfumes y cosméticos.

League of Nations > Liga de las Naciones Organización mundial establecida después de la Primera Guerra Mundial para promover la cooperación pacífica entre los países.

Lee, Robert E. > Lee, Robert E. (1807–1870) General de Virginia que llegó a comandante del ejército confederado durante la Guerra Civil. El 9 de abril de 1865, Lee rindió su ejército ante el ejército de la Unión dirigido por el general Grant en Appomattox Court House. Después de la guerra, fue el presidente de Washington College, actualmente conocido como Washington and Lee University, en Lexington, Virginia.

Lend-Lease Act > Ley de Préstamo y Arriendo Ley aprobada en 1941 que permitió al presidente Franklin Roosevelt vender o prestar suministros bélicos a cualquier país cuya defensa se considerara vital para la seguridad de los Estados Unidos.

Lenin, Vladimir > Lenin, Vladimir (1870–1924) fundó el Partido Comunista en Rusia y dirigió la Revolución Rusa. Se convirtió en dictador de la Rusia soviética y promovía el comunismo siempre que podía. Lenin creía que para lograr revoluciones comunistas exitosas era necesario un partido dedicado de revolucionarios, en oposición a la población en general.

LGBT > LGBT siglas de Lesbiana, Gay, Bisexual y Transgénero

liberal > liberal Persona que tiende a apoyar la intervención gubernamental en la ayuda a los necesitados y favorece las leyes que protegen los derechos de las mujeres y las minorías.

Liluokalani, Queen > Liluokalani, reina (1838–1917) sucedió a su hermano el rey Kalakaua en 1891 como líder del pueblo de Hawái. Fue la primera y única reina hawaiana y la última soberana en gobernar las islas. Aunque Liluokalani trató de recuperar el control de las tierras propiedad de los dueños de las plantaciones, fue derrocada en 1893 y los Estados Unidos se anexaron Hawái en 1898.

limited war > guerra limitada Guerra peleada para alcanzar objetivos específicos.

Lincoln, Abraham > Lincoln, Abraham (1809–1865) Nació en una granja de Kentucky. Fue autodidacta y llegó a ser abogado. Se unió al partido Whig y fue elegido para servir en la legislatura estatal de Illinois. En 1858, se presentó sin éxito como candidato a un cargo en el Senado de los Estados Unidos ante Stephen A. Douglas. Durante esa campaña obtuvo reconocimiento nacional por su desempeño en una serie de debates y por su firme postura en contra de la expansión de la esclavitud. Aunque perdió la carrera hacia el Senado, llegó a ser Presidente en 1861. Dirigió al país durante la Guerra Civil y fue asesinado en abril de 1865.

Lindbergh, Charles > Lindbergh, Charles (1902–1974) fue un piloto estadounidense que se convirtió en un héroe internacional cuando hizo el primer vuelo sin escalas en solitario a través del Océano Atlántico en 1927. Antes de que Estados Unidos entrara a la Segunda Guerra Mundial, Lindbergh se convirtió en una voz líder aislacionista, que argumentó firmemente que los Estados Unidos deberían permanecer neutrales y evitar ser arrastrados a la guerra.

literacy test > prueba de alfabetismo Prueba de lectura y escritura antiguamente usada en algunos estados sureños para evitar que los afroamericanos votaran.

localism > localismo Política de la que dependió el presidente Hoover a principios de la Depresión para que los gobiernos locales y estatales actuaran como los principales agentes de asistencia económica.

Locke, John > Locke, John John Locke (1632–1704) fue un filósofo inglés que escribió *Dos tratados sobre el gobierno*.

Lodge, Henry Cabot > Lodge, Henry Cabot (1850–1924) fue un destacado senador republicano que dirigió con éxito la lucha para evitar que los Estados Unidos se unieran a la Liga de las Naciones después de la Primera Guerra Mundial. Antes de ser senador había servido en el Congreso. Previamente había trabajado como editor de revistas e historiador.

Long, Huey > Long, Huey (1893–1935) Fue elegido gobernador de Luisiana en 1928, donde ganó por una amplia mayoría al proporcionar reformas para ayudar a los pobres durante la Depresión. Mientras servía en el Senado de los Estados Unidos (1932–1935), llegó a ser un crítico vehemente del Nuevo Trato de Roosevelt y pidió la redistribución de la riqueza de la nación. En 1935, anunció su plan para postularse a la presidencia pero fue asesinado ese mismo año.

Lost Generation > Generación Perdida Término usado para referirse a escritores estadounidenses de la década de 1920 marcados por su desilusión con la Primera Guerra Mundial y la búsqueda de un nuevo sentido de la vida.

Louisiana Purchase > Compra de Luisiana Compra que hicieran los Estados Unidos a Francia en 1803 del territorio entre el río Mississippi y las montañas Rocosas.

Lusitania > *Lusitania* Trasatlántico británico hundido por un submarino alemán durante la Primera Guerra Mundial.

M

MacArthur, Douglas > MacArthur, Douglas (1880–1964) Dirigió las tropas estadounidenses en la Primera Guerra Mundial, donde desarrolló su reputación de valor. Como comandante supremo de las fuerzas aliadas del Pacífico (1942–1945) aceptó la rendición de Japón al final de la Segunda Guerra Mundial. En 1950 se convirtió en comandante de las fuerzas de la ONU en la Guerra de Corea. Se jubiló después de su controvertida retirada del mando en 1951, después de una discusión con el presidente Harry Truman.

Maddox, Lester > Maddox, Lester (1915–2003) nació en Atlanta, Georgia. Desertor escolar, dirigió un restaurante en la ciudad de 1947 a 1964, cuando lo cerró porque se rehusó a servir a afroamericanos. Elegido gobernador (1967–1971), luchó en contra de la desagregación escolar.

Madison, James > Madison, James (1751–1836) Fue un patriota que representó a Virginia en el Congreso Continental. En 1787 participó en la Convención Constitucional y fue una voz destacada en el reemplazo de los Artículos de la Confederación por un nuevo plan de gobierno. Por su contribución al ganar la aprobación de la Constitución de 1787, fue conocido como el Padre de la Constitución. Madison siguió ejerciendo como secretario de Estado de Thomas Jefferson y luego fue el cuarto presidente de los Estados Unidos.

Magna Carta > Carta Magna Documento inglés de 1215 que limitó el poder del rey y dio derechos básicos a los ciudadanos.

Mahan, Alfred T. > Mahan, Alfred T. (1840–1914) fue un oficial de la Marina e historiador estadounidense que instó a los líderes estadounidenses a construir una armada más fuerte y obtener bases navales en Cuba, Hawái y Filipinas. Mahan fue también de los primeros en proponer la construcción de un canal en América Central para permitir que los navíos estadounidenses se movieran rápidamente entre los océanos Atlántico y Pacífico.

Malcolm X > Malcolm X (1925–1965) sirvió como portavoz y ministro de la Nación del Islam. Cuando fue liberado de prisión en 1952, su trabajo ayudó a la Nación del Islam, que tenía solo 400 miembros, a crecer hasta los 40,000 miembros para 1960. Dejó el grupo poco antes de su asesinato en 1965.

Mandela, Nelson > Mandela, Nelson (1918–2013) Hijo de un jefe de la tribu africana de los tembús, se convirtió en el primer presidente negro de Sudáfrica en 1994. Como abogado, Mandela comenzó su lucha en contra del apartheid en 1952. En 1964, fue condenado a cárcel de por vida por su activismo anti-apartheid. Fue liberado en 1990. En trabajo conjunto con el presidente sudafricano F.W. de Klerk, Mandela ayudó a terminar con el sistema de segregación racial del país. Compartió el Premio Nobel de la Paz en 1993.

Manhattan Project > Proyecto Manhattan Nombre en clave del proyecto que desarrolló la bomba atómica.

Manifest Destiny > Destino Manifiesto Doctrina del siglo XIX que establecía que la expansión hacia el Oeste de los Estados Unidos no sólo era inevitable sino un derecho divino.

Mao Zedong > Mao Zedong (1893–1976) Líder chino que dirigió con éxito una revolución comunista en China continental. Fue presidente de la comunista República Popular China de 1949 a 1959 y jefe del Partido Comunista del país hasta 1976.

March on Washington > Marcha en Washington Manifestación de más de 200,000 personas que en 1963 marcharon a favor de la igualdad económica y los derechos civiles.

Marshall Plan > Plan Marshall Política económica y exterior que ofreció ayuda a los países de Europa Occidental después de la Segunda Guerra Mundial.

Marshall, George > Marshall, George (1880–1959) llegó a ser el jefe del ejército en 1939. Marshall usó su fuerza tranquila, habilidades de negociación y genio en la planeación para desarrollar un ejército combatiente lo más rápidamente posible. Como secretario de Estado después de la guerra, aconsejó un plan de ayuda, llamado el Plan Marshall, para ayudar a la recuperación de Europa Occidental. En 1950, regresó como secretario de Defensa al comienzo de la Guerra de Corea y ayudó a preparar el ejército una vez más.

Marshall, John > Marshall, John (1755–1835) Fue el cuarto presidente de la Corte Suprema de los Estados Unidos. Después de servir bajo George Washington en la Guerra de Independencia, incluyendo el invierno en Valley Forge, Marshall ocupó varios puestos jurídicos y políticos. Como presidente de la Corte Suprema, participó en más de 1,000 fallos, redactando él mismo más de 500 de ellos, a menudo promoviendo y defendiendo el poder judicial y los principios del federalismo estadounidense.

Marshall, Thurgood > Marshall, Thurgood (1908–1993) llegó a ser consejero de la Asociación Nacional para el Progreso de la Gente de Color (NAACP, por sus siglas en inglés) en 1938 y ganó 29 de los 32 principales casos de derechos civiles que discutió en los siguientes 23 años. En 1967, fue el primer afroamericano en sentarse en la Corte Suprema y ocupar un cargo hasta que algunos problemas de salud le obligaron a retirarse en 1991.

Martí, José > Martí, José (1853–1895) Fue un escritor cubano exilado que se convirtió en el símbolo de la lucha de Cuba por su independencia de España. Martí ayudó a establecer el Partido Revolucionario Cubano y fue elegido su líder en 1892. En 1895 ayudó a comenzar la guerra de la independencia contra España. Murió un mes más tarde en batalla en las llanuras de Dos Ríos.

mass culture > cultura de masas Patrones similares de cultura en una sociedad como resultado de la propagación del transporte, comunicación y publicidad.

mass production > producción en masa Producción de bienes en grandes cantidades mediante el uso de maquinaria y líneas de montaje.

mass transit > transporte de masas Sistemas de transporte público que llevan a grandes cantidades de personas.

massive retaliation > represalia masiva Política de amenazar con el uso de fuerza masiva en respuesta a una agresión.

Mayflower Compact > Pacto del Mayflower Documento para establecer el sistema de autogobierno de la colonia de Plymouth firmado en el barco *Mayflower* en 1620.

McCarthy, Eugene > McCarthy, Eugene Candidato presidencial demócrata antibelicista en 1968.

McCarthy, Joseph R. > McCarthy, Joseph R. (1908–1957) fue un senador de los Estados Unidos que llevó a una serie de investigaciones de alto perfil a los estadounidenses a quienes él acusaba de ser desleales a los Estados Unidos. Sus tácticas, conocidas como macartismo, ayudaron a definir el Temor Rojo de la década de 1950.

McCarthyism > macartismo Lema negativo que expresa acusaciones extremas e irresponsables de deslealtad.

McKay, Claude > McKay, Claude (1890–1948) fue un poeta y novelista jamaiquino cuya obra, de gran influencia durante y después del Renacimiento de Harlem, buscó definir una identidad negra distintiva.

McKinley, William > McKinley, William (1843–1901) Fue el 25° presidente de los Estados Unidos, sirviendo de 1897 a 1901. En 1898 lideró a los Estados Unidos durante la Guerra Hispano-Estadounidense. Su segundo mandato como presidente fue breve porque fue asesinado en 1901.

Meat Inspection Act > Ley de Inspección de Carnes Ley de 1906 que permitió al gobierno federal inspeccionar la carne vendida entre los estados y que exigió la inspección federal de las plantas de procesamiento de carne.

median family income > mediana del ingreso familiar Medida del ingreso familiar promedio.

Medicaid > Medicaid Programa federal creado en 1965 para brindar seguro de salud de bajo costo a los estadounidenses de escasos recursos de cualquier edad.

Medicare > Medicare Programa federal creado en 1965 para brindar seguro hospitalario básico a la mayoría de los estadounidenses mayores de sesenta y cinco de edad.

Mellon, Andrew > Mellon, Andrew (1835–1937) fungió como secretario del Tesoro desde 1921 hasta 1932. Desempeñó un papel importante en la reforma de la estructura fiscal de los Estados Unidos al disminuir las tasas fiscales marginales para individuos y empresas.

Melting pot > crisol de razas Sociedad en la que las personas de diferentes nacionalidades se asimilan para formar una cultura.

Meredith, James > Meredith, James (1933–) asistió a una universidad para personas negras antes de ser el primer estudiante negro en la Universidad de Mississippi en 1962. Después de graduarse, obtuvo una licenciatura en leyes y participó en la política del Partido Republicano. En 1966 le dispararon durante una manifestación en Mississippi. Después de recuperarse, continuó siendo un miembro activo en el movimiento de los derechos civiles.

migrant farmworker > trabajador agrícola del campo Persona que viaja de una granja a otra, algunas veces de un estado a otro, para la recolección de frutas y vegetales.

Milk, Harvey > Harvey Milk (1930–1978) fue uno de los primeros funcionarios por elección abiertamente gay de los Estados Unidos. Después de servir en la Marina de los Estados Unidos, Milk trabajó en Nueva York en una serie de trabajos que incluieron maestro y empleado bancario. Milk se mudó a California, donde fue elegido para formar parte de la Junta de Supervisores de San Francisco, en 1977. La ordenanza de derechos de los homosexuales que fue aprobada bajo su supervisión reveló el creciente poder político de la comunidad gay. Sin embargo, el año siguiente, Milk y el alcalde de San Francisco, George Moscone, fueron asesinados.

militarism > militarismo Glorificación de lo militar.

Model T > Modelo T Automóvil fabricado por Henry Ford para que fuera asequible en el mercado masivo.

modernism > modernismo Movimiento artístico y literario desencadenado por una rotura con las convenciones del pasado.

monetary policy > política monetaria Control de la oferta monetaria realizado por una autoridad central, incluyendo las tasas de interés influyentes para promover el crecimiento y la estabilidad económica.

monopoly > monopolio Control exclusivo de una industria por una sola compañía.

Monroe Doctrine > Doctrina Monroe Doctrina de política exterior establecida por el presidente Monroe en 1823 que desalentaba la intervención europea en el hemisferio Occidental.

"Moral diplomacy" > "diplomacia moral" Aseveración de Woodrow Wilson en cuanto a que los Estados Unidos no usarían la fuerza para ejercer su influencia en el mundo, sino que trabajaría en la promoción de los derechos humanos.

Moral Majority > Mayoría Moral Organización política establecida por el reverendo Jerry Falwell en 1979 para promover objetivos religiosos.

Mott, Lucretia > Mott, Lucretia (1793–1880) estaba profundamente comprometida con el ideal de la reforma. Conocida por su eficaz forma de hablar en público, viajó por el país promoviendo la abolición. En la década de 1840, frustrada por los intentos de limitar la participación de las mujeres en la reforma, Mott dirigió su atención a los derechos de las mujeres. Trabajó con Elizabeth Cady Stanton para organizar la Convención de Seneca Falls.

muckraker > muckraker Escritor que descubre y expone la mala conducta de políticos o empresas.

Muir, John > Muir, John (1838–1914) emigró con su familia desde Escocia en 1849. En 1876, instó al gobierno federal a adoptar una política de conservación de los bosques y más tarde fue un elemento clave en el establecimiento de los parques nacionales de Yosemite y Sequoia en California.

En 1892, Muir fundó Sierra Club, una de las organizaciones conservacionistas líderes de la actualidad.

multinational corporation > corporación multinacional Compañía que produce y vende sus bienes y servicios alrededor del mundo.

multinational corporations > corporaciones multinacionales Compañías que producen y venden sus bienes y servicios alrededor del mundo.

Munich Pact > Pacto de Múnich Acuerdo de 1938 entre Alemania, Italia, Gran Bretaña y Francia que sacrificó los Sudetes para preservar la paz.

mural > mural Pintura de grandes dimensiones realizada directamente sobre una pared o cielo raso.

Mussolini, Benito > Mussolini, Benito Líder y dictador fascista de Italia entre 1922–1945. Le llamaban Il Duce ("el líder") y estableció una dictadura totalitaria que promovía el nacionalismo extremo. Durante su dictadura, Italia invadió Etiopía y se asoció con Alemania durante la Segunda Guerra Mundial.

mutualistas > mutualistas Grupos organizados de mexicoamericanos para ofrecer préstamos y asistencia legal a miembros de su comunidad.

mutually assured destruction > destrucción mutua asegurada Política con la que los Estados Unidos y la Unión Soviética esperaban evitar la guerra nuclear al acumular suficientes armas para destruirse mutuamente.

My Lai > My Lai Villa en Vietnam del Sur donde en 1968 fuerzas estadounidenses dispararon contra civiles desarmados.

N

Nader, Ralph > Nader, Ralph (1934–) es un abogado estadounidense y defensor de los consumidores que ha participado en una variedad de temas, entre ellos seguridad automotriz, uso de la tierra, regulación de los pesticidas y procesamiento seguro de la carne.

napalm > napalm Gasolina gelatinizada lanzada en latas que explotaban al impactar y dejaban en llamas grandes áreas; lanzadas por aviones estadounidenses durante la Guerra de Vietnam.

Nation of Islam > Nación del Islam Organización religiosa afroamericana fundada en 1930 que defendía la separación de las razas.

National Aeronautics and Space Administration (NASA) > NASA Agencia gubernamental formada para coordinar los esfuerzos estadounidenses en el espacio.

National American Woman Suffrage Association (NAWSA) > Asociación Nacional Americana para el Sufragio Femenino Grupo fundado en 1890 que funcionó a nivel tanto estatal como nacional para que se otorgara a las mujeres el derecho al voto.

National Association for the Advancement of Colored People (NAACP) > Asociación Nacional para el Progreso de la Gente de Color Organización fundada en 1909 para suprimir la segregación y la discriminación y avanzar en los derechos políticos y civiles de los afroamericanos.

National Consumers League (NCL) > Liga Nacional de Consumidores Grupo organizado en 1899 para investigar las condiciones en que se fabricaban y vendían los bienes, así como promover condiciones seguras de trabajo y un salario mínimo.

national debt > deuda interna Cantidad total de dinero que el gobierno federal debe a los dueños de bonos de gobierno.

National Organization for Women (NOW) > Organización Nacional de Mujeres Organización establecida por Betty Friedan para derribar las barreras de la discriminación contra mujeres.

National Reclamation Act > Ley Nacional de Reclamaciones Ley de 1902 que otorgó al gobierno federal el poder para decidir adónde y cómo se distribuiría el agua, mediante la construcción y administración de represas y proyectos de irrigación.

National Recovery Administration (NRA) > Administración para la Recuperación Nacional Agencia del Nuevo Trato que promovió la recuperación económica al instaurar nuevos códigos para controlar la producción, precios y salarios.

nationalize > nacionalización Poner un recurso bajo control gubernamental.

nativism > nativismo Creencia a favor de los habitantes nativos en oposición a los inmigrantes.

Nazism > nazismo Discriminación institucional legal en contra de los judíos.

Neutrality Act of 1939 > Ley de Neutralidad de 1939 Ley que permitía que las naciones en guerra compraran bienes y armas a los Estados Unidos si pagaban en efectivo y transportaban la mercadería en sus propios barcos.

New Deal > Nuevo Trato Programas y leyes establecidos por Franklin D. Roosevelt durante la Gran Depresión para promover la recuperación económica y reforma social.

New Deal coalition > Coalición del Nuevo Trato Fuerza política formada por grupos diversos unidos para apoyar a Franklin D. Roosevelt y su Nuevo Trato.

New Freedom > Nueva Libertad Programa de Woodrow Wilson para establecer controles gubernamentales sobre las corporaciones a fin de brindar más oportunidades a las pequeñas empresas.

New Frontier > Nueva Frontera Plan del presidente Kennedy dirigido a mejorar la economía, al combatir discriminación racial, y avanzar el programa espacial.

"New" immigrants > "nuevos" inmigrantes Inmigrantes del Sur y Este de Europa que llegaron a los Estados Unidos en una gran oleada entre 1880 y 1920.

New Nationalism > Nuevo Nacionalismo Plan del presidente Theodore Roosevelt para restaurar el poder del gobierno de disolver monopolios.

New Right > Nueva Derecha Movimiento político apoyado por grupos conservadores revigorizados durante la última mitad del siglo XX.

Niagara Movement > Movimiento Niágara Grupo de pensadores afroamericanos fundado en 1905 que presionó para obtener reformas raciales inmediatas, particularmente en cuanto a la educación y el voto.

Nimitz, Chester > Nimitz, Chester (1885–1966) Tomó el mando de la flota del Pacífico de los Estados Unidos poco después del ataque a Pearl Harbor en 1941. Bajo su liderazgo, el ejército de los Estados Unidos ganó las batallas de Midway, Tarawa, Marianas e Iwo Jima, entre otras. El liderazgo tranquilo de Nimitz fue clave para la victoria estadounidense en el Pacífico durante la Segunda Guerra Mundial.

Nineteenth Amendment > Decimonovena Enmienda Enmienda constitucional que otorgó a las mujeres el derecho al voto.

Nixon, Richard M. > Nixon, Richard M. (1913–1994) sirvió como miembro republicano del Congreso y del Senado así como Vicepresidente bajo Dwight D. Eisenhower. Se presentó para Presidente en 1960 y perdió ante John F. Kennedy pero ganó el cargo en 1968. Su presidencia fue marcada por significantes logros en relaciones exteriores. En 1974, renunció en lugar de ser desacreditado por encubrir actividades ilegales en el asunto Watergate.

No Child Left Behind Act > Ley Que Ningún Niño Se Quede Atrás Ley del año 2002 destinada a mejorar el desempeño de escuelas primarias y secundarias particularmente mediante sanciones por mandato contra las escuelas que no cumplan las normas federales de desempeño.

Noriega, Manuel > Noriega, Manuel (1938–) es un exoficial militar panameño que obtuvo el control del ejército en 1983, convirtiéndose en el líder controlador de Panamá. Acusaciones de fraude electoral, tráfico de drogas, lavado de dinero y espionaje en contra de los Estados Unidos llevó a su captura por tropas de los Estados Unidos. Fue encontrado culpable en 1992 y condenado a 40 años de prisión.

North American Free Trade Agreement (NAFTA) > Tratado de Libre Comercio de América del Norte Acuerdo firmado en 1993 para la remoción de las restricciones comerciales entre Canadá, México y los Estados Unidos.

North Atlantic Treaty Organization (NATO) > Organización del Tratado del Atlántico Norte (OTAN) Alianza militar formada para contrarrestar la expansión soviética.

Northwest Territory > Territorio del Noroeste Vasto territorio al norte del río Ohio y al oeste de Pennsylvania hasta llegar al río Mississippi.

nuclear family > núcleo familiar Hogar ideal o típico con un padre, una madre y niños.

Nuclear Test Ban Treaty > Tratado de Prohibición de Pruebas Nucleares Acuerdo de 1963 sobre armas nucleares que prohibió las pruebas nucleares en la superficie de la Tierra.

nullification > anulación Teoría de que los estados podrían anular o vetar cualquier ley federal que consideraran inconstitucional.

Nuremberg Trials > Juicios de Nuremberg Juicios en los que se acusó a los líderes nazis de crímenes de guerra.

O

Obama, Barack > Obama, Barack (1961–) fue elegido el 44° Presidente de los Estados Unidos en 2008, convirtiéndose en el primer afroamericano en ocupar el cargo. Obama sirvió en la legislatura estatal de Illinois y en el Senado de los Estados Unidos antes de ser Presidente. Enfrentó las guerras en Afganistán e Irak, así como una recesión financiera después de asumir la presidencia. En 2009, fue galardonado con el Premio Nobel de la Paz.

O'Connor, Sandra Day > O'Connor, Sandra Day (1930–) Recibió su diploma en leyes de la Universidad de Stanford pero, por ser mujer, no podía encontrar trabajo en un bufete de abogados. En lugar de eso encontró trabajo como fiscal general adjunta en Carolina del Norte. Después de distinguirse durante años en una cantidad de campos, como "fiscal general adjunto, senadora, jueza de la Corte Superior y jueza de la Corte de Apelaciones (todo en el estado de Arizona)", se convirtió, en 1981, en la primera mujer en la Corte Suprema de Justicia de los Estados Unidos.

Office of War Information (OWI) > Oficina de Información de Guerra Agencia gubernamental que impulsaba el apoyo al esfuerzo bélico durante la Segunda Guerra Mundial.

Okies > Okies Término general usado para describir a los refugiados del Dust Bowl.

Olmsted, Frederick Law > Olmsted, Frederick Law (1822–1903) fue un arquitecto paisajista estadounidense mejor conocido por diseñar Central Park en la Ciudad de Nueva York. Olmsted también contribuyó a la conservación del parque Yosemite en California, los espacios boscosos alrededor de las cataratas del Niágara así como un gran sistema de parques públicos en Boston.

Open Door Policy > política de puertas abiertas Declaración estadounidense que proclamaba que el gobierno no deseaba colonias en China, pero favorecía el libre comercio.

open-range system > sistema de campo abierto Método de cría en granjas en el que el ganadero permitió a su ganado pastar libremente en una vasta zona de pastizal.

Operation Desert Storm > Operación Tormenta del Desierto Ataque que comandaron los estadounidenses en 1991 contra las fuerzas iraquíes luego que Irak rehusó retirar sus tropas de Kuwait.

Oppenheimer, J. Robert > Oppenheimer, J. Robert El físico estadounidense J. Robert Oppenheimer (1904–1967) fue el director del Proyecto Manhattan, el proyecto de investigación del gobierno de los Estados Unidos durante la Segunda Guerra Mundial que produjo las primeras bombas atómicas. Después de la guerra, fue director del Instituto para Estudios Avanzados en Nueva Jersey, un centro para la investigación teórica.

Organization of Petroleum Exporting Countries (OPEC) > Organización de Países Exportadores de Petróleo (OPEP) Grupo de países que vende petróleo a otras naciones y que coopera en la regulación del precio y suministro del crudo.

Otis, Elisha > Otis, Elisha (1811–1861) fue un estadounidense que inventó el elevador seguro en 1852. El "montacargas de seguridad" de Otis fue primero diseñado para carga pero pronto se adaptó para el servicio de pasajeros. El primer elevador para pasajeros se instaló en una tienda de la Ciudad de Nueva York en 1857. Otis también desarrolló un elevador impulsado por vapor que llegó a ser la base de la Otis Elevator Company.

P

Palmer Raids > Redadas Palmer Redadas de principios de la década de 1920 iniciadas por el fiscal general del estado A. Mitchell Palmer contra personas sospechosas de ser radicales o comunistas.

Panama Canal > Canal de Panamá Vía acuática artificial que une el Atlántico y el Pacífico a través del istmo de Panamá.

Panic of 1837 > Pánico de 1837 El comienzo de una prolongada desaceleración en la economía estadounidense desencadenada por los cambios en la política del gobierno.

pardon > indulto Perdón oficial de un delito y su castigo.

Paris Peace Accords > Acuerdos de Paz de París Acuerdo de paz de 1973 entre los Estados Unidos, Vietnam del Sur, Vietnam del Norte y el Vietcong que finalizó efectivamente la Guerra de Vietnam.

Parks, Rosa > Parks, Rosa (1913–2005) comenzó la protesta del autobús de Montgomery en 1955 cuando se negó a ceder su asiento a un pasajero blanco. Continuó siendo activa dentro del movimiento de los derechos civiles mientras trabajaba para un miembro del Congreso y comenzó una organización sin ánimo de lucro para ayudar a los jóvenes.

patent > patente Derechos oficiales otorgados por el gobierno a un inventor para que tenga los derechos exclusivos y desarrolle, use y venda un invento durante un plazo establecido.

Patton, George S., Jr. > Patton, George S., Jr. Con una original personalidad y siendo un líder enérgico admirado por las tropas bajo su mando, George S. Patton (1885–1945) dirigió los tanques estadounidenses durante la Primera Guerra Mundial y rápidamente demostró su habilidad para liderar unidades de combate móviles. Durante la Segunda Guerra Mundial, dirigió las tropas de los Estados Unidos en el norte de África y Europa, avanzando rápidamente por Francia y Alemania en los meses finales de la guerra.

Paul, Alice > Paul, Alice (1885–1977) se unió al liderazgo de la Asociación Nacional Americana para el Sufragio Femenino en 1912 pero pronto lo dejó para fundar una organización más militante, que se convirtió en el Partido Nacional de las Mujeres en 1917. Después de la aprobación de la Decimonovena Enmienda, Paul amplió su trabajo a los derechos de las mujeres. En 1923 introdujo en el Congreso la primera enmienda por la igualdad de derechos.

Peace Corps > Cuerpo de Paz Organización del gobierno de los Estados Unidos que envía voluntarios para que brinden servicios técnicos, educativos y médicos en países en vías de desarrollo.

Pearl Harbor > Pearl Harbor Base militar estadounidense atacada por los japoneses el 7 de diciembre de 1941.

Pendleton Civil Service Act > Ley Pendleton del Servicio Civil Ley que creó un sistema de servicio civil para el gobierno federal en un intento por contratar empleados con un sistema de méritos en lugar del clientelismo.

Pentagon Papers > Documentos del Pentágono Estudio clasificado del gobierno de los Estados Unidos que reveló que los líderes estadounidenses intencionalmente involucraron a su nación en Vietnam sin haber informado completamente a la ciudadanía; fue filtrado al *New York Times* en 1971.

perestroika > perestroika Política de la Unión Soviética de finales de la década de 1980 que abogó por la reestructuración de la estancada economía soviética.

Perot, H. Ross > Perot, H. Ross (1930–) es un multimillonario que hizo su fortuna por sí mismo y que fundó Electronic Data Systems en 1962. Perot se presentó como candidato independiente para Presidente de los Estados Unidos en 1992, logrando 19 por ciento de los votos. En 1995 fundó el Partido de la Reforma y se presentó a la elección presidencial de 1996, pero no ganó.

Perry, Matthew > Perry, Matthew (1794–1858) Oficial de la Marina de los Estados Unidos que dirigió una flota naval de 1853 a 1854 que obligó a Japón a entablar relaciones comerciales y diplomáticas con Occidente después de más de dos siglos de aislamiento. Su viaje abrió aún más la expansión estadounidense en el océano Pacífico.

Pershing, John J. > Pershing, John J. (1860–1948) comandó las Fuerzas Expedicionarias Estadounidenses (AEF) por sus siglas en inglés en Europa durante la Primera Guerra Mundial. Antes había servido en Filipinas y México. Después de la Primera Guerra Mundial, sirvió como jefe del ejército de los Estados Unidos.

personal computer > computadora personal
Computadora pequeña destinada al uso personal.

Pinchot, Gifford > Pinchot, Gifford (1865–1946) fue nombrado jefe del Servicio Forestal de los Estados Unidos, pero fue despedido en 1910 después de una discusión con el secretario del Interior del presidente Taft. En 1912, ayudó a formar el Partido Progresista que nominó a Theodore Roosevelt para Presidente. Pinchot continuó su trabajo de conservación en Pennsylvania, donde fue electo gobernador en 1922.

Platt Amendment > Enmienda Platt Grupo de condiciones con las que se le otorgó la independencia a Cuba en 1902, que incluían restricciones de los derechos de los cubanos y que otorgaban a los Estados Unidos el "derecho de intervenir" a fin de conservar el orden en Cuba.

political machines > máquina política Organización de un partido político que gana la lealtad de los votantes y garantiza el poder a un grupo pequeño de líderes, quienes a menudo abusan de él para su propio beneficio.

Polk, James K. > Polk, James K. (1795–1849) Fue un abogado y político que sirvió como el 11° presidente de los Estados Unidos de 1845 a 1849. Antes de ser elegido presidente, Polk sirvió en la legislatura de Tennessee y fue portavoz de la Cámara de Representantes de los Estados Unidos. Como presidente, Polk lideró a la nación durante la Guerra México-Estadounidense, a raíz de la cual los Estados Unidos ganaron grandes territorios a lo largo de la costa del Pacífico y en el Suroeste.

poll tax > impuesto electoral Suma de dinero a pagar antes que una persona pudiera votar.

popular sovereignty > soberanía popular Principio por el cual las personas son la única fuente de poder gubernamental.

populism > populismo Participación generalizada de los ciudadanos comunes en el proceso político y la inclusión de sus preocupaciones en los debates políticos.

Populist Party > Partido Populista Partido del Pueblo; partido político formado en 1891 para abogar por un mayor suministro de dinero y otras reformas económicas.

Powderly, Terence V. > Powderly, Terence V. (1849–1924) fue un líder sindical estadounidense que dirigió a los Caballeros del Trabajo durante varios años a finales del siglo XIX, con el objetivo de sacar a los trabajadores estadounidenses de lo que él veía como la esclavitud del trabajo asalariado.

Presley, Elvis > Presley, Elvis (1935–1977) fue un músico estadounidense que llegó a ser conocido como el "rey del rock and roll". La música de Presley combinaba elementos de blues afroamericanos, gospel, canciones country y baladas de Tin Pan Alley. Su llamativa personalidad e imagen inconformista hicieron de Presley un ídolo para los adolescentes y una inspiración para los artistas futuros del rock and roll de todo el mundo.

privatizing > privatizar Transferir la propiedad o control gubernamental a intereses privados.

productivity > productividad Velocidad a la que se producen bienes o se brindan servicios.

Progressive Party > Partido Progresivo Partido político surgido de la batalla Taft-Roosevelt que dividió al Partido Republicano en 1912.

Progressivism > Progresismo Movimiento surgido como respuesta a las presiones de la industrialización y urbanización, que promovía nuevas ideas y reformas políticas.

Prohibition > Prohibición Ley para prohibir la fabricación, transporte y venta de alcohol.

protective tariffs > arancel proteccionista Impuestos sobre las mercancías importadas que hacen que el precio sea suficientemente alto para proteger los productos nacionales de la competencia extranjera.

Public Works Administration (PWA) > Administración de Obras Públicas Agencia del Nuevo Trato que brindó millones de empleos en la construcción de obras públicas así como en la de aeropuertos, presas y puentes.

Pulitzer, Joseph > Pulitzer, Joseph (1847–1911) fue un influyente editor de periódicos estadounidense. Pulitzer ayudó a dar el formato de los periódicos modernos e incluyó el reportaje de investigación, cobertura de deportes y moda, tiras cómicas e ilustraciones en sus periódicos.

Pullman Strike > Huelga de Pullman Violenta huelga de los trabajadores ferrocarrileros de 1894 que empezó en las afueras de Chicago y se extendió por todo el país.

pump priming > cebado de bomba Teoría económica que favorece los proyectos de obras públicas porque ponen dinero en manos de los consumidores que comprarán más bienes, estimulando así la economía.

Pure Food and Drug Act > Ley de Alimentos y Fármacos Puros Ley de 1906 que permitió la inspección federal de los alimentos y medicinas y prohibió el transporte y venta interestatal de alimentos impuros así como el rotulado erróneo de alimentos y fármacos.

Q

quota system > sistema de cuotas Acuerdo que limitó el número de inmigrantes provenientes de países específicos que podían ingresar a los Estados Unidos.

R

Radical Republicans > republicanos radicales Congresistas que abogaban por derechos ciudadanos íntegros para los afroamericanos junto con una política dura de Reconstrucción en el Sur.

Randolph, A. Philip > Randolph, A. Philip (1889–1979) fue un destacado líder sindical y del movimiento de los derechos civiles durante décadas. En 1925, llegó a ser el jefe de la Brotherhood of Sleeping Car Porters. Después de más de una década de lucha, consiguió que la Pullman Corporation firmara el primer contrato de la historia entre una compañía importante y un sindicato predominantemente afroamericano. Después Randolph dirigió su atención a la discriminación en la industria de la guerra, convenciendo al presidente Roosevelt de que emitiera la Orden Ejecutiva 8802 en 1941. Después de la guerra, convenció al presidente Truman de que aprobara otra orden ejecutiva para prohibir la discriminación en el ejército. Randolph fue uno de los impulsores de la Marcha a Washington de 1963.

ratify > ratificación Aprobación oficial.

rationing > racionamiento Límites controlados por el gobierno sobre la cantidad de ciertos bienes que podían comprar los civiles en tiempos de guerra.

Reagan, Ronald > Reagan, Ronald (1911–2004) logró su famoso estilo de comunicación sencillo debido a su formación como presentador de deportes en la radio, presentador de programas de televisión y lo que le hizo más famoso, de actor de cine. Aunque fue demócrata de joven, sus puntos de vista se hicieron más conservadores y cambió al Partido Republicano. Fue electo gobernador de California en 1966 donde llevó a cabo una agenda conservadora durante sus dos periodos. En 1980, Reagan fue electo para el primero de sus dos periodos como Presidente.

realpolitik > realpolitik Política exterior promovida por Henry Kissinger durante la administración Nixon con base en intereses nacionales concretos en lugar de ideologías abstractas.

recall > destitución Proceso por el cual los electores pueden remover a funcionarios electos antes de terminar su período.

Reconstruction > Reconstrucción Programa implementado por el gobierno federal entre 1865 y 1877 para reparar los daños al Sur que causó la Guerra Civil y reincorporar los estados sureños a la Unión.

Reconstruction Finance Corporation (RFC) > Corporación de Financiamiento para la Reconstrucción Agencia federal establecida por el Congreso, en 1932, para brindar créditos gubernamentales de emergencia a los bancos, ferrocarriles y otras grandes empresas.

Red Scare > Temor Rojo Miedo a que los comunistas estuviesen empeñados en destruir la forma de vida estadounidense.

Redeemer > Redentor Término con el que denominaban a los demócratas blancos del Sur que regresaron al poder político después de 1870.

referendum > referendo Proceso que permite que los ciudadanos aprueben o rechacen una ley que ha pasado una legislatura.

reparations > reparaciones Pago por los daños causados por la guerra.

repatriation > repatriación Proceso por el cual los funcionarios del gobierno regresan a las personas a sus países de origen.

republican government > república Forma de gobierno en la que el pueblo elige a los funcionarios.

reservationists > reservasionistas Grupo de senadores encabezados por Henry Cabot que se oponía a terminar la Primera Guerra Mundial con el Tratado de Versalles a menos que éste inlcuyera ciertos cambios.

reservations > reservas Tierras públicas donde los indígenas norteamericanos tuvieron la obligación de vivir por orden del gobierno federal.

Riis, Jacob > Riis, Jacob (1849–1914) fue un inmigrante danés que trabajó como reportero periodístico de la Ciudad de Nueva York en 1873. En 1888, como reportero de crímenes para el *New York Evening Sun* tomó fotografías de la vida nocturna en los barrios bajos urbanos. Publicadas en su libro en 1890, *Cómo vive la otra mitad,* las fotografías conmovieron al Comisionado de Polícia de Nueva York, Theodore Roosevelt, y lo llevaron a comenzar la causa de la reforma urbana.

rock-and-roll > rock-and-roll Música originada en las tradiciones del gospel y blues de los afroamericanos.

Rockefeller, John D. > Rockefeller, John D. (1839–1937) fue un empresario y filántropo estadounidense. Comenzó la Standard Oil Company y dominó la industria del petróleo con prácticas de negocio innovadoras y agresivas. También donó dinero para diferentes causas mediante la Rockefeller Foundation.

Roosevelt Corollary > Corolario Roosevelt Replanteamiento del presidente Theodore Roosevelt de la Doctrina Monroe, según la cual la política de los Estados Unidos era mantener al hemisferio occidental libre de la intervención de las potencias europeas.

Roosevelt, Eleanor > Roosevelt, Eleanor (1884–1962) Fue la esposa del presidente Franklin D. Roosevelt. Con la elección de su esposo como Presidente en 1932, Eleanor Roosevelt llegó a ser una figura pública por sí misma. Viajó por el país promoviendo las causas para ayudar a las mujeres, niños y pobres. Después de la muerte de su esposo, fue delegada de los Estados Unidos ante la Organización de las Naciones Unidas (1945–1951), enfocándose en los derechos humanos y temas de la mujer.

Roosevelt, Franklin D. > Roosevelt, Franklin D. (1882–1945) fue Secretario Adjunto de la Marina (1913–1920), antes de postularse sin éxito para Vicepresidente en la convención demócrata en 1920. Afectado por poliomielitis el año siguiente, Roosevelt se recuperó para reasumir su carrera política como gobernador de Nueva York (1929–1933). Elegido Presidente en 1932, dirigió la nación durante la Gran Depresión y la Segunda Guerra Mundial antes de morir en el cargo en 1945.

Roosevelt, Theodore > Roosevelt, Theodore (1858–1919) fue gobernador de Nueva York antes de ser vicepresidente en 1901. Roosevelt fue el hombre más joven en asumir la presidencia. Fue conocido por sus políticas antimonopolio y de conservación. Hizo un intento en 1912 para obtener otro periodo como candidato del Partido Progresista, pero no tuvo éxito.

Rosenberg, Julius y Ethel > Rosenberg, Julius y Ethel Julius (1918–1953) y Ethel Rosenberg (1915–1953) fueron dos civiles estadounidenses acusados de forma controvertida y ejecutados por espionaje durante el Temor Rojo en la década de 1950. Pruebas posteriores de los Documentos Venona confirmaron que ambos habían tenido relación con el espionaje soviético.

Rough Riders > Jinetes Rudos Grupo de hombres fuertes provenientes del Oeste y de la clase alta del Este que pelearon durante la guerra entre España y Estados Unidos.

rural-to-urban migrants > inmigrante del campo a la ciudad Persona que se traslada de las áreas rurales a la ciudad.

Russo-Japanese War > Guerra ruso-japonesa Guerra entre Japón y Rusia durante 1904 por la presencia de tropas rusas en Manchuria.

Ruth, Babe > Ruth, Babe (1895–1948) fue un jugador profesional de beisbol conocido por su talento para el espectáculo y su capacidad para marcar homeruns. Es miembro del Salón de la Fama de Beisbol.

S

Sacco, Nicola > Sacco, Nicola (1891–1927) fue un inmigrante italiano condenado por asesinato y ejecutado en 1927.

SALT II > SALT II Acuerdo propuesto entre los Estados Unidos y la Unión Soviética para limitar la producción de ciertos tipos de armas nucleares. También conocido como Tratado de Limitación de Armas Estratégicas ll no fue ratificado nunca por el Senado de los Estados Unidos.

sanctions > sanción Penalización prevista para obligar a que la gente obedezca las leyes y normas, en particular las medidas adoptadas para obligar a un país a obedecer el derecho internacional.

Sand Creek Massacre > Masacre de Sand Creek Incidente de 1864 durante el cual una milicia de Colorado asesinó a un campamento de indígenas cheyenes y arapajos.

Sanger, Margaret > Sanger, Margaret (1879–1966) fue la primera en acuñar el término "control de natalidad" en un panfleto que publicó en 1914. Una organización médica que ella fundó, el Birth Control Research Bureau, se convirtió en 1942 en Planned Parenthood.

satellite > satélite Dispositivo mecánico que orbita la Tierra y que recibe y envía señales de comunicación o transmite datos científicos.

satellite state > estado satélite Nación independiente bajo el control de una nación más poderosa.

saturation bombing > saturación de bombardeos Táctica de dejar caer cantidades masivas de bombas a fin de infligir el máximo daño.

Savings and Loan crisis > crisis financiera Fracaso en 1989 de cerca de 1,000 bancos de ahorro y préstamo (S&Ls, por sus siglas en inglés) como resultado de prácticas comerciales riesgosas y a veces fraudulentas.

scalawag > *scalawag* Término negativo para referirse a un blanco sureño que apoyó al Partido Republicano después de la Guerra Civil.

Schlafly, Phyllis > Schlafly, Phyllis (1924–), escritora y activista política estadounidense, muy conocida y franca defensora de la familia tradicional. Es la opositora más famosa a la Enmienda de Igualdad de Derechos.

scientific management > administración científica Enfoque para mejorar la eficiencia, en el que los expertos observaban cada paso de un proceso de manufactura y buscaban formas de reducir el tiempo, esfuerzo y costo.

Scopes Trial > Juicio Scopes Juicio al que fue sometido, en 1925, un maestro de Tennessee por enseñar la teoría de Darwin sobre la evolución.

Second Great Awakening > Segundo Gran Despertar Movimiento de renovación religiosa que se dio en la primera mitad del siglo XIX.

segregation > segregación Separación forzada, a menudo con base en la raza.

Selective Service Act > Ley de Servicio Selectivo Ley aprobada por el Congreso en 1917; autorizó el reclutamiento de hombres para el servicio militar.

self-determination > autodeterminación Derecho de las personas de elegir su propia forma de gobierno.

Seneca Falls Convention > Convención de Seneca Falls Primera convención sobre los derechos de la mujer realizada en los Estados Unidos, celebrada en Nueva York en 1848.

service economy > economía de servicio Sistema económico enfocado en la compra y venta de servicios.

service sector > sector de servicios Empresas que brindan servicios en lugar de fabricar bienes.

settlement house > centro comunitario Centro comunal organizado a inicios del siglo XX para ofrecer servicios sociales a los pobres de la ciudad.

Seventeenth Amendment > Decimoséptima Enmienda Enmienda constitucional de 1913 que permitía que los ciudadanos eligieran de manera directa a los senadores de los Estados Unidos.

share-tenancy > arrendamiento por aparcería Similar a la aparcería, excepto que el granjero elige qué cultivar y compra sus propios insumos.

sharecropping > aparcería Sistema en el cual un granjero atiende una porción de la tierra del propietario a cambio de una parte de la cosecha.

Shays' Rebellion > Rebelión de Shays Rebelión de granjeros conducida por Daniel Shays en contra del aumento de impuestos en Massachusetts.

Sherman Antitrust Act > Ley Antimonopolios Sherman Ley de 1890 que prohibió los consorcios que restringían el comercio o negocios interestatales.

Sherman, William T. > Sherman, William T. (1820–1891) Fue el hijo de un juez de Ohio que llegó a ser un renombrado general de la Unión durante la Guerra Civil. Luchó en las Batallas de Bull Run y Shiloh antes de unir sus tropas con las del general Grant para sitiar Vicksburg en 1863. Después de su victoria, Sherman dirigió su "Marcha hacia el mar", 250 millas al este para capturar Savannah, Georgia.

silent majority > mayoría silenciosa Frase introducida por el presidente Richard Nixon para referirse a un número significativo de estadounidenses que apoyaban sus políticas pero eligieron no expresar su opinión.

Sinclair, Upton > Sinclair, Upton (1878–1968) comezó escribiendo para periódicos y completó varias novelas exitosas poco después de graduarse en la universidad en 1897. Su obra más famosa, *The Jungle,* fue publicada en 1906. Sinclair siguió escribiendo obras de denuncia y con el tiempo participó activamente en la política de California, postulándose para gobernador en 1934, pero sin éxito. En 1942, ganó el Premio Pulitzer por su novela *Los dientes del dragon.*

sit-down strike > huelga de brazos caídos Protesta laboral en que los trabajadores dejan de trabajar y ocupan el lugar de trabajo hasta que se satisfacen sus demandas.

sit-in > sentada Tipo de protesta en que los participantes se sientan y rehúsan moverse.

Sitting Bull > Toro Sentado (1831?–1890) fue un jefe guerrero y un importante líder espiritual que se convirtió en el primer jefe de todas las tribus sioux en la década de 1860. Después de rendirse al ejército en 1881, vivió en una reserva donde fue asesinado por la policía indígena enviada a arrestarlo.

Sixteenth Amendment > Decimosexta Enmienda Enmienda constitucional de 1913 que otorgó al Congreso la autoridad para establecer un impuesto a los ingresos.

skyscrapers > rascacielos Edificio muy alto.

Smith Act > Ley Smith Ley que prohibió la enseñanza o defensa de un derrocamiento violento del gobierno estadounidense.

Smith, Bessie > Smith, Bessie (1898?–1937) Fue una cantante de blues conocida como la "Emperatriz del Blues". Cantó con algunos de los grandes músicos del jazz de la época, entre ellos Louis Armstrong.

Social Darwinism > darwinismo social Creencia de algunos a finales del siglo XIX según la que algunas naciones o razas eran superiores a otras y por lo tanto estaban destinadas a gobernar.

Social Gospel > evangelio social Movimiento reformista surgido a finales del siglo XIX cuyo fin era mejorar la sociedad por principios cristianos.

Social Security Act > Ley de Seguridad Social Ley de 1935 que establecía un sistema de pensiones para los jubilados, un seguro de desempleo y un seguro para las víctimas de accidentes laborales; proporcionaba ayuda a las madres y los niños afectados por la pobreza, los ciegos y los discapacitados.

socialism > socialismo Sistema o teoría según la cual los medios de producción son controlados y regulados públicamente en lugar de ser propiedad de individuos.

Sosa, Lionel > Sosa, Lionel (1939–) es un ejecutivo de publicidad que tuvo éxito al ayudar a las compañías a comercializar sus productos para los consumidores latinos. Pero es más famoso por ayudar a los candidatos republicanos a lograr el voto de los latinos. En la elección de 2004, con la ayuda de Sosa, George W. Bush pudo conseguir un estimado de 40% de los votos latinos, un aumento considerable a los anteriores candidatos presidenciales republicanos.

Southeast Asia Treaty Organization (SEATO) > Organización del Tratado del Sudeste Asiático Alianza defensiva orientada a prevenir la agresión comunista en Asia.

southern strategy > estrategia para el Sur Táctica del Partido Republicano para ganar las elecciones presidenciales al asegurarse los votos electorales de los estados del Sur.

space race > carrera espacial Competencia entre los Estados Unidos y la Unión Soviética para aterrizar exitosamente en la Luna.

Spanish Civil War > Guerra Civil Española Conflicto en España en el que las fuerzas nacionalistas dirigidas por el general Francisco Franco se rebelaron contra el gobierno democrático republicano.

speculation > especulación Práctica de hacer inversiones de alto riesgo con la esperanza de obtener grandes ganancias.

spheres of influence > esfera de influencia Región dominada y controlada por un poder externo.

Spock, Benjamin > Spock, Benjamin (1903–1998) Fue un pediatra y autor estadounidense cuyo libro *Common Sense Book of Baby and Child Care,* publicado en 1946, fue uno de los libros más influyentes en la crianza infantil del siglo XX. Spock rompió la tradición al aconsejar a los padres que mostraran afecto, comprensión y flexibilidad y que promovieran y apreciaran la individualidad de cada niño.

spoils system > sistema de prebendas Práctica del partido político en el poder de asignar los puestos y nombramientos a sus seguidores en lugar de basarlos en las calificaciones.

Square Deal > Trato Justo Programa de reformas del presidente Theodore Roosevelt para evitar que los ricos y poderosos se aprovecharan de los propietarios de pequeñas empresas y de los pobres.

stagflation > estanflación Término para la condición económica creada a finales de las décadas de 1960 y 1970 por una alta inflación combinada con el estancamiento del crecimiento económico y el alto desempleo.

Stalin, Joseph > Stalin, Joseph Líder de la comunista Unión de Repúblicas Socialistas Soviéticas (U.R.S.S.) de 1924 a 1953. Sus esfuerzos para transformar la Unión Soviética en una potencia industrial y formar granjas colectivas operadas por el estado provocó penurias extremas y millones de muertes. Asociado con Alemania en 1939, Stalin se unió más tarde a los Aliados en la Segunda Guerra Mundial. Después de la guerra, Stalin se convirtió en un participante agresivo de la Guerra Fría.

Stanton, Elizabeth Cady > Stanton, Elizabeth Cady (1815–1902) Fue una vivaz y a menudo feroz defensora de los derechos de la mujer. Mientras criaba a una familia cada vez más numerosa, trabajaba con Lucretia Mott y otras para organizar la Convención de Seneca Falls. Desde el principio, impulsó a las mujeres para que lucharan por su derecho al voto, ayudando a establecer la dirección que seguiría el movimiento en los años posteriores.

Starr, Kenneth > Starr, Kenneth (1946–) es un abogado estadounidense que sirvió como consejero independiente a cargo de la investigación que intentó obtener la destitución del presidente Bill Clinton en 1998.

steerage > entrecubierta Alojamiento de tercera clase en un buque de vapor.

Steffens, Lincoln > Steffens, Lincoln (1866–1936) Reportero y editor del *New York Post* y más tarde de la revista de denuncias *McClure's.* Escribió artículos y libros exponiendo la corrupción del gobierno en los niveles estatales y municipales.

Steinbeck, John > Steinbeck, John (1902–1968) fue un novelista estadounidense que escribió con frecuencia sobre los trabajadores agrígolas temporales y otros trabajadores durante la Gran Depresión.

Steinem, Gloria > Steinem, Gloria (1934–) es una feminista estadounidense, activista política y escritora-editora, que tuvo un papel influyente en el Movimiento de las Mujeres de finales del siglo XX. En 2013, Steinem fue galardonada con la Medalla Presidencial de la Libertad.

Stonewall Riots > Disturbios de Stonewall Serie de protestas violentas que comenzaron en la madrugada del 28 de junio de 1969, cuando la policía llevó a cabo una redada en un bar LGBT en Greenwich Village, en la Ciudad de Nueva York. Los disturbios marcaron un cambio radical de estrategia para el movimiento por los derechos de los homosexuales, e inspiraron desfiles de orgullo gay cada año en todo el mundo, para conmemorar ese evento.

Stowe, Harriet Beecher > Stowe, Harriet Beecher (1811–1896) Fue una autora abolicionista estadounidense mejor conocida por su novela antiesclavista *Uncle Tom's Cabin,* (La cabaña del tío Tom), publicada en 1852. Comenzó a escribir su novela como una serie de historias, las cuales aparecieron por primera vez entre 1851 y 1852 en el periódico abolicionista *National Era.*

Strategic Arms Limitation Treaty (SALT I) > Tratado de Limitación de Armas Estratégicas Acuerdo de 1972 entre los Estados Unidos y la Unión Soviética para suspender el despliegue de misiles balísticos intercontinentales y limitó los misiles antibalísticos.

strategic bombing > bombardeo estratégico Táctica de dejar caer bombas en blancos políticos e industriales clave.

Strategic Defense Initiative (SDI) > Iniciativa de Defensa Estratégica Plan del presidente Reagan, apodado "Star Wars" para desarrollar defensas innovadoras con el fin de salvaguardar a los Estados Unidos contra ataques de misiles nucleares.

Student Nonviolent Coordinating Committee > Comité Estudiantil Coordinador de la No Violencia Movimiento de base fundado en 1960 por jóvenes activistas a favor de los derechos humanos.

Students for a Democratic Society (SDS) > Estudiantes a Favor de una Sociedad Democrática Organización fundada en 1960 en la Universidad de Michigan para combatir el racismo y la pobreza.

suburbs > suburbios Áreas residenciales que rodean una ciudad.

Suez crisis > crisis de Suez Intento de Francia y Gran Bretaña por apoderarse del control del canal de Suez en 1956.

suffrage > sufragio Derecho al voto.

Sunbelt > Sun Belt Nombre dado a la región de los estados del Sur y Suroeste.

superpowers > superpotencias Naciones suficientemente poderosas para influir en los actos y políticas de otras naciones.

supply-side economics > economía de la oferta Teoría económica que dice que reducir las tasas tributarias estimula el crecimiento económico.

suspension bridges > puentes colgantes Puentes cuya carretera está suspendida por cables.

sweatshops > maquilas Pequeñas fábricas donde los empleados tienen que trabajar largas horas en malas condiciones y por poco dinero.

T

Taft-Hartley Act > Ley Taft Hartley Ley que restringió el poder de los sindicatos de trabajadores.

Taft, William Howard > Taft, William Howard (1857–1930) fue el 27° Presidente de los Estados Unidos de 1909 a 1913. En 1901, se convirtió en el primer gobernador civil de Filipinas. Bajo ese cargo, trabajó para reconstruir la economía y restablecer el orden. En 1921, el presidente Harding nombró a Taft el 10° jefe de justicia de los Estados Unidos, donde sirvió durante 9 años.

Taliban > talibán Fracción fundamentalista islámica que controló la mayor parte de Afganistán entre 1996 y 2001.

Taney, Roger > Taney, Roger (1777–1864) Sirvió como el quinto presidente de la Corte Suprema de los Estados Unidos. Es más conocido por su decisión en el caso *Dred Scott contra Sandford,* en la que establecía que los esclavos no tenían acceso a los derechos garantizados por la Constitución y que el Congreso no estaba facultado para prohibir la esclavitud en ningún territorio, ya que tales leyes privarían a los dueños de esclavos de su propiedad.

Tea Party Movement > movimiento del Tea Party Movimiento informal conformado por grupos locales que quieren reducir el tamaño y el alcance del gobierno federal.

Teapot Dome scandal > Escándalo Teapot Dome Escándalo durante la administración Harding en el cual el secretario del interior arrendó las reservas de petróleo del gobierno a petroleros privados a cambio de un soborno.

televangelist > telepredicadores Ministros que utilizan la televisión para predicar.

temperance movement > movimiento por la templanza Movimiento encauzado a eliminar el abuso del alcohol y los problemas que éste genera.

tenant farming > agricultura de arrendamiento Sistema en el que un agricultor paga un alquiler por el uso de la tierra a un propietario.

tenements > vecindades Edificios de varios pisos divididos en apartamentos para alojar a tantos residentes como sea posible.

Tennessee Valley Authority (TVA) > Autoridad del Valle del Tennessee Agencia gubernamental creada durante el Nuevo Trato, para construir represas en el valle del río Tennessee con el fin de controlar las inundaciones y generar energía eléctrica.

termination policy > política de terminación Política que cerró todos los programas a cargo de la Oficina de Asuntos Indígenas. También dio por terminada la responsabilidad federal en cuanto a la salud y el bienestar de los indígenas estadounidenses.

Tet Offensive > Ofensiva Tet Asalto comunista contra un gran número de ciudades de Vietnam del Sur a principios de 1968.

Thirteenth Amendment > Decimotercera Enmienda Enmienda constitucional de 1865 que abolió la esclavitud en los Estados Unidos.

38th parallel > paralelo 38 Línea divisoria entre Corea del Norte y Corea del Sur.

Tiananmen Square > Tiananmen, Plaza de Lugar en Pekín donde las protestas de los estudiantes chinos a favor de la democracia fueron aplacadas por el gobierno chino en 1989.

Tin Pan Alley > Tin Pan Alley Sección de la Calle 28 de la Ciudad de Nueva York que llegó a ser el centro de la industria musical a finales del siglo XIX; género de una música popular estadounidense.

Tinker v. Des Moines School District > Tinker contra Des Moines School District Caso de la Corte Suprema de 1969 en el que la Corte dictaminó que el derecho a la libre expresión se ampliaba a otros tipos de expresión además de la palabra hablada.

Tocqueville, Alexis de > Tocqueville, Alexis de (1805–1859) fue un aristócrata francés cuyos viajes a los Estados Unidos en la década de 1830 resultaron en la publicación de *Democracia en América,* un análisis de influencia de la política estadounidense.

Tojo, Hideki > Tojo, Hideki (1884–1948) Fue nombrado primer ministro de Japón en octubre de 1941 cuando los planes de atacar a la Marina de los Estados Unidos en Pearl Harbor estaban en marcha. Lideró Japón hasta julio de 1944. Después de la guerra, fue juzgado por crímenes de guerra y ahorcado en diciembre de 1948.

totalitarianism > totalitarismo Teoría de gobierno según la cual un solo partido o líder controla la vida económica, social y cultural de la población.

Trail of Tears > Camino de Lágrimas Marcha forzada de los indígenas cherokee para mudarlos al oeste del Mississippi en la década de 1830.

Transcontinental Railroad > ferrocarril transcontinental Enlace ferroviario entre el Este y el Oeste de los Estados Unidos.

Treaty of Guadalupe Hidalgo > Tratado de Guadalupe Hidalgo Tratado de 1848 que finalizó la Guerra México-Estadounidense; los Estados Unidos adquirieron el territorio de lo que serían los futuros estados de Arizona, California, Colorado, Nuevo México, Nevada, Utah y Wyoming.

Treaty of Paris > Tratado de París tratado de paz de 1783 que dió por finalizada la Guerra de Independencia y estableció la independencia de Estados Unidos

trickle-down economics > economía por goteo Teoría económica que sostiene que el dinero prestado a los bancos y empresas llegará a los pequeños negocios y a los consumidores.

Tripartite Pact > Pacto Tripartito Acuerdo que creó una alianza entre Alemania, Italia y Japón durante la Segunda Guerra Mundial.

Truman Doctrine > Doctrina Truman Promesa del presidente Truman de ayudar a las naciones en lucha contra los movimientos comunistas.

Truman, Harry S. > Truman, Harry S. (1884–1972) Fue presidente de los Estados Unidos de 1945 a 1953. Truman asumió el cargo después de la muerte de Franklin Roosevelt y dirigió la nación durante los últimos meses de la Segunda Guerra Mundial, tomando la decisión de usar armas atómicas en contra de Japón. Durante los primeros años de la Guerra Fría, Truman trabajó para reconstruir Europa y oponerse a la expansión del comunismo. Cuando en 1950 la comunista Corea del Norte invadió Corea del Sur y comenzó la Guerra de Corea, Truman envió tropas estadounidenses al conflicto.

Trump, Donald J. Donald J. Trump nació en la Ciudad de Nueva York en 1946. Su padre era un adinerado promotor de bienes raíces. Después de su graduación en la Universidad de Pennsylvania en 1968, Trump comenzó a trabajar para la empresa de su padre. Para la década de 1990, poseía grandes consorcios de bienes raíces, incluyendo el edificio Empire State, varios hoteles, condominios, edificios de apartamentos y casinos. También participó en el programa de televisión The Apprentice (llamado más tarde The Celebrity Apprentice). Consideró ser candidato a la presidencia en 1999, pero no fue sino hasta 2016 que decidió hacerlo oficialmente. Obtuvo la nominación por el partido republicano en el verano de 2016 y en noviembre de ese año, Donald J. Trump fue elegido como el 45to. Presidente de los Estados Unidos.

trust > trust Grupo de empresas independientes que se colocan bajo el control de un único consejo de administración con el fin de formar un monopolio.

Turner, Frederick Jackson > Turner, Frederick Jackson (1861–1932) fue un historiador estadounidense cuyos trabajos influyeron mucho en los escritos posteriores sobre la historia de los Estados Unidos. Turner promovió el uso de las ciencias sociales en los escritos históricos e hizo hincapié en el empleo de conceptos como inmigración, urbanización, desarrollo económico e historia social y cultural cuando se intenta entender los acontecimientos históricos.

Tuskegee Airmen > Aviadores de Tuskegee Escuadrón de afroamericanos que escoltaba a los bombarderos en la guerra aérea en cielos de Europa durante la Segunda Guerra Mundial.

Twain, Mark > Twain, Mark (1835–1910) fue el pseudónimo de Samuel Langhorne Clemons, un novelista y humorista estadounidense que escribió obras famosas como *Vida en el Mississippi, Las aventuras de Tom Sawyer* y *Las aventuras de Huckleberry Finn*. Las historias de Twain reflejaban la vida estadounidense como él la veía.

Twenty-fifth Amendment > Vigésimoquinta Enmienda Enmienda constitucional ratificada en 1967 que trata de la sucesión presidencial, vacantes de vicepresidentes e incapacidad presidencial.

Twenty-fourth Amendment > Vigésimocuarta Enmienda Enmienda constitucional que prohibió el impuesto electoral como requisito para votar.

U

U-boats > U-boot Submarino alemán.

unconditional surrender > rendición incondicional Darse por vencido completamente sin concesiones.

underground railroad > Tren Clandestino Red secreta de "conductores" que escondían a esclavos fugitivos en vagones agrícolas y en barcazas y luego los trasladaban a destinos en el Norte o en Canadá, y a veces hasta Inglaterra.

unfunded mandate > mandato sin fondos Programa o acción requerido pero que no paga el gobierno federal.

United Farm Workers (UFW) > Trabajadores Agrícolas Unidos Sindicato de trabajadores agrícolas que usó tácticas pacíficas, incluyendo una huelga de trabajadores y un boicot por los consumidores de uvas.

United Nations (UN) > Naciones Unidas (ONU) Organización fundada en 1945 para promover la paz.

Universal Declaration of Human Rights > Declaración Universal de los Derechos Humanos Documento emitido por la ONU para promover los derechos y libertades humanos básicos.

Urban League > Liga Urbana Red de iglesias y clubes que estableció agencias de empleo y ofreció asistencia para que los afroamericanos se asentaran y encontraran empleo en las ciudades.

urban renewal > renovación urbana Programas gubernamentales para el desarrollo de las áreas urbanas.

urbanization > urbanización Expansión de ciudades y/o aumento del número de sus habitantes.

USA PATRIOT Act > Ley Patriótica Ley aprobada después del 11 de septiembre de 2001 que da a las fuerzas de seguridad amplios poderes para monitorear posibles actividades terroristas.

V

Vanzetti, Bartolomeo > Vanzetti, Bartolomeo (1888–1927) fue un inmigrante italiano condenado por asesinato y ejecutado en 1927.

vaudeville > vodevil Tipo de espectáculo que incluye baile, canto y comedia, que se popularizó a finales del siglo XIX.

Venona Papers > Documentos Venona Serie de documentos secretos soviéticos de la era de la Guerra Fría interceptados y más tarde liberados por oficiales de inteligencia de los Estados Unidos.

vertical integration > integración vertical Sistema de consolidación de empresas involucradas en todos los pasos de la manufactura de un producto.

Vietcong > Vietcong Rebeldes comunistas sudvietnamitas que hicieron guerra de guerrillas contra el gobierno de Vietnam del Sur durante la Guerra Vietnamita.

Vietnamization > vietnamización Plan del presidente Nixon para terminar gradualmente la participación estadounidense en Vietnam, a medida que las tropas sudvietnamitas asumían más deberes de combate.

vigilantes > vigilante Persona autonombrada para hacer cumplir la ley.

Villa, Francisco "Pancho" > Villa, Francisco "Pancho" (1878–1923) Fue un revolucionario mexicano líder de la guerrilla. En 1916, su ejército mató a 18 estadounidenses en Nuevo México, lo que hizo que el general estadounidense John J. Pershing liderara una expedición a México con 10,000 soldados para capturarlo y castigarlo. Esta expedición no tuvo éxito.

Violence Against Women Act > Ley Contra la Violencia hacia las Mujeres Ley aprobada en 1994 que aumentó los recursos federales para arrestar y enjuiciar a los hombres culpables de actos violentos contra las mujeres.

Volstead Act > Ley Volstead Ley impuesta por el Congreso para hacer cumplir la Decimoctava Enmienda.

Voting Rights Act > Ley de Derechos Electorales Ley que prohibió las pruebas de alfabetismo y dió poder al gobierno federal de vigilar el empadronamiento de los votantes.

voucher > vales Certificados u otros documentos que pueden ser usados como dinero.

W

Wade-Davis Bill > proyecto de ley de Wade-Davis Proyecto de ley que requería a los votantes de los estados confederados de antes de la guerra jurar lealtad a la Unión para que comenzara la Restauración.

Wagner Act > Ley Wagner Ley del Nuevo Trato que abolió las prácticas laborales injustas, reconoció el derecho de los trabajadores de organizar sindicatos, y dio a los trabajadores el derecho a las negociaciones colectivas.

Wallace, George > Wallace, George (1919–1998) fue gobernador de Alabama de 1963 a 1967. Se postuló para la presidencia en 1968 en la convención del Partido Independiente de los Estados Unidos, abogando por los derechos de los estados y ganando cinco de los estados del sur en la elección. Sirvió tres periodos más como gobernador (1971–1979, 1983–1987), y finalmente renunció a sus creencias segregacionistas.

Walton, Sam > Walton, Sam (1918–1992) fue un pionero estadounidense de la venta minorista que fundó Wal-Mart Stores, Inc., la cual llegó a ser la cadena de venta minorista más grande de los Estados Unidos.

war bond > bono de guerra Bono que se compra para financiar una campaña de guerra, redimible por interés después de un periodo determinado de tiempo.

War on Poverty > Guerra Contra la Pobreza Programas del presidente Johnson enfocados en ayudar a los pobres de la nación mediante la educación, entrenamiento laboral, servicios de salud y nutrición adecuados.

War Powers Act > Ley de Poderes Bélicos Ley aprobada por el Congreso en 1973 que restringió los poderes bélicos del presidente; exigía que el presidente consultara con el Congreso antes de comprometer fuerzas estadounidenses en un conflicto extranjero.

War Refugee Board > Junta de Refugiados de Guerra Agencia del gobierno de los Estados Unidos fundada en 1944 para salvar a los judíos de Europa oriental.

Warren Commission > Comisión Warren Comité que investigó el asesinato del presidente Kennedy.

Warren Court > "Corte Warren" Corte Suprema de la década de 1960 bajo el mandato del presidente de los magistrados Earl Warren, cuyas decisiones apoyaron los derechos civiles.

Warren, Earl > Warren, Earl (1891–1974) fue gobernador de California durante tres periodos antes de servir como Jefe de Justicia de la Corte Suprema de 1953 a 1969. Bajo su liderazgo, la Corte falló sobre varios casos emblemáticos que afectaron los derechos civiles, los procedimientos criminales, los derechos al voto y la separación de iglesia y estado.

Warsaw Pact > Pacto de Varsovia Alianza militar de la Unión Soviética y sus estados satélite.

Washington Naval Disarmament Conference > Conferencia de Desarme Naval de Washington Reunión realizada en 1921 y 1922 durante la cual los líderes mundiales acordaron limitar la construcción de buques de guerra.

Washington, Booker T. > Washington, Booker T. (1856–1915) Nació esclavo y creció en la pobreza después de la emancipación. En 1881, Washington fue escogido para dirigir la Tuskegee Normal and Industrial Institution, donde promovió la educación vocacional para los estudiantes afroamericanos. Animó a los ciudadanos afroamericanos a aceptar la segregación y a enfocarse en mejorarse a sí mismos a través de la educación y de las oportunidades económicas.

Washington, George > Washington, George (1732–1799) fue un oficial y estadista de Virginia que dirigió el Ejército Continental durante la Guerra de Independencia y fungió como el primer Presidente de los Estados Unidos.

Watergate > Watergate Escándalo político que involucró actividades ilegales que al final condujeron a la renuncia del presidente Nixon en 1974.

weapons of mass destruction (WMD) > armas de destrucción masiva (ADM) Armas biológicas, nucleares o químicas destinadas a matar o causar daño a gran escala.

welfare state > estado de bienestar Gobierno que asume la responsabilidad de velar por el bienestar de los pobres, ancianos, enfermos y desempleados.

Wells, Ida B. Wells > Wells, Ida B. Wells (1862–1931) Fue una periodista afroamericana que trabajó toda su vida para terminar con los linchamientos en el Sur. Colaboró con varios periódicos, entre ellos *Memphis Free Speech, New York Age* y *Chicago Conservator*. En 1895 publicó una detallada investigación sobre los linchamientos titulada *A Red Record*.

Western Front > Frente Occidental Frente de batalla entre los Aliados y los Poderes Centrales en Europa occidental durante la Primera Guerra Mundial.

Westmoreland, William > Westmoreland, William De 1964 a 1968, el general William Westmoreland (1914–2005) fue el comandante del ejército de los Estados Unidos en la Guerra de Vietnam. Westmoreland había servido antes en la Segunda Guerra Mundial y en la Guerra de Corea.

Whig Party > Whigs Miembros del partido político nacionalista formado en 1832 en oposición a los demócratas.

Willard, Frances > Willard, Frances (1839–1898) fue una catedrática que se interesó en el movimiento de la templanza en 1874. Se unió a la Unión Cristiana de Mujeres por la Templanza (WCTU, por sus siglas en inglés), donde estuvo en desacuerdo con otros miembros al insistir en unir objetivos con el sufragio de las mujeres. Para 1879, había obtenido apoyo suficiente para ser elegida presidenta de la WCTU, un cargo que ocupó de por vida.

William II > Guillermo II (1859–1941) fue emperador alemán y rey de Prusia hasta el final de la Segunda Guerra Mundial en 1918.

Wilmot Proviso > Cláusula de Wilmot Ley propuesta pero rechazada de 1846 que habría prohibido la esclavitud en los territorios ganados a México en la Guerra México-Estadounidense.

Wilson, Woodrow > Wilson, Woodrow (1856–1924) entró en política en 1910 cuando fue electo gobernador de Nueva Jersey. Sus reformas atrajeron la atención nacional y la nominación presidencial demócrata en 1912. Como Presidente guió a la nación durante la Primera Guerra Mundial y negoció el Tratado de Versalles.

Winfrey, Oprah > Winfrey, Oprah (1954–) trabajó como reportera de noticias y presentadora antes de trabajar como presentadora en su programa matutino de entrevistas. Su show de Chicago, *The Oprah Winfrey Show*, comenzó en 1985 y fue vendido a nivel nacional al año siguiente. El programa tuvo un gran éxito y generó su imperio en los medios y el entretenimiento, que incluye una revista y un canal de televisión por cable. Winfrey es un pilar de la lista de la revista *Forbes* de las personas más ricas de los Estados Unidos. Su valor neto en 2013 fue estimado en $2.9 mil millones de dólares.

Wisconsin v. Yoder > Wisconsin contra Yoder Veredicto de la Corte Suprema en 1972 que ampliaba la libertad de religión para permitir que los padres amish, con base en cuestiones religiosas, retiraran a sus hijos de las escuelas públicas después del octavo grado.

Women's Army Corps (WAC) > Cuerpo Femenino del Ejército Grupo del Ejército de los Estados Unidos establecido durante la Segunda Guerra Mundial para que las mujeres pudieran dar servicio en papeles no combativos.

women's rights movement > movimiento por los derechos de la mujer Campaña por la igualdad de derechos para las mujeres.

Works Progress Administration (WPA) > Administración para el Avance de Obras Públicas Agencia clave del Nuevo Trato que brindó ayuda laboral a través de varios proyectos de obras públicas.

World Trade Organization (WTO) > Organización Mundial del Comercio Organización internacional formada en 1995 para estimular la expansión del comercio mundial.

Wounded Knee > Wounded Knee Enfrentamiento de 1890 entre la caballería de los Estados Unidos y los sioux que marcó el fin de la resistencia indígena.

Y

Yalta Conference > Conferencia de Yalta Reunión sobre estrategia realizada en 1945 entre Roosevelt, Churchill y Stalin.

Yellow Press > prensa amarillista Periódicos que utilizaban titulares sensacionales e historias exageradas para promover su circulación.

Z

Zhou Enlai > Zhou Enlai (1898–1976) Vivió de joven en el extranjero antes de regresar a su China nativa en 1924 para ayudar a Mao Zedong a liderar la revolución comunista allí. Cuando Mao estableció la República Popular China en 1949, Zhou fue primer ministro y ministro de Asuntos Exteriores y más tarde el principal artífice de la política china de la distensión con los Estados Unidos en 1972.

Zimmermann note > Telegrama de Zimmermann Telegrama escrito por el ministro del exterior alemán, Arthur Zimmermann, en el que proponía una alianza entre Alemania y México contra los Estados Unidos en la Primera Guerra Mundial.

murals, 366, 626*i*
Murphy, Audie, 429
Murphy, Edgar Gardner, 190
Murphy, Frank, 352
Murrow, Edward R., 396
music. *See also specific types*
    of African Americans, 303–304, 366
    of baseball, 114
    Civil Rights Movement, 532, 616
    counterculture, 616, 616*p*, 617
    of the Great Depression, 366
    Great Migration of, 303
    morality and, 504*p*
    peace movement, 616
    racial divisions and, 503*p*
musicians
    African American, 303–304
    drug overdoses, 617
music industry, 295–296
music publishing industry, 111
Mussolini, Benito (Il Duce), 341, 384, 384*p*, 386, 388, 410, 413–414, 429
mutualistas, 192
mutually assured destruction, 476
MX missile systems, 684
"My Day" (Roosevelt), 356–357
My Lai, 597
"My People" (Hughes), 307
Myrdal, Gunnar, 521

N

Nader, Ralph, 628, 730, 731
Nagasaki (Japan), bombing of, 433
Nagumo, Chuichi, 402–403
Nairobi, 699, 733
Naismith, James, 101, 114
Nakashima, Ted, 420
Namham River, 474*p*
Nanjing, China, 387
napalm, 582
Nashville, TN, 80
Nasser, Gamal Abdel, 479
Nast, Thomas, 147
National Aeronautics and Space Administration (NASA), 480, 549, 682, 682*p*
National American Woman Suffrage Association (NAWSA), 185–186, 255–256, 297
National Association for the Advancement of Colored People (NAACP), 191, 290, 290*p*, 358, 423, 522–523, 525, 528, 529–530, 531, 537*c*, 538, 747
National Association of Colored Women (NACW), 184
National Association Opposed to Woman Suffrage (NAOWS), 187
National Child Labor Committee, 176

National Consumers League (NCL), 183
National Council of La Raza, 626
national debt, 347, 350, 354, 417, 678
National Defense Act (1916), 251
National Defense Education Act (1957), 480, 500
National Endowment for the Arts and Humanities (1965), 557
National Federation of Independent Business v. Sebelius, 741
National Gay and Lesbian Task Force, 747
National Highway Traffic Safety Administration, 556
National Indian Youth Council (NIYC), 627
National Industrial Recovery Act (1933), 353
National Institute of Health, 707
nationalism
    black, 540
    China, 223
    European, World War I and, 244–245
    in Germany, rise of, 385
    Iraqi, 266
    Lôme letter fueling, 215
Nationalist Party, 388
Nationalists, 443
National Labor Relations Act (1935), 351, 360*c*
National Labor Relations Board (NLRB), 351
National League, 114
National Liberation Front (NLF), 598
national monuments, 200
National Organization for Women (NOW), 619*p*, 620, 771
National Origins Act (1921), 557
National Origins Act (1924), 288–289, 557
national parks, 200, 362
National Park Service, 82, 200
National Reclamation Act (1902), 198*t*, 201
National Recovery Administration (NRA), 346
National Rifle Association (NRA), 683
National Science Foundation, 707
National Socialist German Workers' Party, 385
National Trades Union, 91, 93
National Traffic and Motor Vehicle Safety Act (1966), 556, 628, 628*c*
National Voter Registration Act (1993), 538*c*
National War Labor Board, 418
National Woman's Party (NWP), 186, 187
National Woman Suffrage

Association (NWSA), 185
National Women's Party, 298
National Youth Administration (NYA), 360*c*
A Nation at Risk (DOE), 682
Nation of Islam, 302, 537*c*, 540
Native American culture, forced adaptation of, 128–129, 135
Native American lands
    dam construction, effect on, 363
    fishing rights, 627
    loss of (1850–1890), 129*m*
    reservations, 128–129, 131, 134
    tribal landholding system, 135
Native Americans
    Americanization of, 134–135, 192, 359, 507
    buffalo population decimation and, 129, 132
    citizenship, 192
    Civil Rights Movement, 626–628
    Columbus names "Indians," 6
    conversion attempts, 6
    cultural diversity, 128–129
    discrimination, fighting through litigation, 627–628
    disease, 6
    English colonists and, 6
    Ghost Dance movement, 133
    Indian New Deal, 358–359
    Indian Removal Act, 24
    Indian Wars, 131
    land ownership, 135, 192, 358–359, 627
    militant activism, 627
    military service
        WWI, 192
        WWII, 405, 430, 431*p*
    relocation of, 129, 132, 134, 507
    settlers, conflict with, 130–131
    trade relations, 7, 128, 129
    Trail of Tears, 24
    voting rights, 13, 23, 192
    water use by, 201
    in WWI, 405
    in WWII, 423, 430, 431*p*
Native Americans-U.S. government relations
    termination policy, 507
    trade, regulation of, 128, 129
Native American Wars (1860–1890), 131*m*
Native Son (Wright), 368
nativism, 100, 288–289, 288*p*
NATO (North Atlantic Treaty Organization), 468–469, 469*t*, 698
natural resource protections, 179
natural resources
    Alaska, 211
    imperialism and, 209–210
    of the Industrial Revolution, 74
    Japan's reliance on, 401–402

Acknowledgments

[Photography]

CVR: Johannes Spahn/EyeEm/Getty Images; **iii:** Fotomak/Shutterstock; **v:** Goodluz/Shutterstock; **vi:** Photos 12/Alamy Stock Photo; **vii:** Fuse/Getty Images; **x:** Justasc/Shutterstock; **xi:** akg-images/The Image Works; **xii:** Driving the Golden Spike on 10th May, 1869 (colour litho), American School, (19th century)/Private Collection/Peter Newark American Pictures/Bridgeman Art Kibrary; **xiii:** Everett Collection Inc/Alamy Stock Photo; **xiv:** Everett Collection Historical/Alamy Stock Photo; **xix:** Christian Simonpietri/Sygma/Corbis; **xv:** Dorothea Lange/Stringer/Getty Images; **xvi:** Photos 12/Alamy Stock Photo; **xvii:** Bettmann/Corbis; **xviii:** Francis Miller/The LIFE Picture Collection/Getty Images; **xx:** Cynthia Hart Designer/Corbis; **xxi:** Dirck Halstead/The LIFE Images Collection/Getty Images; **xxii:** Lain Masterton/Age Fotostock; **xxiv(a):** Masson/Shutterstock; **xxiv(b):** Gina Sanders/Fotolia; **xxiv(c):** maxstockphoto/Shutterstock; **xxiv(d):** Andrey Burmakin/Shutterstock; **xxiv(e):** Alterov/Shutterstock; **xxiv(f):** Monkey Business/Fotolia; **xxiv(g):** Garsya/Shutterstock; **xxiv(h):** Gary/Fotolia; **xxvi:** Michael Brown/Fotolia; **xxvii:** 2121fisher/Fotolia; **xxxiv:** Luther Daniels Bradley/Corbis; **xxxvT:** Ho/AP Images; **xxxvB:** Jean-Claude Sauer/Paris Match/Getty Images; **xxxvi:** Swim Ink 2, LLC/Corbis; **xxxviiT:** Tony Freeman/PhotoEdit; **xxxviiB:** Lain Masterton/Age Fotostock; **xxxviii:** Bettmann/Corbis; **xxxix:** Corbis; **xl:** Lightroom Photos/Alamy Stock Photo; **xliB:** Anthony Behar/Sipa USA/Newscom; **xlii:** Justasc/Shutterstock; **lxiii:** Bettmann/Corbis; **001:** Pat Benic/UPI/Newscom; **005:** Fotoluminate LLC/Fotolia; **002–003:** Justasc/Shutterstock; **004R:** Niday Picture Library/Alamy; **005:** Nsf/Alamy Stock Photo; **006:** North Wind Picture Archives/Alamy Stock Photo; **010T:** Historical/Corbis; **010B:** lawcain/Fotolia; **013:** Jean Leon Gerome/Ferris/Private Collection/The Bridgeman Art Library; **015:** North Wind Picture Archives/Alamy Stock Photo; **016T:** North Wind Picture Archives; **016B:** Fotosearch/Getty Images; **017:** Bettmann/Corbis; **019:** Billy Bennight/Photoshot/Newscom; **021:** Everett Collection Inc/Alamy Stock Photo; **031:** Superstock; **033:** North Wind Picture Archives/Alamy Stock Photo; **034T:** Bettmann/Corbis; **034B:** Library of Congress Prints and Photographs Division [LC-USZ62-10476]; **035:** Everett Collection/Newscom; **036T:** Kean Collection/Hulton Archive/Getty Images; **036B:** Photo Researchers, Inc/Science Source; **038T:** Bettmann/Corbis; **038B:** Peter Horree/Alamy; **040:** Archive Pics/Alamy; **041:** Library of Congress Prints and Photographs Division; **042T:** Niday Picture Library/Alamy; **042B:** Library of Congress Prints and Photographs Division [LC-USZ62-86311]; **044:** Library of Congress Prints and Photographs Division [LC-DIG-cwpb-04402]; **045T:** Paris Pierce/Alamy; **045B:** The Art Archive/Alamy Stock Photo; **046T:** The Art Archive/Alamy Stock Photo; **046B:** Archive Images/Alamy Stock Photo; **049:** Library of Congress Prints and Photographs Division [LC-DIG-pga-03898]; **051:** Everett Collection Historical/Alamy; **055:** Everett Collection Inc/Alamy; **057:** North Wind Picture Archives/Alamy; **058T:** Library of Congress Prints and Photographs Division [LC-USZ62-45698]; **058B:** Everett Collection Historical/Alamy; **059:** Marie Hansen/Time Life Pictures/Getty Images; **060:** Everett Collection Inc/Alamy Stock Photo; **062:** Jean Leon Gerome/Ferris/Private Collection/The Bridgeman Art Library; **065:** Bettmann/Corbis; **070–071:** akg-images/The Image Works; **072L:** North Wind Picture Archives/Alamy; **072R:** Fotosearch/Archive Photos/Getty Images; **073:** Bain News Service/Library of Congress; **074:** Chris Hellier/Alamy Stock Photo; **074T:** North Wind Picture Archives/AP Images; **074B:** ArtPix/Alamy; **076:** DIZ Muenchen GmbH, Sueddeutsche Zeitung Photo/Alamy; **077T:** Library of Congress Prints and Photographs Division [LC-USZ62-119565]; **077B:** Library of Congress; **079:** National Child Labor Committee Collection/Library of Congress; **081T:** Corbis; **081B:** Three Lions/Stringer/Hulton Archive/Getty Images; **082:** Detroit Photographic Company/Corbis; **083:** Mary Evans Picture Library/The Image Works; **086:** Everett Collection/Superstock; **087:** Schomburg Center, NYPL/Art Resource, NY; **087T:** Library of Congress; **087B:** Luther Daniels Bradley/Corbis; **088:** Corbis; **089:** North Wind Picture Archives/Alamy; **090T:** Library of Congress; **090B:** Library of Congress; **091:** Sean Sexton/Contributor/Hulton Archive/Getty Images; **092:** Library of Congress; **092T:** Special Collections and Archives/Georgia State University Library; **092B:** Archive Photos/Getty Images; **095:** Fotosearch/Getty Images; **096:** Library of Congress; **098:** Jeff Greenberg/Alamy Stock Photo; **099:** Fotosearch/Archive Photos/Getty Images; **100:** The Art Archive at Art Resource, NY; **101:** Ann Ronan Picture Library/HIP/The Image Works; **103:** Pictorial Press Ltd/Alamy Stock Photo; **104:** FPG/Archive Photos/Getty Images; **106T:** ClassicStock/Alamy Stock Photo; **106B:** Chicago History Museum/Archive Photos/Getty Images; **107:** The Protected Art Archive/Alamy Stock Photo; **108:** North Wind Picture Archives/Alamy Stock Photo;

109: North Wind/North Wind Picture Archives; **110:** Camerique/Corbis; **111:** Hulton Archive/Archive Photos/Getty Images; **112T:** Buyenlarge/Getty Images; **112B:** Library of Congress; **113:** Library of Congress; **114:** Library of Congress; **116:** National Child Labor Committee Collection/Library of Congress; **119:** Everett Collection/Superstock; **124–125:** Driving the Golden Spike on 10th May, 1869 (colour litho), American School, (19th century)/Private Collection/Peter Newark American Pictures/Bridgeman Art Library; **126L:** The Art Archive/Alamy Stock Photo; **126R:** Library of Congress; **127:** Trailing Texas Longhorns (oil on canvas), Remington, Frederic (1861–1909)/Private Collection/Peter Newark American Pictures/The Bridgeman Art Library; **128:** Library of Congress; **130:** Dea Picture Library/DeAgostini/Getty Images; **132T:** Art Resource, NY; **132B:** Bettmann/Corbis; **133T:** The Art Archive/Alamy; **133B:** Smithsonian Institution/Corbis; **134:** Library of Congress; **135:** Everett Collection/Superstock; **136:** The Art Archive/Alamy; **140T:** S.D. Butcher/Historical/Corbis; **140B:** North Wind Picture Archives; **142:** M.E. Jacobson/Corbis; **143:** Private Collection/Bridgeman Art Library; **145:** Library of Congress; **146:** Everett Collection/Newscom; **148:** Library of Congress; **150:** Bettmann/Corbis; **152T:** Library of Congress Prints and Photographs Division [LC-USZC4-769]; **152B:** Library of Congress; **153T:** Bettmann/Corbis; **153B:** Library of Congress; **155T:** AP Images; **155B:** Library of Congress; **157:** Bettmann/Corbis; **160:** Library of Congress; **163:** Library of Congress Prints and Photographs Division [LC-USZC4-769]; **164:** Private Collection/Bridgeman Art Library; **165:** S.D. Butcher/Historical/Corbis; **166:** Bettmann/Corbis; **168–169:** Everett Collection Inc/Alamy Stock Photo; **170L:** akg-images/Newscom; **170R:** Library of Congress; **171:** Niday Picture Library/Alamy Stock Photo; **172:** Library of Congress; **173T:** Library of Congress; **173B:** Bettmann/Corbis; **174T:** Library of Congress; **174B:** Library of Congress; **175:** Corbis; **177T:** AP Images; **177B:** Underwood & Underwood/Corbis; **178:** Library of Congress; **180:** The Protected Art Archive/Alamy Stock Photo; **182:** akg-images/Newscom; **183T:** Lewis W. Hine/Archive Photos/Getty Images; **183B:** Minnesota Historical Society/Corbis; **184:** Everett Collection Historical/Alamy; **187T:** Everett Collection/Newscom; **187B:** Library of Congress; **189:** Everett Collection Inc/Alamy; **191:** Schomburg Center, NYPL/Art Resource; **192:** Buyenlarge/Archive Photos/Getty Images; **194:** Everett Collection Historical/Alamy Stock Photo; **196:** Rockwood Photo Co., photographer/Library of Congress; **197:** Collection Dagli Orti/The Art Archive/Alamy Stock Photo; **199T:** Clifford Kennedy Berryman/Corbis; **199B:** The Art Archive/Alamy Stock Photo; **201:** Everett Collection Inc./Age Fotostock; **207:** Corbis; **209:** The Art Archive/Alamy Stock Photo; **210:** William Vander Weyde/George Eastman House/Getty Images; **211:** North Wind Picture Archives; **212T:** Everett Collection/Newscom; **212B:** akg-images/Newscom; **214:** J.F.Jarvis/Corbis; **215T:** Chronicle/Alamy Stock Photo; **215B:** Niday Picture Library/Alamy Stock Photo; **219T:** Corbis; **219B:** Library of Congress Prints and Photographs Division [LC-DIG-hec-12736]; **222:** Bettmann/Corbis; **224:** AP Images; **230:** Hulton-Deutsch Collection/Corbis; **232:** AP Images; **235:** Clifford Kennedy Berryman/Corbis; **240–241:** Everett Collection Historical/Alamy Stock Photo; **242L:** Bettmann/Corbis; **242R:** Library of Congress; **243:** Hulton-Deutsch Collection/Corbis; **243:** akg-images/Alamy Stock Photo; **249T:** Photo12/The Image Works; **249B:** Ww/Alamy Stock Photo; **250T:** Press Association/The Image Works; **250B:** Library of Congress; **252:** National Archives and Records Administration; **253:** akg-images/Newscom; **255:** Bettmann/Corbis; **257:** Popperfoto/Getty Images; **259:** Bettmann/Corbis; **260:** American Stock/Archive Photos/Getty Images; **261T:** Lightroom/US Army/PhotoShot; **261B:** SOTK2011/Alamy Stock Photo; **263T:** AP Images; **263B:** Niday Picture Library/Alamy Stock Photo; **265T:** TopFoto/The Image Works; **265B:** Library of Congress Prints and Photographs Division [LC-USZ62-36185]; **266T:** Hulton-Deutsch Collection/Corbis; **266B:** AFIP'S National Museum Of Health KRT/Newscom; **268:** Bettmann/Corbis; **269:** TopFoto/The Image Works; **271:** Hulton Archive/Getty Images; **272:** Everett Collection/Newscom; **273:** Science and Society/Superstock; **275:** Jeff Morgan 13/Alamy Stock Photo; **276T:** Riveters attaching a beam, Empire State Building, 1931 (gelatin silver print), Hine, Lewis Wickes (1874–1940)/New York Public Library, USA/Stephen A. Schwarzman Building/Photography Collection, Miriam and Ira D. Wallach Division of Art, Prints and Photographs/Bridgeman Art Library; **276B:** Bettmann/Corbis; **277:** American Stock Archive/Getty Images; **278:** Bettmann/Corbis; **280:** Everett Collection/Newscom; **284:** Buyenlarge/Getty Images; **285T:** Cond Nast Archive/Corbis; **285B:** Bettmann/Corbis; **287T:** akg-images/Newscom; **287B:** Everett Collection/Newscom; **288:** DIZ Muenchen GmbH, Sueddeutsche Zeitung Photo/Alamy Stock Photo; **290:** The Protected Art

Archive/Alamy Stock Photo; **292:** AP Images; **293:** Library of Congress Prints and Photographs Division [LC-USZ62-22847]; **295T:** Everett Collection; **295B:** Blank Archives/Getty Images; **296:** DIZ Muenchen GmbH, Sueddeutsche Zeitung Photo/Alamy Stock Photo; **297:** DaZo Vintage Stock Photos/Images.com/Alamy Stock Photo; **298:** Francis G. Mayer/Corbis; **299:** Snark/Art Resource, NY; **300:** Everett Collection; **301:** Stefano Bianchetti/Corbis; **302T:** AP Images; **302B:** Underwood & Underwood/Corbis; **304T:** Michael Ochs Archives/Corbis; **304B:** Hulton Archive/Stringer; **305T:** Bettmann/Corbis; **305B:** Robert W. Kelley/The LIFE Picture Collection/Getty Images; **306:** Everett Collection/Newscom; **307:** Robert W Kelley/Time Life Pictures/Getty Images; **310:** Francis G. Mayer/Corbis; **313:** Bettmann/Corbis; **315:** Everett Collection/Newscom; **318–319:** Dorothea Lange/Stringer/Getty Images; **298:** Francis G. Mayer/Corbis; **299:** Snark/Art Resource, NY; **300:** Everett Collection; **301:** Stefano Bianchetti/Corbis; **302T:** AP Images; **302B:** Underwood & Underwood/Corbis; **304T:** Michael Ochs Archives/Corbis; **305T:** Bettmann/Corbis; **305B:** Robert W. Kelley/The LIFE Picture Collection/Getty Images; **306:** Everett Collection/Newscom; **307:** Robert W Kelley/Time Life Pictures/Getty Images; **310:** Francis G. Mayer/Corbis; **313:** Bettmann/Corbis; **315:** Everett Collection/Newscom; **320L:** DIZ Muenchen GmbH, Sueddeutsche Zeitung Photo/Alamy Stock Photo; **320R:** AP Images; **321:** Ho/AP Images; **322:** Bettmann/Corbis; **323T:** FPG/Getty Images; **323B:** AP Images; **324T:** Buyenlarge/Getty Images; **324B:** ClassicStock/Alamy; **326T:** Superstock/Glow Images; **326B:** DIZ Muenchen GmbH, Sueddeutsche Zeitung Photo/Alamy; **328:** Underwood Photo Archives/Superstock; **330:** Everett Collection/Newscom; **331T:** Rolls Press/Popperfoto/Getty Images; **331B:** Everett Collection/Newscom; **333T:** DIZ Muenchen GmbH, Sueddeutsche Zeitung Photo/Alamy; **333B:** Arthur Rothstein/Corbis; **335T:** George E. Marsh/NOAA/AP Images; **335B:** Heritage Image Partnership/Alamy; **336:** FPG/Hulton Archive/Getty Images; **338:** Hulton-Deutsch Collection/Corbis; **339T:** MPI/Getty Images; **339B:** Satirical cartoon comment on Herbert Hoover's reaction to the Great Depression, 1935 (litho), Fitzpatrick, Daniel Robert (1891–1969)/Private Collection/Peter Newark American Pictures/Bridgeman Art Library; **341:** MPI/Getty Images; **342:** Everett Collection/Newscom; **344:** Everett Collection/Newscom; **346:** UniversalImagesGroup/Getty Images; **347:** AP Images; **349:** Minnesota Historical Society/Corbis; **350:** AES/AP Images; **355:** Fotosearch/Archive Photos/Getty Images; **356:** Photos 12/Alamy; **357T:** AP Images; **357B:** Corbis; **358:** AP Images; **361:** ho/AP Images; **363:** Everett Collection/Alamy; **364:** Lange/Dorothea/Library of Congress; **365T:** AP Images; **365B:** Hulton Archive/Getty Images; **366:** Bernard Hoffman/Time & Life Pictures/Getty Images; **367T:** David R Frazier Photolibrary, Inc/Alamy; **368T:** Hulton Archive/Getty Images; **368B:** Heritage Image Partnership Ltd/Alamy; **370:** George E. Marsh/NOAA/AP Images; **373:** Universal Images Group/Getty Images; **374:** George E. Marsh/NOAA/AP Images; **378–379:** Photos 12/Alamy Stock Photo; **380L:** Hulton Archive/Getty Images; **380R:** Corbis; **381:** The LIFE Picture Collection/Getty Images; **382:** World History Archive/Newscom; **383T:** Daily Mirror/Mirrorpix/Newscom; **383B:** The Image Works; **384T:** Bettmann/Corbis; **384B:** Henry Guttmann/Getty Images; **385T:** akg images; **385B:** Hulton Archive/Getty Images; **386:** Getty Images; **388T:** Fox Photos/Hulton Archive/Getty Images; **388B:** Private Collection/Peter Newark Military Pictures/The Bridgeman Art Library; **389:** Hulton-Deutsch Collection/Corbis; **390:** RW/AP/AP/Corbis; **391T:** Getty Images; **391B:** Popperfoto/Getty Images; **393T:** Bettmann/Corbis; **393B:** Time Life Pictures/Pictures Inc/The LIFE Picture Collection/Getty Images; **394T:** DIZ Muenchen GmbH, Sueddeutsche Zeitung Photo/Alamy Stock Photo; **394B:** Bettmann/Corbis; **395:** Scherl/Sueddeutsche Zeitung/The Image Works; **396T:** Bettmann/Corbis; **396B:** Swim Ink 2, LLC/Corbis; **398:** Bettmann/Corbis; **399:** Swim Ink 2, LLC/Corbis; **401:** The LIFE Picture Collection/Getty Images; **402:** Corbis; **403T:** Bettmann/Corbis; **403B:** Time Life Pictures/US Navy/The LIFE Picture Collection/Getty Images; **404T:** Stocktrek Images, Inc./Alamy Stock Photo; **404B:** Hulton Archive/Getty Images; **405T:** Bettmann/Corbis; **405B:** Hulton Archive/Getty Images; **406T:** Corbis; **406B:** Everett Collection Inc/Alamy Stock Photo; **408T:** PubImages/Newscom; **408B:** Corbis; **410:** George Rodger/The Life Picture Collection/Getty Images; **411T:** Dpa/dpa/Corbis; **411B:** Corbis; **412T:** akg images/The Image Works; **412B:** Corbis; **413:** Curt Teich Archives/HIP/The Image Works; **416:** Ralph Morse/The LIFE Picture Collection/Getty Images; **417:** Library of Congress; **418:** Newberry Library/Superstock; **419T:** Bettmann/Corbis; **419B:** Bettmann/Corbis; **420T:** Everett Collection/Newscom; **420B:** Lucy Pemoni/Corbis; **421:** Time Life Pictures/National Archives/The LIFE Picture Collection/Getty Images; **422T:** MPI/Getty Images; **422B:** National Archives at College Park Still Pictures; **423T:** Al Gretz/FPG/Hulton Archive/Getty Images; **423B:** Corbis; **424:** Corbis; **425:** Photo12/UIG/Getty Images; **426T:** Paul Popper/Popperfoto/Getty Images; **426B:** Bettmann/Corbis; **428:** Popperfoto/Getty Images; **431T:** AP Images; **431B:** Keystone/Getty Images; **432T:** Science Source/Getty Images; **432B:** Bettmann/Corbis; **433:** Corbis; **434:** Pictorial Press Ltd/Alamy Stock Photo; **435T:** Private Collection/Peter Newark Historical Pictures/Bridgeman Art Library; **435B:** Fox Photos/Hulton Archive/Getty Images; **438:** Bettmann/Corbis; **439T:** Ullstein bild/akg images; **439B:** Bob Daemmrich/The Image Works; **440:** Anne Frank Fonds Basel/Getty Images; **442:** Corbis; **443:** AF archive/Alamy Stock Photo; **444:** Buy Prints/The Image Works; **445T:** Bettmann/Corbis; **445B:** David Coleman/Alamy Stock Photo; **446:** Carl Mydans/The LIFE Picture Collection/Getty Images; **447:** Private Collection/Photo Barbara Singer/The Bridgeman Art Library; **449:** Bettmann/Corbis; **452:** The Life Picture Collection/Getty Images; **455:** Everett Collection Inc/Alamy; **460–461:** Bettmann/Corbis; **462L:** Sovfoto/Universal Images Group/Getty Images; **462R:** J. R. Eyerman/The Life Picture Collection/Getty Images; **463:** CBS Photo Archive/Getty Images; **464:** dpa/picture-alliance/dpa/AP Images; **465T:** Sovfoto/Universal Images Group/Getty Images; **465B:** George Skadding/The LIFE Picture Collection/Getty Images; **466:** AP Images; **467T:** John Rooney/AP Images; **467B:** Bettmann/Corbis; **470:** Harold M. Lambert/Archive Photos/Getty Images; **471T:** AP Images; **471B:** Bettmann/Corbis; **472:** William C. Allen/AP Images; **474:** Park Jin-hee/Xinhua Press/Corbis; **475:** Corbis; **476:** Everett Collection/Newscom; **478T:** Bettmann/Corbis; **478B:** Ulton-Deutsch Collection/Corbis; **480:** Bettmann/Corbis; **481:** CBS Photo Archive/Getty Images; **482T:** David Pollack/Corbis; **482B:** Eileen Darby/The LIFE Images Collection/Getty Images; **483:** Everett Collection/Glow Images; **484:** New York Daily News Archive/Getty Images; **485:** Advertising Archive/Everett Collection; **487:** Marka/Alamy Stock Photo; **489T:** Yale Joel/The LIFE Picture Collection/Getty Images; **489B:** FPG/Archive Photos/Getty Images; **491:** Bettmann/Corbis; **492:** Everett Collection/Newscom; **493:** Bettmann/Corbis; **494:** Popperfoto/Getty Images; **495:** J. R. Eyerman/The LIFE Picture Collection/Getty Images; **496:** J. R. Eyerman/The LIFE Picture Collection/Getty Images; **498:** H. Armstrong Roberts/Corbis; **499T:** akg-images/Newscom; **499B:** Keystone View/FPG/Archive Photos/Getty Images; **500:** Curt Teich Archives/HIP/The Image Works; **502:** Bettmann/Corbis; **503T:** Warner Brothers/Album/Newscom; **503B:** Tony Frank/Sygma/Corbis; **504:** Keystone Pictures USA/Alamy Stock Photo; **507T:** Keystone Features/Hulton Archive/Getty Images; **507B:** Keystone-France/Gamma-Keystone/Getty Images; **508:** FPG/Archive Photos/Getty Images; **511:** Advertising Archive/Everett Collection; **512:** Dpa/picture-alliance/dpa/AP Images; **516–517:** Francis Miller/The LIFE Picture Collection/Getty Images; **518L:** Bettmann/Corbis; **518R:** Joseph Louw/The LIFE Images Collection/Getty Images; **519:** Ivan Massar/Newscom; **520:** Bettmann/Corbis; **521T:** Bettmann/Corbis; **521B:** Everett Collection; **524T:** St Petersburg Times/ZUMAPRESS/Newscom; **524B:** Everett Collection Inc/Alamy Stock Photo; **525:** Bettmann/Corbis; **526:** AP Images; **527:** Lightroom Photos/Alamy Stock Photo; **528:** Al Fenn/The LIFE Picture Collection/Getty Images; **529T:** AP Images; **529B:** File/AP Images; **530:** Bettmann/Corbis; **531:** Buyenlarge/Archive Photos/Getty Images; **532:** The Birmingham News/AP Images; **534:** Francis Miller/The LIFE Picture Collection/Getty Images; **536:** Bettmann/Corbis; **539T:** Rolls Press/Popperfoto/Getty Images; **539B:** Everett Collection/Newscom; **540T:** AP Images; **540B:** AP Images; **541T:** Everett Collection/Newscom; **541B:** Bettmann/Corbis; **542T:** AP Images; **542B:** Joseph Louw/The LIFE Images Collection/Getty Images; **544:** HWC/AP Images; **545:** Popperfoto/Getty Images; **547T:** Byron Rollins/AP Images; **547B:** Keystone View/FPG/Hulton Archive/Getty Images; **550:** King Victor Hugo/Library of Congress; **551:** Popperfoto/Getty Images; **553:** Bettmann/Corbis; **555:** Keystone Pictures USA/Alamy Stock Photo; **556:** ClassicStock/Corbis; **558:** AP Images; **559:** Kim Kulish/Corbis; **560T:** ClassicStock/Corbis; **560B:** St Petersburg Times/ZUMAPRESS/Newscom; **564:** AP Images; **568–569:** Christian Simonpietri/Sygma/Corbis; **570L:** AP Images; **570R:** Michael Boyer/AP Images; **571:** Bettmann/Corbis; **572:** AP Images; **573T:** AP Images; **573B:** Corbis; **575T:** AP Images; **575B:** World History Archive/Alamy Stock Photo; **577:** akg-images/Newscom; **579T:** akg-images/Newscom; **579B:** Everett Collection Inc/Alamy Stock Photo; **580:** Bettmann/Corbis; **581:** USAF/AP Images; **584:** Everett_Glow/Glow Images; **587:** Bettmann/Corbis; **588T:** Pictorial Parade/Archive Photos/Getty Images; **588B:** Bettmann/Corbis; **589:** CBS Photo Archive/Getty Images; **591T:** Tim Page/Corbis; **591B:** NY Daily News/Getty Images; **592:** Michael Boyer/AP

Images; **594:** John Filo/Getty Images; **595T:** White House via CNP/Newscom; **595B:** Block Herbert/Library of Congress; **596:** Frank Curtin/AP Images; **597T:** World History Archive/Newscom; **597B:** Everett Collection Historical/Alamy Stock Photo; **599:** Bettmann/Corbis; **600:** Bill Peters/The Denver Post/Getty Images; **602:** Tim Page/Corbis; **605:** Michael Boyer/AP Images; **606:** World History Archive/Alamy Stock photo; **610–611:** Cynthia Hart Designer/Corbis; **612L:** AP Images; **612R:** Anonymous/File/AP Images; **613:** AP Images; **614:** Henry Diltz/Corbis; **615T:** CBS/Getty Images; **615B:** Henry Diltz/Corbis; **616T:** Underwood & Underwood/Corbis; **616B:** ZUMA Press, Inc/Alamy; **617:** Henry Diltz/Corbis; **618:** Bettmann/Corbis; **619T:** Bettmann/Corbis; **619B:** Bettmann/Corbis; **620:** Arthur Grace/Zuma Press/Newscom; **621T:** Jerry Cooke/Sports Illustrated/Getty Images; **621B:** David Dow/NBAE/Getty Images; **624:** Wally Fong/AP Images; **626T:** Pittsburgh Post-Gazette/Zuma Press/Newscom; **626B:** Laramie Daily Boomerang/Andy Carpenean/AP Images; **627:** Bettmann/Corbis; **629T:** The Art Archive/Alamy Stock Photo; **629B:** Nikolas Georgiou/Alamy Stock Photo; **630:** AP Images; **633:** Block Herbert/Library of Congress; **636:** Xinhua/Landov; **637T:** Benjamin E. "Gene" Forte – CNP/Newscom; **637B:** ChinaFotoPress/Getty Images; **640T:** CSU Archives/Everett Collection; **640B:** Jean-Claude Sauer/Paris Match/Getty Images; **644:** Wally McNamee/Corbis; **645:** Akg-images/Newscom; **647:** Anonymous/File/AP Images; **648T:** Bill Pierce/Time & Life Pictures Collection/Getty Images; **648B:** Dirck Halstead/TIME & LIFE Images Collection/Getty Images; **649T:** AP Images; **649B:** JP Laffont/Sygma/Corbis; **650:** Everett Collection/Newscom; **652T:** Bettmann/Corbis; **652B:** AP Images; **653:** RDA/Hulton Archive/Getty Images; **655:** Panthera/Alamy Stock Photo; **658:** Arthur Grace/Zuma Press/Newscom; **661:** Akg-images/Newscom; **662:** CBS/Getty Images; **666–667:** Dirck Halstead/The LIFE Images Collection/Getty Images; **668L:** Ira Schwarz/AP Images; **668R:** Chuck Kennedy KRT/Newscom; **669:** Dirck Halstead/Time Life Pictures/Getty Images; **670:** Arthur Grace/Zumapress/Newscom; **673:** Lifestyle pictures/Alamy; **676:** Ira Schwarz/AP Images; **679:** Yvonne Hemsey/Hulton Archive/Getty Images; **680T:** PF-(usna)/Alamy; **680B:** Lennox McLendon/AP Images; **681T:** Barry Thumma/AP Images; **681B:** Cond Nast Archive/Alamy; **682:** NASA Archive/Alamy; **683:** Bill Haber/AP Images; **684:** Afp/Getty Images; **686:** Bettmann/Corbis; **688T:** Bettmann/Corbis; **688B:** Lana Harris/AP Images; **690:** Ira Schwartz/AP Images; **692:** Visions of America, LLC/Alamy Stock Photo; **693T:** Wally McNamee/Corbis; **693B:** Kevin Larkin/Afp/Getty Images; **694:** Keystone Pictures USA/Alamy; **699:** Najlah Feanny/Corbis; **700:** Kevin Larkin/Afp/Getty Images; **702:** Steve Eason/Hulton Archive/Getty Images; **703T:** Charles Porter IV/Zuma Press/Newscom; **703B:** John Duricka/AP Images; **706:** Clu/E+/Getty Images; **709L:** Bob Daugherty/AP Images; **709R:** US Army Photo/Alamy Stock Photo; **712:** Wally McNamee/Corbis; **715:** Afp/Getty Images; **717:** Ed Bailey/AP Images; **718:** John Duricka/AP Images; **719:** Kevin McKiernan/ZUMA Press/Newscom; **720–721:** Lain Masterton/Age Fotostock; **722L:** Ed Reinke/AP Images; **722R:** Seamas Culligan/Zuma Press/Newscom; **723:** Anthony Behar/Sipa USA/Newscom; **724:** Nana Buxani/Bloomberg/Getty Images; **727:** Annedde/E+/Getty Images; **730:** Ed Reinke/AP Images; **732B:** Carmen Taylor/AP Images; **732T:** Win McNamee/Reuters; **733B:** Al-Jazeera/Zumapress/Newscom; **733T:** Tom Horan/Ap Images; **734:** Justin Sullivan/Getty Images; **735:** Eric Feferberg/AFP/Newscom; **738:** Chuck Kennedy/Mct/Newscom; **740:** Pete Marovich/Corbis; **742:** Photo by Drew Angerer/Getty Images; **742B:** Photo by Drew Angerer/Getty Images; **744:** Tony Freeman/PhotoEdit; **747:** NiKreative/Alamy stock photo; **749:** Jerry and Marcy Monkman/EcoPhotography.com/Alamy; **750:** Seth Wenig/AP Images; **751:** Stephan Goerlich/Image Broker/Alamy Stock Photo; **754:** Tony Freeman/PhotoEdit; **762:** Stock Connection Blue/Alamy Stock Photo; **804:** The New York Historical Society/Archive Photos/Getty Images;

[Text Acknowledgments]

ABC-CLIO, A History of the U.S. Political System: Ideas, Interests, and Institutions by Richard A. Harris and Daniel J. Tichenor, 2009. Copyright © ABC-CLIO; **ABC-CLIO,** Speech Demanding War Against Great Britain, 1811 by Felix Grundy from The Encyclopedia Of The War Of 1812: A Political, Social, and Military History, 2012. Copyright © ABC-CLIO; **Alfred A. Knopf,** "The Negro Speaks of Rivers," and "My People" from THE COLLECTED POEMS OF LANGSTON HUGHES by Langston Hughes, edited by Arnold Rampersad with David Roessel, Associate Editor, copyright © 1994 by the Estate of Langston Hughes. Used by permission of Alfred A. Knopf, an imprint of the Knopf

Doubleday Publishing Group, a division of Random House LLC. All rights reserved; **Battle of Homestead Foundation,** The Homestead Strike of 1892 by Joe White. Copyright © Battle of Homestead Foundation. Used by permission; **Berghahn Books,** Enemy Images in American History by Ragnhild Fiebig-von Hase and Ursula Lehmkuhl, 1997. Copyright © Berghahn Books; **Cambridge Scholars Press,** American Conservatism: History, Theory and Practice by Brian R. Farmer, 2005. Copyright © Cambridge Scholars Press; **Cambridge University Press,** Al-Umari, Levitzion and Hopkins Corpus of Early Arabic Sources for West African History, 1981. Copyright © Cambridge University Press; **Cambridge University Press – US – Journals,** The Cambridge History of American Foreign Relations: Volume 2, The American Search for Opportunity, 1865–1913 by Warren Cohen. Copyright © 1995 Cambridge University Press, 1995; **Cambridge University Press – US – Journals,** The Cambridge History of American Foreign Relations: Volume 2, The American Search for Opportunity, 1865–1913 by Warren Cohen. Copyright © 1995 Cambridge University Press, 1995; **Constitutional Rights Foundation,** Bill of Rights in Action. 2009: Copyright © Constitutional Rights Foundation. Used by permission; **Cornell University,** A Lecture on the Triangle Shirtwaist Factory Fire by Frances Perkins, 30 September 1964. Copyright © Cornell University; **Cornell University,** A Lecture on the Triangle Shirtwaist Factory Fire by Frances Perkins, 30 September 1964. Copyright © Cornell University; **Council on Foreign Relations,** The League of Nations: Successes and Failures by Eduard Benes. Copyright © Council on Foreign Relations; **David Higham Associates Ltd.,** Esmeraldo de situ orbis by Duarte Pacheco. Copyright © David Higham Associates Ltd. Used by permission; **Doubleday,** Excerpts from "Diary of a Young Girl: The Definitive Edition" by Anne Frank, edited by Otto H. Frank and Mirjam Pressler, translated by Susan Massotty, translation copyright © 1995 by Doubleday, a division of Random House LLC. Used by permission of Doubleday, an imprint of the Knopf Doubleday Publishing Group, a division of Random House LLC. All rights reserved; **Dover Publications,** How the Other Half Lives by Jacob Riis. Copyright © Dover Publications; **East Tennessee State University,** Acceptance Speech for the Democratic nomination for President by William Jennings Bryan, August 8, 1900. Copyright © East Tennessee State University; **George Mason University,** 1895 Atlanta Compromise Speech by Booker T. Washington, 1985. Copyright © George Mason University; **Grove Atlantic, Inc.,** The Earth Shall Weep: A History of Native America by James Wilson, 1998. Copyright © Grove Atlantic, Inc.; **Harold Ober Associates,** The Collected Poems of Langston Hughes by Langston Hughes edited by Arnold Rampersad with David Roessel, Associate Editor. Copyright © 1994 by the Estate of Langston Hughes. Used by permission of Harold Ober Associates Incorporated; **Harvard University Press,** Kill the Indian, and Save the Man: Captain. Richard H. Pratt on the Education of Native Americans. Copyright © Harvard University Press; **Harvard University Press,** Adams Family Correspondence 1963–1993. Copyright © Harvard University Press; **History News Network,** So Henry Cabot Lodge Was One of History's Villains? Copyright © History News Network. Used by permission; **History Today,** The American Revolution Reconsidered by Eric Robson, February 2, 1952. Copyright © History Today. Used by permission; **Houghton Mifflin Harcourt Publishing Company,** Silent Spring by Rachel Carson. Copyright © Houghton Mifflin Harcourt; **Institute of Islamic Knowledge,** English Translation of the Meaning of Al-Qur'an: The Guidance for Mankind translated by Muhammad Farooq-i-Azam Malik. Copyright © 1997 The Institute of Islamic Knowledge. Used by permission; **John Wiley & Sons, Inc,** "Business Leaders: A Historical Sketch of Andrew Carnegie" from Journal of Leadership Studies: Vol. 5, Issue 4, Fall 1998 by Daniel A Wren and Ronald Greenwood. Copyright © John Wiley & Sons; **Leiser, Burton,** Source: Free Inquiry. Volume: 21. Issue: 3, Summer 2001. Burton M. Leiser. Courtesy of Estate of Burton M Leiser; **Linder, Douglas,** The Impeachment Trial of Andrew Johnson by Dr Douglas Linder. Copyright © Dr Douglas Linder. Used by permission; **Macmillan Publishing Company,** Corsi. Edward. 2012.The Shadow of Liberty: The Chronicle of Ellis Island. Macmillan Publishing Company; **Mencken, H. L.,** The Monkey Trial: A Reporter's Account. Copyright © H.L. Mencken; **Miller Center,** Andrew Johnson: A Life in Brief. Copyright © Miller Center. Used by permission; **Mount Holyoke College Art Museum,** In Support of an American Empire by Albert J. Beveridge. Copyright © Mount Holyoke College Art Museum; **National Council of Churches,** "I Corinthians, Chapter 13" from Holy Bible: With the Apocryphal. Copyright © 1989